FLAME
of
YAHWEH

FLAME
of
YAHWEH

Sexuality in the
Old Testament

Richard M. Davidson

HENDRICKSON PUBLISHERS

Flame of Yahweh: Sexuality in the Old Testament
© 2007 by Hendrickson Publishers, Inc.
P. O. Box 3473
Peabody, Massachusetts 01961-3473

ISBN 978-1-56563-847-1

Printed in the United States of America

First Printing — May 2007

Library of Congress Cataloging-in-Publication Data

Davidson, Richard M., 1946–
    Flame of Yahweh : sexuality in the Old Testament / Richard M. Davidson.
        p. cm.
    Includes bibliographical references and indexes.
    ISBN-13: 978-1-56563-847-1 (alk. paper)
    1. Sex—Biblical teaching. 2. Sex—Religious aspects. 3. Bible. O.T.—
    Criticism, interpretation, etc. I. Title.
    BS1199.S45D38 2007
    233'.5—dc22
                        2006027754

To Jo Ann:

lover, partner, wife, theologian, and best friend—par excellence—
with whom the Flame of Yahweh ever blazes more beautifully!

Table of Contents

Acknowledgments

It is impossible to acknowledge by name all those who have played a part in bringing this project to fruition. First and foremost, I extol God himself, El Shaddai, who has imparted the strength and endurance to persist in an endeavor that demanded far more time and energy than I would have ever imagined. I thank my family—my wife, Jo Ann, my children, Rahel and Jonathan, and our new son-in-law, Kirk Schafer (Rahel's husband)—for their steadfast support and patience, wisdom and love, confidence and encouragement, through every stage of the research and writing. Much appreciation goes to Jo Ann's mother, Dr. Alberta Mazat, who has mentored me just like a mother. She is a licensed marriage and family therapist and has kindly provided much-needed input from her vast store of wisdom and experience.

Special kudos to my secretary, Dorothy Show, who has kept this project on track, devoting endless hours to the formatting and proofreading of the manuscript, and often offering valuable suggestions for improvement. Many thanks go to my graduate research assistants over the years, who have helped in bibliographical searches and in ordering, gathering, and photocopying materials; in particular I mention Martin Pröbstle, Afolarin Ojewole, Chun Sik Park, and Jan Sigvartsen. Jan also assisted me greatly in bringing the manuscript into proper SBL style and offering timely suggestions especially in areas related to Second Temple Judaism.

Deep appreciation goes to my colleagues in the Old Testament Department of Andrews University Theological Seminary for their support, in particular Jiří Moskala and Roy Gane, who have read the entire manuscript, offering many valuable suggestions for improvement, flowing forth from their expertise in Old Testament theology and biblical/ancient Near Eastern law. I am also indebted to numerous perceptive graduate students who have provided keen insights regarding the Old Testament theology of sexuality in various doctoral seminars I have conducted on this subject. Countless others have enriched my understanding of this topic as we have shared together in a multitude of contexts. I am grateful to the editorial staff at Hendrickson Publishers for their professionalism in bringing this unwieldy manuscript into publishable form; particular credit goes to my primary editor, Allan Emery, whose wise counsel and sensitive editing have elevated the quality of the manuscript far beyond what it would have been otherwise. I pay special tribute to my *Doktorvater,* the late Gerhard F. Hasel, whose expert guidance prepared me to conduct this research and whose confidence in me opened the way to undertake this project. I offer this monograph as a monument in honor of his life and scholarship. And ultimately, *Soli Deo Gloria!*

Abbreviations

General

abs.	absolute
adj.	adjective
ANE	Ancient Near Eastern
art.	article(s)
B.C.E.	before the Common Era
ca.	circa
C.E.	Common Era
cf.	*confer*, compare
ch(s).	chapter(s)
col(s).	column(s)
const.	construct
d.	died
ed(s).	editor(s), edited by
e.g.	*exempli gratia*, for example
esp.	especially
ET	English translation
fem.	feminine
i.e.	*id est*, that is
impf.	imperfect
inf.	infinitive
Gk.	Greek
HB	Hebrew Bible
Heb.	Hebrew
lit.	literally
LXX	Septuagint
masc.	masculine
MT	Masoretic Text
no(s).	number(s)
p(p).	page(s)
par.	paragraph
pass.	passive
pl.	plural
praef.	*praefatio* (preface)

ptc.	participle
q.	question
rev.	revised (by)
R.M.D.	author Davidson
sect.	section
sg.	singular
suppl.	supplement
s.v.	*sub verbo,* under the word
trans.	translator, translated by
v(v).	verse(s)

Bible Texts and Versions

ASV	American Standard Version
AV	Authorized Version
BVME	Berkeley Version in Modern English
EBR	Emphasized Bible (Rotherham)
ERV	English Revised Version
ESV	English Standard Version
HB	Hebrew Bible
HCSB	Holman Christian Standard Bible
JB	Jerusalem Bible
JPSV	Jewish Publication Society Version (1917)
KJV	King James Version
NAB	New American Bible
NASB	New American Standard Bible (updated 1995)
NEB	New English Bible
NIV	New International Version
NJB	New Jerusalem Bible
NJPS	*Tanakh: The Holy Scriptures: The New JPS Translation according to the Traditional Hebrew Text* (1985)
NKJV	New King James Version
NLT	New Living Translation
NRSV	New Revised Standard Version
NT	New Testament
OT	Old Testament
RSV	Revised Standard Version
RV	Revised Version

Ancient Near Eastern Sources

| BM | British Museum |
| CH | Code of Hammurabi |

HL	Hittite Laws
LI	Lipit-Ishtar
MAL	Middle Assyrian Laws
P.Cair.Zen.	Zenon papyri, Cairo
RS	Ras Shamra
UT	Ugaritic Text(s)

Ancient Jewish Sources

11QT[a]	*Temple Scroll[a]*
b.	Babylonian tractates
m.	Mishna tractates
t.	Tosefta tractates
y.	Jerusalem tractates
Giṭ.	*Giṭṭin*
Ketub.	*Ketubbot*
Moʾed Qaṭ.	*Moʾed Qaṭan*
Nid.	*Niddah*
ʾOhal.	*ʾOhalot*
Sanh.	*Sanhedrin*
Yad.	*Yadayim*
Yebam.	*Yebamot*

Ancient Classical and Christian Sources

Herodotus
    Hist.   *Historiae*
Jerome
    Comm. Ezech. *Commentariorum in Ezecheliem libri XVI*
Origen
    Comm. Cant. *Commentarius in Canticum*
Strabo
    Geogr.   *Geographica*

Secondary Sources

AASOR	Annual of the American Schools of Oriental Research
AB	Anchor Bible

ABD   *Anchor Bible Dictionary.* Edited by D. N. Freedman. 6 vols.
                 New York: Doubleday, 1992
ACEBT   *Amsterdamse cahiers voor exegese en bijbelse theologie*
AcOr   *Acta orientalia*
ACW   Ancient Christian Writers
AfO   *Archiv für Orientforschung*
AJSL   *American Journal of Semitic Languages and Literature*
AJSR   *Association for Jewish Studies Review*
ANEP   *The Ancient Near East in Pictures Relating to the Old Testa-*
                 ment. Edited by J. B. Pritchard. Princeton: Princeton Univer-
                 sity Press, 1954
ANESSup   Ancient Near Eastern Studies Supplement
ANET   *Ancient Near Eastern Texts Relating to the Old Testament.* Ed-
                 ited by J. B. Pritchard. 3d ed. Princeton: Princeton University
                 Press, 1969
ANETS   Ancient Near Eastern Texts and Studies
AOAT   Alter Orient und Altes Testament
AOTC   Apollos Old Testament Commentary
APOT   *The Apocrypha and Pseudepigrapha of the Old Testament.* Ed-
                 ited by R. H. Charles. 2 vols. Oxford: Clarendon, 1913
ASNU   Acta seminarii neotestamentici upsaliensis
ATD   Das Alte Testament Deutsch
ATSDS   Adventist Theological Society Dissertation Series
AUSS   *Andrews University Seminary Studies*
BA   *Biblical Archaeologist*
BAR   *Biblical Archaeology Review*
BASOR   *Bulletin of the American Schools of Oriental Research*
BBB   Bonner biblische Beiträge
BBC   Broadman Bible Commentary
BBR   *Bulletin for Biblical Research*
BCHB   *The Blackwell Companion to the Hebrew Bible.* Edited by Leo
                 G. Perdue. Blackwell Companions to Religion 3. Malden,
                 Mass.: Blackwell, 2001
BDAG   Bauer, W., F. W. Danker, W. F. Arndt, and F. W. Gingrich.
                 Greek-English Lexicon of the New Testament and Other Early
                 Christian Literature. 3d ed. Chicago: University of Chicago
                 Press, 1999
BDB   Brown, F., S. R. Driver, and C. A. Briggs. *A Hebrew and English*
                 Lexicon of the Old Testament. Oxford: Clarendon, 1907
BEATAJ   Beiträge zur Erforschung des Alten Testaments und des
                 antiken Judentums
BHS   *Biblia Hebraica Stuttgartensia.* Edited by K. Elliger and W.
                 Rudolph. Stuttgart: Deutsche Bibelstiftung, 1983
Bib   *Biblica*
BiBh   *Bible Bhashyam*

BibInt	*Biblical Interpretation*
BIS	Biblical Interpretation Series
BJS	Brown Judaic Studies
BK	*Bibel und Kirche*
BKAT	Biblischer Kommentar, Altes Testament. Edited by M. Noth and H. W. Wolff
BLS	Bible and Literature Series
BN	*Biblische Notizen*
BR	*Biblical Research*
BRev	*Bible Review*
BS	Biblical Seminar
BSac	*Bibliotheca sacra*
BSC	Bible Student's Commentary
BSNA	Biblical Scholarship in North America
BT	*Bible Translator*
BTB	*Biblical Theology Bulletin*
BV	*Biblical Viewpoint*
BZAW	Beihefte zur Zeitschrift für die alttestamentliche Wissenschaft
CAD	*The Assyrian Dictionary of the Oriental Institute of the University of Chicago.* Chicago: Oriental Institute, 1956–
CBC	Cambridge Bible Commentary
CBET	Contributions to Biblical Exegesis and Theology
CBQ	*Catholic Biblical Quarterly*
CBRFJ	*Christian Brethren Research Fellowship Journal*
CBS	University Museum, University of Pennsylvania, Philadelphia. Catalog of the Babylonian [now Near Eastern] Section
CHANE	Culture and History of the Ancient Near East
ChT	*Christianity Today*
CML	*Canaanite Myths and Legends.* Edited by G. R. Driver. Edinburgh: T&T Clark, 1956. Edited by J. C. L. Gibson, 1978[2]
COS	*The Context of Scripture.* Edited by W. W. Hallo. 3 vols. Leiden: E. J. Brill, 1997–2002
CovQ	*Covenant Quarterly*
CRBR	*Critical Review of Books in Religion*
CSR	*Christian Scholar's Review*
CTA	*Corpus des tablettes en cunéiformes alphabétiques découvertes à Ras Shamra-Ugarit de 1929 à 1939.* Edited by A. Herdner. 2 vols. Mission de Ras Shamra 10. Paris: Imprimerie Nationale, 1963
CTJ	*Calvin Theological Journal*
CTR	*Criswell Theological Review*
CurTM	*Currents in Theology and Mission*
CWS	Classics of Western Spirituality
DB	*Dictionnaire de la Bible.* Edited by Fulcran Vigouroux. 5 vols. Paris: Letouzey & Ané, 1895–1912

DBI	*Dictionary of Biblical Imagery.* Edited by Leland Ryken, James C. Wilhoit, and Tremper Longman III. Downers Grove, Ill.: InterVarsity, 1998
DCH	*Dictionary of Classical Hebrew.* Edited by D. J. A. Clines. Sheffield, Eng.: Academic Press, 1993–
DOTP	*Dictionary of the Old Testament: Pentateuch.* Edited by T. Desmond Alexander and David W. Baker. Downers Grove, Ill.: InterVarsity, 2003
EBC	*The Expositor's Bible Commentary.* Edited by Frank E. Gaebelein. 12 vols. Grand Rapids: Zondervan, 1976–1992
EgT	*Église et théologie*
Enc	*Encounter*
ERT	*Evangelical Review of Theology*
EvQ	*Evangelical Quarterly*
ExAud	*Ex auditu*
ExpTim	*Expository Times*
FC	Fathers of the Church.
FCB	Feminist Companion to the Bible
FCB²	Feminist Companion to the Bible: Second Series
FCNTECW	Feminist Companion to the New Testament and Early Christian Writings
FemT	*Feminist Theology*
FF	*Forschungen und Fortschritte*
FOTL	Forms of the Old Testament Literature
GHCLOT	*Gesenius' Hebrew and Chaldee Lexicon to the Old Testament Scriptures.* Translated by Samuel P. Tregelles. 1857. Repr., Grand Rapids: Eerdmans, 1949
GKC	*Gesenius' Hebrew Grammar.* Edited by E. Kautzsch. Translated by A. E. Cowley. 2d ed. Oxford: Clarendon, 1910
GTJ	*Grace Theological Journal*
HALOT	Koehler, L., W. Baumgartner, and J. J. Stamm, *The Hebrew and Aramaic Lexicon of the Old Testament.* Translated and edited under the supervision of M. E. J. Richardson. 5 vols. Leiden: E. J. Brill, 1994–2001
HAR	*Hebrew Annual Review*
HBT	*Horizons in Biblical Theology*
Hen	*Henoch*
HKAT	Handkommentar zum Alten Testament
HR	*History of Religions*
HS	*Hebrew Studies*
HTR	*Harvard Theological Review*
HTS	*Hervormde teologiese studies*
HUCA	*Hebrew Union College Annual*
IB	*Interpreter's Bible.* Edited by G. A. Buttrick et al. 12 vols. New York, 1951–1957

IBC	Interpretation: A Bible Commentary for Teaching and Preaching
IBHS	*An Introduction to Biblical Hebrew Syntax.* Bruce K. Waltke and Michael P. O'Connor. Winona Lake, Ind.: Eisenbrauns, 1990
IBS	*Irish Biblical Studies*
ICC	International Critical Commentary
IDB	*The Interpreter's Dictionary of the Bible.* Edited by G. A. Buttrick. 4 vols. Nashville: Abingdon, 1962
IDBSup	*Interpreter's Dictionary of the Bible: Supplementary Volume.* Edited by K. Crim. Nashville: Abingdon, 1976
Int	*Interpretation*
ISBE	*International Standard Bible Encyclopedia.* Edited by G. W. Bromiley. 4 vols. Grand Rapids: Eerdmans, 1979–1988
ITC	International Theological Commentary
JAAR	*Journal of the American Academy of Religion*
JAOS	*Journal of the American Oriental Society*
JATS	*Journal of the Adventist Theological Society*
JBL	*Journal of Biblical Literature*
JBMW	*Journal for Biblical Manhood and Womanhood*
JBQ	*Jewish Bible Quarterly*
JBT	*Jahrbüch für Biblische Theologie*
JCS	*Journal of Cuneiform Studies*
JEA	*Journal of Egyptian Archaeology*
Jeev	*Jeevadhara*
JEOL	*Jaarbericht van het Vooraziatisch-Egyptisch Gezelschap (Genootschap) Ex oriente lux*
JES	*Journal of Ecumenical Studies*
JETS	*Journal of the Evangelical Theological Society*
JFSR	*Journal of Feminist Studies in Religion*
JHSex	*Journal of the History of Sexuality*
JJS	*Journal of Jewish Studies*
JLA	*Jewish Law Annual*
JNES	*Journal of Near Eastern Studies*
JNSL	*Journal of Northwest Semitic Languages*
Joüon	Joüon, P. *A Grammar of Biblical Hebrew.* Translated and revised by T. Muraoka. 2 vols. Subsidia biblica 14/1–2. Rome: Pontifical Biblical Institute, 1991
JPSTC	JPS Torah Commentary
JS	*Journal for Semitics*
JSJ	*Journal for the Study of Judaism in the Persian, Hellenistic, and Roman Periods*
JSJSup	Supplements to the Journal for the Study of Judaism
JSNTSup	Journal for the Study of the New Testament: Supplement Series

JSOT	*Journal for the Study of the Old Testament*
JSOTSup	Journal for the Study of the Old Testament: Supplement Series
JSS	*Journal of Semitic Studies*
JSSEA	*The Journal of the Society for the Study of Egyptian Antiquites*
JTS	*Journal of Theological Studies*
JTT	*Journal of Translation and Textlinguistics*
KAT	Kommentar zum Alten Testament
KBL	Koehler, L., and W. Baumgartner, *Lexicon in Veteris Testamenti libros.* 2d ed. Leiden: E. J. Brill, 1958
K&D	Keil, C. F., and F. Delitzsch, *Biblical Commentary on the Old Testament.* Translated by J. Martin et al. 25 vols. Edinburgh, 1857–1878. Reprint, 10 vols., Peabody, Mass.: Hendrickson, 1996
KTU	*Die keilalphabetischen Texte aus Ugarit.* Edited by M. Dietrich, O. Loretz, and J. Sanmartín. AOAT 24/1. Neukirchen-Vluyn: Neukirchener Verlag, 1976. 2d enlarged ed. of *KTU: The Cuneiform Alphabetic Texts from Ugarit, Ras Ibn Hani, and Other Places.* Edited by M. Dietrich, O. Loretz, and J. Sanmartín. Münster: Ugarit, 1995 (= *CTU*)
Laur	*Laurentianum*
LB	*Linguistica biblica*
LBS	Library of Biblical Studies
LCL	Loeb Classical Library
LKA	*Literarische Keilschrifttexten aus Assur.* E. Ebeling. Berlin: Akademie, 1953
LS	*Louvain Studies*
LT	*Literature and Theology*
LTJ	*Lutheran Theological Journal*
LTQ	*Lexington Theological Quarterly*
Mils	*Milltown Studies*
MQR	*Mennonite Quarterly Review*
NAC	New American Commentary
NCB	New Century Bible
NEA	*Near Eastern Archaeology*
NIBCOT	New International Biblical Commentary on the Old Testament
NICOT	New International Commentary on the Old Testament
NIDNTT	*New International Dictionary of New Testament Theology.* Edited by C. Brown. 4 vols. Grand Rapids: Zondervan, 1975–1985
NIDOTTE	*New International Dictionary of Old Testament Theology and Exegesis.* Edited by W. A. VanGemeren. 5 vols. Grand Rapids: Zondervan, 1997
NIVAC	NIV Application Commentary

NSBT	New Studies in Biblical Theology
NTS	*New Testament Studies*
OBO	Orbis biblicus et orientalis
OBT	Overtures to Biblical Theology
OPBIAA	Occasional Publications of the British Institute of Archaeology at Ankara
OrAnt	*Oriens antiquus*
OSHT	Oxford Studies in Historical Theology
OTA	*Old Testament Abstracts*
OTE	*Old Testament Essays*
OTL	Old Testament Library
OtSt	Oudtestamentische Studiën
Parab	*Parabola*
PD	*Perspective Digest*
PEGLMBS	*Proceedings, Eastern Great Lakes and Midwest Biblical Society*
PEQ	*Palestine Exploration Quarterly*
Presb	*Presbyterion*
Proof	*Prooftexts: A Journal of Jewish Literary History*
PRSt	*Perspectives in Religious Studies*
PTMS	Pittsburgh Theological Monograph Series
PzB	*Protokolle zur Bibel*
RB	*Revue biblique*
ResQ	*Restoration Quarterly*
RevExp	*Review and Expositor*
RevQ	*Revue de Qumran*
RIDA	*Revue internationale des droits de l'antiquité*
RLA	*Reallexikon der Assyriologie.* Edited by Erich Ebeling et al. Berlin: de Gruyter, 1928–
RTR	*Reformed Theological Review*
SAC	Studies in Antiquity and Christianity
SANE	Sources from the Ancient Near East
SBJT	*Southern Baptist Journal of Theology*
SBLDS	Society of Biblical Literature Dissertation Series
SBLMS	Society of Biblical Literature Monograph Series
SBLSP	Society of Biblical Literature Seminar Papers
SBLSymS	Society of Biblical Literature Symposium Series
SBLWAW	Society of Biblical Literature Writings from the Ancient World
SBT	Studies in Biblical Theology
SCB	Storyteller's Companion to the Bible
ScrHier	Scripta hierosolymitana
Scrip	*Scriptura*
SEÅ	*Svensk exegetisk årsbok*
SemeiaSt	Semeia Studies
SHR	Studies in the History of Religions (supplement to *Numen*)
SJOT	*Scandinavian Journal of the Old Testament*

SJT	*Scottish Journal of Theology*
SMRT	Studies in Medieval and Reformation Thought
SNTSMS	Society for New Testament Studies Monograph Series
SR	*Studies in Religion*
StBL	Studies in Biblical Literature
STJ	*Stulos Theological Journal*
StPB	Studia post-biblica
T & S	*Theology and Sexuality*
TBT	*The Bible Today*
TDNT	*Theological Dictionary of the New Testament.* Edited by G. Kittel and G. Friedrich. Translated by G. W. Bromiley. 10 vols. Grand Rapids: Eerdmans, 1964–1976
TDOT	*Theological Dictionary of the Old Testament.* Edited by G. J. Botterweck and H. Ringgren. Translated by J. T. Willis, G. W. Bromiley, and D. E. Green. Grand Rapids: Eerdmans, 1974–
Them	*Themelios*
ThTo	*Theology Today*
TJ	*Trinity Journal*
TLOT	*Theological Lexicon of the Old Testament.* Edited by E. Jenni, with assistance from C. Westermann. Translated by M. E. Biddle. 3 vols. Peabody, Mass.: Hendrickson, 1997
TOTC	Tyndale Old Testament Commentaries
TS	*Theological Studies*
TWOT	*Theological Wordbook of the Old Testament.* Edited by R. L. Harris and G. L. Archer Jr. 2 vols. Chicago: Moody, 1980
TynBul	*Tyndale Bulletin*
UF	*Ugarit-Forschungen*
USQR	*Union Seminary Quarterly Review*
UT	*Ugaritic Textbook.* C. H. Gordon. AnOr 38. Rome, 1965
Vid	*Vidyajyoti*
VT	*Vetus Testamentum*
VTSup	Vetus Testamentum Supplements
WBC	Word Biblical Commentary
WBC	*The Women's Bible Commentary.* Edited by Carol A. Newsom and Sharon H. Ringe. Louisville: Westminster John Knox, 1992
WBE	*The Wycliffe Bible Encyclopedia.* Edited by Charles F. Pfeiffer, Howard F. Vos, and John Rea. 2 vols. Chicago: Moody, 1975
WEC	Wycliffe Exegetical Commentary
WMANT	Wissenschaftliche Monographien zum Alten und Neuen Testament
WO	*Die Welt des Orients*
WS	*Women in Scripture: A Dictionary of Named and Unnamed Women in the Hebrew Bible, the Apocryphal/Deuterocanonical*

	Books, and the New Testament. Edited by Carol Meyers, Toni Craven, and Ross S. Kraemer. Boston: Houghton Mifflin, 2000
WTJ	*Westminster Theological Journal*
WUNT[2]	Wissenschaftliche Untersuchungen zum Neuen Testament: 2. Reihe
WW	*Word and World*
ZA	*Zeitschrift für Assyriologie*
ZAW	*Zeitschrift für die alttestamentliche Wissenschaft*
ZPEB	*Zondervan Pictorial Encyclopedia of the Bible*

Introduction

Sexuality is writ large in the pages of the OT, yet when I first began researching this subject a quarter century ago, it had scarcely entered the footnotes in the literature of OT scholarship. Only in the last few decades—particularly in the wake of the modern feminist movement, the new literary criticism, and the sexual research of social scientists—has there begun a concerted effort to lay down the biblical foundations for understanding human sexuality. At present, despite an abundance of OT research on certain aspects of sexuality (notably the role of women and the feminine dimension of divinity), only scant attention has been given to a wholistic[1] theology of sexuality in the OT.[2]

---

[1] Throughout this study I use the term "wholistic" instead of the more commonly used "holistic" to avoid popular associations of the latter term with New Age holism and also to emphasize a biblical view of "wholism" that in my view is broader than that normally denoted by the term "holism."

[2] Only three monographs deal directly with this subject in any depth and breadth: Phyllis Trible, *God and the Rhetoric of Sexuality* (OBT; Philadelphia: Fortress, 1978); Samuel Terrien, *Till the Heart Sings: A Biblical Theology of Manhood and Womanhood* (Philadelphia: Fortress, 1985); and David M. Carr, *The Erotic Word: Sexuality, Spirituality, and the Bible* (New York: Oxford University Press, 2003). None of these works attempts a comprehensive theology of sexuality in the OT. Some books on sexual ethics present a theology of human sexuality in a very cursory manner, with little or no detailed analysis of relevant biblical passages. See, e.g., Sakae Kubo, *Theology and Ethics of Sex* (Washington, D.C.: Review and Herald, 1980); and Daniel R. Heimbach, *True Sexual Morality: Recovering Biblical Standards for a Culture in Crisis* (Wheaton, Ill.: Crossway, 2004). Some books cover major terminology and phenomena related to sexuality in the HB, but attempt no theology; see, e.g., Athalya Brenner, *The Intercourse of Knowledge: On Gendering Desire and "Sexuality" in the Hebrew Bible* (BIS 26; Leiden: E. J. Brill, 1997). Many books provide a popularized, cursory survey of sex in the Bible. See, e.g., William G. Cole, *Sex and Love in the Bible* (New York: Association, 1959); Michael R. Cosby, *Sex in the Bible: An Introduction to What the Scriptures Teach Us About Sexuality* (Englewood Cliffs, N.J.: Prentice Hall, 1984); Ronald L. Ecker, *And Adam Knew Eve: A Dictionary of Sex in the Bible* (Palatka, Fla.: Hodge & Braddock, 1995); J. Harold Ellens, *Sex in the Bible: A New Consideration* (Psychology, Religion, and Spirituality; Westport, Conn.: Praeger, 2006); Thomas M. Horner, *Sex in the Bible* (Rutland, Vt.: C. E. Tuttle, 1974); Gerald A. Larue, *Sex and the Bible* (Buffalo, N.Y.: Prometheus, 1983); F. L. Perry, *Sex and the Bible* (Atlanta: John Knox, 1982); Otto A. Piper, *The Biblical View of Sex and Marriage* (New York: Charles Scribner's Sons, 1960); and Stephen Sapp, *Sexuality, the Bible, and Science* (Philadelphia: Fortress, 1977).

In the HB there is no general term for "sexuality" that can supply terminological parameters for investigation of the topic. In this study the term "human sexuality" (or "sexuality") is used to encompass both the concepts of human gender differentiation (male and female as a duality and their interrelationships) and sexual endowment (with its various biological, psychological, and social dimensions).[3]

The Purpose of the Work

This study undertakes the Brobdingnagian task of examining every passage in the HB dealing with human sexuality, in an attempt to lay bare the basic contours of a theology of human sexuality in the final (canonical) form of the OT, building on previous research and engaging in original exegesis where necessary. Studies dealing with specific aspects of sexuality in the OT—particularly from a feminist perspective—have become legion in the last twenty-five years, numbering literally in the thousands, but since the turn of the millennium appear to have reached a plateau. The time is ripe for a review and synthesis of this vast corpus of literature.

This study specifically analyzes the theology of the final canonical form of the OT.[4] It utilizes insights from such widely accepted synchronic methodologies

---

[3] See James B. Nelson, *Embodiment: An Approach to Sexuality and Christian Theology* (Minneapolis: Augsburg, 1978), 17–18; and Lisa Sowle Cahill, *Between the Sexes: Foundations for a Christian Ethics of Sexuality* (Philadelphia: Fortress, 1985), passim. Among those who study the social roles of men and women, it is common to distinguish between "sex" (which refers to "the biological differences between males and females, especially in their roles of procreation") and "gender" (which denotes "the culturally specific patterns that are imposed upon these biological differences"). Sex is considered a "natural and hence a universal category" whereas gender is "a socially constructed category that, although not reducible to or directly derived from the biological facts, has some connection to these sex differences" (Ronald A. Simkins, "Gender Construction in the Yahwist Creation Myth," in *Genesis* [ed. Athalya Brenner; FCB[2] 1; Sheffield, Eng.: Sheffield Academic Press, 1998], 35). Cf. John S. Grabowski, *Sex and Virtue: An Introduction to Sexual Ethics* (Catholic Moral Thought; Washington, D.C.: Catholic University of America Press, 2003), 96–97, who points to the common differentiation between "sex" (which denotes "our physicality, our embodiment as male and female"), "gender" (which, mainly in the wake of feminist arguments, "has come to be understood in terms of the way in which education and environment condition us to understand the biological givens of sex"), and "sexuality" (which "refers to how individuals relate to others as men and women because of the dynamic interplay between nature and nurture within their personalities"). In this study I treat all of these aspects wholistically as they emerge from the text of the OT. For a defense of the appropriateness of using the term "sexuality" with reference to ancient Israel (contra those who consider sexuality to be only a modern historical construct), see Hilary B. Lipka, "'Such a Thing is Not Done in Israel': The Construction of Sexual Transgression in the Hebrew Bible" (PhD diss., Brandeis University, 2004), 13 (with bibliography).

[4] For discussion and justification of this approach, with a review of recent proponents, see esp. the article by Johnson T. K. Lim, "Towards a Final Form Approach to Biblical Interpretation," *STJ* 7, nos. 1–2 (1999): 1–11.

as the new literary criticism[5] and the new biblical theology,[6] which focus upon the final form of the OT text. It will not inquire about the possible precanonical history of the text but seek to understand the overriding theological thrust of Scripture wholistically as it now presents itself in the biblical canon. This canonical, close-reading approach does not ignore, however, the unique settings and theological emphases of different sections of the canonical OT. By focusing upon the final form of the OT text, I believe it is possible that the interests of both liberal-critical and evangelical OT scholarship may merge in seeking to understand what constitutes the canonical theological message of the OT regarding human sexuality. Although I have profited enormously from feminist scholarship, this study does not employ the feminist hermeneutic of suspicion and resistance but rather the hermeneutic of consent. In other words, I read not *against* but *with* the grain of the text in its final form.[7]

One of the central premises of this book is that the Edenic pattern for sexuality constitutes the foundation for the rest of the OT perspective on this topic. A radical, even "tectonic," paradigm shift in modern critical scholarship in the last few decades now sees creation, and not just salvation history, as foundational to the rest of the OT canon.[8] It is now widely recognized that in the theological ground plan of the final editor(s) of the OT canon, Gen 1–3 has been situated as the introduction to the canon, and the whole rest of the canon regularly harks back to and builds upon this Edenic pattern. An emerging consensus on this point is apparent within evangelical OT scholarship,[9] as well as within more

---

[5] As pioneered by Robert Alter, *The Art of Biblical Narrative* (New York: Basic, 1981), and developed by numerous recent scholars.

[6] As "fathered" and popularized by Brevard S. Childs, *Biblical Theology in Crisis* (Philadelphia: Fortress, 1970); idem, *Biblical Theology of the Old and New Testaments* (Minneapolis: Fortress, 1992).

[7] See Robin Parry, "Feminist Hermeneutics and Evangelical Concerns: The Rape of Dinah as a Case Study." *TynBul* 53 (2002): 1–28, for a helpful elaboration of these two different approaches as viewed from an evangelical Christian perspective.

[8] This is evidenced, e.g., by William P. Brown and S. Dean McBride Jr., eds., *God Who Creates: Essays in Honor of W. Sibley Towner* (Grand Rapids: Eerdmans: 2000), whose contributors document the "tectonic shift . . . nothing short of a paradigm shift from a once-exclusive stress upon the mighty interventions of God in history to God's formative and sustaining ways in creation" (editors' preface, xi.). The first chapter of that monograph, by S. Dean McBride Jr., is entitled "Divine Protocol: Genesis 1:1–2:3 as Prologue to the Pentateuch." Succeeding essays show how creation theology is foundational to other parts of the HB. See also Jesus M. Arambarri, "Gen 1,1–2,4a: Ein Prolog und ein Programm für Israel," in *Gottes Wege suchend—Beiträge zum Verständnis der Bibel und Ihrer Botschaft: Festschrift für Rudolf Mosis zum 70. Geburtstag* (ed. Franz Sedlmeier; Würzburg: Echter, 2003), 65–86.

[9] Among evangelicals, see, e.g., Dan B. Allender and Tremper Longman, III, *Intimate Allies: Rediscovering God's Design for Marriage and Becoming Soul Mates for Life* (Wheaton, Ill.: Tyndale, 1995), 13–14: "The first three chapters of Genesis provide the picture [of God's plan for sexuality and marriage]. . . . They offer not only a perspective on the problem but all the cure. If I want to know God's design for my marriage, I must begin at the ground floor of the Bible to understand the foundational perspectives that guide my passage through life. . . . Genesis 1–3 establishes crucial principles that are to shape our

liberal scholarship.[10] Phyllis Bird articulates the widespread scholarly position:
"Canonically, the understanding of human nature expressed or implied in the
laws, wisdom literature, narratives, prophetic texts, and other genres of the Hebrew Scriptures may be viewed as commentary on the creation texts. . . . The
Bible's first statement concerning humankind remains the normative statement
that governs all others."[11] John Rankin summarizes, "Whether one is evangelical
or liberal, it is clear that Gen 1–3 is the interpretive foundation of all Scripture."[12]

Within the foundational, normative texts of Gen 1–3, the subject of human
sexuality occupies a surprisingly extensive coverage. "While the topic of sexuality
represents an exceedingly narrow focus within the universe-encompassing question of creation, it is given disproportionate attention in the primary Old Testament texts. By reason of this placement and prominence, the biblical interpreter
is directed to consider the meaning and end of human sexuality in the context of

---

marriages. This story tells us all we ultimately need to know about marriage." Cf. Lilian
Calles Barger, *Eve's Revenge: Women and a Spirituality of the Body* (Grand Rapids: Brazos,
2003), 128: "Its [the book of Genesis's] first three chapters hold the key to understanding
the entirety of the Bible." Evangelical scholars would claim that this biblical phenomenon
exists because of the inspiration of Scripture, the providential placement of Gen 1–3 at
the beginning of the canon, and later individual authors' consistent understanding of the
previous Edenic pattern. Walter Kaiser terms this the "epigenetic" principle, in which
"there was a growth of the record of events, meanings, and teachings as time went on
around a fixed core that contributed life to the whole emerging mass" (Walter C. Kaiser
Jr., *Toward an Old Testament Theology* [Grand Rapids: Zondervan, 1978], 8; cf. 14, 22, 34).
This is my own personal theological/confessional orientation (see Richard M. Davidson,
"Cosmic Metanarrative for the Coming Millennium," *JATS* 11, nos. 1–2 [2000]: 103–4).
My research for this topic was undertaken from a *sola* and *tota Scriptura* perspective that
accepts the historicity, unity, and ongoing authority of the Bible, including both OT and
NT (see idem, "Interpreting Scripture: An Hermeneutical 'Decalogue,'" *JATS* 4, no. 2
[1993]: 95–114). At the same time, this study incorporates insights from, and dialogues
with, the entire theological and methodological spectrum of OT scholarship, offering
analyses and synthesis that, it is hoped, will be of value to all who are interested in a final-
form theology of sexuality in the HB.

[10] Beyond the scholars cited below, see, e.g., Arambarri, "Gen 1,1–2,4a," 65–86; and
S. Dean McBride Jr., "Divine Protocol: Genesis 1:1–2:3 as Prologue to the Pentateuch,"
in *God Who Creates: Essays in Honor of W. Sibley Towner* (ed. William P. Brown and
S. Dean McBride Jr.; Grand Rapids: Eerdmans: 2000), 3–41. Many liberal-critical scholars
would maintain that an overarching general consistency of biblical material has come
about through the editorial shaping and redacting by the final canonical "Master Editor
or Redactor." See, e.g., David Noel Freedman, in David Noel Freedman with Jeffrey C.
Geoghegan and Michael M. Homan, *The Nine Commandments: Uncovering a Hidden Pattern of Crime and Punishment in the Hebrew Bible* (ed. Astrid Billes Beck; New York:
Doubleday, 2000), 168–80 and passim, who sees this "Master Weaver/Editor" responsible
for the "Primary History" of Genesis through Kings, and its "scarlet thread of commandment violations" (p. 180) in which each of the nine books of this Primary History illustrate respectively the violation of the first nine commandments of the Decalogue.

[11] Phyllis A. Bird, "'Bone of My Bone and Flesh of My Flesh,'" *ThTo* 50 (1994):
525, 527.

[12] John Rankin, "Power and Gender at the Divinity School," in *Finding God at Harvard: Spiritual Journeys of Thinking Christians* (ed. Kelly Monroe; Grand Rapids: Zondervan, 1996), 203.

theological reflection on creation."[13] Thus the opening chapters of Scripture may be seen as of "seminal character" and "determinative" for the biblical view of sexuality. Here "the pattern is established and adjudged good. From then until the close of the biblical corpus it is the assumed norm."[14]

The main title of this book, *Flame of Yahweh,* is derived from my own translation and exegesis of Song 8:6 (a passage that I will argue is the climactic biblical statement on human sexuality). Because of my desire to be sensitive to and respectful of the reticence on the part of some to pronounce the Tetragrammaton, I contemplated using other references to the deity in the book title, such as "Yah" (the most literal translation of Song 8:6), "YHWH" (supplying only the consonants of the divine name), or "the Lord" (utilizing English translation). None of these seemed suitable for various reasons. Finally, in consultation with my editor, I have settled on the originally conceived title, *Flame of Yahweh,* because (at least in the Christian tradition) "Yahweh" is probably the most common scholarly way to represent in writing the Hebrew divine covenant name and the title *Flame of Yahweh* seems to most effectively link the contents of the book with the powerful and sublime imagery of the book title's source, the Song of Songs. But I invite readers whose personal convictions or religious tradition avoids pronouncing this name to substitute "Adonai," "Ha-Shem," "YHWH," or some other appropriate circumlocution as they read the title and other references to Israel's God throughout the book.

I have consciously employed the subtitle "Sexuality in the *Old Testament*." I use the term "Old Testament" from my particular confessional stance as a Christian in which the theology of the HB is seen as part of a biblical theology of sexuality that encompasses both Testaments. Granted, the bulk of the present work is focused upon examining the contents of the HB, which I trust will be of value to readers of various theological traditions beyond Christianity. I will occasionally suggest, however, some specific applications of the exegesis to the Christian (and specifically evangelical) community and to issues in contemporary Christian sexual ethics, and an afterword will explore implications of the study for a theology of human sexuality in the NT.

I acknowledge that the OT understanding of human sexuality is a topic hotly debated in pastoral and theological circles—hardly a merely academic topic—and that different theological persuasions digest the exegetical results in different ways, based upon church tradition and councils, science and reason, and so on. I do not claim to have the final or exclusive word on sexual theology in the OT. Hence this work constitutes *a* (not *the*) theology of sexuality in the OT.

At the same time, I set forth a *theology* (not *theologies*) of sexuality in the Old Testament. Although various OT witnesses present different emphases and unique insights, nevertheless I have found that the final canonical form of the HB

---

[13] Phyllis A. Bird, *Missing Persons and Mistaken Identities: Women and Gender in Ancient Israel* (OBT; Minneapolis: Fortress, 1997), 156.

[14] Dennis F. Kinlaw, "A Biblical View of Homosexuality," in *The Secrets of Our Sexuality: Role Liberation for the Christian* (ed. Gary R. Collins; Waco, Tex.: Word, 1976), 105.

presents a unified, consistent, overarching theological portrait of human sexuality.[15] This theology is allowed to emerge from exegetical analysis of relevant passages; thus it is an "exegetical theology,"[16] building upon the exegetical work of others where I have found adequate treatment of the material and providing my own analysis where no satisfactory one has been undertaken.

The Plan and Scope of the Work

In order to provide the full impact of this unified perspective of the OT canon and yet allow for the canonical development of sexual theology, this study is organized both topically and diacanonically (i.e., through the canon).[17] Within the structure of each basic facet of sexual theology that emerges from the foundational chapters of Gen 1–3, it moves systematically through the three divisions of the HB (Pentateuch, Prophets, Writings).

The first major section of this study concentrates on the divine Edenic design for human sexuality as set forth in Gen 1–3. Some ten basic facets of sexual theology emerge inductively from the material in these opening pages of Scripture. As noted above and substantiated throughout this book, the foundational insights set the Edenic pattern for the rest of the OT materials in their final canonical form.

The second major section examines the OT canonical development of the theology of human sexuality "outside the garden," including the further illumina-

---

[15] This conclusion is consistent with the evangelical understanding of *sola Scriptura* and *tota Scriptura* and also with the critical understanding of a master editor or redactor for the entire OT canon. It is contrary, however, to many modern and (especially) postmodern studies of the subject. See, e.g., Carr, *The Erotic Word,* passim, who argues that "the Bible has *multiple* pictures of sexual eros" (p. 87) radically diverging from one another and that today one must selectively move beyond the "childlike existence of rules and regulations" (55), beyond the laws of Torah, which affirm men as "sexual owners and aggressors" (52), and beyond the Prophets, where God is "an abusive male" (87), to the garden scenes of Gen 1–2 and the Song of Songs, where one finds "a picture of love not so dominated by violence, in which God can be male or female, an evocative drama of love that we might wish to enter" (87). So also David Biale, *Eros and the Jews: From Biblical Israel to Contemporary America* (New York: Basic, 1992), 11. I acknowledge that there were divergent attitudes toward sexuality in the culture of ancient Israel. For an attempt to lay bare the "construction of sexuality" within the society of biblical Israel, see, e.g., Lipka, "'Such a Thing Is Not Done in Israel,'" passim. My attempt, by contrast, is not to lay bare the varying attitudes toward sexuality among individuals and groups at different places and times within ancient Israelite society but to set forth the theology of sexuality presented by the final form of the HB, which I have found to be essentially unified and consistent, albeit with different emphases in the various relevant passages.

[16] See Walter C. Kaiser Jr., *Toward an Exegetical Theology: Biblical Exegesis for Preaching and Teaching* (Grand Rapids: Baker, 1981), passim, for a model of exegetical theology that is most useful.

[17] In this approach I am applying (at least part of) the multiplex theological methodology of my Doktorvater, the late Gerhard F. Hasel (see his *Old Testament Theology: Basic Issues in the Current Debate* [rev. and expanded 4th ed.; Grand Rapids: Eerdmans, 1991], 194–208). Hasel favored the term "Old Testament biblical theology" for this approach.

tion of both God's Edenic ideal and humanity's distortion of God's design. The major focus of attention in this section is the pentateuchal narratives and legal material, where I have found virtually all the issues in a theology of sexuality directly and decisively addressed. Elucidation of these constituent elements of sexual theology are further traced as they reemerge and are more fully developed throughout the Prophets and Writings (except the Song of Songs).[18]

The third major section constitutes a "return to Eden," with a theological journey through the Song of Songs, the one book in the HB that is entirely devoted to extolling the beauty and virtue of sexual love. In my estimation, the Song of Songs represents the canonical "holy of holies" in human sexuality, providing a full-orbed theology of sexuality with profound implications for contemporary sexual issues.

An afterword explores the implications of the OT findings for a theology of sexuality in the NT, although a comprehensive NT theology of sexuality is obviously beyond the scope of this work. Furthermore, although this is, for the most part, a biblical theology of sexuality in the OT, not a contemporary handbook of Christian sexual ethics, I do not completely refrain from indicating the relevance of an OT theology of sexuality for current sexual and sex-related issues in the church (and my evangelical tradition in particular) occasionally in the main chapters and particularly in the afterword. I am convinced that the theology of sexuality found in the OT is surprisingly up to date and comprehensive in regard to sexual concerns at the beginning of the third Christian millennium.

Overview of Old Testament Sexual Vocabulary

Before turning to the major sections of this study, we first survey the sexual vocabulary employed in the OT as a whole.[19] As already noted, no single word

---

[18] What scholars have labeled as dissonance and patterns of sexual subversiveness within this material (see, e.g., Biale, *Eros and the Jews,* 11–32) I find largely to be pointers back to the original divine program for sexuality set forth in Gen 1–3.

[19] I am aware of the limitations regarding word studies for biblical theology, as cogently pointed out by James Barr, *The Semantics of Biblical Language* (London: Oxford University Press, 1961), and others, but when conducted cautiously, avoiding the fallacies that Barr exposes, and paying attention to the immediate context of each occurrence of words, word studies can contribute to the overall theology of sexuality in the OT. The lexical work throughout this study represents my own word studies in consultation with the standard lexicons, word books, and Bible dictionaries (such as *ABD,* BDB, *DCH, HALOT, IDB,* KBL, *NIDOTTE, TDNT, TDOT, TLOT,* and *TWOT*) as well as various specialized studies on specific words. Only the specialized studies are normally cited in the footnotes unless a specific quotation from the standard works is cited. All biblical references are to the Hebrew (MT) versification, with English translation (ET) verse numbers in brackets where different from the Hebrew. English citations of Scripture are taken from the NRSV, unless otherwise noted, inasmuch as this translation is particularly sensitive to gender inclusive language, and is so widely recognized within Protestant, Roman Catholic, Orthodox, and Jewish traditions. In quotations of OT poetry, space is frequently saved by not placing the poetry in block format.

exists for the general concept of sex or sexuality despite the numerous manifestations of sexual behavior and relationships in the Hebrew Scriptures. Furthermore, there is practically no sexual terminology proper in the OT. Reference to
sexual organs and activities is almost invariably couched in euphemistic terms.
This is due partly to the limitations of the classical Hebrew language: the modern
range of scientific anatomical vocabulary did not exist. The language limitation
in turn reflects the Hebrew wholistic view of humanity: individual organs often
also refer metaphorically to various attitudinal manifestations of the total self,
and therefore both male and female genitalia are "frequently described in terms
of their relation to the entire body."[20]

Circumlocutions are also employed because of the sense of impropriety and
shame involved in public exposure of the sexual organs. Euphemisms "conceal in
language what must not be exposed in fact—the male and female organs of sexual intercourse and reproduction."[21] The sense of reserve in the euphemistic
mention of sexual organs and acts is often accompanied, however, by a surprisingly frank and free discussion of sexuality and therefore does not support the
contention that the biblical materials reflect a negative view of sexuality itself.[22]

Note first the terminology for the human sexual organs. There is no specific
term for the male organ of regeneration in the OT, only euphemisms. The penis is
sometimes referred to as "flesh" (*bāśār*), as in Gen 17:11: "You shall circumcise
the flesh of your foreskins."[23] Again the word *yārēk*, "thigh" or "loin," indicates
the general region of the body that constitutes the seat of the procreative power,
and serves occasionally as a circumlocution for the male genitalia, especially
when particular refinement of language is called for.[24] Other terms for the male
sex organs are *šopkâ* (Deut 23:2 [ET 23:1]), literally, "outflow" (with reference to
the "fluid duct" of the penis); *mĕbûšîm* (Deut 25:11), the "genitals," literally, "that
which excites shame" (with reference to a woman seizing the "genitals" of a man
fighting with her husband); and *šēt* (Isa 20:4; pl. 2 Sam 10:4), perhaps a term for
the male genitals in general.[25] Additional euphemisms for the penis/genitals include the term *yād* "hand/forearm" (Isa 57:8, 10); *kap* "hand/socket/concavity"

---

[20] R. K. Harrison, *Leviticus: An Introduction and Commentary* (TOTC 3; Downers
Grove, Ill.: InterVarsity, 1980), 248.

[21] O. J. Baab, "Sex, Sexual Behavior," *IDB* 4:298. For discussion of biblical euphemisms in light of recent cross-cultural sociolinguistic research on euphemism, see John
H. Elliott, "Deuteronomy—Shameful Encroachment on Shameful Parts: Deuteronomy
25:11–12 and Biblical Euphemism," in *Ancient Israel: The Old Testament in Its Social Context* (ed. Philip F. Esler; Minneapolis: Fortress, 2006), 161–76.

[22] Contra C. R. Taber, "Sex, Sexual Behavior," *IDBSup* 818; see esp. his discussion
under the heading "Sex is Bad."

[23] See also Gen 17:14, 23–25; Exod 28:42; Lev 6:10 (ET 6:3); 15:2–18, 19; Ezek 16:26;
23:20; 44:7, 9.

[24] See Gen 24:2, 9; 46:26; 47:29; Exod 1:5; Judg 8:30. In one passage, Num 5:21–29, the
female uterus seems to be intended by this term. Although this term is used especially to
describe the male organ of regeneration as a symbol of procreative power, *yārēk* also appears with reference to the female genitalia in Deut 28:57 and Num 5:21, 22.

[25] Brenner, *The Intercourse of Knowledge*, 36.

(Gen 32:26, 33 [ET 32:25, 32], possibly Deut 25:12); *kĕlî* "vessel" (1 Sam 21:6 [ET 21:5]); and *ʿāqēb* "heel/hindpart" (Jer 13:22; possibly Gen 25:26 and Hos 12:4 [ET 12:3]).[26] The word *zeraʿ*, "seed," is employed several times in the sense of "semen."[27] There is one occurrence of the term *zirmâ* (Ezek 23:20), "emission," which may refer to a "phallus" in the sense of "erect penis" or alternatively to "ejaculation," the "emission (of semen)".[28] The term *šĕkōbet*, "lying," in several Pentateuchal passages also probably also means "penis."[29] A crude reference to a man's penis is perhaps found in Rehoboam's reference to his little finger being thicker than his father's *motnayim*, "loins," which may be a slang expression for "(royal) penis" (1 Kgs 12:10 = 2 Chr 10:14).[30] More generally, the word *ʾôn* denotes a man's "generative power" or "virility" (Gen 49:3; Deut 21:7; Ps 78:51; 105:36), and *ḥălāṣayim*, "loins," describes where a man's descendants come from (Gen 35:11; 1 Kgs 8:19; 2 Chr 6:9).

Two precise anatomical terms for parts of the male genitals appear in the OT. The "testicle" (*ʾešek*) is mentioned once in a list of physical deformities excluding the priest from temple service (Lev 21:20), and the "foreskin" (*ʿorlâ*) is referred to repeatedly in Scripture, since circumcision (*mûl*)—the cutting away of the foreskin—played such a central role in Israel's religious life.[31] In this context may also be mentioned castration, described by the expression *pĕṣûaʿ-dakkāʾ*, literally, "wounded by crushing" (Deut 23:2 [ET 23:1]), which implies, but does not explicitly mention, the testicles.

The genitalia of both male and female are sometimes indicated by the euphemisms *raglayim* "feet/legs,"[32] and probably also by *birkayim* "knees" (Judg 16:19, female; Ezek 7:17, 21:12 [ET 21:7], male). The term "flesh" (*bāśār*) can refer euphemistically to the vagina (Lev 15:19). Two other terms—*nablût*, "shame" (Hos 2:12 [ET 2:10]), and *ʿerwāh*, "nakedness"[33]—are employed as circumlocutions for the female sex organs (in the context of their shameful

---

[26] For discussion of the "heel" euphemism in Scripture, see S. H. Smith, "'Heel' and 'Thigh': The Concept of Sexuality in the Jacob-Esau Narratives," *VT* 40 (1990): 464–73.

[27] Lev 15:16; 22:4; Num 5:13, 28; Jer 31:27.

[28] *HALOT* 282, s.v. זִרְמָה.

[29] See Lev 18:20, 23; 20:15; Num 5:20; and discussion in Jacob Milgrom, *Leviticus 17–22: A New Translation with Introduction and Commentary* (AB 3A; New York: Doubleday, 2000), 1550.

[30] Brenner, *The Intercourse of Knowledge*, 37.

[31] The feminine noun occurs fifteen times in the HB: Gen 17:11, 14, 23, 24, 25; 34:14; Exod 4:25; Lev 12:3; 19:23; Deut 10:16; 1 Sam 18:25, 27; 2 Sam 3:14; Jer 4:4; 9:24 (ET 9:25).

[32] The allusion to male genitalia seems most likely in Judg 3:24, 1 Sam 24:4 (ET 24:3), 2 Kgs 18:27, and Isa 36:12, all in the context of urine elimination; and in Isa 7:20, where the reference to the shaving of the "hair of the feet" could well indicate the pubic hair. This interpretation is possible in Exod 4:24 (Zipporah circumcises Moses' son and touches Moses' "feet" with the foreskin) but is far from certain with regard to Ruth 3:1–4, 7–9. For the use of the word "feet" to refer to female genitalia, see Deut 28:57 (in the context of afterbirth coming out between the "feet") and Ezek 16:25 (in the context of Israel's prostitution, offering her "feet" to passersby).

[33] Lev 18:6–19; 20:17–21, 30; Lam 1:8; Ezek 16:37; 23:10, 29.

exposure), and the latter term can also apply to both sexes.[34] A special word, *niddâ*, "menstruation," is coined to denote a woman's menstrual period;[35] this is also described as the "way [*derek*] of women" (Gen 31:35). Menstruation is described by the verb *zûb* or noun *zôb* (lit. "flow, discharge," Lev 15:19–25), an expression that can also refer to both male and female abnormal discharge (Lev 15:2–15, 25–30; Num 5:2; 2 Sam 3:29). The term *mēʿîm* (lit. "intestines, internal body organs") sometimes refers to the male loins[36] or the female womb,[37] denoting the part of the body through which people come into existence. The single occurrence of *nĕḥōšet* (Ezek 16:36), in light of its Akkadian cognate, probably means "female genital 'distillation' produced by sexual arousal" (in the context of lust).[38] In the Song of Songs, a number of other euphemistic expressions—utilizing metaphor, simile, or paranomasia (play on words)—allude to both the male and the female genitalia.[39]

In contrast to the preponderance of euphemisms noted thus far in the biblical references to sex organs, the OT writers speak with candor (and often delight) of the female womb (*reḥem*)[40] and breast (*šad*)[41] or nipple (*dad*).[42] The profound theological significance of uterine imagery is particularly underscored in the Prophets, and the high regard for the beauty and charm of the female breasts becomes especially apparent in Proverbs and the Song of Songs.

Turning to the OT vocabulary for sexual activity leads back into the realm of euphemisms. Sexual intercourse is expressed by various verbs (or verbal phrases). For sexual intercourse approved by God, the verb used is usually "to know" (*yādaʿ*).[43] For emphasis upon sexual intercourse for purposes of procreation, one often finds the verb "to go in unto" (*bôʾ ʾel*).[44] For illicit sexual relations, the terminology includes such expressions as "to approach" (*qārab* or *nāgaš*),[45] "to lie

---

[34] Lev 20:17. See Milgrom, *Leviticus 17–22*, 1534.

[35] Lev 12:2, 5; 15:19, 20, 24, 25 (three times), 26 (two times), 33; 18:19; Ezek 18:6; 22:10; 36:17.

[36] Gen 15:4; 2 Sam 7:12; 16:11; Isa 39:7; 48:19; 2 Kgs 20:18.

[37] Gen 25:23; Num 5:22; Isa 49:1.

[38] See Moshe Greenberg, *Ezekiel 1–20: A New Translation with Introduction and Commentary* (AB 22; Garden City, N.Y.: Doubleday, 1983), 285.

[39] These will be discussed in chs. 13 and 14.

[40] This masculine noun appears thirty-one times in the HB.

[41] This masculine noun appears twenty-one times in the HB, most often in the Song of Songs (eight times).

[42] This masculine noun appears in Prov 5:19 and Ezek 23:3, 8, 21.

[43] The verb can have reference to the man as subject (e.g., Gen 4:1, 17, 25; 24:16; 38:26; Judg 19:25), woman as subject (e.g., Gen 19:18; Num 31:17, 35; Judg 11:39), and homosexual intercourse (Gen 19:5, 6; Judg 19:22; 21:11). The theological significance of *yādaʿ* as a term for sexual intercourse is discussed in connection with the first usage of this term in a sexual sense in Gen 4:1.

[44] Gen 6:4; 16:2, 4; 19:31; 29:21; 29:23, 30; 30:3, 4, 16; 38:2, 8, 9, 16, 18; Deut 21:13; 22:13; 25:5; Josh 15:18; Judg 16:1; 2 Sam 3:7, 12, 24; 16:21, 22; Ezek 17:44; Ps 51:2 (ET 51:1); 1 Chr 2:21; 7:23.

[45] *qārab*: Gen 20:4–6; Lev 18:6, 14, 19; 20:16; Deut 22:14; Ezek 18:6. *nāgaš*: Exod 19:15.

with" (*šākab ʿim*);[46] the related expression *nātan šĕkōbet*, "use [one's] penis for sex";[47] and the further related terminology "lie . . . with a woman" (Lev 18:22) or emission of semen, lit., "lying of seed" (Lev 15:18). Sexual union also is implied in the expression "become one flesh" (Gen 2:24) and is sometimes connoted by the verbs "to love" (*ʾāhab/ʾāhēb*)[48] and "to take [a woman/wife]" (*lāqaḥ*).[49] The clause *gālâ ʿerwat*, "uncover the nakedness of," is used to describe incestuous sexual intercourse (Lev 18:6–17; 20:19; Ezek 22:10) as well as other illicit sexual intercourse (Lev 18:18–19).[50] The term for "ravish" or "sexually violate" is *šāgēl* (Deut 28:30; Isa 13:16; Jer 3:2; Zech 14:2).[51] The sex act of a human female with an animal (bestiality), or of an animal with another animal, utilizes the verb *rābaʿ*, probably an Aramaic loan word meaning "to copulate" (Lev 18:23; 20:16; cf. 19:19).[52] Especially in the Song of Songs, numerous other forms of metaphorical language and plays on words are employed to allude to sexual intercourse.

These various ways of indicating sexual intercourse may be described as euphemistic if it is remembered that such "euphemisms" do not necessarily entail an avoidance of more explicit sexual terminology by substituting less offensive expressions. The "euphemisms" frequently *were* the most precise terminology available. Far from representing an impoverishment of expressive capability, moreover, these euphemistic expressions were often able to connote what modern scientific sexual terms cannot, namely, the essential meaning of the act as well as an objective description. This is true, for instance, in the usage of the verb *yādaʿ*, "to know," to indicate sexual intercourse.

A survey of sexual vocabulary calls for some reference to the larger perspective of sexual differentiation within the OT. This could lead us into a lengthy list of terms denoting the broadest spectrum of vocabulary for aspects of sexuality from

---

[46] Gen 19:32–35; 26:10; 30:15, 16; 34:2; 35:22; 39:7, 10, 12, 14; Exod 22:16; Lev 15:18, 33; 19:20; 20:11–13, 18, 20; Num 5:13, 19; Deut 22:22, 23, 25, 28, 29; 27:20–23; 28:30; 1 Sam 2:22; 2 Sam 11:4; 11:11; 12:11, 24; 13:11, 14; Ezek 23:8. For reference to homosexuality and bestiality, see Lev 18:22; Exod 22:18 (ET 22:19); Deut 27:21.

[47] So, e.g., Lev 18:20 should be translated, "You shall not use your penis for sex." See Milgrom, *Leviticus 17–22*, 1550. See also Lev 18:23; 20:15; Num 5:20.

[48] See, e.g., Gen 24:67; 1 Kgs 11:1; Ezek 16:37. The emphasis of this term, when used of sexual intercourse, is more on the experiencing and desiring of sexual relations than on the act itself. Sometimes a distinction of meaning is connoted by using the active form rather than the stative; this is discussed below in ch. 7 in the contrast between the love of Solomon (1 Kgs 11:1) and Hosea (Hos 3:1).

[49] See esp. Gen 34:2; Exod 2:1; 2 Sam 11:4.

[50] The parallel clause, *rāʾâ ʿerwat*, "see the nakedness of" in Lev 20:17 (bis) also refers to incestuous sexual intercourse. For a discussion of Lev 18:18 (and arguments that, unlike vv. 6–17, this verse does not refer to incest), see ch. 5, below.

[51] The Masoretes thought this term so offensive that the term "to lie with" was substituted in the Qere of the MT. For other terms related to rape, see the discussion in ch. 12, below.

[52] See Milgrom, *Leviticus 17–22*, 1571. Ibn Ezra claimed that the root was related to the Hebrew word for "four" (*ʾarbāʿâ;* derived from the homonym *rbʿ*), since an animal copulates while standing on all fours. In the biblical description of female bestiality, however, it is the woman who crouches on all fours.

pregnancy and birth to death, including the entire range of words denoting human gender.[53] Although such a survey is not provided here, this overview concludes with the basic terms expressing the bipolarity of the sexes: Sexual distinctions in the OT are indicated primarily by the word pairs *zākār/nĕqēbâ*, "male/female," and *ʾîš/ʾiššâ*, "man/woman." The former word pair denotes the gender differentiation of both animals and humans[54] whereas the latter is limited primarily to humans, with the same terms denoting either "man/woman" or "husband/wife," depending upon the context.[55] The significance of these two word pairs with regard to the theology of sexuality is examined in the discussion of their crucial initial appearance in Gen 1 and 2. These foundational chapters of Scripture call for attention in the first chapter of this study.

---

[53] Some of this terminology will be taken up when relevant to the specific topics at hand. E.g., chs. 3 and 7 treat vocabulary of prostitution; ch. 8, terms denoting virginity; ch. 11, vocabulary related to childbearing and childlessness (and ways of dealing with childlessness, such as the levirate marriage and adoption); and ch. 12, verbs associated with rape.

[54] The masculine noun *zākār* appears eighty-two times in the OT, and another three times as an adjective (Num 3:40, 43; Jer 20:15). See also the four occurrences of the related noun *zĕkûr* (Exod 23:17; 34:23; Deut 16:16; 20:13) with the same meaning. The assumed etymology of these words is from the root conception of "to be sharp, pointed"—obviously alluding to the male penis. The feminine noun *nĕqēbâ*, "female," appears twenty-two times in the HB and is derived from the root *nqb*, "to bore, make a hole, pierce"; the etymological reference is no doubt to the female sex organ that is "pierced" by the male penis.

[55] The masculine *ʾîš* appears about 2,160 times in the OT, and *ʾiššâ* occurs about 775 times. Both *ʾîš* and *ʾiššâ* are of uncertain etymology; one suggestion derives the former from the verb *ʾyš*, *ʾwš*, "to be strong," and the latter from *ʾnš*, "to be weak," but these may well be primary nouns not based upon verbal roots (see N. P. Bratsiotis, "אִישׁ *ʾish*; אִשָּׁה *ʾishāh*," *TDOT* 1:222–23). According to most lexicographers, the two terms are related only by popular etymology. If one takes Gen 2:23 at face value, however, this popular etymology was present from the beginning in Eden.

Section 1

Sexuality in Eden
The Divine Design (Genesis 1–3)

1

Sexuality in the Beginning:
Genesis 1–2

The first two chapters of the Bible deal directly and extensively with human sexuality. Not only is human sexuality presented as a basic fact of creation; an elucidation of the nature and theology of sexuality receives central, climactic placement in the Genesis creation accounts. Within the cosmic scope of the creation narratives, the disproportionate amount of space devoted to the subject of sexuality also underscores its special significance in the theology of the HB.[1] As noted in the introduction, above, a central premise of this book builds upon a growing consensus within biblical scholarship that Genesis 1–3 provides the interpretive foundation for the rest of Scripture. Deborah Sawyer represents this consensus assessment: "In the opening chapters of Genesis the triangular relationship of God/man/woman is set in place to explain and inform subsequent narrative and legislation as it unfolds. The reader has the necessary framework to read the codes and recognise proper and improper behaviour."[2]

In particular, the profound portrayal of God's original design for human sexuality at the beginning of the canon constitutes the foundation for the rest of the

---

[1] Phyllis A. Bird, "Genesis 1–3 as a Source for a Contemporary Theology of Sexuality," *ExAud* 3 (1987): 31–44; repr. in *Missing Persons and Mistaken Identities: Women and Gender in Ancient Israel* (OBT; Minneapolis: Fortress, 1997), 155–73. Bird correctly assesses the significance of extensive material on sexuality in these chapters: "While the topic of sexuality represents an exceedingly narrow focus within the universe-encompassing question of creation, it is given disproportionate attention in the primary Old Testament texts. By reason of this placement and prominence, the biblical interpreter is directed to consider the meaning and end of human sexuality in the context of theological reflection on creation" (p. 156).

[2] Deborah F. Sawyer, *God, Gender, and the Bible* (Biblical Limits; London: Routledge, 2002), 29. I disagree with Sawyer, however, in her contention (ibid.) that this "foundational account" only provides the "set sexual/familial/social/political boundaries" as a "necessary counterpart or antithesis to the Bible's central thesis—the *un*bounded power of God." I do not subscribe to her self-described postmodern approach in which "biblical texts will be subject to deconstruction, and understood in the light of their own socio-political contexts, texts that infer a counter-culture, in relation to both the boundaries of their time and those of the Bible itself" (p. 2). Instead of "inconsistencies that posit alternative stances" (p. 1) in Scripture, I have found a basic consistency throughout the biblical witness, albeit with room for development and different emphases.

biblical narrative and discourse on human sexuality and encapsulates the fundamental principles of a theology of sexuality. As pointed out later in this chapter, Gen 2:24 makes explicit that God's original design for sexuality and marriage in the relationship between Adam and Eve is set forth as a pattern for all future sexual relationships. The paradigmatic nature of Gen 1–3 for sexuality has been widely recognized, particularly in the context of marriage. For example, Dan Allender and Tremper Longman argue cogently that the first three chapters of the Bible are like a "North Star" to guide in marriage relationships, providing "God's design" for marriage, and constituting "the ground floor of the Bible" for understanding "the foundational perspectives" and the "Creation foundations" for marriage. "Genesis 1–3 establishes crucial principles that are to shape our marriages. This story tells us all we ultimately need to know about marriage."[3] J. Andrew Dearman expresses a similar conviction: "The two accounts of creation (Gen. 1:1–2:3 and 2:4–3:24) are foundational to the understanding of marriage in the Old Testament. . . . Virtually all aspects of Israelite marriage reflected elsewhere in the Old Testament find their etiological counterpart in the creation accounts."[4]

The multifaceted theology of human sexuality that emerges from my examination of the Genesis creation passages will be organized under ten major subheadings. Within each subheading I first focus upon the summary account of creation (Gen 1:1–2:4a) where applicable and then give attention to the complementary and more detailed narrative (2:4b–25).[5]

---

[3] Dan B. Allender and Tremper Longman III, *Intimate Allies: Rediscovering God's Design for Marriage and Becoming Soul Mates for Life* (Wheaton, Ill.: Tyndale, 1995), 13–14.

[4] J. Andrew Dearman, "Marriage in the Old Testament," in *Biblical Ethics and Homosexuality: Listening to Scripture* (ed. Robert L. Brawley; Louisville: Westminster John Knox, 1996), 54. On the whole issue of a canonical approach to biblical interpretation, see Craig G. Bartholomew et al., eds., *Canon and Biblical Interpretation* (Scripture and Hermeneutics Series 7; Grand Rapids: Zondervan, 2006).

[5] Regardless of one's position regarding presumed preliterary sources underlying the received text of the Pentateuch, canonically it can be affirmed that the final redactor placed these chapters at the beginning of the Torah and the whole HB, and this theology of sexuality focuses upon the final canonical form of the text.

Evidence presented by seminal scholarly studies leads me to the conclusion that Gen 1–2 does not represent separate and disparate sources as argued by proponents of the Documentary Hypothesis. See esp. Jacques B. Doukhan, *The Literary Structure of the Genesis Creation Story* (Andrews University Seminary Doctoral Dissertation Series 5; Berrien Springs, Mich.: Andrews University Press, 1978); William Shea, "Literary Structural Parallels between Genesis 1 and 2," *Origins* 16 (1989): 49–68. For evidence supporting the unity and/or Mosaic authorship of Genesis (and the Pentateuch as a whole), see, e.g., Gleason L. Archer, *A Survey of Old Testament Introduction* (rev. ed.; Chicago: Moody, 1994), 89–189 (esp. 113–26); Umberto Cassuto, *The Documentary Hypothesis* (Jerusalem: Magnes, 1961), passim; idem, *A Commentary on the Book of Genesis* (trans. Israel Abrahams; 2 vols.; Jerusalem: Magnes, 1961), 1:7–20, 84–100; Duane Garrett, *Rethinking Genesis: The Sources and Authorship of the First Book of the Pentateuch* (Grand Rapids: Baker, 1991); R. K. Harrison, *Introduction to the Old Testament* (Grand Rapids: Eerdmans, 1969), 495–541; Gerhard F. Hasel, *Biblical Interpretation Today* (Washington, D.C.: Biblical Research Institute, 1985); I. M. Kikawada and A. Quinn, *Before Abraham Was: The Unity of Genesis 1–11* (Nashville:

Sexuality as a Creation Order

In Gen 1:26–28 "the high point and goal has been reached toward which all of God's creativity from v. 1 on was directed."[6] Here in lofty grandeur is portrayed the creation of humankind (*hā᾽ādām*):

> Then God said, "Let us make humankind in our image, according to our likeness; and let them have dominion over the fish of the sea, and over the birds of the air, and over the cattle, and over all wild animals of the earth, and over every creeping thing that creeps upon the earth." So God created humankind in his image, in the image of God he created him; male and female he created them. God blessed them, and God said to them, "Be fruitful and multiply, and fill the earth and subdue it; and have dominion over the fish of the sea and over the birds of the air and over every living thing that moves upon the earth."

Discussion among theologians over this passage throughout the centuries has mainly focused on the meaning of human creation in the "image of God" and until recently has almost entirely ignored the further affirmation that humankind

---

Abingdon, 1985); Kenneth A. Kitchen, *Ancient Orient and Old Testament* (Chicago: Inter-Varsity, 1968), 112–35; John Sailhamer, *The Pentateuch as Narrative: A Biblical-Theological Commentary* (Grand Rapids: Zondervan, 1992), 1–79; Herbert M. Wolf, *An Introduction to the Old Testament: Pentateuch* (Chicago: Moody, 1991), 51–78.

I find that Gen 1–2, instead of comprising multiple sources, provides a unified dual perspective on creation—and the God of creation. Genesis 1:1–2:4a gives the picture of an all-powerful, transcendent God (Elohim) and a cosmic view of creation. In Gen 2:4b–25 God is further presented as the personal, caring covenant God (Yahweh Elohim), and creation is described in terms of man and his intimate, personal needs. From this unique dual perspective of infinite/personal God and cosmic/man-centered creation emerges a balanced and enriched presentation of the divine design for human sexuality.

[6] Gerhard von Rad, *Genesis: A Commentary* (trans. John H. Marks; OTL; Philadelphia: Westminster, 1961), 57. Similarly, Marsha M. Wilfong, "Human Creation in Canonical Context: Genesis 1:26–31 and Beyond," in *God Who Creates: Essays in Honor of W. Sibley Towner* (ed. William P. Brown and S. Dean McBride Jr.; Grand Rapids: Eerdmans, 2000), 47, argues that "humankind is, in fact the lynchpin that holds creation together." Bruce A. Ware, "Male and Female Complementarity and the Image of God," in *Biblical Foundations for Manhood and Womanhood* (ed. Wayne A. Grudem; Foundations for the Family Series; Wheaton, Ill.: Crossway, 2002), 72, points to seven key internal textual indicators that the creation of "man" (his translation of *hā᾽ādām*, which I would prefer to translate "humankind") was "the pinnacle of God's creative work": (1) only after God creates "man" does God say creation is "very good" (Gen 1:31); (2) the creation of "man" is introduced differently than all other creation with the personal divine deliberative statement "Let us . . ." (1:26); (3) the one God uses the plural "us" as God creates (sg.) "man," who is plural ("male and female"); (4) the phrase "image of God" is used three times in the creation narrative (1:26–27) and only with reference to the creation of "man"; (5) the special term *bārā᾽*, "create," is used three times (1:27) with reference to the creation of "man"; (6) "man" (as male and female) is given rulership over the other created beings on earth (1:26, 28), indicating "man's" higher authority and priority; and (7) only the creation of "man" as male and female is expanded and further developed in the creation account of Gen 2.

is created male and female.[7] In harmony with the concerns of this study, I focus in particular upon the neglected statement—"male and female he created them"— without ignoring the question of the *imago Dei* and the wider context of the chapter.

In the clause concerning humankind's creation as male and female (1:27c), note, first of all, that sexual differentiation is presented as a creation by God and not part of the inherent nature of divinity itself. This emphasis upon the creation of sexual distinction appears to form a subtle but strong polemic against the divinization of sex so common in the thought of Israel's neighbors. Throughout the mythology of the ancient Near East, the sexual activities of the gods form a dominant motif.[8] The fertility myth was of special importance, particularly in Mesopotamia and Palestine. Chapter 3, below, focuses in more detail upon the Canaanite fertility cults, but here note already that in the ANE myths creation was often celebrated as resulting from the union of male and female deities: "Copulation and procreation were mythically regarded as a divine event. Consequently the religious atmosphere was as good as saturated with mythical sexual conceptions."[9] In contrast to this view of creation as divine procreation, there is a radical separation of sexuality and divinity in the Genesis accounts of origins. God stands "absolutely beyond the polarity of sex."[10] The sexual distinctions are presented as a creation by God, not part of the divine realm.

---

[7] Paul K. Jewett, *Man as Male and Female: A Study of Sexual Relationships from a Theological Point of View* (Grand Rapids: Eerdmans, 1975), 19.

[8] Raymond F. Collins, "The Bible and Sexuality," *BTB* 7 (1977): 149–51, conveniently summarizes the major aspects of sexuality (fertility, love-passion, destructive capacity, sacred marriage) in the ANE myths.

[9] Gerhard von Rad, *Old Testament Theology* (trans. D. M. G. Stalker; 2 vols.; New York: Harper & Row, 1962–1965), 1:28. Concrete examples from the ANE literature are provided in ch. 3, below.

[10] Ibid., 1:27–28. At least one modern OT scholar, Johannes C. de Moor, proposes that Gen 1:27 presents a bisexuality in God, as in the many ANE creator-god myths where "bisexuality was seen as a sure sign of exalted divinity, a quality reserved for the highest divine beings who transcended the all too human limitations of split gender" ("The Duality in God and Man: Gen 1:26–27," in *Intertextuality in Ugarit and Israel: Papers Read at the Tenth Joint Meeting of the Society for Old Testament Study and Het Oudtestamentisch Werkgezelschap in Nederland en België, Held at Oxford, 1997* [ed. Johannes C. de Moor; OtSt 40; Leiden: E. J. Brill, 1998], 124). This claim is critiqued by Edward Noort, "The Creation of Man and Woman in Biblical and Ancient Near Eastern Traditions," in *The Creation of Man and Woman: Interpretations of the Biblical Narratives in Jewish and Christian Traditions* (ed. Gerard P. Luttikhuizen; Themes in Biblical Narrative 3; Leiden: E. J. Brill, 2000), 8–9. Noort insightfully points out how throughout Gen 1 the biblical narrator provides a polemic against the ANE creation myths with their creation by sexual procreation of the gods: e.g., the female Tiamat of the Akkadian myth becomes simply "the deep" in Gen 1; the fertile earth of the ANE myths is "only an instrument in the hands of Elohim"; the astral sun and moon gods of the ancient Near East simply "serve as a clock for the (cultic) calendar" and "every connection with an astral religion . . . is cut off here." Noort concludes, "If this overall tendency in the Priestly account of creation [i.e., Gen 1] is correct, then it is unthinkable that the Priestly writer should take over the bisexuality of some gods for a characterisation of Elohim as de Moor suggested" (p. 9).

The accounts of creation in Gen 1 and Gen 2 both assign sexuality to the creation order and not to the divine realm. But whereas Gen 1 does not indicate the precise manner in which God created, Gen 2 removes any possible lingering thoughts that creation occurred by divine procreation. This second chapter of Scripture sets forth in detail God's personal labor of love, forming (*yāṣar*) man from the dust of the ground and "building" (*bānâ*) woman from one of man's ribs.

A Heterosexual Human Duality and Marital Form

A second facet of human sexual theology emerging from Gen 1–2 is that God created the bipolarity of the sexes from the beginning. The popular idea that 1:27 presents *hāʾādām* as an ideal androgynous (or hermaphroditic) being later split into two sexes cannot be sustained from the text of Gen 1.[11] "The plural in v. 27 ('he created them') is intentionally contrasted with the singular ('him') and prevents one from assuming the creation of an originally androgynous man."[12] This is confirmed in the following verse (1:28), where God blessed *them* and commanded *them* to be fruitful and multiply; only a heterosexual couple, not a bisexual creature, could fulfill this command. Further confirmation of an original duality of the sexes and not an androgynous creature is the parallel passage of 5:2, where the plural "them/they" is again employed: "Male and female he created *them*, and he blessed *them* and named *them* 'Humankind' when *they* were created."

The sexual distinction between male and female is fundamental to what it means to be human. To be human is to live as a sexual person. "We cannot say man without having to say male or female and also male and female. Man exists

---

[11] The androgynous interpretation of *hāʾādām* in Gen 1:27 is found already in the medieval Jewish commentator Rashi and is still represented by a number of modern commentators. See, e.g., Rebecca Merrill Groothuis, *Good News for Women: A Biblical Picture of Gender Equality* (Grand Rapids: Baker, 1997), 125; de Moor, "The Duality in God and Man," 112–25; and Pinchas Stolper, "The Man-Woman Dynamic of HA-ADAM: A Jewish Paradigm of Marriage," *Tradition* 27 (1992): 35. For discussion (with bibliography) of the pagan origin of this idea in Plato, and of its inroads into the church via Gregory of Nyssa and others, see Werner Neuer, *Man and Woman in Christian Perspective* (trans. G. Wenham; Wheaton, Ill.: Crossway, 1991), 62–63 and accompanying notes. See below for proponents of the androgynous interpretation of *hāʾādām* in Gen 2.

[12] Von Rad, *Genesis,* 60. See also the arguments presented against the androgynous interpretation of Gen 1:27 by Noort, "The Creation of Man and Woman," 5–8. Noort (p. 7) suggests that the parallel of Gen 6:19 is instructive, where "male and female" means one pair, and thus the well-known explanation that the same expression in Gen 1:27b "means the first pair of mankind, one male and one female, is to be preferred." He also shows (7–8) how this conclusion is supported by the parallel use of the pronoun shift from singular ("it" = humankind) to plural ("them" = the first male and female) in Gen 5:1–2 as in Gen 1:27. Cf. Wayne A. Grudem, *Evangelical Feminism and Biblical Truth: An Analysis of More Than One Hundred Disputed Questions* (Sisters, Ore.: Multnomah, 2004), 111–13.

in this differentiation, in this duality."[13] Whether or not one agrees with Barth that "this is the only structural differentiation in which he [the human being] exists,"[14] the sexual distinction is certainly presented in Gen 1 as a basic component in the original creation of humankind.[15] In Gen 1 "heterosexuality is at once proclaimed to be the order of creation."[16]

Regarding Gen 2, a number of more recent studies have revived an older theory that the original *hāʾādām* described in this chapter was androgynous, one creature incorporating two sexes, or "a sexually undifferentiated earth creature."[17] But such a hypothesis is not supported by the text. According to 2:7–8, 15–16, what God creates before woman is called *hāʾādām,* "the man," better translated as "the human."[18] After the creation of woman, this creature is denoted by the same term (vv. 22–23). Nothing has changed in the makeup of "the human" during his sleep except the loss of a rib. There is no hint in the text of an originally bisexual or sexually undifferentiated being split into two different sexes. The androgynous interpretation suggests that human beings are not intrinsically sexual, a view that contradicts the anthropology of Gen 1–2. According to the biblical text, *hāʾādām,* "the human" formed before woman, was not originally androgynous but was "created in anticipation of the future."[19] He was created

---

[13] Karl Barth, *Church Dogmatics* (ed. G. W. Bromiley and T. F. Torrance; trans. J. W. Edwards et al.; 5 vols. in 13; Edinburgh: T&T Clark, 1956–1969), 3/2:236.

[14] Ibid.

[15] But as already indicated, this does not reflect gender distinctions of male and female back onto the nature of God; God is presented in Scripture as above the polarity of sex.

[16] Samuel H. Dresner, "Homosexuality and the Order of Creation," *Judaism* 40 (1991): 309.

[17] Phyllis Trible, *God and the Rhetoric of Sexuality* (OBT; Philadelphia: Fortress, 1978), 80. Other modern proponents of this view include, e.g., Mieke Bal, *Lethal Love: Feminist Literary Readings of Biblical Love Stories* (Bloomington: Indiana University Press, 1987), 112–14; Sam Dragga, "Genesis 2–3: A Story of Liberation," *JSOT* 55 (1992): 3–4; Mary Phil Korsak, "Genesis: A New Look," in *A Feminist Companion to Genesis* (ed. Athalya Brenner; FCB 2; Sheffield, Eng.: JSOT Press, 1993), 39–52; Azila Talit Reisenberger, "The Creation of Adam as Hermaphrodite and Its Implications for Feminist Theology," *Judaism* 42 (1993): 447–52; Leonard Swidler, *Biblical Affirmations of Woman* (Philadelphia: Fortress, 1979), 76–81; United Church of Christ, *Human Sexuality: A Preliminary Study of the United Church of Christ* (New York: United Church, 1977), 57; and Ellen Van Wolde, *Words Become Worlds: Semantic Studies of Genesis 1–11* (BIS 6; Leiden: E. J. Brill, 1994), 13–31.

[18] As the next section of this chapter will argue, the word *hāʾādām* does not mean "man" in the sense of male gender but "human." It is true that the first specimen of humanity was of male gender, but this is not the meaning of the term *hāʾādām.*

[19] K&D, 1:55. For further argumentation against the view espoused by Trible and others of an originally androgynous earth creature, see esp. Grudem, *Evangelical Feminism and Biblical Truth,* 111–13; Richard S. Hess, "Splitting the Adam: The Usage of *ʾādām* in Genesis I–V," in *Studies in the Pentateuch* (ed. J. A. Emerton; VTSup 41; Leiden: E. J. Brill, 1990), 1–15; Susan Lanser, "(Feminist) Criticism in the Garden: Inferring Genesis 2–3," *Semeia* 41 (1988): 69–72; and Beverly J. Stratton, *Out of Eden: Reading, Rhetoric, and Ideology in Genesis 2–3* (JSOTSup 208; Sheffield, Eng.: Sheffield Academic Press, 1995), 102–4.

with those sexual drives toward union with his counterpart. This becomes apparent in the first human's encounter with the animals, which dramatically pointed up his need of "a helper as his partner" (vv. 18, 20). Such a need is satisfied when he is introduced to woman and he fully realizes his sexuality vis-à-vis his sexual complement. The fact that no sexual companion was found for the man among the animals indicates, among other things, that according to the divine design, human sexual activity is to take place not with animals as sexual partners (bestiality) but only between *human* partners.

According to the description of Gen 2, God arranged for the first marriage, and the divinely-designed marital form involved a heterosexual couple, a "man" and a "woman" (2:22–23). Based upon the experience of the first couple in Eden, Gen 2:24 presents a succinct theology of marriage, the details of which will be explored further in the section on sexuality as relationship. But here note the reference to "a man [*ʾîš*] . . . and . . . his wife [*ʾištô*]" in regard to the marriage relationship. The phrase "man and his wife" indicates a *heterosexual* marriage relationship of a man and woman as the Edenic model for all time. Thus the intrinsic human duality of male and female and the heterosexual marital form involving a sexual union of a man and woman (not man with man, or human with animal) constitute the divine paradigm for humanity from the beginning.

A Monogamous Marital Form

As a third facet of sexual theology found in Gen 1–2, it may be affirmed that the marital form presented by God as paradigmatic for humans from the beginning is a *monogamous* one. In the narrator's description of the first marriage (Gen 2:18–23), the usage of singular nouns and pronouns throughout is significant: God determined to make for "the man" a "helper as his partner" (v. 18); in the process of naming the animals "the man" did not find "a helper as his partner" (v. 20); God took "one of his [the man's] ribs" and fashioned "a woman" and brought "her" to "the man" (vv. 21–22); beholding what God had fashioned, "the man" exclaimed, "this one" shall be called "woman," for out of "man" "this one" was taken (v. 23). Unmistakably this language denotes a marriage between one man and one woman. In 2:24, mentioned above, the phrase "a man [*ʾîš*] . . . and . . . his wife [*ʾištô*]," with both nouns in the singular, clearly implies that the sexual relationship envisioned is monogamous, to be shared between two marriage partners.[20] "Genesis 2:24 is dealing with monogamy: it only mentions explicitly

---

[20] The LXX translation makes the latter point explicit: "they *two* shall become one flesh." Many modern scholars likewise recognize the implication of monogamy from this passage. Note, e.g., Walter Vogels, "Man and Woman—Their Dignity, Mutuality, and Fidelity in Marriage: A Biblical Perspective (Gen 1–3)," *BiBh* 23 (1997): 223–24: "The text [Gen 2:24] certainly proposes a monogamous relationship. . . . The text with or without the 'two' proposes monogamy as the ideal relationship between husband and wife." Cf. William Loader, *The Septuagint, Sexuality, and the New Testament: Case Studies on the Impact of the LXX in Philo and the New Testament* (Grand Rapids: Eerdmans, 2004), 42.

one man and one woman who become one flesh. . . . It refers only to monogamy."[21] According to the creation account, the divine design for marital form is monogamy.

Equality of the Sexes without Hierarchy

A fourth facet of the theology of human sexuality in Gen 1–2 stems from the equal pairing of male *and* female in parallel with *hāʾādām* in 1:27: "So God created humankind [*hāʾādām*] in his image; in the image of God he created them; male and female He created them." Although indeed the terms "male" and "female" connote sexual (biological) differences, there is no hint of ontological superiority/inferiority or functional leadership/submission between male and female.[22] To the contrary, both are explicitly presented as "equally immediate to the Creator and His act."[23] In the wider context of this passage (1:26, 28), both the man and the woman are blessed. Both are to share alike in the responsibility of procreation, to "fill the earth." Both are to subdue the earth. Both are given the same comanagerial dominion over God's nonhuman creation. "Both have been commanded equally and without distinction to take dominion, not one over the other, but both together over the rest of God's creation for the glory of the Creator."[24] Helen Schüngel-Strauman sharpens the implication of 1:26–28: "This statement *explicitly* excludes men's rule over women! Oddly enough, this has not been noticed before. An analysis of the wording of Gen. 1:26–28 results in precisely this, however: man and woman rule over the rest of creation, and this implies only too clearly that one gender may not claim power over the other."[25] The fundamental equality of man and woman is unhesitatingly proclaimed in the first chapter of the Bible.

---

[21] Neuer, *Man and Woman,* 68.

[22] I use the term "leadership" rather than "headship" throughout this book, since the meaning of the term "head" (especially as found in the Pauline writings) has become a matter of dispute in the current debate of the status of the sexes in Scripture (see the afterword). Further support for this use of terms is found especially from Ronald W. Pierce and Rebecca Merrill Groothuis, introduction to *Discovering Biblical Equality: Complementarity without Hierarchy* (ed. Ronald W. Pierce and Rebecca Merrill Groothuis; Downers Grove, Ill.: InterVarsity, 2004), 15–16 (and the entire book).

[23] Helmut Thielicke, *The Ethics of Sex* (New York: Harper & Row, 1964), 7.

[24] Rebecca Merrill Groothuis, *The Feminist Bogeywoman: Questions and Answers about Evangelical Feminism* (Grand Rapids: Baker, 1995), 27. Cf. Noort, "The Creation of Man and Woman," 9: "Gen 1:27 aims at the credo that the separation in male and female belongs to creation from the beginning. There is no priority. Neither male or female have a dominant position here."

[25] Helen Schüngel-Straumann, "On the Creation of Man and Woman in Genesis 1–3: The History and Reception of the Texts Reconsidered," in *A Feminist Companion to Genesis* (ed. Athalya Brenner; FCB 2; Sheffield, Eng.: Sheffield Academic Press, 1993), 75. Allender and Longman, *Intimate Allies,* 20, succinctly state this profound implication for the equality of the sexes: "Both male and female are in essence and status undifferentiated; each is equally and fully the image of God."

David J. A. Clines seeks to counter this conclusion by contending that the reference to "male and female" in 1:27 implies nothing about equality of the sexes but only indicates that there are two kinds of human being just as other creatures are made "according to their kind."[26] But Richard Hess incisively critiques Clines's claim: "Clines fails to demonstrate that male and female are ever understood as the *kinds* (*mîn*) used of different species in Genesis 1:21 and 24. Nowhere in Genesis is ʾādām so described; rather other references to ʾādām connote the species as a whole. There is nothing in this chapter to suggest anything other than equality of male and female created together in the image of God."[27]

Some proponents of male leadership as a creation ordinance agree to an ontological equality between the sexes but find a functional leadership role implied in 1:26, where God identifies male and female as ʾādām, which is translated "man" in some translations. "God cuts right across the grain of our peculiar sensitivities when He names the human race, both man and woman, 'man.' . . . God's naming of the race 'man' whispers male headship."[28] What Ortlund and others who employ this argument fail to recognize is that the word ʾādām never means "man" (in the sense or implication of male gender) in Scripture. The problem is a modern language translation issue, not an aspect of the Hebrew text. The word ʾādām is a generic term meaning "human person" or "humanity."[29] Aside

---

[26] David J. A. Clines, "What Does Eve Do to Help? And Other Irredeemably Androcentric Orientations in Genesis 1–3," in *What Does Eve Do to Help? And Other Readerly Questions to the Old Testament* (ed. David J. A. Clines; Sheffield, Eng.: JSOT Press, 1990), 25–48.

[27] Richard S. Hess, "Equality with and without Innocence: Genesis 1–3," in *Discovering Biblical Equality: Complementarity without Hierarchy* (ed. Ronald W. Pierce and Rebecca Merrill Groothuis; Downers Grove, Ill.: InterVarsity, 2004), 82.

[28] Raymond C. Ortlund Jr., "Male-Female Equality and Male Headship: Genesis 1–3," in *Recovering Biblical Manhood and Womanhood: A Response to Evangelical Feminism* (ed. John Piper and Wayne A. Grudem; Wheaton, Ill.: Crossway, 1991), 97–98. Cf. Ware, "Male and Female Complementarity," 84: "We should resist the movement today in Bible translation that would customarily render instances of ʾādām with the fully non-gender-specific term 'human being.' . . . This misses the God-intended implication conveyed by the masculine generic 'man,' viz., that woman possesses her common human nature only through the prior nature of the man." So also Grudem, *Evangelical Feminism and Biblical Truth*, 34–36.

[29] See *DCH* 1:123–29, which defines ʾādām as "human being, humanity, people, individual person, humans" but avoids the term "man" except for reference to the first human, Adam. Cf. the discussion and bibliography in Victor P. Hamilton, "ʾādām," *NIDOTTE* 1:262–66; and Vogels, "Man and Woman," 216–18. See also the recent debate between James Barr and David J. A. Clines over the semantic nuance of this term. James Barr argues that ʾādām "is essentially a male term" ("One Man, or All Humanity?" in *Recycling Biblical Figures: Papers Read at a NOSTER Colloquium in Amsterdam, 12–13 May 1997* [ed. Athalya Brenner and J. W. van Hentern; Leiden: Deo, 1999; repr. as "Adam: Single Man, or All Humanity," in *Hesed ve-Emet: Studies in Honor of Ernest S. Frerichs* (ed. Jodi Magness and Seymour Gitin; Atlanta: Scholars Press, 1998), 3–12], 3–21, quote at 18). David J. A. Clines responds with an incisive and persuasive critique, "אדם, the Hebrew for 'Human, Humanity': A Response to James Barr," *VT* 53 (2003): 297–310. Clines examines Barr's evidence and finds it wanting. He concludes that "the traditional view that אדם means

from Gen 1–3, where it refers to the first human person, Adam, this term is never in the whole HB used to designate a "man" in the sense of male (as opposed to female). The use of ʾādām does not whisper male headship as a creation ordinance.

The one major question that has dominated the scholarly discussion of sexuality in Gen 2 concerns the relative status of the sexes. The "traditional" view—held by the vast majority of Christian commentators and theologians before the twentieth century—has held that according to Gen 2, woman was created by nature inferior to man and thus women as a class or race are not competent and must be excluded from leadership or exercising authority in the home, church, or society.[30] Many modern scholars—both proponents of male leadership as a creation ordinance and liberal feminists—now acknowledge that Gen 1 emphasizes equality on the ontological, personal, and spiritual level but at the same time maintain that Gen 2 emphasizes hierarchy or leadership/submission on the functional or societal level regarding male-female relationships.[31] Does Gen 2 affirm a fully egalitarian view of the relationship between the sexes, or does it support a

---

'humanity, without distinction of gender' is to be upheld. . . . I deny that in any place [in the HB] אדם means 'a man' in the sense of a male, and affirm that the term is ungendered" (pp. 309–10). I am convinced by Clines's assessment of the evidence.

[30] See esp. Kevin Giles, *The Trinity and Subordinationism: The Doctrine of God and the Contemporary Gender Debate* (Downers Grove, Ill.: InterVarsity, 2002), 145–55, for numerous examples throughout church history illustrating this dominant view since shortly after NT times, including citations from Tertullian, Jerome, John Chrysostom, Augustine, Thomas Aquinas, the early Martin Luther, John Calvin, John Knox, William Gouge and Robert Bolton (Puritans), Matthew Henry, Jonathan Edwards, John Wesley, Charles Hodge, and Adam Clarke. See also John A. Phillips, *Eve: The History of an Idea* (New York: Harper & Row, 1984), passim; and Kristen E. Kvam, Linda S. Schearing, and Valarie H. Ziegler, eds., *Eve and Adam: Jewish, Christian, and Muslim Readings on Genesis and Gender* (Bloomington: Indiana University Press, 1999), passim.

[31] This view, making a clear distinction between Gen 1 and 2, was popular among "first wave" feminists of the late nineteenth century; see, e.g., Elizabeth Cady Stanton, *The Woman's Bible* (New York: European, 1895; repr., Boston: Northeastern University Press, 1993), 20–21. It is also a common view among contemporary liberal feminists, who regard Gen 1 as egalitarian and Gen 2 as hierarchical: e.g., Anne Gardner, "Genesis 2:4b–3: A Mythological Paradigm of Sexual Equality or of the Religious History of Pre-exilic Israel?" *SJT* 43 (1990): 1–18. Many evangelicals also emphasize the difference between ontological equality in Gen 1 and functional hierarchy in Gen 2. See, e.g., Ronald B. Allen and Beverly Allen, *Liberated Traditionalism: Men and Women in Balance* (Portland, Ore.: Multnomah, 1985), 89–117; Mary A. Kassian, *Women, Creation, and the Fall* (Westchester, Ill.: Crossway, 1990), 13–20; Susan T. Foh, "A Male Leadership View: The Head of the Woman Is the Man," in *Women in Ministry: Four Views* (ed. Bonnidel Clouse and Robert G. Clouse; Downers Grove, Ill.: InterVarsity, 1989), 72–73; George W. Knight III, "The New Testament Teaching on the Role Relationship of Male and Female with Special Attention to the Teaching/Ruling Functions in the Church," *JETS* 18 (1975): 83–84; idem, *The Role Relationship of Men and Women: New Testament Teaching* (Chicago: Moody, 1985), 7–9; Richard N. Longenecker, "Authority, Hierarchy, and Leadership Patterns in the Bible," in *Women, Authority, and the Bible* (ed. Alvera Mickelsen; Downers Grove, Ill.: InterVarsity, 1986), 66–67; and Aubrey Malphurs, *Biblical Manhood and Womanhood: Understanding Masculinity and Femininity from God's Perspective* (Grand Rapids: Kregel, 1996), 21–62.

hierarchical ranking in which man is in some way superior to, or in leadership over, the woman at creation?[32]

As already noted, down through the centuries the preponderance of commentators on Gen 2 have espoused the hierarchical interpretation, with notable exceptions such as the later Martin Luther,[33] and a number of modern scholarly studies have reaffirmed some form of hierarchy between the sexes. Liberal-critical scholarship often finds in Gen 2 a chauvinistic or androcentric presentation of the man as superior and the woman as inferior, with the former dominating or even subjugating the latter.[34] Many evangelical scholars, breaking from the

---

[32] There are other options. One is to find the woman superior to the man in these opening chapters of the Bible. For an example of one who comes to this conclusion by reading the text in light of psychoanalytic theory, see P. E. Jongsma-Tieleman, "The Creation of Eve and the Ambivalence between the Sexes," in *God, Biblical Stories, and Psychoanalytic Understanding* (ed. Rainer Kessler and Patrick Vendermeersch; Frankfurt am Main: Peter Lang, 2001), 97–113. Another popular psychoanalytic (Freudian) reading of these chapters maintains that Adam and Eve were both in a "relationship of infantile dependency" (Sawyer, *God, Gender, and the Bible,* 26), while yet another argues that Adam and Eve and the Deity in Gen 1–2 form "the first (among many) dysfunctional families depicted in the Hebrew Bible" (Ilona N. Rashkow, *Taboo or Not Taboo: Sexuality and Family in the Hebrew Bible* [Minneapolis: Fortress, 2000], 10). Such approaches lie outside the focus and method of this interpretive project as described in the introduction.

[33] Martin Luther, as a young monk preaching through the book of Genesis in 1523, still presented the traditional patristic and medieval view. His early view is summarized by Mickey Leland Mattox, *"Defender of the Most Holy Matriarchs": Martin Luther's Interpretation of the Women of Genesis in the "Enarrationes in Genesin," 1535–45* (SMRT 92; Leiden: E. J. Brill, 2003), 252–53: "He accepted without hesitation the traditional notion that Eve was created for submission to her husband, and interpreted Adam's naming of her as a reflection of her derivation from and dependence upon him. He considered the 'weak little woman' her husband's inferior intellectually, and faulted her in a condescending and even insulting way for the weaknesses that left her vulnerable to the devil's attack." The elder Luther's interpretation, however, was radically different. Mattox (p. 253) summarizes: "Eve had become a 'heroic woman,' and excellent philosopher, and played an equal role in the estate of the home and ruled over the creation in equal partnership with her husband before the fall. . . . In his stress on the ways in which Eve was her husband's equal before the fall, Luther's speculations went beyond those of any of his patristic and medieval predecessors examined here." Only in one area did the elder Luther still see the pre-fall Adam as taking the lead: "Adam alone was entrusted with the duty of preaching" (ibid.). See Mattox's full discussion of Luther's views on this subject (with references and citations), pp. 29–33, 67–108. Cf. Martin Luther, *Lectures on Genesis: Chapters 1–5* (trans. George V. Schick; vol. 1 of *Works;* ed. Jaroslav Pelikan; St. Louis: Concordia, 1958), e.g., 117–18, 136–40, 200–203, passim; Susan Karant-Nunn and Merry Wiesner-Hanks, *Luther on Women: A Sourcebook* (Cambridge: Cambridge University Press, 2003), 15–31.

[34] For a bibliography and overview of writers since the latter part of the nineteenth century who regard Gen 2 (and much of the rest of Scripture) as male chauvinist propaganda, see Mary A. Kassian, *The Feminist Gospel: The Movement to Unite Feminism with the Church* (Wheaton, Ill.: Crossway, 1992), passim; Eileen Schuller, "Feminism and Biblical Hermeneutics: Gen 1–3 as a Test Case," in *Gender, Genre, and Religion: Feminist Reflections* (ed. Morny Joy and Eva K. Neumaier-Dargyay; Waterloo, Ont.: Wilfrid Laurier University Press, 1995), 31–46. For specific proponents of this perspective regarding Gen 2, see, e.g., Clines, "What Does Eve Do to Help?" 25–48; Dana Nolan Fewell and David M. Gunn, *Gender, Power, and Promise: The Subject of the Bible's First Story*

traditional Christian view that God made women inferior to men,[35] see in Gen 2 an equality of spiritual and moral worth between the sexes, but at the same time they argue for functional distinctions that include a male leadership role and a female submissive-helper role as creation ordinances.[36] The main elements of the narrative in Gen 2 that are presented to support a creation order involving a hier-

---

(Nashville: Abingdon, 1993), 25–30; Gardner, "Genesis 2:4b–3"; David Jobling, *The Sense of Biblical Narrative: Structural Analysis in the Hebrew Bible* (2 vols.; JSOTSup 39; Sheffield, Eng.: JSOT Press, 1986), 2:17–43; and Lisbeth Mikaelsson, "Sexual Polarity: An Aspect of the Ideological Structure in the Paradise Narrative, Genesis 2:4–3:24," *Temenos* 16 (1980): 84–91.

[35] Evangelicals arguing for a "complementarian" (= hierarchical) interpretation of Gen 1–2 often claim that they are upholding what they call the "traditional" or "historic" Christian interpretation of the functional subordination of women and that this is grounded in the "historic" view of eternal functional subordination of the Son to the Father within the Trinity. A strong critique of this claim is set forth by Giles, *Trinity and Subordinationism*. Giles argues incisively that complementarians are not really upholding the traditional Christian view on women that has been propounded since shortly after NT times (with its interpretation that "God has made women 'inferior' to men, more prone to sin and incapable of leadership" [p. 8]), and he demonstrates that "historical orthodoxy rejects absolutely the eternal subordination of the Son. The Son is not subordinated to the Father either in being or function" (110).

[36] Major modern representatives of the hierarchical, or (their preferred self-designation) "complementarian," position who have set forth substantial arguments from Gen 2 (as well as some from Gen 1), include, e.g., Samuele Bacchiocchi, *Women in the Church: A Biblical Study on the Role of Women in the Church* (Berrien Springs, Mich.: Biblical Perspectives, 1987), 31, 71–79; idem, "Headship, Submission, and Equality in Scripture," in *Prove All Things: A Response to "Women in Ministry"* (ed. Mercedes H. Dyer; Berrien Springs, Mich.: Adventists Affirm, 2000), 65–110; Kassian, *Woman, Creation, and the Fall,* 13–20; Stephen B. Clark, *Man and Woman in Christ: An Examination of the Roles of Men and Women in the Light of Scripture and the Social Sciences* (Ann Arbor, Mich.: Servant, 1980), 23–28; Jack Cottrell, *Gender Roles and the Bible: Creation, the Fall, and Redemption. A Critique of Feminist Biblical Interpretation* (Joplin, Mo.: College Press, 1994), 63–106; Thomas Finley, "The Relationship of Woman and Man in the Old Testament," in *Women and Men in Ministry: A Complementary Perspective* (ed. Robert L. Saucy and Judith K. TenElshof; Chicago: Moody, 2001), 49–58; Susan T. Foh, *Women and the Word of God: A Response to Biblical Feminism* (Phillipsburg, N.J.: Presbyterian and Reformed, 1979), 61–62; W. Robert Godfrey, "Headship and the Bible," in *Does Christianity Teach Male Headship? The Equal-Regard Marriage and Its Critics* (ed. David Blankenhorn, Don S. Browning, and Mary Stewart Van Leeuwen; Grand Rapids: Eerdmans, 2003), 84–85; Grudem, *Evangelical Feminism and Biblical Truth,* 30–42, 102–30; James B. Hurley, *Man and Woman in Biblical Perspective* (Grand Rapids: Zondervan, 1981), 206–14; Malphurs, *Biblical Manhood and Womanhood,* 21–62; Neuer, *Man and Woman,* 69–78; John Piper and Wayne A. Grudem, "An Overview of Central Concerns: Questions and Answers," in *Recovering Biblical Manhood and Womanhood: A Response to Evangelical Feminism* (ed. John Piper and Wayne A. Grudem; Wheaton, Ill.: Crossway, 1991), 66, 81, 87; Thomas R. Schreiner, "Women in Ministry," in *Two Views on Women in Ministry* (ed. James R. Beck and Craig L. Blomberg; Grand Rapids: Zondervan, 2001), 200–210; Michael F. Stitzinger, "Genesis 1–3 and the Male/Female Role Relationship," *GTJ* 2 (1981): 23–44; Clarence J. Vos, *Woman in Old Testament Worship* (Amsterdam: Judels & Brinkman, 1968), 10–19, 28–31; Jerome T. Walsh, "Genesis 2:4b–3:24: A Synchronic Approach," *JBL* 96 (1977): 161–77 (esp. 174); and Ware, "Male and Female Complementarity," 81–92.

archical ranking of the sexes may be summarized as follows: (1) man is created first and woman last (vv. 7, 22), the first is superior (so liberal-critical scholars) or head/leader (so evangelical hierarchicalists), and the last is inferior or subordinate; (2) man, not woman, is spoken to by God and does the speaking (vv. 16–17, 23); (3) woman is formed for the sake of man, to be his "partner" or assistant to cure man's loneliness (vv. 18–20); (4) woman is created from man's rib (vv. 21–22), which implies a derivative and subordinate position or role, and indicates her dependence upon him for life; and (5) the man names the woman (v. 23), which indicates his authority or leadership over her. Do these points in fact substantiate a hierarchical relationship (whether ontological or functional) between the sexes? Let us look at each point in turn.

First, because man is created first and then woman, it has been asserted that "by this the priority and superiority of the man, and the dependence of the woman upon the man, are established as an ordinance of divine creation."[37] Evangelical hierarchicalists today avoid the word "superiority" for man but argue instead for male leadership from this order of creation. But a careful examination of the literary structure of Gen 2 reveals that such a conclusion about hierarchy does not follow from the fact of man's prior creation. Hebrew literature often makes use of an *inclusio* device in which the points of central concern to a unit are placed at the beginning and end of the unit.[38] This is the case in Gen 2. The entire account is cast in the form of an *inclusio* or "ring construction"[39] in which the creation of man at the beginning of the narrative and the creation of woman at the end of the narrative correspond to each other in importance. The narrator underscores their equality of importance by employing precisely the same number of words (in Hebrew) for the description of the creation of the man as for the creation of woman. "The writer has counted his words and been careful to match the lengths of his descriptions exactly."[40] The movement in Gen 2 is not from superior to inferior or from leadership to submission but from incompleteness to completeness. Woman is created as the climax, the culmination of the story, and as Adam's full equal.[41] "The movement of the story beautifully progresses from the utter loneliness of Adam, through the presence of useful living creatures that only accentuate the loneliness by

---

[37] K&D, 1:56.

[38] For discussion of this construction, see esp. James Muilenburg, "Form Criticism and Beyond," *JBL* 88 (1969): 9–10; cf. Mitchel Dahood, *Psalms* (3 vols.; AB 16–17A; Garden City: Doubleday, 1965–1970), 1:5; and Phillis Trible, "Depatriarchalizing in Biblical Interpretation," *JAAR* 41, no. 1 (1973): 36.

[39] Muilenburg, "Form Criticism and Beyond," 9.

[40] Trevor Dennis, *Sarah Laughed: Women's Voices in the Old Testament* (Nashville: Abingdon, 1994), 13. Genesis 2:7 and 2:21b–22 contain sixteen Hebrew words describing the creation of man and woman respectively.

[41] This is recognized already by John L. McKenzie, "The Literary Characteristics of Genesis 2–3," *TS* 15 (1954): 559: "The creation of woman is the climax toward which the whole preceding narrative tends. . . . The narrative treats woman as an equal and a partner of man. This feature does not appear in any ancient Near Eastern story."

their incapacity to be his companions, to the ecstasy of delight in discovering the companionship of an equal [Gen 2:23 cited]."[42]

That reference to man first and then to woman does not thereby imply a patriarchal understanding of male leadership over woman is further supported by comparison with the account of the first marriage in the Akkadian parallel account, the Atrahasis Epic, the extant copy of which is from the seventeenth century B.C.E. Although it is generally recognized that in the patriarchal society of ancient Mesopotamia the subservience of the wife to the husband exceeded that of ancient Israel,[43] it is the woman who is mentioned first, and the man second, in the description of the first marriage and elsewhere throughout the epic where both genders are mentioned.[44] "This indicates that the *sequence* of man's and woman's creation has no significance for implications of the society's view of or assumptions regarding hierarchy."[45]

A second argument concerns the man's priority in speaking and being spoken to in the narrative. It has been claimed that the man's leadership over his wife before the fall is revealed in that God addresses the man, not the woman, and also that the man does the speaking in the narrative of Gen 2, not the woman. Such a claim, however, fails to take into account the movement of the narrative from incompleteness to completeness and climax, as has been pointed out above. As part of the process of bringing the man to realize his "hunger for wholeness," that he is alone and like the other creatures needs a partner, God indeed speaks to him, warning him not to eat of the forbidden tree.[46] As soon as God created a human being, such information was crucial for that being to avoid transgression and to be a free moral agent with the power of choice. But the divine impartation of such knowledge to the man before the woman was created does not thereby reveal the leadership of the man over his partner. "Clearly the man needed to know the rules of the game during the interval before the woman's arrival. . . . This need not imply any superiority on his part; only that he needed to hear the command as soon as he was present in Eden."[47] Likewise, only the man speaking (not the woman) in Gen 2 does not reveal his pre-fall leadership over the woman any more than only Eve speaking (and not Adam) outside the Garden (Gen 4) reveals Eve's leadership over Adam after the fall.[48]

---

[42] Mary Corona, "Woman in Creation Story," *Jeev* 21 (1991): 98–99.

[43] See ch. 6, below; and esp. Sophie Lafont, *Femmes, droit, et justice dans l'antiquité orientale: Contributions à l'étude du droit pénal au Proche-Orient ancien* (OBO 165; Göttingen: Vandenhoeck & Ruprecht, 1999), passim.

[44] Bernard F. Batto, "The Institution of Marriage in Genesis 2 and in *Atrahasis*," *CBQ* 62 (2000): 627.

[45] Hess, "Equality with and without Innocence," 85–86.

[46] The phrase "hunger for wholeness" was coined by Sakae Kubo, *Theology and Ethics of Sex* (Washington, D.C.: Review and Herald, 1980), 19.

[47] Joy Elasky Fleming, *Man and Woman in Biblical Unity: Theology from Genesis 2–3* (Old Tappan, N.J.: Christians for Biblical Equality, 1993), 6.

[48] As the afterword will argue, the interpretation of Gen 2 set forth here does not contradict Paul's reference to this passage in 1 Tim 2:13.

If a hierarchy of the sexes is not implied in the *order* of their creation or the *priority* of speech, is such indicated by the *purpose* of woman's creation, as is suggested in a third major argument for the hierarchical interpretation? Genesis 2:18 records the Lord's deliberation: "It is not good that the man should be alone; I will make him *ʿēzer kĕnegdô* [KJV: 'a help meet for him'; RSV: 'a helper fit for him'; NASB: 'a helper suitable to him']." The Hebrew words *ʿēzer kĕnegdô* have often been taken to imply the inferiority or subordinate status of woman. For example, John Calvin understood from this phrase that woman was a "kind of appendage" and a "lesser helpmeet" for man.[49] More recently Clines argues that the Hebrew word *ʿēzer* refers to someone in a subordinate position.[50] But this is not the meaning conveyed by the Hebrew.

The masculine noun *ʿēzer* is usually translated as "help" or "helper" in English. This is a misleading translation, however, because the English word "helper" tends to suggest one who is an assistant, a subordinate, an inferior, whereas the Hebrew *ʿēzer* carries no such connotation. In fact, of the twenty-one occurrences of *ʿēzer* in the HB, sixteen employ *ʿēzer* to describe a *superordinate*— God himself as the "helper" of Israel.[51] The other three occurrences outside Gen 2 denote military allies.[52] Never in Scripture does the word refer to a subordinate helper (unless Gen 2 is seen as an exception to the consistent usage elsewhere). The word *ʿēzer* is a relational term, describing a beneficial relationship, but in itself does not specify position or rank, whether of superiority or of inferiority.[53] The specific position intended must be gleaned from the immediate context. In Gen 2, where God brings the parade of animals but Adam finds no fitting companion, the "help" intended is clearly "real companionship that can be given only by an equal."[54] This "help" or benefaction is indeed "for the man" (v. 18) in the sense that she "would bring benefit to Adam,"[55] but this does not imply a hierarchy of roles. The benefit brought to the man is that at last he has an egalitarian partner, a soul mate.

---

49 John Calvin, *Commentary on Genesis* (Grand Rapids: Eerdmans, n.d.), 217–18.

50 Clines, "What Does Eve Do to Help?" passim.

51 Exod 18:4; Deut 33:7, 26, 29; Ps 20:3 (ET 20:2); 33:20; 70:6 (ET 70:5); 89:20 (ET 89:19); 115:9, 10, 11; 121:1, 2; 124:8; 146:5; Hos 13:9.

52 Isa 30:5; Ezek 12:14; Dan 11:34.

53 Contra, e.g., C. John Collins, *Genesis 1–4: A Linguistic, Literary, and Theological Commentary* (Phillipsburg, N.J.: P & R Publishing, 2006), 107, who claims: "A 'help(er)' is one who takes a subordinate role (which is why it is so startling to read of God being the 'help' of his faithful ones, as in Deut. 33:7 and Ps. 33:20)." R. David Freedman argues that the Hebrew word *ʿēzer* etymologically derives from the merger of two Semitic roots, *ʿzr,* "to save, rescue," and *gzr,* "to be strong," and in Gen 2 has reference to the latter: woman is created, like the man, "a power (or strength) superior to the animals" ("Woman, a Power Equal to Man," *BAR* 9, no. 1 [1983]: 56–58). Even if Freedman's etymological suggestion is not accepted, the context of Scripture is the final determiner of meaning: an examination of all the other OT passages employing the Hebrew term *ʿēzer*, commonly translated "help(er)," do not present the "helper" in a subordinate role.

54 Corona, "Woman in Creation Story," 99.

55 Grudem, *Evangelical Feminism and Biblical Truth,* 118.

Genesis 2:18 and 20 confirm this equality of ranking with the expression that adjoins ʿēzer, namely, kĕnegdô. The word neged conveys the idea of "in front of," "opposite," or "counterpart," and so a literal translation of kĕnegdô is "like his counterpart." Used with ʿēzer, this prepositional phrase indicates no less than equality without hierarchy: Eve is Adam's "benefactor/helper," one who in position and status is "corresponding to him, i.e., equal and adequate to himself."[56] Eve is "a power equal to man";[57] she is Adam's "soul-mate,"[58] his equal partner both ontologically and functionally. We will return to the implications of this interpretation for the theology of sexuality, but here it can be affirmed that the phrase ʿēzer kĕnegdô in no way implies a male leadership or female submission as part of the creation order.

As a fourth indication of male superiority/leadership and female subordination/submission in Gen 2, it has been argued that since woman came out of man, since she was formed from man's rib, she has a derivative existence, a dependent and subordinate status. That her existence was in some way "derived" from Adam cannot be denied. But derivation does not imply subordination. The text indicates this in several ways. Note, for example, that Adam also was "derived"—from the ground (v. 7)—but certainly one is not to conclude that the ground was his superior or leader.[59] Furthermore, as the first woman was derived from man, every subsequent man comes from woman, and so there is an expression of integration, not subordination, indicated here.

Also, woman is not Adam's rib. It was the raw material, not woman herself, that was taken out of man, just as the raw material of man was "taken" (3:19, 23) out of the ground.[60] In contrast with man, who was merely "formed" or molded (yṣr) from the clay (Gen 2:7), woman was, according to the Hebrew original term, bnh of v. 22, "[architechturally] built" (not just "made," as blandly translated by English versions such as the NRSV and the NIV). The verb bnh, "to build," used in the creation account only regarding the formation of Eve, "suggests an aesthetic intent and connotes also the idea of reliability and permanence."[61] To clinch the

---

[56] BDB 617. So also Noort, "The Creation of Man and Woman," 12–13, who examines the phrase ʿēzer kĕnegdô and concludes that it "means here mutual stimulation, helping each other as equals" (p. 13).

[57] Freedman, "Woman," 56–58. Freedman notes that in later Mishnaic Hebrew kĕneged clearly means "equal," and in light of various lines of biblical philological evidence, he forcefully argues that the phrase ʿēzer kĕnegdô here should be translated "a power equal to him."

[58] Cassuto, Genesis, 1:128.

[59] Cf. Judy L. Brown, Women Ministers according to Scripture (Minneapolis: Christians for Biblical Equality, 1996), 19: "If Adam is better than Eve by virtue of supplying a bone, then the ground is better than Adam by virtue of supplying the dust. The dust and bone were simply raw materials in the hands of the true source of life, the one from whom both Adam and Eve were given their existence."

[60] Trible, God and the Rhetoric of Sexuality, 101.

[61] Samuel Terrien, "Toward a Biblical Theology of Womanhood," in Male and Female: Christian Approaches to Sexuality (ed. Ruth T. Barnhouse and Urban T. Holmes III; New York: Seabury, 1976), 18; cf. idem, Till the Heart Sings: A Biblical Theology of Manhood and

point, the text explicitly indicates that the man was asleep while God created woman. Man had no active part in the creation of woman that might allow him to claim to be her superior or head.[62]

The very symbolism of the rib points to equality and not hierarchy. The word ṣēlāᶜ can mean either "side" or "rib." Since ṣēlāᶜ occurs in the plural in v. 21 and God is said to take "one of" them, the reference in this verse is probably to a rib from Adam's side.[63] By "building" Eve from one of Adam's ribs from his side, God appears to be indicating the "mutual relationship,"[64] the "singleness of life"[65] in which man and woman are joined. The rib "means solidarity and equality."[66] Created from Adam's "rib," Eve was formed to stand by his side as an equal. Peter Lombard was not off the mark when he said, "Eve was not taken from the feet of Adam to be his slave, nor from his head to be his ruler, but from his side to be his beloved partner."[67] This interpretation appears to be further confirmed by the man's poetic exclamation when he sees the woman for the first time (v. 23): "This at last is bone of my bones and flesh of my flesh." The phrase "bone of my bones and flesh of my flesh" indicates that the person described is as close as one's own body. It denotes physical oneness and "a commonality of concern, loyalty and re-sponsibility."[68] Much regarding the theology of sexuality can be deduced from this expression, as will become apparent below, but the expression certainly does not lead to the notion of woman's subordination or submission to man.

The last major argument used to support a hierarchical view of the sexes in Gen 2 is that in man's naming of woman (v. 23) is implied man's authority over

---

Womanhood (Philadelphia: Fortress, 1985), 12: "The use of the verb 'to build' for the woman implies an intellectual and aesthetic appreciation of her body, the equilibrium of her forms, and the volumes and proportions of her figure."

[62] As the afterword will clarify, Paul's argument that "man was not made from woman, but woman from man" (1 Cor 11:8), does not contradict the interpretation set forth here.

[63] BDB 854; *HALOT* 1030.

[64] Claus Westermann, *Genesis 1–11* (Minneapolis: Augsburg, 1974), 230.

[65] Collins, "The Bible and Sexuality," 153. It may be that the Sumerian language retains the memory of the close relationship between "rib" and "life," for the same Sumerian sign TI signifies both "life" and "rib." See Samuel N. Kramer, *History Begins at Sumer* (Garden City, N.Y.: Doubleday, 1959), 146. This is not to say, however, that the detail of the rib in Gen 2 has its origin in Sumerian mythology. The story of creation in Gen 2 and the Sumerian myth in which the pun between "lady of the rib" and "lady who makes live" appears ("Enki and Ninhursag: A Paradise Myth," translated by Samuel Noah Kramer [*ANET* 37–41]) have virtually nothing in common.

[66] Trible, "Depatriarchalizing," 37. Cf. Mary Phil Korsak, "Hebrew Word Patterns Retained in English in Genesis 2:4b–3:24," *ACEBT* 15 (1996): 16: "'Side' expresses man/woman equality."

[67] Quoted in Stuart B. Babbage, *Christianity and Sex* (Chicago: InterVarsity, 1963), 10. A similar statement is attributed to other writers as well, including the earlier church fathers.

[68] Walter Brueggemann, "Of the Same Flesh and Bone (Gen 2:23a)," *CBQ* 32 (1970): 540. For biblical examples of this usage, see esp. Gen 29:14; Judg 9:2–3; 2 Sam 5:1; 19:13 (ET 19:12); cf. Job 2:5; Ps 102:6 (ET 102:5). Terrien, *Till the Heart Sings*, 13, points out that these texts refer to "a psychic bond of covenant loyalty."

her, as his naming the animals implied his authority over the animals.[69] This conclusion is predicated upon the commonly repeated thesis that assigning names in Scripture signifies authority over the one named, but this widely held scholarly assumption has been recently effectively challenged.[70] George Ramsey shows from the OT data of naming that "if the act of naming signifies anything about the name-giver, it is the quality of *discernment*" and not the exercise of authority or control. Even if the man does name the woman in 2:23, "the exclamation in Gen 2:23 is a cry of discovery, of recognition [cf. Jacob's cry in 28:16–17, before bestowing the name Bethel], rather than a prescription of what this creature built from his rib shall be. An essence which God had already fashioned is recognized by the man and celebrated in the naming."[71] That superiority or exercise of leadership authority is not intended here is confirmed from the immediate context, the preceding lines: "This at last is bone of my bones and flesh of my flesh." This clause, as already noted, clearly connotes mutuality and equality, not subordination.[72] The second part of 2:23 also confirms this interpretation: the arrangement in Hebrew is chiastic, with the words for "woman" and "man" placed

---

[69] See, e.g., Schreiner, "Women in Ministry," 206–9.

[70] Biblical examples usually cited in support of the oriental view of naming as the demonstration of one's exercise of a sovereign right over a person include such passages as 2 Kgs 23:34; 24:17; Dan 1:7. Cf. R. Abba, "Name," *IDB* 3:502. George W. Ramsey, "Is Name-Giving an Act of Domination in Genesis 2:23 and Elsewhere?" *CBQ* 50 (1988): 24–35, has challenged this thesis. Examining the major texts where it is claimed that bestowal of a name indicates control or authority over the person named, Ramsey shows that "instead of thinking of name-giving as a *determiner* of an entity's essence, the Hebrews regarded naming as commonly *determined by* circumstances. The naming *results from* events which have occurred" (p. 34). The non-Israelite kings' changing of individual's names cannot be normative for Hebrew thinking (and these do not have the typical naming formula/terminology). Very significant is the fact that Hagar names God (Gen 16:13) by using the typical naming formula. Certainly this does not imply her control/domination over divinity. Again, in 26:17–21 Isaac names the wells even as he relinquishes authority over them. In Gen 2, when the man names the animals, here again "it is more appropriate to understand this as an act of his *discerning* something about these creatures—an essence which had already been established by God" (pp. 34–35). For a similar assessment of the evidence, see also Rick R. Marrs, "In the Beginning: Male and Female (Gen 1–3)," in *Essays on Women in Earliest Christianity* (ed. Carroll D. Osburn; 2 vols.; Joplin, Mo.: College Press, 1995), 2:17–18; and Carol A. Newsom, "Common Ground: An Ecological Reading of Genesis 2–3," in *The Earth Story in Genesis* (ed. Norman C. Habel and Shirley Wurst; Sheffield, Eng.: Sheffield Academic Press, 2000), 66.

[71] Ramsey, "Name-Giving," 34. For further discussion, see ibid., 32–34.

[72] The same point is reaffirmed in Gen 3, where this equality/mutuality is described as recently broken. "By reversing the negatives in God's curse of Adam and Eve, we come to the lost positives of the Garden—and the world as God meant it to be. . . . Reading backwards [from 3:16], we can detect the earlier mutuality between the man and woman, a harmonious relationship expressed by Genesis 2:23. . . . The harmony of the relationship is evident even without the philological argument that the Hebrew words designating Eve as Adam's 'helper as his partner' (Genesis 2:18) does not imply subordination" (Mary Joan Winn Leith, "Back to the Garden," *BR* 18, no. 2 [2002]: 10, 46).

in parallel in the center,[73] "suggesting a corresponding and equal relationship to one another."[74]

Regarding the naming of the animals, the man is not exercising his authority over them but classifying them,[75] and in the immediate context of man's being "alone" and this being "not good" (v. 18), God's bringing of the animals to the man for him to name further implies that the man is entering into a delightful companionship with the animals, only to ultimately discover that such companionship is inadequate to satisfy his quest for complete reciprocity and mutuality.[76]

Furthermore, it appears most probable that Adam does not name the woman before the fall at all. The designation ʾiššâ occurs in the narrative before Adam ever meets her (2:22). She is already called "woman" by the narrator even before the man sees her. Jacques Doukhan has shown that 2:23 contains a pairing of "divine passives," indicating that the designation "woman" comes from God, not man. Just as, in the past, woman was "taken from the man" by God, an action with which the man had nothing to do (he had been put into a "deep sleep"), so in the future she "shall be called Woman," a designation originating in God and not man. Doukhan also indicates how the literary structure of the Genesis creation story confirms this interpretation.[77]

The wordplay in v. 23 between ʾîš ("man") and ʾiššâ ("wo-man") and the explanation that the woman was taken out of man are not given to buttress a hierarchical ranking of the sexes but rather to underscore man's joyous recognition of his second self.[78] In fact, the word ʾîš first appears in this verse; the man becomes

---

[73] J. P. Fokkelman, *Narrative Art in Genesis: Specimens of Stylistic and Structural Analysis* (2d ed.; BS 12; Sheffield, Eng.: JSOT Press, 1991), 37.

[74] Hess, "Equality with and without Innocence," 88.

[75] Ibid., 87.

[76] Paul Borgman, *Genesis: The Story We Haven't Heard* (Downers Grove, Ill.: Inter-Varsity, 2001), 26.

[77] Doukhan, *Literary Structure,* 47, points to "the use of the passive (*niphal, pual*) which conveys the idea of an intervention from outside, hence God, who is still the only 'other' (for the biblical usage of the passive as referring to God, see Lev 13:7; Luke 5:20)." For further discussion of the divine passive in Scripture, see Hans K. La Rondelle, *Perfection and Perfectionism: A Dogmatic-Ethical Study of Biblical Perfection and Phenomenal Perfectionism* (Berrien Springs, Mich.: Andrews University Press, 1975), 127–28; and von Rad, *Old Testament Theology,* 1:247–48, 261–62. For other lines of evidence disaffirming man's authoritative naming of woman in 2:23 in contrast to his authoritative naming of the animals in 2:19–20, see esp. Trible, *God and the Rhetoric of Sexuality,* 99–100; Gerhard Hasel, "Equality from the Start: Woman in the Creation Story," *Spectrum* 7, no. 2 (1975): 23–24; and Fleming, *Man and Woman,* 14–15.

[78] As already noted in the introduction, there is no general consensus among scholars on the etymology of these words. The suggestion by some etymologists that ʾîš has the root idea of "strength" and ʾiššâ the idea of a "weaker" sex could imply that the man was to be the protector-provider for the woman, but this does not connote leadership on the part of the man and submission on the part of the woman. Witness the famous and important people with stronger bodyguards, who are their protectors but certainly do not possess authority or leadership over them. Clearly the intention of the Genesis account in linking this word pair by (popular but inspired) etymology is to emphasize the mutual communion and commonality of the man and the woman.

aware of his own identity as he discerns the identity of ʾiššâ. In his ecstatic poetic utterance, the man is not determining who the woman is—any more than he is determining who he himself is—but delighting in his recognition of what God has done. He is saying yes to God in recognizing his own sexual nature and welcoming woman as the equal counterpart to his sexuality.[79] After the fall Adam did give his wife a name (Eve), but even there it is more probable that he is discerning what she already was by the promise of God, "mother of all living" (3:20), and not exercising authority over her.[80]

In short, none of the arguments advanced from Gen 2 to support a hierarchical relationship between the sexes can stand the test of close scrutiny. In light of the foregoing discussion, I concur with a host of other commentators and scholarly studies—both liberal-critical and evangelical—in their conclusion that Gen 2, like Gen 1, contains no statement of dominance, subordination, or leadership/submission in the relationship of the sexes.[81] The man and the woman before

---

[79] See Barth, *Church Dogmatics,* 3/2:291; Trible, *God and the Rhetoric of Sexuality,* 100.

[80] See Francis Landy, "Mishneh Torah: A Response to Myself and Phyllis Trible," in *A Feminist Companion to the Song of Songs* (ed. Athalya Brenner; FCB 1; Sheffield, Eng.: Sheffield Academic Press, 1993), 261–62; cf. Ramsey, "Name-Giving," 35, n. 38, who points out that in 3:20 the narrator makes clear that Adam is not trying to determine Eve's destiny (i.e., exercise authority over her) or he would have said, "She will be the mother of all living." Instead the narrator reports again what Adam discerns already to be true: "she *was* [*hāytâ*] the mother of all living."

[81] At least fifty major scholarly studies come to this conclusion. The more important analyses of Gen 2 (as well as of Gen 1 and of the various hierarchicalist arguments for male leadership) include Bal, *Lethal Love,* 112–19; Lyn M. Bechtel, "Rethinking the Interpretation of Genesis 2:4b–3:24," in *A Feminist Companion to Genesis* (ed. Athalya Brenner; Sheffield, Eng.: Sheffield Academic Press, 1993), 111–14; Linda L. Belleville, *Women Leaders and the Church: Three Crucial Questions* (Grand Rapids: Baker, 2000), 96–103; Gilbert G. Bilezikian, *Beyond Sex Roles: What the Bible Says about a Woman's Place in Church and Family* (Grand Rapids: Baker, 1985), 21–37; Phyllis A. Bird, "Sexual Differentiation and Divine Image in the Genesis Creation Texts," in *Image of God and Gender Models in Judaeo-Christian Tradition* (ed. Kari Elisabeth Børresen; Oslo: Solum, 1991), 11–31; idem, "'Bone of My Bone and Flesh of My Flesh'"; Brown, *Women Ministers according to Scripture,* 17–34; Corona, "Woman in Creation Story," 95–106; Dennis, *Sarah Laughed,* 8–18; Mary J. Evans, *Woman in the Bible: An Overview of All the Crucial Passages on Women's Roles* (Downers Grove, Ill.: InterVarsity, 1984), 11–17; Fleming, *Man and Woman,* 3–17; Stanley Grenz with Denise Muir Kjesbo, *Women in the Church: A Biblical Theology of Women in Ministry* (Downers Grove, Ill.: InterVarsity, 1995), 160–65; Groothuis, *Good News for Women,* 121–39; Mary Hayter, *The New Eve in Christ: The Use and Abuse of the Bible in the Debate about Women in the Church* (Grand Rapids: Eerdmans, 1987), 84–117; Gretchen Gaebelein Hull, *Equal to Serve: Women and Men in the Church and Home* (Old Tappan, N.J.: Fleming H. Revell, 1987), 152–83; Jewett, *Man as Male and Female,* 33–40, 50, 120–28; (the elder) Luther, *Lectures on Genesis: Chapters 1–5,* 138, 200–203; Marrs, "In the Beginning," 11–12, 18–22, 31–32; Alvera Mickelsen, "An Egalitarian View: There Is Neither Male nor Female in Christ," in *Women in Ministry: Four Views* (ed. Bonnidell Clouse and Robert G. Clouse; Downers Grove, Ill.: InterVarsity, 1989), 181–87; John H. Otwell, *And Sarah Laughed: The Status of Women in the Old Testament* (Philadelphia: Westminster, 1977), 15–18; Ramsey, "Name-Giving," 24–35; J. Alberto Soggin, "The Equality of Humankind from the Perspective of the Creations Stories in Genesis 1:26–30

the fall are presented as fully equal in rank, with no hint of an ontological or functional hierarchy, no leadership/submission relationship between husband and wife.

> Conspicuously absent in Genesis 1–2 is any reference to divine prescriptions for man to exercise authority over woman. Due to the importance of its implications, had such an authority structure been part of the creation design, it would have received clear definition along with the two other authority mandates [God's sovereignty over humans, and human's dominion over all the earth]. The total absence of such a commission indicates that it was not a part of God's intent. Only God was in authority over Adam and Eve. Neither of them had the right to usurp divine prerogatives by assuming authority over each other. Any teaching that inserts an authority structure between Adam and Eve in God's creation design is to be firmly rejected since it is not founded on the biblical text.[82]

This affirmation of the full equality and mutuality of man and woman in the Gen 2 account of creation is all the more important when seen in contrast with the other ANE creation accounts, which contain no separate narration of the creation of woman. The Genesis creation narratives not only give a detailed account of origins but at the same time appear to serve as a direct polemic against the mythological creation stories of the ancient Near East.[83] By its special, lengthy, separate account of the creation of woman in Gen 2, the Bible, with its high valuation of woman on an equal par with man, is unique in ANE literature.

Sexuality and Wholeness

A fifth facet of sexual theology in Gen 1–2 integrates the discussion of "male and female" with the *imago Dei*. In Gen 1:27 the generic term for humankind (*hāʾādām*) includes both male and female. The "man and the woman together make man [human]."[84] The wholistic picture of humankind is complete only

---

and 2:9, 15, 18–24," *JNSL* 23 (1997): 21–33; Ada Besançon Spencer, *Beyond the Curse: Women Called to Ministry* (Nashville: Nelson, 1985), 20–29; Lee Anna Starr, *The Bible Status of Woman* (New York: Fleming H. Revell, 1926; repr., New York: Garland, 1987), 17–26; Swidler, *Biblical Affirmations of Woman*, 75–78; Terrien, *Till the Heart Sings*, 7–17; Trible, *God and the Rhetoric of Sexuality,* 72–105; idem, "Depatriarchalizing," 35–40; Ruth A. Tucker, *Women in the Maze: Questions and Answers on Biblical Equality* (Downers Grove, Ill.: InterVarsity, 1992), 33–42; Vogels, "Man and Woman," 205–27; idem, "It Is Not Good That the 'Mensch' Should Be Alone; I Will Make Him/Her a Helper Fit for Him/Her," *EgT* 9 (1978): 9–35; and Erich Zenger, "Die Erschaffung des Menschen als Mann und Frau: Eine Lesehilfe für die sogenannte Paradies- und Sündenfallgeschichte Gen 2,4b–3,24," *BK* 58 (2003): 14.

[82] Bilezikian, *Beyond Sex Roles*, 41.

[83] For an overview, see esp. Gerhard F. Hasel, "The Polemic Nature of the Genesis Cosmology," *EvQ* 46 (1974): 81–102; cf. Cassuto, *Genesis*, 1:7–177, passim; and Noort, "The Creation of Man and Woman," 8–10.

[84] Johannes Pedersen, *Israel: Its Life and Culture* (4 vols. in 2; London: Oxford University Press, 1926–1940; repr., Atlanta: Scholars Press, 1991), 1:61–62.

when both male and female are viewed together. Both man and woman are made in the image of God, after God's likeness (v. 26). Such a description points to both the individuality and the complementarity of the sexes.[85]

My purpose is not to enter into an extended discussion of the meaning of the *imago Dei*.[86] But it may be noted that the Hebrew words ṣelem, "image," and dĕmût, "likeness," although possessing overlapping semantic ranges, in the juxtaposition of v. 26 appear to emphasize respectively the concrete and abstract aspects of the human being[87] and together indicate that the person as a whole—in both physical/bodily and spiritual/mental components—is created in God's image. Von Rad insightfully concludes regarding 1:26, "One will do well to split the physical from the spiritual as little as possible: the whole man is created in God's image."[88]

Genesis 2 presents an amplification of the twofold meaning of sexual wholeness set forth in Gen 1. First, 2:7 (like 1:26) articulates a wholistic view of humans. According to the understanding of anthropology set forth in this verse, a human being does not *have* a soul, he/she *is* a soul. A human is a living being, a psychophysical unity.[89] There is no room in such a view for a Platonic/Philonic dichotomy of body and soul. Excluded is the dualistic notion of the ascetics that the body is evil and therefore all expressions of body pleasures—including sexual

---

[85] This is not to suggest that a single (unmarried) person is less than fully human. Adam and Eve individually were each made in the image of God. And humankind as a whole (corporately) represents the image of God. At the same time, the text also underscores the wholistic understanding of the *imago Dei* that includes both male and female.

[86] The literature on this subject is voluminous. For a survey of views, see esp. Claus Westermann, *Genesis* (3 vols.; BKAT 1; Neukirchen-Vluyn: Neukirchener Verlag, 1974), 1:203–14; cf. G. C. Berkouwer, *Man: The Image of God* (Grand Rapids: Eerdmans, 1962), 67–118; David J. A. Clines, "The Image of God in Man," *TynBul* 19 (1968): 53–103; Charles Lee Feinberg, "The Image of God," *BSac* 129 (1972): 235–45; Anthony A. Hoekema, *Created in God's Image* (Grand Rapids: Eerdmans, 1986); and Gunnlaugur A. Jónsson, *The Image of God: Genesis 1:26–28 in a Century of Old Testament Research* (Conjectanea Biblica; Old Testament Series 26; Lund: Almquist & Wiksell, 1988).

[87] See BDB 198, 854; Norman W. Porteous, "Image of God," *IDB* 2:684–85; von Rad, *Genesis*, 57–58. Cf. the summary by Rashkow, *Taboo or Not Taboo*, 61: "God says that his intention is to make Adam both 'in our image' (that is, physically similar, whatever that may mean), and 'in our likeness' (having the same abstract characteristics)." Regarding the aspect of outward ("physical" or "bodily") resemblance, which most scholars resist finding in this passage, see also David M. Carr, *The Erotic Word: Sexuality, Spirituality, and the Bible* (New York: Oxford University Press, 2003), 17–26, who counters with solid biblical data the common notion "that Genesis 1 must be talking about something else—anything else—than actual physical resemblance between God and humans" (p. 18).

[88] Von Rad, *Genesis*, 58. For other evidence supporting the wholistic view of what it means to be created in God's image, see also W. Randall Garr, *In His Own Image and Likeness: Humanity, Divinity, and Monotheism* (CHANE 15; Leiden: E. J. Brill, 2003), 117–76 (esp. 166); and Neuer, *Man and Woman*, 65–67 (with references to other scholars).

[89] Hans Walter Wolff, *Anthropology of the Old Testament* (London: SCM, 1974), 10: "Man does not *have* n[epeš], he *is* n[epeš], he lives as n[epeš]." So William Dyrness, *Themes in Old Testament Theology* (Downers Grove, Ill.: Inter Varsity, 1979), 85: "Human beings live as souls; they do not 'possess' souls."

expressions—are contaminated. The wholistic view of humanness presented in 2:7 means that human sexuality cannot be compartmentalized into "the things of the body" versus "the things of the spirit/soul." The human being is a sexual creature, and his/her sexuality is manifested in every aspect of human existence. This wholistic view of sexuality means that the "one flesh" experience of husband and wife (2:24) involves not only the sex act but also a oneness—a wholeness—in all the physical, sensual, social, intellectual, emotional, and spiritual dimensions of life. This wholistic concept of the "one flesh" relationship between husband and wife implies that it is not sufficient to only seek physical compatibility in marriage; equally important is harmony between marriage partners in matters of religious faith.

The meaning of wholeness is also amplified in Gen 2 regarding the differentiation between the sexes. Whereas from Gen 1 it was possible to conclude in a general way that both male and female are equally needed to make up the image of God, Gen 2 indicates more precisely that in "creative complementariness"[90] God designed male and female to participate in this wholeness. The Gen 2 creation story opens with the creation of man. But creation is not finished. The man is alone, he is incomplete. And this is "not good" (v. 18).[91] Man needs an ῾ēzer kĕnegdô—a helper/benefactor who is opposite him, his counterpart. Thus begins man's quest to satisfy his God-instilled "hunger for wholeness."[92] The Lord God brings the animals to the man for him to name (identify), so that he may realize that such hunger is not satisfied by his animal companions. He also evidently recognizes that the animals and birds all have mates but he himself does not.[93] Thus the flow of the narrative leads to the climactic creation of woman, the sexual being God has "built" or "aesthetically designed" (the literal meaning of bnh in v. 22) to be alongside him as his complement. "The woman brings out of the man and to the man the totality of existence. She comes as if he had cried out, 'Help! Help!'"[94] Adam in effect exclaims at his first sight of Eve, "At last, I'm

---

[90] Terrien, "Theology of Womanhood," 18.

[91] This is the only thing in Gen 1–2 that is described as "not good." At the same time, there seems to be a difference of nuance between the Hebrew expressions for "not good" (lō᾽ tôb) and for "evil" (ra῾). See Alexandru Breja, "A Biblical Approach to Transcultural Analysis" (paper presented at the annual meeting of the Evangelical Theological Society, Atlanta, November 21, 2003), 1–19. Breja provides evidence, by means of exegesis of several passages (including the references in Gen 1–2), that throughout the HB something described as "not good" is not "evil," only less than ideal.

[92] Kubo, Theology and Ethics of Sex, 19.

[93] Some critical commentators argue that 2:18–24 describes a series of unsuccessful divine attempts to make an adequate partner for the man. This view is totally out of harmony with the concept of God presented in Gen 1–2, and contrary to the explicit reason given in the text (v. 19): God brings the creatures to Adam to see what he would name them, not to unsuccessfully attempt to provide him a counterpart. See Cassuto, Genesis, 1:127–28, who presents seven different arguments refuting this critical interpretation. He rightly concludes (p. 128), "It would seem that the text intends to tell us only that the Lord God wished to engender in the heart of man a desire for a helper who should correspond to him exactly."

[94] Terrien, Till the Heart Sings, 11.

whole! Here's the complement of myself!" He recognizes, and the narrative instructs us, that "man is whole only in his *complementarity* with another being who is like himself."[95]

Adam and Eve, in their egalitarian complementarity, were to have no interests independent of each other, and yet each had an individuality in thinking and acting.[96] They were bone of each other's bone, flesh of each other's flesh, equal in being and rank, and at the same time they were individuals with differences. "Oneness does not level life to sameness; it allows for distinctions without opposition or hierarchy."[97]

---

[95] Collins, "The Bible and Sexuality," 153 (italics added).

[96] Some may find the juxtaposition of terms "egalitarian complementarity" to be an oxymoron. But I am unwilling to surrender the word "complementarian" to those who use it to describe male leadership and female submission roles as a creation ordinance. The biblical view of egalitarian husband-wife role relations is just as "complementarian"—recognizing differences between the sexes in general and between individual marriage partners but without positing a creation leadership/submission role relationship between man and woman. The definition of complementarity provided by Hyun Chul Paul Kim, "Gender Complementarity in the Hebrew Bible," in *Theological and Hermeneutical Studies* (vol. 1 of *Reading the Hebrew Bible for a New Millennium: Form, Concept, and Theological Perspective;* ed. Deborah Ellens et al.; SAC; Harrisburg, Pa.: Trinity Press International, 2000), 268, is most useful: "The term 'complementarity' . . . implies an idea of the relationship of two distinct parties who share mutual needs, interdependence, and respect. This term is to be distinguished from the connotation of a hierarchical relationship of two parties where one is subordinate to the other. Rather, it is used to include the ideas of mutuality, balance, and equality, while maintaining the uniqueness and distinctiveness of each party rather than homogeneity." For recent further support and elaboration of the terminology of "complementarity without hierarchy," see esp. Pierce and Groothuis, introduction to *Discovering Biblical Equality,* 16–17 (and the entire book). For a popularized elaboration of this concept, see, e.g., H. Dale Burke, *Different by Design: God's Master Plan for Harmony between Men and Women in Marriage* (Chicago: Moody, 2000), 19–51.

[97] Trible, *God and the Rhetoric of Sexuality,* 110. Some have called attention to the different modes of creation between the man and the women—the man's creation out of the ground and the woman's creation out of man—and suggest this may be intimately related to unique differences between the sexes. It is proposed that a man tends to have "an immediate relationship to the world of things" whereas "the woman is primarily directed to the world of persons" (Neuer, *Man and Woman,* 70). It is further pointed out that in Gen 3 the judgments upon Adam and Eve confirm this pattern: Adam's "judgment" involved his work, whereas Eve's involved relationships. This is seen to imply that the man tends to have a physical and internal makeup to protect and provide through his practical, diligent work whereas the woman tends to have a physical and internal makeup to shape, soften, refine, and nurture relationships (Allender and Longman, *Intimate Allies,* 150). These and other differences between males and females (beyond obvious biological functions) are also seen to be supported by recent anthropological research (see esp. Grenz with Kjesbo, *Women in the Church,* 158–60). On the other hand, the divine mandate in Gen 1–2 for both male and female to join in the work of procreation, subduing, having dominion, and tending the garden (1:28; 2:15), reveals that the sexes are not one-dimensional; both sexes are equally directed to the world of things and the world of relationships. These data lead Tikva Frymer-Kensky, *In the Wake of the Goddess: Women, Culture, and the Biblical Transformation of Pagan Myth* (New York: Free Press/Maxwell Macmillan, 1992), to conclude

Although the text of Gen 1–2 implies complementarity between the sexes, it presents no stereotypical roles that constitute the "essence" of manhood and womanhood respectively. Both sexes are made in the image of God; both are given the command to be fruitful and multiply; both are commanded to fill the earth and subdue it; both are commanded to have dominion over all the other creatures (1:27–28). They are equal partners corresponding to each other, with full reciprocity and mutuality and without hierarchy (2:18). Any attempt to distill the essence of the "roles" of man and woman respectively from the opening chapters of Genesis are going beyond the revelation of the text.[98] Complementary wholeness without hierarchy is the portrait of sexuality in Gen 1–2.

Closely connected with egalitarian, complementary wholeness is the concept of wholeness in personal relationship. The juxtaposition of male and female in 1:26 intimates what will become explicit in Gen 2: the full meaning of human existence is not in male or female in isolation but in their mutual communion. The notion of male-female fellowship in Gen 1 has been particularly emphasized by Karl Barth, who maintains that the "I-Thou" relationship of male and female is the essence of the *imago Dei*. For Barth, 1:27b is the exposition of v. 27a. Mankind in fellowship as male and female is what it means to be in the image of God.[99]

Barth's exclusive identification of the sexual distinction with the image of God is too restrictive, but what he asserts is certainly a crucial aspect of the overall picture. The sexual differentiation of male and female (v. 27c) is not identical to the image of God (v. 26a–b), as Barth maintains, but the two are brought into so close connection that they should not be separated, as has been done for

---

that these passages (as well as the rest of the Bible) present a "gender-free" or "gender-blind" concept of humanity. Certainly, gender roles are not hard-and-fast prescribed stereotypes in the creation narratives. Although differences are acknowledged, the emphasis of the stories is on a shared equality of nature and status and responsibility. Since the biblical text in Gen 1–2 differentiates between the sexes (male and female) but does not specify certain role relations that belong exclusively to the male and others that are exclusively the domain of the female, it seems inappropriate to go beyond the biblical evidence at this point and seek to clarify if and to what extent there are gender-specific role relations in addition to the obvious biological differences. For a critique (both from Scripture and the social sciences) of the attempt to establish fixed roles for men and women from Gen 1–2 and the rest of Scripture, see esp. Mary Stewart Van Leeuwen, *Gender and Grace: Love, Work, and Parenting in a Changing World* (Downers Grove, Ill: InterVarsity, 1990); and idem, *My Brother's Keeper: What the Social Sciences Do (and Don't) Tell Us about Masculinity* (Downers Grove, Ill.: InterVarsity, 2002). What can be stated with certainty is that in these opening chapters of the Bible there is no gender status differentiation that gives the man the leadership authority over woman.

[98] Contra a main focus of the Council on Biblical Manhood and Womanhood, represented esp. by Grudem, *Evangelical Feminism and Biblical Truth;* John Piper and Wayne A. Grudem, eds., *Recovering Biblical Manhood and Womanhood: A Response to Evangelical Feminism* (Wheaton, Ill.: Crossway, 1991); and Robert L. Saucy and Judith K. TenElshof, eds., *Women and Men in Ministry: A Complementary Perspective* (Chicago: Moody, 2001).

[99] Barth's discussion of this point extends through major portions of his *Church Dogmatics,* 3/1–3. See the helpful summary of his argument in Jewett, *Man as Male and Female,* 33–48.

centuries. The synthetic parallelism of v. 27c, immediately following the synonymous parallelism of v. 27a–b, indicates that the *mode* of human existence in the
divine image is that of male and female together.[100]

The aspect of personal relationship between the male and female is further
highlighted by the analogy of God's own differentiation and relationship in contemplating the creation of humanity. It is hardly coincidental that only once in
the creation account of Genesis—only in 1:26—does God speak of the divinity in
the plural: "Let *us* make humankind in *our* image, according to *our* likeness."
There have been many attempts to account for this use of the plural, but the explanation that appears most consonant with both the immediate context and the
analogy of Scripture identifies this usage as a plural of fullness. The "let us" as a
plural of fullness "supposes that there is within the divine Being the distinction of
personalities" and expresses "an intra-divine deliberation among 'persons' within
the divine Being."[101]

The juxtaposition of the plurality of the divine "let us" in v. 26 with the plurality of the "them" (male and female) in vv. 26–28 is not without significance. A
correspondence or analogy is intended "between this mark of the divine being,
namely, that it includes an I and a Thou, and the being of man, male and female."[102] The statement of this correspondence "preserves with exceeding care
the otherness of God,"[103] precluding any notion of the bisexuality of God, and yet
at the same time underscores the profound importance of the personal relationship and mutuality of communion in human existence as male and female. Just
as there takes place in the divine being a deliberating over man's creation, "the
differentiation and relationship, the loving coexistence and co-operation, the I
and Thou,"[104] so the same are to be found in the product of God's crowning[105]
creative work, human beings. "The image of God is primarily a relational concept. Ultimately we do not reflect God's image on our own but in relationship.

---

[100] See the argumentation for this point in Jewett, *Man as Male and Female,* 45; cf.
Willem A. M. Beuken, "The Human Person in the Vision of Genesis 1–3: A Synthesis of
Contemporary Insights," *LS* 24 (1999): 6–9.

[101] See Gerhard Hasel, "The Meaning of 'Let Us' in Gen 1:26," *AUSS* 13 (1975): 58–66,
quote at 64. Cf. Derek Kidner, *Genesis: An Introduction and Commentary* (TOTC 1; Downers Grove, Ill.: InterVarsity, 1967), 52. Garr, *In His Own Image and Likeness,* 20, among
many other scholars, also acknowledges that 1:26 involves a "true plural" and "other divine beings," but he interprets these as lesser gods who are God's attendants in God's
heavenly court.

[102] Barth, *Church Dogmatics,* 3/1:196.

[103] Trible, *God and the Rhetoric of Sexuality,* 21.

[104] Barth, *Church Dogmatics,* 3/1:196.

[105] With von Rad, *Genesis,* 57, and Wilfong, "Human Creation in Canonical Context,"
47, I stress that the creation of humans is the "highpoint and goal" (von Rad) and
"lynchpin" (Wilfong) of creation week, and not the Sabbath, even though the Sabbath
comes last in the creation week. As elaborated below, the Sabbath is God's holy gift to humanity in order that they might experience intimate divine-human relationship; humans
are not made in order to keep the Sabbath. As Jesus put it, "The sabbath was made for humankind, not humankind for the sabbath" (Mark 2:27).

Thus the *imago Dei* is not primarily what we are as individuals. Rather, it is present among humans in relationship. In a word, the image of God is found in human community."[106]

Genesis 1 not only indicates God's intention for an I-Thou relationship between male and female made in His image but also begins to fill in the picture of what is involved in that wholistic relationship. Together, in intimate fellowship and relationship with each other and with God, man and woman are to procreate: "Be fruitful and multiply" and "fill the earth" (1:28). Together in relationship they are also to be the creative shapers of the new creation (1:28): "fill the earth and *subdue* [*kābaš*] it"—not by exploitation but by "shaping the creation into a higher order of beauty and usefulness"[107] (as will become more explicit in 2:15). Man and woman in fellowship together are also to be "co-managers" of God's creation (1:28): they are to "have dominion over" (*rādâ*) the animal kingdom, again not by exploitation but by judiciously representing God's sovereignty in the earth (as implicit in their vegetarian diet, free from the slaughter of animals, Gen 1:29).[108] Adam and Eve are not slaves to do the menial work of the gods, as in the ANE stories,[109] but coregents, the king and queen of their earthly dominion. Finally, the Sabbath (2:1–3), given by God at the climax of the creation week, reveals a "palace in time" in which the human family may join together in spiritual fellowship and communion with their Maker.[110]

If Gen 1 provides a melodic statement that human sexuality is for wholistic fellowship in personal relationship, Gen 2 orchestrates this melody with a volume of double forte, and the narrative harmony portrays added richness and beauty in the relational symphony of the sexes.

---

[106] Stanley J. Grenz, "Theological Foundations for Male-Female Relationships," *JETS* 41 (1998): 620.

[107] Allender and Longman, *Intimate Allies*, 80. For a sensitive discussion of the implications of this principle of creative shaping for the marriage relationship, see ibid., 73–125.

The connection between God's creative work and that of humanity is also underscored by the use of the key word *tôlĕdôt*. The term means literally "begettings" or "bringings-forth" (from the verb *yālad* "to bring forth, beget") and implies not only that Genesis is a history/account of beginnings but that in its use throughout the book of Genesis to structure the entire book, it links the creative "begettings" of the heavens and earth by God to the creative work of humans. For further elaboration, see esp. Garr, *In His Own Image and Likeness*, 169, 174–76. Garr (175) summarizes: "God is *creator maior;* humankind is *creator minor.*"

[108] See Cassuto, *Genesis*, 1:58, for a paraphrase of Gen 1:29–30: "You are permitted to make use of the living creatures and their service, you are allowed to exercise power over them so that they may promote your subsistence; but you may not treat the life-force within them contemptuously and slay them in order to eat their flesh; your proper diet shall be vegetable food."

[109] See, e.g., Victor P. Hamilton, *Handbook on the Pentateuch* (Grand Rapids: Baker, 1982), 41–42, for further discussion of this point, comparing the biblical creation narrative with the *Enuma elish* and the Atrahasis Epic.

[110] See Richard M. Davidson, *A Love Song for the Sabbath* (Washington, D.C.: Review and Herald, 1988), 27–32; Abraham Heschel, *The Sabbath* (New York: Harper & Row, 1951), 12–24.

According to Gen 2, the creation of Eve takes place in the context of loneliness. The keynote is struck in v. 18: "It is not good that the man should be alone." Man is a social being; sexuality is for sociality, for relationship, companionship, partnership. In principle this passage may be seen to affirm the various mutual social relationships that should take place between the sexes (as is also true with the "image of God" passage in Gen 1). Singleness, although not God's original ideal, does not prevent an individual from experiencing socialization, including healthy relationship/companionship between both sexes. God provides for those who are single and who are lonely.[111] But more specifically, the Genesis account links the concept of sociality to the marriage relationship. This is apparent from v. 24: "Therefore a man shall leave his father and mother and be joined to his wife, and they shall become one flesh" (NKJV).[112] The introductory "Therefore"

---

[111] As noted above, God's pronouncement that man's being alone was "not good" does not mean that singleness is evil but only that it is not the ideal. From an evangelical Christian perspective, see World Commission on Human Sexuality, "An Affirmation of God's Gift of Sexuality," October 1997, in *God's Good Gift of Sexuality: A Seventh-day Adventist Curriculum Framework for Sexual Education* (Silver Spring, Md.: Department of Family Ministries, General Conference of Seventh-day Adventists, 2002), 6: "Though the creation story establishes marriage as God's primary answer to aloneness (Gen 2:24), in the broader sense aloneness is dispelled through connection with God and fellow human beings in mutually satisfying relationships. . . . All human beings were created for life in community, where persons whose differences would otherwise separate them are bound together as one in Jesus Christ. . . . While some, by choice or circumstance, are single, they may experience wholeness as individuals, connect with others through family and friends, and bring glory to God as single men and women." See ch. 7, below, for further treatment (with bibliography) of an OT theology of singleness.

[112] The majority of biblical commentators throughout the centuries have taken this verse as referring to the institution of marriage. Notable exceptions to this traditional view include Hermann Gunkel in his ground-breaking form-critical commentary, *Genesis* (HKAT, Abteilung 1, no. 1; 3d ed.; Göttingen: Vandenhoeck & Ruprecht, 1910), 13, 41, who saw 2:24 an as an etiology, explaining the mutual sexual attraction of the male and the female as the longing of the two, who had originally been one (androgynous), to become one again. Another exception is Westermann, *Genesis*, 1:232, who argues that 2:18–24 is referring to "personal community between man and woman in the broadest sense" and "is not concerned with the foundation of any sort of institution, but with the primeval event," and thus "is not talking about marriage as an institution for the begetting of descendants, but of the community of man and woman as such." As pointed out below, however, language of formal covenant implies a marriage covenant, and the "Therefore" implies the setting of a pattern for future marriage relationships. A recent study by Batto ("The Institution of Marriage in Genesis 2 and in *Atrahasis*," 621–31) argues forcefully, "This debate over the question whether the author of Gen 2:18–25 invisions the institution of marriage or not can now be settled in the affirmative on the basis of comparative evidence, hitherto overlooked, from the Mesopotamian myth of *Atrahasis*" (p. 623). Batto reviews the now widely recognized evidence that although there are significant differences between the Gen 2 account and the Atrahasis Epic, nonetheless the basic structural flows of the two accounts are in parallel. He then shows how, in the structurally parallel equivalent to Gen 2:18–24 in the Atrahasis Epic, there is reference to *uṣurāt nišī* "regulations for humankind" specifically focusing upon the institution of marriage. Thus, Batto, concludes, the narrator of 2:18–24 "surely intended v. 24 as the equivalent of *uṣurāt nišī* in *Atrahasis,* that is, as a universal law regulating the normative behavior of the sexes

(*ʿal-kēn*) indicates that the relationship of Adam and Eve is upheld as the pattern for all future human sexual relationships.[113] Several significant insights into the nature of the divine ideal for sexual relationships emerge from this verse and constitute separate facets of a theology of human sexuality, to be taken up below in turn.

Sexuality and Exclusivity

A sixth facet of a theology of sexuality, the paradigm for marriage in Gen 2:24 highlights the element of *exclusivity.* The first of three actions described in this verse is that man *leaves* (*ʿāzab*). The verb *ʿāzab* is a forceful term. It means, literally, "to abandon, forsake," and is employed frequently to describe Israel's forsaking of Yahweh for false gods.[114] The leaving of 2:24 indicates the necessity of absolute freedom from outside interferences in the sexual relationship. Barth has pointed out that in a very real sense Gen 2 represents the "Old Testament Magna Charta of humanity," as Adam was allowed to freely and exuberantly recognize and affirm the woman as his partner.[115] Just as this freedom was essential in the garden, so it is crucial in all succeeding sexual relationships.

---

within a community of marriage" (629), and as in the Atrahasis Epic, the Gen 2 narrator is "positing that the institution of marriage is grounded in the very design of creation itself" (631).

[113] See Robert B. Lawton, "Genesis 2:24: Trite or Tragic?" *JBL* 105 (1986): 97–98, for evidence that this is not just an etiological insertion to explain the common prevailing legal custom. Lawton points out, as I will expand further below, that it was not the normal custom for the man to leave his father and mother, but rather for the woman. Therefore the Hebrew imperfect *yāʿăzāb* in this context is best taken not as a frequentative imperfect "he [typically] leaves" (as in, e.g., NJPS, NRSV, and RSV) but as a potential imperfect "he *shall* [= *should*] leave" (as in, e.g., ESV, JPS, KJV, NASB, and NKJV). The verse thus expresses "a description of divine intention rather than of habitually observed fact" (p. 98). For other examples of this usage of the potential imperfect in the HB, see Gen 2:17; 3:14; Exod 20:3–17; 21:12; and Num 15:14. Angelo Tosato, "On Genesis 2:24," *CBQ* 52 (1990): 389–409, provides further evidence that this verse, by means of its introductory *ʿal-kēn* ("therefore"), "speaks of marriage in a normative way" (404). Tosato points out that elsewhere in Scripture there are numerous examples of what he calls "juridical etiologies" (405). The use of the initial *ʿal-kēn* in Gen 2:24 to link a previous action with the divine norm finds a striking parallel in the fourth commandment of Exod 20:11: God rested from his work on the seventh day, and therefore (*ʿal-kēn*) he commands that the sabbath continue to be observed. For other examples, see Exod 13:15; Lev 17:11, 12; Num 18:24; and Deut 5:15; 15:11, 15. See also Sawyer, *God, Gender and the Bible,* 24: "The first couple provide the blueprint for normative citizenship in the theocracy proposed in the Bible's first story." Likewise, Nahum Sarna recognizes that the divine mandate is implicit in 2:24 since "fundamental aspects of the marital relationship are traced to God's original creative act and seen as part of the ordained natural order" (Nahum M. Sarna, *Genesis* [JPS Torah Commentary; Philadelphia: Jewish Publication Society, 1989], 23). Cf. Marrs, "In the Beginning," 22.

[114] See Deut 28:20; Judg 10:13; 2 Chr 34:25; Isa 1:4; and many other passages.

[115] Barth, *Church Dogmatics,* 3/2:291.

What is particularly striking in v. 24 is that it is the *man* who is to leave. It was a matter of course in the patriarchal society at the time Gen 2 was penned that the wife left her mother and father.[116] But for the husband to "leave" was revolutionary.[117] In effect, the force of this statement is that both are to leave—to cut loose from the ties that would encroach upon the independence and freedom of the relationship. This leaving implies not only the outward break to establish a new home but also the inward leaving—the psychological break away from dependence upon parents. It means "starting a whole new relationship in which the core loyalty is not to parents' priorities, traditions, or influence but to an entirely new family that must set its own course, form, and purpose."[118]

This leaving also implies the exclusiveness of the relationship: husband and wife, and no other interfering party, are bone of each other's bones, flesh of each other's flesh. This exclusivity in the marriage relationship is ultimately rooted in the monotheistic nature of God. Just as the one God (Yahweh Elohim) created the whole of humanity for fellowship with himself, so the man and the woman made in God's image were to be exclusively devoted to each other in marriage. The polytheistic pantheon of the ANE pagan religions, on the other hand, engaged in promiscuous sex among themselves, and it is thus not surprising that the civilizations embracing these religions had no standard of monogamous exclusivity within marriage.

Sexuality and Permanence

A seventh facet of a theology of sexuality, the Edenic paradigm for marriage in Gen 2:24 underscores the aspect of *permanence.* The second of three actions

---

[116] Some have seen behind this passage a hint of a matriarchal social structure, but the evidence is insufficient to substantiate such an hypothesis. For modern proponents of matriarchal trends within (and behind) the biblical tradition, see, e.g., Jacques B. Doukhan, "Women Priests in Israel: A Case for Their Absence," in *Women in Ministry: Biblical and Historical Perspectives* (ed. Nancy Vyhmeister; Berrien Springs, Mich.: Andrews University Press, 1998), 32, 41; Savina J. Teubal, *Hagar the Egyptian: The Lost Tradition of the Matriarchs* (San Francisco: Harper & Row, 1990), passim; and Gerda Weiler, *Das Matriarchat im alten Israel* (Stuttgart: Kohlhammer, 1989). For further discussion, bibliographies, and negative assessments of alleged evidence for this theory, see, e.g., Jewett, *Man as Male and Female,* 127; and Hennie J. Marsman, *Women in Ugarit and Israel: Their Social and Religious Position in the Context of the Ancient Near East* (Leiden: E. J. Brill, 2003), 101–2.

[117] "In the ancient Near East and most other cultures, patriarchal lineage prevailed in such a way that the primary bond of solidarity was the duty of a man toward his ancestors in general and to his progenitors in particular. To honor one's father and mother was the most sacred obligation of social responsibility (Exod 20:12; Deut 5:16). By dramatic contrast, [the author of Gen 2]. . . scandalously upsets, even shockingly reverses, this deeprooted principle of tribal morality. Against the cultures of his environment, [the Hebrew author]. . . declares unambiguously that man's first loyalty is to his woman" (Terrien, *Till the Heart Sings,* 14–15).

[118] Allender and Longman, *Intimate Allies,* 218.

described in this verse is that man *clings* (*dābaq*). The Hebrew verb *dābaq* is another robust term, signifying strong personal attachment. The original imagery of the word is that of sticking, clinging, remaining physically close, as skin to flesh and flesh to bone. It is often used in the OT as a technical covenant term for the permanent bond of Israel to the Lord.[119] Applied to the relationship between the sexes in 2:24, it seems to clearly indicate a covenant context, that is, a marriage covenant.

The term "clings" parallels the "oath of solidarity" and language of "covenant partnership" expressed by Adam concerning Eve in the previous verse. When Adam spoke of Eve (2:23a), "This at last is bone of my bones and flesh of my flesh," he was expressing marriage covenant vows.[120] Furthermore, "the third person reference ['this'] in Gen 2:23, with God's presence asserted in the immediate context, implies that Adam was addressing his affirmation not to Eve, nor, presumably to himself but to God as witness."[121] Adam's statement addressed to God regarding Eve was "a solemn affirmation of his marital commitment, an elliptical way of saying something like, 'I hereby invite you, God, to hold me accountable to treat this woman as part of my own body.'"[122] Moreover, God's presentation of the woman to the man implies that God was the officiant at the solemn covenant-making ceremony—the first garden wedding! And "therefore" (*ᶜal-kēn*), the narrator states, as it was with Adam, so the divine intent for every husband and wife is that their marriage be formalized with a clinging—mutual commitment expressed in a formal covenant ceremony.

But more is involved in clinging than a formal covenant. The word *dābaq* also emphasizes the inward attitudinal dimensions of the covenant bond. It "implies a devotion and an unshakable faith between humans; it connotes a permanent attraction which transcends genital union, to which, nonetheless it gives meaning."[123] The word "clings" in 2:24 encapsulates the nuances of Adam's covenant vows in the previous verse. The phrase "bone of my bones and flesh of my flesh" not only affirms the existence of a covenant but expresses "the entire range of intermediate possibilities from the extreme of frailty [flesh] to power [bones]. . . . [It is] a formula of abiding loyalty for every changing circumstance."[124] It is the

---

[119] See, e.g., Deut 10:20; 11:22; 13:5 (ET 13:4); Josh 22:5; 23:8; 2 Sam 20:3; 2 Kgs 18:6.

[120] For further discussion of the covenant language used by Adam, see Brueggemann, "Of the Same Flesh and Bone," 535. Cf. John S. Grabowski, *Sex and Virtue: An Introduction to Sexual Ethics* (Catholic Moral Thought; Washington, D.C.: Catholic University of America Press, 2003), 33–38, for an extended treatment of "the wealth of covenant language" contained in Gen 2, including the language used by Adam. For presentation of evidence from both Gen 1 and 2 that marriage is set forth as covenantal, see John K. Tarwater, "The Covenantal Nature of Marriage in the Order of Creation in Genesis 1 and 2" (PhD diss., Southeastern Baptist Theological Seminary, 2002), passim.

[121] Gordon P. Hugenberger, *Marriage as a Covenant: Biblical Law and Ethics as Developed from Malachi* (VTSup 52; Leiden: E. J. Brill, 1994; repr., Grand Rapids: Baker, 1998), 202.

[122] Ibid., 165.

[123] Collins, "The Bible and Sexuality," 153.

[124] Brueggemann, "Of the Same Flesh and Bone," 534–35.

equivalent to our modern marriage vow "in sickness or in health, in adversity or prosperity." When a man clings to a woman in the marriage covenant, he is vowing to remain in covenant relationship, no matter what may come. The marriage covenant is permanent; it is for keeps.

The permanence implied in the cleaving is not, however, one of ontological indissolubility, as some have inferred from this phrase, thereby concluding that the marriage bond can never be dissolved except by death, even in a context of a spouse's marital unfaithfulness.[125] The covenant connotations of this term must be seen in the light of its covenantal usage elsewhere, such as with Israel's "clinging" to God in covenant faithfulness. Although it was God's intention for the covenant bonding to be permanent, it is clear from the history of Israel that this bond was broken by its unfaithfulness to Yahweh.

Sexuality and Intimacy

An eighth facet of a theology of sexuality, the divine paradigm for all future marriages as set forth in Gen 2:24 stresses the ingredient of *intimacy*. The third of three actions described in this verse is that man and woman "become one flesh" (*wĕhāyû lĕbāśār ʾeḥād*). Note that this one-flesh union follows the "clinging." Thus the Edenic blueprint for sexual relationships underscores that the one-flesh union of sexual intercourse belongs within the context of the marriage covenant. The unitive purpose of sexuality is to find fulfillment inside the marital relationship. Furthermore, as already indicated in previous sections of this chapter, the phrase "man and his wife" indicates that the sexual relationship envisioned is a *heterosexual, monogamous* one.

The "one-flesh" relationship centers in the intimacy of sexual union, sexual intercourse.[126] The physical act of coitus is the primary means of establishing the "innermost mystery" of oneness, and in the covenant context of this verse seems to constitute the sign of the marriage covenant.[127] Notice that according to the "therefore" linking 2:24 with the preceding verses, the "one-flesh" union designed

---

[125] See the biblical examples assembled by William F. Luck, *Divorce and Remarriage: Recovering the Biblical View* (San Francisco: Harper & Row, 1987), 8, and further discussion in ch. 9, below.

[126] See esp. the analysis of biblical data supporting this conclusion by Wayne J. H. Stuhlmiller, "'One Flesh' in the Old and New Testaments," *Consensus* 5 (1979): 3–9, and further discussion in ch. 10, below.

[127] Piper, *The Biblical View of Sex and Marriage,* 52–67, explores the possible dimensions of the "inner mystery" of oneness. For biblical evidence suggesting that sexual intercourse constitutes the sign of the marriage covenant here and elsewhere in Scripture (just as other covenants in Scripture have signs), see, e.g., Hugenberger, *Marriage as a Covenant,* 265–79. Cf. Michael Lawrence, "A Theology of Sex," in *Sex and the Supremacy of Christ* (ed. John Piper and Justin Taylor; Wheaton, Ill.: Crossway, 2005), 137–38: "Now if marriage is a covenant, then that covenant must have a sign, something that makes visible the invisible reality of this one-flesh union.... The sign of that unique covenant relationship is the physical act of becoming one flesh in sexual intercourse."

for all marriages in the future was one which Adam and Eve personally experienced in the Garden of Eden before the fall, and thus sexual intercourse was clearly part of their unitive relationship already before fall as well as during their ongoing relationship outside the Garden (4:1).

The "one flesh" experience is not limited to sexual intercourse. The term *bāśār*, "flesh," in the OT refers not only to one's physical body but as a term to denote human relationship.[128] By "one flesh" is thus connoted a "sexual concourse and psychological concurrence, in the full sense of the conjunction of bodies and minds, at once through *erōs* and *agapē* . . . a psychic as well as physiological gift of loyalty and exchange,"[129] "the deepest harmonious community that exists between people, which is the unity between husband and wife in all its dimensions, emotional, physical, and spiritual."[130] It indicates a oneness and intimacy in the total relationship of the whole person of the husband to the whole person of the wife, a harmony and union with each other in all things.

The creation accounts allude to various dimensions of Adam and Eve's intimacy.[131] I have already pointed out from Gen 1 the sexual intimacy implied by God in the divine command for them to "Be fruitful and multiply," and the creative work intimacy involved in their subduing and ruling the earth. Genesis 2:15 makes more explicit the bold creativity entailed in subduing the earth: they were to "till" (*ʿābad*) and "keep" (*šāmar*) the garden. These terms literally mean to "serve" and "guard" respectively. Man and woman are entrusted with a responsible stewardship of serving and protecting their environment. These two words used as a pair also make up the expression used in Exodus for the service of the priests and Levites in the sanctuary,[132] and there is abundant intertextual evidence that, canonically, the pre-fall garden of Eden is presented as the original sanctuary on earth in parallel to the later Mosaic sanctuary and Solomonic temple.[133] In the context of the suffusion of sanctuary language in Gen 1–2, this

---

[128] See, e.g., Gen 29:14; 37:27; Lev 18:6; 25:49; Judg 9:2; 2 Sam 5:1; 19:13–14 (ET 19:12–13); 1 Chr 11:1; Isa 40:5. Cf. the discussion of this semantic nuance of the term in N. P. Bratsiotis, "בָּשָׂר *bāśār*," *TDOT* 2:319, 326–28. Bratsiotis (328) recognizes that in Gen 2:24 the term "one flesh" refers to "the consummation of the marriage" and also "perhaps an attempt to interpret the relationship formula can also be seen here."

[129] Terrien, *Till the Heart Sings,* 15–16.

[130] Vogels, "Man and Woman," 223.

[131] J. Howard Clinebell Jr. and Charlotte H. Clinebell, *The Intimate Marriage* (New York: Harper & Row, 1970), 23–40, isolate various kinds of marital intimacy; many of these are intimated in the Genesis accounts of creation.

[132] See, e.g., Num 3:7–8; 18:3–7.

[133] For a summary of seventeen lines of intertextual evidence for this conclusion, see Richard M. Davidson, "Cosmic Metanarrative for the Coming Millennium," *JATS* 11, nos. 1–2 (2000): 108–11. Intertextual indicators include, e.g., key terminological linkages ("to plant," "in the midst," God "walking around," "onyx," "bdellium," "light"), thematic parallels (common eastward orientation, three spheres of space in ascending degrees of holiness, river, portrayals of nature), and structural parallels (seven sections concluding with the Sabbath, and the verbal series at the conclusion: "saw the work," "made/did," "finished the work," "blessed"). See also Margaret Barker, *The Gate of Heaven: The History and Symbolism of the Temple in Jerusalem* (London: SPCK, 1991), 68–103; Gregory K. Beale,

phrase clearly implies a sacerdotal function. Adam and Eve are portrayed as creative coparticipants, spiritual intimates—indeed, priests—in the sacred service of the Eden sanctuary.

Genesis 2:24c does not imply that the one-fleshness is an instantaneously achieved state. The phrase *wĕhāyû lĕbāśār ʾeḥād* is better rendered "they will *become* [not *be*] one flesh." "The Hebrew nuance, not usually conveyed in the English translations, indicates that this state of 'unicarnation'—if one may employ a neologism—results from a process of development that deepens in intensity and strengthens itself with the passage of time instead of dissipating like a straw fire."[134]

Genesis 2:24 implies intimacy but at the same time probably also implies forbidden degrees of intimacy within the family. A man (as well as the woman) was to *leave* father and mother, not *marry* one of them. The clinging and becoming one flesh was assumed to be with another partner than parents; thus certain blood relationships were tacitly regarded as off-limits for marriage. From the beginning, at least father-daughter and mother-son relationships were apparently considered as forbidden degrees of closeness for marriage, and perhaps this verse also implicitly precluded all intergenerational liaisons (as is tacitly assumed throughout the book of Genesis; see the discussion in ch. 10, below).

The one-flesh experience of marriage includes the deepest kind of intimacy, a total transparency between marriage partners, described in v. 25: "And the man and his wife were both naked, and *were not ashamed* [*before each other* (*hitpaʿel* of *bôš*)]." (The end of this chapter will discuss the implications of this climactic creation statement on sexuality.)

The Temple and the Church's Mission: A Biblical Theology of the Dwelling Place of God (NSBT 17; Downers Grove, Ill.: InterVarsity, 2004), 66–80; Eric Bolger, "The Compositional Role of the Eden Narrative in the Pentateuch" (PhD diss., Trinity Evangelical Divinity School, 1993); William J. Dumbrell, *The End of the Beginning* (Homebush, N.S.W., Australia: Lancer, 1985), 35–76; Michael Fishbane, *Text and Texture: Close Readings of Selected Biblical Texts* (New York: Schocken, 1979), 12–13; Meridith G. Kline, *Kingdom Prologue* (Southampton, Mass.: M. G. Kline, 1989), 31–32, 54–56; Jon D. Levenson, *Sinai and Zion: An Entry into the Jewish Bible* (Minneapolis: Winston, 1985), 142–45; S. Dean McBride Jr., "Divine Protocol: Genesis 1:1–2:3 as Prologue to the Pentateuch," in *God Who Creates: Essays in Honor of W. Sibley Towner* (ed. William P. Brown and S. Dean McBride Jr.; Grand Rapids: Eerdmans 2000), 11–15; Donald W. Parry, "Garden of Eden: Prototype Sanctuary," in *Temples of the Ancient World: Ritual and Symbolism* (ed. Donald W. Parry; Salt Lake City: Deseret, 1994), 126–51; Terje Stordalen, *Echoes of Eden: Genesis 2–3 and Symbolism of the Eden Garden in Biblical Hebrew Literature* (CBET 25; Leuven: Peeters, 2000), 111–38; and Gordon J. Wenham, "Sanctuary Symbolism in the Garden of Eden Story," in *"I Studied Inscriptions from Before the Flood": Ancient Near Eastern, Literary, and Linguistic Approaches to Genesis 1–11* (ed. Richard S. Hess and David Toshio Tsumura; vol. 4 of *Sources for Biblical and Theological Studies,* ed. David W. Baker; Winona Lake, Ind.: Eisenbrauns, 1994), 399–404.

[134]Terrien, *Till the Heart Sings,* 15. The *waw* consecutive plus the perfect plus the preposition *lĕ* implies a process ("become"), not just a state ("be").

Sexuality and Procreation

A ninth facet of the theology of human sexuality emerging from Gen 1–2 concerns the reference to procreation. In 1:27 humankind is made in God's image: "in the image of God he created him; male and female he created them." Humankind is described as "male and female," and it is noteworthy that "this specific reference [to sexuality] pertains not to procreation but to the image of God."[135] It is clear from the next verse (1:28) that one of the primary purposes of sexuality is procreation, as indicated in the words "Be fruitful and multiply." But it is crucial to recognize that human procreativity "is not seen as an emanation or manifestation of his [the man's] creation in God's image." Rather, human procreative ability "is removed from God's image and shifted to a special word of blessing."[136]

This separation of the *imago Dei* and procreation probably serves as a polemic—like so much of the careful wording of the Genesis creation accounts[137]—against the mythological understanding and orgiastic celebration of divine sexual activity.[138] At the same time a profound insight into the theology of human sexuality is provided. Procreation is shown to be part of the divine design for human sexuality—as a special added blessing. This divine blessing/command is to be taken seriously and acted upon freely and responsibly in the power that attends God's blessing.[139] Adam and Eve are given the joyous privilege of procreativity, emulating (to a limited extent) the creative work of God himself and, in a sense, continuing God's creative work.[140]

Still, sexuality cannot be wholly subordinated to the intent to propagate children. Sexual differentiation has meaning apart from the procreative purpose. The procreative blessing is also pronounced upon the birds and fish on the fifth day (v. 22), but only humankind is made in the image of God. Genesis 1 emphasizes that the sexual distinction in humankind is created by God particularly for fellowship, for relationship, between male and female.

---

[135] Trible, *God and the Rhetoric of Sexuality,* 5.

[136] Von Rad, *Genesis,* 60–61.

[137] See, e.g., Hasel, "The Polemic Nature of the Genesis Cosmology," 81–102; Noort, "The Creation of Man and Woman," 8–10.

[138] See Phyllis A. Bird, "Male and Female He Created Them: Gen 1:27b in the Context of the Priestly Account of Creation," *HTR* 74 (1981): 134. Bird also points out that the very command in itself is a polemic against fertility rituals: "The power of created life to replenish itself is a power given to each species at its creation and therefore is not dependent upon subsequent rites or petitions for its effect" (p. 147).

[139] The Hebrew word for "bless" (*piʿel* of *bārak*) in Gen 1 implies the power to accomplish the task that God has set forth in the blessing. See Josef Scharbert, "ברך *brk,*" *TDOT* 2:306–7; H. Beyer, "εὐλογέω, εὐλογητός, εὐλογία, ἐνευλογέω," *TDNT* 2:755–57.

[140] For further development of this concept of cocreativity mirroring the divine creative work, see esp. Allender and Longman, *Intimate Allies,* 73–87. The uniqueness of the procreative powers of the first human couple should not be overstressed, however, inasmuch as God gives the same blessing, "Be fruitful and multiply," to the fish and fowl (Gen 1:22).

The complete absence of any reference to the propagation of children in Gen 2 highlights the significance of the unitive purpose of sexuality. This omission is not to deny the importance of procreation (as becomes apparent in later chapters of Scripture). But by the "full-stop"[141] after "one flesh" in v. 24, sexuality is given independent meaning and value. It does not need to be justified only as a means to a superior end, that is, procreation. The interpretation given by some that husband and wife become one flesh in the flesh of their children is not warranted by the text. Sexual love in the creation pattern is valued for its own sake.

When viewed against parallel ANE creation stories, this biblical view of marriage also seems to be a polemical corrective to the prevailing ANE perspective represented, for example, by the Atrahasis Epic, which "links marriage and procreation closely as if to suggest that the primary function of marriage is procreation." For the biblical narrator, by contrast, "the communitarian, affective function of marriage takes precedence over the procreative function of marriage."[142]

The Wholesome, Holy Beauty of Sexuality

A final, tenth facet of the theology of human sexuality in Gen 1–2 emerges from God's personal assessment of his creation. According to 1:31, when "God saw everything that he had made"—including the sexuality of his crowning work of creation—"indeed, it was very good." The Hebrew expression *ṭôb mĕʾōd* ("very good") connotes the quintessence of goodness, wholesomeness, appropriateness, beauty.[143] It is that which is both morally and aesthetically pleasing. The syllogism is straightforward. Sexuality (including the act of sexual intercourse) is part of God's creation, part of God's crowning act of creating humans. And God's creation is very beautiful/good. Therefore, declares the first chapter of Genesis, sex is good and beautiful, yes, very beautiful and good. It is not a mistake, a sinful aberration, a regrettable necessity, a shameful experience, as it has so often been regarded in the history of Christian as well as pagan thought. Rather, human sexuality (as both an ontological state and a relational experience) is divinely inaugurated: it is part of God's perfect design from the beginning and willed as a fundamental aspect of human existence.

The narrative of Gen 2 highlights the divine initiative and approbation in the relationship of the sexes. After the formation of woman, the Lord God "brought her to the man" (v. 22). The marriage relationship between man and woman is a divine gift to humanity. The Creator, as it were, celebrated the first marriage. Thus the "very good" that is pronounced upon man and his sexuality in Gen 1 is

---

141 Walter Trobisch, *I Married You* (New York: Harper & Row, 1971), 20.

142 Batto, "The Institution of Marriage in Genesis 2 and in *Atrahasis*," 631. For further discussion see pp. 621–31, where Batto compares the similarities and differences between the understanding of marriage in Gen 2 and that in the Atrahasis Epic.

143 For discussion of the aesthetic as well as moral/ethical dimensions of this term, see esp. Andrew Bowling, "טוב (*ṭôb*) (be) good, beneficial, pleasant, favorable, happy, right," *TWOT* 1:345–46.

in Gen 2 concretized in the divine solemnization of the one-flesh union between husband and wife.

What a joyous celebration that first wedding was. As Adam is introduced to his new wife, the passionate delight exudes from Adam's first recorded words. He breaks forth into poetry (and song?). The opening phrase of Adam (zō't happaʿam) is difficult to translate from Hebrew into equivalent dynamic English. It means something like "Wow! At last! This is the one!" As we have noted above, the woman has been aesthetically designed and well built (bānâ v. 22) just for him—she is dazzlingly beautiful—and he cannot contain his enthusiasm and joy. As Adam recognizes who she is, he also recognizes his true self, and his pun on the words ʾiššâ, "Wo-man," and ʾiš, "Man," constitutes, as already pointed out, a statement of covenant loyalty—his wedding vows. But does this play with words also indicate a spirit of light-hearted play in Adam's heart? As he has seen the animals each romping and playing with their mate, so now Adam senses he is finally whole with an intimate partner—in work, in dominion, yes, but also in sexual intimacy and play. The tone of Adam's response to Eve's creation seems to bespeak not only covenant loyalty but sensuous delight, expectancy of adventure, exuberant celebration.

The last lines of Gen 2 confirm this celebrative interpretation. The final word on God's Edenic ideal for sexuality comes in v. 25: "And the man and his wife were both naked, and were not ashamed." The Hebrew construction of the last English phrase may be more accurately translated, "they were not ashamed *before one another* [hitpaʿel of bôš]."[144] Viewed in contrast with the "utter [shameful] nakedness"[145] mentioned in Gen 3, the intent here is clear: "Shameless sexuality was divinely ordered; shameful sexuality is the result of sin."[146] According to God's original design, sexuality is wholesome, beautiful, and good. It is meant to be experienced between spouses without fear, without inhibitions, without shame and embarrassment. The account of Gen 2 "breathes an atmosphere of unabashed sensuality. There is no puritanical or ascetic disparagement of sexuality. The story contains not the slightest hint of moral or cultic impurity. . . . The coming together of the couple is the healthy fulfilling of the Creator's intention, without shadow or qualification."[147]

This final verse of the creation narratives sets forth the divine approbation upon uninhibited sensuous—yes, erotic—sexuality. Adam and Eve stand before each other, naked and unashamed. They look at each other, delighting in each other's bodies. They are deeply, passionately, romantically, in love.[148] With

---

[144] BDB 102; cf. *HALOT* 117.

[145] See the discussion in ch. 2, below, where I point out that in Gen 3 a different Hebrew for "naked" than that in Gen 2:25 appears, which implies utter and shameful nakedness.

[146] Collins, "The Bible and Sexuality," 154.

[147] Terrien, *Till the Heart Sings,* 16.

[148] See Carr, *The Erotic Word,* 36–48, for elaboration of the erotic passion emphasized in Gen 1–2, which should "impel us to look more broadly at ourselves as passionate beings" (p. 37).

economy of words and delicacy of taste, the narrator paints a scene of human sexuality as God designed it should be.

Just as the one-flesh experience applied to more than the physical union, so the reference to nakedness connotes more than physical nudity.[149] There is implied the ability "to stand in front of each other, stripped and undisguised, without pretensions, without hiding anything, seeing the partner as he or she really is, and showing myself to him or her as I really am—and still not to be ashamed."[150] "Adam and Eve stood before one another naked, and they felt no shame. They were completely vulnerable in each other's presence, and they felt no self-consciousness, no guilt, no shame."[151]

The literary structural placement of the first wedding ceremony and the first married couple's unashamed sexuality at the climax of the creation account in Gen 2 must be viewed in parallel with the placement of the Sabbath at the climax of the first creation account in 1:1–2:4a. Doukhan has shown how these two creation accounts are in a precise literary structural parallelism of seven sections.[152] The narrator has not accidentally paired the Sabbath and marriage—two institutions continuing in salvation history outside Eden. God actualizes Sabbath holiness by his presence (2:3) and solemnizes the marriage covenant by his presence (2:22–23). By linking these two institutions, the narrator implicitly indicates that the marriage relationship is holy like the Sabbath.[153] The covenant bond between husband and wife is sacred, just as is the sacred covenant relationship between God and humanity represented by the Sabbath. Sexuality is sacred not in the sense of the "sacralization/divinization of sex" practiced in the pagan fertility cults but in that it is hallowed by the divine approbation and presence.[154] Human sexuality is thus a divinely created holy mystery.[155] It is apparent already at the

---

[149] See Kidner, *Genesis,* 66, who observes that v. 25 indicates "the perfect ease between them." For a discussion and rejection of the theory that Adam and Eve's nakedness without shame refers to their lack of consciousness of their sexuality, see ch. 2, below.

[150] Trobisch, *I Married You,* 82–83.

[151] Allender and Longman, *Intimate Allies,* 224. Cf. Burke, *Different by Design,* 48–51, who stresses the "freedom to be transparent with the assurance of acceptance" (p. 48) that is implied in this verse.

[152] Doukhan, *Literary Structure,* 35–80.

[153] For further discussion of these interrelated sections of the creation narratives and the links of covenant and relationship, see ibid., 41–42, 223–27. Note the pattern in later salvation history in which God makes something or someone holy by his presence: the burning bush (Exod 3:2–5), the sanctuary (Exod 25:8; 40:34–38), God's appearance to Joshua (Josh 5:13–15), etc. So God makes the Sabbath and marriage holy by his special presence.

[154] Neither in the Genesis accounts of creation nor elsewhere in the canonical Scripture, however, is sexuality explicitly characterized by Hebrew words from the root *qdš,* "sacred/holy." Although the holy nature of sexuality and the marriage institution seems implied by the parallelism with the Sabbath, as discussed above, use of the specific root *qdš* is avoided, probably to avoid any confusion with the sacralization/divinization of sexuality as practiced in the fertility cults.

[155] For recent studies highlighting the sacred nature of sexuality as God designed it, see Tim Alan Gardner, *Sacred Sex: A Spiritual Celebration of Oneness in Marriage* (Colo-

beginning of the biblical canon that the marriage relationship illustrates the divine-human relationship epitomized by the Sabbath and, by the same token, the divine-human intimacy intended for the Sabbath illuminates the intimacy God intended for marriage.

The intimacy within the sacred *space* of the Eden sanctuary (2:15–25) is the counterpart to the climax of the first creation account (2:1–3), where the man and the woman experience intimacy within sacred *time*—the Sabbath. Sabbath, sanctuary, and marriage intersect in the one-flesh experience of the first couple.[156] The first man and woman, created on the sixth day, united in holy wedlock as the first Sabbath draws near, are clearly intended to unite Sabbath holiness with the holy intimacy of married love. That first Friday night in Eden[157]—the eve of the Shabbat[158]—was their wedding night. The references to "one flesh" and their being naked before each other without shame (vv. 24–25), coming immediately after the garden wedding ceremony and appearing in the narrative structure paralleling the Sabbath in the first creation account, all give further evidence that sexual union and Sabbath are not inimical to each other. God, who hallows that first Sabbath with his presence, at the same time hallows the marriage bed on the Sabbath as Adam and Eve share sexual intimacy with each other.

It is not within the scope of this study to draw out the full range of philosophical and sociological implications that follow from the theology of human sexuality set forth in Gen 1–2. Perhaps it may suffice to repeat again the central clause on sexuality in Gen 1—"male and female he created them"—and then exclaim with Emil Brunner,

> That is the immense double statement, of a lapidary simplicity, so simple indeed that we hardly realize that with it a vast world of myth and Gnostic speculation, of cynicism and asceticism, of the deification of sexuality and fear of sex completely disappears.[159]

---

rado Springs, Colo.: Waterbrook, 2000); Daniel R. Heimbach, *True Sexual Morality: Recovering Biblical Standards for a Culture in Crisis* (Wheaton, Ill.: Crossway, 2004), 142–45; and Philip Yancey, "Holy Sex: How It Ravishes Our Souls," *ChT* 47, no. 10 (2003): 46–51, adapted from *Rumors of Another World* (Grand Rapids: Zondervan, 2003).

[156] As I will note in later chapters, after sin, as a safeguard against the sacralization and deification of sex in the fertility cults, God forbade Israel from bringing anything related to sexual activity into the sanctuary where the Shechinah glory was manifested. But as Gen 1–2 make clear, sexuality is not per se inimical to holy space or time, except in the context of polemic against fertility cult distortions of God's original ideal.

[157] The phrase "That first Friday in Eden" is borrowed freely from Alberta Mazat, *That Friday in Eden: Sharing and Enhancing Sexuality in Marriage* (Mountain View, Calif.: Pacific, 1981). As a licensed clinical social worker and marriage, family, and child counselor and as a wonderful mother-in-law and delightful friend, Mazat has had a profound influence in shaping my positive view of sexuality.

[158] The assumption here is that in Gen 1–2 the Sabbath is presented as beginning at sundown Friday night. See H. R. Stroes, "Does the Day Begin in the Evening or Morning? Some Biblical Observations," *VT* 16 (1966): 460–75, for a survey of biblical evidence supporting this conclusion.

[159] Emil Brunner, *Man in Revolt* (Philadelphia: Westminster, 1947), 346.

As with the nature of sexuality depicted in Gen 1, so Gen 2 decidedly does not display a "melancholy attitude toward sex";[160] rather, Gen 2 "gives the relationship between man and woman the dignity of being the greatest miracle and mystery of creation."[161]

---

[160] Cuthbert A. Simpson, "The Book of Genesis: Introduction and Exegesis," *IB* 1:485–86.

[161] Von Rad, *Old Testament Theology,* 1:150.

☙2

Sexuality and the Fall: Genesis 3

Two major issues related to the theology of sexuality call for attention regarding Gen 3. The first concerns the contention by some scholars that Adam and Eve's knowledge of "good and evil" and their knowledge "that they were naked" (3:5, 7) both refer to the awakening of their sexual consciousness. The second issue is the debate over the gender role relationships between Adam and Eve in Gen 3, especially focusing upon the pronouncement of divine judgment concerning Eve (3:16).

The Nakedness of Adam and Eve

Some modern scholars contend that the knowledge of good and evil gained by Adam and Eve as a result of eating the forbidden fruit was actually a consciousness of sex.[1] But Stephen Sapp rightly points out that "such a position assumes that sexuality itself occasions shame by its very nature (once one is aware of it)" and thus "suggests that sexuality was *not* part of God's intention for humans in creation" whereas both Gen 1 and 2, to the contrary, "consider sexuality to be a purposeful part of God's good creation, with no indication whatsoever that sexual experience was jealously withheld from Adam and Eve."[2]

The idea that a consciousness of sex came only after the fall seems to be based mainly on a misunderstanding of the meaning of Gen 3:7 and its relationship to 2:25.[3] It is argued that since, according to 3:7, Adam and Eve knew that they were

---

[1] See, e.g., Sam Dragga, "Genesis 2–3: A Story of Liberation," *JSOT* 55 (1992): 5–8; Anne Gardner, "Genesis 2:4b–3: A Mythological Paradigm of Sexual Equality or of the Religious History of Pre-exilic Israel?" *SJT* 43 (1990): 13; Robert Gordis, "The Knowledge of Good and Evil in the Old Testament and Qumram Scrolls," *JBL* 76 (1957): 114–20; Jacob Milgrom, "Sex and Wisdom: What the Garden of Eden Story is Saying," *BRev* 10, no. 6 (1994): 21, 52; Cuthbert A. Simpson, "The Book of Genesis: Introduction and Exegesis," *IB* 1:485–86.

[2] Sapp, *Sexuality, the Bible, and Science,* 18; cf. 17–19 for further arguments advanced by Sapp against this option.

[3] This study refers to the "fall" in the sense of the traditional Judeo-Christian understanding (a moral fall of Adam and Eve from an original sinless state as the result of their sin in disobeying God's command not to eat of the forbidden fruit), which I see as the view set forth in the final canonical form of the HB and the NT. For a recent defense of this

naked only after the fall, then 2:25 must mean that they were not aware of their nakedness (or sexuality) in the beginning. But this line of argument—and ironically most studies that attempt to counter this argument—fail to recognize that Gen 2 and 3 utilize two different Hebrew words for "naked."[4] In 2:25 the word for "naked" is *ʿārôm,* which elsewhere in Scripture frequently refers to someone not *fully* clothed or not clothed *in the normal manner.*[5] Genesis 2:25 does not explicitly indicate in what way Adam and Eve were without clothes in the normal sense (normal from the postfall perspective), but the semantic range of *ʿārôm* is consonant with the conclusion toward which the parallel creation/paradise passage in Ps 104 points, namely, that Adam and Eve may have been originally "clothed" with "garments" of light and glory.[6] If such is the case in Gen 2:25, then the contrast with Gen 3 becomes clear. In 3:7, 10, 11 the Hebrew word for "naked" is *ʿêrōm,* which elsewhere in Scripture always appears in a context of total (and usu-

---

traditional understanding of the fall in Gen 3 through discourse analysis, see C. John Collins, "What Happened to Adam and Eve? A Literary-Theological Approach to Genesis 3," *Presb* 27, no. 1 (2001): 12–44 (although I disagree with Collins on some specifics of his interpretation regarding the divine sentence in 3:16).

[4] Attention in the commentaries usually focuses upon the similarity of sound and spelling between *ʿărûmmîm,* "naked," in 2:25 (referring to Adam and Eve) and *ʿārûm,* "crafty," in the next verse, 3:1 (referring to the snake). It is usually suggested that the word for "naked" in 2:25 is used for the sake of a literary play on words. A paronomasia may indeed be involved, but this is not all. Elaine Phillips notices that in contrast to the word for "naked" in 2:25, "the word is now [3:6] slightly different in form," and she suggests that "the knowledge they acquired seems somehow to have affected their perception of their nakedness" (Elaine A. Phillips, "Serpent Intertexts: Tantalizing Twists in the Tales," *BBR* 10 [2000]: 237). But this does not get to the heart of the matter. The change to a different word for "naked" in Gen 3 has more specific theological significance, as argued below.

[5] In 1 Sam 19:24, e.g., the term is "used of one, having taken off his mantle, goes only clad in his tunic" (*GHCLOT* 653). Again, in Isa 20:2 the reference is to one "dressed with *śaq* only" (KBL 735; cf. John 21:7). Other passages employ the term in the sense of "ragged, badly clad" (Job 22:6; 24:7, 10; Isa 58:7; *GHCLOT* 653). *HALOT* 883 identifies numerous OT passages where *ʿārôm* denotes "lightly dressed" (Isa 20:2, 4; 58:7; Mic 1:8; Job 22:6; 24:6, 7, 10) and one passage where the term refers to a man without armor (Amos 2:16).

[6] Jacques B. Doukhan, *The Literary Structure of the Genesis Creation Story* (Andrews University Seminary Doctoral Dissertation Series 5; Berrien Springs, Mich.: Andrews University Press, 1978), 81–88, shows how Ps 104 follows exactly the same order as the Genesis creation account, and analyzes the point-by-point parallels between the two passages. What is significant for our discussion here is that in Ps 104, along with the poetic description of God's creative *work,* there appears to be at least one indication of his *appearance* or, rather, his clothing (vv. 1–2): "You are clothed with honor and majesty, wrapped in light as with a garment." If God is portrayed as clothed with "garments" of light and majesty, it is not unreasonable to deduce that man, created in the image and likeness of God both in outward resemblance and in character (as discussed in ch. 1, above) is similarly clothed. Psalm 8:6 (ET 8:5) may also point in this direction. According to this verse describing man in paradise, God "crowned" (NRSV) or "surrounded" (the latter if *ʿāṭar* is taken as *qal* stem) him with glory and honor. See also Gary A. Anderson, "The Punishment of Adam and Eve in the Life of Adam and Eve," in *Literature on Adam and Eve: Collected Essays* (ed. Gary Anderson, Michael Stone, and Johannes Tromp; Leiden: E. J. Brill, 2000), 57–81.

ally shameful) exposure, describing someone "utterly naked" or "bare."[7] As a result of sin, the human pair find themselves "[utterly] naked," bereft of the "garments" of light and glory, and they seek to clothe themselves with fig leaves.

Even this postfall "nakedness" should not, however, be interpreted as causing Adam and Eve to be ashamed of their own bodies before each other. There is no mention of mutual embarrassment of shame before each other. The context is rather one of fear and dread before God. Adam says to God (v. 10), "I heard the sound of you in the garden, and I was afraid, because I was naked, and I hid myself."

Adam's nakedness described in 3:10 is also obviously more than physical nudity, for Adam depicts himself as still naked even though already covered with fig leaves. The nakedness of Gen 3 seems to also include a sense of "being unmasked,"[8] a consciousness of guilt, a nakedness of soul. Likewise, God's clothing of Adam and Eve with skins appears to represent more than a concern for physical covering, more than a demonstration of the "modesty appropriate in a sinful world,"[9] although these are no doubt included. For many Christians in the evangelical tradition, the skins from slain animals are seen to intimate the beginning of the sacrificial system and the awareness of a substitutionary atonement, because of which humans need no longer feel unmasked or ashamed.[10]

The clothing of Adam and Eve by God may have another significance beyond the aspects suggested above. In the previous chapter I referred to studies showing the abundant intertextual evidence within the final canonical form of the Pentateuch that the garden of Eden is to be considered the original sanctuary on earth already before the fall. The intertextual evidence is even more direct and striking for after the fall, representing the garden of Eden (especially its gateway) as a sanctuary, the precursor to the Mosaic sanctuary.[11] After Adam and Eve are expelled, in their sinful state they are no longer able to meet with God face-to-face in the garden's holy of holies. But at the eastern entrance to the garden (Gen 3:24; cf. the eastern entrance to the later sanctuaries) now appear cherubim—the beings associated with the ark in the most holy place of the Mosaic sanctuary (Exod 25:18–22). These cherubim, with a flaming sword, are "placed" (Heb. šākan). The text uses the same specific Hebrew verb for God's "dwelling" among his people (Exod 25:8). The same root is found for "sanctuary" (miškan) and (in extra-biblical Jewish literature) for the Shechinah glory, the visible presence of God in the sanctuary.

---

[7] See Ezek 16:7, 22, 39; 18:7, 16; 23:29; Deut 28:48. Cf. *GHCLOT* 625; BDB 735–36; KBL 702.

[8] Claus Westermann, *Creation* (London: SPCK, 1974), 95.

[9] Stuart B. Babbage, *Sex and Sanity: A Christian View of Sexual Morality* (Philadelphia: Westminster, 1965).

[10] See, e.g., Francis A. Schaeffer, *Genesis in Space and Time* (Downers Grove, Ill.: InterVarsity, 1975), 105–6. Many evangelical Christians see here a typological reference to spiritual covering (the robe of righteousness) provided by the death of the coming substitute, the messianic Lamb of God.

[11] For further discussion of this evidence, see Richard M. Davidson, "Cosmic Metanarrative for the Coming Millennium," *JATS* 11, nos. 1–2 (2000): 108–11.

In light of this intertextual sanctuary background of Gen 3, it is significant to note one more intertextual canonical linkage between Eden and the Mosaic cultus. Before Adam and Eve's expulsion from the garden, God "clothed" (*lābaš*, in the *hip͑il* [causative]) them with "garments of skins" (*kotnôt*, pl. of *kĕtōnet*) (3:21), and these are the very terms used to describe the clothing (*lābaš*, in the *hip͑il*) of the priests—Aaron and his sons (Lev 8:7, 13; Num 20:28; cf. Exod 28:4; 29:5; 40:14). Robert Oden has demonstrated that this phraseology in Gen 3:21— the combination of *lābaš*, in the *hip͑il* with *kotnôt*[12]—describes a divine conferral of status upon Adam and Eve.[13] Jacques Doukhan draws out the implication of the divine ceremony in light of its canonical intertextual parallels: "The rare occasions where God clothes humans in the OT always concerned the dressing of priests. . . . Adam and Eve were, indeed, dressed as priests."[14] The unmistakable and consistent linkage within the HB of this pair of terms—*lābaš*, in the *hip͑il* and *kotnôt*—with the clothing of Israel's priests, viewed in the larger setting of the garden of Eden as a sanctuary, clearly points to Adam and Eve's inauguration as priests in the postfall world. By highlighting God's clothing of Adam and Eve with the skins of sacrificial animals (instead of the fine linen of the later priests), the final canonical form of the text further emphasizes the divine confirmation that Adam and Eve are to be identified as priests, for the skin of the sacrificial animals belonged exclusively to the priests in the Mosaic cultus (Lev 7:8). "By bestowing on Adam and Eve the skin of the sin offering, a gift strictly reserved to priests, the Genesis story implicitly recognizes Eve as priest alongside Adam."[15] The far-reaching implications of this conclusion regarding the divinely ordained sacerdotal status of woman as well as man after the fall will become evident as we proceed through the canonical corpus.

Divine Judgment concerning the Relationship between Eve and Adam

When God comes to the garden after Adam and Eve have sinned, he initiates an encounter that constitutes nothing less than a "legal process," a "trial punish-

---

[12] Note that the significant intertextual linkage is made with the convergence of both of these terms in a single context, not just their isolated occurrence separately.

[13] Robert A. Oden Jr., *The Bible without Theology: The Theological Tradition and Alternatives to It* (San Francisco: Harper & Row, 1987), ch. 3, "Grace or Status? Yahweh's Clothing of the First Humans," 92–105. Oden examines the use of the two key Hebrew words, *lābaš, hip͑il* and *kĕtonet,* both in Scripture and in the ANE literature and shows how these terms are regularly employed in contexts of status marking. See, e.g., Isa 22:21, where God marks the status of Eliakim by clothing him.

[14] Jacques B. Doukhan, "Women Priests in Israel: A Case for Their Absence," in *Women in Ministry: Biblical and Historical Perspectives* (ed. Nancy Vyhmeister; Berrien Springs, Mich.: Andrews University Press, 1998), 36. A full awareness of the nature of canonical intertextuality is needed to be sensitive to this identification.

[15] Ibid., 37.

ment by God."[16] God begins the legal proceedings with an interrogation of the
"defendants," and the defensive and accusatory responses by Adam and Eve (Gen
3:9–14) indicate the rupture in interhuman (husband-wife) and divine-human
relationships that has occurred as a result of sin. Following the legal interrogation
and establishment of guilt, God pronounces the sentence in the form of curses
(over the serpent and the ground, vv. 14, 17) and judgments (for the man and the
woman, vv. 16–19).

What is of particular concern to us for a theology of sexuality is the pronouncement addressed to the woman (v. 16):

(a) I will greatly increase your pangs [ʿiṣṣābôn] in childbearing;

(b) in pain [ʿiṣṣābôn] you shall bring forth children,

(c) yet your desire shall be for your husband [wĕʾel-ʾîšēk tĕšûqātēk],

(d) and he shall rule over you [wĕhûʾ yimšāl-bāk].

The first two lines of poetic parallelism in this verse (a–b) indicate that as a
result of sin, childbearing will involve much ʿiṣṣābôn (NRSV's "pangs," but also
translated, "pain, anguish, [hard] labor") for the woman. Some would separate
the first line into two separate pronouncements and translate, "I will increase
your toil [i.e., the woman's efforts in farming the land] and your childbearing."[17]
But I concur with Linda Belleville that "since the second clause seems to restate
the first clause ('with pain you will give birth to children'), the first clause is more
likely a hendiadys (two phrases expressing one idea): 'I will greatly increase your
toil in childbearing.'"[18] In parallel with the use of ʿiṣṣābôn to mean "toil" (NRSV)

---

[16] Westermann, *Creation*, 96. So also Walter Brueggemann, *Genesis* (IBC 1; Atlanta:
John Knox, 1982), 49: "The scene [Gen 3:8–24] becomes a trial." Phyllis Trible, *God and
the Rhetoric of Sexuality* (OBT; Philadelphia: Fortress, 1978), 117, likewise comments on
this scene: "God becomes the prosecutor in a court of law." Cf. Rick R. Marrs, "In the Beginning: Male and Female (Gen 1–3)," in *Essays on Women in Earliest Christianity* (ed.
Carroll D. Osburn; 2 vols.; Joplin, Mo.: College Press, 1995), 2:27–28, who describes Gen
3:8–13 as a "trial" and "verdict" followed by a "judgment" in 3:14–19; and Aubrey
Malphurs, *Biblical Manhood and Womanhood: Understanding Masculinity and Femininity
from God's Perspective* (Grand Rapids: Kregel, 1996), 99, who summarizes the scene of
3:14–19 thus: "God as the prosecuting attorney probed the two defendants who reluc-
tantly admitted some guilt but shifted the blame to others. Now God moves from the role
of prosecutor to judge and pronounces final judgment." Cf. Calum M. Carmichael, "Law
and Narrative in the Pentateuch," *BCHB* 332–33, who shows how the medieval canonists
found in the divine legal proceedings of Gen 3 the basic principles of human justice and
general rules of judicial procedure.

[17] See Carol Meyers, *Discovering Eve: Ancient Israelite Women in Context* (New York:
Oxford University Press, 1988), 105; cf. Richard S. Hess, "The Roles of the Woman and the
Man in Genesis 3," *Them* 18 (1993): 16.

[18] Linda L. Belleville, *Women Leaders and the Church: Three Crucial Questions* (Grand
Rapids: Baker, 2000), 194, n. 59. See also Claus Westermann, *Genesis 1–11* (Minneapolis:
Augsburg, 1974), 262.

or "(hard) labor" and not "pain" regarding the judgment of the man (3:17; cf.
v. 19, "By the sweat of your face"), I find it preferable to translate the term
ʿiṣṣābôn as "(hard) labor" (and not "pain") regarding the woman's childbearing—
an expression that the English language still retains in the reference to a woman
"going into labor."

But what is the meaning of the last two enigmatic lines (v. 16c–d) of the divine pronouncement concerning the woman? The answer to this question is crucial
for a proper understanding of the nature of God's design for sexual relationships
throughout the rest of Scripture; hence there is need for close examination of the
biblical evidence.

Six major views have been advanced for the interpretation of this pronouncement (in relationship to Gen 1–2 and to the nature of the fall in Gen 3).
The first, and perhaps the most common, position maintains that the subordina-
tion/submission of woman and the supremacy/leadership of man are a creation
ordinance, God's ideal from the beginning (Gen 1–2) and part of the fall consisted in the violation of this ordinance when Eve sought to get out from under
Adam's supremacy/leadership and Adam failed to restrain her (Gen 3).[19] God *describes* in 3:16 the results of sin in the *continued distortion of God's original design
for ontological hierarchy or functional leadership/submission between the sexes*—
with the man's exploitive subjugation of woman and/or woman's desire to control the man (or her "diseased" desire to submit to his exploitations).[20]

---

[19] One could divide this view (and some of the others that follow) into two subcategories, consisting of a liberal-critical version and an evangelical version of the position. Liberal-critical scholars tend to use the terms "supremacy" and "subordination" to
describe the relative status of Adam and Eve respectively, arguing that in the understanding of the narrator there existed a divinely ordained *ontological hierarchy* between the
sexes. Most evangelicals who hold this view, on the other hand, argue for an equality of
ontological status between Adam and Eve at creation but propose that the text presents a
divinely ordained *functional hierarchy* (their preferred term is that it is a "complementarian" relationship) consisting of the roles of male leadership (or "headship," as many
hierarchical complementarians prefer) and female submission respectively. Inasmuch as
both of these views ultimately include a hierarchical ordering of the relationship between
the sexes (whether ontological or functional), they are placed together here for the sake of
schematic synthesis of the major views, using the word pairs "supremacy/leadership" and
"subordination/submission" to represent the two main subcategories within the different
positions. Where only the terms "leadership" and "submission" are employed, this indicates that this is predominately an evangelical position underscoring functional and not
ontological hierarchy.

[20] In this view, the *waw* in *wĕhûʾ* is coordinative ("and") and the *qal* imperfect of
māšal (*yimšol*) is a descriptive future ("he shall rule over you"). Supporting this position,
John Calvin, e.g., sees woman's position before the fall as "liberal and gentle subjection";
after the fall she is "cast into servitude"; nonetheless she still desires what her husband desires (*Commentary on Genesis* [10 vols.; Grand Rapids: Eerdmans, n.d.], 1:172). Carl F.
Keil and Franz Delitzsch similarly understand the original position of man-woman as
rule/subordination rooted in mutual esteem and love but argue that after sin the woman
has "a desire bordering on disease" and the husband exercises "despotic rule" over his wife
(K&D, 1:64). H. C. Leupold describes a morbid yearning on the part of the woman after
the fall that often "takes a perverted form, even to the point of nymphomania" (*Exposition

The second major interpretation also understands the hierarchical relationship between the sexes (submission of woman to the leadership of man) as a creation ordinance (Gen 1–2) and agrees that at the fall this creation ordinance was violated (Gen 3); 3:16 is viewed as a *divine prescription that the man must "rule"— that is, exercise his "godly headship"—to restrain the woman's desire, that is, her urge get out from under his leadership and control/manipulate him.* According to his view, 3:16 should be interpreted along the lines of the similarly worded statement of God to Cain in 4:7. In 4:7, according to this interpretation, God warned Cain that sin's desire would be to control him, but he must master it; in the same way in 3:16, woman's desire would be to control/manipulate man and the husband must master her desire by exercising his godly leadership.[21]

The third major interpretation also views the hierarchical relationship between the sexes as a creation ordinance and the fall as entailing a distortion of this creation ordinance (or a rupture in man-woman relations). Genesis 3:16 is seen as a *divine reaffirmation of the subordination/submission of woman to the supremacy/ leadership of man as it was in the beginning.* According to the evangelical version of this view, Eve at the fall had broken loose from her role of submission to Adam and is now redirected to her former position under the leadership of Adam, not as a punishment but as a continued blessing and comfort to her in her difficulties

---

of Genesis [Columbus, Ohio: Wartburg, 1942], 172). John Skinner speaks of the woman's "desire which makes her the willing slave of the man" (*A Critical and Exegetical Commentary on Genesis* [2d ed.; ICC 1; Edinburgh: T&T Clark, 1930], 82). See also Ronald B. Allen and Beverly Allen, *Liberated Traditionalism: Men and Women in Balance* (Portland, Ore.: Multnomah, 1985), 117–28; Thomas Finley, "The Relationship of Woman and Man in the Old Testament," in *Women and Men in Ministry: A Complementary Perspective* (ed. Robert L. Saucy and Judith K. TenElshof; Chicago: Moody, 2001), 58–61; Wayne Grudem, *Evangelical Feminism and Biblical Truth: An Analysis of More Than One Hundred Disputed Questions* (Sisters, Ore.: Multnomah, 2004), 37–40, 108–10; Mary A. Kassian, *Woman, Creation, and the Fall* (Westchester, Ill.: Crossway, 1990), 21–30; Malphurs, *Biblical Manhood and Womanhood*, 63–112; Robert L. Saucy, "The Negative Case against the Ordination of Women," in *Perspectives on Evangelical Theology: Papers from the Thirtieth Annual Meeting of the Evangelical Theological Society* (ed. Kenneth S. Kantzer and Stanley N. Gundry; Grand Rapids: Baker, 1979), 280; Michael F. Stitzinger, "Genesis 1–3 and the Male/Female Role Relationship," *GTJ* 2 (1981): 38–43; and Clarence J. Vos, *Woman in Old Testament Worship* (Amsterdam: Judels & Brinkman, 1968), 19–27.

[21] In this interpretation, the *waw* in *wĕhûʾ* is adversative ("but") and the *qal* imperfect of *māšal* (*yimšol*) is prescriptive ("he *must* rule over you"). This view is argued most fully by Susan T. Foh, "What Is the Woman's Desire?" *WTJ* 37 (1975): 376–83 (cf. idem, *Women and the Word of God: A Response to Biblical Feminism* [Phillipsburg, N.J.: Presbyterian and Reformed, 1979], 68–69). A similar position is taken by, e.g., Samuele Bacchiocchi, *Women in the Church: A Biblical Study on the Role of Women in the Church* (Berrien Springs, Mich.: Biblical Perspectives, 1987), 79–84; Collins, "What Happened to Adam and Eve?" 36–39; and James B. Hurley, *Man and Woman in Biblical Perspective* (Grand Rapids: Zondervan, 1981), 218–19. Cf. Walter Vogels, "The Power Struggle between Man and Woman (Gen 3,16b)," *Bib* 77 (1996): 197–209, who likewise pictures Gen 4:7 as a negative experience—sin as a wild animal crouching in wait for its prey—although he interprets it as descriptive and not prescriptive like Foh and others. For a critique of Foh's view, see esp. Stitzinger, "Genesis 1–3 and the Male/Female Role Relationship."

as a mother. The meaning of v. 16c–d may be paraphrased, "you will have labor and difficulty in your motherhood, yet you will be eager for your husband and he will rule over you (in the sense of a servant leadership to care for and help and not in the sense of domination and oppression)."[22]

According to the liberal-feminist version of this view, the subordination/ subjugation of women by men is a patriarchal given in Gen 2 (and, many would add, also Gen 1), and what is traditionally called the fall is really Eve's attempt to liberate herself from dominance and control. Genesis 3:16 is seen as the narrator's patriarchal reaffirmation of the subjugation of woman by man. These texts at the beginning of Scripture are viewed as "irredeemably androcentric" throughout, both before and after the fall.[23]

The fourth major view contends that the subordination or subjection of woman to man did not exist before the fall but the original egalitarian relationship between the sexes as designed by God was disrupted at the fall; the mention of such a subordination/subjection in Gen 3:16 is only a *description of the evil consequences of sin*—the usurpation of authority by the man and/or the woman's desire to rule or be ruled (to be removed by the gospel)—and not a permanent

---

[22] Stephen B. Clark, *Man and Woman in Christ: An Examination of the Roles of Men and Women in the Light of Scripture and the Social Sciences* (Ann Arbor, Mich.: Servant, 1980), 35. Clark does not rule out this as a possibility, but he more strongly favors the first view. This interpretation was also the view of Thomas Aquinas, *Summa theologiae* 1a, q. 92, arts. 1–2 (see Thomas Aquinas, *Man Made to God's Image (1a. 90–102)* [trans. Edmond Hill; vol. 13 of *Summa theologiae: Latin Text, English Translation, Introduction, Notes, Appendices, and Glossary;* ed. Thomas Gilby; 60 vols.; New York: McGraw-Hill, 1964], 34–41), who maintained that already before the fall there existed a subordination of the woman (*subjectio oeconomica vel civilis*) that was for the woman's advantage and well-being (*ad . . . utilitatem et bonum*) and this was reaffirmed after the fall. (For full discussion of Aquinas's view of the nature and role of woman, see esp. Kari Elisabeth Børresen, *Subordination and Equivalence: The Nature and Role of Woman in Augustine and Thomas Aquinas* [trans. Charles H. Talbot; Washington, D.C.: University Press of America, 1981], passim). Similarly, Ambrose, *De paradiso* 72, in *Hexameron, Paradise, and Cain and Abel* (trans. John J. Savage; FC 42; New York: Fathers of the Church, 1961), 350: "Servitude, therefore, of this sort is a gift of God. Wherefore, compliance with this servitude is to be reckoned among blessings." See also Irvin A. Busenitz, "Woman's Desire for Man: Genesis 3:16 Reconsidered," *GTJ* 7 (1986): 203–12, who concurs in general with this view but does not agree that the woman's sin consisted in getting out from under the leadership of her husband.

[23] The term "irredeemably androcentric" is that of David J. A. Clines, "What Does Eve Do to Help? And Other Irredeemably Androcentric Orientations in Genesis 1–3," in *What Does Eve Do to Help? And Other Readerly Questions to the Old Testament* (JSOTSup 94; Sheffield, Eng.: JSOT Press, 1990), 25. For representative feminist proponents of this view, see, among others, ibid., 25–47; Danna Nolan Fewell and David M. Gunn, *Gender, Power, and Promise: The Subject of the Bible's First Story* (Nashville: Abingdon, 1993), 22–38; Gardner, "Genesis 2:4b–3"; David Jobling, *The Sense of Biblical Narrative: Structural Analysis in the Hebrew Bible* (2 vols.; JSOTSup 39; Sheffield, Eng.: JSOT Press, 1986), 2:17–43; Pamela Milne, "The Patriarchal Stamp of Scripture: The Implications of Structuralist Analyses for Feminist Hermeneutics," *JFSR* 5 (1989): 17–34; Beverly J. Stratton, *Out of Eden: Reading, Rhetoric, and Ideology in Genesis 2–3* (JSOTSup 208; Sheffield, Eng.: Sheffield Academic Press, 1995), 95–108.

prescription of God's will for man-woman relationships after sin. Proponents of this position underscore the culturally conditioned nature of this passage and vigorously deny that it represents a divinely ordained normative position for sexual relationships after the fall.[24]

The fifth major position concurs with the fourth view that God's original design was for an egalitarian relationship between the sexes (Gen 1–2) and the fall brought a rupture in their relationships. But in the fifth view, 3:16 is to be understood as *prescriptive* and not just descriptive: this verse presents *husband leadership and wife submission as God's normative pattern for the marriage relationship after the fall.*[25]

---

[24] Of the dozens of major studies propounding this position, see esp. Belleville, *Women Leaders in the Church,* 96–108; Gilbert G. Bilezikian, *Beyond Sex Roles: What the Bible Says about a Woman's Place in Church and Family* (Grand Rapids: Baker, 1985), 39–58; Judy L. Brown, *Women Ministers according to Scripture* (Minneapolis: Christians for Biblical Equality, 1996), 35–61; Mary J. Evans, *Woman in the Bible: An Overview of All the Crucial Passages on Women's Roles* (Downers Grove, Ill.: InterVarsity, 1984), 17–21; Joy Elasky Fleming, *Man and Woman in Biblical Unity: Theology from Genesis 2–3* (Old Tappan, N.J.: Christians for Biblical Equality, 1993), 19–42; Stanley J. Grenz with Denise Muir Kjesbo, *Women in the Church: A Biblical Theology of Women in Ministry* (Downers Grove, Ill.: InterVarsity, 1995), 165–69; Rebecca Merrill Groothuis, *Good News for Women: A Biblical Picture of Gender Equality* (Grand Rapids: Baker, 1997), 138–44; Patricia Gundry, *Woman Be Free! The Clear Message of Scripture* (Grand Rapids: Zondervan, 1977), 60–63; Fritz Guy, "The Disappearance of Paradise," in *The Welcome Table: Setting a Place for Ordained Women* (ed. Patricia A. Habada and Rebecca Frost Brillhart; Langley Park, Md.: Team, 1995), 137–53; Mary Hayter, *The New Eve in Christ: The Use and Abuse of the Bible in the Debate about Women in the Church* (Grand Rapids: Eerdmans, 1987), 102–17; Richard S. Hess, "Equality with and without Innocence: Genesis 1–3," in *Discovering Biblical Equality: Complementarity without Hierarchy* (ed. Ronald W. Pierce and Rebecca Merrill Groothuis; Downers Grove, Ill.: InterVarsity, 2004), 79–95; Aida Besançon Spencer, *Beyond the Curse: Women Called to Ministry* (Nashville: Nelson, 1985), 29–42; Lee Anna Starr, *The Bible Status of Woman* (New York: Fleming H. Revell, 1926; repr., New York: Garland, 1987), 27–53; Trible, *God and the Rhetoric of Sexuality,* 105–39; Ruth A. Tucker, *Women in the Maze: Questions and Answers on Biblical Equality* (Downers Grove, Ill.: InterVarsity, 1992), 43–54; and Mary Stewart Van Leeuwen, *Gender and Grace: Love, Work, and Parenting in a Changing World* (Downers Grove, Ill.: InterVarsity, 1990), 42–51.

[25] This position is supported, e.g., by the later Martin Luther, *Lectures on Genesis: Chapters 1–5* (trans. George V. Schick; vol. 1 of *Works;* ed. Jaroslav Pelikan; St. Louis: Concordia, 1958), 137–38, 202–3: "If Eve had persisted in the truth, she would not only not have been subjected to the rule of her husband, but she herself would also have been a partner in the rule which is now entirely the concern of males" (p. 203); "The wife was made subject to the man by the Law which was given after sin" (138); "Eve has been placed under the power of her husband, she who previously was very free and, as the sharer of all the gifts of God, was in no respect inferior to her husband. This punishment, too, springs from original sin" (202). For further discussion of the views of the early and later Luther, see esp. Mickey Leland Mattox, *"Defender of the Most Holy Matriarchs": Martin Luther's Interpretation of the Women of Genesis in the "Enarrationes in Genesin," 1535–45* (SMRT 92; Leiden: E. J. Brill, 2003), 29–33, 67–108. Other more recent proponents of this position include Schaeffer, *Genesis in Space and Time,* 93–94; and Theodorus C. Vriezen, *An Outline of Old Testament Theology* (2d ed. rev. and enlarged; Oxford: Blackwell, 1970), 399.

The sixth view agrees with the fourth and fifth views that God's original plan was an egalitarian relationship between the sexes. It also agrees with the third view that v. 16c–d is a blessing and not a curse, but differs in denying that subordination/subjection of woman to man is a creation ordinance. This position argues, by various means of translation and interpretation, that even in Gen 3 *no hierarchy (leadership/submission) between the sexes is either prescribed or described.* Among proponents of this view, the word for "rule" (v. 16d) is often translated "to be like," emphasizing the equal rank of man and woman.[26]

The major positions are summarized in the chart.

Man-Woman Relationships (Ranking) in the Beginning (Gen 1–3): Major Views

Creation (Gen 1–2)	Fall (Gen 3)	Divine pronouncement concerning Eve (Gen 3:16)
1. Hierarchical (Subordination/submission of woman to male supremacy/leadership)	Violation of male-female hierarchy and/or ruptured relationships	*Description* of the perversion of hierarchical relationships (woman seeks to control man and/or man exploitively subjugates woman)
2. Hierarchical (Submission of woman to male leadership)	Violation of male-female hierarchy and/or ruptured relationships	*Prediction* that woman would desire to get out from under man's authority, and *prescription* that man must exercise his "godly headship" to restrain her urge to control him

---

[26] E.g., John H. Otwell, *And Sarah Laughed: The Status of Women in the Old Testament* (Philadelphia: Westminster, 1977), 18, 197–98; John J. Schmitt, "Like Eve, Like Adam: *Mšl* in Gen 3:16," *Bib* 72 (1991): 1–22; Kowalski Wojciech, "Female Subjection to Man: Is It a Consequence of the Fall?" *African Ecclesial Review* 35 (1993): 274–87. An alternate suggestion is made by Robert Ivan Vasholz, " 'He (?) Will Rule over You': A Thought on Genesis 3:16," *Presb* 20 (1994): 51–52, who contends that the masculine pronoun *hûʾ* should be translated "that" and not "he," referring not to her husband but to the "desire" of the woman (her capacity for affection), which will rule or prevail over her anticipation of suffering. This suggestion is critiqued below. Various feminist interpreters also arrive at an egalitarian view but assume a radical source-critical and sociological reconstruction and/or textual emendation of the passage. See, e.g., Adrien Janis Bledstein, "Was Eve Cursed? (or Did a Woman Write Genesis?)" *BRev* 9, no. 1 (1993): 42–45; Carol Meyers, "Gender Roles and Gen 3:16 Revisited," in *The Word of the Lord Shall Go Forth: Essays in Honor of David Noel Freedman in Celebration of His Sixtieth Birthday* (ed. Carol L. Meyers and M. O'Connor; Winona Lake, Ind.: Eisenbrauns, 1983), 337–54. For a succinct review of these and other hypothetical reconstructions of the life setting in Gen 3, see Hess, "Roles in Genesis 3," 15–19.

3. Hierarchical (Subordinaton/submission of woman to male supremacy/leadership)	Violation of male-female hierarchy and/or ruptured relationships	*Reaffirmation* of original hierarchical roles as a continued divine blessing, or a statement of continued subjugation of woman by man
4. Egalitarian (Full equality with no subordination/submission of woman to male supremacy/leadership)	Ruptured relationship between the sexes	*Predictive description* of the consequences of sin—man usurps authority over the woman—which "curse" is to be removed by the gospel with return to egalitarianism
5. Egalitarian (Full equality with no subordination/submission of woman to male supremacy/leadership)	Ruptured relationship between the sexes	*Permanent prescription* of divine will in order to preserve harmony in the home after sin: wife's submission to her husband's leadership
6. Egalitarian (Full equality with no subordination/submission of woman to male supremacy/leadership)	Egalitarian relationship continues	*Blessing* of equality (no hierarchy of leadership/submission) in the midst of a sinful world and its challenges

In assessing the true intent of this passage, I must immediately call into question the interpretations that proceed from the assumption that a hierarchy (whether ontological or functional) between the sexes existed before the fall (views one, two and three). My analysis of Gen 1–2 has led to the conclusion that no such subordination or subjection of woman to man's leadership was present in the beginning.

Nor is there any indication of male superiority or leadership over the woman, and female inferiority or submission to the man, in the account of the temptation and fall (3:1–7). The temptation of the woman by the serpent is presented in vv. 1–6. In this passage the woman's response to the serpent reveals her to be intelligent, perceptive, informed, and articulate; contrary to frequent assertions in the past that she was feeble-minded, weak, naive, and an easy target for the serpent's wiles.[27] Furthermore, the temptation to which both Adam and Eve yielded was the temptation to become like God—to exercise moral autonomy in acting against the express command of God. God specifically states what the sin of both of them was: not the violation of a man/woman leadership/submission principle but the eating from the tree from which God commanded them not to eat (3:11). "The challenge of the snake is not directed against the man's authority. It is against God's authority."[28] Although the passage may well allow for

---

[27] Trible perhaps exaggerates when she elaborates: "Theologian, ethicist, hermeneut, rabbi, she speaks with clarity and authority" (*God and the Rhetoric of Sexuality*, 110). But her main point is on the mark. And she may well be right when she points out that Eve's addition of the phrase "nor shall you touch it," shows her hermeneutical ability to "build a fence around the Torah," like the later rabbinic exegetes, in order to insure obedience to it (ibid.).

[28] Hess, "Equality with and without Innocence," 89.

the interpretation that Eve wandered from Adam's immediate presence, lingered at the forbidden tree, and later offered the fruit to her husband,[29] there is no warrant in this text for maintaining that their sin consisted of the woman getting out from under the authoritative leadership of her husband, or of her husband failing to exercise his "godly headship" to restrain her.[30]

Neither does the argument have persuasive power that after the fall God approached and addressed the man first because the man was in a position of representative leadership over his wife.[31] God questions the man first for a number of reasons that are apparent in the text: (1) A primary reason no doubt is that the man was created first and the first one to have received the command not to eat from the fruit of the forbidden tree (2:17) and so, since he had been the one directly and personally warned, it was natural for him to be the one God would approach first. But such a choice in no way implies pre-fall male leadership representing his wife. (2) The man clearly is not approached by God on behalf of his wife but solely on his own behalf, since the personal pronoun of God's question in v. 9 is singular, not plural: "Where are you [sg.]?" (3) In the dialogue between God and the man, the man does not function as the woman's overseer; in

---

[29] I prefer this interpretation instead of seeing Eve as the talkative initiator and Adam as the silent bystander (contra Trible, *God and the Rhetoric of Sexuality,* 110–13). The Hebrew clause in 3:6 "she also gave some to her husband, who was *with her* [ʿimmāh]" does not imply that Adam was right by her side at the tree; note the clarification for this preposition in Adam's reply to God (3:12)—"The woman whom you gave to be with me [ʿimmādî]"—showing that it refers to their partnership and not to their proximity of location at any one given time. This interpretation seems to be implied in the last half of 3:12: "she gave me fruit from the tree, and I ate." If Adam had been present and listened to the whole conversation between Eve and the serpent, it seems he would have implicated the serpent as well as the woman in his defense. Similarly, the woman's testimony in 3:13 ("The serpent tricked me") would also seem to have applied to Adam as well (he also would have been deceived) if he had been personally present at the tree next to Eve.

[30] Marrs, "In the Beginning," 32, rightly concludes, "The woman's sin in 3:1–7 has nothing to do with usurping the man's authority; rather, it involves exalting herself above the Creator to determine for herself right and wrong." Marrs, p. 34, n. 90, also correctly points out that God's statement to the man in 3:17 ("Because you have listened to the voice of your wife") does not imply that the man had failed to control his wife or had abdicated his leadership role. Rather, it is simply "an acknowledgment of the man's decision to follow his wife's direction rather than God's command." The sin of Adam was not in "listening to" or "obeying" his wife per se but in "obeying" his wife *rather than* or *in opposition to* God's explicit command not to eat of the fruit. Of course, this is not to deny that there is "strength in numbers" in withstanding temptation and that Eve made herself more vulnerable to the serpent's attack by separating from her husband. But such fortification against temptation by partners standing together is just as applicable in a totally egalitarian relationship (which I see here before the fall) as in a hierarchical one (which I do not find in the narrative before 3:16).

[31] Contra, e.g., Raymond C. Ortlund Jr., "Male-Female Equality and Male Headship: Genesis 1–3," in *Recovering Biblical Manhood and Womanhood: A Response to Evangelical Feminism* (ed. John Piper and Wayne A. Grudem; Wheaton, Ill.: Crossway, 1991), 107–8; Thomas R. Schreiner, "Women in Ministry," in *Two Views on Women in Ministry* (ed. James R. Beck and Craig L. Blomberg; Grand Rapids: Zondervan, 2001), 209.

answer to God's questioning, he explains only his own behavior, not that of the woman, and instead of being her spokesperson, he is her accuser. (4) The woman is summoned to give her own testimony concerning her behavior and answers directly on behalf of herself. (5) The interrogation of vv. 9–13 proceeds in chiastic (reverse) order from that in which the characters in the narrative are introduced in vv. 1–8, with God in the center of the structure (this is in harmony with an overarching chiastic structure of the entire chapter[32] and with another reversal of order in vv. 14–19). (6) In this legal trial investigation, God must examine the witnesses one by one to demonstrate their individual guilt; the man blames the woman, who then naturally in turn is put on the witness stand for divine interrogation. (7) The answers of both man and woman, with their blame of others (the woman and the snake respectively), reveal that "sin's breakdown of the creation order was not an abdication of divinely instituted hierarchy but the loss of loving harmony between the man and the woman."[33] "That no sort of one-way submission could be part of the Ideal Marriage is underscored by what is lost."[34] Thus those espousing the first three views who argue for implications of hierarchy from 3:1–13 are reading into the text what does not exist in the chapter, just as they have done for Gen 1–2.

The fourth view (that 3:16 is only descriptive, not prescriptive), too, is unsatisfactory, despite its popularity, because it fails to take seriously the judgment/punishment context of the passage. The nature of this judgment/punishment is indicated by the text. As already noted, 3:16 comes in a legal trial setting, a "legal process," a "trial punishment by God,"[35] and v. 16 is thus not just a predictive description but a divine sentence.

In fact, the whole context leading up to 3:16 calls for an inference of prescriptive punishment and not just descriptive/predictive information. Numerous stages and conditions in the flow of the narrative lead to this inference: God issues to man a prohibition ("you shall not eat," 2:16–17a); God as the Creator has the authority to impose sanctions if Adam and Eve violate the prohibition ("in the day that you eat," 2:17b); Adam and Eve do violate the prohibition (3:1–6); God then instigates a legal trial (3:8–13) in which God examines the witnesses ("Where are you?" "Have you eaten?" "What is this that you have done?") and they admit their guilt ("I ate"); God then pronounces a legal sentence ("Because you have done *x*, therefore *y*," 3:14–19). In short, "the entire narrative, in which God creates the tree, explicitly forbids *hāʾādām* to eat of it,

[32] Afolarin Ojewole, "The Seed in Genesis 3:15: An Exegetical and Intertextual Study" (PhD diss., Andrews University, 2002), 98.

[33] Hess, "Equality with and without Innocence," 89–90. For the gist of the arguments in this paragraph, I am particularly indebted to Hess (ibid.) and Brown, *Women Ministers according to Scripture*, 45–46.

[34] Paul Borgman, *Genesis: The Story We Haven't Heard* (Downers Grove, Ill.: InterVarsity, 2001), 27. What is lost, Borgman continues, is clarified in v. 16: "The wife, now, must submit to the ruling husband. This is part of the 'curse.'" The interpretation of this verse is explored below.

[35] Westermann, *Creation*, 96.

and then calls the man and woman to account for doing so, creates an overdetermined context in which God is *expected* to deliver punishment long before he does so, and the pronouncements of 3:14–19 fulfill this expectation even if their surface form allows other possibilities."[36] Thus the pronouncement to the woman is "exercitive"—"a decision that something is to be so"—and not "expositive," "a judgment that *is* so."[37]

Not only does the immediate context of the creation-fall narrative point to prescriptive punishment in 3:14–19; also the larger context of Gen 1–11 as a whole confirms this interpretation. David J. A. Clines, building on the previous narrative pattern studies of Gerhard von Rad and Claus Westermann, shows how the entire extended narrative of Gen 1–11 has a recurring motif that climaxes in punishment. In the fall (Gen 3), the story of Cain (Gen 4), the sons of God and the flood (Gen 6–7), and the tower of Babel (Gen 11), the pattern is the same: (1) sin; (2) divine speech announcing or deciding the penalty; (3) mitigation or grace; and (4) the carrying out of the punishment.[38] To Clines's pattern I would add a fifth element. In each of these narratives, after the sin but before the divine speech, there comes a legal trial investigation.[39] It is difficult to avoid the conclusion that Gen 3 is consistent with the other narratives in Gen 1–11, including a legal trial (3:9–13), a divine prescriptive sentence announcing the penalty (3:14–19), and the carrying out of the punishment (3:22–24). Just as in none of the other narratives in Gen 1–11 are the divine pronouncements merely descrip-

---

[36] Susan Lanser, "(Feminist) Criticism in the Garden: Inferring Genesis 2–3," *Semeia* 41 (1988): 75. I am indebted to Lanser for sharpening my thinking regarding inferring punishment from the detailed "stages and conditions" in the narrative that lead up to Gen 3:16.

[37] Ibid., following the nomenclature of J. L. Austin, *How to Do Things with Words* (2d ed.; Cambridge: Harvard University Press, 1975), 155.

[38] David J. A. Clines, *The Theme of the Pentateuch* (JSOTSup 10; Sheffield, Eng.: University of Sheffield Press, 1978), 61–64.

[39] The legal trial setting of Gen 3 has already been noted. The same kind of investigative trial is apparent in the story of Cain (4:9–10): "Where is your brother Abel? . . . What have you done? Listen; your brother's blood is crying out to me from the ground!" (See Victor P. Hamilton, *The Book of Genesis: Chapters 1–17* [NICOT; Grand Rapids: Eerdmans, 1990], 230–31: "Following the crime, comes the divine investigation. . . . God now shifts from interrogator to that of prosecutor." Cf. Kenneth A. Mathews, *Genesis 1–11:26* [NAC 1A; Nashville: Broadman & Holman, 1996], 275: "As in a criminal trial, God presents condemning testimony against Cain.") God comes again for a legal investigation before he brings the flood (6:1–13; see esp. vv. 5, 12–13): "The LORD saw. . . . And God saw. . . . I have determined." (See Sarna, *Genesis,* 46: "This phrase ['The Lord saw'] has juridical overtones, implying both investigation of the facts and readiness for action." Cf. Umberto Cassuto, *A Commentary on the Book of Genesis* [trans. Israel Abrahams; 2 vols.; Jerusalem: Magnes, 1961–1964], 2:57: "[God, as it were, says that] sentence of destruction upon all flesh has been presented before My Court of Justice, and I have already come to a decision concerning it, and I am about to execute it.") The same procedure is described in God's coming down for a judicial investigation of the tower of Babel (Gen 11:5): "The LORD came down to see the city and the tower, which mortals had built." (See Sarna, *Genesis,* 82: "God does not react capriciously; he investigates man's doings").

tive or predictive but also prescriptive of what God has ordained to take place as just punishments for sin, so it is in Gen 3.[40]

The divine origin and prescriptive nature of the judgment upon Eve is underscored by the Hebrew grammar of God's first words in the legal sentencing (3:16): "I will greatly increase" (*harbâ ʾarbeh,* lit. "multiplying I will multiply"). The use of the first person singular "I" refers to the Lord, who is pronouncing the judgment, and the Hebrew infinitive absolute followed by the finite verb implies "the absolute certainty of the action."[41] "The construction 'I will' as a preface to the 'consequences' in 3:15 and 3:16, suggests that God is determining and choosing them."[42] I concur with Carol Meyers's conclusion that the judgment upon Eve represents not just a description but a "divine prescription," a divine "mandate" and "divine oracle."[43] God is not merely *informing* the woman of her fate; God is

---

[40] I underscore the aspect of justice at this point. Each of the narratives in Gen 1–11 that end in divine punishment take pains to reveal God's intimate involvement in the process of evaluating or investigating the nature of the disobedience and sin and in a statement of the nature of that sin, so as to constitute a theodicy revealing God's justice in bringing about the proper punishment to fit the crime. Stratton, *Out of Eden,* 142–44, shows a wide "punishment spectrum" among scholarly interpretations of 3:16—moving through the following options (from one extreme to the other): (1) no punishments are inflicted because there is no remorse or response; (2) an etiology describes the reality the couple chose, with God providing the desired knowledge; (3) though punishment is warranted, God gives grace and mercy; (4) God announces judgments, which are consequences of their actions; (5) punishments are appropriate, not whimsical like those of the ANE deities; (6) unmitigated punishments signal death for the listeners; and (7) punishments are disproportionate to the creatures' misdeeds. (See Stratton's footnotes for specific representatives [with bibliography] of each view.) I find the biblical evidence supporting aspects of options 3–5 to be applicable to 3:16. The punishments are just, as a result of divine investigation, in stark contrast to ANE parallels (option 5); the punishments are also intimately linked with (though not just as natural consequences of) the sinful actions of the creatures (option 4); and as will be shown below, the punishments (although real) are also mitigated by grace and mercy, so that the very punishments become a divine blessing in a sinful world.

[41] See Meyers, *Discovering Eve,* 99.

[42] Lanser, "(Feminist) Criticism," 75.

[43] Meyers, *Discovering Eve,* 110–11. Wojciech ("Female Subjection," 280), in propounding the interpretation that God is only describing and not prescribing, tellingly remarks, "It is very surprising to everyone, that the Yahwist is not interested in finding a judgement of 'guilty' on both man and woman, though so strongly deserved. Rather it seems he intends neither to investigate nor judge the man and woman, but simply scans their future history." It is only "very surprising" if one fails to face the overwhelming evidence that Gen 3 is indeed a divine legal investigation in which God does give a "guilty" verdict upon the couple and pronounce a detailed punitive sentence. Lanser, "(Feminist) Criticism," 75, points out the important "consequence" of accepting 3:16 as divine punishment—a consequence that Trible and Bal and other feminist critics are unwilling to accept: "If in fact the state of affairs described in 3:16 is punishment, then God could be charged with ordaining male dominance, all the more as the man is judged not only for eating but for listening to the woman's voice (3:17). This is the point where Bal's and Trible's readings reach their *aporia*—the impasse, the silence, that unravels the argument. For finally neither can explain why male dominance should be the particular consequence of a transgression for which both man and woman are equally, as they argue, responsible."

ordaining the state of affairs announced in 3:16. God is the Judge announcing his penal sentence for Adam and Eve's guilt.

Just as God destines the snake to crawl on its belly; just as God ordains that woman's childbirth is to entail her going into labor; just as God curses the ground so that it will not produce crops spontaneously but require man's cultivation and labor; just as humankind will inevitably return to dust in death—so God pronounces the sentence upon the woman regarding her future relationship with her husband outside the garden. In the context of the other judgments/punishments of Gen 3 and the use of the generic name for "man" and "woman," it is clear that the biblical writer intended to indicate that this judgment was not applicable to just the first man and woman but was to extend beyond to the human race, to remain in force in perpetuity or as long as the conditions of the fall prevailed.[44]

It also seems clear that according to 3:16c–d, a *change* is instituted in the relationship between the sexes after the fall. God is not simply reiterating or reaffirming a relationship that had already existed in the beginning. The intent of v. 16a is unmistakable: "I will greatly increase your pangs [ˁiṣṣābôn] in childbearing"—there was no pain/anguish/hard labor before sin; this statement is announcing a change in conditions, and it sets the tone for the parallel changes prescribed in the remainder of the verse.[45] This is confirmed by the judgments/

---

[44] Some scholars have suggested that since the punishment of 3:16 is addressed just to Eve and only mention is made of her own husband, this punishment is only limited to the first couple and does not apply to wife-husband relationships in general after the fall. In the context, however, of the other curses/judgments—to the snake, the ground, and the man—it is clear that these judgments are applicable far beyond the single couple Adam and Eve. Since Adam and Eve were the father and mother of the human race, their fall had consequences that passed on to their posterity. As will be pointed out below, inasmuch as these judgments also contain implied blessings to postfall humanity, they apply as long as these blessings are needed (i.e., as long as we are in a sinful world). "The generic names 'man' and 'woman' used throughout the text suggest that the punishment in 3:16 applies to all women. The narrator tells the story as if this verse describes God's current, if not original, intent for women as a group" (Stratton, *Out of Eden,* 208).

[45] Many scholars recognize only one punishment each for serpent, woman, and man, and hence the parallelism in Gen 3:16a–b is often taken as the punishment (increased pain/labor in childbirth), and 3:16c–d is taken as description, not penal prescription, of conditions after sin (see, e.g., Busenitz, "Genesis 3:16 Reconsidered," 206–8). It seems clear, however, that the man receives more than one punishment (although they are all interrelated): pain/hard labor in agricultural pursuits (vv. 17b, 19a); having to deal with thorns and thistles, and a switch to eating the herbs of the field (v. 18); and eventual return to dust in death (v. 19b). Likewise, the woman receives a multiple but interrelated sentence: increased hard labor in childbearing and a new role of voluntary submission to the servant leadership of her husband. Moreover, although the first part of the divine judgment upon Eve and Adam arguably deals with the roles that will be their primary concern (the woman's childbearing and the man's providing for the family's physical needs), both of the judgments end in punishments that broaden to include both male and female. Both Adam and Eve will return to the dust in death, and both Adam and Eve experience a change in role relationships from egalitarian to leadership/submission. For further argumentation in favor of more than one punishment in each of the curses/judgments, see Jerome T. Walsh, "Genesis 2:4b–3:24: A Synchronic Approach," *JBL* 96

curses upon the serpent and the man—both announcing changes from the previous Edenic conditions.

The prescriptive changes in 3:16c–d clearly entail the subjection/submission of the wife to the husband. The force of the last line (v. 16d) is unavoidable: *wĕhûʾ yimšol-bāk*, "he [your husband] shall rule over you."[46] The verb *māšal* in this form in v. 16d means "to rule" (not "to be like" or "to be irresistible") and clearly implies submission/subjection.[47] Theodorus Vriezen correctly concludes from this line that woman's position after the fall is one of subjection to her husband: "This is considered as a just and permanent punishment in Gen iii."[48] Although the text does not explicitly give the reason Eve was placed in submission to her husband rather than vice versa, the implication seems clear from the context: as a result of sin, their mutual egalitarian harmony had given way to accusation and blame (3:12, 13), and the harmony and union of the home could be maintained only by the submission of one or the other. Eve was first in transgression (3:6), and it was by her solicitation that Adam sinned (3:13), and thus she received the sentence of submission to her husband. Umberto Cassuto aptly paraphrases and amplifies the divine sentence: "Measure for measure; you influenced your husband and caused him to do what you wished; henceforth, you and your female descendants will be subservient to your husbands."[49]

(1977): 168–69 (Walsh argues for two punishments for each party, one concerning an essential life function and the other a relationship, with the two punishments mutually related).

[46] Contra Vasholz, "'He (?) Will Rule over You,'" 51, the masculine pronoun *hûʾ* has as its antecedent the masculine *ʾîšēk*, "your husband," and not the feminine *tĕšûqātēk*, "your desire." It is the husband who will "rule" and not the woman's desire. Although Vasholz correctly points out some exceptions in Genesis to the general rule that the masculine pronoun agrees in gender with its antecedent, in this verse there is a natural masculine noun ("your husband") immediately preceding the masculine pronoun, and it strains credibility to suggest that the general rule of gender agreement is broken in this case. The strongest parallel suggested by Vasholz, 4:7, collapses under the explanation provided by Joachim Azevedo (summarized below), since the latter verse does not violate the rule of gender agreement.

[47] Recent attempts by some scholars (see the sixth view in chart on pp. 64–65) to translate *māšal* as "to be like" instead of "to rule" face insurmountable lexical/grammatical/contextual obstacles. It is true that (following BDB nomenclature) the root *mšl^l* in the *nipʿal* stem does signify "to be like, similar," but in 3:16 the root *mšl* is in the *qal*. Both *mšl^l*, "to use a proverb," and *mšl^{II}*, "to rule," occur in the *qal*, but the context of 3:16 seems to preclude the idea of "use a proverb" (*mšl^{II}*). That *mšl^{III}*, "to rule," is intended in this passage is confirmed by the use of the accompanying preposition, *bĕ*, the normal preposition following *mšl^{III}* (cf. BDB 605) and other Hebrew roots of ruling, governing, restraining (*mlk, rdh, šlṭ, ʿṣr*, etc.) but never used with *mšl^l* or *mšl^{II}*. Arguments based largely on the meaning of ANE cognates should not be allowed to override the biblical context, grammar, syntax, and usage. Suggestions of the retrojection of the meaning "to rule" into the fall narrative by later redaction, under the influence of an Egyptian cognate, although they are appealing, unfortunately rest on speculation without textual support. Likewise Trevor Dennis's suggested translation (*Sarah Laughed: Women's Voices in the Old Testament* [Nashville: Abingdon, 1994], 25) of "to be irresistible" is not defensible as a meaning for *mšl* in light of comparative lexical evidence.

[48] Vriezen, *Old Testament Theology*, 399.

[49] Cassuto, *Genesis*, 1:165.

The verb *māšal,* "rule," employed in v. 16, is not, however, the same verb used to describe humankind's rulership over the animals in 1:26, 28. In the latter passages, the verb is *rādâ,* "have dominion over," not *māšal.* A careful distinction is maintained between humankind's dominion over the animals and the husband's "rule" over his wife. Furthermore, although the verb *māšal* does consistently indicate submission, subjection, or dominion in Scripture, "the idea of tyrannous exercise of power does not lie in the verb."[50] Indeed, there are a number of passages where *māšal* is used with the connotation of servant leadership, to "comfort, protect, care for, love."[51] In later usages of *māšal* in scriptural narratives (e.g., the time of Gideon), the people of Israel are eager to have someone to "rule" (*māšal*) over them (Judg 8:22), and the term *māšal* describes the rulership of Yahweh and the future Messiah.[52] Thus *māšal* is predominantly a positive concept, not a negative one.

The semantic range of the verb *māšal* thus makes it possible to understand the divine sentence in v. 16 as including not only punishment but promised blessing, just as the sentence pronounced upon the serpent and the man included an implied blessing in the curse/judgment.[53] "The decrees pronounced by the Lord God mentioned here are not exclusively *punishments;* they are also, and chiefly,

---

[50] Skinner, *Genesis,* 53.

[51] E.g., 2 Sam 23:3; Prov 17:2; Isa 40:10; 63:19; Zech 6:13. See Robert D. Culver, "מָשַׁל (*māshal*) III, rule, have dominion, reign," *TWOT* 1:534: "*Māshal* usually receives the translation 'to rule,' but the precise nature of the rule is as various as the real situations in which the action or state so designated occur." Specific examples follow to support this statement. Note, e.g., that the first usage of *māšal* in Scripture is in reference to the two great lights created by God (Gen 1:16)—they were to "dominate" (NJPS) the day and night. For further discussion of *māšal* in the positive sense here in 3:16 as well as elsewhere in the OT, see Othmar Keel, "Die Stellung der Frau in der Erzählung von Schöpfung und Sündenfall," *Orientierung* 39 (1975): 75.

[52] See, e.g., Judg 8:23; Isa 40:10; Mic 4:14 (ET 5:1); Zech 6:13; 9:10.

[53] Hurley, *Man and Woman,* 216–19, has perceptively recognized how in each of the divine judgments in this chapter there is a blessing as well as a curse. Many from the evangelical Christian tradition maintain that in the curse upon the serpent appears a veiled blessing in the *protoevangelium* (first gospel promise) of Gen 3:15: "The warfare between Satan and the woman's seed comes to its climax in the death of Christ" (Hurley, *Man and Woman,* 217; cf. Walter C. Kaiser Jr., *Toward an Old Testament Theology* [Grand Rapids: Zondervan, 1978], 35–37, and Ojewole, "The Seed in Genesis 3:15," passim, for biblical evidence in favor of this traditional interpretation in contrast to the modern critical tendency to see here only an etiological reference.) Likewise, in the curse of the ground and the "toil" that is the punishment of Adam, there is at the same time a blessing in that God promises that the ground will continue to yield its fruit and man will still be able to eat of it. Furthermore, the expression *ba˓ăbûr,* employed in v. 17, probably means "for the sake of" (NKJV) and not "because of" (NRSV) inasmuch as the meaning of "because" is already expressed by *kî* earlier in the verse. The ground is cursed "for your [Adam's] sake" (NKJV)—that is, the curse is for Adam's benefit. Though it did result from Adam's sin, it also is to be regarded as a discipline rendered needful by his sin, to place a check upon the indulgence of appetite and passion, to develop habits of self-control. According to the biblical text, it was a part of God's great plan for man's recovery from the ruin and degradation of sin.

measures taken for the good of the human species in its new situation."[54] This also fits the pattern of Gen 1–11 as a whole, where, as noted above, each sequence involving divine judgment was also mitigated by grace.[55]

That the element of grace/blessing is especially emphasized in this verse appears to be confirmed by the same synonymous parallelism between v. 16c and v. 16d as occurs between v. 16a and v. 16b.[56] The divine sentence upon Eve concerning her husband's servant leadership is shown to be a blessing by its placement in synonymous parallelism with Eve's "desire" for her husband. The meaning of the Hebrew word *těšûqâ* is "strong desire, yearning,"[57] not "attractive, desirable"[58] or "turning [away]."[59] This term appears only three times in Scripture, and its precise connotation in Gen 3:16 is illuminated by its only other occurrence in a context of man-woman relationship, that is, Song 7:11 (ET 7:10). In this verse, the Shulammite bride joyfully exclaims, "I am my beloved's, and his desire [*těšûqâ*] is for me." As will be observed in the study of the Song of Songs (chs. 13–14, below), this passage is in all probability written as an intertextual commentary on Gen 3:16. Along the lines of this usage of *těšûqâ* in the Song of Songs to indicate a wholesome sexual desire, a desire for intimacy, the term appears to be employed in Gen 3:16c to indicate a positive blessing accompanying the divine judgment.[60] A divinely ordained, intimate (sexual) yearning of wife for

---

[54] Cassuto, *Genesis*, 1:163.

[55] Clines, *Theme of the Pentateuch*, 63–64.

[56] Otwell, *And Sarah Laughed*, 18, cogently argues that the normal structure of Hebrew parallelism is followed here in that 3:16a and b are in parallel and 3:16c and d are likewise in parallel. As the first two parallel members of this verse duplicate content regarding childbearing, so "we may expect . . . that 'he shall rule over you' parallels 'your desire shall be for your husband.'" Otwell's argument is strengthened by the use of the conjunctive *waw*, which serves to unite v. 16a–b with c–d and is best translated by "yet" (NRSV).

[57] See BDB 1003; Victor P. Hamilton, "תשׁוּקָה, *těšûqâ*," *TWOT* 2:913; David Talley, "תשׁוּקָה, *těšûqâ*," *NIDOTTE* 4:341–42.

[58] Bledstein, "Was Eve Cursed?" 42–45, who (mis)translates the noun "desire" (*těšûqâ*) as an adjective, "desirable," based upon a conjectural emendation of the MT that is unconvincing.

[59] Contra earlier (first wave) feminist arguments, represented by, e.g., Katherine C. Bushnell, *God's Word to Women* (London: Women's Correspondence Bible Class, 1912; repr., Mossville, Ill.: God's Word to Women, 1990), lessons 16–19, who followed the translation of most ancient versions (LXX, Theodotian, Syriac Peshitta, Samaritan Pentateuch, Old Latin, Sahidic, Bohairic, Coptic, Ethiopic). Cf. Starr, *The Bible Status of Women*, 28–29. It seems clear that these ancient versions are reading *těšûbâ* ("turning") instead of *těšûqâ* in these passages. There is no good reason to abandon the MT for a misunderstanding of the Hebrew text on the part of the ancient versions. For further discussion, see Roland Bergmeier, "Zur Septuagintaübersetzung von Gen 3:16," *ZAW* 79 (1967): 77–79; Cassuto, *Genesis*, 1:166; Hamilton, *Genesis: Chapters 1–17*, 201; Talley, *NIDOTTE* 4:341–42.

[60] Busenitz, "Woman's Desire for Man," 208–12, gives strong reasons Song 7:11 (ET 7:10) and not Gen 4:7 (where the other occurrence of *těšûqâ* appears) should be the prevailing passage in providing illumination for the sense of *těšûqâ* in Gen 3:16. One must recognize an entirely different context between Gen 3:16 and 4:7 and acknowledge the obscurity of meaning of the latter passage. "To grant Gen 4:7 in its obscurity a determinative

husband will serve as a blessing to sustain the union that has been threatened in the ruptured relations resulting from sin.[61] As Belleville puts it, "The wife's

---

role in the interpretation of Gen 3:16 without permitting the clarity of Cant 7:10 [11] to permeate the exegetical process is to abandon hermeneutical discernment and propriety" (p. 211). J. M. Sprinkle concurs: "The 'desire' (*těšûqâ*) a woman has for her husband (Gen 3:16) is probably sexual attraction or urge (as in Song 7:10 [MT 7:11]) that leads her to marry despite its consequences of painful labor and male domination (pace Foh, 376–83, who interprets as 'woman's desire to dominate' her husband based on the use of *těšûqâ* in Gen 4:7)" (Joe M. Sprinkle, "Sexuality, Sexual Ethics," *DOTP* 742). See also Belleville, *Women Leaders and the Church*, 106; and Fleming, *Man and Woman*, 40.

At the same time, contrary to the claims of those who see a negative connotation of *těšûqâ* in Gen 4:7, a penetrating article by Joachim Azevedo, "At the Door of Paradise: A Contextual Interpretation of Gen 4:7," *BN* 100 (1999): 45–59, argues for an interpretation of this passage in which the use of *těšûqâ* is positive and thus in basic harmony with its usage in 3:16 (although the sexual connotation is not found in the "desire" of 4:7 as in the other two passages where it refers specifically to man-woman relationships). Azevedo points out the serious linguistic problems in the traditional translation/interpretation and argues that the minority view in the history of interpretation is to be preferred—God here is alluding to the positive prerogatives of Cain's birthright, which he would be in no danger of losing if his conduct were such as it should be. The antecedent of the masculine suffixed pronouns in *těšûqātô*, "*his* desire," and *timšol-bô*, "you shall rule over *him*," is not *ḥaṭṭā'ṭ* (usually translated "sin"), which is feminine, but Abel (the nearest male antecedent nominative and the one to whom Cain's anger is directed in previous verses, probably because he had lost his firstborn status by his noncompliance with the prescribed ritual, as pointed out by Gordon J. Wenham, *Genesis 1–15* [WBC 1; Waco, Tex.: Word, 1987], 102). Furthermore, the word *ḥaṭṭā'ṭ* in this context of ritual sacrifice should be translated "sin-offering" or, better, "purification-offering" and not "sin" (as implicit in the LXX translation and as Jacob Milgrom, *Leviticus 1–16: A New Translation with Introduction and Commentary* [AB 3; New York: Doubleday, 1991], 253, points out regarding the word in a similar, intertextually related, context in Leviticus). The masculine participle *rōbēṣ*, "lying down, resting, reposing," provides further evidence of a sacrificial context here, pointing to the male gender of the required male sacrificial animal for the purification offering, as in Lev 4:4, 23. The expression *lappetaḥ*, "at the door," again gives a cultic sacrificial context, referring to the cherubim-guarded door/gate of paradise, where sinful humans were to bring their sacrifices, paralleling the numerous uses of *petaḥ* in the Torah describing the door of the tabernacle. Gathering together the various strands of his exegesis, Azevedo, "At the Door of Paradise," 59, provides the following contextual translation of Gen 4:7b: "A purification-offering [a male sacrificial animal] lies down at the door [of the garden], and to you will be his [Abel's] desire and you will rule [again as the firstborn] over him [your brother]." This interpretation, supported by numerous lines of evidence adduced by Azevedo from grammar, syntax, context, ancient versions (LXX), cognate languages, literary structure, discourse analysis, and ANE parallels, seems plausible and is consistent with the positive interpretation of *těšûqâ* in Gen 3:16 and Song 7:11 (ET 7:10).

[61] It is not possible on the basis of word study alone (see the cautions of James Barr and others) to determine exactly what is the scope of yearning of wife for husband that is implied here. Along the lines of the usage in the Song of Songs (which constitutes a commentary on the Genesis passage; see ch. 13, below), depicting Solomon's desire for the Shulammite, *těšûqâ* no doubt includes a sexual desire (see, e.g., Sprinkle, "Sexuality," 742). This is in harmony with the immediate context of Gen 3:16, which deals with childbearing. In addition, along the lines of Gen 4:7 (which is grammatically parallel with Gen 3:16), with Abel's "desire" for his elder, firstborn brother Cain, it may include a sense of

desire is as God intended—a desire to become 'one flesh' with her husband (Gen. 2:24)."[62]

If 3:16d is seen to be in synonymous parallelism with v. 16c (as v. 16a is with v. 16b), then the emphasis upon promised blessing as well as judgment should also accrue to man's relationship with his wife. The husband's servant leadership in the home, even though it grows out of the results of sin, may be regarded as a divine blessing in preserving the harmony and union of the relationship. As is implied in the semantic range of *māšal,* this is to be a servant leadership of protection, care, and love. In the modern idiom, the husband is to lovingly "take care of" his wife.

Genesis 3:16c and d together also seem to be a combined blessing that relates to the first part of the verse (v. 16a and b). The conjunction *waw* linking the first two lines of this verse with the last two lines should probably be translated as "yet," as in some of the modern versions.[63] God pronounces that even though the woman would have difficult "pangs" in childbearing—an ordeal that would seem naturally to discourage her from continuing to have relations with her husband—"yet," God assures her, "your desire shall be for your husband," and his loving servant leadership will take care of you even through the roughest times. He will be your "strong umbrella" of protection and care.[64] The ruptured relationship between husband and wife, indicated in the spirit of blaming by both man and woman immediately after the fall (3:12–13), is to be replaced by reconciliation and mutual love, with the wife resting in her husband's protective care.

At the same time, the synonymous parallelism between v. 16a–b and v. 16c–d, as well as the parallelism with vv. 17–19, also reveals that it is not inappropriate for humankind to seek to roll back the curses/judgments and get back as much as possible to God's original plan. Few would question the appropriateness of taking advantage of advances in obstetrics to relieve unnecessary pain and hard labor during delivery, or of accepting agricultural and technological advances to relieve unnecessary hard labor in farming, or by scientific and medical advances to delay the process of death. In the same way, it is not inappropriate to return as much as is possible to God's original plan for total egalitarianism ("one flesh," 2:24) in marriage, while at the same time retaining the validity of the husband servant leadership principle, as it is necessary in a sinful world to preserve harmony in the home. Thus it might be better to speak of a

---

respect. It theoretically could also include a maternal desire or instinct for children that a relationship with her husband could fulfill, although, as I point out below, the text emphasizes that her desire will be for her husband, not for children. The point is that *tĕšûqâ* in Gen 3:16 most probably has a positive, not negative, connotation, just as in Song 7:11 (ET 7:10) (and perhaps also as in Gen 4:7, the only other occurrences of this term in the HB).

[62] Belleville, *Women Leaders and the Church,* 106.

[63] See, e.g., NASB and RSV/NRSV.

[64] Note that the woman's "desire" is for her husband, not for children, as some would interpret this verse.

qualified (i.e., remedial or redemptive)[65] prescription in these verses.[66] As husbands and wives learn to live more in harmony through the infusion of divine grace, there is less need to resort to the voluntary submission of the wife to the husband in order to maintain harmony and unity in the home. The result will be a gradual return to egalitarian relationship as before the fall. As will become apparent later in this study, such movement back toward the egalitarian marriage of pre-fall Eden is the canonical thrust of the OT.

Thus I suggest a seventh interpretation of 3:16, one that combines elements of views five and six above. Like view five, there is a *qualified prescriptive divine sentence announcing the voluntary submission of the wife to her husband's servant leadership as a result of sin.*[67] This involves, however, not so much a negative judgment as a *positive promised blessing* (as suggested in view six) *of divine grace designed to lead back as much as possible to the original plan of harmony and union between equal partners without hierarchy.*

For interpreters who hold the pronouncement of 3:16 as still normative for today, three final points may be underscored regarding the potential practical application of this passage. First, as already alluded to above, although in Gen 3 the husband is assigned the role of "first among equals"[68] to preserve harmony and union in the marriage partnership, this does not contradict the original divine ideal of 1:26–28, that both man and woman are equally called to accountable dominion, sociability, and fruitfulness. Nor does it nullify the summary statement of 2:24 regarding the nature of the relationship between husband and wife. Genesis 2:24 is clearly written in such a way as to indicate its basis in the pre-fall ideal ("Therefore," i.e., what has been described before) and its applicability to the postfall conditions. God's ideal for the nature of sexual relationship after the fall is still the same as it was for Adam and his equal partner (*ʿēzer kĕnegdô*) in the beginning—to "become one flesh." The divine judgment/blessing in 3:16 is to facilitate the achievement of the original divine design within the context of a sinful world.[69] As already pointed out, the context of 3:16 reveals that it is entirely ap-

---

[65] The terminology of "remedial hierarchy" utilized by Gilbert G. Bilezikian regarding a temporary mode of local church structure for new church plants "as they attempt to establish their corporate identity under the guidance of directive leadership" is useful (*Community 101: Reclaiming the Local Church as Community of Oneness* [Grand Rapids: Zondervan, 1997], 181). In Gen 3:16 I see God prescribing this "remedial hierarchy" for the home situation to facilitate harmony and unity while all the time aiming toward the pre-fall Edenic ideal of egalitarianism.

[66] In explicit Christian terms, the judgments are ordained by God and are not removed by the cross, but they are tempered or qualified by grace.

[67] I intentionally utilize the term "servant-leadership" rather than "headship" in framing this seventh position, because the term "headship" has become semantically loaded to imply the element of "authority over," which I do not find in the biblical mandate of 3:16.

[68] Gerhard F. Hasel, "Equality from the Start: Woman in the Creation Story," *Spectrum* 17, no. 2 (1975): 26.

[69] I see God's leadership appointment in 3:16 as somewhat like my role as department chair at my seminary. In all committees—at least those constituted after the

propriate for marriage partners to seek to return as much as possible to total egalitarianism in the marriage relationship.

A second point to be emphasized is that the functional roles attached to Adam and Eve in the divine judgments of Gen 3 correspond to what will be their respective primary concerns in a sinful environment, but they do not lock husband and wife into functionally unequal, predetermined, or mutually exclusive roles. As Adam and Eve move outside the garden, Adam's primary concern would be to produce food, and Eve's primary concern would be to produce life. They would share mutually in survival tasks. The text of Gen 3 does not attempt to exhaustively or exclusively define the full scope of either the husband's or the wife's roles in society "but reduces them to their essence for survival. Each has potential and limitation: female production of life is controlled by the male, and male production of food is limited by the uncontrolled aspects of nature. As such, there is a semblance of equality of roles. . . . There is no new human life without women's reproductive power, and human life can not be sustained without men's productive power. The text indicates a mutually dependent relationship and mutual valuation."[70]

Indeed, the woman's role in reproduction is presented as an awesome power to produce life—a direct and inherent power that contrasts with the man's indirect power to sustain life through cultivating the ground. The woman's inherent reproductive power—underscored in God's judgment (3:16a) and Adam's naming of Eve "mother of all living" (3:20)—was much more highly valued at the beginning of this world's history and in ancient Israel than in modern society, where we have overpopulation and a lack of emphasis on the continuation of one's lineal descent. Our modern devaluation of this power of women over life

---

fall—there needs to be a facilitator (the committee chair), and in a committee of equal numbers there must be some way to break a deadlocked tie vote. So God has designated the husband as facilitator and "tie-breaker" to maintain union and preserve harmony of their home "committee of two." The chair (at least in my department) has no power to control the department members; he is the first among equals with the unenviable task of doing the "busy work" to facilitate the smooth performance of the department. So the husband, as first among equals in the home, as 3:16 seems to imply, gets to be first: first to say, "I'm sorry," first to offer to take out the garbage and do other disagreeable jobs, first to take responsibility if something goes wrong. "The husband is to be the first to bleed on behalf of the person whom he has been called to protect: his wife. . . . To be the head is to lead by sacrificing first for those we are called to serve" (Dan B. Allender and Tremper Longman III, *Intimate Allies: Recovering God's Design for Marriage and Becoming Soul Mates for Life* [Wheaton, Ill.: Tyndale, 1995], 165, 192). At the same time, just as a committee works best by consensus and it may rarely or never be necessary for the committee chair to break a tie vote as the members serve together in a harmonious union (I write as a department chair who has the privilege of working with such departmental members), so the husband leadership may rarely need to be exercised (in the sense of tie-breaking or the wife's submission).

[70] Lyn M. Bechtel, "Rethinking the Interpretation of Genesis 2:4b–3:24," in *A Feminist Companion to Genesis* (ed. Athalya Brenner; FCB 2; Sheffield, Eng.: Sheffield Academic Press, 1993), 112. Bechtel has also informed my thinking in the paragraph that follows.

must not be read back into the Genesis account. Instead the focus upon the woman's reproductive power must be seen as further implication of the high status of women upheld in the Genesis text.

Even as the divine judgments in Gen 3 are given separately to Adam and Eve and deal with the aspect of life with which they would have primary concerns, at the same time, as already pointed out, the judgments of both overlapped with and included each other. Their concerns were not to be mutually exclusive. The divine judgments state what will be true regarding Eve's primary concern (child-bearing), and what will be true regarding Adam's primary concern (food production), but the judgment nowhere limits or predetermines that these concerns must remain exclusively (or even primarily) the woman's and the man's respectively. The context of 3:16 reveals the appropriateness of husbands and wives seeking to return as much as possible to pre-fall egalitarianism, including equally shared roles of dominion (work) and fruitfulness (procreation) as described in 1:26–28.[71]

A third point to be emphasized is that the relationship of subjection/submission between Adam and Eve prescribed in v. 16 is not presented as necessarily applicable to man-woman role relationships in general. The context of 3:16 is specifically that of marriage: a *wife's* desire (*tĕšûqâ*) for her own husband and the *husband's* "rule" (*māšal*) over his own wife.

It is common, and probably appropriate, to assume that family is, mutatis mutandis, society, but it is important to recognize that this text describes a *marriage* setting, not a general family setting, and thus the submission of wife to husband prescribed here cannot be automatically broadened into a general prescription mandating subordination of all women to men in society. In contrast to the second point above, where judgments upon the woman (regarding procreation) and the man (regarding work) are spelled out separately and unrelated to each other, the *māšal-tĕšûqâ* prescriptions of 3:16 are specifically linked to the woman's relationship to her own husband, and to the husband's relationship to his own wife. Within the constraints of the poetic parallelism in 3:16 between the husband's "rule" and the wife's "desire," if one attempts to broaden the husband's *māšal* role prescribed in this passage (v. 16d) so as to refer to men's "rule" of women in general (both home and the wider society), then, to be faithful to the poetic parallelism, it would seem necessary to broaden the *tĕšûqâ* of the wife (v. 16c) for her husband to include the (sexual) desire of women for men in general, not just their own husband. Neither broadening seems to be the intent of the passage. Thus any suggestion of extending the marriage-specific prescription of 3:16 beyond the husband-wife relationship to become a divinely prescribed mandate for the leadership of men over women in general does not seem to be warranted by the text. It remains to be seen if the rest of the OT is consistent with this

---

[71] For development of this crucial point from both Gen 1–3 and the social sciences, see esp. Van Leeuwen, *Gender and Grace;* and idem, *My Brother's Keeper: What the Social Sciences Do (and Don't) Tell Us about Masculinity* (Downers Grove, Ill.: InterVarsity, 2002).

position, prescribing (or assuming, at least in a qualified way) *māšal-těšûqâ* for husband and wife as beneficial to preserve the marriage relationship (and ultimately return it to the egalitarian ideal), but not extending *māšal-těšûqâ* beyond the marital relationship and not barring women from roles of authoritative leadership within the covenant community at large. (This will be a focus of chs. 6 and 13, below.)

These conclusions regarding the relative status of the sexes in Gen 1–3 have significant implications for the current debate over the role of women in the home and in the believing community, implications that will be elaborated later, especially in the afterword as it deals with the NT. These conclusions uphold major points of both egalitarians[72] and hierarchicalists[73] in the modern debate and at the same time call both groups to take another look at the biblical evidence. With egalitarians (and against hierarchicalists) it can be affirmed that Gen 1–2 presents God's divine ideal for men and women at creation to be one of equality in both nature and function, with no superiority or leadership of the male and no inferiority or submission of the female. With hierarchicalists (and

---

[72] Represented in Christian evangelicalism esp. by the organization Christians for Biblical Equality (CBE), founded in 1987. See the position paper of CBE drawn up in July 1989 by the evangelical biblical scholars Gilbert Bilezikian, Stanley R. Gundry, W. Ward Gasque, Catherine Clark Kroeger, Jo Anne Lyon, Gretchen Gaebelein Hull, and Roger Nicole. This declaration was made public in July 1989 and published as an advertisement: Gilbert Bilezikian et al., "Men, Women, and Biblical Equality," *ChT* 34, no. 6 (1990): 36–37. Ronald W. Pierce and Rebecca Merrill Groothuis, eds., *Discovering Biblical Equality: Complementarity without Hierarchy* (Downers Grove, Ill.: InterVarsity, 2004), give a comprehensive presentation of this position; see also dozens of individually authored books reviewed in chronological order by Ronald W. Pierce, "Contemporary Evangelicals for Gender Equality," in *Discovering Biblical Equality: Complementarity without Hierarchy* (ed. Ronald W. Pierce and Rebecca Merrill Groothuis; Downers Grove, Ill.: InterVarsity, 2004), 58–75, and the numerous gender-related articles categorized as "egalitarian" in the annual bibliographies of *JBMW*. For a survey of other groups (besides the parachurch CBE) who hold to this egalitarian position, see Grudem, *Evangelical Feminism and Biblical Truth*, 521–23.

[73] Represented in Christian evangelicalism by the organization Council on Biblical Manhood and Womanhood (CBMW), likewise founded in 1987. Its rationale, goals, and affirmations are found in the "Danvers Statement," drawn up by some twenty-four council members (including e.g., James Borland, W. Robert Gundry, Wayne A. Grudem, Mary Kassian, George W. Knight III, Raymond C. Ortland, and John Piper); this statement was finalized in Danvers, Mass., in December 1987, made public in November 1988, and published as an advertisement in *ChT* 33, no. 1, January 13, 1989: 40–41. A comprehensive presentation of this position is given by John Piper and Wayne A. Grudem, eds., *Recovering Biblical Manhood and Womanhood: A Response to Evangelical Feminism* (Wheaton, Ill.: Crossway, 1991); Wayne A. Grudem, ed., *Biblical Foundations for Manhood and Womanhood* (Foundations for the Family Series; Wheaton, Ill.: Crossway, 2002); Grudem, *Evangelical Feminism and Biblical Truth;* and Robert L. Saucy and Judith K. TenElshof, eds., *Women and Men in Ministry: A Complementary Perspective* (Chicago: Moody, 2001); see also numerous gender-related articles categorized as "complementarian" in the annual bibliographies of *JBMW*. For a survey of other groups (besides the parachurch CBMW) who hold to this hierarchical complementarian position, see Grudem, *Evangelical Feminism and Biblical Truth*, 518–21.

against egalitarians) it can be affirmed that God's prescription for harmony and unity *after the fall* does include the wife's submission to the servant leadership of her husband. Against the hierarchical position, however, the evidence in 3:16 already seems to point to the implication that the servant leadership principle is limited to the relationship between husband and wife or at least should not be seen as barring women from roles of leadership over men in the believing community or society at large. Also against the hierarchical position, the evidence of this text points toward a prescription *qualified by grace,* a prescription representing God's less-than-the-original ideal for husbands and wives, thus implicitly including both a divine redemptive call and enabling power to return as much as possible to the pre-fall total egalitarianism in the marriage relationship, without denying the validity of the servant leadership principle as it may be needed in a sinful world to preserve unity and harmony in the home. It is hoped that these conclusions, by moving beyond both hierarchicalism and egalitarianism to a biblical middle ground, may assist in breaking the impasse in the current discussion. It remains for us to see how these conclusions regarding Gen 1–3 work themselves out in the rest of the biblical canon.

Section 2

Sexuality outside the Garden: Old Testament Development (Torah, Prophets, Writings)

💮3

Creation Ordinance versus Cultic Sexuality

As man and woman move outside the garden of Eden and take up life in a sinful world, two distinct trends—or as one scholar has described it,[1] "Rival Plans for God's Sexual Program"—become evident in their understanding of, and experience with, sexuality. Throughout the pages of the OT, one encounters these two tendencies: on the one hand, the positive affirmations of sexuality, upholding and amplifying the Edenic pattern, and, on the other hand, the portrayals of departure from the Edenic plan through the exploitation and distortion of God's intent for sexuality.[2] This section examines the theology of human sexuality as it emerges from the Torah (Gen 4–Deuteronomy), Prophets (Former and Latter), and Writings (Historical Books and Wisdom/hymnic literature excluding the Song of Songs). In order to explore theological continuity and development from the Edenic pattern, the relevant data and discussion have been arranged under the same basic subheadings that structured the first section of this work. Each chapter first directs attention to the positive assumptions and affirmations of sexuality and then examines portrayals of, or legislation concerning, the departures from the divine Edenic norms. I observe in particular how each of the basic facets in the Edenic theology of sexuality has been distorted—always with disastrous consequences. Some of the biblical data is relevant to more than one facet of sexual theology, but the primary discussion is carried out under the subheading where the material seems to make the most significant theological contribution. In each of the major subdivisions within chapters, analysis first focuses upon pentateuchal narratives and legislation, where theological patterns are often

---

[1] Kathy L. Gaca, *The Making of Fornication: Eros, Ethics, and Political Reform in Greek Philosophy and Early Christianity* (Hellenistic Culture and Society 40; Joan Palevsky Imprint in Classical Literature; Berkeley: University of California Press, 2003), 119–57, describing esp. the LXX Pentateuch (and its use by Paul in the NT).

[2] In much current literature on sexuality, it is more politically correct to speak of *"paraphilias"* (unusual or atypical sexual behavior) than "distortions," but I use the latter term because it more accurately represents the biblical stance concerning these practices, within the "Edenic pattern" model that I find pervading the OT. I do, however, generally avoid such terms as "perversion" or "perverted," which have become overloaded with pejorative semantic baggage in modern usage.

established, then illustrative material, fuller treatment, or significant theological development in the Prophets and Writings.

Positive Affirmations of the Edenic Ideal

The narrative of human existence outside Eden begins with an affirmation of human sexuality (Gen 4:1–2): "Now Adam knew [*yādaʿ*, i.e., had sexual intercourse with] his wife Eve, and she conceived and bore Cain. . . . Next she bore his brother Abel." This passage will later be studied more closely regarding its implications for marital intimacy ("knowing") and procreation (see chs. 10 and 11, below), but here I note that this verse presents the actualization of the command of Gen 1:28 to the first man and woman: "Be fruitful and multiply."[3] Sexual activity is thereby linked to creation. At least seven times in the "primeval history" of Gen 1–11, reference is made to the creation of humankind (male and female).[4] Several times in the Pentateuch, God is identified as the Creator/Maker of the "heaven and earth"—a merism for all of creation, including humankind in its sexual differentiation.[5] Such restatements of God's creation of the universe express continuity with the foundational assertions that emerge from Gen 1–3: sexuality is a created ordinance; God the Creator is above and beyond the polarity of sex (see esp. Deut 4:15–16);[6] and thus sexuality is not divinized through intradivine sexual intercourse or sacralized through cultic ritual. Throughout the Torah, these fundamental assumptions are never softened.[7] Sexuality is part of the created order, to be enjoyed and celebrated between man and woman and not to be linked in any way with divine sexual activity or public rituals of the cultus.

---

[3] The narrator does not intend to imply that Adam and Eve did not have sexual relations until after their expulsion from the garden; the commentary of Gen 2:24 ("they become one flesh") makes this apparent. But the use of "to know" is used in this context as a prelude to the description of the conception and birth of Cain.

[4] See Gen 5:2, 3; 6:6, 7; 7:14; 9:1, 6.

[5] See Gen 14:19, 22; Exod 20:11; 31:17; Deut 4:32. For discussion of the expression "heavens and earth" as a merism for all creation, see Richard M. Davidson, "The Biblical Account of Origins," *JATS* 14, no. 1 (2003): 32–33; cf. John Sailhamer, *Genesis Unbound: A Provocative New Look at the Creation Account* (Sisters, Ore.: Multnomah, 1996), 55–56.

[6] For the implication from Deut 4:15–16 that Yahweh "was seen especially to transcend sexual differentiation," see the discussion in Erhard S. Gerstenberger, *Yahweh the Patriarch: Ancient Images of God and Feminist Theology* (Minneapolis: Fortress, 1996), 83, 153–54, quote at 153.

[7] As pointed out in the introduction, a growing consensus of modern scholars recognizes that at least canonically (in its final form), the opening chapters of Genesis set the tone for the rest of the canon. Regarding the Torah, note esp. S. Dean McBride Jr., "Divine Protocol: Genesis 1:1–2:3 as Prologue the Pentateuch," in *God Who Creates: Essays in Honor of W. Sibley Towner* (ed. William P. Brown and S. Dean McBride Jr.; Grand Rapids: Eerdmans: 2000), 3–41.

In the Prophets, God's creation of the universe (including sexuality) is repeatedly affirmed,[8] with specific emphasis upon the creation of humans (including their sexual differentiation) as part of creation.[9] Because humans (and their sexuality) are created by God and are not part of divinity, any attempts to divinize or sacralize sexuality in Israel, as done in the pagan fertility myths and cult practice, is met with the strongest divine denunciation (see below).

The Writings also present numerous statements affirming that humans (including their sexuality) were created by God,[10] often alluding to Gen 1–2 with clear indication that the method of the original creation was by the divine word and not by sex between the gods.[11] The way of sexual wisdom in the Wisdom literature closely parallels the divine pattern set forth in Gen 1–3. It is apparent that in Proverbs the "way of a man with a girl" (Prov 30:19) is set against the sapiential backdrop of a high doctrine of creation (cf. 8:22–31),[12] and thereby sexuality is shown to be a creation ordinance and not part of the divine order.

The Cultic Sacralization/Divinization of Sex in Pagan Worship

Ancient Near Eastern Background

Mesopotamia. In contrast with the Israelite conception of sexuality as a creation ordinance and of a monotheistic God beyond the polarity of sexuality, the Mesopotamian religions abounded with both male and female deities, and their myths often described creation and continuing fertility as occurring by means of sex among these deities.[13] For example, in the Sumerian myth "Disputation between Tree and Reed," An(u), god of heaven, impregnates the earth:

---

[8] See, e.g., Isa 37:16; 40:12–31; 42:5; 43:1–7; 44:24; 45:18; Jer 10:12, 16; 32:17. For discussion of creation in the Prophets, see esp. William P. Brown and S. Dean McBride Jr., eds., *God Who Creates: Essays in Honor of W. Sibley Towner* (Grand Rapids: Eerdmans: 2000), chs. 10–15 (essays by Thomas W. Mann on Isaiah, Walter Brueggemann on Jeremiah, Steven Tuell on Ezekiel, and Robert R. Wilson on Daniel).

[9] See, e.g., Isa 17:7; 29:15–16; 43:7; 45:9–13; 51:13; 54:5; Jer 27:5; Hos 8:14; Zech 12:1; Mal 2:10.

[10] See, e.g., Job 10:9; 31:15; Ps 8:6 (ET 8:5); 89:48 (ET 89:47); 95:6; 104:24, 30; 119:73; 139:15–16; Prov 14:31; 17:5; 22:2; Eccl 3:11; 12:1; and Neh 9:6. For discussions of creation in the biblical Psalms and Wisdom literature, see esp. Brown and McBride, *God Who Creates,* chs. 5–9 (essays by James Luther Mays, Patrick D. Miller Jr., William P. Brown, and Karen Pidcock-Lester).

[11] For allusions to Gen 1–2, see esp. Job 10:9 and Ps 8:6 (ET 8:5); for references to creation by the divine word, see esp. Ps 33:6, 9.

[12] See the discussion of the high doctrine of creation in the Wisdom literature in, e.g., James L. Crenshaw, ed., *Studies in Ancient Israelite Wisdom* (New York: Ktav, 1976), 22–35; and Leo G. Perdue, *Wisdom and Creation: The Theology of Wisdom Literature* (Nashville: Abingdon, 1994).

[13] For a helpful overview and discussion of the Sumerian myths related to divinized sexuality and creation/fertility, including the sacred-marriage rites, see esp. Tikva Frymer-Kensky, *In the Wake of the Goddesses: Women, Culture, and the Biblical Transformation of*

The holy Earth, the pure Earth, beautified herself for holy Heaven,
Heaven, the noble god, Inserted his sex into the wide Earth,
Let flow the semen of his heroes, Trees and Reed, into her womb,
The Earthly Orb, trusty cow, Was impregnated with the good semen of Heaven.[14]

The Sumerian deity Enlil, god of the air, is repeatedly called the "bull that overwhelms"—alluding to the sex act between bull and heifer.[15] In the myth "Enki and the World Order," the Sumerian god of the subterranean water is depicted as creating water for the land of Nippur by impregnating the Tigris River:

He [Enki] stood up proudly like a rampant bull, He lifts the penis, ejaculates,
Filled the Tigris with sparkling water.
The wild cow mooing for its young in the pastures, the scorpion (-infested) stall,
[The Tigr]is is surre[ndered] to him, as (to) a rampant bull.
He lifted the penis, brought the bridal gift, Brought joy to the Tigris,
Like a big wild bull [rejoiced?] in its giving birth.[16]

As a last example, in the royal hymn celebrating the birth of Shulgi, king of Ur (ca. 2094–2047 B.C.E.), there is an oracle predicting Shulgi's birth. This is followed by a description of the birth of King Shulgi resulting from the sexual union of the god Nanna and his wife Ninlil:

To that end, Ashimbabbar [the moon god Nanna] "shone" (?) in the Ekur,
He pleaded (?) with his father, Enlil [the supreme god of the Sumerian pantheon],
    he approached (?) the mother who gave (?) birth (?) to him [i.e., Ninlil, Enlil's
    wife],
In the "good house" made Nanna,
    the noble son, (his) request,
(And) the high-priestess gave birth to a "faithful man,"
    from (the semen) which had been placed in her womb,
Enlil, the powerful shepherd,
    caused the young man to appear,
A child, most suitable for kingship (and) throne-dais—
    it was king Shulgi![17]

Pagan Myth (New York: Free Press/Maxwell Macmillan, 1992), 9–80; cf. Samuel Noah Kramer, *The Sacred Marriage Rite: Aspects of Faith, Myth, and Ritual in Ancient Sumer* (Bloomington: Indiana University Press, 1969). For a broader summary of ANE myths and their divinized sexual elements, see esp. Foster R. McCurley, *Ancient Myths and Biblical Faith: Scriptural Transformations* (Philadelphia: Fortress, 1983), 74–103. For an overview of the goddesses involved in this divinized sexuality in Mesopotamia, see, e.g., Joan Goodnick Westenholz, "Great Goddesses in Mesopotamia: The Female Aspect of Divinity," *JSSEA* 29 (2002): 9–27.

[14] Translation from Samuel Noah Kramer, *From the Poetry of Sumer: Creation, Glorification, Adoration* (Berkeley: University of California Press, 1979), 30.

[15] Stephen Langdon, *Sumerian Liturgical Texts* (Philadelphia: University Museum, University of Pennsylvania, 1917), 292.

[16] Translation from Samuel Noah Kramer, *The Sumerians: Their History, Culture, and Character* (Chicago: University of Chicago Press, 1963), 179.

[17] "The Birth of Shulgi in the Temple of Nippur," translated by Jacob Klein (*COS* 1.172:553).

Gwendolyn Leick summarizes the "cosmological articulation of sexuality" in early Mesopotamia: "While the actual control over the process of primary creation could be ascribed to various agents or gods, depending on the theological slant of the text, the dynamic process of creation, the unfolding diversification, is always symbolized by a male-female pair who mate to produce further offspring, and so on."[18]

In Sumerian mythology there was a whole pantheon of gods and goddesses, often paired as male and female partners. According to Sumerian theology, the fertility of the land is set in motion by sexual action, especially by the annual *hieros gamos,* or sacred-marriage rite, an elaborate ritual that can be reconstructed in considerable detail from allusions in the sacred-marriage songs found in several Sumerian compositions. This sacred marriage is connected with the myth and cult of the vegetation god Dumuzi (in the HB = Tammuz) and his consort Inanna ("Queen of Heaven," also called by the Semitic name Ishtar), goddess of sex and war.[19] The core of this New Year's Festival ritual was the sexual intercourse between the king—who was ritually transformed into the god Dumuzi—and a human female partner (probably a priestess) representing the goddess Inanna. The Iddin-Dagan Hymn describes the sexual union of the king and the goddess:

> The king goes with (eagerly) lifted head to the holy loins,
> goes with (eagerly) lifted head to the loins of Inanna.
> Ama-ushumgal-anna goes to bed with her:
> "O my holy loins! O my holy Inanna!"
> After he on the bed, in the holy loins, has made the queen rejoice,
> after he on the bed, in the holy loins has made holy Inanna rejoice,
> she in turn soothes the heart for him there on the bed;
> "Iddin-Dagan, you are verily my beloved!"[20]

In a Shulgi hymn (Shulgi X) Inanna relates in very intimate terms the experience of sexual intercourse between herself (represented by a human partner) and the king during the sacred-marriage rite: "by his fair hands my loins were pressed," "he [ruffled] the hair of my lap," "he laid his hands on my pure vulva."[21] This explicit language of sex play confirms that there was actual sexual intercourse between the king and a human partner, not just a ritual of the king lying

---

[18] Gwendolyn Leick, *Sex and Eroticism in Mesopotamian Literature* (London: Routledge, 1994), 21.

[19] For a more complete overview of this sacred-marriage ritual, with relevant texts, see esp. Frymer-Kensky, *In the Wake of the Goddesses,* 50–57; Jacob Klein, "Sacred Marriage," *ABD* 5:856–70; Kramer, *The Sacred Marriage Rite,* passim; and Diane Wolkstein and Samuel Noah Kramer, *Inanna, Queen of Heaven and Earth: Her Stories and Hymns from Sumer* (New York: Harper & Row, 1983).

[20] "The Sacred Marriage of Iddin-Dagan and Inanna," translated by Thorkild Jacobsen (*COS* 1.173:558).

[21] Translation from Jacob Klein, ed., *Three Šulgi Hymns* (Tel Aviv: Bar-Ilan University Press, 1982), 124–25. Šulgi was the second king of the Third Dynasty of Ur (ca. 2094–2047 B.C.E.).

with the statue of the goddess, as may have happened in later Mesopotamian sacred-marriage ceremonies.[22] This sexual intercourse between king and goddess-figure were regarded as bringing fertility to the land.

According to the testimony of classical writers, in particular Herodotus, ritual sex was more widespread in ancient Mesopotamia than the annual sacred-marriage rite and also included cult prostitution. Herodotus indicates that every Babylonian woman had to sit in the temple of Aphrodite once in her lifetime and have sexual intercourse with the first man who threw money into her lap. The money was made sacred from the sexual union, and the woman also made herself holy in the eyes of the goddess.[23] Herodotus's account is widely rejected by modern scholars as a sample of early Greek propaganda, although one cannot out-of-hand totally dismiss an element of truth that may lie behind it (i.e., the existence of sacred prostitution).

That cult prostitution was practiced in ancient Mesopotamia has been the dominant scholarly position until the last part of the twentieth century, based not only upon the testimony of classical writers but also upon the evidence from cuneiform texts and ANE iconography.[24] Several studies of the 1980s and 1990s, however, mostly done by feminist scholars, reassessed the evidence and concluded that no such cultic prostitution—either male or female—ever existed in the religions of Mesopotamia (or in Canaan) but only in the imaginations of modern male interpreters affected by the post-Victorian understanding of sexuality.[25] More recently there has been a "reassessment of these reassessments," in

---

[22] See Frymer-Kensky, *In the Wake of the Goddesses*, 53. Frymer-Kensky (pp. 51–52, 221, 223) cites later possible examples of the Mesopotamian sacred marriage involving other goddesses: Baba, a young goddess best known for her connection with the city of Lagash, copulates (by means of her human counterpart) with her mate (the king of Lagash) to ensure the fertility of the city; again, Ninisinna, the city goddess of Isin (Ur III dynasty), is the divine partner of Isin's King Iddingagan in the sacred marriage. For a survey of other traces of the sacred-marriage rite in Mesopotamia during the second and first millennia B.C.E., see esp. Klein, "Sacred Marriage," 5:868–69; and Martti Nissinen, "Akkadian Rituals and Poetry of Divine Love," in *Mythology and Mythologies: Methodological Approaches to Intercultural Influences* (ed. R. M. Whiting; Helsinki: Neo-Assyrian Text Corpus Project, 2001), 93–136.

[23] Herodotus, *Hist.* 1.199 (Godley, LCL).

[24] Wilfried G. Lambert could write in the late 1950s, "No one doubts its [cultic prostitution's] prevalence, esp. in the cult of ISHTAR" ("Morals in Ancient Mesopotamia," *JEOL* 15 [1957–1958]: 195). In 1992 Joseph Healey still confidently asserts, "Sacred prostitution was clearly a part of the religion [of ancient Mesopotamia]" ("Fertility Cults," *ADB* 2:792). For a good summary of the evidence for cult prostitution in the ancient Near East, see esp. Wilfried G. Lambert, "Prostitution," in *Aussenseiter und Randgruppen: Beiträge zu einer Sozialgeschichte des alten Orients* (ed. Volkert Haas; Xenia: Konstanzer althistorische Vorträge und Forschungen 32; Constance: Universitätsverlag, 1992), 127–57; and Edwin M. Yamauchi, "Cultic Prostitution: A Case Study in Cultural Diffusion," in *Orient and Occident: Essays Presented to Cyrus H. Gordon on the Occasion of His Sixty-Fifth Birthday* (ed. Harry A. Hoffner Jr.; AOAT 22; Neukirchen-Vluyn: Neukirchener Verlag, 1973), 213–22.

[25] Representatives of this newer view include Phyllis A. Bird, "The End of the Male Cult Prostitute," in *Congress Volume: Cambridge, 1995* (ed. J. A. Emerton; VTSup 66; Leiden: E. J. Brill, 1997), 37–80; Frymer-Kensky, *In the Wake of the Goddesses*, 199–202;

particular regarding male cult prostitution, with the conclusion that such a practice probably did occur in the Inanna (Ishtar) cult.[26] Despite the "reassessment" that denies female cultic prostitution in the ancient Near East, in my view the cuneiform evidence set forth particularly by W. G. Lambert has not been overthrown.[27] In any case, virtually all scholars who have dealt with this issue, even the feminists who deny the existence of cult prostitution (sex for hire), acknowledge that some kind of ritual sexual intercourse was part of the cultic practice in ancient Mesopotamian religion.[28] Sex was not only *divinized* in the sexual

---

Elaine A. Goodfriend, "Prostitution (OT)," *ABD* 5:507–9; Mayer I. Gruber, "Hebrew *qĕdēšāh* and Her Canaanite and Akkadian Cognates," *UF* 18 (1986): 133–48; S. M. Hooks, "Sacred Prostitution in the Bible and the Ancient Near East" (PhD diss., Hebrew Union College, 1985); Robert A. Oden Jr., *The Bible without Theology: The Theological Tradition and Alternatives to It* (San Francisco: Harper & Row, 1987), 131–53; Karel van der Toorn, "Cultic Prostitution," *ABD* 5:510–13; and Joan Goodnick Westenholz, "Tamar, QĔDĒŠÂ, QADIŠTU, and Sacred Prostitution in Mesopotamia," *HTR* 82 (1989): 245–65.

[26] See esp. the survey of this evidence in Robert A. J. Gagnon, *The Bible and Homosexual Practice: Texts and Hermeneutics* (Nashville: Abingdon, 2001), 48–49, 100–110; David F. Greenberg, *The Construction of Homosexuality* (Chicago: University of Chicago Press, 1988); and Martti Nissinen, *Homoeroticism in the Biblical World: A Historical Perspective* (trans. Kirsi Stjerna; Minneapolis: Fortress, 1998), 28–34. Chapter 5, below, summarizes this evidence for male cult prostitution.

[27] See Lambert, "Prostitution," esp. 135–45. Lambert (p. 142) summarizes his conclusion from the available cuneiform evidence: "Thus in ancient Mesopotamia all prostitution was by definition sacral, because the sexual act was a natural force working for the well being of the human race and was a power personified in the goddess Inanna/Ištar. There were, however, variations within the profession as conceived by the ancients. The high-class priestesses such as the nin-dingir-ra and the corresponding *entus* or *ugbabtus* seem to have copulated with the rulers at major seasonal festivals, at least in some periods and areas, and this would perhaps not be considered prostitution today. At the other end of the scale were the women who were to be found seeking customers in the city squares and streets, but who were still 'sacred' for their functions." Lambert (142) acknowledges that some of these women "had, it seems, unrelated alternative work" and further acknowledges, regarding the *nadītu*, that, although identified as prostitutes in a lexical list probably from Middle Babylonian times, they are not documented in their work as prostitutes. But Lambert aptly points out that "silence in this case is an especially weak argument. The same situation occurs in the modern world. A successful modern Western prostitute might open interest-bearing bank accounts, or invest money in stocks and shares, all of which would be properly documented, but the income from her clients would be either totally undocumented, or at the best documented informally, as in a personal note-book. The present writer is not prepared to reject the lexical evidence, though of course it may not be valid for all periods, and so it follows that at least in some periods and areas the *nadītu* was a prostitute" (137–38). Cf. Leick, *Sex and Eroticism,* 147–56, for a similar assessment.

[28] Eugene J. Fisher, "Cultic Prostitution in the Ancient Near East? A Reassessment," *BTB* 6 (1976): 225–36, distinguishes between "prostitution" (sex for hire) and "ritual intercourse," accepting the biblical and extrabiblical evidence for the latter but not the former. Fisher may be correct that "prostitution" is technically not the most correct word to use for personnel involved in ANE cultic sexual intercourse, since it is not known whether the ritual sex was always for hire. The discussion that follows regarding the cultic sacralization of sex usually avoids using the term "prostitution" to refer to the work of the

activities among the gods themselves but also *sacralized* in the cult through ritual sex (in the annual sacred-marriage rite and possibly much more widespread).

Egypt. In Egypt, as elsewhere in the ancient Near East outside Israel's monotheistic religion, sexuality was divinized as the many deities engaged in sexual activity. For example, in the Pyramid Texts from the Old Kingdom, a spell describes the birth of Shu and Tefnut (god of the air and goddess of moisture respectively) as a result of the masturbation of the god Atum, the single source of all matter: "Atum evolved growing ithyphallic [god with erect penis; lit., 'as one who comes extended'], in Heliopolis. He puts his penis in his grasp that he might make orgasm with it, and the two siblings were born—Shu and Tefnut."[29] A papyrus from the Ptolemaic period expresses this same act of Atum's masturbation:

> I am the one who acted as husband with my fist:
> I copulated with my hand,
> I let fall into my own mouth,
> I sneezed Shu and spat Tefnut.[30]

Other Egyptian texts relate that through the sexual relations of Shu and Tefnut, the god Geb (earth) and goddess Nut (sky) were normally born "from the body." Geb and Nut in turn gave birth to the god Osiris and the goddess Isis; and Osiris and Isis begot the god Seth and the goddess Nephthys. These made up the Great Ennead—the nine ruling gods, with Horus as an added member.[31]

In the cosmogony of Thebes from the time of the New Kingdom, the creator god Amun (the sun god) is described in sexual terms as self-generated: "Who tied his fluid together with his body, to bring about his egg in his secret interior."[32] Although Amun was considered self-created, at the same time he underwent a daily cycle of rebirth. The description of this rebirth utilizes explicit sexual language: every evening at the beginning of the second hour after sunset, the Duat (world space surrounded by the universal waters) becomes pregnant, and the next morning the sun god is reborn; he "parts the thighs of his mother Nut" (the sky goddess), appearing in "redness after birth," and "goes away to the sky."[33]

Whereas the *deification* of sexuality is clear for native Egyptian religions, the evidence for the *sacralization* of sex by means of cult prostitution in Egypt comes only from the late classical texts of Herodotus and Strabo.[34] There is, however,

---

cult functionaries who were involved in ritual sexual intercourse, although my personal (provisional) persuasion, based upon available evidence, is that cult prostitution (both male and female) probably did exist throughout the ancient Near East.

[29] "From Pyramid Texts Spell 527," translated by James P. Allen (*COS* 1.3:7). Reference to the birth of Shu and Tefnut through masturbation (as well as spitting) is repeated in Coffin Text 77 (referred to, but not translated, in *COS* 1:11).

[30] "From Papyrus Bremner-Rhind," translated by James P. Allen (*COS* 1.9:14).

[31] See "The Creation by Atum," translated by John A. Wilson (*ANET* 3); and "The Repulsing of the Dragon and the Creation," translated by John A. Wilson (*ANET* 6).

[32] "From Papyrus Leiden I 350," translated by James P. Allen (*COS* 1.16:23–24).

[33] "From 'The Book of Nut,'" translated by James P. Allen (*COS* 1.1:5).

[34] See Herodotus, *Hist.* 1.182 (Godley, LCL), which describes a woman's sexual intercourse with Zeus of Thebes (Amun), presumably by way of cult prostitutes representing

some evidence for Egyptian festivals in which some type of sacred-marriage rite appears to be involved, a rite that may have involved sexual intercourse between the representatives of the god and goddess.[35] There is also evidence that various Asiatic deities were worshiped in Egypt from the time of the New Kingdom, such as Astarte, Baal, Rešep, and Anat,[36] and the ritual sex apparently involved in these religions would no doubt have been adopted as part of the cultic practice in Egypt. Edwin Yamauchi calls particular attention to the Syrian goddess Qudšu, associated with love and fertility, who is depicted nude in an Egyptian relief, flanked by the ithyphallic Egyptian god Min and the Syrian god Rešeph (both gods also related to fertility), and on one monument is given the title "the Prostitute."[37]

Anatolia/Hittites. The Hittite texts make reference to the "thousand gods" of the Hatti kingdom.[38] As with all the other polytheistic religions surrounding Israel, the Hittite documents reveal a divinization of sex, as the relationships among the deities include references to sexual activity. In the Old Hittite mythology, for example, the myth of the Illuyanka ("Serpent, Snake") was recited as part of the yearly state cult festival. In one version of this myth, the storm god marries a mortal female and has a son, and he gives this son to the Illuyanka's daughter in marriage. In another myth, "Telepinu and the Daughter of the Sea God," the sea god gives the sun god to Telepinu as a marriage gift.

In the New Hittite mythology, numerous other examples of sexual encounters among the gods may be found. Thus in one Hurrian myth, Kumbari (the Hurrian "father of the gods") swallows his "manhood" and eventually gives birth to Tešub (the Hurrian storm god). In the myth of the sun god, the cow, and the fisherman, the sun god apparently falls in love with a cow, comes to the cow in the guise of a young man, and apparently sleeps with her, and a human-looking child is born to the cow. Another Hurrian myth concerns a devouring serpent who falls prey to Ištar's sexual attractions.[39]

---

the deity. Strabo, *Geogr.* 17.1.46 (Jones, LCL): "As for Zeus (Amon), whom they especially revere, a maiden of exquisite beauty and most illustrious family serves him as priestess, [one of those maidens] whom the Greeks designate concubines. She acts as a concubine to, and has intercourse with, whom she will, until her [first?] menstrual purgation takes place. After the purgation she is given to a man in marriage."

[35] Yamauchi ("Cult Prostitution," 217) cites the festival of the fertility god Min at Medinet Habu (Nineteenth Dynasty) and the festival of Hathor and Horus at Edfu (Ptolemaic era).

[36] Edward Frank Wente, "Egyptian Religion," *ABD* 2:410. See below for the implication of this fact with reference to the nature of Israel's apostasy with the golden calf at Sinai as described in Exod 32. Cf. Lise Manniche, "Goddess and Woman in Ancient Egypt," *JSSEA* 29 (2002): 7.

[37] Yamauchi, "Cult Prostitution," 217.

[38] Philo H. J. Houwink ten Cate, "Hittite History," *ABD* 3:224. For an overview of the various Hittite deities, see Hatice Gonnet, "Hittite Religion," *ABD* 3:225–26.

[39] For a summary of these myths, see Gregory McMahon, "Anatolia," *ABD* 1:236–39; for translations, see Harry A. Hoffner Jr., *Hittite Myths* (2d ed.; SBLWAW 2; Atlanta: Scholars Press, 1998), passim.

As a final example, a Canaanite (Northern Syrian) myth, "Elkunirša [transliteration of 'El, Creator of Earth'] and Ašertu [= Astarte]," was translated into Hittite and describes a sexual encounter, as Ašertu apparently rejects the manhood of her husband El and desires to sleep with her son Baal but actually is plotting against Baal:

> [Elkunirša] saw Baal and asked him, "[Why] have you come?" Baal said, "When I came into your house [just then] Ašertu sent girls to me (with the message): 'Come sleep with me!' I refused . . . Ašertu is rejecting your [El's, R.M.D.] manhood.'" . . . (Ašerta said to Elkunirša:) "I will press [down Baal with my word. I will pierce him with my little spindle (?). Then] I will sleep with you . . ." [After Elkurniša turns Baal over to his wife to do with as she wished, R.M.D.] Elkurniša and his wife went to her bed and they slept together.[40]

Although the *deification* of sex is well documented within the Hittite religion, as various gods engage in sexual intercourse with each other, there is no textual evidence of which I am aware that may be interpreted as the *sacralization* of sex through cultic prostitution, or other ritual intercourse, as part of the Hittite cult.

Ugarit/Canaan. In the Ugaritic pantheon, Asherah is the consort of El, the chief god, and it is Anat[41] who is most frequently mentioned as the consort of El's son Baal (the storm god). This diverges slightly from the Canaanite fertility cults referred to in Scripture, where the consort of Baal[42] is usually Astarte[43] (which name the biblical writers distorted by vocalizing it in Hebrew either to sound like Ashtoreth, reflecting the vowels of the Hebrew word *bōšet*, "shame") or sometimes to sound like Asherah.[44]

---

[40] "Elkunirša and Ašertu," translated by Gary Beckman (COS 1.55).

[41] See esp. Neal H. Walls, *The Goddess Anat in Ugaritic Myth* (SBLDS 135; Atlanta: Scholars Press, 1992).

[42] Baal (meaning "lord") is mentioned more than seventy times as a separate epithet for the storm god Hadad ("thunderer") worshiped by apostate Israel during the time of the Judges (e.g., Judg 2:11, 13; 3:7; 6:31–32; 8:33; 10:6, 10; 1 Sam 7:4; 12:10) and the divided monarchy (e.g., Ahab: 1 Kgs 16:31–33; 18:18; Ahaziah: 1 Kgs 22:53; the time of Jehu: 2 Kgs 10:18–28; Athaliah: 11:18; and Manasseh: 21:3). Other times Baal occurs in combination with other terms (e.g., Baal-berith, Judg 8:33; 9:4; Baal of Peor, Num 25:3, 5; Deut 4:3; Ps 106:28; Hos 9:10). See John Day, "Baal," *ABD* 1:545–49.

[43] For references to Astarte (pl. Astartes) in Scripture, see, Judg 2:13; 10:6; 1 Sam 7:3, 4; 12:10; 31:10; 1 Kgs 11:5, 33; 2 Kgs 23:13. See the discussion in John Day, "Ashtoreth," *ABD* 1:491–94. The references to (esp. women's) worship of the "Queen of Heaven" (Jer 7:16–20; 44:15–19, 25) may refer to a syncretistic combination of Ishtar and Astarte, and the "weeping for Tammuz [or Dumuzi]" (Ezek 8:14), the Queen's deceased lover, may be part of that same syncretistic cult (Susan Ackerman, " 'And the Women Knead Dough': The Worship of the Queen of Heaven in Sixth-Century Judah," in *Gender and Difference in Ancient Israel* [ed. Peggy L. Day; Minneapolis: Fortress, 1989], 109–24).

[44] For general discussion of the three great goddesses of the Levant—Anat, Asherah, and Astarte—and how in the course of time their attributes, roles, and functions tended to meld together, see, e.g., Johanna H. Stuckey, "The Great Goddesses of the Levant," *JSSEA* 29 (2002): 28–57. Asherah, understood by the translators of early English versions

Without rehearsing all the details widely recognized by scholars regarding the Canaanite fertility myths and rituals of the second–first millennia B.C.E.,[45] I point to a foundational premise encountered already in the Mesopotamian myths: the processes of nature are controlled by the relations of the gods and goddesses. In particular, the fertility of the earth results from the sexual union of a male god and his consort, a female goddess. In the Baal cult, this (incestuous) sexual relationship is between the storm god Hadad (Baal), who dominates the Canaanite pantheon, and his sister, usually described as Anat (or Baal's consort Asherah).

Since the land is fertilized by the sperm (rain) of Baal, it is crucial that his sexual activity be stimulated. According to Canaanite fertility cult theology, when the divine sex activity of the god is *emulated* at the earthly high place (a place of worship usually set on a hill, sometimes a high or large altar), that same activity is further *stimulated* by means of sympathetic magic. Thus there appeared the cultic offices of "holy man" (*qādēš*) and "holy woman" (*qĕdēšâ*)—male and female personnel who, among other functions, engaged in sacred prostitution or, if not prostitution (sex for hire), at least ritual sex.[46] Worshipers were encouraged

---

(e.g., KJV) as a reference to a "grove" or to a wooden cult symbol, and long thought by scholars (before the discovery of Ugaritic texts) to be the same goddess as Astarte, is now recognized to be a separate goddess. In the Ugaritic material, Asherah is the consort of El, the chief god of the pantheon, but in the Canaanite fertility cult described by the OT, Asherah appears to also be the consort of Baal (see the close linkage of the two in Judg 3:7; 6:25, 28, 30; 1 Kgs 18:18–19; 2 Kgs 23:4). Other references to Asherah as a goddess in the OT include Judg 3:7; 1 Kgs 15:13; 2 Kgs 21:7. Hosea 14:9 (ET 14:8) and Amos 8:14 may also allude to the goddess. Inscriptions found at two sites (Kuntillet ʿAjrud and Khirbet El-Qom) from ca. the eighth century B.C.E. refer to "Yahweh and his Asherah" and suggest the widespread role of syncretistic worship involving this goddess in popular Israelite piety. See Uzi Avner, "Sacred Stones in the Desert," *BAR* 27/3 (2001): 31–41; John Day, "Asherah in the Hebrew Bible and Northwest Semitic Literature," *JBL* 105 (1986): 385–408; J. A. Emerton, "'Yahweh and His Asherah': The Goddess or Her Symbol?" *VT* 49 (1999): 315–37; Frymer-Kensky, *In the Wake of the Goddesses,* 153–61; Judith M. Hadley, *The Cult of Asherah in Ancient Israel and Judah: Evidence for a Hebrew Goddess* (New York: Cambridge University Press, 2000); and Saul M. Olyan, *Asherah and the Cult of Yahweh in Israel* (SBLMS 34; Atlanta: Scholars Press, 1988).

[45] For more detailed description and discussion (representing the predominate view until very recently) and for bibliography dealing with the ancient Canaanite fertility cults, their theology, mythology, and ritual, see Marvin H. Pope, "Fertility Cults," *IDB* 2:265; Healey, "Fertility Cults"; and John Day, "Canaan, Religion of," *ABD* 1:831–37. Despite a strong effort by some recent scholars to dismiss the evidence for ritual sex in fertility cults as indecisive (see the bibliography cited in footnote 25 above), in light of the biblical evidence for ritual sex at the Canaanite high places and terminological parallels between OT expressions and Ugaritic descriptions of cult functionaries at Ugarit (see below), it is premature to abandon the position held by the majority of scholars until very recently.

[46] As indicated in footnote 25 above, some recent (mostly feminist) scholars have sought to demonstrate that these terms do not refer to cultic ritual sex and that, in fact, no cultic ritual sex was ever part of the Canaanite Baal and Asherah worship. Although the cautions against using the term "prostitution" (in its strict sense of "sex for hire") may be sound, I have not been persuaded that the recent research overturns the traditional

to engage in ritual intercourse with the shrine devotees in order to emulate and stimulate the sex activities of the gods. Jackie Naudé summarizes this widely held scholarly interpretation: "Many considered that the processes of nature were controlled by the relations between gods and goddesses. By engaging in sexual intercourse with the devotees of the shrine they believed that this would encourage the gods and goddesses to do likewise, with the result that a person's desire for increase in herds and fields, as well as in his own family, could be realized."[47]

Literary evidence from Ras Shamra (ancient Ugarit) has been seen to give explicit details of the Syro-Palestinian cult ritual that accompanied sacred sex orgies on the high places. The most illuminating is a portion of the Ugaritic sexual/ ritual poem "The Birth of the Gracious Gods," which William F. Albright calls "one of the frankest and most sensuous in ancient Near-Eastern literature."[48] According to John Gray's interpretation, this lurid liturgy was reenacted by the cultic prostitutes in ritual coitus with their "sacramental husbands," who represent the sexually aroused god El. Here is Gray's translation:[49]

> Lo, this maid bows down, lo, this one rises up,
> This one shouts, "Daddy! Daddy!"
> And this one shouts, "Mother! Mother!"
> The organ of El grows long as the sea,[50]
> Yea, the organ of El as the flood.
> The organ of El is long as the sea,
> Yea, the organ of El as the flood.
> El lays down his sceptre,

interpretation of the biblical and extrabiblical (textual and iconographic) evidence that there was widespread ritual sexual intercourse involving cult personnel at the heart of Canaanite fertility worship. For a survey of the evidence, see esp. Yamauchi, "Cultic Prostitution," 213–22.

[47] Jackie A. Naudé, "קדש," *NIDOTTE* 3:886.

[48] William F. Albright, *Archaeology and the Religion of Israel* (5th ed.; Baltimore: Johns Hopkins Press, 1968), 72.

[49] See John Gray, *Legacy of Canaan* (2d rev. ed.; VTSup 5; Leiden: E. J. Brill, 1965), 98–103, for a full translation and interpretation. This text is variously catalogued as *KTU* 1.23 = *CTA* 23 = *UT* 52 = RS 2.002; the portion cited is from lines 31–64. For further discussion of this act of ritual seduction, see Marvin H. Pope, *El in the Ugaritic Texts* (Leiden: E. J. Brill, 1955), 35–42. Pope's interpretation of the scene has the women already inflamed with passion: "The roasting of the bird is not a device to excite the females, who are apparently preheated and anxious for coitus (they are introduced metaphorically as 'torches' . . .), but a ritual intended to remove El's impotence" (idem, review of John Gray, *The Legacy of Canaan*, *JSS* 11 [1966]: 235). For similar translations, see *CML* 123–27; Cyrus H. Gordon, *Ugaritic Literature: A Comprehensive Translation of the Poetic and Prose Texts* (Rome: Pontifical Biblical Institute, 1949), 57–62; and Nicolas Wyatt, *Religious Texts from Ugarit: The Words of Ilimilku and His Colleagues* (BS 53; Sheffield, Eng.: Sheffield Academic Press, 1998), 324–35. Gordon, *Ugaritic Literature*, 57, notes that this text "is the libretto of a religious drama with music . . . which include stage directions." The presence of stage directions in the text makes it very likely that this was reenacted in the rituals of the Canaanite cult.

[50] Pope, *El in the Ugaritic Texts*, 39, points out, "As the Ugaritians ascribed extravagant sexual stamina to their god, e.g., Baal copulates with a heifer 77 or 88 times . . . and 1000 times with Anat . . . , it is natural that they would also endow them with gigantic genitalia."

El puts aside the staff of his hand,
He lifts up (his hand), he shoots into the sky,
He shoots a bird in the sky.
He plucks it and sets it on the coals.
El indeed entices [would tup, i.e., copulate with][51] two women;
Lo, the women cry out.
O goodman, goodman, thy sceptre is laid down,
The staff of thy hand is laid aside.
Behold a bird is roasted at the fire,
But what are being inflamed, are two women,
One wife of El, another wife of El, even the Eternal.[52]
And lo, the two women cry out
O Dad! Dad! thy sceptre is laid down.
The staff of thy hand is laid aside.
Behold a bird is being roasted at the fire,
But what are being inflamed at the coals are two girls,
One girl of El, another girl of El, even the Eternal.
He stoops down and kisses their lips [= the sex act].[53]
Lo their lips are sweet!
Sweet as pomegranates.
By kissing and conceiving,
By embracing and desire they travail.
They bear *šḥr* and *šlm*
Word is brought to El,
My two wives have borne children.
What have they borne?
Two are born, *šḥr* and *šlm*
Take up (and) prepare (an offering for
Lady Sun and the fixed stars.
"He stoops down and kisses their lips.
Lo their lips are sweet
In kissing and conceiving,
In embracing and desire"

To be repeated five times by the company and by the singers of the assembly.[54]

---

[51] Translation of Gordon, *Ugaritic Literature*, 61.

[52] Gray, *Legacy of Canaan*, 101, suggests that "the threefold allusion by the women to the analogy of the roasting of the bird to sexual excitement certainly indicates that this is a rite of imitative magic and an element of the main theme of the text, which is a *hieros gamos*. The 'goodman' (*mt*) or Dad (*'ad*) are possibly burlesque references to El in his domestic capacity, but in our opinion the reference is probably to the husband of the two women or perhaps to several husbands in a common rite of sexual rejuvenation, where the women in ritual coitus with their husbands or those who are declared to be such sacramentally unite with El the Creator (*bny bnwt*) and first progenitor."

[53] Cf. Pope concerning this line (line 49): "At any rate coitus apparently does not take place till when El bends and with a hug and a kiss impregnates the females" (*El in the Ugaritic Texts*, 40).

[54] Gray, *Legacy of Canaan*, 102, suggests, "The repetition of this passage, possibly seven times, reflects the mood of the festal assembly and possibly also the sexual licence in which they indulged on this occasion."

Gray summarizes his understanding of the connection with the OT portrayals: "We may well suppose that this activity of El was sacramentally experienced
by the community in the sexual orgies of the fertility cult which the Hebrew
prophets so vehemently denounced."[55]

Although Gray represents the consensus interpretation of this text and of the
Ugaritic fertility cults as it was held by a previous generation of Ugaritic and OT
scholars, some notable scholars today insist that the evidence from Ras Shamra
does not support the existence of a fertility cult in Ugarit.[56] In light of the biblical
statements that seem to specifically describe ritual sex at the Canaanite high
places and in light of the equivalent terminology (the root *qdš*) describing both
the biblical and Ugaritic cult functionaries (to be examined below), however, it is
premature to abandon the majority position held by scholars until very recently.
Even if "revisionist" scholars of the past few decades prove to be correct, there is
still a general consensus among all who have worked with this material (including
these scholars) that the Ugaritic text "Birth of the Gracious Gods" (*KTU* 1.23)
and perhaps some other Ugartic texts give evidence of a sacred-marriage rite involving ritual intercourse (albeit, for some scholars, on a more limited scale).[57] In

---

[55] Ibid., 101.

[56] See, e.g., the categorical pronouncement made by Dennis Pardee, *Ritual and Cult
at Ugarit* (ed. Theodore J. Lewis; SBLWAW; Atlanta: Society of Biblical Literature, 2002),
234: "The fertility cult so dear to the heart of older generations of Hebrew and Ugaritic
scholars shows up clearly in neither corpus [Ugaritic texts or HB]; the sexual depravity
that some have claimed to be characteristic of the Canaanite cult in general has left no
trace in any of the Ugaritic texts translated above (unless one considers the possibility of a
hieros gamos in text 28 [RS 24.291] to constitute such a trace)." It is revealing to note that
Pardee and Lewis omit from their book the text translated by John Gray (*KTU* 1.23). Although Gregorio del Olmo Lete may help to explain why such omission would occur—
because Ugaritic scholars are now classifying *KTU* 1.23 as "cultic myth" rather than ritual
(*Canaanite Religion according to the Liturgical Texts of Ugarit* [trans. Wilfred G. E. Watson;
Bethesda, Md.: CDL, 1999], 15), such elimination of evidence by redefinition of genre
smacks of special pleading. The categorical denial of any fertility cult rituals in Ugarit or
the Bible by Pardee and Lewis is even more puzzling in light of the fact that Pardee himself
translates this text under the title "Dawn and Dusk (the Birth of the Gracious and Beautiful Gods)" in *COS* 1.87:274–83 and in the introduction acknowledges "the liturgical aspects of the text" and that the interpretation of this text as related to a sacred-marriage rite
in Ugarit "is plausible" (p. 275). Although Pardee's translation plays down the sexual element of the liturgy, in the notes he cannot deny the "general consensus that *yd,* 'hand,'
here is a euphemism for 'penis'" (280, n. 48) or that "the conjunction of words elsewhere
used as euphemisms for the male member with verbs of raising, lowering, and shooting,
with the resultant use of bird flesh, roasted on hot coals, seems to indicate the presence of
sexual allusions in keeping with the following explicitly indicated sexual activity" (281, n.
51). For other scholars who see no cultic prostitution or fertility cult in Ugarit or
anywhere else in the ancient Near East, see the bibliography cited in footnote 25 above, on
Mesopotamian cultic prostitution and ritual sex.

[57] E.g., Wyatt (*Religious Texts from Ugarit,* 324) labels the text "The Birth of the Gracious Gods" as "A Sacred Marriage Liturgy." Again, Lete includes this text in his collection
of Ugaritic liturgical texts, labels it as "sacred marriage," and concludes that it was "probably acted out by the new king and the goddess *Pidrayu* (or her representative) on the
nuptial bed" (*Canaanite Religion according to the Liturgical Texts of Ugarit,* 212).

any case, the Ugaritic materials document both the divinization (among the gods) and the sacralization (ritual intercourse) of sexuality in their cult.

Pentateuch

Already in the Torah are encountered narratives and legislation that reveal the inroads and potential threat of cultic sacralization and divinization of sexuality in the life of God's covenant people.

Narratives. Only a few short months after their exodus from Egypt and only a few weeks after God had given the Ten Commandments from Sinai and entered into a national covenant with his people, the Israelites persuaded Aaron to make for them "gods" (ʾĕlōhîm)[58] while Moses tarried on the mountain. The "molded calf/young bull" [translation mine] (ʿēgel massēkâ, Exod 32:4) probably was not connected with the Egyptian Apis bull deity (which was worshiped as a live bull and not in image form) or with the goddess Hathor (which was symbolized by a heifer, not a bull) but more likely was linked with the bull into which the Canaanite god Baal was thought to have transformed himself and with which the Israelites would have been familiar, since Baal worship was widely known in the Nile Delta at that time.[59] The worship that Aaron instituted with the golden calf/young bull was thus probably not an ad hoc celebration but part of an already well-established worship system. "This is not a casual incident; it is an organized cult, with statue, altar, priest and festival."[60]

The worship of the golden calf/young bull not only constituted a transgression of the second commandment; part of the idolatrous worship also entailed Israel's "breaking loose" sexually. Exodus 32:6b describes the experience of the Israelites' idol worship: "the people sat down to eat and drink, and rose up to revel [lĕṣaḥēq]." The Hebrew verb ṣāḥaq, "laugh, sport, play," here (in light of

---

[58] The expression ʾĕlōhîm can either refer to the appellation for God, Elohim, or represent the pagan plural "gods." Probably connotations of both are ultimately contained in the narrative, and a type of syncretistic worship is described. On the one hand, Aaron indicates that the feast centered on the gold calf was a "festival to the LORD" (ḥag ladonai) (Exod 32:5). On the other hand, the use of the common plural demonstrative adjective "these" (ʾēlleh) in vv. 4 and 8 ("These are your ʾĕlōhîm") implies pagan plural gods. Note that the intertextual references to this narrative emphasize both aspects: Neh 9:18 (with its sg. zeh) highlights the former, and Acts 7:40 (with its pl. theous, "gods") underscores the latter.

[59] R. Alan Cole, Exodus: An Introduction and Commentary (TOTC 2; Downers Grove, Ill: InterVarsity, 1973), 214. Cole cites the Ras Shamra cycle, Baal I. v. 18, where Baal's transformation into a bull is described. The traditional gods of Egypt—including the Apis bull and Hathor—which had just recently been discredited in the ten plagues, would not likely be the gods to which Israel would so soon turn. On the worship of Baal and his consorts in Egypt, even by Egyptians, at the time of the New Kingdom, note the summary of Wente, "Egyptian Religion," 2:410: "Asiatic deities, such as Astarte, Baal, Rešep, and Anat, were accepted in Egypt in the course of the New Kingdom. . . . In Egypt, Asiatic deities were worshiped by Egyptians in accordance with Egyptian cult practices."

[60] Cole, Exodus, 215.

other parallel terms to be discussed below) probably has sexual implications of "drunken, immoral orgies and sexual play."[61] John Davis rightly observes that in this context "the verb translated 'to play' suggests illicit and immoral sexual activity which normally accompanied fertility rites found among the Canaanites who worshiped the god Baal."[62]

God informed Moses of the situation that was transpiring on the plain below Mt. Sinai (Exod 32:7): "Your people, whom you brought up out of the land of Egypt, have acted perversely [šiḥēt, intensive pi'el of šāḥat]." The verb šāḥat is the verb used to describe the corruption of the earth in Noah's day (Gen 6:12), a situation that included sexual corruption (see ch. 4, below). The nature of the corruption at Sinai is further elaborated when Moses poetically responds to Joshua's suggestion that it is the sound of war they hear (Exod 32:18):

> It is not the sound made by victors ['ănnôt gĕbûrâ],
> or the sound made by losers ['ănnôt ḥălûšâ];
> it is the sound of revelers ['annôt] that I hear.

The poem describes three different kinds of "random singing": the first two indicated by the qal infinitive construct plus modifier, and the kind Moses hears denoted by the intensified pi'el infinitive construct alone without modifier. John Durham interprets this third kind of singing as "the disorganized, haphazard singing of a wild debauch."[63] Ariella Deem arrives at a similar conclusion but from a different angle: she suggests that the word 'annôt is the intensive form of a newly discovered Hebrew verb meaning "to make love" and thus in this verse should be translated "the sound of an orgy that I hear."[64] Deem and others also point out the allusion here to the similar sounding name of the goddess Anath— the Canaanite goddess of love and war. Robert M. Good makes clear the implication of this association with Anath: "The ability of Moses' words to multiply meanings has become a mechanism for simultaneously characterizing Israel's apostasy as pagan and implying that it involved sexual license."[65]

---

[61] Walter C. Kaiser Jr., "Exodus," EBC 2:478. So also Leslie C. Allen, "qxc," NIDOTTE 3:797: "More likely it [the verb ṣāḥaq in Exod 32:6] refers to a sexual orgy." Cf. the probable sexual nuance of this term elsewhere in the Torah: Gen 26:8; 39:14, 17.

[62] John J. Davis, Moses and the Gods of Egypt: Studies in the Book of Exodus (Grand Rapids: Baker, 1971), 285. Cf. BDB 850, which points out the nuance of "conjugal caresses" in this verb.

[63] John I. Durham, Exodus (WBC 3; Waco, Tex.: Word, 1987), 425. For a survey of various interpretations of this passage, see, e.g., John Makujina, "Additional Considerations for Determining the Meaning of 'ANÔT and 'ANNÔT in Exod. XXXII 18," VT 55 (2005): 39–46 (although I disagree with Makkujina's conclusion that the first two occurrences of the verb 'ānâ should be translated as "answering" and the third as "singing"; the same word repeated three times in the same verse seems more likely to have the same basic meaning, only intensified in the pi'el).

[64] Ariella Deem, "The Goddess Anath and Some Biblical Hebrew Cruces," JSS 23 (1978): 25–30.

[65] Robert M. Good, "Exodus 32:18," in Love and Death in the Ancient Near East: Essays in Honor of Marvin H. Pope (ed. John H. Marks and Robert M. Good; Guilford, Conn.: Four Quarters, 1987), 141.

Moses' audial assessment on Mt. Sinai is confirmed as he and Joshua near the camp and see the statue of the young bull and the "dancing" (*mĕḥōlōt*) of the idolatrous worship (v. 19). The plural of *mĕḥōlâ* "probably implies a religious ceremony, with devotees whirling ecstatically before the idol and altar."[66] In the context of the worship of the bull cult, this dancing probably had "an orgiastic undertone."[67] The narrator further comments on what Moses witnessed (v. 25): "the people were running wild [*pāraʿ*]"—a verb that has the idea of "loosening" or "uncovering," that is, of nakedness.[68] Most likely, within the canonical form of the Torah, *pāraʿ* should be seen as intertextually linked to the phonetically similar *pĕʿôr* (the same three radicals in different order) in order "to invite comparison with the Baal Pe'or traditions" (Num 25:1ff.). The narrator of the Exodus story has subtly indicated that the offense at the foot of Sinai was sexual and he has virtually embedded the name Pe'or within his narrative."[69] The sexual orgies included in the idolatrous worship were thus not just sensual indulgence. "These, in a Baalized context, would have a religious, not an immoral significance to the worshiper."[70] In other words, sex was sacralized and even divinized as part of the cultic ritual. God's decided punishment of this "breaking loose" reveals God's violent rejection of a distorted theology and praxis that incorporate human sexual activity into religious ritual.

A second incident in the exodus experience refers to spiritual infidelity by utilizing the term *zĕnût,* which means "fornication," here in the spiritual sense of "faithlessness" towards God.[71] In Num 14:33, commenting on Israel's recent rebellion at Kadesh Barnea, Moses pronounces the divine sentence: "And your children shall be shepherds in the wilderness for forty years, and shall suffer for your faithlessness [*zĕnût*], until the last of your dead bodies lies in the wilderness."

Forty years later, on the borders of the promised land, Israel again fell into sacred-sex idolatry, this time at Baal of Peor (Num 25). Gordon Wenham points out the striking literary structural parallels in the narratives about the worship of the golden calf at Sinai and the idolatry on the plains of Moab.[72] By means of these structural parallels in the narrative, the theological point is made clear: the new generation entering the promised land must learn the same lessons as the generation that came out of Egypt. The same test comes around again, and those

---

66 Cole, *Exodus,* 218.

67 Ibid.

68 BDB 828. See Davis, *Moses and the Gods of Egypt,* 285.

69 Good, "Exodus 32:18," 141.

70 Cole, *Exodus,* 216.

71 BDB 276; cf. *HALOT* 276.

72 Gordon J. Wenham, *Numbers: An Introduction and Commentary* (TOTC 3; Downers Grove, Ill.: InterVarsity, 1981), 184–85. Both incidents come immediately after a time of divine revelation (Exod 20; Num 22–24), flout basic covenant principles, and are followed by a census and laws concerning sacrifices and festivals. Internally, the two narratives are also parallel: both include idolatry (Exod 32:8; Num 25:3), the appeasement of divine wrath by the slaughter of the idolaters (Exod 32:26–28; Num 25:7–8), and the setting apart/confirming of Levites/priests for divine service (Exod 32:29; Num 25:11–13).

who failed to learn it the first time are doomed to repeat the mistakes of the past and suffer punishment. Divine judgment at Baal of Peor removed the last of the rebellious wilderness generation that God predicted would not enter Canaan (Num 14:29–34; 26:63–65).

Sexual immorality linked with the pagan fertility cult rituals formed an integral part of the sin at Baal of Peor, as with the worship of the golden calf at Sinai. Numbers 25:1 already hints at the link between sex and cult: "The people [men] began to have sexual relations [*liznôt,* infinitive of *zānâ*] with the women of Moab." The verb *zānâ* can refer either to illicit sexual immorality in general or to practicing prostitution (sex for hire), depending upon the context.[73] But what is striking about Num 25:1 is that this is the only place in the HB where the verb *zānâ* refers to the sexual activity of men, not women. *Men* are committing harlotry/prostitution. By using a term elsewhere reserved to describe the sexual activity of women, the narrator clearly links the sexual activity to the spiritual harlotry of Israel against Yahweh, a phenomenon of "dual harlotry" (religious and carnal) that will appear again and again throughout the OT canon.[74] In Num 25:1 *zānâ* "refers to apostasy from the covenant, expressed in the form of intercourse with the Moabite women. Therefore *zānâ,* which everywhere else has a feminine subject, can have Israel as its subject here, because Israel plays the female role in relationship to Yahweh."[75]

---

[73] Gary H. Hall, "זנה," *NIDOTTE* 1:1123, cautions, "Each usage of *znh* must be evaluated independently on the basis of the literary context and social setting to determine its meaning. In many cases illicit sex, not sex for hire, is in view."

[74] Aron Balorda devotes an entire section to an overview of the dual-harlotry phenomenon in the OT ("The Jealousy of Phinehas in Numbers 25 as the Embodiment of the Essence of Numinal Marriage" [M.A. thesis, Andrews University, 2002], 98–126). These occasions of dual harlotry (and relevant passages) include examples from the antediluvian period (Gen 6:1–4), the patriarchal era (Gen 24:3; 26:34–35; 28:1–5; 34), the period of the exodus and entry into Canaan (Exod 32; 34:15–16; Num 25; Deut 7:3, 4; 17:17; Josh 23:12, 13), the period of the judges and the monarchy (Judg 14:1–3; 16; 1 Kgs 3:1–3; 11:1–8; 16:31; 2 Chr 18:1), and the postexilic era (Ezra 9:1–10:44; Neh 13:23–30; Mal 2:10–16). Balorda concludes from his survey of carnal and religious harlotry that "it is usually the case that the carnal harlotry, esp. when committed collectively, brings about the religious one" (p. 99). Although the present study mainly separates the discussion of the religious "harlotry" from the "carnal" harlotry in order to organize the material, still this intimate connection between the two throughout the OT canon must not be forgotten. The dual-harlotry passages in the Prophets and Writings are discussed later in this chapter.

[75] S. Erlandsson, "זָנָה *zānāh;* זְנוּנִים *z^enûnîm;* זְנוּת *z^enûth;* תַּזְנוּת *taznûth,*" *TDOT* 4:100, 102. Contra Tikva Frymer-Kensky, *Reading the Women of the Bible* (New York: Schocken, 2002), 217, who argues that this story "has nothing to do with sex" because the verb *zānâ* in its basic meaning signifies simply "faithless" or "break the faith" without any sexual connotations. She finds Israel's unfaithfulness in this narrative taking only "the form of eating." Frymer-Kensky apparently fails to recognize that *zānâ* has the primary concrete meaning of "*sexual* unfaithfulness" and only in an etymologically derived sense metaphorically (in the context of the marriage metaphor undergirding the relationship between Yahweh and Israel) comes to mean "exclusive fidelity" in a nonsexual (but still marital) sense. As Hall, *NIDOTTE* 1:1123, puts it, "Since it [*znh*] referred to illicit sex, es-

Numbers 25:2 continues to emphasize the linkage between the sexual entice-
ments of the Moabite women and the worship of Baal. Not obvious in most English versions, the pronouns in this verse are all feminine plural, referring back to
the Moabite women: "These [fem. pl.] invited the people to the sacrifices of their
[fem. pl.] gods, and the people ate and bowed down to their [fem. pl.] gods." A
picture unfolds of Israel's fall into sin: sexual liaisons with pagan women, including
attendance of the fertility cult festivities and finally resulting in full participation
in the degrading sexual rites of Baal worship.

The text does not clarify whether the women of Moab were women priestesses of the Canaanite religion of Baal[76] or common harlots hired by the Moabite
leaders,[77] but it is probable (in light of later biblical references to Baal worship)
that the goddesses in the Baal of Peor fertility cult engaged in licentious sexual activity and that their behavior was to be emulated by their worshipers. "It was this
sort of activity in which the unsuspecting Israelites would be expected to participate once the sacrificial meal had been concluded."[78] Harrison catches the thrust
of the account in the light of ANE archaeological/literary evidence: "The narrative gives some idea of the form the ritual would take. Having eaten a festive meal
at which the wine would flow freely, the Israelites would follow the Moabite
women as they prostrated themselves before the local Baal, their god Chemosh,
and probably his consort Ashtar (mentioned on line 17 of the Moabite Stone), as
a preliminary to indulging in carnal behavior."[79]

What is implicit in Num 25:1–2 becomes explicit in v. 3: "Thus Israel yoked itself [the *nipᶜal* of *ṣāmad*] to Baal of Peor." The religion is here unequivocally identified as Baal worship. The verb *ṣāmad* in the *nipᶜal* means "to be attached to, yoked
together," like a pair of animals (the noun *ṣemed* is a "yoke" or "team" for/of animals). Israel had uninhibitedly adopted the worship of Baal of Peor, apparently not
only at the fertility festival but blatantly bringing such ritual sex practices into the
very camp of Israel (see Num 25:6–8, 14–18). As with the distortion of sexuality at
Sinai, so with the idolatrous sacralization of sex at Baal of Peor: the divine reaction
was swift and unequivocal. "The LORD's anger was kindled against Israel" (Num
25:3), resulting in a plague that killed twenty-four thousand Israelites before it was
stayed by the decisive action of Phinehas (Num 25:7–8, 11–13).

Moses, in his farewell covenant renewal sermon of Deuteronomy, looks back
to the incidents of spiritual harlotry on the part of Israel, including specifically

---

pecially in violation of the covenantal relationship (betrothal or marriage), it could be
used to refer to covenantal unfaithfulness on Israel's part, since this covenant came to be
viewed as a marriage (Hos 2)."

[76] So R. K. Harrison, *Numbers* (WEC; Chicago: Moody, 1990), 337: "The Midianite
women who had, with the Moabites, prostrated themselves before the deities in worship
were evidently cultic prostitutes indulging in the same kind of imitative fertility rituals
mentioned by Herodotus [Herodotus, 1.199]."

[77] The treatment of sexuality in the Prophets, below, will discuss the evidence regarding "sacred prostitution" at the fertility cult sites.

[78] Harrison, *Numbers,* 336. See also 336, n. 52 for Ugaritic literature related to this
situation.

[79] Ibid., 336.

the incident at Baal of Peor (Deut 4:3–4), and as he completes his address to the people, he receives a divine prediction of Israel's future apostasy of Israel, worded in the language of harlotry: "this people will begin to prostitute themselves [wĕzānâ] to the foreign gods in their midst, the gods of the land into which they are going" (Deut 31:16). Narrative, poetry, and prophetic utterance from the rest of the HB will make evident the extent of this apostasy and will refer repeatedly to the incident of Baal of Peor.[80]

Legislation. In the Mosaic legal material, it becomes evident that the biblical legislation formally rejects sacred ritual sex in harmony with the perspective that has emerged from the golden-calf and Baal of Peor narratives. Some of the references containing the root *znh* in the Pentateuch seem to primarily refer to noncultic illicit sex or sex for hire, not cult-related sacralized sexual activity, although it is impossible to rule out a fertility cult context. (Chapter 7, below, will deal with these passages.)

Other pentateuchal occurrences employing some derivative of the root *znh* probably have a metaphorical reference to spiritual harlotry or even a dual reference as in the Baal of Peor narrative—both to the illegitimate sexual activity in the context of fertility cults and to the spiritual harlotry of worshiping other gods. So Exod 34:11–17, following on the heels of the golden-calf worship at Sinai, opens with a stipulation of the renewed covenant that Israel is not to make a covenant with the nations of Canaan (vv. 11–12) but rather to destroy their fertility cult sites (vv. 12–13). The reason is given (vv. 15–16): "You shall not make a covenant with the inhabitants of the land, for when they prostitute themselves [wĕzānû] to their gods and sacrifice to their gods, someone among them will invite you, and you will eat of the sacrifice. And you will take wives from among their daughters for your sons, and their daughters who prostitute themselves [wĕzānû] to their gods will make your sons also prostitute themselves [wĕhiznû] to their gods."

Metaphorical use of words derived from the root *znh* to indicate spiritual unfaithfulness occurs three times in the legal material of the book of Leviticus. Leviticus 17:7 legislates that Israel "may no longer offer their sacrifices for goat-demons [laśśîrîm], to whom they prostitute themselves [zōnîm]." Leviticus 20:5 sets forth the penalty of divine kārēt (being cut off—a divine curse of the extinction of sinner and his progeny)[81] against "all who prostitute themselves [hazzōnîm] . . . to commit harlotry [liznôt] with Molech."[82] The next verse (20:6) announces the same penalty for "any [who] turn to mediums and wizards, prostituting themselves [liznôt] to them."

---

80 See Josh 22:16–18; Ps 106:28–31; Ezek 20:21–26; cf. Rev 2:14.

81 See Donald J. Wold, "The Meaning of the Biblical Penalty *kareth*" (PhD diss., University of California, Berkeley, 1978); and the discussion in ch. 5, below.

82 Quoted from NKJV. Molech was probably not a fertility deity but rather a Canaanite chthonic (underworld) god connected with the cult of the dead ancestors, perhaps related to the ANE god Malik and to the Punic practice of cultic child sacrifice under the term *molk* (see George C. Heider, "Molech," *ABD* 4:895–98). This practice of offering

In contradistinction to the root *znh,* which must be examined contextually in every instance in order to determine whether there is a cultic setting, the masculine noun *qādēš* (and the fem. counterpart, *qĕdēšâ*) seems to invariably refer to male and female personnel of the fertility cults who (among other possible cultic functions) engaged in ritual intercourse at the high places. The term *qĕdēšâ* appears on the lips of the non-Israelite men of Timnah, presumably worshiping in a fertility cult, in the story of Judah and Tamar (Gen 38:21–22) in contrast to the common term for "harlot" (*zônâ*) in the same story on the lips of Judah.[83]

Deuteronomy 23:18 (ET 23:17) specifically forbids an Israelite from becoming a temple prostitute: "None of the daughters of Israel shall be a temple prostitute [*qĕdēšâ,* lit. 'holy one,' fem.]; none of the sons of Israel shall be a temple prostitute [*qādēš,* lit. 'holy one,' masc.]." Although there is currently considerable debate over the exact function of these cultic "holy ones," the evidence is persuasive for the conclusion that they were indeed cultic personnel who (among other possible functions) engaged in ritual sexual intercourse at the high places. John Day summarizes crucial biblical lexical evidence for this position: "That sacred prostitution was a feature of the religion is indicated by the parallelism of the word *zônâ,* 'prostitute,' with *qĕdēšâ,* lit. 'holy one,' in Deut 23:18–19 and Gen 38:15, 22–23 and of *zônôt,* 'prostitutes,' with *qĕdēšôt,* lit. 'holy ones,' in Hos 4:14."[84]

---

child sacrifices to Molech is linked in Israelite history mainly to the Valley of Tophet outside Jerusalem. Other biblical passages referring to Molech and/or child sacrifice include Deut 12:31; 18:10; 2 Kgs 16:3; 17:17, 31; 21:6; 23:10; Isa 57:5; Jer 7:31–32; 19:5, 6, 11; 32:35; Ezek 16:20–21, 36; 20:25–26, 30–31; 23:36–39; Ps 106:37; and 2 Chr 33:6. Although Molech was not a fertility god, the connections with sexuality are implicit because the sacrificing of children robs the family of the results of the sexual union. For further discussion and bibliography, see chs. 5 and 11, below.

[83] This study will analyze the story in more detail in subsequent chapters dealing with prostitution, incest, and levirate marriage (chs. 7, 10, and 11, below), but here in the context of ritual sex it is instructive to note how carefully the words are chosen in this narrative. The terms *zônâ* and *qĕdēšâ* are not used indiscriminately, as some have recently claimed. When the narrator describes what Judah thought the woman (his daughter Tamar disguised as a harlot) was, he uses the common term for "prostitute," *zônâ* (Gen 38:15). In the conversation (and report of the conversation) with the non-Israelite men, who no doubt were worshipers in the Canaanite fertility cults, the operative term is *qĕdēšâ,* "temple prostitute" (38:21–22). (Judah's friend may have also been trying to make Judah look respectable to his Canaanite neighbors.) But when the narrator describes the conversation in which Judah is told of her daughter's "playing the whore" and being "pregnant as a result of whoredom," the terms revert to the root for the common term for "harlotry," *znh* (*zānâ* and *liznûnîm* respectively, 38:24). See Phyllis A. Bird, "The Harlot as Heroine: Narrative Art and Social Presupposition in Three Old Testament Texts," *Semeia* 46 (1989): 125–26, who recognizes this careful narrative distinction.

[84] Day, "Canaan, Religion of," 1:835. See also Naudé, *NIDOTTE* 3:886. Cf. the rendering in BDB 873: "temple-prostitute." The text and footnotes above dealing with cult prostitution in the ancient Near East have already given further substantiation that the terms *qādēš* and *qĕdēšâ* in the HB refer respectively to male and female cult functionaries who (among other duties) performed ritual sex in connection with the fertility cults. Even among feminist scholars who have denied the existence of cultic prostitution in the

The literary context of Deut 23 provides further support for the conclusion that the *qādēš* and *qĕdēšâ* are indeed cultic functionaries of ritual sex and not some form of cultic personnel serving in nonsexual capacities. It is widely recognized that the overall literary structure of Deuteronomy is that of a covenant renewal, following the essential outline of the international suzerainty-vassal treaties of the day:[85]

Preamble	Deut 1:1–5
Historical prologue	Deut 1:6–4:49
General stipulations	Deut 5–11
Specific stipulations	Deut 12–26
Blessings and curses	Deut 27–28
Witnesses	Deut 30:15–20
Deposition of text	Deut 31:9, 24–26
Public reading	Deut 31:10–13
Covenant lawsuit (against rebellious vassals)	Deut 32

Within this overall structure, Deut 24 is situated as part of the specific stipulations of the covenant, Deut 12–26. What has not been as widely recognized is the structuring pattern of these specific stipulations. A penetrating study of this section of Deuteronomy by Stephen Kaufman (among others) has shown that the whole body of material is arranged "with consummate literary artistry" as an expansion and application of the Decalogue of Deut 5, with the various laws grouped within topical units that follow the content and sequence of the corresponding commandments of the Decalogue.[86] Kaufman proposes and substantiates the following arrangement and sequence; see the chart.

Canaanite fertility cults, many "allow for the possibility that rituals of the *qĕdēšôt* may have included sexuality, but may not have been regarded as 'prostitution' by the performers" (Gale A. Yee, " 'She Is Not My Wife and I Am Not Her Husband': A Materialist Analysis of Hosea 1–2," *BibInt* 9 [2001]: 356). See, e.g., Phyllis A. Bird, " 'To Play the Harlot': An Inquiry into an Old Testament Metaphor," in *Gender and Difference in Ancient Israel* (ed. Peggy L. Day; Minneapolis: Fortress, 1989), 87–88; and Renate Jost, "Von 'Huren und Heiligen': Ein sozialgeschichtlicher Beitrag," in *Feministische Hermeneutik und erstes Testament: Analysen und Interpretation* (ed. Hedwig Jahnow; Stuttgart: Kohlhammer, 1994), 135. Karel van der Toorn aptly observes that the issue of sacred prostitution in the ancient Near East (including Israel) is "an area where researchers have difficulty distancing themselves from their own feelings about the matter. For example, we find authors who minimize the occurrence of sacred prostitution in Israel out of hardly concealed apologetic motives, in spite of a number of unequivocal texts" (*From Her Cradle to Her Grave: The Role of Religion in the Life of the Israelite and the Babylonian Woman* [trans. Sara J. Denning-Bolle; BS 23; Sheffield, Eng.: JSOT Press, 1994], 102).

[85] See esp. Meredith G. Kline, *Treaty of the Great King—the Covenant Structure of Deuteronomy: Studies and Commentary* (Grand Rapids: Eerdmans, 1963); and Peter C. Craigie, *The Book of Deuteronomy* (NICOT; Grand Rapids: Eerdmans, 1976), 20–24 and passim, for bibliography and discussion.

[86] Steven A. Kaufman, "The Structure of the Deuteronomic Law," *Maarav* 1–2 (1978–1979): 105–58, quote at 125. That Deut 12–26 represents sequential explications of

Commandment	Deuteronomy Passage	Description
1–2	12:1–31	Worship
3	13:1–14:27 (ET 12:31–14:27)	Name of God
4	14:28–16:17	Sabbath
5	16:18–18:22	Authority
6	19:1–22:8	Homicide
7	22:9–23:19	Adultery
8	23:20–24:7 (ET 23:19–24:7)	Theft
9	24:8–25:4	False charges
10	25:5–16	Coveting

Later chapters will refer to this pivotal study, but the significance of this arrangement for our purposes here is that the instructions regarding the qādēš and qĕdēšâ are found in the section elaborating on the seventh commandment. Therefore these instructions clearly have in view the sexual distortion involved in the functioning of the qādēš and qĕdēšâ. This structural placement, in addition to their usage in a clearly sexual context in Gen 38, forms strong evidence—to be supplemented with additional lines of evidence from the Prophets—that these "holy ones" engaged in ritual sexual intercourse as part of the fertility cult practices of Israel's neighbors. Furthermore, the fact that this legislation prohibiting the qādēš and qĕdēšâ is placed in Deuteronomy as an expansion of the seventh commandment of the moral law (the Decalogue) also gives evidence that cultic prostitution was objectionable not only because it was part of the pagan cult but because it was morally wrong in itself.

The polemic against the divinization of sex in the fertility cults appears to be at least part of the divine rationale for legislation that the priests' clothing be designed so that they do not expose their nakedness (Exod 28:42–43), and that the priests "not go up by steps to my altar, so that your nakedness may not be exposed on it" (20:26). Pictorial representations in the ancient Near East reveal that in the fertility cults of surrounding religions, "the priests were often naked when performing their duties,"[87] and they officiated naked because sexual involvement in the cult was implied in their office.[88] Again, legislation is given to protect against the sacralization or divinization of sex in the Israelite cultus.

---

the Decalogue was recognized in principle as early as Philo of Alexander (who sought to organize all the Mosaic laws according to topics suggested by the Decalogue) and understood by the Protestant Reformers Luther and Calvin, but Kaufman provides a more systematic argument, taking cues from the organizing principles of other ANE law codes. See also Georg Braulik, "Die Abfolge der Gesetze in Deuteronomium 12–26 und der Decalog," in *Das Deuteronomium: Entstehung, Gestalt, und Botschaft* (ed. Norbert Lohfink; Leuven: Leuven University Press, 1983), 252–72; idem, "Zur Abfolge der Gesetze in Deuteronomium 16,18–21,23: Weitere Beobachtungen," *Bib* 69 (1988): 63–92; and Dennis T. Olson, *Deuteronomy and the Death of Moses: A Theological Reading* (OBT; Minneapolis: Fortress, 1994), 62–125, for slight modifications of Kaufman's basic divisions and arrangements.

[87] H. Ringgren, "כֹּהֵן kōhēn," *TDOT* 7:63.
[88] See I. E. S. Edwards, C. J. Gadd, and N. G. L. Hammonds, eds., *Early History of the Middle East* (3d ed.; Cambridge Ancient History 1/2; Cambridge: Cambridge University Press, 1971), 672.

Sacralization of Sex and the Male Priesthood in Israel. Although Scripture does not give us any explicit rationale for the divinely ordained exclusion of female priests from Israelite priesthood, cultural contingencies related to the distortions of sexuality in ANE fertility cults appear to be one of the major factors. This factor seems to be especially significant in view of the larger sweep of salvation history, in which (1) Adam and Eve were designated as priests after the fall in Gen 3 (as noted in ch. 2, above), (2) the whole nation of Israel was considered "a priestly kingdom" before the sexual-idolatrous apostasy at Mt. Sinai (Exod 19:6), and (3) the NT reinstituted the priesthood of all believers (1 Pet 2:5, 9; Rev 1:6; 5:10). The Israelite exclusion of female priests is apparently unique in the whole ancient Near East[89] and therefore seems to be intentional, especially since Israel shared much the same priestly terminology with Canaanite, Ugaritic, and even Babylonian languages.[90] Jacques Doukhan explores several probable rationales for excluding female priests in Israel and argues persuasively—adding his voice to many others—that one of the main reasons was a polemic intention against the sexual distortions in the Canaanite fertility cults with their goddess worship and cultic sexual intercourse.[91]

Hennie Marsman elaborates on this reason by pointing out that in the ancient Near East during the second half of the second and during the first millennium, female priests were primarily, if not exclusively, women of high birth and one of the main priestly functions of these women was to be the wife of the male deity.[92] In Egypt Pharaoh's daughter was a "God's Wife of Amun," and in Mesopotamia the king's daughter was a *nin-dingir,* who "had a kind of marital relationship with the main deity." Marsman summarizes concerning this female priestly role and the contrast with Israel's religion, "They [the female priests] were a wife of the god, whether the interpretation of this function was sexual or not, that is, whether their 'sacred marriage' was a carnally or a symbolically performed rite. In Yahwism, such a function for a woman was out of the question."[93] Thus one of the major reasons for excluding women from the priesthood was that

---

[89] See Roland de Vaux, *Ancient Israel: Its Life and Institutions* (trans. John McHugh; New York: McGraw-Hill, 1961), 183–84.

[90] See Baruch A. Levine, "Priests," *IDBSup*, 688.

[91] Jacques B. Doukhan, "Women Priests in Israel: A Case for Their Absence," in *Women in Ministry: Biblical and Historical Perspectives* (ed. Nancy Vyhmeister; Berrien Springs, Mich.: Andrews University Press, 1998), 31. Cf. Clarence J. Vos, *Woman in Old Testament Worship* (Amsterdam: Judels & Brinkman, 1968), 194; Samuel Terrien, *Till the Heart Sings: A Biblical Theology of Manhood and Womanhood* (Philadelphia: Fortress, 1985), 78.

[92] Hennie J. Marsman, *Women in Ugarit and Israel: Their Social and Religious Position in the Context of the Ancient Near East* (Boston: E. J. Brill, 2003), 544–45, shows that in Egypt and Mesopotamia, although quite a few women were functioning in the role of priestess in the third and first half of the second millennium B.C.E., during the middle of the second millennium and during the first millennium women to a large extent had disappeared from the priesthood and only women of high birth remained active in cultic functions as priestesses.

[93] Ibid., 545.

"in monotheistic Yahwism neither a goddess alongside YHWH, nor a female cultic functionary in the capacity of a 'wife' of the deity could be tolerated."[94] (Other possible rationales will be explored in chs. 6 and 7, below.) Throughout the Pentateuch, by precept and example, God makes unmistakably clear that sexuality is a creation ordinance and is not to be distorted after the manner of the pagan fertility cults.

Prophets/Writings

In the Former Prophets, the author of Judges aptly describes in sexual terms Israel's forsaking the true God and embracing Canaanite idolatry: "They lusted after other gods" (2:17).[95] The depiction of idolatry as harlotry reoccurs elsewhere in Judges[96] and (as shown below) emerges as a major motif in the Latter Prophets' denouncement of Israel's infatuation with participation in the Canaanite fertility cults. Israel's unfaithfulness to God through idolatry is likened to a wife's unfaithfulness to her husband through harlotry, and at the same time the idolatrous participation in the fertility cults also included grossly licentious practices. The nature and extent of this confluence of idolatry and immorality are more apparent in the Latter Prophets, but Judges, Samuel, and Kings are not without references to the decadent sexuality of the fertility cults. Frequent mention is made of the fertility gods—Baal (Hadad the storm god),[97] his consorts Astarte (Ashtoreth)[98] and Asherah, and the presence in Israel of cult objects representing them.[99] The biblical description of Judah's involvement with the fertility cults in

---

[94] Ibid., 547.

[95] Some (esp. from the Scandinavian "myth and ritual school") have suggested the Wisdom literature in the Writings—in particular Prov 1–9—was written to warn against foreign women who are participants in the fertility cults. See the overview with bibliography in John Barclay Burns, "Proverbs 7,6–27: Vignettes from the Cycle of Astarte and Adonis," *SJOT* 9 (1995): 20–36; cf. Robert H. O'Connell, "Proverbs vii 6–7: A Case of Fatal Deception in a 'Woman and the Window' Type-Scene," *VT* 41 (1991): 235–41. This hypothesis is not convincing, although it is possible that there is an implicit polemic against fertility cult ritual by modeling ritual language although this literature intends the descriptions to be taken at face value as warnings against the immoral woman in general. This possibility seems more likely regarding the Song of Songs. But in Proverbs and elsewhere in the Writings outside Song of Songs, the evidence is too speculative to be certain or calls for extended discussion. Hence this section focuses on the Prophets, where references to the fertility cults are reasonably clear.

[96] Judg 8:27, 33.

[97] See the discussion of Ugarit/Canaan, above.

[98] In the Ugaritic texts, the goddess Anat is most frequently mentioned as the consort of Baal, but in the Canaanite fertility cults, Baal's consort is usually Astarte (see the discussion of Ugarit/Canaan, above).

[99] It is not always clear in Scripture when reference is being made to the god or goddess or their visible cultic representation. See, e.g., William L. Reed, "Asherah," *IDB* 1:251–52 and John Day, "Asherah," *ABD* 1:485–87, for examples probably indicating the cult object; see idem, "Canaan, Religion of," *ABD* 1:835 on the likely connection of at least some of the stone cultic pillars (*maṣṣēbôt*) with the phallic symbol representing the male deity.

the time of Rehoboam gives some indication of its permeation throughout the land: "For they also built for themselves high places, pillars, and sacred poles on every high hill and under every green tree; there were also male temple prostitutes [qādēš] in the land. They committed all the abominations of the nations that the LORD drove out before the people of Israel" (1 Kgs 14:23–24).[100] Second Kings 17 also summarizes the extent of the northern kingdom's involvement in the fertility cults. Note especially this description, which parallels that of Judah: "they set up for themselves pillars and sacred poles on every high hill and under every green tree" (2 Kgs 17:10). The reforms of such OT leaders as Asa, Elijah, Jehoshaphat, Jehu, Jehoiada, Hezekiah, and Josiah concentrated upon the uprooting of various elements of the fertility cults from the land by the extermination of the ritual cultic sex personnel and/or the removal of the fertility cult objects and high places.[101]

The Latter Prophets indeed protested against Israel's sexual immorality on the social level and metaphorical adultery/harlotry on the national level,[102] but it

---

[100] Cf. the assessment of Elijah that he alone had not apostatized (1 Kgs 19:14); by the Lord's count, there were only seven thousand faithful to him in all of Judah (v. 18).

[101] Asa: 1 Kgs 15:12–13 (cf. 2 Chr 15:16); Elijah: 1 Kgs 18; Jehoshaphat: 1 Kgs 22:47 (ET 22:46); Jehu: 2 Kgs 10:18–27; Jehoiada: 2 Kgs 11:17–18; Hezekiah: 2 Kgs 18:4 (cf. 2 Chr 31:1); and Josiah: 2 Kgs 23:4, 5, 7, 24 (cf. 2 Chr 34:3–7, 33). A close look at narrative clues may reveal subtle polemic against the goddess worship of Asherah in these accounts. E.g., Jezebel is portrayed as painting her eyes, adorning her head, and looking out the window as Jehu comes to Jezreel (2 Kgs 9:30). Scholars have pointed out the similarity between this narrative portrayal and the iconography of the goddess as sacred prostitute in ANE art (see *ANEP* 131) and suggested that Jezebel is virtually being presented and rejected as the goddess herself. See Peter R. Ackroyd, "Goddesses, Women, and Jezebel," in *Images of Women in Antiquity* (ed. A. Cameron and A. Kuhrt; Beckenham, Kent, Eng.: Croom Helm, 1983), 245–59; cf. Eleanor Ferris Beach, "Transforming Goddess Iconography in Hebrew Narrative," in *Women and Goddess Traditions in Antiquity and Today* (ed. Karen L. King; Minneapolis: Fortress, 1997), 242–49.

For archaeological evidence for the extent of idolatry in 7th–8th century Judah, in harmony with the biblical data, see esp. Jacob Milgrom, "The Nature and Extent of Idolatry in Eighth–Seventh Century Judah," *HUCA* 69 (1998): 1–13.

[102] Numerous expressions and passages in the Latter Prophets speak of Israel's harlotry, utilizing the verb *zānâ* or one of its nominal derivatives: "playing the whore" (Jer 2:20; 3:1, 6, 8; Ezek 16:15, 16, 17, 26, 28, 34, 41; 23:3, 5, 19, 30, 44; Hos 2:7 [ET 2:5]; 3:3; 4:10, 12, 13–14, 15; 5:3; 9:1); "whoring" (Jer 3:2; Ezek 16:36; 23:27; 43:7; Hos 2:4 [ET 2:2]); "whorings" (Ezek 16:15, 20, 22, 33, 34; 23:8, 11, 14, 18, 19, 29, 35); "multiplying whorings" (Ezek 16:25, 26, 29); "become a whore" (Isa 1:21); "forehead of a whore" (Isa 1:21); "deeds of a brazen whore" (Ezek 16:30); "men go aside with whores" (Hos 4:14); "O whore!" (Ezek 16:35); "whoredom" (Jer 3:9; Hos 6:10); "great whoredom" (Hos 1:2); "spirit of whoredom" (Hos 4:12; 5:4); "devote themselves to whoredom" (Hos 4:10–11); "carry on sexual acts" (Ezek 23:43); "go astray after" (Ezek 20:30); "bestow favors upon" (Ezek 23:7); and "indulge in sexual orgies" (Hos 4:18). In Ezek 16 alone, the verb *zānâ* or its nominal derivative occurs twenty times, with another twelve occurrences in ch. 23. As indicated in the discussion that follows in the present chapter, many of these passages probably involve Israel's participation in the fertility cults as part of the national faithlessness toward Yahweh. For further discussion (with secondary literature) of the metaphorical harlotry described by the Latter Prophets (esp. Hos 1–3, Jer 2–3, and Ezek 16 and 23), see ch. 7, below, dealing with prostitution.

was the immoral sexual practices performed on the cultic level that called forth the most vehement denunciation.[103] Although the former practices were also breaches of God's covenant with Israel, the latter struck most directly at the very heart of Israel's existence as God's covenant people.

The OT prophets provide indications of the widespread practice and intense appeal of cultic sexuality in Israel. Several prophetic passages describe how the personnel of cultic sex in Israel had offered their bodies for ritual purposes "on every high hill and under every green tree" (Jer 2:20; 3:6; cf. Deut 12:2; 1 Kgs 14:23; 2 Kgs 16:4; 17:10, 11; Isa 57:5, 7).

Amos portrays the permeation of fertility cult ritual intercourse into the northern kingdom of Israel: "father and son go in to the same girl" and "lay themselves down beside every altar on garments taken in pledge" (Amos 2:7–8). Amos 6:4–7 also could be alluding to fertility cult rituals in his description of the *marzēaḥ*, "revelry" (NRSV) or "cult festive meal," enjoyed among the wealthy class. The *marzēaḥ* is mentioned also in Ugaritic texts and is defined by Marvin Pope as "a social and religious institution which included families, owned property, houses for meetings and vineyards for wine supply, was associated with specific deities, and met periodically, perhaps monthly, to celebrate for several days at a stretch with food and drink and sometimes, if not regularly, with sacral sexual orgies."[104]

Hosea 4 vividly pictures the fertility cult in action on the high places: "They sacrifice on the tops of the mountains, and make offerings upon the hills, under oak, poplar and terebinth, because their shade is good. Therefore your daughters play the whore and your daughters-in-law commit adultery . . . for the men themselves go aside with harlots, and sacrifice with temple prostitutes [*qĕdēšôt*, fem. pl.]; thus a people without understanding comes to ruin. . . . When their drinking is ended, they indulge in sexual orgies"[105] (vv. 13, 14, 18).

---

[103] As pointed out above, there was a trend in the 1980s and 1990s, spearheaded by research into extrabiblical sources from Mesopotamia and Ugarit by some feminist scholars, to deny the existence of any fertility cult with ritual sex in Canaan during the time of Israelite history, in particular, the period of the divided monarchy. The prophet's statements were brushed aside as unhistorical. So, e.g., Gale A. Yee: "Although in the prophet's [Hosea's] mind their rituals involved sexuality, it would be a mistake to accept this at face value" ("Hosea," WBC 197). In light of more recent research, however (see the discussion of extrabiblical evidence above), many feminist scholars are now willing to acknowledge the possibility of ritual sex as part of fertility cult rituals (but not to call this "prostitution"). Thus Yee, "'She Is Not My Wife,'" 356, revises her earlier statement to read, "Although in the prophet's mind these rituals involved *uncontrolled* sexuality or *prostitution,* it is difficult to accept these at face value." In the footnote to this statement, she writes, "This is not to say that female sexuality was never a part of the fertility cults." As another example, already noted above, Bird ("'To Play the Harlot,'" 87–88) also allows for the possibility of ritual sex (but not "prostitution") on the part of the *qĕdēšôt* in the Canaanite cults.

[104] Marvin H. Pope, "A Divine Banquet at Ugarit," in *The Use of the Old Testament in the New and Other Essays: Studies in Honor of William Franklin Stinespring* (ed. James M. Efird; Durham, N.C.: Duke University Press, 1972), 193.

[105] By translating "sexual orgies," the NRSV aptly captures the intensifying force of the Hebrew original, which is a *hipʿil* inf. abs. of the root *znh* followed by a *hipʿil* impf. of the same root. Scholars widely recognize that Hos 4 refers to the fertility cult rituals. See, e.g.,

Jeremiah summarizes the situation in Judah with the cry "Look up to the
bare heights, and see! Where have you not been lain with?" (Jer 3:2).

What at first reading may sound like hyperbole in the prophets' descriptions
of Israel's almost universal acceptance of the fertility cults appears not so exaggerated in the light of archaeological evidence. Figurines and plaques of nude female figures with exaggerated sexual features (often connected with a phallic
symbol) have been discovered at almost every major excavation in Palestine.[106]

The prophets picture the intensity of sexual passion that accompanied the
"orgies on the mountains" (Jer 3:23). Jeremiah 2:23–24 compares the participants
in the fertility cults to wild animals in heat: "How can you say, 'I am not defiled, I
have not gone after the Baals'? Look at your way in the valley; know what you
have done—a restive young camel interlacing her tracks, a wild ass at home in the
wilderness, in her heat sniffing the wind! Who can restrain her lust? None who
seek her need weary themselves; in her month they will find her." Hosea portrays

---

James L. Mays, *Hosea* (OTL; Philadelphia: Westminster, 1969), 75, in his discussion of
"God's indictment of the cult" in Hos 4:11–14: "The sexual rites of the fertility cult, which
gave a foundation of realism to Hosea's constant charge of 'harlotry,' are tersely but
plainly cited. The sacred prostitutes . . . served as cultic personnel at the shrines where fertility rites were practised. Sacrifice accompanied by ritual intercourse with them was
meant to stimulate the sexual activity of the gods for the sake of the land's fertility." Commenting on v. 18, Mays (78) adds, "Along with ritual drunkenness goes the sexual perversion of the fertility cult; the harlotry is the literal sexuality of the rites in which the holy
prostitutes and occasional harlots play a part ([v.]14). Wine and women in the holy place!
Worship has become an orgy!" So also, Francis I. Andersen and David N. Freedman,
Hosea: A New Translation with Introduction and Commentary (AB 24A; New York:
Doubleday, 1989), 369–70: "the cult provided the means for Israelite men and women to
be promiscuous together. . . . [T]he terminology of vv 13–14 suggests that the men resort
to the female prostitutes of the cult shrines and women commit adultery with male
counterparts. . . . The imperfect verbs used in vv 13 and 14 point to habitual activity on
the part of both men and women. . . . The language of v 14b makes it clear that promiscuity and sacrifice were part of a full-scale cult." More recently, the same conclusion is
reached by Duane A. Garrett, *Hosea, Joel* (NAC19a; Nashville, Tenn.: Broadman and
Holman, 1997), 124, commenting on Hos 4:13b–14b: "In this passage Hosea makes his
plainest assertion that the Israelites were engaging in sexual intercourse as part of the worship at the shrines." While the evidence of Hos 4 does not seem to support an earlier hypothesis of Hans Walter Wolff, *Hosea: A Commentary on the Book of the Prophet Hosea*
(Hermeneia; Minneapolis: Fortress, 1974), 86–87, that Israel followed the Babylonian
practice described by Herodotus (ritual deflowering of every woman at the temple, as
summarized above in our discussion of sacred prostitution in the ANE), there does appear to be solid textual evidence in Hosea, as well as other OT passages of the Prophets
(cited above) that ritual sex was performed at cultic sites in Israel as part of a fertility cult
ritual involving temple prostitutes.

[106] For pictures and descriptions, see *ANEP* 160–65, 197–98, 470–73, 597–99. See Ora
Negbi, *Canaanite Gods in Metal: An Archaeological Study of Ancient Syro-Palestinian Figu-
rines* (Tel Aviv: Tel Aviv University, Institute of Archaeology, 1976); Stuckey, "Great God-
desses of the Levant," 36–38, 41–43 (with further bibliography); Miriam Tadmor, "Female
Cult Figurines in Late Canaan and Early Israel: Archaeological Evidence," in *Studies in the
Period of David and Solomon and Other Essays* (ed. Tomoo Ishida; Winona Lake, Ind.:
Eisenbrauns, 1982), 139–74; and Hadley, *The Cult of Asherah*, 188–205.

the inflamed passion by means of a vivid simile from the bakery: "They are all adulterers; they are like a heated oven, whose baker does not need to stir the fire, from the kneading of the dough until it is leavened."[107]

It is not difficult to understand the great sexual fascination of the fertility cults:

> The cult of the Mother Goddess succeeded in merging the sexual drive with the thirst for religious ecstasy and the need for economic security. It offered an overwhelming thrill with physio-psychological effects. The rituals it proposed led to sexual fulfillment, metaphysical satisfaction, and the hope of success in agriculture, viticulture, and animal husbandry. They gratified basic instincts, for they combined erotic pleasure with religious delight, as well as with an escape from the dread of hunger and thirst. They answered human desires at all levels of expectation.[108]

Knowledge of the basic fertility cult theology illuminates our understanding of moments of great crisis in OT Israel such as the showdown between Yahweh and Baal on Mt. Carmel in the ninth century B.C.E. (1 Kgs 17–18). The drought was not simply a general judgment of God against Israel's apostasy but a frontal attack against the fertility cult premise that Baal provided rain when stimulated by ritual sex at the high places. After Yahweh revealed himself by fire as the true God on Mt. Carmel and the false prophets of Baal were slain, the torrential downpour was signal evidence that Yahweh was the true God of fertility. But Yahweh's gift of rain was a gift of grace to repentant Israel, not the result of sympathetic magic in ritual sex.

In the eighth century B.C.E., Hosea became the leading expositor, among the prophets, of God's paradoxical outrage and heartbreak at Israel's participation in the fertility cults. The promiscuity/adultery motif appears repeatedly throughout both the narrative of Hosea's personal experience and the extended recital of the divine covenant lawsuit ($rîb$)[109] against Israel, and the divine assessment of the vile and heinous nature of Israel's departure from God to serve Baal never wavers. "In the house of Israel," God says, "I have seen a horrible thing; Ephraim's whoredom is there, Israel is defiled" (Hos 6:10). The people of Israel "have deeply

---

[107] Hosea 7:4. In succeeding verses Hosea extends the oven simile to describe the passionate political anger, intrigue, and violence in Israel (vv. 5–7). Chapter 12, below, examines how these passions are part of a parody of the true positive fulfillment of human needs.

[108] Terrien, *Till the Heart Sings*, 60.

[109] The word *rîb* introduces the covenant lawsuits of Hosea and Micah: Hos 4:1; Mic 6:1–2. Sometimes the prophets use a synonym, *mišpāt*, "judgment," as in Mal 3:5; Ezek 5:8. The recent scholarly literature on the covenant lawsuit is immense. For introductory discussion, starting bibliography, and numerous biblical examples, see John M. Bracke, "ריב," *NIDOTTE* 3:1105–6; Robert D. Culver, "ריב," *TWOT* 2:845–46; Herbert B. Huffmon, "The Covenant Lawsuit in the Prophets," *JBL* 78 (1959): 285–95; J. Limburg, "The Root *RÎB* and the Prophetic Lawsuit Speeches," *JBL* 88 (1969): 291–304; and Kirsten Nielsen, *Yahweh as Prosecutor and Judge: An Investigation of the Prophetic Lawsuit (rîb-Pattern)* (trans. Frederick Cryer; JSOTSup 9; Sheffield, Eng.: Department of Biblical Studies, University of Sheffield, 1978).

corrupted themselves as in the days of Gibeah" (9:9)—alluding to the vile sexual distortion described in Judg 19.

As the northern kingdom came to the brink of disaster and annihilation because of its national apostasy, God pulled out all the stops, as it were, in an attempt to send a personal, emotion-packed message to change their course before it was too late. He says to Hosea, "Go, take for yourself a wife of whoredom [zĕnûnîm, 'promiscuity, fornication'] and have children of whoredom ['promiscuity'], for the land commits great whoredom ['promiscuity'] by forsaking the LORD" (1:2).[110] Hosea's ensuing relationship with Gomer—including her marital unfaithfulness and his forgiving and enduring love in ransoming the adulteress—becomes a dramatic, pathos-filled life parable of Yahweh's relationship with Israel.[111]

As Gomer committed adultery against Hosea in going after her paramours, Israel has done so against God in following the fertility cult of Baal.[112] In the covenant lawsuit (rîb) of Yahweh against Israel recorded in Hos 2, the basic assumption of the Baal cults—that Baal is the source of the fertility of the land, with the implication of the fusion of divinity and creation—is exposed and refuted. While apostate Israel exclaims, "I will go after my lovers; they give me my bread and my water" (Hos 2:7 [ET 2:5]), God provides the reality check on who is

---

[110] Bird ("'To Play the Harlot,'" 75–94) shows how the RSV rendering of zĕnûnîm as "harlotry" is misguided, as are most commentaries on the word in this context. The reference is not to a professional harlot but to a promiscuous woman/wife: "The use of the abstract plural noun points to habitual behavior and inclination rather than profession" (p. 80).

[111] Scholarly opinion varies considerably regarding a number of issues in Hos 1–3, in particular (1) the status of Gomer when Hosea married her (does the phrase "wife of whoredom" mean that God commanded Hosea to marry someone who was already a harlot, or is another interpretation possible?); (2) the identity of the "adulteress" in Hos. 3:1–5 (is she Gomer or someone else?); and (3) the chronological order of chs. 1 and 3 (does the experience of ch. 1 occur before or after that of ch. 3?). For surveys of views and assessments of evidence, see esp. Harold H. Rowley, Men of God: Studies in Old Testament History and Prophecy (London: Nelson, 1963), 66–97; R. K. Harrison, Introduction to the Old Testament (Grand Rapids: Eerdmans, 1969), 861–68; and Francis I. Andersen and David Noel Freedman, Hosea: A New Translation with Introduction and Commentary (AB 24A; New York: Doubleday, 1989), 118–41. The available evidence leads me to conclude that (1) Gomer was already promiscuous when God told Hosea to marry her; (2) the adulteress in ch. 3 is Gomer; and (3) the experience of ch. 1 is chronologically prior to that of ch. 3. Deconstructionist studies of Hos 1–3 lie outside the focus of this book (e.g., Yvonne Sherwood, The Prostitute and the Prophet: Hosea's Marriage in Literary-Theoretical Perspective [JSOTSup 212; Sheffield, Eng.: Sheffield Academic Press, 1996]).

[112] Bird, "'To Play the Harlot,'" 89, expresses the message pointedly: "It is easy for patriarchal society to see the guilt of a 'fallen women [sic]'; Hosea says, 'You (male Israel) are that woman!'" The arguments of recent scholars who find no evidence for the existence of Baal fertility cults are unpersuasive—e.g., Alice A. Keefe, "Women, Community, and Conflict: Rethinking the Metaphor of Female Adultery in Hosea 1–2" (PhD diss., Syracuse University, 1996), who regards the Baal fertility cult and cultic prostitution as "scholarly fantasies" and chooses instead to read Hosea against a background of "structural violence in Israelite society" (abstract).

the real God of fertility: "She did not know that it was I who gave her the grain, the wine, and the oil, and who lavished upon her silver and gold that they used for Baal" (2:10 [ET 2:8]).

Sexually Related Imagery for God

What emerges as so astounding about the divine repudiation of the fertility cults in the Prophets—especially Hosea—is that God, though vehemently denouncing the cults with their false theology and sexual debauchery, does not avoid sexual language in depicting God's own dealings with Israel, as one might expect God to do. Rather, at the risk of being misunderstood, God indeed counteracts the distorted sexual theology and ritual of the Baal worship with unmistakable sexual imagery to describe the genuine relationship between God and his people.

God as Husband/Bridegroom

Elsewhere in the ANE texts, the deity never is depicted as a "husband" of, or in covenant relationship with, his people,[113] but the Bible clearly portrays Israel's God entering into covenant relationship with his people and often utilizes the imagery of a husband-wife relationship.[114] The concept of God as husband of his people is implicit already in the Torah. "Although the idea of marital love between God and Israel is not explicitly mentioned in the Pentateuch, it seems to exist there in a latent form."[115] Roy Gane describes in modern terms the spiritual marriage relationship between Yahweh and his people in the wilderness:

> After the wedding at Sinai, where God proclaimed the covenant vows (Ten Commandments) with awesome splendor, Israel said "I do," and they built a house (sanctuary) together, there was a journey through the wilderness of real life. Whatever happened, they were in it together. The vows he had given were not only for Israel to keep, they were his vows too. When he had said, "You shall have no other gods before me" (Ex. 20:3)—the equivalent of "forsaking all others"—he not only forbade polytheism, but he also pledged himself to be Israel's God.[116]

Weinfeld shows that this marital relationship is particularly evident in the references to God's "jealousy" (root $qn^>$) and Israel's "harlotry" (root znh): "The term אל קנא as well as the usage of זנה for deviation in the Pentateuch are rooted in the husband/wife metaphor."[117] David Instone-Brewer concurs: "The marriage

---

[113] See Elaine J. Adler, "The Background for the Metaphor of Covenant as Marriage in the Hebrew Bible" (PhD diss., University of California, Berkeley, 1990), passim.
[114] For an overview of these passages, see esp. Victor Armenteros, "'YHWH, el Amante': Modelos de Relación Derivados de la Simbología Matrimonial Veterotestamentaria." *DavarLogos* 3 (2004): 139–66.
[115] Moshe Weinfeld, "בְּרִית. bĕrîth," *TDOT* 2:278.
[116] Roy Gane, *Leviticus, Numbers* (NIVAC 3; Grand Rapids: Zondervan, 2004), 321.
[117] Moshe Weinfeld, "Berit—Covenant vs. Obligation," *Bib* 56 (1975): 125, note 5.

metaphor of Yahweh has very early roots, as seen in the language of jealousy in the Decalogue and other parts of the Pentateuch. The whole language of 'jealousy,' which is central to the picture of God in the Pentateuch, has the connotation of marriage."[118] Several passages in the Pentateuch have already been surveyed earlier in this chapter that employ Hebrew words from the root *znh* with reference to Israel's spiritual (numinal/marital) harlotry against God (Exod 34:15–16; Lev 17:7; 20:5–6; Num 25:1; Deut 31:16). The motif of divine jealousy (root *qn'*), implying God's status as Israel's husband, appears already at the heart of Israel's national-covenant document, the Decalogue, in the commandment prohibiting idolatry: "For I the LORD your God am a jealous God ['*ēl qannā'*]" (Exod 20:5; cf. Deut 5:9). God's marital jealousy is underscored by the double mention of this attribute in the so-called cultic Decalogue of Exod 34: "you shall worship no other god, because the LORD, whose name is Jealous [*qannā'*], is a jealous God ['*ēl qannā'*]" (v. 14). Twice in his farewell address to the Israelites, Moses warns them against spiritual (marital) unfaithfulness to their covenant God by following after idolatry:

> So be careful not to forget the covenant that the LORD your God made with you, and not to make for yourselves an idol in the form of anything that the LORD your God has forbidden you. For the LORD your God is a devouring fire, a jealous God ['*ēl qannā'*]. (Deut 4:23–24)

> Do not follow other gods, any of the gods of the peoples who are all around you, because the LORD your God, who is present with you, is a jealous God ['*ēl qannā'*] among you. The anger of the LORD your God would be kindled against you and he would destroy you from the face of the earth. (Deut 6:14–15)

Building upon these passages, Aron Balorda argues that "the divine sentiment of jealousy/zeal is the supreme marital emotion within the covenant bond"[119] and shows how the motif of divine marital jealousy is particularly highlighted in the Baal of Peor episode of Num 25, where Phinehas is represented as the only human in Scripture to reverberate with the emotion of divine jealousy, in his swift response to Israel's spiritual harlotry.[120] In this chapter the Hebrew *qn'* is employed four times, and the verbal form of this Hebrew root appears only here in the Pentateuch:

---

[118] David Instone-Brewer, *Divorce and Remarriage in the Bible: The Social and Literary Context* (Grand Rapids: Eerdmans, 2002), 34.

[119] Balorda, "Jealousy of Phinehas," 82. Cf. Gerhard von Rad, who regards God's zeal/jealousy as "the most personal of all the manifestations of his being" (*Old Testament Theology* [trans. D. M. G. Stalker; 2 vols.; New York: Harper, 1962–1965], 1:207).

[120] Balorda, "Jealousy of Phinehas," 57–69, 78–86. Gane (*Leviticus, Numbers*, 718–19) notes that the narrator, in describing the place where the Israelite tribal chief Zimri had blatantly taken the Midian woman Cozbi to have sex, utilizes a hapax legomenon for "tent," *qubbâ* (not the usual *'ōhel*), in order to play on words with the woman's impaled *qēbâ*, "stomach" (Num 25:8). "Thus Phinehas penetrates both the *qubbah* and, with his spear, her *qebah*. The punishment fits the crime" (p. 718).

Then the Lord spoke to Moses, saying, "Phinehas the son of Eleazar, the son of Aaron the priest, has turned away My wrath from the sons of Israel in that he was jealous [*bĕqanʾô, piʿel* inf. const.] with My jealousy [*ʾet qinʾātî*] among them, so that I did not destroy the sons of Israel in My jealousy [*bĕqinʾātî*]. Therefore say, 'Behold, I give him My covenant of peace; and it shall be for him and his descendants after him, a covenant of a perpetual priesthood, because he was jealous [*qinnēʾ, piʿel* pf.] for his God and made atonement for the sons of Israel'" (Num 25:10–13, NASB).[121]

One additional possible allusion to Yahweh's relationship with Israel as husband in the Pentateuch may be found in Deut 33:3: "Indeed, O favorite [*ḥābab, qal* ptc.] among peoples, all his holy ones were in your charge; they marched at your heels, accepted direction from you." This verse contains the only occurrence of *ḥābab* in the HB, a verb that in Aramaic means "love" or "make love" and here in Hebrew may contain an allusion to the intimate relationship between Yahweh and his people established at Sinai, parallel to that of a husband's love for his wife.[122]

In the Prophets,[123] a number of references present God as divine husband of Israel. Isaiah explicitly refers to God as Israel's husband: "For your Maker is your husband, the LORD of hosts is his name" (Isa 54:5); "as the bridegroom rejoices over the bride, so shall your God rejoice over you" (62:5). Other allusions to God as married to Judah come in the same context: "but you shall be called My Delight Is in Her, and your land Married; for the LORD delights in you, and your land shall be married" (62:4).

Jeremiah utilizes the marriage metaphor to describe the relationship between God and Israel. In Jer 2:2–3 God reminds Israel of its betrothal to him at the time of the exodus: "I remember the devotion of your youth, your love as a bride, how you followed me in the wilderness, in a land not sown. Israel was holy to the LORD, the first fruits of his harvest." The metaphor is continued throughout Jer 2–3 as God describes Israel's unfaithfulness to him and its harlotry (see the discussion of prostitution in ch. 7, below). The language of married love is continued later in the book of Jeremiah when God speaks of Israel as "my beloved" (*yādîd* [11:15]) and "the beloved (*yĕdidût*) of my heart" (12:7).

Ezekiel extends the divine-husband metaphor throughout a whole chapter (Ezek 16), sharpening the focus by means of explicit sexual/marital imagery, as in, e.g., v. 8: "I passed by you again and looked on you; you were at the age for

---

[121] Cf. Ps 106:31, which gives the added thought that Phinehas's intercessory intervention was "reckoned to him as righteousness from generation to generation forever"—harking back to a similar commendation of Abram for his faith in the Lord (Gen 15:6).

[122] Note that *ḥābab* is the most common term used in later rabbinic tradition for the love between husband and wife. See Michael L. Satlow, *Jewish Marriage in Antiquity* (Princeton, N.J.: Princeton University Press, 2001), 234–35.

[123] For analysis of the marriage metaphor in the Prophets as applied to Yahweh, see esp. Richtsje Abma, *Bonds of Love: Methodic Studies of Prophetic Texts with Marriage Imagery (Isaiah 50:1–3 and 54:1–10, Hosea 1–3, Jeremiah 2–3)* (Assen, Neth.: Van Gorcum, 1999) and Teresa Solà, *Jahvè, Espòs d'Israel: Poderosa Metàfora Profètica* (Barcelona: Claret, 2006).

love. I spread the edge of my cloak over you, and covered your nakedness: I pledged myself to you and entered into a covenant with you, says the Lord GOD, and you became mine." Ezekiel also continues this marital imagery in Ezek 23 as he depicts the spiritual harlotry of Judah and Israel. (See ch. 7, below.)

The most vivid portrayal of God as divine husband of Israel in the HB is found in the book of Hosea. As both husband and plaintiff in the legal proceedings against his wife, God seeks not divorce but reconciliation, not the death penalty but the end of Israel's unfaithfulness. The three "therefores" of Hos 2 display God's "steadfast love" (ḥesed, Hos 2:21 [ET 2:19]) that will not let her go. He considers restraints upon her behavior (vv. 8–10 [ET vv. 6–8]) and deprivations to bring her to her senses (vv. 11–15 [ET vv. 9–13]), then concludes with a determination to "allure her, and bring her into the wilderness, and speak tenderly to her" (v. 16 [ET v. 14]). God is like a lover wooing his beloved and leading her to where they can be alone. The promised recapitulation of the exodus is portrayed as a youthful betrothal of Israel to God. Instead of the tragedy at Achor (Josh 7:26), there will be a door of hope: God is like the bridegroom opening to his wife the door of their new home and new life.[124]

The word "respond" in Hos 2:17 (ET 2:15) ("There she shall respond as in the days of her youth") may be a technical term alluding to personal/sexual intimacy,[125] as is the word "know" in the parallel passage of Hos 13:5 ("It was I who knew you in the wilderness" [RSV]).[126] God vows to betroth Israel to Himself "forever" (2:21 [ET 2:19]) as long as they both shall live. And what a dowry of grace God promises to bestow! "I will take you for my wife in righteousness and in justice, in steadfast love, and in mercy. I will take you for my wife in faithfulness; and you shall know the LORD" (2:21–22 [ET 2:19–20]). But the restored relationship envisioned by God moves beyond the exploitive and dominative view of sexuality engendered by the cultic orgies of the fertility cults. Utilizing a wordplay in the word baʿal (which could mean either the Baal god or simply "husband") and a contrast between the two common Hebrew terms for "husband," God clarifies this advanced understanding. Israel, according to 2:18 (ET 2:16), will no longer call God baʿlî, "My Baal" (lit. "my master"), connoting dom-

---

[124] James Luther Mays, *Hosea: A Commentary* (OTL; Philadelphia: Westminster, 1969), 45.

[125] For the use of ʿānâ in the technical sense of "sexual intercourse by mutual consent" in this passage, see Deem, "The Goddess Anath," 26–27. That God is not intending to communicate literal divine-human cohabitation, however, is made clear by the use of ʿānâ for all the stages of the fertility cycle in Hos 2:23–24 (ET 2:21–22). See Mays, *Hosea,* 52–53, for further discussion. Mays shows how the wordplay involving "Jezreel" and "I [God] will sow" in 2:24–25 (ET 2:22–23) also has sexual connotations in revealing Yahweh as the true source of fertility, providing a polemic against the Canaanite fertility cult.

[126] I here retain the Hebrew yādaʿ "know" from the MT, with the RSV and many other modern versions, and do not follow the LXX and Syriac renderings with the meaning of "feed," as does the NRSV. The dominant theme of "know" and "knowledge" indicates a deep personal relationship throughout Hosea. See esp. Hos 2:22 (ET 2:20); 4:1, 6; 5:4; 6:3; 8:2; 13:4; cf. Amos 3:2, etc. See Gregory Vall, "Hosea and 'Knowledge of God,'" *TBT* 39 (2001): 335–41.

ination, possession;[127] she will call Him *ʾîšî*, "My husband" (lit. "my man"), connoting intimate, personal partnership.[128]

The characteristics of the God-Israel relationship outlined in Hos 2 also by implication apply to human husbands and wives: steadfast love, mutual compassion (suffering with the other), intimacy, and ready response.[129] "The image of God as husband, then, was used by some of the prophets [esp. Hosea] to describe the relationship between Yahweh and Israel, the relationship both as it was at the time and as it was intended to be. The image also provided a better understanding of the character of God—especially of God's faithful, forgiving, and unconditional love."[130] Throughout Hos 1–2 God speaks of his relationship with Israel—as Hosea deals with Gomer, his wayward wife, in Hos 3—"in terms of mutual response and self-giving, a life of genuine sharing, a mutual discovery in each other,"[131] concepts that certainly transcended the pattern of understanding sexuality fostered by the fertility cults. Sexuality is rescued from the land of the enemy and restored by God to its place of value and dignity and holiness as in the beginning, and at the same time, by the use of obvious metaphor, no room is left for a literalistic sexual view of divine-human cohabitation that would lead to the divinization or sacralization of sex.

God as Father

The husband/bridegroom imagery for God is not unfamiliar to us, since it has become one of the central motifs descriptive of divinity in the Judeo-Christian tradition. Equally familiar and significant is another metaphor with clear sexual elements—the representation of God as Father.[132] Contrary to a common misconception, even on the part of biblical scholars, that "the idea of God as Father is essentially a New Testament concept,"[133] the portrayal of God's fatherhood is

---

[127] See the usage of *baʿal* for "married/husband," emphasizing legal rights, in, e.g., Exod 21:3, 22; Deut 22:22; 24:4.

[128] See the usage of *ʾiš* with the more intimate personal connotation in, e.g., Gen 2:23; 3:6, 16.

[129] In reply to the charge by many feminist scholars that Hos 1–3 (along with Jer 2–3 and Ezek 16; 23) depict a divine battering husband who subjects his wife, Israel, to all manner of physical and psychological abuse, see the discussion and critique (with bibliography) in ch. 8, below.

[130] Marguerite Paolantino, "God as Husband," *TBT* 27 (1989): 303.

[131] Joseph Blenkinsopp, *Sexuality and the Christian Tradition* (Dayton, Ohio: Pflaum, 1969), 40.

[132] See esp. John W. Miller, ed., *Calling God "Father": Essays on the Bible, Fatherhood, and Culture* (2d ed.; New York: Paulist, 1999); David R. Tasker, "The Fatherhood of God: An Exegetical Study from the Hebrew Scriptures" (PhD diss., Andrews University, 2001); idem, *Ancient Near Eastern Literature and the Hebrew Scriptures about the Fatherhood of God* (StBL 69; New York: Peter Lang, 2004).

[133] Thomas McGovern, "John Paul II on the Millennium and God as Father," *Homiletical and Pastoral Review* 99, no. 7 (1999): 9. This misconception was fueled esp. by Joachim Jeremias, *The Prayers of Jesus* (trans. John Reumann; Bible Series 8; Philadelphia:

pervasive already in the HB. Eighteen OT passages explicitly mention God as Father; five refer to God's relationship to David and his dynasty, and the rest deal with the relationship of God to Israel, both corporately and in an individual sense.[134] Other passages imply God's parenthood (probably his fatherhood), as they refer to Israel as his "son" or "children."[135]

In the Hebrew canon, the Father imagery for Yahweh is first made explicit in Deuteronomy's Song of Moses:

> Is not he your father, who created you,
> who made you and established you? . . .
> You were unmindful of the Rock that bore you;
> you forgot the God who gave you birth [ḥûl]. (Deut 32:6, 18)

In 2 Sam 7:14 Yahweh promises David that Yahweh would "adopt"[136] David's son Solomon as his own: "I will be a father to him, and he shall be a son to me."[137] Three more times the Chronicler expresses the Father-son relationship between Yahweh and the Davidic king by using this exact wording (1 Chr 17:13), the reverse order ("He shall be a son to me, and I will be a father to him," 22:10), or similar phraseology ("I have chosen him to be a son to me, and I will be a father to him"; 28:6). The psalmist once portrays the Davidic king addressing God as his Father: "He shall cry to me, 'You are my Father, my God, and the Rock of my salvation'" (Ps 89:27 [ET 89:26]).

This paternal image is pressed into service by the prophets Hosea, Isaiah, and Jeremiah:

> Out of Egypt I called my son. (Hos 11:1)

> For I have become a father to Israel, and Ephraim is my firstborn. (Jer 31:9)

> And I thought you would call me, My Father, and would not turn from following me. (Jer 3:19)

Fortress, 1964), 21, who claimed that in the OT references to God's fatherhood are exclusively to a corporate relationship (except when the king was said to have a personal relationship) and that no Jew would have dared to pray individually to God as "Father." See Tasker, "The Fatherhood of God," 264, n. 3, for extensive discussion and bibliography critiquing Jeremias's still widely accepted hypothesis that Jesus introduced something absolutely new when he referred to God as ʾAbbāʾ. Cf. Tasker's briefer treatment in *Ancient Near Eastern Literature*, 114, 135.

[134] In canonical order (of the HB), these passages are Deut 32:6 (cf. 32:18); 2 Sam 7:12–14; Isa 63:16; 64:7 (ET 64:8); Jer 3:4–5, 19–20; 31:7–9; Mal 1:6; 2:10; Ps 68:5–7 (ET 68:4–6); 89:27 (ET 89:26); 103:11–14; Prov 3:11–12; 1 Chr 17:13; 22:10; 28:6; 29:10.

[135] See, e.g., the divine pronouncement to Pharaoh at the time of the exodus: "Israel is my firstborn son" (Exod 4:22). Cf. Deut 14:1; Isa 1:2; Hos 11:1–4; and Jer 31:20.

[136] See ch. 11, below, for a discussion of adoption in the ancient Near East and the HB.

[137] See Ps 2:6–7, where this divine "adoption" of the Davidic king is historically realized at his installation into royal office: "'I have set [or "installed" as in NASB and NIV; nāsak^III] my king on Zion, my holy hill.' I will tell the decree of the LORD: He said to me, 'You are my son; today I have begotten you.'"

For you are our father . . .
>   you, O LORD, are our father . . .
> Yet, O LORD, you are our Father;
>   we are the clay, and you are our potter. (Isa 63:16; 64:7 [ET 64:8])[138]

In the Psalms God is depicted as "Father of orphans and protector of widows" (Ps 68:6 [ET 68:5]), and God's compassion for his people is likened to that of a human father's: "As a father has compassion [*rāḥam,* in the *piʿel*] for his children, so the LORD has compassion [*rāḥam,* in the *piʿel*] for those who fear Him" (103:13). Finally, the wise man in Proverbs compares the Lord's loving discipline to that of a human father: "for the LORD reproves the one he loves, as a father the son in whom he delights" (Prov 3:12).

David Tasker analyzes the ANE portrayals of father deities, engages in careful exegesis of all OT passages mentioning God as Father, and presents a biblical theology of fatherhood.[139] A shorter study by John Miller briefly surveys the same material and arrives at similar conclusions as Tasker.[140] It is shown that in the ANE myths the many father deities are often characterized by their "marginality, cruelty, incompetence, and powerlessness," which "pose dilemmas to which mother, son or daughter deities must respond either by defending themselves or by taking action to uphold the universe in their stead." By contrast, only in biblical tradition is there "one God and one God only to be worshiped and served. He is the divine father, yet not cowardly or withdrawn like so many of his paternal contemporaries, but alert rather, vigorously involved and uniformly just, kind and compassionate."[141] "The basic underlying rationale of God's fatherhood is his passion for his children. The intimate concern and tireless energy he expends in his fathering role is in marked contrast to the largely self-serving detachment of the ANE father-gods, and provide a basis for his role model for human fatherhood."[142] Tasker suggests the following major attributes of God's fatherhood in Scripture: creative, personal and loving, universal, covenantal, powerful, salvific, nurturing, responsible and responsive, educational, vindicating, proactive, relational, and humanitarian.[143]

---

[138] As Tasker makes clear, even though the references to God as Father of Israel have a corporate element, they also often reveal "the possibility of an individual to form a relationship with him" ("The Fatherhood of God," 264).

[139] Tasker, "The Fatherhood of God," abbreviated in idem, *Ancient Near Eastern Literature,* passim.

[140] Miller, *Calling God "Father,"* 35–44, quote at 35.

[141] Ibid., 43.

[142] Tasker, *Ancient Near Eastern Literature,* 207; cf. idem, "The Fatherhood of God," 305.

[143] Tasker, "The Fatherhood of God," 305. Contra those who deconstruct the biblical text and find a negative portrait of divine fatherhood—e.g., Julia M. O'Brien, who argues that in the book of Malachi God's parental relationship with Judah is one of "sheer power": "In Malachi, God is a scolding father who expects reverence—fear. Priests and people have been disrespectful sons, and they must be shamed back into their proper place" ("Judah as Wife and Husband: Deconstructing Gender in Malachi," *JBL* 115 [1996]: 241–50, quotes at 242–43).

Feminine Imagery for God

Not so widely recognized or appreciated is the extent of feminine imagery for God employed in the Hebrew Scriptures.[144] Hints of this imagery are found already in the Pentateuch. Moses' questioning of God in Num 11:12 seems to portray God, by implication, as acting like a mother and nurse to Israel in the pentateuchal accounts of the exodus and the wanderings: "Did I conceive all this people? Did I give birth to them, that you should say to me, 'Carry them in your bosom, as a nurse carries a sucking child,' to the land that you promised on oath to their ancestors?"[145] It has been suggested that 11:15 (in the MT), appearing in the context of the foregoing utilization of feminine imagery, perhaps even has Moses addressing God as "you [fem.]" ("If this is the way you [fem. ʾat] are going to treat me, put me to death at once"), although this is likely a scribal error.[146]

William F. Albright, David Biale, and others have set forth evidence for the conclusion that the divine name Shaddai (šadday), usually translated "almighty," is related to the Hebrew word for "breast" (šad) and implies "the Mighty Breasted One" who nourishes and provides for his people. Albright suggested an etymological derivation from the Akkadian word šadu, "breast," and Biale has shown that each of its six occurrences in Genesis is in a context of fertility blessing or fruitfulness.[147] A more common interpretation is that Shaddai comes from another root ("mountain"?), referring to the "Almighty" God, but its consistent appearance in a context of fertility, the explicit connection with "womb" and "breasts" in Gen 49:25, and the link with other biblical metaphorical references to God "giving birth" (see esp. Deut 32:18; Isa 49:15; 66:7–9, discussed below) may favor the translation as "Mighty Breasted One."

In Gen 49:25 the clear juxtaposition of the divine name shaddai and šad, "breasts," "connotes a maternal aspect in the divine."[148] In Deut 32:13 God is described in terms of a female with breasts who "nursed" (hipʿil of yānaq) Israel, although the metaphorical intent is unmistakable inasmuch as it is "honey from

---

144 See, e.g., Leila Leah Bronner, *Stories of Biblical Mothers: Maternal Power in the Hebrew Bible* (Dallas: University Press of America, 2004), 106–21; Paul R. Smith, *Is It Okay to Call God "Mother": Considering the Feminine Face of God* (Peabody, Mass.: Hendrickson, 1993), 51–77; Leonard Swidler, *Biblical Affirmations of Woman* (Philadelphia: Westminster, 1979), 30–35; Terrien, *Till the Heart Sings,* 51–70; Phyllis Trible, "Depatriarchalizing in Biblical Interpretation," *JAAR* 41, no. 1 (1973): 32–35; idem, *God and the Rhetoric of Sexuality* (OBT; Philadelphia: Fortress, 1978), 31–59.

145 See Trible, *God and the Rhetoric of Sexuality,* 68–69.

146 The notes of *BHS* indicate a scribal error. This is likely, since the other pronouns referring to Yahweh in this same verse are masculine. If this indeed is an instance of a feminine pronoun referring to Yahweh, it would be the only one in the entire HB.

147 The six occurrences of *šadday* in Genesis are 17:1; 28:3; 35:11; 43:14; 48:3; 49:25. For further discussion, see William F. Albright, "The Names Shaddai and Abram," *JBL* 54 (1935): 180–93; David Biale, "The God with Breasts: El Shaddai in the Bible," *HR* 21 (1982): 240–56; idem, *Eros and the Jews: From Biblical Israel to Contemporary America* (New York: Basic Books, 1992), 26.

148 Trible, *God and the Rhetoric of Sexuality,* 61.

the crags" and not milk that Israel suckles from Yahweh. In v.18 of this Song of Moses, there may be a hint of both paternal and maternal imagery: the first reference to "bore" can refer to father or mother, but the Hebrew *ḥûl* literally means "writhe in birth pangs" and is elsewhere used only for a mother in labor, not a father's begetting.[149]

The maternal imagery for Yahweh is more fully developed in the Prophets, particularly in the book of Isaiah.[150] Isaiah boldly describes God as crying out like a woman in birth pangs: "For a long time I have held my peace, I have kept still and restrained myself; now I will cry out like a woman in labor, I will gasp and pant" (Isa 42:14). A few chapters later Israel is represented as borne by God, carried from the womb: "Listen to me, O house of Jacob, all the remnant of the house of Israel who have been borne by me from your birth, carried from the womb" (46:3). Again in Isa 49, God is compared to a nursing mother: "Can a woman forget her nursing child, or show no compassion for the child of her womb? Even these may forget, yet I will not forget you" (49:15). And in the final chapter of Isaiah, God likens himself to a comforting mother: "As a mother comforts her child, so I will comfort you; you shall be comforted in Jerusalem" (66:13).[151]

Phyllis Trible documents the "journey of a metaphor"—the metaphor of the womb—throughout many of these and other biblical passages[152] and points out a theological profundity in the uterus-related terms describing God's "motherly womb-love":

> Difficult to translate in the fullness of its imagery, the Hebrew noun *raḥămîm* connotes simultaneously both a mode of being and the locus of the mode. In its singular form the noun *reḥem* means "womb" or "uterus." In the plural, *raḥămîm*, this

---

[149] Ibid., 62–63; cf. Arthur E. Zannoni, "Feminine Language for God in the Hebrew Scriptures," *Dialogue and Alliance* 2, no. 3 (1988): 5.

[150] See Mayer I. Gruber, "The Motherhood of God in Second Isaiah," *RB* 90 (1983): 351–59, for analysis of the texts. I disagree, however, with with a basic premise of this article that the anonymous Deutero-Isaiah wrote this as a result of realizing the "insensitivity" of Jeremiah and Ezekiel in using only masculine imagery for God and the need to give "positive-divine value" to both masculine and feminine if one was to succeed in conveying the fact that God is above and beyond both sexes (pp. 358–59). From an evangelical perspective, I accept the eighth-century B.C.E. dating for a unified Isaiah, centuries before the writing of either Jeremiah or Ezekiel. For evidence supporting the unity and eighth-century date of the book of Isaiah, see, e.g., John Oswalt, *The Book of Isaiah Chapters 1–39* (NICOT; Grand Rapids: Eerdmans, 1986), 17–28.

[151] For analysis of the maternal allusions in these Isian passages, see esp. Gruber, "The Motherhood of God in Second Isaiah"; and Trible, *God and the Rhetoric of Sexuality*, 64–67. See Sarah J. Dille, *Mixing Metaphors: God as Mother and Father in Deutero-Isaiah* (JSOT Supp 398; Gender, Culture, Theory 13; London: T&T Clark, 2004), passim.

[152] Trible, *God and the Rhetoric of Sexuality*, 31–59. Trible's "journey of a metaphor" with the word-group *rḥm* focuses upon Jer 31:15–22 but also leads through such passages as Gen 20:1–18; 29:31–35; Deut 4:31; 1 Sam 1:1–20; 1 Kgs 3:16–28; Isa 9:17 (ET 9:16); 27:11; 46:3–4; 49:13–15; 63:7–64:12; Jer 1:5; 13:12–14; 20:14–18; Hos 2:23, 25 (ET 2:21, 23); Ps 22:9–10 (ET 22:11–12); 86:16; 103:8, 13; 111:4; 112:4; 139:13–16; 145:8; Job 10:18–19; 31:13–15; Lam 4:10; and Neh 9:17.

concrete meaning expands to the abstractions of compassion, mercy, and love. Further, these abstractions occur in a verb, *rḥm*, "to show mercy," and in an adjective, *raḥûm*, "merciful." Accordingly, our metaphor lies in the semantic movement from a physical organ of the female body to a psychic mode of being. It journeys from the concrete to the abstract. "Womb" is the vehicle; "compassion," the tenor. To the responsive imagination, this metaphor suggests the meaning of love as selfless participation in life. The womb protects and nourishes but does not possess and control. It yields its treasure in order that wholeness and well-being may happen. Truly, it is the way of compassion.[153]

In one passage, Isaiah combines both the maternal/uterine metaphor and paternal imagery—Yahweh is at once God of the womb and God the Father: "[Yahweh, . . .] where is thy zeal and thy might, the trembling of thy womb and thy compassion? [Restrain not thyself,] for thou art our Father, though Abraham does not know us and Israel does not acknowledge us; thou, O Lord, art our Father, our Redeemer from of old is thy name" (Isa 63:15–16).[154]

Although Hosea calls God husband of Israel (see above), he also records God's care of his child Israel in terms of tasks that are normally performed by a mother, not a father, in ancient Israel: "When Israel was a child, I loved him, and out of Egypt I called my son. . . . Yet it was I who taught Ephraim to walk, I took them up in my arms; but they did not know that I healed them. I led them with cords of human kindness, with bands of love, that, with them, I was to them like those who lift infants to their cheeks. I bent down to them and feed him" (Hos 11:1–4).

Trible's detailed rhetorical analysis of Jer 31:15–22 illustrates feminine/uterine imagery underlying the redemptive compassion of God. For example, Trible translates 31:20 thus:

> Is Ephraim my dear son? My darling child? For the more I speak of him, the more I do remember him. Therefore, my womb trembles for him; I will truly show motherly compassion upon him. (*Oracle of Yahweh*)[155]

The hymnic/Wisdom literature of the Writings also makes use of feminine imagery for God. In Job God's ironic rhetorical question intimates both a masculine and a feminine role in the creation: "Has the rain a father, or who has begotten the drops of dew? From whose womb did the ice come forth, and who has given birth to the hoarfrost of heaven?" (Job 38:28–29). The psalmist David depicts Yahweh in the intimate role of a midwife: "Yet it was you who took me from the womb; you kept me safe on my mother's breast. On you I was cast from my birth, and since my mother bore me you have been my God" (Ps 22:10–11 [ET 22:9–10]; cf. 71:6).[156] Again David presents the image of a motherly God who

---

[153] Ibid., 33.

[154] See ibid., 53, for this translation and evidence to support it.

[155] Ibid., 50.

[156] See L. Juliana M. Claassens, "Rupturing God-Language: The Metaphor of God as Midwife in Psalm 22," in *Engaging the Bible in a Gendered World: An Introduction to Feminist Biblical Interpretation in Honor of Katharine Doob Sakenfeld* (ed. Linda Day and Carolyn Pressler; Louisville: Westminster John Knox, 2006), 166–75.

comforts him like a weaned child, on the divine lap: "But I have calmed and quieted my soul, like a weaned child with its mother; my soul is like the weaned child that is with me" (131:2). In one of the psalms of ascent, God is likened to both master and mistress: "As the eyes of servants look to the hand of their master, as the eyes of a maid to the hand of her mistress, so our eyes look to the LORD our God, until he has mercy upon us" (123:2).

In the book of Proverbs (esp. Prov 8:12–36), "Lady" Wisdom (ḥokmâ) seems to be a hypostatization for divinity.[157] Especially impressive is the evidence that Wisdom in Proverbs assumes the very prerogatives elsewhere reserved for Yahweh alone in the HB: giver of life and death (Prov 8:35–36);[158] source of legitimate government (8:15–16);[159] the one who is to be sought after, found, and called (1:28; 8:17);[160] the one who loves and is to be loved (8:17);[161] the giver of wealth (8:18–21)[162] and security (1:33);[163] and perhaps most significantly, a source of revelation (8:6–10, 19, 32, 34; 30:3–5).[164] In 9:1 (cf. 7:6) Wisdom builds herself a temple "as befits a deity of her status."[165] It is also "quite plausible that the plural construction ḥkmwt in Prov 1:20; 9:1 . . . as a *pluralis intensitatis* may be a conscious parallel construction to ʾlhym, as has been proposed."[166]

In Prov 8:12 Wisdom uses the common rhetorical self-asseverating form of "divine self-praise" regularly reserved elsewhere in Scripture and in the ancient Near East for deity: "I am Yahweh your God," "I am Ishtar of Arbela," "I am Isis the divine."[167] For biblical parallels to this divine self-praise with the same

---

[157] For a review of the literature and a defense of this hypothesis, see Richard M. Davidson, "Proverbs 8 and the place of Christ in the Trinity," *JATS* 17 (2006): 34–43.

[158] Cf. Prov 10:27; 14:27 and throughout the biblical canon. "No one but God can say 'He who finds me finds life,' for God is the source of all life" (Elizabeth Achtemeier, *Preaching from the Old Testament* [Louisville: Westminster John Knox, 1989], 173).

[159] Cf. Num 11:16–17; 1 Sam 2:10; 10:1; 1 Kgs 3:4–15; 10:9; Ps 2:7.

[160] Cf. 2 Chr 15:2; Hos 5:6; Amos 5:4–6; 8:12; Ezek 8:18; Deut 1:45; 4:29; Judg 10:11–12; Job 35:12; Ps 22:3 (ET 22:2); 28:1; Isa 1:15; Jer 11:11, 14; 14:12; Mic 3:4; Zech 7:13.

[161] Cf. 1 Kgs 3:3; 1 Sam 2:30; 2 Sam 12:23; Neh 13:26; Isa 48:14.

[162] Cf. 1 Kgs 3:13; 1 Chr 29:12; 2 Chr 1:12; 17:5.

[163] Cf., e.g., Lev 25:18, 19; Jer 32:37.

[164] Cf. Prov 29:18; Ps 19:10 (ET 19:9); 119:1–2. "Wisdom here has become a source of revelation. . . . Such a view contradicts everything we have heretofore learned about the Old Testament, because the created world has here become a source of revelation" (Achtemeier, *Preaching from the Old Testament,* 173–74). Achtemeier points out most of these divine prerogatives assumed by Wisdom but apparently does not recognize the implication for the hypostatization of Wisdom.

[165] Michael D. Coogan, "The Goddess Wisdom—'Where Can She Be Found?'" in *Ki Baruch Hu: Ancient Near Eastern, Biblical, and Judaic Studies in Honor of Baruch A. Levine* (ed. Robert Chazan, William W. Hallo, and Lawrence H. Schiffman; Winona Lake, Ind.: Eisenbrauns, 1999), 203.

[166] Silvia Schroer, *Wisdom Has Built Her House: Studies on the Figure of Sophia in the Bible* (trans. Linda M. Maloney and William McDonough; Collegeville, Minn.: Liturgical Press, 2000), 27.

[167] This kind of self predication is also used by kings, who in some sense claim divinity or an intimate connection with the divine: "I am Azitawadda, blessed by Baal"; "I am Kilamuwa son of Hayya." For analysis of parallels with the Egyptian statements of self

grammatical structure, see, e.g., Ezek 12:25; 35:12; Zech 10:6; Mal 3:6.[168] On the basis of these precise grammatical parallels, Prov 8:12 probably should be regarded as a rhetorical form of aretalogy (i.e., divine self-praise), translated as "I am Wisdom" not "I, wisdom" (NRSV). I concur with Silvia Schroer and other experts that Wisdom here is a hypostatization of God; Wisdom "in the book of Proverbs is a divine figure" who "speaks like a deity, or like the God of Israel."[169] Such scholars have pointed out evidence of Wisdom's self-presentation as a divine being in Prov 8. "This important text about *ḥokmâ* [Prov 8:22–31] at the very beginning of creation leaves no doubt that she is a divine figure. She is not a created work, but rather was present before all created things and is an authoritative participant in the creation of the world."[170] I do not agree, however, that this divine being is presented as a goddess. As argued at length elsewhere,[171] Prov 8:30 portrays Wisdom as a male (masc.) "master craftsman" ("master worker" [NRSV]) (*ʾāmôn*) beside Yahweh at creation. The precise meaning of *ʾāmôn* is debated, but the meaning "workman/craftsman" seems the best supported by the available evidence, set forth by Cleon Rogers, III, among others.[172]

Although Rogers gives strong evidence for translating the word as "master workman," he resists applying this term to Wisdom because he contends that (1)

---

predication on the part of gods and (divine) kings, see the pioneering work of Christa Bauer-Kayatz, *Studien zu Proverbien 1–9* (WMANT 22; Neukirchen-Vluyn: Neukirchener Verlag, 1966), 76–93.

[168] Cf. Terrien, *Till the Heart Sings,* 94–95.

[169] Schroer, *Wisdom,* 27. See also, e.g., Bauer-Kayatz, *Studien,* passim; Carol A. Newsom, "Woman and the Discourse of Patriarchal Wisdom: A Study of Proverbs 1–9," in *Gender and Difference in Ancient Israel* (ed. Peggy L. Day; Minneapolis: Fortress, 1989), 157; Roger N. Whybray, *Wisdom in Proverbs* (SBT 45; Naperville, Ill.: Allenson, 1965), 98–104.

[170] Schroer, *Wisdom,* 28.

[171] See Davidson, "Proverbs 8," 44–48.

[172] See esp. Cleon L. Rogers III, "The Meaning and Significance of the Hebrew Word *ʾāmôn* in Proverbs 8,30," *ZAW* 109 (1997): 208–21; cf. Patrick W. Skehan, "Structures in Poems on Wisdom: Proverbs 8 and Sirach 24," *CBQ* 41 (1979): 365–79. There is much lexical evidence for this meaning in the OT and cognate languages, later Hebrew, and the versions. The Hebrew root occurs elsewhere in the OT as a personal name, "Ammon" (Neh 7:59; 1 Kgs 22:26; 1 Chr 3:14; 2 Chr 33:20–25; Jer 1:2; 25:3; cf. another form of the Hebrew name, "Amnon," 2 Sam 3:2; 13:1; 1 Chr 3:1; 4:20). It is used in Jer 52:15 (though disputed because of the parallel in 2 Kgs 25:11). It is probably a variation of another word, *ʾomān,* which in Song 7:1 clearly means "artist" ("master hand," NRSV). This word probably is found in Phoenician (YMMANAI) as a stamp on a brick, and it clearly appears in Aramaic and Northwest Semitic with the meaning of "architect." It is also clearly attested in Akkadian, probably related to *ummānu,* "workman"—designating a particular class of skilled experts (musicians, skilled craftsmen, sages or scholars). The word is also found in later Hebrew with the meaning "craftsman," and it is clear that the rabbis understood the meaning in Prov 8:30 to be "architect." Versional support for this meaning appears in several Greek versions, the Vulgate, and the Syriac. The MT pointing understood the word to mean "craftsman." So also does the allusion to this text in the Wisdom of Solomon (7:21). Such meaning is also supported by the context in Prov 8, in which the emphasis has been upon the orderly building and craftsmanship in creation. Compare the words "make" (v. 26), "establish" (v. 27), and "foundation" (v. 29).

the motif of co-Creator does not seem applicable to Wisdom and (2) the term ʾāmôn is masculine and, since the antecedent of a word in Hebrew is generally the same gender, one would expect a feminine form of ʾāmôn here. But these obstacles need not cause the interpreter to look for a rare (and in my view improbable) grammatical construction ("accusative of state") to explain the difficulties, as Rogers does. Instead, at least from the perspective of an evangelical Christian, the very dissonances that Rogers points out may be taken as internal textual indicators that Wisdom is here hypostatized and ultimately refers to another person within the Godhead. When Wisdom is interpreted as hypostatization for the Son of God (as was assumed in the christological debates of the early church and throughout most of church history until most recently),[173] the grammatical and contextual difficulties disappear: the Son (masc. in gender indicated by the masc. "master workman") is co-Creator with Yahweh,[174] "rejoicing [měśaḥeqet, lit. 'playing, sporting, laughing'] before him always" (Prov 8:30) and mediating between divinity and humanity (v. 31).[175]

Regardless of one's interpretation of the referent in this passage, however, ultimately one cannot say that Wisdom in Prov 1–9 is either male or female in gender. Francoise Mies presents a fascinating thesis:

> Personified Wisdom in Pr 9 is [widely] considered as a feminine figure. This interpretation is nevertheless corroborated neither by the study of this chapter nor by the analysis of the other passages of the book presenting Personified Wisdom (1,20–33; 8), or of the first seven chapters in which the sexual and gendering atmosphere is nevertheless emphasized. However, Wisdom is not masculine. As God, it exceeds all sexual activity.[176]

---

[173] For the history of interpretation, see Davidson, "Proverbs 8," 34–43.

[174] This inner-textual hint is reinforced in Prov 30:4 (with the allusion to Father and Son co-Creators) and interpreted thus in the NT (1 Cor 1:24, 30; Col 2:2). The language in Prov 8:22–24 for Wisdom's having been "set up" and "brought forth" before the creation of this world is illuminated by parallel language (including the only other biblical occurrence of the Hebrew word nāsakIII, "set") in Ps 2:6–7, where Yahweh installs the messianic king by using the language of birth (= adoption). Thus, from the perspective of a Christian evangelical scholar, I suggest a christological interpretation: the text is not speaking of a time before which Wisdom (the preincarnate Christ) did not exist, but rather seems to refer to the time of his installment into his office of sonship (at the commencement of creation), functioning as the Word or "Mediator" between an infinite God and finite creatures. For further discussion, see Davidson, "Proverbs 8," 44–54.

[175] Many scholars who probably would not accept the christological interpretation proposed here nonetheless see clear evidence of the mediatorial work of this divine figure in Prov 8. See, e.g., Gale Yee: "The whole poem builds structurally to portray Wisdom as the ultimate mediator between God and humanity" ("An Analysis of Prov 8:22–31 according to Style and Structure," ZAW 94 [1982]: 64–65). Cf. Frymer-Kensky, In the Wake of the Goddesses, 181; Samuel Terrien, The Elusive Presence: The Heart of Biblical Theology (San Francisco: Harper & Row, 1978), 355; Shirley Wurst, "Woman Wisdom's Ways: Ecokinship," in The Earth Story in Wisdom Traditions (ed. Norman C. Habel and Shirley Wurst; Earth Bible 3; Cleveland: Pilgrim, 2001), 59.

[176] Françoise Mies, "'Dame Sagesse' en Proverbes 9: Une personification féminine?" RB 108 (2001): 161–83, quote from English abstract, 161.

Mies is indeed correct in pointing out that aside from the feminine gender of the word *ḥokmâ,* "wisdom" (and here there is no choice in the Hebrew language, for the word *ḥokmâ* is invariably feminine in gender and pronouns that refer to *ḥokmâ* must necessarily be feminine), there is simply no indication in the context that Wisdom is to be taken as a feminine figure. Rather, Wisdom as a divine being is presented in a neutral way, beyond the polarity of sexuality.[177] This conclusion has implications for the vigorously debated topic of the "gender" of God as presented in Scripture.

Is God Male or Female?

In recent debate over the gender of the biblical God, Stanley Grenz catalogues at least four different proposals for dealing with the gendered imagery applied to God in Scripture.[178] A first proposal—to use Grenz's nomenclature—*demythologizes* the imagery, declaring that the sexual-related imagery for God utilized by the Bible writers is all anthropomorphic and thus God is beyond the polarity of sex and, in fact, decidedly nonsexual.[179] A second position *literalizes* the imagery and regards the God of the Bible as inherently gendered. This has often led to the conclusion that God is masculine and sometimes even to the further conclusion that God is in actual fact male.[180] A third proposal

---

[177] Mies points out that unlike references to Lady Folly, which repeatedly use the Hebrew word for "woman" (Prov 9:13; 11:16; 12:4), no reference to "the woman Wisdom" appears. There is thus an asymmetry between Folly and Wisdom. Folly is clearly depicted as a woman, but no uniquely feminine activities are described for Wisdom ("'Dame Sagesse' en Proverbes 9," 166–71). In Prov 8 Wisdom speaks in the first person, so that one cannot discern any difference between masculine and feminine grammatically (p. 172). Regarding the contention by many scholars that Wisdom erotically "seduces" her hearers in a sexual context with her use of the word "love," Mies points out that the term "love" throughout the Bible, and in Proverbs in particular, is an expression of polysemy and often does not refer to erotic love (173–74).

This description precisely fits the second Person of the Godhead. Although female imagery is utilized of Yahweh in the HB and Yahweh is denoted by the masculine "he," ultimately Yahweh is presented as beyond the polarity of sexuality.

[178] Stanley J. Grenz, "Is God Sexual? Human Embodiment and the Christian Conception of God," in *This Is My Name Forever: The Trinity and Gender Language for God* (ed. Alvin F. Kimel Jr.; Downers Grove, Ill.: InterVarsity, 2001), 196–208.

[179] E.g., Blenkinsopp, 24–27; Tikva Frymer-Kensky, "Law and Philosophy: The Case of Sex in the Bible," *Semeia* 45 (1989): 90–91; Pamela J. Scalise, "Women in Ministry: Reclaiming Our Old Testament Heritage," *RevExp* 83, no. 1 (1986): 8.

[180] For a defense of the common "traditionalist" position that God is (grammatically) "masculine" but not "male," see, e.g., Paul Mankowski, "The Gender of Israel's God," in *This Is My Name Forever: The Trinity and Gender Language for God* (ed. Alvin F. Kimel Jr.; Downers Grove, Ill.: InterVarsity, 2001), 35–61; and Donald D. Hook and Alvin F. Kimel Jr., "The Pronouns of Deity: A Theolinguistic Critique of Feminist Proposals," in *This Is My Name Forever: The Trinity and Gender Language for God* (ed. Alvin F. Kimel Jr.; Downers Grove, Ill.: InterVarsity, 2001), 62–87. Feminist theologians often take this position as implying that the biblical God is in actual fact male; and the now famous dictum of Mary Daly castigating biblical patriarchy ensues: "If God is male, then the male is god" (*Beyond God the Father: Toward a Philosophy of Women's Liberation* [Boston: Beacon, 1973], 19).

compartmentalizes the divine, ascribing the masculine attributes to the Father and Son and the feminine attributes to the Spirit (or alternatively to the Son).[181] A fourth proposal, suggested by some feminist theologians, *reimages* the divine into a composite feminine image of the deity, either by returning to what is regarded as the most ancient image of the divine in the female "Primal Matrix"[182] or by reconceptualizing the Trinity in light of the wisdom portrayal of a female Spirit-Sophia.[183]

The third and fourth proposals are, however, incompatible with the biblical data as well as with ANE background materials. Regarding the third proposal, the biblical texts of the OT (and more so the NT) do not allow the compartmentalization of the feminine dimension of God in the Spirit (or in the coming messianic Son). The same Yahweh who reveals the compassionate, mothering attributes usually associated with the feminine is often in the same breath revealed as the Father of his people.[184] Regarding the fourth proposal, recent attempts to find an original "Primal Matrix" or "Great Mother" in prehistoric times have not been successful.[185] Within the biblical materials, as surveyed in this chapter, Wisdom (Sophia) is not presented as a female deity, and no other evidence exists to support such a reimaging of the divine.

From a survey of biblical materials utilizing male and female imagery for God, there is no implication that God is ontologically (in essential being) either male or female. As in the Genesis creation accounts and consistently throughout Scripture, the Hebrew deity is above the polarity of sexuality. Although humankind is made in the image of God and participates in the "dynamic that characterizes the social Trinity (unity-in-diversity, mutuality of distinct

---

[181] For a focus on the Spirit as representative of the feminine dimension, see Joan Chamberlain Engelsman, *The Feminine Dimension of the Divine* (Philadelphia: Westminster, 1979), 152 and passim. For the suggestion that the Son is the bearer of the feminine dimension, see Margaret Farley, "New Patterns of Relationship: Beginnings of a Moral Revolution," *TS* 36 (1975): 641–43.

[182] See Rosemary Radford Ruether, *Sexism and God-Talk: Toward a Feminist Theology* (Boston: Beacon, 1983), 67–71.

[183] See Elizabeth A. Johnson, *She Who Is: The Mystery of God in Feminist Theological Discourse* (New York: Crossroad, 1992), 213–14.

[184] See Frymer-Kensky, *In the Wake of the Goddesses*, 164: "We normally think of the father as punitive and the mother as compassionate, and tend to label those passages in which God expresses compassion as 'mother passages,' and those in which God pronounces judgment or announces punishment as 'father passages.' The biblical text itself, however, makes no such division, and God-as-parent transcends our own gendered thinking about parental roles. The same parent is both judgmental and compassionate, punitive and emotional."

[185] For such an attempt, see, e.g., Merlin Stone, *When God Was a Woman* (San Diego: Harcourt Brace Jovanovich, 1978); and Monica Sjöö and Barbara Mor, *The Great Cosmic Mother: Rediscovering the Religion of the Earth* (San Francisco: Harper & Row, 1987). For a critique of the hypothesis of an original "Great Mother" in prehistoric times, see Gary M. Beckman, "Goddess Worship—Ancient and Modern," in *"A Wise and Discerning Mind": Essays in Honor of Burke O. Long* (ed. Saul M. Olyan and Robert C. Culley; BJS 325; Providence: Brown Judaic Studies, 2000), 11–23.

persons, the interaction of sameness and difference)"[186]—at the same time sexuality is part of the structure of creation, and God is totally "other" than all creation. Yahweh is never in Scripture described with genitals, in contrast to the explicit sexual references to the genitals of other ANE deities. Instead of infusing fertility into the earth as with the fertility cult deities, God gave fertility to the earth at creation and continues to bless his creatures with the gifts of fertility, quite apart from any sexual cohabitation among the deities. In the HB, God is never presented as a male god with a female consort at his side. This concurs with the first proposal outlined by Grenz.

At the same time, there is a clear distinction in the OT between the masculine and the feminine language used for God. "The prophets and other Hebrew poets ascribed to Yahweh the moral characteristics of human motherhood, but they never deified the feminine reality. It is this radical distinction that has escaped the notice of most anthropologists and psychologists who have written in modern times on the 'gender of God' in the literature of the Bible."[187] It is crucial to note that (apart from the special case of the hypostatization of Wisdom in Prov 8, discussed above) the feminine imagery for God used in Scripture is invariably in the form of simile (God is *like*) and not metaphor (God *is*).[188] Various aspects of God's activity (such as God's "crying out") are compared to aspects of woman's activity (such her "crying out" in child birth), but God's being is not metaphorically identified with that of a woman. God is *like* a mother but *is* a Father.[189] Consistently throughout Scripture, masculine metaphorical language is used for expressing the nature of God. Feminine imagery used for God does not break the consistent pattern that all gender designations (pronouns and pronominal suf-

---

[186] Grenz, "Is God Sexual?" 212. This harks back to the nature of the image of God according to Gen 1:26–28, discussed in ch. 1, above.

[187] Terrien, *Till the Heart Sings*, 62. Terrien (p. 51) reviews the fundamental difference between Israel and her neighbors regarding sexuality and divinity:

> The religion of ancient Israel differed from the other religions of the classical Near East and Mediterranean antiquity in several aspects, the chief of which was its affirmation of divine transcendence over nature. The Yahwists, the psalmists, the prophets and the sages never identified their God with nature. This is the reason for which they never thought in terms of divine sexuality. God for them was neither male nor female. . . . They were not afraid of human sexuality, but they knew that sexuality could not be a mode of communion with the divine.

> At the same time, the religious language of ancient Israel was derived, of course, from human experience. Therefore, it ascribed to God feminine as well as masculine characteristics.

[188] The representation of divinity by Wisdom in Prov 1–9 is not metaphor but hypostatization and does not contradict the overall biblical pattern. See above and Davidson, "Proverbs 8," passim, for further discussion.

[189] Tasker, "The Fatherhood of God," 238–69; idem, *Ancient Near Eastern Literature,* 173–90. This is not to say that in all aspects the heavenly Father is like an earthly father; for a discussion of what the fatherhood of God teaches us about humanity and the human father-son relationship, see Tasker, "The Fatherhood of God," 269–84; idem, *Ancient Near Eastern Literature,* 191–200.

fixes, adjectives, and verbs) identify God grammatically as masculine.[190] To be consistent with the lead of OT data, it does not appear appropriate to substitute gender-neutral language for God[191] except where the Hebrew terms are intended to express such gender neutrality.[192] On this point I agree with the second proposal categorized by Grenz.

Elizabeth Achtemeier offers a penetrating, plausible, and at least partial explanation of why God defines himself in masculine metaphor and not feminine, in contrast to the other religions of the ancient Near East, where there are both male and female deities. It is not because of the cultural patriarchy of the Bible—as is made clear by the revelation of God in the male Jesus Christ. Instead, Achtemeier argues, it is to minimize the risk of the Creator being identified with creation as in the other ANE religions:

> The basic reason for that designation of God [as masculine] is that the God of the Bible will not let himself be identified with his creation. . . . If God is portrayed in feminine language, the figures of carrying in the womb, of giving birth, and of suckling immediately come into play. . . . A feminine goddess has given birth to the world! But if the creation has issued forth from the body of the deity, it shares in deity's substance; deity is in, through, and under all things, and therefore everything is divine. . . . If God is identified with his creation, we finally make ourselves gods and goddesses—the ultimate primeval sin (Gen. 3).[193]

To the argument by feminists that calling God "she" need not lead to such identification of creation with Creator, Achtemeier points out that "that identification

---

[190] Albert Wolters, "Cross-Gender Imagery in the Bible," *BBR* 8 (1998): 217–28, demonstrates that "in the biblical languages there is a consistent correlation between the masculine and feminine of grammatical gender and the natural gender of persons" (219) and that cross-gender imagery does not affect this correlation. This is true also regarding God: "Masculine gender designators referring to God number in the hundreds of thousands [in the OT and NT], while there is a complete absence of feminine gender designators for God. Grammatically, the God of the Bible is consistently treated as a masculine person" (pp. 224–25). One apparent exception may be Num 11:15, where in the MT Moses uses the second-person singular feminine pronoun to address God when he passionately declares, "If You [fem.] treat me like this, please kill me here and now." But as noted above, the pronominal suffix for God, "*your* sight," in the same verse is masculine, and in the Samaritan text the masculine form appears consistently throughout this verse; thus this one occurrence of the feminine form in the MT is likely a scribal error, as suggested in the notes to *BHS*.

[191] See Hook and Kimel, "The Pronouns of Deity," 62–87; *pace* Smith, *Is It Okay to Call God "Mother,"* passim.

[192] On this point I disagree with Vern S. Poythress and Wayne A. Grudem, *The Gender-Neutral Bible Controversy: Muting the Masculinity of God's Words* (Nashville: Broadman & Holman, 2000), 233–89, who insist on retaining, e.g., the translation "man" for such terms as ʾādām, which elsewhere in Scripture never indicates the male gender but refers to "human being" or "humanity" in general—including both women and men. See esp. David J. A. Clines, "אדם, the Hebrew for 'Human, Humanity': A Response to James Barr," *VT* 53 (2003): 297–310.

[193] Elizabeth Achtemeier, "Why God Is Not Mother: A Response to Feminist God-Talk in the Church," *ChT* 37, no. 9 (1993): 20.

almost automatically comes about when feminine language for God is used. Many feminists argue that that does not necessarily happen. But feminist writings demonstrate it does."[194]

Against Achtemeier's suggestion, it has further been argued that designating the biblical Creator with masculine metaphors can lead to the sacralization and divinization of sex just as much as with feminine metaphors, since in the ANE fertility religions the male deities are just as sexually active as the female ones. Why did God not choose to be designated exclusively as "she" (fem. pronouns and metaphors) and not "he" (masc. pronouns and metaphors)? Although the Bible does not clearly spell out the answer to this question, it appears that Achtemeier is on the right track in suggesting that the danger is greater for the exclusive identification of Yahweh with a goddess to lead to the sacralization/ divinization than identification of Yahweh as a male deity, since the linkage of sexuality and the whole birth process with a female (goddess) seems to be more automatic than the linkage with a male (god). Frymer-Kensky makes this point regarding Sumerian civilization, which also applies throughout the polytheistic ancient Near East:

> The males have nature roles not dependant upon anatomy; for females, their power in nature is defined by sex. The goddesses are in control of the processes of reproduction, fertility, and sexuality. These are anatomical functions, seen as the quintessence and defining characteristic of "female." Society associates the female, whether human woman or goddess, with sex, reproduction, and fertility. In all these, it is the body, particularly the vagina, that performs the functions that only a female can do.[195]

It is opposition to the identification of creation and Creator that lies at the heart of the OT rejection of the Canaanite fertility cults with their sacralization and divinization of sexuality. In its radical opposition to any notion that blurs the distinction between the Creator and his creation, the OT avoids identifying God as feminine in such a way that might open the door to any such error. At the same time, although Scripture identifies the one true God as "he," the biblical material makes clear that the masculine does not exhaust the divine reality. In fact, Yahweh is above the polarity of sexuality and is neither male nor female, and displays within his nature both masculine and feminine dimensions.

The Fertility Cults and Divine Grace

The OT unambiguously, vehemently, and uncompromisingly opposes the sacralization and divinization of sex that appear in fertility cult theology and practice.[196] God's just judgment against such practices is also unmistakable.

---

[194] Ibid., 22.

[195] Frymer-Kensky, *In the Wake of the Goddesses,* 47.

[196] The end of each chapter in section 2 includes a discussion of divine grace as it relates to the various distortions of God's ideal for human sexuality. For a penetrating

Though upholding a consistent picture of divine revulsion and abhorrence at the ritual sex of the pagan cults, the OT at the same time upholds a poignant portrait of divine grace regarding the participants in these degrading rites.[197] For four hundred years, God withholds judgment against the inhabitants of Canaan (Gen 15:16), providing them a time for repentance and witnesses to the truth about God through Abraham and his descendants, Melchizedek, Balaam, and the reports of the forty years of God's miraculous deliverance of Israel at the exodus and in the wilderness.

During the conquest of Canaan, those like Rahab and the Gibeonites who forsook their pagan practices (which well may have included fertility cult rituals) were embraced within the covenant community. Even God's eventual destruction of the Canaanites may be viewed as an act of divine mercy as well as justice. Those who had participated in the most degrading rites imaginable had become unable to respond to the promptings of God's spirit: the cup of their iniquity was full (Gen 15:16), and God in his mercy as well as justice brought to an end the degrading cultic sexual orgies and cruel practices such as child sacrifice.

When Israel "ran wild" in the fertility cult orgies at Mt. Sinai (Exod 32:25), the ones who repented of their activity and took their stand for God were spared, and God forgave their sin (Exod 34). Amazingly, Aaron, the one who oversaw the whole enterprise of building the golden calf, who "had let them run wild, to the derision of their enemies" (32:25), after his repentance was not only forgiven but, by the superabundant grace of God, appointed high priest over Israel (Exod 28, 39).

During the period of the judges, as Israel repeatedly fell back into fertility cult worship, God brought judgments but still condescended to patiently work with his people. The same was true for the period of the monarchy. On Mt. Carmel (1 Kgs 18) at the showdown between Baal and Yahweh, the general populace who had been active participants in the Baal cult watched as the fire descended upon the sacrificial animal instead of on them, who deserved the punishment. God sent prophet after prophet, pleading with the kings and the people to turn from the worship of Baal, Asherah, and the other false gods, and there was occasion for rejoicing (one can imagine in heaven as well as on earth) when such leaders as Asa, Elijah, Jehoshaphat, Jehu, Jehoiada, Hezekiah, and Josiah instituted reforms aimed at eliminating the fertility cult worship in Israel/Judah.

It appears, however, that these reforms were short-lived and superficial, and ultimately God's people refused to respond to divine appeals. The last chapter of the HB summarizes the tragic reaction to God's grace:

> The LORD, the God of their ancestors, sent persistently to them by his messengers, because he had compassion on his people and on his dwelling place; but they kept

---

defense of the thesis that "the hermeneutics of grace" lies at the heart of the OT's "single plot," see esp. J. Clinton McCann Jr., "The Hermeneutics of Grace: Discerning the Bible's 'Single Plot,'" *Int* 57 (2003): 9–15.

[197] For a general orientation to divine grace in the OT, see esp. Jon Dybdahl, *Old Testament Grace* (Boise, Idaho: Pacific, 1990); and Ronald M. Hals, *Grace and Faith in the Old Testament* (Minneapolis: Augsburg, 1980).

mocking the messengers of God, despising his words, and scoffing at his prophets, until the wrath of the LORD against his people became so great that there was no remedy. (2 Chr 36:15–16)

Judah was taken into the Babylonian captivity. Yet even then the grace of God was not withdrawn. God brought his people back home, effectively healed, it seems, from their proclivity to fertility cult worship.[198] Although other temptations still assaulted and overwhelmed them, the empowering divine grace had triumphed in Israel against the divinization and sacralization of sex.

Such triumph was short lived, however, for, as noted in the afterword, below, the various syncretistic religions of the NT milieu included the divinization of sex. Today there is a new movement within radical feminism toward the revival of goddess worship entailing the deification of the female and the the divinization of sex.[199] Such a revival of ancient goddess worship must reckon with the divine condemnation of such worship in OT times, and at the same time those who follow this road are also offered the same forgiving and empowering divine grace when they again choose to embrace the biblical worldview regarding the relationship between sexuality and the divine.

---

[198] The canonical biblical books explicitly identified with the postexilic period give no evidence of problems with idolatry. See Paul E. Dion, "Did Cultic Prostitution Fall into Oblivion during the Postexilic Era? Some Evidence from Chronicles and the Septuagint," *CBQ* 43 (1981): 41–48. Ephraim Stern surveys the archaeological evidence and shows that fertility cult figurines no longer appear in the strata of Israelite sites dating to postexilic times: "In the Persian period (the postexilic period), we find a very strange phenomenon: In the areas of the country occupied by Jews, *not a single cult figurine* has been found! This is despite the many excavations, as well as surveys, that have been conducted in Judea, and, to a somewhat lesser extent, in Samaria. This sharply contrasts with earlier periods, when it was impossible to distinguish between Israelite and pagan areas on the basis of the presence or absence of cult figurines" ("What Happened to the Cult Figurines? Israelite Religion Purged after the Exile," *BAR* 15, no. 4 [1989]: 22–29, 53–54).

[199] See, e.g., Denise Lardner Carmody, *Feminism and Christianity: A Two-Way Reflection* (Nashville: Abingdon, 1982); Carol P. Christ, *Rebirth of the Goddess: Finding Meaning in Feminist Spirituality* (Reading, Mass.: Addison-Wesley, 1997); idem, *She Who Changes: Re-imagining the Divine in the World* (New York: Palgrave Macmillan, 2003); Naomi Goldenberg, *Changing of the Gods: Feminism and the End of Traditional Religions* (Boston: Beacon, 1979); Grace M. Jantzen, *Becoming Divine: Towards a Feminist Philosophy of Religion* (Bloomington: Indiana University Press, 1999); Virginia Ramey Mollenkott, *Godding: Human Responsibility and the Bible* (New York: Crossroad, 1988); Rosemary Radford Ruether, *Woman-Church: Theology and Practice of Feminist Liturgical Communities* (San Francisco: Harper & Row, 1985). For a survey and critique of the entire "goddess movement" and modern feminist writings that have taken this road, see esp. Jo Ann Davidson, "Modern Feminism, Religious Pluralism, and Scripture," *JATS* 10, nos. 1–2 (1999): 401–40; Daniel R. Heimbach, *True Sexual Morality: Recovering Biblical Standards for a Culture in Crisis* (Wheaton, Ill.: Crossway, 2004), 51–88, 297–310; idem, *Pagan Sexuality: At the Center of the Contemporary Moral Crisis* (Wake Forest, N.C.: Southeastern Baptist Theological Seminary Press, 2001); Mary A. Kassian, *The Feminist Gospel: The Movement to Unite Feminism with the Church* (Wheaton, Ill.: Crossway, 1992), 135–248; and Aída Besançon Spencer with Donna F. G. Hailson, Catherine Clark Kroeger, and William D. Spencer, *The Goddess Revival* (Grand Rapids: Baker, 1995).

4

Human Heterosexuality versus Homosexuality, Transvestism, and Bestiality

The Divine Design

Human sexuality according to the Edenic divine paradigm finds expression in a *heterosexual* relationship. This creation pattern of heterosexual human relationships remained the norm throughout the canonical OT Scriptures. As will become apparent in this chapter, the biblical writers portray negatively any deviation from this assumed heterosexual norm. Distortions of the creation norm regarding the heterosexual aspect of human sexual relationships include, in particular, practices connected with homosexuality, transvestism, and bestiality.[1]

---

[1] For a comprehensive survey delineating the spectrum of Christian views (and their representative advocates) on homosexuality, see esp. L. R. Holben, *What Christians Think about Homosexuality: Six Representative Viewpoints* (North Richland Hill, Tex.: Bibal, 1999). I differentiate here between homosexuality as an orientation (propensity, inclination, condition, disposition) and homosexual practice; I do not enter the debate over whether the orientation is inherited or acquired, since no Scripture passage addresses this point. As argued below, the OT condemns homosexual practice and the harboring of homosexual lustful thoughts. Homosexuality as a condition is clearly a sexual disorder, a distortion of the Edenic ideal, but Scripture contains no culpability for homosexual orientation per se, just as it contains no condemnation of natural fallen tendencies and temptations to heterosexual lust if these are not harbored or acted upon. As a pastoral aside, I do not doubt the power of God to bring about a total transformation of both practice and orientation, as sometimes occurs (see the documentation in Stanton L. Jones and Mark A. Yarhouse, *Homosexuality: The Use of Scientific Research in the Church's Moral Debate* [Downers Grove, Ill.: InterVarsity, 2000], 117–51). But just as some people quit smoking and never again have the urge to smoke whereas others quit smoking yet battle the urge all their lives, so some homosexuals have a miraculous change of orientation, and others may have to battle homosexual tendencies all their lives. The culpability is not in the tendencies but in the acting upon (either in imagination or actual practice) those tendencies. For a similar distinction between practice and orientation, see Robert A. J. Gagnon, *The Bible and Homosexual Practice: Texts and Hermeneutics* (Nashville: Abingdon, 2001), 37–38; cf. Thomas E. Schmidt, *Straight and Narrow? Compassion and Clarity in the Homosexuality Debate* (Downers Grove, Ill.: InterVarsity, 1995), 164–65; and

The following pages focus attention on OT passages that refer (or allegedly refer) to these practices, placed in the context of their ANE background and with a view toward assessing the continuing validity of the OT witness regarding these practices for today.

Homosexual Practice

Ancient Near Eastern Background

Mesopotamia. Data regarding ANE attitudes toward homosexuality come largely from Mesopotamian sources.[2] None of the early law codes of Mesopotamia (Urukagina, Ur-Nammu, Eshnunna, and Hammurabi), however, deal with homosexual activity.[3] Only the Middle Assyrian Laws (late second millennium B.C.E.) mention homosexual practice. MAL A §19 refers to a man of aristocratic status, guilty of slandering another man of his same status by charging that the man had repeatedly been penetrated by other men:

> If a man furtively spreads rumors about his comrade, saying, "Everyone sodomizes [lit. 'has sex with'] him," or in a quarrel in public says to him, "Everyone sodomizes you," and further, "I can prove the charges against you," but he is unable to prove the charges and does not prove the charges, they shall strike that man 50 blows with rods; he shall perform the king's service for one full month; they shall cut off his hair; moreover, he shall pay 3,600 shekels of lead.[4]

Stanley J. Grenz, *Welcoming but Not Affirming: An Evangelical Response to Homosexuality* (Louisville: Westminster John Knox, 1998), 119–25.

[2] For further discussion of the ANE background, see esp. Phyllis A. Bird, "The Bible in Christian Ethical Deliberation concerning Homosexuality: Old Testament Contributions," in *Homosexuality, Science, and the "Plain Sense" of Scripture* (ed. David L. Balch; Grand Rapids: Eerdmans, 2000), 173–76; J. Bottéro and H. Petschow, "Homosexualität," *RLA* 4:459–68; Gagnon, *The Bible and Homosexual Practice*, 44–56; David F. Greenberg, *The Construction of Homosexuality* (Chicago: University of Chicago Press, 1988), 124–35; Harry A. Hoffner Jr., "Incest, Sodomy, and Bestiality in the Ancient Near East," in *Orient and Occident: Essays Presented to Cyrus H. Gordon on the Occasion of His Sixty-Fifth Birthday* (ed. Harry A. Hoffner Jr.; AOAT 22; Neukirchen-Vluyn: Neukirchener Verlag, 1973), 81–90; Martti Nissinen, *Homoeroticism in the Biblical World: A Historical Perspective* (trans. Kirsi Stjerna; Minneapolis: Fortress, 1998), 19–36, 144–52 (notes); Ronald M. Springett, *Homosexuality in History and the Scripture: Some Historical and Biblical Perspectives on Homosexuality* (Washington, D.C.: Biblical Research Institute, 1988), 33–48; and Donald J. Wold, *Out of Order: Homosexuality in the Bible and the Ancient Near East* (Grand Rapids: Baker, 1998), 43–61.

[3] One possible reference to homosexuality in these earlier law codes is a provision regarding palace attendants (eunuchs) in CH §187 ("The Laws of Hammurabi," translated by Martha Roth [*COS* 2.131:347; cf. *ANET* 174]): "A child of (i.e., reared by) a courtier who is a palace attendant or a child of (i.e., reared by) a *sekretu* [votary] will not be reclaimed." But even here it is not certain that these palace eunuchs engaged in homosexual practice.

[4] "The Middle Assyrian Laws," translated by Martha Roth (*COS* 2.132:355; cf. *ANET* 181).

This law seems to imply that it was regarded as shameful and degrading in Assyrian society for a man to be penetrated by another man as if he were a woman, whether or not the penetration was voluntary on the part of the one being penetrated. "To be routinely penetrated by other men was to be treated as a 'man-woman' and hence made inferior in honor and status to those doing the penetrating. . . . There was something wrong or strange about *any* man who wanted to be penetrated as if he were a woman."[5] Scholars generally agree that this law does not deal with a case of homosexual rape; the iterative "lain repeatedly" best fits a context of consensual homosexual relationships.

MAL A §20 directly addresses homosexual activity: "If a man sodomizes his comrade and they prove the charges against him and find him guilty, they shall sodomize him and they shall turn him into a eunuch."[6] Many scholars interpret this law as referring only to a situation of homosexual rape, with the implication from the penalty that "a man who played the female role in male-male intercourse lost his manhood. A man who attempted to deprive another man of his manhood, without the latter's consent, would himself be deprived of manhood through castration."[7] David Greenberg argues that "the voice of the verb *na-ku* in this passage implies the use of force. . . . Were the passage to refer to consensual homosexuality, the penalty would make no sense; referring to coercion, it follows the pattern of analogic penalties common to ancient law: 'an eye for an eye,' 'a rape for a rape.'"[8] The fact that the penalty is only applicable to the man who played the dominant (male) role also has been regarded as implying force on the part of the penetrating sexual partner.

Donald Wold, however, counters the interpretation of rape by pointing out that the Akkadian word *nâku* in fact does not imply force; it is the term used for sexual intercourse of various kinds but does not mean "to rape."[9] W. G. Lambert adds that if rape were intended here, the adverb *emūqamma*, "by force," would have been added, as it was in the reference to heterosexual rape in §16.[10] Thus homosexual practice itself is being proscribed, not just homosexual rape. All acts of anal homosexual intercourse are prohibited: "According to this Middle Assyrian law, homosexual conduct is illicit."

Wold further points out that the stiff penalty of *lex talionis* ("eye for an eye") indeed makes sense in this law as applying to consensual homosexuality:

---

[5] Gagnon, *The Bible and Homosexual Practice,* 46.

[6] *COS* 2.132:355; cf. *ANET* 181.

[7] Gagnon, *The Bible and Homosexual Practice,* 55.

[8] Greenberg, *The Construction of Homosexuality,* 126.

[9] Wold, *Out of Order,* 45, citing *CAD* N 1:197, where one finds listed such meanings as "to have illicit sexual intercourse, to fornicate, to have illicit intercourse repeatedly, to permit intercourse," but not "to rape."

[10] See Wilfried G. Lambert, "Prostitution," in *Aussenseiter und Randgruppen: Beiträge zu einer Sozialgeschichte des alten Orients* (ed. Volkert Haas; Xenia: Konstanzer althistorische Vorträge und Forschungen 32; Constance: Universitätsverlag, 1992), 146; cf. Jerrold S. Cooper, "Buddies in Babylonia: Gilgamesh, Enkidu, and Mesopotamian Homosexuality," in *Riches Hidden in Secret Places: Ancient Near Eastern Studies in Memory of Thorkild Jacobsen* (ed. Tzvi Abusch; Winona Lake, Ind.: Eisenbrauns, 2002), 83.

If the offender is brought to trial and convicted, he is given a severe penalty, sufficient enough we may suppose to deter same-gender sexual relations. The penalty consists of two parts: the homosexual is sexually abused by his jurors, perhaps to humiliate him (but not to tacitly legitimize state-sponsored homosexual acts), and then castrated so that he will not perpetrate the crime again. . . . The rationale for the penalty of castration is evident: it is the principle of *lex talionis:* eye for eye, tooth for tooth, act for act.[11]

Martti Nissinen agrees that the key Akkadian term in question, *nâku*, "does not in itself express force or violence on the part of the one who commits the crime." He nuances Wold's position still further: the subject of the law is the "active and dominant partner of the sexual contact," and being repeatedly penetrated as the passive partner was considered shameful; thus the penetrating of another man of equal status "was tantamount to rape and deliberate disgrace, because the penetrating partner effects a change in the other partner's role from active (male) to passive (female)."[12]

The argumentation of Wold and Nissinen is convincing; these Middle Assyrian laws indicate that any homosexual activity—at least outside the cultus, between men from the same aristocratic social status—was regarded as a serious legal offense, with castration as the prescribed penalty for engaging in such practice.[13] Male-male sexual intercourse was considered inherently degrading for the passive partner who was anally penetrated.

The Babylonian magical text *Šumma ālu* (pre–seventh century B.C.E.) contains a manual of omens for divining the future; five of the thirty-eight omens include homosexual intercourse:

If a man has intercourse with the hindquarters of his equal (male), that man will be foremost among his brothers and colleagues.

If a man yearns to express his manhood while in prison and thus, like a male cult-prostitute, mating with men becomes his desire, he will experience evil.

If a man has intercourse with a (male) cult prostitute, care [in the sense of trouble] will leave him.

If a man has intercourse with a [male] courtier, for one whole year the worry which plagued him will vanish.

If a man has intercourse with a [male] slave, care will seize him.[14]

---

[11] Wold, *Out of Order,* 45.

[12] Nissinen, *Homoeroticism,* 25–26, quote at 26.

[13] Although castration is indeed a stiff penalty, it is not as stiff as the death penalty that was sometimes imposed in Mesopotamian law for the crime of adultery. See ibid., 25, for elaboration of this important difference in degree of punishment.

[14] Translation from A. Kirk Grayson and Donald B. Redford, *Papyrus and Tablet* (Englewood Cliffs, N.J.: Prentice Hall, 1973), 149.

At least two of these omens are positive in nature,[15] and none of the omens include any moral condemnation for the homosexual activity itself. Greenberg argues that what is at issue is the status of the partners: to have sex with another male of high social status is favorable and to penetrate another male of slave status is unfavorable; to usurp the prerogatives of a male cult prostitute in prison without license to do so is unfavorable. In particular, the first omen cited above is seen to confirm that in Mesopotamian culture to sexually penetrate one of the same social status lowered the passive partner's status in relation to the active partner.[16]

Wold agrees with this analysis of the issue of dominance and status but also points out that these are magical/omen texts, not legal texts, and one would not expect to find a concern with the morality or immorality of various acts. Although the omens may be good for one who dominates another man of equal status by anal penetration, this does not speak to the issue of the morality of the homosexual act within the Assyrian society.

Whereas the Middle Assyrian Laws seem to indicate that homosexual practice outside the cultus was regarded as illicit, the second omen cited above probably implies that homosexual intercourse *within the cultus,* with a cult functionary ("prostitute"), was societally accepted or at least tolerated. This conclusion is supported by other ANE evidence. The role of the male cult functionaries (termed *assinnu, kurgarrû,* or *kulu'u*) has been debated: earlier scholarly literature refers to them as "cult prostitutes," but more recent research suggests that these functionaries served as musicians, dancers, and thespians (actors) who performed as part of the cultic festivals but were not cult prostitutes.[17] They dressed like women and wore female makeup, usually carried with them the female symbol of a spindle, and took part in ecstatic dances and self-torture. Regardless of their other responsibilities, as highlighted in recent research, and whether or not they regularly engaged in "sex for hire" or prostitution, the evidence seems inescapable that these individuals did participate in ritual homosexual intercourse. Such evidence includes, for example, the following Mesopotamian texts: "When the *kalû* wiped his anus, (he said), 'I must not excite that which belongs to my lady Inanna'"; "When a ['man-woman'] entered the brothel, he raised his hands and said; 'My hire goes to the promoter. You are wealth, I am half'"; "Men take into their houses *kurgarrûs* who deliver them children"; a text from *Šumma ālu* that predicts that a man will find it necessary to have sex with another man "like an *assinnu*"; and a text that describes the detestable lot of these cult functionaries: "Bread from the city's ploughs [a euphemism for penises] shall be your food."[18]

---

[15] There is some question about the appropriate translation of the fourth omen in this list; whereas Grayson and Redford translate positively, others translate negatively: "Terrors will possess him for a whole year and leave him" (see Gagnon, *The Bible and Homosexual Practice,* 47).

[16] Greenberg, *The Construction of Homosexuality,* 127.

[17] See the literature for this debate in ch. 3, above, where cult prostitution in the ancient Near East is addressed more fully.

[18] Cited in Nissinen, *Homoeroticism,* 32–33; Gagnon, *The Bible and Homosexual Practice,* 49. Cf. Wold, *Out of Order,* 48–49, who acknowledges both the wider roles of these

Ancient Mesopotamian theology likely included the belief that a man who had sex with one of these passive cultic homosexual functionaries had direct access to the power of the goddess Ishtar. Although a means to access divine power, these passive homosexual partners were apparently treated with disdain. According to Mesopotamian mythology, they had been turned from men to women by the goddess Ishtar, and thus they were given the designation "man-woman" and even a "dog-woman"—the designation "dog" probably "denoting a disgusting transformation of masculinity and possibly also intercourse in a doglike position."[19] In addition to the epithets of "man-woman," "dog-woman," and "dog," these cultic functionaries were thought to have been created from the dirt lodged under the god Enki's fingernails; they were a mere "broken jar."[20]

Another Mesopotamian magical text, the "Almanac of Incantations," consists of a series of prayers for assistance in matters of love. Three categories are mentioned, apparently on an equal level: "love of a man for a woman," "love of a woman for a man," and "love of a man for a man."[21] Many scholars see the reference to "love of a man for a man" as implying a homosexual relationship and, in this context, as presenting such a relationship in a more positive light than the "power trip by a dominant partner"[22] that is characteristic of the depictions of male homosexual behavior elsewhere in Mesopotamian literature. One cannot be certain, however, that the phrase "love of a man for a man" goes beyond close male friendship and indeed implies a homosexual relationship.

In the Gilgamesh Epic, some have seen a positive homosexual relationship between Gilgamesh, king of Uruk, and Enkidu, the wild, uncivilized man created by the gods as partner for Uruk.[23] Most scholars, however, conclude that the relationship between the two was not sexual.[24] William Moran refers to a letter written

---

cultic functionaries but also continues to use the terminology of "cult prostitute" to describe the legitimate guild in Mesopotamian as well as in Canaanite cultures. Lambert, "Prostitution," 145–53, provides additional cuneiform evidence for male sacred prostitution in ancient Mesopotamia. Joan Goodnick Westenholz provides insight as to why homosexual functionaries were attached to the cult of Ishtar: "As she [Ishtar] is capable of changing sexual roles, so the members of her cult could—and did—copy her, with transsexuals and transvestites taking part in her cult" ("Great Goddesses in Mesopotamia: The Female Aspect of Divinity," *JJSEA* 29 [2002]: 17).

[19] Gagnon, *The Bible and Homosexual Practice*, 49. Cf. Greenberg, *The Construction of Homosexuality*, 127. The Akkadian word *assinnu* is written with the cuneiform sign UR.SAL, "dog-woman," with "dog" probably representing the male element in gender combination. See Bottéro and Petschow, "Homosexualität," 4:7; Springett, *Homosexuality*, 44.

[20] "Ishtar's Descent to the Nether World," lines 218–220, translated by Samuel Noah Kramer (*ANET* 56).

[21] Ibid., 49. See pp. 48–49 for discussion and substantiation of the points related to the male cult prostitutes. Cf. Greenberg, *The Construction of Homosexuality*, 94–97.

[22] Gagnon, *The Bible and Homosexual Practice*, 48.

[23] See esp. Cooper, "Buddies in Babylonia," 73–85. Cooper revives a 1930 suggestion of Thorkild Jacobsen, who himself later abandoned the hypothesis.

[24] For a translation of the part of the epic that may imply Gilgamesh's homosexual relations with Enkidu, see ibid., 77–79 (cf. "The Epic of Gilgamesh" I ii 54–63, 151–64, following the line numbers of C. Wilcke, "Die Anfänge des akkadischen Epen," *ZA* 67 [1977]:

by the wife of Zimri-lin, king of Mari, in which she matter-of-factly states that her husband and also Hammurabi, the king of Babylon, had male lovers.[25]

Wold points out that in the Mesopotamian art, unlike Greek art, there have been found no portrayals of homosexual scenes, even in the victory scenes, where one would expect acts of domination or humiliation. He suggests that the rarity of references to homosexuality in the literature and art of Mesopotamia may be due to the importance of maintaining a nuclear family and the concern to propagate children to carry on the family name. In light of these concerns, Wold provides a fair conclusion regarding the extent of homosexual practice in Mesopotamian society:

> If there was widespread homosexuality in Mesopotamia, it would have stood in sharp opposition to the integrity of the nuclear family, to beliefs in afterlife as they related to having children or adopting them, and to the preservation of these fundamental tenets of society as reflected in the genealogical lists from Babylonian and Assyrian sources. It is not surprising that little reference to homosexuality exists in Mesopotamian literature and art. It is difficult to imagine that the practice was common. Very likely it was limited to the cultus.[26]

The Hittite Empire (Anatolia). In the Hittite Law Code (second millennium B.C.E.), §189 forbids sexual relations between a father and his son: "If a man has sexual relations with (his own) son, it is an unpermitted sexual pairing."[27] This law is found in the context of various forbidden incestuous relationships and therefore should be viewed primarily as prohibiting incest rather than homosexuality.[28] No other Hittite text mentions same-sex intercourse, and thus no conclusion can be drawn about homosexual practice in general in ancient Anatolia.

Egypt. Since no ancient Egyptian law codes have been found and most of the extant Egyptian papyri and inscriptions relate to funerary and religious concerns, it is difficult to assess society's attitude toward homosexual practice. Although no evidence for homosexual cult prostitution has been detected, there are examples of homosexual practice attributed to Egyptian gods. One version of the myth "Contending of Seth and Horus" (ca. 1160 B.C.E.) refers to the god Seth having sex with his younger brother Horus: "Seth made his penis erect, and put it between

---

200–11). Greenberg (*The Construction of Homosexuality,* 112–13) sees hints of a sexual relationship between the two from the sexual puns in the dream episodes. Wold (*Out of Order,* 49), on the other hand, cites evidence from the epic that explicitly points to the heterosexual behavior of both Gilgamesh and Enkidu (*ANET* 97). For representatives and further arguments on both sides of the debate, see esp. Gagnon, *The Bible and Homosexual Practice,* 50–51.

[25] William L. Moran, "New Evidence from Mari on the History of Prophecy," *Bib* 50 (1969): 29–31.

[26] Wold, *Out of Order,* 51; see 50–51 for his full discussion.

[27] "Hittite Laws," translated by Harry A. Hoffner Jr. (*COS* 2.19:118; cf. *ANET* 196).

[28] Hoffner, ibid., clarifies in a footnote to this law: "Since the blood relationship is specified here, this is probably not a blanket prohibition of homosexual sex as in Lev 20:13."

Horus' buttocks, and Horus put his hand between his buttocks, and received Seth's semen."[29] Seth later states that he had "played the male role" with Horus.[30]

Even though there was apparently no cultic homosexual prostitution in ancient Egypt, the culture seems to have held the belief that homosexual intercourse with an Egyptian male deity was auspicious. One coffin text has the deceased vow, "I will swallow for myself the phallus of Rē." Another coffin text refers to sexual relations with the earth god Geb: "his [Geb's] phallus is between the buttocks of his son and heir."[31]

There are also instances of Egyptian pharaohs apparently pursuing homosexual relationships. King Neferkare (Pepi II) of the Sixth Dynasty (ca. 2272–2178 B.C.E.) is described as making regular night visits to see his general Sisene, who was unmarried (or lived without his wife), apparently for sexual intercourse.[32] This evidence by itself, however, is not sufficient for determining the extent of homosexuality in Egypt at large, even among the pharaohs, since the long-lived Pepi II was known for his corrupt reign.[33] Bas-reliefs from the tomb of two manicurists and hairdressers of Pharaoh Niuserre (ca. 2600 B.C.E.) depict the two men in intimate poses, embracing, holding hands, touching noses. Pharaoh Ikhnaton (ca. 1370 B.C.E.) is depicted in scenes of unusual intimacy with Smenkhare, his son-in-law and apparent coregent. The two are pictured nude (highly unusual for conventional Egyptian representations of royalty), with Ikhnaton stroking Smenkhare's chin; Smenkhare is given titles of endearment that are elsewhere reserved for Ikhnaton's queen and concubines. Ikhnaton is depicted with a generally feminine physique, a swollen belly, and no genitals.[34]

As in Mesopotamian literature, several Egyptian texts reveal that the receptive role in male anal intercourse was stigmatized and the aggressive active role was proof of superiority. Thus, in a coffin text (Ninth–Tenth Dynasties) containing magical passages to be recited after death to gain immortality, the deceased man boasts, "Atum [a male deity] has no power over me, for I copulate between his buttocks."[35]

---

[29] Translation from William K. Simpson, *The Literature of Ancient Egypt* (New Haven: Yale University Press, 1972), 120.

[30] Translation from Grayson and Redford, *Papyrus and Tablet,* 76.

[31] Translation from Raymond O. Faulkner, ed. and trans., *The Ancient Egyptian Pyramid Texts* (2 vols. Oxford: Oxford University Press, 1969), 2:162, 264; cf. 1:93–94 for reference to homosexual intercourse with Osiris in these pyramid texts.

[32] Lise Manniche, "Some Aspects of Ancient Egyptian Sexual Life," *AcOr* 38 (1977):14.

[33] So Wold, *Out of Order,* 56. For evidence of Pepi II's corruption, see Donald Redford, *Egypt, Canaan, and Israel in Ancient Times* (Princeton, N.J.: Princeton University Press, 1992), 58.

[34] Greenberg, *The Construction of Homosexuality,* 130, provides references for these data regarding Pharaoh Niuserre's manicurists and hairdressers and Pharaoh Iknaton.

[35] Coffin Texts VI, 258 f–g = Spell 635. Translation in Gagnon, *The Bible and Homosexual Practice,* 52. See Raymond O. Faulkner, ed. and trans., *The Ancient Egyptian Coffin Texts* (3 vols.; Warminster, Eng.: Aris & Phillips, 1973–1978), 2:216, who translates thus: "Atum has no power over me, and I violate his hinder parts."

Several scholars suggest that there was a shift from tolerance of homosexual activity in earlier Egyptian history to a negative attitude later. In the earlier period, only same-sex relations with a male youth appear to be reprehensible. An early text, the "Instructions of Ptahhotep" (Fifth Dynasty, mid–third millennium B.C.E.), warns only against forcing a "vulva-boy" to submit to sexual intercourse after he protests.[36] Similarly, a Heracleopolitan inscription (probably Ninth Dynasty, ca. 2130 B.C.E.) clearly refers to youth-receptive homosexual activity and the possibility of criminal prosecution for an adult who engages in such pederasty; a man declares, "I did not wish to love a youth. As for a respectable son who does it, his (own) father shall abandon him in court."[37] The shift toward a negative assessment of all homosexual practice may be signaled by the "Book of the Dead" (Eighteenth Dynasty, fifteenth century B.C.E.). Chapter 125 of the "Book of the Dead" records a series of negative confessions by which the deceased protests his innocence of a long list of sins. Two of these protestations of guiltlessness refer to homosexuality. John Wilson translates thus:

(A 20) I have not had sexual relations with a boy.

(B 27) O His-Face-Behind-Him, who comes forth from *Tep-het-djat,* I have not *been perverted;* I have not had sexual relations with a boy.[38]

Although many have followed Wilson's translation and taken this text as referring to youth-receptive homosexual acts (pederasty), Greenberg points out that the original text does not indicate the age of the partner and should be translated as "male lover" rather than "boy."[39] Translated thus, this text indicates that all homosexual activity was regarded as reprehensible. By the time of the Edfu Temple inscriptions (Ptolemaic period, third–second centuries B.C.E.), it seems that both the active and the passive roles in homosexual practice were prohibited.[40]

Ugarit/Western Semites/Canaan. No solid evidence for homosexual practice has yet been discovered in the art or literature of Ugarit, although, as will be discussed below, such evidence does appear for bestiality and incest. There is one reference in "The Bow of Aqhat" to the Canaanite goddess Anath as one who "takes away men's bows, that is, who changes men into women"; this may imply, as in the similar Mesopotamian statements about Ishtar, that the goddess has transformed men into homosexuals.[41]

---

[36] Cited in Greenberg, *The Construction of Homosexuality,* 134.
[37] Wold, *Out of Order,* 59.
[38] "The Protestations of Guiltlessness," translated by John Wilson (*ANET* 34–35).
[39] Greenberg, *The Construction of Homosexuality,* 133.
[40] See Gagnon, *The Bible and Homosexual Practice,* 53, who cites an Edfu inscription that "contains a prohibition against coupling with a *nkk* or *ḥmw,* terms associated with either an effeminate coward or a receptive male partner."
[41] See Delbert Hillers, "The Bow of Aqhat: The Meaning of a Mythological Theme," in *Orient and Occident: Essays Presented to Cyrus H. Gordon on the Occasion of His Sixty-Fifth Birthday* (ed. Harry A. Hoffner Jr.; AOAT 22; Neukirchen-Vluyn: Neukirchener Verlag, 1973), 74.

Summary. In the ancient Near East, homosexual practice may be documented in Mesopotamia, Anatolia, and Egypt, and one cannot speak of uniform approval or disapproval. Homosexual activity in the setting of the cultus was apparently accepted within Mesopotamian society. The legal prohibitions of homosexual activity in the Middle Assyrian Laws prescribe the maximum penalty of castration, not death. The early Egyptian culture seems to have been more tolerant of homosexual behavior than later in Egyptian history. The discussion below highlights major differences in attitudes toward homosexuality in the biblical material from those elsewhere in the ancient Near East.

Pentateuchal Narratives

Ham's Sin—a Homosexual Act? Following hard on the heels of the accounts of the flood and the Noahic covenant (Gen 6–9:18) comes the portrayal of Ham's sex-related sin with his father (Gen 9:20–25). Noah was drunk and "lay uncovered [*wayyitgal*] in his tent" (9:21). "And Ham, the father of Canaan, saw the nakedness of [*wayyar* *ʾēt ʿerwat*] his father, and told his two brothers outside" (9:22). The precise nature of Ham's act has been widely debated. Some scholars have contended that it consisted of disrespectful voyeurism—viewing his father's uncovered body.[42] Others argue that the "seeing" (or "uncovering") of the "nakedness of his father" is used here in the technical sense of sexual relations—either homosexual with Noah[43] or heterosexual with Noah's wife[44]—as in the Mosaic legislation (Lev 20:17; cf. Lev 18:14; 20:20–21). In the former case (voyeurism), the sin would be that of filial irreverence in exposing and/or viewing his father's

---

[42] See, e.g., Umberto Cassuto, *A Commentary on the Book of Genesis* (trans. Israel Abrahams; 2 vols.; Jerusalem: Magnes, 1961–1964), 2:151–52; Victor P. Hamilton, *The Book of Genesis: Chapters 1–17* (NICOT; Grand Rapids: Eerdmans, 1990), 322–23; Gordon J. Wenham, *Genesis 1–15* (WBC 1; Waco, Tex.: Word, 1987), 198–201. Cf. H. Hirsch Cohens, *The Drunkenness of Noah* (University: University of Alabama Press, 1974), 13–21, who further elaborates on Ham's "gloating stare" (p. 18), discusses the "taboo of looking," and suggests that "looking" transferred power—by looking on his nude father, Ham acquired his father's potency. Cohens's position cannot, however, be supported by evidence from the passage or elsewhere in Scripture except by "far-fetched etymologizing" (Wenham, *Genesis 1–15,* 200). For other supporters of this interpretation, see Gagnon, *The Bible and Homosexual Practice,* 64, n. 61.

[43] Recent extended arguments in favor of the conclusion that Ham's act was incestuous homosexual rape of his father are found in Wold, *Out of Order,* 65–76; Nissinen, *Homoeroticism,* 52–53; and Gagnon, *The Bible and Homosexual Practice,* 64–71 (see 65, n. 63, for other supporters of this view). Wold follows the suggestion set forth by Rabbi Samuel ben Meir (Rashbam, ca. 1080–ca. 1174), Babylonian Talmudic tractate *Sanhedrin* 70a. The flip side of this thesis is that Noah initiated the incest with his son. Ilona N. Rashkow supports this hypothesis by relying on Freudian psychoanalytic Oedipal theory and by the feminist rejection of the narrator's presumed androcentric perspective ("Daddy-Dearest and the 'Invisible Spirit of Wine,'" in *Genesis* [ed. Athalya Brenner; FCB² 1; Sheffield, Eng.: Sheffield Academic Press, 1998], 82–98).

[44] See Frederick W. Bassett, "Noah's Nakedness and the Curse of Canaan: A Case of Incest?" *VT* 21 (1971): 232–37.

private parts and brashly bragging about it to his brothers. In the latter possibilities, homosexual or incestuous heterosexual activity would be involved.

It is true that the expression "see the nakedness of" is equated with "uncover the nakedness of" in Lev 20:17, which refers to sexual intercourse. One must note, however, crucial grammatical-syntactical-lexical differences between Lev 20:17 and Gen 9:21. Leviticus 20:17 has the construction *yiqqaḥ* (from the verb *lāqaḥ*, "to take") . . . *rāʾâ ʿerwat* ("to see the nakedness of"), whereas Gen 9:21–22 has *rāʾâ ʿerwat* alone without a preceding form of *lāqaḥ*. The expression *rāʾâ ʿerwat,* "to see the nakedness of," by itself never denotes sexual intercourse elsewhere in the HB. Furthermore, the form of *gālâ* in Lev 20:17 is in the *piʿel,* or intensive active, form, implying that a man uncovers someone else, whereas the form of *gālâ* ("to uncover") in Gen 9:21 is the *hitpaʿel,* or reflexive, which should be translated "to expose oneself."[45] In light of these distinct differences between Gen 9:21 and Lev 20:17, the preponderance of modern commentaries have noted—I believe correctly—that the expression "see the nakedness of" in Gen 9:21–22 does not mean "have sexual intercourse with" as in Lev 20:17.

Even more significantly, it has been widely recognized that the interpretation of this phrase as sexual intercourse does not comport with the immediate context of Gen 9. Verse 23 seems to make clear that Ham's sin was that of "seeing," not heterosexual intercourse (with Noah's wife) or homosexual rape (of Noah). The narrator takes pains to slow down the action to clarify the meaning of Ham's action by contrasting it with the action of his brothers: "Then Shem and Japheth took a garment, laid it on both their shoulders, and walked backward and covered the nakedness of their father [*waykassû ʾēt ʿerwat ʾăbîhem*]; their faces were turned away, and they did not see their father's nakedness [*wĕʿerwat ʾăbîhem lōʾ rāʾû*]." Umberto Cassuto rightly notes, "If the covering was an adequate remedy, it follows that the misdemeanor was confined to seeing."[46] Gordon Wenham likewise points out, "The elaborate efforts Shem and Japheth made to avoid looking at their father demonstrate that this was all Ham did in the tent."[47]

Wenham further emphasizes, however, that Ham's "seeing" was not to be taken lightly in "a world where discretion and filial loyalty are supreme virtues."[48] The narrator draws a dramatic contrast between the filial irreverence on the part of Ham and the extreme care to preserve modesty and respect for their father on the part of the other two sons. The next verses underscore the seriousness of Ham's disrespectful action against his father and also seem to imply that the attitude of filial irreverence had already manifested itself in the character of Ham's youngest son: "When Noah awoke from his wine and knew what his youngest son had done [*ʿāśâ*] to him, he said, 'Cursed [is] Canaan; lowest of slaves shall he be [*yihyeh*] to his brothers'" (Gen 9:24–25).[49]

---

[45] *HALOT* 1:192, s.v. גלה.

[46] Cassuto, *Genesis,* 2:151.

[47] Wenham, *Genesis 1–15,* 200.

[48] Ibid.

[49] Alternatively or concomitantly, the father here may be punished through the fate of his descendants, a point that has great narrative significance for later in the Pentateuch

The verb *ʿāśâ,* "to do, make," does not imply a sexual act of abuse, as some have tried to force upon it, but simply refers to the irreverent action of Ham in failing to cover up his father's nakedness and in disrespectfully relating the event to his brothers. The verb "to be" is supplied in the first clause of 9:25 and should probably best be translated as "Cursed *is* [not 'be'] Canaan," whereas the second clause, which has the *qal* impf. of "to be," should be translated as a future: "lowest of slaves *shall he be* to his brothers." The first clause describes a situation that is already present; the second a prediction of what will be in the future. "The evil trait, displayed by Ham in this story, had, no doubt been discerned by Noah as marking Canaan, the son more distinctly. Canaan's whole race will display it more than any of the races of the earth."[50]

This interpretation—that Noah's being "uncovered" and Ham's "seeing his nakedness" refers to Noah's literal (and shameful) exposure and does not present a euphemism for sexual abuse on the part of Ham—is further supported in the light of the larger context of Gen 1–11. Warren Gage has demonstrated that the experience of Noah is presented by the narrator as a recapitulation of the experience of Adam and Eve in the garden of Eden. The events of the flood and its aftermath are placed in parallel order to the creation week, with the waters covering the earth (Gen 7:18–19; cf. 1:1–2), the dove upon the face of the waters (8:9; cf. 1:2), the emergence of dry land and vegetation (8:11; cf. 1:12), and, at the end of the flood, God smelling "the pleasing odor" (*rêaḥ hannîḥōaḥ,* 8:21; cf. *šābat,* 2:2). After the flood, Noah is the new Adam, recommissioned in God's image (9:6; cf. 1:26–27) and commanded to be fruitful and multiply and fill the earth (9:1, 7; cf. 1:28).

Noah's sin in the vineyard parallels Adam's sin in the garden, partaking of what is forbidden (9:20; cf. 3:6); he is shamefully naked like Adam after the fall (9:21; cf. 3:7), and his nakedness is covered by his sons as God covers the nakedness of Adam and Eve (9:23; cf. 3:21).[51] The theological implications of these par-

---

when the people of Israel dispossess the Canaanites. This alternative is explained by a combination of two biblical concepts that David Daube calls "ruler punishment" and "communal responsibility" (*Studies in Biblical Law* [New York: Ktav, 1969], 176 [see 154–89 for a full discussion]). Daube (p. 176) explains that "the head of a house at any given time, and especially the founder or would-be founder of a famous house, was regarded in ancient times as something of the ruler, of the principally interested 'owner,' of the house, even of the as yet unborn generations. Hence it comes that nearly always when a family curse is being announced to an offender, the idea of communal responsibility, of all members of the family being answerable for, and tainted by, his offense, appears side by side with the idea of ruler punishment, of his being punished, as the actually guilty individual, by the disasters to befall his sons and grandsons."

[50] H. C. Leupold, *Exposition of Genesis* (Columbus, Ohio: Wartburg, 1942), 350. Note that the curse is upon Canaan, not upon Ham. Those who have sought to utilize this text as part of the proslavery argument, esp. in the nineteenth century, failed to grasp that only the descendants of Canaan (later known as the Canaanites) were cursed, not the whole Hamitic race. For further discussion, see Willard M. Swartley, *Slavery, Sabbath, War, and Women: Case Issues in Biblical Interpretation* (Conrad Grebel Lectures, 1982; Scottdale, Pa.: Herald, 1983), 33–40.

[51] Warren Austin Gage, *The Gospel of Genesis: Studies in Protology and Eschatology* (Winona Lake, Ind.: Carpenter, 1984), 7–16.

allels are profound, but the pertinent point for our present discussion is that the two falls of Adam and Noah were not sexual sins; furthermore, the result of these falls was physical and shameful exposure or nakedness, and this nakedness is not a euphemism for sexual intercourse or abuse. Gage does not draw the further parallel, but the narrator seems to have implied a link between Adam's sinful response to his nakedness (unsuccessful attempts to cover with fig leaves) and Ham's sinful response to Noah's nakedness (failure to cover the nakedness).

Even though there is no evidence in Gen 9 that Ham's sin was incestuous homosexual rape of his father, at the same time one must explain the intertextual echoes in the canonically received Pentateuch that link Gen 9 with the illegitimate sexual relationships described in Lev 20. Although there was no homosexual *act* in Gen 9, the use of the same expression, *rā'â 'erwat,* in both Gen 9 and Lev 20 is probably not to be taken as accidental. It seems that the narrator wishes the reader to understand that Ham's action did in fact have illicit sexual overtones. The use of *rā'â* with an accusative of person, as in Gen 9:21, often carries the nuance of "to look at (searchingly)."[52] H. C. Leupold has captured this nuance and its implication: Ham's "seeing" "is not a mere harmless and accidental 'and he saw,' but 'he looked at' . . . or 'he gazed with satisfaction.' What ordinary filial reverence should have restrained is given free rein. The unclean imagination feeds itself by gazing."[53]

Likewise Leupold suggests that the clause "[he] told his two brothers" in this context means "and he told with delight."[54] In other words, Ham's sin not only was filial irreverence but may have included impure, homosexual, lingering, lustful thoughts and imagination. The narrator's repetition of the clause "Ham was the father of Canaan" at this juncture in the story may have been "to point more definitely to a kinship of mind between the two. The trait of inclination to the unclean is shared by father and son alike."[55] If this interpretation is correct, then it harks back to the condemnation of humanity even after the flood (Gen 8:21): "the inclination of the human heart is evil from youth." Thus the point is made from the very first hint of homosexual tendencies in Scripture that not only the actual carrying out of the homosexual act but also the harboring of lustful thoughts and imaginations are sin.[56]

Sodom: Homosexual Lust or Inhospitality? The well-known story of Lot and Sodom (Gen 19:1–11) need not be repeated in detail here. The term "sodomy" as a reference to male homosexuality is taken from this story. It has been argued by some, however, that the Sodomites' request to Lot—"Where are the men who came

---

[52] See *HALOT* 3:1159, s.v. ראה, meaning no. 10. For other biblical examples, see Song 1:6; 6:11b.

[53] Leupold, *Genesis,* 346.

[54] Ibid.

[55] Ibid.

[56] The word "harboring" is important here, for, as indicated at the beginning of this chapter, I do not find biblical evidence that individuals are held accountable for the homosexual inclination per se.

to you tonight? Bring them out to us, so that we may know them" (19:5)—did not refer to homosexual activity. For example, D. S. Bailey, followed more recently by John Boswell and others,[57] postulates that Lot, as a resident alien (*gēr*) of Sodom, "either in ignorance or in defiance of the laws of Sodom, had exceeded the rights of a *gēr* in that city by receiving and entertaining two 'foreigners' whose intentions might be hostile, and whose credentials, it seems, had not been examined."[58] According to Bailey, the word *yādaᶜ*, "to know," used in 19:5 does not refer to sexual activity but simply means "get acquainted with," and the request of the Sodomites is to "know" the strangers in the sense of "inquire into their *bona fides*."[59] Lot's decision to surrender his daughters is explained by Bailey as "simply the most tempting bribe that Lot could offer on the spur of the moment to appease the hostile crowd," and not "an offer of heterosexual in lieu of homosexual satisfaction."[60]

As plausible as this hypothesis may sound, the traditional understanding of this passage seems to fit best the immediate context. It is important to recognize that in the Genesis narrative, initial reference to the wickedness of Sodom (13:13) utilizes the term "*men* [*'anšê*] of Sodom," (RSV) not the more generic term "people" (*ᶜam*) used elsewhere in Genesis for a reference to the general inhabitants of a city.[61] In 19:4, the same term, *'anšê*, "men of [a place]," is repeated twice in one verse, again to underscore that these are the males who surround Lot's house. The immediate context also indicates that the wickedness of Sodom goes far beyond (although it does not eliminate) issues of hospitality. The narrator first describes the condition of Sodom's men as "wicked, great sinners against the LORD" (13:13), and then the same message is recorded from the mouth of God: "How great is the outcry against Sodom and Gomorrah and how very grave their sin!" (18:20). Such language could hardly describe merely a spirit of inhospitality.

But the Achilles' heel of the argument of Bailey, Boswell, and others who see only issues of inhospitality in this narrative is the use of "to know" in the immediate context. In v. 8 the verb *yādaᶜ* is used in connection with Lot's daughters and unmistakably refers to sexual intercourse. The close proximity of its usage in v. 5 to this clear sexual meaning of *yādaᶜ* in v. 8 makes it very difficult to conclude

---

[57] John Boswell, *Christianity, Social Tolerance, and Homosexuality: Gay People in Western Europe from the Beginning of the Christian Era to the Fourteenth Century* (Chicago: University of Chicago Press, 1980), 93–95; cf. Daniel A. Helminiak, *What the Bible Really Says about Homosexuality* (San Francisco: Alamo Square, 1994), 35–41.

[58] D. S. Bailey, *Homosexuality and the Western Christian Tradition* (New York: Longmans, Green, 1955; repr., Hamden, Conn.: Archon, 1975), 1–28, quote at 4. A related interpretation is offered by Nissenen (*Homoeroticism*, 48–49) and others, who suggest that the intent of the irate Sodomites was to challenge Lot's honor as a lowly resident alien by dishonoring Lot's guests. Cf. Leland J. White, "Does the Bible Speak about Gays or Same-Sex Orientation? A Test Case in Biblical Ethics, Part I," *BTB* 25 (1995): 20; Daniel Boyarin, "Are There Any Jews in the 'The History of Sexuality'?" *JHSex* 5, no. 3 (1995): 348–53; and others listed in Gagnon, *The Bible and Homosexual Practice*, 77, n. 99.

[59] Bailey, *Homosexuality*, 4.

[60] Ibid., 6.

[61] See Gen 11:6; 14:16, 21. Elsewhere in Genesis, use of *'anšê* regularly seems to emphasize the male gender: 17:27; 24:13; 26:7; 29:22; 34:20, 21; 38:22.

that it has a different, nonsexual meaning in the former. Furthermore, "Bailey's explanation for the reason Lot offers his daughters to the men of Sodom is simply not convincing. . . . It is much more difficult to explain why Lot would offer his daughters to people who came only to demand to check up on two foreigners than if they wanted to abuse them sexually."[62]

James DeYoung shows how the literary macrostructure of Genesis also points to a sexual interpretation for Gen 19. Following the literary analysis of Robert Alter, he points to the three episodes just prior to the birth narrative of Isaac that delay and pose a threat to the fulfillment of God's promise of seed for Abraham—Abraham's intercession and the destruction of Sodom and Gomorrah (Gen 18–19), the incest of Lot and his daughters as the origin of the Moabites and Edomites (Gen 19), and the sister-wife episode involving Abraham, Sarah, and the king of Gerar (Gen 20)—and shows that "each episode relates sexual sin and its punishment. . . . The literary structure of the text demands a homosexual meaning for the sin of Sodom. Illicit sexual enjoyment or opportunism connects all three of the episodes."[63] DeYoung, among others, also points out that scholars generally recognize that the narrator of the book of Judges consciously modeled his telling of the story of the disgrace at Gibeah (Judg 19) after the account in Gen 19, and since the Judg 19 story clearly has reference to homosexual activity, one should interpret the story of Gen 19 the same way.[64]

Most modern interpreters now acknowledge that homosexual activity along with inhospitality is described in Gen 19 but insist that the sexual issue is that of rape or violence and that thus this passage gives no evidence for the condemnation of homosexual practice in general.[65] It is indeed likely that the specific

---

[62] Sakae Kubo, *Theology and Ethics of Sex* (Washington, D.C.: Review and Herald, 1980), 74. James R. White and Jeffrey D. Niell suggest a plausible explanation for why Lot would offer his daughters to the men who surrounded his house, an explanation that recognizes the strong cultural requirement in Lot's day to give protection to those in one's house and at the same time (somewhat) rescues Lot from the charge of being a callous father, willing to offer his daughters to be ravished by the crowd of Sodom's men: "Lot knew these men. He knew their lifestyle, their activities. . . . It is possible that Lot is simply buying time, knowing that, in fact, the offer will not be accepted, for these men simply do not have any desire for women. He may feel his daughters are perfectly safe, for those standing before him had shown a firm and unwavering desire for sexual fulfillment with men, not with women" (*The Same Sex Controversy: Defending and Clarifying the Bible's Message about Homosexuality* [Minneapolis: Bethany House, 2002], 35).

[63] James B. DeYoung, *Homosexuality: Contemporary Claims Examined in Light of the Bible and Other Ancient Literature and Law* (Grand Rapids: Kregel, 2000), 38–40, quote at 39–40.

[64] Ibid., 36. See Gagnon, *The Bible and Homosexual Practice*, 91–92, n. 125, for a bibliography of the many scholars who have recognized the intertextual parallels between these two narratives.

[65] See, e.g., Alice Ogden Bellis and Terry L. Hufford, *Science, Scripture, and Homosexuality* (Cleveland: Pilgrim, 2002), 100; Louis William Countryman, *Dirt, Greed, and Sex: Sexual Ethics in the New Testament and Their Implications for Today* (Philadelphia: Fortress, 1988), 30–31; George R. Edwards, *Gay/Lesbian Liberation: A Biblical Perspective* (New York: Pilgrim, 1984), 42–46; Choon-Leong Seow, "Textual Orientation," in *Biblical*

actions contemplated by the men of Sodom included homosexual rape, but Victor Hamilton points to a fourfold problem with limiting the reference here only to homosexual *rape*.[66] First, the verb *yādaᶜ*, which has been translated by some versions as "to abuse" in this passage (e.g., JB), nowhere else in the HB carries the meaning "abuse" or "violate." Second, elsewhere in Scripture, specific terminology besides *yādaᶜ* is used to describe incidents or cases of rape ("to seize," "to lie with," "to force"; cf. Gen 34:2; 2 Sam 13:14; Deut 22:25–27; see ch. 12, below, for a discussion of these terms and rape in general). Third, translating *yādaᶜ* as "rape" or "violate" in Gen 19:5 would force a different meaning on the word than three verses later, where *yādaᶜ* undeniably means "have intercourse with" regarding Lot's daughters. Finally, Hamilton points out that "such an interpretation forces these incredible words in Lot's mouth: 'Do not rape my visitors. Here are my daughters, both virgins—rape them!'" In light of these problems, Hamilton concludes—correctly, I believe—that "the incident frowns on homosexual relations for whatever reason."[67]

Beyond the significance of the word *yādaᶜ*, one must also recognize that in the overall movement of the narrative, this incident is utilized to characterize the depth of depravity in Sodom and Gomorrah. Thus, "it is likely that the sin of Sodom is not merely inhospitality or even attempted rape of a guest but rather attempted homosexual rape of male guests. . . . What makes this instance of inhospitality so dastardly, what makes the name 'Sodom' a byword for inhumanity to visiting outsiders in later Jewish and Christian circles, is the specific form in which the inhospitality manifests itself: *homosexual* rape."[68]

The larger context of the later prophetic passages that refer to this narrative clearly indicates a sexual interpretation (Ezek 16:43, 50; cf. Jude 6–7; 2 Pet 2:4, 6–8) and a castigation of homosexual activity per se and not just homosexual rape. As will be argued below in the analysis of Ezek 16:49–50, the sin of inhospitality is indeed signaled by the prophet, but this is not all that Ezekiel indicates.

Ethics and Homosexuality: Listening to Scripture (ed. Robert L. Brawley; Louisville: Westminster John Knox, 1996), 22; Johanna Stiebert and J. T. Walsh, "Does the Hebrew Bible Have Anything to Say about Homosexuality?" *OTE* 14 (2001): 129–35. Lyn M. Bechtel also concedes that there may have been an intent on the part of the men of Sodom to engage in homosexual activity, but she insists that this be labeled rape and not homosexuality and further argues that the issue is not lust but a group-oriented xenophobic response of the Sodomites toward Lot and, even more, toward the visitors he entertained ("A Feminist Reading of Genesis 19:1–11," in *Genesis* [ed. Athalya Brenner; FCB² 1; Sheffield, Eng.: Sheffield Academic Press, 1998], 108–28; idem, "Boundary Issues in Genesis 19:1–38," in *Escaping Eden: New Feminist Perspectives on the Bible* [ed. Harold C. Washington, Susan Lochrie Graham, and Pamela Thimmes; BS 65; Sheffield, Eng.: Sheffield Academic Press, 1998], 22–40). Bechtel, however, seems to have exaggerated the concern to exclude outsiders in the biblical materials, and as argued above, the narrator of Gen 19 describes the situation in terms that transcend xenophobia and include an implicit condemnation of homosexual lust and practice as well.

[66] Victor P. Hamilton, *The Book of Genesis: Chapters 18–50* (NICOT; Grand Rapids: Eerdmans, 1995), 34–35.

[67] Ibid., 35.

[68] Gagnon, *The Bible and Homosexual Practice*, 75–76.

Specific terminology in the immediate context of these verses in Ezek 16 also indicates the sexual nature of the sin of Sodom. That the opprobrium attached to the Sodomites' intended activity involved not only rape but the inherent degradation of same-sex intercourse is confirmed by the intertextual linkages between Ezekiel and the sexual "abominations" mentioned in Levitical legislation.[69]

Pentateuchal Legislation

Leviticus 18:22 and 20:13. The Mosaic law strongly condemns, and assigns the most severe sanctions for, homosexual activity. Basic legislation appears in Lev 18:22: "You shall not lie with a male as with a woman; it is an abomination" (wĕ'et-zākār lō' tiškab miškĕbê 'iššâ tô'ēbâ hiw'). Some modern translations (e.g., KJV and NIV) render zākār as "man" or "mankind," which could imply only an adult male or the entire human species, but the meaning of this term is clearly "male," denoting all members of this gender regardless of age. The term "excludes all male sexual relations."[70] Unlike other ANE laws relating to homosexual activity, *both* parties here are penalized, thus clearly implying consensual male-male intercourse, not just a case of homosexual rape. Gagnon summarizes the contrast in comprehensiveness between biblical and other ANE laws regarding homosexual activity: "The absoluteness of the prohibition is unlike anything else found in the ancient Near East or Greece—contexts that made accommodations depending on active role, consent, age or social status of the passive partner (alien, slave, foreigner), and/or cultic association."[71] Roy Gane states regarding this verse, "The language is devastatingly untechnical, leaving no room for ambiguity."[72]

The Hebrew clause lō' tiškab consists of a negative particle followed by the qal imperfect, expressing a permanent negative command. The phrase miškĕbê 'iššâ, literally, "the lying of a woman," has been suggested by some to include only homosexual acts that approximate normal heterosexual coitus and include penile intromission,[73] but the Hebrew is clearly a euphemism for sexual intercourse (cf.

---

[69] For further discussion of Gen 19 besides the studies already cited, see esp. Springett, *Homosexuality*, 55–58; and White and Niell, *The Same Sex Controversy*, 27–51. Another pentateuchal narrative rarely cited in discussions of homosexual practice in the Bible but considered by at least one scholar as including what may be described as homosexual activity—homosexual sex play by children—is the reference to Ishmael "playing" (ṣāḥaq) in the presence of Isaac (Gen 21:9). Jonathan Kirsch, "What Did Sarah See?" *BRev* 14, no. 5 (1998): 2, 49, contends that the verb ṣāḥaq here should be translated "fondle" and that what Sarah saw was incestuous "sex play between Ishmael and his little brother"— incestuous, same-sex child molestation that may have included causing Isaac to masturbate. The term ṣāḥaq can have sexual connotations, as in Gen 26:8 and Exod 32:6, but in this context, it most probably refers to "playing" without sexual implications. See ch. 7, below.

[70] Wold, *Out of Order*, 104.

[71] Robert A. J. Gagnon, "The Bible and Homosexual Practice: Key Issues," in Dan O. Via and Robert A. J. Gagnon, *Homosexuality and the Bible: Two Views* (Minneapolis: Fortress, 2003), 63–64.

[72] Roy Gane, *Leviticus, Numbers* (NIVAC 3; Grand Rapids: Zondervan, 2004), 321.

[73] So Bailey, *Homosexuality*, 58–59.

the male equivalent of this passage in Judg 21:11–12). Thus this passage is a permanent prohibition of all sexual intercourse of a man with another male (zākār). This would also prohibit pedophilia, since the term zākār refers to any male, not just a grown man.

Although this proscription explicitly mentions only sodomy (male homosexual relations), the prohibition of lesbian relationships is probably implicit in the general Levitical injunction against following the abominable practices of the Egyptians or the Canaanites, as recognized in rabbinic interpretation.[74] All the legislation in Lev 18 is in the masculine gender (with the exception of female bestiality, v. 23).[75] The Mosaic legislation in general is considered from a man's (male's) perspective. Even the Decalogue is addressed in the masculine singular, but this certainly does not mean that it applies only to the male gender. The masculine singular is the Hebrew way to express gender-inclusive ideas, much the same as it was in English until the recent emphasis on gender-inclusive language. Since the male is regarded as the patriarchal representative of the family, laws are given as if to him (see, e.g., the tenth commandment of the Decalogue) but are clearly intended for both man and woman where applicable.

Leviticus 20:13 repeats the essential information of 18:22, but in the form of case law followed by the stated sanctions: "If a man lies with a male as with a woman, both of them have committed an abomination; they shall be put to death; their blood is upon them." The penalty for homosexual practice is capital punishment. Leviticus 18:29 mentions an additional sanction, this time phrased generally to include all of the "abominations" mentioned in Lev 18: "For whoever commits any of these abominations shall be cut off [wĕnikrĕtû] from their people." Although many scholars have equated the death penalty with the penalty of being "cut off" (kārēt), Wold has shown that the kārēt penalty was "a conditional divine curse of extinction, obliterating the sinner (and progeny) from any role in the drama of Israel's history."[76] The one who practiced homosexuality faced both of these sanctions.

---

[74] Louis M. Epstein, Sex Laws and Customs in Judaism (New York: Bloch, 1948), 138. Leviticus 18:3 in particular provides the rabbinic basis for condemning lesbianism (Sifra Lev 18:3).

[75] Gagnon (The Bible and Homosexual Practice, 144) suggests that this may have to do with the "primacy of penetration for defining sexual intercourse" in the biblical material; unlike in same-sex intercourse, where two women cannot penetrate each other, regarding bestiality "apparently it was thought that women could be penetrated by male animals" (see further discussion of this legislation against bestiality in this chapter, below). Such a rationale would not, however, eliminate the application of the prohibition against male homosexual activity to female homosexual activity, since, as argued below, all same-sex homosexual activity entails a disruption and degradation of the creation order of gender boundaries. I suggest that the reason that both man and woman are mentioned only with regard to bestiality in Lev 18 and 20 may simply be because in the case of bestiality the gender-inclusive masculine language does not include the animals and thus is not implicitly reversible (applicable to the other gender) in describing human-animal relations like it is with sexual relationships involving only humans. Hence it is necessary to explicitly state the prohibition of bestiality as it applies both to the man and to the woman.

[76] Donald J. Wold, "The Meaning of the Biblical Penalty Kareth" (PhD diss., University of California, Berkeley, 1978), summarized in Wold, Out of Order, 144–47, quote

Leviticus 18:22 and 20:13 reveal the underlying characterization of homosexual practice from the divine perspective: it is considered by God as *tôʿēbâ*, "abomination." This is the term used twice (in the singular) specifically for homosexuality practices, as noted above, and four more times in Lev 18 (in the plural) to summarize all of the sexually related sins (including homosexuality) mentioned in this chapter of Leviticus (vv. 26–27, 29–30). These are the only occurrences of the term in the book of Leviticus. The basic meaning of *tôʿēbâ* is an "abominable, detestable, offensive thing."[77] The fact that among the list of specific prohibitions of sexual acts in Lev 18, the word *tôʿēbâ* is mentioned only regarding homosexual intercourse gives an indication of the degree of revulsion associated with homosexual activity. Indeed, in the entire Pentateuch, the only forbidden sexual act to which the word *tôʿēbâ* is specifically attached is homosexual intercourse.

Some scholars have maintained that the term *tôʿēbâ* refers only to Jewish ceremonial impurity and therefore is linked to the practices of the heathen nations—ritual impurity and cultic prostitution—that would ceremonially defile the sanctuary. Particularly regarding homosexuality, it has been argued that this practice is condemned only because of its association with the idolatrous fertility cults and not because it is considered evil per se.[78] Expressed in different terms, it is suggested that the condemnation of homosexual activity as "abomination" is based solely upon Israel's particular cultic/ritual concerns and not upon universally applicable moral/ethical considerations.[79] The wide-ranging usage, however, of this term, *tôʿēbâ*, in the Torah and elsewhere in the HB reveals that its meaning

---

at 147 (see 146 for a tabulation of the crimes in Scripture for which the *kārēt* penalty was imposed).

[77] Michael A. Grisanti, "תעב," *NIDOTTE* 4:314; cf. *HALOT* 1702, s.v. תּוֹעֵבָה.

[78] For proponents of this view, see, e.g., Bailey, *Homosexuality*, 30; Boswell, *Christianity, Social Tolerance*, 99–102; J. Harold Ellens, *Sex in the Bible: A New Consideration* (Psychology, Religion, and Spirituality; Westport, Conn.: Praeger, 2006), 108–11; Helminiak, *Homosexuality*, 43–54; and Letha Dawson Scanzoni and Virginia Ramey Mollenkott, *Is the Homosexual My Neighbor? Another Christian View* (San Francisco: Harper & Row, 1978), 59–61. Bird, "The Bible in Christian Ethical Deliberation," 160–61, provides arguments against this view of associating the OT prohibitions of homosexual practice with Canaanite fertility cults, but these arguments are based mainly upon the common feminist premise that does not acknowledge the existence of male cult prostitutes among the Canaanites in the time of Israelite history, labeling the clear biblical statements as "polemical constructs that exhibit no firsthand knowledge of the institution they condemn" (p. 173). For a critique of Bird's feminist premise, as well as her other arguments used to support the modern practice of homosexuality in view of the Old Testament witness, see esp. Robert A. Gagnon, "The Old Testament and Homosexuality: A Critical Review of the Case Made by Phyllis Bird," *ZAW* 117 (2005): 367–94.

[79] Boswell, *Christianity, Social Tolerance*, 100–101, along with many others, also describes this legislation in terms of Jewish ritual impurity, as opposed to moral absolutes. Cf. Martin Noth, *Leviticus* (OTL; Philadelphia: Westminster, 1963), 16; and Victor Paul Furnish, "'The Loyal Opposition' and Scripture," in *The Loyal Opposition: Struggling with the Church on Homosexuality* (ed. Tex Sample and Amy E. DeLong; Nashville: Abingdon, 2000), 36–37.

often goes far beyond ritual-cultic contexts. After surveying the various occurrences of the term, P. J. Harland aptly concludes that this word "refers to something which is utterly incompatible with the will of God and which is viewed by him with repugnance because of its evil."[80] As becomes apparent below, this revulsion for homosexual activity goes far beyond its association with the cultic practices of surrounding nations.

Before noting the immediate and wider contexts of the term "abomination" in the relevant biblical passages dealing with homosexual practice, it may be asserted first that "the attempt to place sole responsibility on the Bible for the opprobrium associated with homosexuality hardly reflects the true situation."[81] Joseph Jensen summarizes the evidence for disapproval of homosexuality in ancient Mesopotamia, which has been treated more fully above:

> It was in morally "tolerant" Mesopotamia that we find the homosexual first termed "dog" (used only once in the O.T., Dt. 23:19, and here the context *is* cultic); where he is considered "half a man"; where by transvestism and other means (e.g., symbolically carrying the spindle) he becomes a parody of a woman: where he is, in fact, considered a man who has been turned into a woman by the curse of Ishtar.[82]

Examples of Middle Assyrian and Hittite laws dealing with the penalties for homosexual behavior, also examined above, further substantiate Jenson's point. Given such a view of homosexuality in ANE texts, it does not appear possible to trace the Mosaic prohibition of homosexuality solely to Israel's ritualistic concern for freedom from the cultic defilement of idolatry.

Those who would link the prohibitions of homosexual practice solely to the idolatrous cult prostitution of surrounding nations utilize two main arguments from the context of the Levitical legislation in addition to the reference to the term *tôʿēbâ*.[83] First, it is pointed out that in Lev 18 the prohibition against homosexual intercourse immediately follows the prohibition against sacrificing children to Molech (18:21), thus connecting homosexual practice with idolatry. This argument falters, however, when one recognizes that the repetition of this prohibition in Lev 20 does not follow the reference to child sacrifice but is placed between the prohibitions against incest and bestiality (20:14–16). Furthermore, it is

---

[80] P. J. Harland, "Menswear and Womenswear: A Study of Deuteronomy 22:5," *ExpTim* 110, no. 3 (1998): 73. Ronald F. Youngblood, "תּוֹעֵבָה [*tôʿēbâ*] abominable [custom, thing]," *TWOT* 2:977, points out that "the abomination may be of a physical, ritual, or ethical nature" and especially "includes that which is aesthetically and morally repulsive." Cf. the careful analysis of the usages of this term in the HB in Gagnon, *The Bible and Homosexual Practice,* 117–20; and Grisanti, *NIDOTTE* 4:314–18.

[81] Joseph Jensen, "The Relevance of the Old Testament," in *Dimensions of Human Sexuality* (ed. Dennis Doherty; Garden City, N.Y.: Doubleday, 1979), 7. Jensen is responding particularly to the discussion of homosexuality in the Bible in Anthony Kosnik et al., *Human Sexuality: New Directions in American Catholic Thought* (New York: Paulist, 1977), 188–96.

[82] Jensen, "The Relevance of the Old Testament," 7–8. Jensen's primary source for this summary is Bottéro and Petschow, "Homosexualität," 4:459–68.

[83] For further discussion of both these points, see esp. Gagnon, *The Bible and Homosexual Practice,* 129–32.

now widely recognized that offering children to Molech was prohibited not only because of the idolatrous connection but because child sacrifice threatened the sanctity of the family, or, stated differently, because Molech worship had a sexual aspect: "The Molech cultus . . . consisted of a sexual element and is therefore categorized as *tôʿēbâ;* it is the sexual aspect of the cultus that places it in the list of crimes in Leviticus 18, not its idolatrous element."[84]

The other additional contextual argument for suggesting that homosexual intercourse is prohibited in Leviticus solely because of its connection with idolatry is the oft-repeated warning, found in Lev 18 and 20 (18:1–5, 24–30; 20:22–26), against following Canaanite practices. It is true that the Levitical injunctions regarding homosexuality are placed within the wider setting of the Canaanite abominations. But the deduction of some recent studies—connected with pagan practice, therefore forbidden—does not properly interpret the scriptural context. Jensen turns the "pagan practice" argument on its head when he points out that since much of Israel's cultic ritual coincides with pagan practice (altars, feasts, blood rites, etc.), therefore, "where objection is raised to a pagan rite, some reason *other* than its pagan association must be sought."[85] The context of Lev 18 and

---

[84] Wold, *Out of Order,* 130. Similarly, William J. Webb, *Slaves, Women, and Homosexuals: Exploring the Hermeneutics of Cultural Analysis* (Downers Grove, Ill.: InterVarsity, 2001), 197–98, shows how in the overall structure of this section of Lev 18, the verse concerning sacrificing of children to Molech, with its connection with the subject of offspring from sexual intercourse, comes logically in the transition between prohibitions dealing with *heterosexual* intercourse (vv. 6–20) and those dealing with *nonheterosexual* intercourse (vv. 22–23). James E. Miller hypothesizes a connection between sexuality and Molek worship in that there was a conception vow to Molek in which the human firstborn was dedicated to Molek, much the same way that Hannah dedicated her yet-to-be-conceived child to Yahweh ("Notes on Leviticus 18," *ZAW* 112 [2000]: 402–3). David T. Stewart, "Ancient Sexual Laws: Text and Intertext of the Biblical Holiness Code and Hittite Laws" (PhD diss., University of California, Berkeley, 2000), 236–38, sets forth another possibility. Stewart (p. 236) acknowledges that based upon the content and context of Lev 18:21, "this passage must be about something both idolatrous and sexual." He suggests that already in Genesis both idolatry and adultery were placed in the same category as "great sins" (Gen 20:9; 39:9; cf. Exod 32:21, 30–31) and Lev 20:5 "explicitly describes the practice of the cult [of Molech] as a kind of lust or *zĕnût.*" In light of Isa 57:3–5, which links child sacrifice (to Molech) and adultery, Stewart concludes that from the perspective of Lev 20 and Isaiah, the cult of Molech "has an association—metaphoric or consequential—with fornication" (239). This association between sex and cult is discussed in ch. 3, above. Stewart also points to the intertextual connections between Lev 18:21 and Gen 9 as well as with the creation account, and argues that ultimately this law, like all the others in Lev 18 and 20, prohibits "the misuse of blood and seed, life substances that belong to God. One misuse, in bestial relations, for instance, mimics the creation of species and violates God's prerogative; another misuse, in the *mōlek* cult, undoes the fruit of creation" (259).

[85] Jensen, "The Relevance of the Old Testament," 5. Gagnon, *The Bible and Homosexual Practice,* 130–31, points out another common line of argumentation that is related to the cultic homosexual practice and needs to be turned on its head: "Male cult prostitution was not the only context in which homosexual intercourse manifested itself in the ancient Near East generally. It was merely the most acceptable context for homosexual intercourse

20 provides just such a reason. In 18:24–30 and 20:22–23, God indicates that the sexual distortions described in previous verses (including homosexuality) are defiling in their very nature and not just because they violate Israel's cultic ritual.[86] Because of such practices among the Canaanites—who did not have Israel's cultic ritual—"the land became defiled . . . [and] vomited out its inhabitants" (Lev 18:25). Just as the land vomited out the Canaanites, so God warns that it will vomit out Israel if Israel engages in such abomination (18:27–28).[87] This "natural" law is summarized in 18:29: "Whoever commits any of these abominations shall be cut off from their people." White and Niell recognize that this passage is far from limiting the prohibitions to Jews:

> On the contrary, the text of Leviticus 18:24–30 clearly reveals that God judged the non-Jewish nations who previously lived in the land because they violated His judgments and engaged in the type of sexual immorality that is listed in Leviticus 18:6–23. . . . If

to be practiced in Mesopotamia, certainly for those who played the role of the receptive partner. In our own cultural context we think that the banning of male cult prostitution does not take into account consensual, non-cultic, loving homosexual relationships. In the cultural context of the ancient Near East the reasoning has to be reversed: to ban homosexual cult prostitutes was to ban all homosexual intercourse."

[86] Webb, *Slaves, Women and Homosexuals,* passim, suggests criteria for determining whether a given biblical statement is permanently normative (transcultural), and applies these to the issues of slavery, the role of women, and homosexuality. What is found in Lev 18 and 20, with the contrast between the practices of the surrounding culture and the Levitical legislation, is an example of a persuasive criterion of permanence that Webb, 81–82, labels "Preliminary Movement." As opposed to the widespread acceptance of homosexuality in surrounding ANE cultures, the biblical prohibitions challenge the portrait of the ancient gods, remove homosexual practices from the temple cult, and legislate against homosexual practices within the community life. "Scripture moves in a particular direction relative to these cultures by its broad-sweeping ban of homosexuality within the covenant community" (p. 82). Webb also sees an application of the criterion of "Competing Options" in this case: "A component of a text is more likely to be transcultural, if presented in a time and setting when other competing options existed in the broader culture" (152; see discussion on the applicability to homosexuality, 155–57).

[87] The reference to the "land" in these passages does not imply that the legislation prohibiting homosexual activity pertained only to Jews and non-Jews living in Israel, contra Jacob Milgrom, "Does the Bible Prohibit Homosexuality?" *BRev* 9, no. 6 (1993): 11; idem, "How Not to Read the Bible," *BRev* 10, no. 2 (1994): 14, 48; idem, *Leviticus 17–22: A New Translation with Introduction and Commentary* (AB 3A; New York: Doubleday, 2000), 1568, 1786–90. "If one carried Milgrom's interpretation to its logical conclusion, diaspora Jews and gentiles alike would be exempt from the commands regarding incest, bestiality, and child sacrifice. . . . The text is speaking to the situation of residents in Israel; it is not, however, granting license to all who live outside the land. . . . That it addresses one situation does not make it irrelevant to others, particularly in a case involving gender confusion, a matter that cuts across ethnic lines" (Gagnon, *The Bible and Homosexual Practice,* 116, n. 185). Gane, *Leviticus, Numbers,* 327, further shows that Leviticus has a way of limiting the scope of a law to the promised land by the introduction "When you enter the land . . ." (Lev 14:34; 19:23; 23:10; 25:2); no such limitation of scope, however, is applied to the prohibitions of Lev 18 and 20 (see ibid., 326–29, for further critique of Milgrom's view). The other evidence the present discussion offers for the universality of this prohibition also shows the fallaciousness of this position.

God's prohibitions against homosexuality were restricted to the children of Israel, He would not have judged the surrounding nations for such sinfulness.[88]

That the legislation of Lev 18 constitutes universal moral law, not just ritual law pertaining only to Israel, is also evident from the fact that these laws are explicitly applied to the "alien" (NRSV) (or "stranger," "resident alien") (*gēr*) as well as to the native Israelite (18:26). As elaborated in the afterword to the present study, this applicability to the "alien" becomes a decisive factor for the early NT church in determining which laws beyond the Ten Commandments should be regarded as obligatory for Gentile Christians. In Acts 15 the four categories of prohibitions imposed upon Gentile Christians are precisely the same four, in the same order, as those listed in Lev 17–18 that are applicable to the stranger, with the final prohibition, *porneia,* summarizing the illicit sexual activities described in Lev 18. Clearly the NT covenant community saw this reference to the "alien" as an indication of the transtemporal and transcultural nature of these laws, including the law prohibiting homosexual activity.

Wold has shown how the rationale of the prohibitions in Lev 18—including homosexuality—rests upon the foundational principles of creation order in Gen 1:27–28: the creation of all humanity in the image of God as "male and female," unique and distinct from the rest of God's creation, and the command to "be fruitful and multiply, and fill the earth." "These principles describe the order and structure of humanity in two relationships: to God and to society. All the laws of Leviticus 18 may be understood as violations of these principles."[89] The activities proscribed in Lev 18 and 20 are portrayed as "abominations" because homosexual practice violates the divine order of gender set forth in Gen 1:27 and 2:24.[90]

---

[88] White and Niell, *The Same Sex Controversy,* 68.

[89] Wold, *Out of Order,* 130. So also Gagnon, *The Bible and Homosexual Practice,* 136: "All the laws in Lev 18:6–23; 20:2–21 legislate against forms of sexual behavior that disrupt the created order set into motion by the God of Israel."

[90] For further elaboration of this principle, see Samuel H. Dresner, "Homosexuality and the Order of Creation," *Judaism* 40 (1991): 309–21. Dresner (p. 320) asks this penetrating rhetorical question: "Once the argument from the order of creation and natural law is abandoned and heterosexuality within the marital bond as a norm is dismissed, then how can adultery, pedophilia, incest or bestiality be rejected?" So also Herman C. Waetjen, "Same-Sex Relations in Antiquity and Sexuality and Sexual Identity in Contemporary American Society," in *Biblical Ethics and Homosexuality: Listening to Scripture* (ed. Robert L. Brawley; Louisville: Westminster John Knox, 1996), 105: "There can be no compromise of sexual identity. Created as a male, a man must remain pure and unblemished in his nature of maleness. To surrender it sexually by assuming the role of the opposite sex is a desecration of the divine order of creation." Cf. Deborah F. Sawyer, *God, Gender, and the Bible* (Biblical Limits; London: Routledge, 2002), 35: "The classified list of sleeping partners in Leviticus 18 reinforces the boundaries that are set up in Genesis 1–3." Because of this creation order for gender, "even if the Bible made no reference to homosexual acts, the biblical view [creation/covenant design] of marriage would exclude them" (Maxie D. Dunnam, "The Creation/Covenant Design for Marriage and Sexuality," in *Staying the Course: Supporting the Church's Position on Homosexuality* [ed. Maxie D. Dunnam and

Gagnon points out that this connection with the creation order is implicit in the refrain of Lev 18:22 and 20:13: "*lie[s] with a male as with a woman.*" Such phraseology intertextually links with both Gen 1:27 and Gen 2:24. After surveying several suggested motivations for the prohibition of male same-sex intercourse—connection with idolatry,[91] procreative dead end,[92] contact of semen with excrement[93]—Gagnon concludes that the refrain in 18:22 and 20:13 "is the best indication we have of what the primary concern was; namely, behaving toward another man as if he were a woman by making him the object of male sex-

---

H. Newton Malony; Nashville: Abingdon, 2003], 104). For a proposed theoretical framework providing a scriptural criterion, grounded in creation, for transcultural analysis of biblical passages, see Alexandru Breja, "A Biblical Approach to Transcultural Analysis" (paper presented at the annual meeting of the Evangelical Theological Society, Atlanta, November 21, 2003), 1–19. The creation criterion of permanence for biblical material is specifically related to homosexuality in Webb, *Slaves, Women, and Homosexuals,* 123–45, esp. 131–33.

[91] This view, with its major proponents, is discussed above.

[92] This view suggests that the main reason for prohibiting homosexual intercourse in Levitical law is that such intercourse "wastes seed" and cannot lead to procreation. Major proponents include David Biale, *Eros and the Jews: From Biblical Israel to Contemporary America* (New York: Basic, 1992), 29; Thomas B. Dozeman, "Creation and Procreation in the Biblical Teaching on Homosexuality," *USQR* 49 (1995): 175–76, 179, 189; Sarah J. Melcher, "The Holiness Code and Human Sexuality," in *Biblical Ethics and Homosexuality: Listening to Scripture* (ed. Robert L. Brawley; Louisville: Westminster John Knox, 1996), 98–99; Milgrom, "Does the Bible Prohibit Homosexuality?" 11; idem, "How Not to Read the Bible," 14, 48; idem, *Leviticus 17–22,* 1567–68. Gagnon, *The Bible and Homosexual Practice,* 132–34, acknowledges that the suggested rationale of "procreative dead end" has some merit, given the command in Gen 1:28 to "be fruitful and multiply" and the need to curb any threat to the integrity of the Israelite lineage. But such rationale does not constitute the sole or even primary rationale, because (1) it would not be broad enough to cover the other prohibitions regarding sexual activity in Lev 18, (2) a number of other sexual acts not leading to procreation are not proscribed in Lev 18 (such as heterosexual relations during a woman's pregnancy), and (3) such rationale does not account for the highly emotive reference to male-male intercourse as "abomination." Even more important, I would add that from the beginning of the canon, as discussed in ch. 1, above, even heterosexual intercourse was not limited to the intent to propagate children.

[93] The main proponent is Saul M. Olyan, "'And With a Male You Shall Not Lie the Lying Down of a Woman': On the Meaning and Significance of Leviticus 18:22 and 20:13," *JHSex* 5, no. 2 (1994): 203: "Male-male anal intercourse may have been proscribed in order to prevent the mixing of two otherwise defiling substances [semen and excrement] and thereby prevent the defilement of the land of Israel." A similar position is taken by Stephen F. Bigger, "The Family Laws of Leviticus 18 in Their Setting," *JBL* 98 (1979): 202–3; and Martin Samuel Cohen, "The Biblical Prohibition of Homosexual Intercourse," *Journal of Homosexuality* 19, no. 4 (1990): 3–20; repr. in *Biblical Studies Alternatively: An Introductory Reader* (ed. Susanne Scholz; Upper Saddle River, N.J.: Prentice Hall, 2003), 153–64, who place the laws of Lev 18 under the rubric of "misuse of semen." Gagnon, *The Bible and Homosexual Practice,* 134–35, acknowledges that these rationales may have been a factor, but points out that they are not broad enough to encompass all the prohibitions described in Lev 18 and probably should be subsumed under the larger category of violating the created order—the position discussed below.

ual desires. That is an abomination, an abhorrent violation of divinely sanctioned boundaries—in this case, gender boundaries established at creation."[94] The prohibition of homosexual relations is not an issue of gender status (male honor or hierarchy), as some would claim, but concerns "a distortion of gender itself, as created and ordered by God."[95] B. S. Childs captures this biblical rationale and the implication for today:

> The recent attempt of some theologians to find a biblical opening, if not warrant, for the practice of homosexuality stands in striking disharmony with the Old Testament's understanding of the relation of male and female. The theological issue goes far beyond the citing of occasional texts which condemn the practice (Lev 20:13). . . . The Old Testament views homosexuality as a distortion of creation which falls into the shadows outside the blessing.[96]

Beyond the two main pointers, already emphasized, toward universality and permanent normativeness within the Levitical texts—the absolute, all-encompassing language and the grounding of the legislation in the creation order—Gagnon summarizes five additional biblical indicators that the Levitical legislation concerning homosexual practice is transtemporal and transcultural.[97] First, this legislation is part of the broader and consistent OT witness opposing homosexual practice.[98] Second, the legislation proscribing homosexual activity is grouped

---

[94] Gagnon, *The Bible and Homosexual Practice*, 135–36. See Stewart, "Ancient Sexual Laws," 378, who concludes regarding all the laws of Lev 18: "All these possible sexual violations hark back to the beginning, to the era when God set in motion the ongoing re-creation of humankind."

[95] Gagnon, *The Bible and Homosexual Practice,* 142; contra Nissinen, *Homoeroticism,* 42–44, who claims that the issue is not gender but gender roles or status—the presumption of male superiority and dominance over females in antiquity (see Stiebert and Walsh, "Hebrew Bible," 138–46; and Bird, "Christian Ethical Deliberation," 152, for similar claims). Gagnon, *The Bible and Homosexual Practice,* 140–42, argues (as chs. 1–2, above, have elaborated) that male hierarchy is not grounded in creation but comes after the fall and there is no punishment in Scripture for subversion of male hierarchy. In "The Bible and Homosexual Practice," 46, he further (and correctly) nuances this postfall hierarchy by limiting it to the husband's rule and showing that far from being a rigid insistence upon male superiority and female submission, there is a positive trajectory in the Bible back toward the Edenic ideal of gender equality by placing women in leadership roles. See ch. 6, below, for substantiation of this trajectory. See also Robert A. Di Vito, "Questions about the Construction of (Homo) Sexuality: Same-Sex Relations in the Hebrew Bible," in *Sexual Diversity in Catholicism: Toward the Development of Moral Theology* (ed. Patricia Bettie Jung with Joseph Andrew Coray; Collegeville, Minn.: Liturgical Press, 1989), 116–17, for further argumentation that the issue here is gender differentiation itself and not just status differentiation.

[96] Brevard S. Childs, *Old Testament Theology in a Canonical Context* (Philadelphia: Fortress, 1985), 194.

[97] Gagnon, "The Bible and Homosexual Practice," 62–68. This list is a synthesis and further development of Gagnon's earlier discussion in *The Bible and Homosexual Practice,* 111–46.

[98] Webb, *Slaves, Women, and Homosexuals,* 91, sees here a negative application of his transcultural criterion labeled "Breakouts." According to this criterion, "a component of a

with prohibitions of other sex acts that transcend the culture and setting of ancient Israel: incest, adultery, and bestiality.[99] Third, homosexual intercourse is a "first-tier sexual offense," grouped together with other sexual offenses that are punishable by death sentence (Lev 20:10–16). The death penalty for homosexual practice is unique to biblical law, and the inclusion of this practice among the offenses in Israel that met with capital punishment underscores its seriousness.[100] Fourth, the language of purity used to describe the sexual offenses in Lev 18 and 20, far from relegating these laws to the status of the nonrational, preethical, or merely ritual, in fact buttresses the morality of the laws. In the book of Leviticus, "the conjunction of purity and prohibition often buttresses a moral judgment by focusing on the inherently degrading character of the act for participants and its destabilizing effects for the community. . . . Indeed, one of the hallmarks of the Holiness Code is that it incorporates ethics under the rubric of purity; that is, sin and impurity merge."[101] Finally, the NT appropriates the OT legislation prohibiting homosexual intercourse (see the afterword, below).[102]

---

text may be culturally confined if the social norms reflected in that text are completely 'broken out of' in other biblical texts." Webb notes that, regarding homosexuality, "there are no viable breakouts in the homosexuality texts. . . . Since the movement in all of the homosexual texts relative to the original culture is a complete banning, it is understandable why there is no further movement in that same direction" (103–4).

[99] Webb, *Slaves, Women, and Homosexuals*, 192, labels this transcultural criterion "Contextual Comparisons": "A text or something within a text may be transcultural to the degree that other aspects in a specialized context, such as a list or grouping, are transcultural." Applied to homosexuality, "the context/lists criterion clearly favors a transcultural understanding of the biblical prohibitions. Out of the hundreds of items in the vice and virtue lists, an extremely high percentage of them reflect transcultural values. . . . In view of the repeated inclusion of homosexuality within the vice lists [and here Webb includes the NT lists], the case for not accepting homosexuality in general for today is extremely strong" (p. 196; Webb discusses the Levitical prohibitions amidst the lists in Lev 18 and 20, pp. 197–200).

[100] Webb, ibid., 172, labels this "moderately persuasive" criterion of permanence "Penal Code": "The more severe the penalty, the more likely it is that the prohibited or prescribed action reflects transcultural values." As this criterion is applied to homosexuality, "the placement of homosexuality on the death penalty list argues strongly for the ongoing applicability of divine displeasure against this act in any culture and at any time" (p. 177).

[101] Gagnon, "The Bible and Homosexual Practice," 66. For a helpful discussion of the distinction between ritual and moral purity, see Gane, *Leviticus, Numbers*, 306–8; and Jonathan Klawans, "The Impurity of Immorality in Ancient Judaism," *JJS* 48 (1997):1–16. Based upon Klawans's work, Di Vito, "Questions," 118–22, concludes that the Levitical laws proscribing homosexual activity do not concern ritual defilement at all: "Same sex relations is not 'merely' a matter of ritual purity . . . but an issue of moral purity, a public 'crime,' if you will, that implicates not only the offender and his/her immediate circle but in fact the whole of Israelite society" (p. 122). Cf. Christopher Seitz, "Sexuality and Scripture's Plain Sense: The Christian Community and the Law of God," in *Homosexuality, Science, and the "Plain Sense" of Scripture* (ed. David L. Balch; Grand Rapids: Eerdmans, 2000), 186–89.

[102] This is the transcultural criterion labeled by Webb, *Slaves, Women, and Homosexuals*, 73, as "*absolute movement:* the biblical author has pushed society so far and that is as far as it is supposed to go; further movement is not desired." Thus, in the case of homo-

I fully concur with Gagnon's summary interpretation regarding Lev 18:22 and 20:13:

> In taking such a severe and comprehensive stance toward male homosexual behavior, Lev 18:22 and 20:13 represent a level of revulsion toward same-sex intercourse without parallel in the ancient Near East. . . . [The framer of these laws as part of the so-called Holiness Code] was responding to the conviction that same-sex intercourse was fundamentally incompatible with the creation of men and women as complementary sexual beings. For a man to have sexual intercourse with another male as though the latter were not a male but a female violates God's design for the created order. . . . It is nothing short of a rebellion against the way God made humans to function as sexual beings. . . . [There is solid] evidence for the enduring validity of Lev 18:22 and 20:13.[103]

Deuteronomy 23:18–19 (ET 23:17–18). Chapter 3, above, examines the general issue of cultic prostitution, and chapter 7 discusses noncultic female prostitution. Here we concentrate on the pentateuchal prohibition of male prostitution, which undoubtedly included male-male sexual intercourse.[104] The key passage is Deut 23:18–19 (ET 23:17–18):

> None of the daughters of Israel shall be a temple prostitute [qĕdēšâ]; none of the sons of Israel shall be a temple prostitute [qādēš]. You shall not bring the fee of a prostitute [zônâ] or the wages of a male prostitute [keleb, 'dog'] into the house of the LORD your God in payment for any vow, for both of these are abhorrent to the LORD your God.

As noted in chapter 3, above, 23:18 (ET 23:17) refers to cult functionaries who, among other functions, engaged in ritual sex, probably for hire (sacred prostitution). As also discussed in ch. 3, these cultic functionaries mentioned in v. 18 (ET v. 17) are probably not to be equated with the noncultic prostitution of the "prostitute" (zônâ) and the "dog" (keleb) described in v. 19 (ET v. 18), but at the same time, the close contextual connection confirms the sexual role of the male cultic functionary (qādēš) mentioned in the previous verse. The term

---

sexual practice, "when one comes to the New Testament, there is no softening of Scripture's negative assessment of homosexuality found in the Old Testament" (p. 82).

[103] Gagnon, *The Bible and Homosexual Practice,* 156–57.

[104] If these prostitutes serviced women rather than men, as some have suggested, it would presuppose a custom that cannot be documented elsewhere in the ancient Near East. The discussion above of the ANE background illustrated the same-sex role of the Mesopotamian *assinnu, kurgarrû,* and *kuluʾu;* the fact that these cultic functionaries were usually castrated rendered them unsuitable partners for heterosexual intercourse. Furthermore, as Gagnon points out, "the theory of male-to-female cult prostitution is difficult to harmonize with the attention given by Israelite society to guarding the sexual purity of their women" (*The Bible and Homosexual Practice,* 104). In a paternal society, if women were impregnated by male cult prostitutes, the paternity would belong to these cult functionaries, and this would create havoc regarding issues of legitimacy, inheritance rights, and so forth. Gagnon further argues that "the harsh descriptions of the *qĕdēšîm* in 1–2 Kings . . . along with the epithet of 'dog' in Deut 23:18, suggests a degree of revulsion more suited to *same-sex* male cult prostitution."

qĕdēšîm, "male temple prostitutes," is probably the equivalent of the Mesopotamian *assinnu*, those men "whose masculinity had been transformed into femininity by a goddess . . . and one of whose cultic functions was to offer their bodies to other men for same-sex intercourse."[105] As will become apparent below in the section dealing with the Prophets, one of the major tasks of the reforms in the time of the divided monarchy was to rid the land of the male (as well as the female) cult prostitutes.

If the term *keleb* in Israel refers to noncultic male prostitution, as argued below in ch. 7, then the twin verses of this Deuteronomic passage explicitly prohibit all homosexual activity, both cultic and noncultic. As noted in ch. 3 above, Deut 23:18–19 (ET 23:17–18) is found in the section of Deuteronomy that elaborates upon the seventh commandment; this indicates that any homosexual activity is a violation of the Decalogue.

Homosexual Practice in the Prophets/Writings

Male Cult Prostitution. In addition to the prohibition of male cult prostitution in Deut 23:18 (ET 23:17), five passages in the Prophets/Writings refer to *qĕdēšîm,* "male temple prostitutes." Four of these passages are found in the Prophets. According to 1 Kgs 14:24, in the days of Rehoboam, son of Solomon, "there were also male temple prostitutes [*qādēš*] in the land. They [the people of Judah] committed all the abominations of the nations that the LORD drove out before the people of Israel." According to 15:12, Asa, the grandson of Rehoboam, "put away the male temple prostitutes [*qĕdēšîm*] from the land, and removed all the idols that his ancestors had made." The narrator in 22:47 (ET 22:46) indicates regarding Jehoshaphat, son of Asa, "The remnant of the male temple prostitutes [*qādēš*] who were still in the land in the days of his father Asa, he exterminated." Finally, according to 2 Kgs 23:7, Josiah "broke down the houses [quarters, apartments] of the male temple prostitutes [*qĕdēšîm*] that were in the house of the LORD, where the women did weaving for Asherah." These passages make evident that the problem of male cult prostitution was prevalent during the period of the divided monarchy. Especially telling is the reference in 1 Kgs 14:24 to "all the abominations of the nations that the LORD drove out before the people of Israel"—a striking intertextual linkage with a similar statement in the list of sexual sins in Lev 18:24–30.

One passage in the Writings—Job 36:13–14—refers to *qĕdēšîm.* Elihu declares, "The godless in heart cherish anger; they do not cry for help when he binds them. They die in their youth, and their life ends in shame [*qĕdēšîm,* 'among the temple prostitutes']." Elihu's statement reflects the low estimation placed upon the status of cult prostitutes in ANE society and is consistent with their degrading and debilitating lifestyle, as depicted in ANE texts discussed above. Gagnon recognizes that this passage provides further evidence for concluding that *qĕdēšîm*

---

[105] Gagnon, *The Bible and Homosexual Practice,* 102.

are to be equated with male cult prostitutes: "If the *qĕdēšîm* were simply cultic functionaries who had no connection to profligate sexual acts, it is difficult to see why the author would have used them as the epitome of those who lead short lives." Gagnon also points out that the point of comparison in this passage "is not anger per se but rather the deleterious effects of harbored anger and atrocious sexual immorality, two forms of self-destructive behavior, on the quality and length of life."[106]

Judges 19. There is only one explicit reference to attempted noncultic homosexual activity in the Prophets/Writings. That "text of terror" at the end of the book of Judges portrays men of Gibeah making homosexual advances against the Levite: "While they were enjoying themselves, the men of the city, a perverse lot [lit. 'men of the sons of Belial/worthlessness'], surrounded the house, and started pounding on the door. They said to the old man, the master of the house, 'Bring out the man who came into your house, so that we may have intercourse with him [*yādaʿ*]'" (Judg 19:22). Use of the verb *yādaʿ*, "know," indicates clearly that the meaning is sexual intercourse. Verses 23–25 confirm this as the story continues: the master of the house intervened, offering his virgin daughter and the Levite's concubine for them "to ravish" (*ʿānâ*) instead (v. 24). When the base fellows "would not listen to him," the Levite finally brought out his concubine for them, and "they wantonly raped [*yādaʿ*, 'knew'] her, and abused [*ʿālal*] her all the night until the morning" (v. 25). Certainly the verb "to know" in v. 25 must connote sexual intercourse, and the context of v. 22 demands a similar sexual connotation.

Although no homosexual activity takes place in the story, the narrator makes clear the contemporary perspective on this activity by recording the words of the master of the house to the would-be homosexual assailants: "No, my brothers, do not act so wickedly [*hipʿil* of *rāʿaʿ*]. Since this man is my guest, do not do this vile thing [*nĕbālâ*]. . . . Against this man do not do such a vile thing [*nĕbālâ*]" (Judg 19:23–24). Two issues are involved from the perspective of the man of the house: upholding his responsibility of hospitality to his guest and preserving him from homosexual gang rape. Both are part of the wicked and vile outrage that the assailants demand. Certainly the Gibeahites were inhospitable, but they also attempted homosexual rape. The two themes intertwine, as they did in the closely paralleled account of Sodom and Gomorrah in Gen 19. "The inhospitality is reflected in their attempt at homosexual rape. Inhospitality and homosexuality are not mutually exclusive."[107]

Gagnon counters the oft-repeated claim that this passage condemns only homosexual *rape* and not all homosexual activity. He points to the larger context of the Pentateuch and the so-called Deuteronomistic History, in which a clear stance is taken against homosexual intercourse, and asks this penetrating question: "In these contexts, how is it possible to reasonably argue that homosexual intercourse *per se* did not add to the dimension of horror for the old man, for the

---

106 Ibid., 103.
107 Wold, *Out of Order,* 85. Contra, e.g., Boswell, *Christianity, Social Tolerance,* 95–96.

Levite, and for the narrator of the story?" Gagnon answers his own question: "Repugnance for male penetration of males must have been a significant factor in
twice designating the demand for sexual intercourse with the Levite as a *nĕbālâ*
much greater than that involved in intercourse with the old man's daughter and
the Levite's concubine."[108]

The author of Judges gives his own summary of the outrage contemplated
and committed at Gibeah, in the words of those who were contemporaries of the
event: "Has such a thing ever happened since the day that the Israelites came up
from the land of Egypt until this day? Consider it, take counsel, and speak out"
(Judg 19:30). The narrator also brackets this whole narrative complex (Judg
19–21) with a signal that the events depict a world gone tragically awry. Judges
19–21 begins with the comment "In those days, when there was no king in Israel"
(19:1); and the concluding comment is even more to the point: "In those days
there was no king in Israel; all the people did what was right in their own eyes"
(21:25). Centuries later, Hosea, without explicitly mentioning the attempt at
homosexual rape, nonetheless alludes to this whole event in Israel's history when
he compares it to the moral degradation of Israel in his own day: "They have
deeply corrupted themselves as in the days of Gibeah; he will remember their
iniquity; he will punish their sins" (Hos 9:9; cf. 10:9).

Ezekiel 16 and 18. The discussion of the attempted homosexual activity of the
men of Sodom recorded in Gen 19 referred to Ezek 16:48–50, which alludes to
this incident and compares it to the condition of Ezekiel's Judean contemporaries. Some have argued that this prophetic passage has in view only the display of
inhospitality, and not homosexual practice, in its mention of the sins of Sodom,
but as with the case of the outrage at Gibeah, it is not a matter of "either-or" but
"both-and." Ezekiel does indeed highlight Sodom's nonsexual offenses: "she and
her daughters had pride, excess of food, and prosperous ease, but did not aid the
poor and needy" (Ezek 16:49). But those who argue solely for nonsexual sins at
issue here fail to read this passage in its wider context. In the very next verse
(16:50), mention is made of the "abomination" (NKJV; Heb. *tôʿēbâ,* sg.) committed by Sodom; *tôʿēbâ* is the very term used to describe homosexual practice in Lev
18:22 and 20:13.[109]

Those who regard the sin of Sodom as nonsexual argue that *tôʿēbâ* in Ezek
16:50 simply refers to the social injustice described in v. 49. Gagnon, however,
demonstrates that the term *tôʿēbâ,* (sg.) "abomination," in v. 50 speaks of an additional offense beyond the social injustice of v. 49, and the reference to *tôʿēbôt,*
(pl.) "abominations," in v. 51 is a summary statement of all four sins of Sodom
described in vv. 49–50.[110] The parallel passage that confirms this interpretation is

---

[108] Gagnon, *The Bible and Homosexual Practice,* 95.

[109] See, e.g., Moshe Greenberg, *Ezekiel 1–20: A New Translation with Introduction and
Commentary* (AB 22; Garden City, N.Y.: Doubleday, 1983), 289, who intimates that the
"abomination" of v. 49 refers to "sodomy" and sees the connection with Lev 18:22 and 20:13.

[110] Gagnon, *The Bible and Homosexual Practice,* 80–85; cf. the brief synthesis in idem,
"The Bible and Homosexual Practice," 57–58.

a similar list of vices in 18:10–13, where Ezekiel again uses *tôʿēbâ* (sg.) followed by *tôʿēbôt* (pl.). In the latter passage, it is unmistakable that the use of *tôʿēbâ* refers to an additional act separate and distinct from the oppression of the poor and the needy and *tôʿēbôt* is a summary referring to "all these abominable things" (18:13) of the previous list. Gagnon then shows that this usage of *tôʿēbâ* in Ezek 18 provides a strong intertextual linkage with Lev 18 in general and the practice of homosexuality in particular:

> The explanation for the singular and plural uses of *tôʿēbâ* in [Ezek]18:12–13 probably lies with the similar phenomenon in Leviticus 18, part of the Holiness Code (Leviticus 17–26). A summary following a list of forbidden sexual relations in Lev 18:6–23 characterizes all of the preceding acts as "abominations" (*tôʿēbôt* , 18:24–30, with the plural appearing in 18:26, 27, 29, 30). However, in all of the Holiness Code only homosexual intercourse is singled out for special mention within the list as "an abomination" (18:22 and 20:13). The point is probably the same for Ezek 18:10–13; all of the preceding acts are "abominations," but there is one specific act that deserves the label above all others: homosexual intercourse.[111]

Gagnon further points out that the other two occurrences of *tôʿēbâ* in the singular in Ezekiel (22:11; 33:26), like all the occurrences, both singular and plural, of *tôʿēbâ* in Leviticus, refer to sexual sins. "Therefore, the evidence indicates that the singular *tôʿēbâ* in Ezek 16:50 refers to the (attempted) commission of atrocious sexual immorality at Sodom, probably the homosexual intercourse proscribed in Lev 18:22; 20:13."[112]

In addition to the linkage between the term "abomination" in Ezekiel and homosexual practice proscribed in Lev 18 and 20, one cannot ignore the dominant overtone of sexual immorality throughout Ezek 16, which lends further support to the interpretation that, for Ezekiel, Sodom's sin included sexual immorality.[113] Some scholars have argued that part of Jerusalem's harlotry described in Ezek 16 includes gender reversal, in which the woman Jerusalem "is trying to pass for a male. Like a male, she is associated with war and violence, she seeks multiple sexual partners, she symbolically acquires male genitalia and ejaculates rather than receiving and containing fluids."[114] If this interpretation is correct, then, as part of the woman's spiritual hypersexuality, she (symbolically) reverses gender roles and engages in bisexual behavior, possibly including lesbian sex by means of dildos.[115]

---

[111] Gagnon, *The Bible and Homosexual Practice,* 82–83. Gagnon shows further intertextual linkages between Ezek 18 and Lev 18 in that the phraseology "they committed an abomination" of Lev 20:13 is nearly an exact match in the Hebrew with Ezek 18:12 (p. 83).

[112] Ibid., 83–84.

[113] See chs. 7 and 8, below, for further discussion of the imagery of sexual immorality in the allegory of Ezek 16.

[114] See esp. S. Tamar Kamionkowski, "Gender Reversal in Ezekiel 16," in *Prophets and Daniel* (ed. Athalya Brenner; FCB² 8; New York: Sheffield Academic Press, 2001), 170–85, quote at 182.

[115] Kamionkowski, "Gender Reversal," 177–79, finds in Ezek 16:17 ("You also took your beautiful jewels of my gold and my silver that I had given you, and made for yourself

Whatever the specific revolting sexual activity, according to 16:43 God declares of Jerusalem, "Because you have not remembered the days of your youth,
but have enraged me with all these things; therefore, I have returned your deeds
upon your head. . . . Have you not committed lewdness [*zimmâ*] beyond all your
abominations?" The word *zimmâ*, "lewdness, wickedness, depravity," in this passage is the term used in Leviticus and also often in Ezekiel to refer to "premeditated sexual sins."[116] As with the situation at Gibeah, the inhospitality of the
Sodomites was reflected in homosexual acts (the latter being an abomination
[*tôʿēbâ*] and lewdness [*zimmâ*]). Ezekiel condemns both inhospitality and homosexual activity as part of the deeper sin of pride and rebellion against God.[117]

Ruth and Naomi? Studies of the Bible and homosexuality rarely include a discussion of the possibility that the relationship between Ruth and Naomi was
homosexual in nature. Tom Horner, however, suggests, "There are still not sufficient grounds to say with certainty, however, that a homosexual relationship existed between Naomi and Ruth, but there are enough to point out that the
possibility of such a relationship cannot be overlooked."[118] Horner points in particular to the scenes of physical intimacy (kissing and weeping together [Ruth
1:10]), the intimate statement of devotion on the part of Ruth for Naomi (1:16),
and the experience of these two women living together alone (Ruth 2–3).

This suggestion, perhaps plausible on the surface, finds no solid support in
the overall flow of the book. Ruth's statement of loyalty to Naomi is not one of
homosexual intimacy but of radical faith (like Abraham's) to throw in her lot
with the covenant community of Israel and its God, leaving behind her ties with
Moab.[119] The focus of the two lives of Naomi and Ruth, thrown together by the
bitter misfortunes of their husbands' deaths, is not a homosexual relationship,
but an attempt to find Ruth a husband. Heterosexual, married love, not a lesbian

---

male images, and with them played the whore") an indication of the woman's "usurping
the phallus" by making dildos (phallic images) "as instruments by which to penetrate men
(or perhaps other women)" (p. 8). Verse 36 ("your lust [*nĕḥōšet*, 'juice'] was poured out")
is seen to describe the woman's "ejaculation" by means of the dildo (174–77). Such an interpretation, supported by Akkadian cognates and contextual considerations, is plausible,
viewed as part of the overall portrayal of woman Israel's spiritual hypersexuality. For
further discussion, see chs. 7 and 8, below.

[116] See Lev 18:17; 20:14; Judg 20:6; Ezek 16:27, 58; 22:9; 23:27, 29, 35, 44, 48; 24:13.
Wold, *Out of Order*, 88, points out that the term "is applied to deliberate sin, and sometimes stands parallel to words for lust and harlotry in Ezekiel."

[117] Gagnon, *The Bible and Homosexual Practice*, 85, elaborates on this theocentric
focus of Ezekiel in his depiction of the sins of Sodom: "The two evils [neglecting the poor
and homosexual behavior] are linked by a flagrant disregard of God's own priorities,
putting the human self at the center of the cosmos. In Ezekiel's view, the overarching rubric for the sin of Sodom is not inhospitality or homosexual behavior but human
arrogance in relation to God."

[118] Tom Horner, *Jonathan Loved David: Homosexuality in Biblical Times* (Philadelphia: Westminster, 1978), 43; see 40–46 for elaboration of possible grounds for his
suggestion.

[119] See below, ch. 6, for a more complete discussion of Ruth's act of heroic faith.

relationship, was the experience for both of them before the death of their hus-bands and remains the goal of both throughout Ruth. "Naomi functions as some-thing of a matchmaker for Ruth and Boaz, and Ruth's marriage to Boaz at the end of the book 'fills up' the empty and bitter Naomi. The intimacy between the two women seems fully accounted for in the 'mother and daughter' model that the story presents."[120]

Ron Springett shows how, in the larger context of the book, "the aim of the author was to portray the idyllic scene of a God-fearing pastoral community. The main characters stand out against this background."[121] Springett further summa-rizes main points made by the book—praise of Ruth as a model of virtue, the commendable piety of marriage within kin, and Ruth's inclusion in the ancestry of David—and concludes, "It seems that the last thing the author would wish to do here is to introduce a foreign person whose character could be questioned in any way in the light of Jewish morality."[122] Springett's assessment of the evidence is on the mark: "The homosexual interpretation appears to be a speculation read into the text rather than an interpretation arising from or even suggested by the text and context of the book itself."[123]

David and Jonathan? Some proponents of homosexual practice have argued that the friendship between David and Jonathan was a homosexual relation-ship.[124] According to 1 Sam 18:1, "the soul of Jonathan was bound to the soul of David, and Jonathan loved him as his own soul"; 18:3 adds, "Then Jonathan made a covenant with David, because he loved him as his own soul." First Samuel 19:1 continues in the same vein: "Saul's son Jonathan took great delight in David." And 20:17 restates these assessments of the relationship as David is about to flee from King Saul: "Jonathan made David swear again by his love for him; for he loved him as he loved his own life." Before David's departure, he and Jonathan "kissed each other, and wept with each other; David wept the more" (20:41).

---

[120] Webb, *Slaves, Women, and Homosexuals,* 103.

[121] Springett, *Homosexuality,* 79.

[122] Ibid.

[123] Ibid.

[124] See esp. Horner, *Jonathan Loved David,* 26–39; and Silvia Schroer and Thomas Staubli, "Saul, David, and Jonathan—the Story of a Triangle? A Contribution to the Issue of Homosexuality in the First Testament," in *Samuel and Kings* (ed. Athalya Brenner; trans. Barbara and Martin Rumscheidt; FCB[2] 7; Sheffield, Eng.: Sheffield Academic Press, 2000), 22–36. Cf. Greenberg, *The Construction of Homosexuality,* 114: "The Hebrew Bible underwent extensive editing before being put into final form, and an explicit homosexual relationship between David and Jonathan could easily have been deleted by priestly edi-tors. Nevertheless, homophilic innuendos permeate the story." Yaron Peleg, "Love at First Sight? David, Jonathan, and the Biblical Politics of Gender," *JSOT* 30 (2005): 171–89, sug-gests an "alternative queer reading; one that presents the relations between Jonathan and David not as the relations between two male lovers, but as the attraction and love between a 'man' and a 'woman'" (quote at p. 172). Peleg further explains his view: "In other words, my intention is to read this text not only as a story that justifies David's rise to power by emphasizing his masculinity, but also as a text which disqualifies Jonathan politically by emphasizing his femininity" (ibid.).

Finally, after Jonathan died in battle with his father, Saul, on the mountains of Gilboa, David eulogizes them both. Of Jonathan he poetically exclaims, "I am distressed for you, my brother Jonathan; greatly beloved were you to me; your love to me was wonderful, passing the love of women" (2 Sam 1:26).

Are these descriptions of a homosexual relationship or a close man-to-man friendship? It seems clear that the many wives of David and his adulterous affair with Bathsheba indicate that David had heterosexual urges.[125] Scripture also records that Jonathan was married and had children (1 Sam 20:42; 2 Sam 9). So, were they bisexual? The intertextual and contextual evidence suggests that they were not. Crucial phraseology used to describe the relationship between David and Jonathan intertextually links this passage with earlier pentateuchal narratives. Of Jacob's paternal affection for his youngest son, Benjamin, Judah remarks to Joseph, "his life is bound up in the boy's life" (Gen 44:30). In the various English translations, this does not appear very similar to the relationship described between David and Jonathan, but in Hebrew it is precisely the same expression as found in 1 Sam 18:1: the noun *nepeš*, "soul, life," plus the verbal root *qšr*, "to be knit, bound together," plus the repetition of *nepeš*. In the case of Jacob and his son Benjamin, the phrase undoubtedly refers to a close, affectionate, but not homosexual attachment, and by using precisely the same phraseology regarding David and Jonathan, the narrator of their story also undoubtedly intended to describe a legitimate nonhomosexual bond of affection between the two men.

Again, the terminology "as his own soul/life," utilized twice of Jonathan's affection for David (1 Sam 18:3; 20:17), is illuminated by an intertextual reference to the words of Moses in Deut 13:7, 9 (ET 13:6, 8): "If anyone secretly entices you—even if it is your brother, your father's son or your mother's son, or your own son or daughter, or the wife you embrace, or your most intimate friend [lit. *who is as your own soul*]—saying, 'Let us go worship other gods,' . . . you must not yield." The same terminology is found in this passage—the preposition *kĕ*, "as, like," and *nepeš* plus the appropriate personal pronoun—as in 1 Sam 18:3, describing Jonathan's love for David. Again, in both cases, this is clearly not terminology for a homosexual relationship but for a close friendship (as is captured also by the NLT translations "closest friend" [Deut 13:7 (ET 13:6)] and "best of friends" [1 Sam 18:1]).

The context of the narrative about David and Jonathan also bears out this conclusion. The verb "loved" (*ʾāhab*) in 1 Sam 18:1 is the same word that a few verses later describes the attachment of all Israel and Judah for David: "But all Israel and Judah loved [*ʾāhab*] David; for it was he who marched out and came in leading them" (v. 16). The term does not have any sexual connotations in this context. Likewise, the verb *ḥāpēṣ*, "delight in, take pleasure in," used of Jonathan's regard for David, carries no sexual connotation in this context, as is made clear by its occurrence a few verses earlier in the narrative (18:22): "See, the king is delighted with [*ḥāpēṣ*] you, and all his servants love you; Now then become the

---

[125] See 1 Sam 18:17–29; 25:39–43; 2 Sam 3:2–5, 13–16; 5:13–16; 11.

king's son-in-law." Gagnon shows that the term *ḥāpēṣ* simply means "find favor" and probably includes, in this context, political favor.[126]

Furthermore, the act of a man kissing another man does not necessarily connote sexual attraction. The narratives in the books of Samuel have numerous examples of man kissing man, and never with sexual connotations: Samuel kissing David (1 Sam 10:1), David kissing Absalom (2 Sam 14:33), Absalom kissing the people who visited him (2 Sam 15:5), David kissing his eighty-year-old friend, Barzillai (2 Sam 19:40 [ET 19:39]), and Joab kissing his enemy Amasa (2 Sam 20:9).[127] There is mention of a covenant made between David and Jonathan (1 Sam 18:3), but this is not a covenant of homosexual bonding. "Rather than establishing a sexual union, the 'covenant' between David and Jonathan was a covenant of loyalty and regal recognition set in the context of transferring throne rights to David and symbolized by Jonathan giving David his cloak and armor."[128]

The whole setting of this narrative reveals that despite the political issues that should have interfered with their relationship (with Jonathan, by birth heir to the throne, realizing that David was chosen by God to rule instead), an amazingly close friendship developed between the two. Jonathan, the tender and faithful friend of David, shielded David's life at the peril of his own and gave eloquent witness to the existence and power of unselfish love. This is not a portrait of homosexual relationship but of friends who rose to the heights of self-abnegation.[129]

The Old Testament Wisdom Tradition? Some recent interpreters, recognizing the univocal repudiation of homosexual activity in the HB, have set forth a new strategy by appealing to the wisdom tradition in the OT. Although not explicitly defending homosexual practice, the wisdom tradition is regarded as transcending the appeal to authoritative tradition and divine revelation and opening the possibility for science and experience to guide in matters of homosexuality. "Wisdom

---

[126] Gagnon, *The Bible and Homosexual Practice*, 149. Gagnon (pp. 147–54) argues that many of the expressions of intimate relationship between David and Jonathan are in fact covenant terms describing the political bonding between the two.

[127] Gagnon, ibid., 152, n. 244, gives the statistics for references to kissing throughout the HB: twenty-seven occurrences of the Hebrew verb "to kiss" (*nāšaq* in *qal* and *piʿel*), with the only three having an erotic connotation, those describing the heterosexual kisses between Solomon and Shulammite in Song of Songs (1:2; 8:1) and the harlot's kiss of the naive youth in Prov 7:13.

[128] Webb, *Slaves, Women, and Homosexuals*, 102.

[129] For additional evidence refuting the claim that David and Jonathan shared a homosexual relationship, see Nachum Avraham, "The Nature of David and Jonathan's Relationship (2 Sam 1:26: נִפְלְאַתָה אַהֲבָתְךָ לִי מֵאַהֲבַת נָשִׁים)," Hebrew, *Beit Mikra* 48 (2003): 215–22 (English abstract, 286–87). Martti Nissinen, "Die Liebe von David und Jonatan als Frage der modernen Exegese," *Bib* 80 (1999): 250–63, summarizes the issues in the modern debate over whether the relationship between David and Jonathan was homosexual and concludes that this relationship "may be understood as a socially acceptable male bonding between equals, in which mutual love and affection is depicted with some homoerotic traits but in which the differentiation of active and passive, i.e., male and female sexual roles plays no role" (English abstract). Gagnon, *The Bible and Homosexual Practice*,

is interested in what is natural, and it does not define what is natural or unnatural by what traditions say. Rather the sages turn to nature itself. . . . Here in the wisdom tradition is *scriptural authority* for human beings to make ethical decisions by paying attention to science and human experiences. . . . The wisdom texts of the Bible point us beyond a purely textual orientation in our ethics."[130] Phyllis Bird makes a similar appeal to the OT wisdom tradition: "In this literature [the OT wisdom tradition] . . . we find biblical authorization for the appeal to science to inform our understanding and judgment of homosexual orientation and practice."[131] This marginalizing and muting of the explicit testimony of the biblical canon opens the way for the social sciences to legitimize homosexual practice.

153, aptly concludes, "None of these texts, taken singly or as a collective whole, provide persuasive support for a homosexual relationship between Jonathan and David." Gagnon also points out the absence of any technical terminology for sexual intercourse in this narrative. He counters the claim by Greenberg, *The Construction of Homosexuality,* 114, and others that the story of David and Jonathan once contained explicit reference to their homosexual relationship but later priestly redactors removed these references. Gagnon shows that this theory fails because, "far from censoring, the narrators did their best to play up the relationship between Jonathan and David." He castigates those who seek to find a homosexual relationship in this story: "Only in our own day, removed as we are from ancient Near Eastern conventions, are these kinds of specious connections made by people desperate to find the slightest shred of support for homosexual practice in the Bible" (p. 154).

[130] Seow, "Textual Orientation," 29. Cf. idem, "A Heterotextual Perspective," in *Homosexuality and Christian Community* (ed. Choon-Leong Seow; Louisville: Westminster John Knox, 1996), 19–24.

[131] Bird, "The Bible in Christian Ethical Deliberation," 168. Along with this general appeal to the wisdom tradition for support for homosexuality, at least one author, Uri Wernik, argues that Qoheleth was a homosexual ("Will the Real Homosexual in the Bible Please Stand Up?" *Theology and Sexuality* 11 [2005]: 49, 58–64). Wernik's argument is based upon an assumption regarding the *Sitz im Leben* of the book, that it was produced during the Hellenistic period of Israel's history in which Qoheleth (the philosopher, poet, politician, psychologist) was caught between the anti-homosexual mores of his Hebrew culture and the pro-homosexual attitudes of Hellenistic society (an assumption that I challenge in connection with discussion of the Song of Songs, ch. 13, below). Wernik adduces six lines of evidence to support his conclusion that Qoheleth was a homosexual: (1) Qoheleth's own negative attitude toward women described in Qoh 7:27–29 (which I argue, ch. 6, below, is not the case); (2) use of female verbs related to the masculine term "Qoheleth" in 7:27 and 12:8; (3) the word usually translated "madness, folly" in 10:13, which Wernik translates "libertine" (referring to homosexual activity); (4) use of the language of male "friendship" in the book, esp. the reference to two men lying together to keep warm (4:11), which Wernik sees as implying Solomon's homosexual activity; (5) Qoheleth's admiration of male youth (in true homosexual fashion), e.g., Qoh 9:8; and (6) Qoheleth's pessimism over ageing, betraying a homosexual's fear of losing his attractiveness to male sexual partners and being forced to buy sex. Wernik's arguments are carefully and cogently critiqued by William John Lyons, " 'Outing' Qoheleth: On the Search for Homosexuality in the Wisdom Tradition," *T&S* 12 (2006): 181–202, who finds none of the arguments convincing. Lyons concludes (correctly, in my view) that "there is no compelling evidence to suggest that Qoheleth was a homosexual in the contemporary sense of the term. Rather his sexuality almost certainly matched that defined as the 'norm' by the culture in which he lived. Marriage to a woman was the expectation, both within the Wisdom

Contrary to this position, which seeks to pit the Wisdom literature against the other portions of the HB, I have found in the wisdom tradition no ethic or basis of authority fundamentally different from elsewhere in the biblical canon in matters of sexuality. James Crenshaw, in his classic introduction to OT Wisdom literature, shows that the basic presupposition of the wisdom tradition is a high doctrine of creation with an appeal to the fundamental order of this creation. "Contrary to what would be expected, the wise men do not appeal to creation as direct authority for their counsel. On the other hand, the fundamental premise of their labor to understand the nature of reality is the orderliness of creation. This dependability is grounded in the creative act, at which time an order was established for all time."[132] In precise harmony with this basic premise of wisdom thought, the underlying rationale, as noted above, for the prohibition of homosexual practice is the preservation of the creation order regarding gender boundaries. The witness of the Wisdom literature and the testimony of the rest of the HB (pentateuchal narrative and legislation and prophetic commentary on Torah) thus precisely coincide, and one cannot use the former to overturn the latter.

Summary. Our examination of the relevant passages throughout the HB has revealed a consistent and clear condemnation of homosexual practice. After surveying the evidence (of both OT and NT), Richard Hayes summarizes the biblical witness concerning homosexuality:

> Though only a few biblical texts speak of homoerotic activity, all that do mention it express unqualified disapproval. . . . The biblical witness against homosexual practices is univocal. . . . Scripture offers no loopholes or exception clauses that might allow for the acceptance of homosexual practices under some circumstances. Despite the efforts of some recent interpreters to explain away the evidence, the Bible remains unambiguous and univocal in its condemnation of homosexual conduct.[133]

I fully concur with Hayes's assessment. Not only is there univocal condemnation of homosexual practice throughout Scripture; as shown above, numerous lines of evidence connected to the Levitical legislation point to the universal (transcultural) and permanent (transtemporal) nature of the prohibitions against homosexual activity.

---

tradition and more generally, and Qoheleth's sexuality was most probably expressed within that context (though whether happily or not is perhaps another matter entirely)" (quote at p. 201).

[132] James L. Crenshaw, "Prolegomenon," in *Studies in Ancient Israelite Wisdom* (ed. James L. Crenshaw; New York: Ktav, 1976), 1–60, here 33–34; repr. in *Urgent Advice and Probing Questions: Collected Writings on Old Testament Wisdom* (Macon, Ga.: Mercer, 1995), 90–140.

[133] Richard B. Hays, "The Biblical Witness concerning Homosexuality," in *Staying the Course: Supporting the Church's Position on Homosexuality* (ed. Maxie D. Dunnam and H. Newton Malony; Nashville: Abingdon, 2003), 73, 78. Cf. idem, "Awaiting the Redemption of Our Bodies: The Witness of Scripture concerning Homosexuality," in *Homosexuality in the Church: Both Sides of the Debate* (ed. Jeffrey S. Siker; Louisville: Westminster John Knox, 1994), 3–17.

The biblical materials condemn homosexual *practice* (including a homosexual lifestyle, as with the *qĕdēšîm,* or "male temple prostitutes"), but there is no
castigation of innate homosexual *orientation* per se. The anthropology set forth
in the HB assumes that after the fall all humans have a sinful nature or orientation, whether it be heterosexual or homosexual. The implication of the seventh
commandment and tenth commandment (to be discussed below), however, is
that even the thoughts are to be kept pure, and sexual temptations arising from
the fallen nature/orientation are to be resisted—both heterosexual and homosexual. Likewise, as will become evident regarding temptations to adultery (see
ch. 8, below), divine power is available to enable human beings to live above their
sinful tendencies and natures.

Transvestism (Cross-Dressing)

Deuteronomy 22:5 commands, "A woman shall not wear a man's apparel
[*kĕlî-geber*], nor shall a man put on a woman's garment [*simlat ʾiššâ*]; for whoever
does such things is abhorrent [*tôʿēbâ*] to the LORD your God." The expression
kĕlî-geber utilizes the Hebrew term for "man," *geber,* which emphasizes the male's
strength and prowess;[134] and the broad Hebrew term *kĕlî,* "vessel, utensil," which
elsewhere in the HB may refer to a piece of equipment, an implement, ornament,
garment, or weapon, here in this passage could have in view anything that pertains to a man—a man's "gear." The parallel with the expression *simlat ʾiššâ,*
"woman's garment,"[135] however, seems to imply that the focus in both instances is
the clothing—cross-dressing.

This prohibition is illuminated by the ANE background discussed above regarding homosexual practice: the Mesopotamian male functionaries in the cult
of Ishtar—*assinnu, kurgarrû,* and *kuluʾu*—dressed like women, wore female
makeup, and often carried the female symbol of the (spinning) spindle. The
Deuteronomic injunction against transvestism probably has in view particularly
the male cult prostitutes wearing the garb of the opposite sex, as apparently was
practiced in the Canaanite fertility cults.[136] Harry Hoffner suggests, in light of
ANE evidence, that the condemnation of cross-dressing probably alludes to the
attire and external symbols of masculinity and feminity that were included in the
sympathetic magic of Canaanite fertility cult rituals.[137]

---

[134] BDB 150.

[135] BDB 971.

[136] This is not clearly substantiated from Canaanite (or Ugaritic) sources, but it is
probable on the basis of the parallels with the cult of Ishtar (= Canaanite Astarte/
Asherah) in Mesopotamia. Later writers, such as Lucian of Samosata and Eusebius, refer
to the practice of masquerading (apparently women as men and men as women) in the
religion of Astarte. See James A. Thompson, *Deuteronomy: An Introduction and Commentary* (TOTC 5; Downer's Grove, Ill.: InterVarsity, 1974), 235.

[137] Harry A. Hoffner Jr., "Symbols for Masculinity and Femininity: Their Use in Ancient Near Eastern Sympathetic Magic Rituals," *JBL* 85 (1966): 326–34.

Although the cross-dressing of cult functionaries may have been the predominant background to this prohibition, the wording of the legislation goes beyond a cult setting to include any and all circumstances of men dressing like women and vice versa. The cross-dressing described in this passage is called *tôʿēbâ*, "abomination, detestable thing,"[138] a term that is used in Leviticus and Deuteronomy to refer not only to "cultic taboos that endanger the purity of the religion of Yahweh"[139] but also, as with Lev 18, to violations of the creation order. It seems that both connotations are contained in the prohibition against transvestism. Along with its connections to homosexuality and the fertility cults, this legislation also (and primarily) serves for the "maintenance of the sanctity of the sexes" in opposition to "the tendency to obliterate all sexual distinctions," which "often lends to licentiousness and promotes an unnaturalness opposed to God's created order."[140]

The latter concern is the fundamental rationale for the prohibition. Tikva Frymer-Kensky explains the biblical understanding of deviations from creation categories, including homosexuality and cross-dressing: "Deviations from . . . [creation] categories are dangerous. . . . This extreme aversion to homosexuality is not inherited from other Near Eastern laws, and must make sense in the light of biblical thought. It does not really disturb family lines, but it does blur the distinction between male and female, and this cannot be tolerated in the biblical system. Any thing that smacks of homosexual blurring is similarly prohibited, such as cross-dressing (Deut 22:5)."[141] Harland concurs: "To dress after the manner of the opposite sex was to infringe the natural order of creation which divided humanity into male and female. That distinction was fundamental to human existence and could not be blurred in any way, hence the rule of Dt 22:5."[142]

This blurring-of-the-order-of-creation rationale is supported by the literary structure in which this piece of legislation is placed. According to Steven Kaufman's analysis of Deut 12–27 as elaborations on the Decalogue (addressed in ch. 3, above), Deut 22:5 comes in the transition point between the treatment of the sixth and seventh commandments. He notes a chiastic structure in Deut 22:5–12: (A) dress, v. 5; (B) animals, vv. 6–7; (C) house, v. 8; (C′) field, v. 9; (B′) animals, v. 10; (A′) dress, vv. 11–12. By means of this literary arrangement, the law against cross-dressing is placed in chiastic parallel with the laws against

---

138 BDB 1072–73; Grisanti, *NIDOTTE* 4:314–18.

139 Gerhard von Rad, *Deuteronomy: A Commentary* (trans. Dorothea Barton; OTL; Philadelphia: Westminster, 1966), 141. All the instances of *tôʿēbâ* in Leviticus refer either to Canaanite practices in general (Lev 18:26, 27, 29, 30) or to homosexuality in particular (Lev 20:13). Note these other instances of *tôʿēbâ* in Deuteronomy: Deut 7:25, 26; 12:31; 13:15 (ET 13:14); 14:3; 17:1, 4; 18:9, 12; 20:18; 23:18; 24:4; 25:16; 27:15; 32:16.

140 Walter C. Kaiser Jr., *Toward Old Testament Ethics* (Grand Rapids: Zondervan, 1983), 198.

141 Tikva Frymer-Kensky, "Law and Philosophy: The Case of Sex in the Bible," *Semeia* 45 (1989): 96–97.

142 Harland, "Menswear and Womenswear," 76.

forbidden mixtures.[143] Thus cross-dressing is morally/cultically repugnant to
God not only because of its association with homosexuality and the fertility cult
rituals but also—and primarily—because it mixes/blurs the basic distinctions of
gender duality (male and female) set forth in creation. Because of the grounding
of this prohibition in the creation order, it may be concluded that the intent was
for this legislation to be permanent (transtemporal) and universal (transcultural)
in its application.

Bestiality

Ancient Mesopotamian law codes make no mention of bestiality, but mythological texts in Mesopotamia and Ugarit refer to the practice of bestiality among
the gods. For example, in the Sumerian "Ninegala Hymn," Inanna copulates with
horses.[144] The Gilgamesh Epic may depict bestiality, as Ishtar "loves" a bird, lion,
and stallion.[145] In a Ugaritic poem, Baal is depicted as copulating with a cow and
fathering an ox, a heifer, and a buffalo.[146] The activity of the gods was put into
practice in Egypt, where there is evidence for cultic bestiality at the city of
Mendes (= Dedet).[147] In a dream book probably from the time of Ramesses III,
sex is imagined between a man and a jerboa, a kite, and a pig.[148] The idea of having sex with a donkey is found in a curse: "May a donkey copulate with his wife
and his children."[149] This act is depicted in a faience figurine with a donkey
mounting a woman from behind.[150]

In the Hittite legal system, the copulation of humans and animals is regulated in several different individual case laws. According to Hittite law, human
sexual relations with a cow, sheep, or pig is a capital offence calling for the death
penalty for both man and beast with no right of appeal (although the king may
decide to spare their lives, in which case they are banished from the city),[151]

---

[143] Steven A. Kaufman, "The Structure of the Deuteronomic Law," *Maarav* 1–2
(1978–1979): 105–58, treated in ch. 3, above. For the chiastic structure of Deut 22:5–12,
see ibid., 136; for fuller discussion of the Deuteronomic summary of laws amplifying the
sixth and seventh commandments, see 135–37. Cf. Dennis T. Olson, *Deuteronomy and the
Death of Moses: A Theological Reading* (OBT; Minneapolis: Fortress, 1994), 100–102.

[144] Milgrom, *Leviticus 17–22*, 1570.

[145] "The Epic of Gilgamesh," Tablet VI, lines 48–56, translated by E. A. Speiser
(*ANET* 84).

[146] "Poems about Baal and Anath," translated by H. L. Ginsberg (*ANET* 142).

[147] W. Krebs, "Zur kultischen Kohabitation mit Tieren im alten Orient," *FF* 37 (1963):
20; cf. Milgrom, *Leviticus 17–22*, 1570.

[148] Manniche, "Some Aspects," 16. Manniche points to another dream book, from fifteen hundred years later, in which a woman dreams of having sex with numerous animals,
including a mouse, horse, donkey, goat, ram, wolf, lion, crocodile, snake, baboon, ibis, and
falcon.

[149] Ibid.

[150] Ibid.

[151] HL §§187–188, 199 (*COS* 2.19:118; *ANET* 196). Hoffner, "Incest, Sodomy, and
Bestiality," analyzes other later relevant Hittite texts and shows that the earlier and more

whereas copulation with a horse or mule does not constitute an offense and there is no punishment.[152] There is also legislation concerning cases in which a sexually aroused animal might initiate a sexual relationship with a human, in which cases the human is not punished.[153]

In contrast to the Hittite laws, the biblical legislation regarding bestiality mentions no gradations of punishment or provision for pardon by the king: the crime is absolute, calling for the death penalty for both the human and the beast. The prohibition against bestiality is found in all three major collections of laws in the Pentateuch, in the same context as the laws concerning homosexuality. The book of the covenant (Exod 19–24) sets forth the basic bestiality law: "Whoever lies [šākab] with an animal shall be put to death" (Exod 22:18 [ET 22:19]). In the Holiness Code of Leviticus, Lev 18:23 and 20:15–16 specifically prohibit both men and women from engaging in bestiality and indicate that the animal as well as the human being is to be put to death for engaging in this crime: "You shall not have sexual relations [bĕ . . . lōʾ-tittēn šĕkobtĕkā, lit. 'you shall not inject your penis/flow in']154 with any animal and defile yourself [ṭāmēʾ] with it, nor shall any woman give herself to an animal to have sexual relations [rābaᶜ, 'to lie in position, crouch (on all fours), copulate']155 with it: it is perversion [tebel]"; "If a man has sexual relations [yittēn šĕkobtô, lit. 'injects his penis/flow in'] with an animal, he shall be put to death; and you shall kill the animal. If a woman approaches [kārab] any animal and has sexual relations [rābaᶜ] with it, you shall kill the woman and the animal; they shall be put to death, their blood is upon them." Deuteronomy 27:21 places the prohibition of bestiality among the covenant

---

rigorous penalty for bestiality was later ameliorated so as to make it possible for the human offender to avoid death or banishment without bringing divine wrath against the city. This was accomplished by elaborate rituals to remove the impurity from the offender and the city. These included apparently treating like a bride the animal with whom the offender had copulated—veiling it as a bride and then banishing the animal as a kind of a scapegoat carrying the impurity of the act while the animal's "dowry" is paid back by the offender (as a kind of fine, but how and to whom is unclear). For further discussion of the Hittite texts concerning bestiality, see Stewart, "Ancient Sexual Laws," 288–310.

[152] HL §200a (COS 2.19:119; ANET 197).

[153] HL §199 (COS 2.19:118; cf. ANET 196). If the animal that "leaps on a man (in sexual excitement)" is an ox, the ox shall die, but the man is not executed. Instead, "they shall substitute one sheep in the place of the man and put it to death." If the animal that "leaps on a man (in sexual excitement)" is a pig, there is no punishment. It is not clear why there is this gradation of punishment for bestiality with different animals, but it perhaps parallels the North American world's graded degrees of affinity with various animal species, evidenced in the willingness to eat some kinds of meat (beef, pork, mutton, etc.) but revulsion against some other meat (horse or dog meat, although even these animals are deemed edible by some in the Western world).

[154] The word šĕkobet probably denotes "penis." See the introduction to this study for a discussion of sexual terminology; see Milgrom, Leviticus 17–22, 1550, for the translation of this clause (the text in brackets).

[155] An Aramaic loan word, perhaps related to the Hebrew number four, derived from the homonym rbᶜ and depicting copulation by crouching on all fours. See HALOT 3:1180, s.v. רבעI. Cf. Milgrom, Leviticus 17–22, 1571.

curses to be repeated during the covenant renewal ceremony when Israel enters Canaan: "Cursed be anyone who lies with [šākab] any animal."

According to Lev 18:23, bestiality is defiling (Heb. root ṭmʾ) to the person engaging in the practice. The only other prohibited practice indicated as defiling (ṭmʾ) in Lev 18 is adultery. Jacob Milgrom discusses the significance of this connection of adultery with bestiality: "Adultery [v. 20] and bestiality (v. 23) are the only prohibitions in the entire list containing the root ṭmʾ. . . . Considering that of all the listed prohibitions, this one, adultery, was by far the most widespread, the legist may have purposefully attached the impurity label here [Lev 18:20, referring to adultery] to allude to its grave implications." Milgrom further points out that the defilement from bestiality [ṭmʾ, v. 23], like the defilement for adultery [ṭmʾ, v. 20], "is not cultic, but moral."[156]

Our earlier discussion concerning the relation to "natural law" applies equally to homosexual practices and bestiality. Bestiality is defiling in its very nature as a distortion of the creation order. A Hebrew word describing bestiality serves to underscore the innate defiling nature of this practice and linkage to the creation order. According to Lev 18:23, bestiality is tebel, "perversion." Derived from the verb bālal, "to mix, confuse," tebel refers to a "confusion" or "mixture" of categories—"a violation of the order of nature."[157] Such a violation is not tied to the society of Israel; as a preservation of the creation order, the prohibition has universal and permanent force.[158]

Beyond the foundational rationale grounding this prohibition in the creation order, the intended transcultural and transtemporal scope of the legislation against bestiality is evidenced by many of the other indicators that have already been mentioned regarding homosexual practice: the absolute, all-encompassing language; the grouping with other sex acts that transcend the culture and setting of ancient Israel (adultery, incest, etc.); the use of the term tôʿēbôt "abominations" to describe all these practices; the explicit statement of its applicability to the other nations and the "stranger" as well as to native Israelites; its placement with other supreme offenses that receive the most severe of penalties, capital punishment; and the consistent OT witness opposing the practice of bestiality.

---

[156] Milgrom, Leviticus 17–22, 1551, 1570; see ch. 8, below, on the moral defilement in adultery.

[157] See William A. Bailey, "בלל," NIDOTTE 1:663–64. Cf. Mary Douglas, Purity and Danger: An Analysis of Concepts of Pollution and Taboo (New York: Praeger, 1966), 53. The word tebel only appears twice in the HB, here in Lev 18:23, referring to a violation of the order of nature, and in Lev 20:12, where the marriage of a man to his daughter-in-law brings a violation of the natural social order.

[158] For other suggested rationales for this prohibition, see Stewart, "Ancient Sexual Laws," 124–30. Stewart likewise finds the strongest rationale in its linkage with the creation narratives: "The stories from Gen. 2–3 raise the issue of bestial marriage [when God brings the animals to man in 2:19] and takes up the motif of 'Woman with the Animal' [Gen 3]. Lev. 18 and 20 diagnose the violated categories and supply the consequences" (p. 129).

Distortions of the Heterosexual Marital Form and Divine Grace

Throughout the legislation discussed in this section—as well as the relevant narratives and the prophetic pronouncements alluding to these narratives—the picture is clear that God unequivocally upholds the creation duality between the sexes (Gen 1:26) and the heterosexual norm for marriage (Gen 2:24). Divine judgment is pronounced against those who engage in homosexual practice or bestiality.

At the same time, the grace of God is revealed in the OT portrayals of these distortions. Homosexual practice and bestiality are clearly presented as part of the Canaanite abominations condemned in Lev 18 and 20. Yet, as was pointed out in chapter 3, above, these Canaanites, with their abominable practices, were given four hundred years of probation (Gen 15:16), with many opportunities to learn of the true God and the universal standards of morality, and many did join God's covenant people. Witness also the grace of God to Sodom: Abraham was divinely directed to rescue Lot and the inhabitants of Sodom from the hands of the four invading kings (Gen 14), and very likely some of these rescued individuals were part of the crowd that attempted the homosexual rape at Lot's house (Gen 19). Furthermore, God would have spared the whole city, including the homosexual practitioners, if there had been even ten righteous persons in Sodom (Gen 18:32).

The Mosaic penalty for the abominations of homosexual practice and bestiality was death and being "cut off" (*kārēt*, the divine curse of extinction for sinner and his progeny). God's justice and holy abhorrence of these unnatural crimes called for such severe punishment under the theocracy of Israel. Although the death sentence could not be commuted, this does not mean that there were no grace and forgiveness available. Just as prisoners on death row today may receive the forgiving grace of God before their execution, so God offers to pardon even rebellious sins when the sinner repents (Exod 34:6–7).

According to Ezek 16:51, Judah had multiplied abominations more than Sodom, including the abomination of homosexual practice and also perhaps bestiality. Just two chapters after the allegory of Ezek 16, God bares his heart, revealing his gracious attitude toward Judah: "'Cast away from you all the transgressions that you have committed against me, and get yourselves a new heart and a new spirit! Why will you die, O house of Israel? For I have no pleasure in the death of anyone, says the Lord GOD. Turn, then, and live'" (Ezek 18:31–32). In Ezek 37 God promises a spiritual resurrection from the dead for people who return from Babylonian exile, and in this context, God also promises power to keep his statutes. God even takes responsibility for Israel's obedience: "I will put my spirit within you, and make you follow my statutes and be careful to observe my ordinances" (Ezek 36:27). Even over the most distorted practices and abhorrent abominations, God's forgiving and empowering grace still prevails.

In light of God's gracious attitude toward all sinners, including practicing homosexuals, and in view of the sinful desire that lurks in the heart of every one of us, Thomas Schmidt has provided wise admonition for us today: "We must express our disapproval of homosexual practice in the context of our own sexual fallenness."[159] We must acknowledge that we are all in need of grace and healing in our sexuality, including especially the heterosexual sin of hatred toward homosexuals. We must make a careful distinction between homosexual practice and orientation; if tendencies and temptations to lust are not acted upon or harbored, homosexual orientation is no more condemned by Scripture than a heterosexual sinful nature with its tendencies to lust if not acted upon or harbored. We must emulate the blended justice and grace of God as we continue to uphold the standard of morality concerning the sinfulness of homosexual practice, applying redemptive discipline, and at the same time take a firm and proactive stand for forgiveness and the power to change, for welcoming homosexuals along with all who are sexually wounded into our religious communities, for active involvement in education and helping those who are AIDS victims. In sum, we must show the face of God depicted in the OT (as well as the NT), who is "infinitely knowing, intimately caring, invincibly loving."[160]

---

[159] Schmidt, *Straight and Narrow?* 172. Schmidt (169–75) has provided a very balanced position on the appropriate stance of today's church and synagogue toward homosexuality, a position that upholds both the biblical standard and divine grace.

[160] Ibid., 175. See also, Grenz, *Welcoming but Not Affirming*, passim.

꧁ 5

Monogamy versus Polygamy/ Concubinage

Positive Affirmations of the Edenic Divine Design

The creation design for human sexuality finds expression in a marital form that is heterosexual and *monogamous.* The previous chapter documented that the Edenic pattern of heterosexual relationships between humans remained the norm throughout the canonical OT Scriptures, and examined the distortion of this creation paradigm in homosexual practice, transvestism, and bestiality. Another distortion of the creation design for human sexuality relates to the monogamous aspect of the marital relationship and reveals itself during biblical times in the practice of polygamy (more precisely, polygyny) and concubinage. This chapter surveys the biblical evidence affirming monogamy as the divine creation ideal, examines the prevailing ANE attitudes and practice concerning polygamy and concubinage, analyzes the various OT passages that refer (or supposedly refer) to these practices, and assesses the continuing relevance of the OT witness on this ethical issue for today.

The Edenic divine norm of heterosexual monogamy summarized in Gen 2:24 is assumed throughout the rest of OT Scripture. This continuing standard is apparent in the normal configuration of the nuclear family in the Torah. Witness a sample list of heterosexual monogamous marriage partnerships throughout this period: Adam and Eve (Gen 2–4), Cain and his wife (4:17), Noah and his wife (7:7, 17), Noah's three sons and their respective wives (7:7, 13), Nahor and Milcah (11:29; 24:15), Abram and Sarai (11:29, etc.; regarding Hagar, see below), Isaac and Rebekah (Gen 24, 27, 49:31), Hadar and Mehetabel (36:39), Er and Tamar (38:6), Joseph and Asenath (41:45), Amram and Jochebed (Exod 6:20; Num 26:59), Aaron and Elisheba (Exod 6:23), Eleazar and his wife (6:25), and Moses and Zipporah (2:21; 18:2, 5; Num 12:1).[1]

The pentateuchal legislation mentioning husband and wife together and the prophetic and wisdom portrayals of marriage also assume heterosexual monogamy. This seems to be implied by the use of the singular "wife," and not the plural "wives," as the standard reference to the marriage relationship. For example, the

---

[1] See below for a discussion and affirmation of the monogamy of Moses.

tenth commandment refers to "your neighbor's wife," not "wives" (Exod 20:17).[2]
The prophet Malachi speaks of one who is "faithless to the wife of his youth" (Mal
2:15). Similarly, the wise man Solomon counsels his son to "rejoice in the wife of
your youth" (Prov 5:18), to "enjoy life with the wife whom you love" (Eccl 9:9).[3]

As in the beginning, the monogamous standard is ultimately rooted in the
monotheistic nature of the biblical God and in the concept of *imago Dei*. The
Lord God, who is "alone" (Deut 6:4), is not engaged in promiscuous relationships
within a polytheistic pantheon, and God's creatures are to be united in an exclusive relationship with God alone, and God with them alone (Exod 20:3). In the
same way that humans should worship only one God—in a monotheistic relationship with God—so husbands and wives, created in God's image, are to be
monogamous in their marital relationship with each other. The few deviations
(described in pentateuchal and prophetic narratives) and alleged exceptions (in
Mosaic legislation), upon close reading, in fact serve to confirm the canonical
concern to uphold this Edenic norm.

Plural Marriages (Polygamy/Concubinage)

Ancient Near Eastern Background

In the ancient Near East, where polytheism abounded, the practice of plural
marriage, in particular polygyny (more than one wife), was acknowledged and
accepted within the law codes. According to the earliest known laws of the
Sumerians, the law reforms of King Uru-inimgina of Lagash (Early Dynastic
period of the Sumerians, ca. 2378–2371 B.C.E.), women in earlier times could
marry more than one husband (polyandry), but King Uru-inimgina forbade continuation of this practice and made it a capital crime.[4] In the Sumerian Lipit-
Ishtar Law Code (ca. 1850 B.C.E.), at least four inheritance laws tacitly assume the
social institution of polygyny.[5] The Babylonian Code of Hammurabi (ca. 1700

---

[2] For further examples of pentateuchal legislation that presuppose monogamy as the
normal or ideal marriage form, see Exod 21:5; Lev 18:8, 16, 18; 20:10; 21:13; Num 5:12;
Deut 5:21; 22:22.

[3] For further examples of the assumption of monogamy in the Wisdom literature, see
Prov 12:4; 18:22; 19:13; 31:10–31.

[4] The votive inscriptions containing the law reforms of King Uru-inimgina of Lagash
are translated in Samuel Noah Kramer, *The Sumerians: Their History, Culture, and Character* (Chicago: University of Chicago Press, 1963), 317–23. The law regarding polygamy
reads thus: "The women of former days used to take two husbands, (but) the women of
today (if they attempted this) were stoned with stones (upon which was inscribed their
evil) intent" (p. 322).

[5] See "The Laws of Lipit-Ishtar," translated by Martha Roth (*COS* 2.154:412–13; cf.
ANET 160). LI §24: "If the second wife whom he marries bears him a child, the dowry
which she bought from her paternal home shall belong only to her children; the children
of the first-ranking wife and the children of the second wife shall divide the property of
their father equally." LI §25: "If a man marries a wife and she bears him a child and the

B.C.E.) also acknowledged the practice of polygyny, allowing for a husband to take a concubine if his wife was infertile (as in the case of Abraham) or to take a second wife if his first became diseased or tried to obtain a divorce by means of public scandal.[6] The Middle Assyrian Laws (ca. 1450 B.C.E.) seem to have taken polygamy and concubinage for granted, placing no limit on the number of concubines that a man could have, regardless of his wife's fertility status.[7] Ancient Egyptian texts likewise reveal that the practice of polygamy was common during the second millennium B.C.E. among the pharaohs and the wealthy royal class, who could afford plural wives.[8] Polygamy among the Hittites was apparently

---

child lives, and a slave woman also bears a child to her master, the father shall free the slave woman and her children; the children of the slave woman will not divide the estate with the children of the master." LI §27: "If a man's wife does not bear him a child but a prostitute from the street does bear him a child, he shall provide grain, oil, and clothing rations for the prostitute, and the child whom the prostitute bore him shall be his heir; as long as his wife is alive, the prostitute will not reside in the house with his first-ranking wife." LI §28: "If a man's first-ranking wife loses her attractiveness or becomes a paralytic, she will not be evicted from the house; however, her husband may marry a healthy wife, and the second wife shall support the first-ranking wife."

[6] "Laws of Hammurabi," translated by Martha Roth (*COS* 2.131:344–45; cf. *ANET* 172). CH §148: "If a man marries a woman, and later *la'bum* disease seizes her and he decides to marry another woman, he may marry; he will not divorce his wife whom *la'bum* disease seized; she shall reside in quarters he constructs and he shall continue to support her as long as she lives." CH §145 deals with the special case of a priestess who was forbidden to have children: "If a man marries a *nadītu*, and she does not supply him with children, and that man then decides to marry a *šugītu*, that man may marry the *šugītu* and bring her into his house; that *šugītu* should not aspire to equal status with the *nadītu*." Numerous ANE marriage contracts show that this law applied more generally and reflects actual practice. CH §141: "If the wife of a man who is residing in the man's house should decide to leave, and she appropriates goods, squanders her household possessions, or disparages her husband, they shall charge and convict her; and if her husband should declare his intention to divorce her, then he shall divorce her; neither her travel expenses, nor her divorce settlement, not anything else shall be given to her. If her husband should declare his intention to not divorce her, then her husband may marry another woman and that (first) woman shall reside in her husband's house as a slave woman." For references of relevant marriage contracts and further discussion, see Gordon P. Hugenberger, *Marriage as a Covenant: Biblical Law and Ethics as Developed from Malachi* (VTSup 52; Leiden: E. J. Brill, 1994; repr., Grand Rapids: Baker, 1998), 108–10, n. 100.

[7] "The Middle Assyrian Laws," translated by Martha Roth (*COS* 2.132:357–58; cf. *ANET* 183). MAL A §40: "Wives of a man, or [widows], or [any Assyrian] women who go out into the main thoroughfare [shall not have] their heads [bare]. . . ." MAL A §41: "If a man intends to veil his concubine, he shall assemble five or six of his comrades, and he shall veil her in their presence, he shall declare, 'She is my *aššutu*-wife'; she is his *aššutu*-wife. A concubine who is not veiled in the presence of people, whose husband did not declare, 'She is my *aššutu*-wife,' she is not an *aššutu*-wife, she is indeed a concubine." Despite the lack of legal restrictions, in actual practice, according to many scholars' assessment of the evidence, marriage in ancient Mesopotamia was largely monogamous. See Hugenberger, *Marriage as a Covenant,* 110, n. 101, for bibliography.

[8] See Schafik Allam, *Some Pages from Everyday Life in Ancient Egypt* (Prism Archaeology Series 1; Guizeh, Egypt: Prism, 1985), 27; Alan R. Schulman, "Diplomatic Marriage in the Egyptian New Kingdom," *JNES* 38 (1979): 179–80. With only a couple of exceptions,

similar to the practice in Mesopotamia,[9] and the Ras Shamra texts reveal the widespread practice of polygamy in Ugarit.[10]

Pentateuchal Narratives

In the patriarchal period, there are several biblical examples of plural marriages. Although these biblical narratives provide no explicit verbal condemnation of this practice, the narrator presents each account in such a way as to underscore a theology of disapproval. The record of these polygamous relationships bristles with discord, rivalry, heartache, and even rebellion, revealing the motivations and/or disastrous consequences that invariably accompanied such departures from God's Edenic ideal.[11] Here as elsewhere in the HB, a narrative theology of divine disapproval often speaks even louder, and more eloquently, than explicit condemnation.[12]

---

the evidence for polygamy in the history of ancient Egypt is limited to the royal family. (For an exception, Pierre Montet, *Everyday Life in Egypt in the Days of Ramesses the Great* [London: Edward Arnold, 1958], 54–55, refers to a tomb robber who had four wives.) William A. Ward points out that harems and concubines did not exist even among the royal class during the Old and Middle Kingdoms; only with the New Kingdom and the empire's internationalization did the practice of royal polygyny (not concubinage) become a reality ("Reflections on Some Egyptian Terms Presumed to Mean 'Harem, Harem-Woman, Concubine,'" *Berytus* 31 [1983]: 67–68, 74).

[9] "Hittite Laws," translated by Harry A. Hoffner Jr. (*COS* 2.19:118; cf. *ANET* 196). HL §191: "If a man sleeps with free sisters who have the same mother and their mother—one in one country and one in another, it is not an offence. But if it happens in the same location, and he knows (the relationship, the women are related), it is an unpermitted sexual pairing." HL §194: "If a man sleeps with the slave women who have the same mother and their mother, it is not an offence." Although these texts refer specifically to sexual intercourse with multiple partners in the context of permitted and unpermitted sexual pairing, one may probably infer that multiple wives are also permissible. For further discussion, see Matitiahu Tsevat, "The Husband Veils a Wife (Hittite Laws 197–98)," *JCS* 27 (1975): 235–40.

[10] See A. van Selms, *Marriage and Family Life in Ugaritic Literature* (Pretoria Oriental Series 1; London: Luzac, 1954), 20. Van Selms analyzes UT 119; on the basis of a reasonable reconstruction of the text, there is a list of twenty households, and four of these are mentioned as having two wives, with one having three wives. This would suggest a 25 percent rate of polygyny, although the exact nature of this list is uncertain and additional Ugaritic texts have a much smaller percentage of polygyny. See the summary discussion in Hugenberger, *Marriage as a Covenant*, 106, n. 95.

[11] In the discussion of polygamy in this chapter, I am particularly indebted to my former student (now colleague) Ronald A. G. du Preez, whose D.Min. project dissertation I directed to completion in 1993; his thesis is now published in slightly revised form as *Polygamy in the Bible* (ATSDS 3; Berrien Springs, Mich.: ATS, 1993).

[12] O. Palmer Robertson points out that in narrative theology "theological truth is imbedded in a historical narrative rather than in generalized propositions" (*The Genesis of Sex: Sexual Relationships in the First Book of the Bible* [Phillipsburg, N.J.: Presbyterian and Reformed, 2002], 90). For an introduction to narrative theology, see esp. Robert Alter, *The Art of Biblical Narrative* (New York: Basic Books, 1981). Pamela Tamarkin Reis, *Reading the Lines: A Fresh Look at the Hebrew Bible* (Peabody, Mass.: Hendrickson, 2002), 69, states

The Bigamy of Lamech. In Gen 4 the description of Adam's intimate sexual encounters with Eve (vv. 1, 25) is interrupted with the account of the bigamist
Lamech (vv. 18–24), the first recorded polygamist. Verse 19 records his bigamy:
"Then Lamech took two wives: the name of the one was Adah, and the name of
the other Zillah." Lamech's boasting to his wives makes clear that they were contemporaneous rather than successive wives (vv. 23–24): "Adah and Zillah, hear
my voice; you wives of Lamech, listen to what I say: I have killed a man for
wounding me, a young man for striking me. If Cain is avenged sevenfold, truly
Lamech seventy-sevenfold."

The latter verses not only reveal Lamech's marital status but give an indication of his reprobate moral character, leading to actions filled with violence and
even murder, vengefulness, and insolent boasting. In the parallel genealogies of
Gen 4–5, Lamech appears as the seventh from Adam in the line of Cain, in contrast to Enoch's appearance as the seventh from Adam in the line of Seth. The
narrator clearly pauses in each contrasting genealogy precisely at the seventh generation (seven representing completeness or fullness)[13] for a theological spotlight, as it were, on the fullness of the way of Cain—those who rebelled against
God—and the fullness of the way of Seth—and those who called on the name of
the Lord (Gen 4:26). The poetic boasting of Lamech, with the play on the number
seven, gives some indication that Lamech was even conscious that his reprobate
morality represented the fullness of what it means to rebel against God.

In contrast, the narrator's description of Enoch as one who "walked with
God" so fully—especially after the birth of his son—that "he was no more, because God took him" (Gen 5:21–24). By juxtaposing these two illuminating character portraits and paralleling their position of completeness or fullness as
seventh in the respective genealogical lines, the narrator succeeds in condemning
the practices of Lamech just as effectively as—and perhaps even more so than—
could have been accomplished by an explicit verbal denouncement. In particular,
the narrator highlights Lamech's bigamy by referring three times to this fact of
his marital status (vv. 18, 23a, 23b). Thus the narrative emphatically represents
the practice of plural marriage as a departure from the monogamous order
of creation.

Polygamy at the Time of the Flood. There has been much debate through the
centuries about the interpretation of Gen 6:1–4. Four major theories have been
propounded for the identity of the "sons of God" in this passage: divine beings,
angels, rulers, and Sethites. This is not the place for a comprehensive discussion.[14]

---

well the narrator's technique of disapproval: "The narrator rarely censures or approves
explicitly; rather, the author guides the reader toward correct moral judgment by
inference."

[13] See Jöran Friberg, "Numbers and Counting," *ABD* 4:1145.

[14] For an overview of the arguments for the various interpretations, see, e.g., Kenneth
A. Mathews, *Genesis 1–11:26* (NAC 1A; Nashville, Tenn.: Broadman & Holman, 1996),
323–32; and Willem A. VanGemeren, "The Sons of God in Genesis 6:1–4: An Example of
Evangelical Demythologization?" *WTJ* 43 (1981): 320–48.

Several persuasive recent studies have reviewed the various interpretations and provided cogent evidence that the "Sethite" view best fits the literary context and overall flow of the book of Genesis.[15] The "Sethite" interpretation sees the "sons of God" (*běnê hāʾĕlōhîm*) as the godly line of Seth (described in the genealogy of Gen 5), intermarrying with women from the ungodly line of Cain, who are called "daughters of men" (RSV; Heb. *běnôt hāʾādām*).

In support of this interpretation, note especially the larger context of the early chapters of Genesis, which trace the distinction between the two spiritual "races" of humanity: the spiritual seed of the serpent versus the spiritual seed of the woman (Gen 3:15); the way of Cain versus the way of Abel (Gen 4:1–15); the separation between those who "went out from the presence of the Lord" and those among whom "it was begun [*ḥālal in the hopʿal*, impersonal passive with no stated subject] to call upon the name of the Lord" (Gen 4:16, 26, translation mine); and the genealogy of Cain climaxing in the bigamist and blasphemous Lamech, juxtaposed against the generation of Adam/Seth climaxing in righteous Enoch who was translated without seeing death (Gen 4:16–24; 5:1–32). Immediately after this progressive differentiation of the "two ways," culminating in the genealogies, the moral separation of the two groups of humans is continued contrasting the "sons of God" (*běnê hāʾĕlōhîm*) with the "daughters of men" (*běnôt hāʾādām*).

The immediate context of Gen 6:1–8 and its literary structure also supports the "Sethite" interpretation of the "sons of God." Kenneth Mathews shows how the Genesis flood account is "embedded within the Sethite genealogy, which is not completed until the notice of Noah's death (9:29). This provides the appropriate interpretive key for understanding 6:1–8."[16] I add the following observations, building upon Mathews' insights. The Sethite genealogy is framed by the phrase "begat a son" (*yālad bēn*) plus the naming formula "called his name" (*qārāʾ šěmô*). This terminology is used of Seth and his son Enosh at the beginning of the genealogy (4:25–26) and of Noah, the last of the ante-diluvian Sethite genealogy (5:28–29), but such terminology does not appear at all in the genealogy of Cain. Seth's (not Cain's) begetting (*yālad*) a son is then terminologically linked with God's creating (*bārāʾ*) humanity, both actions containing the key phrase "in the likeness of" (*bidmût;* 5:1, 3). Although the narrator could not state that God "begat" (*yālad*) humanity in the same way as Adam begat Seth without implying God's creation by sexual intercourse, nonetheless the intention of the narrator is evident. The lineage of Adam through his son Seth are to be regarded as function-

---

[15] See esp. Adam Co, "The Probable Identity of the 'Sons of God' in the Literary Context of Genesis 6:1–4" (paper presented at the annual meeting of the Evangelical Theological Society, Danvers, Mass., November 17, 1999), 1–20; and Mathews, *Genesis 1–11:26*, 329–32. See also Gleason L. Archer, *Encyclopedia of Bible Difficulties* (Grand Rapids: Zondervan, 1982), 79–80; K&D, 1:83–87; Gerhard F. Hasel, *Understanding the Living Word of God* (Mountain View, Calif.: Pacific, 1980), 151–52; H. C. Leupold, *Exposition of Genesis* (Columbus, Ohio: Wartburg, 1942), 249–54; and John Murray, *Principles of Conduct* (Grand Rapids: Eerdmans, 1957), 243–49.

[16] Mathews, *Genesis 1–11:26*, 330.

ally equivalent to the "sons of God." Thus the phrase "sons of God" in 6:2 is entirely appropriate and understandable as referring to the godly line of Seth, in light of the immediately preceding context and enveloping literary structure. This is in contrast to the other major scholarly interpretations which do not easily fit the canonical context of the passage.

The reference to "sons of God" (*bĕnê hā'ĕlōhîm*) appropriately applies here to godly humans, since frequently elsewhere throughout the HB God's people are described as God's "sons" (e.g., Deut 14:1; 32:5–6; cf. Exod 4:22; Ps 73:15; Isa 1:2; 43:6; Jer 31:20; Hos 2:1 [ET 1:10]; 11:1–4).

That the term "daughters of men" (*bĕnōt hā'ādām*) refers to a group that are not true worshipers of God is implied by the series of moral contrasts in the preceding chapters of Genesis, as noted above,[17] and perhaps further supported by a similar expression used with regard to people after the flood. In 11:5 the term "sons of men" (RSV; Heb. *bĕnê hā'ādām*) is used to describe the builders of the Tower of Babel. These "sons of men" were clearly comprised of rebels against God, and the term seems to be used in parallel with the "daughters of men" (*bĕnôt hā'ādām*) of 6:2). Although the "sons of God" are not explicitly referred to in 11:1–9, it may well be assumed that there was such a group that did not participate in the rebellion against God. Such seems implied in the genealogy of Shem that immediately follows this story (11:10–32), continuing the genealogy of the godly patriarchal line of Seth (the "sons of God") in Gen 5–6.

If it is accepted that the "sons of God" are the line of Seth, and the "daughters of men" women of the line of Cain, then v. 2 describes a situation in which the godly line has begun to accept the ways of the ungodly: "the sons of God saw [*rā'â*] that the daughters of men were fair [*ṭōb*], and they took [*lāqaḥ*] to wife such of them as they chose" (RSV). Note how the actions of the "sons of God" are described in language intertexually linked to the sin of Eve (Gen 3:6): Eve "saw" (*rā'â*) that the fruit was good (*ṭōb*) and she took (*lāqaḥ*) it. Clearly the narrator intends the reader to see that the marriages described in Gen 6:1–4 were somehow morally tainted.

---

[17] I do not completely eliminate the possibility suggested by Mathews (ibid., 330) that the term "daughters of men" may include ungodly women beyond the line of Cain, in light of the usage of *hā'ādām* "human" in Gen 6:1 to refer to humankind in general ("when humans [*hā'ādām*] began to multiply on the earth"). In Mathews' interpretation, "'Daughters of men,' then, in v. 2 again refers to women regardless of parentage, but among these 'daughters' are the offspring of Cain. 'Any of them they chose' accentuates the Sethite's crime of inclusiveness. Their unrestricted license accelerated the degeneracy of the whole human family." I find more likely, however, that the term *hā'ādām,* when used by itself in this verse (6:1), refers generically to "humankind" in general, but when used as a technical term in the phrase *bĕnôt hā'ādām* "daughters of men" (in parallel with the other contrasting technical term *bĕnê hā'ĕlōhîm* "sons of God," vv. 2, 4) has a more restricted meaning referring to the women in the ungodly line of Cain. The generic meaning of "humankind" is then resumed in v. 5: "The Lord saw that the wickedness of humankind [*hā'ādām*] was great in the earth." This reference to "humankind" in v. 5 encompasses the actions of both "sons of God" and "daughters of men" in vv. 2–4, and both face judgment in the ensuing flood. See K&D, 1:130–31, for further elaboration and defense of this interpretation.

As will be discussed with regard to "mixed" (inter-faith) marriage in ch. 7, below, Gen 6:1–4 depicts a widespread practice of intermarriage with the ungodly among the antediluvian world. But the text also probably indicates a situation which included polygamous marriages. The last part of v. 2 reads: "they [the sons of God] took wives for themselves of all that they chose [*wayyiqḥû lāhem nāšîm mikkōl ʾăšer bāḥārû*]." The Hebrew of this verse, with the partitive preposition *min*, "from," plus the noun *kōl*, "all," seems to imply an introduction of polygamy into the marital practices of Seth's descendants. I concur with David Clines's translation: "taking for themselves wives of as many women as they chose."[18] Emil Kraeling rightly concludes from this verse, "A polygamous situation is here implied in these words."[19] The implication of this translation fits the context of the flood that follows: prevalent polygamy is given as one of the main ingredients in the "corrupt" (*šāḥat*, in the *nipʿal*) condition of the earth that caused the Lord to set a probationary period of 120 years (Gen 6:3) and that finally prompted the divine decision to "destroy" (*šāḥat*, in the *hipʿil*) the earth by the flood (Gen 6:11–13). This narrative in no way countenances polygamy: "It was precisely because of man's autocratic and polygamous ways that God destroyed the earth with a flood. That could hardly be construed as tacit divine approval of polygamy—it is the reverse!"[20]

Abraham's Polygamy/Concubinage. Abraham (then called Abram) came out of a land of idolatry and polygamy. His own brother Nahor was a polygamist (Gen 22:20–24). It is not necessary to retell the familiar story of Abram's divine call, his traveling to Canaan, God's promise of a seed that would become a great multitude, Sarah's (Sarai's) infertility, and her suggestion that Abram have children by her handmaid. Genesis 16:3 summarizes the immediate circumstances of Abram's carrying out of his wife's suggestion and his move into polygamy ten years after his arrival in Canaan: "Sarai, Abram's wife, took Hagar the Egyptian, her slave-girl, and gave her to her husband Abram as a wife." Even though Hagar is called Abram's "wife" (*ʾiššâ*), in reality she still functioned under Sarai as a slave girl. This action of Sarai was a common practice in the ancient Near East at the time of the patriarchs: "If the marriage proved to be infertile, the husband normally took matters into his own hands, but on certain occasions, the wife was able to present one of her slave girls, sometimes specially purchased, to her husband to produce children for their own marriage. . . . The authority over the

---

[18] David J. A. Clines, "The Significance of the 'Sons of God' Episode (Genesis 6:1–4) in the Context of the 'Primeval History' (Genesis 1–11)," *JSOT* 13 (1979): 36. See also David Atkinson, *The Message of Genesis 1–11: The Dawn of Creation* (Leicester, Eng.: InterVarsity, 1990), 131: "Here the 'sons of God' take as many as they choose."

[19] Emil G. H. Kraeling, "The Significance and the Origin of Genesis 6:1–4," *JNES* 6 (1947): 197.

[20] Walter C. Kaiser Jr., *Toward Old Testament Ethics* (Grand Rapids: Zondervan, 1983), 183. As Gen 6:3–13 makes clear, there were many aspects of the antediluvian wickedness besides polygamy that called for divine judgment at the time of the flood.

children resulting from this union belonged not to the slave girl who bore them but to the chief wife."[21]

Although Hagar was humanly regarded as Abram's wife, the narrator carefully records the contrast between human understanding and the divine perspective. Throughout the narrative, God never refers to Hagar as Abram's wife. Although God, in addressing Abram, emphatically speaks of Sarai/Sarah as "your wife" (17:15, 19; 18:9, 10), by contrast he refers to Hagar as "slave-girl of Sarai" (16:8) or "your slave woman" (21:12). Notably, when addressing Hagar after she fled from the presence of Sarah, God told her, "Return to your mistress, and submit to her" (16:9). Nothing was said about her returning to be Abram's wife.[22]

A close look at the narrative intertextuality between the polygamous relationship of Abram with Sarai and Hagar and the fall narrative in Gen 3 is instructive. There are strong verbal parallels between 16:2–3 and 3:6, 16. In the garden of Eden, the woman "took" the fruit and "gave" it to her husband (3:6); so Sarai "took" Hagar and "gave" her to her husband (16:3). The same Hebrew words are used in the same order. Again, Adam "listened to the voice of" his wife (3:17); so Abram "listened to the voice of" his wife, Sarai (16:2). Again identical Hebrew expressions are employed. These verbal parallels may well constitute intentional intertextual echoes on the part of the narrator to indicate that Abram and Sarai in the Hagar scandal fell even as Adam and Eve fell in Eden.[23]

The divine disapproval of Abraham's polygamy is underscored by the narrator's detailed description of the strife and disharmony that polygamy brought to Abraham's household: the rupture in the relationship between Sarai and Hagar (16:4–6), the strife between the children of the two wives (21:9–10), and the deep distress on the part of Abraham (21:11–12). The narrative may also be upholding the divine plan for monogamy by the close juxtaposition of Abraham's return to a monogamous status (Gen 21) with Abraham's supreme test of faith on Mt. Moriah (Gen 22). This juxtaposition perhaps suggests that it was after returning to faithfulness in his marital status that Abraham was prepared to pass the test of loyalty to God and to worship God at the site of the future

---

[21] Martin J. Selman, "Comparative Customs and the Patriarchal Age," in *Essays on the Patriarchal Narratives* (ed. A. R. Millard and D. J. Wiseman; Winona Lake, Ind.: Eisenbrauns, 1983), 137. Selman refers to similar situations in the Code of Hammurabi (§§144, 163) and texts from Nuzi and Nimrud.

[22] In ch. 9, below, on divorce, it also becomes apparent that God never recognized Abraham's divorce because, in the divine perspective, he had never been married to her. Cf. Reis, *Reading the Lines,* 28, 57: "In the story of Sarai, Abram, and Hagar, the words 'husband' and 'wife' are emphasized, highlighting the marital relationships and establishing that, though Hagar becomes Abram's wife, Abram is truly husband only to Sarai. . . . Contrary to prevailing analysis, Hagar does not become a true wife of Abraham."

[23] This intertextual linkage was first suggested to me by Ray McAllister, one of my PhD students at Andrews University, who, despite a handicap of blindness, has memorized the entire book of Genesis in Hebrew and thus is particularly sensitive to intertextual echoes. For scholarly treatment of the intertextual relationships between Gen 16 and Gen 2–3, see esp. André Wénin, "Saraï, Hagar, et Abram: Une approche narrative et contextuelle de Gn 16, 1–6," *Revue théologique de Louvain* 32 (2001): 24–54.

temple. This interpretation seems implied by the inclusion of "After these things" (22:1) following Abraham's return to monogamy and just prior to the test on Mt. Moriah.[24]

Abraham is a prime example of an OT figure who remarried after the death of his first wife. According to Gen 23, Sarah died at the age of 127 and was given an honorable burial. Later, according to 25:1, "Abraham took another wife, whose name was Keturah." In the narrative of Abraham's second marriage after his first wife died, the narrator gives no hint that this marriage was out of the ordinary or contrary to the divine will. Remarriage after the death of the first spouse seems to have been a normal, accepted practice in OT times.

Keturah is called Abraham's "concubine" (*pîlegeš*) in 1 Chr 1:32. The Hebrew term for "concubine" is probably not of Semitic origin and seems most frequently to refer to a secondary or inferior wife or to a slave girl of a Hebrew family who bore children.[25] The term is sometimes used in the HB in clear contradistinction to a wife.[26] On the basis of the biblical and ANE evidence, in these cases it appears that the concubine probably was taken without a legal ceremony or any formalization by means of the dowry and may not have had the same legal status as the wife or wives.[27] In other biblical passages, however, the term *pîlegeš* appears to be used virtually synonymously with *ʾiššâ*, "wife."[28] The only difference in these cases is that the term "concubine" is never used to describe a man's original, first wife. In the case of Abraham, the context makes clear that Keturah was his full and legitimate wife, whom Abraham married after the death of Sarah, but since she was not his original wife, she could also be termed his *pîlegeš*, "concubine."

Jacob's Polygamy/Concubinage. Perhaps the most extended cycle of biblical narratives dealing with polygamous relationships is that of Jacob. Several studies

---

[24] The only other place where this clause occurs in the Abraham cycle of Genesis is in 22:20, immediately after the Mt. Moriah test, when it introduces the divine message to Abraham about his brother's polygamous sexual activity (22:20–24). This narrative frame of polygamous relationships surrounding the Mt. Moriah test seems to highlight the connection. For further discussion of these narrative clues, see Jo Ann Davidson, "Abraham, Akedah, and Atonement," in *Creation, Life, and Hope: Essays in Honor of Jacques B. Doukhan* (ed. Jiří Moskala; Berrien Springs, Mich.: Old Testament Department, Seventh-day Adventist Theological Seminary, Andrews University, 2000), 49–72.

[25] See esp. Chaim Rabin, "The Origin of the Hebrew Word *Pîlegeš*," *JJS* 25 (1974): 353–64.

[26] See, e.g., references to Nahor's wife, Milcah, and his concubine, Reumah, in Gen 22:24; Gideon's wives (Judg 8:30) and concubine (Judg 8:31); David's "concubines and wives" (2 Sam 5:13); Solomon's seven hundred wives and three hundred concubines (1 Kgs 11:3); and his son Rehoboam's wives and concubines (2 Chr 11:21).

[27] For the literature on ANE practice, see Hugenberger, *Marriage as a Covenant*, 107, n. 96.

[28] See, e.g., besides the example of Abraham's relationship with Hagar and Keturah (Gen 16:3; 25:1, 6; 1 Chr 1:32), Bilhah, who is called both Jacob's "concubine" (Gen 35:22) and one of his "wives" (Gen 37:2). The prediction that someone would lie with David's "wives" in broad daylight (2 Sam 12:11) is fulfilled with Absalom going in to his father's "concubines" (2 Sam 16:22).

on polygamy in the Bible have claimed that these narratives not only provide valuable insight into life in a polygamous marriage but also reveal that polygamy was fully acceptable to God.[29]

A close reading of the Jacob cycle of narratives, however, leads to a different conclusion.[30] It is clear that Jacob's original intention was to follow his father's counsel, given before he left home (Gen 28:2), and marry only one wife, taken from his relatives at Paddan-aram. This original choice was Rachel, the beautiful daughter of Laban, with whom he had fallen in love (29:18–25). It is also clear that after being tricked by Laban into marrying his elder daughter, Leah, instead of Rachel, Jacob agreed to enter into a polygamous relationship, taking both Leah and Rachel as wives, in harmony with the local marriage customs (29:26–28). Later, since both of his wives were infertile, they persuaded him to cohabit with the wives' maidservants, Bilhah and Zilpah, in order to bring them children. Bilhah (and also presumably Zilpah) is called both Jacob's "concubine" (35:22) and one of his "wives" (37:2); she (along with Zilpah) seem to have been given the same rights in the household as the legitimate wives, and both Bilhah's and Zilpah's children were given the same status of legal heir as were the children of the legitimate wives.[31] From Jacob's polygamous sexual relationships with his four wives, twelve sons and at least one daughter were born.

The Jacob narratives are filled with details of the disastrous consequences of polygamy in Jacob's family.[32] The strife and discord between Rachel and Leah are meticulously documented (30:1–16). The dispositions of jealousy, revenge, short temper, and lack of self-control on the part of Jacob's children seem to mirror the dysfunctional nature of the polygamous home life (34:13–31; 37:2–34). Jacob himself also experienced the negative effects of the polygamous relationship: the record simply states that Jacob "loved Rachel more than Leah" (29:30); even stronger is the statement that "Leah was unloved [*śĕnûʾâ*, lit. 'hated']" (29:31).

That the narrator is not presenting polygamy in a favorable light is apparent from the depiction of the tensions within the family. God's disapproval is shouting at us, as it were, from every detail of the disastrous results of the polygamous union. But the narrator goes further than this. Careful attention to the radical shift in terminology and characterization following Jacob's life-changing divine encounter at the River Jabbok yields surprising results. After wrestling all night with the divine being, Jacob (meaning "supplanter") had his name changed to Israel ("one who prevails with God"), signifying a change of moral character (32:25–29 [ET 32:24–28]). According to v. 26 (ET v. 25), the divine being also

---

[29] See, e.g., John S. Mbiti, *Love and Marriage in Africa* (Essex, Eng.: Longman, 1973), 190; Clifton R. Maberly, "The Polygamous Marriage variant: The Perspective of Sacred History" (term paper, Adventist Heritage Center, Andrews University, 1975), 12.

[30] See esp. the detailed narrative analysis in du Preez, *Polygamy in the Bible*, 164–72.

[31] See Gen 46, 49; Exod 1; Deut 33.

[32] For analysis of the "inner life of a polygamous marriage" as illustrated in the Jacob cycles, see, e.g., Irmtraud Fischer, *Women Who Wrestled with God: Biblical Stories of Israel's Beginnings* (trans. Linda M. Maloney; Collegeville, Minn.: Liturgical, 2005), 72–90 (quote at 79).

"struck" (*wayyigga^c*) the "hip socket," literally, "the hand of his thigh" (*kap-yĕrēkô*). In light of the usage of *yārēk* elsewhere in the HB to refer to the genital area,[33] it has been suggested that "the hand of the thigh" is a euphemism for Jacob's penis and that God struck his organ of regeneration as an implicit rebuke to his polygamous relationships.[34] In light of 32:32 [ET 32:31], however, which correlates the part of Jacob's body touched by the divine being with the anatomical part of animals not to be eaten by the people of Israel, it seems more likely that *kap-hayyārēk* refers to the "broad part of the thigh" or perhaps the general area of the "groin" on both the animal and Jacob. The narrator also indicates that Jacob's encounter at the Jabbok leaves him "limping because of his hip" (*ṣolēa^c ^cal-yĕrēkô*), which seems to be a clear reference to an anatomical part other than the genitals. Even if the term does not specifically refer to Jacob's genitals, the intentional ambiguity in terminology seems to indicate at least a possible intended play on words with this sexual euphemism, and the disabling blow to Jacob's thigh may allude to divine disapproval of Jacob's polygamous relationship.

Regardless of the decision one makes concerning the meaning of *kap-yĕrēkô*, what is remarkable about the Jacob narrative is the abrupt shift in crucial terminology and characterization describing Jacob's relationship with Rachel, Leah, Bilhah, and Zilpah after the River Jabbok experience. Before the Jabbok wrestling, Jacob's sexual relationship with all four wives is repeatedly mentioned, but after this event the only conjugal relations mentioned are with his wife, Rachel (35:16–19). During the next decade of Jacob's life in Canaan, only Rachel gives birth to a child (35:18). Whereas Jacob called both Rachel and Leah "my wives" (30:26; 31:50) before his name (character) change at the Jabbok, he called only Rachel "my wife" (44:27) after the Jabbok experience. Jacob's use of terminology at the end of his life may point in this same direction. Discussing with his own sons his future burial in the cave of Machpelah, he uses the term "wife" for both Sarah and Rebekah, who were buried there, but simply adds "and there I buried Leah" without using the term "wife" with reference to her (49:31). Most telling of all, in the genealogy of Gen 46, the narrator mentions Leah, Zilpah, and Bilhah as women who "bore to Jacob" children, but only Rachel is classified as his "wife"— "Jacob's wife Rachel" (46:15, 18–19, 25).

Individually these clues might be merely circumstantial, but their cumulative effect seems to point toward the possibility that after Jacob's conversion experience at the Jabbok, he continued to care for Leah, Zilpah, and Bilhah but no longer considered them his wives and that he returned to a monogamous relationship with the wife of his original intention, Rachel.[35] Such hints, if indeed

---

[33] See Gen 24:2, 9; 46:26; 47:29; Exod 1:5; Judg 8:30; and Num 5:21–29. See also the further discussion in ch. 11, below, regarding the theology of circumcision.

[34] See Stanley Gevirtz, "Of Patriarchs and Puns: Joseph at the Fountain, Jacob at the Ford," *HUCA* 46 (1975): 52, 53; Smith, "'Heel' and 'Thigh,'" 463–73.

[35] Zvi Jagendorf points out why Jacob would retain Rachel as his original wife and not Leah: "In the dark Jacob knows Leah sexually, but he knows her *as Rachel*, for the image in his mind prevails over the presence of the woman at his side" ("'In the Morning, Behold, It Was Leah': Genesis and the Reversal of Sexual Knowledge," *Proof* 4 [1984]:

indicating Jacob's forsaking of polygamous relationships after Jabbok, make significant the timing of the divine call for Jacob to return to Bethel to build an altar. God's renewal of the covenant with Jacob (35:11, 12) came after he had repented from his former lifestyle of deceit and polygamy.

But even if Jacob did not return to monogamy, the narrator's negative depiction of the polygamous relationship and his genealogical indicator, which identifies only Rachel as Jacob's wife, eloquently express the divine disapproval and rejection of polygamy as a distortion of God's creation ordinance for marriage.

The Polygamy of Esau and Concubinage of His Son. Of Esau, Jacob's brother, the record states, "When Esau was forty years old, he married Judith daughter of Beeri the Hittite, and Basemath [also apparently called Adah, Gen 36:2] daughter of Elon the Hittite" (Gen 26:34). The narrator then adds, "they made life bitter for Isaac and Rebekah" (26:35). Rebekah's own words are reported: "I am weary of my life because of the Hittite women" (27:46). No doubt, this anguish was in large part due to their pagan (Hittite) ways—that is, Esau's interfaith marriage (discussed in ch. 7, below)—but could also have included a concern for the polygamous situation.

When Esau saw that "the Canaanite women did not please his father Isaac," he proceeded to marry still another wife, this time from the line of Abraham and Ishmael (28:8–9). From a comparison with the genealogical record in 36:2–3, 10–14, it appears that Esau had a total of four wives. Significantly, each of the wives mentioned in the genealogy is stated to be "Esau's wife," in stark contrast to the genealogy of Jacob, in which only Rachel is called his wife. This seems to indicate that Esau, unlike what has been tentatively suggested regarding Jacob, remained a polygamist all his life. From the overall OT record of Esau's life story, coupled with the NT confirmation of his "godless" (Gk. *bebēlos*) ways (Heb 12:16), Esau's polygamy is not surprising and certainly provides no hint of divine approval for the practice. Following in his father's footsteps, Esau's son Eliphaz took a concubine, Timna, in addition to his wife (Gen 36:12). The narrator records the baleful results of disregarding the divine ideal in the lives of the descendants.

Moses a Bigamist? Some commentators suggest that Moses' Midianite wife, Zipporah (Exod 2:21; 4:25; 18:2), and the "Cushite woman whom he had married"

187–92; repr. in *Biblical Patterns in Modern Literature* [ed. David H. Hirsch and Nehama Aschkenasy; BJS 77; Chico, Calif.: Scholars Press, 1984], 51–60, quote at 53). The narrator does make one reference to Zilpah and Bilhah as "Jacob's wives" after his experience at the Jabbok. In Gen 37:2 the narrative stage is set for the Joseph narrative by mentioning that Joseph "was a helper to the sons of Bilhah and Zilpah, his father's wives." But this incidental reference may only serve to identify which sons of Jacob Joseph was helping, without thereby indicating the current marital relationship of Jacob to the women. Joseph's dream, narrated a few verses later (vv. 9–10), which involved a singular moon (along with the sun and the eleven stars) interpreted as a singular "mother" by Jacob, may possibly provide another hint of Jacob's return to monogamy.

(Num 12:1) are two different women, with the implication that Moses was a bigamist.[36] Alternatively, it is suggested that the "Cushite woman" was a wife taken by Moses after Zipporah died.[37] There is, however, no biblical mention of the death of Zipporah prior to the incident recorded in Num 12:1, and there does not seem to be sufficient evidence to substantiate the claim that Zipporah and the "Cushite woman" were different individuals.

It is not unlikely that "Midianite" and "Cushite" are synonymous geographical designations. The Pentateuch contains other examples of a geographical location being given two names (see, e.g., Mt. Horeb and Mt. Sinai). Several commentators point out that geographical evidence is not an obstacle to identifying Zipporah with the Cushite woman of Num 12:1. "It is possible that Zipporah, a Midianite, was also designated a Cushite, for Midian included part of NW Arabia where some Cushite tribes lived. Furthermore, she may have been called a Cushite because her complexion may have been darker than that of most Israelites."[38] Identification of Midian with Cushan also has biblical support. "Favoring the [Cushite] woman's identification with Zipporah is the use in Hab. 3:7 of Cushan and Midian in synonymous parallelism. If the color of skin and shape of facial features was a factor, the term 'Cushite' could also have been applied equally well to the Midianites, who were tanned nomads from northwest Arabia."[39] James Hoffmeier also points to the synonymous parallelism between "Cushan" and "Midian" in Hab 3:7 and suggests that "the 'Cushite' woman of Nu. [2]:1f. could well have been the Midianite Zipporah."[40] I concur with the conclusion of Gerhard Jasper that the view identifying Cush and Midian (and thus Zipporah and the Cushite woman) "is geographically the more probable interpretation."[41] Also, many ancient Jewish and Christian commentators (including Augustine, the Talmud, *Targum Neofiti,* and Ibn Ezra) as well as recent noted OT scholars equate Cush with Midian and Zipporah with the Cushite woman.[42] Finally, reference to Moses' wife under two different appellations (Zipporah and "the Cushite woman") is not unusual for the pentateuchal narratives or extra-

---

[36] So, e.g., Jacqueline Williams, "'And She Became "Snow White"': Numbers 12:1–16," *OTE* 15 (2002): 259–68.

[37] So, e.g., Ronald B. Allen, "Numbers," *EBC* 2:797–98.

[38] John Rea, "Zipporah," *WBE* 2:1848–49.

[39] R. K. Harrison, *Numbers* (WEC; Chicago: Moody, 1990), 194.

[40] James K. Hoffmeier, "Zipporah," *ISBE* 4:1201. See also John Joseph Owens, *Numbers* (BBC 1; Nashville: Broadman, 1970), 118; N. H. Snaith, *Leviticus and Numbers* (NCB; London: Nelson, 1967), 234. Even though the parallel between "Cush" and "Midian" in Habakkuk is later than the time of the exodus purported by the canonical text of Num 12, Habakkuk may well reflect a usage already apparent some centuries earlier.

[41] Gerhard Jasper, "Polygyny in the Old Testament," *Africa Theological Journal* 2 no. 2 (February 1969): 36. Cf. Frank M. Cross, *From Epic to Canon: History and Literature in Ancient Israel* (Baltimore: Johns Hopkins University Press, 1998), 45, 46, 51; and Sten Hidal, "The Land of Cush in the Old Testament," *SEÅ* 41–42 (1976–1977): 102.

[42] For major proponents of this view, see the listings in Edwin M. Yamauchi, *Africa and the Bible* (Grand Rapids: Baker, 2004), 36–37; James L. Kugel, *Traditions of the Bible: A Guide to the Bible as It Was at the Start of the Common Era* (Cambridge: Harvard University Press, 1998), 512–13; and the scholars cited above.

biblical ANE literature of the time.[43] Zipporah's own father is referred to by two different names in the Pentateuch: Jethro (Exod 3:1; 4:18; 18:1, 2, 5, 6, 9, 10, 12) and Reuel (Exod 2:18; 2:14; 10:29).

When we follow the narrative clues regarding Zipporah, it seems apparent that although she started out with Moses to return to Egypt (Exod 4:20), after the "bridegroom of blood" incident (4:24–26), she did not continue to Egypt with Moses but returned to Jethro's house (4:27–31; 18:2) and rejoined her husband when Jethro came to visit Moses at Mt. Sinai (18:1–6). Here Miriam became acquainted with Zipporah, was stirred to jealousy against her (perhaps because of Zipporah's influence on her husband, which left Miriam out of Moses' counsel more than before; cf. Num 12:2), and began to treat her with contempt, employing a racial slur to punctuate her dissatisfaction (Num 12:1).[44] The reference to Moses' wife here as "the Cushite woman" provides a narrative clue that pinpoints the tactic utilized by Miriam to demean and depersonalize Zipporah and bring accusation upon Moses for marrying someone outside the Hebrew nation. Thus Moses' marital arrangement probably does not include bigamy but does constitute an example of exogamy or mixed marriage (see ch. 7, below).

Pentateuchal Legislation

Some scholars assert that several specimens of pentateuchal legislation assume, allow for, and even approve the practice of polygamy. Each of these alleged affirmations of polygamy calls for attention.

Legislation concerning the Female Slave: Exod 21:7–11. One of the case laws in the "book of the covenant" (Exod 19–24) concerns treatment of a female slave. The law reads,

> When a man sells his daughter as a slave, she shall not go out as the male slaves do. If she does not please her master, who designated her for himself, then he shall let her be redeemed; he shall have no right to sell her to a foreign people, since he has dealt unfairly with her. If he designates her for his son, he shall deal with her as with a daughter. If he takes another wife to himself, he shall not diminish the food, clothing, or marital rights of the first wife. And if he does not do these three things for her, she shall go out without debt, without payment of money. (Exod 21:7–11)

Does this law support the practice of polygamy, as is often claimed? A fundamental point to be recognized is that this is a *case law*, describing what should follow if a certain action is taken. Case laws do not legitimize the activity of the case

---

[43] See Harrison, *Numbers,* 177. For Ugaritic and Egyptian examples of paired names, see esp. Cyrus H. Gordon, *Before the Bible: The Common Background of Greek and Hebrew Civilisations* (New York: Harper and Row, 1962), 236–38; and Kenneth A. Kitchen, *Ancient Orient and Old Testament* (Downers Grove, Ill.: InterVarsity, 1966), 121–25.

[44] The grammar of Num 12:1 mentions Miriam and Aaron as subjects of the complaint against Moses' marriage to the Cushite woman, but the verb *dābar,* "speak," is in the feminine singular. Thus one should read, "Then Miriam and Aaron, *she* spoke against Moses." Miriam was the ringleader of the dissatisfaction, and Aaron passively went along.

described but only prescribe what should be done in such cases. Thus this case law legitimates polygamy no more than the case law in Exod 21:37 (ET 22:1, "When someone steals an ox or a sheep . . .") legitimizes theft. The existence of such casuistic legislation does acknowledge the possibility of such circumstances occurring but does not necessarily express approval of these circumstances.

Furthermore, several textual, linguistic, and translational problems in this passage call for special attention. First, most English versions follow the LXX translation of 21:8, which calls for substituting the prepositional phrase *lô,* "for himself," for the Hebrew negative particle *lōʾ,* "not." Textual evidence for such substitution is not strong,[45] and I concur with Walter Kaiser and others that the reading of the MT should be retained.[46] If the Hebrew text is followed, then the man does not take the slave girl as his wife in v. 8. The best translation of this passage is, "If she does not please her master so that he does not betroth her . . ." (translation mine; cf. NIV margin, "master so that he does not choose her").

Verses 9–10 then describe two other circumstances that might follow regarding the slave girl. One is that the man gives her to his son (v. 9). This contingency is straightforward and its meaning not controverted. The other possibility is that the man "takes another [*ʾaḥeret*] wife to himself." Translators have commonly assumed that this refers to another wife in addition to the slave girl mentioned in v. 8. But if v. 8 explicitly states that he does not take the slave girl as his wife, then *ʾaḥeret* in v. 10 has the meaning "another instead of, different" rather than "another in addition to"—the former a well-attested meaning for this word in the MT.[47] The contingency clause of v. 10 thus details the treatment that should be given to the slave girl if her master takes another wife instead of (not in addition to) her. In other words, if v. 8 makes clear that the man does not marry the slave girl, then v. 10 cannot refer to her (sexual) marital rights.

What is the treatment that she deserves? Most modern versions, building on the assumption that v. 8 indicates a marriage between master and slave girl and v. 10 indicates polygamy, are similar to the NRSV in translating thus the three things that he is to continue to provide:[48] "food, clothing, or marital rights [*wĕʿōnātāh*]." The ancient versions understand the Hebrew noun *ʿōnâ* to mean

---

[45] It appears in the LXX, Targum, Vulgate, and Qere, but these substitutions seem to be based upon translational considerations and not manuscript evidence.

[46] Kaiser, *Toward Old Testament Ethics,* 184; cf. du Preez, *Polygamy in the Bible,* 66.

[47] For the meaning of "different" or "distinct from," see Num 14:24; Deut 29:27 (ET 29:28); Judg 11:2; Isa 28:11; Jer 22:26; 36:28, 32. See also BDB 29.

[48] Verse 10 does contain a list of three things. But recent studies of the literary structure of this passage have indicated that "these three things" of v. 11 does not refer back to this list of three in v. 10 but rather refers to the three preceding apodoses in vv. 8b, 9b, and 10b. The structure of Exod 21:2–11 describes two main cases (vv. 2 and 7), each with three subsidiary cases (vv. 3a, 3b, 4 and vv. 8, 9, 10) and a concluding exception case (vv. 5–6 and v. 11). See Hugenberger, *Marriage as a Covenant,* 320–21, who points out that this is also the view of Rashi, Ibn Ezra, and Rashbam. Cf. the foundational literary analysis by Yair Zakovitch, *"For Three . . . and for Four": The Pattern for the Numerical Sequence Three-Four in the Bible* (Hebrew; 2 vols.; Jerusalem: Makor, 1979), 2:452; summarized in Gregory C. Chirichigno, "Debt Slavery in the Ancient Near East and Israel: An Examination of the

"conjugal rights,"[49] but this meaning has questionable linguistic support and is regarded in some important recent studies "to be the least probable of the various alternative suggestions" for translating this *hapax legomenon*.[50] The most likely meaning of this term—accepted by a number of ancient and modern scholars— is "habitation, dwelling," based upon the Hebrew root *'wn* and etymologically related to the Hebrew nouns *māᶜôn, mĕᶜônâ,* "habitation, dwelling."[51] The basic necessities to be supplied the slave girl are, then, "normal food, clothing, and quarters [lodging, shelter]."[52]

This law, then, does not even deal with polygamy, let alone support or legitimize it. It deals with three contingency situations that might arise with a slave girl: (1) if the master rejects her as a wife, she is to be freed by being redeemed (bought back); (2) if the master's son marries her, she is to be treated as the master's daughter; and (3) if the master marries a different woman than her, she is to be assured of her basic necessities: food, clothes, and lodging.[53]

Legislation against Marrying "a Woman to Her Sister": Leviticus 18:18. Leviticus 18:18 reads (NRSV), "You shall not take a woman as a rival [*liṣrōr*] to her sister [*wĕᵓiššâ ᵓel-ᵓăḥōtāh*], uncovering her nakedness while her sister is still alive." Many modern versions translate this verse with explicit reference to polygamy. For example, the NIV translates, "Do not take your wife's sister as a rival wife and

---

Biblical Manumission Laws in Exod 21:6, 7–11; Deut 15:12–18; Lev 25:39–54" (PhD diss., Council for National Academic Awards, 1989), 226–27.

[49] See the LXX, Syriac, and Targumim. For a modern defense of this view, see esp. Robert North, "Flesh, Covering, a Response, Ex. xxi 10," *VT* 5 (1955): 204–6. This translation supposes a connection with the Hebrew root *ᶜnh^III*, "to ravish, oppress, do violence to, humiliate" (although Ibn Ezra relates the term to *ᶜēt*, "time," presuming a reference to "times of sexual relations"). Such connections are questionable and have not met with widespread acceptance by phonologists in recent studies.

[50] Hugenberger, *Marriage as a Covenant,* 320, summarizing the view of other recent studies (see the next footnote). Shalom Paul, "Exod. 21:10: A Threefold Maintenance Clause," *JNES* 28 (1969): 48–53, suggests that the term *ᶜōnâ* should be translated "oil," on the basis of Sumerian and Akkadian texts that speak of "food, clothing and oil" as the basic necessities of life, but this view also does not appear to have strong linguistic support, since the meaning "oil" for *ᶜōnâ* is elsewhere unattested in Hebrew and there is no linguistic relationship between the Akkadian and Sumerian terms for "oil" and the one used in Exod 21:10. Thus the etymology of *ᶜōnâ* is left unexplained.

[51] See Umberto Cassuto, *A Commentary on the Book of Exodus* (trans. Israel Abrahams; Jerusalem: Magnes, 1967), 269, who translates, "conditions of her abode," and adds, "This appears to be the real meaning of the word *ᶜōnātāh*, and not as later tradition interpreted it: times of cohabitation." Nahum H. Sarna, *Exodus* (JPS Torah Commentary; Philadelphia: Jewish Publication Society, 1989), 121, points to medieval Jewish exegetes, such as Rashbam and Bekhor Shor, who came to this same conclusion. Hugenberger, *Marriage as a Covenant,* 321, also favors this view. Cf. Wolfram von Soden, "Zum hebräischen Wörterbuch," *UF* 13 (1981): 159–60.

[52] Cassuto, *Exodus,* 269.

[53] For alternative interpretations of the meaning of this passage that also do not include the assumption of a polygamist relationship, see Hugenberger, *Marriage as a Covenant,* 320–22.

have sexual relations with her while your wife is living." The implication of this translation is that although a certain (incestuous) polygamous relationship is forbidden—to two consanguine sisters while both are living, technically called sororal polygyny—polygamy in general is acceptable within the law. Thus this law is seen to be in harmony with other ANE law codes, where sororate marriage after the death of one of the sisters is deemed acceptable but is forbidden when both sisters are alive.[54]

A close reading of 18:18 in its larger context, however, places this translation of the passage in serious doubt. The crucial phrase is, "a woman . . . to her sister [ʾiššâ ʾel-ʾăḥōtāh]." Does the word "sister" in this passage refer to blood relatives, and thus in this context forbid a specific kind of incestuous polygamous relationship, or does "sister" have a broader reference to a female citizen in general, any additional wife, and thus in this context forbid any kind of polygamy? The following eight considerations—involving semantic, syntactical, literary, contextual, and theological evidence—lead me to conclude that the latter interpretation is to be preferred.[55]

First, the phrase "a woman to her sister" (ʾiššâ ʾel-ʾăḥōtāh) in its eight occurrences elsewhere in the HB always is used idiomatically in the distributive sense of "one in addition to another" and nowhere else refers to literal sisters.[56] The masculine equivalent of this phrase, ʾîš ʾel-ʾāḥîw, "a man to his brother," appears twelve times in the HB and is always used in a similar idiomatic manner with a distributive meaning of "one to another" or "to one another."[57] It would thus not be appropriate to translate this idiomatic expression literally unless the context demands such a departure from the consistent and invariable idiomatic usage elsewhere in the HB.[58]

54 MAL A §31 (COS 2.132:356–57; cf. ANET 182): "If a man presents the bridal gift to his father-in-law's house, and although his wife is dead there are other daughters of his father-in-law, if he so pleases, he shall marry a daughter of his father-in-law in lieu of his deceased wife." HL §192 (COS 2.19:118; cf. ANET 196): "If a man's wife dies, [he may take her] sister [as his wife.] It is not an offence." These laws reveal the approval of sororate marriage after death among the Assyrians and Hittites. HL §194 (COS 2.19:118; cf. ANET 196; translated above in the ANE background section) implies that this type of marriage is forbidden while both sisters are alive.

55 For a detailed examination of this passage, see esp. Angelo Tosato, "The Law of Leviticus 18:18: A Reexamination," CBQ 46 (1984): 199–214; cf. Hugenberger, Marriage as a Covenant, 115–18; and Murray, Principles of Conduct, 250–56.

56 Exod 26:3 (bis), 5, 6, 17; Ezek 1:9, 23; 3:13. This is true whether or not persons are in view. The references in Exod 26 refer to the coupling of curtains and clasps and boards (all fem. words) "to one another," literally, "a woman to her sister." The passages in Ezekiel refer to the wings (fem.) of the cherubim touching "one another," literally, "a woman to her sister." A similar expression, ʾiššâ rěʿûtāh, literally, "a woman with her friend/neighbor," is used to describe the gathering of birds, "each one with its mate" (Isa 34:15–16), and of women teaching "each to her neighbor" (Jer 9:19 [ET 9:20]).

57 Gen 37:19; 42:21, 28; Exod 16:15; 25:20; 37:9; Num 14:4; 2 Kgs 7:6; Jer 13:14; 25:26; Ezek 24:23; 33:30.

58 Milgrom, Leviticus 17–22: A New Translation with Introduction and Commentary (AB 3A; New York: Doubleday, 2000), 1548, claims that taking this expression as referring

Second, if the intention of 18:18 was to describe two women who were literal (consanguine) sisters, this could have easily been done in such a way as to avoid any ambiguity by the use of the conjunction "and" (*wě*) rather than the preposition "to" (*lě*), thus reading, "a woman *and* her sister." This expression would have been precisely analogous to the phrase "a woman and her daughter," used in the immediately preceding verse (and also 20:14), where a literal (consanguine) mother-daughter relationship is described. The fact that this available expression for literal relationship within the nuclear family was not employed lends further contextual support for retaining the distributive sense of the expression *ʾiššâ ʾel-ʾăḥōtāh*, as is found everywhere else in the HB.

Third, it has been argued that the word *ʾāḥôt*, "sister," in 18:18 must refer to a literal sister because elsewhere in Lev 18 it has this meaning (see, e.g., vv. 12–13).[59] Such argument, however, overlooks the fact that "elsewhere in Leviticus 18 we find *ʾāḥôt*, and not as in v. 18 *ʾiššâ ʾ . . . ʾăḥōtāh*. A simple equation between these two philologically different expressions seems to be false."[60] One cannot responsibly confuse the specific idiomatic expression with straightforward references to literal sisters in earlier verses of Lev 18.

Fourth, a number of scholars have suggested that the immediate context of Lev 18 demands a literal translation referring to female siblings (v. 18): it is proposed that the context is literal kinship ties and the prohibition of cases of incest (vv. 6–17). This suggestion, however, fails to take seriously the implications from the literary structure of Lev 18. The literary analysis of Angelo Tosato demonstrates that there is a major literary break between v. 17 and v. 18. Leviticus 18:18 is not to be included with the anti-incest laws of vv. 6–17 but is part of the general prohibitions against various kinds of illicit sexual relationships in vv. 18–23.[61] He shows that this is evident from the consistent sentence structure and content of the laws in the two sections. In vv. 7–17, every verse begins with the identical noun *ʿerwat*, "nakedness of," and culminates in the negative particle plus the imperfect *lōʾ těgallēh*, "you shall not uncover." By contrast, vv. 18–23 each consistently begin with the *waw* conjunctive and some other word besides *ʿerwat* and conclude with a negative particle, *lōʾ*, plus the imperfect of some other verb than *těgallēh*, "uncover." In other words, the first series of laws (vv. 6–17) is

---

to two literal (consanguine) sisters is "the plain meaning of the words." But does following the "plain meaning" ignore a consistent idiomatic distributive use of a given expression throughout the rest of the HB? Furthermore, this expression, "a woman/wife to her sister," even taken "literally" (i.e., not idiomatically in the distributive sense), is far from "plain"; it is a very awkward way to describe two consanguine sisters, especially when another direct way to describe a close blood relationship is used by the writer in the previous verse (see the next point below).

[59] So, e.g., Milgrom, *Leviticus 17–22*, 1549.

[60] Tosato, "Leviticus 18:18," 202, n. 8.

[61] Ibid., 202–8. Cf. Doug C. Mohrmann, "Making Sense of Sex: A Study of Leviticus 18," *JSOT* 29 (2004): 71, who recognizes "a clear shift in the redaction of the sexual laws at v. 18" and argues that the laws mentioned in v. 18 and following "have moved beyond the unit of the family into the larger society" (although unfortunately, he does not see the implication for applying this verse to polygyny in general and not only sororal polygyny).

clearly a unit, composed of laws forbidding relationships on the basis of bonds
of kinship, and the second series of laws (vv. 18–23) is another distinct unit,
covering a broad range of forbidden sexual relationships *not* based on bonds
of kinship.

Fifth, additional evidence that v. 18 belongs to a separate structural unit than
vv. 6–17 comes from the fact that all but one of the anti-incest laws of vv. 6–17
conclude with a nominal clause providing justification for the prohibition on
the basis of the identity of the forbidden individual (vv. 7–8, 10, 12–15, 17; the exception is v. 9). Verse 18 (along with vv. 19–23) does not have this explanatory
clause, which one would expect if it were to be classified with the other laws prohibiting incest.

Sixth, that v. 18 is not part of the laws dealing with incest (vv. 6–17) is also
apparent from the fact that this law contains a time limitation, unlike the permanent nature of the laws in vv. 6–17. The prohibition against taking ʾiššâ ʾel-
ʾăḥōtāh applies only while the first one is alive. This is in stark contrast to the laws
dealing with nearness of kin, which have no such temporary limitation. At the
same time, I do not find convincing the argument advanced by some that v. 18
is placed in literary affinity with the vv. 19–20 only because these verses, unlike vv. 6–17, deal with conditions that can end. It is difficult to understand
how the incestuous relationships of vv. 6–17 are any more or less permanent
than the adulterous relationship of a man with another man's wife (v. 20). Thus
v. 18 does not appear to be in a Janus relationship, looking backward to the permanent incest laws and forward to the time-limited legislation that follows, as has
been argued.[62]

Seventh, the laws of Lev 18 dealing with kinship relationships have specific
defining delimitations of the literal "sister": "your father's daughter or your
mother's daughter" (v. 9), "your father's wife's daughter" (v. 11), "your father's
sister" (v. 12), and "your mother's sister" (v. 13). In stark contrast, the law of v. 18
has no such qualifying delimitation. The alleged parallel between 18:18–19 and
20:17–18—the latter passage containing an unambiguous prohibition of marriage to a literal sister (20:17), followed by reference to sex with a menstruating
woman (20:18, like 18:19)—does not hold any weight in indicating that 18:18 refers to a literal sister, since in 20:17 the literal sister who is mentioned has specific
defining limitations attached ("a daughter of his father or a daughter of his
mother") and refers to 18:9, not 18:18, which has no defining limitation.[63]

Finally, the theological justification for the legislation given in 18:18—"as a
rival to her sister"—does not emphasize the intrinsic wrongfulness but describes

---

[62] For the argument of a Janus relationship, see, e.g., Roy Gane, *Leviticus, Numbers*
(NIVAC 3; Grand Rapids: Zondervan, 2004), 319–20.

[63] As ch. 10, below, points out in detail, the principle of organization for the prohibitions in Lev 18 is entirely different from that of Lev 20: Lev 18 is ordered by family relationships from the closest to the furthest, whereas Lev 20 is arranged according to
punishments based on the crime's severity, from the most severe to the least. Thus, alleged
parallels of placement between the two chapters are not helpful in determining the referent of the term "sister" in 18:18.

a general situation applicable to any bigamous marriage. "The harm which the law wants avoided is such (rivalry, enmity) that any woman (and not necessarily a sister of the first wife) is capable of causing it, once taken as a second wife."[64] The latter point seems confirmed by comparing the use of the Hebrew root *ṣrr,* "to be a rival," found here in Lev 18:18, with the only other OT passage utilizing this Hebrew root to describe an additional wife. This passage is 1 Sam 1:6, which depicts Peninnah as the "rival" wife of Hannah; there is no evidence to suggest that these wives of Elkanah were consanguine sisters. "Accordingly, if the motive for this prohibition was to avoid vexation to one's wife, there is little reason for limiting its prohibition to a literal sister; both the Bible and anthropology provide ample testimony to the unpleasant reality of contention among co-wives, whether sisters or not."[65]

All of these considerations lead to the conclusion that the phrase *ʾiššâ ʾel-ʾăhōtāh* appears in a context of laws dealing with general nonkinship relationships. This nonkinship context strongly favors the translation that retains the consistent general idiomatic meaning found in the rest of Scripture: "one [woman/wife] in addition to another." This phrase refers to any two women, not just two consanguine sisters. The law of 18:18 is thus prohibiting not only sororal polygyny (polygamy involving two consanguine sisters) but also the taking of "two women [fellow citizens] in general."[66] In other words, this legislation prohibits all polygamy.

This law, then, prohibits a man from taking another woman in addition to his first wife, to be a rival wife (*liṣrōr,* lit. "vexer") as long as the first wife is alive. By implication, this law allows for remarriage after the death of the first wife. Thus the monogamous norm of Genesis is upheld in this Mosaic legislation.

Gordon Hugenberger points out that one should not reject this interpretation of Lev 18:18 because of its "impossible idealism," that is, its lack of criminal sanctions (there is no mention of any punishment for transgressing this law in the list of Lev 20 or elsewhere in the Torah). There are many other such cases of "idealistic" stipulations in the Holiness Code (e.g., the prohibition against hatred, 19:17–18), and the very lack of criminal sanction may emphasize the nature of these laws as ethical and not just legal norms. Hugenberger suggests that 18:18 is an example of a *lex imperfecta:* "a law which prohibits something without thereby rendering it invalid (reflecting a society which would have lacked the requisite means of enforcement in any case)."[67] The fact that there is no punishment

---

[64] Tosato, "Leviticus 18:18," 207.

[65] Hugenberger, *Marriage as a Covenant,* 117. It appears like special pleading to argue, as some have done, that the general reference to "rival" is worded in this way so that the law can be expanded by logical extension to refer to any other woman. It does not make sense that the "rival" in this law is allowed to be extended to refer to any other woman while the term "sister" is not allowed such extension, especially when it is a part of the idiomatic phrase "a woman to her sister," which everywhere else in the HB is extended to include all other women.

[66] Ibid., 203.

[67] Ibid., 118.

mentioned in Lev 20 corresponding to this prohibition of 18:18 may be regarded as another indicator that 18:18 is prohibiting polygamy and not another form of incest.[68]

The Qumran community interpreted 18:18 as a law prohibiting polygamy in general.[69] I concur with Tosato that this Qumran interpretation is "more faithful to the original sense that the interpretation commonly given today."[70] As argued in the discussion of homosexual practice and bestiality (ch. 4, above) and in subsequent chapters of this book dealing with other sexually related prohibitions (see esp. chs. 7, 8, and 10), the prohibitions in Lev 18 (including the proscription of polygamy) are set forth as universal law, applicable for all time and for all nations. The legislation prohibiting plural marriages, like the other prohibitions of Lev 18, is ultimately rooted in creation, as it upholds the divine order of monogamous marriage (Gen 2:24).

Legislation regarding the King's Marital Status: Deuteronomy 17:17. In the section of Deuteronomic laws amplifying the fifth commandment (regarding authority, Deut 16:18–18:22),[71] there is legislation governing the activities of a king in Israel should such an institution arise by popular demand to be like the other nations. Amidst these laws is a prohibition that has often been interpreted as condoning a moderate amount of polygamy on the part of the king. Deuteronomy 17:17 reads, "And he [the king] must not acquire many [*yarbeh*, in the *hip͑il* of *rābâ*] wives for himself, or else his heart will turn away." It has been argued that the verb *rābâ*, "increase, multiply," implies acquiring an excessive number of wives, thus abusing the practice of polygamy but not prohibiting it altogether.[72] Others suggest that the law is specifically directed against the king's marrying many *foreign*, idol-worshiping wives, so that they

---

[68] There is one case of incest mentioned in Lev 18—sex with a granddaughter, v. 17a—which also does not find a corresponding punishment mentioned in Lev 20, and so 18:18 could theoretically be another example of such an omission for incest. But in light of all the other lines of evidence cited above, it seems preferable to conclude that the list of punishments of Lev 20 does not refer to 18:18 because indeed it does not deal with incest at all but rather with polygamy, which is condemned by God as immoral although it goes unpunished within the Israelite legal system.

[69] See *Damascus Document*[a] (4QD[a]) 4:20–21 and the discussion in Tosato, "Leviticus 18:18," 202–4, 208–14; 11QT[a] 57:17–19 and the discussion in Yigael Yadin, *The Temple Scroll: The Hidden Law of the Dead Sea Sect* (New York: Random House, 1985), 200; Yigael Yadin, ed., *The Temple Scroll* (3 vols.; Jerusalem: Israel Exploration Society, 1983), 2:258; and David Instone-Brewer, "Nomological Exegesis in Qumran 'Divorce' Texts," *RevQ* 18 (1998): 561–79.

[70] Tosato, "Leviticus 18:18," 208.

[71] See the analysis by Steven A. Kaufman, "The Structure of the Deuteronomic Law," *Maarav* 1–2 (1978–1979): 105–58, discussed in ch. 3, above. Kaufman discusses the Deuteronomic summary of laws amplifying the fifth commandment on pp. 125, 133–34. Cf. Dennis T. Olson, *Deuteronomy and the Death of Moses: A Theological Reading* (OBT; Minneapolis: Fortress, 1994), 78–87.

[72] See, e.g., Jean-Jacques Bouit, "A Christian Consideration of Polygamy" (D.Min. project report, Andrews University, 1981), 79–80.

not turn his heart away from worshiping the true God, and not against royal polygamy per se.[73]

Does this law allow for at least limited royal polygamy? The key term is the Hebrew verb *rābâ* in the causative *hipᶜil,* "to multiply." This verb is found also in the two laws that surround this legislation. In Deut 17:16 Moses specifies that the king "must not acquire many [*yarbeh,* the *hipᶜil* of *rābâ*] horses for himself, or return the people to Egypt in order to acquire more [*harbôt,* the *hipᶜil* of *rābâ*] horses, since the LORD has said to you, 'You must never return that way again.'" In v. 17b the prohibition concerns the accumulation of wealth: "also silver and gold he must not acquire in great quantity for himself [*yarbeh-lô měʾōd*]." The verb *rābâ* in the *hipᶜil* literally means "to cause to increase," with the context determining the extent of this increase.[74]

Hugenberger points out that although the expression "he [the king] shall not increase wives for himself" appears to be "less than precise," this expression "was chosen not to facilitate some more modest level of polygyny, but to achieve an artful parallelism between the three characteristic sins of Canaanite (and Israelite) kingship."[75] An important clue to the meaning of *rābâ* in the context of 17:16–17 is the contrast between the first two laws, on one hand—which use *rābâ* by itself with no adverbial modifier—and the third law, on the other hand, which modifies *rābâ* with the intensifying adverb *měʾōd,* meaning "greatly multiply." By juxtaposing these three laws, the first two with the unqualified prohibition to "increase" and the third with a qualification against *excessive* "increase," it is reasonable to conclude that there is to be *no* increase of horses or wives, in contrast to no *excessive* increase of wealth.[76] In other words, the divine will is that the king have no multiplication of horses (i.e., no chariotry), no multiplication of wives (i.e., no harem), and no amassing of excessive wealth.[77]

The instruction prohibiting multiplication of horses comports well with other biblical statements warning Israel not to trust in horses. So Isa 31:1: "Alas for those who go down to Egypt for help and who rely on horses, who trust in chariots because they are many and in horsemen because they are very strong,

---

[73] So, e.g., Eugene Hillman, *Polygamy Reconsidered: African Plural Marriage and the Christian Church* (Maryknoll, N.Y.: Orbis, 1975), 145.

[74] BDB 916; cf. *HALOT* 1177. See the NIV translation "increase" or "add" for several passages of *rābâ* in the *hipᶜil:* e.g., Deut 1:10 ("increased your numbers"); Lev 26:9 ("increase your numbers [of people]"); Jer 30:19 ("add to their numbers").

[75] Hugenberger, *Marriage as a Covenant,* 119.

[76] One could also interpret this juxtaposition, however, as a contrast between "a lot of" (horses and wives) and "a very lot of" (wealth). The immediate context must be the final determiner; see the discussion below for such context.

[77] One might ask why, if the intent of the prohibition was to forbid all polygyny, the narrator did not simply say regarding the king, "He shall not take more than one wife," or some such statement. But, as Hugenberger notes, such a statement would not take into account "the undeniable right to marry following divorce or the death of a spouse" (*Marriage as a Covenant,* 120, n. 137). Furthermore, such a statement would break the literary flow of the parallelism between the three prohibitions, as diagramed by Hugenberger (ibid., 119).

but do not look to the Holy One of Israel or consult the LORD!" Again, Ps 33:17: "A war horse is a vain hope for victory; and by its great might it cannot save." God wished Israel to put its full confidence in God to bring supernatural deliverance in battle, not in the false security that horses could bring. It seems that the use of the royal mule—not the horse—for the coronation ceremonies of the kings was at least implicit recognition of this regulation (see 2 Sam 18:9; 1 Kgs 1:33, 38, 44), and the multitude of imported Egyptian horses and chariots amassed by King Solomon was in flagrant violation of this command (1 Kgs 5:6 (ET 4:26); 10:26–29).

Likewise, the prohibition of the multiplication of wives comported with the Edenic divine plan of monogamy and with the legislation prohibiting polygamy (Lev 18:18). "The prohibition against 'increasing' wives is not so much concerned with the legality of polygyny in the abstract, but with the inevitable result of *royal* polygyny in apostasy and accommodation to the gods of one's wives: as the text explicitly states, 'lest his heart turn away' (cf. 1 Kgs. 11:1ff.; 16:31–33). . . . This danger can attend diplomatic polygyny practiced to any degree."[78] Solomon's polygamy was in flagrant violation of this command (1 Kgs 11:1–13), with the predicted result of turning away his heart from God. The narrator of Solomon's reign also clearly indicates that Solomon flagrantly violated the command forbidding the excessive amassing of wealth by the king (1 Kgs 10:14–25).

Because of the "less than precise" language of Deut 17:17 taken in isolation, there is not strong enough evidence to say categorically that the law prohibits all royal polygamy. In the very next verses (17:18–20), however, the king is instructed to write for himself a copy of the book of the Torah, "diligently observing all the words of this law and these statutes" (17:19) just like his fellow citizens. The king is not above the law. This would mean that he was also not above the law of Lev 18:18. If Lev 18:18 forbids all polygamy, this would also apply to the king, who is also subject to the commands and prohibitions of Torah.

Recent studies dealing with the instruction regarding the future king of Israel show that the king's behavior was to be a model for all of Israel.[79] The same responsibility placed upon the king to study Torah that he might fear the Lord and obey his law (Deut 17:19) is also placed upon every individual Israelite (6:7; 8:1; 11:1). The same warning given to the king—"neither exalting himself" (17:20)—is given to all Israel (8:14); the same caution against turning aside from the commandment is given to both the king and corporate Israel (17:20; cf. 5:32; 11:28; 28:14).

From the immediate context of Lev 18:18 (esp. vv. 18–20) and the intertextual connections, it is clear that the king in all his behavior—including his monogamous marital status—was to be an example for his subjects to follow. Thus the law prohibiting royal polygamy in Deut 17:17 serves to uphold and further emphasize the similar prohibition given to all Israel in Lev 18:18. The Zadokites

---

[78] Ibid., 120.

[79] See esp. Patrick D. Miller, *Deuteronomy* (IBC; Louisville: John Knox, 1990), 148–49: "Deuteronomy's primary concern was that the king be *the model Israelite*."

and the Qumran community were not misguided when they interpreted this passage as requiring monogamy on the part of the king.[80]

Other Legislation Purportedly Presupposing Polygamy. Several other passages in the pentateuchal legislation have been viewed as giving tacit support to the practice of polygamy. Deuteronomy 21:15–17 deals with the rights of the first-born son:

> If a man has two wives, one of them loved and the other disliked, and if both the loved and the disliked have borne him sons, the firstborn being the son of the one who is disliked, then on the day when he wills his possessions to his sons, he is not permitted to treat the son of the loved as the firstborn in preference to the son of the disliked, who is the firstborn. He must acknowledge as firstborn the son of the one who is disliked, giving him a double portion of all that he has; since he is the first issue of his virility, the right of the firstborn is his.

Interpreters who argue that this law tacitly assumes polygamy must posit that the man has two wives simultaneously. But such is nowhere stated in the legislation. The phrase "If a man has two wives" (*kî-tihyênā lĕʾîš šĕtê nāšîm*) does not at all necessitate an implication of polygamy. "It definitely is wrong to insist that both wives are living, for that would be asking the imperfect verb form (future or continuous action of the verb) to bear a load it was not meant to carry."[81] It has already been shown that the Mosaic legislation recognizes a situation in which a man might lawfully marry two wives: he may marry again after the death of the first wife (Lev 18:18). This legislation might have in view a situation in which one of these wives (either the one now dead or the one a man married after the death of the first) was more highly regarded than the other and thus the man is tempted to give preferential treatment to the offspring of that more highly favored wife.

At the same time, one cannot rule out the possibility that this case law mentions (or includes as possibilities) situations that are not in harmony with God's will (such as polygamy or divorce [as in Deut 24:1–4; see ch. 9, below]), indicating the rights of the firstborn in such cases without sanctioning the practice of polygamy or divorce. As support for this interpretation, one may observe possible allusions in this case law to the Jacob narrative, where the first wife (Leah) is unloved and the second wife (Rachel) is loved and where the birthright is ultimately withheld from Reuben (the firstborn son of Leah) and given to Joseph (the firstborn son of Rachel). This case law would then be seen as a tacit criticism of Jacob's behavior.[82] Even if such is the interpretation, however, this case law, dealing with the rights of the firstborn, cannot be used to legitimize polygamy any more

---

[80] See 11QTᵃ 57:17–19: "And he [the king] shall not take in addition to her another wife, for she alone shall be with him all days of her life; but if she dies, then he can take to himself another"; cf. "Fragments of a Zadokite Sect" 7:4, *APOT* 2:810; Hugenberger, *Marriage as a Covenant*, 120; and Instone-Brewer, "Nomological Exegesis," 566–68.

[81] Kaiser, *Toward Old Testament Ethics*, 187.

[82] See, e.g., Calum M. Carmichael, *Women, Law, and the Genesis Traditions* (Edinburgh: Edinburgh University Press, 1979), 31–32.

than can, for example, Deut 32:18 be used to legitimize prostitution because it prohibits the use of prostitute wages for the payment of vows.

The Pentateuch has two laws dealing with sexual relationships with an unbetrothed woman (Exod 22:15–16 [ET 22:16–17]; Deut 22:28–29; see ch. 8, below, on such relationships and on the following points). Some have pointed out that this legislation allows for, and even forces, polygamy in certain situations. Both of these laws, however, are referring to a case of sexual seduction and not forcible rape (although one may emphasize the psychological more and the other the physical pressure more); thus the Deuteronomy passage is a repetition or extension of the Exodus legislation. The Exodus passage clearly indicates that the father had the right to refuse to let his daughter who had been seduced marry the man who seduced her, and this seems to be assumed also in the Deuteronomy passage. The Exodus passage indicates that in such cases the dowry must still be paid, and the complementary Deuteronomy passage indicates the exact amount of that dowry (fifty shekels of silver). Thus this legislation leaves a way out when the seducer is already married, in that he would be required to pay the dowry of fifty shekels of silver but would not be required to marry the woman. The point is that the father has the first right of refusal regardless of the marital status of the seducer (whether married or single). These laws do not break monogamous pattern set in Eden.

A final piece of Mosaic legislation purportedly presupposing polygamy is the levirate marriage law (Deut 25:5–10; see ch. 11, below, on this law in connection with the issue of procreation and on the following points). What is often overlooked in the discussion of the levirate marriage regulations is the opening dependent clause: "When brothers reside together" (*kî yēšbû ʾaḥîm yaḥdāw*). This introductory statement specifies that it was only when two brothers lived together that the levirate law described in this verse was to be in operation. Commenting on this dependent clause, Anthony Phillips notes, "Until a younger brother married and had children of his own, he would have remained in his father's or elder brother's house."[83] Herbert Leupold draws the implication of this legislation with regard to polygamy: "The brother of the deceased, *if unmarried,* would take the widow to wife."[84] My own detailed analysis of this passage (set forth in ch. 11 below) leads me to concur with these and other scholars (contra Raymond Westbrook) that the brother-in-law who would carry out the levirate marriage law is presumed to be unmarried. The levirate law also has a broader application to other near-of-kin if there is no qualified (unmarried, mature) brother to perform the levirate duty, as in the case of Ruth.

Polygamy in the Prophets/Writings

The Prophets contain several accounts of polygamy and concubinage. Judges 8:30 records the case of Gideon, who "had many wives." The context of this passage makes clear that Gideon's polygamy occurred in the setting of his apostasy

---

[83] Anthony Phillips, *Deuteronomy* (CBC; Cambridge: Cambridge University Press, 1973), 168.

[84] Leupold, *Genesis,* 980 (italics mine).

later in life, in which he not only became polygamous but idolatrous (8:24–28). Thus there is no divine approval for his polygamous relationships. Several other judges may have been polygamous, as they had numerous offspring: Jair (10:3, 4), Ibzan (12:8, 9), and Abdon (12:13).

Judges 19–21, the concluding narrative, is a "text of terror"[85] that all too vividly portrays the explosive nature and destructive capacity of decadent sexuality. The story features a Levite and his concubine. As with the Gideon narrative, this account is clearly not written to express approval for concubinage. To the contrary, the account appears to be deliberately placed at the end of the book of Judges to reveal the depths of degradation to which the people went when, without the acknowledged kingship of God, "all the people did what was right in their own eyes" (21:25). The perspective of the author/editor of Judges condemned the sexual decay of the times; the portrayal of the gruesome details and disastrous results of unlawful sexual activities leads the reader to reject such departures from the divine ideal.

The writers/editors of Samuel–Kings and Chronicles likewise reveal a society that has strayed far from God's ideal. Those who fall prey to the prevailing customs of bigamy, polygamy, or concubinage include even the pious ones, such as Elkanah[86] (1 Sam 1–2), and the political leaders of the united monarchy, Saul (1 Sam 14:50; 2 Sam 3:7), David (2 Sam 5:13; 1 Chr 3:1–9; 14:3), and Solomon (1 Kgs 3:1; 7:8; 11:1–7). Six of the twenty Judean kings of the divided monarchy are mentioned as having more than one wife: Rehoboam (2 Chr 11:18–21), Abijah (13:4, 21), Jehoram (21:14–17), Joash (24:3), Jehoiachin (2 Kgs 24:15), and Zedekiah (Jer 38:23). In the northern kingdom, only the polygamy of Ahab is recorded (1 Kgs 20:3–7), but others no doubt followed this practice. The record of Chronicles also mentions other polygamists: Jerahmeel (1 Chr 2:25–28); Caleb (2:46–48); Ashhur (4:5); Izrahiah and his sons, Michael, Obadiah, Joel, and Isshiah (7:3, 4); and Manasseh (7:14). The biblical narrators faithfully record the anguish and disharmony experienced in having a "rival" (1 Sam 1:6 and the rest of Hannah's story) in disregard of the Lev 18:18 legislation,[87] and the disastrous personal and national results of kings "acquiring many wives" to themselves in blatant disobedience to the divine prohibition in Deut 17:17.[88]

---

[85] See Phyllis Trible's literary-feminist study of the narrative in *Texts of Terror: Literary-Feminist Readings of Biblical Narratives* (OBT; Philadelphia: Fortress, 1984), 65–92.

[86] The motivation for Elkanah's bigamy may well have been Hannah's infertility, as in the case of Abram and Hagar and as attested in ANE law and practice in Mesopotamia.

[87] See esp. 1 Sam 1:7, where the incident of the previous verse (in which the "rival" wife "used to provoke her severely") happened "year by year." Every year "she used to provoke her," and this called forth from Hannah severe anguish: "Hannah wept and would not eat." She was "deeply distressed . . . and wept bitterly" (v. 10); she was "a woman deeply troubled" (v. 15) who experienced "misery" (v. 11). Note that the word for "rival" in the story of Elkanah (1 Sam 1:6) comes from the verbal root ṣrr, echoing the usage of the same root in Lev 18:18, where God prohibits taking a second wife "as a rival" to the first. This intertextual echo employed by the narrator implicitly condemns Elkanah's practice.

[88] The refusal to obey the pentateuchal command against royal polygamy appears to have been mainly responsible for the general apostasy of Israel. See esp. 1 Kgs 11:1–7, where the wording echoes Deut 17:17, signaling the narrator's intent to emphasize that Solomon's actions were in violation of the Mosaic law.

All of these incidences of plural marriage are placed in a context of disobedience and unfaithfulness to God, with two supposed exceptions. Two historical references during the time of the monarchy are frequently cited as giving tacit approval of polygamy. First is the experience of David; it is suggested that God approved of David's polygamy and even called him "a man after his own heart" (1 Sam 13:14) while he was in the polygamous state. Ronald du Preez, however, makes a strong biblical case for the conclusions that (1) this statement of divine approval did not apply to David while a polygamist; (2) the narrator reveals the negative divine assessment of David's polygamous relationships; (3) Nathan's message to David in 2 Sam 12:7–8 does not indicate that God sanctioned and supported David's practice of polygamy; and (4) toward the end of his life, David returned to a monogamous state (with Bathsheba).[89]

A brief look at the biblical evidence adduced for du Preez's conclusions may be helpful. First, it seems clear that it was while David was not yet a polygamist that God called David "a man after his own heart" (1 Sam 13:14); the context of this statement (Saul's presumptuous offering of sacrifice) points to a time when David was probably still unmarried.[90]

Further, du Preez points out the cyclical pattern of David's life, containing several repetitions of a cycle of five successive steps in the narrative: servitude (1 Sam 17; 22:21–23:1; 30:1–5), supplication (17:46; 23:2–4; 30:6–8), salvation (17:50–54; 23:14; 30:16–25), silence (in his relationship with God, 19:12–20:42; 25:21–22; 2 Sam 2:8–3:1), and sin (1 Sam 20:1–21:15; 25:39–43; 2 Sam 3:2–16). The narrator consistently records the references to David's polygamy following a period of silence, in the final step of the cycle, sin. Each of these references in the fifth step is a statement made in the context of some calamity, threat, or judgment (1 Sam 30:1–5; 2 Sam 3:22–37; 5:17; 12:1–14).[91] By such strategic placement of references to David's polygamy within the longer cyclical pattern of the story, the narrator gives a negative assessment of David's polygamous

---

[89] Du Preez, *Polygamy in the Bible,* 183–204.

[90] One should also recognize that Kings and Chronicles also often give generalized eulogizing statements when assessing the overall trend of a king's life, without denying specific, and often very grievous, moral lapses. E.g., 1 Kgs 15:5 reports that "David did what was right in the sight of the LORD, and did not turn aside from anything that he commanded him all the days of his life, except in the matter of Uriah the Hittite." Again, 1 Kgs 14:8 gives a divine eulogy of "my servant David, who kept my commandments and followed me with all his heart, doing only that which was right in my sight." These statements must be seen in the larger context of the divine condemnation of idolatry, marking the contrast between David, who did not disloyally worship other gods, and the idolatrous kings of the divided monarchy, who succeeded him (see 1 Kgs 12:26–33; 14:9; 15:3).

[91] Du Preez, *Polygamy in the Bible,* 192–97, argues that the judgment pronounced upon David by Nathan includes an explicit condemnation of David's polygamy when Nathan accuses him: "You . . . have taken his [Uriah's] wife to be your wife" (2 Sam 12:9). As punishment for his sin of polygamy, Nathan announces the divine predictive sentence that the other wives of David (besides Bathsheba) will be defiled by one close to David (2 Sam 12:11). Although this interpretation is plausible, it is also possible to see the emphasis as upon the adultery of David with Bathsheba (and its aftermath) and not directly addressing his polygamy.

relationships.[92] John Kessler's close reading of the David narratives in the books of Samuel comes to a conclusion similar to du Preez's, that in these accounts the narrator intends to disclose with disapproval the "*progressive descent*" of David into polygamy and here, as in Deuteronomy, polygamy is viewed as "inherently inimical to Yahweh's ultimate will for life and detrimental to those involved."[93]

Again, Nathan's judgment parable in 2 Sam 12 does not support the contention that God sanctions polygamy. The divine statement delivered by Nathan to David in 12:7–8 may, at first glance, give the appearance of such divine approval:

> Thus says the LORD, the God of Israel: I anointed you king over Israel, and I rescued you from the hand of Saul; I gave [*wāʾetnâ*] you your master's house, and your master's wives into your bosom [*běhêqekā*], and gave you the house of Israel and of Judah; and if that had been too little, I would have added as much more.

But notice that only three verses later (12:11) God indicates that he will take David's wives and give (*nātan*) them to one close to him (which turned out to be his son Absalom), who would lie with them. Absalom's defiling of David's wives and concubines (as will be discussed further below) was not only adultery but also incest (called an abomination in Lev 18:8), and certainly God's "giving" (*nātan*) of David's wives to Absalom does not imply divine approval of Absalom's abominable acts. This is, rather, a case of divine accommodation in the use of language, to describe God's permissive will, in which God is said to do what he allows.[94]

Furthermore, in 2 Sam 12:7–8 it is not at all clear that God's "giving" of Saul's wives to David implies that David married them. If the biblical record is complete regarding the marriage status of Saul, he had one wife (Ahinoam, daughter of Ahimaaz and the mother of Michal; 1 Sam 14:50) along with one concubine (Rizpah; 2 Sam 3:7; 21:8). Walter Kaiser points out that if "gave" meant that David took Ahinoam as wife, then "David was authorized, on this supposition, to marry his wife's mother—a form of incest already condemned in the Levitical law, carrying the sanction of being burnt alive (Lev. 18:17)."[95] It is more likely that the phrase "into your bosom" (*běhêqekā*), which applies to Saul's "house" as well as his women/wives, does not speak of marriage but simply indicates that all of Saul's estate/possessions came under David's care and keeping.[96]

---

92 Ibid., 185–86.

93 John Kessler, "Sexuality and Politics: The Motif of the Displaced Husband in the Books of Samuel," *CBQ* 62 (2000): 409–23, quotes at 423, 421.

94 See the parallel where the narrative indicates that God hardened Pharaoh's heart (Exod 4:21; 7:3;10:1, 20, 27; 11:10; 14:4, 8), but this is God's permissive will, since Pharaoh is said to have free choice and harden his own heart (Exod 8:11, 28 [ET 8:15, 32]; 9:34).

95 Kaiser, *Toward Old Testament Ethics,* 188.

96 Kaiser, ibid., suggests translating *nāšîm* as "women," not "wives," and identifying these with Saul's female domestics and courtesans, not his wives. In 2 Sam 12:11, however, David's *nāšîm* are clearly his "wives," and it seems inconsistent and unwarranted by the context to suggest that Saul's *nāšîm* has another meaning. It should be noted that *běhêqekā,* "into his bosom," intertextually echoes the usage of the term in Nathan's parable (12:3), where the poor man's ewe lamb "used to . . . lie in his bosom [*běhêqô*]," and so does not appear to have sexual connotations in this context.

Nathan's judgment parable itself may contain an implicit indication that monogamy was God's divine plan: the poor man in the parable had only "one little ewe lamb," not many (2 Sam 12:3), obviously alluding to the monogamous relationship of Uriah with Bathsheba. "In his parable of the rich man with the flocks and herds and the poor man with the one ewe lamb Nathan clearly indicated his approval of monogamous marriage and at the same time implicitly criticized David's harem."[97]

Finally, du Preez analyzes the episode of Absalom's rebellion, when David fled the palace, leaving behind his ten *nāšîm pilagšîm*, "concubines" (2 Sam 15:16).[98] In light of the earlier divine prediction in 12:11 that David's *wives* (not just his concubines) would be violated and in light of our discussion of the word *pîlegeš*, "concubine," in connection with the Abraham narrative, where it was noted that the term can refer to both concubines and wives (other than the original first wife), it is probable that this expression refers to both the wives and the concubines of David, not just his concubines.

The biblical record mentions exactly ten wives and concubines of David (besides Michal, who apparently was already set aside by this time [2 Sam 6:20–23], and Bathsheba, who appears later in the narrative, apparently still as his wife).[99] These likely were the ten women violated by Absalom (16:21–22). The narrator records that David, upon his return to Jerusalem after the death of Absalom, took his ten wives/concubines "and put them in a house under guard, and provided for them, but did not go in to them" (20:3). It appears probable, then, that David, as part of his attitude of repentance toward God during Absalom's rebellion (see 15:30), recognizing the fulfillment of God's judgment upon him announced by Nathan, now returned to a monogamous state (with Bathsheba, the mother of Solomon) for the rest of his life.[100] "David moves visibly away from the royal ideology [of polygamy] in the direction of the old requirements of covenant [located in Deut 17:14–20]."[101]

Later in the narrative, the narrator seems to go out of his way to underscore David's monogamous status during these later years by emphasizing that he did not have sexual relations with Abishag the Shunammite, who took care of him in his old age (1 Kgs 1:1–4). Thus, according to du Preez's analysis, in the account of David's life, the practice of polygamy is in no way given divine sanction; to the

---

[97] G. N. Vollebregt, *The Bible on Marriage* (trans. R. A. Downie; London: Sheed & Ward, 1965), 23.

[98] Ibid., 197–203.

[99] Second Samuel 3:2–5 mentions six wives (Ahinoam of Jezreel [not to be confused with Ahinoam the daughter of Ahimaaz, Saul's wife, 1 Sam 14:50], Abigail, Maacah, Haggith, Abital, and Eglah), and 2 Sam 5:13 indicates two more wives and two more concubines, making a total of ten.

[100] That Bathsheba was not among the ten women placed in seclusion but was still David's wife is evident from the fact that she is mentioned several times in this part of the narrative (1 Kgs 1:11, 15, 16, 28, 31) as having ready access to the king's bedchamber.

[101] Walter Brueggemann, *First and Second Samuel* (IBC; Louisville: Westminster/ John Knox , 1990), 330.

contrary, the narrative is replete with clues that this practice was not according to the divine will.

Du Preez's analysis may not provide a completely watertight case for David's return to monogamy at the end of his life, but there is intriguing evidence to support this position. Even if David did not turn from his polygyny, there are enough clues of discord and dysfunctionality in the marriages of David to conclude that God worked with David in spite of his failings; God in no wise countenanced these failings of David to live up to the divine ideal.

A second alleged exception to the generally negative assessment of polygamy during the time of the monarchy is the case of the bigamy of Joash in 2 Chr 24:2–3, where many English translations make it appear that the bigamy was included in the divine approval: "Joash did what was right in the sight of the LORD all the days of the priest Jehoiada. Jehoiada got two wives for him, and he became the father of sons and daughters" (cf., e.g., NKJV, NASB, NIV). Several commentators have recognized, however, that these verses from Chronicles, which give a summary introduction to the kingship of Joash,[102] are interpreting the parallel account in 2 Kgs 12:1–4 (ET 11:21–12:3) and indeed follow the same basic structure as the Kings narrative.[103] Note the comparison in the chart.

2 Kgs 12:1–4 (ET 11:21–12:3)	2 Chr 24:1–3
Jehoash [= Joash] was seven years old when he began to reign.	Joash [= Jehoash] was seven years old when he began to reign; he reigned forty years in Jerusalem; his mother's name was Zibiah of Beer-sheba.
In the seventh year of Jehu, Jehoash began to reign; he reigned forty years in Jerusalem. His mother's name was Zibiah of Beer-sheba.	
Jehoash did what was right in the sight of the LORD all his days, because the priest Jehoiada instructed him.	Joash did what was right in the sight of the LORD all the days of the priest Jehoiada.
Nevertheless [raq] the high places were not taken away; the people continued to sacrifice and make offerings on the high places.	[And (waw consecutive)] Jehoiada got two wives for him, and he became the father of sons and daughters.

The Chronicles account closely parallels that of Kings, except that where Kings explicitly indicates (by the term raq, "nevertheless, only, except") the negative aspect of Joash's reign in not removing the high places, the Chronicles account states in the parallel location that Jehoiada took for him two wives. It seems

---

[102] That the first three verses of 2 Chr 24 are a summary statement is apparent from the fact that each of these verses begins with a waw consecutive plus the imperfect whereas v. 4 starts a new section with the more complex statement "Some time afterward" and the verses that follow clearly indicate that Jehoida is still alive and directing the temple repairs (vv. 4–14).

[103] See, e.g., Martin J. Selman, 2 Chronicles: A Commentary (TOTC 10B; Downers Grove, Ill.: InterVarsity, 1994), 450–52; J. Barton Payne, "1, 2 Chronicles," EBC 4:513–14.

likely from this comparison that one should understand the coordinating conjunction *waw* as having the force of "but" or "except" rather than "and" in 2 Chr 24:3—implying divine disapproval for the arranged polygamy: "Joash did what was right in the sight of the LORD all the days of the priest Jehoiada. *But* [or *And yet*] Jehoiada got two wives for him."[104]

Some interpreters have suggested that the allegory of Ezek 23 implies divine approval of polygamy, inasmuch as in the allegory even God is represented as having two wives (Ezek 23:1–4).[105] It must be recognized, however, that this is an allegory, adapted to the historical situation of the divided kingdom of Judah and Israel, and one must concentrate on the point of the allegory—emphasizing Israel's failure and infidelity—and not try to make the allegory "stand on all fours." Robert Hitchens rightly points out that this image of Yahweh's marriage to two sisters in fact "only applies the symbolism of the marriage relationship which was begun before the division of the kingdom. All Jews [Israelites] were still God's chosen and regarded as *one* people, though divided into two kingdoms."[106] The same Ezekiel who recorded the allegory of two sisters in Ezek 23 documented the command of the Lord in Ezek 37 to reunite the two "sticks" of Israel and Judah into one stick: "in order that they may be one in my hand. . . . Never again shall they be two nations, and never again shall they be divided into two kingdoms" (37:19, 22). God's relation with Israel is a "monogamous" one, according to God's consistent plan, even though its apostasy temporarily separated the nation into two parts and called forth an allegorical message to fit the situation. There is no support for bigamous or polygamous marriage in the message of God through Ezekiel.

During and after the Babylonian captivity, the problem of polygamy does not appear to have been an issue among God's people, although two of the heathen kings under whose captivity they lived are mentioned as polygamous in Scripture: Belshazzar the Babylonian (Dan 5:2–3) and Ahasuerus the Persian (Esth 2).[107] The

---

[104] A *waw* consecutive plus the imperfect can have the force of antithesis or contrast ("but" or "and yet"); see GKC §111d–e; and *IBHS* 550 (§33.2.1d). One must recognize that the Chronicler does not use the more forceful term *raq* ("except") in 2 Chr 24:3, as is so frequent in the book of Kings' negative assessment of Joash and many other kings during the period of the monarchy (e.g., 1 Kgs 3:3; 15:5; 2 Kgs 3:2–3; 10:29; 12:42 Kgs 12:1–4 [ET 12:3]; 14:3–4; 15:4, 35; 17:2); the Chronicler employs this term more sparingly for this purpose (e.g., 2 Chr 25:2, 14; 27:2). At the same time, his placement of the reference to bigamy in the same structural position as where the parallel Kings narrative records the negative assessment of Joash's reign seems implicitly to censure Joash's plural marriage. For commentators who recognize that Joash's bigamy was censurable, being opposed to the pentateuchal legislation of Deut 17:17, see, e.g., Jacob M. Myers, *II Chronicles* (AB 13; Garden City, N.Y.: Doubleday, 1965), 137; and Payne, "1, 2 Chronicles," 514. For further discussion, see du Preez, *Polygamy in the Bible*, 213–16.

[105] See, e.g., Robert Holst, "Polygamy and the Bible," *International Review of Missions* 56 (1967): 205–13 (cited in Hugenberger, *Marriage as a Covenant,* 111); Payne, "1, 2 Chronicles," 4:513–14; and Selman, *2 Chronicles,* 450–52.

[106] Robert J. Hitchens, *Multiple Marriage: A Study of Polygamy in Light of the Bible* (Elkton, Md.: Doulos, 1987), 137, n. 11.

[107] Not a single case of polygamy among the Jewish people is mentioned in the biblical record during the postexilic period (with the exception of Esther). The fifth-century

people of Judah seem to have recognized that the Babylonian exile had come upon them because of their sins, in particular their idolatry (cf. Daniel's prayer in Dan 9), and a return to vigorous monotheism (faithfulness to only one true God) was accompanied by a general return to monogamy (faithfulness to only one wife).

In the wisdom/hymnic literature of the Writings, human sexuality in marriage is assumed to be monogamous, a duality of husband and wife. The importance of this point is strikingly revealed in Proverbs by the deafening silence concerning polygamous situations. "In Proverbs the union of one man with one woman is clearly shown to be the norm, both by the absence of any allusion to the discords of polygamy (though we meet other domestic troubles from unfaithfulness to nagging) and by the fully personal bond taken to exist between husband and wife."[108] The wise man in Proverbs calls for faithfulness between a husband and his one wife (not wives):

> Drink water from your own cistern,
> flowing water from your own well. . . .
> Let your fountain be blessed,
> and rejoice in the wife of your youth. (Prov 5:15, 18)

B.C.E. Elephantine community rejected polygamy, as did later sectarian Judaism (Reuven Yaron, *Introduction to the Law of the Aramaic Papyri* [Oxford: Clarendon, 1962], 60). Some scholars, however, find in Mal 2:10–16 an assumption of polygamy. See, e.g., Adam S. van der Woude, "Malachi's Struggle for a Pure Community: Reflections on Malachi 2:10–16," in *Tradition and Re-interpretation in Jewish and Early Christian Literature: Essays in Honor of Jürgen C. H. Lebram* (ed. Jan Willem van Henten et al.; StPB 36; Leiden: E. J. Brill, 1986), 65–71. For a detailed rebuttal of this position, see Hugenberger, *Marriage as a Covenant,* 54–57, 94–95, 121. Hugenberger, 121, concludes, "With respect to the post-exilic period, although Mal. 2:10–16 has been supposed by some scholars to assume . . . or even to commend polygyny . . . , it is far more likely that monogamy was seen as the marital ideal in this period and that actual marital practice was monogamous with few, if any, exceptions." See also the summary statement by Markus Zehnder, "A Fresh Look at Malachi II 13–16," *VT* 53 (2003): 247, regarding the Edenic monogamous ideal underlying the thinking and practice in the postexilic period: "By the same token, the verse [Mal 2:15] provides an argument against a possible polygamous solution of the problem: The desire for another woman cannot . . . be satisfied by engaging in a marriage with a second woman, because such an act would violate the creational unity and exclusiveness of the marriage relationship between one man and one woman." Cf. the discussion of Mal 2:10–16 in ch. 9, below.

[108] Derek Kidner, *The Proverbs: An Introduction and Commentary* (TOTC 15; Downers Grove, Ill.: InterVarsity, 1964), 49. The one possible exception is found in Prov 31:3, where King Lemuel's mother counsels her son: "Do not give your strength to women, your ways to those who destroy kings." It has been suggested that the context of this passage is the king's harem: "The keeping of a harem of wives and concubines was not only a large expense but was also a distortion of the purpose of royal power. The king should use his authority for his people and not to serve himself" (Duane A. Garrett, *Proverbs, Ecclesiastes, Song of Songs* [NAC14; Nashville, Tenn.: Broadman, 1993], 246). However, this warning to the king may have a broader meaning, "not to spend his strength on sensual lust. . . . Whatever the precise meaning, the point of the verse is that while it would be easy for a king to spend his time and energy enjoying women, that would be unwise" (Allen P. Ross, "Proverbs," in *The Expositor's Bible Commentary* [ed. Frank E. Gaebelein; 12 vols.; Grand Rapids: Zondervan, 1976–1992], 5:1127).

In the book of Ecclesiastes, Solomon in his old age, after turning from a dissolute and profligate life, records for later generations the account of his wasted years and the lessons he has learned.[109] He reveals his own vain attempt at finding happiness and meaning in life through hedonistic pursuits (Eccl 2:1): "I said to myself, 'Come now, I will make a test of pleasure, enjoy yourself.' But again, this also was vanity." This experiment apparently included the amassing of a harem of concubines (2:8), although the Hebrew here is not certain.[110] A comparison with 1 Kings confirms the reality of the experiment with polygamous licentiousness:

> King Solomon loved many foreign women. . . . Solomon clung to these in love. Among his wives were seven hundred princesses and three hundred concubines; and his wives turned away his heart. For when Solomon was old, his wives turned away his heart after other gods; and his heart was not true to the LORD his God. (1 Kgs 11:1–4)

No doubt Solomon tasted the bitter and deadly results of a life of immorality he himself had warned against in the book of Proverbs. His own disappointing and devastating sexual encounters with his thousand wives and concubines seem to be at least part of what lies behind his personal confession:

> I found more bitter than death the woman who is a trap, whose heart is snares and nets, whose hands are fetters; one who pleases God escapes her, but the sinner is taken by her. See, this is what I found, says the Teacher, adding one thing to another to find the sum, which my mind has sought repeatedly, but I have not found. One man among a thousand I found, but a woman among all these I have not found. (Eccl 7:26–28)

Still, despite this bitter personal experience with the way of sexual folly in licentiousness, Solomon was not disillusioned with sexuality per se. As will be argued in succeeding chapters, Ecclesiastes has a high view of sexuality and women (even here in these verses).

Summary

In the OT there are thirty-three reasonably clear historical cases of polygamy out of approximately three thousand men mentioned in the scriptural record. Most of these examples were the wealthy patriarchs or Israel's monarchs (the only

---

[109] Many modern scholars question the Solomonic authorship of Ecclesiastes, but the autobiographical statements of the book and intertextual evidence seem to favor the traditional equation of Qoheleth ("the Preacher") with Solomon. In this canonical (final-form) theology of the OT, the internal biblical indicators must be taken seriously. For a summary of this internal (as well as external) evidence, see Gleason L. Archer, *A Survey of Old Testament Introduction* (updated and rev. ed.; Chicago: Moody, 1994), 528–37. For defense of an early (preexilic) date for Ecclesiastes based upon linguistic features, see esp. Daniel C. Fredericks, *Qoheleth's Language: Re-evaluating Its Nature and Date* (ANETS 3; Lewiston, N.Y.: Mellen, 1988).

[110] In favor of *šiddâ wĕšiddôt* referring to the "ladies in a harem," see, e.g., Franz Delitzsch, *Ecclesiastes* (Grand Rapids: Eerdmans, n.d.), 238–41; and most modern versions.

clear case of a commoner having more than one wife is Elkanah, this likely from the motive of Hannah's infertility). In the narratives containing the practice of polygamy or concubinage, invariably the divinely inspired narrators include their tacit condemnation of these practices. Contrary to other ANE legislation, Mosaic legislation condemns all polygamy, both for the people and (at least implicitly) for the king. Unlike in the other ANE law codes and practice, there is no exception for cases of infertility or illness of the wife or for royal diplomatic alliances. None of the pentateuchal legislation concerning marital forms commands or condones polygamous relationships, although remarriage after a man's first wife died is allowed.

As pointed out regarding the legislation concerning homosexuality (ch. 4, above), the prohibitions in Lev 18—including polygamy—are presented as universal law, applicable to all humanity (transcultural) for all time (transtemporal), upholding the order of creation. Thus, although the OT shows the departure from the Edenic model of sexuality in actual practice, this departure is not approved by God, with both narrative and legislation condemning practices that violate the monogamous Edenic norm.[111]

Plural Marriages and Divine Grace

The OT consistently condemns plural marriage either explicitly or implicitly, but at the same time divine grace is consistently extended to the polygamist. God shows his disapproval of the polygamous marital form but does not immediately abandon his children who have fallen into this sinful practice. The antediluvian world was given 120 years in which God's spirit strove with humankind, and Noah, the "herald of righteousness" (2 Pet 2:5), called them to repentance from their rebellion against God and from practices that were not according to God's will including plural marriage (cf. Gen 6:2). The canonical history of the patriarchs shows God's condescension to work with Abraham and Jacob, practicing polygamists, while at the same time prompting and assisting them to come back to the Edenic standard of morality. The tenderness with which God cared for the victims in a polygamous situation is wonderfully displayed in God's treatment of Hagar. Striking evidence of God's amazing grace is that the twelve sons of Jacob, products of a polygamous relationship, become the foundation of the twelve tribes of Israel, God's covenant people. The fact that there is no explicit legal sanction attached to the prohibition of polygamy in Lev 18:18 reveals a God of

---

[111] This conclusion is contra a major trend in modern scholarship which views polygamy as "the biblical model," not condemned but (according to some) even encouraged by God. See, e.g., Ellens, *Sex in the Bible*, 95, 97: "The Bible's model of marriage is not monogamy.... The model for marriage in the Bible is *polygamy*, the term commonly used for what is more correctly called *polygyny*, the practice of a man having numerous wives.... In any case, humans are polygamous by nature. We respond with erotic desire to all others who attract us. That is a God-given response."

grace, expressing his disapproval of polygamous relationships but at the same time condescending to meet his people where they were.

The same divine grace is evident in the canonical history of Elkanah, David, Solomon, and other polygamists during the time of the judges and the monarchy. God does not condone the sin but also does not turn away from the sinner as long as there is any hope of repentant response. "Judgment, though, is not the last word. Yahweh forgave David's sin, gave him a reprieve from death, and granted him the possibility of continued existence. This aspect of David's experience suggests the possibility of hope in divine clemency resulting in the attenuation of merited judgment."[112] Although God cannot bless in fullness the work of those who are disobedient to his revealed will concerning the monogamous marital form, yet he continues to reach out to his people, in grace offering forgiveness and healing, ever seeking to bring them back to his Edenic ideal.

---

[112] Kessler, "Sexuality and Politics," 423.

Elevation versus Denigration
of Women

Leadership/Submission/Equality and Old Testament Patriarchy: An Overview

The divine pattern for husband-wife relationships established in Eden (both before and after the fall) constitutes the assumed paradigm throughout the remainder of the OT. The voluntary submission of the wife to her husband's servant leadership among equals in the home is recognized in precept, in harmony with the qualified prescription of Gen 3:16; at the same time, in practice there is a trend toward parity between the sexes in the marriage as in Eden before the fall. Women are not to be oppressed or denigrated in the family, nor are they barred from positions of influence, leadership, and authority over men in the covenant community.

The leadership of the husband is implicit in the narrative of the life of Abraham and Sarah (Gen 18:12), with Sarah referring to her husband as "my master" (ʾadōnî). The husband's leadership in the marriage relationship is likewise indicated by the use of baʿal ("lord"—both as a verb and a noun) to identify the husband.[1] The meaning of this word must not be pressed too far, however, for it often may simply denote polite respect. As stated earlier regarding a husband's "rule" over his wife in Gen 3:16, the description of husband as "lord" seems to emphasize his legal position as "first among equals," as the "functioning leader of the family," the "epitome of the family," not his domination and supremacy in marriage.[2]

The attendant servant leadership and/or legal responsibility and protection assigned to the man in the husband-wife relationship in Gen 3:16 seems implied in the Mosaic legislation concerning unfaithful wives in Num 5:19–20: "if you have not turned aside to uncleanness while under your husband's authority

---

[1] As a verb: Gen 20:3; Deut 21:13; 22:22; 24:1; Isa 54:1, 5; 62:4–5; Jer 3:15; 31:32. As a noun: Gen 20:3; Exod 21:3, 22; Deut 22:24; 24:4; 2 Sam 11:26; Joel 1:8; Prov 12:4; 31:11, 23, 28; Esth 1:17, 20. The nuance of the Hebrew original is not apparent in most English translations (including the NRSV).

[2] See esp. John H. Otwell, *And Sarah Laughed: The Status of Women in the Old Testament* (Philadelphia: Westminster, 1977), 78, 145.

[*taḥat ʾîšēk*]. . . . But if you [the wife] have gone astray while under your husband's authority [*taḥat ʾîšēk*] . . ." Verse 29 summarizes, "This is the law in cases of
jealousy, when a wife, while under her husband's authority [*taḥat ʾîšāh*], goes
astray and defiles herself." The Hebrew text does not spell out exactly how the
wife is "under" her husband (the NRSV supplies the word "authority" but this is
not in the Hebrew original). In light of the OT evidence (see below), which reveals
many examples of essentially egalitarian husband-wife relations, to supply the
unqualified term "authority"—"under [the authority of]"—as in many English
versions, may be too strong. It seems best to supply the expression "under [the
leadership of]" or perhaps "under [the legal protection of]" or "under [the legal
responsibility of]." In the Prophets, Ezekiel's allegories of Israel as an adulterous
wife of Yahweh uses the same terminology as Num 5. Yahweh announces of Israel
that she was "mine"—literally "under [*taḥat*] me" (Ezek 23:5; cf. 16:32).[3]

There is little question that in ancient Israel (and throughout the ancient
Near East) a patriarchal structuring of society was the norm and the father was
the "titular head of the ancient Israelite family."[4] The family, not the individual,
was the basic unit of society in ancient Israel. In familial/marital situations, the
father assumed legal responsibility for the household—the "father's house" (*bêt
ʾāb*), a large extended family often totaling fifteen to twenty-five members[5] or, in

---

[3] The Hebrew preposition *taḥat* can mean either "under" or "instead of." Most modern translations accept the translation "under" here in Ezek 23:5. E.g., it is suggested by
Moshe Greenberg, *Ezekiel, 1–20: A New Translation with Introduction and Commentary*
(AB 22; Garden City, N.Y.: Doubleday, 1983), 284, that this should also be the translation
in the parallel passage, 16:32: "*Taḥat* means 'under the control, authority of [a husband]'
in 23:5 and Num 5:19f., 29." I would only argue that the terminology of "control" and "authority" may be too strong even here in the divine-human context. See also several passages that utilize the *qal* passive participle of *baʿal* "to rule over, to marry" to describe the
wife who is under the protection and legal responsibility of her husband: Gen 20:3; Deut
22:22; Isa 54:1.

[4] Otwell, *And Sarah Laughed*, 72. Cf. Erhard S. Gerstenberger, *Yahweh the Patriarch:
Ancient Images of God and Feminist Theology* (Minneapolis: Fortress, 1996), passim; and
Gerda Lerner, *The Creation of Patriarchy* (Woman and History 1; New York: Oxford University Press, 1986), passim. Theories of an earlier matriarchal marriage system predating
the patriarchal system throughout the ancient Near East, popular at the turn of the twentieth century (see, e.g., Johann Jakob Bachofen, *Myth, Religion, and Mother Right: Selected
Writings of J. J. Bachofen* [trans. Ralph Manheim; Princeton, N.J.: Princeton University
Press, 1967]), are unconvincing and find little, if any, support among scholars (except
some radical feminists) today. For a comprehensive attempt to substantiate this hypothesis by a radical feminist, see Elizabeth Gould Davis, *The First Sex* (Baltimore: Penguin,
1972). For a critique of the matriarchal hypothesis with further bibliography, see Gary M.
Beckman, "Goddess Worship—Ancient and Modern," in *"A Wise and Discerning Mind":
Essays in Honor of Burke O. Long* (ed. Saul M. Olyan and Robert C. Culley; BJS 325; Providence: Brown Judaic Studies, 2000), 11–23; Gerstenberger, *Yahweh the Patriarch*, 13–23;
and Hennie J. Marsman, *Women in Ugarit and Israel: Their Social and Religious Position in
the Context of the Ancient Near East* (Leiden: E. J. Brill, 2003), 101–2.

[5] For discussion of the vocabulary of family in ancient Israel, see, e.g., Daniel I. Block,
"Marriage and Family in Ancient Israel," in *Marriage and Family in the Biblical World* (ed.
Ken M. Campbell; Downers Grove, Ill.: InterVarsity, 2003), 35–40. There were four basic

the case of a wealthy family, including hundreds of people.[6] His leadership and legal authority are evidenced in such concerns as family inheritance and ownership of property, contracting marriages for the children, and overall responsibility in speaking for his family.[7]

There have been vigorous, varied responses to OT patriarchy and the role of women within this patriarchal system, particularly among feminist writers in the past 150 years.[8] In the first wave of feminism, which swelled in the latter half of the nineteenth century and crested in women's acquiring the right to vote in most Western countries in the 1920s, two widely-divergent approaches were used to counter those who defended from the Bible the subordination of women: (1) the use of opposing proof texts (e.g., Acts 2:17–18 and Gal 3:28) and the study of prominent female biblical characters (such as Miriam, Deborah, Jael, Huldah, Anna, the Samaritan woman, and Mary), to argue that God's ultimate intention in Scripture was that women be equal with men and the concept of subordination of women was largely based upon a faulty (male) translation/interpretation of the Bible;[9] and (2) the assertion that the Bible was fundamentally a patriarchal book with a belief-system based upon the oppression of women, and thus there

---

levels to Israel's kinship structure (in descending order): (1) ʿam, "people"; (2) šēbeṭ or maṭṭeh, "tribe"; (3) mišpāḥâ, "clan"; and (4) bêt ʾāb, "family" (lit. "father's house"). The last level, the "father's house," typically consisted of "a single living male ancestor, his wife/wives, the man's sons and their wives, grandsons and their wives, and conceivably even great grandchildren; any unmarried male or female descendants (married female descendants were excluded, having left the household to live with the families of their husbands) and unrelated dependents; male and female hired servants and slaves, along with their families; resident laborers; and on occasion resident Levites (Judg 17:7–13)" (Block, "Marriage and Family in Ancient Israel," 38). Cf. Joel Drinkard, "An Understanding of Family in the Old Testament: Maybe Not as Different as We Usually Think," *RevExp* 98 (2001): 485–502.

[6] Such was the case with Abraham, who had 318 trained servants, "born in his house" (Gen 14:14), available to fight against Chedorlaomer and his allies to rescue Lot and the other residents of Sodom. When God spoke of Abraham, "No, for I have chosen him, that he may charge his children and his household [*bêtô*] after him" (18:19), this household may well have numbered a thousand people or more.

[7] See James B. Hurley, *Man and Woman in Biblical Perspective* (Grand Rapids: Zondervan, 1981), 33–42. Otwell, *And Sarah Laughed,* 32–37, 143–46, shows that in each of these areas the whole family was involved, although the father, as functioning leader of the family, had formal responsibility.

[8] For incisive typology of feminist responses to the role of women in the Bible in the two major "waves" of feminism, see esp. Carolyn Osiek, "The Feminist and the Bible: Hermeneutical Alternatives," in *Feminist Perspectives on Biblical Scholarship* (ed. Adela Yarbro Collins; Atlanta: Scholars Press, 1985), 93–105. This basic typology is adopted by, among others, Marsman, *Women in Ugarit and Israel,* 1–31. I follow this typology in the discussion below.

[9] E.g., Katherine C. Bushnell, *God's Word to Women* (London: Women's Correspondence Bible Class, 1912; repr., Mossville, Ill.: God's Word to Women, 1990), and Lee Anna Starr, *The Bible Status of Woman* (New York: Fleming H. Revell, 1926; repr., New York: Garland, 1987); cf. the writings of the Grimké sisters—Sarah Grimké and Angelina Grimké Weld—and Frances Willard.

was need to radically cut loose from everything patriarchal in the Bible.[10] These two poles of interpretation are represented in the second wave of feminism which began to swell in the 1960s and crested throughout the next several decades. These two views may be labeled as (1) *loyalist,* which sees the Bible as fully authoritative, and as the Word of God, non-oppressive for women if understood correctly;[11] and (2) *rejectionist,* which sees the entire Bible and Judeo-Christian heritage as androcentric at its core, and suggests the need to transcend patriarchal religion by a sisterhood as cosmic covenant and (often) some kind of Goddess worship.[12] In between these two poles, four additional approaches may be identified: (3) *revisionist* strategies of interpretation, which argue that patriarchal "accidents" of Scripture can be separated from its non-patriarchal essence or core;[13] (4) *sublimationist* theories, which claim that the Bible contains (sublimated) expressions of the divine as the Eternal Feminine (divine Wisdom/Sophia), which must be recovered by the interpreter,[14] or to go further, must be developed into a gynocentric worldview in which every woman embodies the cosmic, creating power of the Goddess;[15] (5) *liberationist* hermeneutics, in which (combining liberation theology with feminist exegesis) the liberation of women is placed at the center as the controlling criterion of the hermeneutical task, and (utilizing a hermeneutic of suspicion or resistance) all that is found in the biblical text to restrict or deny full humanity to women cannot have authority and must be rejected or deconstructed;[16] and (6) *reconstructionist* approaches, involving the diachronic analysis of the text in order to provide an historical reconstruction of the history of the Israelite woman in light of comparative extra-biblical evidence.[17] A third wave of feminism, swelling in the late 1990s, combines the liberation-egalitarian politics of first and second wave feminists with postmodernist, poststructuralist and "cultural studies" emphases.[18]

---

[10] E.g., Elizabeth Cady Stanton, *The Woman's Bible* (New York: European, 1895; repr., Boston: Northeastern University Press, 1993).

[11] E.g., the contributers to the volume edited by Ronald W. Pierce and Rebecca Merrill Groothuis, *Discovering Biblical Equality: Complementarity without Hierarchy* (Downers Grove, Ill.: InterVarsity, 2004; most evangelical feminists would be represented here.

[12] E.g., Mary Daly, *Beyond God the Father: Toward A Philosophy of Women's Liberation* (Boston: Beacon, 1973).

[13] E.g., Phyllis Trible, *God and the Rhetoric of Sexuality* (OBT; Philadelphia: Fortress, 1978).

[14] E.g., Joan Chamberlain Engelsman, *The Feminine Dimension of the Divine* (Philadelphia: Westminster, 1979) and the works of Marie-Theres Wacker.

[15] E.g., Virginia Ramey Mollenkott, *The Divine Feminine: The Biblical Imagery of God as Female* (New York: Crossroad, 1988).

[16] E.g., Letty M. Russell, *Human Liberation in a Feminist Perspective: A Theology* (Philadelphia: Westminster, 1974) and the works of Athalya Brenner and Fokkelien van Dijk-Hemmes.

[17] E.g., Marsman, *Women in Ugarit and Israel;* and the works of Phyllis Bird, Bernadette Brooten, Rosemary Radford Reuther, and Elisabeth Schüssler-Fiorenza.

[18] For discussion of this third wave of feminism, see esp. Leslie Heywood and Jennifer Drake, eds., *Third Wave Agenda: Being Feminist, Doing Feminism* (Minneapolis: University of Minnesota Press, 1997).

Most of the feminist writers represented among these varied responses castigate OT patriarchy, many with utter revulsion.[19] The patriarchal system is often seen to be the major influence behind all subsequent repression and oppression of women. Patriarchy is regularly equated with sexism, the systematic oppression of women.[20] The "generally accepted meaning" of patriarchy among the whole range of feminists is "male dominated" and "oppressive of women."[21] Patriarchy is widely viewed as "the major sin that lies at the root of all systems of oppression."[22]

Guenther Haas presents a helpful overview of the two major hermeneutical perspectives toward OT patriarchy represented by liberal-critical and conservative-evangelical scholars respectively. In the first approach, most liberal-critical feminists (mainline, radical, and post-Christian) hold that OT writers are simply incorporating the patriarchal prejudices of their culture and that this patriarchy is oppressive of women, and they reject all patriarchal themes in Scripture, judging what to accept as authoritative in Scripture according to the critical principle of feminist theology (i.e., what accords with the modern feminist concept of full equality and mutuality of men and women).[23] Second, most evangelical Christian

---

[19] See the collection of strong feminist statements against patriarchy in Carol Meyers, *Discovering Eve: Ancient Israelite Women in Context* (New York: Oxford University Press, 1988), 24–46; and Jo Ann Davidson, "Modern Feminism, Religious Pluralism, and Scripture," *JATS* 10 (Spring–Autumn 1999): 401–40. Additional examples include, Renita J. Weems, *Battered Love: Marriage, Sex, and Violence in the Hebrew Prophets* (Minneapolis: Fortress, 1995); Regina M. Schwartz, *The Curse of Cain: The Violent Legacy of Monotheism* (Chicago: University of Chicago Press, 1997); Carol Delaney, *Abraham on Trial: The Social Legacy of Biblical Myth* (Princeton, N.J.: Princeton University Press, 1998); and Gail Corrington Streete, *The Strange Woman: Power and Sex in the Bible* (Louisville, Ky.: Westminster John Knox, 1997); On the other hand, there are a number of modern feminists not so vitriolic in their castigation of patriarchy, who seek to understand it in its social and historical context. See, e.g., the works of Phyllis Bird, Tikva Frymer-Kensky, and representatives of the evangelical group Christians for Biblical Equality (Catherine Clark Kroeger, Gilbert Bilezikian, Stanley R. Gundry et al.). Mary Kassian (*The Feminist Gospel: The Movement to Unite Feminism with the Church* [Wheaton, Ill.: Crossway, 1992]) provides a helpful historical overview and critique (from an evangelical Christian perspective) of the major waves of modern feminism and their reaction to patriarchy in the Bible.

[20] See, e.g., Letha D. Scanzoni and Nancy A. Hardesty, *All That We're Meant to Be: Biblical Feminism for Today* (3d rev. ed.; Grand Rapids: Eerdmans, 1992), 1.

[21] Alice Ogden Bellis, *Helpmates, Harlots, and Heroes: Women's Stories in the Hebrew Bible* (Louisville, Ky.: Westminster John Knox, 1994), 16.

[22] Guenther Haas, "Patriarchy as an Evil That God Tolerated: Analysis and Implications for the Authority of Scripture," *JETS* 38 (Sept 1995): 322, summarizing various statements by Christian feminists (although not his own view).

[23] Ibid., 327–36. For a discussion of the variety of feminist methodologies based upon a feminist presupposition, see, e.g., Janice Capel Anderson, "Mapping Feminist Biblical Criticism: The American Scene, 1983–1990," *CRBR* 2 (1991): 21–44; Eryl W. Davies, *The Dissenting Reader: Feminist Approaches to the Hebrew Bible* (Aldershot, Eng.: Ashgate, 2003); Athalya Brenner and Carole R. Fontaine, eds., *A Feminist Companion to Reading the Bible: Approaches, Methods, and Strategies* (Sheffield, Eng.: Sheffield Academic Press, 1997); Sarah Heaner Lancaster, *Women and the Authority of Scripture: A Narrative Approach* (Harrisburg, Pa.: Trinity Press International, 2002); Alice Ogden Bellis, "Feminist

feminists likewise view patriarchy as inherently evil but seek to maintain the full authority of Scripture by appealing to the principle of divine accommodation: God accommodated himself to the prevailing culture in Scripture but through progressive revelation makes known in the NT (esp. in Gal 3:28) the redemptive eradication of sexual hierarchy and liberation of women from patriarchal oppression.[24]

I agree that under biblical patriarchy there occurred horrendous incidents of female denigration, oppression, and abuse (see later in this chapter). I also agree with representatives of both liberal-critical and evangelical scholarship who insist that the intention of OT Torah was "neither to create nor to perpetuate patriarchy."[25] The laws of Moses do not unequivocally endorse patriarchy but work within the patriarchal framework and regulate this system, providing a degree of care and protection for women and children.[26]

Instead of regarding patriarchy as inherently evil, however, as so commonly asserted in current literature, I argue that God wisely arranged the institution of

---

Biblical Scholarship," *WS* 24–32; Adela Yarbro Collins, ed., *Feminist Perspectives on Biblical Scholarship* (BSNA 10; Chico, Calif.: Scholars Press, 1985); Elisabeth Schüssler Fiorenza, *Wisdom Ways: Introducing Feminist Biblical Interpretation* (Maryknoll, N.Y.: Orbis, 2001); Jo Ann Hackett, "Women's Studies in the Hebrew Bible," in *The Future of Biblical Studies: The Hebrew Scriptures* (ed. Richard E. Friedman and H. G. M. Williamson; Atlanta: Scholars Press, 1987), 141–64; Letty M. Russell, ed., *Feminist Interpretation of the Bible* (Philadelphia: Westminster, 1985); Pamela Milne, "Feminist Interpretation of the Bible: Then and Now," *BRev* 8/5 (October 1992): 38–43, 52–54; Silvia Schroer and Sophia Bietenhard, eds., *Feminist Interpretation of the Bible and the Hermeneutics of Liberation* (JSOTSup 374; New York: Sheffield Academic Press, 2003); Loraine MacKenzie Shepherd, *Feminist Theologies for a Postmodern Church: Diversity, Community, and Scripture* (American University Studies, Series 7: Theology and Religion 219; New York: Peter Lang, 2002).

[24] See, e.g., Gilbert G. Bilezikian, *Beyond Sex Roles: What the Bible Says about a Woman's Place in Church and Family* (Grand Rapids: Baker, 1985), 59–68, who classes patriarchy with other "sinful conditions" (p. 61); cf. Mary J. Evans, *Woman in the Bible: An Overview of All the Crucial Passages on Women's Roles* (Downers Grove, Ill.: InterVarsity, 1984), 21–32; Ronald W. Pierce, "From Old Testament Law to New Testament Gospel," in *Discovering Biblical Equality: Complementarity without Hierarchy* (ed. Ronald W. Pierce and Rebecca Merrill Groothuis; Downers Grove, Ill.: InterVarsity, 2004), 98–109; and Ruth A. Tucker, *Women in the Maze: Questions and Answers on Biblical Equality* (Downers Grove, Ill.: InterVarsity, 1992), 57–76. The NT references to continuing patriarchy are often considered to be one or more of the following in kind: (1) referring to sub-Christian teaching, (2) referring to situations that fall short of the divine norm, (3) referring to teachings that are related to the rabbinic background, or (4) referring to teachings related to OT creation but not to redemption. See further discussion of NT treatment of patriarchy in the afterword, below. Cf. Meyers, *Discovering Eve*, 322–27.

[25] Phyllis Trible, "Depatriarchalizing in Biblical Interpretation," *JAAR* 41, no. 1 (1973): 31; cited (approvingly) by Pierce, "From Old Testament Law," 105. Support for this position will emerge from the evidence presented in this chapter.

[26] This sentence is a paraphrase from Pierce, "From Old Testament Law," 101. His sentence (in my view wrongly) seems to equate slavery and patriarchy as inherently evil and as dealt with equally by God: "The law of Moses does not endorse slavery (economic or personal) any more than it does patriarchy, but works within these frameworks and regulates them, providing a degree of care and protection for slaves and women."

patriarchy in his condescension to the human fallen condition, as a temporary re-medial and redemptive measure to bring about unity and harmony and integrity in the home in the midst of a sinful world. Patriarchy, as intended by God, was not evil in itself but rather one of those God-ordained remedial provisions, insti-tuted after the fall, that God called "statutes that were not good," i.e., not the ulti-mate divine ideal (Ezek 20:25).[27]

Furthermore, the very term "patriarchy," or the OT phrase "father's house" (*bêt ʾāb*), emphasizes the role of the *father* to his children, not the *husband* to his wife. As will emerge from evidence presented in this chapter, the Hebrew patriarchs of the OT "patriarchal" period were without exception married to a powerful *matri-arch,* and their marital relationships were functionally nonhierarchical and egali-tarian. The OT patriarchy consisted primarily in the *father's* authority over his children, even after they had children of their own, so that the father's descendants were taught to look up to him as their head in both religious and secular matters. This was not the authority of men over women in general but of one patriarchal figure over all of his descendants, male and female. It is fully compatible with this patriarchal model of leadership to have a matriarch functioning in an egalitarian relationship with her husband, the patriarch, and the married children of the pa-triarch and their spouses likewise functioning in an egalitarian marriage. The OT patriarchal system does not imply a husband's authority over his wife.

Some biblical scholars have in recent decades begun to challenge the prevail-ing feminist paradigm that patriarchy is synonymous with the oppression of women. It is widely recognized that biblical patriarchy is not to be equated with the patriarchy, for example, of Assyria or Athens, where there was a strong degree of male domination over women.[28] Carol Meyers seeks to place ancient Israelite

---

[27] See discussion of this crucial passage by Alexandru Breja, "The Meaning and Theological Implications of *chuqqim lo tobim* ('Laws That Were Not Good') in Ezekiel 20:25" (paper presented at the annual meeting of the Evangelical Theological Society, San Antonio, Tex., November 19, 2004). This parallels the use of the term "not good" in Gen 2:18 regarding the man being alone; it is not evil, but it is also not the ultimate divine ideal (see ch. 1, above).

[28] See, e.g., Tikva Frymer-Kensky, *Reading the Women of the Bible* (New York: Schocken Books, 2002), xiv: "Biblical Israel did not invent patriarchy. It was not even the most intense or thorough patriarchy in the ancient world. Other classical societies, like Assyria and Ath-ens, show a much greater degree of domination of women." Regarding the status of women in classical Greece (esp. Athens), see Eva Cantarella, *Pandora's Daughters: The Role and Sta-tus of Women in Greek and Roman Antiquity* (trans. Maureen B. Fant; Baltimore: Johns Hopkins University Press, 1981); Prudence Allen, *The Aristotelian Revolution, 750 B.C.–A.D. 1250* (vol. 1 of *The Concept of Woman;* Montreal: Eden, 1985; repr., Grand Rapids: Eerd-mans, 1997); cf. Linda L. Belleville, *Women Leaders and the Church: Three Crucial Questions* (Grand Rapids: Baker, 2000), 84–86; and Loren Cunningham and David J. Hamilton with Janice Rogers, *Why Not Women? A Fresh Look at Women in Missions, Ministry, and Leader-ship* (Seattle: YWAM, 2001), 71–83. Regarding the status of women in Middle Assyria, see esp. Elisabeth Meier Tetlow, *The Ancient Near East* (vol. 1 of *Women, Crime, and Punishment in Ancient Law and Society;* New York: Continuum, 2004), 125–46, who summarizes regard-ing this period, "The status of women under the Middle Assyrian Laws was far lower than in other ancient Near Eastern societies and legal systems" (p. 141).

women in their historical context and argues forcefully for the necessity to re-evaluate feminist definitions of biblical patriarchy:

> While broadly correct in associating patriarchy with ancient Israel, their assessment of patriarchy as a limiting, harsh, enslaving, or oppressive system, or as a fact that is painful to consider, reveals a serious methodological flaw. They are misusing the term patriarchy as a synonym for male dominance or for a system in which male traits are valued over female ones. Worst of all, their judgmental response to biblical patriarchy unfairly uses contemporary feminist standards (which hope for an elimi-nation of sexist tradition by seeking to promulgate equality between the sexes) to measure the cultural patterns of an ancient society struggling to establish its viability under circumstances radically different from contemporary western conditions.[29]

Meyers, in examining the issue of patriarchy in Israel, exposes a number of faulty assumptions in modern thinking. She points out that although the HB "contains some statements that appear to value men more highly than women or to give men certain legal privileges that are not extended to women," such state-ments, from our contemporary perspective, "give incomplete evidence of biblical patriarchy. They do not tell us how Israelite women felt about differential treat-ment." She further cautions that "in the context of specific social and economic structures that characterized ancient Israel, the existence of gender asymmetry, with men accorded a set of advantages apparently unavailable to most women, must not automatically be perceived as oppressive." The lack of evidence in OT Scripture that the "Eves of ancient Israel felt oppressed, degraded, or unfairly treated in the face of culture asymmetry" leads Meyers to suggest that "gender differences that appear hierarchical may not have functioned or been perceived as hierarchical within Israelite society."[30] Even the patrilineality in ancient Israel (tracing group membership through the father's line) does not imply "the abso-lute control of males over females, or of the male head of the family over his wife and other family members, or of the subservience of women to men."[31]

Meyers shows that the husband's formal "authority" is balanced by the domestic-oriented "power" in the hands of the wife and mother of the Israelite household. "If ever there were a situation in which the condescending phrase 'only a wife and mother' should be expunged from descriptive language, the fam-ily household of early Israel should surely qualify."[32] The household played a cen-tral role in tribal Israel, and social and economic power moved from the bottom (the family household) and not from the top (the tribal rulers). After examining the biblical and the extra-biblical evidence for early Israel (up to the time of the monarchy), Meyers concludes that "there was a functional lack of hierarchy in Is-raelite gender relations."[33] This implies a balance between male and female power, which, although not necessarily including legal or jural equality, at the

---

[29] Meyers, *Discovering Eve*, 25–26.
[30] Ibid., 34.
[31] Ibid., 41.
[32] Ibid., 139.
[33] Ibid., 44.

same time makes the latter irrelevant. "The ability of women to determine the shape of important aspects of personal and group life, and the concomitant hidden value attached to the female persona, make the notion of legal or jural equality a moot point."[34]

Another seminal study, by Tikva Frymer-Kensky, argues that "there is nothing distinctively 'female' about the way that women are portrayed in the Bible. . . . The biblical image of women is consistently the same as that of men."[35] She points out that even though the wife is indeed presented as subordinated to her husband, yet at the same time "the Bible presents a remarkably unified vision of humankind, for the stories show women as having the same inherent characteristics and [*sic*, as] men." Although in ancient Israel the circumstances of women's lives may differ from the circumstances of some men (i.e., those with power), at the same time "there are no innate differences that preclude women from taking men's roles or men taking women's roles should the occasion arise and circumstances warrant it."[36] Frymer-Kensky contrasts the "radically new concept of gender" in the Bible with Mesopotamian society, in which gender roles were fundamental to personal and social identity, and argues for the difference arising from Israel's unique monotheistic religion, in which divinity is beyond gender. She points out how both the traditional Bible interpreters and contemporary feminist criticism have misinterpreted the signs of gender inequality in ancient Israel.

My own research (set forth below) regarding the status of women in the OT has led to similar conclusions and implications. While recognizing the clear OT evidence for the husband's servant leadership in marriage and the family, I have

---

[34] Ibid., 44–45. After the rise of the monarchy, Meyers argues, the centralized sociopolitical structures brought about an institutionalized suppression of both patriarchy and of women. The last part of this chapter will look at the biblical evidence for this development. For an overview of Carol Meyers' historically-based approach, which takes into account not only the biblical text but the extra-biblical artifactual evidence available from the findings of archaeological excavations, see esp. Susan Ackerman, "Digging Up Deborah: Recent Hebrew Bible Scholarship on Gender and the Contribution of Archaeology," *NEA* 66 (2003): 172–84.

[35] Tikva Frymer-Kensky, "Gender and Its Image: Women in the Bible," ch. 11 in *In the Wake of the Goddesses: Women, Culture, and the Biblical Transformation of Pagan Myth* (New York: Free Press/Maxwell Macmillan, 1992), 118–43, quote at 120–21. She continues, "In their strengths and weaknesses, in their goals and strategies, the women of the Bible do not differ substantially from that of men. This biblical idea that the desires and actions of men and women are similar is tantamount to a radically new concept of gender."

[36] Ibid., 120. Frymer-Kensky elaborates: "The Bible presents no characteristics of human behavior as 'female' or 'male,' no division of attributes between the poles of 'feminine' and 'masculine,' no hint of distinctions of such polarities as male aggressivity-female receptivity, male innovation-female conservation, male out-thrusting-female containment, male subjecthood-female objecthood, male rationality-female emotionality, male product-female process, male achievement-female bonding, or any of the other polarities by which we are accustomed to think of gender distinctions" (p. 141). The Bible has a "gender-free concept of humanity"; one may speak of the "gender-blindness of the biblical view of human nature" and the "biblical metaphysics of gender unity" (143).

found throughout the Torah, Prophets, and Writings, in harmony with the divine prescription for the husband's "rule" (servant leadership) in Gen 3:16, that such leadership does not override the basic equality between the marriage partners or imply the husband's ownership, oppression, domination, or control over the wife.[37] The wife does not appear to have viewed such leadership as oppressive; in the Pentateuch and elsewhere in the OT, no examples occur where women rise up in rebellion against the husband's leadership. Furthermore, the submission of the wife to her husband's leadership seems to have been a voluntary act. It is crucial that there is no biblical legislation indicating a punishment for a wife's rebelling against her husband's leadership, as there is for a son rebelling against the authority of his parents (Exod 21:15, 17). The husband leadership, as God designed it after the fall, was an umbrella of protection for the wife that she valued and appreciated, not an oppression under which she chafed and against which she rebelled.

The husband's servant leadership principle, installed by God as a temporary, remedial measure to facilitate harmony and unity in the home after the fall, also does not prevent husbands and wives from returning as closely as possible to the original egalitarian design for marriage before the fall. This move toward the pre-fall ideal is revealed in the descriptions of the day-to-day relationships between OT husbands and wives, in which the "ancient Israelite wife was loved and listened to by her husband, and treated by him as an equal."[38] "The ancient Israelite woman wielded power in the home at least equal to that exercised by the husband . . . ; she participated freely and as an equal in decisions involving the life of her husband or her family."[39]

Furthermore, in ancient Israel the husband's servant leadership in the home is never broadened to constitute a mandated male leadership over women in the public sphere. "The power of husband over wife is not generalized to all men over all females."[40] Although life in ancient Israel was traditionally structured along gender lines, occasioned mainly by "the socioeconomic concerns and physical realities of life,"[41] and leadership positions were usually filled by men, nonetheless husband leadership in the family did not prevent women from holding positions of public leadership over men. Such examples of female leadership were accepted and considered perfectly acceptable. Already in the Pentateuch, the high status of women in religious and civil affairs is evident.

We now turn our attention to a summary of the biblical data that support the generalizations outlined above, examining first the relevant passages in the Pentateuch dealing with the status of women, and then briefly tracing developments in the Prophets and Writings.

---

[37] As will be examined later in this chapter, the HB does depict occasions in which the husband usurps power and exploits his wife, treating her as inferior, as chattel, or even as a nonperson, but these cases are not cited approvingly.

[38] Roland de Vaux, *Ancient Israel: Its Life and Institutions* (trans. John McHugh; New York: McGraw-Hill, 1961), 40.

[39] Otwell, *And Sarah Laughed,* 111–12.

[40] Frymer-Kensky, *In the Wake of the Goddesses,* 128.

[41] Ibid., 143.

The High Valuation of Women in the Old Testament: Pentateuchal Narratives

Much recent discussion has focused on the status of women in the OT.[42] Many biblical scholars have asserted that women had a low status in ancient

---

[42] The literature on women in the HB has burgeoned from being virtually nonexistent a quarter of century ago to an almost bewildering profusion of (mostly feminist) studies at the turn of the millennium. For an overview, with bibliography, of the women in the Bible from a feminist perspective, see esp. *WS*. The signed articles in this classic work on each of the female characters will be taken for granted in the discussion of individual women in the OT and so will not normally be cited separately unless quoted. Cf. Bellis, *Helpmates, Harlots, and Heroes;* Evans, *Woman in the Bible;* idem, "Women," *DOTP* 897–904; the bibliographical study of Mayer I. Gruber, *Women in the Biblical World: A Study Guide* (American Theological Library Association Bibliography Series 38; Lanham, Md.: Scarecrow, 1995); Frymer-Kensky, *Reading the Women of the Bible;* Lillian R. Klein, *From Deborah to Esther: Sexual Politics in the Hebrew Bible* (Minneapolis: Fortress, 2003); Irene Nowell, *Women in the Old Testament* (Collegeville, Minn.: Liturgical Press, 1997); Katharine Doob Sakenfeld, *Just Wives? Stories of Power and Survival in the Old Testament and Today* (Louisville: Westminster/John Knox, 2003); and Luise Schottroff and Marie-Theres Wacker, eds., *Kompendium feministische Bibelauslegung* (Gütersloh: Christian Kaiser/ Gütersloher Verlagshaus, 1998). For a representative collection of influential articles, mostly feminist, on the topic from the past twenty-five years, see Alice Bach, ed., *Women in the Hebrew Bible: A Reader* (New York: Routledge, 1999); note also the comprehensive bibliography of feminist biblical studies, pp. 520–32. Other significant feminist articles are found in the ongoing Sheffield Academic Press series Feminist Companion to the Bible and its Second Series; cf. also *WBC;* and (from an evangelical Christian feminist perspective) Catherine Clark Kroeger and Mary J. Evans, eds., *The IVP Women's Bible Commentary* (Downers Grove, Ill.: InterVarsity, 2002). For sensitive treatment not written by women, see esp. Jon L. Berquist, *Reclaiming Her Story: The Witness of Women in the Old Testament* (St. Louis: Chalice, 1992); Trevor Dennis, *Sarah Laughed: Women's Voices in the Old Testament* (Nashville: Abingdon, 1994); and William E. Phipps, *Assertive Biblical Women* (CWS 128; Westport, Conn.: Greenwood, 1992). For a survey of the history of precritical interpretation of women in the OT, see esp. Thomas L. Thompson, *Writing the Wrongs: Women of the Old Testament among Biblical Commentators from Philo through the Reformation* (OSHT; Oxford: Oxford University Press, 2001). For a survey of narrative analysis concerning the most prominent women in Scripture from an evangelical Christian perspective, see esp. Jo Ann Davidson, "Women in Scripture: A Survey and Evaluation," in *Women in Ministry: Biblical and Historical Perspectives* (ed. Nancy Vyhmeister; Berrien Springs, Mich.: Andrews University Press, 1998), 157–67; and idem, "Modern Feminism" (I owe her a special debt of gratitude for the research and insights she has shared with me). The pages that follow in this chapter cite the most helpful narrative studies on individual biblical women (without, however, subscribing to foundational feminist assumptions about Scripture that undergird much of the research).

For a cross-section of general studies on the status of woman in the OT, see the bibliographies and annotations of Anderson, "Mapping Feminist Biblical Criticism," 21–44; Phyllis A. Bird, "Women in the Ancient Mediterranean World: Ancient Israel," *BR* 39 (1994): 31–79; Gruber, *Women in the Biblical World;* Samuel Terrien, *Till the Heart Sings: A Biblical Theology of Manhood and Womanhood* (Philadelphia: Fortress, 1985), 233–35; Phyllis Trible, "Women in the Old Testament," *IDBSup* 966. Major discussions include esp. Phyllis A. Bird, "Images of Women in the Old Testament," in *Religion and Sexism: Images*

Israel, as elsewhere throughout the ancient Near East,[43] and some (mainly radical feminists) have claimed that the status of women was lower in Israel than in the surrounding ancient Near East because of the oppressive patriarchy engendered by Israel's male-centered monotheism.[44] Studies of women elsewhere in the ancient Near East, however, have begun to reveal that women often had a higher legal status and more rights than usually recognized by modern scholarship.[45]

---

of Woman in the Jewish and Christian Traditions (ed. Rosemary Radford Ruether; New York: Simon & Schuster, 1974), 41–88; idem, *Missing Persons and Mistaken Identities: Women and Gender in Ancient Israel* (OBT; Minneapolis: Fortress, 1997); Athalya Brenner, *The Israelite Woman: Social Role and Literary Type in Biblical Narrative* (Sheffield, Eng.: JSOT Press, 1985); Judy L. Brown, *Women Ministers according to Scripture* (Minneapolis: Christians for Biblical Equality, 1996), 93–108; Grace I. Emmerson, "Women in Ancient Israel," in *The World of Ancient Israel: Sociological, Anthropological, and Political Perspectives* (ed. R. E. Clements; Cambridge: Cambridge University Press, 1989), 371–94; André LaCocque, *The Feminine Unconventional: Four Subversive Figures in Israel's Tradition* (OBT; Minneapolis: Fortress, 1990), 7–20; Inger Ljung, *Silence or Suppression: Attitudes towards Women in the Old Testament* (Acta Universitatis Upsaliensis: Uppsala Women's Studies A, Women in Religion 2; Uppsala: S. Academiae Upsaliensis, 1989); Marsman, *Women in Ugarit and Israel;* Susan Niditch, "Portrayals of Women in the Hebrew Bible," in *Jewish Women in Historical Perspective* (ed. Judith R. Baskin; Detroit: Wayne State University Press, 1991), 25–42; Otwell, *And Sarah Laughed,* passim; and Meyers, *Discovering Eve,* passim.

[43] For cogent examples of this view, see the citations in Otwell, *And Sarah Laughed,* 10. More recent studies with similar conclusions include Paul Avis, *Eros and the Sacred* (Harrisburg, Pa.: Moorehouse, 1989); Mieke Bal, *Lethal Love: Feminist Literary Readings of Biblical Love Stories* (Bloomington: Indiana University Press, 1987); Brenner, *The Israelite Woman;* Evans, *Woman in the Bible,* 11–32; Esther Fuchs, *Sexual Politics in the Biblical Narrative: Reading the Hebrew Bible as a Woman* (JSOTSup 310; Sheffield, Eng.: Sheffield Academic Press, 2000); Kevin Harris, *Sex, Ideology, and Religion: The Representation of Women in the Bible* (Totowa, N.J.: Barnes & Noble, 1984); Meir Malul, *Knowledge, Control, and Sex: Studies in Biblical Thought, Culture, and Worldview* (Tel Aviv–Jaffa: Archaeological Center, 2002); Shlomith Yaron, "The Politics of Sex—Woman's Body as an Instrument for Achieving Man's Aims," *OTE* 15 (2002): 269–92; and Gale A. Yee, *Poor Banished Children of Eve: Woman as Evil in the Hebrew Bible* (Minneapolis: Fortress, 2003).

[44] See esp. Rosemary Radford Ruether, *Sexism and God-Talk: Toward a Feminist Theology* (Boston: Beacon, 1983), 53–54; cf. Daly, *Beyond God the Father,* 19; Judith Ochshorn, *The Female Experience and the Nature of the Divine* (Bloomington: Indiana University Press, 1981), 194–95; Esther Fuchs, "The Literary Characterization of Mothers and Sexual Politics in the Hebrew Bible," in *Feminist Perspectives on Biblical Scholarship* (ed. Adela Yarbro Collins; Chico, Calif.: Scholars Press, 1985), 119. Marsman, *Women in Ugarit and Israel,* in particular addresses this common feminist claim, and in her massive (781-page) monograph demonstrates convincingly that the social and religious status of women in monotheistic Israel was no lower than in neighboring Ugarit (and other surrounding ANE contexts), where polytheistic goddess worship flourished.

[45] For an overview of the status of women in the ancient Near East, see esp. Tetlow, *The Ancient Near East,* passim. Tetlow concludes that women had almost the same rights as men in the oldest civilizations of Sumer and Old Assyria I and that woman's status was still relatively high in Old Babylonia but in later ANE tribal, feudal, military societies (i.e., Hittite, Late Babylonia and Middle/Late Assyria), the status of women declined, reaching its nadir with the Middle/Late Assyrian societies. Cf. James R. Baker, *Women's Rights in Old Testament Times* (Salt Lake City: Signature Books, 1992); Carol R. Fontaine, "A Heifer

Likewise, in contrast with the continued misogynist readings of the OT, a growing number of scholars have reappraised the biblical evidence and concluded "that the status of woman in the Old Testament is high."[46]

---

from Thy Stable: On Goddesses and the Status of Women in the Ancient Near East," in "Ad feminam: Fiftieth Anniversary Volume," ed. Alice Bach, *USQR* 43 (1989): 67–91; Hurley, *Man and Woman*, 21–30; Arthur Frederick Ide, *Women in the Ancient Near East* (Mesquite, Tex.: Ide House, 1982); Elizabeth Mary McDonald, *The Position of Women as Reflected in Semitic Codes of Law* (Toronto: University of Toronto Press, 1931); Patrick Mullins, "The Public, Secular Roles of Women in Biblical Times," *Mils* 43 (1998): 79–111; idem, "The Religious Roles of Women among Israel's Neighbors," *Mils* 45 (2000): 81–113; and Ilse Seibert, *Women in the Ancient Near East* (New York: Abner Schram, 1974). Beckman, "Goddess Worship," 20, summarizes regarding Hittite religious culture, "In sum, we may judge that in the realm of religious practice, the authority of women was approximately equal to that of men." In Mesopotamia the rights and status of women are now recognized to be greater than once thought (esp. in ancient Sumer), although (esp. in Assyrian culture) it still seems that the wife was in much greater subservience to her husband than in Israel; see Rivkah Harris, "Women (Mesopotamia)," *ABD* 6:947–51 (with bibliography); Sophie Lafont, *Femmes, droit, et justice dans l'antiquité orientale: Contributions à l'étude du droit pénal au Proche-Orient ancien* (OBO 165; Göttingen: Vandenhoeck & Ruprecht, 1999), passim; Sarah C. Melville, "Neo-Assyrian Royal Women and Male Identity: Status as a Social Tool," *JAOS* 124 (2004): 37–57; Claudio Saporetti, *The Status of Women in the Middle Assyrian Period* (Monographs on the Ancient Near East 2/1; Malibu, Calif.: Undena, 1979); and Tetlow, *The Ancient Near East,* passim. For ancient Mari, see Bernard F. Batto, *Studies on Women at Mari* (Baltimore: Johns Hopkins University Press, 1974). For Ugarit, see Marsman, *Women in Ugarit and Israel,* passim. For Egypt, see, e.g., Christiane Desroches-Noblecourt, *La femme au temps des pharaons* (Paris: Pernoud, 1986); Leonard H. Lesko, "Women and Priests in Two Egyptian Stories," in *Hesed Ve-Emet: Studies in Honor of Ernest S. Frerichs* (ed. Jodi Magness and Seymour Gitin; BJS 320; Atlanta: Scholars Press, 1998), 217–29; Lise Manniche, *Sexual Life in Ancient Egypt* (London: Kegan Paul, 1987); Alan R. Millard, "The Position of Women in the Family and Society in Ancient Egypt with Special Reference to the Middle Kingdom" (PhD diss., University of London, University College, 1976); and Gay Robins, *Women in Ancient Egypt* (London: British Museum, 1993). For further bibliography, see Gruber, *Women in the Biblical World,* 156–226.

[46] Otwell, *And Sarah Laughed,* 193. A leading proponent of this position is Otwell. But see also other "dissenting voices" from the prevailing view who are cited by him (pp. 10–11, 195–96) and, more recently, e.g., Bronner, *Stories of Biblical Mothers;* Thomas Finley, "The Relationship of Woman and Man in the Old Testament," in *Women and Men in Ministry: A Complementary Perspective* (ed. Robert L. Saucy and Judith K. TenElshof; Chicago: Moody, 2001), 61–88; Daniel Friedmann, *To Kill and Take Possession: Law, Morality, and Society in Biblical Stories* (Peabody, Mass.: Hendrickson, 2002), 218–31; Gerhard F. Hasel, "Equality from the Start: Woman in the Creation Story," *Spectrum* 7, no. 2 (1975): 26–27; Hurley, *Man and Woman,* 20–57; Walter C. Kaiser Jr., *Toward Old Testament Ethics* (Grand Rapids: Zondervan, 1983), 204–8; Faith McBurney Martin, *Call Me Blessed: The Emerging Christian Woman* (Grand Rapids: Eerdmans, 1988), 113–38; Meyers, *Discovering Eve,* passim; Amnon Shapira, "On the Equal Status of Women in the Bible" (Hebrew), *Beit Mikra* 159 (1999): 309–37 (English abstract by Christopher T. Begg, *OTA* 23 [2000]: 195–96); and Savina J. Teubal, *Sarah the Priestess: The First Matriarch of Genesis* (Athens, Ohio: Swallow, 1984), esp. 138–41. Cf. writers of an earlier generation (first-wave feminism) who accepted the high status of women in the OT: e.g., Starr, *The Bible Status of Woman.*

The high valuation of women in the pentateuchal narratives has been the subject of much recent research that has been synthesized elsewhere and thus will be only briefly treated here.[47]

Genesis Matriarchs

Of the twenty-nine women mentioned by name in Genesis, brief attention is given here to the matriarchal figures who figure significantly in the Genesis narratives.[48] Savina Teubal is correct in insisting that this era of the biblical patriarchs and matriarchs deserves reassessment:

> In particular, women have traditionally been depicted as primitive and childish in their aspirations and generally lacking in vision. Fresh study of our female forebears, however, invalidates this view and shows us that the matriarchs were learned, wise women who were highly developed spiritually.[49]

Sarah. Details of Sarah's life in the Genesis narratives reveal the high valuation of this matriarch, as she and her husband are portrayed as equal partners.[50] Con-

---

[47] See esp. Davidson, "Women in Scripture," 161–67; and idem, "Modern Feminism," 415–23; cf. the comprehensive bibliography in Bellis, *Helpmates, Harlots, and Heroes,* 95–98, 110–11.

[48] See esp. Jo Ann Davidson, "Genesis Matriarchs Engage Feminism," *AUSS* 40, no. 2 (2002): 169–78, and idem, "The Well Women of Scripture Revisited," *JATS* 17, no. 1 (2006): 209–20. See the brief discussion/identification of each of these twenty-nine women in Toni Craven, "Women in Genesis," *TBT* 35 (1997): 32–39. Cf. Bronner, *Stories of Biblical Mothers,* 1–25; Irmtraud Fischer, *Women Who Wrestled with God: Biblical Stories of Israel's Beginnings* (trans. Linda M. Maloney; Collegeville, Minn.: Liturgical, 2005), 1–112.

[49] Teubal, *Sarah the Priestess,* xii.

[50] For insightful studies of Sarah, see esp. Bellis, *Helpmates, Harlots, and Heroes,* 70–74; Mark E. Biddle, "The 'Endangered Ancestress' and Blessing for the Nations," *JBL* 109 (1990): 599–611; Adrien Janis Bledstein, "The Trials of Sarah," *Judaism* 30 (1981): 411–17; Katheryn Pfisterer Darr, *Far More Precious than Jewels: Perspectives on Biblical Women* (Louisville: Westminster John Knox, 1991), 85–131; Dennis, *Sarah Laughed,* 34–61; J. Cheryl Exum, "Who's Afraid of 'the Endangered Ancestress'?" in *The New Literary Criticism and the Hebrew Bible* (ed. J. Cheryl Exum and David J. A. Clines; Sheffield, Eng.: JSOT Press, 1993), 91–113; Sharon Pace Jeansonne, *The Women of Genesis: From Sarah to Potiphar's Wife* (SCB 4; Minneapolis: Fortress, 1990), 14–30; Jacques Nicole and Marie-Claire Nicole, "Sara, soeur et femme d'Abraham," *ZAW* 112 (2000): 5–23; Janice Nunnally-Cox, *Foremothers: Women of the Bible* (New York: Seabury, 1981), 5–9; Sakenfeld, *Just Wives?* 7–25; Tammi J. Schneider, *Sarah: Mother of Nations* (New York: Continuum, 2004); idem, "Sarah: The Chosen Mother," *TBT* 44 (2006): 76–80; Teubal, *Sarah the Priestess;* Phyllis Trible, "Genesis 22: The Sacrifice of Sarah," in *Not in Heaven: Coherence and Complexity in Biblical Narrative* (ed. Jason P. Rosenblatt and Joseph C. Sitterson; Bloomington: Indiana University Press, 1991), 170–91; Jack W. Vancil, "Sarah—Her Life and Legacy," in *Essays on Women in Earliest Christianity* (ed. Carroll D. Osburn; 2 vols.; Joplin, Mo.: College Press, 1995), 2:37–68. For studies dealing both with Sarah and Hagar, see Amy-Jill Levine, "Settling at Beer-lahai-roi," in *Daughters of Abraham: Feminist Thought in Judaism, Christianity, and Islam* (ed. Yvonne Yazbeck Haddad and John L. Esposito; Gainesville, Fla: University Press of Florida, 2001), 12–34; Dora R. Mbuwaye-

sider the following: (1) when Sarah and Abraham approach Egypt during a famine, Abraham does not command her to agree to his planned deception but begs her, with an almost apologetic plea, to say she is his sister (Gen 12:13). (2) God protects Sarah from harm at Pharaoh's court and again in the household of Abimelech and returns her to her husband (12:10–20; 20:1–8). (3) Abraham cohabits with Hagar because Sarah wants him to, and expels Hagar again at Sarah's insistence (16:1–4; 21:8–21). (4) God defends Sarah in her demand that Hagar be sent away, telling Abraham, "whatever Sarah says to you, do as she tells you" (21:12). (5) Sarah is regarded as just as critical to the divine covenant as Abraham himself, with God's continued insistence (at least after the birth of Ishmael) that it is *Sarah's* seed that will fulfill the covenant promise (17:18–19; 21:12; cf. Isa 51:2, where the people of Israel are counseled both to "look to Abraham your father and to Sarah who bore you").

(6) Sarah's name is changed from Sarai, just as Abraham's is from Abram, with the accompanying promise that "she shall give rise to nations; kings of peoples shall come from her" (17:16). (7) The literary structure of Gen 17 emphasizes the significance of Sarah by placing her in the middle of the passage concerning circumcision, thus showing that the covenant blessings and promises apply to her—and to women—just as surely as to Abraham and his male descendants.[51] (8) Abraham and Sarah share in the meal preparations when offering hospitality to the three strangers (18:6–8), showing that there is no distinct division of labor by gender. (9) Sarah is the only matriarch with her age indicated when she dies (this is always seen with the patriarchs) (23:1). (10) Her death and burial at Mamre receives extended attention textually: in the sparse historical style characteristic of the Genesis narrator, it is surely remarkable that an entire chapter is devoted to this event (Gen 23) with no more details given of the last forty-eight years of Abraham's life after Sarah's death.

Sarah the matriarch is no wallflower! Janice Nunnally-Cox rightly concludes that, given their social context, Sarah and Abraham are amazingly equal:

> She appears to say what she wants, when she wants, and Abraham at times responds in almost meek obedience. He does not command her; she commands him, yet there seems to be an affectionate bond between them. Abraham does not abandon Sarah during her barrenness, nor does he gain other wives while she lives, as far as we know. The two have grown up together and grown old together, and when Sarah dies, Abraham can do nothing but weep. Sarah is a matriarch of the first order: respected by rulers and husband alike, a spirited woman and bold companion.[52]

---

sango, "Childlessness and Woman-To-Woman Relationships in Genesis and African Patriarchal Society: Sarah and Hagar from a Zimbabwean Woman's Perspective (Gen. 16:1–16; 21:8–21)," *Semeia* 78 (1997): 27–36; and Phyllis Trible, "Ominous Beginnings for a Promise of Blessing," in *Hagar, Sarah, and Their Children: Jewish, Christian, and Muslim Perspectives* (ed. Phyllis Trible and Letty M. Russell; Louisville, Ky.: Westminster John Knox, 2006), 33–69.

[51] See Mary J. Evans, "The Invisibility of Women: An Investigation of a Possible Blind Spot for Biblical Commentators," *CBRFJ* 122 (1990): 37–38, for this analysis.

[52] Nunnally-Cox, *Foremothers*, 9.

Hagar. Hagar is not a matriarch in the covenant line, but God elevates her from a
slave woman to be a matriarch of twelve mighty clans, and thus she deserves consideration among the Genesis matriarchs. Hagar has often been viewed as one of
those "'throw-away' characters whose history have little or no intrinsic significance,"[53] but numerous recent studies show how the Hagar narrative is one of the
many biblical narratives about women that underscore "the inalienable worth of
the human individual" and reveal "Biblical women as moving forces rather than
passive endurers."[54] Poignant details are recorded in Gen 16 and 21: (1) In Gen
16, which describes her flight into the wilderness after she becomes pregnant and
Sarai deals harshly with her, Hagar's significance is emphasized by the sevenfold
repetition of her name, six times by the narrator (vv. 1, 3, 4, 15 [bis], 16) and once
by Yahweh himself (v. 8). (2) In both Gen 16 and 21 the "angel [messenger] of the
LORD/God"—who is God/Yahweh himself—appears for the first time in biblical
history, and the first appearance is to this rejected woman (21:17).[55] Only two
times does the HB describe an angelic messenger "calling from heaven" directly to
a human recipient—here in 21:17 and in the account of Abraham's trial on Mt.

---

[53] Cynthia Gordon, "Hagar: A Throw-away Character among the Matriarchs?" *SBL
Seminar Papers, 1985* (SBLSP 24; Atlanta: Scholars Press, 1985), 271; Gordon (pp. 271–77)
argues that Hagar is not such a character.

[54] Ibid., 277. Beyond Gordon, see esp. Wilma Ann Bailey, "Black and Jewish Women
Consider Hagar," *Enc* 63 (2002): 37–44; idem, "Hagar: A Model for an Anabaptist Feminist?" *MQR* 68 (1994): 219–28; Alan Cooper, "Hagar in and out of Context," *USQR* 55
(2001): 35–46; Dennis, *Sarah Laughed,* 62–83; Philip R. Drey, "The Role of Hagar in Genesis 16," *AUSS* 40 (2002): 179–95; Frymer-Kensky, *Reading the Women of the Bible,* 225–37;
Jo Ann Hackett, "Rehabilitating Hagar: Fragments of an Epic Pattern," in *Gender and Dif-
ference in Ancient Israel* (ed. Peggy L. Day; Minneapolis: Fortress, 1989), 12–27; Scott K.
Nikaido, "Hagar and Ishmael as Literary Figures: An Intertextual Study," *VT* 51, no. 2
(2001): 219–42; Pamela Tamarkin Reis, "Hagar Requited," *JSOT* 87 (2000): 75–109; Nina
Rulon-Miller, "Hagar: A Woman with an Attitude," in *The World of Genesis: Persons,
Places, Perspectives* (ed. Philip R. Davies and David J. A. Clines; JSOTSup 257; Sheffield,
Eng.: Sheffield Academic Press, 1998), 60–89; Savina J. Teubal, *Hagar the Egyptian: The
Lost Tradition of the Matriarchs* (San Francisco: Harper & Row, 1990); Phyllis Trible, "The
Other Woman: A Literary and Theological Study of the Hagar Narratives," in *Understand-
ing the Word: Essays in Honor of Bernhard W. Anderson* (ed. James T. Butler, Edgar W.
Conrad, and Ben C. Ollenburger; JSOTSup 37; Sheffield, Eng.: JSOT Press, 1985), 221–46;
idem, *Texts of Terror: Literary-Feminist Readings of Biblical Narratives* (Philadelphia: For-
tress, 1984), 9–20; Renita J. Weems, *Just a Sister Away: A Womanist Vision of Women's Relationships in the Bible* (San Diego: LuraMedia, 1988), 1–21; Richard D. Weis, "Stained Glass
Window, Kaleidoscope, or Catalyst: The Implications of Difference in Readings of the
Hagar and Sarah Stories," in *A Gift of God in Due Season: Essays on Scripture and Community in Honor of James A. Sanders* (ed. Richard D. Weis and David M. Carr; JSOTSup 225;
Sheffield, Eng.: Sheffield Academic Press, 1996), 253–73; and Delores S. Williams, *Sisters
in the Wilderness: The Challenge of Womanist God-Talk* (Maryknoll, N.Y.: Orbis Books,
1993), 1–33. (Some of these studies, most notably Rulon-Miller and Teubal, though providing helpful insights into the Hagar narrative, also radically reconstruct—or even
deconstruct—the biblical picture.)

[55] According to 16:7–11, it is the "angel [messenger] of the LORD," but v. 13 indicates
that it is Yahweh himself. See also 21:17–19, where the "angel of God" is identified as
God himself.

Moriah (22:11–12). (3) Indeed, the angel even calls her by name (16:8; 21:17). Sarah and Abraham have not granted her this dignity but typically refer to her only by her status as slave.[56]

(4) God does not abandon Hagar in her extremely devastating situation. He pointedly provides for this mother and the son she is due to deliver. God's promise to Hagar regarding her descendants is similar to that given to Abraham regarding the descendants of Isaac: "The angel of the LORD also said to her, 'I will so greatly multiply your offspring that they cannot be counted for multitude'" (16:10; cf. 22:17). This promise parallels Hagar with Abram himself. (5) The experience of Hagar with the angel of the Lord (Gen 16) is the only time a covenantal-type promise is announced to a woman.[57] (6) The whole birth narrative of 16:7–15 may be regarded as the female counterpart to the covenant relationship.[58] (7) God's promise of a son for Hagar (16:11) utilizes phraseology almost identical to the Immanuel prophecy of Isa 7:14 (except in the second person instead of the third). It is a standard annunciation formula. Hagar is the first woman in the Bible to receive such an annunciation.

(8) It is also noteworthy that Hagar is the only woman in the OT, indeed the only person in all of Scripture, to give deity a name: "So she named the LORD who spoke to her, 'You are El-roi'" (Gen 16:13). This passage employs the usual naming formula used for naming individuals in the Bible; and Hagar names God to his face. (9) When God reconfirms the promise to Hagar to make Ishmael a great nation (21:18), God again employs language parallel to the covenant promises to Abraham (12:2). (10) God supplies for Hagar and Ishmael's physical necessities, using language parallel to Abraham's trial of faith on Mt. Moriah.[59] (11) The

---

[56] When Sarah says to Abraham, "go in to my slave-girl" (16:2b), she does not use Hagar's name but refers only to her position. Up to this point only the narrator has given Hagar's name.

[57] Genesis 16 is sandwiched between two chapters explicitly concerned with God's covenant with Abraham, Gen 15 and 17. Drey, "The Role of Hagar," shows that "Genesis 16 functions as an example of the far-reaching effect of the covenant between God and Abram in chapter 15. The covenant episode in Gen 15 states that Abram will have countless descendants. This covenant is fulfilled in Gen 16 through Hagar. . . . Abram is the father [of Ishmael] and, by virtue of the covenant, he will be blessed with countless descendants—including those of Ishmael" (p. 195).

[58] See R. H. Jarrell, "The Birth Narrative as Female Counterpart to Covenant," *JSOT* 97 (2002): 3–18.

[59] "God opened her eyes and she saw a well of water" (21:19); "Abraham looked up and saw a ram, caught in a thicket by its horns" (22:13). For further parallels between Hagar's experience and Abraham's trial on Mt. Moriah, see esp. Nikaido, "Hagar and Ishmael as Literary Figures," 221–29. Nikaido shows that "the stories of Hagar and Abraham are alike in that both culminate with a journey to a desolate place where the child's life is threatened but spared through divine intervention" (p. 223). Besides the call of the angelic messenger in both and the parallel language of "seeing" God's provision for their needs (cited above), both stories begin with exactly the same statement ("So Abraham rose early in the morning") and include a description of Abraham "taking" items necessary for the journey and "putting/laying" them on Hagar/Isaac (21:14; 22:3–6). Both stories also include a naming speech (16:14; 22:14).

story of the travail and deliverance of Hagar finds clear intertextual echoes in the theophany and deliverance of Moses and Israel at the time of the exodus.[60] "As Moses embodies the Israelite people, initiating their release by his lone recognition that Egypt is not the spiritual home of the Hebrews, so Hagar is the embodiment of the downtrodden 'other.' She is not the demeaned and reduced woman as exegetes have maintained but the protypical stranger in name and in fate, an everlasting memorial to mold the conscience of the world."[61] (12) The Hagar narratives conclude with another insight into the forcefulness of Hagar: she is the only woman mentioned in the Bible as choosing a wife for her son (21:21).

Phyllis Trible recognizes Hagar as "a pivotal figure in biblical theology,"[62] and Trevor Dennis concludes that this Egyptian slave woman is "more highly honoured in some respects than almost any other figure in the Bible."[63]

Rebekah. The next matriarch[64] in Genesis, Rebekah, exhibits the same strength of character and high valuation of women by the narrator as Sarah.[65] The following points indicate her prominence: (1) Although she is described as physically beautiful (24:16), she is not appreciated solely for her outward appearance. (2) Her independence, trust, and hospitality parallel those of Abraham: like him, she was willing to take the risk of leaving her family and travel to a strange land; like him, she showed eagerness to perform her hospitable acts.[66] (3) Narrative tech-

---

[60] See Reis, "Hagar Requited," 103–9. Reis not only points to thematic parallels (both Hagar and Moses fleeing, encountering the Lord in the desert, and being told to return to the place from which they fled; the reluctant return; and both Hagar and Israel being thrust out of the house of bondage and being rescued in the desert and provided with water) but also notes key lexical correspondences (e.g., "send," "cast out," "strong hand," "strangers," "slaves," "afflicted," etc.). Cf. Frymer-Kensky, *Reading the Women of the Bible,* 232, elaborating on 231–37: "The story of Hagar parallels the story of Israel; she is the prototype."

[61] Reis, "Hagar Requited," 109.

[62] Trible, "The Other Woman," 238.

[63] Dennis, *Sarah Laughed,* 176.

[64] Keturah, Abraham's wife after Sarah's death, is mentioned only in passing, without any of the impressive detail that the Sarah narratives exhibit.

[65] See esp. Christine Garside Allen, "Who Was Rebekah? 'On Me Be the Curse, My Son,'" in *Beyond Androcentricism: New Essays on Women and Religion* (ed. Rita M. Gross; Missoula, Mont.: Scholars Press, 1977), 183–216; Robert Alter, *The Art of Biblical Narrative* (New York: Basic Books, 1981), 51–54; Frymer-Kensky, *Reading the Women of the Bible,* 5–23; Jeansonne, *Women of Genesis,* 53–70; Donald B. Sharp, "The Courting of Rebecca: A Yahwist Portrait of the Ideal 'Bride-to-Be,'" *IBS* 22 (2000): 26–37; Meir Sternberg, *The Poetics of Biblical Narrative: Ideological Literature and the Drama of Reading* (Bloomington: Indiana University Press, 1987), 136–52; Lieve Teugels, "'A Strong Woman Who Can Find?' A Study of Characterization in Genesis 24 with Some Perspectives on the General Presentation of Isaac and Rebekah in the Genesis Narrative," *JSOT* 63 (1994): 89–104; Mary Donovan Turner, "Rebekah: Ancestor of Faith," *LTQ* 20, no. 2 (1985): 42–49; cf. Mishael Maswari Caspi and Rachel S. Havrelock, *Women on the Biblical Road: Ruth, Naomi, and the Female Journey* (Lanham, Md.: University Press of America, 1996), 38.

[66] Frymer-Kensky, *Reading the Women of the Bible,* 13–14, summarizes, "Rivka is the counterpart to both Abraham and Sarah. Like Sarah, she is the instrument of the promise,

niques such as dialogue, narrative pace, and other literary features suggest the prominence of Rebekah in Israel's history.[67] (4) The Genesis genealogical record highlights the prominence of Rebekah by listing only her as the one begotten by Bethuel (22:23), although later the narrative includes her brother Laban (24:29). (5) The unusual placement of this genealogy immediately after the account of the testing of Abraham with his son Isaac (22:1–19) emphasizes the importance of Rebekah.[68]

(6) In Gen 24, when Abraham directs Eleazar to find a wife for Isaac, he declares that "if the woman is not willing to follow you, then you will be free from this oath of mine" (24:8). Contrary to those who claim that the woman under the patriarchal system had no voice in whom she would marry, here "Abraham assumes the woman will have the final say in the matter."[69] Ultimately it is Rebekah herself who chooses to go with Eleazar. Indeed, in the lengthy narrative of Gen 24, her determination to travel with Eleazar is spoken directly by her in the dialogue and not just reported by the narrator (24:58), and the narrator saves Rebekah's answer for the very climax of the narrative.[70] (7) Upon Eleazar's arrival, Rebekah arranges for his hospitality herself. Eleazar asks for a place in her "father's house," but Rebekah arranges with her "mother's household" (v. 28). Her father says hardly a word throughout this entire narrative. Rebekah's father determines nothing, as might be expected in an oppressive patriarchy.

(8) Most impressive in the Rebekah narratives is the noticeable correspondence of key terms with the Abraham narratives. James Williams highlights this verbal correspondence by suggesting that "with this blessing the narrator quietly moves Rebecca into the cycle of God's promises to the patriarchs."[71] (9) After Rebekah marries Isaac and becomes pregnant, in apparent agony she is anxious enough "to inquire of the LORD" (paralleling the great prophets of the OT); and she does this herself (25:22), receiving a direct oracle from the Lord. (10) Highly

---

the agent through whom Isaac will become the father of a nation. She is also a second Abraham, who, like him, voluntarily chooses to leave Mesopotamia for Canaan. Her 'I will go' answers the four times the issue of going has been raised in the story (vv. 4, 7, 38, and 40) and echoes God's command to Abraham to 'Go!' in Gen. 12:1. . . . Rivka is very much like Abraham. They are both models of hospitality, and the narrator of her story highlights her similarity to him by describing her actions toward the emissary in the same language that describes Abraham's actions toward his angel visitors (Gen. 18:1–8)."

[67] J. P. Fokkelman, *Narrative Art in Genesis: Specimens of Stylistic and Structural Analysis* (2d ed.; BS 12; Sheffield, Eng.: JSOT Press, 1991), 92–93; Jeansonne, *Women of Genesis,* 53–69.

[68] Jeansonne, *Women of Genesis,* 54–55.

[69] Ibid., 57.

[70] Ibid., 61–62, demonstrates this placement and its significance for the narrative.

[71] James G. Williams, *Women Recounted: Narrative Thinking and the God of Israel* (BLS 6; Sheffield, Eng.: Almond, 1982), 44. Danna Nolan Fewell and David M. Gunn concur: "It is she [Rebecca], not Isaac, who follows in Abraham's footsteps, leaving the familiar for the unknown. It is she, not Isaac, who receives the blessing given to Abraham (22:17). 'May your offspring possess the gates of their enemies!' (24:60)" (*Gender, Power, and Promise: The Subject of the Bible's First Story* [Nashville: Abingdon, 1993], 73). Cf. Turner, "Rebekah," 43–44.

significant also is the formula used to announce Rebekah's delivery: "And her days were fulfilled that she should give birth" (25:24, translation mine). This formula is used of only three biblical women: Elizabeth and Mary in the NT and Rebekah in the OT. (11) Later, when Esau marries two Hittite women, the text informs us that "they made life bitter for Isaac *and Rebekah*" (26:35). The inclusion of Rebekah's distress regarding Esau's marriage to pagan women reveals that Rebekah was just as concerned about the covenant line as was Isaac. (12) Finally, the biblical narrator in many ways accents the role of Rebekah the matriarch far beyond that of her husband, Isaac, the patriarch.[72]

By means of all these narrative clues, the narrator has characterized Rebekah as a woman of value with a high degree of autonomy and equality with her husband.

> [This] characterization of Rebekah yields a deeper understanding of her significance. . . . All of these actions are given without a polemical context, and the narrator does nothing to indicate that these were unusual activities for a woman to take. . . . The presentation of Rebekah shows that women in Israel were viewed as persons who could make crucial decisions about their futures, whose prayers were acknowledged, who might know better than men what God designed, and who could appropriately take the steps necessary to support God's plans for the community.[73]

Rachel and Leah. I have already discussed in some detail the situation of Rachel and Leah in regard to their polygamous relationship with Jacob. Note here that the Genesis narratives present them as women fully capable of acting with independent initiative and strength.[74] Both took great initiative in their attempts to

---

[72] Teubal, *Sarah the Priestess,* xv, points out,

> If the narration of events following the death and burial of Sarah was truly patriarchal, it would deal with the life and exploits of the male heir, Isaac. Instead, once again the accent is on the role of a woman, Rebekah. About Isaac, her husband, we are told little relating to the establishment of the religious faith. He is a placid, sedentary man whose life is colored and influenced by the presence of his outstanding wife. Apart from the incident of the Akadah (The Binding of Isaac in which Abraham is commanded to sacrifice his son), we know nothing of the boyhood or youth of the supposed hero. 'His' story begins with a detailed account of Rebekah's betrothal. . . . Rebekah is vividly depicted in Genesis. . . . Rebekah's strength, beauty, and suffering have not been dimmed. The power of her personality is already evident when as a young girl she takes command of her destiny and leaves for Canaan.

Cf. Teugels, "'A Strong Woman Who Can Find?'"
[73] Jeansonne, *Women of Genesis,* 69.
[74] See, e.g., Athalya Brenner, "Female Social Behaviour: Two Descriptive Patterns within the 'Birth of the Hero' Paradigm," *VT* 36 (1986): 257–73; Zvi Jagendorf, "In the Morning, Behold, It Was Leah: Genesis and the Reversal of Sexual Knowledge," *Proof* 4 (1984): 187–92; repr. in *Biblical Patterns in Modern Literature* (ed. D. Hirsch and N. Aschkenasy; BJS 77; Chico, Calif.: Scholars Press, 1984), 51–60; Jeansonne, *Women of Genesis,* 70–86; J. E. Lapsley, "The Voice of Rachel: Resistance and Polyphony in Gen 31:14–35," in *Genesis* (ed. Athalya Brenner; FCB[2] 1; Sheffield, Eng.: Sheffield Academic Press, 1998), 233–48; Ilana Pardes, *Countertraditions in the Bible: A Feminist Approach*

have children, and it was they, and not Jacob, who named their children (Gen 29–30). The narrative regarding the mandrakes (30:14–16) reveals that the women had the power to determine with whom and when their husband would have sexual relations. As Jeansonne ironically points out, "This is astonishing when it is recalled that previously it was their father who determined Jacob's sexual unions."[75] Both dared to stand up against the abuses of their father in withholding their dowry (31:14–16; cf. vv. 34–35), and both in faith urged Jacob to follow God's leading: "now then, do whatever God has said to you" (31:16).[76] The narrative of Leah and Rachel also indicates that a woman in the patriarchal society was valued not only for the sons she bore. It is Rachel who is loved more, regardless of how many sons Leah bore to Jacob (29:32, 34), and it is Rachel, not Jacob, who frets over the lack of sons (30:1).[77] Finally, both Rachel and Leah revealed tremendous courage in being willing to disown their powerful father, Laban, and great faith to leave their homeland for a strange country (Gen 31).

Tamar. The biblical narrator positively characterizes Tamar.[78] Alice Laffey summarizes the aspects of her initiative and resourcefulness:

(Cambridge: Harvard University Press, 1992), 60–78; and Joan Ross-Burstall, "Leah and Rachel: A Tale of Two Sisters [Gen 29:31–30:24]," *WW* 14 (1992):162–70.

[75] Jeansonne, *Women of Genesis*, 86.

[76] Lapsley, "The Voice of Rachel," 233–48, makes the intriguing suggestion that Rachel's words to Laban while she sat on the camel saddle concealing the household gods had a double meaning. On one level. she was speaking of her literal menstrual period: "I cannot rise before you, for the way of women is upon me" (31:35), but on another level, she meant that she could not prevail legally against him (her father) because she was a woman/daughter (and so she was taking an unconventional approach to keep what rightfully belonged to her). Lapsley notes that elsewhere in Scripture "to rise before" someone speaks of confrontation and the term "the way of women" is never used elsewhere in Scripture as a euphemism for menstruation, thus suggesting a double meaning. Without condoning the lie of Rachel, this interpretation, if correct, further shows the resourcefulness of Rachel in seeking justice.

[77] One probable reason for the wives' concern for lack of sons is that apparently in biblical times children were heirs of their mother's estate quite apart from their fathers (Drey, "The Role of Hagar," 187).

[78] Chapters 7 and 11, below, examine the situation of Tamar and Judah (Gen 38) in more detail. For a review of studies on Tamar in ancient Jewish exegesis, see Esther Marie Menn, *Judah and Tamar (Genesis 38) in Ancient Jewish Exegesis: Studies in Literary Form and Hermeneutics* (JSJSup 51; Leiden: E. J. Brill, 1997). For modern studies on the figure of Tamar, see esp. Johanna W. H. Bos, "Out of the Shadows: Genesis 38; Judges 4:17–22; Ruth 3," *Semeia* 42 (1988): 37–67; Joan E. Cook, "Four Marginalized Foils—Tamar, Judah, Joseph, and Potiphar's Wife: A Literary Study of Genesis 38–39," *PEGLMBS* 21 (2001): 115–28; Mordecai Friedman, "Tamar, a Symbol of Life: The 'Killer Wife' Superstition in the Bible and Jewish Tradition," *AJSR* 15 (1990): 23–61; Frymer-Kensky, *Reading the Women of the Bible*, 264–77; Menn, *Judah and Tamar*, 12–106; Susan Niditch, "The Wronged Woman Righted: An Analysis of Genesis 38," *HTR* 72 (1979): 143–49; and Joan Goodnick Westenholz, "Tamar, QĔDĒŠÂ, QADIŠTU, and Sacred Prostitution in Mesopotamia," *HTR* 82 (1989): 245–65.

I do not ignore the element of trickery employed by Tamar in this narrative, but some scholars see even this trait as part of an overall positive, even humorous, perspective.

To fulfill the levirate law—to act "righteously" according to her situation—she chose the time, the place, the circumstances. Had she not thought ahead to keeping Judah's pledge, she would have had no way to prove his paternity. Tamar was also willing to take risks—to disguise herself, to remove her widow's garments, to act as a harlot, the possible consequence of which was to be burned. Tamar might have remained a victim of unfortunate circumstances, a childless widow, had not she used initiative to effect change. . . . Her situation is changeable and, if the men who should intervene— Judah and Shelah—do not willingly do so, she will think of something. She does! And as Judah himself testifies, Tamar proves to be "more righteous than" Judah.[79]

Martin Luther goes beyond praising Tamar's cleverness and initiative; he upholds her chastity and pious faith:

It is clear that Tamar is an upright and honorable woman, for she is not proud nor does she prostitute herself to others. She seeks no illicit pleasures. She makes it her one aim to be able to become a mother in this house into which she has been placed by divine authority. Therefore she lays aside the garments she had put on, clothes herself again in the garments of widowhood and sits in mourning. Although she had been made pregnant, she awaits a further blessing from the Lord.[80]

Similarly, Joan Cook points out how Tamar "demonstrated her integrity by remaining faithful to Judah and Er under extreme circumstances."[81] Paul Noble argues at length for substantial intertextual echoes between the positive narrative characterizations of Tamar and Joseph, who were both wronged by another of the principals but eventually were vindicated when the offenders confess to the wrong committed against their respective victims.[82] In the blessing given to Ruth by the elders and people of Bethlehem during the time of the Judges (Ruth 4:11–12), Tamar is placed alongside the female founders of Israel, Rachel and

---

See, e.g., Melissa Jackson, "Lot's Daughters and Tamar as Tricksters and the Patriarchal Narratives as Feminist Theology," *JSOT* 98 (2002): 29–46. Jackson argues that the writers of these Genesis narratives were in fact perhaps the first feminist theologians: "Precisely in choosing to take their jabs at the patriarchal system, these biblical writers question the base assumptions of the social order and envision a completely inverted reality, where there are no tricksters, because there are no underdogs. It is possible, then, that the writers of the patriarchal narratives were, indeed, the first feminist theologians" (p. 46). Although I do not agree that the narrator of these stories was seeking to completely overthrow patriarchy (as positively conceived), I concur that the narratives were told in such a way as to indict the distortion of the divine plan, and envision a time where there were no inequities between the sexes and where "women were valued for motherhood and also for their intelligence, courage, inventiveness, creativity" (ibid.).

[79] Alice L. Laffey, *An Introduction to the Old Testament: A Feminist Perspective* (Philadelphia: Fortress, 1988), 46.

[80] Martin Luther, *Lectures on Genesis: Chapters 38–44* (trans. Paul D. Pahl; vol. 7 of *Works;* ed. Jaroslav Pelikan; St. Louis: Concordia, 1965), 35.

[81] Cook, "Four Marginalized Foils," 119.

[82] Paul R. Noble, "Esau, Tamar, and Joseph: Criteria for Identifying Inner-biblical Allusions," *VT* 52 (2002): 232–43; cf. idem, "Synchronic and Diachronic Approaches to Biblical Interpretation," *LT* 7 (1993): 138–40.

Leah. Finally, from a Christian perspective, Tamar is one of four women mentioned in Matthew's genealogy of Jesus Christ (Matt 1:3).

Conclusion. The Genesis matriarchs are not wallflowers. They "are not little
housewives; they are the founders of the nation."[83] It would be unfair to the portraits of these women to argue that the Genesis matriarchs bow in submission to
all men or are under the oppressive authority of their husbands. Rather, though
respectful of their husbands, they are intelligent, forceful, and directive. "Far from
conforming to a traditional servitude, these women grace the pages of Genesis
with their laughter, their sorrows, *their strength, and their power.*"[84]

A close reading of Genesis reveals the Genesis matriarchs in roles of individuality and influence. Carol Meyers appears correct in her suggestion that patriarchy itself must be carefully defined in the light of its original context and that
many of the details recorded in the narratives of the matriarchs seem to indicate
a rather equitable situation between male and female—a "functional gender
balance."[85] Feminists are right in demanding redress of the long-accumulating
record of the subjugation of women. But they need to rethink the cause of this repression. The Genesis matriarchs were not suppressed or oppressed women.

Women at the Exodus

Women are featured throughout the OT; but at the most critical junctures of
salvation history—the exodus, the transition to the monarchy, and the incarnation
of Christ—the biblical writers shine a dazzling spotlight upon them. A notable
roster of women are concentrated at the opening of the book of Exodus.[86] "Of all

---

[83] Fischer, *Women Who Wrestled with God,* 148.

[84] Nunnally-Cox, *Foremothers,* 20 (emphasis added).

[85] Meyers, *Discovering Eve,* 45.

[86] For analysis of these narratives, see esp. Dennis, *Sarah Laughed,* 84–114; J. Cheryl
Exum, "'You Shall Let Every Daughter Live': A Study of Exodus 1:8–2:10," *Semeia* 28
(1983): 63–82; idem, "Second Thoughts about Secondary Characters: Women in Exodus
1:8–2:10," in *A Feminist Companion to Exodus to Deuteronomy* (ed. Athalya Brenner; FCB
6; Sheffield, Eng.: Sheffield Academic Press, 1994), 75–87; Fewell and Gunn, *Gender,
Power and Promise,* 93; Fischer, *Women Who Wrestled with God,* 113–28; Frymer-Kensky,
Reading the Women of the Bible, 24–33; Jacqueline E. Lapsley, *Whispering the Word: Hearing Women's Stories in the Old Testament* (Louisville: Westminster John Knox, 2005),
69–88; Moshe Reiss, "The Women Around Moses," *JBQ* 33 (2005): 127–30; Jopie Siebert-
Hommes, "But If She Be a Daughter . . . She May Live! 'Daughters' and 'Sons' in Exodus
1–2," in *A Feminist Companion to Exodus to Deuteronomy* (ed. Athalya Brenner; FCB 6;
Sheffield, Eng.: Sheffield Academic Press, 1994), 62–74; cf. the bibliography in Bellis,
Helpmates, Harlots, and Heroes, 110–11. I do not follow the recent trend among feminist
scholars to deconstruct the biblical text by reading these narratives of the book of Exodus
with a hermeneutic of suspicion or resistance and reaching the conclusion that these narratives constitute a sustained suppression of female voices and an immasculation of
women (so, e.g., Esther Fuchs, "A Jewish-Feminist Reading of Exodus 1–2," in *Jews, Christians, and the Theology of the Hebrew Scriptures* [ed. Alice Ogden Bellis and Joel S.
Kaminsky; SBLSymS 8; Atlanta: Society of Biblical Literature, 2000], 307–26).

the initiatives taken by human beings in Ex 1–14, it is those of the women, how-ever, that display the greatest courage, invite our keenest admiration, and have the most powerful influence on events."[87] Twelve individual "daughters" appear in those opening chapters, perhaps deliberately set forth by the narrator to match the twelve "sons" of Israel.[88] Each of the women plays a vital role in saving Moses' life and that of the Israelite nation, and collectively these assertive women may be seen as helping to lead what has been called an "egalitarian social revolution . . . without parallel in the ancient world."[89]

Shiphrah and Puah. Analysis of the first chapter of Exodus in the traditional commentaries usually focuses upon such details as the growth of the Hebrews in Egypt, the pharaoh who knew not Joseph, and the persecution of, and death de-cree upon, the Hebrew people. Rarely do these commentaries celebrate the cour-age of the two women who are responsible for building up Israel and sparing the life of Moses in the midst of this perilous time for God's people.[90] But only a few verses into the book of Exodus (Exod 1:15–22), the narrator highlights the ac-tions of two Hebrew midwives who make an independent moral decision to dis-obey Pharaoh's command to murder newborn Hebrew baby boys. The midwives have two separate audiences and conversations with Pharaoh, further heighten-ing their position.[91] That these two courageous women are named (in contrast with Pharaoh, who himself remains unnamed) is a highly significant detail in the Hebrew narrative. The unnamed pharaoh is shown to be powerless in his attempt to kill the Israelite children, whereas the named midwives ensure that they can live. Whereas the unnamed pharaoh draws a sex distinction with regard to the newborn, the midwives make no such distinction. Shiphrah and Puah succeed in defeating the policy of genocide. They are the instruments God uses to build up the people of Israel. The narrator points out that because these women feared God, the children were saved alive. And God rewarded their faithfulness: "So God dealt well with the midwives . . . and because the midwives feared God. And because the midwives feared God, he gave them families" (Exod 1:20–21).

---

[87] Dennis, *Sarah Laughed,* 114.

[88] Siebert-Hommes, "But If She Be a Daughter," 62–74, suggests and explores this juxtaposition of the twelve sons with the twelve daughters.

[89] Phipps, *Assertive Biblical Women,* 45. Phipps is building upon the work of Norman K. Gottwald, *The Tribes of Yahweh: A Sociology of the Religion of Liberated Israel, 1250–1050 B.C.E.* (Maryknoll, N.Y.: Orbis Books, 1979), 489–663, and passim. Without subscribing to all of Gottwald's model of Israelite settlement in Canaan and his overall reconstruction of Israel's early history along socialist lines, I think it fair to speak of a trend toward social egalitarianism, revealed in the biblical narrative, in early Israel before the rise of the monarchy.

[90] This anomaly is pointed out esp. by Laffey, *Introduction to the Old Testament,* 47–48.

[91] Laffey, ibid., 48, comments, "Analysis of Exodus 1 usually concentrates on the fact of the Hebrews in Egypt, their ever-growing numbers, the passage of time, the Pharaoh who did not know Joseph, and the Hebrews' persecution. . . . Rarely do traditional com-mentaries point to the midwives. . . . Few celebrate the courage of their decision—to bring forth life rather than death."

The Egyptian Princess. In the continuing narrative of Exod 2, divine providence ironically enlists strategic protection for Israel's future deliverer from an Egyptian princess, a member of the very monarchy that issued the death decree. Astonishingly, "the actions of this non-Israelite are presented in direct parallel to those of the God of Israel: 'she "comes down," "sees" the child, "hears" its cry, takes pity on him, draws him out of the water, and provides for his daily needs' (cf. 3:7–8). What she does for Moses, God is soon to do for Israel."[92]

Jochebed. Jochebed is also intertextually linked with the action of God. Just as God in creation saw that what he made was good (the verb *rāʾâ*, "to see," plus *kî-ṭôb*, "that [it/he] was good," Gen 1:10, 12, 18, 21, 25, 31), so Jochebed saw that Moses was good[-looking] (the verb *rāʾâ*, "to see," plus *kî-ṭôb*, "that [it/he] was good," Exod 2:2, translations mine). Biblical history records the unusual means Jochebed devised to spare her son Moses' life in spite of Pharaoh's grim decree. Her husband, after his brief mention in 2:1, is never referred to again except in genealogical notation. Instead, all attention is focused on his wife. It was Jochebed who saw that he was good-looking, she who hid him for three months, she who made the ark of bulrushes and hid him in it, she who nursed the child, and she who brought him to Pharaoh's daughter when he was grown (2:2–3, 9–10). Between the lines one can also read a mother's teaching her son to be faithful to the ways of Yahweh, preparing him for the temptations in the royal court.[93] Jochebed is also the very first person in the Hebrew canon to be given a theophoric name (i.e., the name Yahweh was attached to the name). To reserve for a woman the first mention of a name containing the name Yahweh appears extremely significant.

Miriam. Miriam, the daughter of Jochebed, exhibits intelligence, diplomacy, and courage in speaking to the Egyptian princess, cleverly suggesting a "nurse" for the baby in the basket (2:1–10). Miriam may not have ever married; the OT includes no record of a husband or names of any children for her as it does for Moses and Aaron. Once the exodus from Egypt commences, the focus of attention among most commentators centers on the lives of her two brothers, Moses and Aaron. Any regard ever granted Miriam concentrates on her errors. Thus this amazing woman's position during the exodus has been underestimated.

Recent (especially feminist) studies, however, have begun to recognize the high profile and valuation of Miriam in Scripture.[94] In the book of Exodus, the

---

[92] Fewell and Gunn, *Gender, Power and Promise*, 93.

[93] For an esp. sensitive treatment of the probably strong influence of Jochebed on Moses for his lifework, see Phipps, *Assertive Biblical Women*, 33–36.

[94] See esp. Rita J. Burns, *Has the Lord Indeed Spoken Only through Moses? A Study of the Biblical Portrait of Miriam* (SBLDS 84; Atlanta: Scholars Press, 1987); Phyllis Silverman Kramer, "Miriam," in *Exodus to Deuteronomy* (ed. Athalya Brenner; FCB² 5; Sheffield, Eng.: Sheffield Academic Press, 2001), 104–33; Carol Meyers, "Miriam the Musician," in *A Feminist Companion to Exodus to Deuteronomy* (ed. Athalya Brenner; FCB 6; Sheffield, Eng.: Sheffield Academic Press, 1994), 207–30; Ursula Rapp, *Mirjam: Eine feministisch-rhetorische Lektüre der Mirjamtexte in der hebräischen Bibel* (BZAW 317; New York: de Gruyter, 2002); and Phyllis Trible, "Bringing Miriam out of the Shadows," *BRev* 5, no. 1 (1989): 14–25, 34.

narrator utilizes the figure of Miriam to bracket the exodus event: she appears at the bank of the Nile as the exodus account begins, and at the end of the story, on the bank of the Red Sea, she reappears (2:1–10; 15:20–21). Thus "the story of salvation of Israel delivered from Egyptian bondage begins and ends with Miriam. . . . Miriam's story brackets the salvation of the Lord! Israel's salvation from Egypt begins when Miriam saves Moses and it ends when Miriam sings her song."[95]

Miriam is presented as a prophet (15:20), only the second person in the Pentateuch so designated thus far in its canonical form. At the crossing of the Red Sea, one finds her in a dual role as prophetess and musician at the side of her two brothers. The Song of Moses and the Song of Miriam are juxtaposed in Exod 15—Moses' song starting with a first-person jussive, "I will sing to the LORD" (v. 1), and Miriam's song commencing with a second-person plural imperative, "Sing to the LORD." This juxtaposition and the use of specific verbal forms imply that "the Song of Moses was meant to be a response to the invocation by the Song of Miriam."[96] Such juxtaposition of songs also indicates that "the prophet Miriam is included along with her fellow musicians, implying the concept of togetherness in the setting of the chorus of both genders and all statuses."[97] Furthermore, the narrator reserves the antiphonal rendition of the Song of Miriam, led by this inspired musician, to be the grand climax of the exodus story (15:20–21).[98] "The subtle emphasis on the importance of the roles of women in

---

[95] Robert Van Kooten, "The Song of Miriam," *Kerux* 16, no. 3 (2001): 38.

[96] Hyun Chul Paul Kim, "Gender Complementarity in the Hebrew Bible," in *Theological and Hermeneutical Studies* (vol. 1 of *Reading the Hebrew Bible for a New Millennium: Form, Concept, and Theological Perspective;* ed. Deborah Ellens et al.; SAC; Harrisburg, Pa.: Trinity Press International, 2000), 273.

[97] Ibid. Kim continues: "Likewise, in the correlation between cohortative and imperative verb forms the reader finds an authorial sketch of the interaction between the two parts of the choir, as if sopranos and altos sing the invitation hymn while tenors and basses echo with the responsive arias, and vice versa. In the corresponding interaction there is a concept of unity and mutuality between Moses and Miriam, between the men and women of Israel. . . . In that unity, though Moses assumes a more prominent role, the two songs imply the concept of complementarity of Moses and Miriam, not only brother and sister, but also coleaders and copartners" (pp. 274, 276). It should be noted that by "complementarity" Kim "implies an idea of the relationship of two distinct parties who share mutual needs, interdependence, and respect. This term is to be distinguished from the connotation of a hierarchical relationship of two parties where one is subordinate to the other. Rather, it is used to include the ideas of mutuality, balance, and equality, while maintaining the uniqueness and distinctiveness of each party rather than homogeneity" (268). I heartily concur with this definition of "complementarity," in contrast to its frequent use in evangelical circles to denote hierarchical roles between women and men.

[98] For examinations of Miriam's Song, see, e.g., Bernhard W. Anderson, "The Song of Miriam Poetically and Theologically Considered," in *Directions in Biblical Hebrew Poetry* (ed. Elaine R. Follis; JSOTSup 40; Sheffield, Eng.: Sheffield Academic Press, 1987), 285–302; J. Gerald Janzen, "Song of Moses, Song of Miriam: Who Is Seconding Whom?" *CBQ* 54, no. 2 (1992): 211–20; Gail R. O'Day, "Singing Woman's Song: A Hermeneutic of Liberation," *CurTM* 12, no. 4 (1985): 203–4; and Van Kooten, "The Song of Miriam." The arguments of some of these authors that the Song of Miriam is primary and the Song of Moses is secondary are based upon source-critical assumptions that are outside the pale

the fate of Moses . . . , and thereby the whole people of Israel, culminates in the duet of Moses and Miriam, where the reader is invited to remember and acknowledge the audacious roles of women, particularly Miriam."[99] Miriam's aesthetic performance as singer-dancer-percussionist has significant implications for her prominence, prestige, and power in Israel.[100]

Most of the passages in the Pentateuch that mention Miriam by name represent her as a leader.[101] Moreover, God insists through Micah (Mic 6:4) that she, along with her brothers, was divinely commissioned as a leader of Israel: "For I brought you up from the land of Egypt, and redeemed you from the house of slavery; and *I sent before you* Moses, Aaron, *and Miriam*." Furthermore, the biblical record of Miriam's death (Num 20:1) highlights her prominence in the estimation of the narrator; most other named figures in the wilderness community disappear without mention. It is not accidental that her death and the deaths of her two brothers coincide with the last three stops in the wilderness wandering.

Scripture also includes a significant genealogical mention of Miriam. First Chronicles 5:29 (ET 6:3) lists Miriam as a child (*bēn*, lit. "son") of Amram. The fact that Miriam is mentioned among Amram's children (lit. "sons") in an entire chapter of fathers and male offspring surely confirms her prominence, implicitly underscoring her parallel status in religious leadership along with her two brothers.

The Seven Daughters of Jethro (Including Zipporah). Just as the two midwives, Moses' mother and sister, and Pharaoh's daughter kept Moses alive for his future mission, so the narrative describes how the seven daughters of the priest of Midian led him into a new phase of his mission by introducing him to the house of their priest father, Jethro/Reuel (Exod 2:18–20). In particular, the daughter Zipporah, who became Moses' wife (2:21–22), was instrumental in keeping Moses alive for that mission. When God sought to kill Moses while he was on his way back to Egypt to rescue the Hebrew people (apparently because he had failed to recognize the covenant obligations symbolized by circumcising his son), Zipporah saved Moses' life by quickly performing the circumcision (4:24–26).[102]

---

of my final-form approach toward the text, but nonetheless these articles rightly maintain the significant position of the Song of Miriam at the climax of the exodus story.

[99] Kim, "Gender Complementarity," 274.

[100] See Meyers, "Miriam the Musician," for examination of the biblical and extrabiblical evidence.

[101] Exod 15:20, 21; Num 12:1, 4, 5, 10 (bis), 15 (bis); Num 20:1; 26:59; Deut 24:9.

[102] Various explanations for this story have been proposed by scholars (some presupposing a non-Hebrew folktale background including demons, and others seeing a literary foreshadowing of the passover blood), but the most straightforward reading of the text connects it with Moses' failure to carry out the covenant sign of circumcision with his own son. It is not clear from the biblical record why Moses neglected this rite; it is possible that Zipporah was to blame for influencing him (this may be implied by Zipporah's flinging of the bloody foreskin at Moses' feet with the twice-repeated shout of apparent revulsion and disgust "Truly you are a bridegroom of blood to me!" [Exod 4:25–26]). Nonetheless, Zipporah's quick and decisive action to save Moses' life in the face of an encounter with divinity must not be overlooked. For further discussion (with the history of

One should not overlook the "mediating role played by Zipporah," which may be seen as "foreshadowing the intercession of Moses, which later saves a rebellious Israel from an angry God (Exod 32–34)."[103] This performance of circumcision by Zipporah is all the more remarkable because she was not from an Israelite background, and may hint at Zipporah's priestlike role, following in the footsteps of her father.[104]

Conclusion. The opening chapters of Exodus (esp. chs. 1–2) reveal attempts on the part of Pharaoh to stop the growth of Israel. In each of these situations, the solution that thwarts Pharaoh's plans centers on the activities of women.

> Exodus begins with a focus on women. Their actions determine the outcome. From its highly positive portrayals of women to its testimony that the courage of women is the beginning of liberation, Exod 1:8–2:10 presents the interpreter with powerful themes to draw on: women as defiers of oppression, women as givers of life, women as wise and resourceful in situations where a discerning mind and keen practical judgment are essential for a propitious outcome.[105]

Exum pithily encapsulates the narrative irony: "Without Moses there would be no story, but without the initiative of these women, there would be no Moses!"[106]

---

interpretation and bibliography), see, e.g., Brevard S. Childs, *The Book of Exodus: A Critical, Theological Commentary* (Philadelphia: Westminster, 1974), 95–101; John I. Durham, *Exodus* (WBC 3; Waco, Tex.: Word Books, 1987), 51–60; Walter C. Kaiser Jr., "Exodus," *EBC* 2:332–34; Pardes, *Countertraditions,* 79–97. Cf. the discussion of circumcision in ch. 11, below, and Godfrey Ashby, "The Bloody Bridegroom: The Interpretation of Exodus 4:24–26," *ExpT* 106 (1995): 203–5; Jeffrey Cohen, "*Hatan Damim*—The Bridegroom of Blood," *JBQ* 33 (2005): 120–26; William H. Propp, "That Bloody Bridegroom (Exodus iv 24–6)," *VT* 43 (1993): 495–518; Bernard P. Robinson, "Zipporah to the Rescue: A Contextual Study of Exodus 4:24–6," *VT* 36 (1986): 447–61.

[103] See Peter F. Lockwood, "Zipporah in the Account of the Exodus: Literary and Theological Perspectives on Exodus 4:24–26," *LTJ* 35 (2001): 121–22. Cohen, "Bridegroom of Blood," 125, notes the irony in this passage: "Ironically, it is Zipporah who stands out here as the one brimming with righteous indignation, and Moses, the future law-giver, is cast as the religious compromiser!"

[104] Susan Ackerman, "Why Is Miriam Also among the Prophets? (and Is Zipporah among the Priests?)," *JBL* 121 (2002): 71–75, defends the hypothesis that "by presenting Zipporah as making a sacrificial-like offering that we normally would have expected to have been made by her priestly father, Exod 4:24–26 provocatively hints at the notion of Zipporah assuming a priest-like role" (p. 75).

[105] Exum, "'You Shall Let Every Daughter Live,'" 82. See her discussion of the threefold thematic structure (pp. 63–82). Beyond the twelve women mentioned individually in the first two chapters of Exodus, in Exod 3:22 the role of women is also highlighted in God's promise that it will be the women who procure the wealth of the departing Israelites: "each woman shall ask her neighbor . . . for jewelry of silver and of gold, and clothing, . . . and so you shall plunder the Egyptians."

[106] Ibid., 75. In her later consideration of the narratives dealing with the women at the Exodus ("Second Thoughts about Secondary Characters"), Exum expresses a more radically-feminist stance, suggesting that the women in these narratives serve largely to stabilize the established gender hierarchy and give support to prescribed gender roles.

Daughters of Zelophehad

One more group of women in the Torah may here serve as a transition from the narratives highlighting women to the legislation relating to women's status. Numbers 27:1–11 and Num 36 record narratives concerning Zelophehad's five daughters, whose names were Mahlah, Noah, Hoglah, Milcah, and Tirzah (27:1). One cannot but be impressed by the outspoken manner of these women.[107] This narrative "makes a remarkable statement about the dignity and value of women and children as members of the congregation of Israel."[108] The narrator highlights the fact that these women are not hesitant to make a move unprecedented in the history of Israel—to publicly take their stand as women "before Moses, Eleazar the priest, the leaders, and all the congregation, at the entrance of the tent of meeting" (27:2) and boldly ask for what they consider is rightfully theirs. Narrative clues suggest that the speech of these daughters was directed toward Yahweh himself, not toward the human court.[109] "This places the daughters in remarkable light. They . . . have the courage and confidence to directly address YHWH before the whole company of Israel as witness."[110]

They make an astonishing request—to be granted a possession among their father's kin (vv. 3–4). Even more astonishing is the fact that Yahweh concurs with their concern (v. 7): "The daughters of Zelophehad are right in what they are saying." And by divine direction their request is written into law (vv. 8–11). The book of Numbers (ch. 36) ends with an elaboration of this law. What is more,

---

Fischer, *Women Who Wrestled with God*, 124, takes seriously Exum's suggestion, but argues that "if we read the entire prologue to the Exodus event and thus also the stories that follow 2:10, a different picture emerges. The man Moses, around whom everything revolves, has to learn from the women what fear of God means, and has to follow a thorny path in working out their strategies for success. The stories in Exodus 1–2 stylize the threat to the male sex. But while the men of the oppressed group, such as Moses' father, remain passive or even turn against each other, the women find a means to act politically and in solidarity with each other." Additional evidence for accepting Exum's earlier and not her later position on these narratives is provided by Lapsley, *Whispering the Word*, 84–88.

[107] For a particularly delightful portrayal of this narrative and how it presents these women in a positive light, see Nunnally-Cox, *Foremothers*, 38–39. Cf. Josiah Derby, "The Daughters of Zelophehad Revisited," *JBQ* 25, no. 3 (1997): 169–71; John D. Litke, "The Daughters of Zelophehad," *CurTM* 29 (2002): 207–18; Zvi Ron, "The Daughters of Zelophehad," *JBQ* 26, no. 4 (1998): 260–62; Katharine Doob Sakenfeld, "Zelophehad's Daughters," *PRSt* 15 (1988): 37–47; Siebert-Hommes, "But If She Be a Daughter," 72–73; Ankie Sterring, "The Will of the Daughters," in *A Feminist Companion to Exodus to Deuteronomy* (ed. Athalya Brenner; FCB 6; Sheffield, Eng.: Sheffield Academic Press, 1994), 88–99; Ilan Tal, "The Daughters of Zelophehad and Women's Inheritance: The Biblical Injunction and Its Outcome," in *A Feminist Companion to Exodus to Deuteronomy* (ed. Athalya Brenner; FCB 6; Sheffield, Eng.: Sheffield Academic Press, 1994), 176–86; and Dean R. Ulrich, "The Framing Function of the Narratives about Zelophehad's Daughters," *JETS* 41 (1998): 529–38.

[108] Litke, "Daughters of Zelophehad," 207.

[109] Ibid., 212.

[110] Ibid.

with consummate artistry, the narrator places the two pericopes about Zelophehad's daughters as "an inclusio which frames the deliberately unfinished story
of the second generation. Zelophehad's daughters exemplified the faith that tena-
ciously clung to the Lord despite adverse circumstances."[111] In contrast with the
shortsighted unbelief of the first generation (which came out of Egypt), "the
daughters' eschatological outlook provided the necessary impetus for obeying
the stipulation of the covenant."[112]

> The gender issue is the key point of the text. . . . In the patriarchal culture of the time
> and in subsequent centuries, it is remarkable that the women are named, that they
> address the deity directly, and that they are called *right* or *just*. A further confirma-
> tion of the status of the daughters is that they are given the status of name bearers of
> their father's family symbolized by the transference of inheritance to them.[113]

This narrative, which upholds the high valuation of women,[114] at the same
time leads us to the question of the pentateuchal legislation dealing with the relative status of women.

The High Status of Women in Pentateuchal Laws

The pentateuchal legal codes have often been interpreted as setting forth a
view of "woman disenfranchised," woman as a "legal nonperson."[115] More current research in pentateuchal law, however, is revealing that the legislation that at
first sight appears to relegate women to a lower status was instead intended as a
protective measure for the more vulnerable members of society, particularly for
women and those who were physically disadvantaged.

Women's Status vis-à-vis That of Men in Pentateuchal Law

Women were participants in the covenant ceremony (Deut 29:9–12 [ET 10–13])
and thus, contrary to some modern claims, were considered full members of the
covenant community.[116] As full covenant members, they were considered under

---

[111] Ulrich, "Framing Function," 538. Cf. Roy Gane, *Leviticus, Numbers* (NIVAC 3;
Grand Rapids: Zondervan, 2004), 476.

[112] Ibid.

[113] Litke, "The Daughters of Zelophehad," 218.

[114] See, e.g., Tal, "The Daughters of Zelophehad," 186, who speaks of "the goodwill toward women displayed by the biblical author, who composed the episode of the daughters
of Zelophehad for the sole purpose of elevating women's legal status within Jewish law."

[115] United Church of Christ, *Human Sexuality: A Preliminary Study of the United
Church of Christ* (New York: United Church, 1977), 36.

[116] Some scholars (e.g., Bird, "Images of Women in the Old Testament," 50) have argued that because the term for "people" (ʿam) is apparently applied only to the male members of the congregation (Exod 19:14–15), only the males were full covenant members. But
Deut 29:9–12 (ET 29:10–13) explodes this hypothesis: all of Israel—including males and fe-

equal obligation to observe the law (Deut 31:12). All Israel, including women and children, were summoned by Moses to hear the law because "Moses recognized that men *and women* must hear and learn in order to practice and propagate the faith and the culture."[117] The laws dealing with major cultic, ethical, and moral prohibitions and infractions are fully egalitarian. The Decalogue is clearly intended to apply to both men and women.[118] The judgments of the chapters following the Decalogue (the Covenant Code) that apply the "ten words" to specific cases make explicit that both male and female are included (Exod 21:15, 17, 20, 26–29, 31–32), and this appears to set the standard for later legal material, where gender inclusiveness is to be implied although masculine terminology is used.[119] "We should reverse our way of thinking—where men are discussed, women are not necessarily excluded. They ought to be included in legal and cultic texts where they are not expressly excluded, or where other issues are not raised."[120]

The legislation of Leviticus and Deuteronomy occasionally contains an explicit reference to both genders, not because both genders are excluded elsewhere but because "it seems to be the importance of the subject that compels the author to such an unusual embellishment of the obvious."[121] Both males and females engaging in the occult receive the same penalty (Lev 20:27; Deut 17:2–7); both male and female cult prostitutes were equally forbidden (Deut 23:18 [ET 23:17]). Both male and female were equally punished for apostasy (Deut 13:7–11 [ET 13:6–10]). Illicit sexual intercourse received the same (death) penalty in the case of both sexes (Lev 18:6–18; 20:10–21; Deut 23:1 [ET 22:30]).

Jonathan Klawans summarizes the situation regarding the issue of gender in both ritual and moral impurity laws. Regarding ritual impurity legislation, the HB presents "a system that is rather even-handed in its treatment of gender."[122] Aside

---

males—were established in the covenant ceremony "as his *people* [ʿ*am*]" (29:12 [ET 29:13]). God's instruction in Exod 19 to the "people" at Mt. Sinai not to go near a woman does not necessarily imply that the women were not counted as part of the covenant congregation; God addresses all Israel—men, women, and children—to "prepare for the third day" and then instructs the husbands not to have sexual intercourse with their wives.

[117] Klein, *From Deborah to Esther,* 31.

[118] This is emphasized by Ellens, *Sex in the Bible,* 86: "Both men and women are addressed as equal agents with power to act independently, and thus to function responsibly on the [*sic*] own. . . . The plural 'you' implies the equality of men and women in and before this set of laws. The relationship of both female and male to the law and to the responsibility to keep it, is the same." See the discussion below on the tenth commandment and the claim that it implies women are only chattel.

[119] On gender inclusiveness in legal terminology in the Torah, see esp. Frank Crüsemann, *The Torah: Theology and Social History of Old Testament Law* (trans. Allan W. Mahnke; Minneapolis: Fortress, 1996), 249–52. As noted below in the discussion of women in the OT cultus, Num 6:2–21 and Deut 29:17–19 (ET 29:18–20) make the gender inclusiveness clear by using both masculine and feminine grammatical forms in the introductory verse and then only masculine in the verses that follow, while implying both genders throughout.

[120] Ibid., 252.

[121] Ibid., 251.

[122] Jonathan Klawans, *Impurity and Sin in Ancient Judaism* (New York: Oxford University Press, 2000), 39.

from menstrual uncleanness, which applies only to women and in fact may be seen "to empower women,"[123] "the other major sources of ritual impurity are clearly gender-blind."[124] Regarding moral impurity, "even though the sexual laws [of Lev 18 and 20] are addressed to men, on the whole they apply equally to men and women."[125] Klawans concludes that "for the most part, the ancient Israelite system of moral impurity applies equally to men and women."[126]

But what about the laws where it seems women are treated differently than men? Many of these laws must be understood against the background of the patriarchal society. As pointed out above, the family, not the individual, constituted the basic unit of society in ancient Israel. One of the chief functions of the pentateuchal laws was "to assure the integrity, stability, and financial viability of the family as the basic unit of society."[127] The family member charged with this responsibility was its "titular head," the husband/father. Much of the legislation that seems to give women a subordinate status or place their sexuality under the "possession" of the male leader of the household should in fact be viewed as setting forth the obligation of the husband/father to protect his wife/daughter's sexuality and thereby the integrity of the family structure. These laws are designed to protect women, not oppress them. This will become clearer in the next section.

Legislation Purportedly Presenting an Inferior Status for Women

Those who see a low status of women reflected in the pentateuchal law codes frequently single out several passages. We examine here these alleged indications of the inferior status of women in ancient Israel.

---

[123] Ibid., 40 (following the suggestion of Ross Kraemer): "The regulations regarding the menstrual taboo actually empower women, by giving them the opportunity to decline sexual relations by claiming that they are ritually impure."

[124] Ibid., 39. Klawans summarizes the evidence regarding ritual impurity: "In the final analysis, one cannot build a very strong case in defense of the argument that the biblical ritual impurity laws were legislated for the purpose of subjugating women" (p. 40).

[125] Ibid., 40. Other chapters of the current study elaborate on this concerning various forms of moral sexual defilement.

[126] Ibid., 40–41. The only exception is regarding menstruation, but even this prohibition (Lev 20:18) "applies equally to men and women" (40). See also Deborah Ellens, "Menstrual Impurity and Innovation in Leviticus 15," in *Wholly Woman, Holy Blood: A Feminist Critique of Purity and Impurity* (ed. Kristin De Troyer et al.; Studies in Antiquity and Christianity; Harrisburg, Penn.: Trinity Press International, 2003), 29–43. Ellens shows how the chiastic literature structure of Lev 15 highlights the equality between man and woman: "The structure pictures the woman equal to the man. She is as responsible as he is for maintaining the laws of purity with respect to genital discharge. Her status as agent in this respect is equivalent to his. Mediation of impurity caused by her genital discharge is equivalent in its significance to mediation of impurity caused by his genital discharge. Her jeopardy in the presence of impurity by genital discharge is equivalent to his. Seminal emission is a normal condition lacking association with illness. So also, according to the structure, is menstruation. In this way, her flow is typologically equivalent to his" (32.)

[127] Bird, "Images of Women in the Old Testament," 51.

Numbers 5. It has often been pointed out that the law in Num 5 concerning the suspected adulteress does not have a reciprocal provision for the wife to bring her husband before the priest if she suspects him of sexual unfaithfulness. But whereas feminists have often referred to this legislation as a prime example of a sexist passage in the Bible,[128] Jacob Milgrom turns the feminist argument on its head: "Ironically, feminists have chosen the worst possible witness. . . . [The woman's] public ordeal was meant not to humiliate her but to protect her, not to punish her but to defend her."[129] In a similar vein, Roy Gane points out that this is the only case in ancient Israel's entire legal system where the Lord himself promises to render a just verdict by supernatural means: "The right to such a Supreme Court trial belongs only to women."[130] As argued in the detailed discussion of this passage below (ch. 8), although God did punish the guilty one, at the same time he protected both guilty and innocent from "a husband's pride, a mob's prejudice."[131] This law, then, does not reflect a lower valuation of women than of men but underscores the motivation to protect the weaker members of society from oppression and abuse.

Leviticus 12:1–8. Many scholars have argued from Lev 12:1–8 that woman was considered inferior in value or status to man, because the time of purification for the woman who gave birth was twice as long for the birth of a female as for a male.[132] Chapter 7, below, on ritual impurity, examines this legislation again, but here it should be noted that this passage does not indicate any inferior status or value of the female. The text is clear that it is not the birth of the newborn child (whether male or female) per se that causes uncleanness but the flow of blood. The newborn is not impure, in contrast with what is implied in Hittite birth ritual texts.[133] Also, the female child is not regarded as attached to greater physical ritual impurity, as an agent of greater intrinsic defilement, as some maintain, since the offerings specified for the end of the purification period are the same as for the male. Further, the legislator intentionally juxtaposes "son" and "daughter" in v. 6—"whether for a son or for a daughter," and places them on the same level. Thereby equality, not lower social status is emphasized.

---

128 See, e.g., Deborah L. Ellens, "Numbers 5.11–31: Valuing Male Suspicion," in *God's Word for Our World, Vol. I: Theological and Cultural Studies in Honor of Simon John De Vries* (ed. J. Harold Ellens, et al.; JSOTSup 388; New York: T&T Clark, 2004), 55–82.

129 Jacob Milgrom, "A Husband's Pride, a Mob's Prejudice: The Public Ordeal Undergone by a Suspected Adulteress in Numbers 5 Was Meant Not to Humiliate Her but to Protect Her," *BRev* 12, no. 4 (1996): 21.

130 Gane, *Leviticus, Numbers,* 526.

131 Ibid.

132 See, e.g., John E. Hartley, *Leviticus* (WBC 4; Dallas: Word Books, 1992), 168; Martin Noth, *Das dritte Buch Mose: Leviticus* (ATD 6; Göttingen: Vandenhoeck & Ruprecht, 1966), 82; Diana Province, "An Examination of the Purity Laws regarding Childbirth and Menstruation in Leviticus" (M.A. thesis, Denver Conservative Baptist Seminary, 1995), 54.

133 Gary M. Beckman, *Hittite Birth Rituals: An Introduction* (SANE 1/4; Malibu, Calif.: Undena, 1978), 135, 137, 143, 219.

Why, then, the difference in time of purification between the births of male and female children? Many proposals have been made, but the suggestion of Jonathan Magonet is the most cogent in light of the biblical data.[134] Magonet points out that the Levitical legislation concerning sexually related ritual impurities carefully distinguishes between normal (physiological) and abnormal (pathological) uncleannesses, indicating the likelihood of a medical rationale behind the difference in the times of impurity. The key to Lev 12:1–8 is found in the phrase "blood purification." It is the blood that defiles. Medical experts point out, and midwives are today still instructed to observe, that vaginal bleeding frequently occurs on the part of the newborn girl as well as her mother. Hence, the phrase "blood purification" likely applies to the discharge of both mother and daughter, and thus the ritual uncleanness of two females must be accounted for. "Since this uncleanness has to be ritually dealt with and the baby cannot do so, the mother with whom the child was formerly united and from whom she has emerged, symbolically bears the uncleanness so that the period is doubled. Thus we are dealing with simple mathematical logic, two generators of uncleanness require two periods of purification."[135]

Carol Meyers points out regarding the "menstrual taboos" of Lev 12–15 that "because these sex-related taboos in the HB are linked with other physical con-

---

[134] Jonathan Magonet, "'But If It Is a Girl She Is Unclean for Twice Seven Days . . .': The Riddle of Leviticus 12:5," in *Reading Leviticus: A Conversation with Mary Douglas* (ed. John F. A. Sawyer; JSOTSup 227; Sheffield, Eng.: Sheffield Academic Press, 1996), 144–52.

Other proposals have included the following: R. K. Harrison suggests that the longer period of time for the female child is in view of the future expectation of the flow of menstrual blood in her case (*Leviticus: An Introduction and Commentary* [TOTC 3; Downers Grove, Ill.: InterVarsity, 1980], 135). Kaiser postulates that in Lev 12 the period of "uncleanness" for a male child is reduced to half the normal time of eighty days for a female child because the male undergoes a second "purification" ceremony at circumcision (*Toward Old Testament Ethics,* 206). David I. Macht points to some scientific evidence that the mother's physiological recovery time is longer after the birth of a girl than of a son ("A Scientific Appreciation of Leviticus 12:1–2," *JBL* 52 [1933]: 253–54). Mayer I. Gruber proposes that since the tendency in patriarchal times was to prefer male children and to wean daughters earlier than sons so that the woman might try again to have a son, Lev 12:1–5 "is meant to counter the notion that the first thought after the birth of a daughter is when to try for a son and that it is meant to provide an extra margin of time for mother and daughter to establish breast-feeding" ("Breast-Feeding Practices in Biblical Israel and in Old Babylonian Mesopotamia," ch. 4 in *The Motherhood of God and Other Studies* [South Florida Studies in the History of Judaism 57; Atlanta: Scholars Press, 1992], 78–79).

[135] Magonet, "'But If It Is a Girl.'" 152. Contrary to most modern translations, the word "her" (i.e., the mother's) does not appear in the phrase "Her time of blood purification" in the Hebrew text of Lev 12:4a. Magonet does not make this point, but it is important. The phrase has exactly the same pointing and pronunciation also in its successive occurrences in vv. 4b and 6 except for the added *mappîq* in the *hê,* indicating "her." In parallel with the first occurrence, which does not have this *mappîq,* I would argue for consistency in these succeeding occurrences comporting with the first usage (i.e., without the "her"), recognizing that the original Hebrew text was not vocalized. But even if the *mappîq* is to be retained in the latter occurrences, one could interpret "her" uncleanness to represent both the mother's and that of her female baby, which she symbolically bears.

ditions, some linked to males and some sexually neutral," this calls "for a re-assessment of menstruation and impurity." Her reassessment leads her to the conclusion that these laws of impurity in Lev 12–15 "are not related at all to the dynamics of gender relations."[136] Thus this law in no way indicates a lower valuation or status of woman.

Leviticus 27:1–8. Some have suggested that Lev 27:1–8 posits a lower social status or inherent value of women as compared with men, because the valuation prices set for the male is consistently greater than for the female. But note that the valuation is also greater for different ages of both males and females. From twenty to sixty years old, a male is valued at fifty shekels of silver and a female thirty shekels; from five to twenty years, a male is twenty shekels and a female is ten shekels; from one month to five years, a male is five shekels and a female is three shekels; and from sixty years and above, a male is fifteen shekels and a female is ten shekels.

Walter Kaiser correctly points out that "the basis for the difference in the valuation of men over against women in the special vows in this chapter is simply the value of their services in the tabernacle" and not "an explicit or even a tacit statement of intrinsic worth."[137] Roy Gane turns the argument against the high valuation of women on its head: "The fact that female valuations of work capacity are as high as they are, taking into account the female responsibility for bearing and raising children, indicates that women were an important part of Israelite labor force."[138] Gane also points out that this law does not take into account an individual's unique physical appearance or particular body strength; rather "the fixed valuations of Leviticus are egalitarian: Everyone of a certain gender and age is worth the same amount."[139]

Women who were vowed to divine service were valued less than their male counterparts for the probable reason that they were generally less physically

---

136 Meyers, *Discovering Eve*, 36–37. See also Kathleen O'Grady, "The Semantics of Taboo: Menstrual Prohibitions in the Hebrew Bible," in *Wholly Woman, Holy Blood: A Feminist Critique of Purity and Impurity* (ed. Kristin De Troyer; Studies in Antiquity and Christianity; Harrisburg, Penn.: Trinity Press International, 2003), 1–28. O'Grady examines Lev 15 and refutes the numerous Jewish and Christian readings of this chapter throughout history "that consign the menstrual prohibitions listed therein to punitive measures against women for the transgression of Eve" or that understand menstruation as "a sinful, unethical, or immoral infraction of the 'natural' order; that is, the menstrual prohibitions are viewed as a divine ordinance against the abnormal and deviant nature of women themselves. A careful reexamination of Lev 15, however, demonstrates that the passage in question does not situate menstruation within the realm of immorality or abnormality, and neither are the regulations detailed as punishments. Rather, the ritual observations of Lev 15 focus, as do the ritual observances for the *nazir* or holy person, on the practice of separation as a means for maintaining the sanctified order" (27–28).
137 Kaiser, *Toward Old Testament Ethics*, 206.
138 Gane, *Leviticus, Numbers*, 468.
139 Ibid., citing Philo, *On the Special Laws* 2.32–34.

strong than males.[140] For the same reason, older people and younger children were valued less than adults in their prime of life. It was ability to perform work in the sanctuary service, not a matter of social status, that was the basis of evaluation. The situation of an elderly man proves this point. An elderly male, who in Israelite society was given the highest social status for his wisdom and influence, was valued here at a relatively low level because his physical strength was not as great as others. Nothing in this text indicates a lower social status for women than men.

Numbers 30:4–17 (ET 30:3–16). Attention has been frequently called to Num 30:4–17 (ET 30:3–16), and the husband's (or father's) right to revoke legal commitments (vows) of his wife or daughter, as evidence of the inferior status of women, but Hurley has shown that "the husband's legal role rather than the women's inferiority or inability to perform forms the basis of his right to revoke her vow."[141] As pointed out above, it is clear that the leadership principle was operative in the homes of ancient Israel, with the husband/father the titular head of the household. But the servant leadership role was one of protective responsibility for those under one's care and not one of oppression or superiority. The husband's/father's right to revoke legal commitments of those in his household was a legal prophylactic mechanism to preserve weaker members of society—in particular, the wife or daughter—from consequences that would bring them harm. The purpose of such legislation was thus not oppression but protection of women. Furthermore, such legislation insured that the interests of the family took precedence over the interests of the cult.[142]

Deuteronomy 25:11–12. The NASB reading of this passage is representative of most modern versions: "If two men, a man and his countryman [lit. 'brother'], are struggling together, and the wife of one comes near to deliver her husband from the hand of the one who is striking him, and puts out her hand and seizes his genitals, then you shall cut off her hand; you shall not show pity." If this is the correct translation, then the punishment in this law constitutes the only biblical example of mandatory physical mutilation. In light of the fact that this law does not specify that the woman has actually crushed the man's testicles, as in a parallel ANE law (MAL A §8),[143] the penalty imposed upon the woman seems a cruel

---

[140] See Harrison, *Leviticus,* 235. Cf. Thomas Finley, "The Relationship of Woman and Man," in *Women and Men in Ministry: A Complementary Perspective* (ed. Robert L. Saucy and Judith K. TenElshof; Chicago: Moody, 2001), 66–67.

[141] Hurley, *Man and Woman,* 44. Hurley notes that "parallels to this sort of authority structure are found in many present-day business situations in which delegated authority is subject to review." He also calls attention to the fact that "when no longer under the authority of a husband, a woman was able to make vows and commitments which were legally binding (Num 30:9)."

[142] Bird, "Images of Women in the Old Testament," 56.

[143] "The Middle Assyrian Laws [Tablet A]," §8, translated by Martha Roth (*COS* 2.132:354; cf. *ANET* 181): "If a woman should crush a man's testicle during a quarrel, they shall cut off one of her fingers. And even if the physician should bandage it, but the second testicle then becomes infected (?) Along with it and becomes . . . , or if she should crush the second testicle during the quarrel—they shall gouge out both her [. . .]-s."

and unusual, that is, unjust punishment. Jerome Walsh recognizes the implications for assessing the biblical attitude toward women: "The uniqueness and extreme severity of Deut. 25:11–12 make it appear in Israelite legal corpora as a particularly egregarious example of violent misogyny."[144]

The discussion of procreation-related issues (ch. 11, below) will examine this law in detail; here we anticipate the conclusion reached in that discussion. I concur with Walsh's analysis of this passage, in which he shows, on philological and lexical grounds, that 25:12 should probably read, "you shall shave [the hair of] her groin" instead of "you shall cut off her hand." With this translation, the basic biblical legal principle of *lex talionis* (just retribution) is preserved, and it addresses the shamefulness of the woman's behavior: "By reducing the severity of the punishment from the permanency of amputation to the temporary humiliation of depilation, it allows the punishment to be seen as both talionic and as responding to the alleged 'shamefulness' of the woman's deed. She has humiliated a man publicly by an assault on his genitalia (presumably without serious injury to them); her punishment is public genital humiliation, similarly without permanent injury."[145] Although the woman is indeed punished, she is not treated any more harshly than her deed deserves. This law is not an example of "violent misogyny."

Woman as Chattel?—the Tenth Commandment and Other Passages. The tenth commandment (Exod 20:17; Deut 5:21) is often cited to demonstrate that a wife was considered a man's chattel, but John Otwell has pointed out that the wife is not here listed as property but as the first-named member of the household.[146] That the wife was not considered chattel or on the level of a slave is confirmed by the fact that an Israelite could sell slaves (Exod 21:2–11; Deut 15:12–18) but never his wife, even if she was acquired as a captive in war (Deut 21:14).

Some scholars have argued that the woman was the property of the husband because, at the time of the marriage, the bridegroom gave the father of the bride the "marriage present," or dowry—thus implying that the husband bought his wife much as he bought other property. The term *mōhar* (used only three times in the OT—Gen 34:12, Exod 22:16 [ET 22:17], and 1 Sam 18:25), however, which is often translated "brideprice" but is more accurately translated "marriage present"[147] probably represents the compensation to the father for the work the daughter would otherwise have contributed to her family,[148] and probably ultimately belonged to the wife, not the father.[149]

---

[144] Jerome T. Walsh, " 'You Shall Cut Off Her . . . Palm'? A Reexamination of Deuteronomy 25:11–12," *JSS* 49 (2004): 48.

[145] Ibid., 58.

[146] Otwell, *And Sarah Laughed,* 76. The parallel in Deut 5:21 makes the distinction unmistakable by placing the wife in a separate clause.

[147] De Vaux, *Ancient Israel,* 26–27; cf. Emmerson, "Women in Ancient Israel," 382–83.

[148] See Carol Meyers, "The Roots of Restriction: Women in Early Israel," *BA* 41 (1978): 98.

[149] De Vaux, *Ancient Israel,* 26–27. De Vaux argues that the father was entitled to the interest accruing to the "wedding present" but the capital itself reverted back to the daughter when her father died, or earlier if her husband died. Hence Leah and Rachel

Several passages in Exodus and Deuteronomy regarding women in situations of premarital or extramarital sex have been seen by some scholars as implying the status of the woman as merely the property of her father or husband, but as pointed out in discussion of these passages below, these do not present the wife/daughter as property of her husband/father but rather serve to protect both the woman and the integrity of the family structure.[150] In contrast to elsewhere in the ancient Near East, where vicarious punishment was carried out (e.g., a man was punished for a crime by having to give up his wife or daughter, or ox or slave) indicating that indeed wives and daughters were viewed as the property of men, in biblical law no such vicarious punishment is prescribed.[151] Likewise, in contrast to other ANE laws, where a husband is permitted to "whip his wife, pluck out her hair, mutilate her ears, or strike her, with impunity," no such permission is given to the husband in biblical law to punish his wife in any way.[152]

Far from being regarded as "chattel," according to the fifth commandment of the Decalogue and repeated commands throughout the pentateuchal codes, the wife/mother was to be given equal honor to the father within the family circle (Exod 20:12; 21:15, 17; Lev 20:9; Deut 21:18–21; 27:16).[153] There is "no discrimination in favor of father and against mother. The mother's authority over the son is as great in the law codes as is that of the father."[154] The same penalty is imposed upon the son for striking or cursing his father or his mother (Exod 21:15, 17). In fact, within a Near Eastern milieu in which the mother was often controlled by the son, Lev 19:3 surprisingly places the mother first instead of the father in the command: "You shall each revere your mother and father." This reversal from normal order clearly emphasizes the woman's right to equal filial respect along

---

refer to it as "the money given for us" (Gen 31:15). For further discussion of the major payments involved in the ANE (and biblical) marriage contract, see ch. 9, below.

[150] See the discussions of rape (ch. 12) and of premarital and extramarital sex (ch. 8) below.

[151] See, e.g., the critique of vicarious punishment in ancient Babylonia by Tetlow, *The Ancient Near East,* 71: "Vicarious punishment was tolerated in a society that regarded men as full persons and citizens and relegated wives and daughters to the category of the property of men." For instances of vicarious punishment in the Ancient Near East, see, e.g., "Laws of Hamurrabi," §§209–210, translated by Martha Roth (*COS* 2.131:348; cf. *ANET* 175): "If an *awīlu* strikes a woman of the *awīlu*-class and thereby causes her to miscarry her fetus, he shall weigh and deliver 10 shekels of silver for her fetus. If that woman should die, they shall kill his daughter." A similar example is in the Middle Assyrian Laws, where an assailant who beats up another woman is punished by having his own wife beaten up to the same extent ("The Middle Assyrian Laws [Tablet A]," §50, translated by Martha Roth [*COS* 2.132:359; cf. *ANET* 184]). Again in the Middle Assyrian Laws, the wife of a rapist could be gang-raped as punishment for her husband's crime (MAL A §55; *COS* 2.132:359; cf. *ANET* 185); for this and related laws, see ch. 12, below.

[152] MAL A §59 (*COS* 2.132:360; cf. *ANET* 185). These are "in addition to the punishments for [a man's wife] that are [written] on the tablet."

[153] See Bird, "Images of Women in the Old Testament," 55: "The ancient command to honor one's parents . . . recognizes the female as the equal to the male in her role as mother."

[154] Otwell, *And Sarah Laughed,* 100.

with her husband. Likewise, the fourth commandment of the Decalogue implicitly places the husband and wife on a par with each other: in Exod 20:10 the masculine "*you* shall not" includes the wife, since she is not mentioned in the list of the household dependents that follows.[155]

When one looks at the empirical evidence of family life as it emerges from the pentateuchal narratives, as summarized above,[156] it is difficult to escape the conclusions that have already been stated and illustrated earlier in this chapter, that the wife was treated by her husband in an egalitarian manner and that the wife exercised an equal power in the home and participated equally in the family decisions. Meyers has rightly concluded that the "functional non-hierarchy" in ancient Israel makes any question of exact legal or jural equality a moot point.[157]

An All-Male Priesthood. Perhaps the most often cited support of the lower status of women in the HB is the fact that the Israelite priesthood was confined only to men. For many liberal feminist writers, this is another indication of male oppression of women. For many evangelical Christian hierarchicalists, this is a crucial indication that women were (and still should be) barred from having a leadership role over men in the covenant community.

First of all, it is important to recognize that the priesthood was barred from most men in Israel as well. Only the males of a single family (Aaron) of a single tribe (Levi) of a single nation (Israel) qualified as priests of the Lord in OT times (Exod 28–29; Lev 8–9). On the other hand, God's original purpose for the priesthood on earth included both male and female. As already argued in section 1, both Adam and Eve had the same role as the Levites and priests in the original Eden sanctuary (Gen 2:15; cf. Num 3:7, 8, 38; 18:2–7), and God himself clothed them as priests (Gen 3:21). Furthermore, in a penetrating study of Exod 19, John Sailhamer has shown that it was God's original purpose for all Israel to be a "kingdom of priests" and for all of them to come up on the mountain to meet God at Sinai. It was only after the people refused to come up on the mountain because of their fearfulness and lack of faith that God introduced the specialized priesthood into the sanctuary equation—replacing the firstborn sons with the Levites and Levitical priesthood.[158] The NT church restored the original ideal, as once more the entire covenant community is a "royal priesthood" (1 Pet 2:4–5, 9).

Some have suggested that women were restricted from the priesthood in Israel because of their regular (monthly) ritual uncleanness, which would have

[155] Tikva Frymer-Kensky, "Deuteronomy," *WBC* 54, points out that the omission of the wife cannot mean she is to continue working, because the inclusion of daughter and maidservant in the fourth commandment indicates that the women stop from work. Rather, "the omission of a phrase 'and your wife' shows that the 'you' that the law addresses includes both women and men, each treated as a separate moral agent."

[156] See also the additional array of evidence in, e.g., Otwell, *And Sarah Laughed,* 67–112.

[157] Meyers, *Discovering Eve,* 44–45.

[158] John Sailhamer, *The Pentateuch as Narrative: A Biblical-Theological Commentary* (Grand Rapids: Zondervan, 1992), 51–59.

prevented their serving in the sanctuary for up to one-fourth of their adult lives; others suggest that the amount of upper-body strength required to lift the sacrificed carcasses or serve as military "guards" of the sanctuary[159] would have made it very difficult for women to serve in the professional capacity as priests.[160] Still another suggestion is that "since women's place in society is determined by their place within the family, women are not normally free to operate for extended periods outside the home."[161] While these and other rationales may have contributed to the exclusion of women from the priesthood in Israel, they do not seem to constitute the main reason.

As pointed out in chapter 3, above, the male priesthood in Israel was in stark contrast to the other ANE cultures where the cultic personnel included priestesses. "Since other peoples in the ancient Near East worshiped in cults which used priestesses, their absence in the Yahwism of ancient Israel must have been deliberate."[162] Yahweh's institution of a male priesthood in Israel—in the immediate aftermath of the worship of the golden calf, linked to Egyptian/Canaanite fertility cults—seems to have constituted a strong polemic against the religions of surrounding nations, which included goddess worship and fertility cult rituals. Since a primary function of the priestesses in the ancient Near East during the last half of the second millennium and in the first millennium was to serve as a "wife of the god," such a function for a woman in the religion of Yahweh was

---

[159] See Roy Gane, *God's Faulty Heroes* (Hagerstown, Md.: Review and Herald, 1996), 50, who interprets Num 3:38 and 18:7 as indicating that "priests had a kind of military function as guards of the sanctuary" and suggests this as at least a partial rationale for God's setting up of an all-male priesthood.

[160] For a summary of these and other suggested rationales, see Mary Hayter, *The New Eve in Christ: The Use and Abuse of the Bible in the Debate about Women in the Church* (Grand Rapids: Eerdmans, 1987), 60–79. Other proposed reasons include the allegedly lower social status of women than men in Israel, which would have meant they lacked the authority and prestige to be priests. But Marsman, *Women in Ugarit and Israel,* passim, demonstrates that Israelite women had no lower social status than in neighboring Ugarit and other ANE societies, where there were female priests. Another reason is proposed by Marsman, who, building upon a reconstruction of the history of Israel with "a professionalization of the priesthood during the monarchic period" that was not present previously, speculates, "Whereas women in earlier times may have fulfilled a priestly role, during the monarchic period such a role seems to have been eliminated" (p. 537). But such hypothetical reconstruction of Israel's history assumes that the regulations regarding the delimitation of the priesthood came later than described in the canonical form of the text, and this cannot be demonstrated to represent the actual course of history. Such a diachronic reconstruction is not explored in this canonical treatment of the biblical theology of sexuality.

[161] Phyllis Bird, "The Place of Women in the Israelite Cultus," in *Ancient Israelite Religion: Essays in Honor of Frank Moore Cross* (ed. Patrick D. Miller Jr., Paul D. Hanson, and S. Dean McBride; Philadelphia: Fortress, 1987), 406. The exception would be women without families (widows, virgins, or women separated from family by a vow) (p. 407). Another exception, not mentioned by Bird, is the upper class of women who had servants to perform the household tasks, and thus to whom the maternal restrictions did not apply.

[162] Otwell, *And Sarah Laughed,* 155.

out of the question.[163] The exclusion of women in the Israelite priesthood helped to prevent syncretistic contamination of Israel's cultus with the introduction of the divinization of sex and sexual immorality, which was so deeply imbedded in Canaanite Baal/Asherah worship.

Thus the restriction of the priesthood to males from the house of Aaron in no way reveals a denigration of women's status and likewise in no way implies that women are barred from leadership (teaching/administrative) roles over men in the covenant community. On the basis of Deut 33:8–10, Jacques Doukhan points to three essential duties of the Levitical priesthood: (1) didactic and administrative leadership functions (judging, teaching), (2) prophetic functions (oracular techniques especially with the Urim and Thummim to determine the future or the will of the Lord), and (3) cultic functions. He then goes on to show that two of the three functions of the priest, the prophetic and the (teaching/administrative) leadership, were allowed women (witness the OT women who functioned as prophet, teacher, and judge).[164] As pointed out above, it was only the cultic function that was barred to women, probably because of the polemical concerns directed against the ANE priestesses' involvement in the divinization of sex.[165]

The High Status of Women in Religious and Civil Affairs

Not only within the family circle but also in religious and civil affairs, the status of woman in Israel was high. Aside from serving as priests—and women "had

---

[163] As mentioned in ch. 3, above, Marsman, *Women in Ugarit and Israel,* 544–45, shows that although in Egypt and Mesopotamia numerous women were functioning in the role of priestess in the third and in the first half of the second millennium B.C.E., women to a large extent had disappeared from the priesthood by the middle of the second millennium and only women of high birth remained active in cultic functions as priestesses during the period matching the period of Israelite history. These women "had a kind of marital relationship with the main deity. They were a wife of the god, whether the interpretation of this function was sexual or not, that is, whether their 'sacred' marriage was a carnally or a symbolically performed rite" (p. 545).

[164] Jacques B. Doukhan, "Women Priests in Israel: A Case for Their Absence," in *Women in Ministry: Biblical and Historical Perspectives* (ed. Nancy Vyhmeister; Berrien Springs, Mich.: Andrews University Press, 1998), 30–33.

[165] Doukhan offers another rationale beyond the polemic concerns against the fertility cults; he suggests that it "may well reflect a Hebrew attitude toward women, who were, from Eve on, traditionally associated with the giving of life [footnote: See Gen 3:20]. And since the woman stands for life, she should be exempt from the act of sacrificing that stands for death. . . . Because of her physiological nature as a provider of life, the woman could not be involved in the cultic act of taking life implied in the ritual of sacrifice" (ibid., 33–34). For Doukhan, this is the most decisive factor in preventing women from becoming priests. The priests were typological pointers to the Messiah, who was to come as the true priest, and women could not function in that typological role—not because of something they lacked but because of something positive they possessed, i.e., "the sign of life and promise," which was incongruent with the slaughter of sacrifices (p. 38). Doukhan points to the occasions in the garden of Eden and in the redeemed community (Rev 1:6; 5:10) when both men and women are priests and notes, "These contexts are both free

reserved to them their own unique and crucial kind of intimacy with God: the bearing of children"—"woman's status in the cult was equal to that of the man."[166]

Women participated in the yearly festivals (Deut 5:14; 16:10–11; 29:9–12 [ET 29:10–13]; 31:12), sharing in the rejoicing, singing, and prayers (Deut 12:18; cf. 1 Sam 2:1–16) and joining in the sacrificial meals (Deut 12:18), although they were also free to remain home and attend to the demands of childbearing as necessary.[167] They brought sacrifices and ate the part returned (Num 18:18). No legislation prohibits women from slaughtering the sacrifices,[168] and some legislation seems to mandate the participation of the woman in bringing sacrifices (see esp. Num 5:6, 8).[169] They participated in performing the rituals connected with ritual cleansing, absolution, and so on (Lev 12:1–8; 13:29–39; 15:19–29). According to

from the threat of ancient Near Eastern cults and from the ceremonial slaughter of sacrifices" (39). As intriguing as this hypothesis is, its Achilles heel is that there is no prohibition against women slaughtering the animal sacrifices in the OT legislation (Doukhan's assertion that no sacrifice by a woman is recorded is an argument from silence and may in fact find exception in 1 Sam 1:25), and the setting of God's conferral of the priestly role upon both Adam and Eve in Eden occurs not only in a pre-fall setting before sin (Gen 2:15) but also after the fall (Gen 3:21), in a context not free from the ceremonial slaughter of sacrifices (see ch. 2, above, for further discussion).

[166] Otwell, *And Sarah Laughed,* 178. Bird samples (with bibliography) the numerous studies in the first half of the twentieth century that maintained (contra Wellhausen's claim that women were disenfranchised in the religious realm in Israel) that "in the religious, if not the political sphere, women were full and equal members, excluded only from the priesthood, from which most males were also excluded." Bird notes that "in the middle decades of this century egalitarian interpretation was the norm." Since that time, feminist critics have exposed what they consider the "androcentric nature of formally neutral or inclusive formulations" (Bird, "Women in the Ancient Mediterranean World," 42–43). Despite feminist concerns over the androcentric perspectives of biblical writers, however, Carol Meyers can still affirm that "late twentieth century scholarship has succeeded in establishing that, in many ways, women were not much more disadvantaged in their participation in *communal* religious activities than were non-priestly males" ("From Household to House of Yahweh: Women's Religious Culture in Ancient Israel," in *Congress Volume: Basel, 2001* [ed. André Lemaire; VTSup 92; Leiden: E. J. Brill, 2002], 279).

[167] Emmerson, "Women in Ancient Israel," 378, points out how often commentators remark that only the male members of Israel were required to attend the feasts and then insightfully comments, "But difference of obligation does not necessarily imply inequality, and in this case probably arose from practical considerations attendant on the birth and care of children."

[168] Contra Bird, "The Place of Women," 408: "Animal slaughter and sacrifice, as an action of the worshiper, was reserved to males." Also contra Doukhan, "Women Priests in Israel," 33–34. For a possible example of a woman slaughtering and offering her sacrifice, see the experience of Hannah (1 Sam 1:25).

[169] Numbers 5:6 reads, "When a man or a woman wrongs another . . ." Crüsemann, *The Torah,* 251–52, comments, "The text explicitly regulates how property offenses are to be handled (restitution plus a fifth of the value as punitive damage), in addition to which a ram is to be offered to God for atonement (v. 8). There can be no doubt that in parallel offenses women were also to bring such a sacrifice. For this reason, we can be sure that women might also be included in the broad range of priestly sacrificial texts where only men are mentioned as making sacrifice. Numbers 5:6, 8 proves that according to priestly sacrificial theology, women were capable of sacrificing."

the pentateuchal record, women at least on one occasion officiated in circumcision (Exod 4:24–26), and they regularly "ministered" (ṣābāʾ) in an official capacity at the door of the sanctuary (Exod 38:8; cf. 1 Sam 2:22).[170] The office of prophetess is attested with Miriam, who also served as a cult singer/musician/leader (Exod 15:20–21; Num 12:1–8).[171] Both males and females could initiate binding religious obligations on their own initiative (Num 6; 30:4–16 [ET 30:3–15]; cf. 1 Sam 1:11, 24–28). Women, as well as men, could participate in the extraordinary consecration of the Nazirite vow (Num 6:2–21). The passage regarding the Nazirite vow is particularly illuminating because it begins with a reference to "either men or women" but in the succeeding verses only the masculine forms appear, indicating that such masculine language is intended in a gender-inclusive sense.[172] In a word, then, both men and woman had an equal standing in God's sight in matters of spiritual privilege and accountability.

Conclusion

The biblical evidence does not support a lowered and oppressed status for women in the pentateuchal legislation and accompanying narratives. Indeed there is a leadership principle operating in the ancient Israelite family consistent with the divine prescription in Gen 3:16: the husband/father is the servant leader of his household, taking responsibility to care and provide for his wife and other family members. But this does not imply that the husband is superior to his wife or that women are oppressed. There is indeed legislation that today one might label "discriminatory" against women, but such legislation, seen in its historical/canonical context, appears to be motivated by the need to provide protection for the weaker and more vulnerable members of society.[173] The "functional

---

[170] Although the exact nature of this "service" remains obscure, Childs notes that the word ṣābāʾ denotes organized service, such as that of the professional Levites (*The Book of Exodus*, 636). Cf. the use of the same technical term regarding Levitical service in the sanctuary (e.g., Num 4:23, 30, 35, 39, 43; 8:24–25). See also Bird, "The Place of Women in the Israelite Cultus," 406, 419; and Janet S. Everhart, "Serving Women and Their Mirrors: A Feminist Reading of Exodus 38:8b," *CBQ* 66 (2004): 44–54. E. L. Greenstein hypothesizes that Exod 38:8 is "but a remnant of an earlier tale" and that the women were forced to give up their mirrors because "there had been some sort of fornication between them and some of the priests" ("Recovering 'the Women Who Served at the Entrance,'" in *Studies in Historical Geography and Biblical Historiography: Presented to Zechariah Kallai* [ed. Gershon Galil and Moshe Weinfeld; VTSup 81; Boston: E. J. Brill, 2000], 165–73, quotes at 168, 173; such speculation goes beyond this final-form analysis of the received text.

[171] See the discussion of Miriam below; cf. the women singers of Ezra 2:65 and Neh 7:67 and the prophetesses Deborah (Judg 4:4), Huldah (2 Chr 31:22; 2 Kgs 22:14), and Isaiah's wife (Isa 8:3)—all to be discussed in later sections of this book.

[172] See also Deut 29:17–19 (ET 29:18–20), where a similar phenomenon appears, with women included in v. 17 (ET 18) but only the masculine grammatical forms in vv. 18–19 (ET 19–20).

[173] "Though there were de facto discriminatory practices against women (exclusion from the priesthood, purity laws, dissolution of 'mixed marriages'), these were not given theological basis in the Old Testament" (Gerstenberger, *Yahweh the Patriarch*, 153).

nonhierarchy" in Israelite gender relations "make[s] the notion of legal or jural equality a moot point."[174] Although women are not often seen in positions of public leadership over men, the examples that do exist are not presented as something unusual or unacceptable. The fact that some public activities—most notably the priesthood—are closed to women is not to be equated with the male oppression of females.[175]

The High Valuation of Women in the Prophets/Writings

The Former Prophets

Throughout the Former Prophets, from Joshua to Kings, the overall canonical structure of these books dramatically highlights the valuation of women in a remarkable way: "Women appear as oracles to announce each stage in the history of Israel. Rahab and Deborah bracket the conquest of Canaan; Hannah and the witch of Endor surround the kingship of Saul; Abigail and Huldah support the Davidic monarchy. . . . The choice of women as the voice of God's decisions makes a powerful statement about how the marginalized can be chosen to convey the word."[176]

Women in Joshua. The book of Joshua highlights the valuation of the harlot Rahab in a remarkable way.[177] The Bible contains several spy stories (Num 13;

Gerstenberger (pp. 153–54) continues by claiming that such theological basis is provided in the NT by appeal to the order of creation, but see the afterword, below, for a rejection of such a claim.

[174] Meyers, *Discovering Eve*, 44–45. After the rise of the monarchy, Meyers argues, the centralized sociopolitical structures brought about an institutionalized suppression of both patriarchy and of women. The last part of this chapter, below, looks at the biblical evidence for this development.

[175] Ibid., 33: "Identifying certain public spheres of activity in ancient Israel as closed to women, or as only exceptionally occupied by them, cannot be equated with the patriarchal control observed in more recent societies that exclude women from the public sphere." Cf. Emmerson, "Women in Ancient Israel," 381: "The legal dependence of women, despite the restrictive inequalities it inevitably imposed, is not, however, to be confused with personal oppression."

[176] Frymer-Kensky, *Reading the Women of the Bible,* xix. For a comprehensive bibliography of studies dealing with women of the Former Prophets, see esp. Bellis, *Helpmates, Harlots, and Heroes,* 136–39 (Joshua and Judges), 157–59 (1 and 2 Samuel), and 176 (1 and 2 Kings). The discussion here includes parallel passages in Chronicles from the Writings.

[177] See esp. Jon L. Berquist, "Expectations and Repeated Climax in the Rahab Story" (paper presented at the annual meeting of the AAR/SBL, San Francisco, November 23, 1992), 1–10; idem, *Controlling Corporeality: The Body and the Household in Ancient Israel* (New York: Rutgers University Press, 2002), 99–102; idem, *Reclaiming Her Story,* 83–89; Phyllis A. Bird, "The Harlot as Heroine: Narrative Art and Social Presupposition in Three Old Testament Texts," *Semeia* 46 (1989): 119–39; repr. in *Missing Persons and Mistaken*

Josh 2; Judg 18). The account in Josh 2 has many allusions to the narrative of the twelve spies in Num 13; the essential elements of the spy story in Num 13 are found in Josh 2.[178] Briefly, in Num 13 the spies are commissioned, enter the land, locate an item of value, return to the people, present the item of value, report their findings, and make a decision to act on the basis of the report. Joshua 2 records all of these elements except, it seems, for two. The spies at Jericho apparently find nothing of value in their reconnaissance mission that they can present upon their return to the people. Or do they? Closer inspection of the story reveals that these elements are not missing after all. The two spies do find an item of value—that item is Rahab herself. Though they do not bring her back immediately, Rahab is brought to the people (Josh 6) before the story is over, into the midst of Israel, is valued and embraced by the covenant community, and ultimately (in the Christian understanding) becomes one of the progenitors of the Messiah.

The Joshua narrative contains a sevenfold valuation of Rahab.[179] First, *Rahab is valued by God for who she is,* even though a "diamond in the rough"—a prostitute not hesitant to tell a lie when she felt it was necessary. Although God does not condone her actions, God nonetheless values her personhood, meeting her where she is. Second, *she is valued as a treasured testimony to the mercy of God upon all humanity, even the so-called heathen.* Of the inhabitants of Canaan who had opportunity to learn the truth about Yahweh, Rahab accepted this truth. Indeed "Rahab makes one of the most impassioned and logical statements of any kind throughout the book of Joshua (vv. 9–13). The spies fade into the woodwork of the brothel wall while Rahab lectures them about the faith in God that enables victories."[180] A detailed analysis of the remarkable parallels between her words and Yahweh's promises of victory to Israel shows that "her words are important because they report the fulfillment of the promises and declaration of YHWH. . . . The words and actions of Rahab move her from the ash heap, as it were, to sit with princes (Ps 113:7, 8)."[181]

Identities: Women and Gender in Ancient Israel (OBT; Minneapolis: Fortress, 1997), 197–218; Richard M. Davidson, *In the Footsteps of Joshua* (Hagerstown, Md.: Review and Herald, 1995), 48–49; Tikva Frymer-Kensky, "Reading Rahab," in *Tehillah le-Moshe: Biblical and Judaic Studies in Honor of Moshe Greenberg* (ed. Mordechai Cogan, Barry Eichler, and Jeffrey Tigay; Winona Lake, Ind.: Eisenbrauns, 1997), 57–67; idem, *Reading the Women of the Bible,* 34–44; Berel Dov Lerner, "Rahab the Harlot and Other Philosophers of Religion," *JBQ* 28 (2000): 52–55; and David Merling, "Rahab: The Woman Who Fulfilled the Words of YHWH," *AUSS* 41, no. 1 (2002): 31–44.

[178] Davidson, *In the Footsteps of Joshua,* 48–49, outlines these, building particularly on the study of Berquist, "Expectations," passim.

[179] For further elaboration, see Davidson, *In the Footsteps of Joshua,* 47–53.

[180] Berquist, "Expectations," 3.

[181] Merling, "Rahab," 37, 43. Cf. Lerner, "Rahab the Harlot," 52–55, who argues, "Among biblical characters, Rahab is uniquely qualified to demonstrate the renown of God's glory. God's miraculous interventions in human affairs are so universally famous that even a Canaanite prostitute speaks the language of Israelite religion. . . . Like Joshua, Rahab does not let the words of the Torah cease from her mouth" (pp. 52–53). Lerner

Third, *Rahab is valued for her awesome courage.* She is willing to stand alone against the whole surrounding culture; in the midst of the prevailing Canaanite religion, she accepts a new God, a Deity totally opposed to the moon god of her city and all the other fertility gods of her land. She well knew that if the king of Jericho found out that she had helped the spies, she and her family would have been executed as traitors, yet she was willing to take the terrible risk to rescue the spies.

Fourth, *Rahab is valued for her faith.* The heart of the Rahab narrative within the spy story is this—Rahab believed. The author of Hebrews highlights her faith in the NT "Hall of Fame" (Heb 11:31). James chooses only two OT figures to illustrate the nature of active faith—Abraham the "friend of God" (Jas 2:21–24) and "Rahab the prostitute" (2:25).

Fifth, *Rahab is valued as an agent of salvation.* She saves the Israelite spies by hiding them, and her speech to the spies is in fact an oracle of salvation for all Israel: "I know that the LORD has given you the land" (Josh 2:9). She is also an agent of salvation for her whole family as she asks the Israelites to show steadfast love (*ḥesed*) to all her next of kin (2:12). The narrative especially highlights the redemptive nature of Rahab's actions in the spies' many allusions to the redemptive event of Passover as they stipulate what Rahab should do. David Madvig points to the "striking similarities to the Passover: compare the scarlet cord with the sprinkled blood and the requirement that Rahab's family remain in the house with the command that the Passover be eaten in family units and that no one was to leave the house (Exod 12:21–23)." Beyond these thematic links, there is also terminological linkage: both narratives point to a "sign" (*ʾôt* [Exod 12:13; Josh 2:12]), both use almost identical language in the prohibition not to the leave the house (compare Exod 12:22 with Josh 2:19), and both emphasize the word "blood" (Exod 12:13; Josh 2:19).[182] The intriguing word for the scarlet "cord" (*tiqwâ*) in the Rahab narrative (Josh 2:18) means "hope" in every other of its thirty-one occurrences in the HB; there seems to be an intentional play on words, in which the scarlet cord hung by Rahab signifies the source of redemptive hope for the spies, all of Israel, and also for Rahab and her household. By the connections with "hope" and the Passover, there also seems to be ultimately a typological prefiguration of the messianic hope, the Lamb of God.

Sixth, *Rahab is valued as an integral part of Israel's community,* as after the fall of Jericho she is brought to dwell "into the midst" (*běqereb*) of Israel. Berquist points out that this term "refers to inward parts, or even the womb. Rahab the prostitute now enters the womb of Israel and the story reaches its climax. The

points out that Rahab's speech (Josh 2:9–11) "is almost an exact quotation from a speech of Moses' that appears in Deuteronomy, but lacks its final monotheistic clause: *The Lord alone is in heaven above and on earth below; there is no other* (Deut 4:39)" (53). Frymer-Kensky, *Reading the Women of the Bible,* 37, points out that her speech also "contains all the essential ingredients of the classic Deuteronomic form of covenants," including preamble, prologue, stipulations, sanctions, oath, and physical sign. "By all these official treaty elements, the narrator conveys the standard nature of the arrangement by which Rahab allies herself with Israel" (p. 38).

[182] Donald Madvig, "Joshua," *EBC* 3:263.

community enfolds Rahab."[183] The spies have finally brought their item of value from the spy mission. Seventh, for Christians, *Rahab is valued as ancestor of Christ.* A comparison of several biblical passages shows that Rahab was the great-great-grandmother of David and thus a progenitor of the Messiah.[184] She is one of five women included in Matthew's genealogy of Jesus. What an affirmation of a harlot turned heroine of faith!

As Rahab appears at the beginning of Joshua, another woman of stellar qualities appears toward the end of the book (Josh 15:16–19). The brief account of Achsah, daughter of Caleb, is repeated in almost the same words at the beginning of Judges. Scholarly attention is focused on the Judges setting of this story.

Women in Judges. The author of Judges gives particular evidence of his high view of the value and dignity of women.[185] The first female figure encountered in the book, Achsah, daughter of Caleb (Judg 1:12–15), "serves as a role model of propriety for later portrayals of women."[186] Even though she appears only in a brief episode, enough narrative is given to characterize Achsah as resourceful and independent in thinking. Her capability for initiating and completing actions is revealed in her persuasion of her husband to ask Caleb for land and in her own tactful petition for "a present"—the water source to accompany the land. Her play on words (v. 15) between "present" (*běrākâ*) and a word with the same consonants meaning "pool, pond" (*běrēkâ*) reveals a literary sensitivity as well as tactful resourcefulness. Lillian Klein points out the play on words in the phrase "as she came" (lit. "in her coming," Judg 1:14, with the root *bwʾ*)—which can express both coming near and sexual intercourse and here seems to refer "both to her coming to her bridegroom and to sexual intercourse. The former connotation informs the reader that Achsah goes to her husband's family in the preferred patrilocal marriage. . . . A second implication of the phrase 'as she came' suggests that Achsah waited until the marriage was consummated to express her wishes;

---

[183] Berquist, "Expectations," 4–5.

[184] Num 7:12; Ruth 4:18–22; 1 Chr 2:11–12; Matt 1:1, 5–6. Rahab married Salmon, son of Nahshon, one of the prominent princes of Judah, and she gave birth to Boaz, great-grandfather of David.

[185] For an overview and characterization (from a feminist perspective) of the nineteen individual and collective female figures in Judges, see esp. Susan Ackerman, *Warrior, Dancer, Seductress, Queen: Women in Judges and Biblical Israel* (New York: Doubleday, 1998); Lillian R. Klein, "A Spectrum of Female Characters in the Book of Judges" and "The Book of Judges: Paradigm and Deviation in Images of Women," in *A Feminist Companion to Judges* (ed. Athalya Brenner; FCB 4; Sheffield, Eng.: Sheffield Academic Press, 1993), 24–33 and 55–71 respectively; idem, *From Deborah to Esther,* 9–40.

[186] Klein, "A Spectrum," 25; cf. idem, "The Book of Judges," 55–60; and idem, *From Deborah to Esther,* 10, 18–23. As a feminist, Klein, however, portrays this ideal model as the "patriarchal ideal of womanhood" (ibid., 10), which is largely rejected by the feminist project. For specific focus upon the Achsah story, see idem, "Achsah: What Price This Prize?" in *Judges* (ed. Athalya Brenner; FCB² 4; Sheffield, Eng.: Sheffield Academic Press, 1999), 18–26; Corinne Lanoir, *Femmes fatales, filles rebelles: Figures féminines dans le livre des Juges* (Sciences Bibliques; Geneva: Labor et Fides, 2005), 119–47; Heidi M. Szpek, "Achsah's Story: A Metaphor for Societal Transition," *AUSS* 40 (2002): 245–56.

more pointedly, she waited until after sexual intercourse to make her wishes known."[187] Thus Achsah "is not depicted as a hesitant, timid little bride in awe of her warrior husband; she is a resourceful and determined woman who knows what she wants and how to realize her objectives in her culture."[188] Roy Gane summarizes the thrust of this narrative: "Achsah assumes the leading role and her men follow."[189] Though respecting her husband, Achsah is not afraid to "urge" (or incite/allure/entice [sût]) him to speak to her father (1:14). The Hebrew also makes clear Achsah's continuing honoring of her father, assuming a posture of respect (1:15), and yet adducing him to her request through gentle, tactful supplication and logic.

If Achsah sets the stage for a model of propriety in Judges, Deborah is set on center stage to reveal the high valuation of women in the book.[190] It cannot be overemphasized that the only judge described in any detail without mentioning serious character flaws (or pointing up how the judge's life "went sour") was a woman.[191] And "the only judge who combines all forms of leadership possible—religious, military, juridical, and poetical—is a woman."[192] That woman, Deborah, is introduced as "wife of Lappidoth"—ʾēšet lappîdôt, which more likely should be translated "woman of torches/lightning" or "woman of spirit."[193] Male

---

[187] Klein, "The Book of Judges," 56–57.

[188] Ibid., 57.

[189] Gane, God's Faulty Heroes, 18.

[190] See esp. Charme E. Robarts, "Deborah—Judge, Prophetess, Military Leader, and Mother in Israel," in Essays on Women in Earliest Christianity (ed. Carroll D. Osburn; 2 vols.; Joplin, Mo.: College Press, 1995), 2:69–86.

[191] "Among the major judges, she escapes unscathed as a spiritual leader" (ibid., 76). See also Daniel I. Block, "Why Deborah's Different," BR 17, no. 3 (2001): 40, who makes the same point: "Not only was she the sole woman in this man's world, with exception of Othniel she was also the only 'judge' with a stainless personal reputation."

[192] Mieke Bal, Death and Dissymmetry: The Politics of Coherence in the Book of Judges (Chicago: University of Chicago Press, 1988), 209.

[193] Frymer-Kensky, Reading the Women of the Bible, 46, points out that this "is a strange-sounding name for a man and, moreover, does not have the standard patronymic 'son of.'" The Hebrew word lappîd literally means "torch" or "lightning" and here (Judg 4:4) in the feminine plural may be a description of the character quality of the woman, much like the phrase ʾēšet-ḥayil, "capable wife" (lit. "woman of strength/valor"), in Prov 31:10. This is the view of a number of scholars. See, e.g., Bal, Death and Dissymmetry, 208–9; Dana Nolan Fewell and David M. Gunn, "Controlling Perspectives: Women, Men, and the Authority of Violence in Judges 4–5," JAAR 58, no. 3 (1990): 391; and the NEB note "fiery woman." Weighty evidence for preferring this interpretation (instead of taking this as the name of her husband) is set forth by Klaas Spronk, "Deborah, a Prophetess: The Meaning and Background of Judges 4:4–5," in The Elusive Prophet: The Prophet as a Historical Person, Literary Character, and Anonymous Artist (ed. Johannes C. DeMoor; OtSt 45; Leiden: E. J. Brill, 2001), 239–40. Spronk points out that the plural of lappîd ("torch") in the MT is normally the masculine lappîdîm, not the feminine lappîdôt. Indeed he could have stated it even more strongly: elsewhere in the HB the plural of lappîd is always masculine. (See Exod 20:18; Judg 7:16, 20; 15:4–5; Ezek 1:13; Nah 2:5 [ET 2:4]; Job 41:11 [ET 41:19]; Dan 10:6. The one alleged exception is Nah 2:4 [ET 2:3], where some scholars conjecture that the word pĕlādôt in the MT should read lappîdôt; the fact, however, that the word lappîdîm with the masculine plural ending appears in the very next verse argues

commentators of the past have often had a difficult time with Deborah. Some have refused to recognize her as a true judge, suggesting that Barak was the real judge; others focus on the battle as the real subject of the narrative and ignore Deborah's leadership as a woman; still others argue that she is only an exception, chosen by God as judge because God could not find a fit man available.[194] Feminist interpreters of the Deborah narrative have also mainly missed the mark, often seeing this as a text of empowerment for women and of subversion of patriarchal oppression.[195] The majority of critical scholars see the narrative of Judg 4 in contradiction with the ancient poem of Judg 5 and posit different redactional sources separated by a long interval of time.[196] Christian evangelical women writers who think the Bible forbids women from occupying leadership positions over men make an effort to show that Deborah deferred to men: she was "not an abrasive or pushy woman" but rather "gave the man [Barak] the opportunity to take the honor of leading the nation to victory all for himself, but was not afraid or hesitant to help him in the leadership role when asked to do so."[197]

---

against the same word appearing in the previous verse with a feminine ending). Spronk suggests that in Judg 4:4 the phrase ʾiššâ něbîʾâ, literally "woman prophet," is in poetic parallelism with the following phrase, ʾēšet lappîdôt, literally "woman of lightning," and the feminine ending of lappîdôt "may be due to the influence of the parallel word" něbîʾâ (p. 239). Since lappîdôt means "lightning" and also the name Barak means "lightning," Spronk postulates that such play on words "denotes Deborah as the counterpart of Barak" or, alternatively, that the name lappîdôt "can be regarded as symbolic for her relation with God, as can be derived from the fact that this word is mentioned in descriptions of the theophany in Gen. 15:17; Exod. 20:18 and Ezek. 1:13" (240). Though favoring the interpretation that the term lappîdôt is used symbolically/metaphorically (to refer to Deborah's character as a "woman of spirit"), I cannot completely rule out the possibility that this word constitutes the name of her husband. Even if married, Deborah does not receive her status in the narrative by virtue of her husband; he is heard of no more in the story.

[194] For a survey of modern commentaries that downplay the role of Deborah in the narrative, see, e.g., Rachel C. Rasmussen, "Deborah the Woman Warrior," in Anti-covenant: Counter-reading Women's Lives in the Hebrew Bible (ed. Mieke Bal; Sheffield, Eng.: Almond, 1989), 79–83; Jo Ann Hackett, "In the Days of Jael: Reclaiming the History of Women in Ancient Israel," in Immaculate and Powerful: The Female in Sacred Image and Social Reality (ed. Clarissa W. Atkinson, Constance H. Buchanan, and Margaret R. Miles; Boston: Beacon, 1985), 27–28; and Gale A. Yee, "By the Hand of a Woman: The Metaphor of the Woman Warrior in Judges 4," Semeia 61 (1993): 110, 117–21. Cf. Herbert M. Wolf, "Judges," EBC 3:404: "Her prominence implies a lack of qualified and willing men."

[195] Others suggest a scenario arising out of a socially dysfunctional society, with Deborah a liminal figure (neither male nor female as customarily defined) on the margins of society (Yee, "By the Hand of a Woman," 99–126); still others deplore a story attempting to justify violence (Fewell and Gunn, "Controlling Perspectives," 389–410). For a convenient survey of these and other major feminist views, see esp. Bellis, Helpmates, Harlots, and Heroes, 115–19.

[196] For a summary of these redaction-critical reconstructions, see esp. Stephen W. Hanselman, "Narrative Theory, Ideology, and Transformation in Judges 4," in Anti-covenant: Counter-reading Women's Lives in the Hebrew Bible (ed. Mieke Bal; Sheffield, Eng.: Almond, 1989), 104–5.

[197] Julia Staton, What the Bible Says about Women (Joplin, Mo.: College Press, 1980), 264. See also Sara Buswell, The Challenge of Old Testament Women (2 vols.; Grand Rapids: Baker, 1987), 1:120.

In contrast to all these misreadings, I find the text straightforward, with the poetry highlighting and amplifying the narrative. In both narrative and poetry, Deborah is unequivocally presented as one of the most powerful woman leaders in the Bible, and she unequivocally exercises authoritative functions over men in Israel. She is the recognized political leader of the nation, "one of Israel's chief executive officers."[198] She is the military leader on an equal footing with the male general Barak.[199] Indeed, "the plot of Judges 4 signals the conceptuality of Deborah's predominant status and superior role in comparison with Barak. . . . Deborah is the initiator and Barak the reluctant follower. Deborah is the strategist and Barak the executor. Against this background the story develops with the subtle implication that the real heroic honor goes to the women, Deborah and Jael, as opposed to the men, Barak and Sisera."[200]

In the narrative of Judg 4 and the song that follows in Judg 5, "the reader finds an unusual and unexpected concept of the status of women, one that ironically surpasses that of men."[201] At the same time, there is compositional evidence of "teamwork and mutuality" between Deborah and Barak in the narrative and accompanying poem: "Both leaders reveal their willingness to be open to and cooperate with each other. Together they build a team with mutual respect, communication, and correction. The only peculiarity is that in spite of the reciprocal relationship, Barak remains a follower."[202] Thus the texts ultimately imply "the concept of balance toward equality by means of the radical paradigm shift and role reversal between Deborah and Barak on the one hand, and through compositional effort to mention the two names together on the other."[203]

---

[198] Hackett, "In the Days of Jael," 22.

[199] Although, as Gane rightly observes, she was not a military general, for a very practical reason: "Generals were combat soldiers who led their armies into battles. Physical size and upper body strength, the main natural advantages possessed by males, were essential for effectiveness in ancient combat. Therefore, women were not used as soldiers and, consequently, they could not be military commanders" (*God's Faulty Heroes,* 50). "Like Moses, Deborah is not a battle commander. Her role is to inspire, predict, and celebrate in song. Her weapon is the word, and her very name is an anagram of 'she spoke' (*dibberah*)" (Frymer-Kensky, *Reading the Women of the Bible,* 49).

[200] Kim, "Gender Complementarity," 277. Kim also shows evidence for this conclusion in the narrative's contrast between the courage of Deborah and the cowardice of Barak. For recognition and elaboration of this same emphasis upon woman's leadership in these chapters, cf. Robert Alter, *The World of Biblical Literature* (New York: Basic Books, 1992), 40–43; and Mark A. Vincent, "The Song of Deborah: A Structural and Literary Consideration," *JSOT* 91 (2000): 64–65.

[201] Kim, "Gender Complementarity," 277.

[202] Ibid., 277–78; see 278–80 for discussion of the compositional balance of the two names. Kim builds upon the detailed analysis of this "structural complementarity" in Judg 4–5 by Athalya Brenner, "A Triangle and a Rhombus in Narrative Structure: A Proposed Integrative Reading of Judges 4 and 5," in *A Feminist Companion to Judges* (ed. Athalya Brenner; FCB 4; Sheffield, Eng.: JSOT Press, 1993), 98–109. As another evidence of this compositional complementarity, note the phrase literally translated "woman of lightning," used of Deborah (Judg 4:4), paralleled with Barak, whose name means "lightning" (see the discussion above).

[203] Kim, "Gender Complementarity," 280.

Deborah is a judge of the same stature as all the other judges in the book of Judges, one to whom men as well as women turn for legal counsel and divine instruction.[204] She is a prophetess, providing spiritual leadership in Israel. Contrary to a common modern claim,[205] the role of prophet(ess) in Scripture entails authoritative leadership over men just a surely as the role of teacher.

A nineteenth-century activist for woman's suffrage provided an apt summary analogy of Deborah's status when she noted that Deborah "appears to have been much the same as that of President of the United States with the additional functions of the judicial and religious offices of the nation. Hence this woman was President, Supreme Judge, and Right Reverend in the theocratic Republic of Israel."[206]

There is no indication in the Judges text that such female leadership over men and women in the covenant community was looked upon as opposed to the divine will for women. "Deborah performs in this authoritative capacity normally and in all its complexity."[207] There is intertextual evidence that Deborah as

---

[204] Contra, e.g., Wayne Grudem, *Evangelical Feminism and Biblical Truth: An Analysis of More Than One Hundred Disputed Questions* (Sisters, Ore.: Multnomah, 2004), 135, who mistakenly seeks to make a distinction between the use of the word "judge" regarding Deborah and its usage with the other (male) judges. Deborah, Grudem claims, never "ruled over God's people or taught them publicly or led them militarily." But such an attempt to circumscribe Deborah's judging to the private sphere with no public leadership over men simply does not square with the full context of the narrative and the subsequent poem. Furthermore, the very claim that a woman's "settling of private disputes" is not exercising leadership over a man but public teaching constitutes such (inappropriate) leadership, is in my understanding a false distinction, resulting in endless casuistic lists of appropriate and inappropriate activities for women today, reminiscent of the Pharisaical hair-splitting lists of appropriate and inappropriate Sabbath observance in Jesus' day (see ibid., 84–101).

[205] E.g., ibid., 137. Grudem seeks to make a distinction between the prophet, who is only a messenger of God and has "no authority on his own to do more than that," and the teacher, who has authority to explain or apply the message. But the prophetic witness throughout Scripture, including the narrative of Deborah, belies this false distinction, showing that if anything, the prophet has *more* authoritative leadership—including the authority to explain and apply the divine message—than the teacher. Grudem fails to satisfactorily answer his own question: "Why then could women prophesy but not teach the people? We may not be able to understand all the reasons, but it is clear that the two roles were distinct, and that God allowed women to be prophets but not teachers." Such clear distinction of roles is not found in Scripture.

[206] W. Kennedy Brown, *Gunethics; or, The Ethical Status of Woman* (New York: Funk & Wagnalls, 1887), 36, cited in Yee, "By the Hand of a Woman," 119.

[207] Yee, "By the Hand of a Woman," 110. See also Ackerman, "Digging Up Deborah," 172–84, argues, based upon the work of Carol Meyers in surveying the biblical, as well as extra-biblical (archaeological, sociological, ethnographic, comparative Semitic) evidence, that "in the domestically-based premonarchic era of ancient Israelite history, women would have been integrally involved in their community's economic social, political and religious affairs" (175). Ackerman suggests the likely possibility "that women in early Israelite villages actually assumed Deborah-like leadership positions in their community's military assemblies" (177).

judge was in fact an elder of Israel.[208] She calls herself a "mother in Israel" (Judg 5:7), which seems equivalent to the "father" imagery used as a "leadership title" in Israel (1 Sam 10:12; 2 Kgs 2:12).[209] Cheryl Exum examines the role of the prominent mother in the OT and finds that such a mother is "one who brings liberation from oppression, provides protection, and ensures the well-being and security of her people." In Judges, Deborah exemplifies these roles in the public arena, providing "counsel, inspiration, and leadership."[210] Her role of mother is "not the soft, gentle, nurturing qualities that are often associated with maternity. Abruptly, we are pushed to associate mother and military commander."[211]

This juxtaposition of military commander with "mother in Israel" is the same as appears in Prov 31 with the description of the ʾēšet-ḥayil, "woman of strength/valor," utilizing the term ḥayil, "strength, might," which usually occurs in the depiction of military warriors.[212] In the public arena, Deborah acts in relative independence of her husband (if she had one), son, or other male kinfolk. The Song of Deborah "celebrates the women who do not wait for sexual violence, capture, or death, women who do not wait to be acted upon, but who take action themselves." At the same time, Deborah "does not stand over against the patriarchy."[213] This story is not about "*female* power directed against patriarchal oppression,"[214] as so many have suggested. As argued above, biblical patriarchy is not oppressive of women: though providing the husband's protection of his wife in the home sphere, it does not prohibit women from assuming positions of leadership over men in the public arena. Such examples of female community leadership are not numerous in the OT, since a woman's "counsel, inspiration, and leadership" were focused upon the raising of her children in biblical times. Nonetheless, the leadership roles of women such as Deborah in the covenant community, clearly accepted by society and given the blessing of God, reveal that such are not opposed to biblical patriarchy or the divine will.

The book of Judges records other explicit, positive affirmations of woman. In the narrative/poetry depicting the slaying of Sisera by Jael (Judg 4:17–24; 5:24–27),[215] Deborah, the prophetess/judge, herself characterizes this non-Israelite

[208] Deuteronomy 1, which melds together Exod 18 (the appointment of judges) with Num 11 (the appointment of the seventy elders) seems to imply that the two chapters are referring to the same office.

[209] Hackett, "In the Days of Jael," 28.

[210] J. Cheryl Exum, "'Mother in Israel': A Familiar Figure Reconsidered," in *Feminist Interpretation of the Bible* (ed. Letty M. Russell; Philadelphia: Westminster, 1985), 73–85, quote at 85. For a thorough study of maternal power in the Hebrew Bible, see esp. Bronner, *Stories of Biblical Mothers,* passim.

[211] Fewell and Gunn, "Controlling Perspectives," 402.

[212] See the many occurrences of this usage as "valiant warrior" in the book of Judges alone: Judg 3:29; 6:12; 11:1; 18:2; 20:44, 46.

[213] Fewell and Gunn, "Controlling Perspectives," 403, 397.

[214] Hanselman, "Narrative Theory," 105.

[215] See esp. Susan Niditch, "Eroticism and Death in the Tale of Jael," in *Gender and Difference in Ancient Israel* (ed. Peggy L. Day; Minneapolis, Minn.: Fortress, 1989), 43–57. Niditch analyzes the sexual nuances in both the prose and the poetry accounts of Jael

woman as "most blessed of women," and again in the same verse she announces, "of tent-dwelling women most blessed" (Judg 5:24). This phraseology is used elsewhere in the Bible only of Mary, the mother of Jesus. Judges 9 depicts the downfall of Abimelech at the hand of a woman of the city of Thebez: 9:53 records that "a certain woman threw an upper millstone on Abimelech's head, and crushed his skull." Abimelech, trying to avoid the humiliation of being killed by a woman, has his armor bearer thrust him through with a sword so that those who would see his corpse would think he was slain in battle and not say, "A woman killed him" (9:54). "His ruse fails, for generations later King David refers to this incident (2 Sam 11:21), and the woman's heroism is vindicated because she is linked to valiant warriors."[216]

In the middle of the book, Judg 13 in its form as well as content concentrates on Manoah's wife. In the matching members of the chiastic structure, it is she who encounters the divine messenger, she reports this encounter to her husband, and Yahweh answers Manoah's prayer by sending the divine messenger to her, not him. Throughout the narrative, the piety and wise discernment of Samson's mother (Judg 13) is portrayed in contrast to the lack of perception on the part of her husband.[217] In the flow of meaning, "the narrative seems intent on stressing the importance of the woman in the events leading to Samson's birth. . . . Good theologian that he is, Manoah recognizes that seeing the deity brings death (v 22). His wife, it seems, is a better theologian, for it is she who calls attention to a divine purpose behind the events (v 23)."[218] Furthermore, the narrator portrays the wife of Manoah as similar to the angel in her insight, in her foreknowledge, and especially in her anonymity: the woman is deliberately left unnamed to link her with the angel, whose self-confessed anonymity highlights his importance.[219] "Far

---

(Judg 4–5; see, e.g., Sisera's position "between Jael's legs," 5:27, [Alter's translation]) and concludes that "Jael is a symbolization of self-assertion, a force of change, one who breaks free heroically from oppressive and suppressive forces" (p. 52). See also the discussion in Mieke Bal, *Murder and Difference: Gender, Genre, and Scholarship on Sisera's Death* (trans. Matthew Gumpert; Bloomington: Indiana University Press, 1988); Bellis, *Helpmates, Harlots, and Heroes*, 119–23; Frymer-Kensky, *Reading the Women of the Bible*, 51–57; Hackett, "In the Days of Jael," 15–38; Pamela Tamarkin Reis, "Uncovering Jael and Sisera: A New Reading," *SJOT* 19 (2005): 24–47; Ellen van Wolde, "Deborah and Ya'el in Judges 4," in *On Reading Prophetic Texts: Gender-Specific and Related Studies in Memory of Fokkelien van Dijk-Hemmes* (ed. Bob Becking and Meindert Dijkstra; Leiden: E. J. Brill, 1996), 283–95; Yee, "By the Hand of a Woman," 114–17, 121–26; Fewell and Gunn, "Controlling Perspectives," 391–96; and Bos, "Out of the Shadows."

[216] Carol Meyers, "Woman of Thebez," *WS* 242.

[217] See esp. Yairah Amit, "'Manoah Promptly Followed His Wife' (Judges 13.11): On the Place of Woman in Birth Narratives," in *A Feminist Companion to Judges* (ed. Athalya Brenner; FCB 4; Sheffield, Eng.: Sheffield Academic Press, 1993), 146–50, for analysis of this contrast. For other studies of Manoah's wife, see, e.g., J. Cheryl Exum, "Promise and Fulfillment: Narrative Art in Judges 13," *JBL* 99 (1980): 43–59; and Adele Reinhartz, "Samson's Mother: An Unnamed Protagonist," in *A Feminist Companion to Judges* (ed. Athalya Brenner; FCB 4; Sheffield, Eng.: Sheffield Academic Press, 1993), 157–70.

[218] Exum, "Promise and Fulfillment," 59.

[219] See esp. Reinhartz, "Samson's Mother," 157–70.

from there being a dissonance between the woman's role, it is her very nameless-
ness [in this narrative, contrary to general norms of biblical literature] which
points to and reinforces her central role."[220]

The book of Judges also contains "texts of terror," such as the account of
Jephthah's daughter and the Levite's concubine—passages that are analyzed in
other contexts in this study. Here we note that recent research has shown how,
even in the midst of the darkest hours of woman's degradation in Judges, the narrator sensitively upholds the nobility of woman.[221]

Women in Samuel and Kings. In the books of Samuel and Kings,[222] "women appear at virtually every prominent juncture. . . . This phenomenon is most striking
in the books of Samuel, where women appear in rapid succession throughout. . . .
These women perform an essential function in the overall schema of 1 and
2 Samuel."[223] Samuel and Kings are also framed by narratives concerning women.

---

[220] Ibid., 169.

[221] See esp. Trible, *Texts of Terror,* 65–116, for a careful rhetorical analysis. John L.
Thompson shows that in the history of interpretation prior to the rise of feminist readings, sensitive treatments of these "texts of terror" expressed sympathy for the female victims in the story ("Preaching Texts of Terror in the Book of Judges: How Does the History
of Interpretation Help?" *CTJ* 37 [2002]: 49–61). For a positive characterization of Jephthah's daughter as a self-assured young woman who choose freely to accept her fate when
she understood the dilemma of her father, see, e.g., Walter Groß, "Jiftachs Tochter," in *Das
Manna fällt auch heute noch. Beiträge zur Geschichte und Theologie des Alten, Ersten Testaments. Festschrift für Erich Zenger* (ed. Frank-Lothar Hossfeld and Ludger Schwienhorst-
Schönberger; Herders biblische Studien 44; Freiburg: Herder, 2004), 273–93.

[222] For bibliography, see esp. Bellis, *Helpmates, Harlots, and Heroes,* 157–59, 176.

[223] Susan M. Pigott, "Wives, Witches, and Wise Women: Prophetic Heralds of Kingship
in 1 and 2 Samuel," *RevExp* 99 (2002): 145–46. Pigott surveys the entire sweep of women in
1 and 2 Samuel, including Hannah (1 Sam 1–2); the women who served at the door of
the tent of meeting (2:22); Phineas' wife (4:19–22); the women at the well who helped
Saul find Samuel (9:11–13); women singers (18:6–7; cf. 21:12 [ET 21:11]; 29:5); Michal, as
Saul's daughter (18:17–29; 19:11–17); Abigail (1 Sam 25); David's first wives (25:43–44;
27:3; 30:5, 18); the witch of Endor (1 Sam 28); more of David's wives (2 Sam 3:2–7; 5:13);
Rizpah, as Saul's concubine (3:7); Michal, as wife of Paltiel (3:12–16); Mephibosheth's
nurse (4:4); Michal, as David's antagonist (6:16, 20–23); Bathsheba, wife of Uriah (2 Sam
11–12); Tamar (13); the woman of Tekoa (14:1–20); David's concubines (15:16; 16:21–22;
20:3); two women providers for David's messengers (17:17–20); the wise woman of Abel
of Beth-maacah (20:1–22); and Rizpah, as intercessor for the dead (21:8–14). Pigott
(p. 163) concludes that "each woman plays an important role (whether she is merely a
passive agent or full-fledged character) in heralding kingship, in legitimizing David's
kingship, and/or in determining his successor. . . . Wives, Witches, and Wise Women—the
humble handmaidens of the Samuel narratives come forth as the prophetic heralds of victory—their words and actions establishing order out of the chaos of the Davidic kingship
and succession." See also David Jobling, *1 Samuel* (Berit Olam: Studies in Hebrew Narrative and Poetry; Collegeville, Minn.: Liturgical Press, 1998), 176–94, who analyzes the role
of women in the books of Samuel in light of his hypothesis that each male leader serves as
a "surrogate father" of the succeeding leader; and Duane L. Christensen, "Huldah and the
Men of Anathoth: Women in Leadership in the Deuteronomic History," *SBL Seminar Papers, 1984* (SBLSP 23; Atlanta: Scholars Press, 1984), 399–404, who explores the roles of
Deborah, Jezebel, Athaliah, and Huldah. For specific characterization of Rizpah and her

The books of Samuel begin with the poignant narrative of Hannah (1 Sam 1–2); at the beginning of 1 Kings, the woman Bathsheba figures prominently in the transition from the reign of David to Solomon (1 Kgs 1).[224] Toward the end of 2 Kings, a queen mother and her son are exiled to Babylon (2 Kgs 24:8–17), and this royal mother symbolizes the fate of the monarchy (cf. Jer 13:18–20; Ezek 19). "In short, the historiographical text block which narrates monarchic Israel and Judah is framed at both its ends by female figures and/or figurations."[225]

The discussion of polygamy in chapter 4, above, has already alluded to the narrative of Hannah; chapter 11 will examine her experience more fully in connection with the motif of barrenness. Like the women mentioned in the Pentateuch at the time of Israel's transition—from slavery to freedom in the exodus—Hannah's life is highlighted at the transition of Israel from the period of judges to the monarchy. The same paradox reoccurs here: "Whereas the important events in Israelite tradition are experienced by men, they are often set in motion and determined by women."[226] Hannah is no ordinary mother; her influence is far-reaching, as by divine providence she gives birth to the leader of Israel, Samuel. She is "the first woman, indeed the *only* woman, in the entire Bible to utter a formal, spoken prayer, and have her prayer quoted in the text for us to read."[227] Her prayer of thanksgiving for Samuel's birth (1 Sam 2:1–10) is no ordinary mother's prayer: it is filled with imagery of warfare and divine judgment, climaxing in an inspired prediction of the coming Messiah, which would be echoed in the NT Magnificat, prayed by the Messiah's mother (Luke 1:46–55).[228] Narrative strategies reveal Hannah's significance in the narrative: her name appears fourteen times in 1 Sam 1–2; she participates in the social authority concerned in naming

---

important role in Samuel narrative, see R. G. Branch, "Rizpah: Catalyst in King-making. An Analysis of 2 Samuel 3:6–11," *JS* 14 (2005): 1–16; and idem, "Rizpah: An Activist in Nation-building. An Analysis of 2 Samuel 21:1–14." *JS* 14 (2005): 74–94.

[224] For discussion of Bathsheba's role in this period of transition, see esp. Elna K. Solvang, *A Woman's Place Is in the House: Royal Women of Judah and Their Involvement in the House of David* (JSOTSup 349; New York: Sheffield Academic Press, 2003), 124–53. Cf. Pigott, "Wives, Witches and Wise Women," 157–58.

[225] Athalya Brenner, "Introduction," in *A Feminist Companion to Samuel and Kings* (ed. Athalya Brenner; FCB 5; Sheffield, Eng.: Sheffield Academic Press, 1994), 14.

[226] Exum, "Mother in Israel," 74.

[227] Dennis, *Sarah Laughed*, 124.

[228] For a particularly sensitive analysis of the Hannah narrative and its highlighting of the value of this woman, see ibid., 115–39. See also Yairah Amit, "'Am I Not More Devoted to You Than Ten Sons?' (1 Samuel 1.8): Male and Female Interpretations," 68–76; Adele Berlin, "Hannah and Her Prayers," *Scrip* 87 (2004): 227–32; Lillian R. Klein, "Hannah: Marginalized Victim and Social Redeemer," 77–92; and Carol Meyers, "Hannah and Her Sacrifice: Reclaiming Female Agency," 93–104, all in *A Feminist Companion to Samuel and Kings* (ed. Athalya Brenner; FCB 5; Sheffield, Eng.: Sheffield Academic Press, 1994); Ken Mulzac, "Hannah: The Receiver and Giver of a Great Gift," *AUSS* 40, no. 2 (2002): 207–17; and Dorothy Kelley Patterson, "Nurturing Mothers," in *Biblical Womanhood in the Home* (ed. Nancy Leigh DeMoss; Foundations for the Family Series; Wheaton, Ill.: Crossway Books, 2002), 161–70.

her son; she makes crucial decisions about the future of her child; she is the only character to figure in all ten of the recorded speeches of 1 Sam 1; except for two poetic verses at the end of the book uttered by her son, her song is the only poetic passage in the book. Most important, Hannah is recorded as having an active part in the Hebrew cultus, making a vow and bringing a sacrifice to the Shiloh tabernacle. "A woman's visibility and centrality in the Hannah Narrative of 1 Samuel 1 and her agency in a ritual act thus reveal an otherwise hidden aspect of women's cultic life."[229]

In the books of Samuel and Kings, we enter the era of the monarchy, and as is noted below, the monarchial structure—which was not ordained by God—took a heavy toll on biblical patriarchy and the status of women. Still, despite the radical shifts in narrative style that betoken the suppression of patriarchy and women in monarchial society, some bright spots in the accounts of the kings reveal the narrator's (and God's) continued high view of women.[230] It must not be overlooked that "the first sages, at least those who left concrete memories in the national heritage, were women."[231] Abigail of Carmel does not receive the explicit title "wise woman," but the record of 1 Sam 25 reveals that she was not only "beautiful" but "of good understanding" (v. 3 RSV; Heb. *ṭôbat-śekel*) and "good sense" (v. 33; Heb. *ṭaʿam*). Her tactful counsel to David reveals her good common sense and intelligent insight as well as her piety. Abigail may be characterized as "intelligent, beautiful, discreet and loyal to her husband (despite his stupidity and boorish character . . .). Prudent, quick-witted, and resourceful, she is capable of independent action."[232] Abigail's qualities include verbal power, strength and decisiveness, and redeemer action and prophecy, the "good-sense wife."[233] Abigail is the

---

[229] Meyers, "Hannah and Her Sacrifice," 104.

[230] For an overview (from a feminist perspective) of the anonymous women in Samuel–Kings and their role in the overall narrative strategy, see Adele Reinhartz, "Anonymous Women and the Collapse of the Monarchy: A Study in Narrative Technique," in *A Feminist Companion to Samuel and Kings* (ed. Athalya Brenner; FCB 5; Sheffield, Eng.: Sheffield Academic Press, 1994), 43–65.

[231] Terrien, *Till the Heart Sings*, 88. For an overview of the woman as sage in ancient Israel and the ancient Near East, see esp. Claudia V. Camp, "The Female Sage in Ancient Israel and in the Biblical Wisdom Literature," in *The Sage in Israel and the Ancient Near East* (ed. John G. Gammie and Leo G. Perdue; Winona Lake, Ind.: Eisenbrauns, 1990), 185–204; Carole R. Fontaine, "The Social Roles of Women in the World of Wisdom," in *A Feminist Companion to Wisdom Literature* (ed. Athalya Brenner; FCB 9; Sheffield, Eng.: Sheffield Academic Press, 1995), 24–49; idem, *Smooth Words: Women, Proverbs, and Performance in Biblical Wisdom* (JSOTSup 356; New York: Sheffield Academic Press, 2002), 51–65; Michael S. Moore, "'Wise Women' in the Bible: Identifying a Trajectory," in *Essays on Women in Earliest Christianity* (ed. Carroll D. Osburn; 2 vols.; Joplin, Mo.: College Press, 1995), 2:87–104; and Silvia Schroer, "Wise and Counseling Women in Ancient Israel: Literary and Historical Ideals of the Personified *ḥokmâ*," in *A Feminist Companion to Wisdom Literature* (ed. Athalya Brenner; FCB 9; Sheffield, Eng.: Sheffield Academic Press, 1995), 67–84.

[232] Bird, "Images of Women in the Old Testament," 65.

[233] Alice Bach, "The Pleasure of Her Text," in "Ad feminam: Fiftieth Anniversary Volume," ed. Alice Bach, *USQR* 43 (1989): 41–58, although I disagree with her reading of a subversive character in Abigail.

first to announce that David will be ruler over Israel, and David sees her as "endowed with the highly valued initiative and efficiency of the *ʾēšet ḥayil* ('ideal woman,' see Prov 31:10–31)."[234] Her prompt and independent action, moving with decision in the way she knew to be the way of the Lord, presents a sterling illustration of womanhood in harmony with the Edenic design—with the wife standing as an equal to her husband, sharing responsibilities while preserving respect for her life partner. "Abigail was a wise woman in a male-dominated, foolish world."[235]

Other women of wisdom recorded by the narrator during the early period of the monarchy include individuals from various parts of the land and beyond. In 2 Sam 14:2 the narrator refers to the woman of Tekoah in the south (14:2–20) as a "wise woman" (*ʾiššâ ḥăkāmâ*),[236] and in her speech to David she displays a perceptive understanding of the nature of justice and mercy and a grasp of exquisite literary techniques.[237] She also speaks with a voice of authority, and men

---

[234] Jon D. Levenson, "1 Samuel 25 as Literature and as History," *CBQ* 40 (1978): 20; but I disagree with his characterization of Abigail as an opportunist who "rides the crest of the providential wave into personal success." See also Adele Berlin, "Characterization in Biblical Narrative: David's Wives," *JSOT* 23 (1982): 69–85; idem, *Poetics and Interpretation of Biblical Narrative* (Sheffield, Eng.: Almond, 1983; repr., Winona Lake, Ind.: Eisenbrauns, 1994), 30–31; Frymer-Kensky, *Reading the Women of the Bible*, 315–23; Ken Mulzac, "The Role of Abigail in 1 Samuel 25," *AUSS* 41, no. 1 (2003): 45–53; J. F. Van Rensburg, "Intellect and/or Beauty: A Portrait of Women in the Old Testament and Extrabiblical Literature," *JS* 11, no. 1 (2002): 112–17; and Ellen Van Wolde, "A Leader Led by a Lady: David and Abigail in 1 Samuel 25," *ZAW* 114 (2002): 355–75. Cf. the beautiful characterization by the nineteenth-century commentator Ellen G. White, *Patriarchs and Prophets* (Mountain View, Calif.: Pacific, 1890; repr., 1958), 667: "These words [of Abigail to David] could have come only from lips of one who had partaken of the wisdom from above. The piety of Abigail, like the fragrance of a flower, breathed out all unconsciously in face and word and action. The Spirit of the Son of God was abiding in her soul. Her speech, seasoned with grace, and full of kindness and peace, shed a heavenly influence.... Abigail was a wise reprover and counselor."

[235] Mulzac, "The Role of Abigail," 53. Mulzac's study provides an especially sensitive treatment of the characterization of Abigail in contrast to her husband, Nabal, and of the wisdom of Abigail in her relationships with Nabal and David.

[236] Several feminist interpreters of this story question whether this woman was really wise or only shrewd, since she is seen to play into the hands of patriarchy (see Bellis, *Helpmates, Harlots, and Heroes*, 153–55, for a summary of views), but such a question ignores the perspective of the final form of the text and the direct statement of the narrator. It is true that according to the narrator and the woman's own testimony, Joab "put the words in her mouth" (2 Sam 14:3; cf. 14:19), but this does not detract from the wisdom of the woman and her ability to communicate the message to David.

[237] See Roy Gane's discussion of the profound understanding of the nature of justice and mercy displayed in her speech (esp. 14:9) in *Altar Call* (Berrien Springs, Mich.: Diadem, 1999), 232–37. For an extended treatment of the proverb/parable (*māšāl*) given by the wise woman of Tekoa to David, with its many intertextual allusions especially to the book of Genesis, see Larry L. Lyke, *King David with the Wise Woman of Tekoa: The Resonance of Tradition in Parabolic Narrative* (JSOTSup 255; Sheffield, Eng.: Sheffield Academic Press, 1997), although I do not subscribe to his postmodern emphasis on multiple readings.

listen.[238] The wise woman of Abel in the far north of Israel (20:14–22) likewise speaks with an authoritative voice, utilizing poetic speech (proverb), and men listen and obey.[239] Her attributes include "sagacity, faithfulness, a commanding presence, and readily acknowledged influence with peers."[240] The wise woman calls herself "a mother in Israel" (20:19), perhaps modeling her role of deliverer with that of Deborah, who used the same title. The queen of Sheba, who comes from Southern Arabia to visit Solomon (1 Kgs 10:1–13; cf. 2 Chr 9:1), is a "spectacularly colorful woman" who "travels freely and interacts with Solomon as an equal;"[241] she has been described as "Woman Wisdom, cast in narrative form."[242] Perhaps the truth-telling harlot of 1 Kgs 3:16–28 should also be considered one of the "wise women."[243]

During the period of the monarchy the "great"[244] woman of Shunem (2 Kgs 4:8–37; 8:1–6) is presented as a woman of wealth and self-reliance.[245] "The portrayal of this unnamed woman is one of the most remarkable in the Bible. Both

---

[238] See Claudia V. Camp, "The Wise Women of 2 Samuel: A Role Model for Women in Early Israel?" *CBQ* 43 (1981): 17–20, for an elaboration of this point. See also Brenner, *The Israelite Woman*, 34–35; and Patricia K. Willey, "The Importunate Woman of Tekoa and How She Got Her Way," in *Reading between Texts: Intertextuality and the Bible* (ed. Dana Nolan Fewell; Louisville: Westminster John Knox, 1992), 115–31.

[239] See Bellis, *Helpmates, Harlots, and Heroes*, 156; Camp, "The Wise Women"; and Frymer-Kensky, *Reading the Women of the Bible*, 58–61.

[240] Camp, "The Wise Women," 26. Camp draws implications for the relative status of women with men: "In the early years of Israel, with its egalitarian principles and desperate need for able minds as well as bodies, such qualities might have placed women not uncommonly in positions of authority in the village-tribal setting."

[241] Bellis, *Helpmates, Harlots, and Heroes*, 163–64. On the background of the queen of Sheba, see Harold M. Parker Jr., "Solomon and the Queen of Sheba," *Iliff Review* 24 (1967): 17–23.

[242] Claudia V. Camp, "1 and 2 Kings," *WBC* 102. It is a fitting title, although I disagree with Camps' denial of the historical basis of the narrative and with her suggestion that there is an "erotic subtext."

[243] So argues William A. M. Beuken, "No Wise King without a Wise Woman (I Kings III 16–28)," in *New Avenues in the Study of the Old Testament* (ed. Adam S. van der Woude; OtSt 25; Leiden: E. J. Brill, 1989), 1–10. The author concludes (p. 10): "In my opinion the good whore of 1 Kings iii may be added to the typology of the wise woman. By listening to the inclinations of her motherly heart she can speak wise words to king Solomon. Thus she creates for him the possibility to judge fairly. The praise of the woman whose value surpasses that of corals is also applicable to her: 'She opens her mouth with wisdom, and the teaching of kindness is on her tongue' (Prov. xxxi 26)."

[244] The narrator uses the adj. *gĕdôlâ*, "great" (2 Kgs 4:8, so translated by the KJV), which may have various nuances, illustrated by modern English translations of the word in this verse, "prominent" (NASB), "notable" (NKJV), "wealthy" (NRSV, RSV, ESV, NLT, NJPS), "well-to-do" (NIV), "[woman] of rank" (NJB), and "[woman] of influence" (NAB). See Bellis, *Helpmates, Harlots, and Heroes*, 173–74.

[245] Frymer-Kensky, *Reading the Women of the Bible*, 64–73, pieces together the biblical clues that lead her to a plausible conclusion that this woman, like the daughters of Zelophehad, inherited land and lived among her own kin: "Owning her own land, she is not dependent upon men for her livelihood." Thus "the Shunammite may be an example of how women act when the *economic* constraints of patriarchy are removed" (p. 72).

independent and maternal, powerful and pious, she brings to mind a number of other female characters, yet surpassed them all."[246] Camp emphasizes this woman's verbal skills and competence, and her initiative and self-reliance (in contrast to her husband)—"a self-sufficiency and an authority independent of motherhood."[247] Several studies argue that in the perspective of the narrator, this great woman in some respects overshadows even the prophet Elisha, with whom she interacts.[248]

The period of the monarchy also produced women of public power, namely, the *gĕbîrôt,* or queen regents.[249] Most of these queen mothers, unfortunately, lent their influence on the side of evil. For example, 2 Chr 22:3 describes Athaliah's relationship to her son Azariah: "his mother was his counselor in doing wickedly." The role of the queen regents in Israel has been vigorously debated among biblical scholars,[250] but Niels-Erik Andreasen's conclusion seems to fit the evidence best. He argues, on the basis of biblical data and Hittite parallels, that "the queen mother was not merely treated with deference by the monarch, but that she held a significant official position superseded only by that of the king himself."[251] This position was that of "lady counselor," giving counsel especially regarding royal succession but also (in the case of Bathsheba at least) in judicial matters and concerns of mediation between political factions (1 Kgs 2:13–25). Ackerman is also probably correct in her assessment that at least four queen mothers—Jezebel in the north, and Maacah, Athaliah, and Nehushta in the south—had an official role in the cult, as

---

[246] Camp, "1 and 2 Kings," 106.

[247] Ibid., 106–8, quote at 107.

[248] See esp. Fokkelien van Dijk-Hemmes, "The Great Woman of Shunem and the Man of God: A Dual Interpretation of 2 Kings 4:8–37," in *A Feminist Companion to Samuel and Kings* (ed. Athalya Brenner; FCB 5; Sheffield, Eng.: Sheffield Academic Press, 1994), 218–30; Burke O. Long, "The Shunammite Woman: In the Shadow of the Prophet?" *BRev* 7, no. 1 (1991): 12–19, 42; Mark Roncace, "Elisha and the Woman of Shunem: 2 Kings 4:8–37 and 8:1–6 Read in Conjunction," *JSOT* 91 (2000): 109–27 (and further bibliography, 109–10, n. 2); Mary E. Shields, "Subverting a Man of God, Elevating a Woman: Role and Power Reversals in 2 Kings 4," *JSOT* 58 (1993): 59–69; Jopie Siebert-Hommes, "The Widow of Zarephath and the Great Woman of Shunem: A Comparative Analysis of Two Stories," in *Samuel and Kings* (ed. Athalya Brenner; FCB[2] 7; Sheffield, Eng.: Sheffield Academic Press, 2000), 98–114; and Uriel Simon, *Reading Prophetic Narratives* (trans. Lenn J. Schramm; Indiana Studies in Biblical Literature; Bloomington: Indiana University Press, 1997), 227–62.

[249] Bathsheba (2 Sam 11:3), Naamah (1 Kgs 14:21), Maacah (15:2, 10), Jezebel (16:31), Azubah (22:42), Athaliah (2 Kgs 11:1, 13–16), Zibiah (12:2 [ET 12:1]), Jehoaddin (14:2), Jecholiah (15:2), Jerusha (15:33), Abi (18:2), Meshullemeth (21:19), Jedidiah (22:2), Hamutal (23:31), and Nehushta (24:8).

[250] See esp. Susan Ackerman, "The Queen Mother and the Cult in Ancient Israel," *JBL* 112 (1993): 385–401; Niels-Erik Andreasen, "The Role of the Queen Mother in Israelite Society," *CBQ* 45 (1983): 179–94; Zafrira Ben-Barak, "The Status and Right of the *gĕbîrâ,*" *JBL* 110 (1991): 23–34; Nancy R. Bowen, "The Quest for the Historical *gĕbîrâ,*" *CBQ* 63 (2001): 597–618; Bronner, *Stories of Biblical Mothers,* 44–58; and Solvang, *A Woman's Place,* passim.

[251] Andreasen, "The Role of the Queen Mother," 180.

they devoted themselves to the worship of the mother goddess Asherah.[252] Athaliah has the distinction of becoming the only woman in the two Hebrew kingdoms to rule as sole monarch, and the narrator criticizes her not for her gender but for conduct equally reprehensible in a male ruler (2 Kgs 11; 2 Chr 22).

Narratives from the time of the monarchy also spotlight a woman of special divine calling, Huldah the prophetess (2 Kgs 22:14–20). Against those who argue that God never calls women to an office that includes a teaching function over men, note that when King Josiah commanded the priest and scribe, "Go, inquire of the LORD" (22:13), regarding the discovery of the book of the law, they went to Huldah the female prophet for divine counsel when the male prophets, such as Jeremiah, could have been consulted. A woman was chosen to authenticate that the scroll found in the temple was authoritative Scripture. According to 2 Kgs 22:14, Huldah lived in Jerusalem in the *mišneh,* which most versions translate as the "Second Quarter" (NRSV) but the NJPS transliterates as "Mishneh" and the KJV translates as "college." The latter translation may be the best inasmuch as some scholars have suggested that this has reference to an academy, perhaps even headed up by Huldah. This was apparently the view of early Judaism, which held Huldah in such high regard that the gates at the southern entrance of the temple were named after her.[253]

These few examples of notable women living for the most part in private life during the period of the Israelite monarchy, prove the exception to the rule. The institution of the monarchy, especially after its bureaucratization during the reign of Solomon, spelled the historical demise of any prominent place for nonroyal women in public life.

> None of Israel's bureaucracies—the palace, the army, the law courts, even the "Sages"—had any room for women. Once the state was consolidated, women had no role in the pyramid of power; they were not leaders outside the domestic sphere.

---

[252] For a discussion of Maacah, see Ktziah Spanier, "The Queen Mother in the Judean Royal Court: Maacah—a Case Study," in *A Feminist Companion to Samuel and Kings* (ed. Athalya Brenner; FCB 5; Sheffield, Eng.: Sheffield Academic Press, 1994), 186–95. For discussion of the story of Athaliah, see, Robin Gallaher Branch, "Athaliah, a Treacherous Queen: A Careful Analysis of Her Story in 2 Kings 11 and 2 Chronicles 22:10—23:21," *IDS* 38 (2004): 537–59. For evidence that Jezebel may have been a high priestess, see Brenner, *The Israelite Woman,* 23–24. For attempts to "revamp" the negative view of Jezebel, see Janet Howe Gaines, "How Bad Was Jezebel?" *BR* 16, no. 5 (2000): 12–23; Mary Joan Winn Leith, "First Lady Jezebel"; and Tina Pippin, "Jezebel Re-vamped," *Semeia* 69–70 (1995): 221–33 *BRev* 20, no. 4 (August 2004): 8, 46. On Jezebel, see also Patricia Dutcher-Walls, *Jezebel: Portraits of a Queen* (Collegeville, Minn.: Liturgical, 2004), and Phyllis Trible, "The Odd Couple: Elijah and Jezebel," in *Out of the Garden: Women Writers on the Bible* (ed. Christina Büchmann and Celina Spiegel; New York: Fawcett Columbine, 1994), 166–79, 340–41.

[253] For further discussion and characterization of Huldah, see esp. Claudia V. Camp, "Female Voice, Written Word: Women and Authority in Hebrew Scripture," in *Embodied Love: Sensuality and Relationship as Feminist Values* (ed. Paula M. Cooey, Sharon A. Farmer, and Mary Ellen Ross; San Francisco: Harper & Row, 1987), 97–113; cf. Bellis, *Helpmates, Harlots, and Heroes,* 174–75; Phipps, *Assertive Biblical Women,* 83–92; and Arlene Swidler, "In Search of Huldah," *TBT* 98 (1978): 1780–85.

They could still be wise, but they were no longer Wise Women. From the standpoint of political power, the days before the state were the good old days to women. Once the state was established, they could exercise considerable family power as wives and mothers—but only queens had an impact on the destiny of the nation.[254]

The Latter Prophets

Specific Women. Few references to specific women occur in the Latter Prophets, and these are mostly wives of the prophets.[255] Still, "the relative paucity of female figures in the prophetic books of the Hebrew Bible . . . should not necessarily be seen as sexist. The type of literature in those books is much less focused on specific persons, male or female; and specific individuals and even generic types of either gender are mentioned far less often than in the historical books."[256] Among such references is the experience of Gomer (Hos 1–3), adulterous wife of Hosea (see ch. 8, below). Also, Isaiah announces to King Ahaz that "the young woman [ʿalmâ] is with child and shall bear a son" (Isa 7:14); this announcement I interpret as having a local fulfillment in the birth of Isaiah's own son born, to his wife, "the prophetess" (Isa 8:3), but, within the overall context of this "Volume of Immanuel" (Isa 7–12), attaining an ultimate messianic fulfillment in the birth of the ultimate Son announced in Isa 9:5–6 (ET 9:6–7).[257] God instructs Jeremiah not to marry, that he might be spared the anguish of seeing the death of his wife and children in the coming Babylonian siege (Jer 16:1–7). Ezekiel 24:15–18 records God's announcement to Ezekiel that his wife—the "delight of your eyes" (24:16)—would die suddenly, and he is forbidden from mourning her death, symbolic of when Judah will be taken into exile and there will be no time to mourn. The language utilized to describe the life partners of these prophets betokens a high view of women and a treatment of them with love and respect on a par with their husbands.

Groups of Women. The Latter Prophets also refer to groups of women. Apostate women (and men) worship the "queen of heaven" and weep for Tammuz (see ch. 3, above). Amos castigates the "cows of Bashan, who are on Mount Samaria, who oppress the poor, who crush the needy, who say to your husbands, 'Bring something to drink!'" (Amos 4:1). Isaiah, his eighth-century B.C.E. contemporary, likewise denounces in language of a covenant lawsuit (Isa 3:13) the haughty "daughters of Zion" (3:16–26) and the "complacent daughters" (32:9–11) and announces their doom along with that of their husbands and their land. About a hundred years later God pronounces judgment against the self-proclaimed

---

254 Frymer-Kensky, *Reading the Women of the Bible,* 63.

255 For a bibliography on women in the Latter Prophets, see esp. Bellis, *Helpmates, Harlots, and Heroes,* 189–90.

256 Carol Meyers, "The Hebrew Bible," *WS* 11.

257 See Richard M. Davidson, "New Testament Use of the Old Testament," *JATS* 5, no. 1 (1994): 17–19; idem, "A ~~Woman~~ Virgin Shall Bear a Child: Isaiah 7:14," *PD* 7, no. 2 (2002): 47–51.

prophetesses in Judah who prophesy falsely and practice divination, thus deceiving the people (Ezek 13:17–23). The prophetic warnings against these groups of women, though not flattering, reveal that there were circles of women with considerable influence, power, wealth, and even religious authority in Judean society during the monarchy.

Other Elevated Valuations of Women. The Latter Prophets uphold the rights and the valuation of women in a number of ways. Isaiah indicates that the mother is due the same respect from her children as is due the father (Isa 45:10). Jeremiah clarifies that women, along with other vulnerable segments of society (the physically impaired and children), must be protected and given the same human rights of freedom as men (Jer 34:9) and promises their safe return from exile (Jer 31:8). Joel predicts that women as well as men will receive the gift of prophecy in the eschatological latter days (Joel 2:3). Allusions to matriarchal figures of the Pentateuch—Rachel (Jer 31:15–22) and Sarah (Isa 51:1–3)—heighten the valuation of women, as these matriarchs become symbols of hope for the eschatological community. The pairing of Sarah with Abraham in Isa 51:2, followed by the grammatically masculine singular language which includes them both, implies that the term "fathers" of Israel refers to Israel's parents, both male and female.[258]

The prophetic literature is also filled with feminine imagery.[259] Earlier chapters of this study have explored the feminine imagery used to describe the divinity; other chapters in section 2 will explore feminine imagery as it relates to various sexually related topics. Here we note general references that have a bearing on the valuation of women. A number of passages compare strong warriors or nations to women; this is not a disparagement of women but a simile or metaphor recognizing the lack of upper-body strength among most women, which disqualified them to serve as combat soldiers.[260] Several poetic passages allude to

---

[258] See discussion in Fischer, *Women Who Wrestled with God*, 3–4.

[259] For feminist interpretation of this imagery, see the overview in *WBC* 161–77, 183–90, 195–202. For specialized studies from a feminist perspective, see, e.g., Angela Bauer, *Gender in the Book of Jeremiah: A Feminist-Literary Reading* (StBL 5; New York: Peter Lang, 1999); idem, "Jeremiah as Female Impersonator: Roles of Difference in Gender Perception and Gender Perceptivity," in *Escaping Eden: New Feminist Perspectives on the Bible* (ed. Harold C. Washington, Susan Lochrie Graham, and Pamela Thimmes; BS 65; Sheffield, Eng.: Sheffield Academic Press, 1998), 199–207; idem, "Dressed to Be Killed: Jeremiah 4:29–31 as an Example for the Functions of Female Imagery in Jeremiah," in *Troubling Jeremiah* (ed. A. R. Pete Diamond, Kathleen M. O'Connor, and Louis Stulman; JSOTSup 260; Sheffield, Eng.: Sheffield Academic Press, 1999), 293–305; and Erin Runions, *Changing Subjects: Gender, Nation, and Future in Micah* (Playing the Text 7; New York: Sheffield Academic Press, 2001), who builds upon the work of postcolonial theorist Homi K. Bhabha.

[260] See, e.g., Isa 3:12;19:16; Jer 50:37; 51:30; and Nah 3:3. I reject the claim of David J. A. Clines, among others, that the Hebrew prophets unconsciously devalued women in their "male texts" ("He-Prophets: Masculinity as a Problem for the Hebrew Prophets and Their Interpreters," in *Sense and Sensitivity: Essays on Reading the Bible in Memory of Robert Carroll* [ed. Alastair G. Hunter and Phillip R. Davies; JSOTSup 348; Sheffield, Eng.:

the special social functions of women in festive vintage singing and dancing[261] and in mourning in the context of divine judgment.[262] Frequently in the prophets (with greatest intensification in Isaiah) Judah is personified as "daughter Zion" or "daughter Jerusalem."[263] Jeremiah cites God's high regard for his people in using this imagery: "I have likened daughter Zion to the loveliest pasture" (6:2).

Finally, Jeremiah makes an enigmatic but powerful statement about the eschatological Day of the Lord: "For the LORD has created a new thing in the earth: a woman encompasses a man" (Jer 31:22). The last clause literally reads, "female [*nĕqēbâ*] surrounds [*poʿel* impf. of *sbb*] (strong) man/warrior [*geber*]." The noun *nĕqēbâ*, "female," which is the generic term for all females used in Gen 1:27, is here "an inclusive and concluding referent" that "encompasses poetically all the specific female images of the poem . . . and it is other than all these images, for it is Yahweh's creation of a new thing in the land."[264] Kathleen M. O'Connor summarizes the possible interpretations and the profound implications:

> Perhaps it refers to future sexual relationships in which women will be active agents in the procreation of a restored people. Perhaps it speaks of a society at peace so that women will be capable of protecting warriors. Or perhaps it anticipates role reversals of a different sort. What is clear is that the surprising new role of women symbolizes a changed order of relationships in a reconstituted and joyous society.[265]

Does this passage, by its clear allusions to the creation-and-fall narrative in Gen 1–3, perhaps envision the reversal of the Gen 3:16 leadership principle

---

Sheffield Academic Press, 2002], 318–22). Clines gives examples from Isaiah in which he considers that women are despised (Isa 4:1), threatened (Isa 3:16–17), blamed (Isa 3:18–24), feared (Isa 4:1–3), stereotyped (Isa 13:8; 21:3; cf. 7:14; 26:17; 42:14; 45:10; 66:12–13), abused (Isa 13:11, 16–17), trivialized (Isa 16:2; 19:16; 32:9–11), marginalized (Isa 3:12), humiliated (Isa 49:15), and ignored (everywhere else in Isaiah). Clines has misread every one of these examples (except the prediction of the historical reality of the rape of Babylonian women in Isa 13:16–17) on the basis of a nonbiblical understanding of masculinity and patriarchy.

[261] See esp. the Song of the Vineyard in Isa 5:1–6, which is sung by a female voice (= the daughter of Zion) to "my beloved" about his vineyard. Cf. Judg 21:16–24.

[262] See, e.g., Jer 9:16–19 (ET 9:17–20); Ezek 32:16.

[263] For usage of "daughter Zion," see, e.g., Isa 1:8; 10:32; 16:1; 37:22; 52:2; 62:11; Jer 4:31; 6:2, 23; Mic 1:13; 4:8, 10, 13; Zeph 3:14; Zech 2:14 (ET 2:10); 9:9. For the expression "daughter Jerusalem," see, e.g., Isa 37:22; Mic 4:8; Zech 9:9. Jeremiah's preferred phrase is "daughter of My people" (so the RSV and several other versions, but not the NRSV): Jer 4:11; 6:26; 8:11, 19, 21–22; 8:23, 9:6 (ET 9:1, 7); 14:17; cf. Isa 22:4. He also refers to Judah as "faithless daughter" (Jer 31:22; 49:4). See also the phrase "virgin Israel": Jer 18:13; 31:4, 21; Amos 5:2. The phrase "daughter(s) [of] . . ." or "virgin daughter(s) [of] . . ." is also used of other nations/cities, such as Tarshish (Isa 23:10), Sidon (Isa 23:12), Babylon (Isa 47:1, 5; Jer 50:42; 51:33; Zech 2:11 [ET 2:7]), Egypt (Isa 46:1; Jer 46:11, 19, 24), Moab (Isa 16:2; 48:18), Ammon (Jer 49:3), Sodom (Ezek 16:48, 53, 55), Samaria (Ezek 16:46, 53, 55), Syria (Ezek 16:57), Philistia (Ezek 16:57), and "the nations" (Ezek 32:16). For discussion, see Frymer-Kensky, "Zion, the Beloved Woman, " ch. 15 in *In the Wake of the Goddesses*, 168–98.

[264] Trible, *God and the Rhetoric of Sexuality*, 48, 50.

[265] Kathleen M. O'Connor, "Jeremiah," *WBC* 176. Cf. the summary of interpretations by Bauer, *Gender in the Book of Jeremiah*, 138–45.

between husbands and wives and the return to the pre-fall Edenic model, a return in which there are no hierarchical relationships and the female again takes a fully egalitarian position, including "encircling" the male with active protection and care?[266]

The Writings: Narratives/History

Among the historical/narrative books of the Writings, Ruth and Esther appear as part of the Megilloth (the five scrolls read during the five respective major Jewish festivals). The books of Ruth and Esther must certainly be placed on center stage for their positive affirmations of sexuality—in particular, the dignity and worth of woman.

Ruth. In her groundbreaking and classic interpretation of the book of Ruth, Phyllis Trible explores major rhetorical elements of the story that reveal a high view of woman in general and underscore the character qualities of Ruth, the "worthy woman" ($^{\circ}\bar{e}\check{s}et\ hayil$) (Ruth 3:11), in particular.[267] Although male char-

---

[266] See Deborah F. Sawyer, "Gender-Play and Sacred Text: A Scene from Jeremiah," *JSOT* 83 (1999): 99–111, who points out the many intertextual linkages between this section of Jeremiah and Gen 1–3 and moves in the direction of my suggestion (albeit with a postmodern deconstructionist approach that I reject). See also William L. Holladay, "Jeremiah xxxi 22b Reconsidered: 'The Woman Encompasses the Man,'" *VT* 16 (1966): 236–39.

[267] See Trible, *God and the Rhetoric of Sexuality,* 166–99. I am indebted to Trible for many of the insights that follow, although I do not subscribe to the same negative view of the patriarchal society as is depicted in her work. Other helpful analyses of the elevated role of women (or even a gynocentric perspective) upheld in the book of Ruth include, e.g., Richard Bauckham, *Is the Bible Male? The Book of Ruth and Biblical Narrative* (Cambridge, Eng.: Grove Books, 1996); idem, "The Book of Ruth and the Possibility of a Feminist Canonical Hermeneutic," *BibInt* 5 (1997): 29–45; Charles P. Baylis, "Naomi in the Book of Ruth in Light of the Mosaic Covenant," *BSac* 161 (2004): 413–31; James Black, "Ruth in the Dark: Folktale, Law, and Creative Ambiguity in the Old Testament," *LT* 5 (1991): 20–36; Darr, *Far More Precious Than Jewels,* 55–84; Fokkelien van Dijk-Hemmes, "Ruth: A Product of Women's Culture?" in *A Feminist Companion to Ruth* (ed. Athalya Brenner; FCB 3; Sheffield, Eng.: Sheffield Academic Press, 1993), 134–39; Irmtraud Fischer, "The Book of Ruth: A 'Feminist' Commentary to the Torah?" in *Ruth and Esther* (ed. Athalya Brenner; FCB² 3; Sheffield, Eng.: Sheffield Academic Press, 1999), 24–49; Frymer-Kensky, *Reading the Women of the Bible,* 238–56; J. Randolph Jaeggli, "Ruth—the Ideal Woman," *BV* 35, no. 2 (2001): 5–10; Judith A. Kates and Gail Twersky Reimer, eds., *Reading Ruth: Contemporary Women Reclaim a Sacred Story* (New York: Ballantine, 1994); LaCocque, *The Feminine Unconventional,* 84–116; Jacqueline E. Lapsley, "Seeing the Older Woman: Naomi in High Definition," in *Engaging the Bible in a Gendered World: An Introduction to Feminist Biblical Interpretation in Honor of Katharine Doob Sakenfeld* (ed. Linda Day and Carolyn Pressler; Louisville: Westminster John Knox, 2006), 102–13; idem, *Whispering the Word,* 89–108; Amy-Jill Levine, "Ruth," *WBC* 78–84; Carol Meyers, "Returning Home: Ruth 1:8 and the Gendering of the Book of Ruth," in *A Feminist Companion to Ruth* (ed. Athalya Brenner; FCB 3; Sheffield, Eng.: Sheffield Academic Press, 1993), 85–114; Mary E. Mills, *Biblical Morality: Moral Perspectives in Old Testament Narratives* (Heythrop Studies in Contemporary Philosophy, Religion & Theology; Burlington, Vt.:

acters appear there, Trible argues that the story belongs to women—to Ruth and Naomi—and to "chance," which is a code for the divine hand of Providence.[268] Women shape their story by bold plans and actions. Ruth and Naomi are women of creative initiative and independence, agents of change and challenge, while functioning within the norms of a patriarchal society. The significance of the bold and assertive actions of Ruth and Naomi are highlighted in bold relief against the backdrop of the "ruthless era"[269] of the judges, in which this narrative is framed—an era that presents some of the most flagrant cases of the denigration of women anywhere in Scripture (to be discussed later in this chapter).

In the time of crisis when Naomi is about to return to her homeland, Ruth becomes a model of the radicality of faith. Her decision to go with Naomi makes no sense—it is a break with her familial, racial, cultural, and religious ties. In her decision "she also reversed her sexual allegiance. A young woman has committed herself to the life of an old woman rather than to search for her husband, and she has made this commitment not 'until death do us part' but beyond death."[270] Her radical decision of faith to leave father and mother and go to a strange land is matched only by that of Abraham (and Rebekah) and perhaps surpasses Abraham, who was wealthy and self-sufficient. It is instructive to note that Boaz's blessing of Ruth (Ruth 2:12) appears to compare her experience with that of the father of the faithful in Gen 12:1–5.

The story indicates the nature of Ruth's *ḥesed,* or steadfast loyalty/love, for Naomi; indeed her loyalty (along with Orpah's) is given as a model for the *ḥesed* of the Lord (Ruth 1:8). She is truly a "worthy woman of strength" (3:11), to be compared with the ancient mothers Rachel, Leah, and Tamar (4:11–12); she is depicted as one more desirable than seven sons (4:15). Amazingly, she is chosen by God ("the LORD made her conceive," 4:13) to be one of the progenitors of the Davidic line (4:18–22), the line of the Messiah (cf. Matt 1:5). In the heart of this narrative, it is Ruth who proposes marriage to Boaz, and not Boaz to Ruth (Ruth 3:9). "This assumes an attitude that ascribes to women the same rights as to men. In the light of this feature, the fact that the book of Ruth is one of the few

---

Ashgate, 2001), 97–116; Alicia Ostriker, "The Book of Ruth and the Love of the Land," *BibInt* 10 (2002): 343–59; Phipps, *Assertive Biblical Women,* 47–67; Christiane Rösener, "'Your People Shall Be My People, and Your God My God': The Shared Life of Ruth and Naomi as a Model for Women Transgressing Intercultural Boundaries," in *Transgressors: Toward a Feminist Biblical Theology* (ed. Claudia Janssen, Ute Ochtendung, and Beate Wehn; Collegeville, Minn.: Liturgical Press, 2002), 1–8; Sakenfeld, *Just Wives?* 27–48; Kristin Moen Saxegaard, "'More Than Seven Sons': Ruth as Example of the Good Son," *SJOT* 15, no. 2 (2001): 257–75; Aldina da Silva, "Ruth, plaidoyer en faveur de la femme," *SR* 27 (1998): 252–57; Norm Wakefield and Jody Brolsma, *Men Are from Israel, Women Are from Moab: Insights about the Sexes from the Book of Ruth* (Downers Grove, Ill.: InterVarsity, 2000); Claus Westermann, "Structure and Intention of the Book of Ruth," *WW* 19 (1999): 285–302; and Johanna W. H. Van Wijk-Bos, *Ruth and Esther: Women in Alien Lands* (Nashville: Abingdon, 2001), 11–63.

[268] Trible, *God and the Rhetoric of Sexuality,* 178.

[269] A pun on the name Ruth, used by Phipps, *Assertive Biblical Women,* 48.

[270] Trible, *God and the Rhetoric of Sexuality,* 173.

narratives in which the thoughts and actions of a woman comprise the events that to a large degree characterize the story takes on enormous weight."[271]

Besides the storyline of the book of Ruth, other features highlight the elevated position of women envisioned in this book. The inspired author utilizes numerous word formulas that normally pertain to a masculine subject but in this book are applied to a feminine subject.[272] At the conclusion of the book occurs a "brilliant celebration in male and female voices" constituting nothing less than "an Old Testament reconciliation of men's and women's roles, wherein Rachel, Leah, Tamar and Ruth are accorded recognition as mothers to a race of kings."[273] Indeed, "the Book of Ruth is a bright spot in Israel's darkest age. Like an oasis in a desert, Naomi and Ruth stand for vital religion and ethics in a time of bigotry and mayhem."[274]

Esther. The story of Esther no less than Ruth indicates the estimate of human worth God places upon woman.[275] In the providence of God (although the name

---

[271] Westermann, "Structure and Intention," 302.

[272] See da Silva, "Ruth, plaidoyer," 252–57.

[273] Black, "Ruth in the Dark," 35.

[274] Phipps, *Assertive Biblical Women,* 67.

[275] For studies dealing with the characterization of Esther (and Vashti), see esp. Mieke Bal, "Lots of Writing," *Semeia* 54 (1991): 77–102; Timothy K. Beal, *The Book of Hiding: Gender, Ethnicity, Annihilation, and Esther* (London: Routledge, 1997); Michael Beckett, *Gospel in Esther* (Carlisle, Eng.: Paternoster, 2002); Adele Berlin, *Esther: The Traditional Hebrew Text with the New JPS Translation* (JPS Bible Commentary; Philadelphia: Jewish Publication Society, 2001), liv–lix; Berquist, *Reclaiming Her Story,* 154–66; Leila Leah Bronner, "Esther Revisited: An Aggadic Approach," in *A Feminist Companion to Esther, Judith, and Susanna* (ed. Athalya Brenner; FCB 7; Sheffield, Eng.: Sheffield Academic Press, 1995), 176–97; idem, "Reclaiming Esther: From Sex Object to Sage," *JBQ* 26, no. 1 (1998): 3–10; Klara Butting, "Esther: A New Interpretation of the Joseph Story in the Fight against Anti-Semitism and Sexism," in *Ruth and Esther* (ed. Athalya Brenner; FCB[2] 3; Sheffield, Eng.: Sheffield Academic Press, 1999), 239–48; Claudia V. Camp, "The Three Faces of Esther: Traditional Woman, Royal Diplomat, Authenticator of Tradition," *Academy: Journal of Lutherans in Professions* 38 (1982): 20–25; John F. Craghan, "Esther: A Fully Liberated Woman," *TBT* 24 (1986): 6–11; Linda Day, *Three Faces of a Queen: Characterization in the Books of Esther* (JSOTSup 186; Sheffield, Eng.: Sheffield Academic Press, 1995); Michael V. Fox, *Character and Ideology in the Book of Esther* (Columbia: University of South Carolina Press, 1991); idem, "Three Esthers," in *The Book of Esther in Modern Research* (ed. Sidnie White Crawford and Leonard J. Greenspoon; London: T&T Clark, 2003), 50–60; Zefira Gitay, "Esther and the Queen's Throne," in *A Feminist Companion to Esther, Judith, and Susanna* (ed. Athalya Brenner; FCB 7; Sheffield, Eng.: Sheffield Academic Press, 1995), 136–48; Lee W. Humphreys, "A Life-style for Diaspora: A Study of the Tales of Esther and Daniel," *JBL* 93 (1973): 211–23; LaCocque, *The Feminine Unconventional,* 49–83; Larry Lichtenwalter, *Behind the Seen: God's Hand in Esther's Life . . . and Yours* (Hagerstown, Md.: Review and Herald, 2001); Rivkah Lubitch, "A Feminist's Look at Esther," *Judaism* 42 (1993): 438–46; Susan Niditch, "Esther: Folklore, Wisdom, Feminism, and Authority," in *A Feminist Companion to Esther, Judith, and Susanna* (ed. Athalya Brenner; FCB 7; Sheffield, Eng.: Sheffield Academic Press, 1995), 26–46; idem, "Short Stories: The Book of Esther and the Theme of Women as a Civilizing Force," in *Old Testament Interpretation Past, Present, and Future: Essays in Honor of Gene M. Tucker* (ed. James Lu-

God never appears in the book), Esther did indeed "come to royal dignity for just such a time as this" (Esth 4:14)—to be a savior of the Jews from the death decree of Haman under King Xerxes. Although Esther was of worth in the king's eyes because of her physical charm, according to the story, the ultimate value of her personhood was in her inner beauty—the character qualities of loyalty, courage, and obedience to God. The character of Esther is a model for life in a severe crisis.

> [The author] respects Esther as a woman of courage and intelligence who does not abandon her dignity even when facing an enemy and struggling to influence the erratic will of a despotic husband. Moreover, the author depicts a successful relationship of power-sharing between male and female, in which both attain prestige and influence in the community. In the pivotal scene in ch. 4, man and woman give each other mutual obedience. What is more, the book takes as its hero a woman whose importance to the Jewish people does not lie in childbearing; there are only a handful of such cases in the Bible.[276]

Similarly, Sidnie Ann White concludes that Esther's "conduct throughout the story has been a masterpiece of feminine skill. From beginning to end, she does not make a misstep. . . . She is a model for the successful conduct of life in the often uncertain world of the Diaspora."[277]

Not only is Esther a model character; she is also a woman of influence and leadership. Starting out as a docile figure, "her personality grows in the course of the biblical story, as she moves from obeying to commanding. It is she who commands the fast, develops a plan and implements it. Ultimately she institutes the festival of Purim. Esther takes charge."[278] In the last half of the book, she is

---

ther Mays, David L. Petersen, and Kent Harold Richards; Nashville: Abingdon, 1995), 195–209; idem, *Underdogs and Tricksters: A Prelude to Biblical Folklore* (San Francisco: Harper & Row, 1987), 126–45; Sakenfeld, *Just Wives?* 49–67; Marie-Theres Wacker, "Tödliche Gewalt des Judenhasses—mit tödlicher Gewalt gegen Judenhass? Hermeneutische Überlegungen zu Est 9," in *Das Manna fällt auch heute noch. Beiträge zur Geschichte und Theologie des Alten, Ersten Testaments. Festschrift für Erich Zenger* (ed. Frank-Lothar Hossfeld and Ludger Schwienhorst-Schönberger; Herders biblische Studien 44; Freiburg: Herder, 2004), 609–37; Sidnie Ann White, "Esther: A Feminine Model for Jewish Diaspora," in *Gender and Difference in Ancient Israel* (ed. Peggy L. Day; Minneapolis: Fortress, 1989), 161–77; idem (now Sidnie White Crawford), "Esther and Judith: Contrasts in Character," in *The Book of Esther in Modern Research* (ed. Sidnie White Crawford and Leonard J. Greenspoon; London: T&T Clark, 2003), 61–76; Bea Wyler, "Esther: The Incomplete Emancipation of a Queen," in *A Feminist Companion to Esther, Judith, and Susanna* (ed. Athalya Brenner; FCB 7; Sheffield, Eng.: Sheffield Academic Press, 1995), 111–35.

[276] Fox, *Character and Ideology,* 210. Fox (pp. 205–11) refutes the feminist critiques of Esther Fuchs, A. L. Laffey, and others who see in this book only a "stereotypical woman in a man's world" in "full compliance with patriarchy." I highlight here the positive valuation of the woman Esther, but she is not without character faults. In ch. 7, below, which discusses her exogamous marriage to Ahasuerus, Esther's compromise of biblical principles will be made clear.

[277] White, "Esther," 173; cf. Crawford, "Esther and Judith," 61–76. For a Christian perspective of Esther as an exemplar of God's servant, see Beckett, *Gospel in Esther,* passim.

[278] Bronner, "Esther Revisited," 194; cf. idem, "Reclaiming Esther." For further demonstration of Esther's role as authoritative, liberating leader, see esp. Berlin, *Esther,*

"assertive, active in the political realm, and full of self-confidence."[279] Esther's influence as a woman is also revealed by an emphasis upon her wisdom: the narrator makes use of intricate intertextual linkages between Esther and the Joseph
narrative to present Esther as a wisdom heroine.[280] And finally, according to the
epilogue of the book (9:16–32, esp. v. 32), Esther is "the one with the authority to
codify and authenticate for later generations the celebratory practices begun by
the Jewish populace at large."[281]

Without ignoring Esther, Vashti must also be recognized as an "unsung heroine" in the book.[282] Vashti was "a rare woman to have retained her sense of dignity and morality to the extent that she was prepared to endanger her life by
refusing her lord and master's bidding to show off her body to the assembled
throng.... [Vashti] demonstrated that moral conscience was the ultimate arbiter
of human behavior, and that human freedom was not to be surrendered under
any circumstances, even the most extreme." She was "a woman to be admired
above all his [the king's] fawning ministers and admiring concubines, the one
person in his entire entourage who could be relied upon to give him wise and objective counsel, rather than—in the case of everyone else—to tell him what they
thought he wanted to hear."[283]

Writings: Hymnic/Wisdom Literature

Job. The book of Job contains no major woman characters, but brief glimpses of
Job's wife and daughters make a profound statement.[284] After the calamities that
strike Job and his family, Job's wife seems to encourage him to give up and die,
perhaps suggesting that he persist in his honesty even to the point of cursing God
(Job 2:9).[285] Job says, "You speak as any foolish woman would speak" (Job 2:10),
but although he criticizes his wife's speech, this should not be interpreted as de-

---

liv–lvii; Craghan, "Esther"; Gitay, "Esther and the Queen's Throne," 136–48; Sakenfeld,
Just Wives? 49–67; and Wyler, "Esther."

[279] Lubitch, "A Feminist's Look at Esther," 441.

[280] For the intertextual linkages and implications, see esp. Butting, "Esther"; and
Niditch, "Esther."

[281] Camp, "Female Voice, Written Word," 106 (see 105–7).

[282] In addition to the sources listed above for characterizations of Esther (many of
which also look at Vashti), see Jeffrey M. Cohen, "Vashti—an Unsung Heroine," *JBQ* 24
(1996): 103–6.

[283] Ibid., 105–6.

[284] For a bibliography on women in the hymnic/Wisdom literature, see esp. Bellis,
Helpmates, Harlots, and Heroes, 204–5.

[285] Carol A. Newsom, "Job," *WBC* 131–32, explores possible interpretations and the
implications connected with the ambiguity of the Hebrew noun *tummâ* ("in complete accord with moral and religious norms" vs. "utter honesty"). Ambiguity in the verbal root
brk used by Job's wife must also be recognized, as pointed out by C. L. Seow, "Job's Wife,"
in *Engaging the Bible in a Gendered World: An Introduction to Feminist Biblical Interpretation in Honor of Katharine Doob Sakenfeld* (ed. Linda Day and Carolyn Pressler; Louisville:
Westminster John Knox, 2006), 148–49: "Should it be taken at face value to mean 'bless,'
or is it a euphemism for 'curse'? Or is it, perhaps, intentionally ambiguous and cannot be

meaning her as a person, and may even be read in a positive way as an ironic statement by Job.[286]

The epilogue of the book reveals an amazing affirmation of female status on the part of both the narrator and Job. The narrator, after portraying Job's recovery of health, lists his new daughters by name (Jemimah, Keziah, and Keren-Happuch), whereas his new sons remain anonymous (42:13–14). "To record the act of naming means, among other things, to accentuate the importance of a given birth, of a given child"[287]—and thus to name the daughters and not the sons is to highlight their importance. Further insight into Job's perhaps newly heightened appreciation of the feminine is indicated by the meanings of the names given to his daughters. He "endows his daughters with captivating names which match their renowned beauty: Bright Day (or possibly Dove), Cassia (a type of perfume), and Horn of Antimony (a black powder used to beautify the eyes). These exotic names have nothing to do with piety. They speak of a new world Job has discovered, a world of beauty, of fragrance, of cosmetics—of feminine grace."[288] Job's daughters also received an inheritance among their

---

decided one way or another? . . . Even those who argue for the literal meaning of the imperative concede, of course, that Job must understand his wife's 'bless' euphemistically, for he rebukes her for what she says. Still, whether or not she means the euphemistic sense remains an open question, and the omniscient narrator provides no clue as to how the reader should take it."

[286] Job does not say his wife *is* a foolish person but that in this particular speech, she is talking *like* one of them. A positive, "ironic" reading of Job's retort to his wife is supported by Seow, "Job's Wife," 149: "He rebukes his wife for what he thinks is outrageous counsel. Yet the vitriol of his own speeches to follow, beginning with his malediction in the next chapter, is certainly no less outrageous, and he will himself long for death to end his suffering, arguably the intent of his wife in the first place." Seow also analyzes the speech of Job's wife, and concludes (149–50): "There are only six forms in the Hebrew of her brief speech, three of them echoing God and three echoing the Adversary. Job's wife gives voice on earth, therefore, to the celestial exchange, giving Job access that he would not otherwise have to God's affirmation along with the Adversary's doubt. . . . She is neither hero nor villain. Her function in the book is, rather, a literary and theological one: to present before mortals a theological dialectic. How a human being like Job responds to that dialectic is another question altogether. It is a question pursued throughout the book, a question with which the reader must grapple." Cf. Victor Sasson, "The Literary and Theological Function of Job's Wife in the Book of Job," *Bib* 79 (1998): 86–90.

[287] Pardes, *Countertraditions*, 153.

[288] Ibid. See also Joan Chittister, *Job's Daughters: Women and Power* (New York: Paulist, 1990), 70, who finds Job's new awareness of the equality of women as paradigmatic of a "new world vision" for today: "The symbol of Job's new world is the symbol of Job's three daughters—Dove, Cinnamon, and Eye-Shadow, the translators call them—not invisible now, but named, not dependent but propertied, not faceless but uniquely gentle, personable, and female. In Job's new world, the feminine is very present and just as powerful, just as established, just as influential as her brothers are. Job's new world, in other words, is the world turned upside down. In this world, equality does not diminish resources, it doubles them. In this world, the development of women does not diminish men, it enhances them. In this world, conflict is not the basis of security and peace and feminism does not signal weakness; it signals the strength of every one."

brothers (42:15), a procedure "unparalleled in the literature of ancient Israel."[289] "There is something enormously satisfying about this prominence of the feminine at the end of *Job*. . . . The daughters have almost the last word. They appear with the luminous power of figures in a dream: we can't quite figure out why they are so important, but we know that they are."[290]

Psalms.[291] The first-person pronouns ("I," "we," etc.) and the first-person verbal forms used throughout the entire collection of the book of Psalms have no gender division, and so these psalms would be fully suitable for both genders equally to sing; there is also the possibility that women, in the tradition of Miriam, Deborah, and Hannah, composed some of the psalms without superscriptions. Several references to women's involvement in the liturgy of Israel may be found. In Ps 148:12–13, the maidens (*bĕtûlôt*, "young women") are particularly singled out to "praise the name of the LORD." Psalm 68:26 (ET 68:25) describes the singers going in procession to the sanctuary, accompanied by players on instruments: "between them girls [*ʿălāmôt*] playing tambourines." The superscription of Psalm 46 contains the directions "According to Alamoth [*ʿălāmôt*, 'young women']."[292] A Song," probably indicating that this psalm was intended to be sung by women. If this is the case, the "women in the community of faith that preserved this psalm are being encouraged to claim that 'God is *our* [women's] refuge and strength' [Ps 46:2, ET 46:1]. . . . When the psalms are sung by women's voices, when women claim the traditions as their own, then the God whom our ancestors called 'the God of Jacob' becomes the refuge and the strength of women."[293] The linkage of women's voices to a psalm of such vigor and power affirms the female singers who are given this special liturgical role.

The Psalms employ numerous other female images. Note the references showing high regard for motherhood (35:14; 48:7 [ET 48:6]; 127:3); God as the defender of afflicted widows (68:6 [ET 68:5]; 78:64; 94:6–7, 20–23; 146:9) and barren women (113:9); feminine imagery used of God (see ch. 3, above); wives, honorable women, and queens (45:10–16 [ET 45:9–15]); daughters (106:37–38; 144:12); virgins/maidens (78:63 in addition to those quoted above); and maids/mistresses (123:2).

Two references in the Psalms stand out with their theological statements regarding the status of women in the community. Psalm 128—one of the Psalms of Ascent to be sung by the pilgrims on their way to the yearly festivals in Jerusalem—

---

[289] Terrien, *Till the Heart Sings,* 90.

[290] Stephen Mitchell, "Introduction," in *The Book of Job* (San Francisco: North Point, 1987), xxx.

[291] See esp. Helen Efthimiadis, "Is There a Place for Women in the Theology of the Psalms? Part I: An Investigation into the Female Imagery of the Ancient Hebrew Psalter," *OTE* 12 (1999): 33–56; cf. Lisa W. Davison, "'My Soul is Like the Weaned Child That Is with Me': The Psalms and the Feminine Voice," *HBT* 23 (2001): 155–67; and Klara Butting, "'Die Töchter Judas frohlocken' (Ps 48,12): Frauen beten die Psalmen," *BK* 56 (2001): 35–39.

[292] BDB 761; *HALOT* 835–36.

[293] Kathleen A. Farmer, "Psalms," *WBC* 138. Other possible interpretations of Ps 46:1 are that it refers to singing "in the style of young girls—soprano" or to "high-pitched musical instruments" (*HALOT* 836).

speaks of the blessing of those who fear the Lord (v. 1). A special blessing is intoned upon a man's wife (v. 3): "Your wife will be like a fruitful vine within [lit. 'in the loins/ innermost recesses,' *yĕrēkâ*][294] your house." The woman's position is placed at the very center—in the very heart or innermost recesses of the home.[295] Finally, Ps 68:12 (ET 68:11)—a verse inexplicably ignored in major feminist treatments of the Psalms—embraces a most powerful affirmation of women as proclaimers of the word of the Lord: "The Lord gives the command; great is the company of those who bore the tidings." The thrust of this verse is largely overlooked perhaps because the feminine gender of "company" is obscured in most modern translations. The NASB, however, catches the import of the Hebrew: "The Lord gives the command; the women who proclaim the *good* tidings are a great host." Here is a portrait of women preacher-evangelists—a great host of them.

Proverbs. In the book of Proverbs, the position of woman is regarded as one of importance and respect. The wife is placed upon an equal footing with the husband in numerous passages. Both have equal authority in the training of children (Prov 1:8, 9; 6:20; 23:25), and the mother is entitled to the same honor as the father (19:21; 20:20; 23:22; 30:17). A lofty view of the true dignity and value of woman in her own right seems implied in the personification/hypostatization of wisdom as a great lady in Prov 1–9.[296] The wife is particularly singled out for praise and honor in 12:4: "A good wife [*ʾēšet-ḥayil*, lit. 'woman of power/strength/ might'] is the crown of her husband." This high valuation becomes concretized in the paean of praise to the *ʾēšet-ḥayil* in Prov 31.[297] Here in an intricately and

---

[294] See Cleon L. Rogers Jr., "יָרֵךְ," *NIDOTTE* 2:543 (cf. Judg 19:1, 18; 2 Kgs 19:23; Isa 14:15; 37:24; Ezek 32:23).

[295] Contra Marc Zvi Brettler, "Women and Psalms: Toward an Understanding of the Role of Women's Prayer in the Israelite Cult," in *Gender and Law in the Hebrew Bible and the Ancient Near East* (ed. Victor H. Matthews, Bernard M. Levinson, and Tikva Frymer-Kensky; JSOTSup 262; Sheffield, Eng.: Sheffield Academic Press, 1998), 29–30, who takes this verse to mean that the woman is "peripheralized" in the corner of the house. Brettler sees this peripheralization and dehumanization of women as characteristic of the entire Psalter, but I disagree.

[296] For discussion of these passages in light of ANE backgrounds, see esp. Gerlinde Baumann, "A Figure with Many Facets: The Literary and Theological Functions of Personified Wisdom in Proverbs 1–9," in *Wisdom and Psalms: A Feminist Companion to the Bible* (ed. Athalya Brenner and Carole Fontaine; FCB² 2; Sheffield, Eng.: Sheffield Academic Press, 1998), 44–78; Mark J. Boda, "The Delight of Wisdom," *Them* 30 (2004): 4–11; Claudia V. Camp, *Wisdom and the Feminine in the Book of Proverbs* (BLS 11; Decatur, Ga.: Almond, 1985); idem, "Woman Wisdom as Root Metaphor: A Theological Consideration," in *The Listening Heart: Essays in Wisdom and the Psalms in Honor of Roland E. Murphy, O. Carm.* (ed. Kenneth G. Hoglund et al.; JSOTSup 58; Sheffield, Eng.: Sheffield Academic Press, 1987), 45–76; Fontaine, *Smooth Words*, 88–149; Terrien, *Till the Heart Sings*, 90–99; and Christine Elizabeth Yoder, *Wisdom as a Woman of Substance: A Socioeconomic Reading of Proverbs 1–9 and 31:10–31* (BZAW 304; New York: de Gruyter, 2001). See Job 28 for a similar personification of wisdom by Job. For a summary discussion of the hypostatization of wisdom in Prov 8, see ch. 3, above.

[297] For studies of this passage, which focus on the characterization of the woman, see esp. Ignatius G. P. Gous, "Proverbs 31:10–31—the A to Z of Woman Wisdom," *OTE* 9

elegantly crafted acrostic and chiastic[298] form, a portrait is provided of the
"capable wife" or (my preferred translation) "woman of valour," (NJPS),[299] who is
"far more precious than jewels" (31:10), a woman of individuality and independence, valued for her own sake and not just as the property of her husband. She is
indeed a loyal and devoted wife: her husband has implicit trust in her, and she meets
his needs (vv. 11–12). She is a model homemaker: a thrifty shopper (vv. 3–14),
superior seamstress (vv. 12–13, 21–22, 24), gourmet cook (v. 15), able adminis-
trator of domestic affairs (v. 15b), and successful in parenting (v. 28). Furthermore,
she is a capable businesswoman: knowledgeable in real estate and agriculture
(v. 16) and an enterprising and farsighted entrepreneur (vv. 18, 24–25). She takes
good care of herself: she is a paragon of physical fitness (v. 17). She dresses be-

---

(1996): 35–51; Tom R. Hawkins, "The Wife of Noble Character in Proverbs 31:10–31,"
BSac 153 (1996): 12–23; Steven R. Key, "A Virtuous Woman," in *Far above Rubies: Today's
Virtuous Woman* (ed. Herman Hanko; Grand Rapids: Reformed Free Publishing Associa-
tion, 1992), 3–15; Bernhard Lang, "The Hebrew Wife and the Ottoman Wife: An Anthro-
pological Essay on Proverbs 31:10–31," in *Anthropology and Biblical Studies: Avenues of
Approach* (ed. Louise J. Lawrence and Mario I. Aguilar; Leiden: Deo, 2005), 140–57; idem,
"Women's Work, Household and Property in Two Mediterranean Societies: A Compara-
tive Essay on Proverbs xxxi 10–31," *VT* 54 (2004): 188–207; Jack P. Lewis, "The Capable
Wife (Prov 31:10–31)," in *Essays on Women in Earliest Christianity* (ed. Carroll D. Osburn;
2 vols.; Joplin, Mo.: College Press, 1995), 2:125–54; Thomas P. McCreesh, "Wisdom as
Wife: Proverbs 31:10–31," *RB* 92 (1985): 25–46; Dorothée Metlitzki, "'A Woman of Vir-
tue': A Note on *eshet ḥayil,*" *Orim* 1 (spring 1986): 23–26; Albert M. Wolters, "Nature and
Grace in the Interpretation of Proverbs 31:10–31," *CTJ* 19 (1984): 153–66; and idem, *The
Song of the Valiant Woman: Studies in the Interpretation of Proverbs 31:10–31* (Waynesboro,
Ga.: Paternoster, 2001); Yoder, *Wisdom as a Woman of Substance.*

Wolters, *The Song of the Valiant Woman,* 59–154, provides a comprehensive survey of
the history of interpretation of this passage, revealing a brief early period of literal reading
in the Talmud and church fathers and then, for over a millennium, the dominance of the
allegorical interpretation (as referring to Scripture or the church) until the return to the
literal interpretation (as the portrait of an exemplary woman) during the Protestant Reformation. Wolters's survey of interpretation also highlights the various strands of feminist interpretation regarding this passage: from Silvia Schroer, *Wisdom Has Built Her
House: Studies on the Figure of Sophia in the Bible* (trans. Linda M. Maloney and William
McDonough; Collegeville, Minn.: Liturgical Press, 2000), 15–51, who assigns divine status
to the valiant woman, and Camp, *Wisdom and the Feminine,* esp. 186–91, who seems to see
reflected in this passage a kind of matriarchal society in Israel, to the majority, who see
here an affirmation of the strong, independent, enterprising female figure (albeit in an
ambiguous setting in which patriarchy is still assumed) and to the other side of the spectrum and those who find this passage hopelessly and irredeemably patriarchal, e.g.,
Denise Lardner Carmody, *Biblical Woman: Contemporary Reflections on Scriptural Texts*
(New York: Crossroad, 1989), 73, who sees in this passage "a good wife who eases the life
of her senatorial husband," a picture in which "woman is the second sex."

[298] See McCreesh, "Wisdom as Wife," 31–36; M. H. Lichtenstien, "Chiasm and Symmetry in Proverbs 31," *CBQ* 44 (1982): 202–11; Bruce K. Waltke, "The Role of the 'Valiant
Wife' in the Marketplace," *Crux* 35 (September 1999): 25–29.

[299] Wolters, among many others, argues convincingly that the term *ʾēšet-ḥayil* in this
context should probably be understood as the female counterpart of the *gibbôrê ḥayil* (the
"mighty men of valor" in the time of David, 1 Chr 12:31 [ET 12:30], etc., RSV) and should
be translated "mighty woman of valor" (*The Song of the Valiant Woman,* 9).

comingly with attention to beauty, quality, and economy (vv. 13, 21–22). She has a high reputation in the community for her liberal philanthropy (v. 20), her noble dignity (v. 25), her wisdom, tact, and kindness (v. 26). It is no surprise that

> her children rise up and call her happy;
>   her husband too, and he praises her:
> "Many women have done excellently,
>   but you surpass them all." (vv. 28–29)

A woman of valor possesses more than physical charm and beauty: she is to be praised ultimately because she is "a woman who fears the LORD" (v. 30).[300] Therefore, concludes the book,

> Give her a share in the fruit of her hands,
>   and let her works praise her in the city gates. (v. 31)

Many scholars have recognized that this *summa summarum* of woman's virtues encompasses all the positive characterization of woman in the book of Proverbs and that at the same time this valiant woman serves as an embodiment of all the wisdom values of the book, "the epitome of all the Lady Wisdom teaches. . . . Throughout the Book of Proverbs women are neither ignored nor treated as inferior to men; in fact the climactic conclusion found in 31:10–31 elevates womanhood to a position of supreme honor."[301] That this woman is elevated to such honor is further indicated by the literary genre of the poem, which, as Wolters incisively analyzes, is reminiscent of Israel's hymnic form (utilizing, e.g., overall hymnic structure, the grammatically unique "hymnic participle," and the theme of incomparability) and forms a part of Hebrew "heroic literature" (utilizing various military terms and themes from the tradition of Hebrew heroic poetry; cf. Judg 5 and 2 Sam 1).[302] Thus here is a "heroic hymn" in praise of a valiant woman.[303]

---

[300] Wolters insightfully argues that "the Song of the Valiant Woman constitutes a critique of the literature in praise of women which was prevalent in the ancient Near East. As a distinct tradition, this literature was overwhelmingly preoccupied with the physical charms of women from an erotic point of view—in a word, with their sex appeal. Against the ideal of feminine perfection reflected in this widespread erotic poetry, which was cultivated in the context of royal courts and harems, the acrostic poem glorifies the active good works of a woman in the ordinary affairs of family, community and business life— good works which for all their earthliness are rooted in the fear of the Lord" (ibid., 13). Wolters (pp. 15–29) also shows how the element of grace ("fear of the Lord") has been interpreted in this passage with regard to the mundane ("secular") activities of the woman and how the four main theological worldviews of the relationship of nature and grace have affected the overall interpretation. I endorse Wolters' fourth category of "grace *restoring* nature" and thus concur that the woman's fear of the Lord "is integral to the poem as a whole. Religion is not restricted to v. 30, but pervades the whole. . . . Here the woman's household activities are seen, not as something opposed to, or even distinct from, her fear of the Lord, but rather as its *external manifestation*" (24–25).

[301] Hawkins, "The Wife of Noble Character," 19.

[302] Wolters, *The Song of the Valiant Woman*, 4–14.

[303] At the same time, Waltke, "The Role of the 'Valiant Wife,'" 30–31, underscores the hermeneutical importance of recognizing that the valiant wife of Prov 31 "is an idealized

This depiction at the end of Proverbs provides a literary model for women "as creative, authoritative individuals, very much in league with men for the well-being of the world in which they lived (though not, primarily, for its perpetuation through reproduction), but not defined by or dependent on them."[304] The woman of Prov 31 stands as "a role model for all Israel for all time. Wise daughters aspire to be like her, wise men seek to marry her, and all wise people aim to incarnate the wisdom she embodies, each in his own sphere of activity."[305]

Ecclesiastes. The attitude of the "Preacher" (Qoheleth) toward women in Ecclesiastes has often been considered to be contradictory: the two major passages in which women are mentioned seem to present two diametrically opposing views.

The assessment of Qoheleth in Eccl 9:9 seems clearly to be a positive one: "Enjoy life with the wife whom you love, all the days of your vain life that are given you under the sun, because that is your portion in life and in your toil at which you toil under the sun." Qoheleth here "emphasizes that life should be enjoyed with the woman, that is, with a wife, who is to be *loved by man* /= you/ and who, at the same time, is *given by God;* the conjugal life is described from the anthropological and theological points of view."[306]

On the other hand, the passage in Eccl 7:26–28 appears on the surface to take a negative view of women. As pointed out in connection with the citation of these verses in the discussion of polygamy (ch. 4, above), the reference to his finding "more bitter than death the woman who is a trap, whose heart is snares and nets, whose hands are fetters" (v. 26), is no doubt an allusion to his own bitter experience with women in his political polygamous profligacy. Such experience does not necessarily imply a negative view of women in general—only that his morally dissolute experience with women was not positive.[307]

---

real woman who incarnates wisdom" and not just "a personification of 'Woman Wisdom.' ... [She is] a real wife ... [who] incarnates wisdom's ideals, without removing her from the historical realm" (p. 30).

[304] Camp, *Wisdom and the Feminine,* 83.

[305] Waltke, "The Role of the 'Valiant Wife,'" 31. See also Lang, "Proverbs XXXI 10–31," 189: "the poem emerges as celebrating a person bursting with energy, a competent and successful woman of Israel's social elite, recommended as a model to emulate."

[306] Johan Yeong Sik Pahk, "A Syntactical and Contextual Consideration of ʾšh in Qoh. ix 9," *VT* 51 (2001): 379. Pahk reviews the various interpretations of this verse, in particular taking issue with those who interpret ʾšh without the article as referring to "any woman" and not one's wife. Pahk gives various lines of evidence for the conclusion that "Qohelet intentionally did not use the definite article before ʾšh. He did not recommend that life be enjoyed with just 'any woman' outside the marital relationship, but because of the linguistic formula *ntn ʾšh l,* in which ʾšh can mean only 'wife,' rather than 'any woman,' Qoh. ix 9b is to be parsed as a relative clause whose proper antecedent is ʾšh rather than 'all the days of futile life'" (ibid.).

[307] Commentators who refuse to take seriously the indicators in the book that it is written by Solomon are at a loss to explain this language and resort to all kinds of verbal gymnastics or textual emendations to explain what is obvious if the life setting of Solomon is accepted at face value. For evidence supporting the Solomonic authorship of Qoheleth, see bibliography cited above, ch. 5.

But what about v. 28? "One man [ʾādām] among a thousand I found [māṣāʾ], but a woman among all these I have not found [māṣāʾ]." Does this not indicate a misogynistic judgment upon women in general? So say many of the commentators.[308] But a closer look reveals something different. First of all, the contrast in this text is not directly between men and women. The word for "man" is ʾādām, which elsewhere in Scripture never indicates the male gender but refers to "human being" or "humanity" in general—including both women and men.[309] David Clines shows that ʾādām in this verse not only "*can* mean 'human' but *must* mean 'human' rather than 'man, male.'"[310] He explains: "Qoheleth must have been considering the whole population of Jerusalem . . . since if he had considered only men, he could not have been surprised that among them were no women. If he had meant that he found only one male among a thousand (whether a thousand of men and women or only of men), it would be a tautology to say that among those (men) there was no woman."[311] That ʾādām refers to "human" and not to "male" in this verse is further confirmed by the use of the same term in the next verse (v. 29), where it unquestionably refers to humanity in general, not males: "See, this alone I found, that God made human beings straightforward, but they have devised many schemes."

V. Philips Long has shown that the determinative word for the understanding of this passage is māṣāʾ, "find."[312] "Although the Hebrew text includes no adjective or other qualifier to make the point of comparison between men and women explicit, most interpreters assume that some virtue or moral quality must be in view."[313] He argues that one should not supply or assume some word such as "good," "wise," "upright" in this verse, which additions imply that women are inferior to men. Building upon the lexical research of A. R. Ceresko, Long shows that the verb māṣāʾ predominately in Ecclesiastes (and also often in other OT passages) means to "find out, comprehend, fathom, or figure out" (see esp. Eccl 3:11; cf. Judg 14:18; Job 11:7). This intellectual sense of the verb clarifies the meaning of Eccl 7:28, and there is no need to take the Hebrew as elliptical in need of a supplied word. Long suggests that Qoheleth "may not at all be asserting that he has found men to be better than women . . . , but, rather, he may simply be admitting that he has *understood* men better than women." Long offers a suggested paraphrase of the passage: "I think I have figured out perhaps one man in a thousand; women, however, remain a mystery to me."[314]

---

[308] See the survey of views on this passage by George M. Schwab, "Woman as the Object of Qohelet's Search," *AUSS* 39 (2001): 73–84.

[309] See esp. David J. A. Clines, "אדם, the Hebrew for 'Human, Humanity': A Response to James Barr," *VT* 53 (2003): 297–310.

[310] Ibid., 302.

[311] Ibid.

[312] V. Philips Long, "One Man among a Thousand, But Not a Woman among Them All: A Note on the Use of *māṣāʾ* in Ecclesiastes vii 28," in *"Lasset uns Brücken bauen . . ."* (ed. Klaus-Dietrich Schunck and Matthias Augustin; BEATAJ 42; Frankfurt am Main: Peter Lang, 1998), 101–9.

[313] Ibid., 101.

[314] Ibid., 107.

Taking *ʾādām* as "human being" instead of "man," I would further paraphrase the Preacher: "I think I have figured out perhaps one human being in a
thousand, but no woman among all these humans have I been able to comprehend." Long shows that this interpretation admirably fits the context of the passage, which emphasizes how little the Preacher has been able to understand. Verse
28 is an aside, indicating that he can barely understand his fellow human beings,
let alone the way the world is governed. Only one thing he truly understands, and
this is stated in the next verse (v. 29): "See, this alone I found, that God made
human beings straightforward, but they have devised many schemes." As Long
puts it, "The one conclusion to which he comes, the one thing he *does understand,*
is that God got it right, and we, his creatures, created the havoc."[315]

With this interpretation of Eccl 7:28, the Preacher is cleared of the charge of
misogyny, and his statement in this verse comports with his positive view of
woman expressed in Eccl 9:9 and with the positive view of women presented by
the other biblical writers.

Distortion of the Divine Ideal: Exploitation, Denigration, and Abuse of Women

This chapter has emphasized the high status of women within the patriarchal
system of the OT Hebrews. At the same time, it must also be recognized that the
OT describes situations of usurpation of power and exploitation of woman in the
society of ancient Israel. Probably the most direct affront to the divine ideal of
equality and mutual valuation between the sexes is the act of rape. But inasmuch
as this sexual distortion also reveals sexuality gone awry in its ugliest manifestation, it is included under the distortion of sexual beauty in chapter 12, below. But
there are numerous other instances of exploitation, denigration, or abuse of
women besides those of rape, and other chapters of this study deal with many of
them. Here our attention is on a few of the most striking examples.[316]

Pentateuch

The Pentateuch contains examples where women are exploited, oppressed,
or otherwise denigrated. These include such situations as Hagar's mistreatment

---

[315] Ibid., 108–9. Long provides a translation of vv. 27–29: " 'Look, this I have understood,' says Qohelet, 'adding one thing to another to understand the sum, which my soul still
sought, but I did not understand. (Oh, I understood maybe one man in a thousand, but not
a woman among them all.) Look, this I alone I have understood: that God made human beings straightforward [or upright], but they have devised many schemes' " (p. 109). Additional support for Long's conclusion (but not set forth by Long) is the parallel idea of Prov
30:18–19, in which Agur also declares his lack of understanding about women (and in particular, how to relate to them): "I do not understand . . . the way of a man with a girl."

[316] For a helpful overview of the distortions of patriarchy that led to the denigration
of women, see Gretchen Gaebelein Hull, *Equal to Serve: Women and Men in the Church
and Home* (Old Tappan, N.J.: Fleming H. Revell, 1987), 76–104.

at the hands of Abram and Sarah (Gen 16:1–16); Abraham and Isaac each lying about their relationship with their wife to save their own skin (12:10–20; 20; 26:6–11); and Judah's failure to provide a levirate marriage for his widowed daughter Tamar and his fall into lust and sexual immorality with one who he thinks is a prostitute (Gen 38, discussed further in ch. 7, below). The distortion of God's plan for the basic equality of the sexes also is in evidence in such practices as polygamy, concubinage, and divorce (see chs. 4, above, and 9, below). Within the context of these distorted sexual relationships, invariably the woman suffers greatly—in loss of status, freedom, and respect (sometimes at the hands of other women, as in the case of Sarah with Hagar).[317] But in each of these cases, God stands on the side of the oppressed women. In the case of Hagar, it is possible that the four hundred years of Israel's oppression in Egypt came, at least in part, as the divine requital of Hagar's mistreatment.[318]

The pentateuchal legislation reveals a deep concern for the oppressed. James Hurley shows that in pentateuchal legislation, "in virtually every case in which strength or power is granted, corresponding warnings about its abuse are also given."[319] Regarding polygamy and concubinage, Mosaic legislation forbids such practices, as discussed earlier, and divorce, although tolerated, is also implicitly shown to be contrary to the divine plan and regulated to minimize the exploitation of the woman, as discussed later.

Prophets/Writings

In the OT development beyond the Pentateuch, many instances of abuse of women occur besides the episodes of rape. "When the treatment of vulnerable women is the measure of worth, the failure of Israel to live up to the mandate of Sinai is revealed in high relief."[320] Some examples have already been explored in

---

[317] For the disparity between man and woman to which such practices lead, see, e.g., Trible, "Women in the Old Testament." For discussion of the oppression of women by other women (in particular, Hagar by Sarah) see Trible, "The Other Woman," 221; and Weems, *Just a Sister Away*, 1–21.

[318] As pointed out above in the discussion of Hagar, strong intertextual links occur between the story of Hagar and the experience of Moses/Israel in the exodus (see Reis, "Hagar Requited," 103–9). Reis draws the possible implication of these parallels: "Because of their faith, Abraham and Sarah merit a peaceful old age, but their descendants will pay for their forebear's maltreatment of Hagar. They will slave under Egyptian affliction as Hagar the Egyptian slaved under affliction. Hagar's nationality, the narrator's second ascription in 16.1, is no coincidence and gains relevance here. For so many people to suffer so long in reparation for the maltreatment of one individual may seem an excessive expiation, but Abraham and Sarah, as the progenitors of God's chosen people, are held to a high standard, and their sins are grave. Hagar will be requited thousands of times over for 400 years, and ever after, all Israel will memorialize her in their laws and practices" (pp. 106–7).

[319] Hurley, *Man and Woman*, 36; see his elaboration of this point, 36–42. I might add that besides warnings, the legislation contains also curbs on the abuse of power.

[320] Frymer-Kensky, *Reading the Women of the Bible*, 170.

the chapters dealing with polygamy/concubinage and homosexuality (chs. 4 and 5); other examples follow in the chapters dealing with prostitution, adultery, divorce, and incest (chs. 7, 8, 9, and 10). One may also point to accounts such as that of Jephthah, "son of a prostitute" (Judg 11:1), who, in fulfillment of his brash vow, apparently sacrifices his virgin daughter (11:34–40) after she has "bewailed her virginity on the mountains" for two months.[321] And it became a custom for the women of Israel to spend a period of four days each year lamenting Jephthah's daughter.[322] The erotic exploits of Samson reveal a decadent sexuality in which woman is no longer the helper/benefactor in a loving relationship but a traitor, a harlot, a temptress.[323] The husband no longer considers his wife an equal partner but chattel, like cattle: "If you had not *plowed with my heifer,* you would not have

---

[321] Although exegetes are not in full agreement on whether Jephthah indeed sacrificed his virgin daughter or only banished her, the former seems more probable in light of the textual data. See Robert G. Boling, *Judges: A New Translation with Introduction and Commentary* (AB 6A; Garden City, N.Y.: 1975), 209; Dale S. DeWitt, "The Jephthah Traditions: A Rhetorical and Literary Study in the Deuteronomistic History" (PhD diss., Andrews University, 1986), 197–236; Frymer-Kensky, *Reading the Women of the Bible,* 102–17; Bernard P. Robinson, "The Story of Jephthah and His Daughter: Then and Now," *Bib* 85 (2004): 331–48; and Trible, *Texts of Terror,* 93–118. Numerous feminist studies of this narrative in one way or another expound negatively upon the "phallogocentric bias in the stories" (J. Cheryl Exum, "Murder They Wrote: Ideology and the Manipulation of Female Presence in Biblical Narrative," in "Ad feminam: Fiftieth Anniversary Volume," ed. Alice Bach, *USQR* 43 [1989]: 36; repr., in *The Pleasure of Her Text: Feminist Readings of Biblical and Historical Texts* [ed. Alice Bach; Philadelphia: Trinity Press International, 1990], 45–67); see Bellis, *Helpmates, Harlots, and Heroes,* 136–39, for a bibliography, and Lanoir, *Femmes fatales,* 149–70. By contrast, Walter Sundberg, "Jephthah's Daughter: An Invitation to Non-lectionary Preaching," *WW* 13 (1993): 85–90, sees the narrative positively as providing a typological portrait of the atonement: "In skeletal form, *the sacrifice of Jephthah's daughter is the story of a father who gives up his only child for the sake of the people Israel.* Does not her story call us to Christ? Does not sacrifice of this daughter remind us of the sacrifice of God's Son?" (p. 87). Such interpretation is speculative, at best. More to the point, David Janzen, in a penetrating analysis of the passage, argues that the inclusion of the sacrifice of Jephthah's daughter into the narrative "teaches yet again the Deuteronomistic lesson that when Israel sacrifices like foreigners it will act like them, as well" ("Why the Deuteronomist Told about the Sacrifice of Jephthah's Daughter," *JSOT* 29 [2005]: 339–57 [quote at p. 354]).

[322] Although it may be argued that the point of the Jephthah narrative was that his daughter was his only child and not that she was female, nonetheless the story points up the vulnerability of females to abuse under the power of patriarchal figures—and all the more so when such figures believe they are doing God's bidding, as in the case of Jephthah's fulfilling of his vow despite the clear prohibition of murder in the sixth commandment of the Decalogue and the clear divine counsel against offering child sacrifices (see ch. 11, below).

[323] See, e.g., James L. Crenshaw, *Samson: A Secret Betrayed, a Vow Ignored* (Atlanta: John Knox, 1978); J. Cheryl Exum, "Samson's Women," in *Fragmented Women: Feminist (Sub)Versions of Biblical Narratives* (JSOTSup 163; Sheffield, Eng.: JSOT Press, 1993), 61–93; Carol Smith, "Delilah: A Suitable Case for (Feminist) Treatment?" in *Judges* (ed. Athalya Brenner; FCB[2] 4; Sheffield, Eng.: Sheffield Academic Press, 1999), 93–116; idem, "Samson and Delilah: A Parable of Power?" JSOT no. 76 (1997): 45–57.

found out my riddle" (14:18). The story of the Levite's concubine at the end of Judges reveals not only the husband's abuse and gang rape of the daughter but a large web of abusive situations in a chaotic society that ends with a whole tribe of Israel decimated and the forced marriage of four hundred virgins of Jabesh-gilead (Judg 21).[324]

The beginning of the monarchy reveals further erosion in the dignified treatment of women, in particular on the part of Israel's leaders. David's interaction with his many wives reveals the monarchial trend to treat women as means to political ends.[325] Absalom's lying with David's ten concubines again reveals women as pawns in the hands of politicians (2 Sam 16:20–22). After a promising beginning under divine wisdom in his affirmation of the Shulammite (insights in Song of Songs; see chapters 13 and 14, below), Solomon's political alliances sealed by marriage to foreign women later in his life likewise bespeak a degradation and abuse of women. Even the wording "King Solomon loved [ʾāhab] many foreign women" (1 Kgs 11:1) may connote an abuse of womanhood. Samuel Terrien points out that the Hebrew verb "to love" may have two different emphases, depending on how it is vocalized. If it is an active pronunciation (ʾāhab), it refers to the act of love but with no implication of duration. Thus when Solomon is said to have "loved many foreign women," the verb ʾāhab indicates "lustful and casual encounters." In contrast, when Hosea is commanded to "Go again, love a woman [Gomer]" (Hos 3:1 RSV), the stative pronunciation (ʾāhēb) is used, which indicates a state of being, implying a lasting relationship. The LXX translators recognized this distinction, rendering the active ʾāhab as erōs and the stative ʾāhēb as agapē.[326]

---

[324] Trible, *Texts of Terror,* 65–92. Cf. Alice Bach, "Rereading the Body Politic: Women and Violence in Judges 21," 143–59, and Ilse Müllner, "Lethal Differences: Sexual Violence as Violence against Others in Judges 19," 126–42, both in *Judges* (ed. Athalya Brenner; FCB[2] 4; Sheffield, Eng.: Sheffield Academic Press, 1999); J. H. Coetzee, "The 'Outcry' of the Dissected Woman in Judges 19–21: Embodiment of a Society," *OTE* 15 (2002): 52–63; and Lapsley, *Whispering the Word,* 35–67. For all of these stories dealing with daughters in Judges, see Willien C. G. Van Wieringen, "De wederwaardigheden van de dochters in het boek Richteren als teken van verval" (The Experiences of the Daughters in Judges as a Sign of Decline), in *Richteren* (ed. Klaas Spronk et al.; Amsterdamse cahiers voor exegese van de Bijbel en sijn tradities 19; Maastricht: Shaker, 2001), 125–38. For an overview of the abuse of women in the book of Judges, see Daniel I. Block, "Unspeakable Crimes: The Abuse of Women in the Book of Judges." *SBJT* 2, no. 3 (Fall 1998): 46–55.

[325] See esp. Tod Linafelt, "Taking Women in Samuel: Readers/Responses/Responsibility," in *Reading between Texts: Intertextuality and the Hebrew Bible* (ed. Danna Nolan Fewell; Louisville: Westminster John Knox, 1992), 99–113. "David no longer struggles with any individuals for power. His political power in Israel is now absolute, as demonstrated by his ability to take women from throughout Jerusalem at will" (p. 102). Cf. Lillian R. Klein, "Michal, the Barren Wife," in *Samuel and Kings: A Feminist Companion to the Bible* (ed. Athalya Brenner; FCB[2] 7; Sheffield, Eng.: Sheffield Academic Press, 2000), 37–46.

[326] See Terrien, *Till the Heart Sings,* 55. For discussion of Solomon's relationship with women, including his treatment of his many wives, see, e.g., Irmtraud Fischer, "Salomo und die Frauen," in *Das Manna fällt auch heute noch. Beiträge zur Geschichte und Theologie des Alten, Ersten Testaments. Festschrift für Erich Zenger* (ed. Frank-Lothar Hossfeld and Ludger Schwienhorst-Schönberger; Herders biblische Studien 44; Freiburg: Herder, 2004), 218–43.

Carol Meyers has set forth evidence suggesting that during the rise of the monarchy there entered both a systematic abuse of patriarchy and the exploitation of women.[327] God had warned of the dire consequences to the nation should Israel insist on having a king (1 Sam 8). The king and his court—and not the patriarchal system—would become absolute in its control over the lives of the populace (8:11–18). God's prediction came true. With its "centralized mechanism for redistributing resources and for establishing a strong military presence" came a high price: it meant a "hierarchical structure" with "a complete break with the social, political principles on which tribal society is based."[328] Thus "the locus of power moved from the family household, with its gender parity, to a public world of male control."[329]

This shift from patriarchy to state control is portrayed in the bureaucratic restructuring of the kingdom carried out by Solomon, which was accompanied by a demographic shift from rural areas to the cities (see 1 Kgs 9–10; 2 Chr 8–9). The wealthy wives of the urban bureaucrats no doubt led lives of leisure and boredom but lost the former parity with men in the maze of bureaucracies and political hierarchies; they are probably among the referents of the negative comments against women in the Prophets and Wisdom literature (esp. Proverbs). There also developed a strong contrast between the upper and lower classes, with the inequalities that accompany such a situation. In the rural areas the egalitarian ideals were probably maintained for some time, although the restructuring of trade into a market economy and the burden of taxation and indenture certainly affected the patriarchal households there as well, especially by the eighth–seventh century B.C.E. (note the protestations of the eighth-century prophets against all forms of injustice, including toward widows and other women [e.g., Isa 1:17, 23; Mic 2:9]).

The radical sociological shift that may be observed with the rise of Israel's monarchy is highlighted by an intertextual reference that seems to further confirm our suggestion (in ch. 2, above) regarding the interpretation of the word *māšal*, "to rule," in Gen 3:16, that it was God's intention for the *māšal* relationship to be confined to the family setting, with the husband exercising servant leadership as necessary to preserve the unity and harmony of the home and that the text contains is no justification for the *māšal* role of husband regarding his wife to be extended to men in general in the public sphere. It is significant that during the time of the judges, the people requested that Gideon rule (*māšal*) over them and Gideon refused, stating emphatically, "I will not rule [*māšal*] over you, and my son will not rule [*māšal*] over you; the LORD will rule [*māšal*] over you" (Judg 8:23). Even more significant, the first time Scripture utilizes the term *māšal* to de-

---

[327] Meyers, *Discovering Eve*, 189–96. Cf. LaCocque, *The Feminine Unconventional*, 4.

[328] A. D. H. Mayes, *Judges* (OTG 8; Sheffield, Eng.: JSOT Press, 1985), 90.

[329] Meyers, *Discovering Eve*, 190. Cf. Frymer-Kensky, *Reading the Women of the Bible*, xvii–xviii: "When there is no centralized power, when political action takes place in the household or village, then women can rise to public prominence. . . . When a strong government is established, a pyramid of power extends from the top down through the various hierarchies and bureaucracies. At such a time, women in Israel were frozen out of the positions of power, and relegated to the private domain."

scribe someone in Israel ruling in the public sphere comes with the rise of the monarchy, in connection with the reign of Solomon: "Solomon was sovereign [*māšal*] over all the kingdoms from the Euphrates to the land of the Philistines, even to the border of Egypt" (1 Kgs 5:1 [ET 4:21]).[330] Intertextually and canonically, it does not seem to be mere coincidence that the first extension of the *māšal* role from the husband in the family to the public arena of the covenant community is found with the rise of the monarchy and Solomon's political shift from patriarchy to state control. This intertextual linkage with Gen 3:16 seems to indicate that although God condescended to work with the institution of the monarchy, at the same time such an extension of the *māšal* role to the public arena was not God's will for Israel. In this extension of the role of *māšal* to men in the wider covenant community, women inevitably suffered.

Despite the systematic abuse of patriarchy and the exploitation of women resulting from the establishment of the monarchy, women as a class were never deemed inferior in the HB, even during the time of the monarchy and beyond. The OT writers maintained the Edenic ideal, and despite the moral degradation of society, the biblical narrators continued to portray the dignity and value of womanhood both by the narrative clues in the texts and by the employment of strong female imagery. Despite the monarchal setting, in which male dominated, women still occasionally appear in leadership roles—especially in the capacity of prophetess and wisdom figure—implying a continuing "intrinsic acknowledgment of female worth and even authority."[331]

Tamara Eskenazi presents important evidence (from the Elephantine papyri and Ezra–Nehemiah) that after the Babylonian exile, with the dissolution of the monarchy there was a trend back toward gender parity on the part of the postexilic Jews.[332] Eskenazi shows that women in the fifth-century B.C.E. Jewish community in Elephantine were able to divorce their husbands, buy and sell, inherit property even when there were sons, and even rise from slavery to an official temple role. Ezra–Nehemiah provides hints of a trend in this direction of gender parity in the contemporaneous community of Jerusalem: the probable mention of a female scribe (Ezra 2:55; Neh 7:57); a clan that appropriated the mother's, not the father's, family name (Ezra 2:61; Neh 7:63); female as well as male singers (Ezra 2:65; Neh 7:67); descendants of a possible famed princess, Shelomith (Ezra 8:10 MT; 1 Chr 3:19); women who repaired the walls of the city together with men (Neh 3:12); a woman prophetess, Noadiah (Neh 6:14); and religious egalitarianism,

---

[330] The term *māšal* is also used by David in his inspired "last words," reporting what God instructed him, that "one who rules [*māšal*] over people justly, ruling [*māšal*] in the fear of God" (2 Sam 23:3). But the narrator does not employ *māšal* to describe the reigns of either Saul or David.

[331] Meyers, *Discovering Eve,* 196.

[332] Tamara C. Eskenazi, "Out from the Shadows: Biblical Women in the Postexilic Era," *JSOT* 54 (1992): 25–43. Cf. Joan E. Cook, "Women in Ezra and Nehemiah," *TBT* 37 (1999): 212–16, who also points out "egalitarian roles" (216) of the women mentioned in Ezra–Nehemiah.

with women's participation in the congregation to hear the reading of the Torah (Neh 8:2–4).

At the same time, oppression of women by means of totalitarian and sexist structures continued in the monarchial regime of Medo-Persia and is dramatically revealed in the book of Esther in the royal decree ordering the submission of women to their husbands (Esth 1:17–22) and in the sexual exploitation of virgins through the royal beauty contest (Esth 2).[333]

As Meyers points out, the radical lowering of woman's status in Israel did not come about until after OT times. The "superimposition of Greco-Roman thought and cultural forms on the biblical world" brought a "dualistic way of thinking to the Semitic world: pairs such as body and soul, evil and good, female and male became aligned," with woman becoming "the victim of this alignment: female was linked with body and evil. Relegated to a position of decreasing power as the household lost its prominence, she then became associated with negative aspects of life."[334]

The Denigration of Women and Divine Grace

In this chapter it has been argued that the OT witness elevates, not denigrates, the status of women, ever pointing back toward the Edenic ideal, and that God

---

[333] For analysis of this sexist totalitarianism and the relationship of sexism to racism, see esp. Butting, "Esther," 241–48; and Wyler, "Esther," 116–18.

[334] Meyers, *Discovering Eve,* 190. Cf. the similar assessment by Richard N. Longenecker: "In the fourth or third centuries B.C., however, an ominous note arose within Judaism, which widened the traditional division between men and women and provided a twisted rationale for male chauvinistic attitudes. . . . The joining of sexuality with sin is not an Old Testament motif, but it was probably a Hellenistic intrusion into Jewish thought" ("Authority, Hierarchy, and Leadership Patterns in the Bible," in *Women, Authority, and the Bible* [ed. Alvera Mickelsen; Downers Grove, Ill.: InterVarsity, 1986], 69). The extremely low status of, and misogynist attitudes toward, women during this Hellenistic period are illustrated in the writings of Ben Sira (book of Sirach, ca. 180 B.C.E.), analyzed by Warren C. Trenchard, *Ben Sirah's View of Women: A Literary Analysis* (BJS 38; Chico, Calif.: Scholars Press, 1982), passim; and A. A. Di Lella, "Women in the Wisdom of Ben Sira and the Book of Judith: A Study in Contrasts and Reversals," in *Congress Volume: Paris, 1992* (ed. J. A. Emerton; VTSup 61; Leiden: E. J. Brill, 1995), 39–53. E.g., Ben Sira was the first to claim that women caused the fall of humanity (Sir 25:24); he omitted all women in his eulogy of major biblical figures, except those who sullied Solomon's honor; and he waxed eloquent about the virtues of Moses and Aaron without even mentioning Miriam (Sir 44–50). Although women in Hellenistic society (esp. the elite) were granted some significant rights, there was still a prevailing negative view of women as inferior to men. See esp. the summary of such negativism in Allen, *The Aristotelian Revolution,* passim; Vern L. Bullough with Bonnie Bullough, *The Subordinate Sex* (Urbana: University of Illinois Press, 1973), 50–76; Cantarella, *Pandora's Daughters,* passim; Cunningham and Hamilton with Rogers, *Why Not Women?* 71–92; and Nancy Tuana, *The Less Noble Sex: Scientific, Religious, and Philosophical Conceptions of Woman's Nature* (Race, Gender, and Science; Bloomington: Indiana University Press, 1993), passim.

takes the side of women in OT history who were oppressed, often requiting their mistreatment. The radical decline of woman's status in Israel did not come until after the OT times with the introduction of Hellenistic dualistic thinking into Judaism. Jesus and NT writers began the task of cutting through all the then-current dualistic misogynist interpretations of the OT and the denigration of women,[335] and ancient Jewish sources and practices likewise reveal a trend toward a higher view of women.[336] It remains for the church and the synagogue to complete this task of restoration back to Eden. Divine grace is available to restore the home to the original egalitarian model, while allowing for servant leadership of the husband as it may be temporarily necessary along the way to preserve unity and harmony in the family; divine grace will empower the covenant community to utilize and officially recognize the Spirit-endowed leadership gifts of women in the church and synagogue. May the day of complete restoration come soon.

---

[335] See the afterword for a brief discussion and bibliography.

[336] See, e.g., Bernadette J. Brooten, *Women Leaders in the Ancient Synagogue: Inscriptional Evidence and Background Issues* (BJS 36; Williston, Vt.: Society of Biblical Literature, 1982); Toni Craven, "Women as Teachers of Torah in the Apocryphal/Deuterocanonical Books," in *Passion, Vitality, and Foment: The Dynamics of Second Temple Judaism* (ed. Lamontte M. Luker; Harrisburg, Pa.: Trinity Press International, 2001), 275–89; Tal Ilan, *Integrating Women into Second Temple History* (Tübingen: Mohr Siebeck, 1999; repr., Peabody, Mass.: Hendrickson, 2001); idem, *Jewish Women in Greco-Roman Palestine* (Peabody, Mass.: Hendrickson, 1995); Amy-Jill Levine, ed., *"Women Like This": New Perspectives on Jewish Women in the Greco-Roman World* (Williston, Vt.: Society of Biblical Literature, 1991); Michael L. Satlow, *Jewish Marriage in Antiquity* (Princeton, N.J.: Princeton University Press, 2001); Shulamit Valler and Judith Hauptman, *Women and Womanhood in the Talmud* (trans. Betty Sigler Rozen; BJS 321; Atlanta: Scholars Press, 1999).

7

Wholeness versus Fragmentation (Prostitution, Mixed Marriages, Masturbation, Sexual Blemishes, and Impurities)

Positive Affirmations of the Edenic Ideal for Sexual Wholeness

Four major aspects of sexual wholeness emerge from the OT Scriptures outside Gen 1–3, affirming and amplifying the basic contours encountered in Eden.

Wholistic Anthropology

First, the same wholistic view of humanity as was apparent in the Eden narratives continues throughout the OT. In the Hebrew thinking behind the OT, human beings do not *have* souls, they *are* souls.[1] Thus within the OT canon there is no room for any kind of Platonic dichotomy, no room for a compartmentalization of the things of the body and the things of the soul. Sexuality is wholistic, involving the whole being. When Joseph was tempted to commit adultery with Potiphar's wife, he recognized that such a physical act had spiritual as well as social implications: "How then could I do this great wickedness, and sin against

---

[1] See, e.g., Richard Ngun, "Theological Implications of the Concept of *nephesh* in the Pentateuch," *STJ* 7 (1999): 13–25. Ngun concludes his word study with the following statement representative of the scholarly understanding of OT anthropology: "The Scripture presents a holistic view of man. While Scripture distinguishes some psychological aspects of man, it neither suggests a dualistic view of man (Greek anthropology) or dichotomy, nor teaches a trichotomy view of man, but rather a holistic view of man. . . . This means that we must maintain the unity of man's immaterial 'parts' with the diversity of its functions. No part of man is independent of the whole because the whole man stands as a complete unit as a creaturely dependent being before the Creator, and among the creatures. . . . Man is viewed as a totality, though he has both a material aspect and manifests something which is not material. The unitary view must always be maintained since the immaterial aspect cannot function without the material aspect. Hence, the immaterial and the material aspects are inseparable, though distinguishable" (p.23).

God?" (Gen 39:9). The narrator places this act of moral integrity at the chiastic center of the last half of Genesis, along with the reprehensible sexual activity of Judah in the previous chapter.[2] The juxtaposition of Gen 38 and 39 contrasts the sexual wholeness in the life of Joseph with sexual fragmentation in the experience of Judah. Sexual integrity/wholeness or the lack thereof reveals the spiritual/moral character of an individual. As in Eden, wholistic sexuality not only includes the sex act but is manifested in every aspect of human existence—physical, mental, social, and spiritual.

Portraits of various individuals throughout Scripture explicitly uphold this wholistic view of sexuality by ascribing to men and women both physical beauty and wisdom (e.g., Rachel, Joseph, Abigail). The Song of Love in Ps 45 (see the superscription) intones to the royal bride that "the King will desire your beauty" (45:12 [ET 45:11] NASB) but in the next breath reveals that "the King's daughter is all glorious within" (45:14 [ET 45:13] NASB).[3] This wholistic view of sexuality is especially emphasized in the book of Proverbs. Proverbs 5:19 refers to the physical attractions of the married sexual relationship. But in wholistic tension with this emphasis stands the description of the "woman of valour" (NJPS) in Prov 31. Albert Wolters points out that this "heroic poem" at the conclusion of Proverbs is a corrective to the overwhelming and exclusive emphasis upon the physical in other ANE literature: "As a distinct tradition, this [ANE] literature was overwhelmingly preoccupied with the physical charms of women from an erotic point of view, but this heroic poem [Proverbs 31] celebrates her activity in the ordinary affairs of family, community and business life."[4] King Lemuel's mother in Prov 31:30 stresses that physical charms are transitory whereas the spiritual qualities endure.

The Whole Family

A second aspect of wholistic sexuality is that the whole family is involved, not just the couple. Although, according to the Eden pattern, a man was to leave father and mother to cleave (NRSV "cling") to his wife (Gen 2:24), this did not mean leaving the parents in the lurch or leaving them out of the decision-making processes. The fifth commandment, "Honor your father and mother," does not cease to be applicable after a son or daughter grows and marries. The children were to value particularly their parents' counsel and direction in selection of a

---

[2] Warren Johns, personal communication, February 12, 1997.

[3] Some versions supply the word "palace" after "within" to put the emphasis upon external/spatial aesthetics (so, e.g., NKJV, "the royal daughter is all glorious within the palace"), but such addition is not in the original, and I prefer to take the MT as it reads and see this as a reference to the inner beauty of the royal daughter. Cf. Peter C. Craigie, *Psalms 1–50* (WBC 19; Waco, Tex.: Word, 1983), 396, who translates this passage as "A princess is all honor within," and who points to other evidences that the emphasis of the psalm is upon the "inner worth of the princess" (340).

[4] Albert M. Wolters, "Proverbs XXXI 10–31 as Heroic Hymnaic: A Form-Critical Analysis," *VT* 38 (1988): 456–57.

spouse. The Torah spotlights the intimate involvement of the patriarchs in directing their sons toward godly wives—and, in the case of Abraham, even sending his
servant to choose the wife for Isaac.

The amount of involvement is varied enough in the narratives of the Pentateuch, however, that one cannot extrapolate from one story occurring under
unique circumstances—Isaac in a foreign land with no God-fearing eligible
women to choose from—to conclude that parents should always choose the bride
for their sons. The narrative of Gen 24 makes abundantly clear that Isaac was
the special son of promise, Eleazar's mission to Abraham's kindred was divinely
superintended (v. 7, "he will send his angel before you"), and the choice of bride
was supernaturally revealed (vv. 12–28). Yet even in this narrative, Rebekah, after
receiving counsel from her family, was given free choice to accept or reject the
nuptial offer (v. 58). Thus Torah highlights the family as part of a theology of
sexual wholeness.

The involvement of the family in wholistic sexuality is revealed throughout
the Prophets in the stories of men and women who continue to interact with their
parents (or in-laws) both before and after their marriage (e.g., Joseph and Jacob,
Moses and Jethro, David's children with their father). This theological point is
also punctuated by setting forth the tragedy of those who do not seek or value
their parents' counsel in matters of sexuality (Samson and Esau).

The Writings underscore this aspect of wholistic sexuality especially in the
stories of Ruth and Esther. Ruth habitually seeks counsel regarding her relations
with Boaz from her mother-in-law, Naomi. Likewise Esther listens to the counsel
of Mordecai regarding her relationship with the king. Similarly, in the book of
Proverbs, counsel on sexual matters, among other things, is repeatedly passed on
from the father (Solomon)[5] to his children (the term "my child" or "children" appears more than twenty times in the book),[6] and the children are advised to listen
to the teaching (*tōrâ*) of their father and mother (Prov 1:8; cf. 4:1; 23:22, 25).

Complementarity—Whether Married or Single

A third aspect of sexual wholeness outside Gen 1–3 is the complementarity
of the sexes as in the creation narratives. Examination of the experience of the
Genesis matriarchs (ch. 6, above) revealed the numerous ways the narrator
underscored the reciprocal relationship between the matriarchs and their husbands. Such reciprocity also was implicit in the portraits of other married couples described at the time of the exodus and wilderness wandering.

---

[5] See Andrew E. Steinmann, "Proverbs 1–9 as a Solomonic Composition," *JETS* 43
(2000): 659–74, for a defense of the Solomonic authorship of Prov 1–9 and of the other
portions of Proverbs that claim to originate with Solomon.

[6] The Hebrew word translated "child" (pl. "children") by the NRSV (also the NJB and
the NLT) many places in Proverbs is *bēn* (pl. *bānîm*), and literally means "son" (pl. "sons").
But in Proverbs (as often elsewhere in the HB) this expression probably refers to both sons
and daughters (where applicable).

In the Former Prophets, the story of Manoah and his wife vividly illustrates the complementary status of husband and wife. Cheryl Exum's penetrating literary analysis shows how the narrative structure stresses the importance of Manoah's wife, but "having made its point about the key role of the woman, the narrative now insists on the importance of her husband. At the same time, it never allows him to take on significance at the expense of the woman."[7]

In the Writings, the author of the book of Ruth strongly affirms this complementarity in depicting the story's characters. Richard Bauckham's analysis of the narrator's stance toward gender in Ruth reveals a deliberate "strategy of complementing androcentricity with gynocentricity": "While the male and female perspectives are deliberately juxtaposed and contrasted, the purpose is evidently not to reject the former so much as to complement it. The women's perspective exposes the men's as one-sided, relatively true for the men, but missing completely what matters for the women."[8]

The book of Proverbs also points out this complementarity aspect of wholistic sexuality. Husband and wife need each other to be whole, and Proverbs especially emphasizes how much the husband needs his spouse. The wife is the making or breaking of her husband. A good and prudent wife is the "crown" of her husband (Prov 12:4), the source of divine favor (18:22) and family stability (14:1). On the other hand,

> she who brings shame is like rottenness in his bones. . . .
> It is better to live in a corner of a housetop
>   than in a house shared with a contentious woman. . . .
> It is better to live in a desert land
>   than with a contentious and fretful wife. (Prov 12:4; 21:9 [= 25:24], 19)

The complementarity of the sexes is particularly pertinent in the marriage relationship, but as noted in the discussion of Gen 1–2 (ch. 1, above), God intends such complementarity and mutuality also in the wider arena of social relationships between the sexes. Christians understand that part of what it means for humanity to be made in the image of God is the capacity for an I-Thou relationship on the human level as God experiences an I-Thou relationship among the members of the Godhead. It takes both male and female together to most adequately represent the image of God.[9] The mutuality between the sexes in this wider sphere of interpersonal relationships can be

---

[7] J. Cheryl Exum, "Promise and Fulfillment: Narrative Art in Judges 13," *JBL* 99 (1980): 43–59, here 58–59.

[8] Richard Bauckham, "The Book of Ruth and the Possibility of a Feminist Canonical Hermeneutic," *BibInt* 5 (1997): 29–45, here 39. Cf. Denise Dick Herr, "How a Modern Bestseller Illuminates the Book of Ruth," *BRev* 14, no. 3 (1998): 34–41, 54–55.

[9] Although in one sense every person, whether male or female, married or single, alone represents the image and likeness of God, in another sense the I-Thou relationship of the Godhead is represented by humans in their wider relationships with each other, and in the most complete sense male and female together most fully represent the *imago Dei*.

experienced by single people before they marry, if they never marry, or after the death of a spouse.[10]

Scripture contains possible examples of singles who never married—Miriam, Ebed-melech (Jer 38–39), Nathan-melech (2 Kgs 23:11), Daniel (and his three friends Hananiah, Mishael, and Azariah), Jeremiah, Nehemiah, Mordecai, not to mention the many unnamed individuals who were made to be eunuchs (ch. 11, below). At least one individual, Jeremiah, was commanded by God not to marry, because of the horrors about to befall Jerusalem in its destruction (Jer 16:1–3). Others who were married moved into single lives because of circumstances that came upon them, such as Hagar when sent away from the house of Abram and Sarai. When God calls to a life of celibacy or when circumstances force celibacy upon individuals (as may have been the case with Daniel and his three friends, Nehemiah, and Mordecai if they were castrated like many other royal officials in the Neo-Babylonian and Medo-Persian empires),[11] at the same time God gives sufficient grace and a sense of fulfillment and often even empowers for a special task of service (as with all the above-named singles in the OT).[12] Contemplate especially the singleness of Hagar, whose difficult

---

[10] Single people in OT times generally may be grouped under six different categories: (1) widows (see ch. 11, below); (2) eunuchs (see ch. 11); (3) those who could not marry or are separated from a spouse because of disease or severe economic difficulties (probably King Uzziah after contracting leprosy, 2 Chr 26:19–21); (4) those who did not marry because of some kind of divine call (e.g., Jer 16:1–4); (5) those divorced (see ch. 9); and (6) unmarried young men and women (many examples in the OT, discussed in several chapters of this study). See Andreas J. Köstenberger with David W. Jones, *God, Marriage, and Family: Rebuilding the Biblical Foundation* (Wheaton, Ill.: Crossway, 2004), 174–76, for further illustrations and discussion of these six categories.

[11] For evidence suggesting that all three of these individuals were eunuchs, see Janet S. Everhart, "The Hidden Eunuchs of the Hebrew Bible: Uncovering an Alternate Gender" (PhD diss., Iliff School of Theology and University of Denver, 2003), 152–56. In brief, Daniel and his three friends may have been castrated in fulfillment of Isa 39:7 (= 2 Kgs 20:18); the likelihood of this is stronger in that their overseer was called *rab sārîsāyw*, "master of his [the king's] eunuchs" (Dan 1:3 NKJV), or *śar haśśārîsîm*, "chief of the eunuchs" (Dan 1:7–11, 18 RSV). Evidence for Nehemiah being a eunuch centers in his position as the king's "cupbearer" (Neh 1:11, which, as additional evidence, the Codex Sinaiticus and the Codex Vaticanus of the LXX both replace with the Greek word for "eunuch") and appointment as "governor" (Neh 5:14), both positions usually filled by eunuchs. Evidence for Mordecai's status as eunuch is weaker, although he is depicted as one of the king's servants sitting at the gate, in association with others who are eunuchs (Esth 2:21), and his liminality throughout the narrative seems to give him access to Esther and to the other women of the court to an extent not likely if he were not a eunuch.

[12] The evidence that these individuals were actually eunuchs is inconclusive, at best, since the term *sārîs* can mean either "eunuch" (as translated by the RSV and the NKJV) or "court official" (as in Dan 1:3 NIV; cf. "palace master" NRSV), and since many officials in the Babylonian and Medo-Persian courts were not eunuchs. See ch. 11, below. For a theology of singleness, and practical biblically based counsel for singles, see esp. Albert Y. Hsu, *Singles at the Crossroads: A Fresh Perspective on Christian Singleness* (Downers Grove, Ill.: InterVarsity, 1997); cf. the chapter "Fearlessly Single," in Jani Ortlund, *Fearlessly Feminine: Boldly Living God's Plan for Womanhood* (Sisters, Ore.: Multnomah, 2000), 95–103; Köstenberger with Jones, *God, Marriage and Family*, 173–99; and O. Palmer Robertson,

circumstances God understood; twice God drew near to encourage and bless her in the wilderness (Gen 16:8–12; 21:14–21). She came to experience God as "the God who sees me" (Gen 16:13 NLT).

For those who had wished to marry but were forced to stay single—as eunuchs—God gave a special eschatological promise: "and do not let the eunuch say, 'I am just a dry tree.' For thus says the LORD: 'To the eunuchs who keep my sabbaths, who choose the things that please me and hold fast my covenant, I will give, in my house and within my walls, a monument and a name better than sons and daughters; I will give them an everlasting name that shall not be cut off'" (Isa 56:3–5).[13]

Wholeness of Sexual Organs and Freedom from Ritual Impurities

A fourth aspect of sexual wholeness in the OT is found in the legislation that the physical sexual organs be intact (whole) and free from ritual impurities. This concern is of such importance that participation in the sanctuary ritual requires meeting certain standards of sexual "wholeness" (e.g., Deut 23:1; Lev 15).[14] This aspect of wholeness will become apparent below, in the examination of pentateuchal legislation aimed at preserving such wholeness and of narratives and prophetic literature alluding to such legislation.

Each of these four aspects of wholeness has been distorted outside Eden. To these post-Eden accounts—and legislation that deals with these situations—we now turn our attention.

Fragmentation of Sexual Wholeness

Prostitution/Harlotry

In contrast to the Eden norm, in which sexuality involves the whole being—physical, mental, social, and spiritual—sexual wholeness was fractured after the fall by the practice of prostitution/harlotry. Cultic ritual sex has already been discussed (ch. 3); here the focus is upon noncultic prostitution as sex for hire (although it is not always possible to separate the two). The verb zānâ (as noted in ch. 3) can refer either to illicit sexual immorality in general or to practicing prostitution (sex for hire), depending upon the context; the concern here is the latter.

The Genesis of Sex: Sexual Relationships in the First Book of the Bible (Phillipsburg, N.J.: Presbyterian and Reformed, 2002), 127–31.

[13] For discussion of this passage as an eschatological reversal of the prohibition of Deut 23:2 (ET 23:1), see esp. Everhart, "The Hidden Eunuchs," 146–51.

[14] For elaboration on the concept of "wholeness" regarding freedom from physical defects and ritual impurities, see esp. Jon L. Berquist, *Controlling Corporeality: The Body and the Household in Ancient Israel* (New York: Rutgers University Press, 2002), 18–50. Berquist, passim, takes the imagery of Israel as a "body" and applies it to various aspects of the household in ancient Israel.

The form *zônâ* (*qal* fem. ptc. of *zānâ*) is the regular Hebrew expression for a prostitute; sometimes it appears in the phrase *ʾiššâ zônâ*, "woman of prostitution/harlotry." Since prostitution is extramarital (which includes premarital) sex, its practice could be discussed along with other extramarital sexual relations (ch. 8, below). But prostitution, unlike other forms of extramarital sexual encounters, usually reduces sexuality to a business proposition and almost always to a promiscuous focus upon the physical sex act itself, fragmented from the wholistic links of the intellectual, emotional, and especially the spiritual dimensions. Sexuality is thereby indeed "prostituted" (put to base or unworthy use) from its wholistic theological purpose. Thus the discussion of prostitution/harlotry is included under this facet, wholeness versus fragmentation, of sexual theology.

Ancient Near Eastern Background. In Egypt there is considerable evidence, both literary and archaeological, for nonreligious prostitution.[15] For example, at the workmen's village of Deir el-Medina, numerous documents tell of "women who were neither wives nor mothers, but belonged with 'the others,'"[16] and among these documents are also found numerous portrayals, on flakes of limestone, of scantily clad women with a tattoo on the thigh, probably prostitutes wearing a protection against venereal disease.[17] As another example, a special cemetery for women and children was found at Abydos in Middle Egypt from the Ramessid period; the women were called "songstresses of the god," probably prostitutes.[18] The historian Herodotus reports that King Cheops, builder of the Great Pyramid, also forced his daughter to be a prostitute.[19]

In ancient Mesopotamia, prostitution was not only tolerated but even legally recognized as a social institution. The opening story of the Gilgamesh Epic, depicting the uncivilized Enkidu being enticed by a prostitute, indicates that "the gods in the beginning laid down that prostitution should exist in human society, as much as sexual intercourse exists."[20] The rights and restrictions of the prostitute are set forth in the law code of Lipit-Ishtar and the Middle Assyrian Laws. LI §27 reads as follows: "If a man's wife does not bear him a child but a prostitute from the street does bear him a child, he shall provide grain, oil, and clothing

---

[15] See Lise Manniche, *Sexual Life in Ancient Egypt* (London: Kegan Paul, 1987), 15–20.

[16] Ibid., 15.

[17] Ibid., 17–18.

[18] Ibid., 18.

[19] Herodotus, *Hist.* 2.126 [Godley, LCL]: "And so evil a man was Cheops that for lack of money he made his own daughter to sit in a chamber and exact payment (how much, I know not; for they did not tell me this). She, they say, doing her father's bidding, was minded to leave some memorial of her own, and demanded of everyone who sought intercourse with her that he should give one stone to set in her work; and of these stones were built the pyramid that stands midmost of the three, over against the great pyramid; each side of it measures one hundred and fifty feet."

[20] Wilfried G. Lambert, "Prostitution," in *Aussenseiter und Randgruppen: Beiträge zu einer Sozialgeschichte des alten Orients* (ed. Volkert Haas; Xenia: Konstanzer althistorische Vorträge und Forschungen 32; Constance: Universitätsverlag, 1992), 128. For a full discussion of the institution of prostitution in ancient Babylon, see ibid., 127–57.

rations for the prostitute, and the child whom the prostitute bore him shall be is heir; as long as his wife is alive, the prostitute will not reside in the house with his first-ranking wife."[21] The relevant Middle Assyrian Laws are the following:

§40: . . . A prostitute shall not be veiled, her head shall be bare. Whoever sees a veiled prostitute shall seize her, secure witnesses, and bring her to the palace entrance. They shall not take away her jewelry, but he who has seized her takes her clothing; they shall strike her 50 blows with rods; they shall pour hot pitch over her head. And if a man should see a veiled prostitute and release her, and does not bring her to the palace entrance, they shall strike that man 50 blows with rods; the one who informs against him shall take his clothing; they shall pierce his ears, thread them on a cord, tie it at his back; he shall perform the king's service for one full month.

§49: [. . .] like a brother [. . .]. And if the prostitute is dead, because (?) Her brothers so declare they shall divide shares [with (?)] the brothers of their mother (?).

§52: If a man strikes a prostitute causing her to abort her fetus, they shall assess him blow for blow, and he shall make full payment of a life.[22]

A prayer to be prayed by the prostitutes at the local café, requesting the deity that the local clientele be pleased, illustrates the practice of prostitution among Babylonians and even its divine protection:

Ishtar of the lands, heroine of goddesses,
this is your storeroom: exult and rejoice!
Come, enter our house,
and may your handsome companion come with you,
your lover and your man of pleasure.
My lips—may they be pure honey,
my hands—may they be wholly charming,
may my labia (?) be lips of honey.
Just like the birds twitter and assemble
over the snake that comes out of its hole,
may people crowd around me in the same way!
Seize him in the storehouse of Ishtar,
in the . . . residence of Ninlil, among the flock of Ningizzida,
bring him to me, make him willing!
May the distant one return to me,
and the angry one come back to me.
May his heart be again (undividedly)
devoted to me like pure gold.[23]

---

[21] "The Laws of Lipit-Ishtar," translated by Martha Roth (*COS* 2.154:413; cf. *ANET* 160).

[22] "The Middle Assyrian Laws [Tablet A]," translated by Martha Roth (*COS* 2.132:357–59; cf. *ANET* 183–85).

[23] Karel van der Toorn, *From Her Cradle to Her Grave: The Role of Religion in the Life of the Israelite and the Babylonian Woman* (trans. Sara J. Denning-Bolle; BS 23; Sheffield, Eng.: JSOT Press, 1994), 104; cf. Richard I. Caplice, *The Akkadian Namburbi Texts: An Introduction* (SANE 1/1; Los Angeles: Undena, 1974), 23.

In light of the general toleration, even legal recognition and divine protection, of prostitution elsewhere in the ancient Near East, we turn now to the practice of, and legislation concerning, prostitution in ancient Israel.

Pentateuchal Narratives. Genesis 34:31 contains the Torah's first reference to a *zônâ*, "whore"; the verse speaks volumes with one short question on the mouths of Simeon and Levi, "Should our sister be treated like a whore?" The context is the rape of Dinah, sister of Simeon and Levi, by Shechem the Hivite (a narrative examined in detail in ch. 12, below). Jacob's two sons compare rape to a sexual encounter with a prostitute. The comparison seems to accentuate the bruteness (even brutality?) of the physical sex act in prostitution to relieve a man's sexual drives—devoid of emotional and spiritual attachment and relationship.

In Gen 38 the narrative of Judah and Tamar further illustrates the reductionism and fragmentation of wholistic sexuality in prostitution. Judah meets Tamar in an open place on the way to Timnah; she is disguised as a prostitute. With deft strokes the narrator paints the portrait of Judah yielding to his lustful passions and his ensuing "business proposition" (38:15–16): "When Judah saw her, he thought her to be a prostitute, for she had covered her face. He went over to her at the roadside, and said, 'Come, let me come in to you,' for he did not know that she was his daughter-in-law. She said, 'What will you give me, that you may come in to me?'" After Judah and Tamar had struck a bargain on the price and the security pledge, "so he gave them [the items of pledge] to her, and went in to her, and she conceived by him" (v. 18). The narrator's terseness indicates the truncated sexuality entailed in an encounter with a prostitute, and this is reinforced by the use of the expression *wayyābō' 'ēlêhā*, "he went in to her" or even "he entered her," not "he knew [*yāda'*] her," thus indicating only the sexual penetration with no implication of intimacy.[24]

It is apparent from this passage that the practice of prostitution was a common one at that time and among the Canaanite neighbors of Judah was an accepted social institution (probably related to the fertility cults, in light of the use of the term *qĕdēšâ* in vv. 21–22 by the Canaanite speaker).[25] A certain dress with facial covering may have signaled the presence of a prostitute (v. 15),[26] and Judah

---

[24] See Robert Alter, *The Art of Biblical Narrative* (New York: Basic Books, 1981): 8–9.

[25] See discussion of this term in ch. 3, above. It is possible that Judah's friend asks where the *qĕdēšâ* is, seeking to put a better (religious) spin on his actions but thereby implying that Judah engaged in Canaanite religious practice. That Judah had indeed engaged in Canaanite practices is not hard to imagine, given the fact that he had left his father's house and married a Canaanite woman (Gen 38:1–2).

[26] Some see v.15 as alluding to the presence of a veil as standard dress for a prostitute, but this is not certain. According to the ancient Near Eastern parallel recorded in MAL A §40 (quoted above), a common prostitute was not to veil herself. It is possible that the custom was different in Palestine at the time of Tamar than in Middle Assyrian Mesopotamia; it is also possible that MAL A §40 refers only to a common prostitute, whereas a cultic prostitute, in Mesopotamia as well as Palestine, could be veiled (note that vv. 21–22 indicates by use of technical terminology that at least the Canaanite speaker thought of a cultic prostitute). Another plausible explanation is that "her situation [not her veiling]

spoke frankly and matter-of-factly with the men of the place about the presence of a prostitute in the area (vv. 20–23). At the same time, it is clear from the narrative that this was not an acceptable practice for the women of Israel. When Judah was told that Tamar his daughter-in-law had "played the harlot" (*zāntâ*) and that she was "with child by harlotry" (*hārâ liznûnîm*), his response was immediate and unequivocal: "Bring her out, and let her be burned" (v. 24 NKJV).[27]

In the narrative, Judah himself never acknowledges any guilt or wrongdoing in having sex with a prostitute, but only that he had not kept his promise to Tamar. The narrator, however, "is thoroughly disapproving of Judah and correspondingly sympathetic toward Tamar" and presents an "implicit moral indictment against Judah."[28] This disapproval is indicated by intimating the sense of shame that Judah senses as he sends a friend to pay off the harlot; the shame becomes unmistakable when his friend returns unsuccessful and Judah advises to give up the search for the prostitute, "otherwise we will be laughed at [*bûz*, 'to be shamed, disgraced, disdained']" (v. 23).

The inspired narrator also implies a condemnation of Judah's sexual activity by carefully juxtaposing it with the sexual purity of Joseph (Gen 39) in the center of the chiastic arrangement of Gen 25–50 (as pointed out above). At the same time, the narration of the later life of Judah appears to point out Judah's spiritual reformation as it traces his character development through a time of repentance and renewed accountability (44:18–34) to the blessing of the spiritual birthright in Jacob's deathbed blessing of his children (49:8–12).[29]

Pentateuchal Legislation. In contrast to the legal recognition of prostitution outside Israel (as noted above), pentateuchal legislation clearly prohibits this practice.

The divine legislation of the Torah makes explicit the implicit condemnation of prostitution in the Genesis narratives (as seen above). Several laws prohibit "prostitution" in the sense of noncultic sex for hire. Lev 19:29 gives the general prohibition: "Do not profane [*ʾal-tĕḥallēl*] your daughter by making her a prostitute [*lĕhaznôtāh*], that the land not become prostituted [*tizneh*] and full of depravity [*zimmâ*]." The reference to the social implications of prostitution, that the *land* would become full of wickedness, indicates that this legislation is not

---

suggested her vocation because a crossroads (v 14) is a traditional place for a harlot to sit (Jer 3:2; Ezek 16:25), and because Tamar's face was covered, Judah could not identify her as his daughter-in-law" (Elaine Adler Goodfriend, "Prostitution [OT]," *ABD* 5:506).

[27] In this context, Judah's use of the verb *zānâ* to describe the activity of his daughter may well refer to what he assumes is her promiscuity, not necessarily her practice of prostitution (sex for hire).

[28] Gordon P. Hugenberger, *Marriage as a Covenant: Biblical Law and Ethics as Developed from Malachi* (VTSup 52; Leiden: E. J. Brill, 1994; repr., Grand Rapids: Baker, 1998), 324.

[29] See Anthony J. Lambe, "Judah's Development: The Pattern of Departure-Transition-Return," *JSOT* no. 83 (1999): 53–68; cf. Bryan Smith, "The Role of Judah in Genesis 37–50: Tangential or Central?" *BV* 37, no. 1 (2003): 73–90; and Paul Borgman, *Genesis: The Story We Haven't Heard* (Downers Grove, Ill.: InterVarsity, 2001), 189–210.

just aimed at the parents but constitutes legislation safeguarding the social fabric of the nation as a whole.

Leviticus 21:9 reemphasizes the basic prohibition (adding the penalty for disobedience) concerning specifically a priest's daughter: "When the daughter of a priest profanes herself [*tēḥēl*] through prostitution [*liznôt*], she profanes [*mēḥallelet*] her father; she shall be burned to death." In light of the possible wider meaning of *zānâ* to refer to sexual promiscuity as well as prostitution (depending on the context), this case law may include any premarital sexual activity of a priest's daughter as well as sex for hire (premarital sex is discussed in ch. 8, below).

Even though the Mosaic law categorically condemns prostitution, Lev 21:7 gives a hint of recognition that despite strict legislation, prostitution would remain a temptation and even a reality within Israel's pagan neighbors and indeed within the covenant community. Hence God prohibits a priest from marrying a harlot: "They [the priests] shall not marry a prostitute [*zōnâ*] or a woman who has been defiled [*ḥălālâ*]." Prohibited as well was the bringing of earnings of a (female) harlot (*zōnâ*) or male prostitute (*keleb*, lit. "dog")[30] to the sanctuary as an offering to God (Deut 23:19 [ET 23:18]). The Mosaic law stops short of making prostitution a capital crime and in fact does not spell out the nature of punishment for this practice (aside from the case of a priest's daughter). Perhaps this is in part a divine accommodation to possible circumstances of male abuse that would virtually force a woman into prostitution, so that she would not be primarily to blame.

At the same time, the legislation gives no license for anyone to practice prostitution. Contrary to some who suggest from the above verses that prostitution was a recognized social institution in Israel, the evidence seems to suggest that although among Israel's neighbors prostitution was indeed a recognized social institution, in Israel the practice was officially proscribed, despite the reality that individuals too often fell into pagan practice. The situation may be aptly described as "*de jure* prohibition of prostitution in Israel, whatever the case *de facto*."[31]

Prophets/Writings. From the scattered references to prostitutes and prostitution throughout the OT, particularly in the Prophets and Writings, a general picture of a harlot's status in Israel emerges. The prostitute is consistently portrayed as a woman of low repute.[32] In the narrative description of Ahab's death, the bathing of harlots is paralleled with the dogs licking up blood (1 Kgs 22:38). Having one's

---

[30] Some have suggested that "dog" here refers to cultic male prostitutes, but the parallelism with *zōnâ* seems to point to a more general designation for male prostitutes. See N. Kiuchi, "כֶּלֶב," *NIDOTTE* 2:640.

[31] Elaine A. Goodfriend, "Prostitution (OT)," *ABD* 5:506. Cf. James B. Hurley, *Man and Woman in Biblical Perspective* (Grand Rapids: Zondervan, 1981), 39–42.

[32] See Phyllis A. Bird, "The Harlot as Heroine: Narrative Art and Social Presupposition in Three Old Testament Texts," *Semeia* 46 (1989): 119–39; repr. in *Missing Persons and Mistaken Identities: Women and Gender in Ancient Israel* (OBT; Minneapolis: Fortress, 1997), 197–218.

wife become a harlot as a result of Samaria's fall was considered among the most horrible of events (Amos 7:17). The harlot was proverbially known as a brazen, impudent woman without any sense of shame (Jer 3:3; Ezek 16:30).

It is in light of this stereotypical characterization of the prostitute that the story of Rahab the harlot (Josh 2; 6) shines so brilliantly. Rahab was certainly a prostitute: in 2:1 (cf. 6:17, 25) she is called a ʾiššâ zônâ, "prostitute," and the spies find her in "the house of a prostitute" (lit. "house of" ʾiššâ zônâ), which would normally, then as now, be associated with an inn or public house. It is clearly not her own family home because later in the narrative she has to bring her family to this house to be saved (2:18). Corresponding to the status of prostitution, this house is found in the outer periphery of the city, "on the outer side of the city wall," perhaps the red-light district of Jericho (2:15). In describing the spies' visit to Rahab's "house," the narrator employs various sexual innuendos, adding an aura of uncertainty about this disreputable character's intentions.[33]

In Rahab's status as a prostitute, "the reader does not expect anything from her, or at least not anything of moral strength, courage, or insight. For she is the lowest of the low." But just such negative expectations heighten the sense of wonder and surprise when these expectations are not met: "In her display of loyalty, courage, and altruism, she acts out of keeping with her assumed character as a harlot and thus reveals her true character as a person."[34] The outcast harlot turns out to be a heroine of faith. She leaves her prostitution and is embraced by the community of Israel, becoming a progenitor of the Messiah (as pointed out in ch. 6, above). This narrative contains a message of divine grace, healing, and acceptance for the prostitute. Would that all stories of prostitution in the Bible had such a happy ending.

The narrator of Judges spotlights the story of Jephthah, placing this narrative in a position that some have suggested is the chiastic center of the book.[35] Jephthah is introduced as the "son of a prostitute" (Judg 11:1). Because of his dubious past, his half-brothers throw him out of their house (v. 2), thus depriving him of their father's inheritance. Later, when the Gileadite elders need his military leadership, Jephthah responds (v. 7), "Are you not the very ones who rejected me and drove me out of my father's house?" Apparently the driving out by the brothers includes obtaining court action by the local elders who served as judges. It seems that Jephthah's father, Gilead, legitimated this son though begotten by a prostitute, but the brothers win their legal case to declare him illegitimate and thereby not eligible for his father's inheritance. Jephthah agrees to become leader

---

[33] See ibid., 128–29. For example, in Josh 2:1 the spies entered the brothel and "spent the night there" (lit. "lay down there")—an expression that can have sexual connotations, as pointed out elsewhere. Again, in 2:3–4 the king's messengers ask Rahab about the men who "have come to you," and she replies that they indeed "came to me"; both phrases could refer to sexual entry in intercourse. The context indicates that it was not sexual intercourse, but the narrator thereby creates the atmosphere of sexual innuendo.

[34] Ibid., 130–31.

[35] See Dale S. DeWitt, "The Jephthah Traditions: A Rhetorical and Literary Study in the Deuteronomistic History" (PhD diss., Andrews University, 1986), 261–313.

of the Gileadites only if the elders "bring him home" (v. 9), that is, reinstate him to his father's inheritance.[36] Thus the narrative illuminates the low social status of the prostitute and those born to her.

Judges also presents the narrative of Samson, who formed various erotic attachments in the indulgence of unrestrained or unlawful sexual passions. This narrative records a display of physical lust outside marriage: in an affair in which love has no part, Samson has sexual relations with a harlot of Gaza (16:1–3). The erotic exploits of Samson reveal a decadent sexuality in which the wholistic divine ideal has been hopelessly fractured. Wholesome sexuality degenerates into sensuality and sentimentality; the spiritual dimension is ignored in the self-centered search for what "pleases me well" (14:3 RSV).[37]

First Kings presents a story of prostitutes (see ch. 6, above). The two prostitutes of 1 Kgs 3 apparently lived together in a brothel (note the reference to a single house and the mention of "strangers" [3:18 NASB; Heb. *zār*]). This story once again reveals prostitutes' "marginal status and their reputation for lying and self-interest."[38] At the same time it reveals a prostitute's heart still soft toward her child; her profession has not quenched the feelings of the deepest emotional bonds of affection for the fruit of her womb.

In the Wisdom literature of the Writings, the book of Proverbs contains several warnings concerning prostitutes (*zōnôt*). These passages are to be seen as part of the larger counsel against being seduced by the "strange woman" (2:16 NASB)—who is probably a married woman seeking adulterous affairs (and hence discussed in more detail in ch. 8, below, on adultery, and in the discussion of the parody of beautiful and wholesome sex, ch. 12). Proverbs 6:26 has been interpreted as about a prostitute and an adulteress either in synonymous parallelism or in contrast to each other (antithetical parallelism): "for a prostitute's [*iššâ zônâ*] fee is only a loaf of bread, but the wife of another [an adulteress] stalks a man's very life." I take it as synonymous parallelism in light of the similar comparisons elsewhere in the book.

Proverbs describes the adulteress (7:19) or "loose woman" (v. 5), "decked out like a prostitute [*zônâ*]" (v. 10). This woman approaches an unsuspecting youth, "She seizes him and kisses him, and with impudent face she says to him: 'I must

---

[36] See David Marcus, "The Bargaining between Jephthah and the Elders (Judges 11:4–11)," *JNES* 19 (1989): 95–100; idem, "The Legal Dispute between Jephthah and the Elders," *HAR* 12 (1990): 105–13; followed by Roy Gane, *God's Faulty Heroes* (Hagerstown, Md.: Review and Herald, 1996), 90.

[37] See James L. Crenshaw, *Samson: A Secret Betrayed, a Vow Ignored* (Atlanta: John Knox, 1978), 65–98, for identification and analysis of the various kinds of erotic attachments in Samson's career. This view is contra the postmodern reading of David M. Gunn, "Samson of Sorrows: An Isaianic Gloss on Judges 13–16," in *Reading between Texts: Intertextuality and the Hebrew Bible* (ed. Danna Nolan Fewell; Louisville: Westminster John Knox, 1992), 225–53, who deconstructs the biblical text to rehabilitate Samson into a noble servant of Yahweh (compared repeatedly to the Servant in Isaiah) who enters into wholesome and loving relationships but is bullied and forsaken by Yahweh. Gunn's reading clearly goes against the grain of the text in its final form.

[38] Bird, "The Harlot as Heroine," 133.

provide a sacrificial meal, / today I must fulfill [*šillamtî*] my vows'" (vv. 13–14).[39] In light of the fact that the adulteress tells the young man that her husband has taken the money bag (v. 20), Karel van der Toorn argues that this woman "implies that she does not have access to the money she needs in order to discharge her religious obligations. The only way out that she can think of, or so she suggests, is prostitution. Of course she is no common whore! Under normal circumstances she would not dream of doing such things. But necessity knows no law."[40]

Proverbs 23:27 clearly seems to place "prostitute" and "adulteress" in synonymous parallelism, although not thereby implying that the two terms are exactly equivalent: "For a prostitute [*zônâ*] is a deep pit; an adulteress [*nokriyyâ*, lit. 'foreign woman'] is a narrow well." The last mention of prostitutes in Proverbs is 29:3: "A child who loves wisdom makes a parent glad, but to keep company with prostitutes [*zônôt*] is to squander one's substance."

Metaphorical References. Metaphorical references to harlotry/promiscuity/prostitute (the verb *zānâ* and its nominal derivatives, including *zônâ*) constitute the majority of appearances in the OT. These occur in a context depicting Israel's spiritual apostasy by "playing the whore" with other gods and/or other nations. Our discussion of the fertility cults has already alluded to this usage found throughout the OT but concentrated in the Latter Prophets. We saw that "metaphorical" harlotry cannot be separated from physical prostitution in Israel, inasmuch as the fertility cult rituals probably included sexual intercourse with temple prostitutes. Whereas chapter 3, above, examined a sample of these passages to illuminate the nature of the fertility worship and the use of husband imagery for God, here we look at the major passages to glean theological insight into the practice of prostitution. Passages dealing with spiritual (metaphorical) prostitution on the part of Israel shed light on the distortion of sexuality through physical prostitution. Our exploration spotlights the writings of three biblical prophets—Hosea (esp. Hos 1–3), Jeremiah (esp. Jer 2–3), and Ezekiel (esp. Ezek 16; 23)—where the contours of harlotry are most vividly thrown in relief.[41]

---

[39] The translation for v. 14 is adopted from Karel van der Toorn, "Female Prostitution in Payment of Vows in Ancient Israel," *JBL* 108 (1989): 193–205. Following suggestions of G. Boström and W. McKane, van der Toorn has made a strong case for translating *šillamtî* as "I must fulfill" (future), not "I have fulfilled" (past). She points out that the Perfective in Hebrew can refer to "an action expected to occur in the near future" (p. 198, citing Joüon §112g).

[40] Van der Toorn, "Female Prostitution in Payment of Vows," 199.

[41] For the passages in Hosea and Jeremiah, see esp. Richtsje Abma, *Bonds of Love: Methodic Studies of Prophetic Texts with Marriage Imagery (Isaiah 50:1–3 and 54:1–10; Hosea 1–3, Jeremiah 2–3)* (Assen, Neth.: Van Gorcum, 1999); for all the passages, see esp. Raymond C. Ortlund Jr., *Whoredom: God's Unfaithful Wife in Biblical Theology* (Grand Rapids: Eerdmans, 1996; repr. as *God's Unfaithful Wife: A Biblical Theology of Spiritual Adultery* [NSBT 2; Downers Grove, Ill.: InterVarsity, 2002]); and Ruben Zimmermann, *Geschlechtermetaphorik und Gottesverhältnis: Traditionsgeschichte und Theologie eines Bildfelds in Urchristentum und antiker Umwelt* (WUNT[2] 122; Tübingen: Mohr Siebeck, 2001), 104–52. Brief use of prostitution/harlotry terminology regarding Israel's apostasy is also found in Isa 1:21 ("How the faithful city [Jerusalem] has become a whore!"), Mic 1:7 ("All

Hosea, Jeremiah, and Ezekiel refer to Israel's apostasy both as "whoredom" (zānâ) and "adultery" (nā'ap), but the former is by far the more frequent metaphor here and throughout the Prophets.[42] Elaine Goodfriend suggests cogent reasons that zānâ is the preferred prophetic term even though Israel's apostasy, strictly speaking, more accurately consisted of adultery with relations outside her "marriage covenant" with Yahweh. She points out that in contrast with nā'ap, "adultery," zānâ implies (1) habitual illicit activity, (2) a motive of personal gain, (3) a multiplicity of partners, (4) a treacherous and hardened woman, and (5) illicit sex only by females. Thus "the root znh, while strictly speaking less appropriate for symbolizing Israel's covenant breaking, was therefore a more effective rhetorical tool."[43] I suggest a sixth reason: in prostitution, as noted above, there is a fragmented emphasis upon the physical aspects of sex—animal passions of raw and even vulgar sexuality—devoid of the wholistic contexts of commitment, exclusivity, and loving relationship. All six of these aspects of "whoredom" (zānâ) are represented in the Prophets' elucidation of Israel's apostasy. There is also a progression of intensity as one moves from eighth-century B.C.E. Hosea to seventh-century Jeremiah and finally to Ezekiel (seventh to sixth century).

First, all these prophets indicate the habitual, iterative nature of Israel's spiritual harlotry. God makes this clear to Hosea when God asks the prophet to take a "wife of whoredom [zĕnûnîm, 'promiscuity, fornication']" (Hos 1:2)—the abstract plural indicating the habitual nature of the practice. This is confirmed by God's explanation of the symbolism contained in the request: "for the land commits *great* whoredom" (1:2). It is further illustrated in the reference to Israel's penchant to "pursue her lovers" (2:7) and by the divine observation that Israel possessed a "spirit of whoredom" (4:12; 5:4) that tended to "take away the understanding" ("enslave the heart" [4:11 NKJV]) and thus the people of Ephraim "commit harlotry continually" (4:18 NKJV). Jeremiah likewise makes clear that Israel has played the harlot "on every high hill and under every green tree" (Jer 2:20; 3:6) "days without number" (2:32). Ezekiel's language is the strongest. In the allegory of Jerusalem's harlotry, Yahweh points out that her harlotry is "multiplied" (Ezek 16:25), "insatiable" (v. 28), "not satisfied" (v. 29). In the allegory of the two sisters Oholah (Samaria) and Oholibah (Jerusalem), Yahweh testifies that

---

her images shall be beaten to pieces, all her wages ['etnan, a technical term for the wages of a prostitute] shall be burned with fire"), and Joel 4:3 (ET 3:3) ("[They] cast lots for my people, and traded boys for prostitutes"). The latter passage shows how low the morality of Israel had sunk, that a son could be sold as payment to hire a harlot. Two more passages describe Tyre (Isa 23:15–18) and Nineveh (Nah 3:4–6) as committing harlotry with other nations. Tyre's commercial harlotry was comparable to professional prostitution inasmuch as both have an indiscriminate attitude toward prospective customers. Nineveh's harlotry was in the form of seductive enchantments by which Nineveh lured and exercised power over other nations.

[42] Verbal and nominal forms of the root znh appear in the Prophets about eighty times whereas terms from the verbal root n'p occur only a couple of dozen times in the same corpus.

[43] Goodfriend, "Prostitution (OT)," 5:509.

their harlotry already started in their youth (23:3) and Oholah "did not give up her whorings" (v. 8). Moreover, Oholibah "was more corrupt than she [her sister] in her lusting and in her whorings, which were worse than those of her sister" (v. 11).

Second, Hosea and Ezekiel allude to the "prostitute's hire"—the motive of personal gain in the spiritual prostitution of Israel/Judah. Hosea mentions that Israel "played the whore, departing from your God. You have loved a prostitute's pay [ʾetnan, the technical term for the wages of a prostitute] on all threshing floors" (Hos 9:1). Hosea also states, "Ephraim has bargained [tānâ] for lovers" (8:9), and alludes to the gifts (2:7–8 [ET 2:5–6]) and "pay" (ʾetnâ) (2:14 [ET 2:12]) of Israel's lovers. Ezekiel likewise refers to the prostitute's hire but intensifies the imagery: contrary to the normal harlot, who receives payment for her services, Jerusalem "scorned payment [ʾetnan]" and instead "gave your gifts to all your lovers, bribing [šāḥad] them to come to you from all around for your whorings" (Ezek 16:31, 33). Thus Yahweh tells Jerusalem, "So you were different from other women in your whorings: no one solicited you to play the whore; and you gave payment [ʾetnan], while no payment [ʾetnan] was given to you; you were different" (16:34).

Third, the threefold witness of these Latter Prophets agrees that Israel/Judah had a multiplicity of sexual partners. Hosea repeatedly uses the plural "lovers" (Hos 2:7, 14–15 [ET 2: 5, 12–13]). Jeremiah speaks of "strangers" (pl.) as her lovers (Jer 2:25), "many lovers" (3:1), "she took her whoredom so lightly [lit. 'lightness of her harlotry']" (3:9), "All your lovers" (30:14), and "trooping to the houses of prostitutes" (5:7). Ezekiel again presents the ultimate in charges of promiscuity: "But you [Jerusalem] . . . lavished your whorings on any passer-by . . . offering yourself to every passer-by, and multiplying your whoring" (Ezek 16:15, 25). Political sex partners (for Israel/Judah) included the Egyptians (16:26; 23:3), the Assyrians (16:28; 23:5–10, 12), and the Babylonians (23:14–21). Interspersed between the presentations of these sex partners is the pulsating refrain "multiplying your whoring" (16:25, 26, 29; 23:14, 19), describing the increasing heinousness of the prostitute's offenses.

Fourth, the "whore" Israel/Judah is depicted as a treacherous, hardened woman. This is not so apparent in Hos 1–3 inasmuch as the word "whore" (zônâ) is not used in these chapters. But the hardened harlot comes into full view in Jeremiah. She is so wicked "that even to wicked women you have taught your ways" (Jer 2:33). Yet she claims that she has done no sin (2:35). The prophet depicts her sitting by the road, waiting with cunning calculation to entice her victims (3:2). Her stubborn, unrepentant brazenness is captured in the divine accusation: "you have the forehead of a whore, you refuse to be ashamed" (3:3). Ezekiel provides the bald description: "How sick is your heart, says the Lord GOD, that you did all these things, the deeds of a brazen whore" (Ezek 16:30). The prophet zooms in on her wanton exterior: "For them [your lovers] you bathed yourself, painted your eyes, and decked yourself with ornaments; you sat on a stately couch" (23:40–41).

Fifth, the harlot imagery of the Prophets highlights illicit sex by females. Yahweh has been a loyal, faithful, and pure husband; His wife, Israel/Judah, has become a promiscuous harlot. Numerous passages speak of Israel's harlotry: "great whoredom" (Hos 1:2), "playing the whore" (Hos 2:7 [ET 2:5]; 4:12, 15; 9:1; Jer 2:20; 3:1, 8; Ezek 16:15–16; 23:5, 44), "committing harlotry" (Hos 4:13–14, 18; 5:3; Ezek 16:26; 20:30; 23:3, 7, 43), and "whorings" (Ezek 16:22, 25). In Ezek 16 alone, the verb *zānâ* or its nominal derivative occurs twenty times, with another twelve occurrences in Ezek 23. Harlotry is no doubt the key term and key subject of these allegories.

Finally, these portrayals of prostitution contain an exaggerated emphasis upon the driving animal passions behind the physical sex act, often utilizing intentionally crude and even vulgar language to highlight the fragmented view of sexuality in prostitution, which has interest only in satisfying sensual urges. It may be that this language (esp. in Ezekiel) is even borrowed from the contemporaneous "argot [special vocabulary] of whoring"; lurid images are masterfully created and crafted for their overall "shocking impact."[44]

Hosea likens the spiritual harlotry of Israel to "a wild ass wandering alone" in heat (Hos 8:9). Jeremiah also portrays the insatiable sexual lust of Israel for her paramours to "a wild ass at home in the wilderness, in her heat sniffing the wind! Who can restrain her lust?" (Jer 2:24). The previous verse compares Israel's urges for the Baals to a camel in heat: "a restive young camel interlacing her tracks" (2:23). Jeremiah also likens Israel's spiritual sexual urges to horses in heat: "They were well-fed lusty stallions" (5:8); "I have seen your . . . adulteries and neighings, your shameless prostitutions" (13:27). The sexual urges of the prostitute are equated with untamed animal passion: fiery lust and no love.

Ezekiel paints the most lurid portrait of raw sex in prostitution, using what is perhaps the slang vocabulary in the brothels of that day. The harlot described in Ezek 16 and 23 is no ordinary harlot; she is a nymphomaniac.[45] Ezekiel 16:25 speaks of the harlot (literally) "opening [*pāśaq*] your legs" (Greenberg) to anyone

---

44 Moshe Greenberg, "Ezekiel 16: A Panorama of Passions," in *Love and Death in the Ancient Near East: Essays in Honor of Marvin H. Pope* (ed. John H. Marks and Robert M. Good; Guilford, Conn.: Four Quarters, 1987), 145, 143.

45 For further discussion of these terms and the prostitute's nymphomania, see esp. Moshe Greenberg, *Ezekiel 1–20: A New Translation with Introduction and Commentary* (AB 22; Garden City, N.Y.: Doubleday, 1983), 270–306; and idem, *Ezekiel 21–37: A New Translation with Introduction and Commentary* (AB 22A; Garden City, N.Y.: Doubleday, 1997), 471–94. The translations in this section are, for the most part, from Greenberg. A further suggestion regarding the woman's sexual activities comes from S. Tamar Kamionkowski, "Gender Reversal in Ezekiel 16," in *Prophets and Daniel* (ed. Athalya Brenner; FCB2 8; New York: Sheffield Academic Press, 2001), 170–85. Kamionkowski argues that woman's sexual crime primarily consists in inverting the divine order of gender distinctions: "At a subtle level within the text of Ezekiel 16, wife Israel's crime is that she is trying to pass for a male. Like a male, she is associated with war and violence, she seeks multiple sexual partners, she symbolically acquires male genitalia and ejaculates rather than receiving and containing fluids" (p. 182). See further discussion of this possibility in ch. 4, above. Although the use of phallic symbols as dildos (which Kamionkowski sees implied in Ezek 16:17) may have been included in wife Israel's (metaphorical) criminal sexual behavior, it seems that such is only part of the larger portrait of hypersexuality described by Greenberg and others.

who passed by. The next verse indicates that "you [Jerusalem] harloted with the Egyptians, your big-membered [*gidlê bāśār,* lit. 'big of flesh/penis'] neighbors" (v. 26, Greenberg). The sexual arousal of the prostitute is presented in graphic terms: "your juice [*nĕḥuštēk,* 'your female genital distillation'] was poured out" (v. 36, Greenberg).[46] The same verse depicts the prostitute's "nakedness [the Targum reads, 'pudendum'] uncovered" in the sex act. The divine punishment ironically fits the crime: "I [Yahweh] will expose your nakedness to them [her 'lovers'] and they shall gaze upon your nakedness" (v. 37, Greenberg).

In Ezek 23 the description of lurid hypersexuality is even heightened. Verse 3 graphically portrays Oholah and Oholibah's harlotry with Egypt, begun already while they are youths: "there their breasts [*šĕdêhen*] were squeezed, and there they pressed their virgin nipples [*daddê bĕtûlêhen*]" (Greenberg). Verse 8 makes explicit that during this time the fondling of the girls' breasts awakened sexual urges and seduced them to venery in sexual intercourse: "they [the Egyptians] had bedded her [*šākab* + direct object, lit. 'lay her' = a vulgar reference to intercourse] in her youth, they had pressed her virgin nipples and poured [*šāpak*] their fornication [*taznûtām*] on her" (Greenberg). The latter phrase, "poured out their fornication," clearly is meant to evoke genital emissions. Still again, the allegory alludes to the onset of prostitution: "You reverted to the depravity of your youth, when your nipples were pressed in Egypt on account of your young breasts" (v. 21, Greenberg). After Oholah's marriage to Yahweh, she again "lusted [*ʿāgab*] after her lovers" (v. 5, Greenberg). The verb *ʿāgab,* "lust," employed here (and five more times in vv. 7, 9, 12, 16, and 20), is a rare Hebrew word meaning "to have inordinate affection, to desire carnally, lust," and its nominal derivative *ʿăgābâ,* used only in v. 11, means "lustfulness." Its recurrence throughout this allegory underscores raw sexual desire without loving relationship.

In vv. 14–16, "the prophet escalates his wanton's lewdness: if at first she lusted for the Assyrians in the flesh, the next stage of her degeneracy is conceiving a passion for Babylonians from mere pictures of them, and inviting them to an orgy from afar."[47] Pornographic voyeurism is added to prostitution. Verses 17–18 describe the orgy that follows: "Then the Babylonians came to her, into the bed of lovemaking [*dōdîm*], and they defiled her with their immorality.... She revealed her harlotry and uncovered her nakedness" (translations mine). But yet again "she increased her harlotry" (v. 19, Greenberg), once more on the Egyptians. Verse 20 contains perhaps the most vulgar comparisons of the allegory: "She lusted after concubinage to them [the Egyptians], whose members [*bāśār',* 'flesh' = penises] were like those of asses and whose discharge [*zirmâ,* semen from ejaculation] was like that of horses" (Greenberg). The oversize genitals of the Egyptians are here compared to those of the proverbial lascivious horses, as in Jeremiah (see Jer 5:8, above), but here the vocabulary is blatantly coarse and bald. The most shocking imagery, however, is saved for the end: the divine punishment

---

[46] Alternatively, Kamionkowski, "Gender Reversal," 174–77, takes this expression to refer to the woman's "ejaculation" (using a dildo) as part of her gender reversal.

[47] Greenberg, *Ezekiel 21–37,* 478.

includes handing the harlot over to her lovers: "They shall treat you with hatred and take away all you have toiled for and leave you stark naked. Your harloting nakedness shall be exposed and your depravity and your harlotry" (Ezek 23:29, Greenberg). In a "paroxysm of self-loathing," the shamed prostitute will engage in an act of "self-mutilation."[48] The extravagantly shocking v. 34 reads, "You . . . shall tear out your breasts; for I have spoken, says the Lord GOD" (NRSV).

The ultimate irony: "the woman's breasts—organs of seduction and in the end objects of self-mutilation."[49] Could more shocking and revolting language be employed to describe the brokenness of promiscuous physical sex without love?[50]

Grace. The discussion of prostitution in the OT cannot end on a negative note, however. Astonishingly, all three OT allegories of prostitution conclude with an assurance of divine grace (Hos 2:14–15; Jer 3:11–18; Ezek 16:53–63). God promises to take back his wayward wife, forgive her, and restore the wholistic marriage relation. Divine mercy is the prostitute's hope.

Mixed (Interfaith) Marriages

God's design for spiritual wholeness in marriage was threatened in patriarchal and Mosaic times by the practice of marriages between worshipers of God and those who did not fear the true God. We turn to OT examples of mixed marriage and warnings against the practice.

At the Time of the Flood (Gen 6:1–4). In ch. 5 above, I summarized the evidence which has persuaded me that the "Sethite" interpretation of this passage best fits the overall flow and literary context of the early chapters of Genesis. The "Sethite" interpretation takes the "sons of God" (*běnê hāʾĕlōhîm*) as the godly line of Seth (described in the genealogy of Gen 5), who took as wives the "daughters of men" (RSV; Heb. *běnôt hāʾādām*)—women (primarily from the ungodly line of Cain) who were not worshipers of the true God. Our discussion in ch. 5 above concluded that Gen 6:1–4 probably alludes to the practice of polygamy, as the "sons of God . . . took wives for themselves of all that they chose" (v. 2). But here we point out that the main focus of this passage is upon the intermarriage between the godly line of Seth and those who were not worshipers of God. In terms borrowed from Ezra 9:2, the "holy seed" had "mixed itself" with idol worshipers.

The implication of these verses is that the ungodly wives of the "sons of God" turned the hearts of Seth's descendants away from the worship of the true God. Although not presented as a prohibition in this narrative, nonetheless the message would be clear to the people of Israel in light of the immediate judgment

---

[48] Ibid., 484.

[49] Ibid., 491.

[50] See ch. 8, below, for discussion, bibliography, and critique of the now popular feminist deconstruction that finds in these texts the depiction of a divine battering husband who subjects his adulterous/promiscuous wife, Israel, to all manner of physical and psychological abuse.

context and later explicit pentateuchal prohibitions of interfaith marriage: "This Sethite incident of intermarriage with the ungodly leads to the deterioration of the godly family; as a forewarning it alerts the holy seed of Israel not to neglect God's prohibition."[51]

As noted in ch. 5 above, there are strong intertexual echoes between the actions of Eve at the forbidden tree in Gen 3 and the actions of the "sons of God" in Gen 6. Eve "saw" (*rāʾâ*) that the fruit was good/beautiful (*ṭôb*) and she took (*lāqaḥ*) it (3:6). The "sons of God" "saw" (*rāʾâ*) that the "daughters of men" were good/beautiful (*ṭôb*), and they took (*lāqaḥ*) to wife as many of them as they chose (6:2). Ken Mathews suggests a conceptual parallel intended by the narrator: "As a consequence of believing the snake, she [Eve] rebels by unlawfully choosing the forbidden fruit. Similarly, these 'sons of God' stumble by choosing wives from the forbidden lineage."[52]

By juxtaposing Gen 6:1–4 with the flood narrative that immediately follows, the narrator makes evident that the flood was a divine judgment upon the antediluvian world because of, among other things, their departure from the Edenic plan for marriage, which called for a complementary wholeness of two partners in spiritual faith as well as other significant values (see ch. 1, above).[53]

Patriarchal Warnings. A deep concern for spiritual as well as physical wholeness in marriage seems to underlie the determination of the patriarchs that their children would not take wives from the pagan neighbors but will marry worshipers of the true and living God. Abraham emphatically warned his servant, indeed requiring him to swear an oath with his hand under his "thigh," that he would not involve his son Isaac in a mixed marriage: "you will not get a wife for my son from the daughters of the Canaanites, among whom I live, but will go to my country and to my kindred and get a wife for my son Isaac" (Gen 24:3–4). The narrator of Genesis takes pains to highlight this point by devoting several chapters to describing the patriarchal planning and the search for a God-fearing wife. Abraham's sending of Eleazar to find a wife for Isaac occupies a full sixty-seven verses of Gen 24.

Likewise Isaac counseled Jacob against marrying a wife who did not worship Yahweh: "You shall not marry one of the Canaanite women. Go at once to Paddan-aram to the house of Bethuel, your mother's father; and take as wife from there one of the daughters of Laban, your mother's brother" (28:1–2). Isaac's charge to Jacob not to marry a Canaanite wife is followed by a poetic blessing (28:3–5), and Jacob's obedience to his father's counsel occupies an entire chapter (Gen 29). The contrast is all too apparent in the description of Esau's marriages with Canaanite wives and the grief that it caused his father and mother (26:34; 28:6–9). Isaac expressed his displeasure at Esau's mixed marriages: "Esau saw that

---

[51] Kenneth A. Mathews, *Genesis 1–11:26* (NAC 1A; Nashville, Tenn.: Broadman & Holman, 1996), 331.

[52] Ibid., 331–32.

[53] See Chun Sik Park, "Theology of Judgment in Genesis 6–9" (PhD dissertation, Andrews University, 2005), 43–48, 57–58.

the Canaanite women did not please his father Isaac" (28:8). The account of the rape of Dinah in Gen 34 (see ch. 12, below) not only reveals the divine and societal revulsion against rape; in the refusal of Dinah's family to allow the rapist Shechem to marry Dinah, there is also a vehement rejection of the notion of intermarriage between Israelite women and non-Israelite males.[54]

Other marriages to foreigners mentioned in the Pentateuch may have brought about compromise with the worship of Yahweh, although not enough details are provided in the narrative to be certain: Judah's wife, Bathshua, was Canaanite (38:2; 1 Chr 2:3); Tamar, wife of Er (and daughter-in-law of Judah) was also probably Canaanite (38:6). The genealogical lists during this time record further instances of foreign wives/concubines (1 Chr 2:34–35; 7:14).

At the same time, there are examples of exogamous marriages—marriages to individuals outside the covenant line of Abraham—that seem to be approved by God. These include Abraham's second wife, Keturah (Gen 25:1, 4; 1 Chr 1:32–33), whom he married after Sarah's death; Joseph's Egyptian wife, Asenath (Gen 41:45, 50; 46:20); and Moses' Midianite/Cushite wife, Zipporah (Exod 2:21; 4:25; 18:2; Num 12:1). All of these instances, however, concern men who lived in a foreign country for an unusually long period of time and women who presumably were fearers of the true God. The issue was not one of ethnic purity but of faithfulness to Yahweh. Individuals of foreign ethnic origin who accepted the religion of Yahweh were incorporated into the covenant community and became fully recognized as part of ethnic/tribal Israel.[55]

Mosaic Legislation. The pentateuchal legislation reaffirms the warning of the patriarchs against intermarriage between Israelites and the pagan nations around them. Exodus 34:11–16 lists the nations that God was driving out before Israel, and commands Israel to avoid making a covenant with these nations lest someone of them invite Israel to idolatrous festivals "And you will take wives from among their daughters for your sons, and their daughters who prostitute themselves to their gods will make your sons also prostitute themselves to their gods" (34:16). Deuteronomy 7:1–4 uses similar language. Moses lists the seven nations inhabiting Canaan that Israel was to dispossess and destroy (7:1) and then adds this divine prohibition (7:3–4): "Do not intermarry with them, giving your daughters to their sons or taking their daughters for your sons, for that would turn away your children from following me, to serve other gods. Then the anger of the LORD would be kindled against you, and he would destroy you quickly."

---

[54] On this point, I concur with Helena Zlotnick, *Dinah's Daughters: Gender and Judaism from the Hebrew Bible to Late Antiquity* (Philadelphia: University of Pennsylvania Press, 2002), 66, although her hypothetical reconstruction of the redaction process of Gen 34 and of the attempts of the final redactor to suppress the earlier worldview of the story's protagonists (pp. 34–56) are problematic. In any case, we are focusing upon the theology of the final form of the narrative without speculating on earlier redactional history.

[55] For discussion and bibliography on the issue of tribal ethnicity during biblical times, see esp. Randall W. Younker, "The Emergence of the Ammonites: Socio-cultural Transformation on the Transjordanian Plateau during the Late Bronze/Iron Age Transition" (PhD diss., University of Arizona, 1997), 68–74.

The focus of this legislation is not on racial intermarriage per se but upon marriage to those outside Israel who follow idolatry. The intent of the prohibition is not to ban all intermarriage but protect against racial intermarriages that would lead the followers of Yahweh to turn after other gods at the instigation of nonbelieving spouses.[56]

Prophets. Several references in the Prophets echo the pentateuchal counsel against mixed (interfaith) marriage. Judges 3:5–6 records Israel's failure to follow the divine counsel, with disastrous results: "So the Israelites lived among the Canaanites, the Hittites, the Amorites, the Perizzites, the Hivites, and the Jebusites; and they took their daughters as wives for themselves, and their own daughters they gave to their sons; and they worshiped their gods." The book of Judges also brings us face-to-face with Samson's Philistine wife and his relationship with a Philistine prostitute,[57] both of whom apparently were not believers in Yahweh, and it is apparent that his exogamous affairs (Judg 14–16) had a destructive influence upon Samson's own life and upon the lives of the nation at large.

At least two of David's wives were non-Israelite (2 Sam 3:3; 1 Chr 3:2) and may have contributed to the downward moral spiral in the lives of David and his family. Note especially the experience of Absalom, who was son of Maacah—David's wife, daughter of Talmai, king of Geshur—and may have been influenced by his mother in his path of pride and rebellion. Likewise Solomon had many foreign wives (see earlier chapters of this study). The text states plainly, "King Solomon loved many foreign women" (1 Kgs 11:1). Not only were they many (polygamy); they were "foreign women" (*nāšîm nokriyyôt*). True to the biblical warning (Exod 34:16; Deut 7:3,4), these foreign wives "turned his heart away after other gods" (1 Kgs 11:5).

The time of the divided monarchy presents further examples of mixed marriage,[58] reaching a nadir in Judah with the reign of the Phoenician queen mother Athaliah (2 Kgs 8:26; 11) and in Israel with the marriage of Ahab to Jezebel, daughter of the Sidonian king (e.g., 1 Kgs 16:13). The worship of fertility cult deities fostered by these heathen queen mothers virtually neutralized the religion of Yahweh and in the north climaxed in the showdown of Elijah on Mt.

---

[56] See Jacob Milgrom, *Leviticus 17–22: A New Translation with Introduction and Commentary* (AB 3A; New York: Doubleday, 2000), 1584–85: "There is no absolute ban against intermarriage in preexilic times. . . . Endogamy is not a prerequisite for holiness. . . . God has separated Israel from the nations so that Israel will not follow their ways ([Lev] 20:23, 24b). Otherwise, contact with them—presumably including intermarriage—is not proscribed." This openness to intermarriage seems hinted at in Deut 21:10–14, where a soldier is permitted to take a wife of one of the female captives from a battle against Israel's "enemies" (v. 10), which presumably would consist of another nation, and thus constitute intermarriage. The concern in this legislation is not the intermarriage per se, but the protection of a defenseless captured slave girl (see discussion above, ch. 9).

[57] Delilah, with whom Samson also had an affair, is not mentioned in the narrative as Philistine and may well have been an Israelite from the "valley of Sorek" (see Judg 16:4–20).

[58] See ch. 6, above, for a listing of the various "queen regents" of the divided monarchy, many of whom clearly worshiped gods other than Yahweh.

Carmel against the priests of Baal. Worship of Baal and Asherah/Astarte was not successfully rooted out of either the northern or the southern kingdom, and as a result, both nations went into captivity.

Again, the issue in these marriages is not the rejection of foreigners per se if these foreigners or "aliens" have identified with Israel, accepted Israel's God, and been integrated into the community. The record of the Prophets spotlights individuals, such as Rahab from Jericho and Uriah the Hittite, who had ethnic origins outside Israel but were fully incorporated into Israel's tribal society. What happened de facto in a tribal society is concretized into eschatological legislation in Ezek 47:21–23: the aliens or strangers who sojourned in Israel "shall be to you as citizens of Israel; with you they shall be allotted an inheritance among the tribes of Israel" (47:22). Persons who have adopted Israel's God as their own and are assimilated into Israelite society are not those who are in view in the prohibition against intermarriage with foreigners.

Writings. Some scholars have suggested that the "loose (lit. 'strange, foreign') woman" (*nokriyyâ*) of Proverbs 1–9[59] refers to a foreign woman (of another country), inasmuch as the same terminology (*nāšîm nokriyyôt*) is employed in the account of Solomon's marriage to "foreign women" (compare, e.g., 1 Kgs 11:1 with Prov 2:16). As argued in chapters 8 and 12, below, however, the term *nokriyyâ* ("foreign" or "strange") applied to the immoral woman of Proverbs refers not to her ethnicity but to her departure from the worship and law of God and the covenant with her husband and to her following unacceptable moral practices within Israel. "Within the context of Proverbs, nothing warrants our taking these Hebrew terms as references to foreign nationality. . . . The *nokriyyâ* is the 'outsider,' not on a national level but in respect to the married couple. Her adulterous intentions, not her country of origin, make her a stranger."[60]

The Writings record at least one individual who had an ethnic origin outside Israel but was fully incorporated into Israel's tribal society. Ruth specifically voiced her intent to become part of Israel and the worship of Yahweh—"your people shall be my people, and your God my God" (Ruth 1:16)—and she became a progenitor of King David and the Messiah.

Among those who chose to remain behind in Persia after the Babylonian exile, there occurs a notable biblical example of an exogamous marriage: that of Queen Esther with King Ahasuerus.[61] This occurred while God's people

---

[59] In Prov 1–9, *nokriyyâ* appears several times: 2:16; 5:10, 20; 6:24; 7:5.

[60] Van der Toorn, "Female Prostitution in Payment of Vows," 199, who acknowledges that there are other passages, such as Ezra 10, where the term "strange woman" appears, but rightly warns that "it would be improper exegesis, however, to read the same meaning into the Proverbs passages, without paying due attention to the difference in context."

[61] Zlotnick, *Dinah's Daughters,* 84–92, discussing the intermarriage between Ahasuerus and Esther, argues that "Esther's redactor cleverly avoided the thorny subject of the acceptability (or unacceptability) of intermarriage" (p. 88). She also points out that "With the exception of the Dinah affair, the scroll of Esther provides the only example [in the HB] of a Jewish woman allied to a non-Jew" (91). The ultimate irony (and what Zlotnick calls the "stunning silence") of the book of Esther is also underscored: "Plainly put, only by violating

sojourned in a foreign land for a lengthy time and among Jewish exiles who did not heed the providential openings and prophetic calls to return to their homeland. Esther's shining example of faithfulness and courage are exemplary (as argued in ch. 6, above), and God condescended to work through this less-than-ideal arrangement to bring deliverance to his people. But Esther's exogamous marriage with a pagan king is not held up as an example for all to follow.

That Esther's action was not to be followed by Israelites is clear from the narratives dealing with the Jewish exiles who returned to their homeland. Malachi 2:10–12 depicts the situation in postexilic Judah where Jewish men enter into marriage with a pagan wife, "the daughter of a foreign god." Such marriages have "profaned [ḥālal] the sanctuary [qōdeš] of the LORD, which he loves" (v. 11). Malachi registers God's disapproval of the mixed marriage with an idolatrous wife by pronouncing judgment: "May the LORD cut off from the tents of Jacob anyone who does this" (v. 12).

The last two chapters of Ezra describe a similar, perhaps identical, state of affairs in which Ezra, upon returning from exile in the summer of 457 B.C.E., confronted leading Jews who had married pagan [nokrî, "foreign, alien"] wives. It was not the ecclesiastical but the civil leaders ("officials") who brought this situation to Ezra's attention a short time after he came from Babylon. The Jewish leaders' report to Ezra summarizes the situation:

> The people of Israel, the priests, and the Levites have not separated themselves from the peoples of the lands with their abominations, from the Canaanites, the Hittites, the Perizzites, the Jebusites, the Ammonites, the Moabites, the Egyptians, and the Amorites. For they have taken some of their daughters as wives for themselves and for their sons. Thus the holy seed has mixed itself with the peoples of the lands, and in this faithlessness the officials and leaders have led the way. (Ezra 9:1b–2)

The issue here is a blatant disregard, on the part of postexilic Jews, of the explicit instructions found in the Torah (Deut 7:1–5, discussed above). The officials' full citation of the Deuteronomic legislation, including explicit reference to the "abominations" of the pagan nations, indicates that the motivation was not ethnic purity but preservation of the true worship of Yahweh from distortion by pagan religions. The pagan wives of the Jews were apparently not in the category of aliens who had renounced their idolatrous worship and fully embraced the worship of Yahweh and been integrated into the covenant community. They were still pagan idolaters, probably part of the syncretistic religious opposition group against whom Ezra and Nehemiah had to contend.[62]

---

the very law that had been devised to create and perpetuate Jewish identity [i.e., prohibiting intermarriage] could the Jewish people survive in the Persian environment conjured up in the scroll" (92). The believer in divine providence might also counter that God would have brought deliverance in another way if the prohibition against intermarriage had been followed in Esther's case (cf. Mordecai's words along this trajectory of thought, Esth 4:14).

[62] See the evidence summarized by Hyam Maccoby, "Holiness and Purity: The Holy People in Leviticus and Ezra–Nehemiah," in *Reading Leviticus: A Conversation with Mary Douglas* (ed. John F. A. Sawyer; JSOTSup 227; Sheffield, Eng.: Sheffield Academic Press, 1996), 153–70. This is contra, e.g., Helena Zlotnick, "The Silent Women of Yehud: Notes

Ezra, recognizing that "the holy seed [of God's people in postexilic Jewry] has mixed itself" with pagan wives, tore his robe, plucked out some of his hair (Ezra 9:3), and offered a corporate prayer of repentance on behalf of his people (vv. 6–15) in which he cites the commandment of Deut 7:1–5 (Ezra 9:11–12) and expresses his dismay: "shall we break your commandments again and intermarry with the peoples who practice these abominations?" (9:14). Shechaniah, one of the lay leaders, counsels, "Now therefore, let us make a covenant with our God to put away [yāṣ'ā, in the hip'il, 'to cause to go out'] all [these] wives and those who have been born to them, according to the counsel ('ēṣâ) of the Lord[63] and of those who tremble at the commandment of our God; and let it be done according to the law" (10:3, translation mine).

Deuteronomy 7:1–5 did not indicate the procedure for dealing with a situation in which foreign/pagan wives had been taken. The clause "let it be done according to the law" appears to imply that by putting away the wives, the offenders would be considered to have complied with the law. Ezra concurred with this counsel and made the people all swear an oath that they would "do as has been said" (Ezra 10:5). The people were gathered together in the open square of the house of God on a rainy day in the winter of 457 B.C.E. to hear Ezra admonish, "You have trespassed and married foreign women, and so increased the guilt of Israel. Now make confession to the LORD the God of your ancestors, and do his will; separate yourselves [bādal, in the nip'al, reflexive] from the peoples of the land and from the foreign wives." The congregation agreed: "It is so; we must do as you have said." Then followed a three-month investigation into the situation, and the ones found with pagan wives "pledged themselves to send away [yāṣ'ā, in the hip'il] their wives" (10:10–12, 19). As a result of these reforms, 113 Jewish men (17 priests, 10 Levites, and 86 laypersons) put away their wives.

The terminology for divorce in these Ezra passages is different from any other passage in the OT. Both yāṣ'ā (in the hip'il, "to cause to go out, put away") and bādal (in the nip'al, "to separate oneself") are used nowhere else in the biblical

---

on Ezra 9–10," *JJS* 51, no. 1 (2000): 3–18, who implies throughout her article that the problem is "foreignness" per se that is rejected by Ezra: "Foreigners, especially foreign women cannot be integrated into the painstakingly reconstructed fabric of society" (p. 18). This is also contra Harold C. Washington, "Israel's Holy Seed and the Foreign Women of Ezra-Nehemiah: A Kristevan Reading," *BibInt* 11 (2003): 427–38, who regards the expelling of the foreign women as "the outcome of Ezra-Nehemiah's conjunction of the feminine with the unclean" which "signifies an irreparable trauma at the core of Judean identity, a trauma that the text both records and tries unsuccessfully to repress" (p. 428). See the discussion in ch. 6, above, for evidence that Ezra-Nehemiah uphold, not denigrate, the status of women.

[63] I translate "the Lord" with the Masoretic pointing of the Hebrew text, not "my lord/master" (i.e., Ezra) as is suggested by many translations. The context appears to be one of following the commandment of the Lord in Deut 7:1–5; many other passages from the Prophets and Wisdom literature speak of the 'ēṣâ ("counsel," NKJV) of the Lord (Ps 33:11; Prov 19:21; Isa 19:17; Jer 49:20; 50:45). By this juncture in the narrative, Ezra had not given any counsel. For further discussion supporting this interpretation, see Edwin M. Yamauchi, "Ezra–Nehemiah," *EBC* 4:669.

canon for divorce. A different terminology could have been in vogue at that time, but this possibility seems weakened by the contemporary prophet Malachi's use of the appropriate technical terminology for divorce. It seems more likely that these marriages, once they were recognized to be in direct violation of the command of the Torah, were not considered legitimate, valid marriages. Ezra, the "scribe skilled in the law of Moses" (7:6), who certainly knew the technical terminology for divorce, deliberately used terminology that was out of the ordinary for both the "marrying" (*nāśāʾ* and *yāšab*)[64] and the "putting away" of the wives. The "putting away" of the wives was not in fact a divorce procedure but the dissolution of invalid marriages.[65] "In Ezra's eyes this was not a question of breaking up legitimate marriages but of nullifying those which were contrary to the law."[66]

Such actions on the part of postexilic Israel "were more than racial or cultural measures and were necessary to preserve the spiritual heritage of Israel."[67] Edwin Yamauchi points to the example of the Elephantine settlement of Jews in Egypt—contemporary with Ezra and Nehemiah—who allowed intermarriage with pagan worshipers both on the lay and the priestly levels. There soon developed a syncretistic religion that included the worship of Yahweh and his pagan consort, the goddess Anat.[68]

Ezra 10:11 states that in this particular situation the "putting away" of the pagan wives was according to "his [the Lord GOD's] will."[69] Inasmuch as the

---

[64] Although Ezra knows and uses the ordinary *lāqaḥ*, "to take," for marriage elsewhere in the book (Ezra 2:61), in the case of the "marriage" to the foreign women, he uses other terms for marriage: *nāśāʾ*, "to take up" (9:2, 12; 10:44), and *yāšab*, "to give a dwelling to" (10:2, 10, 14, 17–18). The word *nāśāʾ* for marriage always refers to marriages with foreigners, multiple wives, and/or concubines elsewhere in the OT (Ruth 1:4; 2 Chr 11:31; 13:21; 24:3; Neh 13:25), and *yāšab* appears with reference to marriage only here in Ezra and in Neh 13:24, 27, again always with reference to foreign wives. Allen Guenther, "A Typology of Israelite Marriage: Kinship, Socio-Economic, and Religious Factors," *JSOT* 29 (2005): 401–2, 405, suggests that this latter kind of marriage denoted by *yāšab* in the *hipʿil* may have involved a kind of common-law marriage as found elsewhere in the ANE, "a live-in arrangement" (402) or "cohabitation which may eventuate in formal marriage" (405), a situation in which "the possessions and children gained in the period of their cohabitation are equally divided between the cohabitants" (ibid.).

[65] For additional supporting arguments for this conclusion, see esp. William A. Heth and Gordon J. Wenham, *Jesus and Divorce: The Problem with the Evangelical Consensus* (Nashville: T. Nelson, 1985), 163–64. Because these were not viewed as valid marriages, it was not a matter of choosing the lesser of two evils, as often claimed.

[66] Ibid., 163. Heth and Wenham cite the earlier statement of George Rawlinson, *Ezra and Nehemiah: Their Lives and Times* (New York: Randolph, 1890), 42: "It is quite clear that [Ezra] read the Law as absolutely prohibitive of mixed marriages (Ezra ix.10–14)— i.e., as not only forbidding their inception, but their continuance. Strictly speaking, he probably looked upon them as unreal marriages, and so as no better than ordinary illicit connections. For the evils which flow from such unions, those who make them and not those who break them, are responsible."

[67] Yamauchi, "Ezra–Nehemiah," 677.

[68] See Yamauchi, "Ezra–Nehemiah," for further discussion and relevant bibliography.

[69] This conclusion stands in tension with feminist interpretation of Ezra's action such as that of Zlotnick, *Dinah's Daughters*, 63, who contends that "Ezra's marital

Torah gave no specific command for what to do in such a situation, it would probably be too hasty to generalize and insist that the extreme measures taken by Ezra are a pattern for all future situations in which a believer marries a non-believer. "These were special one-time circumstances. The Messianic line ['the holy seed'] was in jeopardy of extinction, and God commanded severe, drastic action."[70] Not only the messianic line was in jeopardy; the integrity of the entire community of God's elect people was at risk at this critical moment of their return from exile.

The account of Nehemiah's reforms in Jerusalem provides a third witness to the problem of interfaith marriages in postexilic Judaism, probably coming later than the situation faced by Ezra (depending upon how one relates the chronology of Ezra and Nehemiah).[71] The last reform recorded in Nehemiah's account concerned those who had married pagan wives: "In those days also I saw Jews who had married women of Ashdod, Ammon, and Moab" (Neh 13:23). Nehemiah took the direct approach: "And I contended with them and cursed them and beat some of them and pulled out their hair; and I made them take an oath in the name of God, saying, 'You shall not give your daughters to their sons, or take their daughters for your sons or for yourselves.'" Instead of citing support for his contention in Deuteronomy, Nehemiah invokes the example of Solomon's intermarriage with pagan wives: "Did not King Solomon of Israel sin on account of such women? Among the many nations there was no king like him, and he was beloved by his God, and God made him king over all Israel; nevertheless, foreign women made even him to sin." Nehemiah then draws home the point for his contemporary situation: "Shall we then listen to you and do all this great evil and act treacherously against our God by marrying foreign women?" (13:25–27). One of the leading figures of the postexilic community, the son of the high priest Joiada, had taken a pagan wife; Nehemiah records his response to this situation: "I chased him away from me." Nehemiah does not explicitly state how he resolved the situation of interfaith marriages that were already formed; there is no explicit mention of annulling the relationships as in Ezra, although this cannot be ruled out. Nehemiah simply summarizes: "Thus I cleansed them from everything pagan" (13:28, 30).

The NT (1 Cor 7; see the afterword to this study) sets forth yet a different approach to dealing with marriage to unbelieving spouses from that taken by Ezra and Nehemiah, but the same basic biblical truth is upheld, underscoring the problems and dangers inherent in intermarriage with unbelievers.

---

ideology strives, then, to undermine the role of women as potential mediators of peace and prosperity."

[70] Edward G. Dobson, *What the Bible Really Says about Marriage, Divorce, and Remarriage* (Old Tappan, N.J.: Fleming H. Revell, 1986), 47.

[71] For a survey of chronological options and defense of the chronological priority of Ezra over Nehemiah (Ezra's arrival in Jerusalem before Nehemiah), see, e.g., F. Charles Fensham, *The Books of Ezra and Nehemiah* (NICOT; Grand Rapids: Eerdmans, 1982), 5–9; and Derek Kidner, *Ezra and Nehemiah: An Introduction and Commentary* (TOTC 11; Downers Grove, Ill.: InterVarsity, 1979), 146–58.

Grace. God's grace, so profusely presented in the OT as well as the NT, will empower those who have married unbelievers to live a life of faithfulness and devotion to both God and spouse in spite of the heartaches and pains that may accompany the marriage relationship. Already implicit in the OT (see the principle, e.g., in Hos 1–3) and even more apparent in the NT (see the afterword), the divine word of encouragement is that the winsome ways of the believing spouse under the power of the Spirit can melt the heart of the unbeliever and draw that spouse to God.

Masturbation

The practice of masturbation is included in this chapter because, at least as usually defined, it refers to an activity of genital self-stimulation/manipulation to orgasm, thus falling short of the wholistic Edenic model of sexual intercourse between a heterosexual married couple.

There appears to be no general prohibition against masturbation per se by the general population, either in Egypt or elsewhere in the ancient Near East. In ancient Egyptian mythology, the Heliopolitan cosmogony features creation by masturbation on the part of the hermaphroditic sun god Atum (Ra): "Atum is he who (once) came into being, who masturbated in On. He took his phallus in his grasp that he might create orgasm by means of it, and so were born the twins Shu and Tefenet."[72] According to a later (fourth-century B.C.E.) papyrus, this entailed ejaculating the semen into his own mouth and then spitting it out as the stuff of creation.[73] One cannot help wondering if what was described of the sun god was reenacted by the priests in the Egyptian cultic rituals, although I am not aware of any unequivocal evidence to support this possibility. One possible piece of evidence pointing in this direction is the pharoah's negative confession recorded in the Book of the Dead, which includes this enigmatic sentence: "I have not masturbated in the temples of my city god."[74] It is possible but not certain that this implies that he participated in cultic masturbation in the precincts of the supreme deity, Ra, but not the shrines for the local deities.

Scholars have suggested several biblical passages as referring to the practice of masturbation, but the evidence presented in each case is unconvincing. For example, 2 Sam 3:29 refers to one "who holds the spindle." Although some have taken this to refer to masturbation,[75] more likely it alludes to those who are unable or unwilling to perform "manly" tasks, that is, the effeminate. Another possibility is that it is an allusion to "cripples."[76]

---

[72] Utterance 527 (Pyr.1248) in Raymond O. Faulkner, ed. and trans., *The Ancient Egyptian Pyramid Texts* (Oxford: Clarendon, 1969), 198.

[73] The Bremmner-Rhinds papyrus records the statement of Ra-Atum: "I was the one who with my fist stimulated desire; I masturbated with my hand and I spat it [the semen] from my mouth." See Larue, *Sex and the Bible*, 144.

[74] Ibid.

[75] E.g., R. H. Pfeiffer, *The Hebrew Iliad* (New York: Harper, 1957), 75.

[76] See Peter R. Ackroyd, *The Second Book of Samuel: Commentary* (CBC; Cambridge: Cambridge University Press, 1977), 47.

Another passage allegedly referring to masturbation (or related sex play by children) is the reference to Ishmael "playing" (ṣāḥaq) in the presence of Isaac (Gen 21:9). Jonathan Kirsch contends that the verb ṣāḥaq here should be translated "fondle" and that what Sarah saw was incestuous "sex play between Ishmael and his little brother"—incestuous child molestation that may have included causing Isaac to masturbate.[77] Phyllis Trible suggests the translation "play with oneself" and sees a possible reference to masturbation.[78] But this interpretation is unlikely. The term ṣāḥaq can have sexual connotations in certain contexts, as in Gen 26:8 and Exod 32:6, but in this context most probably refers to "mocking/scoffing" without sexual implications.[79]

The passage most frequently regarded as referring to masturbation is the narrative concerning Onan in Gen 38:9. The detailed examination of this passage in chapter 11, below, in connection with the levirate marriage practice, however, concludes that onanism in this passage is not masturbation but coitus interruptus on the part of Onan to avoid his levirate duty to raise up children for his deceased brother.[80]

In short, there is no clear reference to masturbation in the OT. Since masturbation is not specifically mentioned in either narrative or legislation, one cannot be certain about the biblical stand regarding this practice. But in light of the fact that the seventh commandment forbids harboring sexually impure thoughts as well as engaging in sexually immoral acts (see ch. 8, below), it is safe to say that sexual lust or sexual fantasies about a person other than one's spouse is prohibited, and thus the act of masturbation—if accompanied by illicit sexual fantasy—is opposed to the will of God. It is also safe to conclude that habitual substitution of masturbation for regular sexual relations with one's spouse when the latter is available is not fulfilling the highest ideal for sexual wholeness in marriage.

Sexual Blemishes and Ritual Uncleanness Related to Sexuality

Pentateuchal Legislation. In the pentateuchal legislation, entrance into the assembly of the Lord is forbidden of one "whose testicles are crushed [peṣûaʿ-dakkāʾ, lit. 'emasculated by crushing'] or whose penis [šapkâ] is cut off" (Deut 23:2 [ET

---

[77] Jonathan Kirsch, "What Did Sarah See?" *BRev* 14, no. 5 (1998): 2, 49.

[78] Phyllis Trible, "The Other Woman: A Literary and Theological Study of the Hagar Narratives," in *Understanding the Word: Essays in Honor of Bernhard W. Anderson* (ed. James T. Butler, Edgar W. Conrad, and Ben C. Ollenburger; JSOTSup 37; Sheffield, Eng.: JSOT Press, 1985), 244, n. 46.

[79] I concur with Derek Kidner, *Genesis: An Introduction and Commentary* (TOTC 1; Downers Grove, Ill.: InterVarsity Press, 1967): 140, that the term "should be translated 'mocking' (AV, RV). This is the intensive form of Isaac's name-verb 'to laugh,' its malicious sense here demanded by the context and by Galatians 4:29 ('persecuted')."

[80] If one takes "masturbation" in its most widely accepted definition to mean "self-gratification via self-stimulation," then clearly onanism is not masturbation. "Masturbation" has sometimes been defined, however, as "incompleted coitus as a birth control technique," in which case the term "masturbation" would apply to this situation. But already in talmudic literature there is a clear distinction between coitus interruptus and masturbation; see *b. Nid.* 13ab; *Yebam.* 34b.

23:1]). Almost all scholars agree that this passage not only speaks of injury to one's genitals but also includes castration.[81] The legislation forbidding the sexually blemished from entering the assembly of Yahweh may include a protest against acts of mutilation among the fertility cults,[82] but beyond this it seems to rest on a reason similar to that for the prohibition against mutilating oneself in 14:1: "The deliberate mutilation of the nature which God has given to man is inconsistent with the character of Jehovah's people."[83] The immediate context of both these prohibitions provides an explicit rationale: "For you are a people holy [qādôš] . . . therefore your camp must be holy [qādôš]" (14:2; 23:15 [ET 23:14]). Holiness (the Heb. root qdš—which many scholars recognize as signifying wholeness for God, as well as separation unto him[84]—required in ancient Israelite cultus a concrete statement of this wholeness in unmutilated members of the covenant tribal assembly. As Janet Everhart summarizes with regard to 23:15 (ET 23:14), "The intent of the passage seems clear: men who are not physically whole because of some disfigurement of their sexual organs are not to be admitted to the assembly of YHWH."[85]

This legislation, while theologically pointing to a divine call for holiness, may be seen as a ritual regulation, intrinsically bound up with the presence of the holy Shechinah dwelling in the midst of Israel. Consequences for violating this ritual regulation included exclusion from the assembly of Yahweh, which presumably met in session at the cultic center of the sanctuary. When the sanctuary and Shechinah no longer existed on earth, however, this ritual exclusion no longer retained its applicability.[86] This is in contrast with, for example, the sexually related

---

[81] See Everhart, "The Hidden Eunuchs," 158–60.

[82] Being forbidden to enter the "assembly of the LORD" did not mean being banished from the camp of Israel. Jacob Milgrom shows that "assembly of the LORD" is "an ancient technical term for the sociopolitical body that was called into session by Israel's tribal chieftains whenever a national transtribal issue arose" (*Leviticus 1–16: A New Translation with Introduction and Commentary* [AB 3; New York: Doubleday, 1991], 242). Cf. Jeffrey H. Tigay, *Deuteronomy* (JPS Torah Commentary; Philadelphia: Jewish Publication Society, 1996), 210–11.

For ANE references to self-mutilation by cultic functionaries in connection with cultic rituals, see, e.g., Robert A. J. Gagnon, *The Bible and Homosexual Practice: Texts and Hermeneutics* (Nashville: Abingdon, 2001), 49; cf. the self-mutilation in the Baal cultic practices described as taking place on Mt. Carmel at the time of Elijah: "*as was their custom,* they [the prophets of Baal] cut themselves" (1 Kgs 18:28). See also Deut 14:1; Jer 16:6; 41:5; 47:5; and possibly Jer 5:7 and Mic 4:14 (ET 5:1).

[83] S. R. Driver, *A Critical and Exegetical Commentary on Deuteronomy* (ICC; New York: Charles Scribner's Sons, 1902), 260.

[84] For discussion of the root qdš signifying both "separation" and "wholeness," see esp. Jiří Moskala, *The Laws of Clean and Unclean Animals of Leviticus 11: Their Nature, Theology, and Rationale (an Intertextual Study)* (ATSDS 4; Berrien Springs, Mich.: Adventist Theological Society, 2000), 220–27; cf. Mary Douglas, *Purity and Danger: An Analysis of Concepts of Pollution and Taboo* (New York: Praeger, 1966), 51–53; Milgrom, *Leviticus 1–16,* 721, 730–31.

[85] Janet S. Everhart, "The Hidden Eunuchs," 159.

[86] At the same time, the principle behind this legislation, i.e., the importance of keeping one's body physically as whole as possible, seems still to have application today.

laws found in Lev 18–20, which are explicitly given universal status and not restricted only to Israel and the Israelite cultus.

Several Mosaic laws deal with sexual matters specifically in the context of ritual uncleanness. For example, Lev 12:1–5, as already mentioned, prescribes the length of time a mother is ceremonially unclean after childbirth (forty days with the birth of a son and eighty days with the birth of a daughter). The focus here is not on the alleged difference in time of uncleanness with the birth of male versus female babies but rather on the blood itself as a source of ritual uncleanness.

First, it must be underscored that the uncleanness described in Lev 12 (as well as the genital discharges in Lev 15) is a ritual, not moral, uncleanness.[87] Such genital discharges are not seen as morally defiling, that is, as a sin. "The Hebrew text does not use terms for moral faults (e.g., *ḥaṭṭāʾt* ['sin'], *pešaᶜ* ['transgression'], *ᶜawōn* ['iniquity/culpability']) or forgiveness (e.g., verb *slḥ* ['forgive'] with reference to physical ritual impurities."[88] Gane, following Milgrom, shows that the sacrifices brought by the woman after her time of impurity had passed (12:6, 8), as with the ritual sacrifices for genital discharges (Lev 15), are not a "sin-offering" (as many English versions translate) to remove moral fault but a "purification offering" to remove physical ritual impurity.[89]

---

[87] For a careful articulation of the difference between moral and ritual impurity in the HB and the biblical support for such a distinction, see esp. Jonathan Klawans, *Impurity and Sin in Ancient Judaism* (New York: Oxford University Press, 2000), 21–42. Klawans (p. 23) summarizes three main characteristics of "ritual impurity": "(1) The sources of ritual impurity are generally natural and more or less unavoidable. (2) It is not sinful to contract these impurities. And (3) these impurities convey an impermanent contagion." Regarding "moral impurity," Klawans (26) summarizes five areas of distinction from ritual impurity: (1) "moral impurity is a direct result of grave sin," such as the sexual sins of Lev 18:24–30, idolatry (e.g., Lev 19:31; 20:1–3), and bloodshed (e.g., Num 35:33–34), whereas ritual impurity is generally not sinful; (2) "there is no contact-contagion associated with moral impurity" as in ritual impurity; (3) whereas "ritual impurity leads to impermanent defilement, moral impurity leads to long-lasting, if not permanent, degradation of the sinner, and eventually, of the land of Israel"; (4) moral impurity cannot be "ameliorated by rites of purification" as with ritual impurity, but rather "moral purity is achieved by punishment, atonement, or, best of all, by refraining from committing morally impure acts in the first place"; and (5) whereas the term "impure" (*ṭāmēʾ*) is used for both ritual and moral impurity, the terms "abomination" (*tôᶜēbâ*) and "pollute" (*ṭānap*) "are used with regard to the sources of moral impurity but not with regard to the sources of ritual impurity." See also idem, "The Impurity of Immorality in Ancient Judaism," *JJS* 48 (1997): 1–16; and Roy Gane, *Leviticus, Numbers* (NIVAC3; Grand Rapids: Zondervan, 2004), 306–8.

[88] Gane, *Leviticus, Numbers,* 225.

[89] Gane summarizes regarding the woman's sacrifices of Lev 12:6, 8, "She has not sinned, as shown by the fact that the goal of her pair of sacrifices is to expiate (*kipper*) for her so that 'she will be ceremonially clean from (privative *min*) her flow of blood' (12:7; cf. v. 8). The goal/meaning of the ritual procedure is to remove physical ritual impurity from the woman so that she is ritually pure, not to remove moral fault from her in preparation for divine forgiveness (contrast 4:20, 26, 31, 35). So her *ḥaṭṭāʾt* is a 'purification offering'" (ibid., 221). See esp. Gane, *Leviticus, Numbers,* 306–8, and Jonathan Klawans, "The Impurity of Immorality in Ancient Judaism," *JJS* 48 (1997): 1–16.

Leviticus 12:2 reveals that the uncleanness after childbirth is of a similar kind as during the menstrual period: "as at the time of her menstruation, she shall be unclean." Hence understanding the nature of the ritual uncleanness in Lev 12 depends upon an understanding of the menstrual discharge and its uncleanness detailed in Lev 15. Leviticus 15 deals with five basic categories of ceremonial uncleanness: (1) a man's prolonged genital discharge (vv. 2b–15) or (2) (nocturnal) emission of semen (vv. 16–17); (3) both man's and woman's engagement in sexual intercourse (v. 18); and (4) a woman's menstruation (vv. 19–25) or (5) prolonged bleeding (vv. 25–30). Leviticus 18:19 and 20:18 build upon these basic laws of ritual impurity found in Lev 15, prohibiting sexual intercourse during menstruation; 22:4–6 applies the legislation of Lev 15 in the context of the priesthood, describing the ceremonial uncleanness ("until evening") of a priest after sexual intercourse.

Clearly Lev 15 is the core of legislation upon which the other laws of ritual uncleanness related to sexuality depend, and so must be the major focus of attention for understanding the theology of sexually related ritual uncleanness. The laws of uncleanness resulting from bodily discharges in Lev 15 are arranged in a carefully crafted chiastic structure. Richard Whitekettle summarizes this chiastic arrangement of the contagions and the means of cultic resolution:[90]

A. Verses 2b–15—abnormal, long-term male discharges—he/they wash(es) and he sacrifices

B. Verses 16–17—typical, transient dysfunctional male discharges—he washes

C. Verse 18—normal discharge of sexual intercourse—both wash

B'. Verses 19–24—typical, transient dysfunctional female discharges—she washes[91]

A'. Verses 25–30—abnormal, long-term female discharges—she washes and sacrifices

Several features of this structure should be pointed out. The concern of each member of the chiasm is only with sex-related discharges, not with other discharges such as excretion of waste or blood flow from a cut or wound. Furthermore, there is a decrease in impurity as one moves toward the center of the

---

[90] Richard Whitekettle, "Leviticus 15:18 Reconsidered: Chiasm, Spatial Structure, and the Body," *JSOT* 49 (1991): 31–41.

[91] Although the text does not explicitly state that the woman is to bathe after her monthly period, this can be assumed because bathing is necessary even for more minor impurities, such as a man's emission of semen, Lev 15:16 (Gane, *Leviticus, Numbers*, 259). Milgrom, *Leviticus 1–16*, 934–35, gives additional weighty evidence that "all statements regarding the duration of impurity [in Leviticus] automatically imply that it is terminated by ablutions."

chiasm. The literary members in the extremities of the chiasm (A and A') are abnormal, pathological conditions, requiring a sacrifice when the discharge ceases. Moving inward in the chiasm, parallel members B and B' deal with typical discharges (menstruation and emission of semen) that render the physiological system temporarily dysfunctional in terms of reproduction. No sacrifice is required for ritual resolution. The central section, C, concerns the emission of semen in normal sexual intercourse, which likewise requires no sacrifice in the ritual resolution.

The placement of normal sexual intercourse in the heart of the chiastic structure is not just a rhetorical device devoid of theological significance. "Only the setting of v. 18 is akin to the ideal sexual relationship described in Gen 2:20–25."[92] The structure of this collection of sexually related laws draws the reader toward this fulcrum of the Edenic ideal in sexuality. And within this fulcrum of v. 18, which forms a hinge between the male discharges of vv. 2–18 and the female discharges of vv. 19–30, a surprising grammatical reversal in the Hebrew puts the woman rather than the man first as the subject. Thus v. 18 is an "inverted hinge" that "binds male and female together rather than simply putting them beside each other. This structure reflects the creation ideal of equal responsibility in the sexual act"[93] and captures "in literary form the unification of man and wife as 'one flesh' (Gen 2:24)."[94]

But why are the various genital discharges described in Lev 12 and 15 (and related passages) defiling? And especially, why does even normal sexual intercourse, approximating most closely the divine Edenic ideal, render both sexual partners "unclean" (*ṭāmēʾ*) until evening? Various suggestions have been made,[95] and the answer seems to be multifaceted.

A verse in the concluding summary of Lev 15 gives an explicit answer (v. 31): "Thus you shall keep the people of Israel separate [the *hipʿil* of *nāzar*] from their uncleanness, so that they do not die in their uncleanness by defiling [the *piʿel* inf. const. of *ṭāmēʾ*] my tabernacle that is in their midst." The motifs of "separation" and "defilement of sanctuary" lead to the overarching rationale of holiness. Several facets of the holiness rationale seem evident from Scripture. The first is built on the meaning of holiness as "separation [from and to]."[96] As noted in ch. 3, above, God radically separates sexuality from any ritual activity in the cultus. As part of a polemic against the divinization of sex in the fertility cults, God makes a clear and distinct separation between sex and the sanctuary. Thus even those perfectly normal and typical genital functions/activities connected with sexual activity or the birthing process were distanced from the sanctuary to signify a clear separation between sex and cult. This appears to be at the heart of the reason abstinence from sexual intercourse was required for those entering into the holy

---

92 Whitekettle, "Leviticus 15:18 Reconsidered," 37.

93 Gane, *Leviticus, Numbers*, 263.

94 Milgrom, *Leviticus 1–16*, 930–31, who cites a term paper of J. Randolph.

95 See ibid., 766, for a summary of views.

96 Ibid., 731: "Holiness means not only 'separation from' but 'separation to.'"

presence of Yahweh at Mt. Sinai or in the midst of sanctuary (Exod 19:10–11, 14–15; cf. 1 Sam 21:4–7; 2 Sam 11:11). This also explains why even nocturnal emission rendered a soldier ritually unclean in the holy presence of Yahweh, who "travels along with your [war] camp, to save you and to hand over your enemies to you, therefore your camp must be holy, so that he may not see anything indecent among you and turn away from you" (Deut 23:15 [ET 23:14]; cf. vv. 11–14 [ET 10–13]. "All hints of sexuality were kept far away from cultic life and religious experience. The separation of sexuality and cult is also embedded in the impurity provisions of the sacral laws. Israel's impurity rules were intended to keep intact the essential divisions of human existence: holy and profane, life and death."[97]

Hyam Maccoby broadens the polemical restriction to include the whole birth-death cycle of mortality.

> Everything that is a feature of the cycle of birth and death must be banished from the Temple of the God who does not die and was not born. Not that there is anything sinful about birth and death, which are the God-given lot of mankind. But the one place in the world which has been allotted for the resting of the Divine Presence must be protected from mortality. When entering the Temple, one is entering the domain of eternity.

> [T]his cycle of birth and death . . . is the basis of chthonic [underworld-related] religion, in which the deity himself/herself is subject to the cycle of birth and death, thereby providing salvation to worshipers, who thereby become divinized. By bringing God down into the world of birth, death and rebirth, the worshiper hopes to escape the cycle, cross the barrier between the human and divine, and achieve immortality.

> . . . Judaism divested the cycle of birth and death of divine significance and thereby released humans from the quest for divinity. They were released into humanity, accepting birth and death as their lot, but pursuing human aims as sanctified by the God of Heaven, who did not ask them to transcend humanity, but instead to worship Him as the sole transcendent Being.[98]

This leads to a second aspect of holiness: "wholeness"[99] or "fullness of life."[100] "The holiness/uncleanness contrast is seen essentially as an opposition

---

[97] Tikva Frymer-Kensky, "Law and Philosophy: The Case of Sex in the Bible," *Semeia* 45 (1989): 91.

[98] Hyam Maccoby, *Ritual and Morality: The Ritual Purity System and Its Place in Judaism* (Cambridge: Cambridge University Press, 1999), 207. Cf. Gane, *Leviticus, Numbers,* 262: "Divine regulation of human sexuality had the purpose of protecting God's holiness from association with human mortality by carefully delineating the impure/moral category and separating it from the sacred category." At the same time, as Gane notes, "while distancing himself from human mortality, God did not attach any moral stigma to bodily sexual functions per se."

[99] Milgrom, *Leviticus 1–16,* 1001: "That wholeness (Hebrew *tāmîm*) is a significant ingredient of holiness cannot be gainsaid." Cf. Douglas, *Purity and Danger,* 51, who defines holy as "wholeness and completeness."

[100] Gordon J. Wenham, "Why Does Sexual Intercourse Defile (Lev 15:18)?" *ZAW* 95 (1983): 434.

between life and death. . . . According to cultic law, the poles of existence are life and death."[101] Blood is a symbol of life: "the life of the flesh is in the blood" (Lev 17:11). Likewise semen is in Hebrew literally *zera*ᶜ "seed" (15:16, 18) and thus clearly identified as a life-giving fluid. Various scholars have recognized what may be implicit in the connections of genital discharges with the realm of life: "The loss of vaginal blood and semen, both containing seed, meant the diminution of life and, if unchecked, destruction and death. And it was a process unalterably opposed by Israel's God, the source of its life [18:5 is quoted]."[102] "God, who is perfect life and perfect holiness, can only be approached by clean men who enjoy fulness of life themselves. The unclean are those who in some way have an aura of death about them in that they manifest less than physical wholeness. Therefore those who suffer the loss of 'life liquids,' whether it be blood or semen, are debarred from worship until they have recovered from that loss."[103]

This life/death opposition not only is linked to the motif of holiness but ultimately goes back to creation and the separation of boundaries between life (creation) and death (uncreation), as Jiří Moskala has also demonstrated regarding the laws of clean/unclean foods.[104] A major difference, however, between the laws of ritual sexually related uncleanness and the laws of clean/unclean food must be recognized. The laws of Lev 12–15—dealing with uncleanness from genital discharge (as well as the laws of leprosy and scale disease)—all concern *temporary* uncleanness whereas the laws of clean and unclean foods deal with *permanent* uncleanness.[105] The laws of temporary uncleanness in Lev 12–15, unlike the laws

---

[101] Ibid., 433.

[102] Milgrom, *Leviticus 1–16,* 767; cf. 732–33; 766–68; 1000–1004. A weakness to this hypothesis is pointed out by Maccoby, *Ritual and Morality,* 31: "Normal loss of semen hardly comes into the category of life-diminishing discharge. . . . Involuntary loss of semen might be regarded as life-diminishing, but a discharge that produces new life cannot be so regarded." In light of this criticism, it is possible, although not provable, that the loss of semen referred to in Lev 15 is that which is not deposited in the vagina of the woman and is therefore "wasted," i.e., life-diminishing seed. (This suggestion was made to me in an oral conversation with my colleague Angel Rodriquez of the Biblical Research Institute in Silver Springs, Md.)

[103] Wenham, "Why Does Sexual Intercourse Defile?" 434. I might add that they are debarred not only from worship but also from holy war. Whitekettle, "Leviticus 18:15 Reconsidered," 31–45, agrees with Wenham and others on the basic polarity between life and death but disagrees that semen is a "life fluid" and that the loss of semen places one in an "aura of death." He prefers to see the loss of "fullness of life" in an emission of semen as defiling in that the penis is used both to ejaculate semen and to expel urine, a nonlife waste liquid. Thus "as an anatomical structure it is functionally ambiguous, confusing features of both the production of life and the production of waste, features of the center and of the periphery. . . . Thus sexual intercourse, when there is the emission of semen, defiles because with the emission of semen, that which structurally unites husband and wife as one flesh, crosses functional boundaries" (p. 44). Although this thesis is creative, I find no evidence within the biblical text to support this view of the ambiguous function of the male sex organ.

[104] Moskala, *The Laws of Clean and Unclean,* 193–96, 316–18, 359, 363–69.

[105] See the summary and discussion of this data, ibid., 169–76.

of the clean and unclean foods of Lev 11, are also inextricably connected with divine prohibitions to enter the sanctuary until the uncleanness has been resolved.
Thus this kind of uncleanness may correctly be called "ritual"[106] (or ceremonial)
uncleanness—uncleanness that prevents participation in the rituals of the sanctuary services. Such a connection, as in the case of the sexual blemishes discussed
above, would seem to imply a built-in statute of limitations that rendered the
laws inapplicable or obsolete when the sanctuary and the resident Shechinah
were no longer present with his people.

Identifying the context of these laws as "ritual uncleanness" does not, however, thereby necessarily or automatically indicate their irrelevance for Christians
today. A third aspect of the "holiness" rationale explains how some, if not all, of
the laws of ritual uncleanness related to sexuality may also have continuing relevance at least in principle. In Hebrew there is no word that specifically means
"health." The Hebrew term qōdeš, "holiness," includes the concept of "wholeness"
in the sense of "health/wellness."[107] God's concern for the holiness of Israel includes a wholistic concern for its health and well-being (cf. Exod 15:26; Deut
7:15). The explicit "holiness" rationale may include a hygienic or humane component in the case of at least some of these laws of sexual uncleanness, some understanding of which has more recently been reenforced by the results of modern
scientific investigation, and other issues that have yet to be fully understood.[108]

One law concerning menstruation has a continuing universal applicability
that transcends a ritual context. According to Lev 18:19; 20:18, a man is not to
have sexual intercourse with a woman during her menstrual period. This prohibition is placed alongside other laws of universal significance, applicable to both Israelites and the gēr, "stranger/alien" (as discussed esp. in ch. 4, above). There is no
provision for ritual cleansing if this prohibition is willfully violated; it is not related to ritual uncleanness.[109] As noted below in the treatment of sex-related

---

[106] Roy Gane, *Ritual Dynamic Structure* (Gorgias Dissertations 14; Piscataway, N.J.:
Gorgias, 2004), 60, gives a helpful definition of ritual: "an activity system of which the
components/subsystems are fixed in terms of their inclusion, nature, and relative order,
and in which the activity is believed to interact with an entity that is ordinarily inaccessible to the material domain." A ritual is thus a (physical) activity conveying (spiritual)
meaning and leading to interaction with the spiritual/divine world and usually related to
the services of the sanctuary, such as festivals, purification rites, and sacrifices. See
Moskala, *The Laws of Clean and Unclean*, 175.

[107] See Moskala, *The Laws of Clean and Unclean*, 223–27. Moskala aptly defines the
biblical view of health: "Biblically speaking health is total well-being, a comprehensive
wholeness" (p. 223).

[108] For suggestions of hygienic and humane reasons for the laws dealing with menstruation, see, e.g., R. K. Harrison, *Leviticus: An Introduction and Commentary* (TOTC 3;
Downers Grove, Ill.: InterVarsity, 1980), 163–64; and R. Laird Harris, "Leviticus," *EBC*
2:586–87. For a full discussion of menstruation in the OT, see Deborah Klee, "Menstruation in the Hebrew Bible" (PhD diss., Boston University, 1998).

[109] It seems clear that Lev 15:24 refers to an experience of sexual intercourse that does
not deliberately occur during menstruation; only after the sexual union is the fact of menstruation ascertained, and then it requires seven days of ritual cleansing. According to

uncleanness in the Prophets, Ezek 18:6; 22:10 places this prohibition in the midst of a list of ethical/moral, not ritual, laws.

Leviticus 20:18 states that a man who had sexual intercourse with a woman during her menstruation has "laid bare [lit. 'make naked,' from the *hip‘il* of *‘ārâ*] her flow [lit. 'fountain,' *māqôr*] and she has laid bare [from the *pi‘el* of *gālâ*] her flow ['fountain,' *māqôr*] of her blood." Whitekettle has sought to explain this "fountain/wellspring" terminology by suggesting that in Levitical thought the womb was viewed as a physiological microcosm of the primeval cosmology.[110] But it seems far more likely that the expressions are used euphemistically for sexual intercourse as elsewhere throughout the chapter and that "fountain of blood" is a common expression for menstrual flow, as in 15:19–24. The period of abstinence from sexual activity as prescribed in the biblical text is seven days from the onset of menstruation, that is, during the time of bleeding, not fourteen days (with an extra week after the menstrual flow has stopped) as in later rabbinic literature.[111]

In this legislation, prohibiting sex with a menstruating woman seems to concern an issue of the woman's physical and psychological well-being. This may be inferred from 20:18, where the woman with a genital flow is described as *dāweh*, "faint, i.e., in a state of malaise." The implication is that "this is a women's rights issue. The law protects 'the woman from unwanted advances by her husband during her period of weakness (R. Gane).'"[112] "Her liminal status gives her rest: from labor, from male touch, and from conjugal duties."[113]

18:19; 20:18, deliberate or willful sexual activity during a woman's menstruation results in both partners being "cut off" by divine *kārēt* from the congregation. For a survey of this and other suggested explanations of the differences between Lev 15 and Lev 18 and 20 concerning menstruation (with proponents and rationale for each suggestion), see O'Grady, "The Semantics of Taboo," 9–11.

[110] Richard Whitekettle, "Levitical Thought and the Female Reproductive Cycle: Wombs, Wellsprings, and the Primeval World," *VT* 46 (1996): 376–91. Whitekettle draws on the homology between "well-spring" and "womb" in Akkadian (both *idim*) and shows the interconnections between primeval Mesopotamian cosmology (*apsû*, the Mesopotamian mythological subterranean ocean) and Mesopotamian reproductive thought. He then seeks to establish that this same interconnection between primeval macrocosm and uterine microcosm exists in Levitical thought. But his evidence is unconvincing; the whole tenor of pentateuchal thought (both in creation/flood and Levitical legislation) is polemical against ANE mythology.

[111] See Maccoby, *Ritual and Morality,* 44, for discussion of the deliberate shift to fourteen days in the Talmud.

[112] Gane, *Leviticus, Numbers,* 325 citing himself in Milgrom, *Leviticus 17–22,* 1755. See also Harrison, *Leviticus,* 164: "By placing the woman in what amounted to a state of isolation, the legislation made it possible for her to enjoy some respite from her normal duties, and gave her an opportunity of renewing her energy. The life of the woman in the ancient Near East was normally very arduous, and these regulations enabled younger females in Israel to rest legitimately during the menses."

[113] David T. Stewart, "Ancient Sexual Laws: Text and Intertext of the Biblical Holiness Code and Hittite Laws" (PhD diss., University of California, Berkeley, 2000), 54.

A growing body of scientific evidence seems to point toward a health-related (i.e., holiness/wholeness–related) rationale for this legislation. For example, studies have revealed a markedly lower incidence of cervical cancer among observant Jewish women, who refrain from sexual intercourse during menstruation, compared with the general population.[114] Regardless of the rationale, a biblical theology of sexuality must highlight what is often overlooked in modern sexual ethics: the prohibition against sexual intercourse with a menstruating spouse is placed on the same universal level with the prohibitions of incest, polygamy, homosexuality, and bestiality.[115]

Prophets/Writings. The discussion above has alluded to several references in the Former Prophets about refraining from sexual intercourse while entering or partaking from the stores of the sanctuary or during a time of holy war. David comes to Ahimelech requesting bread from the sanctuary for soldiers with him, and the priest agrees provided that "the young men have kept themselves from women." David assures him, "Indeed women have been kept from us as always when I go on an expedition; the vessels of the young men are holy" (1 Sam 21:5–6 [ET 21:4–5]). This refraining from sexual intercourse during divinely directed war, alluding to Deut 23:10–14 (ET 23:9–13), is also implied in Uriah the Hittite's refusal to have sexual intercourse with his wife during the time of his service in the army's war against Ammon (2 Sam 11:11). These narratives concern ritual prohibitions against bringing sex into proximity with the Shechinah glory (either in the sanctuary or in the war camp), as a protective polemic against the fertility cults. Thus they do not represent a model for Christians today, prohibiting sexual intercourse before attending church or before participating in the Communion service, as some have claimed.

The Latter Prophets contains a few references to ritual impurity; most are limited to the priestly writing of Ezekiel, and most refer to the pentateuchal laws regarding menstruation. Ezekiel 18:6 defines a just and law-abiding man as one who, among other things, does not "approach a woman during her menstrual period"; Ezek 22:10 lists among the sins of Jerusalem those of men who "violate women in their menstrual periods." Both of these assume the legislation set forth in Lev 15:24, 18:19, and 20:18 (discussed above). Ezekiel 36:17 compares Israel's spiritual defilement of the land to a woman's defilement during her menstrual period: "Mortal, when the house of Israel lived on their own soil, they defiled it with their ways and their deeds; their conduct in my sight was like the unclean-

---

[114] See, e.g., S. L. Heering et al., "A Cohort Analysis of Cervical Cancer in Israeli Jewish Women," *Gynecologic Oncology* 39, no. 3 (1990): 244–48; and M. Glezerman, B. Piura, and V. Insler, "Cervical Cancer in Jewish Women," *American Journal of Obstetrics and Gynecology* 161, no. 5 (1989): 1186–90. The results of these studies may also point to the hygienic basis for circumcision.

[115] As noted in the afterword, the NT implies the applicability of the legislation in Lev 17–18, including sexual intercourse with a menstruating woman; the practices forbidden to the Gentile Christians (Acts 15:29) are a summary of the practices forbidden to both Jew and Gentile (*gēr*, "stranger") listed in Lev 17–18—in the exact same order, with the word *porneia* constituting a summary of all the types of illicit sexual intercourse catalogued in Lev 18.

ness of a woman in her menstrual period." Several other possible allusions to the defilement of menstruation occur in the Latter Prophets (Isa 30:22; 64:5 [ET 64:6]; Ezek 7:19–20; 36:7). Finally, the pentateuchal law regarding a priest's defilement of himself by approaching a corpse (Lev 21:1–4) is restated in Ezek 44:25: "They [the priests] shall not defile themselves by going near to a dead person; for father or mother, however, and for son or daughter, and for brother or unmarried sister they may defile themselves."

As noted above, references to these sexual impurities are all (except the universalized nonritual prohibition against having sex during a woman's menstruation) clearly in the context of ritual uncleanness, intrinsically bound up with the visible presence of the Shechinah glory. They thus have a built-in statute of limitations and are no longer binding/applicable with the disappearance of the earthly sanctuary and Shechinah.

Grace. Previous sections of this chapter have explored the elements of divine grace regarding prostitution and exogamous marriages. Here we discuss the divine grace operative with reference to sexual blemishes and ritual uncleanness related to sexuality. Regarding sexual blemishes, in particular male castration, as remarked above in the discussion of singleness, the prophet Isaiah foretells an eschatological time of salvation when the eunuchs will be accepted into the congregation of the Lord and will be given special honor and recognition in God's house (Isa 56:3–5).[116]

Regarding ritual uncleanness related to sexuality, as pointed out earlier, these states of uncleanness were temporary in nature, and God in his grace provided a ritual means of removing such uncleannesses. The law forbidding sexual intercourse with a menstruating women occurs in a universalized context, indicating that this legislation has continuing applicability transcending a ritual uncleanness. But as part of that catalogue of illicit sexual relationships in Lev 18, this prohibition is couched in the same undergirding framework of grace as the other prohibitions in Lev 18 that are explored in other chapters of this study. While upholding his divine will for sexuality, God graciously condescends to work with his people even as they falter, but God ever calls them up to a higher standard, ever summons them back to his divine ideal. Although Ezekiel, in the context of castigating Israel for their sins, mentions the universalized nonritual statute prohibiting having sex with a menstruating woman (Ezek 18:6, cf. Lev 18:19, 20:18), yet the conclusion of this chapter a few verses later constitutes one of the most sublime statements of divine grace for the sinner who repents: "Cast away from you all the transgressions that you have committed against me, and get yourselves a new heart and a new spirit! Why will you die, O house of Israel? For I have no pleasure in the death of anyone, says the Lord God. Turn, then, and live" (Ezek 18:31–32). God's amazing grace.

---

[116] This does not appear to have in view only a special situation of extenuating circumstances but to envision a fundamental change in the theological nature of the elect community, as recognized by the early Christian church leaders at the Jerusalem Council in their interpretation of the similar OT passage in Amos 9:11–12 (see Acts 15:12–21).

8

Exclusivity versus Adultery and Premarital Sex

Genesis 2:24 provides the model for relationships in marriage outside the garden of Eden, as elaborated in chapter 1, above. Man and woman are to (1) "leave" any outside interfering relationships, that is, preserve *exclusivity* between themselves; (2) "cling" to each other, that is, enter into a covenant relationship of *permanence;* and (3) "become one flesh," that is, experience a profound *intimacy* as husband and wife in the marriage relationship. The OT material beyond Gen 1–3 upholds these basic components of a sexual relationship, expresses disapproval for distortions of this Edenic ideal, and provides legislation prohibiting sexual relationships that would compromise this ideal. The next three chapters of this study take up these components of the Edenic relational model for marriage, along with their respective distortions.

Affirmations of the Divine Ideal of Exclusivity

Exclusivity in the Marriage Relationship

God's Edenic design for exclusivity in marital sexual relations is assumed in portraits of married couples in the Pentateuch as well as the rest of the OT (chs. 4 and 6, above). In the Prophets the marriage metaphor is employed frequently to describe the relationship between God and his people (ch. 3). Throughout these metaphorical references to marriage (and references to Israel's marital unfaithfulness, ch. 7), there is a powerful emphasis upon the exclusivity of the marriage relationship according to the divine ideal. "The figure of Israel as YHWH's wife derives from the cardinal commandment that Israel worship YHWH alone. To that demand of exclusive fidelity, the obligation of a wife to her husband offered a parallel."[1] As noted in chapters 1 and 4, the call to exclusive fidelity in marriage is ultimately based upon Israel's concept of monotheism. This belief in one God

---

[1] Moshe Greenberg, "Ezekiel 16: A Panorama of Passions," in *Love and Death in the Ancient Near East: Essays in Honor of Marvin H. Pope* (ed. John H. Marks and Robert M. Good; Guilford, Conn.: Four Quarters, 1987), 146.

and in God's fidelity to his people shapes the understanding of marital fidelity on the human level. Israel's true concept of sexual exclusivity is based upon its true conception of the exclusive monotheistic God and upon the concept of *imago Dei.*

As discussed in chapter 3, the motif of divine jealousy (the Hebrew root *qnʾ*)—implying God's exclusive relationship with Israel, his wife—appears at the heart of the Decalogue, in the commandment prohibiting idolatry: "For I the LORD your God am a jealous God [*ʾēl qannāʾ*]" (Exod 20:5; cf. Deut 5:9). God's marital jealousy is underscored by the double mention of this attribute in the so-called cultic Decalogue: "you shall worship no other god, because the LORD, whose name is Jealous [*qannāʾ*], is a jealous God [*ʾēl qannāʾ*]" (Exod 34:14). Twice more in his farewell address to Israel, Moses indicates that God is *ʾēl qannāʾ*, "a jealous God" (Deut 4:24; 6:14).

In chapter 3 it was further noted that "the divine sentiment of jealousy/zeal is the supreme marital emotion within the covenant bond."[2] We also examined how the motif of divine marital jealousy is highlighted in the Baal of Peor apostasy of Num 25, where the Hebrew root *qnʾ* is employed four times and Phinehas is represented as reverberating with the emotion of divine jealousy in his swift response to Israel's spiritual harlotry.

In the Prophets as well as the Pentateuch, Yahweh is portrayed as a "Jealous Lover" (e.g., Josh 24:19; Nah 1:2). God will jealously, zealously bring judgment upon his wife, Israel, when she follows after other lovers and thus breaks the covenant vow to exclusive faithfulness (see, e.g., Ezek 16:38, 42; 23:25), thus revealing that the human marital relationship likewise demands exclusive fidelity to one's spouse.

The Writings also uphold the exclusivity of the marriage relationship. Proverbs 1–9 elaborates on the marital unfaithfulness of the immoral woman who "forsakes the partner of her youth and forgets her sacred covenant" (Prov 2:17). The wise man in Proverbs also emphasizes marital exclusivity on the part of the husband as well as the wife: "Drink water from your own cistern, flowing water from your own well. . . . Let them be for yourself alone, and not for sharing with strangers. Let your fountain be blessed, and rejoice in the wife of your youth" (Prov 5:15–18). The "exclusivity of marriage" is a recurring theme and one of the two "dominant concerns" of this passage.[3] This is revealed in such expressions as *"your own* cistern" and *"your own* well" (v. 15); "Let them be *for yourself alone,* and not for sharing with strangers" (v. 17); "wife of *your* youth" (v. 18). Verse 15 represents "the sexual satisfaction produced by the wife, symbolized by the cistern/well," and vv. 16–17, consistent with this picture, indicate that "the wife is capable of attracting and satisfying many men, just like a prostitute or adulteress."

---

[2] Aron Balorda, "The Jealousy of Phinehas in Numbers 25 as the Embodiment of the Essence of Numinal Marriage" (M.A. thesis, Andrews University, 2002), 82.

[3] Walter C. Kaiser Jr., "True Marital Love in Proverbs 5:15–23 and the Interpretation of the Song of Songs," in *The Way of Wisdom: Essays in Honor of Bruce K. Waltke* (ed. J. I. Packer and Sven K. Soderlund; Grand Rapids: Zondervan, 2000), 107–11, quotes at 111.

But despite her tremendous capabilities, her streams of sexual satisfaction belong solely to the son (v. 17a). They are off limits to other men . . . (v. 17b)." Thus in this section "the father offers the antidote to promiscuity as he urges his son to intoxicate himself with the sexual satisfaction that marriage has to offer."[4]

The High Value of Virginity

In order to uphold this sexual exclusivity in marriage, the legislation of the Pentateuch and the commentary of the Prophets/Writings highlight the value of virginity. The feminine noun *bĕtûlâ*, "virgin," appears fifty-one times in the HB (both sg. and pl.), and the related abstract feminine plural *bĕtûlîm*, "[tokens of] virginity," appears another nine times. Gordon Wenham and others have challenged the traditional translation, claiming that these terms do not mean "virgin/virginity" but simply "girl of marriageable age/teenager"[5] or "girl under the guardianship of her father/adolescence."[6] Reexamination of the biblical evidence by Tom Wadsworth and others, however, convincingly supports the position that the meaning and translation "virgin/virginity" is still to be preferred.[7]

Wadsworth shows how the exegesis and argumentation of Wenham and others are flawed and that in all biblical occurrences the term *bĕtûlâ* refers to an unmarried woman with her marital integrity intact (i.e., a virtuous girl)—a virgin. His main arguments are the following: (1) The use of the term in the legal passages, such as Exod 22:15–16 (ET 22:16–17), clearly points to the translation

---

4 Robert B. Chisholm Jr., "'Drink Water from Your Own Cistern': A Literary Study of Proverbs 5:15–23," *BSac* 157 (2000): 397–409, quotes at 401, 400, and 398.

5 Gordon J. Wenham, "*Bᵉtûlāh* 'a Girl of Marriageable Age,'" *VT* 22 (1972): 326–48; cf. Tikva Frymer-Kensky, "Virginity in the Bible," in *Gender and Law in the Hebrew Bible and the Ancient Near East* (ed. Victor H. Matthews, Bernard M. Levinson, and Tikva Frymer-Kensky; JSOTSup 262; Sheffield, Eng.: Sheffield Academic Press, 1998), 79–80; and John J. Schmitt, "Virgin," *ABD* 6:853–54. Frymer-Kensky, unlike Wenham, acknowledges that often the term in context in the HB—especially in the sexual legislation examined below—must be translated "virgin/virginity."

6 John H. Walton, "בְּתוּלָה," *NIDOTTE* 1:781–84.

7 Tom Wadsworth, "Is There a Hebrew Word for Virgin? *Bethulah* in the Old Testament," *ResQ* 23 (1980): 161–71; Duane A. Garrett, "Song of Songs," in Duane Garrett and Paul R. House, *Song of Songs, Lamentations* (WBC 23B; Nashville: Nelson, 2004), 164–68 (his excursus "Virginity in the Bible and the Ancient World"). Cf. M. Tsevat, "בְּתוּלָה *bĕtûlāh*; בְּתוּלִים *bĕtûlîm*," *TDOT* 2:340, who suggests that "there was an original common Semitic word *batūl(t)*, and that it meant a young girl at the age of puberty and the age just after puberty. Then very gradually this word assumed the meaning of 'virgo intacta' in Hebrew and Aramaic. . . . It is not surprising that this process of narrowing the meaning and of making it more precise is discernible in legal language." In my estimation, Wadsworth and Garrett have shown that the contextual evidence does not demand translating the term in a different way from "virgin/virginity" even outside the legal usage.

8 Exodus 22:1–16 (ET 22:16–17) is discussed further below, but here note that according to this law, even though the unbetrothed virgin was seduced (statutory rape) and lost her virginity, yet her father could still command the full "bride-price for virgins [*bĕtûlōt*]." (22:16 [ET 22:17]). This text implies that although the girl who had been deflowered was no longer a *bĕtûlâ* and thus her value had been diminished, nonetheless her

"virgin/virginity."[8] (2) Wenham's interpretation of *bĕtûlîm* in Deut 22:13–21 as "evidences of *menstruation*" instead of "tokens of virginity" does not fit the facts of the legislation: it is the girl's virginity, not her pregnancy, that is in question (see detailed discussion of this legislation below). (3) Supposedly redundant phrases, such as "whom no man had known," added to the term *bĕtûlâ* (Gen 24:16; Lev 21:3; Judg 11:39; 21:12) are a common literary device in the HB to give emphasis to an important point and do not throw in question the basic meaning of the word so emphasized.[9] (4) The parallelism between *bĕtûlâ* and *bāḥûr*, "young man," does not imply that the former term cannot mean "virgin." (5) The word *bāḥûr* comes from the root *bāḥar*, "to choose," and denotes a "choice" young man, one "in the prime of manhood." The parallelism is between ideal marriage partners, both with a special status: the girl a virgin and the boy in the height of manhood. (6) The story of Tamar in 2 Sam 13 clearly points to the use of *bĕtûlâ* to mean "virgin," as also in Esth 2. (7) Likewise Job 31:1 is referring to a "virgin" (see discussion below), and Joel 1:8 most probably refers to a virgin who is betrothed to a man in her youth but not yet married (as in the case of Joseph and Mary, Matt 1:18, 20, 24).

The high value of virginity is underscored in the story of the rape of Dinah in Gen 34 (see discussion of the rape in ch. 12, below). Shechem's sexual intercourse with Dinah was a shameful act of ravishing a young virgin. The virginity of Dinah, an unmarried girl, was to be guarded faithfully by her father and brothers, and robbing her of her virginity not only defiled the girl but disgraced the family, who were expected to protect her. The unmarried girl had no right of consent, not as a sign of the low status of women in that day and their subjection to men (as many authors claim) but as with minors today for a protection of their chastity and personhood. For a man to violate a woman's virginity was to treat her as a harlot (Gen 34:31) who shunned her family's protection and took her sexuality into her own hands. "Only the prostitute owned her sexuality. By sleeping with her, Shechem was acting as if she had no family to protect, guard and marry her. As the brothers say, 'should our sister be treated as a whore'? He has disgraced her, and through her, her whole family."[10]

The elevated valuation of virginity is highlighted in Lev 21:13–14, in the instructions to the high priest that his marriage partner be limited to a virgin. Leviticus 21:10–12 gives the rationale for this restriction: the high priest is consecrated to wear the holy garments, and his position of utmost holiness must encompass his marriage through the choice of a partner who is of utmost "wholeness," that is, a virgin. The importance of premarital chastity is also em-

---

father could still obtain the bride money as if she were a *bĕtûlâ*. Such inner logic of the text would not make any sense if the meaning of *bĕtûlâ* here were merely "girl of marriageable age," because such status would not have changed even if she had lost her virginity. Hence Wenham's case fails.

[9] See, e.g., Gen 24:1 ("old, well advanced in years"), 38, 40 ("from my kindred, from my father's house"); Judg 11:34 ("only child; he had no son or daughter except her").

[10] Frymer-Kensky, "Virginity in the Bible," 89.

phasized in several of the laws regarding adultery/premarital sexual intercourse (examined below).[11]

Although virginity is prized as an indication of freshness and purity and the beauty and appropriateness of remaining a virgin until marriage is extolled, at the same time virginity is never held up in canonical Scripture as a permanent virtue, along the lines of the platonic virgin in Greek thought. There is a sense of looking forward to more beyond virginity, in the consummation of sexuality in marriage, and a sense of loss and sadness is portrayed in virginity when by tragedy a virgin is prevented from fulfilling or completing her sexuality. This is illustrated in particular in the case of Jephthah's daughter, who, when faced with imminent death, asked for two months to "bewail" her virginity (Judg 11:37).

This sense of loss and tragedy and lack of fulfillment appears to be behind the metaphorical use of the Hebrew word bĕtûlâ, "virgin," in the Prophets. The term bĕtûlat yiśrāʾēl "virgin of Israel" (RSV) is utilized metaphorically (Amos 5:2; Jer 18:13; 31:4, 21) to refer to the people of Yahweh, represented by their capital cities Samaria and Jerusalem respectively,[12] and seems to personify "the nation as a maid cut off before the consummation of her life, a girl violated by the ravaging assault of a military foe."[13] In the Prophets, a similar term, bĕtûlat bat "virgin daughter," is frequently applied to God's people (represented by the city Jerusalem) under the titles of Zion (Isa 37:22; Lam 2:13; 2 Kgs 10:21 [= Isa 37:22]), Judah (Lam 1:15), and "my people" (Jer 14:17); the phrase is also applied to Sidon (Isa 23:12), Babylon (Isa 47:1), and Egypt (Jer 46:11). "Virgin daughter" here appears to allude to "the ancient practice by which an unmarried woman continued to live under the protection of her father,"[14] and appears to connote (negatively) a "sense of helplessness, lack of power and sometimes abuse or a fallen condition" or (positively) a sense of "being prized by God and yet looking forward to future blessings."[15]

In the Writings, one observes that the virgins in the Song of Love (Ps 45) are the rough equivalent of "bridesmaids" in modern weddings (and so translated in NLT). They are companions of, but upstaged by, the bride, in whom they rejoice (45:15–16 [ET 45:14–15]). In Ps 78:63 divine judgment against Israel is characterized by the tragedy that their "virgins had no wedding songs" (NASB). In Ps 148:12 the two categories of "young men [bahûrîm 'choice ones'] and virgins

---

[11] For further substantiation of the high value placed on virginity in ancient Israel, see also Hilary B. Lipka, "'Such a Thing Is Not Done in Israel': The Construction of Sexual Transgression in the Hebrew Bible" (PhD diss., Brandeis University, 2004), 340 and passim.

[12] See John J. Schmitt, "The 'Virgin' of Israel: Referent and Use of the Phrase in Amos and Jeremiah," CBQ 53 (1991): 365–87, for analysis of these usages, although I disagree with his conclusion that the term refers exclusively to the capital cities and does not also by metonymy stand for the whole of the people symbolized by the cities.

[13] James Luther Mays, Amos: A Commentary (OTL; Philadelphia: Westminster, 1969), 85.

[14] Schmitt, "Virgin," 6:854.

[15] DBI 917–18, s.v. "Virgin, Virginity."

[*bĕtûlôt*]" (NASB) are placed in poetic parallelism, as pointed out above, to emphasize ideal marriage partners, the boys in the height of manhood and the girls
virgins. Significantly, the term "virgin" does not appear in the book of Proverbs;
the contrast of the "two ways" in morality is not between the immoral women
and a platonic virgin but between the immoral woman and a loving and faithful
wife with children and an adoring husband (e.g., Prov 5:15–20; 31:10–31).

Distortions of the Divine Ideal: Adultery and Premarital Sexual Intercourse

Ancient Near Eastern Background

The prohibition of adultery, the sense that is it a "great sin/crime"[16] against
the gods,[17] and the death penalty for committing adultery are found almost universally in the ancient Near East. Legislation related to adultery/premarital sex is
found in most of the extant ANE law codes.

Laws of Ur-Nammu [§§6–8]:[18]

§6: "If a man violates the rights of another and deflowers the virgin wife of a young
man, they shall kill that male."

§7: "If the wife of a young man, on her own initiative, approaches a man and initiates
sexual relations with him, they shall kill that woman; that male shall be released."

§8: "If a man acts in violation of the rights of another and deflowers the virgin slave
woman of a man, he shall weigh and deliver 5 shekels of silver."

Laws of Eshnunna [§§28, 31]:[19]

§28: "If he [a man] concludes the contract and the nuptial feast for (?) her father and
mother and he marries her, she is indeed a wife; the day she is seized in the lap of another man, she shall die, she will not live."

---

[16] Pnina Galpaz-Feller, "לא תנאף ! עיונים במקרא ובתרבות מצרים הקדומה" *Beit Mikra* 49
(2004): 159–73 (in Hebrew); William L. Moran, "The Scandal of the 'Great Sin' at Ugarit,"
JNES 18 (1959): 280–81; Jacob J. Rabinowitz, "The 'Great Sin' in Ancient Egyptian Marriage Contracts," *JNES* 18 (1959): 73; "The Story of Two Brothers," translated by John A.
Wilson (*ANET* 24); cf. the Akkadian texts that use the word "sin" (cognate to Hebrew root
ḥṭᵓ) with reference to adultery: *CAD* 6:153, 157. For a summary of evidence from a wide
variety of Egyptian documents indicating that adultery was considered a moral failing
and prohibited in ancient Egyptian society, see Pnina Galpaz-Feller, "Private Lives and
Public Censure—Adultery in Ancient Egypt and Biblical Israel," *NEA* 67 (2004): 153–61.

[17] For summary of evidence, see esp. Jacob Milgrom, "The Betrothed Slave-Girl, Lev
19:20–22," *ZAW* 89 (1977): 45–46.

[18] "The Laws of Ur-Namma (Ur-Nammu)," translated by Martha Roth (*COS*
2.153:409–10; cf. *ANET* 524).

[19] "The Laws of Eshnunna," translated by Martha Roth (*COS* 2.130:333–34; cf.
ANET 167).

§31: "If a man should deflower the slave woman of another man, he shall weigh and deliver 20 shekels of silver, but the slave woman remains the property of her master."

Code of Hammurabi [§§129, 133b]:[20]

§129: "If a man's wife should be seized lying with another male, they shall bind them and cast them into the water; if the wife's master allows his wife to live, then the king shall allow his subject (i.e., the other male) to live."

§133b: "If that woman [the wife of a man who has been captured] does not keep herself chaste but enters another's house, they shall charge and convict that woman and cast her into the water."

Middle Assyrian Laws [A §§13–16, 23, 56]:[21]

A §13: "If the wife of a man should go out of her own house, and go to another man where he resides, and should he fornicate with her knowing that she is the wife of a man, they shall kill the man and his wife."

A §14: "If a man should fornicate with another man's wife either in an inn or in the main thoroughfare, knowing that she is the wife of a man, they shall treat the fornicator as the man declares he wishes his wife to be treated. If he should fornicate with her without knowing that she is the wife of a man, the fornicator is clear; the man shall prove the charges against his wife and he shall treat her as he wishes."

A §15: "If a man should seize another man upon his wife and they prove the charges against him and find him guilty, they shall kill both of them; there is no liability for him (i.e., the husband). If he should seize him and bring him either before the king or the judges, and they prove the charges against him and find him guilty—if the woman's husband kills his wife, then he shall also kill the man; if he cuts off his wife's nose, he shall turn the man into a eunuch and they shall lacerate his entire face; but if [he wishes to release] his wife, he shall [release] the man."

A §16: "If a man [should fornicate] with the wife of a man [. . . by] her invitation, there is no punishment for the man; the man (i.e., husband) shall impose whatever punishment he chooses upon his wife. If he should fornicate with her by force and they prove the charges against him and find him guilty, his punishment shall be identical to that of the wife of the man."

A §23: "If a man's wife should take another man's wife into her house and give her to a man for purposes of fornication, and the man knows that she is the wife of a man, they shall treat him as one who has fornicated with the wife of another man; and they treat the female procurer just as the woman's husband treats his fornicating wife. And if the woman's husband intends to do nothing to his fornicating wife, they shall do nothing to the fornicator or to the female procurer; they shall release them. But if the man's wife does not know (what was intended), and the woman who takes her

---

[20] "The Laws of Hammurabi," translated by Martha Roth (*COS* 2.131:344; cf. *ANET* 171).

[21] "The Middle Assyrian Laws (Tablet A)," translated by Martha Roth (*COS* 2.132:354–56, 359–60; cf. *ANET* 181, 185).

into her house brings the man in to her by deceit (?), and he then fornicates with her—if, as soon as she leaves the house, she should declare that she has been the victim of fornication, they shall release the woman, she is clear; they shall kill the fornicator and the female procurer. But if the woman does not so declare, the man shall impose whatever punishment on his wife he wishes; they shall kill the fornicator and the female procurer."

A §56: "If a maiden should willingly give herself to a man, the man shall so swear; they shall have no claim to his wife; the fornicator shall pay 'triple' the silver as the value of the maiden; the father shall treat his daughter in whatever manner he chooses."

Hittite Laws [§§197–198]:[22]

§197: "If a man seizes a woman in the mountain(s) (and rapes) her, it is the man's offence, but if he seizes her in (her) house, it is the woman's offence; the woman shall die. If the (woman's) husband (lit. the man) finds them (in the act), he may kill them without committing a crime."

§198: "If he brings them to the palace gate (i.e., the royal court) and says: 'My wife shall not die,' he can spare his wife's life, (but) he must also spare the lover and 'clothe his head.' If he says, 'Both of them shall die,' they shall 'roll the wheel.' The king may have them killed or he may spare them."

The particulars of this extrabiblical ANE legislation will be discussed below after the analysis of pentateuchal legislation in order to highlight both the similarities and the stark contrasts between the biblical understanding of adultery and that elsewhere in the ancient Near East.

Pentateuchal Narratives Related to the Theme of Adultery

Several pentateuchal narratives deal with the theme of adultery. In Gen 12:10–20 one finds Abram's attempt to deceive Pharaoh into believing Sarai was his sister, not his wife (a half-truth since she was his half-sister, 20:12), and Gen 20 records that the patriarch tried the same tactic with Abimelech, king of Gerar. A few chapters later, 26:1–11 indicates that Abraham's son Isaac attempted the same deception with another king of Gerar by the same name (or title). In each of these narratives, it is clear that the foreign king and his people considered adultery a "great sin" (RSV, Heb. *ḥāṭāʾâ gĕdôlâ*, the term used by Abimelech in 20:9) and they would rather kill the husband of Sarai/Sarah or Rebecca than that he commit adultery (12:12; 20:3–5; 26:6). The narratives also record God's divine disapproval of adultery, bringing plagues (in the case of Pharaoh) or threatening capital punishment (in the case of Abimelech) upon those who were about to (unknowingly) commit the adulterous act (12:17; 20:3; cf. 26:10). The record also makes clear that Yahweh's (threatened) punishment was collective, extending beyond the adulterer to his family and kingdom (12:17; 20:7, 17; 26:10). Finally, the

---

[22] "Hittite Laws," translated by Harry A. Hoffner Jr. (*COS* 2.19:118; cf. *ANET* 196).

divine speeches in these narratives also underscore that the sin of adultery is ultimately a sin against God himself. Note especially God's speech to Abimelech in a dream: "Yes, I know that you did this in the integrity of your heart; furthermore it was I who kept you from *sinning against me*. Therefore I did not let you touch her [Sarah]" (20:6).[23]

Genesis 35:22 records an incident of adultery in which Reuben had sexual relations with Bilhah his father's concubine. Since this also constituted a case of incest, we will deal with this situation in ch. 10 below. Here we point out the severe consequences for Reuben (and his lineage) of this immoral act: he lost the birthright normally reserved for the firstborn (Gen 49:4; cf. 1 Chr 5:1). In Gen 39 a false accusation of adultery is narrated, this time of Joseph by Potiphar's wife. Here again is encountered the recognition that adultery is not just a crime on the human level but ultimately a sin against God. Joseph resists temptation with the words "How then could I do this great wickedness, and *sin against God?*" (39:9). Ronald Wallace also points out that Joseph's prompt and firm resistance of the temptation to adultery implies that giving in to sexual lust, in addition to the outward act of adultery, is opposed to the morality of Scripture.[24]

Pentateuchal Legislation regarding Adultery

The Decalogue. The foundational principles of sexual fidelity and purity are set forth in the Decalogue. The seventh commandment presents a categorical prohibition of adultery in the form of apodictic law: *lōʾ tinʾāp*, "You shall not commit adultery" (Exod 20:14; Deut 5:18). The tenth commandment categorically prohibits sexual lust: *lōʾ taḥmōd ʾēšet rēʿekā*, "you shall not covet your neighbor's wife" (Exod 20:17; Deut 5:21).[25] Even though the Decalogue is written in the

---

[23] See ch. 7, above, regarding the issue of prostitution in the account of Judah and Tamar in Gen 38. Elaine Goodfriend, "Adultery," *ABD* 1:85, suggests the possibility that Judah sentenced his daughter to be burned not only for alleged prostitution (or promiscuity) but for what he surmised was adulterous sexual relations while she waited for Judah's son Shelah, to whom she was apparently promised according to the law of levirate marriage (Gen 38:11), to come of age. The text of Gen 38, however, does not make clear that Tamar was already betrothed to Shelah; in fact, my reading of the text seems to point in the opposite direction, that she was not yet betrothed, which precipitated Tamar's drastic action.

[24] Ronald S. Wallace, *The Story of Joseph and the Family of Jacob* (Grand Rapids: Eerdmans, 2001), 34: "[Joseph's reply to Potiphar's wife] is a reminder to us that not only the sin of actual adultery but the type of free sexual lust to which she was tempting him was then, and still is, abhorrent to the God we know in Christ, and can hinder our ability to be of service to him in his kingdom."

[25] Attempts have been made to explain away the language of the tenth commandment so that it is made to refer to concrete acts and not thoughts and desires. Bernard S. Jackson, "Liability for Mere Intention in Early Jewish Law," *HUCA* 42 (1971): 197–225, examines these theories in detail, shows how all such attempts fail to take the Hebrew verb *ḥāmad*, "to desire, covet," in its clear and normal OT meaning, and concludes that "there is no adequate reason to doubt the traditional meaning of the 10th commandment" (p. 205). Brevard S. Childs, *The Book of Exodus: A Critical, Theological Commentary*

masculine singular, it is clear that this is utilized as a generic gender and that the ten words are intended to apply to all humankind. Thus the act of adultery is prohibited for both men and women. And thus both men and women are called to a standard of purity that excludes even impure thoughts and desires. Stephen Kaufman, in his analysis of the Deuteronomic amplification of the tenth commandment in Deut 25:13–15, points to a powerful strategy for avoiding lust, a strategy embedded in the legislation: "Avoid tempting situations."[26]

Other Legislation. The prohibition of adultery with another man's wife is repeated several times in the pentateuchal legal material. In Lev 18:20; 20:10 the prohibition is placed amid the universal-level legislation applicable to both Israelites and foreigners/other nations, legislation dealing with "abominations" that defile the land and cause it to "vomit out its inhabitants" (18:20, 24–25, as discussed above in the chapters dealing with polygamy, homosexuality, and bestiality). According to 20:10, the punishment for adultery is death for both parties: "both the adulterer and the adulteress shall be put to death." As in the Decalogue, Lev 18 and 20 emphasize that adultery transgresses religious boundaries as a violation of divine law.[27]

(Philadelphia: Westminster, 1974), 425–28, points out that this conclusion is reinforced in the Deuteronomy version of the tenth commandment: the second use of *ḥāmad* in the Exodus passage is substituted with *ʾāwâ* in Deut 5:21—the latter term unequivocally referring to subjective desire and not concrete action—thus strengthening the emphasis already present in the original command. Furthermore, Steven A. Kaufman, "The Structure of the Deuteronomic Law," *Maarav* 1–2 (1978–1979): 143–44, in his analysis of the structure of the Deuteronomic law in Deut 12–25 (which follows precisely the order of the Decalogue), shows that the legislation placed under the rubric of the tenth commandment (Deut 25:5–16) supports this conclusion; *ḥāmad* "means to desire something so strongly that you want to take it, but it neither refers to nor implies the act of taking itself; *pace* all those who so argued (and that includes most everyone from the Tannain onward). . . . I have no doubt that the author or authors of the Decalogue actually intended to 'prohibit' (that is to say, strongly discourage) even patterns of thought that might lead to commit any of the civil crimes subsumed under the preceding rubrics of murder, adultery, theft and false witness. Anyone thinking such thoughts is to know that they are divinely prohibited and therefore to be eschewed." See also David L. Baker, "Last But Not Least: The Tenth Commandment," *HBT* 27 (2005): 3–24; Umberto Cassuto, *A Commentary on the Book of Exodus* (trans. Israel Abrahams; Jerusalem: Magnes, 1967), 248–49; J. Philip Hyatt, *Commentary on Exodus* (NCB; London: Oliphants, 1971), 216; William L. Moran, "The Conclusion of the Decalogue," *CBQ* 95 (1967): 543–54; and David Talley, "חמד," *NIDOTTE* 2:167–69.

[26] As an example of how Deuteronomic law, in the section expanding on the tenth commandment, attempts to solve the problem of wrong thoughts, Kaufman, "The Structure of the Deuteronomic Law," 144, notes that Deut 25:13–15 forbids not the use of false weights (which would be theft) but even their possession, because only if you have them in your possession would you be tempted to use them. Thus the elaboration on the tenth commandment gives an effective strategy for avoiding lust, applicable to areas of sexual temptation: avoid even the situations that might give rise to a temptation. As discussed below, the book of Proverbs develops this theme significantly.

[27] See esp. Lipka, " 'Such a Thing Is Not Done in Israel,' " 158. Lipka (pp. 54–225) analyzes all the passages in the HB dealing with adultery, showing that the transgression is consistently a violation of religious boundaries. Whereas the Decalogue and Lev 18 and

Deuteronomy 22:22 also prescribes capital punishment for both parties who commit adultery[28] and, by the use of the phrase *gam šěnêham,* "both of them," underscores that this law seeks to uphold the demand for equal justice. The context of related laws in Deut 22 seems to imply that the means of execution is death by stoning (cf. Deut 22:21, 24 and below).[29]

Adultery in Israel in Contrast with Other Ancient Near Eastern Legislation. A comparison of the biblical legislation regarding the rape or seduction of married or betrothed women with parallel laws in other ANE codes reveals that the biblical law holds a man to a higher level of responsibility for his sexual misbehavior. As noted above, the recognition that adultery is a "great sin/crime" against the gods, deserving of the death penalty, is found almost universally in the ancient Near East. But although the religious aspect of adultery was present in ANE thought, it seems to have had little or no effect upon the legislation outside the Bible. The extrabiblical ANE law codes do not seem to regard adultery as an unconditional "violation of a divinely ordained statute with a death penalty, as in Israel."[30] This is evident in that these extrabiblical law codes often made provision for the husband to mitigate the sentence of both his wife and the adulterer from death to mutilation, monetary compensation, or total forgiveness if he so chose.[31] By contrast, there is no specific provision in the Mosaic legislation for commuting the

---

20 focus exclusively on the violation of religious boundaries, the passages in Deuteronomy and Numbers dealing with adultery (discussed below) reveal adultery to be a violation of both religious and communal boundaries.

[28] Contra Anthony Phillips, *Ancient Israel's Criminal Law: A New Approach to the Decalogue* (Oxford: Basil Blackwell, 1970), 110, who argues that originally only the adulterer was executed while the woman, "who was not subject to Israel's criminal law," would either be forgiven or divorced by her husband but that after the Deuteronomic reform ("whereby women were made equal members of the covenant community with men") the adulteress was also tried, convicted, and executed. This view rests on the mistaken view that the Decalogue applied only to male Israelites (see ch. 6, above) and on the Documentary Hypothesis (with Deuteronomy written at the time of the Josianic reform), which goes beyond this canonical study of the final form of the OT text. See Goodfriend, "Adultery," 1:84, for refutation of linguistic arguments used by Phillips to support his conclusions.

[29] See Goodfriend, "Adultery," 1:84.

[30] Moshe Greenberg, "More Reflections on Biblical Criminal Law," in *Studies in Bible, 1986* (ed. Sara Japhet; ScrHier 31; Jerusalem: Magnes, 1986), 3.

[31] Laws of Eshnunna §31 (*COS* 2.130:334; *ANET* 162), CH §129 (*COS* 2.131:346; *ANET* 171), MAL A §14–16, 23 (*COS* 2.132:355–56; *ANET* 181). But premeditated adultery, when the man knows the marital status of the woman (that she is either married or betrothed), does seem to receive a mandatory death penalty in the ANE law codes: Laws of Ur Nammu §6 (*COS* 2.153:409; *ANET* 524), CH §133b (*COS* 2.131:344; *ANET* 171), MAL A §13 (*COS* 2.132:354; *ANET* 181). For this insight, distinguishing between premeditated and unpremeditated adultery in the Mesopotamian laws, see Roy Gane, "Biblical and Ancient Near Eastern Penalties for Sexual Misconduct" (PhD preliminary examination in biblical law, University of California, Berkeley, November 1988, in Gane's 1995 syllabus for the Andrews University Theological Seminary course Covenant-Law-Sabbath, 139–45). The Hittite Laws also provide for the husband or the king to spare the adulterer and adulteress from the death penalty, but also add a provision for the husband to kill them while in the act if he so chooses: HL §§197–198 (*COS* 2.19:118; *ANET* 196).

death sentence of this sin against God when conviction came through due process by two or three witnesses (Deut 17:6).[32] Also in contrast to the ANE law codes, whereas the adulterer's ignorance that the woman he impregnated was married brought his acquittal,[33] in biblical laws the adulterer's ignorance of the woman's marital status made no difference in assigning the penalty. In other words, the Mesopotamian law codes have "a complex and subjective approach to adultery," with distinctions made "between types of adultery on the basis of degree of intention, and therefore circumstances may be a mitigating or aggravating factor in the fixing of penalties." This is in contrast with biblical law, in which "the act was viewed in absolute terms, with no distinctions based on different kinds of intentions."[34] The Mosaic legislation thus seems to go beyond other ANE law codes in treating adultery as primarily a *moral crime against God* and not merely a personal injury to the husband.[35] "In YHWH's eyes, the guilt of adultery is absolute."[36]

---

[32] See Moshe Greenberg, "Some Postulates of Biblical Criminal Law," in *Yehezkel Kaufmann Jubilee Volume* (ed. M. Haran; Jerusalem: Magnes, 1960), 12: "There is no question of permitting the husband to mitigate or cancel the punishment." A contrary view is presented by Samuel E. Loewenstamm, "The Laws of Adultery and Murder in Biblical and Mesopotamian Law," in *Comparative Studies in Biblical and Ancient Oriental Literatures* (Neukirchen-Vluyn: Neukirchener Verlag, 1980), 146–53; Henry McKeating, "Sanctions against Adultery in Ancient Israelite Society, with Some Reflections on Methodology in the Study of Old Testament Ethics," *JSOT* 11 (1979): 62–65; and others, who maintain that the law represented an idealized presentation of the seriousness of adultery but in practice the husband was given the right of pardon as in other ANE laws. Evidence in Scripture for the latter assertion is deduced from the lack of any biblical reference to the enforcement of capital punishment for adultery and from hints in the OT that are seen to point toward the husband's right of pardon (to be mentioned below). The conclusion of this chapter (in the section on grace) will argue that although the pentateuchal legislation regarding adultery and other illicit sexual practices calling for the death penalty does not include any explicit provision for commuting the sentence, thus emphasizing the absolute sin against God in such behavior, nonetheless a recognition is implicit in the Pentateuch (as well as the Prophets and Writings) that mitigation of the death sentence through grace or pity was possible for most sex-related crimes.

[33] See MAL A §§13–14 (*COS* 2.132:354; *ANET* 181).

[34] Gane, "Biblical and Ancient Near Eastern Penalties," 144–45.

[35] So Greenberg, "Some Postulates," 12: "Adultery is not merely a wrong against the husband, it is a sin against God, an absolute wrong." This is also the view of Louis M. Epstein, *Sex Laws and Customs in Judaism* (New York: Bloch, 1948), 199; James B. Hurley, *Man and Woman in Biblical Perspective* (Grand Rapids: Zondervan, 1981), 41–42; Shalom M. Paul, *Studies in the Book of the Covenant in the Light of Cuneiform and Biblical Law* (Leiden: E. J. Brill, 1970), 98; and Anthony Phillips, "Another Look at Adultery," *JSOT* 20 (1981): 3–25. This position has been challenged especially by McKeating, "Sanctions against Adultery," but his argumentation is based upon an acceptance of the hypothetical reconstruction of the pentateuchal text according to the Documentary Hypothesis, with D[Deuteronomist] and H[Holiness Code] no earlier than the seventh/sixth centuries. We are examining the theology of the final canonical form of the biblical text, not the theology of conjectured source-critical reconstructions. I also disagree with Patrick G. D. Riley, *Civilizing Sex: On Chastity and the Common Good* (Edinburgh: T&T Clark, 2000), passim, who argues that the entire Decalogue is "*purely* civil law" and not moral in character (p. 56).

[36] Goodfriend, "Adultery," 1:84.

Anthony Phillips rightly concludes, "Israel's law of adultery rested on a distinctive principle found nowhere else in the ancient Near East."[37] This principle is that adultery in Israel is "a crime [against God] and not just a civil offence." More important, Phillips points out why Israel's laws on adultery were different from elsewhere in the ancient Near East in demanding the death penalty with no exceptions: "This situation could only have arisen because ancient Israel came into being through accepting a distinctive law which, regardless of any covenant theology . . . made her a peculiar people among the other ancient Near Eastern peoples. . . . This could only have been the Decalogue."[38] Jacob Milgrom points out that all Israel was corporately bound by the Decalogue at Mt. Sinai, and any breach of its provisions could be regarded as a *mā'al*, "act of faithlessness, breach of trust," against God. In effect, then, "the Bible predicates a collective oath against adultery when Israel became covenanted with God."[39] An act of adultery desecrated the Sinaitic oath and constituted a "great sin" of offense against God.

But an even deeper question remains: why was adultery in Israel so heinous in God's eyes? Christopher Wright suggests that it has to do not only with personal morality but with the sociotheological importance of the family, which forms the focal point of the social, economic, and theological realms in Israel.[40] He argues that God takes adultery (and other offenses threatening the stability of the household) so seriously because a stable relationship in the household was the social basis upon which the people's relationship with God rested and therefore any attack upon the stability of the family in Israel constituted a potential threat to Israel's relationship with God. "Adultery strikes at the very heart of the stability of the household by shattering the *sexual integrity* of the marriage." Thus a twofold theological concern is addressed in the laws against adultery. "From the general perspective of biblical sexual ethics, adultery is an act of immorality condemned on the basis of the biblical concept of marriage. But from the particular, historical perspective of Israel's relationship with Yahweh and the central importance of the household to it, adultery acquired an additional dimension of gravity which transcended private sexual morality . . . and raised it to the level of national concern."[41]

The "Trial of Jealousy" in Numbers 5. A striking legal case, revealing the sin of adultery as a crime directed against God himself, is recorded in Num 5:11–31, where a special "trial of jealousy" procedure that includes drinking the *mê*

---

[37] Phillips, "Another Look at Adultery," 3.

[38] Ibid., 19.

[39] Milgrom, "The Betrothed Slave-Girl," 49.

[40] One might also add that a pregnancy via adulterous relationships upsets the patrilineal system upon which not only the family inheritance but also the whole societal order was built. Eventually the entire fabric of Israelite society could be turned upside down.

[41] Christopher J. H. Wright, "The Israelite Household and the Decalogue: The Social Background and Significance of Some Commandments," *TynBul* 30 (1979): 123; cf. 102–24 for his full argument. For a summary of other suggested rationales for the adultery prohibition, see David T. Stewart, "Ancient Sexual Laws: Text and Intertext of the Biblical Holiness Code and Hittite Laws" (PhD diss., University of California, Berkeley, 2000), 216–18.

hammārîm, "water of bitterness" or "water of revelation,"[42] is prescribed to determine the guilt or innocence of a wife whom her husband suspects of unfaithfulness.

Recent literary studies have demonstrated that this passage constitutes a coherent whole with a logical composition and intricately designed literary structure.[43] The passage is arranged in a chiastic structure: (A) introduction (vv. 12–14); (B) preparation (vv. 15–18); (C) the oath (vv. 19–24); (B′) execution (vv. 25–28); and (A′) summary/recapitulation (vv. 29–30).[44] Verse 15 repeats the verb "[the man] brings" (*hipᶜil* of *bôʾ*); vv. 16, 18 repeat the verb "[the priest has the woman] stand" (*hipᶜil* of *ᶜāmad*); vv. 19, 21 repeat the verb "[the priest] adjures [the woman]" (*hipᶜil* of *šābaᶜ*); and vv. 24, 27 repeat the verb "[the priest has the woman] drink" (*hipᶜil* of *šāqâ*).[45] Thus each of these sections—which at first glance appears to indicate that key actions were performed twice—actually utilizes a literary *inclusio* repetition in which a key action word at the beginning forms a heading that "headlines" the purpose of the section, followed by a repetition of the same key word in its proper place, where the "prime act" occurs in the descriptive flow of that section.[46]

The law of Num 5:11–31 has in view two possible circumstances, stated clearly in the introduction (vv. 12–14). Verses 12–14a describe a first situation in which the husband's suspicions are aroused (lit. "becomes jealous/zealous" [*qinnēʾ*]) after his wife commits adultery: she "goes astray" (*śaṭâ,* whence the rabbinic title "suspected *Sotah*"), and "is unfaithful" (*māᶜal*) toward her husband; another man lies (i.e., had sexual intercourse) with her, and she thereby "has defiled herself" (*nipᶜal* of *ṭāmēʾ*). Verse 14b describes a second situation in which the husband's suspicions are aroused even though his wife has not been unfaithful to her husband. The "jealousy" referred to here "was not a selfish, sinful, or

---

[42] See Herbert Chanan Brichto, "The Case of the *Sōṭā* and a Reconsideration of Biblical Law," *HUCA* 46 (1975): 59, n. 1, who suggests that *mê hammārîm* does not mean "water of bitterness" but rather "water of knowledge/revelation," with *hammārîm* deriving from the verb *yārâ* (in the *hipᶜil*), "to teach." Tikva Frymer-Kensky, "The Strange Case of the Suspected Sotah (Numbers V 11–31)," *VT* 34 (1984): 26, after surveying the various suggestions for translating the phrase *mê hammārîm,* also finds this "the most attractive suggestion." The water would then refer to its function in the ritual—to provide the "revelation" of guilt or innocence. If the traditional interpretation is maintained, that *hammārîm* means "bitterness," then R. K. Harrison, *Numbers* (Wycliffe Exegetical Commentary; Chicago: Moody, 1990), 110, is probably correct in explaining, "The water she would drink was 'bitter' in terms of the awful potential consequences that would become actual if she were in fact guilty."

[43] See, among others, Brichto, "The Case of the *Sōṭā*"; Michael Fishbane, "Accusations of Adultery: A Study of Law and Scribal Practice in Numbers 5:11–31," *HUCA* 45 (1974): 25–45; Frymer-Kensky, "The Strange Case of the Suspected Sotah"; Jacob Milgrom, "The Case of the Suspected Adulteress, Numbers 5:11–31: Redaction and Meaning," in *The Creation of Sacred Literature: Composition and Redaction of the Biblical Text* (ed. Richard Elliott Friedman; Berkeley, Calif.: University of Berkeley Press, 1981), 69–75.

[44] Milgrom, "The Case of the Suspected Adulteress," 70–71.

[45] The translations are mine.

[46] Frymer-Kensky, "The Strange Case of the Suspected Sotah," 13–18.

petty feeling of envy (as in Gen. 30:1; 37:11), for which the husband deserved censure. Rather it was a rightful *zeal* to protect the exclusively intimate covenant relationship of marriage as God had instituted it."[47]

The crucial point in this law is that in either case scenario the husband has no
proof of any wrongdoing on the part of his wife. This key point is underscored by
repeating this concept four different times in one verse (Num 5:13): "it is hidden
from her husband"; "she is undetected though she has defiled herself"; "there was
no witness against her"; and "she was not caught in the act." Because the allegedly
guilty woman was not apprehended, she is not subject to the jurisdiction of the
human court. Deuteronomy 17:6–7 is explicit that one could not be put to death
without at least two witnesses. Note that the law avoids describing the woman's
sin as "committing adultery" (*nāʾap*), since the biblical penalty for a clear case of
adultery is invariably death.

At the same time, this law reveals how serious is the divine displeasure with
unfaithfulness to the marriage vow—how this sin is seen as an offense against
God himself. Although the lack of human witnesses precludes a sentence of death
for adultery, the stability of the social structure of the household (and thus Israel's societal relationship with God as well) is at stake, and Israel gives this situation over to God, who takes the "trial" and punishment into his own hands. "The
society has relinquished its control over the woman to God, who will indicate his
judgment by punishing her if she is guilty. Not only does God decide whether she
is guilty, but even the right of punishment is removed from society and placed in
the hands of God."[48]

That this sin is an offense against God himself is also emphasized by where
this law is placed in the Pentateuch. In contrast with the Code of Hammurabi,
where a similar law follows immediately after the other laws relating to adultery,[49]
in the biblical material this law is not placed amid the various other adultery-
related laws concentrated in Deut 22 (examined below), but within the corpus of
ritual practices found in Lev 1–Num 6. The placement seems motivated by the
fact that the trial of jealousy is performed by a priest (Num 5:15) in the sanctuary
(v. 17) and is associated with various ritual offerings (vv. 15, 18, 25–26); thus this
is a *sanctuary* ritual, conducted in the presence, and under the direct control, of
Yahweh himself.[50]

The oath (vv. 19–24) forms the central focus of the legislation, as indicated by
its location in the chiastic apex of the passage. This oath, taken by the woman before she drinks the "water of bitterness/revelation," may recall the marriage vow
taken by the woman to be faithful to her husband[51] and with the accompanying

---

[47] Roy Gane, *Leviticus, Numbers* (NIVAC 3; Grand Rapids: Zondervan, 2004), 528.
[48] Frymer-Kensky, "The Strange Case of the Suspected Sotah," 24.
[49] CH §§129–130 (*COS* 2.131:344; *ANET* 171) are the laws concerning adultery, and
this is followed by §§131–132 with the cases of unsubstantiated accusations of adultery.
[50] I am indebted to Fishbane, "Accusations of Adultery," 26–27, for this insight.
[51] We have a hint of the marriage "vows" in Gen 2:23 (see ch. 1, above) and a further
hint in reference to marriage as a "covenant" (implying a covenant-making oath) in Mal
2:14 (see ch. 9, below).

curse may also allude to the collective "vow" made by Israel at Sinai to obey the covenant stipulations of the Decalogue (Exod 19:8; 24:7) under threat of covenant curse for disobedience (Lev 26).[52]

The verdict in the divine trial reveals God's concern for *lex talionis* (just retribution): if the woman has allowed another man to put (*qal* of *nātan*) his penis (*šĕkōbet*) in her (Num 5:20), the Lord will put/set (*qal* of *nātan*) her as a curse among her people by putting (*qal* of *nātan*) physical maladies upon her reproductive organs (vv. 21–22).[53] "The adulteress who acquiesced to receive forbidden seed is doomed to sterility for the rest of her life."[54] Frymer-Kensky presents a detailed examination of the expression *wĕṣābtâ biṭnāh wĕnāplâ yĕrēkāh* ("her womb shall discharge, her uterus drop") in v. 27 and concludes that it probably refers to a prolapsed uterus in which "the pelvic floor . . . collapses, and the uterus literally falls down. It may lodge in the vagina, or it may actually fall out of the body through the vagina. If it does so, it becomes edematous and swells up like a balloon. Conception becomes impossible, and the woman's procreative life has effectively ended."[55]

This is the only biblical law where the outcome depends upon a miracle. It is not coincidental that this unique instance of divine jurisprudence directly dependent on miraculous divine intervention concerns marital unfaithfulness. Thus this ordeal emphasizes the uniquely high regard that God has for the integrity of the marriage relationship.

At the same time, this legislation also aims at protecting the woman from abuse and injustice—whether she is guilty or innocent. The whole case is taken out of human hands and placed before the Judge of the universe, who promises to judge righteously and render the verdict himself by supernatural means. "The right to such a Supreme Court trial belongs only to a woman."[56] Milgrom points out that this law forestalls the possibility of her being "lynched by mob rule or its legal equivalent, a kangaroo court."[57] If the woman is innocent, the "water of bitterness/revelation"—a nonpoisonous potion—would not harm her, and her accusers also could not punish her. If she is guilty, God gives her just retribution, and no human court can add to that sentence by putting her to death.

The biblical trial of jealousy is thus much less drastic (and life-threatening) than its parallels in other ANE law codes. For example, in the Code of Hammurabi, the trial of jealousy included the command for the woman to "throw herself into the sacred river." If she sank, she was guilty, and if she survived, she was innocent.[58] Whereas the "water of bitterness/revelation" required a miracle in

---

[52] Cf. Milgrom, "The Betrothed Slave-Girl," 45, and the discussion above.

[53] Gane, *Leviticus, Numbers,* 522.

[54] Milgrom, "The Case of the Suspected Adulteress," 75.

[55] Frymer-Kensky, "The Strange Case of the Suspected Sotah," 21. Cf. Harrison, *Numbers,* 112–13, for other possible medical conditions that might have resulted from the curse.

[56] Gane, *Leviticus, Numbers,* 526.

[57] Milgrom, "The Case of the Suspected Adulteress," 74.

[58] CH §132 (*COS* 2.131:344; *ANET* 171); see CH §2 (*COS* 2.131:337; *ANET* 166) for the full account of the "river ordeal"; it is noteworthy that the cuneiform word for "[Euphrates] river" in these cases has the determinative sign for deity, showing that the judge

order to condemn the woman in the biblical legislation, being thrown into the life-threatening river required a miracle in order for the woman to be regarded as innocent in the Mesopotamian version. The biblical law of the suspected adulteress thus presumed innocence until proven guilty, whereas the Mesopotamian counterpart presumed guilt until proven innocent.[59]

Furthermore, in the Mesopotamian trials by ordeal, the god's decision was manifested immediately (if she drowned, she was guilty), whereas in the biblical legislation the verdict appeared some time later (in connection with the woman's fertility or barrenness).[60] In addition, the biblical text makes very clear that there is no magic involved in the "water of bitterness/revelation," in contrast to the magical associations connected with much ANE religious ritual. The text is unequivocal (v. 21): "the LORD makes your uterus drop, your womb discharge." Because of these differences, it seems "unwarranted and misleading" to speak of Num 5:11–31 as a trial by ordeal.[61] It is a divine "ritual trial," which most nearly parallels the "classic purgatory oath, in which the individual swearing the oath puts himself under divine jurisdiction, expecting to be punished by God if the oath-taker is guilty."[62]

As noted above on the status of women (ch. 6), feminists have often cited this legislation as their coup de grace proving the sexist nature of the OT. But as Milgrom insightfully argues, this is "the worst possible witness" for such a claim because the woman's "public ordeal was meant not to humiliate her but to protect her, not to punish her but to defend her" from "a husband's pride, a mob's prejudice."[63] The final verse of the legislation (v. 31) indeed underscores

---

in these cases was considered to be the deity. See also MAL §17 (*COS* 2.132:355; *ANET* 181); and other citations of actual drowning in the Mari river ordeal in Milgrom, "The Case of the Suspected Adulteress," 75.

[59] Harrison, *Numbers*, 120–21, makes the same point.

[60] Frymer-Kensky carefully analyzes the structural flow of the legislation and points out that with the meticulous details of the procedure to be followed, it is significant that such details terminate with the drinking of the potion. "The ritual trial of the Sotah ended with the drinking of the potion. Nothing further was done, and we can assume that the woman went home to await the results at some further time" ("The Strange Case of the Suspected Sotah," 22).

[61] I concur with Frymer-Kensky, ibid., 24, on this caution.

[62] Ibid. Note that in CH §§131–132 (*COS* 2.131:344; *ANET* 171), the oath before the deity and the river ordeal are placed in separate laws dealing with different circumstances. CH §131, which contains the "affirmation by god," refers to the case where the man becomes suspicious and accuses his wife of adultery (apparently with no external evidence except his own suspicion), whereas §132 (containing the river ordeal) refers to the case where "the finger was pointed at" his wife (i.e., some public denouncement of her unfaithfulness exists although she was not apprehended in the act of adultery).

[63] Jacob Milgrom, "A Husband's Pride, a Mob's Prejudice: The Public Ordeal Undergone by a Suspected Adulteress in Numbers 5 Was Meant Not to Humiliate Her but to Protect Her," *BRev* 12, no. 4 (1996): 21. This is not to suggest that there is total egalitarianism in the biblical treatment of men and women, as pointed out in ch. 6, above. This trial of jealousy apparently was available only for the husband to apply to his wife and not vice versa. At the same time, in contrast with ANE applications of trial by ordeal, this

the protection for both the suspected woman (even when guilty) and her suspicious husband. For the husband: "[t]he man shall be free from iniquity." That is, he will not be charged with false accusation even if the woman is ultimately acquitted in the divine trial. For the woman (if guilty): "the woman shall bear her iniquity" (*tiśśāʾ ʾet-ʿăwōnāh*). This expression does not refer to additional action taken by the community (the death penalty, as often assumed) but, as elsewhere in the Torah, conveys the idea of "leaving the punishment to God."[64]

The provision for dealing with the suspected adulteress, like the prohibitions for adultery as a whole, seems to have had the intended purpose of striking terror into the heart of one contemplating unfaithfulness to one's marriage partner, thus constituting a powerful incentive to guard the exclusiveness of the marriage bond. In light of this strong deterrent in Mosaic legislation, it might be asked how often adultery was punished in ancient Israel. There is no biblical evidence for an individual being put to death for adultery, although such omission does not indicate that it never happened. Inasmuch as a capital offense had to be sustained by at least two witnesses (Deut 17:6–7), legal conviction of adultery may not always have been easy, and the trial of jealousy would have been necessary in such cases. But even the trial of jealousy was dependent upon the husband becoming suspicious and deciding to bring the case to court. Furthermore, as argued in the concluding section of this chapter, implicit in the pentateuchal legislation (and elsewhere in the OT) seems to be some allowance for the commutation of the death penalty in cases of most sex-related offenses. In practice, then, carrying out the death penalty or the trial of jealousy for adultery may have been quite rare.

Pentateuchal Legislation Dealing with Premarital/Pre-betrothal Sexual Intercourse

Several pentateuchal laws deal directly with premarital/pre-betrothal sexual intercourse. Indeed, in Deut 22:13–29—the single coherent unit of Deuteronomic case laws[65] that contains the amplification of the seventh commandment,

---

legislation presumed the woman's innocence and served to protect the woman—who was the more vulnerable party in the marriage—against false charges of infidelity brought by her husband.

[64] Frymer-Kensky, "The Strange Case of the Suspected Sotah," 22–24. See, e.g., the laws receiving the *kārēt* punishment, discussed above, and Num 30:16 (ET 30:15); Lev 5:1.

[65] See Carolyn Pressler, *The View of Women Found in the Deuteronomic Family Laws* (Berlin: de Gruyter, 1993), 20, for the similarities of content, form, and wording that mark this section of six laws as a discrete textual unit. These include, among other things, the similar content of sexual offenses; the same casuistic form (If . . . then . . .) in contrast to the apodictic laws ("You shall not . . .") that precede and follow; repeating terms and phrases (*yāṣāʾ* in the *hipʿil* "bring out," [vv. 14, 15, 19, 21, 24], *māṣaʾ* "find" [vv. 14, 17, 20, 22, 23, 25, 27, 28], *ʾiššâ* "wife" [vv. 13, 14, 16, 19, 22, 24, 29], *naʿărâ* "young man" [vv, 15, 16, 21, 23, 24, 26], and *bĕtûlâ* "virgin" [vv. 19, 23, 28], the death penalty and the expurgation phrase "So you shall purge the evil from your midst" [vv. 21, 22, 24]); and an *inclusio* beginning and ending with cases concerning premarital, pre-betrothal sexuality (22:13–19, 28–29).

concerning improper sexual relations[66]—all but one verse (v. 22) deals with situations that today we would call premarital sexual relations.[67] These laws are recorded in this chapter in a general descending order of gravity (i.e., penalty).

Premarital Sex with a Betrothed Virgin (Deut 22:23–27). After the case law concerning our modern definition of full-fledged adultery between a man and another man's wife (Deut 22: 22), which was discussed above, there follows further legislation concerning sex with a man's betrothed virgin, which we today would call premarital sex but which was apparently considered equivalent to adultery in biblical terms, although the term "commit adultery" is never used regarding these situations.[68]

Deuteronomy 22:23–27 describes a situation in which a man has sexual relations with a virgin who is betrothed to another man; that is, he violates a virgin for whom the bride money (*mōhar*) has already been paid but who still lives in

---

[66] Kaufman, "The Structure of the Deuteronomic Law," 113. Kaufman shows that the Deuteronomic code amplifies the seventh commandment under several different topics: (1) Deut 22:9–11, prohibited mixtures; (2) 22:13–23:1 (ET 22:30), regulations concerning improper sexual relations; (3) 23:2–9 (ET 23:1–8), sexual wholeness and genetic purity as requirements for membership in God's community; (4) 23:10–15 (ET 23:9–14), sexual purity and cleanness in the military camp; and (5) 23:18–19 (ET 23:17–18), prohibition of cultic prostitutes. As noted in the previous footnote, section 2 is further subdivided, with the bulk of the material constituting casuistic laws related to adultery (22:13–29), and the single added verse (23:1, ET 22:30) dealing with incest (probably included by attraction to the mention of "father" in v. 29, as Kaufman, p. 139, suggests).

[67] As will become apparent below, however, some of these concern sexual relations with a betrothed woman, who in ancient thinking was already legally bound to her future husband by the payment of the bride money even though the marriage was not yet formally consummated, and thus the premarital sexual offense would have been considered adultery.

[68] This seems to be the consensus of scholarship (see Pressler, *The View of Women,* 31; Goodfriend, "Adultery," 1:82). We could just as well have dealt with this legislation concerning illicit sexual relations with a betrothed virgin under the section on adultery, above, inasmuch as the betrothed virgin was in a real sense already considered to be a man's wife even though the marriage was not yet consummated (see esp. Deut 22:24, where raping a woman betrothed to another man is considered "violating his neighbor's wife"). The legislation concerning a betrothed virgin is included together with pre-betrothal sex in a separate section because the term "commit adultery" is never used to characterize this illicit sexual activity and because some of the legislation in this section involves situations that include both pre-betrothal and post-betrothal premarital sexual activity. In addition to the pentateuchal legislation concerning sexual relations with a woman engaged to someone else, there is another pentateuchal reference to an engaged woman being violated, but this probably occurs in the context of Israel's being defeated in battle. If Israel should fail to stay loyal to the covenant with Yahweh, one of the "futility curses" which would befall them was, "You shall become engaged to a woman, but another man shall lie with [lit. 'ravish', *šāgal*] her" (Deut 28:30). This passage does not make clear whether the engaged man would be still alive (as a war captive) or would have died in battle when the one to whom he had been engaged was ravished by another. The point of this passage, as with the other "futility curses" in Deut 28:30–33a, is that proper enjoyment is frustrated (J. G. McConville, *Deuteronomy* [AOTC 5; Downers Grove, Ill.: InterVarsity, 2002], 406).

her father's house while waiting for the consummation of the marriage.[69] The punishment in this case depends upon whether the woman has consented to the sexual encounter. If they are discovered in the city, it is presumed that she is guilty (or she would have cried out), and both of them are executed by stoning, "the young woman because she did not cry for help in the town and the man because he violated his neighbor's wife. So you shall purge the evil from your midst" (v. 24). If a man finds a betrothed woman in the countryside and lies with her, it is presumed that the man "forced" (NASB; *hipᶜil* of *ḥāzaq*) her (i.e., raped her), and whereas the man is executed, the woman is declared innocent, "since he found her in the open country, the engaged woman may have cried for help, but there was no one to rescue her" (v. 27).[70] In the latter case, the legislation employs five separate clauses to emphasize that the woman is not guilty.[71] Several scholars have pointed out that this general principle of location implying the woman's consent/nonconsent was probably intended to apply also to the case of the married woman as well as the betrothed.[72]

The Case of the Slandered Bride (Deut 22:13–21). According to this law, if a man takes a wife and, after having sexual relations with her, "dislikes" (lit. "hates" [*śānēʾ*]) her and spreads false rumors about her[73] (lit. "brings a bad name on her") by claiming that she was not a virgin when he married her, the parents of the woman can bring the "evidence of the young woman's virginity" (*bĕtûlîm*, i.e.,

---

[69] This can be inferred from texts such as Exod 22:15–16 (ET 22:16–17); Deut 20:7; and comparative ANE material (e.g., CH §130 [*COS* 2.131:344; *ANET* 171] and Laws of Eshnunna §26 [*COS* 2.130:333; *ANET* 162]).

[70] For the ANE parallel to this use of location to determine a woman's consent/nonconsent, see HL §197 (*COS* 2.19:118; *ANET* 196). For further discussion of this passage as involving rape, see ch. 12, below.

[71] They are the following: (1) "the man who lay with her shall die"; (2) "You shall do nothing to the young woman"; (3) "the young woman has not committed an offense punishable by death"; (4) "because this case is like that of someone who attacks and murders a neighbor"; and (5) "the engaged woman may have cried for help, but there was no one to rescue her."

[72] See, e.g., Raymond Westbrook, *Studies in Biblical and Cuneiform Law* (Paris: J. Gabalda, 1988), 6; Jacob J. Finkelstein, "Sex Offenses in Sumerian Laws," *JAOS* 86 (1966): 366–68.

[73] Some have suggested that this law contradicts the law of the malicious witness in Deut 19:16–19: whereas the latter prescribes that the false witnesses shall suffer the same penalty as the wrongly accused party would have received if convicted (i.e., a strict *lex talionis*, "eye for eye, tooth for tooth," etc.), the law in Deut 22:13–21 does not demand a talionic death penalty if the accusing husband should prove to be a false witness. Pressler, *The View of Women*, 24, however, points out that the structure of the law in 22:13–21 is similar to those in Deut 21:18–21 and 25:5–10, in which the persons instructed to come before the court are clearly the plaintiffs; this would seem to imply that it is the parents of the slandered girl who are the plaintiffs in this case as well. If such implication is valid, the situation in 22:13–21 is different from that in 19:16–19: the latter concerns false accusations in court whereas 22:13–21 concerns a husband (potentially) guilty of "spreading malicious rumors but not of false testimony before the elders."

the bloody sheet/garment from the wedding night)[74] as evidence before the elders at the city gate that she was indeed a virgin. Such evidence clears the woman of the husband's slanderous claims. The husband is then "chastised/admonished" (*yāsar*),[75] fined one hundred shekels of silver (to be paid to the woman's father), and forbidden to divorce the woman "as long as he lives." If the evidence of the young woman's virginity" is not found, however, then the woman is to be stoned by the men of the city at the door of her father's house "because she committed a disgraceful act [*nĕbālâ*] in Israel by prostituting herself [*zānâ*] in her father's house. So you shall purge the evil [*raʿ*] from your midst" (Deut 22:21).[76]

In the case where the husband is guilty of slandering his bride, the penalty of one hundred shekels—twice the normal bride money of fifty shekels (cf. vv. 28–29)—shows that there are financial concerns related to this law. Other ANE laws provided that a groom should reclaim double the bride money for a father-in-law's breach of contract (failing to give over his daughter in marriage),[77] and this same breach of contract seems to apply in a case where the bride is not a virgin (as will become apparent in vv. 28–29). The husband, if he has falsely slandered his bride, is thus fined the amount that his father-in-law would have had to pay if the charges were true. That the fine is paid to the girl's father shows that he is viewed as an injured party.

But the sanctions in this legislation go beyond financial concerns and offense to the father. The husband, in spreading false rumors, "has slandered a virgin of Israel" (v. 19). The law prohibits the husband from ever divorcing the wife he has

---

[74] See esp. Pressler, *The View of Women*, 27–28, and Wadsworth, "Is There a Hebrew Word for Virgin?" 165–66, for refutation of Wenham's thesis that *bĕtûlîm* refers to menstrual blood and that the husband's legal charge is that he had failed to find signs that she was menstruating (and therefore she was pregnant and guilty of adultery). Pressler shows the implausibility of this view by paraphrasing the husband's charge: "I had sexual intercourse with my wife and now, some weeks later, she shows signs of being pregnant" (p. 27). Why, Pressler asks, would this show that someone other than the husband was the father of the child? Why could her lack of menstruation (i.e., pregnancy) not be due to her sexual intercourse with her husband on the wedding night? Further, the use of the term *qārab* "come near" (RSV) in Deut 22:14 certainly refers to "sexual intercourse" and not merely to the husband's coming close to his wife to see if she were menstruating, as Wenham claims. Finally, in Wenham's reading of this law, it is a specific case of adultery; but this offense is discussed later in 22:23–24, and a repetition of essentially the same law in the same chapter is highly unlikely (no other example of such repetition is found in Deut 19–25). I conclude with Pressler, "The traditional reading, that the husband accuses his wife of not being a virgin at the time of their wedding, is much more likely" (28).

[75] Many of the modern versions (including the NASB) translate this verb as "punished," implying the infliction of corporal punishment, but it seems preferable to take *yāsar* in its normal usage elsewhere in Scripture as "admonish" or "chastise" (so NASB). Where the meaning of corporal punishment is meant in Deuteronomy, a different Hebrew verb, *nākâ*, occurs (Deut 25:1–3). For further discussion, see Phillips, "Another Look at Adultery," 9.

[76] The Hebrew *hārāʿ* should be translated "the evil" and not "the evil person." It is the act, not the individual, that is the object of outrage in the passage.

[77] Laws of Eshnunna §25 (*COS* 2.130:333; *ANET* 162); CH §160 (*COS* 2.131:345; *ANET* 173); HL §29 (*COS* 2.19:109; *ANET* 190).

slandered and spurned and thus provides her with social/economic security. In a society where a man could divorce his wife rather easily (although, as noted in ch. 9, below, on divorce, not without implicit divine condemnation), "the prohibition is to be seen as a penalty imposed on the husband which protects the wife. The law thus also treats the girl as an injured party. . . . [The law] penalizes the slanderer by forcing him to provide for the woman for the rest of their lives."[78]

In the case where the bride is guilty of what her husband claims, several indicators in the text show the gravity of her offense. First, the penalty is death. Second, she is to be executed by all the men of the city, indicating that this is an offense against the social order of the whole community as well as against her husband and father.[79] Shame has been brought upon the honor of the community.[80] Third, her act is described as *nĕbālâ*, a term used for serious disorderly and unruly conduct that violently threatens a breakdown in the social order.[81] Fourth, the seriousness of this offense is also underscored by describing the woman's action as "prostituting herself" (*zānâ*, having illicit sexual relations) while in her father's house (i.e., under his legal protection/jurisdiction). Finally, the gravity of the sexual offense is even further reinforced by the expurgation formula of v. 21: "So you shall purge the evil from your midst."

This law does not specifically indicate whether the guilty bride's premarital sexual relations occurred before or after her betrothal, but in light of the fact that there are separate laws later in the chapter explicitly spelling out both of these situations, it seems that the premarital sex envisaged in this law is general, encompassing possible sexual encounters both before and after betrothal. The punishment for this illicit premarital sexual activity is considerably more strict than a clear case of consensual premarital sex on the part of an unmarried, unbetrothed girl (to be examined below): it is equivalent to that of adultery by a married or betrothed woman. Apparently what makes the punishment equivalent to that for adultery even if the sexual intercourse took place before betrothal is that the girl *concealed* from her husband her premarital sexual activity, and in such case it was to be assumed that it was illicit sex after betrothal. The serious, but not capital, offense of premarital sex thus becomes a capital offense because of the element of

---

[78] Pressler, *The View of Women,* 29.

[79] "Stoning, moreover, is a very special penalty, reserved for those offenses which completely upset the hierarchical arrangements of the cosmos. In these cases, the entire community is threatened and endangered, and the entire community serves as the executioner" (Tikva Frymer-Kensky, "Law and Philosophy: The Case of Sex in the Bible," *Semeia* 45 [1989], 93).

[80] See further discussion in Victor H. Matthews, "Honor and Shame in Gender-Related Legal Situations in the Hebrew Bible," in *Gender and Law in the Hebrew Bible and the Ancient Near East* (ed. Victor H. Matthews, Bernard M. Levinson, and Tikva Frymer-Kensky; JSOTSup 262; Sheffield, Eng.: Sheffield Academic Press, 1998), 97–112.

[81] Anthony Phillips, "NEBALAH—a Term for Serious Disorderly and Unruly Conduct," *VT* 25 (1975): 237–42. Other sexual offenses referred to by this term are the rape of Dinah (Gen 34:7), the rape of the concubine and threatened rape of her master (Judg 19:23; 20:26), and the rape of Tamar by Amnon (2 Sam 13:12). It is significant that only in this law is the term applied to a woman's offense.

deceit and false pretense to premarital chastity: she has entered into marriage without acknowledging her prior loss of virginity.[82]

Seduction of a Single Woman (Deut 22:28–29; cf. Exod 22:15–16 [ET 22:16–17]). The section on plural marriage in chapter 5, above, briefly referred to the final case law in Deut 22:28–29 and its parallel in Exod 22:15–16 (ET 22:16–17). Exodus 22:15–16 (ET 22:16–17) provides basic case law regarding the seduction of a single (unbetrothed) woman: "When a man seduces [*pātâ*] a virgin [*bětûlâ*] who is not engaged to be married, and lies with her, he shall give the bride-price [*māhar*] for her and make her his wife. But if her father refuses to give her to him, he shall pay an amount equal to the bride-price [*māhar*] for virgins." Deuteronomy 22:28–29 is probably an extension and expansion of the same law: "If a man meets a virgin [*bětûlâ*] who is not engaged, and seizes [*tāpaś*] her and lies with her, and they are caught in the act, the man who lay with her shall give fifty shekels of silver to the young woman's father, and she shall become his wife. Because he violated [*ʿānâ*, in the *piʿel*,] her he shall not be permitted to divorce [*šālaḥ*] her as long as he lives." The law of 22:28–29 does not consider the case of a ravisher who is already married, but the comparative evidence from the fuller treatment of punishment for ravishers found in Middle Assyrian Laws (from about the same era) provides an exception clause for the ravisher who is already married.[83]

The law in Exod 22:15–16 (ET 22:16–17) concerns most likely a situation of verbal persuasion or enticement (the meaning of *pātâ*), but commentators differ on whether Deut 22:28–29 describes a case of forcible rape or seduction (statutory rape).[84] The latter passage indicates that the man "seizes" (*tāpaś*) and "violates" (*ʿānâ*, in the *piʿel*) the woman. The verb *tāpaś* usually implies taking hold of with force, and the verb *ʿānâ* in the *piʿel* ("humble" or, better, "mishandle, afflict, violate") is used several times elsewhere in the OT to describe clear cases of forcible rape.[85] The passage in Deut 22, however, also seems to indicate that the woman had acquiesced and was a willing partner in the sexual encounter, when it notes that "*they* [not just he] are caught in the act [*wěnimṣāʾû*]" (v. 28).

Both of these laws are probably speaking of a similar (but perhaps not identical) situation of sexual seduction (statutory rape) of a virgin (*bětûlâ*) who is not betrothed (*ʾāraś*, in the *puʿal* pf.), the former emphasizing more the psychological

---

[82] See Pressler, *The View of Women*, 31, n. 28, for support of this conclusion. The question of paternity versus maternity seems to come into play here. It was easy for a woman to know whether the baby was hers, but in biblical society the husband could not know for sure whether her child was also his. So the family integrity depended upon the absolute fidelity of the wife. For men, the situation was precarious—the situation was completely out of their hands; the stability of the entire family structure was dependent upon the wife being a virtuous, faithful sexual partner to her husband.

[83] MAL A §55 (*COS* 2.132:359; *ANET* 185).

[84] So, e.g., Gerhard von Rad, *Deuteronomy: A Commentary* (trans. Dorothea Barton; OTL; Philadelphia: Westminster, 1966), 143, labels it "rape"; in contrast, J. A. Thompson, *Deuteronomy* (TOTC 5; Downers Grove, Ill.: InterVarsity, 1974), 236, calls it "seduction."

[85] See Gen 34:2 (Shechem's rape of Dinah); Judg 19:24; 20:5 (the men of Gibeah's rape of the Levite's concubine); and 2 Sam 13:12, 14, 22–32 (Amnon's rape of Tamar).

pressure (he "seduces" [*pātâ*] her) and the latter the physical pressure (he "catches, takes, seizes" [*tāpaś*] her).[86] The two laws are complementary (the Deuteronomy passage an extension of the Exodus law), and together they give the whole picture of circumstances and legal consequences.[87] The point here is that the woman in this situation has never been married or betrothed: the seduction includes premarital sexual intercourse. And such activity constitutes an illicit sexual encounter.[88]

The penalty for such distortion of the divine design for sexuality is not death or *kārēt* (being "cut off"), since there has been no breach in a relationship, such as in adultery. Nonetheless the legislation makes clear the seriousness of the offense.[89] "A man cannot just 'love her and leave her': by sleeping with her, he has assumed the obligation to marry her. And he must pay a normal bride-price: he cannot obtain a girl cheaply by first sleeping with her, thus dishonoring her, and lowering her bride-price."[90] Deuteronomy 22:29 tells us the amount of the bride wealth—fifty shekels of silver—and adds that the man "shall not be permitted to divorce her as long as he lives." The limitation of the man's right to divorce, as in the law of 22:13–19, serves to protect the woman and provide for her social and financial security. At the same time, such a penalty—the high bride wealth price and the knowledge that no matter how miserable one might try to make the other, they could not divorce—would certainly cause the unmarried, both men and women, to give serious pause before engaging in premarital sex.

Exodus 22:16 (ET 22:17) adds the provision that the father of the violated girl was not required to consent to his daughter getting married to her seducer, apparently in the case where he was already married to another woman (as in the ANE parallel containing an exception clause for the married ravisher, cited above). Presumably this also applied to other situations where the father did not deem such a marriage wise. It should not be assumed that a girl who has been seduced and lost her virginity would not be able to marry—there is no hint of this in Scripture—but

---

[86] That these two laws are "variants of the same case" (Pressler, *The View of Women*, 35–41, quote at 36) is recognized by a number of scholars. See, among others, Ronald A. G. du Preez, *Polygamy in the Bible* (ATSDS 3; Berrien Springs, Mich.: ATS, 1993), 93–97; and Jan Ridderbos, *Deuteronomy* (trans. Ed M. van der Maas; Grand Rapids: Zondervan, 1984), 227.

[87] Westbrook states this principle in dealing with biblical law: "It is therefore by combining the partial discussion in each of the separate codes that we are able to reconstruct the complete original problem, and we are entitled to assume prima facie that all the rules of the reconstructed problem applied in each of the systems that have contributed to it" (*Studies in Biblical and Cuneiform Law*, 6).

[88] Phillips, "Another Look at Adultery," 12, points out that the use of the passive perfect rather than the passive participle in Exod 22:15 (ET 22:16) and Deut 2:28 makes plain that the girl is one who *has never been* betrothed, not just (as the RSV renders it) one who is not at present betrothed.

[89] Cf. the similar treatment in other ANE law codes: CH §130 (*COS* 2.131:344; *ANET* 171) and MAL A §§55–56 (*COS* 2.132:359–60; *ANET* 185). MAL A §55, however, adds a talionic element in which "the father of the virgin shall take the wife of the virgin's ravisher and give her to be ravished." In the biblical view, it seems that both the sanctity of marriage and the rights of the innocent wife preclude prescribing a *lex talionis* of equivalent ravishing.

[90] Frymer-Kensky, "Virginity in the Bible," 91.

her father would not normally be able to command the full bride wealth price. In the case described here, however, the father was still entitled to the full bride-price—which would ultimately belong to the daughter (see chs. 6 and 9 of this study).[91] Thus the daughter was further protected from the sexual advances of a man who would try to seduce her so that she would be forced to marry him. By the same token, the law also preserved an unmarried daughter from her own immaturity by preventing her from circumventing her father's protective jurisdiction and impulsively choosing her own husband by having sex with him.

The provision that the father was not required to have his daughter marry the one who seduced her seems also to provide further evidence within Scripture for the conclusion that sexual intercourse per se does not constitute a marriage. As with God's ideal in Eden, the "cleaving" (or marriage covenant) was to come before the "becoming one flesh" (sexual intercourse). But even if there is sexual intercourse before the formalizing of the marriage covenant, this does not automatically mean that the sexual partners are married.

The pentateuchal legislation contains no reference to a situation in which a virgin seduces a man, unlike other ANE legal systems (as noted above). It appears that biblical law holds men strictly liable in all cases of seduction, in contrast to legal provisions elsewhere in the ancient Near East. The biblical system of law thus serves to protect women, who were more vulnerable to the stigmatizing effect of sexual impropriety than men in a society that tended toward male dominance and where virginity was so highly prized.

The pentateuchal legislation regarding pre-betrothal or postbetrothal premarital sex contains concerns common with those elsewhere in the ancient Near East: to protect the father's economic interests (if the girl is not yet married or betrothed) and to protect the exclusive domestic rights of the husband toward his betrothed. But the biblical laws go beyond these common concerns, consistently placing full responsibility upon individuals for their own sexual behavior and equitably distinguishing between consensual sex (involving an unbetrothed virgin) and the more reprehensible offense of statutory or forcible rape.[92]

Sexual Intercourse with a Betrothed Slave Girl (Lev 19:20–22). A final piece of legislation related to premarital sexuality is found in Lev 19:20–22:

> If a man has sexual relations with a woman who is a slave, designated for another man but not ransomed or given her freedom, an inquiry shall be held. They shall not be put to death, since she has not been freed; but he shall bring a guilt offering for himself to the LORD, at the entrance of the tent of meeting, a ram as guilt offering. And the priest shall make atonement for him with the ram of guilt offering

---

[91] Because the deflowering of the virgin daughter resulted in loss of her value due to loss of virginity, for which the seducer had to compensate her father, this law is situated at the end of a series of laws in Exod 22 dealing with property damage. This is not to say, however, that the daughter was considered mere chattel, the property of her father, as ch. 6, above, points out.

[92] For further discussion of rape, both what we would today term statutory and forcible, see ch. 12, below.

before the LORD for his sin that he committed; and the sin he committed shall be forgiven him.

In the case where a man had sexual intercourse with a slave girl who was betrothed (*neḥĕrepet*, lit. "assigned"),[93] there was to be an "inquiry" (*biqōret*, not "punishment/scourging," "compensation," "differentiation," or "indemnity").[94] Neither the betrothed slave girl nor her lover is executed for illicit sexual intercourse. The reason is given: "since she has not been freed." This has commonly been interpreted to mean that the usual law of adultery does not apply because she is a slave girl and, as in other ANE law codes, "her sexual violation is treated as a transgression of her owner's property for which he would seek compensation, not prosecution."[95] The inquest probably determined the exact status of the woman and may have included a determination of the amount of compensation due her owner, although there is no explicit reference to compensation in the legislation.

Moreover, a built-in protection for the vulnerable woman also seems to be implied in the reference to her slave status. "The law in Leviticus 19:2–21 protects a female of inferior legal status by recognizing that her ability to withhold consent is seriously compromised. She suffers no punishment, whether she offers consent or gives in to sexual harassment."[96] This principle of protection (and exoneration) for vulnerable women who are sexually harassed is seen to be operative in such narratives as David's power rape of Bathsheba (see ch. 12, below).

Because in this case the guilty parties are not put to death and there is no compensation mentioned, this law makes clear—indeed perhaps more so than any of the other adultery-related laws, since here the property and paternity issues do not apply or are not addressed—that adultery is morally wrong per se and meets with God's divine disapproval. The moral nature of the offense is confirmed in that it must be expiated by sacrifice. "The seducer of the betrothed slave-girl is indeed guilty of adultery and though her slave status renders the death penalty inoperable, the 'great sin' against God still must be expiated. As in all cases of desecration where sacrificial expiation is allowed, the offender must bring an *ʾāšām* [reparation offering]."[97] The seducer brings the *ʾāšām* offering of a ram to the sanctuary, and "the priest shall make atonement for him with the

[93] See Jacob Milgrom, *Leviticus 17–22: A New Translation with Introduction and Commentary* (AB 3A; New York: Doubleday, 2000), 1666–67, for defense of this translation and for cogent arguments against Raymond Westbrook's suggestion (*Studies in Biblical and Cuneiform Law,* 101–9) that this legislation refers to a married woman who is betrothed to her owner.

[94] See Jacob Milgrom, "The Betrothed Slave-Girl," 44, for compelling reasons that the Hebrew term *biqōret*, from the verb *bāqar*, "to seek, investigate" (found in Lev 13:36; 27:33), should here be taken in its natural meaning of "investigation" or "inquiry." Milgrom suggests that this term implies "that her paramour was tracked down, judged, and found guilty" (p. 45). More recently, see Milgrom, *Leviticus 17–22*, 1668–71.

[95] Goodfriend, "Adultery," 1:83; cf. Finkelstein, "Sex Offenses," 360.

[96] Gane, *Leviticus, Numbers*, 354.

[97] Milgrom, "The Betrothed Slave-Girl," 49. For a discussion of the *ʾāšām* offering, see Jacob Milgrom, *Leviticus 1–16: A New Translation with Introduction and Commentary* (AB 3; New York: Doubleday, 1991), 339–78.

ram of guilt [ʾāšām] offering for his sin that he committed; and the sin he committed shall be forgiven him" (Lev 19:22).

A Double Standard of Sexual Faithfulness in the Pentateuch?

Contrary to a widespread interpretation,[98] the Mosaic laws concerning adultery should not be seen as creating a double standard in the sense usually claimed—that is that the wife is circumscribed but the husband is free to engage in extramarital sexual activity. It is true, however, that the pentateuchal legislation regarding adultery focuses upon the wife's faithfulness or unfaithfulness. This is probably due to a fundamental concern regarding procreation within Israel's patriarchally oriented and covenant-centered setting, a concern to safeguard the purity of a male's bloodline by the determination of paternity.[99] There may also be a practical consideration in that it was much easier to regulate females, whose sexual activity would have provable, observable, physical results.

Despite this primary emphasis upon the wife's faithfulness, further Mosaic legislation effectively curtails the husband's extramarital affairs also. As already concluded above (ch. 5), polygamy is prohibited. Moreover, a man is forbidden to have sexual relations with an unmarried virgin (unless he subsequently marries her and pays her father the bride money), with another man's betrothed virgin, or with another man's wife (see above). Both cultic prostitution and common harlotry are also proscribed (see ch. 7, above), and this prohibition (as with all other Mosaic legislation) applies also to foreigners within Israel.[100] As will become apparent in chapter 10, below, throughout the ancient Near East, including Israel, incestuous relations of various kinds were prohibited. The accumulative effect of the legislation just mentioned was to safeguard the sanctity of sexual relationships within the marriage on the part of the husband as well as the wife. It must be concluded that "while the law does not speak directly to the promiscuous man, neither does it leave him any legitimate partner."[101]

Both adultery and premarital sexuality constitute an assault upon the divinely ordained sacred circle of the nuclear family as set forth in Gen 2:18–24. Frymer-Kensky correctly concludes regarding the adultery laws, "Beyond the

---

[98] See, e.g., Tikva Frymer-Kensky, "Sex and Sexuality," *ABD* 5:1144: "As in the rest of the ANE, there was a double standard: males could have sex outside of marriage, most notably with prostitutes: 'adultery' meant copulation with a *married* woman."

[99] See Goodfriend, "Adultery," 1:82.

[100] According to Exod 12:49, foreigners within Israel were to be treated the same as native Israelites and were subject to the same legal jurisdiction and protection. Cf. Deut 31:10–12. It might be argued that biblical legislation does not prescribe a penalty for a man having sex with a prostitute, but the counterargument is that there is also no penalty prescribed for being a common prostitute. Both are explicitly condemned by God but apparently not punishable under the Mosaic legal system. As pointed out in ch. 7, above, whereas elsewhere in the ancient Near East prostitution was a recognized social institution, in Israel the practice was officially proscribed, although individuals too often fell into pagan practice. There was a de jure prohibition of prostitution in Israel, including both women functioning as prostitutes and men frequenting prostitutes, whatever might have been the case de facto.

[101] Hurley, *Man and Women*, 40.

concern for property rights or clear paternity, the demand for sexual exclusivity for wives sought to prevent married women from establishing bonds that would weaken the family unit."[102] I would add that the Mosaic legislation also demanded sexual exclusivity for husbands and sought to prevent married men from engaging in any extramarital sexual unions, which would weaken the family unit. Furthermore, this legislation also demanded sexual exclusivity by penalizing sexual intercourse before marriage. The biblical sanctions against adultery and other premarital and extramarital sexual activity must ultimately be viewed as divine provisions to protect the exclusive sacred bonds between husband and wife within the Edenic institution of marriage.

Adultery in the Prophets

The most striking example of adultery in the Prophets is the story of David and Bathsheba (examined in detail in ch. 12, below, since it involves rape as well as adultery). Although the narrative does not use the Hebrew word nāʾap, "to commit adultery," David's power rape of Uriah's wife clearly constituted adultery.[103] David deserved death, but Nathan's sentence against David seems to imply that the death penalty was commuted to the unborn son of the adulterous union.[104] David's deep experience of repentance, his sense of the depth and breadth of his sin against God, and the joy of divine forgiveness and restoration are the subjects of Ps 51 (see below).

The verb nāʾap, "to commit adultery," and its nominal derivatives occur twenty-four times in the Prophets. These usages are clustered in Hosea, Jeremiah, and Ezekiel—the same three books as contain the allegories of prostitution discussed in chapter 7, above.[105] Here we note that the spiritual "whoring" of Israel/Judah to God described so vividly in these allegories was not only a case of prostitution—fracturing the wholistic nature of sexuality—but also a case of adultery, breaking the exclusive bonds of the covenant relationship. God points

---

[102] Frymer-Kensky, "Sex and Sexuality," 5:1144.

[103] See Regina M. Schwartz, "Adultery in the House of David: The Metanarrative of Biblical Scholarship and the Narratives of the Bible," *Semeia* 54 (1991): 35–55, for an overview of the "adultery/rape" scenes which mark ruptures in the story of David and suggest instability in Israel's national politics.

[104] See the linkage between David's sin and the death of the child in 2 Sam 12:14: "because by this deed you [David] have utterly scorned the LORD, the child that is born to you shall die." Apparently no human being would dare carry out the death sentence against the king, and by this transfer of penalty, justice was upheld; at the same time, David no doubt suffered even greater anguish with his son dying in his place than if he had died himself. As another (or related) suggestion, David Daube argues that this is a case of "ruler punishment" in which the ruler is punished by causing him to lose a person under his jurisdiction (*Studies in Biblical Law* [New York: Ktav, 1969], 163–64 [see 154–89 for full discussion of this biblical concept]).

[105] Hos 2:4 (ET 2:2); 3:1; 4:2, 13–14; 7:4; Jer 3:8–9; 5:7; 7:9; 9:1 (ET 9:2); 13:27; 23:10, 14; 29:23; Ezek 16:32, 38; 23:37 (bis), 43, 45 (bis). For scholarly discussion of these passages of the metaphorical adultery of Israel against her "Husband," Yahweh, see the footnotes in connection with these passages in ch. 7, above.

out to Hosea that Gomer committed adultery just like Israel, "who turn to other gods" (Hos 3:1). Jeremiah records Yahweh's charge against Judah: "I have seen your abominations, your adulteries and neighings [after other 'lovers']" (Jer 13:27). Ezekiel records a similar charge: "Adulterous wife, who receives strangers instead of her husband!" (Ezek 16:32). And the judgment meted out upon un-faithful Israel is fashioned after the pentateuchal penalty for adultery: "I will judge you as women who commit adultery. . . . They shall bring up a mob against you, and they shall stone you and cut you to pieces with their swords" (Ezek 16:38, 40). Apparently, in the time of the divided monarchy, the punishment for adultery also included the husband's public (physical) exposure of his unfaithful wife, as illustrated in ANE parallels,[106] and several of the prophets also employ this imagery to express divine judgment of unfaithful Israel.[107] As will be empha-sized in the final section of this chapter, divine grace, forgiveness, and restoration accompany the divine judgment/punishment in each of these allegories.

A number of feminist scholars have in recent years deconstructed these and other prophetic portrayals of Israel's spiritual adultery and, using the "herme-neutic of suspicion," have concluded that in these passages Yahweh is to be re-garded as a battering husband subjecting his wife to all manner of physical and psychological abuse.[108] Hosea 1–3 is interpreted as portraying an independent

---

[106] For ANE parallels to the punishment of stripping a woman naked and publicly exposing her, see Moshe Greenberg, *Ezekiel 1–20: A New Translation with Introduction and Commentary* (AB 22; Garden City, N.Y.: Doubleday, 1983), 287. Greenberg also notes that this punishment in the context of Ezek 16 "echoes the childhood nakedness of the woman in vs. 7."

[107] See Ezek 16:35–42; 23:10, 22–35. Cf., e.g., Isa 20:2; 32:11; Nah 3:5.

[108] See, among others, Gerlinde Baumann, *Love and Violence: Marriage as Metaphor for the Relationship between YHWH and Israel in the Prophetic Books* (trans. Linda Maloney; Collegeville, Minn.: Liturgical Press, 2003); Athalya Brenner, *The Intercourse of Knowledge: On Gendering Desire and "Sexuality" in the Hebrew Bible* (BIS 26; Leiden: E. J. Brill, 1997), 153–74; idem, "Some Reflections on Violence against Women and the Image of the Hebrew God: The Prophetic Books Revisited," in *On the Cutting Edge—the Study of Women in Biblical Worlds: Essays in Honor of Elisabeth Schüssler Fiorenza* (ed. Jane Schagerb, Alice Bach, and Esther Fuchs; New York: Continuum, 2003), 69–81; Tristanne J. Conolly, "Metaphor and Abuse in Hosea," *FemT* 18 (May 1998): 55–66; Peggy L. Day, "Adulterous Jerusalem's Imagined Demise: Death of a Metaphor in Ezekiel XVI," *VT* 50, no. 3 (2000): 285–309; idem, "The Bitch Had It Coming to Her: Rhetoric and Interpreta-tion in Ezekiel 16," *BibInt* 8 (2000): 231–53; Carol J. Dempsey, "The 'Whore' of Ezekiel 16: The Impact and Ramifications of Gender-Specific Metaphors in Light of Biblical Law and Divine Judgment," in *Gender and Law in the Hebrew Bible and the Ancient Near East* (ed. Victor H. Matthews, Bernard M. Levinson, and Tikvah Frymer-Kensky; JSOTSup 262; Sheffield, Eng.: Sheffield Academic Press, 1998), 57–78; Fokkelien van Dijk-Hemmes, "The Metaphorization of Woman in Prophetic Speech: An Analysis of Ezekiel XXIII," *VT* 43 (1993): 162–70; repr. in *On Gendering Texts: Female and Male Voices in the Hebrew Bible* (ed. Athalya Brenner and Fokkelien van Dijk-Hemmes; BIS 1; Leiden: E. J. Brill, 1993), 167–76; J. Cheryl Exum, "The Ethics of Biblical Violence against Women," in *The Bible in Ethics: The Second Sheffield Colloquium* (ed. John W. Rogerson, Margaret Davies, and M. Daniel Carroll R.; JSOTSup 207; Sheffield, Eng.: Sheffield Academic Press, 1995), 248–71; rev. and updated in "Prophetic Pornography," in *Plotted, Shot, and Painted: Cultural Representations of Biblical Women* (JSOTSup 215; Gender, Culture, Theory 3;

woman doggedly pursued by an obsessive and dangerous individual (Yahweh), who is "a despotic oppressor god" acting like "a controlling, jealous wife-batterer."[109] Even Yahweh's attempts at reaching out in romantic love to his promiscuous wife is seen as part of the cycle—characteristic of battering husbands—of abuse followed by romance. The prophetic statements in these passages are viewed as representing a blatant androcentric viewpoint and seen to imply the subjugation of women to the control of males (humans and the male God) and to suggest that women are the source of evil and pollution. Special anger is vented against the Yahweh of Ezek 16 and 23 for his subordination and public physical abuse of his wife, his "sexualized rage against females,"[110] which is regarded as an implicit sanctioning for human husbands to treat their wives in the same way.

Sheffield, Eng.: Sheffield Academic Press, 1996), 101–28; Naomi Graetz, "God Is to Israel as Husband Is to Wife: The Metaphoric Battering of Hosea's Wife," in *A Feminist Companion to the Latter Prophets* (ed. Athalya Brenner; FCB 8; Sheffield, Eng.: Sheffield Academic Press, 1995), 126–45; Erin Runions, "Violence and the Economy of Desire in Ezekiel 16:1–45," in *Prophets and Daniel* (ed. Athalya Brenner; FCB[2] 8; New York: Sheffield Academic Press, 2001), 156–69; Katharine Doob Sakenfeld, "How Hosea Transformed the Lord of the Realm into a Temperamental Spouse," *BRev* 20, no. 1 (February 2004): 28–33, 52; T. Drorah Setel, "Prophets and Pornography: Female Sexual Imagery in Hosea," in *Feminist Interpretation of the Bible* (ed. Letty M. Russell; Philadelphia: Westminster, 1985), 86–95; Mary E. Shields, "Circumcision of the Prostitute: Gender, Sexuality, and the Call to Repentance in Jeremiah 3:1–4:4," in *Prophets and Daniel* (ed. Athalya Brenner; FCB[2] 8; New York: Sheffield Academic Press, 2001), 121–33; idem, "Circumscribing the Prostitute: The Rhetorics of Intertextuality, Metaphor, and Gender in Jeremiah 3:1–4:4" (PhD diss., Emory University, 1996); idem, "Multiple Exposures: Body Rhetoric and Gender in Ezekiel 16," in *Prophets and Daniel* (ed. Athalya Brenner; FCB[2] 8; New York: Sheffield Academic Press, 2001), 137–53; Gail Corrington Streete, *The Strange Woman: Power and Sex in the Bible* (Louisville: Westminster John Knox, 1997), 76–100; Rut Törnkvist, *The Use and Abuse of Female Sexual Imagery in the Book of Hosea: A Feminist Critical Approach to Hosea 1–3* (Acta Universitatis Upsaliensis: Uppsala Women's Studies A, Women in Religion 7; Uppsala: Uppsala University Library, 1998); Renita J. Weems, "Gomer: Victim of Violence or Victim of Metaphor?" *Semeia* 47 (1989): 87–104; idem, *Battered Love: Marriage, Sex, and Violence in the Hebrew Prophets* (OBT; Minneapolis: Fortress, 1995), esp. 58–64 and 96–104; Shirley Wurst, "Retrieving Earth's Voice in Jeremiah: An Annotated Voicing of Jeremiah 4," in *The Earth Story in the Psalms and the Prophets* (ed. Norman C. Habel; Sheffield, Eng.: Sheffield Academic Press, 2001), 172–84. For an overview of these positions with regard to Hos 2, see Willem Boshoff, "The Female Imagery in the Book of Hosea: Considering the Marriage Metaphor in Hosea 1–2 by Listening to Female Voices," *OTE* 15 (2002): 23–41. With regard to Ezek 23, see Corrine L. Patton, "'Should Our Sister Be Treated Like a Whore?' A Response to Feminist Critiques of Ezekiel 23," in *The Book of Ezekiel: Theological and Anthropological Perspectives* (ed. Margaret S. Odell and John T. Strong; SBLSymS 9; Atlanta: Society of Biblical Literature, 2000), 221–38.

[109] Törnkvist, *Use and Abuse*, 72, 64.

[110] Streete, *The Strange Woman*, 94, citing David J. Halperin, *Seeking Ezekiel: Text and Psychology* (University Park: Pennsylvania State University Press, 1993), 207, who in fact uses this phrase to describe Ezekiel, not Yahweh, as Streete intimates, "a man overwhelmed by sexualized rage against females." Halperin continues, however, in his psychoanalysis of Ezekiel, indicating that Ezekiel "makes absolutely clear" that his words of rage are not his own words but the words of Yahweh (p. 208).

In response to this feminist deconstruction of the materials in the Prophets on
spiritual adultery and of Ezek 23 in particular, Moshe Greenberg's critique (and
justification for his own approach in his commentary) deserves citation at length,
as it expresses precisely my sentiments regarding the radical feminist project:

> There can be no doubt that such readings are authentic expression of the pain and
> outrage experienced by feminists searching Scripture for reflections of their con-
> structions of reality and meeting with Oholah and Oholibah. The feminist project,
> promoting a new female reality, necessarily clashes with Scripture—one of the fash-
> ioners of the reality to be superseded. At bottom, what feminists criticize is not what
> the texts meant to those who composed and received them in their historical context,
> but what the text means in today's context. . . . [The feminist] demands a text that
> reflects her identity; for that purpose Ezekiel is but a negative countertext, whose
> male-centered agenda must be exposed and disarmed in terms of today's values, psy-
> chology, and anthropology.
>
> Whether aiming to savage Scripture or to salvage it, feminists are judgmental. They ap-
> plaud or decry, approve or disapprove. They write to promote a new gender reality.
>
> Their project differs fundamentally from the (quixotic?) historical-philological
> search for the primary, context-bound sense of Scripture that is the project of this
> commentary. Hence reference to feminist criticism will be as rare in the following
> pages as it has been in the preceding ones.[111]

Corrine Patton has provided a thoughtful response to the feminist critiques
of Ezek 23 and its parallel biblical passages dealing with the divine judgment
upon Israel's spiritual adultery.[112] Like Greenberg, Patton acknowledges a theological presupposition far different from the feminist critiques, a presupposition
with which I identify: "I read this text [Ezek 23] as part of the canon and do not
entertain feminist strategies of reading that would strip it of its authoritative
status."[113] Patton points out that these feminist studies "expressly reject reading
the text solely as a metaphor generated by historical events" and thus offer little or
no analysis of the historical situation that gave rise to these metaphors. After examining the historical setting of Ezek 23, Patton concludes that "this text does
not substantiate domestic abuse; and scholars, teachers, and preachers must continue to remind uninformed readers that such an interpretation is actually a mis-
reading." Rather, "the theological aim of the passage is to save Yahweh from the
scandal of being a cockolded husband, i.e., a defeated, powerless, or ineffective
god. . . . It is a view of a God for whom no experience, not even rape and
mutilation in wartime, is beyond hope for healing and redemption."[114]

---

111 Ibid., 494. This search for the primary, context-bound sense of Scripture is likewise the project of the present study. See also R. R. Reno, "Feminist Theology as Modern
Project," in *This Is My Name Forever: The Trinity and Gender Language for God* (ed. Alvin
F. Kimel Jr.; Downers Grove, Ill.: InterVarsity, 2001), 161–89. For a critique of the feminist
project in the study of Hosea, see Duane A. Garrett, *Hosea, Joel* (NAC; Nashville,
Broadman and Holman, 1997), 124–33.
112 Patton, " 'Should Our Sister?' " 221–27.
113 Ibid., 227.
114 Ibid., 238.

Some scholars have argued that the references in the Prophets to adultery in the indictments against Israel all concern covenant unfaithfulness in connection with the fertility cults. But it is clear that noncultic sexual crimes are violations of the covenant between Yahweh and his people just as surely as ritual immorality. So, for example, in the covenant lawsuit of Yahweh against his people Israel, the eighth-century prophet Hosea lists "adultery" along with other breaches of the second table of the Decalogue (Hos 4:2). The prophet Jeremiah describes the men of Judah as "well-fed lusty stallions, each neighing for his neighbor's wife" (Jer 5:8) and, in the great "temple sermon" that follows and elsewhere, lists adultery as one of Judah's crimes that constitutes a rupture in the covenant relationship with God (7:8; cf. 13:27; 29:23). The prophet Ezekiel mingles cultic and social abuses in his indictment of Jerusalem and in one passage delineates such sexual crimes as adultery and incestuous relations with mother, daughter-in-law, and sister (Ezek 22:9–11; cf. 33:26). Malachi also records the divine threat of judgment against adultery, clearly in a setting of noncultic crimes: "Then I will draw near to you for judgment; I will be swift to bear witness against the sorcerers, against the *adulterers,* against those who swear falsely, against those who oppress the hired workers in their wages, the widow and the orphan" (Mal 3:5). The conclusions of Carroll Stuhlmueller seem inescapable: "The religious covenant is fractured when Israel breaks the apodictic laws in her secular life. . . . Many secular crimes are condemned as immoral *in se* and not for any cultic connection. . . . The prophets condemned all adultery and prostitution, literally as such."[115]

One passage in the Prophets has been called a "landmark in moral history by its refusal to treat a man's sexual sins more leniently than a woman's."[116] Hosea 4:14 records God's intent: "I will not punish [only] your daughters when they play the whore, nor your daughters-in-law when they commit adultery; for the men themselves go aside with whores, and sacrifice with temple prostitutes; thus a people without understanding comes to ruin."[117] This text is not reversing the

---

[115] Carroll Stuhlmueller, "Prophetic Ideals and Sexual Morality," in *Dimensions of Human Sexuality* (ed. Dennis Doherty; Garden City, N.Y.: Doubleday, 1979), 13, 15, 16. The word "secular," however, does not seem appropriate in speaking of the noncultic arena of Israel's life; ancient Israel's existence was not compartmentalized into categories of secular versus religious as in modern society.

[116] Derek Kidner, *Love to the Loveless: The Message of Hosea* (Bible Speaks Today; Downers Grove, Ill.: InterVarsity, 1981), 53.

[117] Supplying the word "only" brings out the intent of the author, in parallel flow with such passages as Deut 5:3, where God does not make a covenant (only) with the fathers at Sinai but also with the ones being addressed by Moses forty years later. For this interpretation of Deut 5:3, see Moshe Weinfeld, *Deuteronomy 1–11: A New Translation with Introduction and Commentary* (AB 5; New York: Doubleday, 1991), 237–38. This interpretation may also be arrived at by translating Hos 4:14a as a question: "Should I not punish . . . ?" (So Francis I. Andersen and David Noel Freedman, *Hosea: A New Translation with Introduction and Commentary* [AB 24A; New York: Doubleday, 1989], 369). Alternatively, the text is stating that "the women are not to blame, because the men foster and encourage such worship" (Thomas Edward McComiskey, "Hosea," in *Hosea, Joel, and Amos* [vol. 1 of *The Minor Prophets: An Exegetical and Expository Commentary;* ed. Thomas Edward McComiskey; Grand Rapids: Baker, 1992], 67).

pentateuchal legislation against adultery with its accompanying penalty but insisting that the men are just as responsible to be faithful to their marriage vows as are the women.[118] Proposals of a double standard of sexual faithfulness in the canonical OT flounder on this passage.

Adultery in the Writings

Psalms. The hymnic literature of the Psalms confronts us with a radicalization of the seventh and tenth commandments of the Decalogue. The divine covenant lawsuit against Israel in Ps 50 condemns those who "keep company with adulterers" (Ps 50:18). But this is radicalized in the next psalm. Psalm 51 reveals that adultery consists of much more than an external act of sexual transgression against a human being. On the one hand, David grasps the enormity of his sin with Bathsheba—he senses that he has sinned against God himself. On the other hand, he recognizes God's desire for "truth in the inward being" (51:8 [ET 51:6]), not just correct external behavior; he realizes that the motivation, the inward lustful desire, is already sin. David pleads for a supernatural (re-)creation within himself: "Create in me a clean heart, O God, and put a new and right spirit within me" (51:12 [ET 51:10]). Compare the entrance liturgy of Ps 24, in which only those with "clean hands and pure hearts" will "ascend the hill of the Lord" (24:3–4; cf. Ps 15:1–2). The two ways in sexuality—sin and purity—are thus radicalized to include the spiritual intent of the heart.

Job. In the Wisdom literature, the book of Job presents the same concentration upon purity of thought, attitude, and motivation rather than merely the overt act in matters of sexual purity. In Job's catalogue of wickedness in the earth in Job 24, the furtive way of the adulterer is revealed: "The eye of the adulterer also waits for the twilight, saying, 'No eye will see me'; and he disguises his face" (Job 24:15). But the sin of adultery is radicalized beyond the external act in Job 31. In his final desperate argument, his "oath of clearance"[119] before God and his friends, Job maintains his innocence of sexual offenses regarding unmarried (31:1–4) and married women (vv. 9–12). Under oath, he asserts (v. 1), "I have made a covenant with my eyes; how then could I look upon a virgin?" The verb for "look" here is *ʾetbônēn* (*hitpoʿlel* of *bîn*) and signifies "show oneself attentive to, consider diligently"[120] or "look out for."[121] Job pleads innocence from

---

[118] For analysis of this passage, see Kidner, *Love to the Loveless,* 52–54; and Douglas Stuart, *Hosea–Jonah* (WBC 31; Nashville: Thomas Nelson, 1987), 83–84, who likewise argues that both women and men are held accountable here by God for their sexual sins. Alternatively, the men are held even more—indeed, entirely—accountable for the women's actions: "The guilt is not really theirs [the women's], but has its source in what their men do in the fertility cult" (James Luther Mays, *Hosea: A Commentary* [OTL; Philadelphia: Westminster, 1969], 75).

[119] See, e.g., Francis I. Andersen, *Job* (TOTC 13; Downers Grove, Ill.: InterVarsity, 1976), 238–40, for discussion of this literary genre.

[120] BDB 107.

[121] *HALOT* 122.

lusting after unmarried women.[122] Again in vv. 9–10 he calls down a curse upon himself should he be found guilty of adultery:

> If my heart has been enticed by a woman,
>   and I have lain in wait at my neighbor's door;
>   then let my wife grind for another,
>   and let other men kneel over her.

The protestations of innocence reveal a high degree of sensitivity to the attitudinal aspects of sexual purity: it is again a radicalization of the seventh and tenth commandments. Sexual purity is a matter of a pure mind, a pure look, pure motives, as well as abstinence from the immoral act. Sexual impurity likewise is seen as a "heinous crime" (v. 11), "a fire consuming down to Abaddon, and it would burn to the root all my harvest" (v. 12).

Proverbs. The strong emphasis in Proverbs (esp. Prov 2:17; 5:15–18) on exclusivity in the marriage relationship has already been encountered in the introduction to this chapter. It is crucial to reiterate that no text in the Writings, as there is none in the Pentateuch or the Prophets, supports the commonly assumed position of a double standard in which the man is free to engage in unfaithfulness to the marriage exclusiveness. After surveying all the alleged OT passages to the contrary, I concur with Gordon Hugenberger, who concludes after his extensive survey, "There are, in fact, no texts which condone a husband's sexual infidelity."[123] This is most apparent in Proverbs, where the husband is singled out with warnings against sexual promiscuity.

In the book of Proverbs, there is also the recognition that adultery not only applies to the external act but includes the desire of the heart. Hence Wisdom warns against even lusting after the adulterous woman: "Do not lust in your heart after beauty or let her captivate you with her eyes" (Prov 6:25, NIV). The verb "lust/covet" (ḥāmad), used here in Proverbs, is the same as found in the tenth commandment of the Decalogue (Exod 20:17). The warning against sexual lust in Proverbs is especially directed to men.

In Prov 7:13 the adulteress is depicted as brazen or impudent (ʿāzaz in the hipʿil). Proverbs 7:13–14 depicts her as feigning a religious posture in order to entrap her prey: she needs to have sex for hire in order to earn money to pay her

---

[122] See esp. the arguments supporting this traditional interpretation in Gordon P. Hugenberger, *Marriage as a Covenant: Biblical Law and Ethics as Developed from Malachi* (VTSup 52; Leiden: E. J. Brill, 1994; repr., Grand Rapids: Baker, 1998), 331–33. Contra Schmitt, "Virgin," 6:853, who insists that "the reference is to the Canaanite goddess and not any young woman." Walter L. Michel, "*Btwlh,* 'Virgin' or 'Virgin (Anat)' in Job 31:1?" *HS* 23 (1982): 59–66, summarizes the Ugaritic evidence for translating as "Virgin (Anat)." The immediate context, however, must take precedence over alleged extrabiblical parallels. The context of Job 31:1 is clearly that of adultery (cf. vv. 9–12), not the fertility cults.

[123] Hugenberger, *Marriage as a Covenant,* 338. Hugenberger provides a careful examination of the alleged examples of biblical indifference to a husband's sexual fidelity (pp. 313–38).

religious vows.[124] "Clearly, this woman from outside is using her—fictitious?—
situation as an excuse for her desire of sensual enjoyment. Yet her arguments presumably impress her potential companion. Of course, adultery is wrong, but do
not the ends justify the means in this case? He would not be merely buying a pleasure, but contributing to a good cause."[125]

One descriptive verse in Proverbs utilizes the term "adulteress" in its characterization of her lack of conscience: "This is the way of an adulteress: she eats, and
wipes her mouth [a euphemism for sexual activity],[126] and says, 'I have done no
wrong'" (30:20). Other qualities of the seductive adulteress portrayed in Proverbs
include such attributes as "wily [*nāṣar, qal* pass. ptc., crafty/secretive] of heart"
(7:10); "loud [*hāmâ, qal* ptc., boisterous brashness]" (7:11; 9:13); "wayward
[*sārar, qal* ptc., rebellious stubbornness]" (7:11); "lying in wait [*ʾārab,* with
hostile purpose, lurking]" (7:12);[127] "insolence, stupidity [*kĕsîlût*]" (9:13); and
"thoughtlessness, lacking in understanding [*pĕtayyût*]" (9:13).[128]

Proverbs most vividly characterizes the enticing seductiveness (*ḥēleq,* 7:21)
of the loose woman. To man's natural drives and inclinations, the path of adultery
is alluring (see ch. 12, below). There are the "smooth words" (2:16) from lips that
seem to "drip honey" (5:3), the lure of the eyelashes and voluptuous beauty
(6:25), the sexual advances (7:13), flattery (7:15), tempting offers of forbidden
pleasure (6:16–18), and assurances of secrecy (7:19–20). Just as vividly is depicted
the young man losing his senses and succumbing to the seductive speech in a
moment of passion (7:21–23).

What is particularly noteworthy is the sapiential support for the seventh commandment by the articulation of the devastating results of adultery. To commit
sexual sin is to squander one's honor and one's years (5:9, 11; 6:33), one's strength
and health (5:10–11), one's possessions (6:26; 29:3), and freedom (23:27–28). Although the way of adultery may appear appealing, it is really "an exchange of true
intimacy for its parody" (5:19–20; see ch. 12, below).[129] The stolen waters of the
loose woman may seem sweet for the moment (9:17), but "in the end she is bitter as
wormwood" (5:4). The fiery passion of illicit sexual relations will in the end sear
the adulterer inescapably (6:27–29). The way of sexual sin is the way of death:

> For her way leads down to death,
>   And her paths to the shades;
> those who go to her never come back,
>   nor do they regain the paths of life. (2:18–19)

> Her feet go down to death;
>   her steps follow the path to Sheol. (5:5)

---

[124] See ch. 7, above; and Karel van der Toorn, "Female Prostitution in Payment of
Vows in Ancient Israel," *JBL* 108 (1989): 193–205.

[125] Ibid., 199.

[126] Cf. Prov 9:17; see Allen P. Ross, "Proverbs," *EBC* 5:1124.

[127] *HALOT* 489.

[128] *HALOT* 989.

[129] Derek Kidner, *The Proverbs: An Introduction and Commentary* (TOTC 15; Downers Grove, Ill.: InterVarsity, 1964), 50.

For by means of a harlot
A man is reduced to a crust of bread;
And an adulteress will prey upon his precious life. (NKJV 6:26)[130]

Right away he follows her,
    and goes like an ox to the slaughter,
    or bounds like a stag toward the trap
until an arrow pierces its entrails.
    He is like a bird rushing into a snare,
    not knowing that it will cost him his life. . . .
for many are those she has laid low,
    and numerous are her victims.
Her house is the way to Sheol,
    going down to the chambers of death. (7:22–23, 26–27)

But he who commits adultery has no sense;
    he who does it destroys himself. (6:32)

In light of the destructive nature of sexual sin, much of the counsel of the wise man to his "son" is directed at preserving him from following its path. The deadly results of sexual immorality are vividly portrayed, and the reminder is given that there is no secret before God: "For human ways are under the eyes of the LORD, and he examines all their paths" (5:21). The counsel not only warns against the overt act but indicates the importance of a pure mind or heart (22:11). The heart must not be allowed to "stray into her paths" (7:25) or "desire her beauty" (6:25).[131]

---

[130] The Hebrew of this verse is difficult. Many versions have translated baʿad "on account of" or "by means of" (e.g., KJV, NKJV, NASB) although such usage of the term is not attested elsewhere in the OT; such language as "one is brought down/reduced to" is then supplied. See, e.g., K&D, 6:110–11. Other versions render baʿad in this context as "price" (NRSV, ESV; cf. HALOT 1:141) and translate the verse along the following lines: "Although the price of a prostitute may be as much as a loaf of bread, / [another] man's wife hunts the precious life." For support of this translation, see, e.g., Duane A. Garrett, Proverbs, Ecclesiastes, Song of Songs (NAC 14; Nashville: Broadman, 1993), 100. Regardless of which translation is chosen, this verse does not encourage a man to seek prostitutes (whose fee is only a crust of bread) rather than be tempted by the wife of another. Garrett, ibid., aptly remarks, "The man's life, which the wayward woman hunts, is called 'precious' [i.e., valuable] in contrast to meager payment the prostitute demands. This obviously is not meant to endorse going to a prostitute as opposed to having an affair with another man's wife but to show the complete folly of getting involved with another man's wife."

[131] Two alleged examples of pre-marital sex in the Writings (outside of Song of Songs) may be briefly noted: the case of Esther's presumed sexual relations with the King Xerxes as he invited her to spend the night with him as part of the beauty contest (Est 1:12–18), and the case of Ruth's night encounter with Boaz at the threshing floor (Ruth 3), which many interpret as involving sexual relations. As for the case of Esther, although it is indeed likely that Esther (and the other participants in the beauty contest) did have sexual relations with the king, this was not pre-marital sex, but rather the process by which the king took to himself concubines (note that according to v. 14 the women who spent the night with the king emerged the next morning as concubines). As for the case of Ruth, see

Adultery, Extramarital Sex, and Divine Grace

The pentateuchal legislation makes clear that adultery calls for the death penalty and that the various situations of extramarital sex also call for appropriate, just punishments. At the same time, there appears to be allowance for showing "pity" (*ḥûs*) or "compassion" (*ḥāmal*), that is, grace, in commuting the sentence for sex-related offenses. This is implicit in the book of Deuteronomy as one looks at the repeated references to situations in which this directive appears: "your eye shall not pity (*ḥûs*)" [translation mine] or "you shall not spare/show compassion (*ḥāmal*) to" [translation mine] the one facing criminal charges. These absolute prohibitions of pity/compassion (i.e., commutation of sentence) are attached to cases of apostasy into idolatry (Deut 7:16; 13:9 [ET 13:8]), premeditated murder (19:11), a malicious witness (19:21), and a woman who seizes a man's genitals as he is fighting her husband (25:12; discussed below in ch. 11). The fact that these situations do not allow for commutation of the sentence implies that legal sentences for other offenses (including adultery and extramarital sex) that are not thus restricted, may indeed be commuted as circumstances might warrant. Proverbs 6:35 seems also to hint at this as it describes the jealous and furious husband who, upon learning of a man's adultery with his wife, "will accept no compensation [*kōper*], and refuses a bribe no matter how great." The very mention of the enraged husband's refusal to accept a ransom seems to imply that such ransom would be theoretically possible within the law.[132]

That the husband could exercise a right of pardon toward his adulterous wife in Israel is illustrated in the case of Gomer, when God directs Hosea to forgive his wayward wife and take her back (Hos 3:1–3). In NT times, the intent of Joseph (who is specifically characterized as a "righteous man" [Matt 1:19], no doubt implying his unswerving obedience to God's law) to break off his engagement with Mary when she was found to be pregnant implies that leniency was available. It seems that such issues of family law belonged to the sphere of private litigation.

Even in cases where the strict execution of the legal penalty under the civil law of the theocracy was carried out regarding sexual offenses and the scars remained in the lives of the offender and/or others affected, forgiveness was nonetheless available to the repentant sinner (Exod 34:6–7). The narrative of David's adultery with Bathsheba and especially David's inspired prayer in Ps 51 illustrate

---

our discussion in chapter 11, below, for evidence that according to the narrative of Ruth 3, Ruth and Boaz did not have sexual relations that night at the threshing floor, but only after their marriage did the two "come together" sexually (Ruth 4:13).

[132] For further discussion of the evidence for leniency in the case of adultery and other sex-related offenses, see esp. Joe M. Sprinkle, "The Interpretation of Exodus 21:22–25 (*Lex Talionis*) and Abortion," *WTJ* 55 (1993): 237–43; and idem, "Sexuality, Sexual Ethics," *DOTP* 744, following Bruce Wells, "Adultery, Its Punishment, and the Nature of Old Testament Law" (paper presented at the annual meeting of the Evangelical Theological Society, Orlando, Fla., November 20, 1998). See also Lipka, "'Such a Thing Is Not Done in Israel,'" 220–23.

divine grace and the assurance of forgiveness and cleansing for the one who repents of his sin, no matter how heinous it might be. This psalm is full of significance in showing the steps of the adulterer—and this includes all who have
committed spiritual adultery by unfaithfulness to one's divine Husband—from
repentance to forgiveness, cleansing, joy, witness, ever-deepening repentance,
and worship.[133]

The Latter Prophets give vivid examples of spiritual adultery committed by
Israel against their divine "spouse." God the divine marriage partner, who has
been so often rejected by his spouse, himself a victim of adultery, can understand
the pain in the heart of the one victimized by a spouse's unfaithfulness. "It was essential for Hosea to experience the pain of betrayal. He would then know the pain
of God when Israel was unfaithful to the covenant, worshiping other gods and refusing to embrace the divine law. Hosea's experience of betrayal would enable
him to deliver the call to repentance and fidelity with an inner dynamism that expressed the very heartache of God; Hosea's pain and struggle would mirror the
anguish and sorrow of God that came from Israel's fickle fidelity."[134]

Although such marital unfaithfulness brings consequences in divine judgment, at the same time God himself models forgiveness for his adulterous spouse
and offers divine forgiveness for human partners who have been unfaithful. The
Prophets are replete with promises to the repentant sinner (including the adulterer and fornicator), for example, Isa 55:7: "Let the wicked forsake their way, and
the unrighteous their thoughts; let them return to the LORD, that he may have
mercy on them; and to our God, for he will abundantly pardon." The promises
made to unfaithful Israel that beyond her "death penalty" (the Babylonian exile)
there await a resurrection to newness of life (Ezek 37) and a renewal of the marriage to Yahweh in exclusivity forever (Isa 54:5–10; Jer 3:14–25; Ezek 16:6–63; Hos
2:16–25 [ET 2:14–23]) also seem to intimate that beyond even the civil death sentence upon repentant individuals in OT Israel was the hope of resurrection and
eternal life.

The promise of divine grace that transcends the death penalty appears especially in Hosea. Although most of the message of Hosea is framed as an extended
covenant lawsuit (see the term *rîb* in Hos 4:1; 12:3 [ET 12:2]), the purpose of this
covenant lawsuit is not to condemn but "to return Israel to Yahweh. The pivotal
text is 11:8, in which God's heart turns against himself and toward Israel, even in
her disobedience."[135] In 2:16–25 (ET 2:14–23) there is a marvelously unexpected
reversal: Yahweh offers to his adulterous spouse what may be called "revirgini-
zation," as in the days of her youth. Such an attitude on the part of Yahweh, also

---

[133] From an evangelical Christian perspective, one can also see the possibility that
God's apparent commutation of David's death sentence to his unborn son foreshadowed
the coming of the Son of God to bear the death sentence that all (spiritual as well as physical) adulterers deserve.

[134] Gregory J. Polan, "Hosea's Interpretation of Israel's Traditions," *TBT* 39 (2001): 331.

[135] Craig D. Bowman, "Prophetic Grief, Divine Grace: The Marriage of Hosea," *ResQ*
43 (2001): 236–37.

illustrated in Hosea's treatment of Gomer (see above), gives a model for the spouse whose partner has been unfaithful. God reveals that he can work the miracle to renew "the unspoiled newness of their union. The ugly past will be forgotten and they will start over again, as if nothing had ever gone wrong."[136]

As we have seen above, the book of Proverbs contrasts the way of legitimate, exclusive marital sexuality with the way of adulterous sexual sin. And it provides a radical solution to man's bent toward sinning: the divine gift of grace. Sexual exclusivity within marriage, in both act and heart, the wise man recognizes, cannot be achieved on one's own. Man is not left to the mercy of his natural resources. The book of Proverbs, along with other OT hymnic/Wisdom literature, provides "aids to obedience" of the Torah, especially in avoiding adultery.[137] The same Lord who is said to watch all of man's ways (Prov 5:21) is also presented as the one who freely gives wisdom (2:6) to him who diligently seeks and asks for it (2:1–5). This wisdom, informed by the divine law, will serve to preserve man from sexual sin (2:16; cf. 6:24; 7:4–5).[138]

---

[136] Raymond C. Ortlund Jr., *Whoredom: God's Unfaithful Wife in Biblical Theology* (Grand Rapids: Eerdmans, 1996; repr. as *God's Unfaithful Wife: A Biblical Theology of Spiritual Adultery;* NSBT 2; Downers Grove, Ill.: InterVarsity, 2002), 70.

[137] See David L. Brooks, "The Ideological Relationship between Old Testament Law and the Book of Proverbs" (PhD diss., Dallas Theological Seminary, 2000), 252: "On the matter of adultery Proverbs aids obedience to the Law's standard by giving practical steps to resist temptation. Where the law prohibits and would punish adultery, Proverbs attempts to serve as a preventative." Brooks discusses at length these "aids to obedience" (pp. 135–74). See the next footnote for my own list of practical steps from Proverbs and other OT hymnic/Wisdom literature.

[138] The hymnic/Wisdom literature of the OT gives very practical steps for availing oneself of empowering divine grace to preserve moral purity in both thought and action. Although this material is more pastoral and application-oriented than exegetical, I include it here because the theology of the hymnic/Wisdom literature is in fact oriented toward the practical, everyday life, presenting wisdom as practical advice on how to succeed in life. Here is a summary of steps toward moral integrity that have emerged from my study of this literature: (1) daily consecration and prayer for God to create a pure heart (Ps 51:12 [ET 51:10]); (2) trusting in God's keeping power by faith (Prov 3:5–6); (3) meditation upon the character of God and focusing upon pure thoughts (Ps 16:8; Prov 23:7); (4) avoiding situations that contain temptations to impurity (Prov 5:8); (5) constant "watchfulness" (Prov 4:23, 26 [NASB]; 8:34); (6) earnest prayer and claiming of God's promises (Prov 2:1–6, 16); (7) dependence upon the abiding influence of the Holy Spirit (Ps 51:13 [ET 51:11]; 143:10; Prov 1:23); (8) diligent study and internalizing of the word (Ps 119:9, 11; Prov 2:1–13; 6:20–24; 7:2–3); (9) cultivating a sense of God's presence and the certainty of future judgment (Ps 139:7; Prov 2:18–19; 5:3–4, 20–22); (10) cultivating a sense of the ennobling power of pure thoughts (Prov 22:11); (11) cultivating intimacy and sexual satisfaction with one's own spouse (Prov 5:15–19); and (12) realizing the cosmic-conflict context in which the enemy "stalks" victims (Prov 6:26). The hymnic/Wisdom literature presents these twelve steps in order that the wise—the ones who follow these steps—may experience success in the path of moral integrity.

9

Permanence versus Divorce/
Remarriage

Affirmation of the Divine Ideal

According to the Edenic model for marriage, husband and wife were to "cling" (*dābaq*) to one another in a permanent relationship (Gen 2:24). This "clinging" included a lasting covenant bond between husband and wife, implied not only by the covenant term *dābaq* but by the "covenant oath" made by Adam concerning Eve with God as witness: "This at last is bone of my bones and flesh of my flesh" (Gen 2:23).[1]

Outside the garden the divine ideal is upheld throughout OT Scripture. Marriage is set forth as a permanent covenant bond between husband and wife. Gordon Hugenberger's comprehensive OT study of marriage as covenant reveals a number of texts where these covenantal ideas are present.[2] The most explicit passage is Mal 2:14, appearing in the context of disputations between God and those among the returned exiles who (as argued later in this chapter) had divorced Judean wives to marry pagans: "Because the LORD was a witness between you and the wife of your youth, to whom you have been faithless [*bāgad*], though she is your companion and your wife by *covenant* [*běrît*]." Hugenberger shows that this passage clearly indicates (1) the covenantal nature of marriage, (2) that the covenant is clearly between the husband and wife and not outside parties, and (3) that Yahweh is the divine witness to the marriage vows.[3] All three of these aspects emphasize the solemn obligation to permanence in the relationship. The use of the term *bāgad,* "to deal treacherously, unfaithfully," in this passage also implies an intended permanent faith commitment that has been broken.[4]

---

[1] See Walter Brueggemann, "Of the Same Flesh and Bone (Gen 2:23a)," *CBQ* 32 (1970): 535; Gordon P. Hugenberger, *Marriage as a Covenant: Biblical Law and Ethics as Developed from Malachi* (VTSup 52; Leiden: E. J. Brill, 1994; repr., Grand Rapids: Baker, 1998), 165, 202; and the discussion of this phraseology in ch. 1, above.

[2] Hugenberger, *Marriage as a Covenant,* 280–312.

[3] Ibid., 27–47.

[4] The divinely intended permanence is not, however, one of ontological indissolubility, in which the marriage bond can never be dissolved except by death, even in a context of a spouse's marital unfaithfulness, as some have claimed. This becomes clear in the discussion that follows in this chapter.

Other OT passages also refer to the marriage covenant between husband and wife.[5] In Prov 2:17 Wisdom warns against the immoral woman "who forsakes the partner of her youth and forgets her sacred covenant." Especially in the Prophets the concept of permanence becomes explicit as God likens his covenant relationship with Israel to a marriage covenant.[6] Hosea 2:18–22 (ET 2:16–20) describes God's intent to reaffirm the covenant with Israel after her unfaithfulness to him. Notice the covenant language of permanence: "I will take you for my wife *forever*" (2:21 [ET 2:19]). Another eighth-century prophet, Isaiah, also expresses the permanence of the marriage covenant between God the Husband and his bride: "For your Maker is your husband, the LORD of hosts is His name. . . . For the mountains may depart and the hills be removed, but my steadfast love [*ḥesed*, 'steadfast covenantal love'] shall not depart from you, and my covenant of peace shall not be removed" (Isa 54:5, 10).

Ezekiel 16:8 mentions Yahweh swearing an oath (his marriage vows), entering into a marriage covenant with Israel (at Sinai): "I pledged myself to you and entered into a covenant with you, says the Lord GOD, and you became mine." The divine oath is surely a sign of permanence. Although Israel proves unfaithful (described in vv. 15–43) and "despised the oath, breaking the covenant" (v. 59), God reiterates his intention for a permanent marriage covenant: "yet I will remember my covenant with you in the days of your youth, and I will establish with you an everlasting covenant. . . . I will establish my covenant with you, and you shall know that I am the LORD" (vv. 60, 62).

The understanding of marriage as a covenant is not unique to the Bible; throughout the ancient Near East, marriage was regarded as a covenant or contract.[7] The ANE marriage contract included a number of elements—the payments, the contract stipulations, and the penalties incurred if the stipulations were broken. Payments varied throughout OT times, but generally there were two

---

[5] See Hugenberger, *Marriage as a Covenant*, 280–312. Besides the passages cited in the text of the discussion below, Hugenberger, pp. 311–12, mentions 1 Sam 18–20, where the narrative analogy is drawn between David's covenant with Jonathan and David's marriage covenant with Michal. Hugenberger, 309–10, also looks at two potential but doubtful examples of the covenantal nature of marriage (Gen 31:50; Jer 31:32).

[6] For discussion of the intertextual linkages between the human-marriage formulas and the divine-covenant formulas, see Seock-Tae Sohn, " 'I Will Be Your God and You Will Be My People': The Origin and Background of the Covenant Formula," in *Ki Baruch Hu: Ancient Near Eastern, Biblical, and Judaic Studies in Honor of Baruch A. Levine* (ed. Robert Chazan, William W. Hallo, and Lawrence H. Schiffman; Winona Lake, Ind.: Eisenbrauns, 1999), 255–372. Sohn also presents a helpful collection of ANE materials revealing a pervasive legal pattern for the marriage ceremony, which included proclaiming or reciting a covenant-ratifying oath in the presence of witnesses.

[7] See esp. David Instone-Brewer, "The Ancient Near East: Marriage is a Contract," ch 1 in *Divorce and Remarriage in the Bible: The Social and Literary Context* (Grand Rapids: Eerdmans, 2002), 1–19, to whom I am indebted for his excellent summary of the research on the contents and nature of the ANE marriage covenant. See also the exhaustive analysis of Hugenberger, *Marriage as a Covenant*, 168–213, for decisive refutation of those who claim that marriage in Scripture and the ancient Near East should not be regarded as a covenant.

major payments (as well illustrated in Old Babylonian documents).[8] First, the "bride wealth" (Old Babylonian *terḫatu*, Heb. *mōhar,* sometimes [I believe mistakenly] called the "bride-price"), averaging about ten months' wages (ten shekels), was paid by the groom to the father of the bride and served to seal the betrothal.[9] This payment, representing a considerable amount of money, contributed toward insuring that the marriage was not entered into flippantly.

Second, the dowry (Old Babylonian *širiktu*), normally much in excess of the bride wealth, was paid by the bride's father to the bride; this was "equivalent to the daughter's share of the family estate, held in trust for her by her husband."[10] The dowry gave personal financial security to the bride, since it continued to belong to her even after the consummation of the marriage and could be used by her to support herself and children in case of the husband's death or if he divorced her. Both these payments not only gave financial security to the marriage but also constituted a legal seal of the marriage covenant.

The various stipulations in an ANE marriage covenant were sometimes written down in a formal marriage contract, especially in cases when the payments had been unusually large or there were unusual stipulations. But most often there was no written document; the covenant stipulations were stated verbally before witnesses.[11] Beyond the stated stipulations, fundamental unwritten and unspoken rights/responsibilities were assumed applicable in every marriage (such as the agreement to remain sexually faithful). In the Babylonian written marriage documents (seventh–third centuries B.C.E.), one of the common additional stipulations was that a man was not to take a second wife to the neglect of his first.[12] Another recorded stipulation contained details of settlement should a divorce occur (see below).

Still another regular additional stipulation in the ANE marriage documents is that the husband is obligated to provide food, clothing, and anointing oil for his wife.[13] We will examine below the apparent similarity of language of this

---

[8] See Edwin M. Yamauchi, "Cultural Aspects of Marriage in the Ancient World," *BSac* 135 (1978): 241–52.

[9] The term *mōhar* occurs several times in the OT (Gen 34:12; Exod 22:17; 1 Sam 18:25), and the bride wealth is alluded to at other times when the word *mōhar* does not appear (Gen 24:53; Hos 3:2).

[10] Instone-Brewer, *Divorce and Remarriage,* 5. Cf. Martha T. Roth, *Babylonian Marriage Agreements: 7th–3rd Centuries B.C.* (AOAT 222; Kevelaer, Ger.: Butzon & Bercker, 1989), 9.

[11] Roth, *Babylonian Marriage Agreements,* 1–2, points out that among the tens of thousands of cuneiform documents so far discovered, only forty-five are marriage covenants. Even these written documents read like transcripts of an oral ceremony. E.g., "The groom said . . . then the bride's father said . . ."

[12] See "The Laws of Lipit-Ishtar," §28, translated by Martha Roth (*COS* 2.154:413): "If a man's first-ranking wife loses her attractiveness or becomes a paralytic, she will not be evicted from the house; however, her husband may marry a healthy wife, and the second wife shall support the first-ranking wife." (Samuel Noah Kramer [*ANET* 160] provides a slightly different translation but the same overall sense.) Cf. Roth, *Babylonian Marriage Agreements,* 66.

[13] See Shalom M. Paul, "Exod. 21:10: A Threefold Maintenance Clause," *JNES* 28 (1969): 48–53.

threefold maintenance clause with Exod 21:10, but here note the precise parallelism with the items Israel is quoted as receiving from her lovers:

> She [Israel] said, "I will go after my lovers;
> they give me my *bread and my water,*
> my *wool and my linen,* my *oil* and my drink." (Hos 2:7 [ET 2:5])

The marriage covenant, whether written or spoken, was probably ratified in the context of a public wedding ceremony. Although the evidence is scant for what exactly happened in the typical ANE wedding ceremony, MAL A §41 gives some insight (at least regarding a man's marriage to his concubine):

> If a seignior wishes to veil his concubine, he shall have five (or) six of his neighbors present (and) veil her in their presence (and) say, "She is my wife," (and so) she becomes his wife. A concubine who was not veiled in the presence of the men, whose husband did not say, "She is my wife," is not a wife; she is still a concubine.[14]

The wedding ceremony for a man marrying his concubine probably was different from that for marrying a free woman; the latter would no doubt also include the statement of agreement with the wife's parents. The necessity of such parental assent is explicitly indicated in the Laws of Eshnunna:

> §27 If a man marries the daughter of another man without the consent of her father and mother, and moreover does not conclude the nuptial feast and the contract for (?) her father and mother, should she reside in his house for even one full year, she is not a wife.

> §28 If he concludes the contract and the nuptial feast for (?) her father and mother and he marries her, she is indeed a wife.[15]

The laws just cited also make clear the necessity of the public ceremony and the legal contract in order for there to be a marriage. Contrary to what has sometimes been assumed, sexual intercourse between a man and woman, or the two living together, without a formal covenant or wedding ceremony did not thereby make them husband and wife. Another explicit statement of this principle appears in the Code of Hammurabi: "If a man marries a wife but does not establish a contract for her, that woman is not a wife."[16]

Although some scholars have argued against the existence of *verba solemnia* (declaration formulae, roughly equivalent to our contemporary marriage vows) in the typical ANE marriage ceremony, the weight of evidence makes it "highly probable that *verba solemnia* were in fact normally employed in Israelite marriage"

---

[14] "Middle Assyrian Laws," A§41, translated by Theophile J. Meek (*ANET* 183). Cf. *COS* 2.132:358.

[15] "The Laws of Eshnunna," §§27–28, translated by Martha Roth (*COS* 2.130:333–34). Cf. *ANET* 162.

[16] "The Laws of Hammurabi," §128, translated by Martha Roth (*COS* 2.131:344). Cf. *ANET* 171.

and throughout the ancient Near East.[17] Scholars have attempted to recover the original (or typical) oral formula in the ANE marriage covenant;[18] in light of the language of MAL A §41 (cited above) and especially the parallel with the language of divorce formulae in ANE marriage contracts and with the apparent divorce formula of Hos 2:4 [ET 2:2]), it seems likely that the marriage *verba solemnia* included a statement such as "She is my wife" on the part of the groom.

Although the written marriage certificates were written from the perspective of the man, both the man and the woman probably participated in the oral ceremony.[19] In light of the language of many ANE formulae of divorce, often given mutually for both the man and the woman ("She is not my wife and I am not her husband" and "He is not my husband and I am not his wife" [discussed below]), the typical *verba solemnia* at an ANE wedding may well have been the positive equivalent of the divorce formulae. Thus the groom may have declared, "I [groom's name] will be your husband and you [bride's name] will be my wife"; and likewise the bride may have declared, "I [bride's name] will be your wife and you [groom's name] will be my husband."[20] There is also evidence that along with the declaration "You will be my wife/husband . . . ," there probably was the added phrase ". . . this day, and forever"[21]—signifying the intended and promised permanence of the marital relationship. The participation of the wife as well as the husband in the mutual verbal affirmation of permanency in their marriage may be alluded to in Hos 2:16–22 (ET 2:14–20).[22]

Verbal affirmations between spouses may at times have been accompanied by a covenant oath that solemnized the marriage in the presence of the deity, or the verbal affirmations alone may have been regarded as the equivalent of a covenant oath and by themselves constituted the *verba solemnia* of the wedding.[23] The

---

[17] Hugenberger, *Marriage as a Covenant,* 216. The definitive study is Samuel Greengus, "The Old Babylonian Marriage Contract," *JAOS* 89 (1969): 505–32. Hugenberger, *Marriage as a Covenant,* 216–37, reevaluates the evidence presented by Greengus, in light of arguments against this position presented by Raymond Westbrook, *Old Babylonian Marriage Law* (AfO 23; Horn, Austria: Berger & Söhne, 1988), 120–25. Although Westbrook has made some valuable observations, Hugenberger's refutation of Westbrook's overall critique is decisive. Hugenberger shows that the evidence from the ancient Near East, the OT, and later Jewish texts all supports the existence of *verba solemnia* as part of the marriage ceremony.

[18] See esp. Mordecai A. Friedman, "Israel's Response in Hosea 2:17b: 'You Are My Husband,'" *JBL* 99 (1980): 199–204; and Roth, *Babylonian Marriage Agreements,* passim.

[19] Ibid., 202–3.

[20] For this suggested wording on the part of the groom, see Daniel I. Block, "Marriage and Family in Ancient Israel," in *Marriage and Family in the Biblical World* (ed. Ken M. Campbell; Downers Grove, Ill.: InterVarsity, 2003), 45 (he does not address the probability that the *verba solemnia* were also spoken by the bride).

[21] See Instone-Brewer, *Divorce and Remarriage,* 13; and John J. Collins, "Marriage, Divorce, and Family in Second Temple Judaism," in Leo Perdue et al., *Families in Ancient Israel* (Louisville: Westminster John Knox, 1997), 108. Parallels are cited from Ugaritic materials and the Elephantine marriage contracts of the fifth century B.C.E.

[22] See Friedman, "Israel's Response"; Hugenberger, *Marriage as a Covenant,* 233–36.

[23] See Hugenberger, *Marriage as a Covenant,* 168–239, for discussion and ANE/ biblical evidence of *verba solemnia* and/or a covenant oath that solemnized the marriage.

statement of Adam in Gen 2:23 probably served as *verba solemnia,* indeed, a covenant oath before God in the Edenic wedding of the first human couple (as noted
in ch. 1, above, and earlier in this chapter). Hugenberger discusses other OT passages that may contain or allude to *verba solemnia* or the covenant oath of the
wedding ceremony: Hos 2:4 (ET 2:2); Hos 2:17–19 (ET 2:15–17); Prov 7:4–5; and
Song 2:16; 6:3; 7:11 (ET 7:10).[24]

Based upon ANE background material in general and upon the parabolic description of Israel/Judah's marriage to Yahweh in Ezek 16:8–13 in particular,
Daniel Block infers the following series of elements in a wedding of OT times:[25]
(1) the groom covers the bride with his garment, symbolizing his intent to protect and provide for her in the new relationship (cf. Ruth 3:9); (2) the groom
(and, I would add, likely also the bride) swears an oath of fidelity, probably raising the right hand, thus invoking the deity as witness and guarantor of the marriage covenant; (3) the groom (and, I would add, likely also the bride) enters into
the marriage covenant with *verba solemnia;* (4) the bride is bathed by the groom
and anointed with oil by him, expressing his love and devotion to her; (5) the
bride is dressed by the groom in the finest clothing and ornaments that he can afford (cf. Ps 45; Isa 61:10); and (6) a sumptuous feast provided by the groom
ensues at the groom's house (cf. Gen 29:22; Judg 14:10).

During the feast, which could last an entire week (Gen 29:27; Judg 14:12) or
even two weeks (Tob 8:20–9:2; 10:7), there was elaborate celebration, with singing and dancing, praises of the bride and groom, and a spirit of great joy (Ps
78:63; Isa 5:1; Ezek 33:32; Song 4–7; cf. Matt 9:15; Mark 2:19; Luke 5:34). The
husband also seems to have worn a crown on the wedding day (Song 3:11). The
bride remained veiled until she and the groom were alone in the bridal chamber
(*ḥeder*), where, during the first night of the feast, the night of the wedding, on the
bridal bed with its canopy, they physically consummated their marriage (Gen
29:23; Song 3:4; 4:16; 5:1).[26] The evidence that the bride was a virgin was the

---

Among the forty-five Neo- and Late Babylonian marriage contracts analyzed by Roth,
Babylonian Marriage Agreements, 19, eight invoke a curse against the one who would
break the stipulations of the marriage covenant. Hugenberger, *Marriage as a Covenant,*
187–88, provides several other possible ANE examples of "a mutual oath by which both
bride and groom are bound to the terms of the contract" (p. 187). On the other hand,
Hugenberger notes that the presence of an oath in the written form of the marriage
contract is not to be expected, since the written version of the contract usually states the
extraordinary stipulations not normally assumed in the oral contract. "Hence," Hugenberger concludes, "the lack of an explicit stipulation of a ratifying oath in marriage need
occasion no surprise" (191).

[24] Hugenberger, *Marriage as a Covenant,* 231–39.

[25] Block, "Marriage and Family in Ancient Israel," 44–45.

[26] For ANE and biblical evidence for the bridal chamber, see Steven C. Horine, *Interpretive Images in the Song of Songs: From Wedding Chariots to Bridal Chambers* (Studies in
the Humanities: Literature–Politics–Society 55; New York: Peter Lang, 2001), 73–121. See
Hugenberger, *Marriage as Covenant,* 240–79, for evidence that "sexual union is the indispensable means for the consummation of marriage both in the Old Testament and elsewhere in the ancient Near East." Less clear, but possible, is Hugenberger's suggestion that
"sexual union functioned in this manner precisely because it was viewed as an oath-sign."

sheet stained with virginal bleeding produced by the first sexual intercourse of the couple, and the bride's parents apparently kept this in case their daughter's virginity at the time of marriage should ever be questioned (Deut 22:13–21).

In the wedding ritual, one crucial aspect mentioned (but not emphasized) by Block is the formal occasion in which the groom, accompanied by his friends and musical instruments, singing and dancing, brought his bride from her father's house to his own (Gen 24:67; Ps 45; 1 Macc 9:39; Jer 7:34; 16:9; 25:10; Song 3:6–11). In the OT it is not clear when this joyous procession to the groom's house normally occurred, but from NT evidence it appears to have taken place after the formal covenant ceremony of the wedding (the oaths of fidelity/*verba solemnia*), usually in the evening; the groom brought his bride to his house for the wedding feast and the physical consummation of the wedding (Matt 25:1–13; Luke 12:35–38).

The activities of the wedding just described should be placed within the larger context of the formation and cementing of the marital union between a man and a woman. Samuel Greengus has defined at least five stages of this wider process in Old Babylonian laws: (1) "deliberative," during which the families planned and negotiated for the marriage; (2) "prenuptial," during which the husband sends the bride wealth to the bride's home; (3) "nuptial," or the actual wedding proceedings and celebrations, including the formal marriage pact, the nuptial feast, physical consummation of the marriage, and honeymoon; (4) "connubial," beginning when the husband brings his bride back from the honeymoon to their new home; and (5) "familial," with the birth of the first child.[27] These stages are well represented in the marriages of various OT couples, although the critical moment when the couple becomes legally bound in a permanent marriage covenant seems clearly to occur at the time of the *verba solemnia* as the mutual covenant declaration/oath is made before God and human witnesses.

The permanence implied in the covenantal nature of marriage is the assumed pattern in the illustrations of lives of married couples throughout the OT, as surveyed here and in previous chapters.[28] The biblical testimony surveyed

---

[27] Samuel Greengus, "Redefining 'Inchoate Marriage' in Old Babylonian Contexts," in *Riches Hidden in Secret Places: Ancient Near Eastern Studies in Memory of Thorkild Jacobsen* (ed. Tzvi Abusch; Winona Lake, Ind.: Eisenbrauns, 2002), 123–39. Greengus shows that each of these stages is mentioned in Old Babylonian laws, with a view toward the impact of a given stage (or of the aborting of the marriage at such stage) on marital property. For another helpful overview of this whole process, see esp. Victor H. Matthews, "Marriage and Family in the Ancient Near East," in *Marriage and Family in the Biblical World* (ed. Ken. M. Campbell; Downers Grove, Ill.: InterVarsity, 2003), 6–14.

[28] Besides the normal contexts of marriage in the Old Testament, there are other kinship, socio-economic, and religious factors that play a role in Israelite marriages. For an examination of these factors from a sociological point of view, and a preliminary attempt to establish a typology of Israelite marriage, see Allen Guenther, "A Typology of Israelite Marriage: Kinship, Socio-Economic, and Religious Factors," *JSOT* 29 (2005): 387–407. Guenther identifies five special types of marriage situations in addition to the basic marriage type (which normally uses the terms "give" [*nātan*] and "take" [*lāqaḥ*]), each of which employs distinct Hebrew terminology: (1) the *ḥātan*-type marriage, which involves "a peace covenant, ratified by oath by which a kinship group representative designates a

includes the call to covenant faithfulness on the part of both husband and wife. Contrary to common scholarly opinion, the biblical record gives no license to the husband any more than to the wife to break the covenant by unfaithfulness to the marriage vows.[29]

Distortion of the Divine Ideal: Divorce/Remarriage

The distortion of the divine mandate for permanence in marriage led to the practice of divorce. The wide range of OT passages related to the issues of divorce and remarriage includes at least six different Hebrew expressions referring to divorce and occurring altogether about twenty-seven times,[30] plus several references to remarriage.[31] Despite the numerous occurrences of Hebrew terms referring to divorce in the OT, the surprising fact is that the OT contains no legislation dealing directly with divorce. Divorce is tolerated, conceded, permitted but never commanded, commended, or approved by divine legislation. This is true even of the most prominent OT passage in recent discussions of divorce, Deut 24:1–4.

---

man or leading members of an exogamous group of significant social standing as affines, paving the way to intermarriage" (p. 404; see Gen 34:9; Deut 7:3; Josh 23:12; 1 Sam 18:21, 22, 23, 26, 27; 1 Kgs 3:1; Ezra 9:14; and 2 Chron 18:1); (2) the *yābam*-type or levirate marriage in which "the next of kin assumes the responsibility of taking (marrying) his widowed sister-in-law to produce a male heir to preserve the family's possession of its original land grant" (p. 404; see Gen 38:8; Deut 25:5, 7; Ruth 1:15; we will examine this type in ch. 11 below); (3) the *nāśāʾ*-type marriage, "in which, because of poverty or through the exercise of power, a man takes a wife without the exchange of the usual bride wealth or dowry" (p. 405; see Judg 21:23; Ruth 1:4; Ezra 9:2; 12:10, 44; Neh 13:25); (4) the *hôšîb* [*hipʿil* of *yāšab*]-type marriage, involving "cohabitation which may eventuate in formal marriage" (p. 405; see Ezra 10:2, 10, 14, 17, 18; Neh 13:23, 27; and our discussion of these passages in ch. 7, above); and (5) a *bāʿal*-type marriage situation, involving an act after marriage and its consummation in which the wife is "*bāʿal*-ed" by her husband; this act marks "an elevated marriage status and attendant responsibility for the household, conferred on the wife by her husband who himself bears the social honorific" title *baʿal* (p. 405; see Gen 20:3; Deut 22:22; Isa 54:1; 62:4). This sociological classification of marriage types in the OT calls for further study.

[29] See ch. 8, above; cf. Hugenberger, *Marriage as Covenant,* 313–38, where the various passages are examined that have often been interpreted as instituting a double standard giving the man license to engage in extramarital sexual activity without penalty. Hugenberger shows that none of these passages supports the claimed indifference of the OT to a man's sexual fidelity.

[30] The Hebrew terms and their occurrences are as follows: (1) *šālaḥ* in *piʿel,* "to send away, divorce," Gen 21:14; Deut 21:14; 22:19, 29; 24:1, 3–4; Isa 50:1; Jer 3:1, 8; Mal 2:16; (2) *gāraš,* "to drive out, cast/thrust out, banish, divorce," *piʿel,* Gen 21:10; *qal* passive, Lev 21:7, 14; 22:13; Num 30:10 (ET 30:9); Ezek 44:22; (3) [*sēper*] *kěrîtût,* "[document] of cutting off or divorce," Deut 24:1, 3; Isa 50:1; Jer 3:8; (4) *yāṣaʾ* in *hipʿil,* "to cause to go out = divorce," Ezra 10:3, 19; (5) *bādal* in *nipʿal,* "to separate oneself = divorce," Ezra 10:11; (6) *bāgad,* "to deal treacherously with, break faith with = divorce," Mal 2:14–16.

[31] See Gen 25:1; Deut 24:1–4; Judg 14:20–15:2; 1 Sam 25:44; perhaps Isa 7:14; 8:3.

The rest this chapter first surveys the ANE background regarding divorce, then examines passages dealing with divorce/remarriage in the pentateuchal narratives and legal material, and finally discusses divorce/remarriage passages in the Prophets and Writings of the OT.

Ancient Near Eastern Background

Specific ANE laws and practices regarding divorce are discussed below in connection with the corresponding biblical divorce passages they illuminate. Here a general overview provides illustrations of ANE divorce law and practice not directly paralleled in Scripture and points out the major differences between ANE and biblical laws regarding divorce.

The ANE law codes indicate various grounds for divorce, but it seems that often in practice the husband did not need any further grounds to divorce his wife than simply his choice to do so. The ANE marriage contracts often contain divorce formulae and clauses describing penalties if the one who divorces has no legal grounds.[32] A major function of the ANE laws concerning divorce was to regulate the financial and property issues, much as divorce proceedings today. The major complicating factor in these proceedings was whether the couple had children. If the wife had given birth to children, the penalties upon the husband for initiating the divorce were generally greater.[33]

As noted above, the standard divorce formula that dissolved the marital ties formed in marriage was the declaration (for the husband) "You are not my wife" or (for the wife) "You are not my husband." As the groom clothed his bride during the wedding rituals, so in the divorce proceedings that dissolved the marriage the husband cut the hem of his wife's garment, "thereby sundering their association and making it possible for them to establish new marriage links."[34] More drastic symbolic action was taken if the wife had committed serious violations of the marriage agreement: she was stripped naked and driven from the house.[35]

Contrary to a common misconception that women in the ANE had very little freedom to initiate a divorce until the Persian period (when Jewish marriage contracts in fifth-century B.C.E. Elephantine contain mutual divorce rights),

---

[32] See Matthews, "Marriage and Family," 24–25; Westbrook, *Old Babylonian Marriage Law,* 78.

[33] See, e.g., CH §§137–140, 159 (*COS* 2.131:344–45; *ANET* 172–73); and the discussion of the issue of divorce settlements involving children in Westbrook, *Old Babylonian Marriage Law,* 78–79, 85.

[34] Matthews, "Marriage and Family," 25; cf. Jacob J. Finkelstein, "Cutting the *sissiktu* in Divorce Proceedings," *WO* 8 (1976): 236–40. This procedure was not carried out to shame the wife, but it seems to have sometimes symbolized that she was forfeiting her dowry as part of the price for gaining freedom from the marriage.

[35] Matthews, "Marriage and Family," 25; cf. Meir Malul, *Studies in Mesopotamian Legal Symbolism* (Kevelaer, Ger.: Butzon & Bercker, 1988), 122–38; and the parallels with Hos 2:2–3. Grounds for such proceedings included repudiating her husband, giving family property to outsiders, or other flagrant violations of social norms.

Lipinski has shown that there was a strong Semitic legal tradition in the ancient Near East throughout the biblical period that gave mutual rights to both the husband and the wife to divorce if there were legal grounds, and equal penalties for both as well.[36] Lipinski traces this tradition from a wide array of ANE Semitic sources: Neo-Sumerian, Old Assyrian, Old Babylonian, West Semitic (Khana and Alalakh), Middle Assyrian, and Neo-Assyrian besides the Aramaic marriage contracts from fifth-century B.C.E. Elephantine.[37] It also appears that according to Hittite law, women had similar rights to divorce as men.[38] In light of this strong ANE tradition, due consideration must be given to the possibility that such rights were afforded women in the Israelite society as well (as will be argued below).

According to the Code of Hammurabi, a woman had a right to divorce her husband if he neglected her—in case he was taken captive and did not beforehand make adequate provision for her well-being. If he returned from his captivity, however, he could take her back even if she had remarried.[39] A Middle Assyrian law

---

[36] E. Lipinski, "The Wife's Right to Divorce in the Light of an Ancient Near Eastern Tradition," *JLA* 4 (1981): 9–27.

[37] The clearest example, from the ANE laws, of the woman's right to divorce when the husband is at fault is probably CH §142 (*COS* 2.131:344; cf. *ANET* 172): "If a woman repudiates her husband, and declares, 'You will not have marital relations with me'—her circumstances shall be investigated by the authorities of her city quarter, and if she is circumspect and without fault, but her husband is wayward and disparages her greatly, that woman will not be subject to any penalty; she shall take her dowry and she shall depart for her father's house." This "freedom," presented in theory in CH §142, is severely circumscribed in practice, however, by the law that follows (CH §143 [*COS* 2.131:344]): "If she is not circumspect but is wayward, squanders her household possessions, and disparages her husband, they shall cast that woman in the water" (cf. *ANET* 172). With the threat of death by drowning hanging over her head should she not win her case in court to prove her husband at fault, a wife in reality probably did not often take the risk in exercising her right to take the initiative in seeking divorce. Many of the examples cited by Lipinski are found in written marriage contracts, where the mutual rights of both husband and wife to divorce are stated in the contract stipulations. As noted earlier in this chapter, the stipulations of written contracts often state unusual circumstances that would not normally be assumed, and so the occurrence of mutual right to divorce in these contracts does not allow us to assume that the wife's equal right to divorce with her husband was automatic or universal in the ancient Near East. Nonetheless, there are enough examples, and enough chronological spread of these examples throughout ANE history, that the possibility, and even the probability, cannot be ruled out that such mutuality of divorce rights existed in Israelite society well before the fifth century B.C.E.

[38] "Hittite Laws," §§26a and b, translated by Harry A. Hoffner Jr. (*COS* 2.19:109): §26a, "If a woman re[fuses] [another manuscript reads 'divorces'] a man, [the man] shall give [her . . .], and [the woman shall take] a wage for her seed. But the man [shall take the land] and the children [. . .]"; §26b, "But if a man divor[ces] a woman, [and she . . . s, he shall] s[ell her.] Whoever buys her [shall] pa[y him] 12 shekels of silver." Cf. *ANET* 190, translated by Albrecht Goetze, which begins the translation of §26a with "If a woman sends away a man . . ." and §26b with "If a man divorces a woman . . ." Instone-Brewer points out that although the text is fragmentary, the parallelism between what is said of the woman and what is said of the man seems to point to similar rights (*Divorce and Remarriage*, 24).

[39] CH §§133–136 (*COS* 2.131:344; *ANET* 171).

code included the stipulation that a woman who was neglected by her husband, even if he were not taken captive, could not divorce him and seek another husband until five years had passed.[40] Some have suggested that Exod 21:10–11 provides a parallel to these ANE laws providing for a woman's divorce on grounds of neglect and have further argued that the biblical law is more generous to the woman than its ANE counterparts;[41] but as argued in chapter 5, above, and discussed further below, 21:10–11 probably does not deal with a situation of divorce at all, and thus no comparison of this passage with the ANE laws should be drawn.

There are, however, at least two areas in which the laws of the Bible related to divorce clearly provide women greater equality with men than comparable laws elsewhere in the ancient Near East (see also below in connection with the relevant biblical passages). The first area is a woman's right to remain married. According to a Middle Assyrian law, a rapist must give up his own wife to be raped, may not receive his first wife back again, must marry the raped woman (if her father agrees), must give the bride wealth for a virgin, and may not divorce her.[42] The biblical law (Deut 22:28–29) is similar but does not sanction "rape for rape" or take away the rapist's original wife. The biblical legislation upholds the dignity of the woman even if she is a rapist's wife, and does not punish the wife for the crime of her husband.

Also in this first area, a woman's right to remain married, biblical law includes another provision for women that has no parallel in other ANE laws. This is the right for a woman who has been accused of not being a virgin on her wedding night to prove her virginity by having her parents exhibit the blood-stained sheets of the wedding night (Deut 22:13–19), thereby gaining the right to remain married, countering the unfounded charges of her husband.

A second area in which divorce-related biblical laws provide more equality to women than other ANE laws is the woman's right to remarry. As further elucidated in chapter 12, below, levirate marriage (Deut 25:5–9) guaranteed this right to remarry for all widows, and nothing quite the same as levirate marriage is found elsewhere in the ancient Near East (except perhaps among the Hittites). But the biblical law also provided for the right of remarriage to all divorced women by means of the divorce certificate. The mandatory giving of a divorce certificate within Israelite society "is unique in ancient Near Eastern sources" (see the discussion, below, of Deut 24:1–4).[43] Inasmuch as "the right of a woman to a divorce certificate is equivalent to the right of a woman to remarry,"[44] such mandatory practice in Israelite society, assumed in the law of 24:1–4, gave women greater freedom and security in remarriage than any other ANE law.

In contrast with other ANE laws, which (as noted above) permitted a man to neglect his wife for up to five years and then reclaim her even if she was married

---

[40] MAL A §36 (*COS* 2.132:357; *ANET* 183).
[41] See, e.g., Instone-Brewer, *Divorce and Remarriage*, 25–26.
[42] MAL A §55 (*COS* 2.132:359; *ANET* 185).
[43] Instone-Brewer, *Divorce and Remarriage*, 28.
[44] Ibid.

to another man, the mandatory biblical law assumed in 24:1–4, on the other hand, "gave divorced women the documentary evidence of their divorce, which enabled them to remarry without fear of counterclaims some time in the future from their former husbands."[45] Thus 24:1–4 "stands in stark contrast to other ancient Near Eastern laws. This law forbids a man from remarrying a woman whom he has divorced. This, in effect, gives the woman the right to remain remarried to her second husband." The divorce certificate, "which was a right of a few privileged women in some ancient Near Eastern legal systems, was extended by the Pentateuch [in 24:1–4] to all divorced women."[46]

To the biblical laws and practice regarding divorce, with particular focus upon 24:1–4, we now turn our attention.

Divorce in Pentateuchal Narratives

Patriarchal "Divorce": Genesis 21:9–14. The book of Genesis contains one example of what some have labeled "divorce": Abraham and Hagar (see the discussion of Abraham's polygamous relationship with Sarah's handmaid in ch. 5, above). The peace of the household had been broken because of the polygamous marriage. After Hagar had borne Ishmael, "she looked with contempt on her mistress" (Gen 16:4). Sarah in turn "dealt harshly with her, and she ran away from her" (16:6). In Gen 21 the narrative has progressed to the point when, in fulfillment of the divine promise, Sarah now also bears a son, Isaac.

After Isaac was born and weaned, Ishmael was caught making fun of or scoffing at (lit. "laughing at") Isaac, and Sarah said to Abraham, "Cast out [gāraš] this slave woman with her son; for the son of this slave woman shall not inherit along with my son Isaac" (21:10). As Abraham delayed in deciding what to do, God said to him, "Do not be distressed because of the boy and because of your slave woman; whatever Sarah says to you, do as she tells you, for it is through Isaac that offspring shall be named for you" (21:12). Abraham obeyed God's instructions and, after providing Hagar with food and water, "sent her away" (šālaḥ). Thus Abraham divorced Hagar.

The question arises whether in this passage God does not indeed countenance, even command, divorce. But it should be remembered what the narrator makes plain (and was highlighted ch. 5, above): God never recognized the relationship between Abraham and Hagar as a legitimate marriage in the first place. In God's perspective, Abraham had only one wife, Sarah. The narrator is careful to record that God did not tell Abraham to "divorce" Hagar. God rather uses the circumlocution "whatever Sarah says to you, do as she tells you." Thus, although, in Abraham's terms, he had divorced—"cast out" (gāraš) and "sent away" (šālaḥ)—Hagar, there had never been a valid marriage in God's eyes, and so there was really no divorce, only the dissolving of an illegitimate polygamous

---

[45] Ibid., 31.
[46] Ibid., 32, 33.

relationship. God had condescended to bear with Abram during this time but also gently led him to realize the divine ideal for marriage (see ch. 5, above).

Patriarchal Remarriage: Genesis 25:1. Abraham is a prime example of an OT figure who remarried after the death of his first wife. According to Gen 23, Sarah died at the age of 127 and was given an honorable burial. Later, according to 25:1, "Abraham took another wife, whose name was Keturah." In the narrative of Abraham's second marriage after his first wife died, the narrator gives no hint that this marriage was out of the ordinary or contrary to the divine will. Remarriage after the death of the first spouse seems to have been a normal, accepted practice in OT times.

Pentateuchal Legislation Related to Divorce: Deuteronomy 24:1–4

Deuteronomy 24:1–4 is the most prominent OT passage appearing in recent discussions of divorce. This passage is of crucial importance in understanding the divine instruction regarding divorce (in both OT and NT). In the scholarly discussion of 24:1–4, crucial grammatical-syntactical and intertextual features of the legislation have been mostly overlooked, features that provide keys for recognizing the implicit divine disapproval of divorce in pentateuchal legislation.[47]

Translation. Deuteronomy 24:1–4 reads as follows (with verse divisions marked):

> 1 Suppose a man enters into marriage with a woman, but she does not please him because he finds something objectionable about her, and so he writes her a certificate of divorce, puts it in her hand, and sends her out of his house; she then leaves his house 2 and goes off to become another man's wife. 3 Then suppose the second man dislikes her, writes her a bill of divorce, puts it in her hand, and sends her out of his house (or the second man who married her dies); 4 her first husband, who sent her away, is not permitted to take her again to be his wife after she has been defiled; for that would be abhorrent to the LORD, and you shall not bring guilt on the land that the LORD your God is giving you as a possession.

Literary Form and Structure. The legal portions of the Pentateuch contain two major literary types of law: apodictic and casuistic. In the former, there is an absolute command or prohibition, "You shall" or "You shall not." In the latter, the case laws, there first appears the protasis, or description of conditions, usually starting with Hebrew words best translated by "If" or "When." This is followed by the apodosis, or the legislation proper, best signaled in English translation by the word "then." Following the protasis and apodosis, a case law (as well as an apodictic law) sometimes has one or more motive clauses giving the rationale for the law.

---

[47] See a detailed exegesis of this passage in Richard M. Davidson, "Divorce and Remarriage in Deuteronomy 24:1–4," *JATS* 10, nos. 1–2 (1999): 2–22. The most salient points of that study, revised to include more recent literature, and my further reflections on the passage are presented here.

Deuteronomy 24:1–4 is a case law that has all three elements just described. Verses 1–3 contain the protasis, with several conditions: the grounds and procedure for divorce (v. 1), the remarriage of the woman (v. 2), and the divorce or the death of the second husband (v. 3). Only after describing all of these conditions in vv. 1–3 does the Hebrew word *lōʾ*, "not," at the beginning of v. 4 signal the start of the apodosis, or legislation proper. Thus the only legislation in this passage is in v. 4a, forbidding the woman's former husband to take her back to be his wife under the circumstances described in vv. 1–3.[48] The implication is clear: God is in no wise legislating divorce in this passage. In fact, it is conceivable that the whole passage may be expressing tacit divine disapproval although the divorce is tolerated and not punished. That this is indeed the case will become evident from further analysis below.

Following the protasis and apodosis of 24:1–4a comes the third major part of the case law, the motive clauses of v. 4b, containing the multiple rationales for the prohibition: the woman has been "defiled"; it would be a "abhorrent" to the Lord; and "guilt" should not be brought upon the land. These all call for attention in order to understand the purpose of the legislation.

Grounds for Divorce (v. 1a). Deuteronomy 24:1 describes two conditions that lead the husband to "send out" (*šālaḥ*) or divorce his wife. First, "it happens that she finds no favor [*ḥēn*, 'approval' or 'affection'] in his eyes" (NASB). The phrase "to find/not find favor in one's eyes" is the ordinary Hebrew expression for "like/dislike" or "please/displease." It describes the subjective situation—the husband's dislike, displeasure, or lack of approval/affection for his wife.

But the grounds for divorce are not limited to the subjective element. There are also concrete grounds for the disapproval: "because he finds something objectionable [*ʿerwat dābār*] about her." The Hebrew expression *ʿerwat dābār* may be translated literally as "nakedness of a thing." But to what does it refer? This question has been widely debated among scholars both ancient and modern. The word *ʿerwat*, "nakedness," elsewhere in the OT most often refers to the nakedness of a person's private parts or genitals, which should not be uncovered or exposed (*gālâ*) to be seen by those who should not see them; and the uncovering of one's

---

[48] This is the near unanimous consensus of modern biblical scholarship, represented in most modern versions. In contrast, some earlier English translations of this passage (e.g., KJV, ERV, and ASV) have the apodosis (the legislative portion) beginning already with v. 1b ("then let him write her a bill of divorcement"), implying that the law enacts the permission to divorce. Andrew Warren, "Did Moses Permit Divorce? Modal *wĕqāṭal* as Key to New Testament Readings of Deuteronomy 24:1–4," *TynBul* 49 (1998): 39–56, has more recently defended this translation. Although the latter interpretation is theoretically possible, J. G. McConville points out "the very specific focus of the law, in which the need for proper procedure as a prelude to the prohibited case is crucial. A general law of divorce can hardly be embedded here" (*Deuteronomy* [AOTC 5; Downers Grove, Ill.: InterVarsity, 2002], 358). Even according to Warren's interpretation, God still did not command divorce but only permitted it by way of concession ("Did Moses Permit Divorce?" 54–55).

nakedness usually has sexual connotations.[49] The word *dābār* can mean "word [speech, saying]" or "thing [matter, affair]"[50] and in the context of 24:1 surely means "thing" or "matter."

The phrase *ʿerwat dābār* occurs only once in the OT besides 24:1, and this is in the previous chapter, 23:15 (ET 23:14). There it clearly refers to the excrement mentioned in the previous verse, which should be covered (Heb. *gālâ*) so that the Lord "may not see anything indecent [*ʿerwat dābār*] among you and turn away from you." The "nakedness of a thing" is something that is uncovered that should have been covered, something that is indecent, repulsive, disgusting, or shameful when left exposed. It appears that the phrase *ʿerwat dābār* in 24:1 has a similar meaning to that in the preceding chapter but refers to the "nakedness of a thing" with regard to a wife. It seems probable, given the preceding context and the usual sexual overtones of the term *ʿerwâ* when referring to a woman, that the phrase in 24:1 describes a situation of indecent exposure (of private parts) by the woman.[51] Theoretically, the phrase could probably include illicit sexual intercourse (i.e., adultery), in parallel with the phrase "uncover nakedness" (*gillâ ʿerwâ*) describing such behavior in Lev 18:6–19 and 20:11–21.[52] Since adultery (and other illicit sexual intercourse), however, received the death penalty (or that of being "cut off" from the congregation) according to the law (Deut 22:22; Lev 20:10–18), the indecent exposure referred to here in Deut 24:1 must be something short of these sexual activities,[53] but a serious sexual

---

[49] See, e.g., Gen 9:22–23; Exod 20:23; 28:42; figuratively, uncovering of one's nakedness in punishment: Isa 20:4; 47:3; Ezek 16:37; 23:10, 29. The term "uncovering the nakedness of" is often used euphemistically for sexual intercourse: Lev 18:6, 8, 10, 16; 20:17; Ezek 16:36. See BDB 788–89 for a full list of passages; and see Roy Gane, "Old Testament Principles Relevant to Divorce and Remarriage," *JATS* 12, no. 2 (2001): 41–49, for careful analysis of the meaning and usage of this word and the whole phrase, *ʿerwat dābār,* in the OT.

[50] For the various nuances, see BDB 182–84; *HALOT* 211–12.

[51] Cf. Abel Isaksson, *Marriage and Ministry in the New Temple: A Study with Special Reference to Matt. 19.13[sic]–12 and 1 Cor. 11.3–16* (trans. N. Tomkinson with J. Gray; ASNU 24; Lund, Swed.: Gleerup, 1965), 26, who concurs that the phrase is a euphemism for indecent exposure of the wife's private parts: "All other exposure of his wife's pudendum than that which the husband himself is responsible for arouses his loathing." See also Eugene H. Merrill, *Deuteronomy* (NAC 4; Nashville: Broadman & Holman, 1994), 317: "The noun *ʿerwah* bears the meaning of both 'nakedness' and 'pudenda' [i.e., the sexual organs], meanings no doubt to be combined here to suggest the improper uncovering of the private parts."

[52] I agree with Merrill, *Deuteronomy,* 317: "Surely this circumlocution is to be understood as a euphemism that may or may not include adultery. . . . It is likely that *ʿerwat dābār* is a phrase broad enough to include adultery but not synonymous with it."

[53] See John Murray, *Divorce* (Grand Rapids: Baker, 1961), 10–11, who gives six cogent reasons why Deut 24:1 cannot refer to adultery. The OT legislation is here in contrast with elsewhere in the ancient Near East, where adultery under certain circumstances could provide legitimate grounds for divorce. See Jacob J. Rabinowitz, "The 'Great Sin' in Ancient Egyptian Marriage Contracts," *JNES* 18 (1959): 73; William L. Moran, "The Scandal of the 'Great Sin' at Ugarit," *JNES* 18 (1959): 280–81; Gane, "Old Testament Principles,"

indiscretion nonetheless.[54] The phrase *ʿerwat dābār* in 24:1 thus describes some type of serious, shameful, and disgraceful conduct of indecent exposure probably associated with sexual activity but less than illicit sexual intercourse.

Procedure of Divorce (v. 1b). According to 24:1b, there were three major elements in the divorce proceedings. First, the husband wrote a "certificate of divorce" (lit. "document of cutting off" [*sēper kĕrîtut*]). Other legal documents are mentioned in the OT,[55] and other passages that will be examined shortly also allude to the certificate of divorce. Although there is no OT example of the wording of such a document, it has been suggested that the central divorce formula is contained in what some have considered to be Yahweh's statement of divorce proceedings against Israel in Hos 2:4 (ET 2:2): "she is not my wife, and I am not her husband."[56] Such a statement would mean the legal breaking of the marriage covenant just as surely as the death of the marriage partner. The document no doubt had to be properly issued and officially authenticated, thus ensuring that the divorce proceedings were not done precipitously.

The bill of divorce may have also contained what in rabbinic times was considered "the essential formula in the bill of divorce," that is, "Lo, thou art free to marry any man."[57] This would provide for the freedom and right of the woman to be married again. The document would be indicating that although the woman had been guilty of some kind of indecent exposure, she was not guilty of adultery or other illicit sexual intercourse and therefore not liable to punishment for such

---

45. In light of the conclusion reached in ch. 8, above, however, that pentateuchal law may have implicitly given a husband the right to commute the death sentence of his adulterous wife, the possibility is not eliminated that in practice the "nakedness of a thing" may have included adultery. See Joe M. Sprinkle, "Sexuality, Sexual Ethics," *DOTP* 744, following Bruce Wells, "Adultery, Its Punishment, and the Nature of Old Testament Law" (paper presented at the annual meeting of the Evangelical Theological Society, Orlando, Fla., November 21, 1998).

54 See S. R. Driver, *A Critical and Exegetical Commentary on Deuteronomy* (ICC; New York: Charles Scribner's Sons, 1902), 271, who concludes regarding this phrase, "It is most natural to understand it of *immodest* or *indecent behavior.*" Gane, "Old Testament Principles," 45, concludes that the " 'indecent exposure' could be understood literally to mean that a wife improperly uncovers herself without physical contact of her sexual body parts with those of another person." Following a suggestion pointed out to him by Westbrook, Gane further suggests that it could be understood figuratively to mean " 'improper conduct with a man other than her husband,' e.g., kissing him, allowing him to fondle her, acting in a lewd or sexually suggestive manner, or otherwise flirting, thereby tempting him to covet her (in violation of the tenth of the Ten Commandments)" (ibid.).

55 See 2 Sam 11:14–15, the legal correspondence (*sēper*) of David to Joab delivered via Uriah the Hittite; Jer 32:11, the purchase deed (*sēper*) of Jeremiah.

56 The discussion of this passage below will argue, however, that most probably Yahweh did not in fact divorce his "wife," Israel, in Hos 2.

57 *Giṭ.* 9:3. From the scattered references to the divorce document in the Mishnah, it is possible to reconstruct its hypothetical form, which closely resembles the form recorded in the twelfth century by Maimonides (treatise *Gerushin* 4.12). See D. W. Amram, *The Jewish Law of Divorce* QĔDĒŚÂ, QADIŠTU (London: David Nutt, 1897; repr., New York: Sepher-Hermon, 1975), 156–58, for the reconstructed document.

sexual activity. Thus she was protected from abuse or false charges by her former husband or others at a subsequent time.

David Instone-Brewer provides examples of this kind of provision in other ANE divorce documents outside the OT and Judaism but points out that whereas elsewhere in the ancient Near East such a divorce certificate indicating the woman's freedom to remarry after the divorce is rare and optional, in the biblical legislation (and later Jewish practice based upon this legislation) the divorce certificate is mandatory for any woman who has been divorced.[58] Instone-Brewer summarizes regarding the "absolute distinctiveness" of the biblical divorce certificate, "There is no equivalent to the divorce certificate in any ancient Near Eastern culture outside Judaism."[59] The mandatory divorce certificate afforded the woman after a divorce in Israelite society freedom and protection unprecedented elsewhere in the ancient Near East. Parallels from Code of Hammurabi and the Jewish Mishnah suggest that the certificate of divorce would also contain mention of the financial settlement, unless the woman was guilty of misconduct, in which case no financial compensation was awarded her.[60] Probably the latter (no financial compensation) was the case in Deut 24:1.

The second step of the divorce proceedings was to "put it [the bill of divorce] in her [the wife's] hand" (24:1). She must receive notice of the divorce directly in

---

[58] David Instone-Brewer, "Deuteronomy 24:1–4 and the Origin of the Jewish Divorce Certificate," *JJS* 49 (1998): 235–43. According to Instone-Brewer (pp. 236–37), the only two surviving ANE divorce documents (Kirkuk 33 and Meissner 91) both speak about the freedom of the wife after her husband has divorced her. He summarizes the reason such documentation was needed: "A certificate of freedom was necessary in the social context of the ANE where a husband had the legal rights to reclaim a wife even after he had deserted her for a number of years" (237, citing CH §135 and MAL A §36 as evidence). Instone-Brewer (241–42) compares the divorce document of Deut 24:1 with the only other mandatory ANE document giving a woman the right to remarry, i.e., the "widow's tablet" issued to women whose husbands were missing in war and presumed to be dead (mentioned in MAL A §45, dated to the second millennium B.C.E.). This document was given only after the husband was missing two years and probably was not given to every widow but only to those whose widowhood was in question. Also cited is evidence from divorce provisions in two marriage documents of Jews at Elephantine in the fifth century B.C.E. (Papyrus G = Cowley 15 and Kraeling Papyrus 7), which refer to the woman's freedom after divorce, stating, "She may go wherever she wishes" (ibid., 240).

[59] Instone-Brewer, *Divorce and Remarriage*, 32.

[60] CH §§141–142 (*COS* 2.131:344; cf. *ANET* 172). CH §141: "If the wife of a man who is residing in the man's house should decide to leave, and she appropriates goods, squanders her household possessions, or disparages her husband, they shall charge and convict her; and if her husband should declare his intention to divorce her, then he shall divorce her; neither her travel expenses, nor her divorce settlement, not anything else shall be given to her. If her husband should declare his intention to not divorce her, then her husband may marry another woman and that (first) woman shall reside in her husband's house as a slave woman" (CH §142 is cited above in the discussion of ANE precedents for women seeking divorce). Cf. *m. Ketub.* 7:6 (and other regulations regarding giving the *kĕtûbâ* [financial settlement] in this tractate; and discussion of this and other evidence in Raymond Westbrook, "The Prohibition on Restoration of Marriage in Deuteronomy 24:1–4," in *Studies in Bible, 1986* [ed. Sara Japhet; ScrHier 31; Jerusalem: Magnes, 1986], 393–98).

order for it to be effective. The Mishnah tractate *Giṭṭin* concerns various situations that might not qualify as putting the divorce certificate in the hand of the woman.[61] The effect, again, is the protection of the wife by ensuring that she has access to, and concrete notification of, the divorce document.

The third step is that the husband "sends her out of his house" (24:1). The word "send" (*šālaḥ* in the *pi'el*) is elsewhere in the OT virtually equivalent to a technical term for "divorce."[62] Sending the wife away is intended to be the effectuation of the divorce process. The break is final and complete.

Remarriage and the Second Divorce or Death of a Second Husband (vv. 2–3). The third condition specified in the protasis of Deut 24:1–3 is that the divorced woman remarries and then her second husband either divorces her or dies. Raymond Westbrook seeks to establish that the grounds for the second divorce are not the same as those for the first divorce. The second husband is said to "detest" or "dislike" (*śānē'*, lit. "hate") her, which term is not employed in the grounds for the first divorce.[63] Some of the evidence Westbrook cites may, however, in fact militate against his conclusion, for he shows that in ANE sources and later Jewish material (e.g., the Elephantine marriage contracts), the formula "I hate [*śānē'*] my husband/wife" is a summary of the longer standard divorce formula "I hate and divorce my husband/wife."

Westbrook's argument that "hate/dislike" in 24:3 refers to divorce without objective grounds in contrast to divorce with objective grounds in 24:1, though plausible, is not persuasive. Besides the elements of conjecture that he must introduce (that this legislation is about finances, when no such indication is given in the text, and that the first divorce provided no financial compensation but the second divorce did), Westbrook's thesis that the law is merely to prevent the first husband from profiting financially twice from the woman, though possible, does not match the severe language used in the motive clauses to describe the "abhorrence" and "guilt" of this action. This will be discussed further below.

In light of the fact that *śānē'* is used elsewhere in ANE materials as the technical term to summarize the grounds for divorce, whatever they might be, it seems preferable to take the term "hate/dislike" (*śānē'*) as summarizing the same situation as the first divorce, mentioned in 24:1. This interpretation is strengthened by the summary reference in Jer 3:1, where Deut 24:1–4 is interpreted as a general statement forbidding one who has divorced and remarried to return to her previous husband, not as positing a distinction between two different types of divorce (see discussion of Jer 3 below). The divorce procedure in Deut 24:3 is the same as described in 24:1: the husband writes his wife a certificate of divorce, puts

---

[61] E.g., *m. Giṭ.* 4.1 states that if the bill of divorcement is intercepted by the husband before it reaches his wife, then it is void, but if he tries to intercept it after she receives it, it is not void.

[62] This is already apparent in 24:4, where the Hebrew term simply means "divorce." The other usages of *šālaḥ* with reference to divorce are examined below.

[63] Westbrook, "The Prohibition," 399–405. See Instone-Brewer, "Deuteronomy 24:1–4," 232–35, who finds Westbrook's overall hypothesis convincing.

it in her hand, and sends her away out of his house. Or as an alternative situation, the second husband dies.

Legislation: The Apodosis (v. 4a). After the lengthy statement of conditions, the legislation itself is short and simple: "her first husband, who sent her away [*šilḥāh*], is not permitted [*lōʾ yûkal*] to take her again to be his wife after she has been defiled" (Deut 24:4a). Although the legislation is clear, the rationale for this legislation is far less certain. Already in the legislation, however, one part of the rationale is given: "after she has been defiled." Two additional aspects of the rationale for the prohibition appear in the motive clauses. All of these aspects will be examined in the next section.

Rationale for the Legislation (v. 4a–d). The first indicator of the reason for this legislation comes in the explanation why the first husband is not permitted to remarry (Deut 24:4a): "she has been defiled." The Hebrew for this clause is a single word, *huṭṭammāʾâ*, from the verb *ṭāmēʾ*, "to be or become unclean or defiled." But the grammatical form employed in this verse, the *hotpaʿal*, is very unusual in the HB, used nowhere else with *ṭāmēʾ* and only three other times with another verb.[64] This form is the passive of the *hitpaʿel*. Since the *hitpaʿel* normally conveys the reflexive idea and the *hitpaʿel* of *ṭāmēʾ* is invariably used reflexively ("to defile oneself") elsewhere in the HB,[65] the passive of this reflexive (*hotpaʿal*) in Deut 24:4 is best translated, "she has been made/caused to defile herself."[66] The implications of this will become apparent after an examination of the nature of the woman's defilement.

Intertextual usage of the verb *ṭāmēʾ* in the reflexive elsewhere in the HB, occurring in the context of sexual activities, leads us to Lev 18, which contains not only the reflexive form of this word (18:24, 30) but also the other two terms/concepts used in the motive clauses of Deut 24:4: the term "abomination" (*tôʿēbâ*) (Lev 18:22, 26, 29, RSV) and the idea of bringing defilement/sin upon the land (18:25, 27–28). Leviticus 18 is the only other chapter of the HB that combines these three terms/ideas in one context, and seems undoubtedly to be intertextually connected with Deut 24:4 in the final form of the Pentateuch.

---

[64] The three other occurrences of the *hotpaʿal* are Lev 13:55–56 and Isa 34:6. See *IBHS* 432; GKC 150 (§54 h).

[65] Lev 11:24, 43; 18:24, 30; 21:1, 3–4, 11; Num 6:7; Ezek 14:11; 20:7, 18; 37:23; 44:25. See BDB 379; *HALOT* 376.

[66] Contra John H. Walton, "The Place of the *hutqattel* within the D-Stem Group and Its Implications in Deuteronomy 24:4," *HS* 32 (1991): 7–17, who translates as a declarative: "she has been made to declare herself to be unclean." Walton suggests that this alludes to a public judicial statement the woman was obliged to declare at the time of her first divorce, that she was unclean. There is, however, no biblical evidence for such a judicial procedure, and the reflexive "defiled herself" is more in keeping with the usual grammatical sense (*hotpaʿal* being the passive of the reflexive *hitpaʿel*) than translating it as a declarative. In a footnote Instone-Brewer alternatively suggests that "this form could also be translated 'she has been caused to be unclean.' This would mean that her second marriage made her unclean to her first husband" ("Deuteronomy 24:1–4," 233, n. 15). This translation likewise fails to capture the reflexive meaning of the *hotpaʿal*.

In Lev 18 a person "defiles oneself" by having illicit sexual relations with another (vv. 20, 24, including at least adultery, bestiality, and homosexual practice). Deuteronomy 24:4 also probably should be seen in intertextual linkage with Num 5:13–14, 20, which refers to the wife as having "defiled herself" (nip‿al reflexive of ṭāmē᾽) by having illicit sexual relationships with another man than her husband. The implication of this intertextuality between Deut 24:4, Lev 18, and Num 5 is that in Deut 24:4 the sexual activity of the divorced woman with the second husband is tantamount to adultery or some other illicit sexual intercourse even though she does not incur the death penalty or other punishment as in the cases of Lev 18.

Various commentators have recognized this implication. C. F. Keil and Franz Delitzsch write on Deut 24:4, "Thus the second marriage of a divorced woman was placed *implicite* upon a par with adultery."[67] S. R. Driver concurs that "the union of a divorced woman with another man, from the point of view of her first husband, [is] falling into the same category as adultery."[68] Likewise Peter C. Craigie comments, "The sense is that the woman's remarriage after the first divorce is similar to adultery in that the woman cohabits with another man."[69] And Earl Kalland remarks, "So here [Deut 24:4] it refers to whatever defilement is associated with adultery."[70]

If the sexual intercourse of the woman with her second husband defiles her and is tantamount to adultery, why is she free from punishment? The answer is found in the meaning of the *hotpa‿al* form: she "*has been caused* to defile herself" (translation mine). The one she has had sexual intercourse with (i.e., her second husband) is not the "cause" of defilement, as would be the case if a *nip‿al* or even *hitpa‿el* grammatical form were used.[71] With the utilization of the rare *hotpa‿al* (pass. reflexive) form, another cause than the immediate defilement with her second husband is implied. This is highlighted by a comparison of this occurrence of the *hotpa‿al* with its other three occurrences in the HB, where the same dynamic is functioning.[72] The ultimate cause, implicit in this rare grammatical form, must

---

[67] K&D, 1:951.

[68] Driver, *Deuteronomy*, 272.

[69] Peter C. Craigie, *The Book of Deuteronomy* (NICOT; Grand Rapids: Eerdmans, 1976), 305.

[70] Earl S. Kalland, "Deuteronomy," *EBC* 3:146.

[71] See, e.g., *nip‿al*, Lev 18:24; Num 5:13, 14 (bis), 20, 27; *hitpa‿el*, Lev 18:24, 30. Whether one translates these passages reflexively (as I prefer) or passively (or a mixture of both), the person "defiles himself/herself" with, or "is defiled" by, the sexual partner.

[72] So in Lev 13:55–56. In the case of leprous garments, the priest "shall *command* them to wash the article in which the disease appears" (v. 54), and then the priest examines the plague after "it had been caused to be washed" (*hotpa‿al*; vv. 55–56, translation mine). It was "they" who actually washed the garment, but the priest was the "cause." Likewise in Isa 34:6, "The sword of the Lord is filled with blood, it is *caused to be made fat* (*hotpa‿al*) with fat (i.e., the fat of the kidneys of rams" [translation mine]). The object that makes it fat is the fat of the rams' kidneys, but the Lord (who wields the sword) is the one who causes it to happen. In each case another cause prior to what does the action (washing, making fat) is in view.

be the first husband. The legislation subtly implicates the first husband for divorcing his wife. Even though his action is not punished, and therefore it is legally tolerated, the law makes clear that his action does not have divine (moral) approval. The first husband's putting away of his wife has in effect caused her to defile herself in a second marriage in a similar way to committing adultery.[73]

Thus, although Deut 24:1–4 does not legislate divorce or remarriage and even tolerates it to take place on certain moral grounds that are less than illicit sexual intercourse, at the same time within the legislation is an internal indicator that such divorce brings about a state tantamount to adultery and therefore ultimately is not in harmony with the divine will. Though not illegal, it is not morally pleasing to God. Already in 24:4 it is indicated that breaking the marriage bond on grounds that are less than illicit sexual intercourse causes the woman to defile herself, that is, commit what is tantamount to adultery. By providing an internal indicator of divine disapproval of divorce, the legislation in 24:1–4 is pointing back to God's Edenic ideal for permanency in marriage. God's concession to less than ideal situations in Israel did not supplant the divine intention set forth in Gen 2:24. This legislation is also in harmony with the later summary statement of Yahweh (examined below), "I hate divorce" (Mal 2:16).

The second indicator of rationale for the legislation lies in the reason given in Deut 24:4: "for that is an abomination before the LORD" (RSV). As noted above, the term *tôʿēbâ,* "abomination," occurring in context with the other two rationales found in 24:4, links unmistakably with Lev 18. As the various types of illicit sexual intercourse mentioned in Lev 18 are "abominations" (RSV, Heb. *tôʿēbôt*), so is a woman's returning to the first husband after having been married again. Craigie rightly points out that if the woman's remarriage after her first divorce is similar to adultery, remarriage to her former husband is even more so: "If the woman were then to remarry her first husband, after divorcing the second, the analogy with adultery would become even more complete; the woman lives first with one man, then another, and finally returns to the first."[74]

What is more, it appears that the prohibition does in effect bring indirect "punishment" upon the first husband for divorcing his wife. Even though his divorcing her is not directly censured, yet since she "has been caused [by him] to defile herself" (translation mine) through his action, he is indirectly punished by not being allowed to take her as a wife again. To do such would be "abhorrent." Though the punishment for failing to follow this prohibition is not given in the text, it could be assumed that such an abomination would not just be *similar* to adultery but treated *as* adultery and punished accordingly.

The third rationale for the legislation comes in the command of Deut 24:4d: "You shall not bring sin on the land" (NASB). This last motive clause once again brings us to Lev 18. The idea that illicit sexual intercourse defiles the land is mentioned three times in Lev 18 (vv. 25, 27–28). Because the land is defiled, God says

---

[73] For further arguments, see William F. Luck, *Divorce and Remarriage: Recovering the Biblical View* (San Francisco: Harper & Row, 1987), 62.

[74] Craigie, *Deuteronomy,* 305.

that "I punished it for its iniquity [ʿāwôn], and the land vomited out its inhabitants" (v. 25). The same concept is found in Deut 24:4b, even though the noun
"iniquity" (ʿāwôn) is replaced with the verbal idea of "sin" being brought on the
land (ḥāṭāʾ in the hipʿil, "to bring sin"). The verbal root ḥṭʾ "sin" (to "miss a
mark, go astray")[75] may have been substituted to imply a somewhat less serious
infraction than the "iniquity" (ʿāwôn, "crooked behavior, perversion")[76] of Lev
18, but it also may here have been considered virtually synonymous.[77]

A man is not to remarry his wife when she has been married again to someone else for the same reason that Israel is not to engage in other illicit sexual intercourse. As already noted, to commit this abomination defiles the land and will
eventually lead to divine punishment as God causes the land to vomit out its inhabitants. As also noted in previous chapters of this study, this intertextual linkage to defiling the land in Lev 18 brings us to the realm of universally applicable
law. The "abominations" mentioned in Lev 18 (and reiterated in Lev 20) are forbidden not only for the native Israelite but also explicitly for the non-Israelite
"stranger" or "alien" (gēr) who sojourns among the children of Israel. Furthermore, as also pointed out earlier, these abominations caused the non-Israelite pagans who inhabited Canaan before Israel to be vomited out when they committed
these acts. Therefore the "abomination" and "defiling" quality of these acts clearly
are not simply ritual in nature, applying only to Israel, but timeless and universal,
applying to whoever practices them. Since Deut 24:4 is placed in the same category as the practices of Lev 18, it may be assumed that the prohibition against
marrying a former wife who has been married again is universal and of contemporary relevance in its application. Disregarding such prohibition will not only
bring defilement and sin upon the land of Israel, which God was giving to them
as an inheritance, but will also presumably defile any land where such practice is
carried out.

The Overall Purpose of the Legislation. There have been many suggestions regarding the overall purpose of the legislation in Deut 24:1–4. Eight major views
may be categorized and summarized:[78]

(1) *To ensure the proper legal procedure of divorce.* This assumes the translation of
     the KJV and other versions that place the apodosis already in v. 1a.

---

[75] BDB 306; HALOT 305. Cf. Alex Luc, "חָטָא," NIDOTTE 2:87–93.

[76] BDB 730; HALOT 800. Cf. Alex Luc, "עָוֹן," NIDOTTE 3:351.

[77] Cf. Lev 5:1, where the root ḥṭʾ, "to sin," results in ʿāwôn, "iniquity," from the same
action. See also Baruch J. Schwartz, "The Bearing of Sin in the Priestly Literature," in
*Pomegranates and Golden Bells: Studies in Biblical, Jewish, and Near Eastern Ritual, Law,
and Literature in Honor of Jacob Milgrom* (ed. David P. Wright, David Noel Freedman, and
Avi Hurvitz; Winona Lake, Ind.: Eisenbrauns, 1995), 8–17.

[78] For a listing/critique of many of these views, see esp. Hugenberger, *Marriage as a
Covenant,* 76–77; J. Carl Laney, "Deuteronomy 24:1–4 and the Issue of Divorce," BSac 149
(1992): 9–13; Westbrook, "The Prohibition," 388–91, 404–5; and Luck, *Divorce and Remarriage,* 63–65.

(2) *To discourage easy divorce (protect the first marriage).* This is the argument of John Murray and S. R. Driver, among others.[79] "The whole point of the four verses in question is to forestall hasty action by making it impossible to rectify the situation when divorce and remarriage to another takes place."[80]

(3) *To inhibit remarriage (avoid legalized adultery).* Craigie argues that the text treats subsequent remarriages as defilements similar to adultery. He regards the grounds for the divorce as perhaps just some type of "physical deficiency in the woman." The legislation restricts current divorce practices so that it does not become simply a "'legal' form of committing adultery."[81]

(4) *To protect the second marriage.* Reuven Yaron suggests that the legislation inhibits the social tensions that might arise from a "lover's triangle."[82]

(5) *To prevent a "type of incest."* Gordon Wenham argues that marriage creates a kind of indissoluble "kinship bond" between husband and wife, and thus after a divorce and remarriage to return to the first husband is a kind of incest that is forbidden in Lev 18:6–18.[83]

(6) *To "protect a stigmatized woman from further abuse by her offending first husband."*[84] According to William Luck, "Deuteronomy deals not with a sinning wife but a sinning husband."[85] In his view, the wife's action of *'erwat dābār* was not a sexual offense at all but some "embarrassing condition," and the husband was "so hard-hearted that he cast the woman from himself" and was "so unrepentant that he allowed her to be sexually coupled to another man."[86]

(7) *To codify the "natural repulsion" or taboo against having sexual intercourse with a woman who has cohabited with another man.* This view has found support in Calum Carmichael, who seeks to show evidence that such an attitude existed in ancient Israel.[87]

---

[79] Murray, *Divorce*, 3–16; Driver, *Deuteronomy*, 272.
[80] Jay Adams, *Marriage, Divorce, and Remarriage in the Bible* (Phillipsburg, N.J.: Presbyterian and Reformed, 1980), 62.
[81] Craigie, *Deuteronomy*, 305–7, quote at 305. Cf. John Calvin, *Commentaries on the Four Last Books of Moses Arranged in the Form of a Harmony* (trans. Charles William Bingham; 4 vols. Edinburgh: Calvin Translation Society, 1852–1855; repr., 4 vols. in 2; Grand Rapids: Baker, 1989), 3:94.
[82] Reuven Yaron, "The Restoration of Marriage," *JJS* 17 (1966): 1–11.
[83] Gordon J. Wenham, "The Restoration of Marriage Reconsidered," *JJS* 30 (1979): 36–40; William A. Heth and Gordon J. Wenham, *Jesus and Divorce: The Problem with the Evangelical Consensus* (Nashville: T. Nelson, 1984), 105–11 and passim.
[84] Luck, *Divorce and Remarriage*, 57–67, and passim.
[85] Ibid., 65.
[86] Ibid., 60–63.
[87] Calum M. Carmichael, *The Laws of Deuteronomy* (Ithaca, N.Y.: Cornell University Press, 1974), 203–7; idem, *Women, Law, and the Genesis Traditions* (Edinburgh: Edinburgh University Press, 1979), 8–21.

(8) *To deter greedy profit (unjust enrichment due to estoppel) by the first husband.*[88] Raymond Westbrook contends that this legislation is about property. In the first divorce (Deut 24:1), since there were moral grounds, the wife received no financial settlement, whereas in the second divorce (24:3) there were no moral grounds and so the wife received financial remuneration. The legislation is to keep the first husband from profiting twice, once to divorce her (and give her nothing) and once to remarry her (and obtain her financial settlement from her second husband). Westbrook notes that this interpretation fits nicely with the structural placement of this law in the section of Deuteronomic legislation dealing with theft.[89]

In light of the foregoing exegesis of this passage, we can evaluate the above proposals, underscoring what is consistent with the text and critiquing the points that stand in tension with exegetical data presented heretofore.[90]

The first view, that the law ensures a proper legal divorce procedure, is based upon a misunderstanding of the structure of the passage. As already pointed out, 24:1–4 does not legislate divorce or even sanction it. The legislation proper deals only with the prohibition of remarriage to the first husband after an intervening marriage. In fairness to this first view, however, it must be said that the very mention of certain conditions in the divorce proceedings does at least indicate that these conditions would have to be met in order for the legislation to apply. In the very toleration of divorce under these conditions, the passage gives some tacit recognition of a set procedure for divorce, including the mandatory inclusion of a divorce certificate for the wife who has been sent away.

The second view, that the purpose was to discourage hasty divorce, has more to commend it. The mention of specific divorce proceedings in the protasis of the legislation would have some tacit influence to this effect (as mentioned under view 1), but the apodosis, or legislation proper, would have further underscored this point. When the first husband contemplated a divorce, he had to reckon with the fact that such action would be final once the woman had remarried. He could never change his mind and try to woo her back. But Westbrook points out a weakness in the idea that this was the only purpose for the legislation: "The divorcing husband is hardly likely to have in mind the possible circumstances following the dissolution of a subsequent marriage by his wife."[91]

---

[88] Estoppel is the principle that a man who benefits from asserting certain facts may not then benefit a second time by conceding that these facts were otherwise than first asserted.

[89] Westbrook, "The Prohibition," 392–405.

[90] Others also find a combination of these rationales plausible. E.g., see John A. Thompson, *Deuteronomy: An Introduction and Commentary* (TOTC 5; Downers Grove, Ill.: InterVarsity, 1974), 245, who speaks favorably of views 2 and 4 above; and K&D, 1:950–53, who hold to a combination of views 2 and 6.

[91] Westbrook, "The Prohibition," 389. Against this view see also Thompson, *Deuteronomy,* 244; Wenham, "The Restoration of Marriage Reconsidered," 36; and Yaron, "The Restoration of Marriage," 5–6.

The third view, that the purpose was to inhibit remarriage, contains elements that find support in the text. Craigie is correct to argue that the remarriage of the woman (after a divorce on lesser grounds than extramarital sexual intercourse) is presented as tantamount to adultery in that she "defiles herself" (although she is not punished). He is also on the right track in seeing the legislation as curbing the excesses of divorce so that it becomes "legalized adultery." But Craigie broadens the meaning of *ʿerwat dābār* far too much when he sees it probably referring to a "physical deficiency" in the woman and not "indecent exposure." Craigie also misses the implication that it is the first husband who is ultimately culpable for having caused his wife to defile herself by the second marriage relationship.

The fourth view, that the purpose was to protect the second marriage, not the first, also has merit. If the divorced wife who has married again knows that she cannot get back together with her first husband, she would certainly be discouraged from planning any intrigue against her second husband so that he would divorce her. The first husband would likewise be prevented from trying to obtain his first wife back. Although these aspects seem to be part of what the law accomplished, this view "fails to explain why the rule would apply after the death of the second husband when the second marriage would no longer be in jeopardy."[92]

The fifth view, that the purpose was to prevent a type of incest, does not, as indicated above, have the weight of evidence from the text and context to support it. "The major difficulty with this view is that it seems to reach beyond what is clear to the reader. One wonders how many Israelites would have seen the connection between the 'one flesh' of the marriage union and the incest laws of Leviticus 18:6–18."[93] Westbrook moves closer to the main objection to Wenham's "type of incest" view: "[Wenham's] analysis cannot possibly apply to the Deuteronomic law because it completely ignores the intervening marriage. The law does not, as Wenham assumes, prohibit remarriage as such, and there is no way that we can see of the second marriage being a factor in the creation of an incestuous affinity."[94] The major problem of Wenham's position, as Westbrook already hints, is that it is founded on an erroneous view of the marriage covenant. Wenham assumes that the "one flesh" relationship in the marriage covenant is absolutely indissoluble, even by divorce and remarriage. Such a position is not supported in Gen 1–3 or elsewhere in Scripture.[95]

---

[92] Laney, "Deuteronomy 24:1–4," 10; cf. Westbrook, "The Prohibition," 390, for a similar critique. A possible rejoinder to this objection is that with the inclusion of the death of the second husband as a possibility for which the law is still in force, there would be no attempt on the life of the second husband by his wife or her former husband. But this does not seem to cover clear cases of the second husband's natural death. Against this view, see also Carmichael, *The Laws of Deuteronomy,* 204; and Wenham, "The Restoration of Marriage Reconsidered," 37.

[93] Laney, "Deuteronomy 24:1–4," 11.

[94] Westbrook, "The Prohibition," 390–91.

[95] Against this view, see also Harold W. Hoehner, "A Response to Divorce and Remarriage," in *Applying the Scriptures: Papers from ICBI Summit III* (ed. Kenneth Kantzer; [a paper read by Willam A. Heth]; Grand Rapids: Zondervan, 1987), 243.

The sixth view, that the purpose was to protect a stigmatized wife from further abuse from her offending first husband, has many points that square with the exegesis presented above. Luck is correct that the law implicates the first husband as the offending party (even though Luck arrives at this conclusion by a different route from what I have suggested).[96] He states, "the stigma [of 'defilement'] of the woman in Deuteronomy 24:4 does not so stigmatize her that the moral guilt hangs about her marriages to men other than her former husband. The stigma instead reflects back upon the man who caused the problem, that is, her first husband."[97] In emphasizing the first husband's culpability, however, Luck has tended to trivialize the grounds for divorce by indicating that ʿerwat dābār in 24:1 simply refers to "embarrassing circumstances" instead of "indecent exposure" as I have concluded.[98]

The seventh view, that the prohibition reflects a "natural repulsion" or taboo against having sexual relations with one who has cohabited with another, does not stand up to a rigorous scrutiny. Westbrook reexamines Carmichael's evidence for such a taboo in the OT and finds it wanting.[99] "We would suggest that, far from there being a natural repulsion, both biblical and ancient Near Eastern sources find nothing untoward in a man resuming relations with his wife after she has had relations with another, even amounting to marriage, providing no other factor makes resumption of the marriage improper."[100]

The eighth view, that the purpose was to deter greedy profit by the first husband, points in a promising direction, although it appears to go beyond the evidence in its specifics. Westbrook's distinction between two kinds of divorce functioning in 24:1–3 (the first based on moral grounds and the second only out of aversion) may find support from parallels in the Code of Hammurabi and the Mishnah[101] but, in my view, has no basis in the biblical text. As indicated above,

---

[96] Luck, *Divorce and Remarriage*, 62, instinctively recognizes the importance of the word "defiled" in the *hotpaʿal*, correctly labels it a "reflexive passive," and even states, "Moses went out of his way to make this form unusual!" But he does not draw out the implications of his observations.

[97] Ibid. Luck's argument rests on making an analogy with the rapist who causes his victim to be "defiled" even though she is an innocent party. "The 'defilement' of the woman reflects upon the rapist." In a similar manner the "defilement" of the woman in Deut 24:4 reflects upon the one who caused her to get into this situation of being defiled, i.e., her first husband by divorcing her and refusing to remarry her. Luck also rightly and significantly notes (ibid., based on Murray's observation) that "the defilement only seems to be taken into account with regard to the first husband—when the issue is of a remarriage to that one, after a marriage to another has occurred." This would be an additional support to the conclusions I reached earlier based on the *hotpaʿal* form of the word ṭāmēʾ in 24:4.

[98] Against this view, see also Hoehner, "A Response," 242.

[99] Westbrook, "The Prohibition," 392–93.

[100] Ibid., 392. Against this view, see also Wenham, "The Restoration of Marriage Reconsidered," 37.

[101] CH §§141–142 (*COS* 2.131:344; *ANET* 172), and *m. Ketub.* 7:6 (see the discussion above).

the divorce formula of 24:3 is probably an abbreviated version of the same type of divorce in 24:1.

Westbrook's position, in addition to being speculative, does not appear to take seriously enough the double condemnation of "abomination" (*tôʿēbâ*) and "bring sin [*ḥāṭāʾ* in the *hipʿil*] on the land" used with reference to the action prohibited in this legislation (24:4, NASB). If the legislation deals only with issues of property, there does not seem warrant for the strong terminology to condemn the action. Westbrook's view also assumes that the first divorce is not only legal but also under no divine condemnation, contrary to what I have argued is implied in the clause "she has been caused to defile herself" (translations mine). Finally, Westbrook's hypothetical distinction between two kinds of divorce in this passage does not square with the later canonical reference to this law in Jer 3:1, where the legislation of Deut 24:1–4 is clearly summarized as describing the general principle that a woman may not return to a former husband after she has been married to someone else, not as making a distinction between legitimate and illegitimate grounds for divorce. Aside from the weakness of Westbrook's proposal in its details, he does seek to make sense out of the placement of this law within the section of Deut 12–26 dealing with theft. If it does not deal with theft in the way that Westbrook suggests, he must be credited with attempting to wrestle with the larger issue of the theological context for this legislation.

The key to the overall purpose of the legislation in 24:1–4 is found in its placement within the larger context of Deuteronomic law. As just pointed out, this legislation is not placed within the section of Deuteronomy amplifying the seventh commandment, as one might expect, but within the section dealing with theft. The relationship between this legislation and theft should be placed in a much larger perspective than Westbrook proposes. The law of 24:1–4 prevents a man from treating a woman as mere chattel, property, to be swapped back and forth at will.[102] Her dignity and value as an individual person are upheld in this law. The focus of the law makes it illegal for the first husband to remarry his wife after he has divorced her and she has been married to another. What is more, the *hotpaʿel* of *ṭāmēʾ* in 24:4a seems to imply that the first husband, who caused his wife to defile herself by divorcing her, is causing her to commit what is tantamount to adultery and such divorce is not in harmony with the divine will, even if legally tolerated. The law is aimed, in its final placement within the larger context, to protect the woman from being robbed of her personhood.

This conclusion is reinforced by the very next law in this section of Deuteronomy (24:5): "When a man is newly married, he shall not go out with the army or be charged with any related duty. He shall be free at home one year, to be happy with the wife whom he has married." This law clearly indicates that its ultimate purpose is to enable the newly wedded man to stay at home "to be happy with the wife whom he has married." The law protects against robbing the newly

---

[102] As Christopher J. H. Wright puts it, she is to be protected from being "a kind of marital football, passed back and forth between irresponsible men" (*Deuteronomy* [NIBCOT 4; Peabody, Mass.: Hendrickson, 1996], 255).

married couple of their intimacy and happiness, and it especially protects the happiness of the wife.

The way is now prepared to see how 24:1–4 fits into the progression of thought in the section of Deuteronomic laws dealing with the eighth commandment, or theft. As Stephen Kaufman points out regarding the organization of the various laws within the thought units of a given commandment, they "are arranged according to observable principles of priority."[103] In Kaufman's insightful analysis of the Deuteronomic laws arranged under the eighth commandment, he notes that there are six paragraphs (which he labels A through E) in this section. The structure of the section starts with the theft of property (paragraphs A [23:20–21 (ET 23:19–20)], B [23:22–24 (ET 23:21–23)], and C [23:25–26 (ET 23:24–25)]). Then it moves to the theft of "life" (*nepeš*) in a metaphorical sense (paragraphs D [24:1–4 and 5] and E [24:6]). Finally, it deals with the theft of physical *nepeš* (kidnapping, paragraph F [24:7]).

Kaufman rightly points out that 24:1–4 and 5 belong together as one paragraph with a common theme. "Perhaps the current position of paragraph D within Word VII [the eighth commandment] offers an insight into the compiler's (or author's) understanding of the very essence of the two laws which comprise it. Both, like paragraph E and F that follow, were apparently seen as preventing the theft of *nepeš*—of the services and devotion of a groom to his bride, and of the self-respect of a divorced woman."[104]

Therefore, without ignoring other possible rationales for the legislation referred to above, 24:1–4 in its larger Deuteronomic context should be viewed primarily as serving to protect the rights of women. These include the rights of women to be remarried and protected from possible counterclaims by a former husband, yes, but more than this, the law serves to protect women's right to dignity and self-respect, especially in circumstances in which they may appear powerless. The law, in its implicit disapproval, although temporary toleration, of inequalities afforded women due to the hardness of men's hearts, points toward the day when such inequalities will be resolved by a return to the Edenic ideal for marriage.

Jesus announces such a day in his teaching on divorce. Deuteronomy 24:1–4 contains far-reaching implications for understanding the interpretation of Jesus' divorce pronouncements in Matt 5 and 19 and for properly recognizing the hermeneutical relationship between OT and NT divorce/remarriage legislation (see the afterword to this study).

It appears that the potentially abusive and male-dominated practices such as divorce must be understood along the same lines as institutions such as slavery, which God regulated by means of legislation but did not totally abolish in the social life of OT Israel. Because they "were so hard-hearted," God tolerated certain situations to continue while making very clear in Gen 1–3 and in the context of the laws themselves that "from the beginning it was not so" (Matt 19:8). God

---

[103] Stephen A. Kaufman, "The Structure of the Deuteronomic Law," *Maarav* 1–2 (1978–1979): 115.

[104] Ibid., 156–57, n. 109.

revealed his great patience and condescension in meeting Israel where she was and yet calling her up to a higher standard. The divinely given Mosaic legislation was revolutionary for the times, lifting the standard of ethics in Israel (particularly the view of sexuality and the treatment of women) above the ethics of the Egypt from which the Israelites had come and the Canaan to which they were going. And overarching the illustrative case laws of the Mosaic code stand the broad principles of the Decalogue, the full application of which to the area of sexuality would lead an enlightened Israel back to the Edenic ideal.

Other Pentateuchal Legislation Dealing with Divorce

Prohibitions of Divorce. In two Deuteronomic passages—both in the section of Deuteronomic laws amplifying the seventh commandment[105]—divorce is prohibited under certain circumstances. The first passage, Deut 22:13–19, deals with the case of a husband's slander against his wife, in which he claims that she concealed from him that she was not a virgin when he married her (see ch. 8, above). If these charges are proven false by presentation of the "evidence of the young woman's virginity" (i.e., the blood-spotted bedclothes or garments), then the husband is fined, and "She shall remain his wife; he shall not be permitted to divorce [*šlḥ*] her as long as he lives" (22:19). Thus the newly married bride is protected from the whims and slander of her husband.[106]

The second case in which divorce is prohibited is when a man is caught raping/seducing an unbetrothed/unmarried virgin (22:28–29): "If a man meets a virgin who is not engaged, and seizes [*tāpaś*] her and lies with her, and they are caught in the act, the man who lay with her shall give fifty shekels of silver to the young woman's father, and she shall become his wife. Because he violated her [*ʿānâ*, in the *piʿel*] he shall not be permitted to divorce [*šālaḥ*] her as long as he lives." This law is an extension of the parallel law in Exod 22:15–16 (ET 22:16–17); both deal with what we could today call statutory rape, in which the unmarried woman acquiesced and was a willing partner in the sexual encounter (see ch. 8, above, regarding premarital sex). An almost identical law is found in the Middle Assyrian Laws, including the provision that "her ravisher shall marry her and not cast her off" unless the father of the one ravished objects.[107] As pointed out above in the overview of divorce in the ancient Near East, however, the Middle Assyrian law further provides that the rapist's wife shall be raped and not given back to the rapist. In contrast, the biblical law does not sanction rape even as a *lex talionis* provision against a rapist. The biblical law respects the personhood of the

---

105 Ibid., 138.

106 From the perspective of the twenty-first-century reader, the legislation which prohibits the husband from divorcing his wife may not seem to respect the personhood of the wife, if she is bound to spend the rest of her life with the man who slandered her. But, as will be argued below, this passage does not forbid the wife from divorcing her husband, if circumstances warrant, and such provision seems likely in the context of other pentateuchal passages.

107 MAL A§55 (*ANET* 185; cf. *COS* 2.132:359).

woman even if she is the wife of a rapist. The rapist's wife is not punished for the crime of the rapist.

The question may be asked, How is it respecting a woman's personhood when she has to marry, and spend the rest of her life with, the man who raped her? First, it must be emphasized that these two biblical passages do not deal with what we could consider forcible rape, but rather with statutory rape, i.e., cases in which both man and woman were consenting partners (although she was seduced). Thus the woman is not forced to marry and spend the rest of her life with a stranger who forcibly overpowered and raped her, but to marry a sexual partner with whom she willingly had sexual relations. This penalty served to discourage premarital sex and highlight the seriousness of the offense. Second, as pointed out above in ch. 8, Exod 22:16 [ET 22:17] adds an exception clause in which the father of the violated girl may not consent to her marrying the one who seduced her (presumably in cases where he was already married or where he would not make a good husband). Third, the limitation of the man's right to divorce served to protect a woman from the whims of a man who might want to just "love her and leave her." By engaging in premarital sex, the man was under obligation to marry his sexual partner and continue to provide for her social and financial security. Such protection was especially crucial in a patriarchal society in which a divorced woman would find herself defenseless and unlikely to find another marriage partner after having been cast off by her husband. Finally, although the husband is forbidden ever to divorce the woman, there is no prohibition of the woman divorcing the man, if circumstances warrant. As will be argued below, such "right" of the woman in divorce, although not explicit in the pentateuchal passages, was very likely assumed in pentateuchal law and practiced in Israelite society.

Prohibitions against Marrying Divorced Women. Leviticus 21 describes two special prohibitions against priests marrying divorced women. Verse 7 speaks of the common priests: "They shall not marry a prostitute [zōnâ] or a woman who has been defiled [raped] [wahălālâ],[108] neither shall they marry a woman divorced [gāraš, in the qal pass.] from her husband. For they are holy to their God." Verse 14 speaks of the high priest: "A widow, or a divorced [gāraš, in the qal pass.] woman, or a woman who has been defiled, a prostitute, these he shall not marry. He shall marry a virgin of his own kin."

Note the progression in holiness, from common person, who could presumably marry any of the aforementioned classes of women denied to the priests; to the common priest, who could not marry a prostitute or a divorcee but could marry a widow; to the high priest, who must only marry a virgin of his own house who has never been married. "We meet here [in the OT] the

---

[108] See Jacob Milgrom, *Leviticus 17–22: A New Translation with Introduction and Commentary* (AB 3A; New York: Doubleday, 2000), 1806–8, for a summary and critique of the various suggested meanings of this term. I follow his interpretation that this word is probably best translated "desecrated pierced one," referring to a woman who has been raped. See also ch. 12, below.

higher standard demanded of God's special ministers which we shall find again in the New Testament."[109]

Exclusion of divorced women does not necessarily mean there was a strong stigma attached to being divorced. Milgrom points out that in the list of prohibited women for the common priest to marry, which is given in descending order of defect, the reference to the divorced woman comes last on the list. Similarly, for the high priest, the list of prohibited women moves (chiastically) in ascending order of defect, and next to the innovated reference to a widow, the divorced woman comes first.[110] Thus the divorced woman was the least objectionable on the list for the common priest, and next-to-least objectionable on the list for the high priest. The exemption of the widow for the common priest seems to indicate "that the prohibition focuses on reputation, not on virginity."[111] The fact that there is a distinction between the widow (whom the common priest could marry) and the divorcee (whom he could not marry) may imply, moreover, a recognition that divorce, even though legally tolerated in Deut 24:1–4, was not God's moral ideal.

Similar restrictions on the priests are repeated in the legislation of Ezek 44:22 for the service in the new temple: "They shall not marry a widow, or a divorced woman, but only a virgin of the stock of the house of Israel, or a widow who is the widow of a priest."

Rights of Divorced Women. Two pentateuchal passages speak to the issue of divorced women's rights. This first is Lev 22:12–13: "If a priest's daughter marries a layman, she shall not eat of the offering of the sacred donations; but if a priest's daughter is widowed or divorced [*gāraš*, in the *qal* pass., lit. 'one driven out'], without offspring, and returns to her father's house, as in her youth, she may eat of her father's food. No lay person shall eat of it." According to this legislation, if the divorced woman has no children, she may return to her premarital status in her father's house. Here is clearly a provision to care for the divorced woman if she has no other means of support. The second passage is Num 30:10 (ET 30:9), part of a chapter containing various laws concerning vows: "But every vow of a widow or of a divorced [*gāraš*, in the *qal* pass.] woman, by which she has bound herself, shall be binding upon her." This law upholds the right of a divorced woman to be accountable for herself in legal affairs, in contrast to a married woman, who is under the legal protection of her father or husband (see Num 30:4–9 [ET 30:3–8]).

A Woman's Right to Divorce. At least two passages seem to imply a woman's rights to a divorce, but these case laws concern the very special circumstances of a master's marriage to his female servant. The first, Exod 21:26–27, states, "When a slaveowner strikes the eye of a male or female slave, destroying it, the owner shall let the slave go, a free person [*laḥopšî yĕšallĕḥenû*, lit. 'shall send him/her to (be)

[109] Andrew Cornes, *Divorce and Remarriage: Biblical Principles and Pastoral Practice* (Grand Rapids: Eerdmans, 1993), 139.

[110] Milgrom, *Leviticus 17–22*, 1807, 1819–20, 1834–36.

[111] Ibid., 1808.

free'], to compensate for the eye. If the owner knocks out a tooth of a male or female slave, the slave shall be let go, a free person [*laḥopšî yĕšallĕḥenû*, lit. 'shall
send him/her to (be) free'], to compensate for the tooth." Although this law deals
in general with the right of a servant, male or female, to be released if assaulted by
his/her master, who thereby causes permanent physical injury, one may undoubtedly assume that "covered under this law would be the case of a maidservant who
suffered such abuse and who happened to be married to her master. Her release
would end not only her servitude, but also her marriage."[112] The verb *šālaḥ* in this
context seems to imply both sending her away from the marriage (i.e., the right to
a divorce) and sending her away from servitude (i.e., the right to be set free).

The second passage is Deut 21:10–14, coming under the general heading of
laws pertaining to manslaughter (presumably because of its context, dealing with
treatment of prisoners of war).[113] The essence of the law is that if a man sees a female prisoner of war after a battle and desires to take her as a wife, then she is to
be brought to his house and allowed to mourn for her father and mother for a
month, after which time he may take her as his wife and have sexual relations
with her. "But if you are not satisfied with her, you shall let her go free [*šillaḥtāh
lĕnapšāh*, lit. 'send her according to her soul'] and not sell her for money. You
must not treat her as a slave [or 'as merchandise' (*ʿāmar*, in the *hitpaʿel*)],[114] since
you have dishonored [*ʿānâ*] her" (21:14).

This legislation provides protection for the defenseless captured slave girl.
Immediate marriage or sexual relations with her is forbidden. This would temper
the lust of the soldier to rape a female prisoner of war. She is allowed a month to
mourn for her father and mother (who are probably either dead or left behind)
and adjust to her new situation in a new land. Such provision for delay would also
make the Israelite soldier slower to marry the slave girl. The provision concerning
divorce also works toward this end while upholding two rights for the woman.
The verb *šālaḥ* in this context, as in Exod 21:26–27 above, seems to imply both
sending her away from the marriage (i.e., the right to a divorce) and sending her
away from servitude (i.e., the right to be set free). These provisions would certainly give the prospective husband pause before marrying and before divorcing
the captive girl: if he divorces her, he also loses her as a slave and receives no financial profit from her leaving. Thus this law gives the woman prisoner of war
some protection and potential compensation for having been "dishonored" (or
"violated," i.e., subjected to both the forced marriage and the forced divorce).

---

[112] Gane, "Old Testament Principles," 55–56.

[113] See discussion in Kaufman, "The Structure of the Deuteronomic Law," 134–37.

[114] This Hebrew word is found only here and in Deut 24:7. Various suggestions have
been made for the precise meaning: "to trade with" (*HALOT* 849); "to treat as merchandise" (Craigie, *Deuteronomy,* 282); and "to deal tyrannically with, treat someone brutally"
(Ignatius Swart and I. Cornelius, "עמר," *NIDOTTE* 3:441). On the basis of the context,
Swart and Cornelius (ibid.) summarize the probable semantic range of the word in Deuteronomy: "an oppressive deed that has devastating physical and psychological impact on
the afflicted person. The latter is mistreated, forced to submit to the will of a stronger
party, reduced to servile existence, and his or her whole person degraded."

Some scholars have suggested that a third passage, Exod 21:7–11, also speaks of circumstances under which a maidservant had a right to divorce from her master. It is claimed that this legislation upholds the right of a slave girl to "go out free [both from slavery and from being wife]" (v. 11 NKJV) if her master/husband marries another wife and fails to provide for his first (slave) wife's basic needs: her "food, clothing, or marital rights" (v. 10). But as concluded regarding this passage in the discussion of polygamy (ch. 5, above), the word often translated "conjugal rights" or "marriage rights" in v. 10 ('*ōnâ*) is a hapax legomenon in the OT and should probably instead be translated "oils/ointments" or "habitation/shelter." Furthermore, this passage probably does not deal with either the marriage of the slave woman or of her right to a divorce for neglect (passive abuse, i.e., failure to provide for her) (see ch. 5, above). In v. 8 many translators follow the LXX and translate, "he betroths her *to himself* [*lô*]," but the better reading, with most Hebrew manuscripts, is, "he does *not* [*lōʾ*] betroth her" (translation mine). If he does not betroth her, then "If he takes another wife" (v. 10) would not mean a second wife but another wife in her stead. Thus the context favors the interpretation that the master does not betroth the woman (for himself), does not cohabit with her, but takes another woman as his wife instead. Thus this text is probably not discussing a divorce/remarriage situation.

Although there are no pentateuchal passages mentioning a free (nonslave) woman's right to divorce, this right cannot be categorically ruled out and in fact is highly likely. As observed in previous chapters, the bulk of legal material in the Pentateuch is written in the masculine gender, and yet many of these laws are clearly intended to apply to both men and women. It is possible that gender inclusivity was intended also in the case of divorce legislation. Such was clearly the practice of the fifth-century B.C.E. Jewish community in Elephantine, in which women were able to divorce their husbands (see the conclusion of ch. 6, above), and as indicated above in the discussion of ANE practices regarding divorce, a strong Semitic tradition throughout biblical history from as early as the second millennium B.C.E. gives the wife equal rights with her husband to initiate divorce if there are grounds for this divorce. Such also seems to have been the case in Hittite society. In light of this strong ANE tradition of mutual rights for both husband and wife in divorce, this very likely was also true in the Israelite culture. At the same time, as argued regarding Deut 24:1–4, any "right" to divorce, on the part of either man or woman, though tolerated within the Israelite legal system, is presented as ultimately morally opposed to the will of Yahweh.

Divorce/Remarriage in the Preexilic Prophets

The two passages in the preexilic prophets that directly mention the term "divorce"—Isa 50:1 and Jer 3:1, 6–8—are both allusions to Deut 24:1–4 (which is discussed above). The discussion here of these two passages will be limited mainly to clarifying what advances or developments, if any, are made in the prophetic passages over the Deuteronomic legislation. A third passage in the Prophets may allude to divorce without using the term: Hos 2:4 (ET 2:2). Two additional

passages in the Former Prophets (1 Sam 25:44; Judg 14:20–15:2) give narrative
evidence for a woman's remarriage after abandonment by her husband. We will
first examine the possible divorce passages (starting with Hos 2:4, since chronologically it probably comes first of the three), with particular focus upon the
phraseology that seems to denote divorce proceedings and/or remarriage. Then
we will briefly look at the cases of a woman's remarriage after abandonment by
her husband.

Hosea 2:4. We have already looked at Hos 2 in the context of the fertility cults
and prostitution (in chs. 3 and 7, above). The major question to be answered here
is the following: did God divorce Israel in Hos 2? Commentators have brought to
bear strong arguments on both sides of this question.[115] Maria Dass, surveying
the precise wording of the marriage and divorce formulae throughout the ancient
Near East and Second Temple Judaism, has shown that the formula in Hos 2:4a
(ET 2:2a) has no precise parallel with any of these sources and should probably
not be taken as a divorce formula. Rather it is a negated statement of the marriage
formula such as is found in the Elephantine texts, and she suggests it should be
regarded as "a formula of separation."[116] "This formula itself does not effect a
legal divorce but is a prelegal or extralegal act. It indicates a temporary break in
the relationship, which can eventually lead to judicial action."[117] In light of the
larger context of Hos 2, Dass's conclusions are convincing. God threatened to divorce Israel but did not in fact do so, and Hosea did not divorce Gomer.

As divine Husband of Israel and plaintiff in the legal proceedings against his
wife, God contemplates divorce as one of the possibilities but does not follow
through on his threat. Instead God seeks not divorce but reconciliation, not the
death penalty but the end of Israel's unfaithfulness. God invokes a time of temporary separation but envisions a renewed relationship, a new beginning, with his
estranged bride.[118]

---

[115] For the major arguments in favor of there being a divorce described in Hos 2, see,
e.g., Markham J. Geller, "The Elephantine Papyri and Hosea 2,3: Evidence for the Form of
the Early Jewish Divorce Writ," *JSJ* 8 (1977–1978): 139–48; Paul A. Kruger, "The Marriage
Metaphor in Hosea 2:4–17 against Its Ancient Near Eastern Background," *OTE* 5 (1992):
7–25; and Cornes, *Divorce and Remarriage,* 142–45. For the most complete argument that
Hos 2 is not speaking of a divorce, see Francis I. Andersen and David Noel Freedman,
Hosea: A New Translation with Introduction and Commentary (AB 24A; New York:
Doubleday, 1989), 221–24. Cf. A. A. Macintosh, *A Critical and Exegetical Commentary on
Hosea* (Edinburgh: T&T Clark, 1997), 41: "Since the mother [in Hos 2] is herself effectively the agent of this process and since appeal to her reason is urged in order to impede
it, the statement 'she is not my wife etc.' cannot be understood as a quotation of a divorce
formula." See also Dwight Harvey Small, "The Prophet Hosea: God's Alternative to Divorce for the Reason of Infidelity," *Journal of Psychology and Theology* 7 (1979): 133–40.

[116] Maria Dass, "The Divorce (?) Formula in Hos 2:4a," *Indian Theological Studies* 34
(1997): 59–67, quote at 67.

[117] Ibid., 68.

[118] If one asks how God could refrain from divorcing Israel when the Deuteronomic
law called for even more than divorce—the death penalty—Andersen and Freedman, *Hosea,*
219, answer, "The speech is full of recriminations, and punishments are threatened. But the

Although it seems probable that there is no actual divorce in Hos 2, later in the covenant lawsuit of this book (beginning in 4:1) it appears that the northern kingdom (called Ephraim) spurns all of God's appeals and there is no option left but divorce. Divorce seems to be alluded to in such passages as 4:17: "Ephraim is joined to idols—let him alone." So also 11:8 seems to describe the anguishing struggle of God as Lover as he is forced to let her go her way: "How can I give you up, Ephraim? How can I hand you over, O Israel?" That a "divorce" between God and the northern kingdom was inevitable is confirmed in other prophetic references to this situation (particularly in Jeremiah, as noted below).

Isaiah 50:1. In Isa 50:1, tucked in amid the Servant Songs of Isa 42–53, the Lord asks Judah (the southern kingdom),

> (A) Where is your mother's bill of divorce [*sēper kĕrîtût*]
>   with which I put her away [*šālaḥ*]?
>
> (B) Or which of my creditors is it to whom I have sold you?
>
> (B′) No, because of your sins you were sold,
>
> (A′) and for your transgressions your mother was put away [*šlḥ*].

This poetic verse is clearly in a chiastic structure, ABB′A′. The divorce theme occupies the outer two members of the verse, and the selling to the creditors the inner two members.

The larger context of this passage is Yahweh's legal defense in view of the charges made against him by the exiles. The main charge is recorded in 49:14: "But Zion said, 'The LORD has forsaken me, my Lord has forgotten me.'" Although 50:1 mentions the terms for divorce and the bill of divorce, it seems most likely that there is no actual divorce. Yahweh asks, in other words, "Where is the legal divorce document [as mentioned in Deut 24:1–4] to prove your charges?" The preponderance of commentators on this passage recognize that the hypothetical question here demands a negative answer.[119] There is no

---

way remains open for forgiveness, a possibility beyond law. We remember that death was the penalty for adultery. The laws of marriage are intersected here by the provisions of the covenant between Yahweh and Israel. The broken covenant could be mended because Yahweh's love was stronger than his wrath." It is also possible that there is a parallel to the experience of Gomer, and her experience was not adultery. She may well have been involved in cultic ritual sex or prostitution and gone back to her old profession. Hosea then bought her back. Prostitution did not carry the death penalty. Likewise Israel's metaphorical prostitution would not require the death penalty.

[119] See, e.g., J. Ridderbos, *Isaiah* (BSC; Grand Rapids: Zondervan, 1985), 447: "Concerning Zion (Israel) the Lord points out, in a rhetorical question to which only a negative reply can be given, that he has given her no certificate of divorce (proof of a formal divorce) in order to renounce her with it." See also John L. McKenzie, *Second Isaiah: A New Translation with Introduction and Commentary* (AB 20; Garden City, N.Y.: Doubleday, 1968), 112: "The question here is a denial that there has ever been a divorce. Yahweh remains faithful to Israel." Cf. Edward J. Young, *The Book of Isaiah* (3 vols.; NICOT; Grand Rapids: Eerdmans, 1972), 3:295: "To the first question a negative answer is expected. Zion

divorce document. No divorce document—no divorce. Yahweh's response to the charge against him is thus to the effect that he has not in fact divorced Judah. It appears that the Lord is playing upon the twofold meaning of the word *šālaḥ*, "to send away." It can have the technical meaning of legal "divorce." This God claims he has not done to the southern kingdom of Judah as he did to the northern kingdom of Israel (as will become apparent in Jer 3:8). At the same time, in the chiastic parallel to this in the A' member of Isa 50:1, Yahweh acknowledges that Judah has been "put away" (*šālaḥ*) for their transgressions. In this case, the Lord apparently uses the nontechnical sense of *šālaḥ*, "sent away" not in the sense of divorced but in the sense of going away into exile.[120] In the case between Yahweh and Judah, there is only "an informal separation or 'sending away,' and consequently [there is] no hindrance to subsequent resumption of the marriage."[121]

The sequel to this courtroom scene is found in Isa 54:5–6. Verse 5 assures Judah that "your Maker is your husband, the LORD of hosts is His name." Verses 6–8 describe the "reconciliation of a broken marriage": " 'For the LORD has called you like a wife forsaken [lit. 'left'; *ʿāzab* does not necessarily imply blame to the one who leaves] and grieved in spirit, like the wife of a man's youth when she is

---

has no writing of divorcement and hence cannot produce one, for God has never sent her away." As a last example, note the summary of J. Alec Motyer, *The Prophecy of Isaiah: An Introduction and Commentary* (Downers Grove, Ill.: InterVarsity, 1993), 397: "The thrust of the two hypothetical situations, divorce and sale, is to ask if something irretrievable has happened, terminating a relationship. . . . The absence of a *certificate,* however, would indicate that this procedure [of divorce] had not even been started and that, therefore, the door was open to reconciliation." Not only does the hypothetical question itself call for a negative answer; the combination of the interrogative *ʾê*, "where?" with the enclitic *zeh* at the beginning of the sentence, to be translated something like "Where, I wonder . . . ?" (*IBHS* §18.4b), gives an even greater force of implausibility to Yahweh's question receiving a positive answer. Despite the evidence for a negative answer to Yahweh's question (i.e., no divorce of Israel on God's part), John N. Oswalt, *The Book of Isaiah, Chapters 40–66* (NICOT; Grand Rapids: Eerdmans, 1998), 318, on the basis of the chiastic parallelism with "was put away" (*šālaḥ*) later in the same verse, argues that Yahweh has indeed divorced Israel's mother, Zion, but not arbitrarily: "God tells them to produce the certificate of divorce, on which they will see that it was because of their rebellions that God had put away their *mother,* Zion." Oswalt rightly recognizes the chiastic parallel in this verse, involving a repetition of *šālaḥ*, but in light of the strong evidence (presented above) from the hypothetical question, which expects a negative answer, and its introduction of implausibility, I find it is preferable to see in this verse a play on the twofold meaning of *šālaḥ* as explained below, rather than positing a divorce as Oswalt does.

[120] Cf. Isa 27:8, where *šālaḥ* is used in the sense of "exile."

[121] Roger N. Whybray, *Isaiah 40–66* (NCB; London: Oliphants, 1975), 149. Cf. George A. F. Knight, *Servant Theology: A Commentary on the Book of Isaiah 40–45* (ITC; Grand Rapids: Eerdmans, 1984), 143: "What God is saying here to Zion's children—in the plural—is this: 'I didn't *divorce* your mother (when I sent Zion into exile), and the proof of that is that she can show no certificate to that effect. . . . [But] I had to deal with you in some way for your transgressions,' God explains. 'It was not that I was bankrupt of love. Yet I had to make a plan. My plan was to allow you to leave home, and so to let you suffer a just punishment (40:2) for your unfaithfulness; but I vowed to have you back thereafter.' "

cast off,' says your God. 'For a brief moment I abandoned you, but with great compassion I will gather you. In overflowing wrath for a moment I hid my face from you, but with everlasting love I will have compassion on you,' says the LORD, your Redeemer." There was no divorce with the southern kingdom; it was more like a brief separation due to Judah's sins. But now God is bringing her to himself in covenant reconciliation (cf. 54:9–10).

This extended Isaianic passage thus presupposes Deut 24:1–4 and develops the imagery of that passage in applying it to the relationship between God and Judah. On the basis of what is indicated as part of a divorce proceeding in Deut 24:1–4, God argues that since there was no bill of divorce, there was no divorce. Instead of divorce, God desires reconciliation after a time of estrangement and separation.

Jeremiah 3:1, 6–8. Jeremiah 3 comes on the heels of Yahweh's legal indictment of Judah because of her sins in Jer 2. The time of writing, probably the early years of Jeremiah's ministry, represents the period of Josiah's reformation, probably before the finding of the book of the law in the temple in 621 B.C.E.[122] In its canonical position within the book, Jer 3:1–5 represents a transition from the legal covenant indictment of Jer 2 to a passionate call to repentance in 3:6–4:4. We focus first upon 3:1:

> If a man divorces [šālaḥ] his wife
> and she goes from him
> and becomes another man's wife,
> will he return to her?
> Would not such a land be greatly polluted?
> You have played the whore with many lovers;
> and would you return to me?
>   says the LORD.

The people's words in this verse corresponds precisely with the law of Deut 24:1: a woman may not be remarried to her former husband after she has been married to someone else, for this would pollute the land. The answers to the questions of whether such a woman could return to her first husband and whether the land would be polluted are obvious to Jeremiah's hearers; they would heartily agree with the Deuteronomic legislation as it applies to marriage/divorce situations on the human level. But God now takes this human analogy and applies it to the covenantal relationship between himself and his people. He utilizes a *qal wāḥômer* or a fortiori argument.[123] If it is against the law for a wife to return to her first husband after a subsequent marriage, how much more monstrous is it for the people of Judah to imagine that they can return to Yahweh after having

---

[122] For discussion of the historical background to this passage, see, e.g., James A. Thompson, *The Book of Jeremiah* (NICOT; Grand Rapids: Eerdmans, 1980), 186–87.

[123] See discussion of this argument in Mary E. Shields, "Circumscribing the Prostitute: The Rhetorics of Intertextuality, Metaphor, and Gender in Jeremiah 3.1–4.4" (PhD diss., Emory University, 1996), 126.

affairs with many lovers. They want to have their cake and eat it too: to "whore" after the Baal fertility cults and at the same time make a pretense of "returning" to Yahweh.

One cannot expect that the analogy between the human marital situation and the divine-human covenantal relationship will stand on all fours.

> It would be unwise to press the opening analogy of marital law, for as the prophet develops the theme, he freely adapts it to his immediate purpose. (Thus, though the legal summary indicates that the original husband cannot *return* to the original wife, in the development of the theme, the concern is with the return of Israel, the wife, to the Lord, the husband. But the purpose of the chapter is not legal; the summarized legislation merely provides the starting point for the elaboration of unfaithfulness and the invitation to return to God that follows.)[124]

In the verses that follow (vv. 2–5), Yahweh elaborates on the extent of Judah's unfaithfulness. Then Jeremiah develops the "whoring" theme in a different direction from Hosea, who had written a century earlier. Verses 6–8 record Yahweh's dialogue with the prophet:

> The LORD said to me in the days of King Josiah: Have you seen what she did, that faithless one, Israel, how she went up on every high hill and under every green tree, and played the whore there? And I thought, "After she has done all this she will return to me"; but she did not return, and her false sister Judah saw it. She saw that for all the adulteries of that faithless one, Israel, I had sent her away with a decree of divorce; yet her false sister Judah did not fear, but she too went and played the whore.

In addressing his Judaite hearers, the Lord alludes to the experience of the northern kingdom of Israel in the time of Hosea (eighth century B.C.E.). God confirms to Jeremiah a century later what was implicit in Hosea (not in Hos 1–3 but later in the lawsuit, 4:17 and 11:8), that he indeed did eventually divorce Israel. He had called to her to return (*šûb*, which means both "return" and "repent") to him (v. 7; cf. the pleas of Hosea), but she had spurned his appeals. Finally, nothing was left but a divorce. This "divorce" undoubtedly refers to the fall of the northern kingdom of Israel to the Assyrian army, climaxing in the capture of the capital city of Samaria in 722/721 B.C.E. The majority of the population was deported to distant lands and replaced by foreigners.

In this passage the Lord clearly refers to this collapse and exile of the northern kingdom as divorce: "I had sent her away with a decree of divorce." But according to the Mosaic law, the acts of harlotry/adultery called for more than divorce, as already pointed out. The punishment should have been death. Why, then, does God speak of divorcing Israel? Several possible reasons may be advanced. The reference to the divorce/remarriage law of Deut 24:1–4 in Jer 3:1 may have set the tone for the analogy, and the Lord continues the analogy of divorce here. Another possibility follows from what was already implicit in the

---

[124] Peter C. Craigie, Page H. Kelley, and Joel F. Drinkard Jr., *Jeremiah 1–25* (WBC 26; Dallas: Word, 1991), 51.

pentateuchal legal system: an allowance for a husband to commute the death sentence of his wife in cases of sexual infidelity (as was concluded at the end of ch. 8, above). It may be that in the time of Jeremiah the death penalty was not normally carried out in cases of adultery or harlotry but divorce was the accepted substitute punishment instead and that God is depicting consequences of a ruptured relationship in terms familiar to his listeners.

Furthermore, as noted, God, in dealing with the covenant relationship with Israel, does not bind himself in this passage to follow exactly the analogy of the human marital laws in all their provisions. Finally, and what is probably most to the point, indeed the "divorce" that befell the northern kingdom was nothing less than a death penalty in practice. The northern kingdom of Israel was destroyed and ceased to exist; the majority of the population was either killed or taken into exile. So, although the terminology for divorce is utilized, in historical reality the punishment corresponds more precisely with the death penalty that was legally prescribed for adultery. The depiction of this situation by Ezek 23:5–10 consistently portrays Israel's sin as harlotry/adultery and the divine punishment as death/destruction. The main point made by both Ezekiel and Jeremiah in referring to the experience of the northern kingdom is to stir up the southern kingdom of Judah to repent/return to wholehearted covenant faithfulness to Yahweh. Both prophets point out that the treachery and unfaithfulness of the people of Judah, who witnessed what happened to Israel, were even worse than their northern neighbors'.

Despite the divine indictment of Judah's unfaithfulness recorded by Jeremiah, there is no mention of divorce regarding Judah—Yahweh seeks instead reconciliation as she returns to him:

> Return, O faithless children,
>> says the LORD,
>> for I am your master;
>> I will take you, one from a city and two from a family,
>> and I will bring you to Zion.

> I will give you shepherds after my own heart, who will feed you with knowledge and understanding. And when you have multiplied and increased in the land, in those days, says the LORD, they shall no longer say, "The ark of the covenant of the LORD." It shall not come to mind, or be remembered, or missed; nor shall another one be made. At that time Jerusalem shall be called the throne of the LORD, and all nations shall gather to it. (Jer 3:14–17)

In summarizing the essence of the Deuteronomic legislation regarding divorce, Jer 3:1 accurately reflects the meaning of Deut 24:1–4. In later verses, however, Jeremiah makes a metaphorical application of this law to the situation between God and Israel/Judah. It is important hermeneutically not to utilize this metaphorical application of the legislation in an attempt to interpret Deut 24:1–4 or vice versa, as some have mistakenly attempted to do.

> Jer 3:8 is a prophetic passage, not a legal passage. It reflects legal practice, but in an extended sense and for a theological purpose. We are dealing here with historical

relationships between YHWH and nations, which are analogous to, but not identical with, relationships between human husbands and wives as governed by law. . . . Thus, it is clear that Pentateuchal legal practice cannot be safely extrapolated from a theological prophetic oracle.[125]

Judges 14:20–15:2. According to this narrative, when Samson returned to his father's house in anger after his newly wedded bride had revealed his riddle to her countrymen, "Samson's wife was given to his companion, who had been his best man" (Judg 14:20). Judges 15:2 reports that Samson's father-in-law interpreted Samson's return to his father's house as a case of abandoning his wife: "I was sure," said the father-in-law, "that you had rejected [qal inf. abs. plus qal pf. of śānēʾ, lit. 'thoroughly hated'] her; so I gave her to your companion." Although this incident may reflect Philistine practice of the time, it gives no indication of the divine will of Yahweh regarding the right of divorce after abandonment.

1 Samuel 25:44. After David fled from King Saul, Saul gave "his daughter Michal, David's wife, to Palti [or Paltiel, 2 Sam 3:15] son of Laish, who was from Gallim" (1 Sam 25:44). Although Saul possessed royal power and thoroughly detested David, nonetheless it does appear from the narrative that a husband's abandonment of his wife was regarded in Israel, as in Philistia, as grounds for dissolving the marriage (at least under certain circumstances) and leaving the abandoned wife free to remarry. In David's case, however, he abandoned Michal because he was forced to and not through any fault of his own, and thus David did not consider that his marriage to her was legitimately dissolved.[126] Apparently reflecting the prevailing Israelite custom, under which only willful desertion of one's wife was grounds for dissolving a marriage, David later employed his political power to dissolve Michal's marriage with Palti and to take her back (2 Sam 3:13–16). David would most likely not have viewed this move as a violation of Deut 24:1–4 (prohibiting taking back one's wife after an intervening marriage; see above), since he had not divorced Michal or even willfully abandoned her.

Some may wish to deduce from the above narratives concerning Samson and David that God in OT times allowed the practice of divorce on the grounds of abandonment. But there is no pentateuchal legislation setting forth such grounds for divorce. Further, the narrator in these stories seems to give no clues that such a practice receives the divine sanction. Hence it seems unwarranted to allow these passages to determine one's understanding of the (permissive) will of God regarding grounds for divorce/remarriage in the OT.

---

[125] Gane, "Old Testament Principles," 51. For a summary of the major departures from the law of Deut 24:1–4 (which is accurately restated in Jer 3:1) and its historical application to Israel/Judah in later verses of the Jeremiah passage, see Shields, "Circumscribing the Prostitute," 126–28 (Shields terms these departures "transgressions" of the law).

[126] See the parallel in CH §§135–136 (COS 2.131:344; ANET 184), which makes a distinction between involuntary capture of a man and willful desertion of his wife.

Divorce and Remarriage in the Postexilic Prophets and the Writings

Ezra 9–10; Nehemiah 9:2; 13:3, 30. The discussion of mixed (interfaith) marriages (ch. 7, above) examined the situation of Jewish men who had married pagan wives. We concluded that the reforms of Ezra and Nehemiah enforcing the pentateuchal legislation against such marriages were not intended to address a normal case of divorce, because the normal terms for divorce are never used. Rather their enforcement concerned the dissolution of invalid marriages.[127] Hence these passages are not discussed further here.

Malachi 2:13–16. Malachi, a contemporary of Ezra and Nehemiah, writes about the same time as they do and faces a similar set of problems. His book is presented largely in the form of (rhetorical) disputations, arranged chiastically, in which God carries on a legal dispute or dialogue with the people of Israel.[128] Malachi points out the various areas where they are being unfaithful to the covenant relationship with Yahweh as established in the Torah, invoking the covenant curses for continued disloyalty and the covenant blessings for repentance and obedience.[129]

Malachi 2:10–16 presents the flip side of the problem encountered in Ezra 9–10. Malachi encounters a number of cases in which a Jewish man has entered into marriage with a pagan woman, "the daughter of a foreign god" (Mal 2:11) (see the discussion of these interfaith marriages in ch. 7, above). Probably the incidents of interfaith marriage described in vv. 11–12 should be viewed as integrally connected with the incidents of divorce described in vv. 13–16.[130] A man who married a pagan wife apparently first divorced his Jewish wife in order to avoid polygamy (see ch. 5, above). Malachi insists that such marriages have "profaned (ḥālal in the piʿel) the holy institution (qôdeš) of the LORD, which He loves" (v. 11 NKJV). This situation clearly involves a divorce (šālaḥ, v. 16), not a

---

[127] This is not to deny that from a human perspective those who took pagan wives may well have considered these unions as legal marriages, but such was not the case in God's eyes.

[128] See esp. Douglas Stuart, "Malachi," in *Zephaniah, Haggai, Zechariah, and Malachi* (vol. 3 of *The Minor Prophets: An Exegetical and Expository Commentary;* ed. Thomas Edward McComiskey; Grand Rapids: Baker, 1998), 1247–52, 1263.

[129] Ibid., 1257–62.

[130] See esp. the penetrating study by Markus Zehnder, "A Fresh Look at Malachi II 13–16," *VT* 53 (2003): 230–31. Zehnder sets forth cogent reasons for assuming that the two aspects (marriage to pagan wives and divorcing the Jewish wives) are interrelated. First, "the text does not give the impression that different groups of men are being addressed in the two passages [Mal 2:10–12 and 13–16]" (p. 230). This is supported by the second point, that "both actions are combined in verse 10 under the same heading of faithlessness [bāgad] against the 'brother' and desecration of the 'covenant of the fathers'" (230). Third, "no other possible reasons for the divorces appear in the context save the relationship with women of foreign faiths" (231). Finally, "such a picture fits well in the horizon of what is said about the problem of mixed marriages in Ezra/Nehemiah" (231). Zehnder acknowledges the possibility, however, that in not every case was the marriage to a pagan woman connected with the separation from an Israelite wife.

dissolution of an illegitimate marriage with pagan wives (as in Ezra 9–10). The Jewish returnees are dealing treacherously/faithlessly (*bāgad*) with their Jewish marital partners of their youth (v. 14).

As noted in the introduction to the present chapter, v. 14 makes clear the covenantal nature of marriage. God indicates why he has not heard their prayers or accepted their sacrifices (v. 13): "Because the LORD was a witness between you and the wife of your youth, to whom you have been faithless, though she is your companion and your wife by covenant" (v. 14). The Lord's response to this activity is forthright: "So look to yourselves, and do not let anyone be faithless [*bgd*, 'deal faithlessly'] to the wife of his youth" (v. 15). Then comes the most forceful statement in the whole OT on God's attitude toward divorce, an attitude already expressed implicitly in Deut 24:1–4 and other passages: "For I hate divorce [*šālaḥ* = *šlḥ*, *piʿel* inf. const.], says the LORD, the God of Israel, and covering one's garment with violence [*ḥāmās*], says the LORD of hosts. So take heed to yourselves and do not be faithless [*bāgad*]" (Mal 2:16).

The proper translation/interpretation of Malachi 2:16 has been the subject of considerable debate.[131] Hugenberger has succinctly summarized four categories of interpretation: the first denies any reference to divorce in this verse; the second interprets the verse as requiring or permitting divorce (the "traditional Jewish interpretation"); the third interprets this passage as an absolute prohibition of divorce ("the traditional Christian interpretation"); and the fourth limits the kind of divorce prohibited in this passage. Hugenberger has convincingly set forth weighty reasons to reject the first two categories of interpretation.[132] Though not

---

[131] For a comprehensive survey of the various views, see esp. Hugenberger, *Marriage as a Covenant*, 51–76.

[132] Ibid., 51–62. Most of those who deny any reference to divorce in Mal 2:16 regard this passage as a case of hopeless textual corruption, but Hugenberger aptly queries, "May this textual agnosticism be a rather too convenient means of eliminating contrary evidence?" (p. 52). As argued below, the MT of 2:16 makes good sense without necessitating any textual emendation. Hugenberger (53–54) further shows that those who argue that this text condemns idolatrous (Tammuz) worship rather than marital offenses (e.g., I. G. Matthews) posit a textual emendation and suggest a meaning for *šālaḥ* ("stripping off" rather than "send/divorce") that is found nowhere else in the HB among its 847 occurrences. Against the view of A. S. van der Woude that this verse deals with the abuse of secondary (Jewish) wives, not with divorce, Hugenberger, 54–57, shows that van der Woude's suggestion that *šālaḥ* is an abbreviation of the longer expression *šālaḥ yād*, referring to a morally detestable hostile act, requires emendation of the text and is not supported by the alleged biblical parallels or by ANE parallels.

Regarding the second category of interpretation (that this passage commends divorce), Hugenberger, 59, points out that although it finds apparent support among some versions, "the reading of the versions with their approval of divorce is considered by many scholars to be tendentious." Among the many objections Hugenberger cites to this interpretation, perhaps the most weighty is that stated by Joyce G. Baldwin: "Such a reading undermines all that the prophet is seeking to convey" (*Haggai, Zechariah, Malachi: An Introduction and Commentary* [TOTC 24; Downers Grove, Ill.: InterVarsity, 1972], 241). This proposed interpretation does not comport with the forceful conclusion of v. 16: "So take heed to yourselves and do not be faithless."

eliminating the possibility of the third interpretative strategy, Hugenberger prefers the fourth alternative.

The fourth alternative finds its most vigorous modern defender in Raymond Westbrook.[133] He examines the Akkadian parallels to 2:16 and argues that the statement "I hate divorce" refers to divorce motivated by hatred/aversion alone, that is, divorce without justification. Westbrook interprets the reference to "hate" and "divorce" in 2:16 in harmony with the Akkadian parallels, as a statement of the human partner (not Yahweh), yielding the following translation: "For he (the unfaithful Jewish husband) has hated, divorced . . . and covered his garment in injustice." Hugenberger follows this basic interpretation except that he translates the initial *kî* conditionally as "if," not causally as "for."[134]

Hugenberger acknowledges several problems in this interpretation.[135] First, one must repoint *šallaḥ* (*piˁel* inf. const. of *šālaḥ*) to a *piˁel* perfect to form an asyndetic construction with *śānēʾ*, "he has hated"; without this repointing, the biblical phraseology does not correspond to the grammar of the alleged Akkadian parallels.[136] A second problem is apparent in the ellipsis of Westbrook's translation. The clause "says Yahweh, God of Israel" intrudes right in the middle of Westbrook's suggested translation, awkwardly breaking up the flow of the three parallel actions proposed by Westbrook. A third problem is the awkward shift from second person in 2:15b to third person in 2:16a, leaving one to wonder who is the antecedent of "he" in 2:16a. A fourth problem is that with this translation/interpretation, it is not clear how the assertion "he has hated, divorced . . . and covered his garment . . ." comports with the last part of the verse: "Therefore take heed to your spirit, that you do not deal treacherously."

Besides the problems admitted by Hugenberger, the most difficult is found in the very argument that ultimately leads Hugenberger to embrace Westbrook's basic hypothesis instead of the traditional Christian interpretation. Hugenberger recognizes and affirms the "wide scholarly consensus that Malachi is heavily indebted to the Deuteronomic perspective."[137] He also correctly notes that the

---

133 Westbrook, "The Prohibition," 402–3.

134 Hugenberger, *Marriage as a Covenant*, 68–69. See also Martin Shields, "Syncretism and Divorce in Malachi 2, 10–16," *ZAW* 111 (1999): 76–86; Stuart, "Malachi," 1342–44; and Instone-Brewer, *Divorce and Remarriage*, 56–57 (one of the options cited with approval).

135 Hugenberger, *Marriage as a Covenant*, 68–69.

136 Ibid., 72: "the Akkadian formula which Westbrook cites has both verbs in the I/1 durative, while the MT of Mal. 2:16 involves one perfect and one infinitive construct."

137 Ibid., 48. Hugenberger, 48–50, summarizes major points of comparison between Malachi and Deuteronomy. Only Malachi and Deuteronomy among the OT books commence with an address to all "Israel," and Malachi concludes his work with a Deuteronomic injunction (3:22 [ET 4:4]; cf. Deut 4:10–14). Further, note the interest of both Malachi and Deuteronomy in Yahweh's elective love for Israel in spite of their doubts of that love (cf. Deut 4:37; 7:6–8), Yahweh's "name" (Mal 1:6; cf. the "name" theology of Deuteronomy), the fatherhood of God (Mal 1:6; 2:10; cf. Deut 8:5; 14:1; 32:6), the "covenant with Levi" (Mal 2:4, 8; cf. Deut 33:8–11), the tithe (Mal 3:8–10; cf. Deut 26:12–15), and Israel as God's "special possession" juxtaposed with Israel's sonship (Mal 3:17; cf.

traditional interpretation of Mal 2:16 "necessarily involves a conflict with the seemingly lenient attitude toward divorce in Deut 24:1–4."[138] But Hugenberger cuts this Gordian knot of difficulty by following Westbrook's hypothesis regarding the interpretation of both Deut 24:1–4 and Mal 2:16, as distinguishing between two different rationales for divorce, one with justification (which is approved) and one out of mere aversion (which is condemned). Thus he concludes that "Deut. 24:3 in reality reflects a disapprobation of divorce when grounded in mere aversion similar to what is attested in Mal. 2:16."[139]

As argued above, however, Westbrook's interpretation of Deut 24:1–4 does not comport with the full range of evidence in this passage. Deuteronomy 24:1–4 does not imply a lenient attitude toward divorce, as commonly suggested. Instead, by use of precise terminology and rare grammatical construction, this legislation implies a divine condemnation of all divorce—justified and unjustified—even as God at the same time condescends to Israel's hardness of heart and tolerates such practice. If my interpretation is correct for 24:1–4, then the consistent interpretation for Malachi, who clearly follows a Deuteronomic perspective throughout his book, would be to unconditionally condemn divorce. Such an interpretation of Mal 2:16 is the traditional Christian one, to which we now turn.

The "traditional Christian interpretation" is in fact just as well represented among early Jewish interpreters as the second of Hugenberger's categories.[140] My own survey of the evidence leads me to the conclusion that the traditional Christian interpretation is most faithful to the text of Mal 2:16, requiring no emendation of the MT, and is most congruent with the context of 2:10–16 and the legislation of Deut 24:1–4, upon which Malachi is generally considered to have depended.

Many who have espoused the traditional Christian interpretation posit a minor shift in the translation of Mal 2:16 from the third person, "He [Yahweh] hates divorce," to the first person, "I [Yahweh] hate divorce."[141] Those suggesting the latter translation usually presuppose a slight revocalization of the MT from the *qal* perfect *śānēʾ*, "he hates," to the *qal* participle *śōnēʾ* with the assumption of an elided first-person singular pronominal subject.[142] But several scholars

---

Deut 14:1–2). Finally, "perhaps the most notable evidence of Deuteronomic influence within Malachi is the prominence of covenant concepts throughout this brief work. . . . This goes far beyond the six explicit references to 'covenant' (Mal. 2:4, 5, 8, 10, 14; 3:1), to include the Deuteronomic vocabulary of covenant (e.g., 'love,' 'hate,' 'father,' 'son,' 'cursed,' 'great king,' etc.) as well as characteristic perspectives and themes" (ibid., 50).

[138] Ibid., 65.

[139] Ibid., 81.

[140] Hugenberger, ibid., 62, cites early Jewish supporters of this view, including, e.g., Rabbi Johanan (mentioned in *b. Git.* 90b), Al-Qumisi, Jephet Ben Eli, and Ibn Ezra (who mentions this as one option).

[141] Modern versions representing this majority view include, e.g., NASB, NIV, NJB, NJPS, NLT, and NRSV. For further discussion of textual challenges in Mal 2:10–16, see, e.g., Ralph Smith, *Micah–Malachi* (WBC 23; Waco, Tex.: Word, 1984), 318–25.

[142] See, e.g., K&D, 10:653; and Verhoef, *Haggai and Malachi*, 278. For discussion, bibliography, and critique, see Hugenberger, *Marriage as a Covenant*, 64.

have suggested that there is no need for any revocalization if *śānēʾ* is taken as a verbal adjective (employed here as a participle) and the elided first-person pronoun is assumed.[143] This translation is grammatically defensible but not without problems.[144]

I suggest that a straightforward translation of this verse as preserved in the MT, without resort to emendation or to conjectured elision of pronouns, makes the best sense of the text and best fits the context. If we take the introductory *kî*, "that," in its usage as the standard grammatical marker indicating that the subject of the subordinate clause is made the object of the principal sentence,[145] this clause may be translated, "Yahweh, the God of Israel says that He hates divorce."[146] Some have objected that it seems strange to find the third person "He hates divorce" followed by the usual expression for direct address, "says Yahweh, the God of Israel,"[147] but such objection falls to the ground when one recognizes that just such usage is found elsewhere in Malachi. Malachi 1:9 presents a precise parallel to 2:16: a description of the divine activity in the third person is followed by the clause "says the LORD of hosts." Further, "it must also be taken into consideration that the whole passage of Mal. ii 10–16 is constructed not as a word of YHWH, but as a speech of the prophet."[148]

Whether one translates this verse as "He [Yahweh] hates divorce" or "I [Yahweh] hate divorce," the intent remains the same. As with Deut 24:1–4, the legality of divorce is not denied, but such practice is presented as morally repugnant to God.[149] As Zehnder states regarding the men addressed by Malachi, "Their practice is not illegal, but the expulsion of their wives in order to marry another woman of foreign faith is a moral wrong in the eyes of YHWH."[150]

I concur with the majority of modern commentators and versions that this verse presents an unconditional divine condemnation of divorce. Peter Verhoef sums up the wide consensus among scholars: "nowhere else in the OT do we find such an elevated view of marriage as in Mal. 2:10–16. Nowhere else is divorce

---

[143] These include, e.g., Wilhelm Rudolph and Clemens Locher. For discussion, bibliography, and critique, see Hugenberger, *Marriage as a Covenant*, 64.

[144] Hugenberger, ibid., points out that *śānēʾ* as a verbal adjective is unattested elsewhere in the MT and the appeal to an elided first-person singular pronoun is problematic, with no other first-person pronouns in the immediate context.

[145] *HALOT* 471, s. v. כִּי, meaning 6.

[146] This is essentially the translation represented by the NKJV. In the Hebrew text the predicate object of the sentence "that He hates divorce" is placed first for the sake of emphasis.

[147] So, e.g., Zehnder, "A Fresh Look," 253.

[148] Ibid.

[149] Some scholars have argued that the use of the verb *śānēʾ*, "hate," in this context harks back to Deut 24:3, where *śānēʾ* refers to the husband who divorces his wife, and thus *śānēʾ* in Mal 2:16 should refer to the Jewish husband who divorces his wife, not to Yahweh as the One who hates divorce. The verb *śānēʾ* elsewhere in Malachi, however, is used exclusively of Yahweh (1:3), and the immediate context of 2:10–16 seems to point to Yahweh, not a Jewish husband, as the subject of *śānēʾ*.

[150] Zehnder, "A Fresh Look," 256.

condemned in such explicit terms. . . . The prophecy of Malachi . . . provides in this respect [regarding divorce] the ultimate in OT revelation."[151]

Block presents the spiritual and covenantal implications of divorce emerging from Mal 2 and its declaration "of fundamental divine aversion to divorce": (1) prevalent divorce is "evidence of a fundamental lack of reverence and fear toward Yahweh"; (2) divorce is "an act of treachery against one's companion, and a fundamental breach of covenant commitment to one's wife" (v. 14); (3) divorce, along with marriage to pagans, is "an act of treachery against the community ('brothers') and a profanation of God's covenant with Israel" (v. 10); (4) divorce disrupts the stability of the home, which is "prerequisite to producing 'godly offspring'" and "indispensable for the continuation of a people of faith" (v. 15); (5) divorce "absolves God of his covenantal obligations" to the person who divorces, and "God rejects the offerings of those guilty of marital treachery" (v. 13); and (6) "treachery is committed in the spirit (rûach) before it is committed in action. God is not fooled by external acts of devotion when the spirit is fundamentally treacherous" (vv. 15–16). In sum, "this passage treats divorce not as a moral right enjoyed by males but as a moral offense committed by males."[152]

This passage is a fitting one with which to end this survey of the OT passages relating to divorce/remarriage. This statement is not an innovation, not an advance coming late in the OT growth and development of understanding on divorce. Since the beginning in Gen 1–3, the divine ideal was clear. Scholars have argued persuasively that the use of the term "one" ($^\circ eh\bar{a}d$) in Mal 2:10 for God and in 2:15 for the "one flesh" of marriage ("But did He not make them one . . . ?" Hugenberger) is an intertextual linkage with the "one flesh" divine ideal for marriage in Gen 2:25.[153] "What could be more natural in a disputation on covenant-breaking divorces than for the prophet to return to the originating passage where the biblical norm for marriage had been set forth?"[154] The sovereign Lord calls for a return to the divine ideal in Eden.

Divorce/Remarriage and Divine Grace

God's condescension to human hardness of heart in the inspired OT legislation regarding divorce surely intimates divine grace and forgiveness for those today who have already irrevocably taken the step of divorce. The Prophets especially show the element of grace in the attitude of the divine Husband to his wayward adulterous wife, Israel. He is a jealous Husband indeed, jealous for the exclusive and faithful affection of his spouse. But also he is a broken-hearted Hus-

[151] Verhoef, Haggai and Malachi, 280.
[152] Block, "Marriage and Family in Ancient Israel," 51–52.
[153] Walter Kaiser Jr., "Divorce in Malachi 2:10–16," CTR 2 (1987): 73–84; Hugenberger, Marriage as a Covenant, 124–67. Cf. Zehnder, "A Fresh Look," 244: "The verse is much richer in content if its conception is related to God's creation in Gen. i–ii and understood as an additional reason for the admonition to be faithful to the 'wife of one's youth.'"
[154] Kaiser, "Divorce in Malachi 2:10–16," 75.

band, yearning for his wife to return to him; he seeks reconciliation, not divorce (Hos 2; Jer 3–4). He is also the weeping Husband, sobbing almost inconsolably in his grief over his unfaithful spouse (Jer 8:18–9:22).[155] The divine attitude provides a model of grace for the husband or wife today who finds that his or her spouse has been unfaithful.

To the one who is divorced, who may have contributed to the demise of the marriage, who may have been an innocent victim of consequences beyond his/her control, or who may be feeling like a complete failure because of the divorce—God has a word of grace for all these situations. As demonstrated in the lives of those going through divorce in OT times, God works with the failures of the past. He picks up the broken pieces and lets those divorced make a new beginning.

God's own forgiving grace and the grace he asks human spouses to display to an unfaithful partner pervade the OT. At the same time, it does not nullify nor mute the word of the Lord God, implicit in Eden, audible throughout the OT in law and practice, and a thundering shout at the end of the OT era, that "I hate divorce."

---

[155] Interpreters debate who is weeping in Jer 8:18–9:22. For a strong case that it is God who is weeping in these passages, see Kathleen M. O'Connor, "The Tears of God and Divine Character in Jeremiah 2–9," in *Troubling Jeremiah* (ed. A. R. Pete Diamond, Kathleen M. O'Connor, and Louis Stulman; JSOTSup 260; Sheffield, Eng.: Sheffield Academic Press, 1999), 387–401. But even if it is Jeremiah, Jeremiah is here undoubtedly full of the grief of the Lord, just as he is "full of the wrath of the Lord" in Jer 6:11.

❧10

Intimacy versus Incest

Affirmations of the Divine Ideal of Marital Intimacy

Pentateuch

The first statement about humans outside the garden of Eden concerns their sexual activity: "Now the man knew Eve his wife, and she conceived and bore Cain" (Gen 4:1).[1] The use of the word "know" (*yādaʿ*) in this first explicit biblical reference to sexual intercourse conveys a psychological profundity regarding the significance of sexual encounter. The word *yādaʿ* in the OT is fundamentally a relational term and often refers not just to objective knowledge but also (and particularly) to existential experience. It implies a deep personal relationship with the one known.[2] The choice of *yādaʿ* here to indicate sexual intercourse emphasizes, as often elsewhere in the OT, that in sexual union the man comes to know his wife in the deep intimacy of her being.[3] And the wife shares equally in this sexually intimate knowledge.[4] The sexual encounter "provides

---

[1] This verse does not imply that Adam and Eve had sexual intercourse only after the Fall, outside the Garden, as some have argued. See Nahum M. Sarna, *Genesis* (The JPS Torah Commentary; Philadelphia: Jewish Publication Society, 1989), 31: "The Hebrew construction here employed usually indicates a pluperfect sense; that is, it would normally be rendered 'the man had known.' This leads Rashi to conclude that coition had already taken place in the Garden of Eden before the expulsion, an interpretation that finds support in 3:20. There is nothing to sustain the idea that sexual activity first occurred outside Eden. A text like 1 Samuel 1:19—'Elkanah knew his wife Hannah'—shows that the Hebrew phrase in our text does not need to imply that we have here the first occurrence of sexual experience."

[2] See Terence E. Fretheim, "ידע," *NIDOTTE* 2:409–14. "In the broadest sense, *ydʿ* means to take various aspects of the world of one's own experience into the self, including the resultant relationship with that which is known. The fundamentally relational character of knowing (over against a narrow intellectual sense) can be discerned, not least in that both God and human beings can be subject and object of the vb." (p. 410).

[3] Fretheim describes this kind of knowledge as "sexual intimacy" (ibid., 2:411). Occurrences of *yādaʿ* for sexual intimacy of a man with a woman include Gen 4:1, 17, 25; 38:26; Judg 19:25; 1 Sam 1:19; 1 Kgs 1:4.

[4] See Gen 19:8; Judg 11:39; contra a common scholarly misconception that the verb is used only with a male as the subject in Scripture (e.g., Francis I. Andersen and David Noel Freedman, *Hosea: A New Translation with Introduction and Commentary* [AB 24A; New York: Doubleday, 1989], 284).

the most complete, most accurate, and most fulfilling knowledge of one another available to humans."[5]

The book of Genesis also provides amazingly candid glimpses into the intimate sexual activities of the patriarchs and matriarchs that bespeak a wholesome
and positive view of sexuality in this period. Particular attention is called to the
stunning physical beauty of Sarah (12:11; 20:11), Rebekah (24:16), and Rachel
(29:17). There is reference to Sarah's "pleasure" in sexual intercourse and having a
child (18;12), and one to Isaac's intimate "fondling" of Rebekah (26:8). Equally
touching and beautiful are the expressions of Isaac's loving sexual relation with
Rebekah (24:67) and Jacob's great love for Rachel (29:20).

Prophets/Writings

In the Prophets the language of marital intimacy comes to the fore in describing the relationship between Yahweh and his people. The discussion of sexually related imagery for God in chapter 3, above, highlighted this language of
marital intimacy between God and Israel in Hos 2, and the implications for husbands and wives. In Jer 2 Yahweh likewise uses terms of intimate endearment to
speak of his bride, Israel. He recalls the time of the betrothal: "I remember the devotion [ḥesed] of your youth, your love [ʾāhăbâ] as a bride, how you followed
[hālak ʾaḥărê] me in the wilderness, in a land not sown. Israel was holy to the
LORD" (Jer 2:2–3). Three terms of intimacy appear here: ḥesed, "devotion, steadfast love"; ʾāhăbâ, "love"; and hālak ʾaḥar, "follow after." Yahweh is an intimate
"Lover" with his bride, Israel. After Israel's harlotry and unfaithfulness, Yahweh's
tender desire for intimacy has not waned: "Return, faithless Israel, . . . for I am
merciful. . . . Return, O faithless children, . . . for I am your master; I will take you,
one from a city and two from a family, and I will bring you to Zion. . . . Return, O
faithless children, I will heal your faithlessness" (3:12, 14, 22).

In Ezekiel's allegory of God's marital relationship with Jerusalem/Judah,
Yahweh likewise speaks with tender love to his bride at the time of her betrothal:
"I passed by you again and looked on you; you were at the age for love. I spread
the edge of my cloak over you, and covered your nakedness" (Ezek 16:8). In almost the same breath, God speaks to Ezekiel regarding the imminent death of the
prophet's wife, whom God describes as "the delight of your eyes" (24:16). Evidently Ezekiel and his wife had an intimate relationship.

In the Writings, according to Proverbs, sexuality is designed for relationship,
fellowship, intimate partnership between husband and wife. The breaking of the
marriage vow is visualized as a sin against an ʾallûp—a term in Scripture for the
closest of friends, a comrade.[6] The wise man describes this loving marriage relationship in terms of continual affection and deepest intimacy: "a lovely deer, a
graceful doe. May her breasts satisfy [rāwâ] you at all times; may you be intoxicated [šāgâ] always [tāmîd] by her love" (Prov 5:19). The term rāwâ literally

[5] Sapp, *Sexuality, the Bible, and Science,* 21.
[6] Prov 2:17; cf. 16:28; 17:9; Ps 55:14 (ET 55:13).

means "to be satiated, saturated"; *šāgâ* literally means "to be intoxicated." And *tāmîd* means "continually"—without ceasing. Such is the hyperbole piled upon hyperbole for the enjoyment of deepest physical intimacy between husband and wife. Proverbs describes not only physical erotic intimacy but intimacy expressed in words of praise and appreciation by husband for wife: "Many women have done excellently, but you surpass them all" (31:29). The husband also is described as having the peace of perfect trust: "The heart of her husband trusts in her" (31:11).

Intimacy in marriage has been distorted in a sinful world through various counterfeits, involving most of the distortions of sexuality examined thus far in this book. (These are reviewed in chapter 12, below, which looks at the parody of true intimacy and beauty, especially as suggested by the immoral woman of Prov 1–9.) The remainder of this chapter focuses upon another kind of distortion of marital intimacy not yet discussed: incest.

Forbidden Degrees of Intimacy: Incestuous Relationships

In contrast with divinely approved intimacy within marriage, there were forbidden degrees of closeness concerning sexual relationships with near of kin. This section examines the ANE background and OT narratives/legislation dealing with incest.

Ancient Near Eastern Background

Throughout the entire ancient Near East, there are countless examples of gods and goddesses and humans of royal descent engaged in incest. "Incest is attributed to pagan goddesses and gods, and to humans of royal or similar descent and social status; myths and legends from Mesopotamia, Canaan, Ugarit, and Egypt are replete with such incestuous stories which are far from pejorative in tone."[7]

Paradoxically, on the level of law for the common citizen, incestuous relations of various kinds are prohibited. Two extant ANE law codes address the issue of incest. The Code of Hammurabi enumerates several forbidden degrees of relationship: father-daughter (§154), father–daughter-in-law (§155), son-mother (§157), and son–foster mother (§158).[8] The Hittite Laws prohibit sexual relationship of a man with his mother, daughter, or son (§189), with his stepmother while his father is still alive (§190), with his sister-in-law while his brother is still alive (§195), with both a free woman and her mother (§195), and with both a free woman and her sister (§195).[9]

---

[7] Athalya Brenner, "On Incest," in *A Feminist Companion to Exodus to Deuteronomy* (ed. Athalya Brenner; FCB 6; Sheffield, Eng.: Sheffield Academic Press, 1994), 116.

[8] "Laws of Hammurabi," translated by Martha Roth, §§154–158 (*COS* 2.131:345; cf. *ANET* 172–73).

[9] "Hittite Laws," translated by Harry A. Hoffner Jr., §§189–190, 195 (*COS* 2.19:118; cf. *ANET* 196).

In these laws, different punishments are prescribed for different forbidden relationships. According to the Code of Hammurabi, in cases of incest between father and daughter, the father is banished from the city (CH §154); in case of incest between father and daughter-in-law, the father is bound and thrown into the river (§155); in case of incest between son and mother (after his father's death), both of them shall be burned (§157); in case of incest between a son and his foster mother (after his father's death), the son shall be banished from the parental home (§158).[10]

According to the Hittite Laws, all of the incestuous relationships mentioned in the laws were capital crimes. Harry Hoffner shows, however, that the illegal couplings of bestiality and incest, called ḫurkel, originally (in the Old Kingdom, ca. 1650 B.C.E.) demanded the death penalty but the king could spare the life of his subject, in which case the guilty one was banished from his city.[11] Later Hittite texts (fifteenth or fourteenth century B.C.E.) reveal that various Hittite-controlled cities and towns had different customs regarding punishment of these offenses: some executed and some banished. In these cases of ḫurkel, the offence is against the city: the act has brought impurity upon the townsfolk and made them liable to divine wrath, which must be appeased either by execution or by banishment. After the guilty one was banished, rituals were performed in the town to remove the impurity. In still later Hittite texts, there seems to be a further development (probably due to Hurrian influence) in which "the human offender need not be killed or banished. . . . The earlier and more rigorous treatment of the offender was ameliorated, giving way to a purification ritual and the payment of a fine."[12]

Pentateuchal Narratives concerning Incest

Immediately after the Fall. According to the divine plan for marriage established in Eden and summarized in Gen 2:24 as applicable also after the fall, a man was to leave his father and mother and be joined in marriage to his wife. This probably implies, among other things, that from the beginning certain blood relationships were off-limits for marriage—a man (and presumably also a woman) was to *leave* father and mother, not *marry* them. Thus at least father-daughter and mother-son relationships were considered forbidden degrees of closeness for sexual relationships, and perhaps this verse also implicitly precluded all intergenerational liaisons.

In the canonical depiction of the early history of humankind, at the beginning of this world's history, when the whole human race consisted of a single nuclear family, it was obviously necessary for Adam's sons (Cain, Seth, and all the other males who were married) to marry their sisters (see 4:17; 5:4, 6), although

---

[10] CH §§154–158 (*COS* 2.131:345; *ANET* 172–73).

[11] Harry A. Hoffner Jr., "Incest, Sodomy, and Bestiality in the Ancient Near East," in *Orient and Occident: Essays Presented to Cyrus H. Gordon on the Occasion of His Sixty-Fifth Birthday* (ed. Harry A. Hoffner Jr.; AOAT 22; Neukirchen-Vluyn: Neukirchener Verlag, 1973), 85–90.

[12] Ibid., 90.

this is not explicitly mentioned in Scripture.[13] At the time of Abraham, it apparently was still considered appropriate for a man to marry his half-sister; Abraham was the paternal brother of his wife, Sarah (20:2, 12).[14]

James Miller shows that in the book of Genesis only intergenerational liaisons are considered incestuous; intragenerational liaisons are tacitly accepted.[15] At the time of the exodus, the marriage of an aunt and her nephew apparently was considered acceptable, since, according to Exod 6:20, this was the status of Moses' mother and father. But as will become apparent below, by the time the Levitical code concerning forbidden sexual practices was formalized, these relationships were regarded as incestuous and forbidden by law (Lev 18:11–12; 20:17, 19). To the biblical evidence for this development we turn our attention.

Ham and His Mother? The discussion of homosexuality (ch. 4, above) considered the possibility of sexual relations between Ham and his father (Gen 9:22). The text indicates that Ham "saw the nakedness of his father." Frederick Bassett, among others, has argued that since in Lev 18 the expression "to uncover the nakedness of" a man sometimes refers to having sexual intercourse with his wife

---

[13] If one accepts the historicity of the Genesis account of the early history of humankind, it might be surmised that immediately after the fall, the genetic makeup of humans was no doubt less susceptible to the negative effects of inbreeding and such relationships were thus apparently not forbidden. So O. Palmer Robertson, *The Genesis of Sex: Sexual Relationships in the First Book of the Bible* (Phillipsburg, N.J.: Presbyterian and Reformed, 2002), 88: "The simple answer to the perplexing question concerning Cain's wife is that Cain married his sister. Though this degree of consanguinity in marriage is forbidden later in the Bible because of the degenerating effects of sin, these principles were not in effect from the beginning."

[14] E. A. Speiser, *Genesis* (AB 1; Garden City, N.Y.: Doubleday, 1964), 91–93, points out that the "wife-sister" custom was especially popular among the Hurrians, in the region of Haran, where Abraham and Sarah lived after moving from Ur of the Chaldeans. "In Hurrian society, the bonds of marriage were strongest and most solemn when the wife had simultaneously the juridical status of a sister, regardless of actual blood ties. This is why a man would sometimes marry a girl and adopt her at the same time as his sister, in two separate steps recorded in independent legal documents. . . . The practice . . . gave the adoptive brother greater authority than was granted the husband. By the same token, the adopted sister enjoyed correspondingly greater protection and higher social status" (p. 92). Commenting on the implications for Abram and Sarai's situation, Speiser continues: "[Genesis 20:12] describes her indirectly as the daughter of Terah, but not by Abraham's own mother. This alone would make Sarah eligible for 'sistership' status under the law of the land from which Abraham had set out on his journey to Canaan, with all the attendant safeguards and privileges which that law afforded" (92–93).

From the perspective of the Mosaic law, the relationship between Abram and Sarai was forbidden. See Gershon Hepner, "Abraham's Incestuous Marriage with Sarah: A Violation of the Holiness Code," *VT* 53 (2003): 143–55, who argues for intertextual relationships between Lev 20:17 and (among others in Genesis) the narrative of Abraham's marriage with Sarai. His conclusion is that "Genesis narratives often allude to biblical laws" (p. 154). The allusion could go the other way (i.e., the laws alluding to the narratives), however, depending on one's theory of source criticism; and based upon a canonical reading of the texts, the Genesis narratives occur before the giving of the Mosaic Law.

[15] James E. Miller, "Sexual Offences in Genesis," *JSOT* 90 (2000): 41–53.

(see vv. 7, 8, 14, 16), and since in Lev 20:17 the expression "to uncover the nakedness of" is used synonymously with the expression "to see the nakedness" of that
person, therefore the latter expression, which appears in Gen 9:22, implies an incestuous relationship between Ham and his mother.[16] But as Bassett rightly recognizes, the text as it now reads "pictures the offense as nothing more than an
accidental case of Ham's viewing his father naked. . . . This understanding of the
offense is now clearly demanded by v. 23 which describes how Shem and Japheth
walk backward into Noah's tent with a garment over their shoulders and cover
their naked father. They avoid Ham's offense by keeping their faces turned away
from Noah." Bassett's son-mother incest interpretation requires a hypothetical
reconstruction of the history of the text in which "the redactor, or perhaps a later
editor, has missed the idiomatic meaning of the tradition that Noah's son saw his
father's nakedness and has added the reference to the brothers' covering their father's nakedness with a garment."[17] Since this study deals with the theology of the
final form of the text, such suggestions based upon redaction-critical conjectures
are outside its purview. Accepting the text as it stands and as concluded above
(ch. 4), it is far more likely this was an incident of filial disrespect (a "gloating
stare"), not sexual relations.

Although the narrative of Ham's relation with Noah includes only "viewing,"
not incestuous sexual intercourse, Miller points out a number of parallels in language and motif with the stories of incest that follow in Genesis (discussed
below). As with the other cases of incest in Genesis, this is intergenerational. As
with the story of Lot and his daughters, the incident takes place after an escape
from destruction; both cases include the inebriation of the parent, with offspring
taking advantage of his inebriated state; both Noah and Lot needed to be ignorant of the act for it to take place. As with the narrative of Reuben's incest, "the
conclusion of the story is a repudiation of the activity and a curse which places
the descendants of the offender in the service of the descendants of his siblings."[18]
In light of these intratextual parallels, it is possible, as Calum M. Carmichael suggests, that Ham's "viewing" of his father's nakedness is itself considered by the
narrator as a species of incest.[19] This suggestion is further supported by the role
of nakedness and clothing in Gen 2–3, which "strengthens the narrative force of
viewing another's nakedness in this passage. In a way, viewing nakedness is a form
of sexual contact." Miller postulates that the phraseology of "uncovering the
nakedness" of an offended relative (in Lev 18 and 20) could not only be a euphemistic prohibition of incest but also include a prohibition of the literal act of uncovering (or viewing uncovered) that relative's nakedness.[20] Understood this way,
one might term this incident a case of "visual" incest.

---

[16] Frederick W. Bassett, "Noah's Nakedness and the Curse of Canaan: A Case of Incest?" *VT* 21 (1971): 232–37.

[17] Ibid., 232, 234.

[18] Miller, "Sexual Offences in Genesis," 44–45.

[19] Calum M. Carmichael, *Law, Legend, and Incest in the Bible: Leviticus 18–20* (Ithaca,
N.Y.: Cornell University Press, 1997), 16; cf. Miller, "Sexual Offences in Genesis," 43.

[20] Miller, "Sexual Offences in Genesis," 45.

Lot and His Daughters (Gen 19:30–38). In the aftermath of the destruction of Sodom and Gomorrah (Gen 19:23–29), the narrator records the case of incest of Lot's daughters with their father. The incestuous acts of Lot's daughters were apparently not because of lustful passions but, as made explicit by the firstborn daughter's speech (19:32), an attempt to keep their father's lineage from dying out in the face of desperate circumstances.[21] But the effects of living in wicked Sodom were apparent in their incestuous acts as well as in the capacity for drunkenness to the point of insensibility on the part of their father. As apparent regarding other sexual sins described in the biblical narratives, even though there is no explicit condemnation of the acts, yet the narrative "contains indirectly a severe judgment on the incest in Lot's house."[22] By means of simple narrative devices, the narrator establishes the inappropriateness of the act. Most notably, "the fact that the daughters resorted to getting Lot drunk in order to accomplish their plans indicates that the intercourse was not legitimate in their code of mores."[23]

Carol Smith observes that the account of 19:30–38 contains "the closest approximation possible to a female's rape of a male"; Lot is "a helpless victim of a sexual assault."[24] She further points out that "the events in the second part of the chapter are the events of the first half turned completely upside down": whereas in the first part of Gen 19 Lot "intended to render his daughters passive victims when he blandly offered them to the mob to do with whatever they chose," in the second part "it is his [Lot's] turn to be violated."[25] Both parts of the story, Smith

---

[21] The firstborn daughter of Lot says to her younger sister, "we will lie with him, so that we may preserve offspring through our father." In the introduction to this stated reason, the firstborn says, "there is not a man on earth to come in to us after the manner of all the world" (Gen 19:31). Some critical scholars take this statement to indicate that this story was originally an alternative to the flood story, implying that there were no more living persons on earth after the destruction of Sodom and Gomorrah. But such certainly does not fit the context of the story in its canonical form, and the statement need not be interpreted thus. The NIV attempts to capture the intent of the Hebrew in modern idiom: "there is no man around here to lie with us, as is the custom all over the earth." They had lost their fiancés in Sodom (v. 14), and so they took matters into their own hands to insure that they had children. K&D, 1:152, suggest a similar explanation: "Not that they imagined the whole human race to have perished in the destruction of the valley of Siddim, but because they were afraid that no man would link himself with them, the only survivors of a country smitten by the curse of God." Alternatively, it may indeed be possible that the two daughters, hiding with their father in a cave (v. 30) after the conflagration that devastated the five cities of the plain, thought they were the only survivors of a cosmic catastrophe; for this view, see Hoffner, "Incest, Sodomy, and Bestiality," 81.

[22] Gerhard von Rad, *Genesis: A Commentary* (trans. John H. Marks; OTL; Philadelphia: Westminster, 1961), 224.

[23] Miller, "Sexual Offences in Genesis," 43.

[24] Carol Smith, "Stories of Incest in the Hebrew Bible: Scholars Challenging Text or Text Challenging Scholars?" *Hen* 14 (1992): 236, 239. Contra Ilona N. Rashkow, "Daddy-Dearest and the 'Invisible Spirit of Wine,'" in *Genesis* (ed. Athalya Brenner; FCB[2] 1; Sheffield, Eng.: Sheffield, 1998), 98–107, who argues that despite the clear statement of the narrator, Freudian psychoanalytic theory suggests (and Renaissance artists discerned) that "the unconscious desires of Lot seem to have surfaced" (106).

[25] Smith, "Stories of Incest," 237.

rightly contends, are intended to shock the reader with the "outrageous and un-precedented" actions taken by the participants. By recognizing the linkage be-tween the first and last parts of the chapter, and the intended shock tactics of the narrator, the reader may begin to appreciate how far both of these actions were from God's ideal for sexuality. The baleful result of these incestuous relation-ships—the birth of Moab and Ben-ammi, fathers of the Moabites and Ammo-nites respectively—is clearly traced in the long-standing conflict between these "brother" nations and the people of Israel.[26] These nations became the source of "the worst carnal seduction in the history of Israel (that of Baal-Peor, Num 25) and the cruellest religious distortion (that of Molech, Lev 18:21)."[27]

Reuben and Bilhah (Gen 35:22; 49:4). Genesis 35:22 records another incident of incest, this time Reuben's incest with his father's concubine: "While Israel lived in that land, Reuben went and lay with Bilhah his father's concubine; and Israel heard of it." This verse implies that Jacob (Israel) was ignorant of the incestuous act until after it had happened. The immediate context of the short narrative no-tice does not comment further on this incident, but in the poetic blessing of his twelve sons toward the end of both the book of Genesis and Jacob's life, the patri-arch reveals his extreme displeasure with Reuben's incestuous act (49:4): "Un-stable as water, you shall no longer excel because you went up onto your father's bed; then you defiled it—you went up onto my couch!" Even though Bilhah was Jacob's concubine and not a full wife, nonetheless Reuben is said to have defiled his father's bed, that is, committed incest. Jacob's deathbed denunciation of Reu-ben's sinful act cites this incest as the reason for the prediction that he would no longer excel (or have preeminence [*yātar* in the *hip*^c*il*], in contrast to his former excellency [*yeter*] of dignity and excellency [*yeter*] of power prior to his moral fall, 49:2). That is, Reuben would no longer have the rights of the firstborn son. This is made explicit in the genealogy of Reuben in 1 Chr 5:1: "The sons of Reu-ben the firstborn of Israel. (He was the firstborn, but because he defiled his fa-ther's bed his birthright was given to the sons of Joseph son of Israel, so that he is not enrolled in the genealogy according to the birthright." Reuben's incestuous act cost him his birthright.

Judah and Tamar (Gen 38)? Chapters 3, 7, and 11 of this study also examine this narrative; here we explore the question whether the relationship between Judah and Tamar should be considered incest. Some scholars have argued that Judah in-deed committed incest—with his daughter-in-law Tamar (Gen 38), albeit with-out knowledge of her identity.[28] By the standards of Lev 18 and 20, this is

---

[26] See Num 22:4–20; Deut 23:4 (ET 23:3); Judg 3:12–30; 11:4–33; 1 Sam 11:1–11; 2 Sam 8:2; 10:1–19; 2 Kgs 3.

[27] Derek Kidner, *Genesis: An Introduction and Commentary* (TOTC 1; Downers Grove, Ill.: InterVarsity, 1967), 136. This is not to say that no good can come from an in-cestuous relationship—even progenitors of the Davidic Messiah (i.e., Tamar). What I speak of here are major observable trends.

[28] See, e.g., Miller, "Sexual Offences in Genesis," 43–44.

undoubtedly true. What would otherwise be considered incest is not regarded as such, however, if the sexual activity is in fulfillment of the levirate responsibility (Deut 25:5–10) (see ch. 11, below). Genesis 38 describes a situation in which Tamar—frustrated that her father-in-law had neglected to provide his son Shelah as her husband to perform the duty of the *levir* so that she might have children— decided to take matters into her own hands. It is possible (but by no means certain) that in patriarchal times there was a custom that the levirate duty could be performed by the father-in-law as well as by the brother-in-law, and that Tamar's desperate action to cause Judah to have sex with her was to force him to carry out his levirate responsibility to make her pregnant. A practice similar (but not identical) to the levirate marriage and carried out in other ANE societies (attested particularly in the Hittite laws) does allow the father-in-law to perform such service so that his daughter-in-law may have progeny. If this is also the understanding of the Genesis patriarchs, then from Judah's perspective his relationship with Tamar would not have been considered incestuous.

On the other hand, if the patriarchs of Genesis were following the same basic tradition as later codified in Deut 25:5–10, which does not provide for a father-in-law to perform the role of a *levir,* then "Judah did not consider this [the father-in-law as *levir*] to be an option." Assuming that the patriarchs were following the later biblical legal tradition, thus making Judah ineligible to act as *levir* to his daughter-in-law,[29] Miller argues that Judah is clearly presented throughout this narrative as the father-in-law of Tamar. Thus "there is no doubt that it is definitely an incest taboo which motivates this story. It is modern commentators, not the ancient narrator, who fear treating the case of Tamar as a case of incest."[30]

There may be a middle ground between these two positions. According to the biblical record, Judah's first wife was Canaanite (Gen 38:2), and it also possible that Tamar was Canaanite (no record of her parentage is given, 38:6) or at least influenced by Canaanite culture through her mother-in-law. In light of ANE parallels in which the father-in-law could be one of the levirate relatives, Miller suggests that "it is possible that Tamar is portrayed as playing by different rules than Judah and the family of Jacob."[31] If this hypothesis should prove true, then both of the above suggestions (incest or no incest) have validity. From Tamar's perspective, following an ANE custom that allows the father-in-law to fulfill the levirate role, there was no incest. But from Judah's perspective, in line with later

---

[29] Miller essentially makes this assumption with no supporting evidence, but it appears that one possible piece of evidence pointing in this direction is the fact that in the laws of Lev 18 and 20 sexual relations between father-in-law and daughter-in-law are one of the capital crimes whereas sexual relations between a man and the wife of his (deceased) brother is presented as the least serious of the forbidden sexual unions (see the discussion below). Such high-level aversion to the father-in-law having relations with his daughter-in-law may indicate that this tradition has a long-standing and deeply rooted place in Israel's history, going back perhaps to the patriarchal period and even before, to the beginning.

[30] Miller, "Sexual Offences in Genesis," 43.

[31] Ibid.

Deuteronomic law, which forbade the father-in-law to be a *levir,* incest did occur (albeit without Judah's knowledge at the time). There are thus enough narrative clues to strongly suggest that an incest taboo somehow lies in the background of the story (at least from the perspective of later Deuteronomic law), but there is not enough information given for us to know for sure whether the patriarchal custom in the time of Jacob allowed for a father-in-law to perform the levirate duty without being guilty of incest.

As we conclude this survey of pentateuchal incest passages, it is significant to note that the two most prominent examples of incest in Genesis—Lot's daughters with their father—involve the one kin relationship that is strangely omitted from the list of forbidden near-of-kin sexual relationships in pentateuchal legislation. Why are father-daughter sexual relations omitted from the detailed list of various prohibited incestuous relationships? Or are they really omitted? We turn now to that legislation for a closer look.

Pentateuchal Legislation against Incestuous Relations

Biblical legislation concerning incest is omitted in the book of the covenant (Exod 19–24) but found in the Holiness Code (Lev 18:6–17; 20:11–12, 14, 17, 19–21) and the Deuteronomic amplification of the seventh commandment (Deut 23:1 [ET 22:30]).

The apodictic ("You shall not") laws concerning incest in Lev 18:7–17 all follow the same sentence pattern: every verse begins with the identical construct noun, *ʿerwat,* "the nakedness of," and culminates in the negative particle plus the imperfect *lōʾ tĕgallēh,* "you shall not uncover."[32] The expression "uncover the nakedness of" is clearly a euphemism for sexual intercourse, and thus this legislation forbids copulation with close relatives (as defined further below). But the legislation also, in effect, proscribes marital unions formed between these close relatives, since in biblical law there is no free sex: the couple who engages in sex must marry (Exod 22:15–16; Deut 22:28–29).[33] "The truth, however, is that the interdictions fall on both copulation and marriage. Incest can never be legitimated by marriage. . . . The question, therefore [of whether these prohibitions deal with copulation or marriage], is academic."[34]

Forbidden sexual liaisons listed in Lev 18:7–17 (and Deut 23:1 [ET 22:30]; 27: 20, 22–23) include those of a man with his

---

[32] Leviticus 18:18–24 has a very different, consistent structural sentence framework. For this and many other reasons, I reject the common assumption that Lev 18:18 continues the discussion of incest, referring to a case of incestuous polygamous marriage to consanguine sisters. Instead the verse should be seen as a categorical prohibition of polygamy (bigamy). See ch. 5 (in the section on polygamy), above, for full discussion.

[33] The term *lāqaḥ,* "take," used in the prohibition of incest in Lev 18:17b, probably here refers to marriage.

[34] Jacob Milgrom, *Leviticus 17–22: A New Translation with Introduction and Commentary* (AB 3a; New York: Doubleday, 2000), 1532. Milgrom documents (with bibliography) the scholarly debate over whether these laws prohibit marriage or copulation, summarizes the arguments, and clearly shows that it is a both-and, not either-or, situation.

1. mother (v. 7)[35]

2. stepmother ("your father's wife," v. 8; cf. Deut 23:1 [ET 22:30]; 27:20)[36]

3. half-sister ("your father's daughter [and stepmother] or your mother's daughter [and her previous husband]," v. 9; cf. Deut 27:22)[37]

4. granddaughter ("your son's daughter or . . . your daughter's daughter," v. 10)

5. stepsister ("your father's wife's daughter," v. 11)

6. paternal aunt ("your father's sister," v. 12)

7. maternal aunt ("your mother's sister," v. 13)

8. paternal aunt by marriage (dôdâ, "aunt," i.e., "your father's brother['s wife]," v. 14)[38]

9. daughter-in-law (kallâ, "daughter-in-law," i.e., "your son's wife," v. 15)

10. sister-in-law ("your brother's wife," v. 16)

11. stepdaughter ("a woman and her daughter," v. 17a)[39]

12. stepgranddaughter ("her son's daughter or her daughter's daughter," v. 17b)

13. mother-in-law (ḥōtenet, Deut 27:23)

---

[35] The verse is best translated, "the nakedness of your father, which is the nakedness of your mother." This verse shows the principle often employed in the euphemism: uncovering the nakedness of the father is actually having sexual relations with his wife. (See below for the probable rationale of this principle.) This prohibition presumably has in view marital union with one's mother after one's father (her husband) has died (or divorced). The point is that the kinship ties established by marriage (with the spouse's close kin) continue even after the spouse dies.

[36] This would cover any additional wife of one's father after the first wife's death or divorce.

[37] Some commentators take the phrase "the nakedness of your sister ['erwat ăḥôtkā]" to cover both full sister and half-sister, but the modifying phrases that follow— "your father's daughter or ['ô] your mother's daughter"—with the intervening "or," seem to imply that it is a half-sister (either on the father's side or the mother's), and not a full sister that is intended. If the first phrase, "your father's daughter," referred to a full sister (as often suggested), then the law would not cover one's half-sister on one's father's side. Verse 9 adds the clause "whether born at home [môledet bayit] or born abroad [môledet ḥûṣ]." The word môledet is a verbal noun that should probably be translated here "family," as in, e.g., Gen 12:1; 24:4. The clause then indicates that the half-sister is forbidden whether she is a member of one's own family or not.

[38] This follows the principle, set down in v. 7, that uncovering the nakedness of a man refers to sexual intercourse with his wife (see the note above). Presumably this law has in view marriage with one's paternal aunt after her first husband has died or divorced. The same principle would hold for the daughter-in-law and sister-in-law in succeeding verses: the prohibited liaison implies a situation after the first husband has died or divorced. As noted above, kinship ties established in marriage are not dissolved when the spouse dies or is divorced.

[39] Again, this most probably presumes not polygamy but marriage to a woman (who had been married before and whose husband died or divorced her), and then marriage to her daughter (by the previous marriage) after the woman's death or divorce.

All of the above forbidden relationships are based on two basic principles: "A man may not marry any woman who is a close blood relation, or any woman who has become a close relative through a previous marriage to one of the man's close blood relations."[40] The latter principle assumes that marriage makes the husband and wife as closely related as parents and children, so that the wife's blood relations are considered also the husband's (and vice versa). The prohibitions referring to marriage kinship are often described as "uncovering the nakedness" of a male relative (Lev 18:7, 8, 14, 16). For example, having sexual relations with one's father's wife is described as "uncovering the nakedness of your father." Wenham explains the rationale in terms of the assumption just enunciated: "Foreign to our way of thinking is the idea that a wife's nakedness is her husband's nakedness and vice versa. . . . In other words, marriage, or more precisely marital intercourse, makes the man and wife as closely related as parents and children. In the words of Gen 2:24, 'they become one flesh.'"[41]

With such a detailed list of forbidden relationships found in the Mosaic law codes, why does the legislation fail to mention the incestuous relationship between father and daughter—the most universally abhorrent and yet probably the most common type of incest in ancient times as well as today?[42] Many suggestions have been made to answer this question:[43] some posit a mistake or inadvertent omission by the redactor;[44] others hypothesize an intentional schematic of editing to make up a certain number of cases to fit an incest decalogue or duodecalogue;[45] still others attempt to derive the father-daughter incest prohibi-

---

[40] Gordon J. Wenham, *Leviticus* (NICOT; Grand Rapids: Eerdmans, 1979), 255. As noted in ch. 4 above with regard to homosexual practice, Lev 18 is written in the default male gender, but implicit in these prohibitions, as in the seventh commandment of Exod 20 which they elaborate, is the applicability to both genders. Thus a woman is tacitly prohibited from having sexual relations with the male equivalent of the close relatives contained in the list.

[41] Ibid., 255.

[42] As noted above, the extrabiblical ANE laws include prohibition of this incestuous relationship. Tirzah Meacham summarizes the modern situation and sharpens the question to be asked of the Hebrew text: "From the point of view of reality, at least as documented in modern times, daughter-father incest not only exists but is also the most common form of incest. We must, therefore, ask: how could the incest code have neglected to mention father-daughter incest?" ("The Missing Daughter: Leviticus 18 and 20," *ZAW* 109 [1997]: 254–55).

[43] For a concise overview of opinions, see, e.g., ibid., 254–56.

[44] See, e.g., Ephraim Neufeld, *Ancient Hebrew Marriage Laws: With Special References to General Semitic Laws and Customs* (New York: Longmans, 1944), 191–92; Arie Noordtzij, *Leviticus* (trans. Raymond Togtman; BSC; Grand Rapids: Zondervan, 1982), 185. But this explanation would require an omission on the part of the biblical authors as well as the redactors; furthermore, it does not explain its omission also in Lev 20, where it is impossible to argue for haplography.

[45] See, e.g., Stephen F. Bigger, "The Family Laws of Leviticus 18 in Their Setting," *JBL* 98 (1979): 187–203; K. Elliger, "Das Gesetz Leviticus 18," *ZAW* 26 (1955): 1–7. This suggestion does not account for why the daughter would have been omitted instead of more distant relatives.

tion from other related Levitical passages.[46] None of these approaches has been entirely successful. It might also be asked why the incestuous relationship with one's mother is mentioned and not with one's daughter when the son-mother incest is (at least today) the rarest type of incest to occur and the father-daughter is the most common?[47] Furthermore, why are other close kin relationships, such as with one's full sister, omitted? Why also are no penalties given in Lev 20 for incest with one's mother, full sister, or daughter?

Susan Rattray has convincingly shown that the key to these issues is found in the opening verse of the incest prohibitions of Lev 18.[48] Rattray calls attention to 18:6, where it is stated, "None of you shall approach anyone near of kin. None of you shall approach [*qārab*, i.e., have sexual intercourse with] anyone near of kin to him [*šĕʾēr bĕśārô*]" (RSV). Rattray points out that the term "close kin" (Rattray's translation, *šĕʾēr bĕśārô*, lit. "flesh of his flesh") in Lev 18:6 is equivalent to the term "close relative" (*šĕʾērô haqqārōb ʾēlāyw*, lit. "his flesh near to him") in 21:2[49] and that the latter passage explicitly spells out who these "close kin" are: mother, father, son, daughter, brother, and virgin (unmarried) sister. Thus "mother, sister and daughter, as close kin, are automatically forbidden by Lev 18:6. The purpose of the list of Lev 18 is to indicate *who else* is forbidden by extension from these basic relationships." In other words, the prohibitions of sexual union with mother, sister, and daughter are implicit in the phrase "close kin [flesh of one's flesh]" (*šĕʾēr bĕśārô*) of Lev 18:6. This phrase is not just a heading for the list that

---

46 This was the approach of the Jewish sages. Meacham, "The Missing Daughter," 255, summarizes four major avenues of derivation that were attempted: (1) from Lev 18:17, "a woman and her daughter" (although the Hebrew strongly implies no biological connection between the daughter and the man); (2) from a *qal wāḥômer* (*a fortiori*) argument based on 18:10, that "your son's daughter and your daughter's daughter" must include one's own daughter (but this was only applied to a daughter born by a woman the man had raped); (3) parallelism between 18:17, "her son's daughter or her daughter's daughter," and 18:10, "your son's daughter or your daughter's daughter" (although this also was restricted to a case of rape); and (4) from 19:29, "do not defile your daughter to prostitute her" (which, however, refers to giving a daughter over to prostitution, not to father-daughter incest).

47 See Robin Fox, *Kinship and Marriage: An Anthropological Perspective* (Harmondsworth, Eng.: Penguin, 1967), 71.

48 Susan Rattray, "Marriage Rules, Kinship Terms, and Family Structure in the Bible," in *SBL Seminar Papers, 1987* (SBLSP 26; Atlanta: Scholars Press, 1987): 537–44. See also Milgrom, *Leviticus 17–22*, 1527–29, who is convinced that Rattray has "satisfactorily accounted for the ostensible omission of the full sister and, esp., of the daughter from the list" (p. 1527). Cf. Madeline G. McClenney-Sadler, "Re-covering the Daughter's Nakedness: A Formal Analysis of Israelite Kinship Terminology and the Internal Logic of Leviticus 18" (PhD diss., Duke University, 2001), who agrees with Rattray that Lev 18:6 implies the daughter, but argues further that v. 17 explicitly supplies the prohibition of the "missing" daughter (pp. 140–43, 156–57). The arguments for interpreting v. 17 as forbidding relations between a man and his own daughter are plausible but not as convincing as the arguments advanced regarding v. 6.

49 Rattray, "Marriage Rules," 542, n. 24, points out that both of these phrases are also used with the meaning of "next of kin" (with the restricting phrase "from his clan" [*mimmšpatô*]) in Lev 25:49 and Num 27:11.

follows; it is a technical term that already implies the obvious instances of incest that involve the nuclear family members.

But why, then, include the mother at the start of the list if the mother is already implicit in the term "close kin [flesh of one's flesh]"? "The reason for beginning the list with the mother is to establish the principle with the one case least likely to occur and the most universally abhorred. In other words, just as one would 'not expose the nakedness of one's father, that is of one's mother' so one must not expose the nakedness of father's wife, half sister, etc."[50] According to Jacob Milgrom, an even more satisfactory explanation is to recognize that "mother and father have been placed in tandem in order that this law may serve a heuristic function, to classify all the following incestuous unions as a violation of either one's father or one's mother."[51] Whichever explanation is preferred, Milgrom finds confirmation in Lev 20 for the basic point common to both suggestions: "That the mother was exceptionally singled out in order to head the list . . . and normally would be taken for granted is proved, in my opinion, by the fact that she is absent from the corresponding list of prohibitions in ch. 20, where a different order prevails and there is no need for the mother to head the list."[52]

Rattray's study also gives a rationale for the selection of the relationships by extension from the basic "close kin." Leviticus 18:7–17 extends to include, in effect, "close kin" of one's "close kin," literally, "flesh" of the "flesh of one's flesh." This is made apparent in various verses where the clarifying statement of relationship indicates that the extended relative is šĕ'ēr, "flesh of," one of those nuclear family members who is "flesh of flesh" to the laws' addressee. Thus one's father's sister is (literally) "flesh of your father" (v. 12); one's mother's sister is (literally) "flesh of your mother" (v. 13); a wife's grandson or granddaughter is her "flesh" (v. 17). In other words, the term "flesh of one's flesh" in 18:6 refers not to "people who are consanguineous to the first and second degree," as often assumed,[53] but only to those who are consanguineous to the first degree, that is, the nuclear family. The succeeding verses (vv. 7–17) spell out who are considered "flesh" (or near of kin) to the "flesh of one's flesh" (i.e., one's nuclear family).

Rattray shows that vv. 7–17 move out in a "hierarchy of closeness: wives, then parents and children, then collateral relatives (siblings and parents' siblings)."[54] The prohibitions extend only to four generations.[55] Regarding one's *wife*

---

[50] Ibid., 542.

[51] Milgrom, *Leviticus 17–22,* 1529, following Fred L. Horton, "Form and Structure in Laws Relating to Women: Leviticus 18:6–18," in *SBL Seminar Papers, 1973* (SBLSP 1; Missoula, Mont.: Scholars Press, 1973), 29–31; and John E. Hartley, *Leviticus* (WBC 4; Waco, Tex.: Word Books, 1992), 287.

[52] Milgrom, *Leviticus 17–22,* 1529–30.

[53] See Wenham, *Leviticus,* 254.

[54] Rattray, "Marriage Rules," 542. Rattray includes also v. 18, but as I have argued earlier, this verse starts a different section of the chapter and deals with the prohibition of bigamy, not incest.

[55] Meacham, "The Missing Daughter," 254, categorizes these four generations: "1) the father's generation, that is, the mother, father's wife, father's sister, mother's sister, father's

(who, in light of Gen 2:24, is so closely connected with the husband that her relatives are treated as "flesh of his flesh"), sexual relations are prohibited with
her mother, daughter, or granddaughter (Lev 18:17; Deut 27:23). Regarding the
next level of hierarchy, *parents and children,* sexual relationships are prohibited
(within a range of four generations) with: (1) one's father's "close kin" (i.e., his
wife, daughter, and sister, Lev 18:8–9, 12); (2) one's mother's "close kin" (i.e., her
daughter and sister, 18:9, 13); (3) one's son's "close kin" (i.e., his wife and daughter, 18:15, 10); and (4) one's daughter's "close kin" (i.e., her daughter, 18:10). In
the final level of the hierarchy, the *collateral relatives* include those related to one's
wife: her brother's wife (18:16) and, by "patrilateral extension," her father's
brother's wife (18:14). On this level the stepsister on the father's side is also prohibited (18:11). Beyond these restrictions, other female relatives, such as one's
first cousin or niece, are permitted as potential marriage partners.

Milgrom succinctly states the natural flow in the order of sexual prohibitions
in 18:6–17: 18:6–11 includes one's *own* closest blood relations; 18:12–14 includes
one's *parents'* closest blood relations and affines; 18:15–16 includes one's *relatives
by marriage;* and 18:17 includes one's *wife's* closest relatives.[56]

The penalties for incest described in Lev 20 are ordered in this same hierarchical pattern, moving from closest relationships to farthest, and it becomes apparent from this ordering that the closer the relationship, the more severe the
penalty. "Incest with near affines was punished by execution while incest with
blood relatives was punished by *kārēt* and incest with collateral affines by *kārēt*
and barrenness."[57]

---

brother's wife, and woman and her mother; 2) the generation of the addressee: sister from
his father, sister from his mother, daughter of father's wife, brother's wife, a woman and
her daughter or a woman and her mother; 3) the generation of children: the daughter-in-
law, and a woman and her daughter; 4) the generation of grandchildren: the son's daugh-
ter, the daughter's daughter, the daughter of the wife's son, the daughter of the wife's
daughter."

[56] Milgrom, *Leviticus 17–22,* 1526. Milgrom's analysis encompasses the entire chapter
and includes v. 18 as one of the forbidden (incestuous) relations; but as concluded above
in ch. 5, this verse constitutes the beginning of a new section of the chapter and forbids
polygyny, not incest. See also the analysis of the incest laws of Lev 18 by Clenney-Sadler,
"Re-covering the Daughter's Nakedness," passim, who argues that "the kinship system of
ancient Israel was *normal Hawaiin*" (p. v), and that the internal logic of Lev 18 is as follows: "Close sexual relations are not permitted between 1) Ego and Ego's close kin
(vv. 7–11); 2) Ego and Ego's close kin's kin (vv. 12–16); 3) Ego and two people who are
close kin to each other (vv. 17–18)" (194). As with Milgrom's analysis, I concur with all
but the interpretation of v. 18.

[57] Rattray, "Marriage Rules," 543. In terms of the overall structure of Lev 20 in comparison to the overall structure Lev 18, Milgrom, *Leviticus 17–22,* 1742, notes also contrast
of arrangement. Whereas the entire chapter of Lev 18 is ordered by family relationships
from the closest to the farthest (moving from incestuous relationships in the first part of
the chapter to forbidden sex with nonrelatives in the second half), in Lev 20 all the prohibitions are arranged according to punishments, based on the crime's severity, from the
most severe to the least, thus lumping all the capital sex crimes in the first section (including mother-daughter incest, adultery, sodomy, and bestiality), all the crimes punished by

For participating in any of the "abominations" mentioned in Lev 18, including the various degrees of incest, the general punishment mentioned (18:29) was
kārēt, to be "cut off" (i.e., to receive a divine curse of extinction for both sinner
and progeny, as discussed above).[58] In addition, the case laws of Lev 20 mention
capital punishment for some of these incestuous relations: with one's mother,
mother-in-law, or daughter-in-law (20:11, 12, 14). The incestuous relationship
with one's daughter-in-law is called *tebel*, "perversion, confusion"—a violation of
the natural order (20:12). This word is employed only one other time in the HB: in
the prohibition against bestiality (18:23; see ch. 4, above). Particular abhorrence
against incest with one's mother-in-law after being married to her daughter is indicated by use of the term *zimmâ*, "depravity, wickedness, lewdness,"[59] and the
prescribed penalty of burning up the offenders (20:14): "If a man takes ['takes'
(*lāqaḥ*)][60] a wife and her mother also, it is depravity [*zimmâ*]; they shall be
burned to death, both he and they, that there may be no depravity [*zimmâ*]
among you."

On the second level of the crimes' severity, relations with one's half-sister,
mother's sister, or father's sister result in both parties being "cut off [*kārēt*, divine
curse of extinction] in the sight of their people" (20:17). Milgrom points out the
legal implication of *kārēt:* since it is a punishment administered by God himself,
it "cannot be punished by a human court."[61] But the addition of the phrase "in
the sight of their people" seems to imply "that the community will witness that
they will die prematurely . . . : they will not receive a proper burial, and/or their
children will die before them; that is, their line will be cut off."[62]

As a result of relations with one's aunt (mother's sister or father's sister),
both parties "shall be subject to punishment" (20:19); the expression *nāśā'*
ʿāwōn, "bear iniquity/punishment," probably "is not a penalty but a declaratory
formula stating that punishment is sure to follow."[63] The penalty for incest with

---

kārēt in the second section, and all the crimes punishable by childlessness in the third section. Thus the punishments for incestuous relationships are mixed with punishments for
other crimes of equal severity throughout Lev 20.

[58] See the discussion of *kārēt* in ch. 4, above; cf. Milgrom, *Leviticus 17–22*, 1458, 1758;
and idem, *Leviticus 1–16: A New Translation with Introduction and Commentary* (AB 3;
New York: Doubleday, 1991), 457–61.

[59] The term *zimmâ*, "wickedness, foul deed, lewdness," "is predominantly used to depict certain acts as shameful and repugnant to God. . . . [The term] occurs a few times in a
declaratory formula used to pronounce certain sexual relations as potently defiling. . . .
Such lewd acts were so defiling that over the course of time they so polluted the Promised
Land that it disgorged its inhabitants" (John E. Hartley, "זִמָּה," *NIDOTTE* 1:1113). Cf. S.
Steingrimsson, "זָמַם *zmm*," *TDOT* 4:89, who tallies twenty-two occurrences of *zimmâ* in
the OT with the meaning of "wickedness, lewdness."

[60] Again, this most likely presumes not polygamy but marriage to a woman and then,
after the woman died or was divorced, marriage to her mother-in-law. The point is that
the kinship relationship established by marriage continues even after the man is no longer
married to his wife and that the wife's near of kin continue to be the man's near of kin.

[61] Milgrom, *Leviticus 17–22*, 1754.

[62] Ibid.

[63] Ibid., 1757; cf. 1488–90 for further discussion.

one's aunt is not specified, but since it immediately follows the preceding punish-ment of *kārēt* in v. 18 and since the same phrase, "be subject to punishment" (*nāśā² ²āwōn*), is used in v. 17 in connection with the *kārēt* punishment, probably the *kārēt* punishment applies here in v. 19 as well.

Finally, on the third level of (lessening degree of) punishment, an aunt (un-cle's wife) or sister-in-law (brother's wife) both receive the penalty of being *²ărîrîm*, "childless"[64] (20:20–21). The difference between the punishment of *kārēt* and childlessness (*²ărîrîm*) is not entirely clear. The rabbis' distinction is plausi-ble: they defined *kārēt* as premature death (before the age of sixty) plus the ex-tinction of one's bloodline whereas the punishment of being childless (*²ărîrîm*) meant the extinction of one's bloodline but not premature death.[65]

The prohibition of relations with one's brother's wife (Lev 20:21) is the last of the prohibitions mentioned in Lev 20. It is the last of a list of sexual offenses that proceeds in descending order of seriousness, and thus this prohibition is considered the least serious of all the illicit sexual relations mentioned in Lev 20. Regarding this sexual relationship, there appear none of the strong terms of moral disapproval and/or portrayals of the various means of capital punishment to fit the crime that accompany other prohibited sexual liaisons of Lev 20; rather, the text only describes it as *niddâ*—which is elsewhere in the Pentateuch a cere-monial uncleanness. Only regarding this relationship in Lev 20 is the word "un-clean" (*niddâ*) used. By means of such textual clues, 20:21 not only gives a general rule forbidding a man to marry and have sex with the wife of his deceased brother (and states the punishment of childlessness for such action) but at the same time utilizes specialized language that allows for the exception in case of levirate mar-riage as described in Deut 25:5–10 (in which case the punishment of childlessness is turned into a blessing of fertility).[66] (See ch. 11, below, for a full discussion of these points.)

Unlike the adultery-related extramarital sexual distortions (homosexual practice, bestiality, adultery) that are presented in Scripture as absolute crimes against God and invariably demanding the death penalty, the penalties for incest become less severe as one moves to lesser degrees of intimacy. This gradation of penalty, coupled with the fact that brother-sister marriage was once unavoidable

---

[64] See ibid. for a summary of the debate over the meaning of this word and a defense of the traditional translation.

[65] *b. Mo²ed Qat.* 28a, cited in Milgrom, *Leviticus 17–22*, 1758. Milgrom's other sug-gestion is unconvincing: the one who is "cut off" "not only suffers the termination of his lineage, but is 'excised' from joining his ancestors." The one punished with childlessness, on the other hand, "joins his ancestors. But what good does it do him?" Milgrom asks rhe-torically. Ultimately, if this interpretation is taken, there is no difference in punishment between the two.

[66] Milgrom, ibid., 1545, also acknowledges the strong possibility that Lev 18:16 and 20:21 provide the general rule and Deut 25:5–10 the exception, but in my view he fails to recognize the implication of the use of *niddâ* here, despite the testimony of ancient Jewish sources he himself cites (p. 1758) that do (*Sipra, parashat Qedoshim, pereq* 12:7; Ibn Ezra). See my more detailed discussion and critique in the following chapter.

(at the beginning of this world's history, in order for Adam and Eve's children to "be fruitful and multiply") and for some time apparently not forbidden (as in the case of Abraham and Sarah), seems to imply that at least some forms of close-kin marriage are not inherently immoral of themselves. As mentioned above (and further elucidated in ch. 11, below), an exception is made to the prohibition against sexual intercourse with one's sister-in-law if one's brother has died without children (Deut 25:5). At the same time, some kinds of incestuous relationships—including probably the forms for which the mandatory death penalty was attached—seem to have been greatly offensive to God from the beginning.

Although no special rationale is given for these laws in the text, one may infer that they came, at least in part, as attempts to improve the lot of humanity, especially for women. These laws in Leviticus had "the objective of improving the status of women within the framework of ancient Israel's patriarchal family structure."[67] They may also have served to limit birth defects that came from close inbreeding. The devastating effects of close-relative marriages is apparent today in situations where there have been centuries of close inbreeding.[68] Robert Gagnon summarizes four possible aims of the laws against incest:

> (1) protecting females (both blood relations and in-laws), including girls, in the intimate context of an extended family from the predatory sexual habits of male family members; (2) reducing sexual temptations within the family and preventing infidelity, which breeds alienation and distrust in one's spouse and could result in the dissolution of a family; (3) reducing intergenerational conflict, disorder, and dishonor that would arise through sexual rivalry within the family; and (4) ensuring healthy offspring by limiting inbreeding.[69]

Along with (or among) these various suggested rationales for the laws against incest, is there a single theological issue undergirding the forbidden degrees of kinship marriages? I suggest that the expression šěʾēr běśārô (lit. "flesh of one's flesh") in Lev 18:6 not only provides the key to explaining the individuals

---

[67] Jonathan R. Ziskind, "Legal Rules on Incest in the Ancient Near East," *RIDA* 35 (1988): 104; cf. idem, "The Missing Daughter in Leviticus xviii," *VT* 46 (1996): 128–29. The question of whether this "reform" was an attempt to improve on existing law codes at the time this legislation was written, as implied by Ziskind and Milgrom, takes us beyond a final-form theology of the text.

[68] A striking example of the long-term effects of close inbreeding is found in the Samaritans of Israel. With only about 600 Samaritans remaining (see www.the-samaritans .com.), there is of necessity much inbreeding, and the effects are seen in the numerous kinds of physical and psychological defects permeating the Samaritan population. See R. K. Harrison, *Leviticus: An Introduction and Commentary* (TOTC 3; Downers Grove, Ill.: InterVarsity, 1980), 189 (and the scientific sources he cites), for other studies showing that inbreeding "is accompanied by an increase in congenital malformations and perinatal mortality" and for a delineation of risk rates illustrating the principle that "the closer the relationship between those who marry, the more frequent is the incidence of harmful or lethal genes."

[69] Robert A. J. Gagnon, *The Bible and Homosexual Practice: Texts and Hermeneutics* (Nashville: Abingdon, 2001), 137.

missing from, and the hierarchical pattern behind, the list of forbidden sexual relationships but also shows the linkage with the divine ideal for marriage in Gen 2 and highlights the foundational rationale for these sexual prohibitions. A fundamental principle of these laws goes back to the "one flesh" of husband and wife in Gen 2:24. "The regulations [concerning incest] interpret relationships of affinity (connection by marriage) in terms of the principle that man and wife are 'one flesh' (Gn. 2:24), *i.e.*, kin or blood relations."[70] The expression *šĕʾēr bĕśārô* in Lev 18:6 also recalls Adam's statement regarding Eve when she was first created from his rib (Gen 2:23): "This at last is bone of my bones and *flesh of my flesh*." The latter term, as highlighted in the discussion of sexuality in Eden (ch. 1, above), refers to the intimate bond of solidarity and intimacy between the first married couple. The incest laws, echoing terminology for intimacy from Gen 2, thus constitute a prohibition of forbidden degrees of intimacy. As Hoffner defines incest, it concerns "partners who are *too intimately related* by blood or by marriage to allow sexual intercourse."[71] (Hence a discussion of incest is included in this chapter on marital intimacy and its distortions.) The undergirding theological rationale integrating these laws is to prevent any illicit (incestuous) intimacy from interfering with or distorting the legitimate and sacred intimacy between husband and wife.

All of the illicit sexual relationships enumerated in Lev 18 are considered *tôʿēbâ*—an "abomination" or "detestable thing" (Lev 18:29). The laws proscribing incestuous relationships are included among the laws that, as stressed in this chapter, Lev 18–20 elevates to a status of ongoing, universal validity: laws applicable to both Israelites and the strangers from other nations who live among them, laws prohibiting activities that caused the land to vomit out the Canaanites and other nations (and would vomit out Israel and any other nation that violated them). The ultimate theological rationale for the incest laws, as well as all the other legislation regarding sexuality in Lev 18–20, is the preservation of community holiness in sexual conduct (Lev 20:26). Thus they must be taken as seriously today by God's "holy people" as the legislation against polygamy, homosexual practices, bestiality, and adultery.

Incest in the Prophets

Amnon and Tamar (2 Sam 13). The one incident of incest that is treated at any length in the Prophets is that of the incestuous rape of Tamar by Amnon recorded in 2 Sam 13 (discussed further in ch. 12).[72] Along with a portrayal of the shocking

---

[70] Harrison, *Leviticus*, 186.
[71] Hoffner, "Incest, Sodomy, and Bestiality," 83.
[72] Some scholars have suggested another instance of incest between David and his half-sister Abigail. See, e.g., Jon D. Levenson and Baruch Halpern, "The Political Import of David's Marriages," *JBL* 99 (1980): 507–18; and Hepner, "Abraham's Incestuous Marriage," 153. This hypothesis, however, posits the hypothetical reconstruction of an allegedly corrupt and reedited Hebrew text and claims that later biblical tradition suppressed the memory of this incestuous union. As Levenson and Halpern admit, their conclusions are "highly reconstructive . . . , speculative, and quite possibly incorrect" (pp. 507–8). Such

horror of rape, the narrative also seems to focus on the aspect of incest.[73] Throughout the narrative the terms "my brother" and "my sister" occur repeatedly. In the introductory scenes, Amnon refers to Tamar as "my sister Tamar" (vv. 5, 6), and Amnon is referred to as "her/your brother" (vv. 7, 8) The dialogue at the moment preceding the incestuous rape also may highlight the brother-sister relationship: "[Amnon her brother] took hold of her, and said to her, 'Come, lie with me, my sister.' She answered him, 'No, my brother, do not force me'" (vv. 11–12). And the aftermath of the violent act likewise is marked by repeated familial references: "Her brother Absalom said to her, 'Has Amnon your brother been with you? Be quiet for now, my sister; he is your brother; do not take this to heart'" (v. 20).[74]

The text also seems to explicitly indicate that incest was regarded at that time as inappropriate behavior. The narrator states at the outset of the story, "and it seemed impossible [or 'inappropriate,' nip^cal of $p\bar{a}l\bar{a}$']"[75] to Amnon to do any-

---

speculative reconstructions are outside the purview of this canonical theology. On the basis of the final form of the OT canon, the references to Abigail in the biblical accounts indicate two different individuals (one is Nabal's wife, who married David [1 Sam 25; 27:3; 30:5, 18; 2 Sam 2:2, 3 (= 1 Chr 3:1)], and the other is David's sister [1 Chr 2:16–17; 2 Sam 17:25]) and do not describe an incestuous relationship involving David. For plausible explanations for the apparent contradiction in the biblical passages concerning who was the latter Abigail's father, see Edward Mack, "Abigail," ISBE 1:7–8.

[73] Most critical/feminist scholars reject the conclusion that the issue of incest is present in this passage, because of their source-critical assumption that the books of Samuel predate the Pentateuch. At least one critical scholar, however, Pamela Tamarkin Reis ("Cupidity and Stupidity: Woman's Agency and the 'Rape' of Tamar," JNES 25 [1997]: 43–60), argues that the final redactor intended the story to be read as an integrated whole with the Pentateuch and that the clues for the presence of incest must be taken seriously (although, unfortunately, her unconvincing hypothesis that the incest was consensual and not rape overshadows her strong arguments in favor of incest in this passage).

[74] Hilary B. Lipka, "'Such a Thing Is Not Done in Israel': The Construction of Sexual Transgression in the Hebrew Bible" (PhD diss., Brandeis University, 2004), 275–80, provides an alternative reading. Lipka suggests that incest is not a factor at all in the minds of Tamar and Amnon, since this is never explicitly mentioned as an objection by Tamar against Amnon's advances. The language emphasizing brother-sister relationships, argues Lipka, must be seen in light of the culture in which a brother was responsible for protecting the sexual purity of his sister and avenging any sexual transgressions against her. Tragically, Tamar's brother, instead of protecting her, raped her. Although I still lean toward the reading in which the narrator emphasizes the incestuous nature of the crime as well as the rape, this alternate interpretation cannot be altogether ruled out. Kenneth A. Stone, Sex, Honor, and Power in the Deuteronomistic History (JSOTSup 234; Sheffield, Eng.: JSOT Press, 1996), 107, also sees the reference to brother-sister relations as primarily emphasizing the brother's responsibility to protect his sister's sexual purity but does not rule out a reference to incest as well: "'Incest' does not seem to be the primary sexual issue at stake in the story, although the incestuous relation may have intensified an already volatile situation, that is, the rape of another man's sister."

[75] BDB 810; cf. HALOT 927. In this verse I also prefer to separate the reason that it is inappropriate/impossible for him to have relations with her from the statement that Tamar was a virgin. It does not make sense that he could do nothing if she was any other virgin than his sister—she would be fully eligible for him to woo. Alternatively, Lipka,

thing to her" (v. 2). This apparently alludes back to the pentateuchal legislation against incest with one's half-sister (Lev 18:9; 20:17; Deut 27:22). The impropriety/ impossibility of an incestuous sexual encounter also may be behind Tamar's re- fusal of her half-brother's request to come and lie with him. She replies, "No, my brother, do not force [ʿinnâ in the piʿel, 'violate/rape/degrade'] me; for such a thing is not done in Israel; do not do anything so vile [něbālâ]!" (2 Sam 13:12). She speaks of the "shame" (ḥerpâ) that would be hers and the reputation of being an "impious and presumptuous fool [nābāl]"[76] that would be his (v. 13). It is also possible that Tamar is referring to the aspect of rape and not incest.

From the perspective of a canonical reading of this narrative, it is not clear why Tamar says to Amnon, "Now therefore, I beg you, speak to the king; for he will not withhold me from you" (13:13b). Perhaps she somehow thinks that her royal father has the power to waive the Mosaic prohibition, perhaps justifying his action by the precedent of Abraham's marriage to his half-sister (Gen 20:12). Per- haps the moral state of the royal court had fallen so low in the aftermath of Da- vid's adultery that Tamar felt her father could not object to the request for an incestuous marriage in light of his own moral indiscretions. Perhaps during the period of the Davidic monarchy, at least in the royal court, marriage between brother and half-sister was not regarded as incestuous, regardless of any taboo or prior legislation. Perhaps Tamar was genuinely unaware of the law prohibiting sexual relations with a half-brother.[77] Or perhaps she was trying to buy time to avoid the incident, confident that the king would say no. The narrative does not give us sufficient information to decide for sure. (See ch. 12, below, for the baleful results of Amnon's treatment of his sister.)

Absalom and His Father's Concubines (2 Sam 15–16). Another case of incest oc- curred during the time of Absalom's rebellion against his father, King David. When David was forced to flee from Jerusalem, he left ten concubines, members of his royal harem, to take care of the palace (2 Sam 15:16). When Absalom occu- pied Jerusalem, his counselor Ahithophel advised Absalom, "Go in to your fa- ther's concubines, the ones he has left to look after the house; and all Israel will hear that you have made yourself odious to your father, and the hands of all who are with you will be strengthened" (16:21). Absalom heeded his counselor's sug- gestion: "So they pitched a tent for Absalom upon the roof; and Absalom went in to his father's concubines in the sight of all Israel" (16:22). This act was clearly a blatant social act to demonstrate his authority supplanting that of David. The

---

"'Such a Thing Is Not Done in Israel,'" 278, and others translate the nipʿal of pālāʾ here as "to be difficult" and understand that Amnon found it to be difficult to be alone with his sister because she was probably protected by a guardian and by her full brother, Absalom. In this reading, Amnon was not interested in wooing his sister but only in having sex with her. This interpretation is plausible but not preferable.

[76] BDB 614.

[77] Many critical scholars would maintain that the relevant pentateuchal legislation came later than the incident described in this narrative, but even from that perspective, the Levitical rules regarding incest may have been in effect in Tamar's time. Here I seek to make sense of a final-form reading of the text set within the context of the entire canon.

disastrous results of this rebellious and incestuous act are clear in the circumstances of the civil war that ensued and the tragic end of Absalom.

Other Cases of Incest. Incestuous relationships are also recorded during the divided monarchy. The prophet Amos describes an apparent case of incest that was prevalent in the eighth century, perhaps in connection with the fertility cult rites: "father and son go in to the same girl, so that my holy name is profaned" (Amos 2:7; cf. Lev 18:7–8, 15, 17; 20:10–11; Deut 27:20). Such activity should not be surprising in the Canaanite fertility cult setting inasmuch as in the Baal cult mythology, there is an incestuous sexual relationship between the storm god Hadad (Baal), who dominates the Canaanite pantheon, and his sister, usually described as Anat (or Baal's consort Asherah).

Before the Babylonian exile, incest still was a problem in Israel. Ezekiel mingles cultic and social abuses in his indictment of Jerusalem and delineates in one passage such sexual crimes as adultery and incestuous relations with mother, daughter-in-law, and sister: "In you they uncover their fathers' nakedness. . . . One commits abomination with his neighbor's wife; another lewdly defiles his daughter-in-law; another in you defiles his sister, his father's daughter" (Ezek 22:10–11; cf. 33:26). After the Babylonian exile, there is no written record of incestuous relationships among God's covenant people in the remainder of OT history.

The treatment of incest in the Prophets is consistent with that of the Pentateuch.[78] All of the narratives and legislation in the OT dealing with incest reveal that incestuous relationships are out of harmony with the divine will for sexuality. By prohibiting incest, God seeks to eliminate the intimacy of close relations that would subvert the original divine design for intimacy in marriage set forth in Gen 1–2.

Incest and Divine Grace

To those who have committed incest the OT proffers the same word of divine grace and forgiveness and empowerment for purity as to those who have committed other sexual sins (see ch. 8, above, regarding adultery and extramarital sex). To the victims of incest God offers the same comfort and consolation as to other victims of sexual abuse, as God assists them to work through their pain and brokenness.[79] But the severe sanctions against incestuous relations in the OT legislation provide clear evidence of God's abhorrence of this sexual distortion and a solemn foreshadowing of end-time divine judgment upon those who take lightly these ongoing and universal moral prohibitions.

---

[78] I have not found any references to incest in the Writings.

[79] For description of this pain and how Scripture can be misused or correctly used to facilitate healing, see, e.g., Catherine Clark Kroeger and James R. Beck, eds., *Women, Abuse, and the Bible: How Scripture Can Be Used to Hurt or to Heal* (Grand Rapids: Baker, 1996), passim. Cf. Peter Rutter, *Sex in the Forbidden Zone: When Men in Power—Therapists, Doctors, Clergy, Teachers, and Others—Betray Women's Trust* (Los Angeles: Jeremy P. Tarcher, 1989).

🪷11

Procreative Sexuality versus Problems/Distortions (Childlessness, Children Born out of Wedlock, and Abortion)

Positive Affirmations of the Edenic Ideal

The First Children

In the first narrative about life outside Eden, sexuality is not only positively affirmed by the terminology employed to denote intercourse but also by the value placed upon the conception and birth resulting from the sexual encounter (Gen 4:1). The birth of Cain brought to Adam and Eve the realization of that special added divine blessing of procreation that was promised and commanded at creation. What is more, Cain was welcomed into the world as a child of destiny; Eve seems to have at first thought he was the messianic seed promised by God after the fall (3:15).[1] Even after the death of Abel and the banishment of Cain, it appears that Eve remained unshaken in her messianic hope, with confidence that Seth was "appointed" by God as "another seed" (NKJV)—if not the ultimate seed,

---

[1] For substantiation of the messianic interpretation of Gen 3:15, see esp. Afolarin Ojewole, "The Seed in Gen 3:15: An Exegetical and Intertextual Study" (PhD diss., Andrews University, 2002), passim. Eve's words recorded in Gen 4:1 should probably be translated, "I have gotten a man—the Lord!" See Walter C. Kaiser Jr., *Toward an Old Testament Theology* (Grand Rapids: Zondervan, 1978), 37, 79, for the linguistic basis for the translation. Cf. Gen 36:24, where an identical grammatical construction occurs, with a second direct object (a proper noun) following in apposition to the first (a common noun). I find unconvincing the recent feminist/deconstructionist interpretation that sees here Eve in an "expansive mood" celebrating her cocreation ("With Yahweh I have made a man") and presenting an "ironic retort" to her husband, saying in effect, "You claim to have made *ishah,* but I have made *ish*" (Mark G. Brett, *Genesis: Procreation and the Politics of Identity* [Old Testament Readings; London: Routledge, 2000], 27, 30). Cf. Ilana Pardes, "Beyond Genesis 3: The Politics of Maternal Naming," in *A Feminist Companion to Genesis* (ed. Athalya Brenner; FCB 2; Sheffield, Eng.: Sheffield Academic Press, 1993), 178–93.

the Messiah, at least a link in the genealogy of that seed.[2] The genealogies of Gen 5 and 11 carry forward the record of that line of holy seed, the sons of God. After the flood, the original command to Adam and Eve in Eden is repeated to Noah, the "new Adam": "Be fruitful and multiply, and fill the earth" (9:1; cf. 1:28).[3]

Procreative Fruitfulness, Covenant, and Circumcision

In the patriarchal narratives of Genesis, there are openness and frankness in dealing with various sexual subjects related to procreative function, such as menopause (18:11); conception, birth, nursing, and weaning (21:1–8); menstrual periods (31:34–35); use of aphrodisiacs (36:15); and the problem of infertility (16:1; 25:21; we will return to the latter problem below). Free use of procreative descriptions and metaphors continues throughout the rest of the OT, with a concentrated emphasis upon a woman's labor and the child-birthing process.[4]

With the call of Abraham, the blessing of procreative "fruitfulness" becomes a central part of God's everlasting covenant with his chosen people.[5] Procreation is held in high regard not merely for the economic advantage of having children but because of "the idea that by means of descendants the People of the Covenant would be kept in existence and thereby the blessing to the man and to the woman would be perpetuated."[6] And there is more. L. L. Walker writes of the "expectation of every mother [in ancient Israel] that she might be the mother of the Messiah."[7] I concur: Yahweh's climactic promise of "offspring" (*zera*[c], lit. "seed") to Abraham after the test on Mt. Moriah includes not only the assurance of numerical multiplication of seed (collective)—"I will make your offspring as numerous as the stars of heaven and as the sand that is on the seashore"—but narrows to the one messianic seed, who "will possess the gate of *his* [sg.] enemies" (22:17, translation mine). Most modern versions (with the notable exceptions of the KJV, ESV, and the margin of the NASB) fail to capture the crucial nuance of the move from collective to singular. But comparison with other usage of personal pronouns with the word *zera*[c] "offspring" throughout

---

[2] Gen 4:1–3, 25; cf. 5:3. For discussion of these verses and the messianic "seed" motif in the Hebrew Bible, see esp. Ojewole, "The Seed in Gen 3:15," 251–351.

[3] For substantiation of the parallels between the original Adam in Eden and Noah as a "new Adam" in a postdiluvian "new creation," see Warren Austin Gage, *The Gospel of Genesis: Studies in Protology and Eschatology* (Winona Lake, Ind.: Carpenter Books, 1984), 7–16.

[4] Note the following examples of labor/childbirth imagery in the Prophets: Isa 13:8; 21:3; 26:17; 42:14; 66:6–7; Jer 4:31; 6:24; 13:21; 20:14–18; 22:23; 30:6; 48:41; 49:22, 24; 50:43; Hos 13:13; Mic 4:9–10.

[5] E.g., Gen 12:2; 13:16; 15:4–5; 17:2–8, 20; 22:16–18; 26:3–4; 28:3–4; 35:11–12; 48:4. For an overview of the covenantal promise of "offspring" in the Pentateuch and beyond, see esp. Thomas Edward McComiskey, *The Covenants of Promise: A Theology of the Old Testament Covenants* (Grand Rapids: Baker, 1985), 17–38.

[6] Piper, *The Biblical View of Sex and Marriage*, 33.

[7] L. L. Walker, "Barren, Barrenness," *ZPEB* 1:479, providing, however, no biblical substantiation.

the Hebrew Bible reveals the significance of this nuance: when *zera*ᶜ "offspring" is to be taken in a collective idea, the modifying pronouns are always plural, but when *zera*ᶜ "offspring" refers to a single individual, the pronouns are singular (as here and Gen 3:15).[8]

In light of God's special purpose for Abraham in becoming "exceedingly fruitful" (17:6) and having descendants as numerous as the particles of dust (13:16) or the stars (15:5), ultimately issuing in the coming of the messianic seed, it is not surprising that God chooses the male organ of regeneration upon which to place the sign of his covenant with his chosen people. Numerous theories have been advanced for the origin and significance of circumcision among various ancient peoples, but a practice common elsewhere in the ancient Near East was infused with new meaning in the OT.[9] Whereas in other ANE cultures circumcision

---

[8] See discussion of this consistent usage in the HB by Ojewole, "The Seed in Genesis 3:15," 191–94; cf. Jack Collins, "A Syntactical Note (Genesis 3:15): Is the Woman's Seed Singular or Plural?" *TynBul* 48 (1997): 143. Note that the verse immediately following this narrowing to the individual seed is the messianic promise: "In your seed all the earth shall be blessed" (Gen 22:18 NASB)—the very verse cited by Paul in Gal 3:8 as embodying the gospel regarding Christ. Paul's insight that Gen 22 ultimately does not refer to "offsprings" but to the "offspring" surely indicates that he was aware of this narrowing from the many "descendants" to the one "offspring" and was engaged in careful close reading of the plain sense (*peshat*) of the Hebrew text, not an eisegetical midrash. For further discussion, see C. John Collins, *Genesis 1–4: A Linguistic, Literary, and Theological Commentary* (Phillipsburg, N.J.: P & R Publishing, 2006), 178–80; idem, "Galatians 3:16: What Kind of Exegete Was Paul?" *TynBul* 54, no. 1 (2003): 75–86; Jo Ann Davidson, "Abraham, Akedah, and Atonement," in *Creation, Life, and Hope: Essays in Honor of Jacques B. Doukhan* (ed. Jiří Moskala; Berrien Springs, Mich.: Old Testament Department, Seventh-day Adventist Theological Seminary, Andrews University, 2000), 69–71; and Richard M. Davidson, "New Testament Use of the Old Testament," *JATS* 5, no. 1 (1994): 30–31.

[9] For a survey of rationales for circumcision in the ancient Near East and beyond, see Michael V. Fox, "The Sign of the Covenant: Circumcision in the Light of the Priestly 'ôt Etiologies," *RB* 81 (1974): 557–96; Erich Isaac, "Circumcision as a Covenant Rite," *Anthropos* 59 (1964): 444–56; T. Lewis and C. E. Armerding, "Circumcision," *ISBE* 1:701–2; and Charles Weiss, "Motives for Male Circumcision among Preliterate and Literate People," *Journal of Sex Research* 2 (1966): 76–84.
    In the ancient Near East, circumcision was practiced among the West Semitic peoples of Syro-Palestine (Hebrews, Moabites, Ammonites, Edomites) but not among the East Semites of Mesopotamia (Babylonians and Assyrians), nor in Canaan among the Philistines or (later) among the Greeks. In Egypt circumcision was practiced among the upper (esp. priestly) class but consisted of slitting the foreskin and letting it hang free, instead of removing it altogether, as among West Semitic peoples. For further discussion and bibliography, see esp. David L. Gollaher, *Circumcision: A History of the World's Most Controversial Surgery* (New York: Basic Books, 2000); Robert G. Hall, "Circumcision," *ABD* 1:1025–31; J. Philip Hyatt, "Circumcision," *IDB* 1:629–31; and Jack M. Sasson, "Circumcision in the Ancient Near East," *JBL* 85 (1966): 473–76. Jason S. Derouchie argues, on the basis of biblical and extrabiblical evidence, that although circumcision by amputation of the foreskin was known outside Israel, "from the Middle Bronze Age (2000 B.C.) through the early Roman period (A.D. 125)—the time roughly associated with biblical Israel, Israel alone amputated the foreskin" ("Circumcision in the Hebrew Bible and Targums: Theology, Rhetoric, and the Handling of Metaphor," *BBR* 14 [2004]: 187). In light of Jer 9:24–25 (ET 9:25–26), Derouchie suggests that slitting, not removing, the

was apparently performed on males at the onset of puberty, probably "as a rite of initiation for manhood and marriage,"[10] the Hebrews were required to circumcise their males on the eighth day after birth (17:12). The theological meaning of the rite in the OT is explained to Abraham (17:11): "You shall circumcise the flesh of your foreskins, and it shall be a sign of the covenant between me and you."[11] Circumcision marks Abraham and his descendants (and others not biologically related to Abraham who wished to become part of the covenant community) as participants in the covenant. The Jew who is circumcised "carries in his flesh a constant reminder of the fact that his own self-perpetuation is also the perpetuation of Israel's mission and that the offspring which he begets are not merely his own heirs, but also the prospective agents and witnesses of an eternal God."[12] Circumcision is a private, not public, covenant sign: "the all-seeing God beholds the mark beneath the clothes and recognizes the bearer as his own. And the man, every time he sees his nudity, recalls his obligations to God under the covenant."[13]

Meredith G. Kline argues that the "cutting off" of the flesh in the act of circumcision is in fact an implicit act of covenant commitment (although the infant has no say in the matter), equivalent to the statement of a wish to be personally "cut off" if one fails to keep the covenant (something like "God do this to me and more, if I am not faithful to the covenant"); the cutting of the male organ of regeneration implies even the "cutting off" of one's descendants as well as their consecration.[14]

In the context of Gen 17, it appears that the cutting of the male sex organ also had a significance beyond the making of a covenant oath that included future descendants. Abraham had attempted to fulfill God's promise of descendants by means of his own sexual prowess (Gen 16), and now circumcision required the cutting of the part of his body through which God's promise of descendants would be fulfilled. Surely this symbolized that the divine blessing does not depend upon human sexual prowess for accomplishment; the covenant promises depend upon God's faithfulness and the human's total dependence upon God.

---

foreskin may have been the kind of circumcision practiced among Israel's West Semitic neighbors, as in Egypt (p. 188).

[10] Leslie C. Allen, "Circumcision," *NIDOTTE* 4:374.

[11] Cf. 17:13: "So shall my covenant be in your flesh an everlasting covenant." For an overview of the origin, practice, and significance of circumcision as presented in the Pentateuch and beyond, see esp. Paul R. Williamson, "Circumcision," *DOTP* 122–25. See also Andreas Blaschke, *Beschneidung: Zeugnisse der Bible und verwandter Texte* (Texte und Arbeiten zum neutestamentlicher Zeitalter 28; Tübingen: Francke, 1998); and Klaus Gründwaldt, *Exil und Identität: Beschneidung, Passa, und Sabbat in der Preisterschrift* (BBB 85; Frankfurt am Main: Anton Hain, 1992).

[12] Theodore Gaster, *The Holy and the Profane: Evolution of Jewish Folkways* (New York: W. Sloane Associates, 1955), 53.

[13] William H. Propp, "Circumcision: The Private Sign of the Covenant," *BibRev* 20, no. 4 (August 2004): 25.

[14] Meredith G. Kline, *By Oath Consigned* (Grand Rapids: Eerdmans, 1968), 39–49, 86–89.

God is demanding that Abram concede, symbolically, that fertility is not his own to exercise without divine let or hindrance. A physical reduction in the literal super-abundance of Abram's penis is a sign with an intrinsic relationship to what it signifies. . . . The organ and the power behind it now belong partly to God.[15]

John Goldingay moves this theological rationale even further, advancing the fascinating thesis that circumcision, far from being a sign of those who are fit to be God's special people, instead indicates those "who embody spiritual and mental *unfitness* to belong to the people of promise." And those who are unfit are the males. This conclusion is supported by the circumcision stories in the Bible, which highlight men's state of unfitness at the time the circumcision takes place. Such, as already noted, was the situation of Abram: "Abraham was supposed to see the fulfilment of God's promise through his sexual activity, but before that happens his sexual activity is the means whereby he seeks to engineer his own fulfilment of God's promise." Moses likewise, in the account of Exod 4:24–26, was "in breach of the crucial covenant requirement in Genesis 17," and "he had not taken seriously the significance of the sign of circumcision" when he failed to circumcise his son; the Lord sought to kill him until Zipporah performed the required rite upon their son.[16] For sons of Israel as a whole, circumcision is "a sign of a disciplinedness which the Israelite community actually lacks." Viewed in this way, circumcision does not militate against women in the covenant relationship. To the contrary, it signifies that "men in particular lack the moral and spiritual commitment and discipline that make holiness possible . . . and that their sexuality is a focus of that lack." It is important, Goldingay urges, not to rob circumcision of its "cutting edge with regard to men."[17]

Other indicators in the biblical text make clear that male circumcision did not imply noncovenantal status for the women of Israel. It is not accidental that the narrative introducing circumcision in Gen 17 has Sarah placed in the literary center of the story—to affirm that women are included in the covenant although not physically circumcised.[18] Furthermore, ultimately the covenant sign is about spiritual circumcision—circumcision of the heart—an experience open to both men and women. Although Deut 10:16 calls for the people of Israel themselves to "circumcise . . . the foreskin of your heart," Deut 30:6 promises that the "the LORD your God will circumcise your heart and the heart of your descendants." All of Israel—men, women, and children—may experience this promised divine covenantal blessing.

The Prophets continue to refer to both the physical and the spiritual dimensions of circumcision. Joshua 5 describes the circumcision of the children of

---

[15] Jack Miles, *God: A Biography* (London: Simon & Schuster, 1995), 53, 90.

[16] For further discussion of this incident (with bibliography), see ch. 6, above, in connection with the characterization of Zipporah.

[17] John Goldingay, "The Significance of Circumcision," *JSOT* 88 (2000): 16.

[18] See the discussion of this narrative strategy in Mary J. Evans, "The Invisibility of Women: An Investigation of a Possible Blind Spot for Biblical Commentators," *CBRFJ* 122 (1990): 37–38.

Israel after the covenant curse of the wilderness wandering is over and they are about to cross the Jordan into the promised land. There are numerous references to uncircumcised nations, especially the Philistines.[19] Habakkuk speaks of those in Judah who become intoxicated and find themselves "exposed as uncircumcised" (Hab 2:16 NKJV). Jeremiah records God's call to the men of Judah: "Circumcise yourselves to the LORD, remove the foreskin of your hearts" (Jer 4:4). Yahweh also speaks of Judah, whose "ear is uncircumcised, and they cannot give heed" (Jer 6:10 NKJV), and warns of coming judgment in which Yahweh "will attend to all those who are circumcised only in the foreskin [nations are listed]. For all these nations are uncircumcised, and all the house of Israel is uncircumcised in the heart" (Jer 9:24–25 [ET 9:25–26]).

God's choice of a sexual symbol, the male sex organ, upon which to place the symbol of religious identity also certainly constitutes an affirmation of the Hebrews' high regard for human sexuality. The Abrahamic narrative provides further supporting evidence for this conclusion in the description of the procedure for solemnizing an oath. In the oath-making ceremony of Abraham and his servant (Gen 24:9) and later Jacob and Joseph (47:29), the one swearing the oath put his hand under the "thigh" of the one before whom he was swearing. As already indicated in the introduction to this study in the survey of OT sexual terminology, the word "thigh" probably here refers to the genital area in general, and perhaps to the male sex organ in particular. The sex organ is not an object of shame or repulsion; it is the most sacred part of one's body, which God employs as a sign of his covenant with Israel.

The Cherishing of Children

Throughout the OT, children are highly cherished.[20] Parents pray that they may have children (e.g., Gen 15:2–3; 16:1–2; 20:17; 1 Sam 1:27; 2:20), and celebrate when they are born (Jer 20:15). Sensitive fathers such as Jacob "lead on softly" in deference to the children (Gen 33:14). Parents save up to provide for their children (Ps 17:14). With the psalmist, Israel sings, "Sons are indeed a heritage from the LORD, the fruit of the womb a reward. Like arrows in the hand of a warrior are the sons of one's youth. Happy is the man who has his quiver full of them" (Ps 127:3–5). The sapiential counsel concerning family and children pervades the OT Wisdom literature, particularly the book of Proverbs.[21] Prophets speak of "precious [taʿănûg] children (Mic 1:16 NKJV, lit. 'children of your exquisite delight')" and "the cherished [maḥmad] offspring of their womb" (Hos 9:16). Specific legislation is aimed at cherishing children and protecting them from

---

[19] For references to the "uncircumcised" Philistines, see Judg 14:3; 15:18; 1 Sam 14:6; 17:26, 36; 18:25, 27; 31:4; 2 Sam 1:20; 3:14; 1 Chr 10:4. References to other nations include Isa 52:1; Jer 9:24–25 (ET 9:25–26); Ezek 28:10; 31:18; 32:19, 21, 24–30, 32.

[20] See esp. Roy B. Zuck, *Precious in His Sight: Childhood and Children in the Bible* (Grand Rapids: Baker, 1996).

[21] See Derek Kidner, *The Proverbs: An Introduction and Commentary* (TOTC 15; Downers Grove, Ill.: InterVarsity, 1964), 50–52, for a summary of this motif.

abuse (Lev 18:21; 20:3–4; Deut 33:9; Josh 1:14; Mal 3:24 [ET 4:6]). God himself promises to defend the cause of the children (Ps 72:4; Hos 11:10; Isa 49:25), especially the defenseless and fatherless (Ps 10:14, 18; 68:6 [ET 68:5]; 146:9). The divine revulsion and wrath is particularly aroused when children are sacrificed in connection with pagan fertility worship (see the discussion below). The divine affirmation of procreation and children reaches its zenith in the OT with God describing himself in the imagery of a loving father or mother, as highlighted in ch. 3, above, and with God himself becoming the ultimate Child/Son—the Messiah (Isa 7:14; 9:5 [ET 9:6]).

Though stressing the important place of children in the family, at the same time the OT is clear that sexual relations are not wholly subordinated to the intent to propagate. As stressed in chapter 6, above, women are cherished and valued for their own person, and not just for their ability to procreate (Miriam, Deborah, Hannah, Esther). In the descriptions of physical intimacy in the Writings (esp. Prov 5:18–19), sexuality is given meaning and value independent of procreation. Sexual intimacy may be enjoyed for its own sake, for the beauty and ecstasy, for the sheer enjoyment by the partners; it needs no justification as a means to a superior end, that is, propagation of children.

Childlessness

Orientation and Terminology

We have noted the profound significance attached to procreation among the Hebrew people, not only in the creation ordinance to "be fruitful and multiply" but especially in the covenantal and messianic import attached to the perpetuation of the family line of descendants. It is thus understandable that childlessness was considered a great misfortune, and more than misfortune, even a reproach and humiliation (Gen 18:12; 30:1), indeed a curse by God (16:2; 20:18).

The OT employs a number of terms to denote the condition of childlessness: the adjectives *ʿāqār* (masc.) and *ʿăqārâ* (fem.), "childless, barren, sterile";[22] the adjective *ʿărîrî*, "stripped, childless";[23] the adjective *galmûd*, "barren";[24] the verb *šākal* in the qal, "to be bereaved [of children]"[25] or *piʿel* "to make childless, cause barrenness";[26] and several adjectives and nouns derived from the latter verb.[27]

---

[22] Gen 11:30; 25:21; 29:31; Exod 23:26; Deut 7:14 (the only masc., referring to male childlessness); Judg 13:2–3; 1 Sam 2:5; Isa 54:1; Ps 113:9; Job 24:21.

[23] Gen 15:2; Lev 20:20–21; Jer 22:30.

[24] Isa 49:21; Job 3:7; 15:34; 30:3.

[25] Gen 27:45; 43:14; 1 Sam 15:33; Isa 49:21.

[26] Gen 42:36; Exod 23:26; Lev 26:22; Deut 32:25; 1 Sam 15:33; 2 Kgs 2:19–21; Jer 15:7; Ezek 5:17; 14:15; 36:12–14; Hos 9:14; Lam 1:20.

[27] The adjective *šakkûl*, "robbed of" or "childless" (2 Sam 17:8; Jer 18:21; Hos 13:8; Prov 17:12; Cant 4:2; 6:6); the adjective *šākûl*, "bereaved"(Isa 49:21); the noun *šĕkôl*, "loss of children" or "forlorn" (Isa 47:8–9; Ps 35:12); and the plural abstract noun *šikkulîm*, "bereavement" (Isa 49:20).

Other expressions include "having no child" (Gen 11:30); "prevented (or 'shut up' [ʿāṣar]) from bearing" (16:2); "closed fast [ʿāṣōr ʿāṣar] the wombs" (20:18); "barren womb" (Prov 30:16, lit. 'restraint [ʿōṣer] of the womb'); and "withholding (mānaʿ) the fruit of the womb" (Gen 30:2).

Pentateuch

It is astonishing that all the matriarchs of the Hebrew people—Sarah, Rebekah, Rachel, and Leah—experienced the anguish of childlessness.[28] The literary analysis of Robert Alter and others has suggested that the narratives of the Hebrew matriarchs, like the three other narratives in the OT featuring childless women (the wife of Manoah, Hannah, and the Shunammite woman), follow a pattern that Alter classifies as an "annunciation type-scene" and contain the following common elements: (1) indication of the woman's childlessness; (2) divine promise that the woman's childlessness would end; and (3) the conception and birth of the promised son.[29]

The patriarchal narrative states that God closed the wombs of the house of Abimelech as a sign of divine displeasure (Gen 20:17–18), and even records on the lips of both matriarch (16:2) and patriarch (30:2) that it was the Lord who had shut up their wombs, but the narrator does not indicate any culpability on the part of the childless matriarchs for their condition. They are not under a divine curse. They are still able to enjoy sexual pleasure and intimacy with their husbands for its own sake, regardless of whether it leads to the propagation of children. At the same time, the narrative several times indicates that it is the Lord who opens the matriarchs' wombs so that they might bear (21:1–2; 29:31; 30:22), especially in answer to intercessory prayer, as in the case of Isaac for his wife (25:21).

The great OT statement of righteousness by faith—15:6, "He believed the LORD; and the LORD reckoned it to him as righteousness"—concerns a divine

---

[28] Sarah, Gen 11:30; 21:1–2; Rebekah, 25:21; Leah, 29:32–33; Rachel, 29:31; 30:1–2, 22.

[29] Robert Alter, "Biblical Type-Scenes and the Uses of Convention," *Critical Inquiry* (1978): 355–68; idem, "How Convention Helps Us Read: The Case of the Bible's Annunciation Type-Scene," *Proof* 3 (1983): 115–30; cf. James G. Williams, "The Beautiful and the Barren: Conventions in Biblical Type-Scenes," *JSOT* 17 (1980): 107–19. Cf. Susan Ackerman, "Child Sacrifice: Returning God's Gift," *BRev* 9, no. 3 (1993): 20–28, 56, who adds a fourth element, that the promised child, after birth, experiences a threat to his life. Although analyzing the type-scene is helpful, I disagree with the basic presupposition behind these analyses that sees the type-scene as only a literary convention with little or no basis in historical reality. I do not see these narratives only as literary conventions, but as the way, in fact, in which salvation history plays out—while not denying the literary genius of the narrator in crafting profound narrative-theological masterpieces. For analysis of the motif of barrenness in Scripture and in later Jewish midrash on the biblical texts, see esp. Mary Callaway, *Sing, O Barren One: A Study in Comparative Midrash* (SBLDS 91; Atlanta: Scholars Press, 1986). For a more popular and homiletical treatment of the childlessness narratives in Scripture (including that of the Genesis matriarchs), see Frank Damazio, *From Barrenness to Fruitfulness* (Ventura, Calif.: Regal Books, 1998), 63–107, for the Genesis matriarchs.

promise to eliminate Abram's childlessness. Abraham and Sarah's great lack of faith centered on their failure to trust this divine promise and on taking matters into their own hands via a surrogate (16:1–2), following contemporary custom.[30] And the divine miracle for the father of the faithful centered on sexuality and the relief of childlessness: the Lord visited Sarah in her old age so that she conceived and bore Abraham a son, Isaac—"son of the promise" (21:1–5).

From the threefold elaboration of the childlessness motif among the Hebrew matriarchs in the "annunciation type-scenes" of Genesis, one may ask why each of the matriarchs was childless? Is it only coincidental that the foremothers of the Hebrews were all unable to conceive without supernatural intervention? Although the narrative never explicitly answers this question, the same powerful lesson comes through in each childlessness narrative: it is not ultimately human ambition or human services that suffice to carry on the line of promise. God's covenant people do not come into being naturally but by faith in the divine promise, by special intervention from the Lord.

Yahweh is not only concerned about, but ultimately sovereign over, the procreative function of human sexuality. The patriarchal narratives concerning childlessness reveal that though above the differentiation of sex, "Yahweh is the true and only God of Fertility, the only god upon whom Israel should depend for the fulfillment of the promise of descendants and, consequently, the continuation and growth of the chosen people."[31] In an age when the teraphim, or household gods, were seen to ensure fertility (this form of idolatry was present even in the patriarchal household, 31:20–35; 35:1–2)[32] and the land of Canaanites was rife with fertility cults, God revealed himself as the One who opens the childless womb at will even when it seems physiologically impossible for a woman in menopause to bear a child. God has the last word in the patriarchal narratives about childlessness (18:14): "Is anything too wonderful for the LORD?"

Beyond the book of Genesis, the Pentateuch continues the theme of childlessness, especially in connection with the covenant blessings and curses. The blessings attendant upon covenant faithfulness focus mainly upon promised

---

[30] See "The Laws of Hammurabi," §146, translated by Martha Roth (*COS* 2.131:345; cf. *ANET* 172); and esp. the Nuzi parallels, as discussed by E. A. Speiser, *Genesis* (AB 1; Garden City, N.Y.: Doubleday, 1964), 120–21. Yahweh's insistence upon the child of promise (i.e., Isaac) being the one designated to continue the covenant line instead of an adopted or surrogate son should not be seen as divine opposition to the practice of adoption per se. As will become apparent in the Writings—particularly in Ps 2—Yahweh himself "adopts" the Davidic king as his "son."

[31] Donald B. Sharp, "On the Motherhood of Sarah: A Yahwistic Theological Comment," *IBS* 20 (1998): 14. Although accepting the critical assumptions of the Documentary Hypothesis on the "Yahwist" source, Sharp, pp. 2–14, nonetheless insightfully points out how the Sarah narrative serves as a polemic against the fertility cults of Canaan.

[32] See Miriam Tadmor, "Female Cult Figurines in Late Canaan and Early Israel: Archaeological Evidence," in *Studies in the Period of David and Solomon and Other Essays* (ed. Tomoo Ishida; Winona Lake, Ind.: Eisenbrauns, 1982); and Judith M. Hadley, *The Cult of Asherah in Ancient Israel and Judah: Evidence for a Hebrew Goddess* (New York: Cambridge University Press, 2000), 188–205.

fruitfulness and absence of any childlessness (Exod 23:26; Deut 7:14; 28:1–4, 15–18), apparently including cases of congenital conditions, injury inhibiting pregnancy, and a lack of spouse. At the same time, the covenant curses include childlessness, especially emphasizing the parents being bereaved of their children (Lev 26:2; Deut 32:25). Divine punishment for certain forms of incestuous or "near of kin" sexual relationships also include childlessness (Lev 20:20–21; see ch. 10, above).

Prophets/Writings

The same basic contours appear in the Prophets as in the Pentateuch in discussing childlessness. Three classic examples of the childless woman in the Prophets have been alluded to above—the wife of Manoah (Judg 13), Hannah (1 Sam 1–2), and the woman of Shunem (2 Kgs 4). We have examined the high valuation of these women (ch. 6, above) and noted the pattern of the annuncia-tion type-scene that is present here as well as in the matriarchal narratives (see above). In each case God is active in relieving the distress of childlessness, and this is followed by great joy on the part of the parents who receive the gift of a child from the Lord. Manoah's wife and Hannah provide illustrations of godly women willing to surrender ownership and control of God's gift for the service of the nation, and Hannah's experience models the power of intercessory, peti-tionary prayer in breaking childlessness.[33]

Threats of divine judgment for disobedience in the Prophets, as in the Penta-teuch, include the covenant curse of childlessness and miscarriage.[34] Michal, the daughter of Saul and wife of David, is an example of one stricken with childless-ness, apparently as a divine judgment for her pride and arrogance in despising David's dancing before God at the return of the ark to Jerusalem (2 Sam 6:20–23).[35] At the same time, in the Prophets, God's promise of future eschato-logical salvation incorporates the covenant blessings of fertility and fruitful-ness,[36] blessings that cause the childless woman to "burst into song and shout" (Isa 54:1).

In the hymnic/Wisdom literature of the Writings, the psalmist praises the Lord because "He gives the barren woman a home, making her the joyous mother of children" (Ps 113:9), and invokes the covenant curse of childlessness in his im-precation of the wicked (Ps 58:9 [ET 58:8]). Job in his misery wishes his mother had been childless or that he had been stillborn (Job 3:7, 16), decries the violence of the wicked against the childless (24:21), and indicates childlessness as a pun-ishment for the wicked (30:3; cf. 15:34). At the same time, as emphasized above, the Wisdom literature describes the sexual relationship as having independent

---

[33] See Damazio, *Barrenness to Fruitfulness,* 109–32.

[34] See, e.g., Jer 15:7; Ezek 5:17; Hos 9:14; cf. Lam 1:20.

[35] See, e.g., Lillian R. Klein, "Michal, the Barren Wife," in *Samuel and Kings* (ed. Athalya Brenner; FCB² 7; Sheffield, Eng.: Sheffield Academic Press, 2000), 37–46.

[36] See, e.g., Isa 49:20–21; Ezek 36:12–14.

meaning and value of its own, quite apart from procreation, to be enjoyed for its own sake with no need to be justified as a means to have children (see esp. Prov 5:18–19 and ch. 13, below).

Adoption

One of the ways to deal with the problem of childlessness in the ancient Near East was adoption. The practice of adoption provided care for children without families (orphans, illegitimately conceived children, and foundlings). Documentation for adoption is found in several ANE law collections[37] and in adoption contracts (mostly from the Old Babylonian and Middle Babylonian times)[38] and some other ANE texts,[39] including a few from Egypt.[40] The adoption contracts in Mesopotamia characteristically contain a statement of the adoptive relationship, dissolution clauses, a record of the oath taken by the adoptive parties, names of the witnesses, and the date.[41]

---

[37] See CH §§170–171, 185–193 (COS 2.121:346–48; ANET 173–75); "The Laws of Eshnunna," §35, translated by Martha Roth (COS 2.130:334; cf. ANET 162); "The Middle Assyrian Laws," A §28, translated by Martha Roth (COS 2.132:356; cf. ANET 182); and, doubtfully, MAL A §41 (COS 2.132:358; cf. ANET 183) and "The Laws of Lipit-Ishtar," §27, translated by Martha Roth (COS 2.154:413; cf. ANET 160).

[38] For Old Babylonian texts, see Elizabeth C. Stone and David I. Owen, *Adoption in Old Babylonian Nippur and the Archive of Mannum-mešu-lissur* (Winona Lake, Ind.: Eisenbrauns, 1991); and Maria deJ. Ellis, "An Old Babylonian Adoption Contract from Tell Harmal," *JCS* 27 (1975): 130–51. For Nuzi texts, see E. A. Speiser, "New Kirkuk Documents Relating to Family Laws," *AASOR* 10 (1930): 1–73; E. M. Cassin, *L'adoption à Nuzi* (Paris: Adrien-Maissoneuve, 1938); and B. L. Eichler, "Nuzi and the Bible: A Retrospective," in *DUMU-E2–DUB-BA-A: Studies in Honor of Åke W. Sjöberg* (ed. Hermann Behrens, Darlene Loding, and Martha T. Roth; Philadelphia: Babylonian Section, University Museum, 1989), 107–19.

[39] See Frederick W. Knobloch, "Adoption," *ABD* 1:76–79, for additional cuneiform sources. These include "The Legend of Sargon," translated by E. A. Speiser (*ANET* 119); the lexical series *ana ittišu* (see Benno Landsberger, *Die Serie ana ittišu* [vol. 1 of *Materialien zum sumerischen Lexikon;* ed. Benno Landsberger; Rome: Pontificium Institutum Biblicum, 1937–]), and some litigation records regarding custody and/or inheritance rights.

[40] For a possible example of adoption, see "The Story of Sinuhe," translated by John A. Wilson (*ANET* 19–20), which may describe the adoption of a son-in-law in Syro-Palestine. See also "The Extraordinary Adoption" text (ca. 1100 B.C.E.), which describes a wife's adoption by her childless husband as his daughter and heir (Thomas L. Thompson, *The Historicity of the Patriarchal Narratives: The Quest for the Historical Abraham* [BZAW 133; Berlin: de Gruyter, 1974], 229; A. H. Gardiner, "Adoption Extraordinary," *JEA* 26 [1940]: 23–27). See also Schafik Allam, "De l'adoption en Egypte pharaonique," *OrAnt* 11 (1972): 277–95. Records of Jewish adoption at fifth-century B.C.E. Elephantine include an Aramaic papyrus referring to the adoption/freeing of a Jewish slave (Emil G. H. Kraeling, ed., *The Brooklyn Museum Aramaic Papyri* [New Haven: Yale University Press, 1953], 224–31 [papyrus no. 8]).

[41] Knobloch, "Adoption," 1:79, gives this summary of the major elements of the contract. See MAL A §28 for reference to this "adoption tablet" in the ANE laws codes.

In the most common form of adoption, a couple adopted one or more sons (or daughters). The written contract would typically indicate that in exchange for his inheriting their property, the adopted son would agree to responsibilities such as providing food for his new parents, paying off debts owed by them, and managing their financial affairs. Severe penalties were attached to the contract in cases where the adopted son did not comply with the terms of the agreement, including monetary fines, the cancellation of the adoption, and even being sold as a slave.[42]

The Code of Hammurabi contains particular provisions designed to protect the well-being of both the adopted child and the ones doing the adopting. For instance, if a man adopted a child from birth and reared him, then the child could not be reclaimed later by his parents (CH §185); but if he adopted a young child and the child wished to return to his biological parents, he could do so (CH §186). If a man adopted a child and taught him a trade, the child could not be reclaimed (CH §188), but if he neglected to teach him a trade, the child would be sent back to his father's house (CH §189). Again, if the one who adopted the child did not treat him as equal with his other children, then the one adopted could return to his biological father (CH §190). And if the adopted child was raised by a man who had no children of his own but, when he had his own children, wanted to disinherit the adopted son, the adopted child had to be given the same-size inheritance as the natural-born sons (except the firstborn, who received a double portion, CH §191).

Regarding foundlings, in the ancient Near East a couple surrendered their legal rights to an infant if they abandoned their child without cleansing its amniotic fluid and blood (cf. Ezek 16:4–5), and such abandoned children could be legally adopted without fear of the biological parents later claiming it.[43] The ANE practice of adopting foundlings is illustrated not only outside Scripture[44] but also probably in the life of Moses (Exod 2:1–10). Ezekiel 16:1–7 seems to allude to this practice of adopting foundlings; in light of ANE parallels, the

---

[42] See Victor H. Matthews, "Marriage and Family in the Ancient Near East," in *Marriage and Family in the Biblical World* (ed. Ken M. Campbell; Downers Grove, Ill.: InterVarsity, 2003), 20 (and sources cited in notes); cf. the examples given in Stone and Owen, *Adoption in Old Babylonian Nippur*, 38–42.

[43] See the translation of CH §185 by Meir Malul, "Adoption of Foundlings in the Bible and Mesopotamian Documents: A Study of Some Legal Metaphors in Ezekiel 16–17," *JSOT* 46 (1990): 106: "If a man has taken in adoption an infant while still (bathed in) his amniotic fluid and raised him up, that adopted child shall not be (re)claimed!" Malul summarizes the evidence from this and other Old Babylonian documents regarding adoption of foundlings: "In summary, when a legal document reports the adoption of an infant still lying in its amniotic fluid and birth blood, it is intended to specify that it is an exposed child, abandoned by its parents soon after its birth. Anyone adopting it in this state acquires full right to it, for the adopter is considered to have taken possession of an ownerless child. The child's natural parents can no longer reclaim it from its adopter" (pp. 109–10).

[44] Cf. Ibid., 106–10. According to legend, Sargon of Akkad was an adopted foundling ("The Legend of Sargon," translated by E. A. Speiser [*ANET* 119]).

mention of the exposed girl (= Israel) lying in her birth blood (16:6) is "a formal hint of the existence of adoption relationships between her and God," and the expression "in your blood, live!" (*bĕdāmayik ḥăyî*) may be interpreted "as a formal declaration of adoption."[45]

Scripture also alludes to the ANE practice of a childless older couple adopting an adult slave to be their son and care for their needs in old age. According to Gen 15:2, the childless and aged Abram suggests to God that he might adopt Eliezer his servant to be his heir;[46] parallels to this procedure are found in second-millennium B.C.E. Nuzi texts.[47] According to ANE custom, the adopted slave was to serve the couple while they were alive and to care for their burial and mourning rites, and in return for this, the slave would be designated heir of the couple's possessions. Should the couple then have children of their own, the adopted slave would no longer be the chief heir but would still inherit as a penultimate heir.

The texts from ancient Mesopotamia illustrate many other types of adoption: individuals adopted into the role of brother, sister, or even father; individuals adopted into apprenticeship; slaves freed by adoption; illegitimately conceived children legitimated; females adopted in order to give them away in marriage; cowives adopted as sisters to promote family harmony; son-in-laws adopted by a childless father to retain the property within the family; even "sale adoptions" in which a buyer was adopted and "given" land to circumvent prohibitions against selling ancestral property outside the family.[48]

The expression for "adopt" in cuneiform literature was formulated in several different ways: "to make as a son" (*ana māri epēšu*); "to make into the status of sonship" (*ana mārūti epēšu*); "to enter into sonship" (*ana mārūti erēbu*); "to bind into son/sonship" (*ana māri / mārūti rakāsu*); "to appoint/designate for sonship" (*ana mārūti nadānu*); "to record (in a tablet) for sonship" (*ana mārūti šaṭāru*); "to establish for the status of heir" (*ana mārūti šakānu;* cf. the biblical counterpart in Jer 3:19); and "to take into the status of sonship" (*ana mārūti leqû*).[49] For the last example, note the close parallel with the Hebrew *lĕqāḥāh . . . lĕbat,* "he adopted her as his own daughter," in Esth 2:7 (cf. 2:15), describing Mordecai's adoption of Esther.

The adoption formula could take different forms. As a proclamation or declaration formula, ANE examples include the following wording: "You are my

---

[45] Malul, "Adoption of Foundlings," 111 (see 97–112 for a full discussion of the adoption metaphor in this passage).

[46] Yahweh's insistence upon the child of promise (i.e., Isaac) being the one designated to continue the covenant line, instead of an adopted or surrogate son, should not be seen as divine opposition to the practice of adoption per se.

[47] See E. A. Speiser, "Notes to Recently Published Nuzi Texts," *JAOS* 55 (1935): 435–36; and Cyrus H. Gordon, "Biblical Customs and the Nuzi Tablets," *BA* 3 (1940): 2–3.

[48] Knobloch, "Adoption," 1:77.

[49] For cuneiform sources of these expressions (and the Sumerian equivalents when applicable), see Shalom M. Paul, "Adoption Formulae: A Study of Cuneiform and Biblical Legal Clauses," *Maarav* 2 (1979–1980): 180–81.

son"; "He is your son"; "[You are] my children"; "I, the king, called him my son"; "Behold, Muršiliš is now my son"; "My son he shall be."[50] As a descriptive formula, the typical wording in Old Babylonian Nippur adoption contracts was, "A [adopter] has adopted B [the adoptee] as his son."[51] Another form has the son say orally and put in writing this statement: "He adopted him as his father."[52] Parallels to these adoption formulae are found in Scripture. When Yahweh metaphorically adopts the messianic Davidic king as his son, he utters a declaration formula: "I will tell of the decree of the LORD: He said to me, 'You are my son; today I have begotten you'" (Ps 2:7). An alternative adoption formula appears in 2 Sam 7:14 (the divine promise to which Ps 2 probably alludes): "I will be a father to him, and he shall be a son to me." Another allusion to the adoption formula may be found in the account of the exodus, when Yahweh tells Moses to proclaim to Pharaoh, "Israel is my firstborn son" (Exod 4:22; cf. Deut 8:5; 14:1; Jer 3:19; 31:9; Hos 11:1). A descriptive formula is found in Esth 2:7, 15, referring to Mordecai's adoption of Esther: "when her father and her mother died, Mordecai adopted her as his own daughter. . . . Esther daughter of Abihail the uncle of Mordecai, who had adopted her as his own daughter."

It is noteworthy that no clear-cut OT case of actual adoption is found taking place in Israelite society in Palestine.[53] The biblical illustrations referred to above either are metaphors (Yahweh's adoption of Israel and the Davidic king) or occurred in the patriarchal period before Israel became a people (Abram's reference to Eliezer as a potential adoptee) or in a foreign culture (Moses in Egypt, Esther in Persia).[54] This paucity of biblical evidence for cases of adoption in ancient Israel, coupled with the fact that no biblical laws deal with the issue, has led some scholars to conclude that the institution of adoption did not even exist in ancient Israel.[55] As Daniel Block points out, however, the frequent reference to Yahweh's adoption of the nation of Israel and the Davidic king "reinforces the impression

---

[50] For cuneiform sources of these formulae, see ibid., 179–80.

[51] Sohn, "'I Will Be Your God and You Will Be My People,'" 371.

[52] D. J. Wiseman, The Alalakh Tablets (OPBIAA; London: British Institute of Archaeology at Ankara, 1953), 16:3; see Paul, "Adoption Formulae," 179–81.

[53] Knobloch, "Adoption," 1:77–78, suggests other possible examples: children of the surrogate mothers for Sarai, Rachel, and Leah (Gen 16:1–4; 30:1–13); Jacob by Laban (Gen 29–31); children of the foreign wives in the time of Ezra (Ezra 10:44); grandchildren by Jacob (Gen 48:5–6), Joseph (Gen 50:23), and Naomi (Ruth 4:16–17); the illegitimately conceived son Jephthah (Judg 11:1–2); son-in-laws Jarha (1 Chr 2:34–35) and Barzillai (Ezra 2:61; Neh 7:63). Thomas Rees, "Adoption," ISBE 1:53, mentions one additional example from Egypt: Genubath (1 Kgs 11:20). None of these suggestions are clear-cut cases of adoption. Victor P. Hamilton, "Adoption," NIDOTTE 4:363, indicates that the alleged examples of adoption in the OT "may involve only inheritance matters and not represent adoption in its fullest sense."

[54] Hamilton, NIDOTTE 4:363, questions even whether the cases of Moses and Esther should be termed adoption or instead constituted more of a foster child arrangement.

[55] So, e.g., H. Donner, "Adoption oder Legitimation? Erwägungen zur Adoption im Alten Testament auf dem Hintergrund der altorientalischen Rechte," OrAnt 8 (1969): 87–119.

that adoption must have been a relatively common experience—the metaphor would have been meaningless otherwise!"[56]

It is likely, nonetheless, that adoption was not all that prevalent in Israel.[57] Such infrequency may be due, in part, to "(1) the fact that close-knit tribal consciousness created artificial family ties, and (2) the pervasive practice of polygamy, which rendered adoption almost unnecessary."[58] Another possible explanation may be that in cases where the husband died without having children, a special institution obtained in Israel to provide for the situation of childlessness—the levirate marriage.

Levirate Marriage, Related Legislation, and the Sin of Onan

The prime importance of progeny in fulfilling God's covenantal promise to successive generations (e.g., Gen 17:7–9) is highlighted in the practice of levirate marriage. This practice provided that a surviving brother should marry the childless wife of his deceased brother in order to provide an heir for the dead brother. The ancient Near East had practices similar to the levirate marriage in Israel but apparently nothing exactly the same.[59] The term "levirate" derives from the Latin

---

[56] Daniel I. Block, "Marriage and Family in Ancient Israel," in *Marriage and Family in the Biblical World* (ed. Ken M. Campbell; Downers Grove, Ill.: InterVarsity, 2003), 88.

[57] Knobloch suggests another piece of evidence for this conclusion: "The absence of adoption in postbiblical Jewish law, however, suggests that it was not prevalent in Israel, at least in later periods" ("Adoption," 1:79).

[58] Hamilton, *NIDOTTE* 4:363. Knobloch suggests other possible explanations: "the importance of blood lineage to the Hebrews, . . . and the belief that fertility or barrenness reflected God's will, which adoption would circumvent" ("Adoption," 1:79).

[59] Babylonian law contains nothing resembling the levirate marriage practice, apparently because the problem of childlessness was solved in other ways, such as adoption or the legitimization of children by a concubine or slave girl. MAL A §§30, 33, 43 (*COS* 2.132:356–58; *ANET* 182, 184) describes practices containing formal points of contact with the Israelite levirate, but whereas the Israelite law was primarily concerned with continuing the name of the deceased, the Assyrian laws focused almost exclusively on the (property) rights of the (future) husband's family that brings the bride into their household (as spelled out in the marriage contract) and apparently do not refer to a woman whose marriage was consummated. As with the Babylonians, the Assyrians obtained the same end as the levirate in Israel by polygamy, legitimization of children by concubines or slave wives or the wife's maid, or by adoption. (See the discussion of these laws in G. R. Driver and John C. Miles, *The Assyrian Laws* [Oxford: Clarendon, 1935], 176–78, 227–29, 240–50; Raymond Westbrook, *Property and the Family in Biblical Law* [JSOTSup 113; Sheffield, Eng.: Sheffield Academic Press, 1991], 88–89.) The Hittite law code contains one law similar to the Israelite levirate marriage. "The Hittite Laws," §193, translated by Harry A. Hoffner Jr. (*COS* 2.19:118; cf. *ANET* 196), although the text is uncertain in places, reads thus: "If a man has a wife and the man dies, his brother shall take his widow as wife. (If the brother dies,) his father shall take her. When afterwards his father dies, his (i.e., the father's) brother shall take the woman whom he had." There is no mention of the wife being childless, although some scholars argue that this is the case. (See discussion with bibliography in Donald A. Leggett, *The Levirate and Goel Institutions in the Old Testament, with Special Attention to the Book of Ruth* [Cherry Hill, N.J.: Mack, 1974], 21–24;

levir, "brother-in-law," and represents the Hebrew *yābām,* "husband's brother"—
specifically the husband's brother who qualifies to perform the levirate duty. This
noun, its feminine counterpart, *yĕbēmet,* "sister-in-law"[60] (referring to his dead
brother's widow), and the verb *yābam,* in the *piᶜel,* "to do the duty of the *levir,*"
are all found only in connection with the three references to the levirate institution in the HB: in the narrative of Tamar (Gen 38), in the legal regulation regarding this institution (Deut 25:5–10), and in the book of Ruth.[61]

Levirate and "Onanism" in the Pentateuchal Narrative

Genesis 38. Chapter 10, above, analyzed the narrative of Tamar and Judah regarding the nature of (apparent) prostitution in which Tamar was engaged in
order to entice Judah to have sexual relations with her. Here we focus upon the
motivation that led Tamar to go to such lengths to get pregnant. According to the
narrative (Gen 38:6–8), Judah's firstborn son, Er, died (by divine judgment for his
wickedness) and left his wife, Tamar, childless. Hence, according to the custom of
levirate marriage that was apparently already in existence in patriarchal times,
Er's brother Onan was responsible to perform the duty of the *yābām* for Tamar
and raise up offspring to Er's memory and for an heir to his inheritance.

In 38:8 Judah does not tell Onan to marry Tamar, only to "go in to your
brother's wife and perform the duty of a brother-in-law [*yābām*] to her; raise up
offspring for your brother." Hence some interpreters conclude that the levirate
obligation, at least in the time of the patriarchs, only mandated impregnating the

---

Westbrook, *Property and the Family,* 87.) Some scholars have also argued for a levirate
practice implicit in the political testament of the Ugaritic king Arihalbu; this inference,
unlike the concerns of the other ANE parallels, does appear to have concern for continuation of the line of the dead as in Israel (but not, apparently, a concern for inheritance).
(See Leggett, *Levirate,* 25–27; and Matitiahu Tsevat, "Marriage and Monarchical Legitimacy in Ugarit and Israel," *JSS* 3 [1958]: 237–43.) Millar Burrows, "The Ancient Oriental
Background of Hebrew Levirate Marriage," *BASOR* 77 (1940): 15, summarizes: "Except
among the Hebrews and perhaps the Canaanites, levirate marriage was not in the ancient
Near East a means of securing a son for the dead. It was rather a part of the whole system of family relationships, authority, and inheritance. At the same time, the object
sought by the Hebrews through levirate marriage was sought by other peoples also, but in
different ways."

[60] On the basis of the usage of this term in the cognate language of Ugaritic as an epithet for the goddess Anat, some scholars have suggested that the nouns *yābām* and
yĕbēmet originally meant "progenitor" and "progenitress" respectively and later began to
refer to the brother-in-law and sister-in-law as the ones who performed the function to
produce progeny for the deceased. For discussion and bibliography, see, e.g., Burrows,
"The Ancient Oriental Background," 6–7; and Thomas Thompson and Dorothy Thompson, "Some Legal Problems in the Book of Ruth," *VT* 18 (1968): 84–85.

[61] The noun *yābām,* "brother-in-law" or "husband's brother," appears in Deut 25:5,
7; the noun *yĕbēmet,* "brother's widow," "brother's wife," or "sister-in-law," is found in
Deut 25:7 (bis), 9 and Ruth 1:15 (bis); and the denominative verb *yābam* (in the *piᶜel*),
"perform the duty of a brother-in-law," or "perform the duty of a husband's brother,"
occurs in Gen 38:8 and Deut 25:5, 7.

brother-in-law's widow, not necessarily marrying her.[62] A narrative is not to be expected, however, to include all the details at the beginning. In light of what follows in this narrative, and especially 38:14, where the point is specifically made that Judah had not done his duty as father-in-law in that "she had not been given to him [Shelah, the next brother in line] in *marriage*," it seems more likely that the duty of the *yābām* at least normally included not only making his widowed sister-in-law pregnant but also marrying her.[63]

This duty was shamefully disregarded by Onan, Judah's son (see the next section for further comment), and God put him to death. When Judah failed to give Tamar his next son, Shelah, as a husband to perform the duty of the *levir,* Tamar decided to take matters into her own hands. Some interpreters have suggested that in patriarchal times the levirate duty could be performed by the father-in-law as well as by the brother-in-law and that Tamar's trickery to cause Judah to have sex with her was to force him to carry out his levirate responsibility to make her pregnant.[64] A practice similar to the levirate marriage and carried out in other ANE societies (attested particularly in the Hittite Laws)[65] did allow for a father-in-law to perform such service. This interpretation of Gen 38 is possible. The text specifically states that Judah's wife had died (38:12) and thus (assuming that polygamy was frowned upon) he would be free to marry again, and in light of what is suggested below regarding pentateuchal legislation, such an action seems in harmony with a broader interpretation of that later law if no eligible brother is available.

At the same time, such an interpretation does not seem to me to integrate all the data of Gen 38. After the disclosure to Judah that Tamar was pregnant by him and his admission that "she is more in the right than I" (38:26), the narrator makes clear that Judah "did not lie with her again"—that is, he never had sexual relations with her and thus presumably he never married her. If, as argued above, 38:8 implies that the levirate custom in patriarchal times normally entailed marriage as well as sexual impregnation, then Judah was probably not envisioned as performing a full levirate function, at least not in the regular sense of the current custom.

It is possible, as suggested in the discussion of incest in ch. 10, above, that when Tamar saw that Judah was not going to give his son Shelah to her as a husband/*levir,* as he had promised (38:11), she may have acted by rules different from the normal pattern of levirate marriage, perhaps more in line with Hittite standards, where a father-in-law could be engaged as a substitute for a brother-in-law. Judah had promised her a *levir;* she was causing him to fulfill his promise through a substitute: himself. Another possibility is that Tamar's goal was not necessarily to find a normally legitimate *levir* but, by any emergency

---

[62] See, e.g., Leggett, *Levirate,* 39, and sources cited by him.

[63] For further support for this conclusion, see esp. Eryl W. Davies, "Inheritance Rights and the Hebrew Levirate Marriage," *VT* 31 (1981): 143.

[64] For proponents and opponents of this view, see Leggett, *Levirate,* 35–36.

[65] HL §193 (*COS* 2.19:118; *ANET* 196), quoted in full in n. 59, above.

means, obtain a son who could carry on her dead husband's line and assure an heir to his inheritance, in which case the conclusion of Walter Kaiser would apply: "Tamar's act [with Judah] was not a levirate relationship; rather, it was a desperate act of a woman who desired children from the same stock as her husband."[66]

There is not enough information in the narrative to decide definitively on this question. From the perspective of later biblical law, Judah was certainly not a legitimate *levir,* but it is unclear exactly what the prevailing levirate custom was in the time of the patriarchs. The narrative of Gen 38 does not seem to end neatly, with Tamar finally being impregnated by one who legitimately and completely performs the duty of a *levir.*[67] But although there was no regular levirate relationship, she nonetheless achieved her desired goal: a son—no, two sons!—are born to fulfill the intended function of the levirate in "raising up offspring" for her deceased husband.

Genesis 38:8–10: "Onanism." According to Gen 38:9–10, "Once Onan knew that the offspring would not be his, he [regularly] spilled his semen on the ground [lit. he 'spoiled it groundward']68 whenever he went in to his brother's wife, so that he would not give offspring to his brother. What he did was displeasing in the sight of the LORD, and he put him to death also."

Onan's deliberate activity of coitus interruptus was not a one-time event but a repeated, regular occurrence, a point clear in the Hebrew[69] but obfuscated in most English translations. Furthermore, the sin of Onan was clearly not the act of coitus interruptus per se, since such practice is nowhere prohibited in biblical law and since the context makes it evident that his coitus interruptus was motivated by his determination not to "give offspring to his brother" (38:9). Moreover, Onan's sin was probably not even his refusal to perform the duty of the *levir* for his dead brother. In the legislation of Deut 25 regarding levirate marriage, which

---

66 Walter C. Kaiser Jr., *Toward Old Testament Ethics* (Grand Rapids: Zondervan, 1983), 191.

67 See D. R. G. Beattie, "The Book of Ruth as Evidence for Israelite Legal Practice," *VT* 24 (1974): 260–61, who rejects the conclusion that the levirate obligation extended to the father-in-law in this story. He points out "that Judah's vindication of Tamar's action is cast in relative, and not absolute, terms—'She is more in the right than I,' he said (v. 26)—and there is no hint in the story that her actions were sanctioned by law or custom" (p. 261). This is contra George W. Coats, "Widow's Rights: A Crux in the Structure of Genesis 38," *CBQ* 34 (1972): 461–66, who argues that at this stage in history, the levirate custom only "concerns the widow's right to conceive a child" and so the ending of the story "fits": "Tamar is satisfied. Judah is satisfied . . . The reader knows that justice . . . finally wins out" (p. 466).

68 R. Lansing Hicks, "Onan," *IDB* 3:602, rightly points out that the verb šāḥat (*pi*ᶜel) in this verse should be translated "spoil," not "spill" as in the KJV and RSV. Rather than raise up offspring for his brother, whenever he had intercourse with his brother's wife, he would let his semen "'spoil on the ground'—i.e., make it ineffective" (ibid.).

69 For discussion of the use of *ʾim* with the perfect as a "frequentative perfect," see GKC §§159o, 112gg; and Victor P. Hamilton, *The Book of Genesis: Chapters 18–50* (NICOT; Grand Rapids: Eerdmans, 1995), 430, 436.

is examined below, it was not absolutely required for a brother to perform this duty, although a shaming ritual was attached to his refusal, and this same option may well have been available in patriarchal times, even though not explicitly mentioned in this narrative. Most likely, what brought upon Onan the divine judgment was his *pretending* to perform the levirate responsibility when in fact he did not consummate the sex act and thus did not give Tamar the chance to have progeny, since such progeny would one day deprive Onan of his brother's inheritance and of the opportunity for the family line to pass through him.[70] By his act of subterfuge, Onan was in effect causing the extinction of his brother's entire line of descendants (i.e., the line that would be reckoned to his brother). By pretending but not in fact performing the levirate duty, he also deprived Tamar of her right to be free and marry someone else (of close kin) who would give her children as heirs to her first husband.

The modern English usage of the term "onanism" to describe masturbation is misleading inasmuch as there is no masturbation (at least in the usual meaning of self-gratification via self-stimulation) envisaged in this verse. (For discussion of masturbation, see ch. 7, above.) Even the use of "onanism" as coitus interruptus has often been taken in a negative sense as an activity forbidden by God in light of Gen 38:9, but such disparagement of this sexual act per se is not warranted in the wider context of the Genesis narrative and the HB.

Levirate in the Pentateuchal Legislation: Deuteronomy 25:5–10

We now turn to the Mosaic legislation regarding the institution of levirate marriage, found in Deut 25:5–10. Verses 5–6 give the basic legislation:

> When brothers reside together, and one of them dies and has no son, the wife of the deceased shall not be married outside the family to a stranger. Her husband's brother shall go in to her, taking her in marriage, and performing the duty of a husband's brother to her, and the firstborn whom she bears shall succeed to the name of the deceased brother, so that his name may not be blotted out of Israel.

Verses 7–10 then describe the course of action if the brother fails to perform his levirate duty: his wife is to take his case publicly before the elders, and they in turn will attempt to persuade him. If he is not persuaded, then the wife is to pull his sandal off and spit in his face, declaring, "This is what is done to the man who does not build up his brother's house." This brother's house from then on will be called "the house of him whose sandal was pulled off." Several difficult and widely debated issues arise in this passage.

Why Levirate Marriage? First, what is the purpose of this legislation? Genesis 38:8 has already partially answered this question: it is to "raise up offspring for your

---

[70] This is explained by Fischer, *Women Who Wrestled with God,* 106: "Tamar is supposed to be the mother of the firstborn of Judah's oldest son. Judah's genealogical line is supposed to be continued through her son. Onan refuses her this because he wants to be the heir himself."

brother." The Deuteronomic legislation gives the same answer: the firstborn[71] of the levirate marriage "shall succeed to [lit. 'rise upon'] the name of the deceased brother, so that his [the dead brother's] name may not be blotted out of Israel" (Deut 25:6). Verse 7 echoes this reason when the wife before the elders points out that her brother-in-law "refuses to perpetuate his brother's name in Israel" and, as she spits in his face, she reiterates his failure to "build up his brother's house" (v. 9).

Raymond Westbrook argues that the term "name" in these passages should be fully equated with "title to . . . [one's] landed inheritance," and he interprets the whole purpose of the levirate in terms of the legal inheritance of property.[72] There is undoubtedly an inheritance issue involved, but it is significant that nowhere is property or inheritance mentioned explicitly in these verses, although very good legal terms are available for these concepts in Hebrew law. As with his interpretation of the case of divorce in the preceding chapter of Deuteronomy (24:1–4), Westbrook here again seems to have interpreted the law too narrowly by limiting it to issues of property and inheritance.[73]

As noted above, there was great concern in ancient Israel for ensuring the continuation of the family line; it was viewed as a great tragedy for a man to die without a descendant. The issue was not about just property or inheritance, contrary to the ANE parallels (except perhaps Ugarit); it is first and foremost about preserving the line of descent and the memory of that line.[74] The firstborn of the levirate marriage would represent the deceased brother's name—that is, "he would be equivalent to the son of the deceased and he would provide the deceased man with a posterity in Israel."[75] The greatest punishment provided for

---

[71] Although the word *bēn*, "son," (v. 5) often refers to male progeny in the HB, sometimes it is used in the generic sense of "offspring." It is debated among scholars whether this passage refers to a deceased man with no offspring (male or female) or with no son (see Leggett, *Levirate,* 49–50, for a survey of viewpoints and their representative advocates). I am inclined to take it in the generic sense in light of the legislation formulated in Num 27 (after the case of the daughters of Zelophahad was considered), that if there were no sons, the daughters could inherit the estate. I concur with Meredith G. Kline, *Treaty of the Great King—the Covenant Structure of Deuteronomy: Studies and Commentary* (Grand Rapids: Eerdmans, 1963), 117: "In view of the provision of Numbers 27:4 ff., there would be no need for the levirate marriage if the deceased had daughters."

[72] Westbrook, *Property and the Family,* 69–89, quote at 77.

[73] Westbrook uses questionable logic when he deduces "by a simple process of inversion" from the facts of Gen 38, Ruth 4, and Deut 25 that "the main purpose of the levirate was to provide the deceased with a successor in his estate" (ibid., 74). Just because these cases involve a childless deceased brother and land available to inherit, it does not follow that the inheritance of the land is the main purpose of the levirate institution.

[74] This is made clear, e.g., in the story of Absalom: he has a pillar set up for himself in the King's Valley, for he said, "I have no son to keep my name in remembrance" (2 Sam 18:18). For further discussion and support for the conclusion that the "original and primary motive of levirate marriage in Israel" was "the desire to raise up a son for the dead man," not to deal with the issue of inheritance, see esp. Millar Burrows, "Levirate Marriage in Israel," *JBL* 59 (1940): 23–33, quote at 33; and Davies, "Inheritance Rights," 139–41.

[75] Peter C. Craigie, *The Book of Deuteronomy* (NICOT; Grand Rapids: Eerdmans, 1976), 314.

the sinner in Israel was that he be *kārēt*, "cut off" (a divine curse of extinction not only for himself but especially for his progeny).[76]

This is not to say that inheritance rights were not an important part of the picture here—as a secondary reason for the legislation. The Abrahamic promise of seed and land go together (e.g., Gen 12:7). The land ultimately belonged to God (Lev 25:23), and God assigned it to each tribe by lot in perpetuity (Num 26:52–56; 33:54; 34:13).[77] The case of Zelophahad's daughters (Num 27:1–11; 36:1–13) reveals a concern that the "name" of an Israelite not be "taken away" (*gāra*, v. 4) because he had no son, and this entailed assigning the inheritance to his descendants and a concern to keep the inheritance of each Israelite and his descendants within the tribe and family assigned originally by God. Likewise the wife of the deceased husband in Deut 25 was not to marry outside her family/clan, so that the inheritance would not be taken away from the family of the deceased.

Along with insuring the continuation of the line of descent and the implication of providing an heir to the deceased man's estate and thus perpetuating the family property within the immediate family, a third (and related) implied purpose of the levirate marriage seems to have been to provide for the protection and security needs of the widow. Although this purpose is not explicitly mentioned in the legislation of Deut 25, v. 5 does clearly state that her husband's brother was to "take her in marriage." The most natural way to provide for the widow of the deceased would be marriage. This reason was also implied in the narrative regarding Tamar (Gen 38:14) and is certainly part of the picture in the story of Ruth and Boaz, which is examined below.[78]

Who Qualified as *Levir*? A second issue in the levirate marriage concerns the scope of the institution: who could qualify as the *yābām* to perform the levirate duty? An appropriate answer to this question must take into account the intent of the dependent clause that introduces the legislation (Deut 25:5): "If[79] brothers live together" (RSV). What is the meaning of this clause? Various suggestions have been advanced;[80] probably the most widely accepted today is that articulated by Westbrook, building upon an earlier explanation of David Daube.[81] Westbrook,

---

[76] See Donald J. Wold, "The Meaning of the Biblical Penalty *kareth*" (PhD diss., University of California, Berkeley, 1978); cf. ch. 3, above.

[77] See Eryl W. Davies, "Land: Its Rights and Privileges," in *The World of Ancient Israel: Sociological, Anthropological, and Political Perspectives* (ed. R. E. Clements; Cambridge: Cambridge University Press, 1989), 349–69, esp. 358.

[78] For further discussion of the threefold purpose for the levirate as surveyed above, see esp. Davies, "Inheritance Rights," 138–44.

[79] Some modern translations instead render *kî* as "when," but this may well be one of those occurrences, "oft[en] in laws," where the preposition "has a force approximating to *if*," although it usually describes a case that is more likely to occur than the preposition *ʾim* (BDB 473).

[80] For a survey of options, see Leggett, *Levirate,* 42–48; Westbrook, *Property and the Family,* 77.

[81] Westbrook, *Property and the Family,* 78–80; cf. David Daube, "*Consortium* in Roman and Hebrew Law," *Juridical Review* 62 (1950): 71–91. The idea of "coparcenary"

following Daube, argues that "the phrase refers to the period after the father's death when his sons have not yet taken each his share of the inheritance but continue to live together on the undivided estate."[82] He further buttresses Daube's proposal by pointing to what he sees as parallels in Mesopotamian law where there is mention of a "special legal position of sons prior to their division of the inheritance."[83] According to this hypothesis, before the property is divided, there is common ownership in which each partner (before the inheritance is divided) theoretically owns the whole.

Westbrook's general hypothesis seems plausible on the surface, but a closer look reveals that his fundamental supposition is faulty and the ANE parallels far from conclusive.[84] Although Westbrook's hypothesis cannot be completely ruled

---

or "co-owners of an inheritance by descent" in both the Middle Assyrian Laws and in Deut 25:5–10 is discussed at some length in Driver and Miles, *The Assyrian Laws,* 194–98, 295–300.

[82] Westbrook, *Property and the Family,* 78.

[83] Ibid. Laws cited include MAL A §25 (*COS* 2.132:356; cf. *ANET* 182), which refers to brothers who "have not yet divided their inheritance"; Laws of Eshnunna §16 (*COS* 2.130:333; cf. *ANET* 162), which speaks of the coparcener, or "son of a man who has not yet received his inheritance share" (see Reuven Yaron, *The Laws of Eshnunna* [2d rev. ed.; Jerusalem: Magnes, 1988], 159–60); and CH §165 (*ANET* 173), which refers to the time "when the brothers divide the estate after the father goes to his fate." Westbrook finds three stages at which the levirate operates in Israel, represented respectively by the three biblical sources alluding to the practice: Gen 38, the situation before the father dies; Deut 25, the situation immediately after the father dies but before the brothers have divided the inheritance; and Ruth 4, a situation "where the land has been alienated, but the nearest relative (who would theoretically be the deceased's brother if he died without issue) buys it back" (*Property and the Family,* 79). In all of these cases, according to Westbrook's hypothesis, the surviving brother is not heir to the dead one, since he is already the (co-)owner; the dead brother thus drops out of the inheritance picture unless there is a levirate to "establish the deceased's title by a legal fiction, so that his title 'be not extinguished from Israel'" (p. 80). Westbrook suggests a fourth situation that arises if a married brother dies childless *after* the brothers divide their father's inheritance: the surviving brother now inherits as natural heir of the deceased, and since the name of the deceased would be listed as a former owner of the family estate, his name would not be lost and thus no levirate marriage would be required "to perpetuate his brother's name" (lit., "to raise up a name" to him).

[84] Westbrook's hypothesis is built upon the supposition that "name" in this passage is equivalent to "title to property" and thus the ANE materials dealing with property inheritance are relevant parallels to the biblical law. But as seen above, the primary concern in this biblical legislation is preservation of a line of posterity for the deceased, which is never mentioned in the ANE allegedly parallel laws. Furthermore, the ANE phraseology denoting coparceners (co-owners) is totally different from the terminology used in the biblical levirate legislation: the laws of the ancient Near East mention a time before the brothers have "divided [the inheritance]," whereas the biblical law simply speaks of brothers "residing together." What is more, parallel biblical passages, such as Gen 13:1–6; 36:6–7, that mention "brothers" living together do not have in view coparceners: neither Abram and Lot nor Jacob and Esau owned the land on which they grazed their flocks, and thus there is no co-ownership or inheritance issues involved in their living together. It is merely a matter of geographical closeness. In sum, the ANE texts cited by Westbrook in favor of his hypothesis have no demonstrable commonality of vocabulary or purpose

out, there seems to be a simpler explanation that follows from a straightforward reading of the Mosaic law and its intertextual parallels. Another expert in biblical and ANE law, Anthony Phillips, comments on the clause "when brothers reside together": "Until a younger brother married and had children of his own, he would have remained in his father's or elder brother's house."[85] Phillips takes the clause in its plain sense of geographical proximity, describing a situation where a younger unmarried brother lives with his elder married brother until he establishes a household of his own, and thus concludes that the levirate marriage legislation assumes an unmarried status for the levirate brother. Phillips summarizes his interpretation of the scope and meaning of the levirate institution: "[Deut 25:5–10] required that when a man died childless, his *unmarried* brother living with him should marry the widow and the first son of the union would be regarded as the son of the deceased brother and so bear his name and inherit his property."[86]

Even if one interprets this clause as referring to coparcenery (common ownership) as Westbrook maintains, identification of the eligible *levir* as the younger unmarried brother still seems to make most sense. Phillips points out that only an unmarried brother could realistically be persuaded to do the duty of the *levir* without fear of jeopardizing his own family's security and inheritance.[87] Other scholars—both evangelical and critical—have advocated or implied that the *levir* is an unmarried brother.[88]

---

with the Deuteronomic law. Whereas the ANE laws speak of "before they divided [the inheritance]" the biblical text speaks of "residing together" (which elsewhere in Scripture refers to geographical proximity, not inheritance); whereas the ANE texts say nothing about the practice of levirate, such is the focus of the biblical law; whereas the point of the ANE laws is inheritance, the focus of the biblical law is preservation of a posterity for the deceased.

[85] Anthony Phillips, *Deuteronomy* (CBC; Cambridge: Cambridge University Press, 1973), 168.

[86] Anthony Phillips, "The Book of Ruth—Deception and Shame," *JJS* 37, no. 1 (1986): 3, emphasis added.

[87] Ibid., 4.

[88] Besides Phillips, see, e.g., Gordon P. Hugenberger, *Marriage as a Covenant: Biblical Law and Ethics as Developed from Malachi* (VTSup 52; Leiden: E. J. Brill, 1994; repr., Grand Rapids: Baker, 1998), 114–15; H. C. Leupold, *Exposition of Genesis* (Columbus, Ohio: Wartburg, 1942), 980: "The brother of the deceased, *if unmarried,* would take the widow to wife" (emphasis mine); cf. Victor P. Hamilton, "Marriage: Old Testament and Ancient Near East," *ABD* 4:567, who states that the brothers who dwell together are ones "who have not yet established families of their own." Other supporters of the position that an unmarried brother is in view here include, e.g., Lyle M. Eslinger, "More Drafting Techniques in Deuteronomic Laws," *VT* 34 (1984): 224; Matthew Henry, *Commentary on the Whole Bible* (6 vols.; Old Tappan, N.J.: Fleming H. Revell, n.d.), 1:827; Henri Lesètre, "Lévirat," *DB* 4, col. 215; and Cuthbert Lattey, *The Old Testament: The Book of Ruth* (London: Longmans, Green, 1935), xxvi. Indirect support for this position comes from scholars who take the phrase "the son of a man who is not separated [or, has not been given a share]" in the Laws of Eshnunna §16 (*COS* 2.130:130; *ANET* 162; which law Westbrook cites in support of coparcenry) as referring to a minor. See Yaron, *The Laws of Eshnunna,* 159, n. 101, for bibliography. In light of the conclusion reached in ch. 5, above, that the

This interpretation is also perhaps supported by analogy with the law of Deut 22:28–29 and its ANE parallels, which require a ravisher to marry his victim. As noted in ch. 8, above, the law of 22:28–29 does not state the marital status of the ravisher in question, but the comparative evidence of the fuller treatment of punishment for ravishers that is found Middle Assyrian Laws from about this same time in history provides an exception clause for the ravisher who is already married. This suggests the possibility that biblical law presumed a similar exception clause in cases where the brother was already married, although one must always be cautious in arguing from comparative ANE evidence.[89]

Although the clause "When brothers reside together" seems to refer primarily to an unmarried brother as the normal one to perform the duty of levirate, a broader interpretation may also be implied in light of intertextual linkages with Gen 13:1–6 and 36:6–7. Genesis 13:6 twice uses the same phrase, "dwell/live together," as in Deut 25:5, and in Gen 13:8 Abraham says to his nephew Lot, "we are brothers" (NASB), again employing the same plural noun, "brothers," as in Deut 25:1. Genesis 36:6–7 likewise contains the phrase "dwell/live together" and the noun "brother." These are the only passages in Scripture (aside from the later Ps 133:1) that contain this common phraseology.

It seems likely that the intertextual connection between Deut 25:5–10 and Gen 13 and 36 provides a clue to the semantic range of "brothers" in the Deuteronomy law. The "brothers" Jacob and Esau (described in Gen 36) were male offspring with the same parents in common. On the other hand, the "brothers" (NASB) Abraham and Lot (described in Gen 13) were not male siblings but close relatives. Does Deut 25:5–10, by its intertextual linkage with these two Genesis narratives, hint that reference to the "brothers" who "reside together" (i.e., in close proximity) refers primarily and theoretically to male siblings (as with Jacob and Esau) but, if an unmarried sibling is not available, may in principle (but not mandatorily) refer to "brothers" in the sense of close blood relatives (such Abraham and Lot)? This broader application may also be implicit in the use of the term *yābām* for the *levir,* a term that, as pointed out above, originally designated "progenitor" and not just "brother-in-law." If this wider semantic range

---

pentateuchal legal system proscribed the practice of polygamy in Israel (Lev 18:18; Deut 17:17), this interpretation regarding the levirate marriage laws is consonant with pentateuchal legislation concerning polygamy. Such a conclusion, however, is not reached merely in the interest of "harmonization." As a critical scholar, Anthony Phillips, the most articulate recent proponent of the view that the prospective *levir* was unmarried, has no stake in upholding a conservative conclusion and no particular concern to harmonize the levirate laws with legislation concerning polygamy.

[89] That the levirate law was considered not applicable for a married brother may also be the interpretation implied in the Aramaic *Targum Ruth* 4:6: "Because I have a wife, I have no right to marry another in addition to her lest there be contention in my house and I destroy my inheritance" (D. R. G. Beattie, trans., *The Targum of Ruth: Translated, with Introduction, Apparatus, and Notes* [Aramaic Bible 19; Collegeville, Minn.: Liturgical Press, 1994], 30). It could be argued, however, that this statement falls under the provision in Deut 25 for next of kin not wanting to take her, and not that the law was inapplicable to him.

for "brother" in Deut 25:5 is accepted, then the application of the levirate marriage law to a more distant relative in the book of Ruth would be consistent with the extended meaning of the Deuteronomic law.[90] We will examine Ruth's situation below.

Does Levirate Marriage Entail Incest? This brings us to a third and related issue: how does one reconcile the law of the levirate marriage, which calls for the marriage of a man to his brother's wife, when such a relationship is proscribed as incestuous elsewhere in pentateuchal law? As noted in the discussion of incest (ch. 10, above), this constituted one of the "forbidden degrees" of kinship sexual relationships described in Lev 18 and 20. Leviticus 18:16 reads, "You shall not uncover the nakedness of your brother's wife; it is your brother's nakedness." Leviticus 20:21 adds, "If a man takes his brother's wife, it is impurity; he has uncovered his brother's nakedness; they shall be childless."

Some have attempted to cut the Gordian knot of difficulty by positing that what is prohibited in these Levitical verses is sexual relations between a man and his brother's wife *while the brother is still alive*[91] and that such a relationship after the brother dies is not prohibited. But cohabitation between a man and his brother's wife while the brother was still alive would constitute adultery, punishable by *kārēt* (a divine curse of extinction for sinner and progeny) and death, which is covered by 18:20 and 20:10, and thus does not seem to be what is in view here. Furthermore, 20:21 uses the verb *lāqaḥ*, "take" ("If a man *takes* his brother's wife"), which clearly indicates marriage, and thus the woman must be single (either divorced or widowed).

A closer look at the text of 20:21 (in comparison to the other verses dealing with forbidden degrees of kinship sexual relationships) provides a clue to the

---

[90] Another option would likewise lead to this broader interpretation of the levirate situation. Westbrook may be correct in his argument that Deut 25:1–4 does not present the only legislation under which the levirate marriage would be applicable, as many have claimed. Westbrook, *Property and the Family*, 70–71, suggests that the various attempts to highlight contradictions among the three biblical references to the levirate and thus prove historical development in levirate practice all operate on a basic faulty assumption: that Deut 25 "contains a comprehensive account of the law of the levirate" (p. 71). He illustrates, from the OT and ANE law codes, how this law may be seen as part of a collection of decisions in individual cases and refers only to a particular aspect of the levirate institution. From the individual case laws, combined with the picture presented in narratives dealing with the levirate practice, it is the task of the interpreter to piece together the essential features of the levirate institution. He further hypothesizes that the reason there is only one case concerning the levirate in the Deuteronomic legislation is that the institution of levirate marriage is really a family matter, not a public legal duty, and it only comes into public concern (hence into Deuteronomic law) because the father is no longer alive to exercise his patriarchal authority in this matter. Because it is a family matter, the law provides no sanctions of criminal law but only the procedure of public humiliation (71, 82). For further evidence and discussion of the typical incompleteness of ANE and biblical law codes, see Raymond Westbrook, "Biblical and Cuneiform Law Codes," *RB* 92 (1985): 247–64.

[91] So, e.g., Davies, "Inheritance Rights," 267.

solution. It is not without significance that only with regard to this relationship is the word "impurity" (*niddâ*) used. Elsewhere in the Pentateuch, *niddâ* always refers to ceremonial, not moral, uncleanness/impurity—in particular, to the "uncleanness" of menstruation and the "water for cleansing [i.e., for removing ceremonial impurity]" of touching a corpse.[92] These ceremonial uncleannesses are unavoidable, expected states—of the woman and the warrior. There is no moral fault contained in such uncleanness; the sin is only if one fails to be ceremonially purified in the proper way and time.

In Lev 20, as pointed out in the discussion of incest (ch. 10, above), the prohibition of relations with one's brother's wife is the last of a list of sexual offenses that proceeds in descending order of seriousness. Thus this prohibition is considered the least serious of all the illicit sexual relations mentioned in that chapter. The other "forbidden degrees" of kinship sexual relationship are called "perversion" (v. 12), "depravity" (v. 14), "a disgrace" (v. 17), a "sin" (v. 20 RSV), with punishments of being "put to death" (v. 12), "burned to death" (v. 14), or "cut off in the sight of their people" (v. 17), with "their blood . . . upon them" (vv. 11–12), bearing "punishment" (vv. 17, 19) and "the consequences of their guilt" (v. 20 NJB). Regarding the relationship between a man and his brother's wife, there appears none of these strong terms of moral disapproval and/or portrayals of the various means of capital punishment to fit the crime. The text instead only describes it as *niddâ*—which is elsewhere in the Pentateuch a ceremonial uncleanness.

Why is this particular sexual relationship singled out for special treatment, described only as *niddâ*? The wording regarding this relationship is uniquely and carefully chosen to make room for the levirate marriage as a legitimate exception to this prohibition. On the one hand, the prohibition of sexual relations with one's brother's wife is lumped together with all of the other illicit sexual relationships of Lev 18, and the same punishment of *kārēt* is mentioned for all these relationships (18:29), thus indicating that, as a general rule, having sex with one's brother's wife is considered a moral defilement. On the other hand, there appears to be an intent to make allowance for an exception in the case of performing the duty of the *levir* in the levirate marriage, by the choice of the word *niddâ*, which elsewhere in the Pentateuch denotes an "uncleanness" that is unavoidable and even expected in certain situations.

Thus the prohibition of 18:16 and 20:21 indeed upholds the integrity of the family structure in general intrasocial relationships and shows respect for the sex-

---

[92] For menstrual ceremonial uncleanness, see Lev 12:2, 5; 15:19, 20, 24, 25 (three times), 26 (bis), 33; 18:19. For the "water for cleansing" for touching a corpse, see Num 19:9, 13, 20, 21 (bis); 31:23. See BDB 622, which recognizes *niddâ* as "ceremonial impurity." This is contra Jacob Milgrom, *Leviticus 17–22* (AB 3A; New York: Doubleday, 2000), 1758, who argues that the Holiness Code departs from the usage of the Priestly source and uses *niddâ* only metaphorically to mean "a foul, odious, repulsive act." By positing such a change in meaning within the canonical book of Leviticus, Milgrom has missed the significant implication of the usage of this term for reconciling Lev 18:16 (and Lev 20:21) with Deut 25:5–10.

uality of the sister-in-law, as it indicates that, as a general rule, a man is not allowed to marry and have sexual relations with his brother's wife after the brother dies, under penalty of (divinely imposed) childlessness if such happens. At the same time, the unique wording of these passages allows (and even make provision) for an exception in the case of levirate marriage (Deut 25:5–10), which institution likewise maintains the integrity of that same family structure in a particular situation when it is threatened by death, and indeed shows respect, rather than disrespect, for the sexuality of the sister-in-law.[93] When a man marries and has sexual relations with the wife of his deceased brother in order to fulfill the duty of a *levir,* such exception to the prohibitions of Lev 18:16 and 20:21 is not punished by childlessness but rather rewarded with progeny to carry on the line of the dead brother. Childlessness is turned to fertility.[94]

What Does the "Sandal Ceremony" Symbolize? A fourth issue in Deut 25:5–10 is the nature and purpose of the public procedure for dealing with the one who refuses to perform the levirate duty for his deceased brother. This is the only example of shame punishment in the pentateuchal legislation. Calum Carmichael has made a case that the whole ceremony has sexual symbolism reenacting what Onan did to Tamar,[95] but this sensational hypothesis is too fanciful, speculative, and forced.[96] A more straightforward interpretation is that the shoe is a symbol of authority/responsibility; removing the shoe "indicates that the brother had abandoned his responsibility," and spitting symbolizes the "shame" the brother deserved.[97] Although this is a matter of family customary law, in which the court has no direct punitive jurisdiction, the failure of the brother-in-law to take seriously his responsibility to avert the childlessness of his brother calls forth public and perpetual shame upon his name and house.

---

[93] Milgrom, *Leviticus 17–22,* 1545, acknowledges that a possible solution is that Lev 18:16 and 20:21 provide the general rule and Deut 25:5–10 constitutes the exception, although he fails to grasp the significance of the use of the term *niddâ* to substantiate this solution. Milgrom here would have done well to follow the lead of the rabbis he cites, who do recognize that *niddâ* provides the clue to link Deut 25:5–10 with Lev 18:16 (and 20:21) without contradiction. See *Sipra, parashat Qedoshim, pereq* 12:7; cf. Ibn Ezra.

[94] That, according to this legislation, it was permissible for a man to marry the wife of his dead brother if she had not born him children does not imply that a childless marriage was somehow considered not fully consummated (as seems to be implied in later rabbinic rulings, where a man could divorce his wife if she had not been able to provide him offspring, in order to take a new wife). See ch. 9, above.

[95] Calum M. Carmichael, "A Ceremonial Crux: Removing a Man's Sandal as a Female Gesture of Contempt," *JBL* 96 (1977): 321–36. Carmichael suggests that the sandal represents the woman's genitals; removing it (as in Arab divorce ceremonies) from the foot (a symbol of the male sexual organ) symbolizes exposing the man's genitals and signifies the man's (like Onan's) withholding conception; the woman's spitting imitates (Onan's) spilling of seed; and the whole ceremony symbolically "confers a particularly bold sexual freedom upon a woman" (p. 332).

[96] Anthony Phillips, "The Book of Ruth," 12–13, provides cogent arguments to show that Carmichael's "attempt to explain the shame ritual of Deut. 25:5–10 as figuratively a re-enactment of the Onan incident is unconvincing."

[97] Craigie, *Deuteronomy,* 215.

The placement of this ceremony at the heart of a chiastic structure running from v. 4 to v. 14 provides even greater emphasis on the shame and contempt that one deserves who refuses to use his procreative powers to "build up" his brother's house.[98] Furthermore, it seems probable that the ceremony was as much designed for the benefit of the widow as for shaming the brother-in-law, since at the same time as it released the latter from his responsibility as *levir,* "the widow herself was no longer bound by the family of her deceased husband and she became free to marry whom she wished."[99]

Moreover, the "shaming" ceremony speaks to the issue of women's status and rights. This ceremony is powerful biblical evidence against "the concept [apparently present in other ANE societies] of the woman as being part of the family property, so that she is inherited by the dead man's kinsman along with his estate. . . . The active role played by the woman in the levirate in Deut 25 militates against this view of the woman as passive chattel being passed from hand to hand."[100] Verses 7–9 reveal that in this public procedure the woman clearly has the right to act in the legal sphere, representing her deceased husband: she brings the legal complaint before the elders; she acts as the plaintiff in the legal case; she carries out the punishment against the one who refuses to be a *levir.*[101]

Why Is This Law Placed Here in Deuteronomy? A final issue regarding the levirate marriage legislation is its placement in the flow of the book of Deuteronomy. I here follow Stephen Kaufman's analysis of the literary structure of Deuteronomic law, particularly Deut 12–26, which he shows to be "a highly structured composition whose major topical units are arranged according to the order of the laws of the Decalogue—more specifically the Decalogue as it appears in ch. 5 of that book."[102] Earlier chapters of this book have referred to Kaufman's study in noting that, for example, various sexually related crimes are organized under the section that elaborates on the seventh commandment, prohibiting adultery, and, as another example, that the law regulating divorce is surprisingly

---

[98] For analysis of the chiastic structure, see Eslinger, "More Drafting Techniques," 221–25.

[99] Davies, "Inheritance Rights," 262.

[100] Robert Gordis, "Love, Marriage, and Business in the Book of Ruth: A Chapter in Hebrew Customary Law," in *A Light unto My Path: Old Testament Studies in Honor of Jacob M. Myers* (ed. Howard N. Bream, Ralph D. Heim, and Carey A. Moore; Philadelphia: Temple University Press, 1974), 248.

[101] Carolyn Pressler, *The View of Women Found in the Deuteronomic Family Laws* (BZAW 216; Berlin: de Gruyter, 1993), 73–74. The sandal ceremony also brings up the connection between the levirate law and Num 27:8–11, where the inheritance of a man with no male heir passes (in order) to his daughters, then his brothers, and then the next nearest kin. Numbers 27:8–11 has no mention of the levirate law. J. G. McConville points out that "the Numbers legislation would be intelligible in circumstances in which levirate marriage had been refused (as Deuteronomy anticipates), or had otherwise not produced the necessary son" (*Deuteronomy* [AOTC 5; Downers Grove, Ill.: InterVarsity, 2002], 369).

[102] Steven A. Kaufman, "The Structure of the Deuteronomic Law," *Maarav* 1–2 (1978–1979): 108–9.

placed under the amplification of the eighth commandment, forbidding theft (i.e., the theft of the woman's dignity and self-worth).

The placement of the levirate marriage legislation in the flow of Deuteronomy yields another (at least initial) surprise: it is situated, of all places, under the section amplifying and illustrating the tenth commandment ("You shall not covet").[103] Kaufman points out that careful thought grasps the eminent appropriateness of this placement and brings admiration for the ingenuity of the inspired compiler. According to Kaufman, the levirate marriage is a "social institution that provides a sanctioned exception to the basic prohibition of the Tenth Commandment. There does, he [the compiler of Deuteronomy] tells us, exist an institution through which a man may rightfully claim the wife of his brother."[104] As Kaufman points out, the connection depends on the recognition that the word "brother" can mean "neighbor, fellow Israelite" and also one's literal blood relative (sibling).[105]

Though following much of Kaufman's argumentation, Michael Matlock asks whether the consummation of levirate marriage is a "sanctioned exception" to the tenth commandment or constitutes, more properly, "a way to show true obedience to the intent of the tenth commandment."[106] Matlock's reasoning has convinced me that the latter is true.

> The *levir* is faced with the decision to desire what is lawful or unlawful, that is, what is right and honorable in the sight of Yahweh or displeasing and sinful in his sight. He can choose to act honorably: ensure an heir for his dead brother thereby continuing the deceased's name, preserve the proper property distribution among clan heads, and provide for the widow. Or he can also choose to act shamefully: seek the wealth of his dead brother's estate and maintain his own present children's future inheritance. If he does the latter, it seems he has also broken the essence of the tenth commandment.[107]

Just as the tenth commandment forbade coveting one's neighbor's ("brother's") property, so in the levirate marriage situation, the property of his brother, no matter how desirable it might be in his own eyes, remains in his brother's estate. Just as the prohibition against covetousness in the tenth commandment was impossible to effectively police, so the law of the levirate marriage could not be legally enforced (except by the social pressure of a shaming ceremony).

---

103 The section dealing with the tenth commandment is Deut 25:5–16. See the analysis of Kaufman, ibid., 142–44.

104 Ibid., 143.

105 Ibid.

106 Michael D. Matlock, "Disobeying or Obeying the First Part of the Tenth Commandment: Alternative Meanings from Deuteronomy 25:5–10," *PEGLMBS* 21 (2001): 99.

107 Ibid. For a full discussion see 91–103. See also Dvora E. Weisberg, "The Widow of Our Discontent: Levirate Marriage in the Bible and Ancient Israel," *JSOT* 28 (2004): 403–29, who examines the sense of discomfort on the part of men who are asked to do the duty of the *levir*. She summarizes the reason for the reluctance: "Concerns for the self trump fraternal loyalties" (p. 429).

The temptation to covet the deceased brother's inheritance was strong—and that covetousness could lead a brother to refuse to perform the duty of the *levir* and thereby usurp his deceased brother's estate. Conversely, being willing to do the duty of the *levir* meant resistance to the temptation to covet. Thus the levirate marriage legislation not only served to provide a son and heir for the deceased and support for the widow but ultimately served as a check against the sin of covetousness among the families of Israel.

The "Immodest and Violent Lady Wrestler" of Deuteronomy 25:11–12

An intriguing piece of legislation immediately follows the law concerning levirate marriage, which, as will become apparent, is closely connected to the issue of childlessness, and is thus treated here.[108] Deuteronomy 25:11–12 reads in the NASB,

> If [two] men, a man and his countryman [lit. "brother"], are struggling together, and the wife of one comes near to deliver her husband from the hand of the one who is striking him, and puts out her hand [*yād*] and seizes [*ḥāzaq* in the *hipʿil*] his genitals [*mĕbušim*], then you shall cut off her hand [*kap*]; you shall not show pity.

If one accepts the traditional rendering of this passage (as in the NASB and most English versions), this law constitutes the only explicit example of mutilative punishment in the Israelite legal system.[109] This traditional reading mandates the amputation of the woman's hand as her punishment for crushing the testicles of a man while she is defending her husband. A parallel is envisaged in the Middle Assyrian Laws (MAL A §8): "If a woman should crush a man's testicle in a quarrel, they shall cut off one of her fingers. And even if the physician should bandage it, but the second testicle then becomes infected (?) Along with it and becomes . . . , or if she should crush the second testicle during the quarrel—they shall gouge out both her [. . .]'s."[110] According to this interpretation, the *hipʿil* of *ḥāzaq* is taken to imply an intensely violent act, entailing permanent damage to the man's testicles, thus rendering him unable to father children.[111]

---

[108] "Immodest and Violent Lady Wrestler" is a title adapted from Lyle M. Eslinger, "The Case of an Immodest Lady Wrestler in Deuteronomy XXV 11–12," *VT* 31 (1981): 269–81.

[109] The general principle of *lex talionis* is also found in Deut 19:21; cf. Exod 21:24 and Lev 24:19–20. Craigie argues cogently that the punishment in this law is "an extension of the *lex talionis* . . . ; for obvious reasons, given the different sexes of the persons involved in the incident, the *lex talionis* could not be applied literally. It may be that this very particular piece of casuistic law is intended as an example of how *lex talionis* was able to be interpreted when it could not be applied literally" (*Deuteronomy*, 316). For the widespread use of mutilation in ANE law outside Israel, see, e.g., CH §§195–200 (*COS* 2.131:348; *ANET* 175).

[110] MAL A §8 (*COS* 2.132:354). Theophile J. Meek's translation of this law (*ANET* 181) supplies the word "eyes" for the break at the end of the sentence.

[111] See, e.g., Anthony Phillips, *Ancient Israel's Criminal Law: A New Approach to the Decalogue* (Oxford: Basil Blackwell, 1970), 95: "It must be assumed that this action caused permanent injury, for it would seem unlikely that this mutilation was inflicted merely for the woman's immodesty."

If the traditional reading and interpretation are correct, then, when viewed in the light of the importance of procreation and offspring among the Hebrews, this legislation would constitute a powerful positive affirmation of sexuality. What is indicated would be along these lines: "The adversary male's reproductive power is more important than a wife's 'natural' instinct to help her husband in any way she can. The importance of progeny to a man is so great that absolute priority is given to the protection of the organs that permit him to reproduce."[112] The traditional interpretation seems to explain the placement of this law immediately after—indeed, in an intricate chiastic structure linking it to—the law of levirate marriage.[113] Both of these laws would be seen as dealing with the same basic subject—threats to procreation that would lead to childlessness. "The sanctity of procreation and its implements lies at the center of these strange laws in Deuteronomy."[114] Whereas the levirate marriage seeks to avoid the threat of childlessness by providing a *levir* to raise up progeny to the deceased brother and his wife, the law concerning "the immodest lady wrestler" seeks to avoid the threat of childlessness that would result from a man whose organs of regeneration were mutilated. In both cases it is suggested that the punishment would be seen to involve a public and permanent shaming of the offender, designed to provide an effective deterrent against violation of the law.[115]

Lyle Eslinger suggests an alternate interpretation for this passage.[116] Building upon Carmichael's symbolic sexual interpretation of the levirate shaming procedure (as discussed above), Eslinger argues that the "hand" (*kap*) here refers to the woman's genitals and that this is a case of exact *lex talionis,* in which mutilation of the man's genitalia calls for punishment in kind for the woman (probably by a clitoridectomy). His argument is based upon interpreting Gen 32:26, 33 as referring to Jacob's underhanded technique to gain the advantage over his opponent by grasping his private parts (this requires textual emendation to implicate Jacob and not the one he was wrestling with) and upon interpreting *kap* in Song 5:5 as a reference to the phallus. My examination of these texts elsewhere in this book

---

[112] Sapp, *Sexuality, the Bible, and Science,* 30. To this list of prohibitions may also be added the verbal command of Moses to the men of Israel in preparing them to encounter God at Sinai: "Prepare for the third day; do not go near a woman" (Exod 19:15).

[113] Eslinger, "More Drafting Techniques," 222–25.

[114] Ibid., 225.

[115] On the shame-based punishment operative in these laws (as well as throughout Israel's legal system), see P. Eddy Wilson, "Deuteronomy xxv 11–12—One for the Books," *VT* 47 (1997): 220–35. I do not agree, however, with Wilson's attempt to downplay the retributive nature of the law and its guilt-based legal basis (alongside the shame-based element) or with his suggestion that this law is a "substantively just law" (distinguished from procedurally just laws) that is so exaggerated in its statement of punishment that it serves as an effective deterrent but is not intended to be enforced. Cf. John H. Elliott, "Deuteronomy—Shameful Encroachment on Shameful Parts: Deuteronomy 25:11–12 and Biblical Euphemism," in *Ancient Israel: The Old Testament in Its Social Context* (ed. Philip F. Esler; Minneapolis: Fortress, 2006), 161–76.

[116] Eslinger, "The Case of an Immodest Lady Wrestler."

finds both of these conclusions wanting,[117] although the apparently intentional ambiguity of the term *kap* in these passages may indeed suggest sexual overtones.

Jerome Walsh summarizes the traditional view and other more recent interpretations of this passage,[118] all of which assume that the passage refers to permanent severe physical maiming of the woman, either the amputation of her hand or genital mutilation (with the word *kap* being used euphemistically for the genitals). Although the interpretations of this passage presupposing physical mutilation of the woman have a degree of cogency (especially the traditional view), Walsh shows that a closer look at the text reveals serious philological and lexical difficulties with these views, in addition to highlighting the anomaly that this is the only law in the Hebrew legal corpus to mandate physical mutilation.

First, it is important to note that the law specifically describes a quarrel between "a man and his countryman (lit. 'brother' NASB)" and not an attack from an outside enemy; thus the likelihood that the one attacked is in mortal harm is lessened. Second, the verbal root *ḥāzaq* in the *hipʿil* does not necessarily imply the infliction of damage to the testicles; if it did imply such here, the amount of damage would be variable (as would the amount of punishment), and there would be a need for the law to deal in detail with these variations, as in the Middle Assyrian Laws (cited above). The fact that there is no such detailed treatment in the biblical legislation seems to imply that this law does not concern a case of permanent injury to the man's testicles but rather the shameful act of the woman grasping the man's private parts. This interpretation is strengthened by the Hebrew word used here for "testicles," *mĕbušîm,* which is related to the Hebrew verb meaning "shame."[119]

Third, the word used for "hand" in the punishment of Deut 25:12 is *kap,* not *yād,* the word for used in the previous verse describing her crime. In the HB the term *kap* normally denotes the cupped palm of the hand, and if literally referring to the woman's hand, this would entail in 25:12 an "odd image of trying to amputate the palm of someone's hand."[120] Are there other possible meanings of *kap* besides "cupped palm of the hand"? If we turn to the various extended meanings of *kap,* it can refer to the arched instep of the foot (2 Kgs 19:24; cf. Isa 37:25); the bowl of an open container such as a dish, bowl, or spoon (concentrated in the book of Numbers); curved fronds of a palm tree (Lev 23:40); or the pocket of a sling (1 Sam 25:29). In all these usages, as Walsh points out, the common element is "the image of an open, concave curve."[121] Walsh finds that Eslinger is on the

---

[117] See chs. 5 and 14 in this study. Likewise, since Carmichael's view of the woman's symbolic "bold sexual freedom" in the levirate shaming procedure appears to be unlikely, I cannot concur with his assessment that this law in Deut 25:11–12 "is an expression of the lawgiver's desire to communicate that such freedom in the case of levirate is absolutely intolerable in any other circumstances" ("A Ceremonial Crux," 332).

[118] Walsh, " 'You Shall Cut Off,' " 47–53.

[119] This is an OT *hapax legomenon,* related to the verbal root *bwš,* "shame," probably chosen by the legislator "to emphasize the villainy of the woman's method" (Eslinger, "The Case of an Immodest Lady Wrestler," 271). The plural probably constitutes a euphemism for the testicles.

[120] Walsh, " 'You Shall Cut Off,' " 58.

[121] Ibid., 54.

right track to see an allusion to the genital area in the use of the word *kap* in Gen 32:26, 33 and Song 5:4–5 but faults his "excess of ingenuity" in trying to identify the precise anatomical part labeled *kap*,[122] which suggestions lose the basic element of "open concavity" that seems to be characteristic of other uses of *kap*. It makes more sense, according to Walsh, to read both of these verses "as general references to the pelvic area rather than to particular organs," and in these two passages *kap* "would be the open concave curves of the pelvic region, and would correspond most closely to the English word 'groin' or perhaps 'crotch.'"[123]

Is there any contextual or lexical evidence in Deut 25:11–12 that would point to the denotation of *kap* as "groin" or "crotch"? This question is answered in the affirmative by a fourth—for me, the decisive—piece of evidence adduced by Walsh. The Hebrew verb *qāṣaṣ* in 25:12 has regularly been translated "cut off" in the modern versions, but Walsh points out that although such is the meaning of the verb in the *piʿel*,[124] in this verse the verb is in the *qal*. The three occurrences of the verb *qāṣaṣ* in the *qal* outside Deut 25 all are used in reference to a group of desert dwellers in Jeremiah's day who had the fashion of "clipping" or "shaving" (*qāṣaṣ* in the *qal* pass. ptc.) the hair on their temples, and thus a reasonable inference is that in the *qal* the verb *qāṣaṣ* means "to cut or shave [the hair]," not "to amputate," particularly when used of a part of the body that contains hair. If the meaning of *qāṣaṣ* (in the *qal*) in 25:12 is "cut/shave [the hair]," then it makes good sense to understand the *kap* in 25:12 to refer to the place where hair grows, that is, the "groin," instead of the cupped palm of the hand (where no hair grows). Deuteronomy 25:12 is then best translated, "You shall shave [the hair of] her groin." Elsewhere in the HB, shaving someone's pubic hair, as well as exposing their genitals, appears in contexts of punishment by humiliation (2 Sam 10:4–5; Isa 7:20; cf. Isa 3:17; 20:4; Ezek 16:37),[125] and this is also true elsewhere in the ancient Near East.[126]

---

[122] Eslinger, "The Case of an Immodest Lady Wrestler," 274, 276, sees *kap* in Gen 32 as the scrotum, whereas in Song 5:5 *kap* is identified with the labia minora and majora of the woman's vagina.

[123] Walsh, "'You Shall Cut Off,'" 55.

[124] The verb appears fourteen times in the HB, of which ten are in the *piʿel*. In the *piʿel* the basic meaning is indeed to "sever into parts," in such senses as "cut off" (Judg 1:6–7; 2 Sam 4:12), "cut in pieces" (2 Kgs 24:13; 2 Chr 28:24; Exod 39:3; Ps 129:4), "cut off/ strip" (2 Kgs 16:17; 18:16), or "cut in two" (Ps 46:10 [ET 46:9] NASB).

[125] In Isa 7:20 the phrase is literally "the hair of the feet," a euphemism for pubic hair. In 2 Sam 10:4–5 the reference to shaving off "half the beard of each," coupled with cutting off their garments at their hips, seems to imply that the "beard" be taken euphemistically for the pubic hair. See Walsh, "'You Shall Cut Off,'" 57, for further discussion.

[126] CH §127 (*COS* 2.131:344; *ANET* 171) refers to the shaving of a person convicted of making a false accusation of sexual impropriety, but it is not clear what hair is shaved. A Sumerian document (CBS 10467) indicates that the punishment of a woman convicted of adultery included shaving her genitalia, boring a hole in her nose, and leading her through the city in public humiliation. See discussion (with bibliography) in Martha T. Roth, "The Slave and the Scoundrel: CBS 10467, a Sumerian Morality Tale?" *JAOS* 103 (1983): 275–82; and Raymond Westbrook, "Adultery in Ancient Near Eastern Law," *RB* 97 (1990): 542–80; cf. Walsh, "'You Shall Cut Off,'" 57.

I agree with Walsh's conclusion (cited also in ch. 6, above): "By reducing the severity of the punishment from the permanency of amputation to the temporary humiliation of depilation, it allows the punishment to be seen as both talionic and as responding to the alleged 'shamefulness' of the woman's deed. She has humiliated a man publicly by an assault on his genitalia (presumably without serious injury to them); her punishment is public genital humiliation, similarly without permanent injury."[127] His explanation for the basic concern behind the legislation is, however, not entirely satisfactory. Walsh joins others who regard the law as addressing "the gravity of the offense of a married woman initiating sexual contact with another man."[128] But in the context that in the law of levirate marriage (Deut 25:5–10) that immediately precedes it, the concern was a threat to procreation that would lead to childlessness, the issue here appears to be similar—protecting a man's sexual organs in order to preserve his power of procreation (as elaborated above in discussing the traditional interpretation of this passage).

If one accepts the traditional interpretation, then the punishment is severe and permanent—amputation of the hand. If Walsh's interpretation is adopted, then the penalty is still serious, as it applies the law of *lex talionis* and utilizes a shame-based punishment common elsewhere in the ancient Near East. Regardless of which interpretation one adopts, the seriousness of the crime is underscored by the final climaxing clause, which proscribes leniency: "show no pity [on her]" (v. 12).[129] Yahweh potently protects the power of procreation.

Levirate in the Prophets/Writings: The Book of Ruth

The third OT passage concerning levirate marriage is the book of Ruth. Although some have questioned whether levirate marriage even appears in this book,[130] several studies have persuasively shown the numerous intertextual links between Deut 25:5–10 and the book of Ruth.[131] Terminological linkages include such expressions as "wife of the deceased" (Deut 25:5; Ruth 4:5); "go in to her,

---

[127] Walsh, "'You Shall Cut Off,'" 58.

[128] Ibid., 49, citing Pressler, *The View of Women,* 99.

[129] The same prohibition of leniency is found in connection with homicide (Deut 19:13; cf. Num 35:31–32), enticement to the worship of other gods (Deut 13:9 [ET 13:8]), and the malicious false witness (Deut 19:21); the implication seems to be that leniency may be possible with other penalties. For discussion and bibliography supporting this conclusion, see above, chapter 8.

[130] E.g., Gordis, "Love, Marriage, and Business," 241–62, sees "virtually no similarity between" Ruth 4 and Deut 25:5–10 and concludes, "The transaction described is not an instance of the levirate, but a genuine example of the redemption of land, which had been sold under the stress of economic want to an outsider" (246, 259).

[131] See esp. Michael D. Goulder, "Ruth: A Homily on Deuteronomy 22–25?" in *Of Prophets' Visions and the Wisdom of Sages: Essays in Honour of R. Norman Whybray on His Seventieth Birthday* (ed. Heather A. McKay and David J. A. Clines; JSOTSup 162; Sheffield, Eng.: Sheffield Academic Press, 1993), 307–19, although I disagree with the implications Goulder draws on the basis of his critical redating of Deuteronomy.

taking her in marriage" (Deut 25:5; cf. Ruth 4:13); "succeed to the name of the deceased brother, so that his name may not be blotted out" (Deut 25:6; cf. Ruth 4:5, 10); "go up to the elders at the gate" (Deut 25:7; cf. Ruth 4:1–2); "pull his sandal off his foot" (Deut 25:9; cf. Ruth 4:7); and "build up his brother's house" (Deut 25:9; cf. Ruth 4:11). Goulder correctly concludes, "So many verbal contacts with Deut 25:5–10 cannot be accidental."[132] Donald Leggett shows that Ruth contains allusions to the levirate marriage not only in the parallels cited by Goulder but also in Ruth 2:20; 3:10, 13; and 4:12.[133] And Calum Carmichael suggests parallels in sexual symbolism between Deut 25 and Ruth.[134] It seems clear that the book of Ruth is dealing with the levirate marriage.

At the same time, there appears at first glance to be a number of differences between the Deuteronomic levirate legislation and the book of Ruth. Instead of the deceased's brother marrying the widow as in Deuteronomy, it is a distant relative. Whereas Deut 25 focuses upon perpetuating the name of the deceased, Ruth 4 centers on the redemption of property. In Deuteronomy the duty of the *levir* is compulsory; in Ruth it is not. Deuteronomy speaks of the "brother-in-law" (*yābām*) whereas Ruth speaks of a "kinsman-redeemer" (NIV; *gōʾēl*). Whereas the

---

132 Ibid., 313.

133 Leggett, *Levirate*, 246.

134 See Calum M. Carmichael, " 'Treading' in the Book of Ruth," *ZAW* 92 (1980): 248–66; idem, "A Ceremonial Crux," 321–36. I have already reviewed earlier in this chapter Carmichael's view of sexual symbolism in Deut 25 and found it unconvincing. Some of his suggestions regarding Ruth (esp. the reenactment of the sin of Onan in the sandal ceremony and the "treading" symbolizing sexual intercourse) also appear forced. But Ruth's uncovering of Boaz's feet at the threshing floor and the fourfold mention of her lying at them could well be a symbolic gesture representing the uncovering of his genitals ("feet") in sexual intercourse, and the request for Boaz to "spread his skirt over" Ruth is perhaps a symbolic request to cover her (nakedness) in marriage (Carmichael, " 'Treading' in the Book of Ruth," 332–33). Although the sexual symbolism may be present in these gestures, I do not concur with some commentators that Ruth actually uncovered Boaz' genitals and engaged in sexual intercourse with him that night. Such seems totally out of harmony with the overall characterization of Ruth in the book as a virtuous woman and with Boaz's statement about her in the immediate context (Ruth 3:11): "for all the assembly of my people know that you are a worthy woman." In this immediate context, Boaz speaks in language completely foreign to a midnight sexual rendezvous—referring to Ruth as "blessed by the LORD" and full of *ḥesed* ("loyalty") (v. 10) and announcing his willingness to perform the act of near kinsman in the future if such duty is not performed by the one who is nearer of kin (vv. 11–13). As the narrator continues the story, Boaz's dealings at the gate are not those of a man afraid he may have made a woman pregnant who was not his wife. Furthermore, Holly M. Blackwelder Carpenter shows that the "foot" motif runs through the entire book of Ruth, referring elsewhere always to the literal foot (not a euphemism for the genitals) ("A Comprehensive Narrative Analysis of the Book of Ruth" [M.A. thesis, Andrews University, 2004], 72). With the majority of commentators, I conclude that what is described is Ruth's uncovering of Boaz's feet (not genitals), without denying the possible sexual symbolism that this action may have implied. See Shadrac Keita and Janet W. Dyk, "The Scene at the Threshing Floor: Suggestive Readings and Intercultural Considerations on Ruth 3," *BT* 57 (2006): 17–32, for a straightforward reading of Ruth 3 without any erotic overtones.

sandal ceremony has a clear stigma attached in Deuteronomy, there appears to be none in Ruth. But these alleged contradictions between the two accounts are more apparent than real. As indicated above in the discussion of Deut 25:5–10, the levirate legislation is focused upon male siblings, but the intertextual clues point to a possible wider application when no sibling is available or willing. In the case of Ruth, both of the sons of Naomi were dead, and therefore the wider application to more distant relatives applies.

As concluded above in the discussion of the Deuteronomic legislation, the levirate institution was concerned with both progeny and property together. Several scholars have recognized that this dual purpose of the Deuteronomic legislation provides a crucial key to understanding the situation in Ruth.[135] Because one of the primary functions of the $g\bar{o}\,\bar{e}l$ "kinsman-redeemer" (NIV) in ancient Israel concerned property (see Lev 25:25), it is natural that under certain circumstances the levirate and kinsman functions may coalesce, as is the case in the book of Ruth. "In those cases where the childless widow was connected to property which was in danger of being lost to the family through poverty, the deceased's name was not merely revived through the birth of a son but through the redemption of his patrimony as well. . . . The dual purpose involved in the levirate law—to raise up descendants for the deceased, thereby preventing the alienation of the family property—is that which is fulfilled by Boaz when he married Ruth and redeems the property."[136] "Boaz was simply making explicit what had always been implicit in the levirate duty."[137]

Regarding the sandal ceremony, it has become clear from the discussion of Deut 25 that a shaming stigma is attached to the procedure of removing the sandal. But the basic meaning of the procedure was to symbolically indicate that the levirate responsibility was being relinquished by the brother. The same basic meaning is found in the ceremony of Ruth 4. The one nearest of kin, by removing his sandal, was symbolically relinquishing/abandoning his responsibility to Boaz to redeem the property and marry Ruth. "The measure of the stigma would be in direct ratio to the nearness of the relationship to the next-of-kin";[138] this makes sense inasmuch as there are no natural siblings to perform the levirate duty, and thus the responsibility becomes more optional as it moves beyond the theoretical meaning of the legislation to the principle of near of kin.

Thus the levirate marriage portrayed in the book of Ruth is in full accord with the legislation of Deuteronomy but complicated by the need of a $g\bar{o}\,\bar{e}l$ to redeem property and by the lack of a sibling to perform the levirate duty. "There is no contradiction between the legislation in Deuteronomy and in Ruth; it is merely a question of the case portrayed by the latter being more complex. Deuter-

---

[135] See esp. Eryl W. Davies, "Ruth iv 5 and the Duties of the $g\bar{o}\,\bar{e}l$," VT 33 (1983): 231–34; Leggett, Levirate, 244–45; Thompson and Thompson, "Some Legal Problems," 87.

[136] Leggett, Levirate, 244–46.

[137] Davies, "Ruth iv 5," 233.

[138] Harold H. Rowley, The Servant of the Lord and Other Essays on the Old Testament (London: Lutterworth, 1952; repr., Oxford: Blackwell, 1965), 173.

onomy speaks of a widow without children, but the book of Ruth adds to that the situation of a widow about to be dispossessed of the land which belonged to her husband."[139]

As observed above, fulfilling the levirate marriage responsibility was not mandatory even in OT times, although there was a stigma attached for not fulfilling one's duty as *levir*. If the eligible *levir* was an unmarried brother of the deceased, as argued above, there is theoretically nothing preventing the continuation of the practice of levirate marriage beyond OT times. But the basic purposes of the levirate marriage—to raise up descendants for the deceased and prevent the alienation of the family property—are no longer such pressing concerns in modern society as in biblical times, and contemporary society has ways of meeting these concerns without resorting to the institution of levirate marriage. The overarching principle of caring for the widow's needs, however, still remains a definite concern.

Caring for the Widows and Orphans

Along with caring for the childless widow through the institution of levirate marriage, the OT and other ANE texts contain many references to the care of the widow[140] and the orphan. The protection of the widow, the orphan, and the poor

---

[139] Leggett, *Levirate*, 245.

[140] See, e.g., Paula S. Hiebert, "'Whence Shall Help Come to Me?' The Biblical Widow," in *Gender and Difference in Ancient Israel* (ed. Peggy L. Day; Minneapolis: Fortress, 1989), 125–41; and Karel van der Toorn, *From Her Cradle to Her Grave: The Role of Religion in the Life of the Israelite and the Babylonian Woman* (trans. Sara J. Denning-Bolle; BS 23; Sheffield, Eng.: JSOT Press, 1994), 134–40. On the basis of the relevant biblical data, Carolyn S. Leeb, "The Widow: Homeless and Post-menopausal," *BTB* 32 (2002): 162, identifies the widow (ʾalmānâ) thus: "The biblical 'widow' is a post-menopausal woman whose husband has died and who has no secure attachment to a household headed by an adult male, in which she can be protected and represented." Further support for this basic position was given earlier by John Rook, "Making Widows: The Patriarchal Guardian at Work," *BTB* 27 (1997): 10–15; and idem, "When Is a Widow Not a Widow? Guardianship Provides the Answer," *BTB* 28 (1998): 4–6. This definition is widened by Karel van der Toorn, "Torn between Vice and Virtue: Stereotypes of the Widow in Israel and Mesopotamia," in *Female Stereotypes in Religious Traditions* (ed. Ria Kloppenborg and Wouter J. Hanegraaff; SHR 66; Leiden: E. J. Brill, 1995), 1–13, who identifies the "widow" in Israel and the ancient Near East as "the woman whose husband has died; it need not imply poverty or lack of male support" (5–6), although she acknowledges that the term was so commonly associated with poverty and lack of support that "it was apparently felt to be a redundancy to speak of the 'poor widow'" (6). Three categories of "widow," represented by different Hebrew expressions, are distinguished by Naomi Steinberg, "Romancing the Widow: The Economic Distinctions between the ʾALMĀNÂ, the ʾIŠŠ̌ʾ-ʾALMĀNÂ, and the ʾŠET-HAMMĒT," in *God's Word for Our World, Vol. I: Theological and Cultural Studies in Honor of Simon John De Vries* (ed. J. Harold Ellens et al.; JSOTSup 388; New York: T&T Clark, 2004), 327–46. Steinberg concludes: "I suggest that henceforth we distinguish between the ʾalmānâ widow, a woman without economic resources after the death of her husband, and what I have labeled, the inherited widow, an ʾiššâ-ʾalmānâ, an inherited

was a common public policy in the ancient Near East and considered a virtue of gods, kings, and judges.[141] Although there are too many variations in ANE practice to make generalizations about the treatment of widows, it is clear that ANE law attempted to provide the widow, if she needed it, sufficient protection to ensure that she could live a comfortable life.[142] In the pentateuchal laws, oppression of the widow and the orphan is forbidden (Exod 22:20–23 [ET 22:21–24]); their protection is linked with the supreme Judge, Yahweh (Deut 10:18); they must be allowed to "eat their fill" from the (second) tithe of produce brought to the festivals (Deut 14:28–29; cf. 16:11, 14; 26:12–13); their rights to glean the harvests must be maintained (Deut 24:17–22; cf. Ruth 2); and a curse is given upon anyone who abuses their rights (Deut 27:19).[143] In the Wisdom literature, God himself is said to be the protector of the widow (Ps 146:9; Prov 15:25), and anyone who abuses the rights of widow or orphan is said to reproach his Maker (Prov 14:31) and is called an evildoer (Job 24:1–4). The Prophets repeatedly call for the people to "defend the orphan; plead for the widow" (Isa 1:17; cf. Jer 7:6; 22:3; Zech 7:10) and denounce those who have oppressed them (Isa 1:23; Ezek 22:7). We need to heed their call today.

Children Born out of Wedlock

Pentateuchal Legislation

Deuteronomy 23:3 (ET 23:2) forbids the entrance of a *mamzēr*, traditionally taken to mean "one born out of wedlock," into the assembly of the Lord. The term *mamzēr* appears only twice in the HB (here and in Zech 9:6) and the precise meaning is uncertain. Other pentateuchal legislation (discussed above) mandated that the man who raped, or engaged in consensual premarital intercourse

---

widow with sons, or an *ʾšet-hammēt*, a woman who is transferred by levirate procedures to the nearest patrilineal kin of her husband" (p. 342). Steinberg points out that, regardless of these distinctions, "in ancient Israel all widows, mothers of sons and mothers without sons, or simply childless widows, whether they were landed or landless, had to depend on others for support of one form or another" (p. 343).

[141] See F. Charles Fensham, "Widow, Orphan, and the Poor in Ancient Near Eastern Legal and Wisdom Literature," *JNES* 21 (1962): 129–39; and van der Toorn, *From Her Cradle to Her Grave,* 135–37.

[142] For further discussion and literature, see Matthews, "Marriage and Family," 22–24.

[143] See, e.g., Anna Norrback, *The Fatherless and the Widows in the Deuteronomic Covenant* (Åbo, Finland: Åbo Akademis Forlag, 2001). Contra Harold V. Bennett, *Injustice Made Legal: Deuteronomic Law and the Plight of Widows, Strangers, and Orphans in Ancient Israel* (Grand Rapids: Eerdmans, 2002), who claims that the Deuteronomic code "used a category of socially weak but politically useful persons [i.e., the widows, strangers, and orphans] as pawns in a scheme to siphon off percentages of produce and livestock from overburdened peasant farmers and herders in the biblical communities during the Omride administration" (173). Bennett's thesis is not convincing.

with, a woman must marry her, and this would have prevented children born out of wedlock as a result of rape (Deut 22:29). Hence the term *mamzēr* may refer to the result of certain incestuous relationships not calling for the death penalty (e.g., Lev 20:19).[144] As another possibility, *mamzēr* may be etymologically derived from the verb *nāzar*, "to dedicate" (*hipᶜil* ptc.), and may thus refer to a child "'dedicated' to a foreign god, by reason of its conception during some kind of temple fertility ritual."[145] The latter interpretation, even if the etymology is uncertain, is supported by the second occurrence of this term in Zech 9:6, where the term seems to refer to the mixed population after the exile that were partly worshipers of other gods, including the fertility cult gods.[146] If such an interpretation is correct, it is entirely understandable that "the children would have been conceived and born in an environment directly related to the cult of a foreign religion, and therefore would be an abomination in the eyes of the Israelites and God."[147] (The divine revulsion against fertility cult sexuality is discussed in detail in ch. 3, above.)

The exclusion of illegitimately conceived[148] children—whatever situations are specifically targeted by the legislation—from the assembly of Israel[149] until the tenth generation seems to underscore God's high regard for the sanctity of marriage and the divine disapproval of illicit sexual relations. Even though such a law seems unfair to the illegitimately conceived child, who had no fault in the situation, in the divine perspective the integrity of the family and sexuality within those family bounds is regarded as so vital to the ongoing survival of the covenant community that the consequences of violating this integrity must be made abundantly manifest.

Prophets/Writings

Judges 11:1 records that Jephthah was the "son of a prostitute," and further provides evidence of the disdain in Israelite society for children born out of wedlock. The record states, "Gilead's wife also bore him sons; and when his wife's

---

[144] Victor P. Hamilton, "מַמְזֵר," *NIDOTTE* 2:971: "*mamzēr* here [in Deut 23] does not mean one born out of wedlock . . . but one born of an incestuous union." Cf. the definition of *mamzēr* given by BDB 561: "bastard, specif. child of incest."

[145] Craigie, *Deuteronomy*, 297. Walter C. Kaiser Jr., "מַמְזֵר," *TWOT* 1:498, supports this etymological derivation.

[146] See Kaiser Jr., *TWOT* 1:498: "It is possible that the Deut reference also refers to a child of mixed parentage—Hebrew and pagan."

[147] Ibid.

[148] The term "illegitimate children" is not used here because it is the parents' relationship that is illegitimate, not the children themselves.

[149] The term "assembly" (*qāhāl*) may be used here, like "congregation" (*ᶜēdâ*) elsewhere, as "an ancient technical term for the sociopolitical body that was called into session by Israel's tribal chieftains whenever a national transtribal issue arose" (Jacob Milgrom, *Leviticus 1–16: A New Translation with Introduction and Commentary* [AB 3; New York: Doubleday, 1991]: 242). Thus those who are barred from the "assembly of the LORD" are still "part of the community" but, like resident aliens, "not full members of it" (Craigie, *Deuteronomy*, 296).

sons grew up, they drove Jephthah away, saying to him, 'You shall not inherit anything in our father's house; for you are the son of another woman'" (v. 2).[150] Apparently this was no casual request, for the next verse states that "Jephthah fled
[bārah, 'flee, run away, hurry away'] from his brothers and lived in the land of
Tob" (v. 3). Verse 7 indicates that the disdain and forced expulsion involved the
whole city as well as the brothers, as Jephthah questions the city elders, "Are you
not the very ones who rejected me and drove me out [gāraš in the pi'el, 'cast out,
drive out'] of my father's house?" Despite this aversion to Jephthah as an illegitimately conceived child, his abilities at leadership and warfare overshadowed his
shady birth, and he was chosen head of the city of Gilead and commander of its
army. Eventually he became a divinely chosen and divinely empowered judge
over Israel (Judg 11–12).

Other examples of children born out of wedlock may include some of the sons
of Gomer, wife of Hosea, "a wife of whoredom" who bore "children of whoredom"
(Hos 1:2). It is possible that one or more of the children named in Hos 1 were born
out of wedlock by Gomer in her extramarital sexual relationships. In Hosea's announcement of impending judgment upon Israel and Judah, he indicts the people
for having "dealt faithlessly [bāgad] with the Lord; for they have borne illegitimate
[lit. 'strange, foreign'; Heb. zār] children" (Hos 5:7). This no doubt refers to the
spiritual apostasy in which the people had largely chosen Baal, and not Yahweh, as
their "Father," and thus were considered by Hosea to be spiritually born out of
wedlock.[151] It may also include reference to literal children born from illegitimate
sexual unions that were carried out in connection with Canaanite fertility cult ritual.[152] The mention of the abandoned female baby of Ezek 16:4–6, representing
Judah, may have alluded to the pagan practice of abandoning children (especially
girls) born out of wedlock in connection with fertility cult rituals, common prostitution, and other extramarital sexual encounters. To this and other "birth control"
practices and related issues we now turn our attention.

Reproduction/Population Control and Abortion-Related Issues

Reproduction/Population Control

In the ancient Near East, a number of methods of reproduction/population
control were utilized, including sterilization/castration, celibacy, sexual abstinence,

---

150 The brothers did not refer to the other woman as a harlot. Since, according to the
narrative, there was a possibility that Jephthah would share in the inheritance, this seems
to indicate that his father recognized him as his son. As suggested above in the discussion
of adoption, it is possible that Jephthah's father had "legitimized" him as his son by adoption. For further analysis of this historical situation surrounding Jephthah's social standing (with bibliography), see ch. 7, above.

151 McComiskey, "Hosea," 78–79.

152 See Garrett, Hosea, Joel, 144–46. For discussion of the Canaanite fertility cults, see
ch. 3 above.

alternative intercourse, contraception (through chemical antispermicides), coitus interruptus, infanticide (through exposure at birth), and abortion.[153] Given the high regard for having "a quiver full" of children in Hebrew society (Ps 127:5) as well as elsewhere in the ancient Near East, these birth control methods were probably not widely practiced. The problems related to reproduction were infertility, childlessness, and infant mortality,[154] not having too many children. There were times, however, when pregnancy was unwanted, unexpected, or illegal (e.g., for some of the ANE priestesses who took vows that they would not have children),[155] and various birth control practices were carried out (see ch. 7, above, on the practices of celibacy and coitus interruptus). Sexual abstinence seems to have been more the exception than the rule,[156] other than during times of ritual impurity for the woman, when sexual intercourse was not permitted (see ch. 7 on abstinence during menstruation). Alternative forms of sexual intercourse in the ancient Near East may have served, among other things, as birth control strategies (e.g., prostitution, discussed in ch. 7), particularly homosexual practice for the cult functionaries of the Sumerian and Babylonian religions (see ch. 4).

Mechanical contraceptions, found particularly among the Egyptians, included exotic potions (such as a willow bark potion mixed with the burned testicles of a castrated ass), used as chemical antispermicidal douches, and shields inserted into the vagina (e.g., a wool swab dipped in honey).[157] Such practices may well have been familiar to the Hebrews, and the OT silence on the utilization of such mechanical contraception devices probably indicates that "either contraception of this type was never an issue with Israel because of their high regard for children . . . or that the practice was accepted as normal and not considered worth mentioning."[158] Since sexual intercourse, for the Hebrews, had independent value

---

[153] For further discussion of all these forms of birth control in the ancient Near East, see Andrew E. Hill, "Abortion in the Ancient Near East," in *Abortion: A Christian Understanding and Response* (ed. James K. Hoffmeier; Grand Rapids: Baker, 1987), 31–48.

[154] According to ancient Mesopotamian records, an average of only two to four children in a nuclear family lived beyond early childhood (K. R. Nemet-Nejat, *Daily Life in Ancient Mesopotamia* [Westport, Conn.: Greenwood, 1998], 126–27); although the average total number of children born in a nuclear family is unknown, it no doubt was considerable more than this. Cf. also the references in ANE law codes to the possibility of a miscarriage due to someone striking a pregnant woman (see below for a discussion of ANE laws relating to miscarriage).

[155] See Michael C. Astour, "Tamar the Hierodule: An Essay in the Method of Vestigial Motifs," *JBL* 85 (1966): 188: "These priestesses were sexually active, though in a way unnatural for women. The goal of it was to prevent conception, for no women consecrated to gods were allowed to bear children, even in marriage."

[156] Some cases of sexual abstinence in Sumerian culture are inferred from Sumerian proverbs, such as "Conceiving is nice, being pregnant is irksome," and another in which a husband boasts that his wife has given birth to eight sons and is still ready to have sex with him, presumably in contrast to other wives who demand sexual abstinence (see H. W. F. Saggs, *The Greatness That Was Babylon* [New York: Hawthorn, 1962], 187, 407; cf. Hill, "Abortion," 33).

[157] See Hill, "Abortion," 34, for references.

[158] Ibid.

for the pleasure and sexual fulfillment of the married couple and was not subordinated to the intent to have children,[159] there appears to have been no theological impediment preventing Hebrew couples from utilizing such contraceptives
if they were ever needed. But inasmuch as large families were highly regarded
in order to supply the labor force around the estate and facilitate the inheritance
of property, the use of contraceptives may have been, for the most part, a
moot issue.

One ANE practice of birth control that may have found its way into Hebrew
society, especially at the royal court, is castration. The Hebrew term *sārîs* is an
Akkadian loanword that in preexilic times referred to a court official or royal
steward, with no necessary implication of castration,[160] but in exilic and postexilic times came to indicate a eunuch who was appointed royal steward and/or
harem guard.[161] The practice of castration was forbidden by pentateuchal law
(Lev 21:20; Deut 23:2 [ET 23:1]), as noted in the discussion of sexual blemishes in
ch. 7, above. Hence the term *sārîs* with the meaning "eunuch" probably refers
mainly (but not exclusively) to foreigners (Assyrians, Babylonians, and Persians)
or to Judean males castrated in exile.[162] The royal courts of the Neo-Assyrian and
Neo-Babylonian and Persian empires regularly employed eunuchs as royal attendants of the harem. The one recorded biblical example of this practice during the
time of the united monarchy in Israel appears to have been during the reign of
Ahab, when Queen Jezebel had eunuch attendants (*sārîsîm*) who threw her down
from the window of the royal palace to Jehu (2 Kgs 9:32–33). This use of intentionally castrated men underscores Jezebel's blatant disregard of the law of Yahweh. Such a practice may have been continued during the reigns of other Israelite
or Judaite kings who "did what was evil in the sight of the LORD."[163] As empha-

---

[159] See ch. 1, above. This is contra the prevailing understanding of the purpose of sexual intercourse in rabbinic and Philonic Judaism and the early church fathers. See Charles
E. Cerling, "Abortion and Contraception in Scripture," *CSR* 2 (1971): 44–45.

[160] Potiphar is an example of a court official called by the narrator *sārîs* (Gen 37:36;
39:1), but he was clearly married and perhaps not castrated (although Jewish tradition
suggests that he was indeed castrated, and this contributed to his wife's sexual attraction
to Joseph). See Janet S. Everhart, "The Hidden Eunuchs of the Hebrew Bible: Uncovering
an Alternate Gender" (PhD diss., Iliff School of Theology and University of Denver,
2003), 109–14.

[161] For a full discussion of eunuchs in the Hebrew Bible and the ancient Near East,
see ibid., passim.

[162] See 2 Kgs 9:32; 18:17; Esth 1:10, 12, 15; 2:3, 14–15, 21; 6:2, 14; 7:9; Dan 1:3, 7–11,
18; and Gordon H. Johnston, "סָרִיס," *NIDOTTE* 3:288–95; and B. Kedar-Kopfstein, "סָרִיס
sārîs," *TDOT* 10:344–50. As argued in ch. 7, above, it is possible, but not certain, that Daniel was a eunuch, inasmuch as the term could refer to royal officials as well as eunuchs in
Babylon.

[163] There are a number of references to *sārîsîm* in lists of court personnel and/or relatives of the kings of Israel and Judah other than the time of Ahab and Jezebel: 1 Sam 8:15;
2 Kgs 23:11; 24:12, 15; 25:19; 1 Chr 28:1; 2 Chr 18:8; Jer 29:2; 34:19; 38:7; 41:16; and 52:25.
Some of these occurrences (esp. preexilic) may only refer to a "court official" and not necessarily a eunuch, but in Jer 38:7 the Hebrew construction makes certain that Ebed-
melech the Ethiopian was a eunuch.

sized in ch. 7, above, in the discussion of sexual wholeness, God promises the eunuch who feels like a "dry tree" that he will be specially honored in God's house with a "monument and a name better than sons and daughters" and with "an everlasting name that shall not be cut off" (Isa 56:3–5).

Another ANE birth control method that also found its way into Israelite society was the practice of exposing unwanted female babies to die. The practice of parents exposing their children seems to have been quite widespread throughout ancient Mesopotamia during the entire period of biblical history. Meir Malul has collected illustrations of children being exposed in places such as the street, in the woods, on mountains, in rivers or wells, even in swamps or puddles.[164] Most of these children were exposed immediately after birth, with their birth blood still on them.[165] This seems to be the allegorical allusion in Ezek 16:4–5, where Yahweh depicts to Israel how he found her "thrown out in the open field, for you were abhorred on the day you were born. I passed by you, and saw you flailing about in your blood. As you lay in your blood, I said to you, 'Live!' Yes, I said to you in your blood, 'Live!'" The divine abhorrence of such action is shown in Yahweh's response to the abandoned infant: for all children, even abandoned ones, God seeks life, not death.

Just as abhorrent to Yahweh was the practice of child sacrifice. Although human sacrifice was carried out intermittently in various parts of the ancient Near East, especially in earlier periods, child sacrifice in the second millennium B.C.E. seems to have been limited mainly to Canaan.[166] This practice seems to have taken place in times of national danger, such as when a Canaanite city was being besieged, but the most horrible setting for infant sacrifice was in connection with the worship of Molech in Canaan.[167] Numerous biblical passages denounce this

---

[164] See Malul, "Adoption of Foundlings," 104–6.

[165] Ibid., 106.

[166] For a general discussion of infant sacrifice in the ancient Near East, see James K. Hoffmeier, "Abortion and the Old Testament Law," in *Abortion: A Christian Understanding and Response* (ed. James K. Hoffmeier; Grand Rapids: Baker, 1987), 50–53. See also A. R. W. Green, *The Role of Human Sacrifice in the Ancient Near East* (American Schools of Oriental Research Dissertation Series 1; Missoula, Mont.: Scholars Press, 1975). Cf. M. Popović, "Bibliography of Recent Studies [on Gen 22]," in *The Sacrifice of Isaac: The Aqedah (Genesis 22) and Its Interpretations* (ed. Edward Noort and Eibert Tigchelaar; Leiden: E. J. Brill, 2002), 211, 219, which provides a comprehensive bibliography of recent works dealing with human (including infant) sacrifice.

[167] For surveys of literature and defenses of the existence of Molech as a deity related to the ANE god Malik and the existence of child sacrifice in the Molech cult, see esp. John Day, *Molech: A God of Human Sacrifice in the Old Testament* (University of Cambridge Oriental Publications 41; Cambridge: Cambridge University Press, 1989); George C. Heider, *The Cult of Molek: A Reassessment* (JSOTSup 43; Sheffield, Eng.: University of Sheffield Press, 1985); idem, "Molech," in *Dictionary of Deities and Demons in the Bible* (ed. Karel van der Toorn, Bob Becking, and Pieter Willem van der Horst; Leiden: E. J. Brill, 1995), 1090–97; idem, "Molech," *ABD* 4:895–98; and Edward Noort, "Genesis 22: Human Sacrifice and Theology in the Hebrew Bible," in *The Sacrifice of Isaac: The Aqedah (Genesis 22) and Its Interpretations* (ed. Edward Noort and Eibert Tigchelaar; Leiden: E. J. Brill, 2002), 11–14.

abominable Canaanite practice.[168] Infant sacrifice was also very prevalent in the city of Carthage in North Africa (ca. 750–146 B.C.E.), as evidenced by excavation of a huge cemetery filled with infant sacrifice victims (a place called Tophet, the same word as used for the place of similar atrocities in Jerusalem, 2 Kgs 23:10; Jer 7:31–32; 19:6, 11–14). Although infant sacrifice does not seem to have had population control as its primary function in Palestine or in the early years of Carthage, it seems that ritual infanticide was indeed used to regulate population by the fourth through the third centuries B.C.E.[169] As will be clarified below, child sacrifice, and not abortion, was the real issue that the Israelites faced in Canaan.

There is ANE evidence for the practice of abortion. Both cuneiform texts[170] and Egyptian sources[171] reveal that chemical concoctions were employed to end a pregnancy before full term, and it is also possible that given the level of sophistication in surgical procedures for other medical cases, surgical methods of abortion were also employed (although these are not mentioned in extant ANE texts).

It appears, however, that prevailing views on abortion shifted over time in the ancient Near East, as implied especially in the Mesopotamian law codes concerning miscarriage. In dealing with miscarriage, as discussed further below, the earlier law codes, such as the Sumerian laws and the Code of Hammurabi, do not appear to regard the unborn fetus as a person, and thus, as might be expected, no prohibition of abortion appears in these earlier codes. By the time of the Middle Assyrian Laws (considered to represent Assyrian ideology as far back as the fifteenth century B.C.E., and promulgated ca. 1400–1200), however, legislation concerning miscarriage indicates that the unborn fetus was considered a person, and thus, as expected, terminating the life of the fetus by means of abortion was legally prohibited.

The only ANE law collection to deal with abortion is the Middle Assyrian Laws (ca. 1400 B.C.E.). MAL A §53 explicitly prohibits abortion, and the punishment implies a radical repudiation of the practice: the woman guilty of abortion was to be impaled alive without burial, and if she died while attempting the abortion, she still was to be impaled and denied a proper burial.[172] The kind of pun-

---

168 For references to child sacrifice, see esp. Lev 18:21; Deut 12:31; 18:10; 2 Kgs 16:3; 17:17, 31; 21:6; 23:10; Isa 57:5; Jer 6:11; 9:20 (ET 9:21); 18:21; 32:35; Ezek 16:21, 36; 20:26, 31; 23:37; Ps 106:37; 2 Chr 33:6.

169 Hoffmeier, "Abortion," 51–53.

170 For reference to an herb that was taken to induce miscarriage, see *CAD* 11/1:79; cf. Matthews, "Marriage and Family," 21.

171 See, e.g., Cyril P. Bryan, *Ancient Egyptian Medicine: The Papyrus Ebers* (Chicago: Ares, 1974; repr. of *The Papyrus Ebers* [London: G. Bles, 1930]), 83, for a summary of the remedy given in the Ebers papyrus (written ca. 1500 B.C.E.) to bring about an abortion: "Dates, Onions, and the Fruit-of-the-Acanthus, were crushed in a vessel with Honey, sprinkled on a cloth, and applied to the Vulva. It ensured abortion either in the first, second or third period."

172 MAL A §53 (*COS* 2.132:359; cf. *ANET* 185): "If a woman aborts her fetus by her own action and they then prove the charges against her and find her guilty, they shall impale her, they shall not bury her. If she dies as a result of aborting her fetus, they shall impale her, they shall not bury her."

ishment indicates the seriousness of this crime. "From the savagery of the punishment, namely impalement, and from the refusal of burial it seems certain that the act is regarded as a most heinous and presumably sacrilegious offence." Driver and Miles conclude that in Assyrian law impalement "is prescribed for the worst offence that a mother can commit, namely to procure the death of the unborn child in her womb." Although no reason is given in the law for such revulsion, Driver and Miles suggest, "as in the case of suicide, that the woman by her offence has caused the sacred blood of the family to flow and has thereby called down the wrath of heaven not only on herself but also on the whole community."[173]

As far as is presently known, abortion was not generally practiced in Canaan, which may explain why there is no explicit reference to abortion in Scripture, either in biblical law or in narrative. In light of the radical denunciation and repudiation of abortion implied in the Middle Assyrian Laws from the late second millennium B.C.E., the absence of any pentateuchal legislation dealing directly with abortion may be significant. It must be remembered that the biblical law collections, like their counterparts elsewhere in the ancient Near East, were incomplete and did not deal with every facet of life and practice.[174] David Instone-Brewer articulates a general principle regarding silence in the biblical legislation on a given practice: "Because of the similarity of the Pentateuch with other ancient Near Eastern law codes, we must assume that where the Old Testament is silent, there was broad agreement with the prevailing culture."[175] Andrew Hill applies this principle to the practice of abortion when he points out that instead of viewing silence in Scripture concerning abortion as signifying consent of the practice, "it is more probable that the Hebrews accepted and assumed this kind of anti-abortion legislation to be the norm in the cultural milieu, especially since the actual practice of abortion appears to have been an exceptional activity in the ancient world. Hence, they saw no need to condemn such an obvious criminal act."[176] Meredith Kline comes to a similar conclusion: "It was so unthinkable that an Israelite woman should desire an abortion that there was no need to mention this offense in the criminal code."[177]

The Status of the Human Fetus and Implications for Abortion

Ancient Near Eastern Background. As alluded to above, the earlier law codes, such as the Sumerian laws and the Code of Hammurabi, when dealing with possible cases of miscarriage, do not seem to give the unborn fetus the legal status of

---

173 Driver and Miles, *The Assyrian Laws,* 116–17.

174 This has already been noted above regarding levirate marriage law and parallel laws elsewhere in the ancient Near East; for further discussion of the characteristic incompleteness of these law codes, see Westbrook, "Biblical and Cuneiform Law Codes."

175 David Instone-Brewer, *Divorce and Remarriage in the Bible: The Social and Literary Context* (Grand Rapids: Eerdmans, 2002), 21.

176 Hill, "Abortion," 46.

177 Meredith G. Kline, "*Lex talionis* and the Human Fetus," *JETS* 20 (1977): 193.

a person, since the penalty for the miscarriage is simply a monetary fine, with no mention of the principle of *lex talionis*. According to the Laws of Lipit Ishtar (ca. 1934–1924 B.C.E.), one who struck a man's daughter, causing miscarriage but not the death of the pregnant woman, was penalized thirty shekels of silver (§d),[178] and one who struck a man's slave woman, causing miscarriage but not the woman's death, had to pay five shekels (§f).[179] According to the Sumerian laws (ca. 1800 B.C.E.), accidental striking of a woman resulting in miscarriage carried a fine of ten shekels of silver (§1),[180] whereas deliberate striking resulting in miscarriage called for a fine of twenty shekels (§2).[181] The Code of Hammurabi (ca. 1760–1750 B.C.E.) gives similar stipulations (but graded according to high, middle, and lower class): the penalty for an aristocrat (*awīlu*) causing a miscarriage in another aristocrat's daughter but not death to the daughter was ten shekels of silver (§209);[182] causing miscarriage in a commoner's daughter but not the daughter's death carried the penalty of five shekels (§211);[183] and causing miscarriage to an aristocrat's female slave but not the slave's death carried the penalty of two shekels (§213).[184] Finally, the Hittite Laws (ca. 1650–1500 B.C.E.) prescribe the penalty of ten shekels of silver if the miscarriage of a free woman is caused in her tenth month, and five shekels if the miscarriage is in her fifth month (§17)[185] or if it is a female slave who is caused to miscarry in her tenth month (§18).[186]

---

[178]LI §d (*COS* 2.154:411): "If [a . . .] strikes the daughter of a man and causes her to lose her fetus, he shall weigh and deliver 30 shekels of silver."

[179]LI §f (*COS* 2.154:411): "If a . . . strikes the slave woman of a man and causes her to lose her fetus, he shall weigh and deliver 5 shekels of silver."

[180]"Sumerian Laws," translated by J. J. Finkelstein (*ANET* 525), §1: "If (a man accidentally) buffeted a woman of the free-citizen class and caused her to have a miscarriage, he must pay 10 shekels of silver."

[181]"Sumerian Laws," §2 (*ANET* 525): "If (a man deliberately) struck a woman of the free-citizen class and caused her to have a miscarriage, he must pay one-third mina of silver [i.e., twenty shekels]."

[182]CH §209 (*COS* 2.131:348; cf. *ANET* 175): "If an *awīlu* strikes a woman of the *awīlu*-class and thereby causes her to miscarry her fetus, he shall weigh and deliver 10 shekels of silver for her fetus." Note, however, that if the woman of this class dies after being struck and miscarrying, the penalty was to kill the daughter of the assailant (CH §210 [*COS* 2.131:348; cf. *ANET* 175]: "If that woman should die, they shall kill his daughter").

[183]CH §211 (*COS* 2.131:348; cf. *ANET* 175): "If he should cause a woman of the commoner-class to miscarry her fetus by the beating, he shall weigh and deliver 5 shekels of silver."

[184]CH §213 (*COS* 2.131:348; cf. *ANET* 175): "If he strikes an *awīlu*'s slave woman and thereby causes her to miscarry her fetus, he shall weigh and deliver 2 shekels of silver."

[185]HL §17 (*COS* 2.19:108; cf. *ANET* 190): "If any causes a free woman to miscarry, [if] it is her tenth month, he shall pay 10 shekels of silver, if it is her fifth month, he shall pay 5 shekels of silver. He shall look to his house for it." §XVI (a late version of §17) reads, "If anyone causes a free woman to miscarry, he shall pay 20 shekels of silver" (*COS* 2.19:108).

[186]HL §18 (*COS* 2.19:108; cf. *ANET* 190): "If anyone causes a female slave to miscarry, if it is her tenth month, he shall pay 5 shekels." HL §XVII (a late version of §18) reads, "If anyone causes a female slave to miscarry, he shall pay 10 shekels of silver" (*COS* 2.19:108).

By contrast to these earlier law collections, which merely mention a monetary penalty, the Middle Assyrian Laws (ca. 1400 B.C.E.) invoke the *lex talionis* principle, thus apparently implying that the unborn fetus was given the legal status of a person, a human being. MAL A §50 states that if a man strikes a woman and causes her to abort her fetus, "they shall treat him as he treated her; he shall make full payment of a life for her fetus"; if the husband of the woman whose fetus was aborted had no sons, then "they shall kill the assailant for her fetus."[187] MAL A §52 indicates, "If a man strikes a prostitute causing her to abort her fetus, they shall assess him blow for blow, he shall make full payment of a life." Although Westbrook may be correct that the term to "pay a life" refers to "payment of a fixed sum representing the value of a person,"[188] this does not alter the conclusion that the fetus is considered "a person" and that the *lex talionis* principle is applied in these cases involving the death of the fetus.

Exodus 21:22–25. Although no Mosaic legislation directly addresses the issue of abortion, one passage, Exod 21:22–25, is concerned with the most crucial question in the abortion debate: is the fetus to be considered fully a human being? The NRSV represents a popular interpretation of this passage:

> When people who are fighting injure [lit. "strike," *wĕnāgpû* (from *nāgap*)][189] a pregnant woman so that there is a miscarriage [lit. "children[190] come out," *wĕyāṣᵊʾû*

---

[187] MAL A §50 (*COS* 2.132:359; cf. *ANET* 184): "[If a man] strikes [another man's wife thereby causing her to abort her fetus, . . .] a man's wife [. . .] and they shall treat him as he treated her; he shall make full payment of a life for her fetus. And if that woman dies, they shall kill that man; he shall make full payment of a life for her fetus. And if there is no son of that woman's husband, and his wife whom he struck aborted her fetus, they shall kill the assailant for her fetus. If her fetus was a female, he shall make full payment of a life only."

[188] Raymond Westbrook, "*Lex talionis* and Exodus 21,22–25," *RB* 93 (1986): 64.

[189] The verb *nāgap* means "to strike or smite" (BDB 619), "to injure by striking" (*HALOT* 669), and although it implies serious and sometimes even fatal injury, the term cannot be necessarily equated with "death" in this passage, contra Kline, "*Lex talionis* and the Human Fetus," 198. Kline's reference to the use of the word in Exod 21:35 for the "fatal attack of the goring ox" fails to recognize that in this verse the verb *nāgap* indicates the "striking/hitting" of the other ox but the death of the victim is indicated by a separate, added word, *wāmēt*, "and it died." The modern English versions that translate it as "hit" (NIV), "strike" (NASB), or "hurt" (NKJV, NRSV) seem to have best captured the nuance implied in this verse. The verb is in the plural ("they hit/strike/hurt") probably because it is a generic plural, referring to "one of the combatants, which ever of them it be" (Umberto Cassuto, *A Commentary on the Book of Exodus* [trans. Israel Abrahams; Jerusalem: Magnes, 1967], 275).

[190] The plural "children" in this clause should probably be taken in the sense of a generic plural inasmuch as potentially "male or female, one or two" might be born (Cassuto, *Exodus,* 275). Cf. Gleason L. Archer, *Encyclopedia of Bible Difficulties* (Grand Rapids: Zondervan, 1982), 247: "The plural is used here because the woman might be pregnant with twins when this injury befalls her." H. Wayne House, "Miscarriage or Premature Birth: Additional Thoughts on Exodus 21:22–25," *WTJ* 41 (1978): 114, suggests the plural may be "to indicate natural products in an unnatural condition," since the maliciously induced premature birth involves an irregularity; here House follows a use of the plural discussed in Ronald J. Williams, *Hebrew Syntax, an Outline* (Toronto: University of Toronto Press, 1967), 8 (par. 10).

yĕlādêhā],[191] and yet no further harm [*'asôn*] follows, the one responsible shall be fined what the woman's husband demands, paying as much as the judges determine [*biplilîm*].[192] If any harm [*'asôr*] follows, then you shall give life [*nepeš*] for life [*nepeš*], eye for eye, tooth for tooth, hand for hand, foot for foot, burn for burn, wound for wound, stripe for stripe.

A number of interpreters throughout history,[193] including some pro-choice advocates among evangelicals,[194] have found in Exod 21:22–25 support for their

---

[191] The LXX here makes a distinction between a child who comes out "not yet fully formed" (*mē exeikonismenon*) (v. 22) and one that is "fully formed" (*exeikonismenon*) (v. 23); in the former case there is only a fine; in the latter the guilty party is punished by the principle of *lex talionis*, "life for life." But there is no support for this distinction in the Hebrew text.

[192] In an attempt to bolster the "miscarriage" interpretation of this verse, some interpreters suggest emending this word to *bannĕpālîm*, "for the miscarriage" (see BDB 813; Karl Budde, "Bemerkungen zum Bundesbuch," *ZAW* 11 [1891]: 108–11), but there is no need to emend the text when the Hebrew makes sense in its canonical form. E. A. Speiser, "The Stem *pll* in Hebrew," *JBL* 82 (1963): 301–6, esp. 303, suggests that the root *pll* has the meaning "to estimate, assess, calculate," but Westbrook, "*Lex talionis* and Exodus 21, 22–25," 58–61, shows that this hypothetical translation does not fit the evidence. Westbrook's own hypothesis—translating the term as "alone"—also seems forced, and in order to substantiate his entire "miscarriage" hypothesis (that the contrast is between knowledge and ignorance of the identity of the miscarriage's perpetrator), Westbrook in the end must assume that the *lex talionis* parallel in Lev 24:17–21 is a later "strained" exegetical distortion of the Exodus passage (p. 68). Kline, "*Lex talionis* and the Human Fetus," 195–96, suggests that the preposition *bĕ* is a *bêt* of equivalence and *pĕlilî* is an adjective meaning "liability to death" (with the -*m* as an emphatic enclitic, not an abstract plural), so that *biplilîm* refers to payment equivalent "for his forfeited life" or "as one deserving of death" (196). There does not seem to be a compelling reason, however, to depart from the traditional understanding of *pālil* as "judge, umpire" (BDB 813) and *biplilîm* as "in [the presence of or accordance with] the judges" (with the majority of modern translations).

[193] These include talmudic allusions to this text, which uniformly interpret it as referring to a miscarriage, with the fetus having the value of a property loss on the part of the father. See *m. 'Ohal.* 7:6; *b. Sanh.* 72b (cf. the comments of Rashi). Many modern critical commentators take Exod 21:22 as referring to miscarriage mainly because of the ANE laws that seem to parallel this biblical passage. The examination of all these laws above found that most accept a sum of money for the loss of a fetus through miscarriage. But as will be argued below, unlike the alleged ANE parallels, Exod 21:22 does not deal with miscarriage but with premature live birth. Furthermore, the closest ANE parallels are the Middle Assyrian Laws, which, as pointed out above, seem to give an unborn fetus the legal status of a human person. In the final analysis, supposed ANE parallels (or lack of parallels) cannot override the weight of exegetical evidence from the biblical text.

[194] See, e.g., Bruce K. Waltke, "The Old Testament and Birth Control," *ChT* 13, no. 8 (1968): 3–6; idem, "Old Testament Texts Bearing on the Issues," in *Birth Control and the Christian* (ed. Walter O. Spitzer and Carlyle L. Saylor; Wheaton, Ill.: Tyndale House, 1969), 10–11; and Nancy Hardesty, "When Does Life Begin?" *Eternity* 22, no. 2 (1971): 19, 43. Bruce Waltke, however, in his presidential address at the 1975 annual meeting of the Evangelical Theological Society, reversed his former position on the status of the human fetus, concluding that "the fetus is human and therefore to be accorded the same protection to life granted every other human being" (Bruce K. Waltke, "Reflections from the Old Testament on Abortion," *JETS* 19 [1976]: 13).

contention that a fetus is not a fully human person and thus has less inherent value than an already born person. Most of these interpreters take the clause *wĕyāṣᵓû yĕlādêhā* as a reference to a miscarried fetus, that is, a stillborn child (v. 22a). Since the fetus is not fully human, only a fine is required of the offender as compensation for the loss of fetus (v. 22b). Only if further harm follows—that is, the woman herself suffers serious injury or death—is the principle of *lex talionis* (equivalent punishment) applicable.

But this interpretation fails to take seriously the precise linguistic evidence of the text. Particularly at issue are several Hebrew expressions. First, the clause *wĕyāṣᵓû yĕlādêhā* (v. 22a) literally means "when children come out." The noun *yeled*, "child," is the common OT term for a fully human child from infancy to the age of twelve;[195] the word for "stillborn child"—not used in this passage—is *nēpel*, "untimely birth," not *yeled*.[196] The verb *yāṣāᵓ*, "to go or come out," is a term regularly used to describe the ordinary live birth of children.[197] When referring to a stillbirth, the verb is always accompanied by some form of the verb *mût*, "to die";[198] the latter verb does not appear in 21:22. Furthermore, the technical word for miscarriage in the OT is not *yāṣāᵓ* but *šākāl*, "to miscarry,"[199] and the latter verb is employed only two chapters later in the Covenant Code of Exodus (23:26). Had Moses intended to mean "miscarriage" in this passage, he certainly would have used the technical term *šākāl*, which he employed later in the same Exodus code. It is difficult to escape the conclusion that the expression *wĕyāṣᵓû yĕlādêhā* refers to a live premature birth, not miscarriage, as is recognized by numerous commentators and exegetical studies.[200] Recent evangelical translators of the OT have taken seriously the above lexical evidence and translated the clause as referring to premature birth.[201]

The second expression calling for more detailed analysis in context is the word *ᵓāsôn*, "harm/calamity/hurt."[202] This word is used only three times in the HB outside the two occurrences in this passage, and all three of those appear in the Joseph narrative expressing Jacob's concern that some kind of "harm" would come upon his son Benjamin if he was allowed to go down to Egypt (Gen 42:4,

---

195 BDB, 409; cf. Archer, *Encyclopedia of Bible Difficulties*, 247.

196 See Job 3:16; Ps 58:9 (ET 58:8); Eccl 6:3; BDB 658.

197 See, e.g., Gen 15:4; 25:25–26; 38:28–30; 46:26; 1 Kgs 8:19; Job 1:21; 3:11; Eccl 5:14 (ET 5:15); Isa 39:7; Jer 1:5; 20:18.

198 See, e.g., Num 12:12; Job 3:11.

199 BDB 1013; *HALOT* 1492. See Gen 31:38; 2 Kgs 2:19, 21; Job 21:10.

200 See, e.g., Cassuto, *Exodus*, 275; Jack W. Cottrell, "Abortion and the Mosaic Laws," *ChT* 17, no. 12 (1973): 7–8; Ronald A. G. du Preez, "The Status of the Fetus in Mosaic Law," *JATS* 1, no. 2 (1990): 5–21; House, "Miscarriage or Premature Birth," 110–14; Bernard S. Jackson, "The Problem of Exod. xxi 22–25 (*ius talionis*)," *VT* 23 (1973): 292–93. Contra, e.g., Joe M. Sprinkle, "The Interpretation of Exodus 21:22–25 (*Lex Talionis*) and Abortion," *WTJ* 55 (1993): 248–53; and idem, *Biblical Law and Its Relevance*, 69–90.

201 The NKJV, NIV, and updated NASB translate, "she gives birth prematurely." The NLT translates, "her child is born prematurely." (The original NASB had the translation "miscarriage," but this was changed in the 1995 update.)

202 BDB 62; Eugene H. Merrill, "אָסוֹן," *NIDOTTE* 1:467.

38; 44:29). The term appears to be a general one, denoting any kind of serious harm, including mortal accident.[203] The pertinent issue in Exod 21:22–23 is not so much the meaning of the word but its referent: who is envisioned as receiving the harm? Those who interpret v. 22 as describing a miscarriage assume that harm was already done in the abortion of the fetus, and thus they are forced to supply the word "further" or "other" before "harm" in vv. 22–23 to indicate additional hurt done to the mother that calls for *lex talionis* punishment, even though such a word is not in the original.[204] But if what is in view is a premature live birth of the child, as argued above, then there is no need to supply the word "further" because no serious or fatal injury was incurred in the premature birth. Thus the term *ʾāsôn*, appearing immediately after the clause "her children come out," with no Hebrew expression *lāh*, "to her," restricting the harm to the woman, is indefinite, referring at least to the prematurely born child and probably to either mother or child.[205]

In v. 22, then, if no harm has come to either mother or child, only a fine is imposed upon the striker, presumably to compensate for the physical or mental discomfort he has caused or "because of the danger to which mother and child are exposed and the parents' distress in connection with the unnaturally premature birth."[206] In v. 23, if harm (from serious to fatal injury) has come to either mother or child, then the law of *lex talionis* comes into effect.[207]

---

[203] Westbrook, "*Lex talionis* and Exodus 21,22–25," 56–57, hypothesizes that *ʾāsôn* refers to "damage caused by an unknown perpetrator," i.e., "cases where responsibility cannot be located." But such meaning does not seem to follow from Jacob's use of this word to describe the "harm" that might come upon Benjamin: Jacob is concerned with harm in general, regardless of whether the perpetrator of the crime is known. As noted above, in order to sustain his overall hypothesis, Westbrook is forced to posit a later distortion of this Exodus legislation in Lev 24.

[204] See, e.g., the NRSV, NJB, original NASB, JPSV, NEB, and Schocken Bible (Everett Fox).

[205] Cottrell, "Abortion and the Mosaic Laws," 8, points out that the contrast in these verses is not between harm to the mother and harm to the child but between no harm to either mother or child and harm to either one or the other. See also Archer, *Encyclopedia of Bible Difficulties*, 248; Cassuto, *Exodus*, 275; John M. Frame, "Abortion from a Biblical Perspective," in *Thou Shalt Not Kill: The Christian Case against Abortion* (ed. Richard L. Ganz; New Rochelle, N.Y.: Arlington House, 1978), 55; House, "Miscarriage or Premature Birth," 118; Kaiser, *Toward Old Testament Ethics*, 103, 172.

[206] Cottrell, "Abortion and the Mosaic Laws," 8; cf. House, "Miscarriage or Premature Birth," 120.

[207] The language of this statement of *lex talionis* is clearly formulaic, since the kinds of injuries mentioned (e.g., "burn for burn") are not the likely injuries to occur in this situation. Kline, "*Lex talionis* and the Human Fetus," 197, points out that this "fossilized formula" is meant "to express only the general principle that the offense must receive a just punishment." This just punishment is in contrast to the ANE laws where the wealthy or people in the higher social strata simply paid fines and escaped punishment. Shalom M. Paul, *Studies in the Book of the Covenant in the Light of Cuneiform and Biblical Law* (Leiden: E. J. Brill, 1970), 75–77, shows that the *lex talionis* principle, far from being a primitive or barbaric form of punishment, as often claimed, was an important advance in the history of jurisprudence, an advance that in the Bible served to "curb unlimited retribution, personal vendetta, and excessive retaliation" (76) by instituting a system of equal

In summarizing this crucial passage, two main exegetical points emerge: (1) the clause *wĕyāṣᵊʾû yĕlādêhā* refers to premature live childbirth and not miscarriage, and (2) the term *ʾāsôn* includes harm to the child as well as the mother. From these two points, the conclusion is straightforward: the *lex talionis* (law of just retribution) of vv. 23–24 applies to the fetus equally as much as to the mother, and the fetus is therefore granted under the law the status of a full human being just as is the mother.[208] And if the fetus is fully human, then the implication for abortion is also straightforward: the passage gives no support to the legitimacy of this practice. In fact, taking the life of a human fetus is considered homicide, just as is taking the life of the mother.

Other Old Testament Passages Dealing with the Status of the Human Fetus. A number of other OT passages provide evidence that God considers the unborn child fully human. A whole series of passages reveal God's personal involvement in the development of the fetus in the womb. Job declares that God personally fashioned each individual person in the womb:

> Your hands fashioned and made me;
>   and now you turn and destroy me.
> Remember that you fashioned me like clay;
>   and will you turn me to dust again?
> Did you not pour me out like milk
>   and curdle me like cheese?
> You clothed me with skin and flesh,
>   and knit me together with bones and sinews.
> You have granted me life and steadfast love,
>   and your care has preserved my spirit. (Job 10:8–12)

Again, Job declares regarding God's part in the creation of both himself and his fellow human beings, "Did not he who made me in the womb make them? And did not one fashion us in the womb?" (Job 31:15).

---

justice and fairness for all. In the case of the "life for life" death penalty, it is also important to recognize that a ransom was probably possible. Numbers 35:31–32 forbids a ransom in the case of homicide, which seems to imply the possibility of ransom in other cases (see Jackson, "The Problem of Exod. xxi 22–25," 283–84). Westbrook, "*Lex talionis* and Exodus 21,22–25," 64–66, suggests that "life for a life" should be understood against the background of ANE references: "The phrase 'pay a life' refers to the payment of a fixed sum representing the value of a person" (64). Though appealing at first glance and probably applicable elsewhere, Westbrook's hypothesis denies the reality of the death penalty in this passage, and thus he cannot reconcile this passage with Lev 24:17–21, where he must admit that literal retaliation—the death penalty—is in view (68).

[208] Kline, "*Lex talionis* and the Human Fetus," 193–201, arrives at the same conclusion (that the human fetus is fully human) but from a different exegetical base. According to Kline, the "striking" (NASB) of Exod 21:22a indicates that either the mother or the fetus is killed; the "harm" of v. 22b is the premature live birth of the fetus; the "harm" of vv. 23–25 is a miscarriage; and the penalty of both v. 22b and vv. 23–25 is the same: "death (as at least one possibility) . . . demanding a ransom for the offender's forfeited life" (p. 197). Contra Kline, as already noted, the verb "strike" in v. 22a does not refer to death but a premature live birth, and the penalties of v. 22b and vv. 23–25 do not appear to be essentially the same.

The psalmist gives a similar inspired testimony:

For it was you who formed my inward parts;
  you knit me together in my mother's womb.
I praise you, for I am fearfully and wonderfully made.
  Wonderful are your works;
  that I know very well.
My frame was not hidden from you,
  when I was being made in secret,
  intricately woven in the depths of the earth.
Your eyes beheld my unformed substance [or 'fetus,' gōlem].[209]
  In your book were written
  all the days that were formed for me,
  when none of them as yet existed. (Ps 139:13–16)

William Brown, after analyzing the motif of *creatio corporis* ("the creation of the individual") in Ps 139, summarizes, "Every physical thread woven in secret contains the moral fiber of the psalmist's being. In conception was established both the physical and moral constitution of a human being."[210] Brown then comments on the implications of both Ps 139 and Job 10: "From the perspective of both authors, the womb is the home of God's creation and sustenance. It is here that the physical nature and moral nurture coalesce. The womb is a refuge, impregnable from both physical and moral harm. . . . Whether for weal or for woe, both Job and the psalmist regard *creatio corporis* as the sign and seal of God's unconditional pledge of support. It is God's covenantal grant *in utero*."[211] John Stott captures the thrust of Ps 139:13–16: "The fetus is not a growth in the mother's body (which can be removed as readily as her tonsils or appendix), nor even a potential human being, but a human life who, though not yet mature, has the potentiality to grow into the fullness of the humanity he already possesses."[212]

Isaiah repeats a similar declaration as the Psalmist: "Thus says the LORD, your Redeemer, who formed you in the womb: I am the LORD, who made all things" (Isa 44:24). Jeremiah likewise records the divine testimony of God's personal work of creating Jeremiah from the womb: "Before I formed you in the womb I knew you, and before you were born I consecrated you, and I appointed you a prophet to the nations" (Jer 1:5).

John Davis summarizes the implication of these passages: "All these texts indicate that God's special dealings with human beings can long precede their awareness of a personal relationship with God. God deals with human beings in an intensely personal way long before society is accustomed to treat them as per-

---

[209] For the meaning of *gōlem* as "embryo," see BDB 166; *HALOT* 194; and Leslie C. Allen, *Psalms 101–150* (WBC 21; Waco, Tex.: Word, 1983), 252.

[210] William P. Brown, "*Creatio corporis* and the Rhetoric of Defense in Job 10 and Psalm 139," in *God Who Creates: Essays in Honor of W. Sibley Towner* (ed. William P. Brown and S. Dean McBride Jr.; Grand Rapids: Eerdmans, 2000), 114.

[211] Ibid., 122–24.

[212] John R. W. Stott, "Does Life Begin before Birth?" *ChT* 24, no. 15 (1980): 50.

sons in the 'whole sense.' . . . God's actions present a striking contrast to current notions of personhood."[213] Paul Fowler adds, "God's personal involvement with the unborn provides the foundation for their personal worth. If we are persons because God has related to us in a personal way, then the unborn are also persons since God's care for them obviously begins in the womb."[214]

Additional evidence that biblical writers considered human the fetus with whom God is personally involved in forming in the womb is found in references to the unborn possessing a spiritual/moral nature already before birth. Psalm 58:4 (ET 58:3) speaks of the sinful nature as already present in the fetus: "The wicked go astray from the womb; they err from their birth, speaking lies." Psalm 51:7–8 (ET 51:5–6) in particular supports the concept that a human's spiritual moral nature is already present in the fetus from the moment of conception. After being confronted by Nathan regarding his adultery with Bathsheba, David confesses, "Indeed, I was born guilty, a sinner when my mother conceived me." Edward Dalglish captures the implication of this verse: "In Psalm li. 7 [ET 51:5] the psalmist is relating his sinfulness to the very inception of life; he traces his development beyond his birth . . . to the genesis of his being in his mother's womb—even to the very hour of conception."[215]

Fowler summarizes the implication of these passages regarding a fetus's moral nature and the relationship with the image of God: "Putting all this together, we may conclude that man's moral, spiritual faculty is already present in the fetus before birth. If the image of God pertains to man's moral nature, then that nature has been passed on from Adam (Genesis 5:3). It is hard to argue that someone is not a person who has moral attributes."[216]

Another set of biblical data shows that the OT writers assumed a basic continuity between prenatal and postnatal human life. In Ps 139, already cited above, "David sees *himself* as having existed in his mother's womb (Psalm 139:13ff.)."[217] As John Stott states regarding Ps 139 as a whole: "The psalmist surveys his life in four stages: past (v. 1), present (vv. 2–6), future (vv. 7–12), and before birth (vv. 13–16), and in all four refers to himself as 'I.' He who is writing as a full-grown man has the same personal identity as the fetus in his

---

[213] John J. Davis, *Abortion and the Christian: What Every Believer Should Know* (Philadelphia: Presbyterian and Reformed, 1984), 49.

[214] Paul W. Fowler, *Abortion: Toward an Evangelical Consensus* (Portland, Ore.: Multnonah, 1987), 144. Cf. Harold O. J. Brown, *Death before Birth* (Nashville: Nelson, 1977), 127, who, after surveying these passages, concludes, "In short, there can be no doubt that God clearly says the unborn child is already a human being, made in the image of God, and deserving of protection under the law."

[215] Edward R. Dalglish, *Psalm Fifty-One in the Light of Near Eastern Patternism* (Leiden: E. J. Brill, 1962), 121. Dalglish goes on to argue that in the next verse, "inward parts" and "hidden part" more likely refer "to the womb where the psalmist's being was initiated" than to the inner parts of the (adult) psalmist, and v. 8 (ET v. 6) is interpreted to mean "that truth and wisdom were, alas, also part of his natal endowment," thus implying that the moral nature is already present in the fetus from conception (p. 124).

[216] Fowler, *Abortion*, 142.

[217] Ibid., 144.

mother's womb."[218] The same could be said for many of the other verses already cited, where the prophet uses the personal pronouns ("I," "me," "my," etc.) to describe the fetus in the womb as well as the postnatal human life.

Especially telling is the fact that often the biblical writers used the same nouns to label prenatal and postnatal life. Thus, for example, the term *geber,* normally referring to a "young, strong, man,"[219] is employed to describe the embryo at conception in Job 3:3: "Let the day perish in which I was born, and the night that said, 'A man-child [*geber*] is conceived.'" Again, *yeled* is the term regularly referring to a "child" from infancy to the age of twelve,[220] and this term is used in Exod 21:22, as noted above in discussion of that passage. Again, the term *bēn* is the normal Hebrew term for "son,"[221] and Gen 25:22 uses this term in the plural to describe the unborn fetuses in Rebekah's womb: "The children [*habbānîm*] struggled together within her."

From the above OT data on the status of the unborn fetus,[222] the conclusion articulated by Bruce Waltke after his survey of the same data is inescapable: "The image of God is already present in the fetus. . . . We conclude then, on both theological and exegetical grounds, that the body, the life and moral faculty of man originate simultaneously at conception." Waltke then proceeds to "give a clear statement regarding the morality of induced abortion based upon God's Word. The fetus is human and therefore to be accorded the same protection to life granted every other human being. Indeed, feticide is murder, an attack against a fellow man who owes his life to God, and a violation of the commandment, 'You shall not kill.'"[223]

This study is not the place to apply the biblical principles regarding procreative sexuality to a number of ethical issues facing the church today, including stem cell research, cloning, genetic engineering, artificial insemination, sex selection by sperm sorting—the list could go on and on. But the OT does give basic principles that can provide a foundation to guide our ethical thinking.

Problems/Distortions of Procreative Sexuality and Divine Grace

The grace of God is revealed throughout the various problems and distortions of procreative sexuality surveyed in this chapter. God's grace shines out in

---

[218] Stott, "Does Life begin Before Birth?" 50.

[219] *HALOT* 175; cf. BDB 149.

[220] BDB 409; cf. Archer, *Encyclopedia of Bible Difficulties,* 247.

[221] BDB 119; *HALOT* 137.

[222] For extended discussion and rebuttal of the various attempts by those advocating abortion rights to discount the biblical evidence cited above, see Francis J. Beckwith, *Politically Correct Death: Answering Arguments for Abortion Rights* (Grand Rapids: Baker, 1993), 137–50; cf. Randy Alcorn, *ProLIFE Answers to ProCHOICE Arguments* (rev. and enl. ed.; Sisters, Ore.: Multnomah, 2000), passim. For a comprehensive annotated bibliography on the issue of abortion from a religious or moral perspective, see esp. George F. Johnston, *Abortion from the Religious and Moral Perspective: An Annotated Bibliography* (Bibliographies and Indexes in Religious Studies 53; Westport, Conn.: Praeger, 2003).

[223] Waltke, "Reflections," 13.

the rite of circumcision, as he recognizes humanity's helplessness to offer acceptable obedience and announces through the rite that his strength is made perfect in our weakness. God's grace shines brightly amid the numerous instances of childlessness, sometimes providing a miraculous gift of fertility, always providing care and a sense of his presence to the ones who are childless. To the widows and orphans, God provides his gracious care. God takes personal responsibility for the welfare of all needy widows and orphans. To the childless widows he offers the institution of levirate marriage. To the orphans he offers adoption: human adoption, or the realization that God himself is in the business of adopting those who have been abandoned (Ezek 16:1–7). To those born out of wedlock, God performs a miracle whereby they become in God's eyes legitimately conceived children, and the parents who conceived out of wedlock are spiritually "revirginated" and in God's constant care (Hos 1–3).

To children who, through the inscrutable wisdom of God, are allowed to suffer abuse by the hand of the enemy, God offers comfort, healing, and indeed the promise of divine retribution upon the abusers. Similar divine retribution is promised to someday make right the unspeakable wrongs done to innocent children through child sacrifice, but at the same time, God offers forgiving grace to those who repent of their heinous crimes of sacrificing innocent blood, even the blood of his own children (cf. Manasseh; 2 Kgs 21:6, 16; 2 Chr 33:10–17).

God's grace is available for forgiveness and cleansing for those who have performed or undergone abortion, just as for any other person who has committed murder. David's inspired prayer in Ps 51 records his repentance not only from his adultery with Bathsheba but also from his "bloodshed" or murder (51:16 [ET 51:14]), and the same picture of grace as is drawn in this psalm in reference to adultery (see ch. 8, above) applies to murder. Grace did not, however, deliver David from the consequences of his sins, losing four sons.

Although I wish to emphasize the power of divine grace, in view of the widespread disregard of the biblical evidence on the status of the unborn fetus in the church and society today, I am constrained to end this chapter not on a note of grace but with a biblical warning cry of alarm. God's voice on this issue is clear: abortion is feticide, a violation of the sixth commandment, "You shall not murder." Who among the followers of God will hear the cry of the unnumbered unborn humans whose voices are silenced in death before they even have a chance to speak? The same God who brought the people of ancient Israel to judgment for murdering their little children by passing them through the fire to pagan gods will bring before his judgment bar the current generation who turns a deaf ear to his cry and the cry of his unborn precious ones.[224]

---

[224] See esp. John O. Anderson, *Cry of the Innocents: Abortion and the Race towards Judgement* (South Plainfield, N.J.: Bridge, 1984).

🪷12

Beauty versus Rape and the
Parody of Beauty

Positive Affirmations of the Edenic Ideal

Pentateuchal Narratives

The Hebrew *ṭôb mĕ'ōd* ("very good")—connoting the quintessence of goodness, wholesomeness, appropriateness, and beauty—was applied to all God's creation in Gen 1:31, including the sexuality of humans. The very first verse depicting humans outside Eden attests to the continuing "very good" of sexuality after the fall: "Now the man knew his wife Eve, and she conceived and bore Cain" (Gen 4:1). As noted in ch. 10 of this study, the word *yādaʿ*, "to know," often implies a deep personal relationship with the one known, and the reference to conception and birth affirms the commencement of the divine blessing upon the human race to "be fruitful and multiply." Sexuality is still intended by God to be beautiful, wholesome, and good outside Eden.

The narratives of Genesis do not provide many glimpses into the daily sexual lives of the patriarchs and matriarchs to reveal their affirmations of the wholesome beauty of sexuality, but the few closeups included by the narrator speak volumes. Sexual beauty is by no means a subject ignored. Particular attention is called to the stunning physical beauty of Sarah: Abram tells his wife, "I know well that you are a woman beautiful in appearance [*yĕpat-mar'eh*]" (Gen 12:11), and the Egyptians likewise "saw that the woman [Sarai] was very beautiful [*yāpâ . . . mĕ'ōd*]" (12:14). The narrator records his similar assessment of Rebekah's physical appearance when Abraham's servant met her: "The girl was very fair to look upon [*ṭōbat mar'eh mĕ'ōd*]" (24:16), and this was also Isaac's thinking about his beloved wife: "she is attractive in appearance [*ṭōbat mar'eh*]" (26:7). The narrator describes Rachel as "graceful and beautiful" (*yĕpat-tō'ar wiypat mar'eh*) (29:17), and the exact masculine counterpart to this description is given of Joseph in the context of his sexual temptation by Potiphar's wife: "Now Joseph was handsome and good-looking [*yĕpēh-tō'ar wiypēh mar'eh*]" (39:6). The context of each of these affirmations of beautiful/handsome physical appearance reveals a beauty of character as well (as already observed in the analysis of the matriarchal narratives; see below for Joseph).

Accompanying the physical attraction between patriarch and matriarch was a loving relationship. Sometimes this emerges explicitly from the narrative. Thus Moses writes not only that Isaac "took Rebekah, and she became his wife" but also that "he loved [ʾāhēb] her" (24:67). Three times the narrator mentions that Jacob loved Rachel, with the verb ʾāhēb in 29:18, 30 and the noun ʾahăbâ in 29:20.

Isaac's love for Rebekah is fleshed out in a fleeting snapshot of their uninhibited, erotic, sensuous love play. The king sees Isaac through his window in Gerar, "fondling [mĕṣaḥēq] his wife Rebekah" (26:8). The piʿel participle mĕṣaḥēq is a play on words with Isaac's name (which contains the same consonants and carries the same meaning of "sport, play") and implies an intense and elongated exchange of "conjugal caresses."[1] Behind the references to Jacob's love for Rachel is the intimation of a delightful and passionate romance between the two, so much so that Jacob's seven-year service for her hand in marriage "seemed to him but a few days because of the love he had for her" (29:20).

That the narrator of Genesis wishes to uphold a high view of the wholesome beauty and purity of human sexual love is demonstrated by his careful crafting of the last half of Genesis (Gen 25–50). As pointed out in ch. 4, above, on wholeness, the central apex of the chiastic megastructure is found in Gen 38–39. It seems clear that Moses wished to contrast the distortion of sexuality in the account of Judah and Tamar with Joseph's recognition of the purity and dignity of sexual love and faithfulness. "Finally, when we return from Judah to the Joseph story (Gen 39), we move in pointed contrast from a tale of exposure through sexual incontinence to a tale of seeming defeat and ultimate triumph through sexual continence—Joseph and Potiphar's wife."[2] Genesis 39 contains the lofty account of Joseph's sexual purity and integrity in refusing the sexual advances of Potiphar's wife and in particular highlights the recognition by Joseph that a sexual sin is really a sin against God. To the insistence of Potiphar's wife that he commit adultery with her, he responds (39:9): "How then could I do this great wickedness, and sin against God?"

Pentateuchal Legislation

When we turn to sex-related Mosaic legislation, the evidence for affirmation of the wholesomeness and beauty of sexuality must be viewed in light of the general nature of legal material. The legislation analyzed thus far in preceding chapters has all been in the form of prohibitions. Such is the tendency of law in general: it safeguards "life, liberty and the pursuit of happiness" by restricting activities that would jeopardize such fundamental rights.

The Mosaic legislation regarding sexuality is not conspicuous because of inordinate volume or emphasis within the legal material of Exodus through Deuteronomy. Sexual sins are not singled out as special or more heinous than other sins. Furthermore, in the legislation concerning sexuality, sex itself is never

---

[1] BDB 850. Cf. HALOT 1019, which gives the meaning "fondle a woman."
[2] Robert Alter, The Art of Biblical Narrative (New York: Basic Books, 1981), 10.

considered evil in any way. Rather, the intent of the sexually related laws (as with laws concerning nonsexual matters) seems to be that of providing safeguards and restrictions so as to prevent the damaging of intrahuman (familial) and divine-human (cultic) relationships. The earlier discussion of pentateuchal laws regulating sexual behavior has noted repeatedly how the legislation was designed to uphold a high view of the holiness and dignity of human sexuality.

A list of prohibitions, however, could be mistaken to mean that sexuality itself was somehow bad and only barely tolerated by God with severe restrictions attached. That such was not the intent of the Mosaic legislation governing sexual conduct is clear from at least one law that contains a positive commandment regarding sexuality. This is found in Deut 24:5: "When a man is newly married, he shall not go out with the army or be charged with any related duty. He shall be free at home one year, to be happy with [or 'to bring happiness to' (wĕśimmaḥ, pi'el of śāmaḥ)] the wife whom he has married." No doubt one concern in this legislation is procreation, that a man have the opportunity to produce progeny before being subjected to war. But the wording of the phrase "be happy with [or 'to bring happiness to'] the wife whom he has married" transcends procreative considerations and emphasizes God's concern for the establishment of a strong family life and the enjoyment of sexual pleasures between spouses.[3]

The placement of this law in the Deuteronomic code is significant. As Stephen Kaufman has shown, 24:5 is one of the amplifications of the eighth commandment—laws against theft (23:20 [ET 23:19]–24:7). As with the immediately preceding law dealing with divorce (24:1–4), Kaufman argues that this law is concerned to "prevent the theft of nepeš [life, soul, livelihood]." In the latter case, it is theft "of the services and devotion of a groom to his bride."[4] The immediately succeeding law prohibiting the taking of only one of a pair of millstones in pledge (24:6) is seen by Kaufman to be linked with the law protecting bride and groom. The millstone law is placed in this position because of its analogy with bride and groom: the upper millstone (rekeb, lit. "rider") is not to be separated from its mate, just as a groom is not to be separated from his bride. There also may be a sexual connotation included in "grinding" in biblical Hebrew that links these two laws together.[5]

In short, 24:5 is positive legislation protecting the beauty and happiness of married sexual love while it is still a tender plant among newlyweds, so that the bonds of love may be solidified and thus sexual joy and beauty may be prolonged even after the special first year is completed. No one and nothing is to rob

---

[3] Another passage that has been suggested as a possible positive command regarding sexuality is Exod 21:10–11. If the word 'ōnâ in v. 10 is interpreted as "conjugal rights" (see BDB 773) and the 'aḥeret ("another") in question as a rival wife, then what is true for her is a fortiori even truer of a sole wife: the husband "shall not diminish the food, clothing, or conjugal rights of the first wife." But as the study, above, of this passage has argued, the translation of 'ōnâ as "conjugal rights" and 'aḥeret as "rival wife" should be rejected.

[4] Steven A. Kaufman, "The Structure of the Deuteronomic Law," Maarav 1–2 (1978–1979): 156–57, n. 109.

[5] See Job 31:10; Kaufman, "The Structure of the Deuteronomic Law," 156, n. 108.

newlyweds of the unfettered happiness of sexual love in the context of marriage. No more should they be robbed of this "one-flesh-ness" than the upper millstone should be taken away from its "grinding" mate.

Prophets/Writings

The wholesome and holy beauty of sexuality is revealed in the Prophets most dramatically when God describes his own relationship with Israel in terms of a marriage. Eighth-century Isaiah records God's self-portrait of joy in his marriage and in his bride: "but you shall be called My Delight Is in Her, and your land Married; for the LORD delights [ḥāpēṣ] in you, and your land shall be married. . . . and as the bridegroom rejoices over the bride, so shall your God rejoice over you" (Isa 62:4–5). The verb ḥāpēṣ means "to take pleasure in, to delight in, to desire" and implies the deep joy in the human marriage relationship as God designed it.

Another eighth-century prophet, Hosea, likewise reveals God's intention for the beauty and joy of married love. As noted in chapter 10, above, discussing intimacy, God, the romantic Lover, shares his plans for his beloved wife: "Therefore, I will now allure her, and bring her into the wilderness, and speak tenderly to her [lit. 'to her heart']. . . she shall respond [or 'sing,' Heb. ʿānâ] as in the days of her youth" (Hos 2:16–17 [ET 2:14–15]). Romantic allurement and responsive songs of love!

In the hymnic/Wisdom literature of the Writings, one encounters Ps 45, which is designated in its superscription "A love song." Probably composed for the royal wedding of an Israelite (or Judean) king, perhaps Solomon himself,[6] this psalm contains explicit references to the beauty of both bridegroom and bride. Of the bridegroom it is written, "You are the most handsome of men; grace is poured upon your lips; therefore God has blessed you forever" (45:3 [ET 45:2]). The bride is described thus: "and the king will desire your beauty. . . . The princess is decked in her chamber with gold-woven robes" (45:12, 14 [ET 45:11, 13]).

A recent study by William Propp argues that Ps 45 constitutes "one of the Bible's sexiest poems"—with numerous sexual double entendres "relieving the tension by suggestively teasing bridegroom and bride."[7] Among the possible sexual allusions suggested by Propp are the following. The term šōšānîm, "lilies," in the tune name to which this song of love is to be song (v. 1), is seen as an erotic symbol, as in the Song of Songs (e.g., Song 2:16; 6:2–3). The "sword" (Ps 45:4 [ET 45:3]) and "arrows" (v. 6 [ET v. 5]) are viewed as erotic allusions, since "long, piercing implements of bloodshed like swords, spears and arrows are phallic symbols throughout Near Eastern literature."[8] Associated with this warfare

---

[6] Note the reminiscences in the description of the procession described in Ps 45 with the Song of Songs (3:6–11; 5:10–16); see below, ch. 13, for defense of Solomonic authorship of the Songs of Songs.

[7] William H. Propp, "Is Psalm 45 an Erotic Poem?" *BR* 20, no. 2 (2004): 33–42, quotes at 33, 42.

[8] Ibid., 35.

terminology are references to the "thigh" (*yārēk,* v. 4 [ET v. 3]), which here, as elsewhere in Scripture, is taken as a euphemism for "penis" (e.g., Gen 46:26; Exod 1:5; Judg 8:30), and the Hebrew verb *rākab,* "ride, mount, lie atop" (Ps 45:5 [ET 45:4]), which is used in Akkadian in a sexual sense and here, according to Propp, has erotic overtones. Propp also sees a phallic association in the psalmist's use of the term "right hand" (*yāmîn,* v. 5 [ET v. 4]), in light of Ugaritic parallels where the word "hand" can connote the genitals. Likewise, for Propp, the phrase in v. 7 (ET v. 6) *šēbeṭ mîšōr,* "staff of righteousness/straightness" (Propp's translation), within the context of a wedding psalm, is a blatant innuendo of sexuality. The references to perfumed "oil of gladness" (v. 8 [ET v. 7]), "myrrh and aloes and cassia" (v. 9 [ET v. 8]), also are seen to evoke erotic connections, "for, then as now, scent and sex were inextricably linked, as any devotee of the Songs of Songs will recall (see also Proverbs 7:17)."[9] Finally, use of the rare term *šēgal* for "queen" (v. 10 [ET v. 9]) may be regarded as an erotic double entrendre, since "it chimes with the unrelated Hebrew verb *šāgal,* 'sexually ravish.'"[10]

Propp summarizes the main terms that may constitute sexual double entendres and admits his own ambiguity over whether such sexual allusions are in fact present in the text:

> With some effort, I can read the poem with a straight face. Sometimes a sword is just a sword, a thigh is just a thigh, a conquest is just a conquest, a mount is just a mount, a bow is just a bow, a hand is just a hand, a foot is just a foot, and a straight scepter is just a straight scepter. But in a marriage song? . . . I cannot but think that the raunchy *double entendre* that I detect in Psalm 45 is real and deliberate. And also fun.[11]

Although some of Propp's suggestions of erotic imagery seem clear (such as the reference to lilies and amorous spices), his evidence for many of the proposed sexual allusions is too slender to be unambiguously affirmed as the poet's intention in this psalm. On the other hand, it is possible, as Propp suggests, that "the poem's allusions to the ancient language of love and lust are too subtle and obscure for today's audience,"[12] including myself. If Propp should prove right in his assessment of most or all of the sexual allusions in Ps 45, such sexual double entendres do not need be interpreted as "raunchy" or lacking divine inspiration or referring to lust, as Propp suggests;[13] rather they provide the tastefully chosen, beautifully wrought, joyously erotic backdrop of this lofty and inspired "Song of Love."

The most vivid—and unambiguous—portrayal of the beauty and joy of sexuality is found in the book of Proverbs. Chapter 10, above, on intimacy noted the endearing expressions found in Prov 5:15–23, which not only describe intimacy but denote the wholesome beauty of married love. The wise man is not ashamed

---

9 Ibid., 37.
10 Ibid.
11 Ibid., 42.
12 Ibid., 33.
13 Ibid., 42, 32.

to employ expressions of frank eroticism and ecstatic pleasure to describe the divinely designed sexual relationship. He counsels without hesitation,

> Let your fountain be blessed,
>   and rejoice in the wife of your youth,
> a lovely deer, a graceful doe.
>   May her breasts satisfy you at all times;
>   may you be intoxicated always by her love. (5:18–19)

Physical sensuousness, a husband's joyous satisfaction (*rāwâ, piʿel*, lit. "drenching, saturation")[14] with his wife's breasts, and exhilarating pleasure, his continuous (*tāmîd*) staggering intoxication (*šāgâ*)[15] with her love—such is the portrait of wholesome, God-ordained sexuality.

Walter Kaiser analyzes the five different words for water used in 5:15–20, each referring to a different but related water source—cistern, well, springs, streams, and fountain—and together serving "as metaphors of connubial love." He points out that in a land that is characteristically hot and where water is not plentiful, the wise man "compares a drink of cool, refreshing water to the thirst-quenching delight that comes from enjoying one's own spouse.... The images of a cistern, well, fountain, spring, and stream are used because one's spouse, like water, satisfies desire."[16] As noted above, the Hebrew word for "satisfy" (*rāwâ*) has the connotation of "drenching, drinking to one's fill," probably alluding to the satisfying water sources and reinforcing the joyous fulfillment in sexuality.

Furthermore, the wife is described in v. 19 as "a lovely deer, a graceful doe [or 'mountain goat']"—symbols of "agility, grace form, and beauty."[17] Again, in the same verse the reference to the woman's breasts (*dad*) is a wordplay on the Hebrew word for "love" (*dôd*). Verse 18a describes the "fountain" (of wholesome married sexuality) as "blessed," echoing the original blessing of sexuality in the garden of Eden. And finally, the central thrust of the passage is contained in v. 18b: "rejoice in [*śāmaḥ min*] the wife of your youth." "This programmatic exhortation ('rejoice in') captures the purpose of the entire proverb."[18] Wholesome married sexual love as God designed it to be is indeed a gift that calls for exultant rejoicing.

According to the wise man (Prov 30:18–19), wholesome and beautiful human sexuality, which he describes as "the way of a man with a girl," is "wonderful," "amazing" (NIV; *nipʿal* of *pālāʾ*)—in fact, too wonderful and amazing to fully understand. Sexuality is beautiful, and beauty is more than skin deep.

---

14 The Hebrew verb *rāwâ* in the *piʿel* means to "drench, water abundantly," and even "be intoxicated, drunk" (BDB 924).

15 The Hebrew *šāgâ* here literally means to "stagger because of (as a consequence of) wine" (*HALOT* 1413).

16 Walter C. Kaiser Jr., "True Marital Love in Prov 5:15–23 and the Interpretation of the Song of Songs," in *The Way of Wisdom: Essays in Honor of Bruce K. Waltke* (ed. J. I. Packer and Sven K. Soderlund; Grand Rapids: Zondervan, 2000), 107, 109–10.

17 Ibid., 108.

18 Ibid.

Inextricably bound up with the erotic and the sensuous, the book of Proverbs emphasizes the moral/spiritual dimension, without which the physical attractiveness has no ultimate significance. Thus, on the one hand, "a gracious woman gets honor," (11:16), but on the other,

> Like a gold ring in a pig's snout
>   is a beautiful woman without good sense. (11:22)

The final chapter of Proverbs puts the physical component of sexuality in proper perspective with the spiritual:

> Charm is deceitful, and beauty is vain,
>   but a woman who fears the LORD is to be praised. (31:30)[19]

The way of wisdom is the fear of the Lord, and with this as the foundation of the marital relationship, sexuality in all its dimensions becomes wholesome, beautiful, and good.

The book of Ecclesiastes affirms that there is also the way of wisdom in a wholesome sexual relationship. According to Qoheleth, God "has made everything suitable for its time" (Eccl 3:11), and this includes sexuality. Sex is beautiful. Therefore there is "a time to embrace" (3:5) and "a time to love" (3:8); therefore he encourages, "Enjoy life with the wife whom you love" (9:9).

Throughout the HB, but particularly in the Prophets/Writings, the love of God is consistently described in sexual metaphors. This phenomenon received attention in ch. 3, above. A penetrating study by Larry Lyke sets forth a case study of the imagery of springs and wells in the HB, revealing that "the theological and human registers of these metaphors are essentially inseparable."[20] Lyke shows that the "simultaneity of the theological and human registers" in the language of love throughout the HB provides one "of the primary vehicles for the sanctifying of human sexuality."[21] Human sexuality in the OT is holy, not in the sense of being divinized or sacralized in the cultus but in the sense that it reflects the holy character of God's love.

Thus, throughout the OT canon, the wholesome and holy beauty of human sexuality is affirmed and extolled. But distortions of this lofty portrait of the divine ideal for beautiful sex are also apparent, and to these we now turn our attention.

Distortions of the Beauty of Human Sexuality: Rape

Although other distortions of God's ideal for sexuality mar its wholesome and holy beauty, none so directly distorts God's plan by transforming sexuality

---

[19] See ch. 6, above, on "The Song of the Valiant Woman" of Prov 31.

[20] Larry L. Lyke, "The Song of Songs, Proverbs, and the Theology of Love," in *Theological Exegesis: Essays in Honor of Brevard S. Childs* (ed. Christopher Seitz and Kathryn Greene-McCreight; Grand Rapids: Eerdmans, 1999), 222; see his full argument in 208–23.

[21] Ibid., 223.

into unvarnished and horrendous ugliness as that of rape. Its vile violence strips
away all semblance of beauty.

Ancient Near Eastern Background

The ANE laws dealing with rape usually appear in the context of adultery,
and the case laws are concerned with two major variables: the marital status of
the one raped and whether she consented. Regarding the rape of an unattached
woman (i.e., a virgin, not betrothed or married), MAL A §55 states that her father
is to take and hand over the assailant's wife to be raped and that the father has the
right to demand that the rapist marry his daughter with no right of divorce and
also pay the bride money or, if the father so chooses, the father can receive the
bride money but give his daughter to someone else.[22]

Regarding the rape of a betrothed girl (for whom the bride money has already been paid), since betrothal has the legal status of being already inchoately
married, the rapist is punished by death, but the woman goes free (Code of Ur-
Nammu §6; Code of Eshnunna §26; CH §130).[23] Likewise the rapist of a fully
married woman also receives the death penalty, and the woman is not punished
(MAL A §§12, 23; HL §197).[24]

---

[22] "The Middle Assyrian Laws (Tablet A)," §55, translated by Martha Roth (*COS*
2.132:359; cf. *ANET* 185): "If a man forcibly seizes and rapes a maiden who is residing in
her father's house, [. . .] who is not betrothed (?), whose [womb (?)] is not opened, who is
not married, and against whose father's house there is no outstanding claim—whether
within the city or in the countryside, or at night whether in the main thoroughfare, or in a
granary, or during the city festival—the father of the maiden shall take the wife of the fornicator of the maiden and hand her over to be raped; he shall not return her to her husband, but he shall take (and keep?) her; the father shall give his daughter who is the victim
of fornication into the protection of the household of her fornicator. If he (the fornicator)
has no wife, the fornicator shall give 'triple' the silver as the value of the maiden to her
father; her fornicator shall marry her; he shall not reject (?) her. If the father does not desire it so, he shall receive 'triple' silver for the maiden, and he shall give his daughter in
marriage to whomever he chooses."

[23] "The Laws of Ur-Namma (Ur-Nammu)," §6 (§5 in *ANET*), translated by Martha
Roth (*COS* 2.153:409; cf. *ANET* 524): "If a man violates the rights of another and deflowers
the virgin wife of a young man, they shall kill that male." "The Laws of Eshnunna," §26,
translated by Martha Roth (*COS* 2.130:334; cf. *ANET* 167): "If a man brings the bridewealth
for the daughter of a man, but another, without the consent of her father and mother, ab-
ducts her and then deflowers her, it is indeed a capital offense—he shall die." "The Laws of
Hammurabi," §130, translated by Martha Roth (*COS* 2.131:344; cf. *ANET* 171): "If a man
pins down another man's virgin wife who is still residing in her father's house, and they seize
him lying with her, that man shall be killed; that woman shall be released."

[24] MAL A §12 (*COS* 2.132:354; cf. *ANET* 181): "If a wife of a man should walk along
the main thoroughfare and should a man seize her and say to her, 'I want to have sex with
you!'—she shall not consent but she shall protect herself; should he seize her by force and
fornicate with her—whether they discover him upon the woman or witnesses later prove
the charges against him that he fornicated with the woman—they shall kill the man; there
is no punishment for the woman." MAL A §23 (*COS* 2.132:355–56; cf. *ANET* 181): "If a
man's wife should take another man's wife into her house and give her to a man for

Regarding the issue of the woman's consent, MAL A §12 assumes that the woman tried to fight off the assailant and was forced (and thus innocent) if the act took place on the street (where presumably the woman was engaged in legitimate business); if the rapist is caught in the act or if witnesses later prove that rape occurred, the rapist is to be killed, and the woman receives no punishment. HL §197 assumes that if the act is committed in the mountains, the woman is innocent; but if the act occurs in her house, the woman is presumed guilty and given the death penalty. If the woman's husband finds them in the act, he has the option of killing them on the spot without being guilty of any crime.

The Sumerian laws add additional variables: the social status of the one raped (and whether the rapist was of aware of this status) and whether the parents knew that their daughter was "in the street." Sumerian Law §7 states that if the (free-class) parents of the raped virgin daughter are unaware that she was in the street but the daughter insists that she was raped, the parents may force the rapist to marry their daughter.[25] Sumerian Law §8 indicates that if the (free-class) parents of the virgin daughter knowingly allowed her to be out in the street and her rapist swore under oath that he did not know she was of the free-citizen class, then the rapist was not punished.[26]

On the basis of the above texts, Jacob Milgrom points out that "in the ANE, rape was considered a stigma." By contrast, as will become evident below, Milgrom notes that normally "in Israel, however, there was no stigma attached to a raped (or seduced) single girl" (unless she is the daughter of a priest).[27]

purposes of fornication, and the man knows that she is the wife of a man, they shall treat him as one who has fornicated with the wife of another man; and they treat the female procurer just as the woman's husband treats his fornicating wife. And if the woman's husband intends to do nothing to his fornicating wife, they shall do nothing to the fornicator or to the female procurer; they shall release them. But if the man's wife does not know (what was intended), and the woman who takes her into her house brings the man in to her by deceit (?), and he then fornicates with her—if, as soon as she leaves the house, she should declare that she has been the victim of fornication, they shall release the woman, she is clear; they shall kill the fornicator and the female procurer. But if the woman does not so declare, the man shall impose whatever punishment on his wife he wishes; they shall kill the fornicator and the female procurer." "Hittite Laws," §197, translated by Harry A. Hoffner Jr. (*COS* 2.19:118; cf. *ANET* 196): "If a man seizes a woman in the mountain(s) (and rapes) her, it is the man's offence, but if he seizes her in (her) house, it is the woman's offence; the woman shall die. If the (woman's) husband (lit. the man) finds them (in the act), he may kill them without committing a crime."

[25] "Sumerian Laws," §7, translated by J. J. Finkelstein (*ANET* 526): "If (a man) deflowered the daughter of a free citizen in the street, her father and her mother not having known (that she was in the street), and she (then) says to her father and mother: '*I was raped*,' her father and her mother may give her to him (forcibly) as a wife."

[26] Sumerian Law §8 (*ANET* 526): "If (a man) deflowered the daughter of a free citizen in the street, her father and her mother having known (that she was in the street) but the man who deflowered her denied that he knew (her to be of the free-citizen class), and, standing at the temple gate, swore an oath (to this effect, he shall be freed)."

[27] Jacob Milgrom, *Leviticus 17–22: A New Translation with Introduction and Commentary* (AB 3A; New York: Doubleday, 2000), 1807.

Pentateuchal Narratives

Lot's Daughters (Gen 19). Chapter 4, above, examined the story of Lot in Gen 19 and concluded that the men of Sodom were desirous of homosexual activity with the two guests.[28] Here I add that it was male homosexual *gang rape* that was in the minds of the Sodomites.[29] The story also alludes to the rape of women, as Lot offers the men of Sodom his two virgin daughters to rape instead of the (angel) visitors (19:8), and this offer might have been carried out if not for the angelic intervention. The narrator's depiction of these stories clearly underscores the violence, vileness, and horror of rape.

Dinah (Gen 34). A forceful example of rape that was carried out appears in the narrative of Gen 34. The narrator records the incident succinctly (vv. 1–2): "Now Dinah, the daughter of Leah, whom she had borne to Jacob, went out to see the daughters of the land. And when Shechem the son of Hamor the Hivite, prince of the country, saw her [*wayyar² ²ōtāh*], he took her [*wayyiqqaḥ ²ōtāh*] and lay with her [*wayyiškab ²ōtāh*] and violated her [*wayᶜannehā*]." The steps in the rape are described in swift succession: Dinah ventures into association with pagan women, Shechem lusts after her, and in the heat of his desire he takes her and lies with her, thus violating her person.

Is this really a case of rape? Some commentators argue that Dinah probably consented to the illicit sexual union.[30] Several arguments for this position have

---

[28] In addition to the two narratives clearly involving rape, which are discussed at some length in this study, brief mention may also be made of the article by Helena Zlotnick, "The Rape of Cozbi (Numbers XXV)," *VT* 51 (2001): 69–80, which claims that Phinehas in effect raped Cozbi the Midianite as he killed her: "Phinehas kills Cozbi by piercing her belly. . . . By wielding a spear Phineas uses a weapon that resembles a male sexual organ. By selecting her womb as a target he rapes her. To be precise, he impregnates her in a manner calculated not only to inflict death but also to degrade her legal relationship to a level of arbitrary passion" (74). Such a reading is part of Zlotnick's hypothesis that regards the rapes of Dinah (Gen 34) and Cozbi "as two bookends, one signaling the demise of the last matriarch, the other effecting the elimination of a potential matriarch. . . . Ultimately, such stories also provide negative stereotypes of behavior: a Jew is not to marry outside the group; a Jew-ess behaves neither like Dinah who leaves the domestic space to encounter a 'rapist' nor like Cozbi who enters her own bedroom to encounter a murderer." In order to arrive at this conclusion, the author must reconstruct the narrative of Cozbi far beyond what is provided in the text, and ultimately in such a way as to read against the narrator himself. For an evangelical critique of such kinds of reading including a feminist orientation of suspicion, see Robin Parry, "Feminist Hermeneutics and Evangelical Concerns: The Rape of Dinah as a Case Study," *TynBul* 53 (2002): 1–28.

[29] See esp. Lyn M. Bechtel, "A Feminist Reading of Genesis 19:1–11," in *Genesis* (ed. Athalya Brenner; FCB[2] 1; Sheffield, Eng.: Sheffield Academic Press, 1998), 108–28, who assumes, however, as noted in ch. 4, above, that a reprisal against outsiders in a group-oriented society, not homosexual lust, was the issue. It seems best to conclude, however, that both were at issue.

[30] See, e.g., Lyn M. Bechtel, "What If Dinah Is Not Raped? (Genesis 34)," *JSOT* 62 (1994): 19–36; Mayer I. Gruber, "A Re-examination of the Charges against Shechem Son of Hamor," *Beit Mikra* 157 (1999): 119–27; Hilary B. Lipka, " 'Such a Thing Is Not Done in

been advanced. First, the narrative employs the more neutral verb "take" (*lāqaḥ*) for Shechem's act (v. 2) rather than the stronger word *ḥāzaq*, "force" (as in the clear case of forcible rape in Deut 22:25–27). Second, the *piᶜel* verb *ᶜinnâ*, "violate," can sometimes imply a case of "statutory rape" rather than "forcible rape"; that is, "a man who has sex with a woman without proper arrangements is said to 'rape' [*ᶜinnâ*] . . . the woman even if she consents."[31] Alternatively, it is argued that this verb does not refer to any sort of rape in this text but serves "as an evaluative term in a juridical context denoting a spatial movement downwards in a social sense . . . [and] should be translated as 'debase.'"[32] Third, it is suggested that the circumstances that follow the sexual activity do not seem to fit the pattern of forcible rape: Shechem falls in love and speaks tenderly to Dinah, and some time after the rape took place, Dinah was still in Shechem's house (Gen 34:26) and apparently had to be removed (unwillingly?) by her brothers when they plundered the city.[33]

At first glance, this evidence seems persuasive (and I originally held this view). But a closer look at the grammar of this narrative—especially "the exact use of prepositions" in comparison with the rape narrative of Tamar and Amnon (2 Sam 13)—has led me to a different conclusion.[34] The narrator in Gen 34:2 says that Shechem (literally) "lay her" (using the verb *šākab*[35] in its transitive sense plus the direct object *ʾōtāh* rather than the usual intransitive sense of *šākab* plus the prepositional phrase *ᶜimmāh*, "lay *with* her"), thus emphasizing the use of force in the sexual crime.[36] The preposition *ᶜim*, "with," implies permission, as when Potiphar's

---

Israel': The Construction of Sexual Transgression in the Hebrew Bible" (PhD diss., Brandeis University, 2004), 247–69; Burton L. Visotzky, *The Genesis of Ethics* (New York: Crown, 1996), 197; Ellen van Wolde, "The Dinah Story: Rape or Worse?" *OTE* 15 (2002): 225–39; and Nicolas Wyatt, "The Story of Dinah and Shechem," *UF* 22 (1990): 433–58.

[31] E.g., Deut 22:24, 29; cf. Tikva Frymer-Kensky, "Sex and Sexuality," *ABD* 5:1145.

[32] Ellen van Wolde, "Does *ᶜinnâ* Denote Rape? A Semantic Analysis of a Controversial Word," *VT* 52 (2002): 528–44, quote at 543.

[33] For elaboration of these arguments, see esp. ibid.; and Wyatt, "The Story of Dinah and Shechem," 435.

[34] Mishael Maswari Caspi, "The Story of the Rape of Dinah: The Narrator and the Reader," *HS* 26, no. 1 (1985): 32, points out, "From the phrasing and the exact use of prepositions, it is possible to interpret the narrator's perspective and his relation to the whole event." Caspi's discussion (pp. 32–33) broke the impasse in my own thinking about this text.

[35] "When used to denote sexual relations, the idiom 'lie with' and its derivatives denote sexual relations that are illicit (Gen 30:15–16 and 2 Sam 11:11 are exceptions)" (William C. Williams, "שכב," *NIDOTTE* 4:102). Williams also points out that "the expression denotes rape in Gen 34:2."

[36] This crucial grammatical detail is highlighted by, e.g., Meir Sternberg, *The Poetics of Biblical Narrative: Ideological Literature and the Drama of Reading* (Bloomington: Indiana University Press, 1987), 446: "What for lack of an equivalent I translated as 'lay with' is in fact a transitive verb (*va'yishkab otah*, i.e., 'laid her') that reduces the victim to a mere object and thus exceeds the properly intransitive construction 'lay with' (*va'yishkab ittah*)." Cf. Susanne Scholz, *Rape Plots: A Feminist Cultural Study of Genesis 34* (New York: Peter Lang, 2000), 136–37; and idem, "Through Whose Eyes? A 'Right' Reading of Genesis 34," in *Genesis* (ed. Athalya Brenner; FCB[2] 1; Sheffield, Eng.: Sheffield Academic Press, 1998), 165–68. Van Wolde, "The Dinah Story," 228, seeks to counter this interpretation by citing results of the study by Harry Orlinsky, "The Hebrew Root ŠKB," *JBL* 63 (1944): 19–44, who

wife pleads with Joseph to "lie with me [*immî*]" (Gen 39:7). In the narrative of the rape of Tamar, Amnon first asked Tamar's permission when he says, "Come, lie with me [*immî*]" (2 Sam 13:11), but after she refused, Amnon "forced her and lay her [*ʾōtāh*]" (13:14, translation mine). This clear distinction in usage in the parallel rape narrative, coupled with the contextual clues within the narrative itself, points toward the conclusion that Shechem employed force in his sexual encounter with Dinah. Several modern versions have captured this nuance by translating this phrase in Gen 34:2 as "he lay with her by force."[37] This deliberate use of precise terminology seems to imply that Dinah was a victim of forcible (and not just statutory) rape. (Perhaps it is an instance of what we might call date rape.)

The verb *innâ* (in the *piʿel*), "violate," is a technical term for illicit sexual intercourse; it is "used in juridical contexts to confirm that penetration (and ejaculation) actually took place."[38] The term refers to an illegitimate sex act (or its consequences) but does not by itself indicate whether the woman gave her consent. In a number of other OT passages, however, this verb is used in a setting of forcible rape[39] and probably is best translated "violate" or "rape." In the context of Gen 34—especially in light of the grammatical construction in 34:2 discussed above and the fact that "at *no* point in the chapter is Dinah blamed for what has happened"[40]—I conclude that Dinah did not consent. Thus the violation of Dinah as a result of forcible rape is in view.

The rapid succession of the three verbs—he "took" her, he "laid" her, and he "violated" her—probably serve as a hendiadys (two or more words serving to describe one activity) to "express the single action of rape. The use of this device underscores the act. On another level the three words suggest a progressive severity. They emphasize Shechem's increasing use of violence against Dinah in v. 2b."[41]

---

concludes that "there is no semantic difference" between *šākab ʾēt* and *šākab ʿim*. This may be true when *ʾēt* is used as a preposition (in parallel with the preposition *ʿim*), but contra Orlinsky (pp. 23–27), who claims that all suffix forms vocalized as *ʾōt-* refer back to the preposition and not to the sign of the direct object. Sternberg, Scholz, and others have, in my view, correctly recognized that in Gen 34:2 *šākab ʾēt* occurs in precise parallelism with (and is flanked on each side by) two other verbs unmistakably followed by the direct-object marker, and thus the narrator's intent here (as in the parallel rape story in 2 Sam 13) is for *ʾōtāh* to be taken as the direct-object marker (plus the fem. sg. accusative suffix) indicating the use of force and not as the preposition "with" (plus fem. suffix).

[37] So the NRSV, NJPS, NAB, and NASB. Cf. NJB: "[he] forced her to sleep with him."

[38] So David Noel Freedman, "Dinah and Shechem, Tamar and Amnon," *Austin Seminary Bulletin: Faculty Edition* 105 (1990): 54. Van Wolde argues that this term highlights the juridical consequences of social debasement that accompanied the sexual activity ("Does *ʿinnâ* Denote Rape?" 528–44). But although rape may have implied social debasement in other ANE cultures, as Milgrom points out (*Lev 17–22*, 1807), there was no stigma attached to rape in Israelite society (except in the case of a priest's daughter). More on this below.

[39] See Judg 19:24; 2 Sam 13:12, 14, 22, 32; Ezek 22:11; Lam 5:11.

[40] Parry, "Feminist Hermeneutics," 16. Parry continues, "Blame is always placed squarely on Shechem's shoulders."

[41] Scholz, *Rape Plots*, 138. Cf. Sternberg, *The Poetics of Biblical Narrative*, 446. Contra Tikva Frymer-Kensky, *Reading the Women of the Bible* (New York: Schocken Books, 2002),

After the rape, Shechem apparently abducted Dinah, brought her to his own house (v. 26), and tried to woo her (v. 3): "His soul was drawn [lit. 'clung' (*watidbaq*)] to Dinah daughter of Jacob; he loved [*wayyeʾĕhab*] the girl, and spoke tenderly [lit. 'to/upon the heart' (*ʿal-lēb*)] to her."[42] The same word, *dābaq* "to cleave/cling", is used here as in 2:24 (where it describes the covenant bond of marriage), but the meaning is significantly changed: here the cleaving comes after sexual intercourse but outside the marriage covenant. The phrase *dibbēr ʿal-lēb* (lit. "to speak upon the heart") is used ten times in the HB, and always "in less than ideal situations, where there is a sense of guilt or repentance, where A attempts to persuade B of his feelings."[43] Shechem's subsequent attempts to woo Dinah, the offers of his father to Jacob to arrange for a marriage between Shechem and Dinah, even the character assessment that Shechem "was the most honored of all his family" (34:19)—none of these facts lessen the heinousness of the rape crime that was committed.[44]

182, who argues that "in rape, the word *ʿinnah* ["degrade"] comes before the words 'lay with'; in other forms of illicit sexual intercourse, *ʿinnah* comes after the words 'lay with.'" Frymer-Kensky considers this word order important because, "in rape, abuse starts the moment the rapist begins to use force, long before penetration. In other illicit sexual encounters, the act of intercourse may not be abusive." Frymer-Kensky, however, has not taken into account the precise use of the terminology of the verb "to lay" plus the direct object to indicate forcible rape, as discussed above, or the use of hendiadys in this passage, which is more probable than her hypothesis.

[42] Scholz, *Rape Plots,* 138–42, seeks to demonstrate that these three verbs, in the context of rape, do not speak positively of Shechem's "wooing" Dinah but rather refer respectively to his continued sexual desire, lust, and attempt to soothe/calm her after the rape. Scholz, however, stretches the semantic possibilities of these terms beyond reasonable limits, and I concur with Sternberg, *The Poetics of Biblical Narrative,* 447, and others that these are "three verbs of endearment."

[43] Victor P. Hamilton, *The Book of Genesis: Chapters 1–17* (NICOT; Grand Rapids: Eerdmans, 1990), 355. Besides this passage, see Gen 50:21; Judg 19:3; Ruth 2:13; 1 Sam 1:13; 2 Sam 19:8 (ET 19:7); 2 Chr 30:22; 32:6; Isa 40:2; Hos 2:16. According to Danna Nolan Fewell and David M. Gunn, "Tipping the Balance: Sternberg's Reader and the Rape of Dinah," *JBL* 110 (1991): 211, the phrase "speak to/upon the heart" implies that Shechem managed to win Dinah's affections. But as Meir Sternberg points out: "Fewell and Gunn have confused the agent-oriented 'speak [*dbr*] to the heart of somebody' with the patient-oriented 'touch [or reach, *ngʿ*] the heart of somebody.' . . . [The phrase 'speak to the heart of somebody' does not] have any special romantic bearing. . . . It just means to speak good words of some kind—for example, of cheer, benevolence, tenderness, gratitude, encouragement—designed to move the addressee's 'heart.' Designed to move, I would emphasize, without necessarily achieving it" ("Biblical Poetics and Sexual Politics: From Reading to Counter-reading," *JBL* 111 [1992]: 476–77).

[44] According to Joseph Fleishman, "Shechem and Dinah in the Light of Non-Biblical and Biblical Sources," *ZAW* 116 (2004): 12–32, although Shechem abducted and forced sexual relations upon Dinah, this was not a case of rape (as he narrowly defines it), but rather a case of marriage by abduction. Perhaps this was the way the people of Shechem viewed the matter, but the reaction of Jacob's sons seems to indicate that the Hebrews did not accept the validity of such an arrangement, and regarded Shechem's act as a heinous crime of rape.

Although the evidence points toward forcible rape on the part of Shechem, this evidence is admittedly not coercive. But even if Dinah did consent to have sex with Shechem, it still would constitute, in today's terminology, statutory or power rape. If Shechem did not physically force Dinah, his position of power as "son of Hamor the Hivite, prince of the region" (34:2), should be regarded a psychological forcing of Dinah.[45]

Susanne Scholz's articles on Gen 34 and her published dissertation reveal that many, if not most, modern interpretations of Gen 34, even if they agree that it was forcible rape, nonetheless "contain numerous assumptions complicit with a contemporary belittlement of rape."[46] But a close reading of the narrative, already begun in Christian interpretation by Martin Luther, brings us face-to-face with the horrible nature of the rape crime.[47] The narrator calls the violation of Dinah *nĕbālâ*, "an outrage" (v. 7), a term often used elsewhere in the OT to describe various sexual crimes or other kinds of "serious disorderly and unruly action resulting in the breakup of an existing relationship whether between tribes,

---

[45] See below for further discussion of power rape in connection with David's sin against Bathsheba. Those who deny that Gen 34 constitutes rape define "rape" more narrowly than I do. E.g., Lipka, "'Such a Thing Is Not Done,'" 242, defines "rape" as having two essential elements: (1) the sexual act is forced against someone's will, and (2) the sexual act violates the victim on a personal level (psychological effects). I argue that the coercion may be psychological (power rape) as well as (or instead of) physical and that the psychological effects on the victim need not be spelled out by the narrator in order for the sexual act to be identified as rape.

[46] Susanne Scholz, "Was It Really Rape in Genesis 34? Biblical Scholarship as a Reflection of Cultural Assumptions," in *Escaping Eden: New Feminist Perspectives on the Bible* (ed. Harold C. Washington, Susan L. Graham, and Pamela Thimmes; BS 65; Sheffield, Eng.: Sheffield Academic Press, 1998), 182–98, quote at 195; idem, "Through Whose Eyes?"; and idem, *Rape Plots,* 105–47. Scholz shows that by means of textual arguments, historical considerations, source-critical reconstructions, or anthropological comparisons, the majority of treatments of this passage "obfuscate" rape by diverting attention to some other part of the story than the rape itself as the major issue in the passage or minimize its seriousness. Scholz summarizes the common approaches/conclusions: "Scholars suggested that the rapist 'really' loved Dinah. They find rape less harmful in ancient Israel. They maintain that in ancient Israel a marriage could redeem the rape, that the story reflects a tribal conflict with Canaanite neighbors or that similar to other ANE texts Gen 34 narrates a sacred marriage ritual. Further, interpreters identify an original love story and relegate the rape to a later edition. They explain the events with the dynamics of group-oriented societies in which sexual intercourse is only problematic when it threatens the community" ("Was It Really Rape?" 195).

[47] Luther broke with a whole millennium of medieval commentators who allegorized the narrative, making the story of Dinah a warning example of the punishment that will come when women through pride, foolishness, or curiosity fall into sin and are seduced by the devil. Luther, in contrast, underscored the historicity of the narrative and viewed Dinah as the victim of forcible rape—she was unwilling. For a discussion of Luther's view in contrast with the prevailing medieval interpreters, see Joy A. Schroeder, "The Rape of Dinah: Luther's Interpretation of a Biblical Narrative," *Sixteenth Century Journal* 28, no. 3 (1997): 775–91. Luther as well as Calvin, however, still deflect the full force of the rape amid their moralizing. See Michael Parsons, "Luther and Calvin on Rape: Is the Crime Lost in the Agenda?" *EvQ* 74 (2002): 123–42.

within the family, in a business arrangement, in marriage or with God."[48] It is "the worst kind [of crime]—something absolutely unthinkable in Israel."[49] The narrator also implies that (at least in the minds of Dinah's brothers) the whole city was corporately guilty for the defiling of their sister. The Hebrew of 34:27 reads, "Jacob' sons came upon the slain and looted the city, because *they* [i.e., the city] had defiled [*ṭimmᵊʾû*] their sister."[50] Although Dinah's brothers were not justified in the slaughter of the inhabitants of Shechem in retribution for this terrible act—one violent act does not justify another—nonetheless, their reaction correctly assesses the reprehensibleness of the violating rape, and the sense of moral outrage at an act that disrupted the whole social order.[51]

The account of Dinah's violation not only decries her rape by Shechem; the carefully crafted narration perhaps emphasizes by its silence the denigration and oppression of the woman in the story.[52] Dinah never speaks. Even though she is raped, feminist interpreters point out, she is given no voice to protest. Even in the brother's retaliation for the heinous crime done against their sister,[53] Dinah is apparently not given the full respect of her personhood.[54]

---

[48] See Anthony Phillips, "Nebalah—a Term for Serious Disorderly and Unruly Conduct," *VT* 25 (1975): 241. For the other sex-related crimes described using this term, see Deut 22:21; Judg 19:23–24; 20:6, 10; 2 Sam 13:12; Jer 29:23.

[49] Freedman, "Dinah and Shechem," 62.

[50] The updated NASB translates this way; many other modern versions translate as a passive "she had been defiled," but the Hebrew could have easily used the *nipʿal* if a passive were intended. It seems best to understand it as referring to the corporate guilt that the brothers ascribed to the whole city for Shechem's "wanton deed" against their city. In other words, the crime went beyond a sexually offensive immoral act: it disrupted the social order of the whole city and their relationship with Jacob's family.

[51] See Scholz, *Rape Plots*, 160, 168.

[52] Feminist interpreters of the story make this point. See, e.g., Fewell and Gunn, "Tipping the Balance," 211; van Wolde, "The Dinah Story," 237 and passim; and Visotzky, *The Genesis of Ethics*, 197. Although the silence of Dinah may be an important point in the narrative, I disagree with feminists who find fault not only with Jacob and Dinah's brothers but also with the narrator. For defense of the reliability of the narrative voice, see Sternberg, *The Poetics of Biblical Narrative*, 463–73 (esp. 464: "Regarding point of view, whatever the narrative voice brings to the surface is always reliable, though rarely complete").

[53] Some scholars argue that Dinah's brothers had no concern for their sister, only for their own honor. See, e.g., Fewell and Gunn, "Tipping the Balance," 202. But I concur with Sternberg, *The Poetics of Biblical Narrative*, 472, that the brothers' concern was "selfless and single-minded: to redress the wrong done to their sister and the whole family, which includes the prevention of an exogamous marriage, by hook or by crook." Fewell and Gunn, "Tipping the Balance," 211, also argue that Dinah responded positively to the wooing of Shechem, indeed desired to marry him, and had to be "taken" by force by her brothers back into their home. As noted above, Sternberg shows that this conclusion is based upon a faulty understanding of the phrase "speak to the heart of somebody." Sternberg marvels at this "dangerous, existential premise: that a little sweet talk after the event will turn round the heart of a woman (a virgin, possibly still bleeding, included) toward the man who has just 'taken her and lain with her and abused her.' All this on the authority of feminism, no less. Tell it not to rapists, publish it not in the streets" ("Biblical Poetics and Sexual Politics," 476).

[54] I do not wish to totally pass over the remark at the beginning of the narrative that Dinah "went out to visit the women of the region" (Gen 34:1), thus putting herself in a

As a sequel to the story, Jacob remonstrates with his sons for having made him and his household "odious to the inhabitants of the land" by slaughtering the men of the city of Shechem in revenge for their sister's victimization (34:30).[55] The sons respond with a rhetorical question: "Should our sister be treated like a whore?" (34:31). The text does not say that the violation of Dinah's sexuality had made her the equivalent of a harlot, as some commentators maintain. Rather, "the sons are asserting that *their failure to defend their sister's honor* would be tantamount to regarding her as if she were a harlot. . . . The sons see very clearly that *in rape—a man, or a community, treats a woman the way a harlot treats herself.*"[56] That is, rape denigrates and violates a woman's whole being—body, mind, and spirit.[57]

----

vulnerable position that might have been avoided if she had not sought social intercourse with the idolatrous nations that surrounded her. See, e.g., Naomi Graetz, "Dinah the Daughter," in *A Feminist Companion to Genesis* (ed. Athalya Brenner; FCB 2; Sheffield, Eng.: Sheffield Academic Press, 1993), 312, who recognizes the possibility that "the text itself criticizes Dinah's behavior by using the verbal stem * yṣ'* 'to go out.'" But so many of the commentaries focus on this and other aspects of the story and thereby (subconsciously) belittle the rape crime itself that I put this comment in a footnote. Leon R. Kass, "Regarding Daughters and Sisters: The Rape of Dinah," *Commentary* 93, no. 4 (1992): 36, points out the kinds of argument that are, "to this day, advanced in defense of accused rapists: 'Look how she dresses.' 'She sleeps around.' 'What was she doing in his apartment, or in that fraternity house?' 'She was asking for it.' Even granting their possible relevance, such complaints of 'provocation' never constitute an adequate defense for rape."

[55] In the deathbed blessing of Jacob upon his twelve sons, Simeon and Levi are characterized together as "weapons of violence" (Gen 49:5–6), and the mention that "in their anger they killed men" no doubt referred to the Shechem incident. Their actions disqualified them from receiving the patrimony. Freedman, "Dinah and Tamar," 59, draws the lesson: "While the rape criminal or violator will not escape the consequences . . . those who take the law into their own hands will suffer consequences as well and just as severe."

[56] Kass, "Regarding Daughters and Sisters," 36. Scholz offers another plausible and compatible explanation of this expression: "The brothers saw through Shechem's attempt to turn rape into paid sex. They insisted that Dinah was not a prostitute who offered sexual favors and then received payment. . . . Dinah could not be bought like prostitutes in ancient Israel who needed economic support" (*Rape Plots,* 166–67). Still another plausible and compatible explanation of the brothers' question is given by Paul R. Noble, "A 'Balanced' Reading of the Rape of Dinah: Some Exegetical and Methodological Observations," *BibInt* 4 (1996): 194: "The specific point of the brothers' comparison (I would suggest) is that a prostitute receives payment for providing sex, and this is effectively the position into which Shechem has put Dinah by offering 'gifts' for her *without acknowledging that he had previously abused her.* The brothers' objection, then, is not to the offer of money *per se,* but to it being offered as a routine bridal payment (rather than as compensation or restitution) which simply ignores the fact that Shechem has already *forced* her to have sex with him."

[57] For further emphasis upon rape as sexual violence in this narrative, see Scholz, "Through Whose Eyes?" My final-form treatment of the rape of Dinah does not deal with speculative diachronic studies such as Helena Zlotnick, *Dinah's Daughters: Gender and Judaism from the Hebrew Bible to Late Antiquity* (Philadelphia: University of Pennsylvania Press, 2002), 33–56, who attempts a hypothetical reconstruction of redactional layers in the tradition history of the story, with the final redactor seeking (without complete success) to suppress the worldview of the protagonists in earlier stages of the tale.

Pentateuchal Legislation concerning Rape

Exodus 22:15–16 (ET 22:16–17) and Deuteronomy 22:28–29. These two penta-teuchal passages, which were addressed above in the discussions of plural marriage (ch. 4) and premarital sex (ch. 8), are best regarded as dealing with statutory, not forcible, rape (with the woman voluntarily submitting to the man's pressure to have sexual intercourse). But even though the woman apparently consents to engage in sexual intercourse with the man in these situations, the man nonetheless has "afflicted/oppressed/humbled her" (*ʿinnāh*). The divine plan that a woman's purity be respected and protected has been violated. The penalty imposed was that either the rapist had to marry the one he had seduced and support her financially all her life (without possibility of divorce) or else the girl's father (as legal guardian) could on her behalf exercise the right of refusal and demand monetary payment equivalent to the dowry even though the seducer did not marry her.

Even though the woman may have acquiesced to her seducer, nonetheless, according to the law, the dowry is "equal to the bride-price for virgins" (Exod 22:16 [ET 22:17]): she is treated financially as a virgin would be. Such treatment upholds the value of a woman against a man taking unfair advantage of her and at the same time discourages rape. It also implies, as Milgrom points out, that in Israel there was no stigma attached to a raped virgin.

Deuteronomy 22:25–27.[58] This passage gives legislation that clearly refers to forcible rape: "But if a man finds [*yimṣāʾ*] a betrothed young woman in the countryside, and the man forces her [*wĕhehĕzîq-bāh*] and lies with her [*wĕšākab ʿimmāh*], then only the man who lay with her shall die" (22:25 NKJV). In this passage a stronger word than either *pātâ,* "seduce," or *tāpaś,* "catch, take, seize," is employed; the verb *ḥāzaq* (*hipʿil* with the preposition *bĕ*), "force," often denotes the overpowering of the weaker by the stronger.[59] The next verses (26–27) verify that this is the case: the young woman was not guilty, since she was forced against

---

[58] In addition to this passage from Deuteronomy dealing with rape, Harold C. Washington argues that Deut 21:10–14 constitutes "an institutionalized form of rape" ("Violence and the Construction of Gender in the Hebrew Bible: A New Historicist Approach," *BibInt* 5 [1997]: 344); cf. idem, " 'Lest He Die in the Battle and Another Man Take Her': Violence and the Construction of Gender in the Laws of Deuteronomy 20–22," in *Gender and Law in the Hebrew Bible and the Ancient Near East* (ed. Victor H. Matthews, Bernard M. Levinson, and Tikva Frymer-Kensky; JSOTSup 262; Sheffield, Eng.: Sheffield Academic Press, 1998), 202–7. But Washington's claim to see rape in this passage is part of his larger "construction of gender" in the war laws of Deut 20–22, which laws, according to Washington, all "valorize violent acts, construe them as essential to male agency, and define licit conditions for their exercise" ("Violence and the Construction of Gender," 344). Washington therefore interprets all these laws as "a discourse of male power" (ibid.) and characterizes Israel as a "rape culture" (p. 352). Such a reading, however, seeks to evaluate the biblical material by reading *against,* rather than *with,* the intention of the biblical author and is beyond the purview of my final-form, friendly-to-the-text theology.

[59] E.g., Gen 19:16; Judg 19:25; 1 Sam 15:27; 17:35; 2 Sam 2:16; 13:11; Dan 11:7, 21. See BDB 304; *HALOT* 303–4, s.v. חזק.

her will (like a victim in a murder) and since she is presumed to have cried out in the countryside but there was no one to hear.

"Biblical law assumes her innocence without requiring witnesses [v. 27]; she does not bear the burden of proof to argue that she did not consent. . . . If the woman *might* have been innocent, her innocence must be assumed."[60] But the man who violates the woman in this way receives the death penalty. Thus the Mosaic law protects the sexual purity of a betrothed woman (and protects the one to whom she is betrothed) and prescribes the severest penalty to the man who dares to sexually violate her. "It sent a message to the man: Sex is an act of covenantal intimacy only proper in the context of a committed relationship. If you are going to have sex with someone, you must be prepared to support her for the rest of your life."[61]

Leviticus 21:7, 14. Leviticus 21:7–9 lists prohibitions concerning marriage for priests, and vv. 10–15 enumerate prohibitions for the high priest. These verses have been examined in chapter 9, above, regarding divorce, but here note the prohibition regarding one who is defiled by rape. "They [the common priests] shall not marry a prostitute [or promiscuous woman (*zōnâ*)] or a woman who has been defiled [*ḥălālâ*]; neither shall they marry a woman divorced from her husband. For they are holy to their God. . . . A widow, or a divorced woman, or a woman who has been defiled [*ḥălālâ*], a prostitute [or a promiscuous woman (*zōnâ*)], these he [the high priest] shall not marry. He shall marry a virgin of his own kin" (vv. 7, 14). Some commentators have taken *ḥălālâ* as a reference to a woman's defilement by (cultic) prostitution, but Milgrom, after critiquing this and other interpretations, has made a strong case for translating this term as "one who was raped."[62] Milgrom shows that v. 7 lists the prohibited women in *descending* order of defect, and thus the *ḥălālâ* must be less offensive than promiscuity (*zōnâ*) but more offensive than being divorced. This pattern is confirmed by v. 14, which lists the prohibited marriage partners for the high priest in *ascending* order of defect. If *zōnâ* refers to a woman who willingly has illegitimate sex, then *ḥălālâ* refers to a woman who is forced, that is, raped. Milgrom further suggests a semantic coalescence, in this term, of the meaning of the verbal root *ḥll*[I], "desecrate," with *ḥll*[II], "pierce;" thus the *ḥălālâ* is " 'the desecrated pierced one,' or 'raped.' "[63] Although a rape victim was not stigmatized in ancient Israel in terms of being an appropriate marriage partner for a layperson, this passage, as was pointed out regarding divorce in ch. 9, below, indicates a progression in holiness from the common person, who could presumably marry any of the aforementioned classes of women denied to the priests, to the common priest, who could not marry a prostitute or a divorcee but could marry a widow, to the high priest,

---

[60] Craig S. Keener, "Some Biblical Reflections on Justice, Rape, and an Insensitive Society," in *Women, Abuse, and the Bible: How Scripture Can Be Used to Hurt or to Heal* (ed. Catherine Clark Kroeger and James R. Beck; Grand Rapids: Baker, 1996), 126.

[61] Ibid., 127.

[62] Milgrom, *Leviticus 17–22*, 1806–8, 1819.

[63] Ibid., 1807.

who could marry only a virgin of his own house who had never been married. As noted also in ch. 9, these prohibitions focus on reputation, not on virginity.[64] There is simply a higher standard of purity (of reputation) demanded of a priest's bride than of the bride of a common person. Such "higher standard demanded of God's special ministers"[65] will be seen also in the NT (see the afterword to this study).

Rape in the Prophets/Writings

Outside the Pentateuch there are several passages in which the prophet predicts or records a foreign army conquering a nation (Judah, Babylon) and "ravishing" or raping the women.[66] In the Song of Deborah and Barak, King Sisera's mother, waiting at the window for her son to return from battle with the spoils of victory, muses, "Have they not found and divided the spoil?—A womb [*raḥam*] or two for every man . . . ?" (Judg 5:30 ESV). "Sisera's mother callously and crudely refers to Israelite girls as 'wombs,' that is, physical objects to be raped by Sisera and his Canaanite soldiers."[67] Aside from these general references to rape, three episodes are recorded in detail where the rape of a woman is a key event in the narrative: the gang rape of the Levite's unnamed concubine (Judg 19), the rape of Bathsheba by David (2 Sam 11), and the rape of Tamar, daughter of David, by her half-brother Amnon (2 Sam 13).

The Levite's Concubine (Judg 19). The discussions of concubinage (ch. 4) and homosexuality (ch. 5) briefly alluded to the gang rape of the Levite's concubine. Here we focus upon the horror of the violent act itself and the equal horror of the callous indifference of the men who abetted the violence.[68] The laws of hospitality

---

[64] Ibid., 1808.

[65] Andrew Cornes, *Divorce and Remarriage: Biblical Principles and Pastoral Practice* (Grand Rapids: Eerdmans, 1993), 139.

[66] Regarding Babylonian wives being raped, see Isa 13:15. For women of Judah being raped by Babylonian soldiers, see Jer 13:22 (cf. 13:26); Lam 5:11 (cf. 1:1–22); and perhaps Mic 4:11. For women of Judah being raped in the eschatological battle against the nations, see Zech 14:2. For discussion of the motif of rape in Lamentations, see F. W. Dobbs-Allsopp and Tod Linafelt, "The Rape of Zion in Thr 1,10," *ZAW* 113 (2001): 77–81 (although I do not accept one of the central premises of this article, i.e., that Yahweh himself is a rapist of Zion); and Lipka, "'Such a Thing Is Not Done,'" 327–35. Lipka, pp. 315–22, also suggests that the divine punishment of Judah at the hands of Babylon (Ezek 23:29) implies that Judah will be raped, but this is not explicit and far from certain.

[67] Roy Gane, *God's Faulty Heroes* (Hagerstown, Md.: Review and Herald, 1996), 56. Robert Alter points out that the twice-repeated description, in the previous verse, of Sisera falling (literally) "between her [Jael's] feet" (Judg 5:27) is "a hideous parody of soldierly sexual assault on the woman of a defeated foe" (*The Art of Biblical Poetry* [New York: Basic Books, 1985], 46).

[68] For analysis of this narrative with particular attention to the rape, see esp. Phyllis Trible, *Texts of Terror: Literary-Feminist Readings of Biblical Narratives* (OBT; Philadelphia: Fortress, 1984), 65–92; and Alice Bach, "Rereading the Body Politic: Women and Violence in Judges 21," in *Judges* (ed. Athalya Brenner; FCB[2] 4; Sheffield, Eng.: Sheffield

522 FLAME OF YAHWEH

clearly do not pertain to the concubine; the lord of the house offers the guest's concubine and even his own virgin daughter to the mob outside and gives them permission to ravish the women: "Ravish them, and do whatever you want to them" (Judg 19:24). The narrator captures the unfeeling violence already in the actions of the Levite as he "seized (*ḥāzaq* in the *hipʿil*) his concubine and pushed to them outside" (v. 25b).[69] When the Levite brought out his concubine to the waiting mob, "They wantonly raped her, and abused her all through the night until the morning. And as the dawn began to break, they let her go." (v. 25). By the combination of the verbs "know sexually" (*yādaʿ*) and "abuse/torture" (*hitpaʿel* of *ʿālal*), the ghastly reality of gang rape is described, and by the reference to "all night till morning," the multiple acts of unrelenting terror are indicated.

But the strong Hebrew terminology for gang rape is not forceful enough for the narrator to drive home the shock he wishes to elicit from his readers. The last desperate attempts of the raped woman to secure help are vividly recorded: "As morning appeared, the woman came and fell down at the door of the man's house where her master was, until it was light." Here is a "post-rape portrait of a devastated, nearly dead woman, that leaves no room for any commentator to imagine that she might secretly have enjoyed her evening with the mob. . . . Lying there, 'with her hands on the threshold' (Judg 19:27), she seeks refuge with her last bit of strength. She has no voice, but the description is heavy with the violence she has endured."[70]

Shocking as this scene appears, perhaps even more shocking is the callousness of the Levite, who casually wakes up the next morning, opens the door as if to leave alone without regard for his concubine, and, upon seeing her with her hands on the threshold, barks the two-word (in Hebrew) order: "Get up, we are going" (v. 28). No bending down to see if she is alive. No "words to speak to her heart" as he had earlier intended to give (v. 3). When she does not respond (the Hebrew ambiguity does not indicate whether she is dead or exhausted), she is flung onto his donkey's back like a sack of flour, taken home, and dismembered into twelve pieces. (The Hebrew here is written for maximum shock value to catch the attention of the readers.) No mourning for the man; no burial for the woman. She is distributed among the tribes of Israel like pieces of an animal—as the pieces of oxen that Saul would later send out as a call to war (1 Sam 11:7). "Of

---

Academic Press, 1999), 143–59. Cf. J. H. Coetzee, "The 'Outcry' of the Dissected Woman in Judges 19–21: Embodiment of a Society," *OTE* 15 (2002): 52–63; Lapsley, *Whispering the Word*, 35–67; and Ilse Müllner, "Lethal Differences: Sexual Violence as Violence against Others in Judges 19," in *Judges* (ed. Athalya Brenner; FCB[2] 4; Sheffield, Eng.: Sheffield Academic Press, 1999), 126–42.

[69] This translation by Trible, *Texts of Terror*, 76, captures the hurried and callous roughness of the Levite denoted by the Hebrew word *ḥāzaq* in the *hipʿil* and the lack of the direct object "her" after the verb.

[70] Alice A. Keefe, "Rapes of Women/Wars of Men," *Semeia* 61 (1993): 90. Cf. Coetzee, "The 'Outcry' of the Dissected Woman," 55–60 (although I cannot agree with Coetzee's implicating the narrator in addition to the male participants in the rape for reflecting the contemporary societal attitude of "silencing all women completely" [55]).

all the characters in Scripture, she is the least. . . . She is property, object, tool . . . Without name, speech, or power, she has no friends to aid her in life or mourn her in death. . . . Captured, betrayed, raped, tortured, murdered, dismembered, and scattered—this woman is the most sinned against."[71]

The narrator preserves the commentary of the people of Israel who witnessed this deed; it serves as a timeless response both to the "vile outrage" (Judg 20:6) of gang rape and the male insensitivity to women's suffering: "Consider it, take counsel, and speak out" (19:30).

Bathsheba (2 Sam 11). The next incidence of rape in the Former Prophets is found in David's act of adultery with Bathsheba, the wife of Uriah the Hittite. Chapter 8, above, referred briefly to this incident when discussing adultery; here we address the issue of whether David's act was also one of rape.

The historical narrative of David's adultery with Bathsheba (2 Sam 11) is one of the prime biblical examples of a sophisticated and intricately written literary masterpiece, calling for careful attention and sensitivity to the inspired narrator's artistic techniques in order for the interpreter to grasp the theological truths highlighted in the narrative. The following eighteen lines of evidence have convinced me, contrary to a common interpretation implicating Bathsheba as a coconspirator,[72] that Bathsheba was a victim of power rape on the part of David, and that the narrative indicts David, not Bathsheba.[73]

1. Literary structure. Yehuda Radday's literary analysis of 1–2 Samuel reveals a chiasm encompassing each book.[74] David's sin involving Bathsheba (recorded in 2 Sam 11) is placed at the chiastic center of 2 Samuel, just as Saul's failure to destroy the Amalekites (1 Sam 15) forms the chiastic apex of 1 Samuel. The first

---

[71] Trible, *Texts of Terror,* 80–81.

[72] E.g., Randall C. Bailey, *David in Love and War: The Pursuit of Power in 2 Samuel 10–12* (Sheffield, Eng.: JSOT Press, 1990), 86, argues at some length that Bathsheba is "a willing and equal partner to the events that transpire"; H. W. Hertzberg, *I and II Samuel: A Commentary* (OTL; London: SCM, 1964), 309, suggests a possible element of "feminine flirtation." So also Cheryl A. Kirk-Duggan, "Slingshots, Ships, and Personal Psychosis: Murder, Sexual Intrigue, and Power in the Lives of David and Othello," in *Pregnant Passion: Gender, Sex, and Violence in the Bible* (ed. Cheryl A. Kirk-Duggan; SemeiaSt 44; Atlanta: Society of Biblical Literature, 2003), 59: "The text seems to imply that Bathsheba asked to be 'sent for' and 'taken.'" Similarly, Klein, *From Deborah to Esther,* 56, speaks of "Bathsheba's complicity in the sexual adventure." Cf. idem, "Bathsheba Revealed," in *Samuel and Kings* (ed. Athalya Brenner; FCB[2] 7; Sheffield, Eng.: Sheffield Academic Press, 2000), 47–64; George G. Nicol, "Bathsheba, a Clever Woman?" *ExpTim* 99 (1988): 360–63; idem, "David, Abigail and Bathsheba, Nabal and Uriah: Transformations within a Triangle," *SJOT* 12 (1998): 130–45.

[73] These careful narrative analyses also support this conclusion: Trevor Dennis, *Sarah Laughed: Women's Voices in the Old Testament* (Nashville: Abingdon, 1994), 144–55; and Moshe Garsiel, "The Story of David and Bathsheba: A Different Approach," *CBQ* 55 (1993): 244–62.

[74] Yehuda T. Radday, "Chiasm in Samuel," *LB* 9–10, no. 3 (1973): 23; idem, "Chiasmus in Biblical Hebrew Narrative," in *Chiasmus in Antiquity: Structures, Analyses, Exegesis* (ed. John W. Welch; Hildesheim: Gerstenberg, 1981), 78–80.

half of each book depicts the successful rise to power of Saul and David respectively; the central chapters of the chiasm delineate each king's pivotal moral failure, his "great sin;" and the last half of each book portrays the decline of the king as a result of his sin. Thus 2 Sam 11 serves as the fulcrum event that spelled David's descent from integrity and power. The emphasis within the overall literary structure of 2 Samuel points to David's moral fall as the critical turning point in his life and implicitly lays the blame for this moral fall squarely at his feet.

2. Historical context (vv. 1–2). Already in the introduction to this narrative, the ironic contrast is set forth with a long sentence about the war—"In the spring of the year, the time when kings go out to battle, David sent Joab with his officers and all Israel with him; they ravaged the Ammonites, and besieged Rabbah"—juxtaposed with a short, three-Hebrew-word statement about David: "But David remained at Jerusalem." The Hebrew word order of this last clause places emphasis upon the subject, "David," by placing it first in the clause instead of the usual order of verb followed by subject, which is roughly equivalent in English to highlighting David's name with italics. At the time of year when *kings* normally go forth to war, David's general and his army, yes "all Israel" are risking their lives on the battlefield, but *King David himself* stays at home in Jerusalem. The contemporary readers were aware that in the world of the books of Samuel, people expected their king to "go out before us and fight our battles" (1 Sam 8:20), and they remembered that David gained his initial prestige for strong and daring leadership when he went out to battle in contrast to the stay-at-home King Saul (1 Sam 18:19; cf. 2 Sam 5:2). "It therefore leaps to the eye that this is the first war in which David fails to lead the army in person."[75] The irony is intensified in 2 Sam 11:2 when, in contrast to the nation fighting at Rabbah, the narrator describes David in relative isolation, "leading a life of idleness in Jerusalem, taking his leisurely siesta, getting up in the evening, and strolling about on his roof."[76]

3. Archaeological/topographic and architectural data (vv. 2, 8–10, 13). The archaeological excavations in the city of David have unearthed what is thought by some to be the Millo, the nearly vertical retaining wall supporting the royal palace in David's time.[77] The elevated placement of the royal palace makes clear that David would have had a commanding view over the dwellings in the Kidron Valley directly below. (One can still stand atop this wall, frequently described as the "stepped-stone structure" [probably the "Millo" of 2 Sam 5:9 of the city of David], and have a clear view into the courtyards of the houses in the modern village of Silwan below—I did while contemplating this narrative). The text indicates that Bathsheba's house was among those dwellings in the valley below the palace (vv. 8–13 repeat five times the necessity of Uriah to "go down" [*yārad*] to his house from the palace). The architectural reconstructions of the

---

[75] Sternberg, *The Poetics of Biblical Narrative,* 194.
[76] Ibid., 197.
[77] See 2 Sam 5:6–9. Cf. David Tarler and Jane M. Cahill, "David, City of," *ABD* 2:55–56; G. J. Waightman, *The Walls of Jerusalem: From the Canaanites to the Mamluks* (Mediterranean Archaeological Supplement 4; Sydney, Australia: Meditarch, 1993), 27–37.

typical Israelite four-room house reveal an open courtyard where household residents probably bathed.[78] All these data combine to make the point that from his rooftop David could have seen a woman bathing without her being deliberately provocative.

4. The time of day (v. 2) and the purpose of Bathsheba's bathing (vv. 2, 4). It is not merely incidental that the narrator mentions the time of day when David sees Bathsheba bathing. It is early evening (the Hebrew narrator punctuates this with deliberateness: *lĕ^cēt hā^cereb*, lit. "to the time of the evening"). Verse 4 makes clear the purpose of Bathsheba's bathing: she is engaging in a ritual washing, purifying herself from ritual impurity incurred during her monthly period, as required in Lev 15:19, 28.[79] According the Levitical legislation, a woman was "in her impurity

---

[78] For descriptions of the four-room house, see Amihai Mazar, *Archaeology of the Land of the Bible, 10,000–586 B.C.E.* (New York: Doubleday, 1990), 486; Philip J. King and Lawrence E. Stager, *Life in Biblical Israel* (Louisville: Westminster John Knox, 2001), 28–35. Regarding the likelihood of Bathsheba's full-body bath in the courtyard, see, e.g., Oded Borowski, *Daily Life in Biblical Times* (Archaeology and Biblical Studies 5; Atlanta: Society of Biblical Literature, 2003), 78: "Bathsheba, the wife of Uriah the Hittite, was taking a full-body bath, possibly in her courtyard, when David, who was on the roof of his house, saw her and liked her (2 Sam 11:2)." Cf. Garsiel, "The Story of David and Bathsheba," 255.

[79] The NRSV places the following in parentheses near the end of v. 4: "She was purifying herself [*hitpa^cel* ptc. of *qādaš*] after her period." Since is the sole occurrence of a participial clause (introduced by the *waw* conjunctive/disjunctive) in the verse, interrupting four sequential verbs (*waw consecutive* plus the imperfect), it is best taken as a parenthetical flashback to v. 2, explaining as the purpose of Bathsheba's bathing a ritual cleansing from her menstrual period. Versions such as the NJPS capture the intent of the Hebrew text of this verse even more vividly than the NRSV: "David sent messengers to fetch her; she came to him and he lay with her—she had just purified herself after her period—and she went back home." (See also the NIV, NLT, NJB, and ESV for similar translations.) Some modern versions (e.g., the NASB) have taken v. 4 to indicate that after Bathsheba had sex with David, she engaged in a ritual postcoital purification and then returned to her house (so also, e.g., Frymer-Kensky, *Reading the Women of the Bible,* 147; and Klein, *From Deborah to Esther,* 57), but this reading does not take into account the disjunctive placement of the participial clause amid the grammatical flow of sequential verbs in the verse. Such an interpretation is based in part on the assumption that since Lev 15:19, 28 does not explicitly mention a ritual ablution after a woman's menstrual period is complete, this cannot be what is referred to by the narrative (but "is anachronistically based on later rabbinic law" [Frymer-Kensky, *Reading the Women of the Bible,* 147]). Jacob Milgrom, however, gives weighty evidence showing that "all statements regarding the duration of impurity [in Leviticus] automatically imply that it is terminated by ablutions" (*Leviticus 1–16: A New Translation with Introduction and Commentary* [AB 3; New York: Doubleday, 1991], 934). Those who seen no connection between Bathsheba's bathing and her purification after her menstrual period fail to recognize that this otherwise inconsequential detail is in fact a parenthetical statement reserved for this location to establish beyond question that Bathsheba's pregnancy, mentioned in the next verse, is due to the sexual impregnation by David that has just occurred. Since she had just been purified from her monthly period before this sex act, there is no possibility that Bathsheba was pregnant from Uriah, her husband. "What was previously taken as an objective and impartial recording of external facts now turns into covert indictment" of David, and there is an even

for seven days" (Lev 15:19), and the counting of the days ended in the evening (at sunset, the biblical beginning of the next day). Hence the evening, right after sunset, would be the expected time for a woman completing her menstrual period to engage in the ritual washing. This part of the narrative records no hint of a deliberate ploy on the part of Bathsheba. Rather, while Bathsheba was seeking to faithfully discharge the requirements of Torah regarding prescribed ceremonial cleansing from ritual uncleanness, David was lustfully watching her.

5. *David's walking around on the palace rooftop (v. 2)*. The fact that David is "walking about" (*hitpaꜥel* of *hālak*, v. 2) and happens to see Bathsheba bathing also implies chance circumstances, not a plot. That David was not stalking Bathsheba is indicated in v. 3, in that he did not know the identity of Bathsheba at the time he saw her bathing, and needed to inquire concerning her.

At the same time, David's strolling about on the palace rooftop at this very time of day reveals already the first deliberate steps in his moral fall. The generally accepted code of decency in David's day no doubt included the unwritten understanding that it was inappropriate to look out from one's rooftop or upper story down into the courtyards of neighbors' property at this time of day, out of respect for their privacy, since this was the normal time for baths to be taken. Still today this is part of an unwritten but strictly enforced code of ethics prevalent in Middle Eastern culture. For David to stroll on his rooftop at this time of day was to be in the wrong place at the wrong time, inviting temptation to impure thoughts and actions.

That David's sin started on his rooftop is made clear later in the narrative when Yahweh decrees judgment upon David for his sin. Nathan predicts the divine punishment of *lex talionis* ("measure for measure" retributive justice): "I will take your wives *before your eyes,* and give them to your neighbor, and he shall lie with your wives in the sight of this very sun" (2 Sam 12:11b). Moshe Garsiel points out the narrative parallel of David's rooftop lust and his son's rape of David's wives on the same rooftop:

> To look at a woman who is bathing and covet her constitutes a deviation from the modesty usual between the sexes (Gen 24:64; Job 31:1), and so the narrator invokes the principle of "measure for measure" upon the location where the sin commences. From his roof David sees the woman with whom he later commits adultery, and on that same roof Absalom takes his father's concubines.[80]

The narrator's description of David's walking about on the rooftop of his palace, by sight invading the privacy of his subjects below, also has the effect of putting him "in the position of a despot who is able to survey and choose as he pleases."[81]

---

greater irony: "the very detail that might at first have been interpreted as the sole meritorious feature of David's act ('and he did not transgress the laws of menstrual purity') twists around to condemn him" (Sternberg, *The Poetics of Biblical Narrative,* 198).

[80] Garsiel, "The Story of David and Bathsheba," 253.

[81] J. P. Fokkelman, *King David (II Sam 9–20 and 1 Kings 1–2)* (vol. 1 of *Narrative Art and Poetry in the Books of Samuel;* Assen, Neth.: Van Gorcum, 1981), 51.

6. The identity of the bather (v. 3). When David inquires as to the identity of
the one he has lusted after, he is told, "This is Bathsheba daughter of Eliam, the
wife of Uriah the Hittite" (v. 3). The information concerning Bathsheba's identity
takes on enormous significance when one realizes that both Bathsheba's father
(Eliam) and her husband (Uriah) are listed among the select group of soldiers
called David's "thirty chiefs" (2 Sam 23:13, 34, 39). These men were David's close
comrades, trench buddies who had fought together before David was king. Furthermore, Eliam was the son of Ahithophel, David's personal counselor (2 Sam
15:12; 1 Chr 27:33). The statement "This is Bathsheba daughter of Eliam, the wife
of Uriah the Hittite" should have pricked David's conscience and restrained his
lustful desires. Such intimate ties between David and Bathsheba's husband and
father and grandfather make the sexual sin of David against Bathsheba all the
more audacious and appalling. He took the wife/daughter/granddaughter of his
close friends.

7. Accelerated narrative tempo (v. 4). The fast narrative flow of v. 4 depicts David's impulsive succumbing to lust as he "sent messengers, and took her, and she
came to him, and he lay with her" (RSV). The string of verbs in this narrative sequence ("saw . . . sent . . . inquired . . . sent . . . took her . . . lay with her") indicates
that it is David's initiative throughout, not Bathsheba's. These verbs "speak his
power, and tell, surely, of his abuse of that and of Bathsheba herself. There is a terrible abruptness and stark quality to his actions. There is no time for speech or conversation, no time for care, and certainly none for love, no time for even courtly
etiquette. . . . Bathsheba's verbs in v. 4, by way of contrast, merely describe the setting for those actions of David, and their immediate prelude and aftermath."[82] In
particular, her action of coming to David (v. 4, "she came to him") is in obedient
response to the explicit command of her sovereign lord, the king. "Summoned by
the king, she must obey."[83] This interpretation is later confirmed by use of the same
expression with reference to her husband, Uriah, who, after being summoned by
David, obediently "came to him" (v. 7). That the authority of David's command
was not to be trifled with is also confirmed in the later experience of Uriah: "Uriah's
noncompliance with David's suggestions, commands, and manipulations cost him
his life."[84] Bathsheba is portrayed as "a powerless woman who was victimized by
the conglomeration of David's power, gender, and violence."[85]

8. Verbs of initiative indicating David's power rape (v. 4). Two verbs found at
the heart of this action-packed scene have David as their subject: David "takes
her" and he "lies with her" (RSV). The word *lāqaḥ* "take," in this context (of sending royal messengers) should probably be understood in the sense of "fetch" (NJB)

---

[82] Dennis, *Sarah Laughed,* 148.

[83] Ibid., 149.

[84] Hyun Chul Paul Kim and M. Fulgence Nyengele, "Murder S/He Wrote? A Culture
and Psychological Reading of 2 Samuel 11–12," in *Pregnant Passion: Gender, Sex, and Violence in the Bible* (SemeiaSt 44; Atlanta: Society of Biblical Literature, 2003), 114.

[85] Ibid., 115. So also Kenneth A. Stone, *Sex, Honor, and Power in the Deuteronomistic
History* (JSOTSup 234; Sheffield, Eng.: JSOT Press, 1996), 97: "Bathsheba's action is no independent initiative (unlike David's), but the response to a royal command."

or "summon,"[86] and clearly implies psychological power pressure on the part of David and not voluntary collusion on the part of Bathsheba. According to the text, David sends "messengers" (pl.), but the verb "to take" has a singular masculine subject ("he took her"). Although many modern versions are ambiguous at this point, giving the impression that it was the messengers who "took" Bathsheba to the palace, the Hebrew unambiguously indicates that "he," that is, David himself (by means of the messengers, to be sure), "took" Bathsheba.[87] By using the term lāqaḥ, "took," the narrator clearly implies that "the primary emphasis is on the responsibility of the subject for that act."[88] David's "taking" Bathsheba makes him responsible for her coming to him. The whole narrative flow here suggests Bathsheba's vulnerability once she is inside the palace and, indeed, even before. "Who is there who might protect her from the designs of the king? We are made to feel there is no one."[89]

The expression "lay with" (šākab ʿim), used for the sexual intercourse between David and Bathsheba, does not stress the use of overpowering physical brutality on the part of David, as in the case of the terminology used for the rape of Dinah (Gen 34) and Tamar (2 Sam 13).[90] As evidenced in the pentateuchal legal material (Deut 22:25–27), however, the term "lay with" employed here can indeed imply rape if the context indicates such. Given the context of psychological pressure by a man in power in this passage, the best term to describe David's action is probably "power rape," in which a person in a position of authority abuses that power to victimize sexually a subservient and vulnerable person, whether or not the victim appears to give "consent." David, the king, who was appointed by God to defend the helpless and vulnerable, becomes a victimizer of the vulnerable. Just as intercourse between an adult and a minor, even a "consenting" minor, is today termed statutory rape, so the intercourse between David and his subject Bathsheba (even if Bathsheba, under the psychological pressure of one in power over her, acquiesced to the intercourse) is understood in biblical law,

---

[86] See P. J. J. S. Els, "לקח," NIDOTTE 2:814, meaning 1(m), for examples of this common semantic nuance when lāqaḥ is used of humans.

[87] While it true that sometimes in Hebrew grammar the use of a Hebrew predicate in the singular does not always call for a singular subject (GKC § 145), in this context, the string of masculine singular verbs taking David as the subject are clearly employed by the narrator to point the finger of accusation against the king. As Dennis, Sarah Laughed, 148, puts it, "David is the subject of the two verbs at the center of it all, the verbs that matter more than any of the others. He 'takes her'; he 'lies with her'. He taker her. He lies with her. That is how the storyteller puts it. In doing so he tells us all we need to know" (emphasis his).

[88] Douglas W. Stolt, "לקח lāqaḥ," TDOT 8:17.

[89] Dennis, Sarah Laughed, 5. See Fischer, Women Who Wrestled with God, 93: "if the woman [Bathsheba] were to cry for help, no one would dare force his or her way into the royal chambers to rescue the woman from the hands of her rapist!"

[90] The narrators in Gen 34:2 and 2 Sam 13:14 use the verb plus the direct object (ʾōtāh), "he lay her," rather than the usual indirect object (prepositional phrase ʿimmāh), "he lay with her," to indicate the brutality of the rape. Here in 2 Sam 11:4 we find the usual indirect object with the prepositional phrase ʿimmāh.

and so presented in this narrative, to be a case of rape—what today would be called power rape—and the victimizer, not the victim, is held accountable.[91]

9. Bathsheba's response to the power rape (v. 4). The narrator stresses that after the sexual intercourse Bathsheba on her own initiative returned to her house and did not try to stay in the palace (v. 4b); she desired to go back to her status as Uriah's wife. Her response to David after she knows she is pregnant is a mirror image of what David had done to her: as he sent messengers to fetch her, so now she sends a message to him that she is pregnant. By this means the narrator gives to Bathsheba some dignity of her own:

> She is doing what David did. She is sending him a message. She is answering his show of power with hers. He asserted her power over her by raping her. She asserts her power over him by conveying to him the words: 'I am pregnant.' . . . To David they [these two words in Hebrew] are devastating. He will never be the same again. On them the plot of his whole story, from 1 Samuel 16 to 1 Kings 2, turns. They are not the triumphant cry of a woman who knows she bears the probable heir to the throne. They are the plain speaking of a woman who has been raped and discarded, and who wishes most courageously to make clear to her rapist the consequences of his act.[92]

10. David's continued use of royal power to summon Uriah (v. 6). Verse 6 contains only one verb, "to send" (*šālaḥ*), and this verb is utilized three times in the verse to describe David's use of kingly power to summon Uriah: "So David sent [*šālaḥ*] word to Joab. . . . 'Send [*šālaḥ*] me Uriah the Hittite.' And Joab sent [*šālaḥ*] Uriah to David." The parallel between David's action toward Bathsheba and his actions toward her husband in this same paragraph of the narrative cannot be overlooked. Just as Uriah's wife was sent for, so her husband is sent for. Just as Uriah is helpless and must do what the king orders, so Bathsheba was constrained by the same power pressure of the king's orders. David's power rape of Bathsheba is paired with his power murder of Uriah.

---

[91] For a helpful discussion of the sexual abuse of power in the case of David with Bathsheba and in modern counterparts, see Larry W. Spielman, "David's Abuse of Power," *WW* 19 (1999): 251–59. Cf. Peter Rutter, *Sex in the Forbidden Zone: When Men in Power— Therapists, Doctors, Clergy, Teachers, and Others—Betray Women's Trust* (Los Angeles: Jeremy P. Tarcher, 1989), 21: "*Any sexual behavior by a man in power within what I define as the forbidden zone* [i.e., 'a condition of relationship in which sexual behavior is prohibited because a man holds in trust the . . . woman' (p. 25)] *is inherently exploitive of a woman's trust. Because he is keeper of that trust, it is the man's responsibility, no matter what level of provocation or apparent consent by the woman.*" See also Deut 22:25–26 for a situation parallel to that of David with Bathsheba: "But if the man meets the engaged woman in the open country, and the man seizes her and lies with her [the verb *šākab* and the indirect object (prepositional phrase *ʿimmāh*), just as in 2 Sam 11:4], then only the man who lay with her shall die. You shall do nothing to the young woman; the young woman has not committed an offense. . . . there was no one to rescue her." Deuteronomy 22:25–27 speaks of no one to save the woman, who presumably cried out in the countryside; the narrative of David and Bathsheba presents a similar situation, in which "all Israel" has gone off to war and Bathsheba, alone without her husband, finds herself coerced by the psychological power of the king, with "no one to rescue her."

[92] Dennis, *Sarah Laughed*, 149.

11. Bathsheba's response to word of Uriah's death (vv. 26–27). The strong emotive language used to describe Bathsheba's grieving for Uriah when she heard he was killed assures us that she was not a co-conspirator with David: she does not engage in customary "mourning" (*ʾēbel,* v. 27) but wails/laments with loud cries (*sāpad,* v. 26). The narrator here "uses a strong verb to express her wailing and lamentation, much more heavily freighted with emotion than the one he uses in the next verse of the rites of mourning."[93]

12. References to Bathsheba and Uriah at the time of Uriah's death (v. 26). The fact that the narrator still here calls her "the wife of Uriah" implies her continued fidelity to her husband, as does the reference to Uriah as "her husband." By using the term *baʿal,* "lord," to denote her husband, the narrator intimates that "if Uriah is her 'lord,' then David is not."[94] Furthermore, it is important to notice that the narrator carefully avoids using the name of Bathsheba throughout the entire episode of David's sinning, making her character more impersonal and thus perhaps further conveying the narrator's intent that Bathsheba was not personally responsible.

13. Imagery of David's ruthlessness regarding Bathsheba (v. 27). According to v. 27, after her mourning rites were over, David again sent for Bathsheba and "harvested" her; the Hebrew word *ʾāsap,* usually used for harvesting a crop or mustering an army.[95] By use of this military/agricultural term devoid of any implication of endearment or sensitivity, the narrator further implies King David's ruthlessness.

14. The narrator's explicit indictment of David, not Bathsheba (v. 27). In this same verse is a crucial statement of culpability: "The thing that David had done displeased the LORD." "David is here condemned by God, but Bathsheba is not. The most natural way to interpret that is to suppose that Bathsheba has indeed been the innocent party all along, and David's victim, not his co-conspirator."[96] Those who set forth arguments such as "She could/should have said no!" are simply not hearing the overriding theological message of the narrative.

15. Nathan's parable and interpretation indicting David and not Bathsheba (2 Sam 12:1–15). The parable told by the prophet Nathan to David in the next chapter confirms the conclusion that it is David who is indicted for his victimization of both Bathsheba and Uriah. Nathan equates the "little ewe lamb" with Bathsheba,[97] who had (like the lamb) "lain in his bosom." Dennis rightly draws the implication: "Now there can be no doubt left. The lamb in Nathan's parable is an innocent victim. Nothing could be clearer. And that means Bathsheba in

---

[93] BDB 704. Dennis, *Sarah Laughed,* 151–52.

[94] Dennis, *Sarah Laughed,* 152.

[95] BDB 62; *HALOT* 74.

[96] Dennis, *Sarah Laughed,* 152–53.

[97] Dennis, ibid., 154, points to a number of narrative details that confirm this equation. E.g., the phrase "lie in his bosom," referring to the lamb, also has sexual connotations of Bathsheba lying in the bosom of her husband, Uriah (cf. 2 Sam 12:8; 1 Kgs 1:2; Mic 7:5). Again, the mention of the lamb being like the *bat,* "daughter," is probably a play on words with the beginning of the name Bathsheba.

ch. 11 was also an innocent victim. Unless, of course, both Nathan and God have seriously misjudged the events!"[98]

Furthermore, the death of the child conceived from David's intercourse with Bathsheba is announced by Nathan as divine judgment upon David's sin, not upon the sin of both David and Bathsheba (12:13–14). Nathan could easily have used the plural pronoun—"Now the LORD has put away your [pl.] sin"—implicating both David and Bathsheba, as in other biblical narratives when the couple are indicted together, but Nathan utilizes the singular consistently throughout this passage, referring only to David's sin.

16. *The honoring of Bathsheba as progenitor of the Davidic line (2 Sam 12:24–25).* After David's repentance and the forgiveness of his sin, David and Bathsheba have another son, Solomon, and the narrator makes the striking statement that "the LORD loved him" (12:24). It is the son of Bathsheba, not of another of David's wives, who becomes the divinely appointed successor to David and part of the ongoing Davidic royal line (1 Kgs 1). Although David's part in the sexual encounter incurs sharp rebuke by Yahweh, Bathsheba is blessed by bearing the next king of Israel.

17. *Bathsheba the faithful one in the time of revolt against David (1 Kgs 1).* Far from her being a sinister character throughout the narratives of Samuel–Kings, as some have surmised, the narrator presents Bathsheba as consistently faithful to David and the concerns of the kingdom even when close associates betray the king. During the attempt by Adonijah, Solomon's older brother, to usurp the kingship, Bathsheba is one of the few individuals faithful to David in the royal court. Bathsheba, Zadok the priest, Nathan the prophet, and a few others remain faithful when even General Joab and Abiathar the priest side with Adonijah, and Bathsheba plays a decisive role, under the encouragement of Nathan, in motivating David to appoint Solomon as his coregent before it is too late (1 Kgs 1:11–31). In a later attempt by Adonijah to usurp Solomon's throne, Bathsheba reveals her trusting and forgiving spirit, even willing to ask a favor of her son Solomon on behalf of Adonijah, clearly unaware that this favor (that Adonijah be allowed to marry Abishag) is an attempt by Adonijah to take over Solomon's throne (2:13–22). The conclusion of this episode of the narrative makes apparent that King Solomon does not hold Bathsheba responsible but rather his conniving half-brother, who took advantage of Bathsheba's innocent willingness to do a favor even for one who had earlier sought to usurp the throne from her son (2:23–25).

18. *Bathsheba as progenitor of the Messiah (Matt 1:6).* Christians may add another piece of evidence regarding the character of Bathsheba. Bathsheba is chosen by the evangelist Matthew as one of five women to be included in the genealogy of Jesus the Messiah.[99] She is placed among the honored women in the line of the Messiah.

---

[98] Ibid., 155.
[99] All of these women were misunderstood, maligned, mistreated, or denigrated in some way: Tamar was wronged by Judah; Rahab was despised as a prostitute; Ruth the Moabitess was seen as a foreigner; Bathsheba has often been accused of seducing David; and Mary was suspected of marital unfaithfulness to Joseph.

In light of the evidence presented above, I conclude that Bathsheba was not a sinister character, nor an accomplice in the events described in 2 Sam 11, but an innocent victim of power rape on the part of King David. By means of numerous narrative techniques in this literary masterpiece, the narrator communicates powerfully—perhaps more powerfully than the explicit pentateuchal legal prohibitions—the divine indictment against rape, and in particular "power rape" by a person in authority.

Tamar (2 Sam 13). The last incident with rape as the focus of the narrative is the incestuous rape of Tamar by Amnon, recorded in 2 Sam 13.[100] The discussion of incest (ch. 10, above) and the discussion of the rape of Dinah above have already referred to this narrative. We also noted that this account employs specific wording for forcible rape. In this final account spotlighting rape in the OT, Amnon, David's eldest son, becomes lovesick over his beautiful virgin stepsister, Amnon, sister of Absalom, and following the advice of his crafty friend, Jonadab, he feigns sick and arranges with his father, David, that she care for and be alone with him. She prepares and serves food "in his sight" (v. 8).[101] "Voyeurism prevails."[102] But he is not satisfied with an illicit lustful look; he "took hold of [ḥāzaq in the hipʿil, 'seized'] her, and said to her, 'Come, lie with me, my sister'" (v. 11). She answers,

---

[100] For discussion of this incident, see esp. Shimeon Bar-Efrat, *Narrative Art in the Bible* (JSOTSup 70; Sheffield, Eng.: JSOT Press, 1989), 239–82; Frymer-Kensky, *Reading the Women of the Bible,* 157–69; Keefe, "Rapes of Women/Wars of Men," 79–97; Victor H. Matthews and Don C. Benjamin, *The Social World of Ancient Israel, 1250–587 B.C.E.* (Peabody, Mass.: Hendrickson, 1993), 182–86; Carol Smith, "Stories of Incest in the Hebrew Bible: Scholars Challenging Text or Text Challenging Scholars?" *Hen* 14 (1992): 227–42; and Trible, *Texts of Terror,* 37–63. Pamela Tamarkin Reis, "Cupidity and Stupidity: Woman's Agency and the 'Rape' of Tamar," *JNES* 25 (1997): 43–60, argues that this incident included incest but not rape; she concludes that "the sexual intimacy of Amnon and Tamar is consensual, and that their incestuous union is encouraged by Tamar's flirtatiousness and supported by her easy virtue, persistent ambition, and implacable stupidity" (43). Although I concur with her assessment that incest is involved, her arguments against the presence of rape are not convincing.

[101] It has been suggested by some, e.g., Reis, that since the food prepared by Tamar was *lĕbibôt,* which may be literally translated "heart-cakes," a romantic relationship between Tamar and Amnon is implied. But although it is true that *lĕbibôt* refers to "heart-cakes," probably made in the shape of a heart (*HALOT* 516), this kind of cake was particularly requested by Amnon, not brought spontaneously by Tamar. Such a request would not have carried any connotation of romantic relationship, since the word for "heart-cakes" probably indicates its function as well as (or even instead of) its shape, i.e., "to 'enhearten' the sick person and make his life force flow" (Frymer-Kensky, *Reading the Women of the Bible,* 159). This interpretation is confirmed by comparing this word with the specific term used by Amnon's friend Jonadab for "food" in his suggestion of what Amnon could request that Tamar bring to his house (2 Sam 13:5); the term is *biryâ,* "patient's food" (*HALOT* 156), a word that comes from the root meaning "fat" or "healthy" and well may refer to a "healing substance." Thus, as Frymer-Kensky notes, "The *birya* is not simply a food, and making it is not simply an act of cooking; it is the preparation of a medicinal concoction" (*Reading the Women of the Bible,* 158).

[102] Trible, *Texts of Terror,* 43.

"No, my brother, do not force [ʿinnâ, violate/rape] me; for such a thing is not done in Israel; do not do anything so vile [nĕbālâ]!" (v. 12). Tamar, like Joseph, "tries to speak from the high moral ground."[103] She appeals to her would-be assailant that his doing such an act would be a moral outrage in Israel.

Tamar also speaks (v. 13) of the personal "reproach" (or 'shame' [ḥerpâ]) that would be hers and the reputation of being an "impious and presumptuous fool [nābāl]"[104] that would be his. Then she tries to talk Amnon into delaying the gratification of his sexual desire, by suggesting that he speak to the king, their father, "for he will not withhold me from you."[105] But Amnon will not be dissuaded, and in the heat of his lustful passion, "being stronger than she, he forced [ʿinnāh] her and lay with her ['raped,' lit. 'lay her,' without the preposition, to stress the brutality]" (v. 14). Then his so-called love—which is really lust—turns to spiteful hate. "The crime is despicable; the aftermath, ominous."[106] He says, in effect, "Get up and get out!" Over her futile protestations, despite her pleading, in broken sentences of shock and anguish, not to be stripped of her last vestige of dignity,[107] Amnon tells his servant to "Put this woman [lit. 'put *this* (no mention of 'woman')] out of my presence, and bolt the door after her" (v. 17). "She has become for him solely a disposable object."[108]

In this passage, narrative space is given not only to the violent act but also to the woman's psychological experience of rape. Several authors have pointed out that the narrative is carefully crafted in a chiastic structure, with the central focal point drawing attention to the brutality and violation inflicted upon Tamar and showing how this tragedy was the turning point in her life.[109] The story, with its revelation of multidimensional violence on the part of Amnon—physical, emotional, and social—serves to call forth from the reader a sense of outrage against such violence and sympathy for Tamar the victim. This account, unlike the other rape cases, provides space to reveal the woman's personal torment after the rape and brutal ejection from the rapist's presence like a piece of unwanted trash (see vv. 15–18): "But Tamar put ashes on her head, and tore the long robe that she was wearing; she put her hand on her head, and went away, crying aloud as she

---

103 Frymer-Kensky, *Reading the Women of the Bible*, 160.

104 BDB 614. Cf. *HALOT* 663, referring to "infamous people in a misdirected profession."

105 For the interpretation of this suggestion, and the ramifications regarding the current practice of brother-sister incest and what Tamar may have been implying with this statement, see the discussion of this narrative in ch. 10, above.

106 Trible, *Texts of Terror*, 47.

107 Frymer-Kensky translates literally with the added words to make sense in brackets: "Don't [do this]! Concerning this great evil—[it is greater] than the one which you did to me.—Sending me away [is worse than the other evil you did by raping me]" (*Reading the Women of the Bible*, 164).

108 Trible, *Texts of Terror*, 48.

109 See George Ridout, "The Rape of Tamar: A Rhetorical Analysis of 2 Sam 13:1–22," in *Rhetorical Criticism: Essays in Honor of James Muilenberg* (ed. Jared J. Jackson and Martin Kessler; PTMS 1; Pittsburgh: Pickwick, 1974), 81–83; Trible, *Texts of Terror*, 43–44; cf. Keefe, "Rapes of Women/Wars of Men," 91.

went" (v. 19).[110] Her full brother Absalom was no comfort; as too often in cases of domestic rape, where the family tries to belittle the seriousness of the rape and cover up the crime, Absalom minimizes what happened to her by not identifying the offense as rape ("Has Amnon your brother been with you?"), and then he tries to silence her: "Be quiet for now, my sister; he is your brother; do not take this to heart" (v. 20). "Like so many other victims of domestic rape, she joins the conspiracy of silence that dooms her";[111] for two years she "remained, a desolate woman, in her brother Absalom's house" (v. 20). The word for "desolate" (root *šmm*), when used elsewhere in Scripture for people, refers to those who have been destroyed by an enemy or torn to pieces by an animal (Lam 1:16; 3:11; Isa 54:1). Tamar is a broken woman.

King David, her father, paralyzed by his own moral indiscretions, allows the shameful crime of Amnon to pass unrebuked and unpunished. But the rape ultimately leads to murder—Absalom kills his brother Amnon to avenge his sister's rape (2 Sam 13:23–34)—thus partially fulfilling David's unwitting sentence upon himself that "he shall restore the lamb fourfold" (12:6) after hearing Nathan's parable. The second of David's four sons falls as a result of his sin.[112] As if to pay tribute to this violated daughter, the narrator provides information about Absalom's children—three sons and one daughter—and only the daughter is named: "one daughter whose name was Tamar; she was a beautiful woman" (14:27). The narrator records that a living memorial has been raised for Absalom's raped sister.

These stories reveal rape to be (both then and now) "a particular kind of human violence . . . in which women's bodies, always implicitly subject to male possession, are objectified, fetishized, and freely violated. The threat of rape appears for us as a perpetual assault upon woman's autonomy, power and personhood."[113] In the face of such violation of the dignity and personhood of woman, what should be our reaction? Contrary to many scholarly warnings to remain "objective" and emotionally detached and avoid terminology such as "revolting" to describe these incidents, the text insists that we respond in shock and horror

---

[110] Frymer-Kensky, *Reading the Women of the Bible,* 185, points out that this public spectacle may be understood in light of a Middle Assyrian law (MAL A §23; *COS* 2.132:355–56; cited above in the section on ANE backgrounds) indicating that if a woman was tricked into adulterous sex, she must make public declaration immediately that she was victimized or she would be treated as an adulteress. Perhaps in a parallel situation, by crying out, Tamar made public declaration of her innocence in addition to expressing her personal torment after the rape. Lipka, " 'Such a Thing Is Not Done in Israel,' " 295, suggests that Tamar's robe of many colors symbolized her special status of virgin princess and her tearing of the robe signaled her loss of virginity.

[111] Frymer-Kensky, *Reading the Women of the Bible,* 167.

[112] The first was the child of the adulterous affair with Bathsheba (as noted in ch. 8, above); Amnon was the second to die, Absalom the third (2 Sam 18), and Adonijah the fourth (1 Kgs 2). See Dominic Rudman, "Reliving the Rape of Tamar: Absalom's Revenge in 2 Samuel 13," *OTE* 11 (1998): 326–39, for evidence that "Absalom's murder of his brother is in fact a replaying of the circumstances surrounding Tamar's rape, with Amnon as the principle victim" (327).

[113] Keefe, "Rapes of Women/Wars of Men," 79.

against the crime and in sympathy for the victim. "If the reader is not moved to some sort of emotion—whether it is horror, sympathy, or anger—one can only feel that the biblical writer has failed in what he intended to do. . . . Surely we are meant to see that the behavior of Amnon was as totally and utterly repugnant then as it is now (Absalom certainly regarded it as repugnant). Why else include the episode at all?"[114] Trible concludes her discussion of the Tamar narrative with a rhetorical question: "Who will preserve sister wisdom from the adventurer, the rapist with his smooth words, lecherous eyes, and grasping hands? In answering this question, Israel is found wanting—*and so are we.*"[115]

Rape and Divine Grace

In the HB, God is portrayed as the defender of the oppressed, including victims of rape. Never is there any hint in Scripture that the rape victim is assigned guilt. "Anyone who attributes to the rapist anything less than *all* the blame is making up his or her own ideas, not reflecting those of the Bible."[116] According to the biblical witness, God is always on the side of the rape victim. Although judgment is sometimes delayed against the perpetrators of abuse and rape, God promises that ultimately those who have suffered unjustly will be vindicated.[117] Scripture "also offers a deeper hope to victims of rape and other major traumas: If they continue to cultivate their relationship with God, *God can turn their pain into healing for themselves and for others.*"[118]

Although the severe legal penalty for rape reveals God's revulsion for this distortion of sexuality, those who have committed rape are proffered the same word of divine grace and forgiveness and empowerment for purity as those who have committed other sexual sins (see ch. 8, above, regarding adultery and extramarital sex). Scripture is explicit that God offers forgiveness for the repentant rapist. Note the prophetic word to David after he repented of his power rape of Bathsheba: "Now the LORD has put away your sin; you shall not die" (2 Sam 12:13). But forgiveness here did not mitigate divine justice; thus, for example, in the case of David, his son born out of the illegitimate sexual encounter died as judgment for David's sin (12:14).[119]

---

114 Smith, "Stories of Incest," 238, 241.

115 Trible, *Texts of Terror,* 57.

116 Keener, "Some Biblical Reflections," 129.

117 Keener, ibid., provides the following biblical passages to support the concept of divine vindication of the oppressed: Deut 32:43; 2 Kgs 9:7; Ps 79:10; cf. Rev 6:10; 16:6; 19:2.

118 Ibid., 130.

119 Many evangelical Christians see in this narrative an intimation of the ultimate Son of David, the Messiah, who died to take the penalty of all repentant sinners. Keener provides an evangelical Christian perspective on the substitutionary death of Jesus regarding repentant rapists: "According to biblical teaching, when Jesus died on the cross, God was not ignoring justice; God was punishing Jesus in our place. That is the greatest act of avenging justice on our behalf possible" ("Some Biblical Reflections," 129).

Sexuality as Unwholesome, Ugly, and Evil

Besides the clear and unmixed ugliness of rape, one may argue that, in a sense, all of the distortions of sexuality that have been discussed in previous chapters of this study are ultimately attacks upon the wholesomeness, beauty, and goodness of sexuality as presented in the Edenic ideal. The recital of sexual misconduct as recorded in the pentateuchal narratives serves to point up the explosive and potentially disruptive force of human sexuality after the fall. It is no surprise that in order to preserve the moral integrity of the individual, the family, and society, according to the canonical text of Scripture, God provided detailed legislation—at Sinai (Exodus and Leviticus) and on the borders of the promised land (Deuteronomy)—regulating the sexual practices of Israel.

The narratives of the Former Prophets depict in grim detail the distortion of sexuality from the wholesome beauty that God intended. The sexual tragedies surrounding Samson's life, mentioned in earlier chapters of this study, are a prime exemple. The Samson narrative in Judges displays beautiful sexuality gone awry, focusing mainly on various erotic attachments formed in the indulgence of unrestrained or unlawful sexual passions. First is the marriage based solely on physical attraction: Samson demands of his father after seeing a daughter of the Philistines at Timnah, "Get her for me, because she pleases me" (Judg 14:3). Next comes a display of physical lust outside marriage: in an affair in which love has no part, Samson enjoys sexual relations with a harlot of Gaza (16:1–3). Finally, Samson indeed "loves" a woman (Delilah—"darling"), but it is an unrequited love in which the blind passion that enslaved him finally led to total physical blindness and enslavement by the Philistines.[120]

The erotic exploits of Samson reveal a decadent sexuality in which the beautiful divine ideal has been hopelessly marred. Wholesome sexuality degenerates into sensuality and sentimentality; the spiritual dimension is ignored in the self-centered search for what "pleases me well." Woman is no longer the helper/benefactor in a loving relationship but a traitor, a harlot, a temptress. The husband no longer considers his wife an equal partner but chattel, like cattle: "If you had not plowed with my heifer, you would not have found out my riddle" (14:18). The multifaceted loving and lasting relationship between husband and wife has evaporated in the fires of lust and distrust.

The concluding narrative in Judge 19–21 is a "text of terror"[121] that all too vividly portrays the explosive nature and destructive capacity of decadent sexuality. In its outworking, the story runs virtually the entire gamut of sexual aberrations, discussed in this and previous chapters of this study. A Levite engages in concubinage, and the concubine "became angry with him"

---

[120] See James L. Crenshaw, *Samson: A Secret Betrayed, a Vow Ignored* (Atlanta: John Knox, 1978), 65–98, for identification and analysis of these three kinds of erotic attachments in Samson's career.

[121] See Trible's literary-feminist study of the narrative in *Texts of Terror,* 65–92.

(19:1–2);[122] the men of Gibeah, "a perverse lot," make violent homosexual advances against the Levite (v. 22); and both the Levite and his host are willing to subject women (the concubine and/or the virgin daughter) to the ravishing of the mob to save their own lives (vv. 23–24). The concubine is sexually abused (gang raped) all night and dies at the doorstep in the morning (vv. 25–28). Her body is mutilated—and sent throughout Israel as a call to action against the "wanton crime" committed in Gibeah. After describing the decimation of the tribe of Benjamin in their attempt to defend the city of Gibeah, the book concludes with a shocking solution to a sexual problem. In order to take care of the lack of eligible women for the surviving men of Benjamin, four hundred young virgins are spared in the mass slaughter of Jabesh-gilead and given to the Benjaminites, and the men of Benjamin still without wives are told to "come out of the vineyards and each of you carry off a wife for himself from the young women of Shiloh" (21:21) who are dancing at the yearly festival. Beautiful sexuality has turned ugly, violent, and repulsive.

The books of Samuel and Kings reveal wholesome sexuality gone awry (see previous chapters in this study). David and Solomon fall prey to the prevailing customs of bigamy, polygamy, or concubinage. The author faithfully records the anguish and disharmony experienced in having a rival wife, and the disastrous personal and national results of kings multiplying wives to themselves. Samuel and Kings also present a checkered account of extramarital sexual aberrations during the time of the monarchy. From the sexual promiscuity of Eli's sons (1 Sam 2:22) to David's power rape of Bathsheba and the incestuous rape of Tamar by Amnon, to Absalom's blatant affairs with David's concubines, to the matter-of-fact stories of harlots and eunuchs[123] and possible allusions to effeminate men and male prostitutes (lit. "dogs," 2 Kgs 8:13)—throughout the period wholesome sexuality is in decay. The parallel narratives in Chronicles likewise "chronicle" the sordid saga of decadent sexuality. Throughout this whole period, sexuality is distorted as it is juxtaposed with violence[124] and as it becomes a manipulative political tool in the hands of powerful men.[125]

---

[122] According to the MT, the concubine *wattizneh ʿālāyw* (usually translated "played the harlot against") the Levite, i.e., was unfaithful to him. But the LXX reads *ōrgisthē autō*, "became angry with him," which is preferred by many recent commentators and some modern translations (e.g., the NJB and NRSV). See Robert G. Boling, *Judges: A New Translation with Introduction and Commentary* (AB 6a; Garden City, N.Y.: Doubleday, 1975), 273–74; G. F. Moore, *Judges* (ICC; Edinburgh: T&T Clark, 1895), 409–10. J. Alberto Soggin, *Judges* (OTL; Philadelphia: Westminster, 1981), 284, following KBL, suggests that *zānâ* here in the MT is possibly a separate root related to the Akkadian cognate *zenū*, "to be angry, hate." (So also *HALOT* 275, s.v. זנהII, which translates the term in Judg 19:2 as "to feel repugnance against.") All of these interpretations make good sense in this context, making it difficult to decide which is the preferred reading/interpretation.

[123] 1 Kgs 3:16–28; 22:38; 2 Kgs 9:32; 23:11.

[124] For exploration of this juxtaposition of sex and violence throughout Scripture, see, e.g., Cheryl A. Kirk-Duggan, ed., *Pregnant Passion: Gender, Sex, and Violence in the Bible* (SemeiaSt 44; Atlanta: Society of Biblical Literature, 2003).

[125] Among the many studies of "sexual politics" in the HB, focused esp. upon the period of the Former Prophets, see, e.g., Bailey, *David in Love and War;* Danna Nolan

In the Latter as well as the Former Prophets, God's original design for sexuality as a beautiful creation ordinance has also been distorted in the divinized sex of the fertility cult orgies. Israel's departure from a wholesome, beautiful relationship with God is compared by the prophets to sexual infidelity, the prophets even utilizing the vulgar terminology of the brothel (see esp. Ezek 16 and 23, discussed in ch. 7, above) to portray the vile distortion of the divine ideal. Beautiful sexuality is twisted into heinous distortions of God's character and the divine-human relationship.

Distorted Sexuality as a Parody of Beauty

The Wisdom literature of the Writings presents the "two ways": (1) the way of divine wisdom, the way of the fear of the Lord, which leads to life (Prov 1:6, 4:22–23); and (2) the way of men's natural foolish inclinations, the "way that seems right to a person, but its end is the way to death" (14:12; 16:25). The book of Proverbs may accurately be called "The Book of the Two Ways."

The two ways enter into every sphere of man's practical existence, and man's choice of whether to have "your ear attentive to wisdom" (2:2) decides his destiny. Perhaps nowhere are the two ways more evident then in areas of sexuality: hence the extolling of wholesome sexuality interwoven with warnings against destructive sexual relationships; hence the extended juxtapositioning of Lady Wisdom with the "loose woman."[126]

Fewell and David M. Gunn, *Gender, Power, and Promise: The Subject of the Bible's First Story* (Nashville: Abingdon, 1993); Esther Fuchs, *Sexual Politics in the Biblical Narrative: Reading the Hebrew Bible as a Woman* (JSOTSup 310; Sheffield, Eng.: Sheffield Academic Press, 2000); John Kessler, "Sexuality and Politics: The Motif of the Displaced Husband in the Books of Samuel," *CBQ* 62 (2000): 409–23; Klein, *From Deborah to Esther;* Jon D. Levenson and Baruch Halpern, "The Political Import of David's Marriages," *JBL* 99 (1980): 507–18; Spielman, "David's Abuse of Power," 251–59; Sternberg, "Biblical Poetics and Sexual Politics"; Stone, *Sex, Honor, and Power,* passim; and Shlomit Yaron, "The Politics of Sex—Woman's Body as an Instrument for Achieving Man's Aims," *OTE* 15 (2002): 269–92. Some of these studies define "sexual politics" to include far more than the abuse of sex by men in power; the term refers "more specifically to the economic, social, and ideological arrangements whereby males have traditionally controlled females.... 'Biblical sexual politics' refers to the ways which the Bible promotes the idea of woman's subordination to man" (Esther Fuchs, "The Literary Characterization of Mothers and Sexual Politics in the Hebrew Bible," in *Feminist Perspectives on Biblical Scholarship* [ed. Adela Yarbro Collins; Chico, Calif.: Scholars Press, 1985], 117). I strongly affirm that the abuse of sex by powerful men is clearly seen when one reads *with* the biblical text, but I do not follow the feminist agenda of counterreading the narratives in order to lay bare what is regarded as the narrators' own androcentric sexual politics.

[126] See esp. Claudia V. Camp, *Wisdom and the Feminine in the Book of Proverbs* (Decatur, Ga.: Almond, 1985); idem, "Wise and Strange: An Interpretation of the Female Imagery in Proverbs in Light of Trickster Mythology," *Semeia* 42 (1988): 14–36; idem, "Woman Wisdom and the Strange Woman: Where Is Power to Be Found?" in *Reading Bibles, Writing Bodies: Identity and the Book* (ed. Timothy K. Beal and David M. Gunn;

The first part of the present chapter examined the way of beautiful married sexuality portrayed in Proverbs. There is, however, another way—the way of the fool, the way of destructive sexual relationships. To man's natural drives and inclinations, this path is alluring. As evident in the discussion of adultery (ch. 8, above), the way of illicit sexuality lures by offering secret and forbidden pleasure. But its appeal can ultimately gain legitimacy only because it parades itself as beautiful and attractive. In fact, however, illicit sex is a parody of beauty. The alluring and entrapping power of the "strange," "loose," or "foreign" woman lies in her presentation of a counterfeit to the real thing. A close literary analysis of the speeches of the foreign woman—who is a figure combining the characteristics of "the alien, harlotrous, evil, adulterous, and foolish woman"[127]—shows that this immoral woman is intentionally portrayed by the author of Proverbs as the antithesis of Lady Wisdom. "Both women are described in dangerously similar terms; both speak perilously similar messages to beckon the young man to their respective houses."[128]

In the extended instruction of Prov 1–9, the father warns his son against the wiles of the ʾiššâ zārâ, "loose woman," by showing how closely her allurements resemble the way of Lady Wisdom. Depicting the loose woman and Wisdom with the same terminology, the father teaches that "the greatest seduction to evil consists in inviting the foolish with the same words that summon one to good."[129] The ʾiššâ zārâ is portrayed as lying in wait in the streets and market places (7:11–12), and Wisdom also is in the streets and market places, crying out loudly (1:20–21). The seductress calls out, "Come," as does Wisdom (7:18; cf. 9:5); both invite the naive to their houses (7:15–20; 9:4) for a banquet (9:17; 9:5). Indeed, the two women allure with the same phrase, "You who are simple, turn in here!" (9:16; 9:4). Both describe their way as nʿm, "pleasant" (9:17; 3:17); both seek to be ʾhb, "loved" (7:18; 4:6), and ḥbq, "embraced" (5:20; 4:8).

The immoral woman speaks to the naive young man as would a genuine lover to her beloved or a spouse to her real husband. She tells of seeking her lover and finding him (7:15); of preparing the perfumes of the bed for making love (7:16–17); and of beckoning her lover, "Come, let us take our fill of [rāwâ] love until morning; let us delight ourselves with love" (7:18). The same word, rāwâ, "to take

London: Routledge, 1997), 85–112; Cosby, *Sex in the Bible,* 35–40; Gail Corrington Streete, *The Strange Woman: Power and Sex in the Bible* (Louisville: Westminster John Knox, 1997), 101–19; and Gale A. Yee, "'I Have Perfumed My Bed with Myrrh': The Foreign Woman (ʾiššâ zārâ) in Proverbs 1–9," *JSOT* 43 (1989): 53–68; repr., pages 110–30 in *A Feminist Companion to Wisdom Literature* (ed. Athalya Brenner; FCB 9; Sheffield, Eng.: Sheffield Academic Press, 1995).

[127] Yee, "'I Have Perfumed My Bed,'" 53–68, substantiates that the various epithets—alien woman, evil woman, harlot, adulteress, and foolish woman—are used in parallelism in Prov 1–9 and all refer to one woman described variously rather than to different women. The ʾiššâ zārâ, "loose woman," is the immoral seductress with a unity of attributes. This parallels the personification of Wisdom, who is also depicted under the attributes of knowledge, discretion, and understanding.

[128] Ibid., 53.

[129] Ibid., 62.

one's fill of, to be saturated with," is used of the husband's satisfaction with his wife (5:19).[130]

Although there are numerous terminological similarities, there are major theological differences. The parody distorts the true. The most obvious difference is that what Wisdom offers—the way of wholesome, joyous married sexuality—continues to satisfy whereas the way of illicit sex with an immoral woman does not last. "The love of the true wife will fill her beloved at all times. The love of the ʾiššâ zārâ is transitory. It lasts until morning, until the return of her cuckolded husband."[131] But there is a more ominous difference. The way of Wisdom (and wise, wholesome sexuality) leads to life whereas the way of the fool (and illicit sex) leads to death. This point is subtly indicated, for example, in 7:16–17, where the choice of wording to describe the luxury and sensual enjoyment of the seductress's bed simultaneously depicts the imagery of burial: "The fool of Prov. vii is lured by the woman's choice wording in vv. 16–17, all the while oblivious to her intention to prepare him for burial. . . . These mortuary aspects of the seductress's bed chamber become explicit at the end of the passage (vv. 26–27)."[132]

The same point is perhaps most forcefully made in 5:15–23 by means of the threefold repetition of the verb šāgâ, "to stagger, become intoxicated." As noted above, this term is used for the intoxifying captivation of this husband for the wife of his youth (v. 19). But the term also appears in v. 20, describing the sensuous experience of being "intoxicated" (šāgâ) by an immoral woman. Not apparent in most English translations, the same term appears also in v. 23 to describe the result of the one who succumbs to the wiles of the immoral woman: "They die for lack of discipline, and because of their great folly they are lost [šāgâ, 'stagger/be intoxicated']." "The husband may choose to be intoxicated and stagger in the pleasure that his wife gives (v. 19) or choose to embrace the bosom of another woman and stagger into the arms of death (v. 23a)."[133] The destructive results of illicit sex are described in great detail in Proverbs (see ch. 8, above on adultery).

---

[130] Note, however, that rāwâ appears in the simple qal in the mouth of the seductress (7:18), while the description of the wholesome lovemaking within the confines of marriages utilizes rāwâ in the intensive piʿel stem, which can mean not only "be saturated," but "be intoxicated, drunk." By shifting from qal to piʿel, the wise man may be highlighting the superiority of beautiful married love over its parody in extra-marital relations.

[131] Ibid., 63. Unfortunately, Yee's radical-feminist bias does not enable her to see the implication of this fact for her thesis. She ultimately focuses only on the similar language for the two kinds of women, which she thinks shows the hopelessly patriarchal stance of the author with his "pervasive suspicion of the words of woman," which "cast[s] aspersions on anything prophetic a woman might say to rock the patriarchal boat," and, what is more insidious, "what might be accepted as wisdom from the mouth of one woman can by the same token be discerned by men as destructive in the mouth of another woman" (p. 66). For her, Prov 1–9 leaves unresolved crucial questions: "Can a woman ever seek and ultimately find Wisdom? Or does she simply suffer the fate of the ʾiššâ zārâ, an object of aversion and ever condemned?" (67).

[132] For a discussion of the mortuary aspects (linen burial cloth, burial spice mixes) in this passage, see Robert H. O'Connell, "Proverbs VII 16–17: A Case of Fatal Deception in a 'Woman and the Window' Type-Scene," VT 41 (1991): 235–41.

[133] Kaiser, "True Marital Love," 109.

Underneath the erotic veneer of the parody presented by the immoral woman is a totally different atmosphere from that of wholesome married sexual love. Several studies have compared the way of the immoral woman of Proverbs with the view of wholesome and beautiful sexuality in 5:15–23 and/or the Song of Songs (the book to which we turn shortly).[134] Striking is the contrast in fundamental outlook between the joyful sexual relationship of married love in both Song of Songs and Prov 5:13–23 and the immoral and ominous liaison with the seductress described by Solomon especially in Prov 7. Although both contain the motif of eroticism, with the language of love (breasts/nipples, intoxication, bed of spices, terms of endearment) and the hide-and-seek-and-find theme (seeking, finding, grasping, kissing, locale of the search, night setting, the sexual goal), there is an entirely different tone. Whereas licit married love emphasizes reciprocity, mutuality and equality between both of the lovers (evidenced by actions, speech, and interchangeability of roles), in the illicit affair this is subverted.

Daniel Grossberg notes nineteen actions of the loose woman in Prov 7:

> The woman is the sole initiator of the action and the prime actor. The young man is largely passive and acted upon, whereas she speaks smoothly, comes toward him, is boisterous, is rebellious; she lurks, she grabs, she kisses, she acts defiantly, she finds him, she decks her couch, she sprinkles her bed, invites him to drink deeply of love and to revel in love, she sways him, she leads him astray, and she strikes many dead.[135]

The young man, by contrast, is the subject of only four verbs in the twenty-six verses of the chapter ("passing along the street near her corner, taking the road to her house" [Prov. 7:8]; "Right away he follows her" [v. 22]; "not knowing" [v. 23]). Note also that the young man utters no words in the whole of Prov 7.

Whereas there is exclusiveness and uniqueness in the divinely designed relationship of Prov 5 and Song of Songs, the seductress is indiscriminate in Prov 7. Although the temptress feigns exclusivity to her victim—"I have come out to meet you, to seek you eagerly, and I have found you!" (Prov 7:15)—the reader knows what the young man learns too late: "for many are those she has laid low, and numerous are her victims" (7:26). Whereas Prov 5 and the Song of Songs speak of peace and harmony (the *šlm* root appears eighteen times in the Song of Songs) and blessing and joy (Prov 5:18–19), the affair with the loose woman in Prov 7 is filled with conflict, contention, exploitation, domination, and violence (see esp. 7:23). Whereas Prov. 5 affirms the family and household (5:18; cf. 31:11,

---

134 See esp. Alter, *The Art of Biblical Poetry,* 179–84; Brevard S. Childs, *Biblical Theology in Crisis* (Philadelphia: Fortress, 1970), 184–202; Daniel Grossberg, "Two Kinds of Sexual Relations in the Hebrew Bible," *HS* 34 (1994): 7–25; Kaiser, "True Marital Love," 106–16; and Martin Paul, "Die 'fremde Frau' in Sprichwörter 1–9 und die 'Geliebte' des Hohenliedes: Ein Beitrag zur Intertextualität," *BN* 106 (2001): 40–46.

135 Grossberg, "Two Kinds of Sexual Relations," 12. For a more popularized "portrayal of a foolish woman" based on Prov 7, see Nancy Leigh DeMoss, "Portrait of a Foolish Woman," in *Biblical Womanhood in the Home* (ed. Nancy Leigh DeMoss; Foundations for the Family Series; Wheaton, Ill.: Crossway, 2002), 83–100.

15, 23, 27–28), in Prov 7 all ties with family are severed: "her feet do not stay at home" (7:11); the one reference to her husband is to "my husband," who has gone on a long trip (7:19–20). Finally, as already noted, in the Song and Prov 5, love is preeminent, stronger than death, leading to life (Prov 5:19; cf. 8:35); but in Prov 7, the end of all is death (7:22–27). The way of immorality is indeed a pernicious parody of true intimacy and beauty in sexual love.

⚜ ⚜ ⚜

The wholesome beauty and joy of married sexual love as described in Prov 5:15–23 has been recently described as "a convenient entry point into the interpretation of the Song of Songs (the 'greatest' of songs)" and, even more, "an interpretative key to the entire book of Song of Songs."[136] Kaiser suggests, in light of the strong terminological parallels, which he examines (especially in the metaphors of cistern, well, and fountain), and an assumed common author, that "if the purpose of Prov 5:15–23 is to teach the importance of the exclusiveness of marriage and the joys and benefits of marital fidelity, there is every confidence that this is the best way to understand the Song."[137] The testing and outworking of this hypothesis will occupy our attention in the last chapters of this study.

"And I will show you a still more excellent way" (1 Cor 12:31). What Paul said of the love chapter in the NT applies equally to the one book in the Writings—and in all of Scripture—that deals directly, exclusively, and comprehensively with sexuality. This book, the most beautiful Song of Songs, provides the climax and capstone to the OT theology of sexuality. Let us return to Eden—to the holy of holies.

---

[136] Kaiser, "True Marital Love," 112, 111.
[137] Ibid., 113.

Section 3

Return to Eden

𝕀13

Sexuality in the Song of Songs: The Holy of Holies

"For in all the world there is nothing to equal the day on which the Song of Songs was given to Israel, for all the writings are Holy, but the Song of Songs is the Holy of Holies."[1] Thus Rabbi Akiba in the council at Yavneh (ca. 90 C.E.) purportedly expressed his vision of the exalted importance of the Song of Songs (also called the Canticle of Canticles). According to tradition, Akiba's speech reconfirmed the Song's place in the already established canon of Hebrew Scripture.[2]

Allegorization of the Song of Songs

Unfortunately, the speech did not also serve to reconfirm a lofty conception of sexuality. Even the Jewish rabbis, with their basically healthy and robust view of sexuality, apparently had great difficulty seeing how what seemed to be a purely secular love song such as the *Shir Hashirim* (Song of Songs) could be included in the sacred canon. Therefore they adopted and developed an elaborate allegorical interpretation of the Song that downplayed the literal sense in favor of a hidden, spiritual meaning. When Akiba said the Song of Songs was the holy of holies, what he probably had in mind was that the Song was a detailed allegory of the historical relationship between the divine presence (the Shechinah, in the holy of holies) and the people of Israel from the exodus onward to the coming of

---

[1] *m. Yad.* 3:5.

[2] See esp. Jack P. Lewis, "Jamnia Revisited," in *The Canon Debate* (ed. Lee Martin McDonald and James A. Sanders; Peabody, Mass.: Hendrickson, 2002), 146–63. Lewis shows that the critical consensus of the last century—of a three-stage closing of the Hebrew canon, with the Writings closed in the council at Yavneh—is no longer viable. Rather, according to the new consensus, there is evidence of a tripartite canon already closed well before the first century C.E., and the discussion held in the council at Yavneh regarding Ecclesiastes and the Song of Songs confirmed the canonical status of what had already been recognized as such in pre-Christian times. In other words, the discussions at Yavneh had only haggadic, not halakic (legal), force. Cf. Gerhard F. Hasel, "Divine Inspiration and the Canon of the Bible," *JATS* 5, no. 1 (1994): 90–91; and Magne Sæbø, "On the Canonicity of the Song of Songs," in *Texts, Temples, and Traditions: A Tribute to Menahem Haran* (ed. Michael V. Fox et al.; Winona Lake, Ind.: Eisenbrauns, 1996), 267–77.

the Messiah.[3] Thus Akiba warned against taking the Song of Songs only as a human love song: "He who trills his voice in the chanting of the Song of Songs and treats it as a secular song has no share in the world to come."[4] According to rabbinic tradition, the Song of Songs was not to be read until one reached the age of thirty.[5]

Christian allegorists went even further than the rabbis: they not only downplayed but virtually rejected the literal sense altogether. Influenced by the pagan Greek philosophers of Platonic dualism, Stoicism, and the Hellenistic-Roman cults, they posited a dichotomy between things of the flesh and things of the spirit.[6] Purity was associated with sexual renunciation, and all expressions of

---

[3] See Marvin H. Pope, Song of Songs (AB 7C; Garden City, N.Y.: Doubleday, 1977), 89–112, for a description of the development and content of the normative Jewish interpretation of the Song of Songs as pioneered by Akiba and found full-flowered in Targum Song of Songs. In the latter the following historical periods appear to be the allegorical referents of the major divisions:

1. exodus and entry into Canaan—Song 1:2–3:6
2. Solomon's temple—Song 3:7–5:1
3. sin and exile—Song 5:2–6:1
4. rebuilding of the temple—Song 6:2–7:11 (ET 6:2–7:10)
5. Roman diaspora and coming of the Messiah—Song 7:12–8:14 (ET 7:11–8:14)

Specific details of the Song have been interpreted variously. Thus, e.g., the Shulammite's two breasts were seen by different Jewish authors to represent Moses and Aaron, the two Messiahs (son of David and son of Ephraim), Moses and Phinehas, and Joshua and Eleazar (see Dennis F. Kinlaw, "Song of Songs," EBC 5:1203). For further discussion of Jewish interpretation of the Song of Songs, see Duane A. Garrett, "Song of Songs," in Duane A. Garrett and Paul R. House, Song of Songs, Lamentations (WBC 23B; Nashville: Nelson, 2004), 60–64; Christian David Ginsburg, The Song of Songs and Coheleth (Commonly Called Ecclesiastes): Translated from the Original Hebrew, with a Commentary, Historical and Critical (2 vols.; 1857–1861; repr., 2 vols. in 1; LBS; New York: Ktav, 1970), 20–60; Tremper Longman III, The Song of Songs (NICOT; Grand Rapids: Eerdmans, 2001), 24–28; Roland E. Murphy, The Song of Songs: A Commentary on the Book of Canticles or the Song of Songs (Hermeneia; Minneapolis: Fortress, 1990), 12–16, 28–32; Jacob Neusner, Israel's Love Affair with God: Song of Songs (Bible of Judaism Library; Valley Forge, Pa.: Trinity Press International, 1993), passim; and Weston W. Fields, "Early and Medieval Jewish Interpretation of the Song of Songs," GTJ 2 (1980): 221–31. Fields shows that the earliest Jewish interpretations of the Song (LXX, Ben Sira, Wisdom of Solomon, Josephus, 4 Ezra) do not allegorize; the allegorical hermeneutic enters only in the Christian era and becomes the accepted method of interpretation in the Talmud, midrashim, and Targumim.

[4] t. Sanh. 12:10. William E. Phipps, Recovering Biblical Sensuousness (Philadelphia: Westminster, 1975), 47, alternatively argues that Akiba was opposed to the use of the Song as a "vulgar" or "bawdy" song outside the context of marital love.

[5] Jerome, Comm. Ezech. 1.praef., preserves the record of this tradition. The Song of Songs was one of four portions of Scripture that were regarded as forming a more advanced course of study for students. Besides the Song, these scriptural portions included the beginning of Genesis (the account of creation), Ezek 1 and 10 (the description of the cherubim), and Ezek 40–48 (the description of the building of the temple).

[6] The influence of Platonic dualism and gnostic thinking is emphasized, e.g., by Harry Austryn Wolfson, The Philosophy of the Church Fathers: Faith, Trinity, Incarnation

bodily pleasure—including sexual expression—were considered evil. In the Song of Songs all erotic imagery was allegorized as the yearning of the soul for union with God or as an expression of Christ's love for his church. As by allegory the Greek philosophers had succeeded in transforming the sensuous gods of Homer and Hesiod into ethereal, spiritual ideals, so the celibate church theologians were "able by allegory to unsex the Sublime Song and make it a hymn of spiritual love without carnal taint."[7]

Origen of Alexandria (d. 254 C.E.), one of the foremost early Christian proponents of the allegorical method of biblical interpretation, wrote a ten-volume commentary of nearly twenty thousand lines on the Song of Songs. In the prologue to his commentary, he warns that the Song of Songs is safe reading only for mature persons no longer troubled by sexual desires: "I advise and counsel everyone who is not yet rid of the vexations of flesh and blood and has not ceased to feel the passion of his bodily nature, to refrain completely from reading this little book and the things that will be said about it." Origen refers to a Jewish tradition "to allow no one even to hold this book in his hands, who has not reached a full and ripe age." In his commentary Origen warns against taking literally the sexual content of the Song: "Wherefore we also, from the position where we find ourselves, earnestly beg the hearers of these things to mortify their carnal senses. They must not take anything of what has been said with reference to bodily functions but rather employ them for grasping those divine senses of the inner man."[8]

For Origen, as with other early Christian allegorists, the literal sense of the text—the human love relationship between Solomon and the Shulammite (usually recognized as Pharaoh's daughter)—though often meticulously analyzed, ultimately constituted the worthless "husk" to be stripped away allegorically to find the "kernel," the "true" meaning, that is, the love relationship between God and his covenant community (whether corporate church or individual soul).[9] Thus,

---

(Cambridge: Harvard University Press, 1970), 270–80, 571–73. Cf. Murphy, *Song of Songs,* 19–20; and Iain W. Provan, *Ecclesiastes, Song of Songs* (NIVAC; Grand Rapids: Zondervan, 2001), 243.

[7] Pope, *Song of Songs,* 114; for a discussion of early Christian allegorical interpretation of the Song and samples of the specific exegesis, see esp. 112–21. Cf. Mark W. Elliott, *The Song of Songs and Christology in the Early Church, 381–451* (Studies in Texts in Antiquity and Christianity 7; Tübingen: Mohr Siebeck, 2000); Garrett, "Song of Songs," 64–69; Longman, *Song of Songs,* 28–32; Murphy, *Song of Songs,* 14–21; and Richard A. Norris Jr., ed. and trans., *The Song of Songs: Interpreted by Early Christian and Medieval Commentators* (Church's Bible 1; Grand Rapids: Eerdmans, 2003), passim. Without denying the role of Platonic thought and the contribution of Christian ascetic values and goals, Murphy is quick to point out that the patristic and medieval allegorical interpretation of the Song "cannot be adequately explained as an exercise in pathological rejection of human sexuality." He indicates the broader soteriological purpose, "providing the intellectual mechanism to effect a synthesis between Old Testament witnesses to God's providential love for humankind and what was confessed to be the preeminent display of that love in the Christ event" (p. 16).

[8] Origen, *Comm. Cant.* Prologue (Lawson, 23) and 1.4 (Lawson, 79).

[9] Origen propounded a threefold sense of Scripture, corresponding to the body, soul, and spirit of humans. The "bodily" (or literal) meaning, readily discernible even to neophytes, was the least important and was often excluded altogether (if a scriptural passage

for example, the kiss of Solomon was seen to allegorically represent the incarnation; the cheeks of the bride, outward Christianity or good works; the golden chain, faith; spikenard, redeemed humanity; hair like flocks of goats, nations converted to Christianity; the navel of the Shulammite, the cup from which God gives salvation; the two breasts, the OT and the NT. Other Christian allegorists interpreted various details differently. For example, the two breasts of the Shulammite have been interpreted as the church from which Christians feed, the twin precepts of love of God and neighbor, the blood and water that flowed from Christ's chest at the crucifixion, and the outer and inner person.[10]

For fifteen centuries the allegorical method held sway in the Christian church, and the Song of Songs became "the favorite book of the ascetics and monastics who found in it, and in expansive commentaries on it, the means to rise above earthly and fleshly desire to the pure platonic love of the virgin soul for God."[11] The crowning achievement of allegorical interpretation was perhaps reached by Bernard of Clairvaux (1090–1153), who wrote eighty-six eloquent sermons on the Song and did not even reach the end of its second chapter.[12] During these one and a half millennia, only one church leader of stature dared to protest against the allegorical interpretations. Theodore of Mopsuestia (d. 428) asserted in his commentary that the Song should be understood according to its plain and literal sense—as a love song in which Solomon celebrates his marriage to Pharaoh's daughter. This view was considered so radical that even his student Bishop Theodoret considered Theodore's literal interpretation "not even fitting

---

seemed unworthy of God or useless to humans in its literal meaning); the "psychical" (or moral) sense could be grasped by those with more advanced insight; and the "spiritual" (allegorical) could be apprehended only by those with mature faculties of spiritual wisdom. This threefold sense of Scripture was expanded by the time of John Cassian (d. 435) into the *Quadriga* (lit. "four-horse chariot"), or fourfold sense of Scripture: the literal and three spiritual senses—the allegorical (mystical or christological), the tropological (moral), and the anagogical (heavenly or eschatological). This "four-horse chariot" was driven through the Song of Songs for over a millennium in Christian thought. For further discussion (with bibliography) of Origen and the Alexandrian exegetical school with its allegorical method, in contrast to the Antiochene school of exegesis, which emphasized the literal sense of the text, see Richard M. Davidson, *Typology in Scripture: A Study of Hermeneutical τύπος Structures* (Andrews University Dissertation Series 2; Berrien Springs, Mich.: Andrews University Press, 1981), 21–27.

[10] Kinlaw, "Song of Songs," 5:1203.

[11] Pope, *Song of Songs,* 114; for a comprehensive bibliography of major extant or known commentaries on the Song of Songs during this long period of history, see 236–51. For discussion of the allegorical use of the Song of Songs during medieval times, see Ann W. Astell, *The Song of Songs in the Middle Ages* (Ithaca, N.Y.: Cornell University Press, 1990); Mary Dove, "Sex, Allegory, and Censorship: A Reconsideration of Medieval Commentaries on the Song of Songs," *LT* 10 (1996): 317–28; E. Ann Matter, *The Voice of My Beloved: The Song of Songs in Western Medieval Christianity* (Philadelphia: University of Pennsylvania Press, 1990); and Norris, *Song of Songs,* passim. Cf. Murphy, *Song of Songs,* 21–28; and Pope, *Song of Songs,* 121–25.

[12] Bernard of Clairvaux, *On the Song of Songs* (trans. Kilian Walsh and Irene M. Edmonds; 4 vols.; Spencer, Mass.: Cistercian, 1971–1980).

in the mouth of crazy women."[13] The Second Council of Constantinople (553) anathematized Theodore and condemned his views as unfit for human ears.

The allegorical interpretation of the Song continued to be dominant in the modern history of Roman Catholicism until very recently and was the generally accepted approach even among Protestant scholars until the past century. Luther, though breaking formally with the allegorical method, still criticized those who attempted to interpret the song literally.[14] The Westminster Assembly in the seventeenth century censured blasphemous Presbyterians who "received it as a hot carnal pamphlet formed by some loose Apollo or Cupid."[15] John Wesley wrote to his Methodist followers that

> the description of this bridegroom and bride is such as could not with decency be used or meant concerning Solomon and Pharaoh's daughter . . . that many expressions and descriptions, if applied to them, would be absurd and monstrous; and that it therefore follows that this book is to be understood allegorically concerning that spiritual love and marriage which is between Christ and his church.[16]

The Literal Interpretation of the Song of Songs

The allegorical interpretation still has its representatives today, in both traditional[17] and critical[18] venues, but fortunately it is no longer anathema (at least in

---

[13] Johannes Quasten, *Patrology* (4 vols.; Westminster: Newman, 1953–1986), 3:540.

[14] Martin Luther, *Lectures on Ecclesiastes, Song of Solomon, and Last Words of Daniel* (trans. Ian Siggins; vol. 15 of *Works;* ed. Jaroslav Pelikan; St. Louis: Concordia, 1972), 192–95; cf. Phipps, *Recovering Biblical Sensuousness,* 57–58.

[15] Westminster Assembly, *Annotations upon All the Books of the Old and New Testaments* (2d ed.; London: John Legatt, 1651), n.p., quoted in Phipps, *Recovering Biblical Sensuousness,* 58.

[16] John Wesley, *Explanation Notes upon the Old Testament* (3 vols.; Bristol, Eng.: William Pine, 1765), 3:1926, quoted in Phipps, *Recovering Biblical Sensuousness,* 58.

[17] See, e.g., A. B. Simpson, *The Love-Life of the Lord* (Harrisburg, Pa.: Christian Alliance, n.d.); the notes in the JB (see Murphy, *Song of Songs,* 93, for the literary history of these notes); Marian G. Berry, *The Prophetic Song of Songs* (Albia, Iowa: Prophetic Song of Songs, 1985); and Theodore E. Wade Jr., *The Song of Songs: Tracing the Story of the Church* (Auburn, Calif: Gazelle, 1992).

[18] See, e.g., Raymond J. Tournay, *Word of God, Song of Love: A Commentary on the Song of Songs* (trans. J. Edward Crowley; New York: Paulist, 1988), who postulates that the writer of the Song lived in the Persian period, selected old Egyptian love poetry, and recast it as a love song between Solomon and his Egyptian princess; at the same time he utilized double entendres to refer to the coming Messiah (the new Solomon) and the Messiah's relationship with his covenant people. Besides the more traditional allegorical interpretation (the Messiah and his people), the mythological interpretation of the Song (as described more fully below) is insightfully identified by some recent critics as a form of allegorization. So, e.g., Jack M. Sasson, "Unlocking the Poetry of Love in the Song of Songs," *BRev* 1, no. 1 (1985): 16, in his review of Pope, *Song of Songs,* comments on Pope's method (and that of the mythological interpretation upon which he builds): "The Song was not about Solomon and the Shulamite, it was suggested [in the mythological interpretation], but about the love shared between the goddess Ishtar and her consort, identified

most circles!) to interpret the Song according to its plain and literal sense. Already with John Calvin came the break with the traditional allegorical view. The Reformer maintained that the Song is both inspired by God and a song of human love. The English Puritan Edmund Spencer seems to have been the first to concur with Calvin, and two centuries later the German romanticist Johann G. Herder also interpreted the Song as a natural expression of human love.[19] Since the time of Herder, a number of novel interpretations of the Song have arisen, attracting some adherents,[20] but in recent decades "there has been a notable trend toward the interpretation of the Song of Songs as human love poetry."[21] Although diverging in a number of significant details, contemporary interpreters in general no longer feel constrained to "unsex the Sublime Song." In 1952 Harold Rowley, after a thorough review of the Song's hermeneutical history, gave a judgment consonant with the literal interpretations of Theodore, Spencer, and Herder and

---

with Shulmanu or with Tammuz. Later, in our own century, recovery of Sumerian myths allowed scholars to substitute for these deities the passionate goddess Inanna and her fickle consort, Dumuzi. These transformations too are essentially allegorical; they simply replace the allegory advanced in orthodox circles, in which God or Christ was said to display his affection for Israel or the Church, with an allegory of a pagan god and goddess. Although Marvin Pope wants us to read the Song itself literally, his interpretation is also essentially allegorical . . . [and] is merely an adaptation of Theophile J. Meek's allegorical readings of 50 years ago." Fiona C. Black points out similarities between the traditional allegorical interpretations and the modern feminist readings ("Unlikely Bedfellows: Allegorical and Feminist Readings of the Song of Songs 7:1–8," in *The Song of Songs* [ed. Athalya Brenner and Carole R. Fontaine; FCB[2] 6; Sheffield, Eng.: Sheffield Academic Press, 2000], 104–29).

[19] See John D. Baildam, *Paradisal Love: Johann Gottfried Herder and the Song of Songs* (JSOTSup 298; Sheffield, Eng.: Sheffield Academic Press, 1999); Phipps, *Recovering Biblical Sensuousness,* 59–61; Pope, *Song of Songs,* 126–27, 131–32.

[20] For an overview and critique of the various drama and dream theories, cultic/liturgical/funerary interpretations, wedding week theory, and psychological/political and feminist/deconstructionist interpretations, see C. Hassell Bullock, *An Introduction to the Old Testament Poetic Books* (rev. and expanded ed.; Chicago: Moody, 1988), 208–15; Garrett, "Song of Songs," 76–84; R. K. Harrison, *Introduction to the Old Testament* (Grand Rapids: Eerdmans, 1969), 1052–58; Longman, *Song of Songs,* 39–47; and Pope, *Song of Songs,* 133–92. The discussion that follows refers to some of these theories and indicates where they are incompatible with the evidence of the text of the Song. I am indebted to constructive feminist analyses of the Song conducted during the 1980s and 1990s, but disappointed to see feminist analyses of the Song take a generally negative turn around the turn of the new millennium, arguing (contra most earlier feminist studies) that it is misguided to see an egalitarian or even gynocentric perspective in the Song because the Song is actually a subversive text—subversive of feminist ideology. See, e.g., Black, "Unlikely Bedfellows," 104–29; J. Cheryl Exum, "Ten Things Every Feminist Should Know," in *Song of Songs* (ed. Althaya Brenner and Carol R. Fontaine; FCB[2] 6; Sheffield, Eng.: Sheffield Academic Press, 2000), 24–35; Daphne Merkin, "The Woman in the Balcony: On Rereading the Song of Songs," in *Out of the Garden: Women Writers on the Bible* (ed. Christina Büchmann and Celina Spiegel; New York: Fawcett Columbine, 1994), 238–55; and D. C. Polaski, "'What Will Ye See in the Shulamite?' Women, Power, and Panopticism in the Song of Songs," *BibInt* 5 (1997): 64–81.

[21] Pope, *Song of Songs,* 192.

in harmony with today's prevailing scholarly assessment: "The view I adopt finds in it nothing but what it appears to be, lovers' songs, expressing their delight in one another and the warm emotion of their hearts. All of the other views find in the Song what they bring to it."[22]

As the conclusion of the last chapter suggests, the terminological linkages between the Song of Songs and Prov 5 add confirming evidence that the Song was intended to be interpreted literally. If one takes the Song according to its plain and literal sense, then one must conclude that a whole book of the OT is devoted to celebrating "the dignity and purity of human love."[23] How could Scripture more forcefully proclaim that human sexuality is not cheap, ugly, and evil but beautiful, wholesome, and praiseworthy! Here is a book that overturns the thinking of much of Christian history (represented by traditional allegorizers): the ideal of virginity, exalted in Christian asceticism and monasticism, is stood on its head, as celibacy is shown not to be God's ideal, a path toward achieving a more exalted spiritual state. Here is "a beautiful, rich, yet compact presentation of the Bible's teaching on human sexuality."[24] Here is a whole book extolling the beauty of human sexual love, which, as will be argued, the Songs presents as a precious gift from Yahweh himself. The "theology of sexuality" set forth in the Song of Songs is not somehow less than "real theology," as some maintain, as if the exaltation of sexual love as a marvelous gift from God somehow "falls short of a profound theology."[25] This chapter and the next contend that the theology of sexuality in this Song is the quintessence of profound theology in the OT—the holy of holies.

---

[22] Harold H. Rowley, "Interpretation of the Song of Songs," in *The Servant of the Lord and Other Essays on the Old Testament* (London: Lutterworth, 1952; repr., Oxford: Blackwell, 1965), 243. For a succinct and penetrating analysis of the problems with the traditional (and more recent critical/feminist) allegorical approaches to the Song, see esp. Garrett, "Song of Songs," 74–76, 84–90. Regarding the latter approaches, Garrett does not mince words: "Feminist readings of the Song labor under a heavy weight of ideological baggage. . . . The Song is subjected to a higher law, the political and theological agenda of feminism, and judgments about the Song's value, validity, and usefulness in social criticism are made on the basis of whether the text, or a 'reading' of the text, supports that agenda. If not, the Song by default supports the agenda of terrorizing women—the patriarchy. Those seem to be the only two alternatives. Feminist readings, no less than ancient allegorizing interpretations, explicitly and intentionally pass the text through a grid, albeit a postmodern political and philosophical grid rather than a traditional theological grid. . . . In such circumstances, the Song is not a poem to be appreciated and interpreted; it is grist for a mill" (pp. 86–87).

[23] Edward J. Young, *An Introduction to the Old Testament* (Grand Rapids: Eerdmans, 1949), 336.

[24] Michael A. Eschelbach, "Song of Songs: Increasing Appreciation of and Restraint in Matters of Love," *AUSS* 42 (2004): 305.

[25] See the somewhat surprising comments of Garrett: "Is a 'theology of sexuality' all that the Song has to offer? Does Song of Songs have any real theology? Is it a nontheological love song from which one can get a theological message only by an exegetical tour de force? . . . . According to Song of Songs, love and sex are good. For all the beauty and pathos the Song brings to that blunt statement, it falls short of a profound theology"

Return to the Garden of Eden

In the Song of Songs we have come full circle in the OT back to the garden of Eden. Several recent studies have penetratingly analyzed and conclusively demonstrated the intimate relationship between the early chapters of Genesis and the Song of Songs.[26] In the "symphony of love," begun in Eden but gone awry after the fall, The Song constitutes "love's lyrics redeemed."[27] Phyllis Trible summarizes how the Song of Songs "by variations and reversals creatively actualizes major motifs and themes" of the Eden narrative:

("Song of Songs," 98, 107). To be fair to Garrett, these statements come in the context of his objection to those who view the Song as only affirming that sex and love is good, without any connection to spirituality or ethics. But by citing my article (Richard M. Davidson, "Theology of Sexuality in the Song of Songs: Return to Eden," *AUSS* 27 [1989]: 1–19) in this same context ("Song of Songs," 98), he makes it appear that my theology of sexuality in the Song is devoid of a spiritual-theological dimension. As will become even more apparent in the discussion that follows (chs. 13–14) than in my earlier short article, such could not be further from what I attempt to establish. Both Garrett and I agree that the Song has a powerful spiritual message that comes from within the Song and not by an "exegetical tour de force." But I have not been convinced by Garrett's attempt to draw out from the Song his "theology of the transformation of the soul" (107) by means of the structural linguistics of Lévi–Strauss, which finds deep structures of the "heroic quest and transformation" in the language of myth that represents the structure of human existence. Not only do I question the foundational presupposition of structuralism, that "deep structures" deterministically impose themselves upon the text (see Grant R. Osborne, *The Hermeneutical Spiral: A Comprehensive Introduction to Biblical Interpretation* [Downers Grove, Ill.: InterVarsity, 1991], 371–77, for a succinct critique of structuralism); I also find Garrett's attempted leap of genres from myth to lyric poetry to be a hermeneutical gymnastic move that is suicidal to his overall enterprise. It requires, among other things, positing that the overarching focus of the Song is the "woman's experience of losing virginity" ("Song of Songs," 117), with the man serving as her redeemer figure as he persuades his bride to yield herself to him (186). Garrett's basic thesis, that "the woman's experience in the Song of Songs brings out the deep structure of the human soul" (117), seems to let return through the back door the same allegorical interpretation that he banished through the front door (he even calls his thesis a "true allegory of love" [107]), despite his attempts to distance himself from the common understanding of allegorization (117). Garrett's commentary on the Song provides a good introduction and many fine exegetical insights into the text, but unfortunately, he does not recognize the textual clues (such as in Song 8:6) that in my view point to a spiritual undergirding (and typological message) for the Song. These clues will be analyzed in detail in ch. 14, below.

[26] See Nicholas Ayo, *Sacred Marriage: The Wisdom of the Song of Songs* (illustrated by Meinrad Craighead; New York: Continuum, 1997), 37–53; Francis Landy, "The Song of Songs and the Garden of Eden," *JBL* 98 (1979): 513–28; idem, *Paradoxes of Paradise: Identity and Difference in the Song of Songs* (Sheffield, Eng.: Almond, 1983), esp. ch. 4, "Two Versions of Paradise," 183–265; William E. Phipps, *Genesis and Gender: Biblical Myths of Sexuality and Their Cultural Impact* (New York: Praeger, 1989), 90–95; Phyllis Trible, "Depatriarchalizing in Biblical Interpretation," *JAAR* 41, no. 1 (1973): 42–47; and idem, *God and the Rhetoric of Sexuality* (OBT; Philadelphia: Fortress, 1978), 145–65.

[27] Trible, *God and the Rhetoric of Sexuality,* 144.

Female and male are born to mutuality and love. They are naked without shame; they are equal without duplication. They live in gardens where nature joins in celebrating their oneness. Animals remind these couples of their shared superiority in creation as well as their affinity and responsibility for lesser creatures. Fruits pleasing to the eye and tongue are theirs to enjoy. Living waters replenish their gardens. Both couples are involved in naming; both couples work.... Whatever else it may be, Canticles is a commentary on Gen. 2–3. Paradise Lost is Paradise Regained.[28]

Jill Munro depicts even more directly how sexuality in the Song of Songs is a return to Eden:

The garden, which in the Genesis story becomes an inaccessible place from which humanity is exiled, in the Song is rediscovered in the woman; it is in union or communion with her that her lover rediscovers the bliss of which the Eden story spoke. As a result, the world around is also recreated; it too becomes a garden, a garden of love which the reader too may enter for a time.[29]

The Song of Songs is a return to Eden, but the lovers in the Song are not to be equated in every way with the pre-fall couple in the garden. The poetry of the Song reveals the existence of a world of sin and its baleful results: there are the angry brothers (1:6), the wet winter (2:11), "the little foxes, that ruin the vineyards" (2:15), the anxiety of absence from one's beloved (3:1–4; 5:6–8; 6:1), the cruelty and brutality of the watchman (5:7), and the powerful presence of death (8:6). Yet the lovers in the Song are able to triumph over the threats to their love.

In parallel with Gen 2:24, the Song depicts the ideal of "woman and man in mutual harmony after the fall."[30] This inspired reflection and elucidation of the divine ideal for postfall sexuality may be discussed under the same ten subheadings employed in the treatment of sexuality in the beginning (chs. 1–2, above concerning Gen 1–3). The first nine of these subheadings are explored in the present chapter, and the final—and major—theological statement on sexuality in the Song is treated in the next chapter.

---

[28] Idem, "Depatriarchalizing," 47.

[29] Jill M. Munro, *Spikenard and Saffron: The Imagery of the Song of Songs* (JSOTSup 203; Sheffield, Eng.: Sheffield Academic Press, 1995), 105–6. See also David Blumenthal, "The Shulamite Is Not the Woman of Valor," in *Relating to the Text: Interdisciplinary and Form-Critical Insights on the Bible* (ed. Timothy J. Sandoval and Carleen Mandolfo; JSOTSup 384; New York: T&T Clark, 2003), 230: "there is something edenic about the Song of Songs. Its love is without the burdens and temptations of real life; it is direct, naïve, touching, erotic. The woman is forthcoming, playful, attentive and the man responds in the same vein. Bodily love in the Song of Songs is central, not peripheral; she evokes and he responds, bodily, embodied. Sex is in the context of erotic love, not possession and procreation; it is enchantment, delight, joy." Blumenthal also underscores that in the Song there is a return to Eden, which he describes as messianic: "As there is something edenic about the Song of Songs, so there is something messianic about it. The cycle of Eden *will be* completed, so says the Song of Songs. We *will* return to a fuller, more loving, erotic state" (ibid., emphasis his).

[30] Trible, "Depatriarchalizing," 48.

Sexuality as a Creation Order

Underlying the entire Song is the same high doctrine of creation as forms the backdrop for biblical Wisdom literature in general.[31] Though without explicit mention that God "has made everything suitable for its time" (Eccl 3:11), the beauty of God's handiwork made during the six days of creation week is concretely described by the Song in the natural surroundings of the lovers—brilliant light, fountains and springs, many waters, mountains and hills, pastures and vineyards, trees and flowers, sun and moon, birds and animals.[32] As in the cre-

---

[31] For a discussion of the doctrine of creation in Wisdom literature, see, e.g., James L. Crenshaw, "Prolegomenon," in *Studies in Ancient Israelite Wisdom* (ed. James L. Crenshaw; New York: Ktav, 1976), 1–60, here 22–35; repr. in *Urgent Advice and Probing Questions: Collected Writings on Old Testament Wisdom* (Macon, Ga.: Mercer, 1995), 90–140; and Roland E. Murphy, "Wisdom and Creation," *JBL* 104 (1985): 3–11. Many scholars (represented, e.g., by Crenshaw, "Prolegomenon," 5) exclude the Song from biblical books classed as Wisdom literature, but Brevard S. Childs unhesitatingly (and I think correctly) asserts, "The Song is to be understood as wisdom literature" (*Introduction to the Old Testament as Scripture* [Philadelphia: Fortress, 1979], 574). Childs points out that "the ascription of the Song of Songs to Solomon by the Hebrew canon sets these writings within the context of wisdom literature. Indeed this song is the 'pearl' of the collection. . . . The Song is to be understood as wisdom literature." He further remarks that "reflection on human experience without resort to the religious language of Israel's traditional institutions of law, cult, and prophecy is characteristic of wisdom" (ibid.). Roland E. Murphy argues that although not technically Wisdom literature, the Song "emphasizes values which are primary in wisdom thought (cf. Prov 1–9)" (*Wisdom Literature: Job, Proverbs, Ruth, Canticles, Ecclesiastes, Esther* [FOTL 13; Grand Rapids: Eerdmans, 1981], xiii). Murphy cites a number of scholars who are becoming "open to ascribing the preservation and transmission of these poems [the Song] to the sages of Israel." Murphy's later book, *The Tree of Life: An Exploration of Biblical Wisdom Literature* (2d ed.; Grand Rapids: Eerdmans, 1996), 106–7, points to several factors that link the Song in its canonical form to Wisdom literature: its attribution to Solomon (Song 1:1) and placement along with the wisdom books of Solomon (Proverbs and Ecclesiastes); its emphasis of wisdom values of fidelity and mutuality between lovers (as in Prov 5:15–20); the connection between wisdom and eros in Proverbs (4:6–8; 7:4; 9); and the wisdom statement in Song 8:6–7. See also the similar sentiments expressed by Duane A. Garrett, *Proverbs, Ecclesiastes, Song of Songs* (NAC 14; Nashville: Broadman, 1993), 367: "The Song of Songs celebrates love, but it also teaches love; in this respect it must be counted as wisdom literature." Cf. the defense of the Song as Wisdom literature by Christopher W. Mitchell, "The Song of Songs: A Lutheran Perspective," in *"Hear the Word of Yahweh": Essays on Scripture and Archaeology in Honor of Horace D. Hummel* (ed. Dean O. Wenthe, Paul L. Schrieber, and Lee A. Maxwell; St. Louis: Concordia, 2002), 81–82.

[32] The six days of creation are profusely represented in the Song:

1. Light: "flashes of fire" (8:6) of Yahweh (see ch. 14, below).

2. Water and air: springs and fountains or wells of fresh water (4:12, 15), streams from Lebanon (4:15), rivers of water (5:12), many waters and floods (8:7), wind (north and south; 4:16); dew (5:2); rain (not present) (2:11).

3. Land and vegetation: Mountains and hills—Lebanon (4:8, 11, 15; 7:5 [ET 7:4]), Amana and Senir and Hermon (4:8), Gilead (4:1; 6:5), Carmel (7:6 [ET 7:5]). Pas-

ation narrative of Gen 2, special emphasis is placed upon the paradisaical garden home of the lovers.[33] Likewise sexuality is assumed to be a creation ordinance, given by God for man to enjoy.[34] In lofty love lyrics, "the voices of the Song of Songs extol and enhance the creation of sexuality in Gen 2."[35]

At the same time, as in the Genesis account of creation, the Song radically separates sexuality and divinity; sexuality belongs to the creation order, not the divine realm. "Israel's opposition to the mythically satiated atmosphere of its environment is nowhere more clearly and simply expressed [than in the Song of Songs].... The love poems of the Song of Songs confidently presuppose that Yahwism is incompatible with a divinization of sex."[36] Far from being a reenactment of the fertility cult mythology, as some have claimed,[37] the Song of Songs may in

---

tures (7:12 [ET 7:11]). Vineyards (1:6; 7:13 [ET 7:12]; 8:11), vines (2:13, 15; 6:11; 7:9 [ET 7:8]), raisins (2:5), and wine (1:2; 4:10; 7:10 [ET 7:9]; 8:2). Trees/fruit—palm (7:8 [ET 7:7]), cedar (1:17; 3:9; 5:18; 8:9), pine/fir (1:17), apple (2:3, 5; 7:9 [ET 7:8]; 8:5), fig (2:13), pomegranate (4:3, 12; 6:7, 11; 7:13 [ET 7:12]; 8:2). Nuts (6:11) and mandrakes (7:14 [ET 7:13]). Spices/fragrances—in general (4:10, 14, 16; 5:1, 13; 6:2; 8:14), nard (1:12; 4:13), saffron and calamus and aloes and cinnamon (4:14), frankincense (3:6; 4:6, 14), henna (1:14; 4:13), and myrrh (1:13; 3:6; 4:6, 14; 5:1, 5 [bis], 13). Flowers—in general (2:12), rose/crocus (2:1), lily/lilies [lotus flowers] (2:1, 2, 16; 4:5; 6:2, 3; 7:3 [ET 7:2]).

4. Luminaries: sun (1:6; 6:10), moon (6:10), sunrise/daybreak (2:17; 4:6), night (3:1, 8; 5:2), morning (6:10).

5. Birds: turtle doves (2:12), ravens (5:11), doves (1:15; 2:14; 4:1; 5:1, 12; 6:9).

6. Animals: gazelles (2:7, 9, 17; 3:5; 4:5; 7:4 [ET 7:3]; 8:14), young stags (2:9, 17; 8:14), hinds of the field (2:7; 3:5), flocks of goats (1:8; 4:1; 6:5), sheep (1:7; 4:2; 6:6), foxes (2:15), lions and leopards (4:8).

This list is not meant to imply that the author of the Song intended to follow intertextually the order of creation week—he does not—or that he intended a direct parallel to the details of what was created in the beginning. Rather the list points out the breadth of creation background that encompasses all six days of creation week. It is also tempting to see an echo between the divine Sabbath rest (*wyšbt*) on the seventh day in Gen 2:1 and the woman's sitting down (*wyšbty*) under the shade of the apple tree (= her lover) in Song 2:3, but this is not certain.

[33] See esp. 1:16–17. The "garden" motif is a dominant one in the Song: 4:12, 15–16; 5:1; 6:2 (bis); 8:13. For discussion of this motif in Genesis and the Song of Songs, see Landy, *Paradoxes of Paradise,* 189–210. Parts of his analysis are more convincing than others.

[34] See ch. 14, below, for a discussion of the divine origin of love in the Song.

[35] Trible, *God and the Rhetoric of Sexuality,* 145.

[36] Gillis Gerleman, *Ruth: Das Hohelied* (Neukirchen-Vluyn: Neukirchener Verlag, 1965), 84–85; this quotation is translated into English in Othmar Keel, *The Song of Songs: A Continental Commentary* (trans. Frederick J. Gaiser; Minneapolis: Fortress, 1994), 33.

[37] The mythological interpretation was first argued strongly by T. J. Meek, "Canticles and the Tammuz Cult," *AJSL* 39 (1922–1923): 1–14; cf. his later elaboration of the theory in idem, "The Song of Songs: Introduction and Exegesis," *IB* 5:89–148. For later proponents of some form of this mythological interpretation, including Pope himself, see Pope, *Song of Songs,* 145–53 and passim. For incisive critiques of the various mythological interpretations, see esp. Rowley, *Servant of the Lord,* 213–32; and Garrett, "Song of Songs," 82–83.

fact, like Gen 1–3, constitute an intentional (or at least implicit) polemic against the fertility cults. In a provocative article, Connie Whitesell summarizes the striking parallels between the Sumerian fertility cult myth and the Song and suggests that the latter presents a "repudiation of the fertility goddess paradigm" and "works to wrest sexuality from its mythicomagical roots and to establish it within the confines of mundane human experience."[38] Unlike the Mesopotamian myths, where the gods are engaged in orgiastic rites connected with the fertility of nature, in the Song "sexuality has no magical force and no connection with the goddess; romantic love participates in and is analogous to the fecundity of nature, but it does not cause it."[39]

A Heterosexual Human Duality and Marital Form

A second major facet of the theology of sexuality in the Song of Songs underscores that sexuality is for heterosexual human couples. The man and the woman in the Song are a heterosexual duality as in the world's beginning at creation (Gen 1–2).[40] Hypotheses that suggest a lovers' triangle or multiple affairs in the Song are

---

[38] Connie J. Whitesell, "'Behold, Thou Art Fair, My Beloved,'" *Parab* 20 (1995): 95, 97. Whitesell (p. 94) summarizes the main features of the Sumerian Inanna-Dumuzi fertility cult myth, highlighting a number of intriguing parallels with the Song of Songs: Inanna is a virgin and rustic, as is the Shulammite; her suitor Dumuzi is first described as a shepherd and then later after their marriage is king, as Solomon is depicted as both shepherd and king; following a separation Inanna misses her husband and, on her way to find him, is stripped and humiliated by the "Keeper of the Gate," as the Shulammite is struck and wounded by the "keepers of the wall" while searching for her lover. They are reunited, as in the Song. Whitesell (ibid.) shows that in each of these points of contact, the Song "immediately silences the mythological reference." For full discussion of the Inanna goddess and reconstruction of the fertility myth surrounding her, see esp. Diane Wolkstein and Samuel N. Kramer, *Inanna, Queen of Heaven and Earth: Her Stories and Hymns from Sumer* (New York: Harper & Row, 1983).

[39] Ibid., 98. "Contrary to the cultic and funerary interpretations, it [the Song] has no allusions to love play among the gods. It never implies that the sexuality of the couple has any cultic or ritual significance or that their joining promotes the mythical powers of fertility in the renewal of nature. Simply put, the act of sex is not a religious act. . . . It has no ritual powers" (Garrett, *Proverbs, Ecclesiastes, Song of Songs,* 378).

[40] Attempts to provide a "gay reading" of the Song constitute, in the colorful words of Garrett, "the most violent kind of an imposition of extrinsic values on the Song" ("Song of Songs," 103). For such a gay reading, see, e.g., Roland Boer, "The Second Coming: Repetition and Insatiable Desire in the Song of Songs," *BibInt* 8 (2000): 276–301; so also the "queer reading" of Virginia Burrus and Stephen D. Moore, "Unsafe Sex: Feminism, Pornography, and the Song of Songs," *BibInt* 11 (2003): 24–52, who argue that traditional allegorical exegesis of the Song down through the centuries has sanctioned "queer" interpretation of the Song: "With astonishing ease, these austere male interpreters were seduced by the Song in to whispering Shulamith's white-hot words of passion into the ear of the divine male personage in whose muscular arms they had eagerly taken refuge" (24). Burrus and Moore have mistaken the allegorical interpretation of the Song for the Song's plain sense and have imputed to the Christian allegorists a homosexual outlook completely foreign to their interpretive intent. Garrett, "Song of Songs," 103, incisively cri-

not convincing. The most popular of these is the "shepherd" hypothesis, which argues for three main characters in the Song: the Shulammite, her shepherd lover, and King Solomon, who carries the Shulammite by force to his harem and, after unsuccessfully attempting to seduce her, allows her to return home to her rustic lover.[41] The main support for this hypothesis—the apparent description of two male characters, a shepherd and a king—disappears when it is realized that the poet portrays Solomon as both king and shepherd. In the Psalms God himself is portrayed as both King and Shepherd (compare Pss 95–97 with Ps 23). Acceptance of this hypothesis forces one to arbitrarily interpret many of the beautiful descriptions of the Shulammite as perverse. "The three-character drama is arbitrary in nature; its advocates tend to see what they want to see in the lyrics. If an interpreter assigns a love song to the 'shepherd,' the words are ardent and pure; if another interpreter assigns the same text to Solomon, it is lustful and manipulative."[42]

Equally unconvincing is the popular suggestion that the book is simply an anthology or collection of various unrelated love songs and hence has no specific couple in mind.[43] If one takes seriously the data from the canonical text,

---

tiques these gay readings against the claims of the Song itself: "Not only are the central lovers in the Song male and female, but it is understood that this is the outlook of the community at large. At the beginning of the Song, when the splendors of the man's love are being praised, the woman responds that the girls 'rightly' love the man (Song 1:3–4)."

[41] This view was suggested by Ibn Ezra in the twelfth century, popularized by H. Ewald in the nineteenth century, and accepted by S. R. Driver, C. G. Ginsburg, C. Hassell Bullock, and many others. For a recent evangelical commentary espousing this view, see Provan, *Ecclesiastes, Song of Songs,* passim. This hypothesis is discussed (with bibliography of other major proponents of this view) and critiqued in, e.g., Garrett, "Song of Songs," 77–79; Harrison, *Introduction to the Old Testament,* 1054; Murphy, *Song of Songs,* 58, 64, 80–85; and Pope, *Song of Songs,* 136–41. Cf. the hypothesis of Michael D. Goulder, *The Song of Fourteen Songs* (Sheffield, Eng.: JSOT Press, 1986), 4, 55, who suggests that the Shulammite is actually Abishag the Shunammite, who competes with the Princess of the Song for the affections of Solomon. Goulder also interprets many of the poetic lines of the Song as describing Solomon's sexual adventures with other women of his harem. I will argue below, however, in harmony with the traditional view of the Song, that the Shulammite is Solomon's bride who speaks throughout the Song and that the love relationship in the Song is exclusively between Solomon and his one and only, the Shulammite.

[42] Garrett, "Song of Songs," 77.

[43] For example, in 1902 Paul Haupt wrote that the book was "simply a collection of popular love-ditties, and these erotic songs are not at all complete . . . neither are they given in their proper order" ("The Book of Canticles," *AJSL* 18 [1902]: 205). The following more recent commentaries espouse this view: W. Rudolph, *Das Buch Ruth, Das Hohe Lied, Die Klagelieder* (KAT 17; Gütersloh: Gerd Mohn, 1962), 97–98; Harold L. Ginsberg, "Introduction to the Song of Songs," in *The Five Megilloth and Jonah: A New Translation* (Philadelphia: Jewish Publication Society of America, 1969), 3; Robert Gordis, *The Song of Songs and Lamentations: A Study, Modern Translation, and Commentary* (New York: Ktav, 1974), 17–18; Pope, *Song of Songs,* 40–54 (who also discusses earlier commentators with this view); Marcia Falk, *Love Lyrics from the Bible: A Translation and Literary Study of the Song of Songs* (BLS 4; Sheffield, Eng.: Almond Press, 1982), 3, 69; Robert Davidson, *Ecclesiastes and the Song of Solomon* (Daily Bible Study Series; Philadelphia: Westminster, 1986), 98; Keel, *Song of Songs,* 17–18; and Longman, *Song of Songs,* 55 (although Longman acknowledges that it is "a single Song composed of many different Songs").

including the superscription, the book constitutes "The Song of Songs" (Song 1:1)—a typical Hebrew expression for the superlative, meaning something like "The Most Sublime Song"—and indicating a unified song, not an anthology.[44] Furthermore, a number of studies in the last few decades point to strong evidence within the Song itself for its integral unity, rather than as a collection of unrelated love poems. Roland Murphy points to recurring refrains, themes, words, phrases, and elements of dialogical structure.[45] J. Cheryl Exum analyzes numerous stylistic and structural indications of "a unity of authorship with an intentional design."[46] Michael Fox elaborates on four factors that point to a literary unity (and the same couple throughout the Song): (1) a network of repetends (repetitions), (2) associative sequences, (3) consistency of character portrayal, and (4) narrative framework.[47] Monroe demonstrates the psychological unity and the narrative progression of numerous poetic images throughout the Song.[48]

The most comprehensive exploration of the literary unity of the Song of Songs is by M. Timothea Elliott.[49] Building upon her detailed microstructural

---

[44] See Murphy, *Song of Songs,* 119: "The Hebrew idiom, comprised of the singular and plural forms of the same noun in construct, is a typical expression of the superlative." See GKC §133i. For biblical examples, see Gen 9:25; Exod 29:37; Deut 10:17; Eccl 1:2; 12:8; and the Aramaic of Ezra 7:12 and Dan 2:37. This is contra those who would see the phrase as a sign of the composite nature of the Song. Thus, e.g., Longman, *Song of Songs,* 88, interprets this phrase as "a single poem composed of many poems, literally, then, a song of songs"; and Garrett, "Song of Songs," 124, takes the expression to mean "a single musical production that is a collection of smaller songs." Such interpretation, however, runs roughshod over straightforward Hebrew syntax, as it uses horseshoes studded with English-language idiom and is often goaded on by the predetermined hypothesis of a composite origin for the Song.

[45] Roland E. Murphy, "The Unity of the Song of Songs," *VT* 29 (1979): 436–43; idem, *Song of Songs,* 64–67.

[46] J. Cheryl Exum, "A Literary and Structural Analysis of the Song of Songs," *ZAW* 85 (1973): 47–79. See Exum's more recent, more nuanced, but similar assessment: "If the Song exhibits cohesiveness, homogeneity, consistency of character portrayal and a distinctive vision of love—and I believe it does—is there any need to posit an editor at all? Perhaps the Song was composed by a single author, working within a poetic tradition, and was only lightly edited in the process of its transmission. If the Song is an anthology of love poems, one might reasonably expect it to feature different protagonists and exhibit different attitudes toward love, sex, and the body. But this is by no means apparent. . . . [F]or my part, I have become increasingly convinced that an inspired poetic vision of love has guided the composition of the Song. The present commentary assumes that only by reading it as a whole can we do justice to its poetic accomplishment" (*Song of Songs* [OTL; Louisville, Ky.: Westminster John Knox, 2005], 35, 37).

[47] Michael V. Fox, *The Song of Songs and the Ancient Egyptian Love Songs* (Madison: University of Wisconsin, 1985), 209–22. Note his conclusion: "There is no reason to posit an editor to explain the Song's cohesiveness and stylistic homogeneity. The most likely explanation of these qualities is that the Song is a single poem composed, originally at least, by a single poet" (p. 220).

[48] Munro, *Spikenard and Saffron,* 144–47.

[49] M. Timothea Elliott, *The Literary Unity of the Canticle* (European University Studies, Series 23, 371; New York: Peter Lang, 1989). This study is a revision of Elliott's doctoral dissertation in biblical science at the Pontifical Biblical Institute in Rome, defended in 1988.

analysis of the entire Song, Elliott sets forth an array of formal and stylistic evidence for the unity of the Song of Songs. On the formal level, Elliott shows that "a multiplicity of correspondences among the various parts [of the Song]" indicates "a tightly woven tissue of interrelated parts. The formal structure is indeed an organic one."[50] Especially persuasive is her overwhelming evidence that the prologue (1:2–2:7) and epilogue (8:5–14) form an *inclusio* to the entire Song, sharing many verbal and structural correspondences. On the stylistic level, Elliott traces "eleven major elements of style which pervade the work, unify it, and argue strongly in favor of a single poet."[51] Elliott's work is a tour de force affirming the unity of the Song of Songs.[52]

A number of recent literary-structural analyses demonstrate an overarching symmetrical or chiastic structure for the entire Song.[53] My own literary

---

[50] Ibid., 236.

[51] Ibid., 260. These elements include (1) setting, (2) focus, (3) theme, (4) dialogue, (5) motifs and imagery, (6) mirroring dynamics, (7) paradigms of enclosure and protection, (8) consistency of characterization, (9) the epithets, (10) associated sequences as a principle of organization, and (11) function and integration of refrains. Elliott allows for the possibility of the poet using some previous materials but nonetheless insists on an organic unity in the final canonical form: "Even if this anonymous poet borrowed extensively from already existing material, brief love songs or even collections, his unique combination of all these elements constitutes an individual artistic creation of remarkable beauty and genius. As a new, organically unified entity, it demands its own particular interpretation" (ibid.).

[52] See the concise summary of the more salient features of her argumentation in Garrett, "Song of Songs," 28. See P. W. T. Stoop-van Paridon, *The Song of Songs: A Philological Analysis of the Hebrew Book* שִׁיר הַשִּׁירִים (ANESSup 17; Louvain: Peeters, 2005), 476, whose comprehensive philological analysis of the book leads her to support Elliott's conclusion regarding the unity of the Song of Songs: "Each verse and each passage is understandable and meaningful, provided the details of grammar and lexicography are respected and allowance is made for veiled language. The intrinsic entity is confirmation and support for a literary entity which has already been proposed by others on the grounds of various literary criteria. This removes any basis for the frequently expressed suggestion that the Song of Songs is made up of a collection of individual songs (cf., e.g., Dorsey [1990]; Longman [2001])."

[53] G. Lloyd Carr, *The Song of Solomon: An Introduction and Commentary* (TOTC 17; Downers Grove, Ill.: InterVarsity, 1984), 44–49; idem, "Song of Songs," in *A Complete Literary Guide to the Bible* (ed. Leland Ryken and Tremper Longman III; Grand Rapids: Zondervan, 1993), 284; David Dorsey, "Literary Structuring in the Song of Songs," *JSOT* 46 (1990): 81–96; cf. idem, *The Literary Structure of the Old Testament: A Commentary on Genesis–Malachi* (Grand Rapids: Baker, 1999), 199–213; Garrett, "Song of Songs," 30–35; Andrew Hwang, "The New Structure of the Song of Songs and Its Implications for Interpretation," *WTJ* 65 (2003): 97–111; Leland Ryken, *Words of Delight: A Literary Introduction to the Bible* (2d ed.; Grand Rapids: Baker, 1992), 279–82; William H. Shea, "The Chiastic Structure of the Song of Songs," *ZAW* 92 (1980): 378–96 (Murphy, *Song of Songs,* 63–64, points to some weaknesses in Shea's analysis, but his critique does not overturn Shea's general thesis); Edwin C. Webster, "Pattern in the Song of Songs," *JSOT* 22 (1982): 73–93; Ernst R. Wendland, "Seeking a Path through a Forest of Symbols: A Figurative and Structural Survey of the Song of Songs," *JTT* 7, no. 2 (1995): 13–59; and the chiastic structure of R. L. Alden, reproduced in Garrett, *Proverbs, Ecclesiastes, Song of Songs,* 376. For a survey and critique of the various macrostructural analyses before

analysis[54] identifies twelve macrounits indicated by refrains (repetends) that denote the boundaries within these sections. The twelve sections form an artistic symmetrical macrostructure, composed of reverse parallelism (i.e., chiasm) and block parallelism (i.e., panel writing) in a doubled-seven pattern (including the two-verse central climax): A–B–CDEF–GG'–C' D' E' F'–B'–A'. The more detailed outline is as follows:

A. 1:2–2:7 Mutual love
   B. 2:8–17 Coming and going
      C. 3:1–5 Dream I: lost and found
         D. 3:6–11 Praise of groom, I
            E. 4:1–7 Praise of bride, I
               F. 4:8–15 Praise of bride, II
                  G. 4:16 Invitation by bride
                  G'. 5:1 Acceptance of invitation by groom
                    and divine approbation
      C'. 5:2–8 Dream II: found and lost
         D'. 5:9–6:3 Praise of groom, II
            E'. 6:4–12 Praise of bride, III
               F'. 7:1–10 (ET 6:13–7:9) Praise of bride, IV
   B'. 7:11–8:2 (ET 7:10–8:2) Going and coming
A'. 8:3–14 Mutual love

A detailed examination of the extremely intricate symmetry between each of the parallel pairs in the above structure seems to rule out the possibility of a redactor imposing an artificial structure upon a miscellaneous collection of love poems.[55] Furthermore, as argued in a later section of this chapter, in addition to

---

2003, see Richard M. Davidson, "The Literary Structure of the Song of Songs *redivivus,*" *JATS* 14, no. 2 (2003): 44–50. The literary structure proposed by Garrett ("Song of Songs," 32–35) is similar to mine in many ways, including a symmetrical pattern of paired members A–F, the "wedding-night songs" of 3:1–4:15 paired in block parallelism with the "wedding-night songs" of 5:2–6:10 (though I would see this block parallelism extending to 7:10 [ET 7:9]), and with the central verses (4:16–5:1) constituting the apex of the Song (although I subdivide this central member, G, into G and G'). My major difficulty with his analysis is in the beginning and ending portions of the Song (1:2–2:17 and 6:11–8:14), which he subdivides into far more (and far too short) macrostructural sections than indicated by the refrains. In other words, he allows the individual "cantos" (indicated by changes of voice), which, in my estimation, point to different subsections and not the major macrosections, to override what I see as the basic macrostructural indicator in the Song: the refrains. Hence the chiastic parallels he proposes for some of these sections I do not find convincing.

[54] Davidson, "Literary Structure," 50–65.

[55] See ibid., 52–64. According to my analysis, the first two outer-paired members of the Song are designed in chiastic arrangement (ABB'A'); next come four paired panel (block parallelism) structures (CDEFC'D'E'F'), with members E/E' and F/F' containing not only panel but chiastic features (E–F' and F–E'); and the climactic two central verses of the Song (members GG') are paired in both chiastic and block parallelism. "Such detailed and multidimensional macrostructure surely displays the overarching unity and stunning literary beauty of Scripture's Most Sublime Song" (p. 64).

the overall symmetrical macrostructure, a horizontal, linear, quasi-narrative structure is also inherent in the Song. Such detailed and multifaceted structuring, along with the other arguments already noted, surely points to the unity of the Song of Songs.

In a unified song, then, the love relationship between a specific heterosexual couple—man and woman—is extolled and celebrated.

A Monogamous Marital Form

A third facet in the theology of sexuality is the identity and marital status and form depicted in the Song. Who is this couple in the Song of Songs? Addressing this question is not just a matter of historical curiosity; it is crucial for interpreting the Song's theology of sexuality. The answer is inextricably related to the issues of authorship, dating, and life setting of the Song. In harmony with the aim of this canonical-form study of the Song, I take the superscription of the Song of Songs in Song 1:1 seriously with its formula *ʾăšer lišlōmōh*, "which is Solomon's [lit. 'which is to Solomon']." This phrase most probably means "authored by Solomon." Gleason Archer rightly points out that "this preposition *lĕ*, 'to,' is the only convenient way of expressing possession or authorship in Hebrew where the same author may have composed many other works."[56] Even critical scholars, who regularly dismiss the superscription out of hand as unhistorical, at the same time generally agree that the most natural way to read the *lĕ* in Song 1:1 is a *lamed* of authorship.[57] So, for example, Marvin Pope: "It is, nevertheless, most

---

[56] Gleason L. Archer, *A Survey of Old Testament Introduction* (updated and rev. ed.; (Chicago: Moody Press, 1994), 537–38. If the construct form were used, it would imply that the Song of Songs was *the* Song of Solomon, i.e., the only song he wrote, which would not be true in light of his 1,005 songs mentioned in 1 Kgs 5:12 (ET 4:32).

[57] See, e.g., Murphy, *Song of Songs,* 119: "The construction אֲשֶׁר לִשְׁלֹמֹה (so **M** [= MT] with the full support of the ancient versions) is quite intelligible as a relative clause attributing the work to Solomon. . . . The preposition ל is most easily taken to be the *lamed auctoris.* . . . Just as many editorial superscriptions in the psalter exhibit לְדָוִד to claim Davidic authorship (e.g., Ps 3:1; 4:1; 5:1), so Solomon is named as the Song's author." Murphy refers to the standard grammar, Joüon §130b.

Some scholars who do not accept the Solomonic authorship of the Song argue that the use of a different relative pronoun for "which" in the superscription from that in the Song itself (*ʾăšer* in the superscription and *še* in the Song) indicates that the superscription was added later, but this argument is not persuasive. The Pentateuch and the Former Prophets display the same phenomenon as one moves from the narrative material to the poetry: the early poetic passages (such as Gen 49; Exod 15:1–19; Num 23:7–10, 18–24; 24:5–9, 15–24; Judg 5:2–31; 1 Sam 2:1–10) avoid using the relative *ʾăšer* even though it appears repeatedly in the narratives immediately surrounding them (the only exception I have found is the one occurrence of *ʾăšer* in Deut 32:38). Judges 5 is particularly instructive: the relative pronoun *še* appears twice in the poem (Judg 5:7) but not *ʾăšer*, even though *ʾăšer* occurs repeatedly in the surrounding narrative (e.g., 4:22, 24; 6:10, 11, 13). Landy, *Paradoxes of Paradise,* 282, n. 27, though not defending a Solomonic authorship, nonetheless sees an underlying principle that applies here: "Another factor that in my

likely that the intent of the superscription was to attribute the authorship to
Solomon."[58] A final-form theology does not easily dismiss the intended identity
of the author within the Song.

Numerous lines of external and internal evidence support the superscription's
assertion of Solomonic authorship in the tenth century B.C.E.[59] In brief, note especially the following: (1) six other references to Solomon by name in the book
(1:5; 3:7, 9, 11; 8:11, 12); (2) three references to "the king" (1:4, 12; 7:6 [ET 7:5]);
(3) references to the royal wedding of Solomon (3:7–11), paralleling the wedding
of Solomon to Pharaoh's daughter (1 Kgs 3:1); (4) the historical reference to
Solomon's writing of 1,005 songs (1 Kgs 5:12 [ET 4:32]) (it would be strange if
not one were preserved); (5) the historical reference to Solomon's expansive
knowledge of natural history (1 Kgs 5:13 [ET 4:33]) (cf. the profusion of flora
[twenty-one varieties of plant life] and fauna [fifteen species of animals] mentioned in the Song); (6) mention of Pharaoh's chariotry (Song 1:9), according
with Solomon's importing of horses from Egypt (1 Kgs 10:28); (7) depictions of
royal luxury throughout the Song (e.g., Song 1:12, 13; 3:6, 9) and expensive imported products (spices, gold, silver, purple, ivory, beryl, cedar), comporting with
the historical description of Solomon's fabulous wealth (1 Kgs 10:14–23) and extensive trading (1 Kgs 9:26–28); (8) the geographical references, which fit only a
time when the northern and southern kingdoms were not divided, that is, the

view determined the choice between ''ăšer' and 'še' is genre and style: ''ăšer' suits historical
narrative such as Esther, while 'še' is most apt for lyric compression, and has a powerful al-
literative function." This could explain why in the superscription ʾăšer is used and in the
Song itself še is used.

[58] Pope, Song of Songs, 296. It is rather ironic that liberal-critical scholars, who have
no stake in accepting as accurate and normative the superscription to the Song, generally
agree that the superscription assigns authorship of the Song to Solomon, whereas evangelical scholars, who for the most part accept the superscription as genuine and normative, seek by hook or crook to evade the most natural reading in favor of theoretically
possible but unusual or even unattested meanings of the Hebrew expression. This smacks
of special pleading.

[59] Although this is a subject of heated debate today, I accept the basic historicity of
the Davidic-Solomonic empire in the tenth century B.C.E. as depicted in the narratives
of 2 Samuel through 1 Kgs 11 (and 1 Chr 11 through 2 Chr 9). For a summary of archaeological evidence that corroborates the biblical perspective of this period, see, e.g., William Dever, What Did the Bible Writers Know and When Did They Know It? (Grand
Rapids: Eerdmans, 2001), 131–57. (This sampling of evidence is all the more telling
since it comes from one who explicitly denies having any burden to uphold the reliability of the Bible.)
For a general survey of evidence for Solomonic authorship of the Song, see esp.
Christopher W. Mitchell, The Song of Songs (Concordia Commentary: A Theological Exposition of Sacred Scripture; Saint Louis: Concordia, 2003), 98–127. Cf. Franz Delitzsch,
Das Hohelied untersucht und ausgelegt (Leipzig: Dörffling & Franke, 1851), passim (summarized in Archer, Survey of Old Testament Introduction, 538–41); K&D, 6:504–7; and
Edward J. Young, An Introduction to the Old Testament (rev. ed.; Grand Rapids: Eerdmans,
1960), 332–33. Strong support of a tenth-century B.C.E. date for the Song (and that
the Song was written either by Solomon or for Solomon) is found in Garrett, "Song of
Songs," 16–25.

united monarchy (esp. the reference to the splendorous city of Tirzah, implying authorship "during the narrow window of history when Tirzah had prominence but was not yet the domain of an enemy state . . . [that is,] the Solomonic period";[60] locations in both north and south mentioned indiscriminately whereas the city of Samaria is not mentioned at all); (9) extensive parallels with the Proverbs of Solomon (e.g., Song 4:5 = Prov 5:19; 4:11 = Prov 5:3; 4:14 = Prov 7:17); (10) extensive similarities of vocabulary and syntax with the book of Ecclesiastes, which is also traditionally attributed to Solomon (e.g., the profusion of the relative pronoun *še*);[61] (11) use of archaic grammatical and poetic features;[62] and (12) extensive parallels with the Egyptian love poetry from the Eighteenth to the Twentieth Dynasty (1400–1070 B.C.E.), in themes and motifs, terms of endearment, imagery, vocabulary, and the use of superscriptions (in contrast to only sparse and superficial parallels to the later Hellenistic poetry).[63]

Contrary to the claims of scholars a few decades ago and more, there are now no substantive stylistic or lexical barriers preventing the adoption of an early date for the book. "Arguments for a late dating, which would preclude Solomonic authorship, have been largely exploded. Even some liberal-critical scholarship is now insisting that the book could have originated in the Solomonic era."[64] Robert Alter concurs: "All the supposed stylistic and lexical evidence for a late date is ambiguous, and it is quite possible, though not demonstrable, that these poems originated, whatever subsequent modifications they may have undergone, early in the

---

[60] Garrett, "Song of Songs," 228, who summarizes the archaeological and biblical data supporting this conclusion (20–21, 228).

[61] For discussion of an early (preexilic) date for Ecclesiastes based upon linguistic features, see esp. Daniel C. Fredericks, *Qoheleth's Language: Re-evaluating Its Nature and Date* (ANETS 3; Lewiston, N.Y.: Mellen, 1988); cf. Archer, *Survey of Old Testament Introduction*, 528–37.

[62] See, e.g., William F. Albright, "Archaic Survivals in the Text of Canticles," in *Hebrew and Semitic Studies Presented to Godfrey Rolles Driver* (ed. D. Winton Thomas and W. D. McHardy; Oxford: Clarendon, 1963), 1–7.

[63] For an analysis of parallels, see esp. Fox, *Song of Songs,* passim (although Fox, while noting the strong parallels to Egyptian love poetry, nonetheless dates the Song to a postexilic period on the basis of linguistic criteria that, as pointed out below, no longer are an obstacle to an early date); cf. G. Lloyd Carr, "The Love Poetry Genre in the Old Testament and the Ancient Near East: Another Look at Inspiration," *JETS* 25 (1982): 491–97; and Murphy, *Song of Songs,* 42–48. Garrett, "Song of Songs," 21, points to the inconsistency of critical scholars' acceptance of parallels with Egyptian love poetry but rejection of an early date for the book: "If the Hebrew and Egyptian texts are not directly related, one must say that it is peculiar that so many scholars give so much attention to analyzing correspondence between the two. Yet these very scholars will date the Song almost a millennium after the Egyptian texts. That is, instead of dating the Song near the time that the Egyptian love poetry of this kind flourished and to a time when, according to the Bible, Egyptian influence was strong in Jerusalem, these scholars date the Song to a time many hundreds of years after the passing of the Egyptian love songs and to a time when the Jewish community was a tiny department of the Persian Empire."

[64] Kinlaw, "Song of Songs," 5:1210. For a list of (mostly Israeli) critical scholars who now argue for a date in the Solomonic era (though not for King Solomon himself as author), see Landy, *Paradoxes of Paradise,* 281, n. 22.

First Commonwealth period."[65] The major lines of evidence, summarized above, and the removal of former linguistic roadblocks lead to the conclusion that Solomon was the author of the Song of Songs.

With acceptance of Solomonic authorship of the Song in the tenth century B.C.E., the evidence is most persuasive for the traditional view that the couple in the Song are King Solomon and Pharaoh's daughter.[66] Major lines of evidence include the following: (1) Solomon was a great lover of many women (1 Kgs 11:1–2), but although the various other women are lumped together, one is singled out, Pharaoh's daughter. (2) The importance of Pharaoh's daughter is underscored by her mention five times in the narrative of 1 Kings (1 Kgs 3:1; 7:8; 9:16, 24; 11:1–2). (3) The only clear reference to any wedding of Solomon in the historical narrative is that concerning his wedding to Pharaoh's daughter (1 Kgs 3:1). (4) An intertextual link seems to be evident in that the same verbal root ḥtn is used in the descriptions of the wedding of Solomon in 1 Kgs 3:1 and in Song 3:6. (5) First Kings 3:1 states of Pharaoh's daughter that Solomon "brought [bôʾ in the hipʿil] her into the city of David," and Song 1:4 is intertextually linked by the use of this same word, "The king has brought [bôʾ in the hipʿil] me into his chambers." (6) The "city of David" mentioned in 1 Kgs 3:1 is clearly Jerusalem, and the Song contains frequent interchange between the lady and the "daughters of Jerusalem" (e.g., Song 1:5; 2:7; 3:5, 11; 5:8, 16; 6:9; 8:4); the distinction between the woman in the song and the daughters of Jerusalem may suggest that she was not a native of Jerusalem. (7) Solomon's comparison of his beloved "to a mare among Pharaoh's chariots" (Song 1:9) would speak in familiar Egyptian terms to the heart of Pharaoh's daughter, and it constitutes another intertextual link to

---

[65] Robert Alter, *The Art of Biblical Poetry* (New York: Basic Books, 1985), 185. For a summary of the allegedly late linguistic features and a display of extrabiblical evidence showing that these features also existed early (even before the time of Solomon), see Archer, *Survey of Old Testament Introduction*, 538–39; Garrett, "Song of Songs," 16–18; and Ian Young, *Diversity in Pre-exilic Hebrew* (Tübingen: Mohr [Siebeck], 1993), 73–96, 157–65.

[66] I continue to maintain my former position (Davidson, "Theology of Sexuality," 11) that Solomon is the male lover in the Song, but I have changed (or broadened) my thinking on the probable identity of the Shulammite. I currently lean toward the traditional view, having been especially influenced by Victor Sasson's insightful article "King Solomon and the Dark Lady in the Song of Songs," *VT* 39 (1989): 407–14. Sasson states his thesis, which has become my own: "Increasingly I have come to conclude that the woman in question was Pharaoh's daughter whom Solomon loved and took for a wife" (p. 407). As a critical scholar, Sasson does not take Solomon and the lady in the Song as historical characters but as "poetic characters based on, or linked to, biblical historical records, both known and unknown to us" (ibid.). He also takes no position on the date or authorship of the Song. Nonetheless, he marshals strong evidence in favor of Solomon and Pharaoh's daughter being the principal characters intended in the Song. The evidence summarized below builds upon Sasson's study but goes beyond it (and against it) in some points. Assuming the beginning of Solomon's reign ca. 970–960 B.C.E. (see Tomoo Ishida, "Solomon," *ABD* 6:105), I suggest that the pharaoh who gave his daughter in marriage to Solomon was probably Siamun (978–959 B.C.E.), the next-to-last ruler in the Twenty-First (Tanite) Dynasty of Egypt (see Alfred Hoerth, *Archaeology and the Old Testament* [Grand Rapids: Baker, 1998], 291; cf. Kenneth A. Kitchen, *The Third Intermediate Period in Egypt, 1100–650 B.C.* [2d ed. with suppl.; Warminster, Eng.: Aris & Phillips, 1986], 280–83).

1 Kgs 3:1. (8) Song 7:2 (ET 7:1) seems to connect the woman to royal lineage; cf. the reference to her being "prince's daughter" (*bat-nādîb*) (7:2 [ET 7:1] NASB), paralleling the "princess" (*bat-melek*) in the Song of Love, Ps 45 (v. 14 [ET v. 13]), which psalm is likely connected to Solomon along with Ps 72.[67] (9) In Song 6:12 occurs the enigmatic mention of *markĕbôt ʿammî-nādîb* "the chariots of my royal/noble people" (translation mine), which could well refer to her royal lineage and link with the famous chariots of Egypt (cf. 1:9). (10) The play on words between Solomon, the Shulammite, and *šālôm*, "peace" (7:1 [ET 6:13]; 8:10–11),[68] all based on the same Hebrew root *šlm*, suggests that the lover in the Song, the partner of the Shulammite, is King Solomon.[69] All this evidence makes it more

---

[67] Psalm 45:11 (ET 45:10) advises the royal wife, "forget your people and your father's house," which may imply a foreign (Egyptian?) descent from at least her father's lineage. The question naturally arises as to how the Song can depict the Shulammite as a royal princess at the same time that she is described as a country girl from Northern Palestine. One possibility seems not to have been considered before: with many references to the "mother" and "mother's sons" and going to the "mother's house" but no reference to the father, could it be that the princess was one of Pharaoh Siamun's daughters whom he fathered in "one-night stands" with village women while he was on campaigns or visits in northern Palestine? There is biblical evidence for his conquering Gezer to give the city as a dowry to his daughter (1 Kgs 9:16), and this may not have been his only campaign or visit into Palestine. Some cities in northern Palestine, such as Beth-shan, constituted an Egyptian presence from the fifteenth century B.C.E. for several hundred years and probably were still under Egyptian influence in the time of the united monarchy (see Patrick E. McGovern, "Beth-Shan," *ABD* 1:694–95). Could it be that shortly after his coronation or even before, Solomon met one of these daughters of Pharaoh who might have grown up in northern rural Palestine with her mother and that he fell in love with her and married her for love (and not primarily for political alliance, as apparently with many of his later marriages)?

One indirect line of evidence favoring this suggestion comes from the fact that until this time in Egyptian history, state policy allowed only a prince, and not a princess, to be given in marriage to the ruler of another country but, starting about the time of Solomon, princesses were also given in marriage to foreign rulers (see Hoerth, *Archaeology and the Old Testament,* 291–92, for further discussion). During this period of weakness in Egyptian political history (two dynasties rivaling each other, one in Lower and one in Upper Egypt), with the rise in power of Israel's empire to the north, could it be that Pharaoh Siamun felt the need to establish a treaty with Solomon and, by providing a "local" princess for him to marry, succeeded in upholding the previous long-standing Egyptian policy? (Another possibility is that the Egyptian princess moved from Egypt to northern Palestine with her mother and brothers sometime before her courtship with Solomon.) These suggestions regarding the circumstances of Solomon's courtship and marriage to Pharaoh's daughter are admittedly speculative but seem to best account for all the evidence in the book. One is thereby able to posit the traditional view that Shulammite is Pharaoh's daughter, and at the same time incorporate the data from the Song that imply her identity as a country shepherd maiden of northern Palestine, which was my former position. At any rate, the overall thrust of the theology of sexuality in the Song does not depend on these hypotheses.

[68] See discussion of this paronomasia in Tom Gledhill, *The Message of the Song of Songs* (Bible Speaks Today; Downers Grove, Ill.: InterVarsity, 1994), 237.

[69] I concur with Sasson, "King Solomon and the Dark Lady," 410, that it does not make good sense to "fictionalize" all of the references to royalty in the Song by stating that the lovers are really shepherds "pretending" to be king and queen, along the lines of alleged parallels in extrabiblical Egyptian love poetry (contra Murphy, *Song of Songs,* 47;

than "mere guesswork"[70] to identify Shulammite with Pharaoh's daughter; the weight of evidence, if not compelling, is to me substantive and persuasive.

Since Solomon's marriage to Pharaoh's daughter took place at the beginning of his reign, even before he had built his house and the house of the Lord (1 Kgs 3:1; 7:8), the Song was probably written early in Solomon's reign, before he apostatized into idolatry and polygamy (1 Kgs 11:1–8). The narrative in 1 Kings implies that Solomon's marriage to Pharaoh's daughter was his first marriage, not only by the timing at the beginning of his reign, just mentioned above, but also by the description of Solomon's building projects. First Kings 7:7 describes Solomon's house for himself and then states (7:8), "Solomon also made a house like this hall for Pharaoh's daughter, whom he had taken in marriage." First Kings 9:24 indicates that "Pharaoh's daughter went up from the city of David to her own house that Solomon had built for her." The clear implication is that he was building a house for himself and a house for his sole wife. If at this time he had other wives, it would seem strange not to mention the provisions for them as well. The mention of Pharaoh's daughter five times in the narrative, with no mention of any previous wives, also seems to imply that this was his first wife. The parallel passage in 2 Chr 8:11 adds Solomon's own words when he brought up Pharaoh's daughter to her house, and also makes explicit that she is his sole wife: "My wife shall not live in the house of King David of Israel." Finally, in the context of Solomon's marriage to Pharaoh's daughter (1 Kgs 3:1), the narrator is careful to point out that Solomon had not yet apostatized from following God's statutes and commandments: "Solomon loved the LORD, walking in the statutes of his father David; only, he sacrificed and offered incense at the high places" (1 Kgs 3:3). Only in 1 Kgs 11:1–2 does the narrator mention the many other wives that Solomon, who turned his heart away from God, later took in violation of God's command.

Fox, *Song of Songs,* 98; and many other scholars). Most, if not all, of these Egyptian parallels of "literary fiction" are unconvincing: in the Egyptian love poetry cited by these authors, the context regularly makes it clear that the lovers are *wishing* they were someone else ("If I were appointed doorkeeper" [no. 7]; "If only I were her Nubian maid" [no. 21A]; "If only I were the laundryman" [no. 21B]), or using simile ("If only you would come [to your sister swiftly] like a royal horse" [no. 39]), or expressing feelings of the heart ("prince of my heart" [no. 17]; "I am the Mistress of the Two Lands [i.e., the queen of Egypt] *when I am with you*" [no. 8]), or using a term of affection ("[Give me] my prince tonight" [no. 13]). Furthermore, Murphy, *Song of Songs,* 47, acknowledges that "the persona of a 'king' is not mentioned in these texts" in contrast to the Song's repeated reference to Solomon as king. The Song is simply too saturated with royal figures and royal backdrop to fictionalize it all away. See Sasson, "King Solomon and the Dark Lady," 410, for other weighty arguments in favor of identifying the couple in the Song as a real royal couple. Sasson also suggests that this royal couple "act as shepherds because they feel impelled to return to nature's naked, fundamental realities. In nature the royal couple's love is divested of the trappings of the palace which can only act as a barrier to their expression of love for each other. In nature their love finds its true and innocent self." I would add that probably the woman was a shepherdess before her marriage to Solomon and that Solomon, son of David the once-shepherd, would also be well acquainted with shepherd's ways.

[70] As claimed by Garrett, "Song of Songs," 25.

The Song of Songs seems to underscore that the Shulammite was Solomon's one and only at this time, inasmuch as her name/epithet, "*the* Shulammite" = "*the* Solomoness" (see below for verification of this linkage), would hardly have been appropriate if there had been many Solomonesses at the time.

Not only does Scripture imply that Solomon's marriage to Pharaoh's daughter (whom I take to be the Shulammite of the Song of Songs) is his first marriage; also, as argued below, the woman in the Song is depicted as being a virgin at the time of the wedding (Song 4:12). Thus the marriage and sexual activity of Solomon and Shulammite in the Song are set in the context of a monogamous relationship.[71] Contrary to the common perception that Solomon fell into a

---

[71] Some scholars have argued that the reference to "sixty queens and eighty concubines" in Song 6:8 implies that Solomon already had quite a harem by the time of the experience described in the Song, but this need not be the case at all. Joseph C. Dillow postulates that this harem was inherited from his father, David, and "Solomon may not have been sexually involved with those many concubines until later in his reign, when we know he began to degenerate into lustful polygamy" (*Solomon on Sex: The Biblical Guide to Married Love* [New York: Thomas Nelson, 1977], 121). Carr, *Song of Solomon*, 148, argues that it is not necessary to equate this harem with Solomon's: "More probably, no particular harem is being considered. Note the text does not say 'Solomon has' or 'I have,' but it is a simple declaration: '*There are* . . . , and my beloved is unique' (v. 9, NIV)." Fox, *Song of Songs,* 152–53, concurs: "The verse [Song 6:8] does not refer to any particular group of women, such as Solomon's wives and concubines. The youth is saying: There are numerous queens and noble ladies around, but my beloved is one of a kind. None of them can compare to her, and what's more, even *they* recognize her majesty." Garrett, "Song of Songs," 228–29, points out that "the rounded numbers . . . indicate that this is an artificial device for the sake of hyperbolic comparison. The device is similar to the numerical pattern in Wisdom literature, 'there are three things . . . , there are four' ('sixty' and 'eighty' represent 3 x 20 and 4 x 20). . . . In the fashion of Wisdom literature, the man is proclaiming that however many other women of whatever status there may be, his beloved is still by far the best."

Still others point to the fact that Solomon reigned for forty years and then his son Rehoboam took over the throne at the age of forty-one (1 Kgs 11:42–43; 14:21), implying that Rehoboam was born the year before Solomon became king. But the LXX records in 1 Kgs 12:24a (in an extended section not found in the MT) that Rehoboam was sixteen years of age when he began to reign (not forty-one) and that he reigned twelve years. The LXX may well preserve the correct chronological data, since these data make more sense of the statement in 1 Kgs 12:8 that Rehoboam "consulted with the young men [*hayĕlādîm*] who had grown up with him and now attended him." The Hebrew term used for "young men" is *yeled,* "boy, (male) child, youth." If those who grew up with him were called "boys/youths," then Rehoboam himself was a "boy/youth" when he became king, and this would seem to apply more to a sixteen-year-old than to a forty-one-year-old. If Rehoboam was only sixteen when he ascended Solomon's throne, there would be ample chronological space for the twenty-plus years of Solomon's monogamous marriage to Shulammite before he married Rehoboam's mother and she gave birth to Rehoboam. As an alternate interpretation, one may note that according to 1 Kgs 14:21 Rehoboam's mother was "Naamah the Ammonite." It is possible that Naamah had already given birth to Rehoboam by an Ammonite father before her political marriage to Solomon and that Solomon simply adopted Rehoboam as his own (eldest) son (a practice hinted at from about this very time in Ps 2:7). David's bloodline, in this case, would be passed on through Rehoboam's wife Maachah (the granddaughter of Absalom, David's son), who gave birth to Rehoboam's successor, Abijam (1 Kgs 15:1, 2; 2 Chr 11:21).

polygamous lifestyle early in his reign, the record implies a long-lasting monogamous marital relationship between Solomon and the wife of his youth. As noted
above, Solomon's marriage to Pharaoh's daughter occurred before his extensive
building projects began (1 Kgs 3:1). The building of the temple took seven years
(6:38), and the building of his own house and the house for Pharaoh's daughter
another thirteen years (7:1), for a total of twenty years of building activity (9:10)
before he brought his sole wife, Pharaoh's daughter (Shulammite), to her house
in Jerusalem (9:24). Thus the monogamous marriage between Solomon and
Shulammite lasted at least twenty years and perhaps a number of years longer
(depending upon when he married Shulammite and when he started his polygamous lifestyle, neither of which chronological data is stated precisely in the
text). The text simply states that Solomon loved and married many other women
and that "when Solomon was *old,* his wives turned away his heart after other
gods" (11:1–4).

Of course, as the later account of Solomon's polygamous apostasy makes
clear (11:1–8), the historical reality of Solomon's later life is dissonant with what
is present in his earlier years as portrayed in the Song. But one must not allow the
later dark history of Solomon to detract from the ideal (and the reality of his earlier years) depicted in the "narrative frame" of the Song of Songs, the Sublime
Song. The Song has a happy, monogamous literary ending.

Although there is good evidence for identifying the couple in the Song as
Solomon and Pharaoh's daughter, the possibility is not entirely eliminated that
this poem depicts an idealized couple and their love relationship. But even if
one does not accept the identification of the Song's lovers as Solomon and the
daughter of Pharaoh, nonetheless the Song itself provides sufficient evidence
for the conclusion that the relationship between the lovers is envisaged as monogamous. Garrett, who sees an idealized and not historical couple portrayed
in the Song, summarizes the internal evidence for this conclusion and its
implications:

> This love is monogamous in nature. The woman is to the man "my sister, my com-
> panion, my bride" (e.g., Song 5:1). She is the lotus blossom; all other women are
> thorns (Song 2:2). Among sixty queens and eighty concubines, and an endless num-
> ber of girls, "my dove" is perfect and unique (Song 6:8–9; the figures represent a con-
> trived comparison; the man is not saying that he has other queens, concubines, and
> girl-friends . . .). To the woman, the man is simply "my lover" and the one "whom
> my soul loves" (e.g., Song 1:7; 5:10). He is an apple tree; all other men are just trees in
> the forest (Song 2:3). He is the best among ten thousand men (Song 5:10). Most pow-
> erfully, the woman proclaims, "My lover is mine and I am his" (e.g., Song 2:16). To
> dismiss all this as white lies and empty "sweet talk" (as when a man who has several
> girlfriends tells one of them, "You're the only girl for me!") is to indulge in the kind
> of cynicism that is set against. The song portrays an idealized, perfect love; when
> these idealized lovers express their absolute devotion to each other, we can assume
> that they mean it.[72]

---

[72] Garrett, "Song of Songs," 103.

Beyond this catena of passages from the Song upholding monogamy, Garrett also cites three other passages in the Song that point toward a monogamous (and married) relationship between the lovers. First, in Song 2:7 (and parallel passages 3:5 and 8:4) the women tells the girls, in effect, "Do not enter into a sexual relationship until the right time . . . that is, the woman asserts that girls should remain virgins until marriage."[73] Second, 3:6–11 describes a wedding. "An ancient audience would have recognized this and understood that this is not a couple engaging in extramarital sex."[74] Third, in 8:6–7 "fidelity to one's bride is here equated with fidelity to Wisdom herself."[75] In the third passage also the woman sings in the imperative to her husband, "Set me as a seal upon your heart, as a seal upon your arm," and by her "unashamedly possessive and exclusive" statement, "infidelity and even polygamy are here excluded."[76] (Later sections of this chapter and chapter 14, below, discuss these passages further.)

Equality of the Sexes without Hierarchy

A fourth major facet in the Song's theology of sexuality is the highlighting of egalitarianism, mutuality, and reciprocity between the lovers. The Song "reflects an image of woman and female–male relations that is extremely positive and egalitarian."[77] Indeed, Othmar Keel rightly asserts, "nowhere in the OT is the equality of the sexes . . . as real as in the Song."[78] Phipps gives a similar, even more sweeping, assessment: "Nowhere in ancient literature can such rapturous mutuality be paralleled."[79] The keynote of egalitarianism is struck in Song 2:16: "My beloved is mine and I am his." The same refrain recurs in 6:3, "I am my beloved's and my beloved is mine," and a third time in 7:11 (ET 7:10), "I am my beloved's, and his desire is for me." Scholars have not failed to point out the implication of this thrice repeated refrain: "Love-eros is mutual; it puts the two partners on a perfectly equal footing";[80] "The present verse [7:11] speaks of a relationship of

---

[73] Ibid., 103–4.

[74] Ibid., 103.

[75] Ibid.

[76] Ibid., 256.

[77] Leonard Swidler, *Biblical Affirmations of Woman* (Philadelphia: Westminster, 1979), 92.

[78] Keel, *Song of Songs,* 32.

[79] Phipps, *Genesis and Gender,* 94; see 94–95 for a rich discussion of the equality/mutuality theme in the Song. See also David M. Carr, *The Erotic Word: Sexuality, Spirituality, and the Bible* (New York: Oxford University Press, 2003), 134: "This bond, however is not one of the male claiming power over his wife's reproduction. Instead, this is a mutual passion between a man and a woman who are as equal as they can be in their social context." And Alicia Ostriker, "A Holy of Holies: The Song of Songs as Countertext," in *The Song of Songs* (ed. Athalya Brenner and Carole R. Fontaine; FCB[2] 6; Sheffield, Eng.: Sheffield Academic Press, 2000), 49–50, assesses, "What is extraordinary in the Song is precisely the absence of structural and systemic hierarchy, sovereignty, authority, control, superiority, submission, in the relation of the lovers."

[80] André LaCocque, *Romance She Wrote: A Hermeneutical Essay on Song of Songs* (Harrisburg, Pa.: Trinity Press International, 1998), 37.

mutuality, expressed in a formula of reciprocal love like that in 2:16, 6:3. In the Song, sex is free of notions of control, dominion, hierarchy."[81]

This egalitarianism/mutuality/reciprocity is revealed throughout the Song in a number of ways. Several recent studies have pointed to literary techniques in the Song that highlight the gender mutuality between the lovers.[82] Perhaps most obvious is the frequent use of echoing, in which the words or actions of the one lover are repeated or patterned on the other's.[83] Especially significant are the mutuality of actions and the statements in reversal of stereotypical gender conceptions, which usually place the woman in a passive-receptive and dependent role with the man taking the independent initiative. Thus, for example, the woman, like the man, is portrayed as a person of capability, independence, and self-reliance. She, like the man, is gainfully employed—(1:6, 7; cf. 6:11). Even after the marriage—at the conclusion of the Song—she continues to display her business acumen and retain her self-reliance: like Solomon, she owns a vineyard and is not totally dependent upon her husband for sustenance (8:11–12). The lovers see each other as having eyes like doves (4:1; 5:12); both are proud and tall like trees (5:15; 7:8 [ET 7:7]); both describe parts of the other's body as rounded and crafted like artworks (5:14, 15a; 7:2b, 3a [ET 7:1b, 2a]).

Again, the woman is just as active in the lovemaking as the man. She brings him to the love chamber (3:4) just as he brings her (1:4; 2:4). She sexually arouses

[81] Ariel Bloch and Chana Bloch, *The Song of Songs: A New Translation with an Introduction and Commentary* (New York: Random House, 1995), 207.

[82] See, e.g., Dorsey, *Literary Structure of the Old Testament,* 199–213; Fox, *Song of Songs,* 318–21; Kinlaw, "Song of Songs," 1234; and Carol Meyers, "Gender Imagery in the Song of Songs," *HAR* 10 (1986): 209–23.

[83] A partial list of gender parallel or "echoing" passages includes 1:2 = 4:10 (his love and her love are better than wine); 1:4 = 3:4 (he brings her into his chamber, she brings him into the chamber of her mother); 1:4 and 3:11 and 7:6 [ET 7:5] = 7:1–2 [ET 6:13 and 7:1] (he is King Solomon and she is Shulammite, royal daughter); 1:7, 8 and 3:1–4 and 5:6–7 = 2:9, 14 (she searches for him and he searches for her); 1:12–14 = 4:6, 13 (he is nard, myrrh, and henna, and she is nard, myrrh and henna); 1:15 = 1:16 and 7:7 [ET 7:6] (he calls her beautiful and she calls him beautiful); 1:15 and 4:1 and 7:5 [ET 7:4] = 5:12 (her eyes are doves and pools in Heshbon and his eyes are doves beside springs of water); 2:2 = 2:3 (she is better than other women and he is better than other men); 2:3 = 7:8–9 [ET 7:7–8] (he is an apple tree, she is a palm tree); 2:4 = 8:2 (he brings her into the house of wine and she brings him to the house and gives him wine); 2:8 = 4:8 (he comes from the mountains and she comes from Mt. Lebanon); 2:9, 17 and 8:14 = 4:5 and 7:4 [ET 3] (he is like a gazelle and her breasts are like two fawns, twins of a gazelle); 2:10–13 = 7:12, 13 [ET 7:11, 12] (he invites her for a walk in springtime and she invites him for a walk in springtime); 2:16 and 6:3 = 4:5 (he grazes in the lilies and her breasts graze in the lilies); 4:11 = 5:15 (the scent of her garment is like the scent of Lebanon and his appearance is like Lebanon); 4:11 = 5:13 (her lips are dripping honey and his lips are dripping myrrh); 5:16 = 7:10 [ET 7:9] (his mouth is sweet and her mouth is like "sweet wine" [NJB]. Note also the longer echoing *wasf*s (praise descriptions): 3:6–11 and 5:9–16 = 4:1–15 and 6:4–10 (she describes his beauty and he describes hers). Elliott, *Literary Unity,* 246–51, calls this technique "mirroring dynamic," and presents some twenty examples in the Song, including some not listed above which involve single-term descriptive metaphors applied to both the lover and the beloved.

him (8:5) just as he has aroused her (2:3–4; 5:2–5). She uses expressions of endearment and praise for him just as he does for her (e.g., "my beloved" [raʿātî/rēʿî], 5:2, 16, etc.), "Ah, you are beautiful" [hinnāk yāpâ/hinnĕkā yāpeh] (1:15–16). Both use similar language to praise the beauty of the other (e.g., eyes like doves [1:15; 4:1; 5:12], "beautiful, . . . truly lovely" [1:16; 7:2, 7 (ET 7:1, 6)], lips dripping honey/ myrrh [4:11; 5:13], and whole matching sections with extended praise of the other's beauty [4:1–16; 6:4–10; 7:2–10 (ET 7:1–9)]). She invites him to come with her into the fields (7:12–14 [ET 7:11–13]) just as he invites her (2:10–14). In the Song, "where the lovers take turns inviting each other, desire is entirely reciprocal. Both are described in images that suggest tenderness (lilies/lotus flowers, doves, gazelles) as well as strength and stateliness (pillars, towers). In this book of the Bible, the woman is certainly the equal of the man."[84]

Daniel Grossberg's assessment of the reciprocity and mutuality of roles between man and woman is not an overstatement:

> In all of Canticles there is hardly a thought, idea or deed that is not attributed to *both* the male and the female. Almost all expressions (spoken both inwardly, outwardly, and acted) are shared by the two lovers in the Song of Songs. . . . Sexism and gender stereotyping, so prevalent in ancient (and modern) literature is totally lacking in Canticles. Instead, undifferentiated, shared roles and positions are the rule. Harmony, not domination, is the hallmark of the Song of Songs. . . . In Canticles, neither one of the couples is subordinate; neither is minor. The Song revolves around them both equally. They are costars sharing the spotlight.[85]

David Dorsey's literary structural analysis of the Song demonstrates how each of its seven sections reinforces and enhances the theme of reciprocity/mutuality by means of various structuring devices, including alternation of speeches, initiations, and invitations, and the numerous matchings of reciprocal expressions of love.

> These structuring techniques underscore the point that the two lovers are equally in love, equally adore one another, and are equally ready to initiate, to suggest, to invite. The ideal conveyed by the author's structure (as well as by the contents of the speeches) is an egalitarianism and mutuality in romantic love that is virtually unparalleled in ancient Near Eastern literature. In a world that was strongly patriarchal, where love lyrics often portrayed the man as a "bull" and the woman as something less than his equal, the Song of Songs represents a surprisingly high view of woman and a remarkable vision of the ideal of equality and delightful reciprocity in the marriage relationship.[86]

Indeed, apparently to accentuate this mutuality and equality in dramatic reversal of gender stereotypes prevailing at that time, the woman is given the predominant role in the Song.[87] Landy aptly calls "the dominance and initiative of the

---

84 Bloch and Bloch, *Song of Songs,* 4.

85 Daniel Grossberg, "Two Kinds of Sexual Relations in the Hebrew Bible," *HS* 34 (1994): 12, 15. See Ayo, *Sacred Marriage,* 40, for a similar assessment.

86 Dorsey, *Literary Structure of the Old Testament,* 213; see his discussion in 200–213.

87 See Bloch and Bloch, *Song of Songs,* 4–6; LaCocque, *Romance She Wrote,* 39–53; Meyers, "Gender Imagery," 209–21; and Trible, *God and the Rhetoric of Sexuality,* 144–65.

Beloved [the woman] the most astonishing characteristic of the Song."[88] The Song
of Songs begins and closes with the woman speaking (1:2–4a; 8:14). The image of
the garden, representing the woman, falls at the midpoint of the Song, emphasizing her predominance.[89] The woman carries almost twice the amount of dialogue
as the man.[90] A number of the man's lines are in fact quotations of him made by
the woman (2:10–14; 5:2), whereas the man never quotes the woman's words. It is
the woman who interrelates with the other major and minor protagonists in the
Song. The woman initiates most of the meetings with her lover. In these rendezvous, she repeatedly takes the initiative.[91] The woman's invitations to love are
more forceful and outspoken than the man's (4:16; 7:13 [ET 7:12]; 8:2). Most of
the first-person verbs have reference to the woman; she is the only one who uses
the emphatic "I" (ʾănî) (twelve times); and the significant introspective term
"soul, self" (nepeš) is applied only to her (seven times).[92] Only she makes dra-

---

[88] Francis Landy, "The Songs of Songs," in *The Literary Guide to the Bible* (ed. Robert
Alter and K. Kermode; Cambridge, Mass.: Belknap, 1987), 317.

[89] Munro, *Spikenard and Saffron,* 109, elaborates: "The image of the garden, developed over a number of verses (4:12–5:1), falls at the midpoint of the Song. The position of
the image not only emphasizes the predominance of the woman, who throughout the
Song plays the major part, but also echoes structurally the relationship of the woman to
the world beyond, in the eyes of her beloved one; the natural world and the abundance of
life visible there is recreated in her, for she, to him, is the personification of its beauty."

[90] The count may vary depending upon the interpretation of the sometimes ambiguous first-person statements and unmarked sections. Athalya Brenner, *The Israelite
Woman: Social Role and Literary Type in Biblical Narrative* (Sheffield, Eng.: JSOT Press,
1985), 44–50, analyzes in detail the distribution of male and female voices in the Song and
concludes that the female voice(s) account(s) for approximately 53 percent of the text
whereas the male voice(s) account(s) for only 34 percent. Carr, "Love Poetry Genre," 494,
counts lines: out of 227 lines, 114 are for the girl, 54 for the lover, 31 of mixed dialogue,
and 28 lines by a third party. My own count comes to 74 verses or parts of verses where the
woman speaks and only 38 where the man speaks, giving the woman about twice as many
lines as the man. (I include in the woman's speeches her citations of the man [2:10–14;
5:2] and 3:7–11 [following the arguments of Bloch and Bloch, *Song of Songs,* 161–62].)
Carr, ibid., cautions that these statistics must not be made to prove too much, inasmuch as
the same two-to-one ratio of female-to-male speeches also occurs in the ANE love poems
of Egypt and Mesopotamia. The preponderance of the woman's speech throughout the
Song, however, is much more than elsewhere in the ancient Near East if one eliminates the
four lengthy *waṣfs* (descriptions and praise of the physical beauty of the man and woman:
4:1–15; 5:10–16; 6:4–9; 7:2–10 [ET 7:1–9]): the woman still has 61 verses or parts of verses
of dialogue whereas the man only has 7 verses, a ratio of more than eight-to-one.

[91] She *invites* the man: "Draw me after you, let us make haste" (1:4). She *commands*
the man, using the imperative: "Turn, . . . be like a gazelle" (2:17); "Make haste, . . . and be
like a gazelle . . . !" (8:14). She *grasps* the man and will not let him go (2:15). She *leads* the
man to her mother's house and love chamber (3:4; 8:2). She *gives* the man her love (7:13
[ET 7:12]). She sexually *awakens* the man under the apple tree (8:5).

[92] The occurrences of ʾănî are 1:5, 6; 2:1, 5, 16; 5:2, 5, 6, 8; 6:3; 7:11 (ET 7:10); 8:10. The
term *nepeš* is found in 1:7; 3:1, 2, 3, 4; 5:6; 6:12. See M. Deckers, "The Structure of the Song
of Songs and the Centrality of *nepeš* (6:12)," in *A Feminist Companion to the Song of Songs*
(ed. Athalya Brenner; FCB 1; Sheffield, Eng.: Sheffield Academic Press, 1993), 172–96;
and Grace I. Emmerson, "The Song of Songs: Mystification, Ambiguity, and Humour," in

matic, self-assured statements about her beauty and character: "I am black and[93] beautiful" (1:5); "I am the [glorious, beautiful] rose of Sharon, the [single, special][94] lily/lotus of the valleys" (2:1 translation mine);[95] "I was a wall, and my breasts were like towers"[96] (8:10). Only she commands the elements: "Awake, O north wind, and come, O south wind! Blow upon my garden" (4:16). The Shulammite is the one who pronounces the great wisdom sayings about love (8:6–7; cf. 2:7; 3:5; 8:4). Dianne Bergant summarizes the attributes of the Shulammite not traditionally ascribed to women: "She is assertive, taking the initiative in this relationship. She is undaunted, risking misunderstanding and censure as she pursues her love. She is responsible, being accountable for her actions. She is protective, shielding her lover and the love they share from the prying eyes of others."[97]

Crossing the Boundaries: Essays in Biblical Interpretation in Honour of Michael D. Goulder (ed. Stanley E. Porter, Paul Joyce, and David E. Orton; New York: E. J. Brill, 1994), 101–2.

[93] The Hebrew conjunction *wĕ* can be translated either "and" or "but." In this case, the meaning comes out essentially the same. She is saying, in effect, "I am dark from the sun, and/but whatever you may think about it, I think it is beautiful!"

[94] The use of the *-at* ending of *šôšannâ* in this verse (contrasted with the masc. pl. in other occurrences in the Song) denotes "singularity." See Bruce K. Waltke and Michael P. O'Connor, *An Introduction to Biblical Hebrew Syntax* (Winona Lake, Ind.: Eisenbrauns, 1990), 105: "Single components of a collective unit often appear with *-at* suffix: such a form is called a *nomen unitatis* or singulative." Waltke and O'Connor give *šôšannâ* as an example of this phenomenon. The woman is a singular, special lily out of all the others in the valleys.

[95] Most commentaries wrongly interpret this line as having a tone of self-depreciation. But Bloch and Bloch, *Song of Songs*, 148–49, rightly point out that the very two flowers mentioned in Song 2:1, "rose" (*ḥăbaṣṣelet*) and "lily" (*šôšannâ*), are the ones mentioned in the prophecies of Israel's restoration to her former glory (Isa 35:1–2; Hos 14:6–8 [ET 14:5–7]), and the mention of Sharon probably links with "the majesty of Carmel and Sharon" in Isa 35:2. They conclude, "Seen in this light, 2:1 is an expression of a young woman's proud awareness of her blossoming beauty. The Shulamite is not presenting herself—either modestly or coyly—as a common ordinary flower of the field ('I am a mere flower of the plain,' as Ginsburg and others would have it). Quite the contrary, she is identifying herself with the *ḥăbaṣṣelet* and *šôšannâ*, two flowers that are the very epitome of blossoming in the symbolism of the Bible." Many modern versions retain the translation "lily" for *šôšannâ* in the Song, but recent studies have presented weighty evidence for translating this Hebrew term as "lotus" rather than "lily." See esp. Blažej Štrba, "שׁושׁנה of the Canticle," *Bib* 85 (2004): 475–502; and W. Derek Suderman, "Modest or Magnificent? Lotus versus Lily in Canticles," *CBQ* 67 (2005): 42–58. If the correct translation is "lotus" and not "lily," then, as Suderman points out, with regard to Song 2:1, "Rather than drawing on the most abundant and common flower as an 'expression of humility,' by comparing herself to a lotus the woman calls up an image of exceptional beauty, sweet fragrance, and rich symbolic imagery. From this perspective the second line builds incrementally on the first so as to heighten rather than diminish the woman's self-description. . . . Thus, the woman's self description is transformed from an expression of her common character into a bold statement of her singular, spectacular status as beautiful and without comparison in 'the valleys'" (p. 50, 52).

[96] For further discussion of the symbolism of self-assured inaccessibility in this clause, see below in the section on intimacy.

[97] Dianne Bergant, *The Song of Songs: The Love Poetry of Scripture* (Spiritual Commentaries; Hyde Park, N.Y.: New City, 1998), 158.

The woman is also described with imagery that is normally connected with the male. Carol Meyers has shown that "the Song as a whole presents a significant corpus of images and terms derived from the military—and hence the male—world. Without exception these terms are applied to the female. . . . Since military language is derived from an aspect of ancient life almost exclusively associated with men, its use in the Song in reference to the woman constitutes an unexpected reversal of conventional imagery or of stereotypical gender association."[98] Meyers also examines the use of animal imagery in the Song and notes that although some animals (such as the dove and the gazelle) depict the character of both the male and the female, the wild beasts—lion and leopard—with their wild habitations are associated exclusively with the female (4:8). "Nothing would be further from a domestic association for a female. Nor does the wildness, danger, might, strength, aggressiveness, and other dramatic features of these predators fit any stereotypical female qualities."[99] Combining both military and faunal imagery, the woman is also compared to a "mare among Pharaoh's chariots" (1:9). This connotes a powerful military ploy: "The female horse set loose among the stallions of the chariotry does violence to the military effectiveness of the charioteers. The female has a power of her own that can offset the mighty forces of a trained army."[100] Again, the military term *ʾăyummâ* "terrifying"[101] or "awe-inspiring" (NAB) is twice linked with the woman in the Song: she is "terrible [*ʾăyummâ*] as an army with banners" (6:4, 10).[102]

What is more, the woman in the Song possesses not only awesome power but power over the man. She ravishes (*lbb* in the *piʿel*) his heart with one look of her eyes (4:9). Her eyes overcome or overwhelm him—elicit his fear (*rāhab* in the *hipʿil*) (6:5). Amazingly, the king—one of the most powerful humans on earth—is held captive/bound/imprisoned (*qal* pass. of *ʾāsar*) by the tresses of her hair (7:6 [ET 7:5]). Clearly "the reversal of conventional gender typing is again evident."[103]

Moving beyond the predominance of the female lover herself, one can recognize throughout the Song that a "gynocentric mode"[104] prevails. The third set of

---

[98] Meyers, "Gender Imagery," 215. The imagery of military architecture (pp. 212–15) include the military tower, armory, and shields (4:4); the military tower, outpost "tower of Lebanon," pools of Heshbon (probably for military purposes), and defensive gate of Bathrabbim (all in 7:5 [ET 7:4]); and the towers and wall with "a battlement" or "buttresses" or "turrets" (again in a military context, 8:9–10).

[99] Ibid., 216.

[100] Ibid., 217. This military ploy and the fact that Egyptian chariots were drawn by stallions, not mares, are discussed in detail, with illustrations from ANE literature, esp. by Pope, *Song of Songs,* 336–41.

[101] *HALOT* 41.

[102] The word for "army" does not appear in the MT of this verse, but the poetry allows the translator to supply the kinds of banners clearly implied.

[103] Meyers, "Gender Imagery," 218. This is not to imply that the woman possesses magical powers or that she literally domineers over the man. This is the language of metaphor, not magic or manipulation.

[104] Ibid.

voices is the "daughters of Jerusalem," who play no small role in the movement of the Song.[105] The mother of the woman or man is mentioned seven times in the Song,[106] but never the father. The king is crowned by his mother for his wedding (3:11).[107] Furthermore, the Song twice mentions the "mother's house" (3:4; 8:2), never the masculine equivalent. This is very significant, even startling, in view of the importance of the term "father's house" elsewhere in Scripture.

The emphasis upon the woman—and women—in the Song does not, however, imply the superiority or dominance of woman over man. Rather, in light of prevailing stereotypical biases that placed women in a subservient or subordinate role, the Song sets right the stereotypical gender imbalance by highlighting the woman's powers. At the same time, the Song pictures the woman desiring the man to draw her away after him (1:4). She is pictured leaning upon, and resting under the protecting shadow of, her lover. Thus 2:3: "As an apple tree among the trees of the wood, so is my beloved among young men. With great delight I sat in his shadow, and his fruit was sweet to my taste." Francis Landry catches the intent of the imagery: "The apple-tree symbolizes the lover, the male sexual function in the poem; erect and delectable, it is a powerful erotic metaphor. It provides the nourishment and shelter, traditional male roles—the protective lover, man the provider."[108] Song of Songs 8:5 seems to continue the male-protector motif: "Who is that coming up from the wilderness, leaning upon her beloved?"[109] Song of Songs 8:2 may also describe the woman being instructed (in lovemaking) by her husband.[110]

By highlighting both the woman's initiative/power and the protecting, providing role of the man, the Song paints a balanced portrait of full mutuality and egalitarianism, captured by the refrain already quoted from the woman: "My beloved is mine and I am his" (2:16; cf. 6:3; 7:11[ET 7:10]). "The Song has a

---

[105] The daughters of Jerusalem/Zion sing or are addressed numerous times in the Song: 1:4, 5, 11; 2:7; 3:5, 10, 11; 5:8, 9, 16; 6:1, 8–9; 8:4. By contrast, the brothers are only alluded to—and with the term "My mother's sons," not "brothers"—in 1:6 and perhaps (but far from certain) have lines in 2:15 and 8:8–9. For discussion of the significance of the daughters of Jerusalem in the structure, content, and flow of the Song, see esp. Munro, *Spikenard and Saffron*, 43–48.

[106] Song 1:6; 3:4, 11; 6:9; 8:1, 2, 5.

[107] If the groom in the Song is Solomon, as I have argued, then the mother is the famous Bathsheba, known for her great beauty (2 Sam 11:2).

[108] Landy, "Song of Songs and the Garden of Eden," 526.

[109] The very next line (8:5c) reintroduces the "apple tree" metaphor, but it is now the woman who awakens the man under the apple tree. Thus juxtaposed in two lines are the images of female initiative/independence and male protection. Certainly the author wished this balanced perspective to be held together. Some have claimed that this verse does not refer to an apple tree but to some other kind of fruit tree (such apricot or even citrus), because it is claimed that the edible apple was not known in ancient Israel. But for evidence of the antiquity of the apple tree and for arguments of the probable existence of edible apples in the time of Israel, see, e.g., Garrett, "Song of Songs," 149–50.

[110] The Hebrew is ambiguous whether the Shulammite is instructed by her mother or her husband. Perhaps there is an intentional ambiguity to imply both, as will be explored below in the discussion of double entendres in the Song.

preponderance of females, but that situation does not obtain at the cost of a sustained sense of gender mutuality. Neither male nor female is set in an advantageous position with respect to the other. . . . In the erotic world of human emotion, there is no subordination of female to the male."[111] "Although feminist scholars insist that the female 'voice' is very conspicuous in the Song, the male voice is also constantly 'there' and equally strong. Thus, the Song does not celebrate the supremacy of either gender, but praises mutuality and equality."[112]

This balanced perspective of equality between the sexes not only serves to militate against distorted stereotypical gender biases but also may constitute an implicit polemic against the mythological worldview and rituals of the fertility cults, in which the woman was a "deadly, bewitching goddess who must be propitiated, cajoled, and in the end, endured." In the Song, although there are intriguing parallels of language and imagery with the fertility cult rituals, the woman has no divine magical powers that dominate, threaten, and even emasculate the male. She is "no deadly lunar goddess, but only a lovely young woman. . . . [The Song's] repudiation of the fertility goddess paradigm is barely detectable. Yet through it the reader is quietly seduced into rejecting the goddess, and sexual allure is established as a properly human reality."[113] Whitesell, who analyzes the parallels and differences between the Song and the fertility myths, concludes,

> A trend that is operative throughout the Song is that of redressing the imbalance between male and female as they function in the myth. Although the maiden is portrayed paradigmatically, she is everywhere less imposing than the goddess. Her dangerous aspect is all but gone. The lust and promiscuity so conspicuous in the goddess are veiled and transformed in the Shulamite into a deep emotional longing for a single lover. He, conversely, gains in dignity, stability, and prestige, while conforming nominally to the mythical type. The result is a pair of perfectly matched human lovers.[114]

Several modern studies have pointed out that the Song of Songs constitutes a reversal of the divine judgment set forth in Gen 3:16, and a return to Eden before the fall (Gen 1–2) regarding the love relationship between male and female.[115] Such a reversal seems implicit in the Song's echo of Eden's "desire" (*tĕšûqâ*)—a

---

[111] Meyers, "Gender Imagery," 220. Meyers limits this arena of gender mutuality in Scripture only to the situation of domestic, nonpublic, love. My study of the theology of sexuality in the OT, however, has convinced me that God's ultimate ideal throughout OT history has been an egalitarian one for the sexes, although the husband was given the responsibility of servant headship when necessary to preserve harmony in the home.

[112] S. S. Ndoga and Hendrik Viviers, "Is the Woman in the Song of Songs Really That Free?" *HTS* 56, no. 4 (2000): 1286–1307, quote at 1286 (abstract). See their supporting arguments in the remainder of the article.

[113] Whitesell, "'Behold, Thou Art Fair, My Beloved,'" 94–95.

[114] Ibid., 97.

[115] Bloch and Bloch, *Song of Songs,* 207: "Song 7:11 [ET 7:10] reads almost like a deliberate reversal of Gen. 3:16, turning it upside down by making the *woman* the object of desire." Cf. Trible, "Depatriarchalizing," 46; idem, *God and the Rhetoric of Sexuality,* 159–60; and Kinlaw, "Song of Songs," 1239.

term found only in Gen 3:16 and Song 7:11 (ET 7:10) with reference to sexual desire between man and woman. In Song 7:11 (ET 7:10), the third of the woman's three explicit affirmations of mutuality with her lover (along with 2:16 and 6:3, already cited above), the Shulammite says, "I am my beloved's, and his desire [*tĕšûqâ*] is for me." Whereas the judgment of God in Gen 3:16 stated that the woman's desire (*tĕšûqâ*) would be for her husband and he would "rule" (*māšal*) over her (in the sense of servant leadership), now the Song describes a reversal—the man's desire (*tĕšûqâ*) is for his lover. But contrary to the feminist readings that see here a movement away from a distorted use of male power (which is their [misguided] interpretation of Gen 3:16), I find a reaffirmation of the divine ideal of full equality ("one-fleshness") between husband and wife set forth in Gen 2:24, without necessarily denying the validity of Gen 3:16. Song of Songs does not nullify the provision of Gen 3:16 whereby the servant leadership of the husband may be necessary to preserve the harmony in the home. But the Song reveals that after the fall it is still possible for man and woman to experience that mutual, reciprocal love wherein headship/submission is transcended and the egalitarian ideal of Gen 2:24 is completely realized.[116]

We have indeed returned to Eden. This return to full reciprocity is encapsulated in the names of the lovers. Just as in pre-fall Eden the husband and wife were called ʾîš and ʾiššâ (Gen 2:23)—names linked together by sound and (folk) etymology, so in the return to Eden the names of the lovers once again intertwine—*šĕlōmōh* (Solomon) and *šûlammît* (Shulammite/Shulammit = Solomoness).[117]

---

[116] My thinking has developed considerably on the question of egalitarianism since my initial treatment of the theology of human sexuality in the Song (Davidson, "Theology of Sexuality," 8–10). I still consider the divine judgment of Gen 3:16 to be a (qualified) prescription applicable in situations where it is necessary to maintain harmony in the home. But I find that the Song of Songs, like the Gen 1–3 accounts, show us that God's ideal is still Gen 2:24 and that egalitarianism, mutuality, and reciprocity can be experienced by lovers even in a sinful environment.

[117] Many suggestions have been made for the derivation and meaning of *šûlammît* (Song 7:1 [6:13]). For the options in interpretation, see Bloch and Bloch, *Song of Songs*, 197–98; Fox, *Song of Songs*, 157–58; Murphy, *Song of Songs*, 181; and Pope, *Song of Songs*, 596–600. The least problematic solution (without resorting to emendations or Ishtar mythology) is to take the word as the feminine equivalent of Solomon or at least as a name/title related etymologically (or by folk etymology) to Solomon. See the support for this connection of *šûlammît* to Solomon in Harold H. Rowley, "The Meaning of 'The Shulammite,'" *AJSL* 56 (1939): 84–91 (summarized, with additional support from a Ugaritic parallel, in Pope, *Song of Songs*, 596–97). Delitzsch, *Proverbs, Ecclesiastes, Song of Solomon*, 3:120, correctly concludes that the poet purposely used this name "to assimilate her name to that of Solomon." I take the article before the word as the equivalent of the vocative particle, "O Shulamite" (see Joüon 137–38; GKC §126e, note [e]; Pope, *Song of Songs*, 600), and the article also seems to point to a specific woman as *the* Solomoness (implying that she was his one and only wife at this time). It is difficult to know whether the term is to be taken as a personal name (Shulammite or Shulammit) or as an epithet (the Solomoness). As Pope, *Song of Songs*, 600, points out, "The distinction between proper name and epithet is not easy to maintain, since proper names often develop from epithets. The article may be applied to an epithet on the way to becoming a proper noun, or a proper noun with the article may be regarded as an epithet in cases like the Lebanon,

The reciprocation between Solomon and the Solomoness displays the equivalent of the *ʿēzer kĕnegdô* of Gen 2:18: the lovers in the Song return to Eden as egalitarian, mutual, reciprocal partners.

Sexuality and Wholeness

Closely related to the motif of mutuality/egalitarianism is a fifth facet in the theology of sexuality—the concept of wholeness. This is highlighted by "one of the key themes in the Song"—"the presence and/or absence of the lovers to each other."[118] Throughout the Song the fact of physical closeness is obviously important as the lovers speak and cling to each other: "O that his left hand were under my head, and that his right hand embraced me!" (Song 2:6; 8:3). Even more significant is the feeling of loss and anxiety at the absence of the partner. Already in 1:7 the desire of the beloved for a rendezvous with her lover is clear: "Tell me, you whom my soul loves, where you pasture your flock . . . ?" The eagerness to be with the beloved is also evident from both the woman's exclamations of joy and the man's exuberant approach in 2:8: "The voice of my beloved! Look, he comes leaping upon the mountains, bounding over the hills."

But the absence-presence motif reaches its zenith at the matched nocturnal/dream sections[119] of the symmetrical macrostructure of the Song (3:1–5; 5:2–8),[120] in which the woman searches anxiously for her lover:

> Upon my bed at night
>   I sought him whom my soul loves;
>   I sought him, but found him not. . . .
>   "Have you seen him whom my soul loves?" (3:1, 3)

---

the Nile, the Jordan, the Baal, the Christ, etc." Even if the name also denotes "completeness/perfection" (as suggested by various commentators, e.g., Pope, ibid., 599–600), it seems clear that in the Song there is intended a paronomasia between this name and Solomon.

[118] Roland E. Murphy, "A Biblical Model of Human Intimacy: The Song of Songs," in *The Family in Crisis or in Transition: A Sociological and Theological Perspective* (ed. Andrew Greeley; Concilium 121; New York: Seabury, 1979), 63; cf. idem, *Song of Songs,* 101.

[119] For defense of these sections as constituting dreams (and not historical occurrences), see, e.g., Delitzsch, *Proverbs, Ecclesiastes, Song of Solomon,* 3:57, 91. Delitzsch writes regarding 3:1–5, "That it is a dream is seen from this, that that which is related cannot be represented as an external reality. But it at once appears as an occurrence that took place during sleep" (p. 57). Regarding 5:2–8, Delitzsch points out, "To sleep while the heart wakes signifies to dream, for sleep and distinct consciousness cannot be co-existent; the movements of thought either remain in obscurity or are projected as dreams" (91). See also Kinlaw, "Song of Songs," 1225, 1232. I emphasize what Delitzsch implied, that those who deny the dream interpretation (esp. of 5:2–8) must rationalize the woman's explicit statement that she "slept" (*yĕšēnâ*) beyond limits of semantic credibility—e.g., the claim that this expression "may mean little more than she was in bed" (Garrett, "Song of Songs," 206).

[120] For structural analyses of the dream sections (3:1–5 and 5:2–8), see Davidson, "Literary Structure," 55–56; cf. Shea, "Chiastic Structure," 388–89, 396.

I opened to my beloved,
> but my beloved had turned and was gone. . . .
> I sought him, but did not find him;
> I called him, but he gave no answer. (5:6)

In Song 3:1–4 the author utilizes various literary techniques to highlight the intensity of the longing for the presence of the beloved. In this section, the woman four times—once in each verse—repeats an expression showing her deep emotional attachment to her lover: ʾēt šeʾāhăbâ napšî, "him whom my soul loves." The woman's use of three cohortative verbs plus the particle of entreaty (nāʾ) in her self-deliberation (v. 2) further emphasizes her intensity of desire: "I *must* arise *now!* . . . I *must* go around . . . I *must* seek . . ." (NASB). Furthermore, while both the woman and the guards "go about" (sābab) in the city (vv. 2–3), the woman uses the intensive form of the verb (poʿlel) whereas the guards are described with the simple (qal) form: the guards routinely patrol the city, but the woman intensely and desperately roams, indeed combs, the city streets for her beloved. Again, by means of the threefold play on the verb māṣāʾ, "find," the Song's composer sustains the suspense and further accentuates the absence-presence motif: the woman searches for her lover but does not *find* him (v. 2); rather the watchmen *find* her (v. 3); but at last she *finds* the one her soul loved (v. 4). Finally, when she finds her beloved, she grasps or seizes him (ʾāḥaz) and does not let him go (or slip away, rāpâ in the hipʿil).

Song of Songs 5:2–8 utilizes some of the same literary techniques as employed in 3:1–4, but here in Song 5 the eagerness is further underscored by recording the man's bold actions and words and the woman's inner feelings of desire for the presence of the beloved. In 5:2, the man dôpēq, "is knocking." The force of the qal ptc. is "knocks repeatedly." This Hebrew verb dābaq elsewhere in Scripture denotes a vigorous, even violent, beating (cf. Gen 33:13; Judg 19:22). He is not just timidly tapping on the door. And he calls out, "Open to me"—using the imperative. He then addresses her with one of the longest strings of endearment terms anywhere in the Song: "my sister, my love, my dove, my perfect one." His heart is overflowing with eagerness for her. She, in turn, throughout this scene describes her deep emotional desire to be with him: her inner being yearns/thrills for her lover (Song 5:4),[121] her soul faints with love for him (v. 6);[122] she is "faint with love" (v. 8). She is so intense and even frantic in her search for her lover that apparently the watchmen mistake her for a harlot and try to physically restrain her (v. 7). But she manages to adjure her female companions that they tell her lover how lovesick she is for him, should they find him (v. 8). And the ensuing question by the daughters of Jerusalem about her

---

[121] Literally she says, "my inward parts [mēʿîm, 'internal organs, intestines, bowels, belly' = 'the seat of the emotions' (BDB 588–89)] thrilled [hāmâ, 'murmur, growl, roar, be boisterous' = 'the *thrill* of deep compassion or sympathy' (BDB 242)] over him."

[122] She says literally, "My soul went out [yāṣāʾ, here probably = 'fainted' (Murphy, *Song of Songs*, 165)]."

beloved (v. 9) calls forth from her a flowery *wasf* expressing praise of his beauty (vv. 10–16).[123]

"Absence makes the heart grow fonder"—the absence motif serves to heighten the meaning of presence.[124] As in the garden of Eden, lovers need each other to be whole. In the Song man and woman each appear as individuals—capable, inde-

---

[123] The Arabic word *wasf* ("description," pl. *ʾawsāf*, "that which is indescribable," which we will simplify with the English "s"), used to describe the extravagant praise of the physical charms of the bride and groom in modern Syrian wedding customs, has become the common term employed to describe the same kind of description of the physical beauty of the man and woman in the Song. Parallels between the modern Syrian village nuptial practices (including esp. the seven-day festivity cycle) and the Song of Songs were first studied by J. G. Wetzstein, "Die syrische Dreschtafel," *Zeitschrift für Ethnologie* 5 (1873): 270–302; and developed esp. by Karl Budde, "Was ist das Hohelied?" *Preussische Jahrbücher* 78 (1894): 92–117; and "Das Hohelied erklärt," in *Die fünf Megillot* (ed. Karl Budde, Alfred Bertholet, and D. G. Wildeboer; Freiburg im Breisgau: Mohr, 1898), ix–48. For an English summary of Wetzstein's observations, see Delitzsch, appendix, "Remarks on the Song by Dr. J. G. Wetzstein," in *Proverbs, Ecclesiastes, Song of Solomon*, 3:162–76. For further discussion, see also Falk, *Love Lyrics*, 80–87; and Pope, *Song of Songs*, 55–66 (with bibliography).

[124] Garrett misses this whole thrust of the presence-absence motif in these two sections of the Song in his "bizarre, quasi-allegorical view" (to use the words of Longman, *Song of Songs*, 130), which takes these passages as a series of symbolical events centered in the woman's trauma of losing her virginity. According to Garrett, "Song of Songs," 172, the city represents the woman, and the guards are her virginity. In Song 3:1–5, "first, the guards abruptly come upon her as she seeks her lover. That is, as she yearns for her lover, the brute fact of her virginity suddenly presents itself before her mind. Second, she asks the guards if they have seen her lover. That is, she looks on her virginity as a key to finding her lover" (ibid.). Song of Songs 5:2–8, according to Garrett, 206–18, focuses on the traumatic moment of the bride's loss of virginity on her wedding night; the pounding on the "door" by the man (v. 2) is the man's penis beating against her vaginal opening, seeking penetration; the man's "head" is a euphemism for the penis, with the "drops of the night" signifying his semen (v. 2); the "hand" of the man reaching into the "hole" of the door (v. 4) describes his penis penetrating her vagina; the woman's "fingers" are her genitals, wet with oils that represent her vaginal fluids (v. 5); the guards' stripping off her tunic represents the moment her virginity is taken away (v. 7); the guards' "beating" her is the searing pain she experiences after the man withdraws his penis (v. 7); the man's "moving on" signifies his dissipation of interest after the orgasm is over, leaving the woman feeling as if she had expired (i.e., totally deflated, v. 8). Garrett's emphasis on the woman's loss of virginity is surely overdrawn, to the point where he suggests that "in the symbolism of this text of the Song [5:2–8], the woman feels that she has lost her purity, notwithstanding that she lost her virginity in a lawful manner" (214). Although there may indeed be sexual double entendres in these sections of the Song (esp. in the second dream sequence; see ch. 14, below), these cannot be allowed to overshadow or even overcome the basic absence-presence motif that dominates these sections.

Equally problematic in misconstruing the absence-presence motif is the feminist interpretation of 5:2–8 that takes the woman's wet fingers (5:5) to depict the woman masturbating as part of a "nocturnal wet dream" in which the man ultimately vanishes (see, e.g., Carey Ellen Walsh, "A Startling Voice: Woman's Desire in the Song of Songs," *BTB* 28 [1998]: 129–34; and Fiona C. Black, "Beauty or the Beast? The Grotesque Body in the Song of Songs," *BibInt* 8 [2000]: 314–15). The passage is not about female masturbation.

pendent, self-reliant—and at the same time they have become "bone of one's bone, flesh of one's flesh" (cf. Gen 2:23). There is no "smothering love" on the part of either partner. There is a merging yet differentiation and separateness, a belonging yet not possession, a dependence yet independence, a wholeness yet recognition and acceptance of the otherness of each.[125]

This paradoxical wholeness/individuality is encapsulated in the climactic imperative the Shulammite addresses to Solomon: "Set me as a seal upon your heart, as a seal upon your arm" (8:6). The seal over the heart/arm emphasizes the identity of the lovers, and the combination of woman's command ("Set me") with the dependent position/function of the seal on the heart/arm of her lover again expresses the paradox of "dependent independence."

> "Set me"—the imperative, at once, urgent, demanding, and insecure—introduces a compressed formulation of all the ambiguities of identification and difference in the poem. She both commands him and is utterly dependent on him; as a seal, she wills to be his instrument. She is both independent of him, with her own words, and she wishes to be part of him. . . . A seal is a sign of identity, wherewith the person conducts his affairs. She is thus impressed on his heart, i.e. his feelings and thoughts, as his identity; she governs his relations with the world. No closer fusion can be imagined.[126]

The motif of wholeness in the Song not only involves the two lovers eager for each other's presence and becoming fused into one. Also included is the wholistic view of the human person as a sexual being. "The poem [Song of Songs] . . . is fundamentally a critique of . . . the dualism between body and soul prevalent in sophisticated as well as in popular mentalities."[127] Sexuality is not just the sex act;

---

[125] See Landy, *Paradoxes of Paradise,* 272; Robin Payne, "The Song of Songs: Song of Woman, Song of Man, Song of God," *ExpTim* 107 (1996): 333. J. Cheryl Exum, in her 2005 commentary (*Song of Songs,* 13–28 and passim), claims to be "the first to examine systematically gender differences and the role they play in the presentation of the relationship between the lovers in the Song" (p. 81). Exum finds "the Song's portrayal of gender relationships as fairly egalitarian" (p. 68), with "the female and male voices . . . in complete accord" (p. 14), yet she traces differences between the woman's and man's perspectives on romance. According to Exum's analysis, the woman "expresses her desire and explores her feelings for him, and his for her, through stories," while the man "does not tell stories. His way of talking about love is to look at her and tell her what he sees and how it affects him" (p. 14). Again, "the lovers describe differently what it is like to be in love. . . . He is awestruck; she is lovesick" (p. 15). In terms of the metaphors used of each other's body, "his imagery is more vivid and animated than hers, hers is more relational than his" (p. 21). While their desire for each other is mutual, and both take initiative, love is presented "as something she gives and he takes. . . . But he takes what he desires only by invitation" (p. 27). Exum's observations support the conclusion that the relationship between the man and woman in the Song constitutes complementarity without hierarchy. While Exum has rightly noted "the poet's remarkable sensitivity to differences between women and men—differences that, in turn, reflect cultural assumptions about gender differences and roles" (p. 14) she also recognizes ways in which the poem can "challenge certain of these assumptions as well" (ibid.).

[126] Landy, *Paradoxes of Paradise,* 122.

[127] LaCocque, *Romance She Wrote,* 7. I do not agree with the part of his thesis that is omitted with ellipses—that the book is also a critique "of the mores of conformist

it involves the whole inseparable human being: physical, sensual, emotional, and spiritual.[128] In the Song "every human pleasure combines physical, emotional, and spiritual powers, stimulating each of these equally."[129]

Physical attraction includes the whole body—not just the sexual organs. Both the man and the woman describe their lover's beauty from head to foot in the extensive *waṣfs* of praise (5:10–16; 7:2–9 [ET 7:1–9]. All of the senses are involved: "Only here [in biblical poetry] is the exuberant gratification of love through all five senses the subject."[130] The emotions are involved: as already noted above, the woman is "faint with love" (2:5; 5:8), her inner being (lit. "bowels," the seat of the emotions) yearns/thrills for her lover (5:4), her soul faints with love for him (5:6). On Solomon's part, his heart is ravished,[131] and he is even overwhelmed[132] by her eyes (4:9; 6:5), and his strong emotional desire (*tĕšûqâ*) is for her (7:11 [ET 7:10]).

The mutual descriptions of the beauty of the beloved (in the *waṣfs* and elsewhere in the Song) do not always refer only to physical beauty.[133] Several modern

---

societies" with its shameless indulging in premarital and/or extramarital sex. According to LaCocque, "the entire Song strums the chord of 'free love,' neither recognized nor institutionalized" (p. 8). I will argue below that such is not the case.

[128] Hendrik Viviers also points out another kind of dualism that is missing in the Song: "The Western dualism of linking woman, nature and sexuality with the 'lower despicable body' and men with the sublime rational mind . . . is absent in the Song" ("The Rhetoricity of the 'Body' in the Song of Songs," in *Rhetorical Criticism and the Bible* [ed. Stanley E. Porter and Dennis L. Stamps; JSOTSup 195; Sheffield, Eng.: Sheffield Academic Press, 2002], 242).

[129] Keel, *Song of Songs*, 32.

[130] Alter, *Art of Biblical Poetry*, 202. My own list of explicit references to the five senses includes (1) *smell*, 1:3 (fragrance of ointments), 1:12 (fragrance of spikenard), 2:13 (scent of fig and grape blossoms), 3:6 (myrrh and frankincense perfume), 4:10–11, 16 (scent of perfumes), 4:11 (fragrance of garments), 4:16 (scent of the spices in the "garden"), 7:9 (ET 7:8) (scent of apple on the breath), 7:14 (ET 7:13) (fragrance of mandrakes); (2) *taste*, 2:3 (fruit sweet to the palate), 4:11 (honey, honeycomb, and milk), 4:13 (pomegranates and other pleasant fruits), 4:16 (taste pleasant fruits), 5:1 (taste of honey and honeycomb), 7:10 (ET 7:9) (your mouth like the best wine), 7:14 (ET 7:13) (pleasant [fruits] laid up), 8:2 (drink spiced wine and pomegranate juice); (3) *sight*, 1:6 (do not look on me because I am dark), 2:14 (see her "face," which is lovely), 3:11 (see King Solomon), 4:9 (you have ravished my heart with one glance of your eyes), 7:1 (ET 6:13) (look at the Shulammite), plus the many descriptions of physical beauty in the *waṣfs*; (4) *hearing*, 2:8 (voice of beloved), 2:12 (voice of turtledove heard), 2:14 (hear her voice, her voice is sweet), 5:2 (the voice of my beloved! He knocks . . .), 8:13 (hear her voice), plus the speeches themselves in the Song; and (5) *touch*, 1:2 (kiss), 2:6 = 8:3 (caress/embrace), 3:4 (hugging/embrace), 7:8, 9 (ET 7:7, 8) (fondling of breasts), 7:10 (ET 7:9) (kiss), 8:1 (kiss), 8:5 (leaning on her beloved), plus numerous double entendres for sexual physical intimacy (see below). Beyond this list of explicit references, many more allusions to the natural surroundings and experiences of the lovers imply the involvement of all the senses.

[131] *Piʿel* of the denominative verb *lbb*, lit. "to make the heart beat faster," BDB 525. Cf. *HALOT* 515: "to steal, enchant the heart."

[132] *Hipʿil* of *rāhab*, "alarmed, awed, disturbed, overcome," BDB 923. Cf. Mark Anthony Phelps, "רהב," *NIDOTTE* 3:1063, who follows the NIV translation, "overwhelm."

[133] For a helpful typology of the different ways the metaphors of the Song have been interpreted, see esp. Garrett, "Song of Songs," 38–40. His six possibilities include regard-

studies have shown that the imagery employed in the comparisons at times penetrates beyond literalistic description of the physical form[134] or the presentation of general emotional images[135] to also describe dominant and admirable moral qualities of the lovers.[136] The extent to which the comparisons in the *wasfs* move

---

ing the metaphor as (1) "subverting" the genre of love poetry; (2) a deconstruction of the social order; (3) a culturally acceptable way of depicting physical beauty; (4) visibly similar to the thing the metaphor represents; (5) a description of the speaker's feelings; (6) part of the inherent logic of the praise form of the *wasf;* (7) referring not to the woman but (allegorically) to the land of Israel; and (8) larger-than-life idealizations of an archetypal love relationship. I concur with Garrett that possibilities 1, 2, and 7 read into the text what is not there (see below), possibilities 3 through 6 are not mutually exclusive and contain an element of truth, and special emphasis in the Song is placed upon possibility 8 (although, unlike Garrett, I do not minimize or reject the historical basis of the Song in the life of two real lovers—Solomon and Shulammite).

[134] Contra, e.g., Leroy Waterman, *The Song of Songs, Translated and Interpreted as a Dramatic Poem* (Ann Arbor: University of Michigan Press, 1948), who seeks to interpret the imagery throughout the *wasfs* as literalistic comparisons with the color or contour of the physical form. Sometimes this may indeed be the case, especially when the passage specifically gives the point of comparison: "His locks . . . black as a raven" (5:11). But to apply this method of interpretation in a thoroughgoing way contorts the object of comparison (e.g., the woman) into grotesque and comic proportions.

I also reject the even more radical interpretation of a growing number of postmodern/ feminist interpreters who argue that the *wasfs* are indeed to be taken literalistically as grotesque descriptions of the lovers. See, e.g., Black, "Beauty or the Beast?" 302–23, who suggests a "grotesque reading" (322) of the Song, describes the woman as "a creature who is ill-proportioned, odd-looking and impossible" (311), and finds the descriptions of both the man and the woman "comical, puzzling, even repulsive" (317); cf. Athalya Brenner; " 'Come Back, Come Back the Shulammite' (Song of Songs 7:1–10): A Parody of the *wasf* Genre," in *On Humour and the Comic in the Hebrew Bible* (ed. Yehuda T. Radday and Athalya Brenner, JSOTSup 92; Sheffield, Eng.: Almond, 1990), 251–75. Such interpretations are difficult to sustain in light of the explicit statements both of the lovers and of their associates in the Song, attesting to the unparalleled beauty of the man and the woman. Black has unknowingly given an accurate self-critique of her approach: "It could be said that I am merely blind to the 'point' of poetic language—missing the metaphors" ("Beauty or the Beast?" 304). For a critique of these interpretations, see Garrett, "Song of Songs," 38, who correctly concludes, "Such a reading is driven by feminist ideology and has little to support it in the text."

[135] Contra, e.g., Richard N. Soulen, "The *wasfs* of the Song of Songs and Hermeneutic," *JBL* 86 (1967): 183–90; repr. in *A Feminist Companion to the Song of Songs* (ed. Athalya Brenner; FCB 1; Sheffield, Eng.: Sheffield Academic Press, 1993), 214–24, who sees the function of all the imagery as merely evoking a sensation, conveying the delight of the beholder. Soulen's emphasis on "presentational" rather than "representational" or "literalistic" interpretation may be correct regarding some of the imagery, especially where the purpose of the images (e.g., the scenes of flora and fauna) may be to set an erotic mood. But to insist that all the imagery is "unanalytical and imprecise" and used simply to create in the hearers "an emotion [of joy, awe, and delight] congruent with his own in the presence of his beloved" (p. 190) does not do justice to the data in the Song.

[136] Garrett, "Song of Songs," 40: "The metaphors of the Song express the affections of the lovers for one another, but they also express the meaning of love for the reader or audience. They draw us into reflection on the qualities of the man, the woman, and their love as an ideal archetype." For discussion and further substantiation of this

beyond literalistic bodily description or emotional presentation to representation
of functional or moral qualities has been debated, but I have become convinced
that in at least some of the metaphors and similes, in the praise of bodily parts
"there seems to be clear representational intent."[137] The decision whether primarily form (size, shape, color, etc.), emotional sensation (erotic joy, awe, delight), or dynamics (function and power of the symbol) is in view must be made
on an individual basis as one examines each comparison. Keel most convincingly
argues that often the point of the comparison in the metaphors and similes lies
not so much in the form or shape as in the function and power of the symbol, and
he provides a helpful methodology (a "concentric circle model") for grasping the
representational point that is intended.[138]

Thus, for example, the military tower/fortress imagery describing the
woman (4:4; 7:5 [ET 7:4]; 8:10) signifies not only aesthetic beauty and strength
but "insurmountability, inaccessibility, pride, purity, and virginity . . . the proud
inaccessibility of a pure maiden."[139] The description of the woman in some
mountain fastness (4:8; cf. 2:14) likewise portrays "the inaccessible character of
the woman."[140] The dove imagery (1:15; 2:14; 4:1; 5:1, 12; 6:9) in some passages
of the Song may refer primarily to the color or shape of the eye, or even the
sparkle of the "glance" of the eye, but in others seems to move beyond this to
connote spiritual qualities of "innocence, moral purity, and blamelessness."[141]

---

understanding of the Song's metaphors, see esp. Thorleif Boman, *Hebrew Thought Com-
pared to Greek* (New York: W. W. Norton, 1960), 77–89; Fox, *Song of Songs,* 274–77;
Garrett, "Song of Songs," 37–40 and passim; Meyers, "Gender Imagery," 211–21; Munro,
Spikenard and Saffron, passim; Roland E. Murphy, "The Symbolism of the Song of
Songs," in *The Incarnate Imagination: Essays in Theology, the Arts, and Social Sciences in
Honor of Andrew Greeley—A Festschrift* (ed. Ingrid H. Shafer; Bowling Green, Ohio:
Bowling Green State University Popular Press, 1988), 229–34; idem, *Song of Songs,*
70–74; Othmar Keel, *Deine Blicke sind Tauben: Zur Metaphorik des Hohen Liedes*
(Stuttgart: Katholisches Bibelwerk, 1984); idem, *Song of Songs,* 22–30 and passim.

[137] Murphy, "Symbolism," 229.

[138] See esp. Keel, *Song of Songs,* 25–30, for a summary. At the same time, both Boman
and Keel go too far in seeking to press every metaphor and simile into a representation of
function and not form.

[139] Boman, *Hebrew Thought,* 78. Cf. Keel, *Song of Songs,* 147: "The simile 'your neck is
like a tower' describes the beloved as a proud, unconquered city." So also Garrett, "Song of
Songs," 191: "Applied to walls and towers, this language connotes impregnability." Some
commentaries interpret the "tower" of the woman's neck literalistically as referring to a
special type of multiple-layered necklace (like that portrayed on a sixth-century B.C.E.
Cypriotic sculpture), on the basis of the influential article of B. S. J. Isserlin, "Song of
Songs IV,4: An Archaeological Note," *PEQ* 90 (1958): 59–60; but these interpretations
miss the point—the context shows that it is not the jewelry but the woman herself that is
being praised.

[140] Murphy, "Symbolism," 230; cf. Keel, *Song of Songs,* 154–60.

[141] Boman, *Hebrew Thought,* 79. Boman adds, "Purity and innocence are the highest
form of feminine beauty" (p. 80). Regarding the dove imagery, Keel, *Song of Songs,* 69–71,
provides good evidence for rejecting the literalistic interpretations but then unfortunately
allows extrabiblical iconographic parallels (linking the dove to messengers of love in the
realm of the goddess) to override the inner-biblical evidence for the significance of the dove.

These examples illustrate that the lovers each delight in the whole person of their beloved, not just in their body.[142] They are not only "lovers" (*dôdîm*) but "friends" (*rēʿîm*) (5:1, 16).

When the woman says, "your name [*šēm*] is perfume poured out" (1:3), she refers to "the attractiveness of the whole personality of the lover."[143] Likewise the woman's whole being—including her physical beauty and moral integrity— causes her to be viewed in Solomon's eyes "as one who brings peace" (8:10). She is seen to be both physically and morally "perfect" (*tam*) and "flawless" (*bārâ*) (6:9; 5:2).[144] Her whole person ("altogether" [*kullāk*]) has "no flaw" (*ʾên mûm*) (4:7).

> That which attracted her [Shulammite] to him [Solomon] is not her personal beauty alone, but her beauty animated and heightened by nobility of soul. She is a pattern of simple devotedness, naive simplicity, unaffected modesty, moral purity, and frank prudence—a lily of the field, more beautifully adorned than he could claim to be in all his glory. We cannot understand the Song of Songs unless we perceive that it presents before us not only Shulamith's external attractions, but also all the virtues which make her the ideal of all that is gentlest and noblest in woman.[145]

The wholistic view of sexuality in the Song not only entails the pleasant and positive aspects of love but also realistically takes account of negative experiences—potential and real difficulties, frustrations, pain, and suffering.[146] The

---

142 So Bergant, *Song of Songs,* 162: "The explicitness of the imagery in the poems demonstrates that the belonging referred to is unquestionably emotional, profoundly spiritual, and certainly physical. No one of these three aspects is absent, nor is any one of them dominant. Rather, they are three dimensions of the same all-encompassing elemental power of love, a power that permeates every corner of the human soul. As such a love transforms, it integrates. It calls all of the powers and personality traits of the person into play and focuses them on the beloved. One who knows this kind of love can say: 'At last, I'm whole!'"

143 Carr, *Song of Solomon,* 74. Carr rightly points out that "name" in this context "is used in the broader sense for the true being of the person." Cf. S. Craig Glickman, *A Song for Lovers* (Downers Grove, Ill.: InterVarsity, 1976), 30: "When she said that his name was 'perfume poured forth,' she meant that his character was as fragrant and refreshing as cologne poured out of a bottle."

144 For a good summary of the Song's direct and indirect indications of the Shulammite's inner character of purity, see Harold R. Holmyard III, "Solomon's Perfect One," *BSac* 155 (1998): 164–71.

145 Delitzsch, *Proverbs, Ecclesiastes, Song of Solomon,* 3:5.

146 For discussion of this aspect of sexuality in the Song, see esp. Peter Chave, "Towards a Not Too Rosy Picture of the Song of Songs," *FemT* 18 (1998): 41–53; Glickman, *Song for Lovers,* 96–97; Payne, "Song of Songs," 333; and Barry G. Webb, "The Song of Songs: A Love Poem and as Holy Scripture," *RTR* 49 (1990): 96–97. George M. Schwab devotes an entire monograph to the motif of negativity in the Song: *The Song of Songs' Cautionary Message concerning Human Love* (New York: Peter Lang, 2002). Schwab focuses upon seven lines of evidence that "argue the negative component of the Song's message to lovers. Although Love is wassailed in the Song, it is also presented as a jeopardous and risky endeavor, which lovers are adjured to respect" (p. 2). These seven lines of reasoning include: (1) the repeated refrain "do not stir up . . . love" (2:7; 3:5; 8:4), which Schwab interprets to imply that "love is conceptualized as an uncontrollable power that is best left asleep" (45); (2) the comparison in the Song between love and the forces of death (8:6–7),

lovers recognize that disruptive forces will be working against love (the angry brothers, 1:6; the "little foxes, that ruin the vineyards," 2:15; the "many waters" and "floods," 8:7). There is awareness that love can get out of hand (2:7; 3:5; 8:4) and become destructive (8:6). The woman in the Song dreams about love but in the same dream probably also experiences attempted rape (5:7). There is pain as well as pleasure throughout the Song: the pain of insecurity and inferiority (1:6, 7), the pain of longing and fear of unfulfilled love (3:1–4), the pain of conflict and separation (5:2–8). But this "profound realism" is accompanied by a "biblical idealism"—a confidence that love will win out through all the difficulties and challenges: "Many waters cannot quench love, neither can floods drown it" (8:7).

The motif of wholism in sexuality also entails solidarity with the larger units of family and friends. In contrast to the illicit love presented in Prov 7 (where the sexual activity is inimical to home and hearth), in the Song there are strong family ties undergirding the love relationship of the couple. Grossberg analyzes this contrast and shows that in the Song "family members and the house play a role marked by and generally indicating acceptance, approval or affirmation."[147] We have already noted the wide range of passages referring to the positive connection between both the man and the woman and their mothers.[148] The Song also ac-

---

interpreting love in this passage as the negative "jealousy" and the "flame of Yahweh" as a consuming and destructive force; (3) love as a disease (2:5), which "cripples and disables" (66); and (4) love as subjugation (6:4–5, 10; cf. 4:9; 7:6 [ET 7:5]), which "diminishes degrees of freedom" (65); (5) episodes of tension and dismay in the Song (2:15; 3:1–5; 5:2–8; 8:1–4); (6) Solomon's dark side (8:11–12 and other passages in the Song that, in the wider context of 1 Kgs 3, Schwab finds to be an implicit indictment of the king's harem); and (7) the Song's lack of "satisfaction" terminology (e.g., the conclusion of 8:13–14), which Schwab sees as implying that "love is never presented in the Song of Songs as ultimately satisfying or fulfilling" (105). Although Schwab makes many valid points in showing the divine power of love and its potential danger if not kept within the divinely prescribed bounds, he has overstated his basic thesis that in the Song "love itself is portrayed as a negative force in human life, not merely the imperfect realization of it or the absence of it" (6). Although I agree with elements of points 1 and 5 above (and include examples of these points in the main text of this study), I would not classify the other points as negative elements (see the discussion of these alleged examples of negativity elsewhere in this chapter). Schwab has unwittingly provided a valid self-critique of, e.g., his reference to love as a disease: "Is this study merely making a mole out of a molehill? Surely, the desirability and spine-tingling attraction of love is what is being described" (69). I would answer, "Yes!"

[147] Grossberg, "Two Kinds of Sexual Relations," 20–23.

[148] Besides the seven explicit occurrences of the word "mother" in the Song (1:6; 3:4, 11; 6:9; 8:1, 2, 5), referred to above, four additional terms appear as synonyms for "mother": "her who conceived me" (3:4); "her that bore her" (6:9); "she who used to instruct me" (8:2 NKJV); and "she who bore you" (8:5). The Shulammite brings her lover back to her mother's house, where lovemaking (8:2) or dreams of lovemaking (3:4) follow; sexual intimacy is pleasantly associated with the place where Solomon's mother (Bathsheba) bore him (8:5); the mother is seen as providing "both physical continuity in her reproductive function and transmission of teaching in her instructional role" (3:4; 6:9; 8:2, 5); and the mothers have a close bond with son (she crowns him on his wedding day, 3:11) and daughter (who is her "darling" [ˀaḥad in the emphatic position] and "flawless" [bārâ] one, 6:9).

knowledges sibling ties: the brothers, although apparently somewhat overbearing (1:6), are mentioned in a positive and affirming sense (8:1–2) and also seem to serve in a protective, care-taking role (8:8–9)—perhaps taking the place of a missing father (who is never mentioned). The inclusiveness of the love circle also embraces various companions who are actively engaged in supporting the love relationship.[149] "Throughout the Song, Eros is inclusive; the love between two welcomes the love and companionship of many."[150]

The motif of wholeness is perhaps best summarized and sustained throughout the Song in the play on words between Solomon, the Shulamite, and *šālôm* "peace," (1:1, 5; 3:7, 9, 11; 7:1 [ET 6:13]; 8:10–12). This triangulation of words built on the same Hebrew root *šlm* not only demonstrates the mutuality/egalitarianism between the lovers, as noted in our discussion above, but accentuates the concept of wholistic *šālôm* that underlies the lovers' names. Sexual love in the Song is all about *šālôm*—which denotes "full-orbed and total peace and prosperity in body, mind, and soul."[151]

Sexuality and Exclusivity

Although, in one sense, eros in the Song of Songs is inclusive in that it welcomes the companionship of many, in another sense—and this is a sixth facet in the theology of sexuality—paradisaical sexual love means an exclusive relationship. The relational symphony of the sexes in the Song of Songs is a "live performance" of the "score" set forth in Gen 2:24.

As in Gen 2 man "leaves"—he is free from all outside interferences in the sexual relationship—so in the Song the lovers are unfettered by parental prearrangements[152] or political promises.[153] They are in love for love's sake alone. They are free for the spontaneous development of an intimate friendship.[154] In the

---

[149] The many references to the "daughters of Jerusalem/Zion" (1:4, 5, 11; 2:7; 3:5, 10–11; 5:8–9, 16; 6:1, 8–9; 8:4) have already been noted; several passages in the Song also denote Solomon's male companions (*ḥăbērîm*) (1:7; 8:13; cf. 3:7–8; 7:1 [ET 6:13]).

[150] Trible, *God and the Rhetoric of Sexuality*, 159.

[151] Ellens, *Sex in the Bible*, 158. Ellens entitles the final chapter of his book, "Sex and Shalom: What God Had in Mind" (pp. 157–62).

[152] Numerous references in the Song are made to the mother of the lovers (1:6; 3:4, 11; 6:9; 8:1–2, 5), indicating the closeness of ties that continue between parent and son (3:11), and parent and daughter (3:4; 8:2). But in all of this there is no hint of the parents' interfering with the lovers' freedom of choice and action. Thus both the fifth commandment and the "leaving" of Gen 2:24 are upheld.

[153] I concur with Sasson, "King Solomon and the Dark Lady," 409, that even though there was a political alliance that emerged from this marriage with Pharaoh's daughter, yet "the reference in 1 Kings to Solomon's love for Pharaoh's daughter makes it clear that Solomon's marriage to her was not prompted by political considerations." He goes on to add, "The possibility, of course, cannot be excluded that Solomon loved Pharaoh's daughter and also found it opportune to marry her for political reasons." Such a possibility seems a probability in light of 1 Kgs 3:1; 11:1.

[154] The Shulammite is considered as close as a sister by her lover (4:9–10, 12; 5:1–2), and she in turn can say of him, "This is my beloved and this is my friend" (5:16).

freedom from outside interferences, the couple may find mutual attraction in the
physical beauty and inward character qualities of the other.

"Leaving" also implies freedom from any other amorous ties—the exclusivity
of the love relationship between the man and the woman and the inaccessibility
to the advances of any outside party. The exclusivity of the couple's relationship is
apparent from several references in the Song. The man speaks of his beloved as
his "only one" (ʾaḥat hîʾ) (6:9),[155] the "lily [lotus blossom] among brambles [all
other women]" (2:2). Shulammite likewise sees Solomon as "an apple tree among
the trees of the wood [all other men]" (2:3). She refers to exclusivity as well as
mutuality when she says, "My beloved is mine and I am his" (2:16); "I am my beloved's, and my beloved is mine" (6:3); "I am my beloved's, and his desire is for
me" (7:11 [ET 7:10]). Garrett summarizes regarding the last-mentioned passage
(7:11 [ET 7:10]; he also finds it true of its parallels 2:16 and 6:3): "If it means anything at all, it means that the two belong to each other exclusively."[156] We have already noted the imagery of military walls and towers (4:4; 7:5 [ET 7:4]; 8:10) and
mountain fastness (2:14; 4:8), used to denote the inaccessibility of the woman to
any but her lover. She has "laid up" (ṣāpan) her "fruits," new and old, for him
alone (7:14 [ET 7:13]).[157]

The imperative on the lips of Shulammite in 8:6 not only emphasizes "dependent independence," as discussed above, but also exclusivity. When she sings
to her husband, "Set me as a seal upon your heart, as a seal upon your arm,"
Garrett points out that "she now sings of herself as stamped into the body and
mind of her husband. This can only mean that she possesses him as her own and
now demands his complete fidelity. The bond is of course a bond of love, but she
is unashamedly possessive and exclusive about it."[158] This emphasis upon the exclusivity of the relationship further underscores the monogamous nature of the
marital union upheld in the Song, as described above.

---

[155] For discussion of the reference to the "sixty queens and eighty concubines, and
maidens without number" in 6:8, see above under the section "A Heterosexual Duality."
The evidence points to Shulammite being Solomon's first wife, to whom he was monoga-
mously faithful for many years until he started down the road to apostasy.

[156] Garrett, *Proverbs, Ecclesiastes, Song of Songs,* 379. Garrett makes similar statements about the parallel passages in his more recent commentary, "Song of Songs."
Regarding 2:16, he aptly states ("Song of Songs," 162): "This simple sentiment . . . is perhaps the most beautiful line of the Song. . . . True love is monogamous. It implies devotion to the other but also implies that one has the right to expect fidelity from the other."
Regarding 6:3 Garrett remarks, "She now sees herself fully bound to the man in affection and commitment, and she possesses him just as he possesses her. There can be no
question of the love described here being anything other than monogamous. The
woman's claim upon the man here is the counterpart to the man's claim in Gen 2:23
that she is 'bone of my bones and flesh of my flesh' [RSV]. The two have become one
flesh" (p. 225).

[157] For further discussion of the exclusivity motif in Song 7:14 (ET 7:13), see R. B.
Laurin, "The Life of True Love: The Song of Songs and Its Modern Message," *ChT* 6, no. 22
(1962): 10–11.

[158] Garrett, "Song of Songs," 256.

Sexuality and Permanence

Not only is the relationship exclusive; a seventh facet of sexual theology is that the relationship is also permanent. As in the Genesis model, where man and woman are not only to "leave" but also to "cling" to each other in a marriage covenant, so the Song of Songs climaxes in the wedding ceremony. The chiastic structure of the unified Song reveals a symmetrical design focused upon a central section that describes the royal wedding of Solomon and his bride.[159] Song of Songs 3:6–11 clearly portrays the wedding procession of Solomon "on the day of his wedding" (3:11).[160] What follows in 4:1–5:1 appears to encompass the wedding ceremony proper.[161] Only in this section of the Song does Solomon address Shulammite as his "bride" (*kallâ*, 4:8–12; 5:1).[162] The groom also gives an extended public tribute of praise for his bride, paralleling the Arab *wasfs* of modern village weddings in Syria.

Following this come the central two verses of the entire symmetrical structure of the Song (4:16, 5:1).[163] It is hardly accidental that these two verses are situated at the exact physical midpoint of the book: there are 111 lines on either side. These verses contain the most intricate and beautiful literary patterns of the Song, epitomizing its entire macrostructure.[164] Many commentators have noted

---

[159] According to *DBI* 938, this whole section should be identified with a royal epithalamion: "A wedding ceremony occupies the very center of the Song of Songs (3:6–5:1)." For the structural placement of this section, see above, and Davidson, "Literary Structure," 61–64. Cf. Hwang, "New Structure," 102, 105, 111; Shea, "Chiastic Structure," 387–95.

[160] See esp. the arguments presented by Gordis, *Song of Songs,* 19–23, for the conclusion that "we have no song for a rustic wedding but, quite the contrary, an epithalamium for a wedding of great luxury, one possessing even national significance. In fact, all the details cited are easily explained by one assumption—*that we have here a song composed on the occasion of one of Solomon's marriages to a foreign princess,* probably an Egyptian" (20). See also P. B. Dirksen, "Song of Songs III 6–7," *VT* 39 (1989): 219–25; David A. Hubbard, *Ecclesiastes, Song of Solomon* (Communicator's Commentary 15; Dallas: Word Books, 1991), 301; L. D. Johnson, *Proverbs, Ecclesiastes, Song of Solomon* (Layman's Bible Book Commentary 9; Nashville: Broadman, 1982), 136; and Webster, "Pattern," 82. Commentaries who recognize that 3:6–11 portrays a royal wedding procession of Solomon are divided over who is riding in Solomon's palanquin (an enclosed litter suspended by poles and carried on the shoulders of several men), which is coming to the wedding—Solomon, the Shulammite, or perhaps even both. J. Cheryl Exum, "Seeing Solomon's Palanquin (Song of Songs 3:6–11)," *BibInt* 11 (2003): 301–16, presents weighty evidence in favor of the conclusion that it is Solomon who rides in the palanquin on the day of his wedding, and that this scene is described by the woman.

[161] For discussion of supporting evidence for this conclusion, see Shea, "Chiastic Structure," 394. Pope, *Song of Songs,* 508, lists other commentators who have come to similar conclusions.

[162] See Delitzsch, *Proverbs, Ecclesiastes, Song of Solomon,* 3:81, 90–91, for the significance of the term *kallâ* here. There is no evidence that the term *kallâ* in the ancient Near East was ever used loosely to mean "girlfriend" or even "fiancee" rather than "bride."

[163] See Davidson, "Literary Structure," 61–64.

[164] In my analysis of these two verses (ibid.), I have found a stunningly beautiful overlay of poetic patterns—a triplet of bicola superimposed on a couplet of tricola, and a

these verses. For example, Shea waxes eloquent on this point: "Like two resplendent peaks that surmount twin mountains, two short passages appear at the very center of the Song and its chiasm, in 4:16 and 5:1."[165] And Garrett observes, "This moment [described in 4:16–5:1] is the pivot point for the whole book. . . . In the structure of the Song of Songs, this is the centerpiece and crescendo."[166] These verses seem to be equivalent to our modern-day exchange of marriage vows, or alternatively, represent the consummation of the marriage in the marriage bed of the bridal chamber.[167] The groom has compared his bride to a garden (4:12, 15); now the bride invites her groom to come and partake of the fruits of her (now his) garden (4:16), and the groom accepts her invitation (5:1a–d).

The marriage covenant solemnized, an unidentified voice extends approbation as the bride and groom "drink" in the consummate experience of sexual union (5:1e). Commentators have puzzled over the identity of this voice at the center of the Song. Many suggest that it is the groom extending an invitation to the guests to join in the wedding banquet. But this is improbable, since the two

---

chiastic structure superimposed on panel writing—epitomizing the macrostructure of the entire Song, with its combination of matching chiastic members (ABB′A′) and panel members (CDEFC′D′E′F′) and its superimposing of chiasm and panel (EF and E′F′).

[165] Shea, "Chiastic Structure," 394.

[166] Garrett, "Song of Songs," 201–2. Cf. idem, *Proverbs, Ecclesiastes, Song of Songs*, 376 (citing R. L. Alden's chiastic structure of the Song); Carr, "Song of Songs," 294; Hwang, "New Structure," 102; and Wendland, "Seeking a Path," 42.

[167] Shea, "Chiastic Structure," 394, argues for linking 5:1 with what comes before, all as part of "the wedding service proper." On the other hand, Delitzsch, *Proverbs, Ecclesiastes, Song of Solomon*, 3:89, insists that "between iv. 16 and v. 1a the bridal night intervenes." Cf. also Garrett, *Proverbs, Ecclesiastes, Song of Songs*, 407, who is convinced that "this [4:16; 5:1] is the consummation of the marriage." The Hebrew verbs in the perfect in 5:1 could be translated to support either view, as a present (or even future) or as a past tense. Perhaps the text is intentionally ambiguous, blending the public (legal) and sexual (physical) consummation of the marriage. Such ambiguity is present often elsewhere in the Song, especially when allusions are made to sexual intercourse. Glickman, *Song for Lovers*, 84–85, speaks of the "almost formal request and acceptance," the "delicate formality" of 4:16–5:1. Glickman simply attributes it to a certain stiffness of mood in lovemaking on their wedding night, but it could also allude to the formal covenant-making setting of the wedding "vows." The wedding couple is both *saying* "I do" and *acting* on it. See the following section of this chapter.

Stephen C. Horine interprets 5:1 as the entrance of the couple into the "garden," i.e., their bridal chamber, to consummate their marriage (*Interpretive Images in the Song of Songs: From Wedding Chariots to Bridal Chambers* [Studies in the Humanities: Literature-Politics-Society 55; New York: Peter Lang, 2001], 42). Horine arrives at this conclusion, however, by positing a shift in metaphor between 4:16 (where the garden is the woman's sexual anatomy) and 5:1 (where the garden becomes the bridal chamber). This shift in the referent of the "garden" metaphor is forced at this point, as is Horine's exegesis that identifies "bridal chamber" imagery in many other places throughout the Song (esp. 1:4, 16–17; 2:4; 3:4, 7, 9; 8:13), so that this imagery in fact constitutes the "central metaphor of the Song" (p. 3). Although Horine's attempt to show that marriage is the context of the entire Song is laudable, in opposition to those who in recent decades have argued that the Song is devoid of nuptial connotations, he has stretched the evidence to make this the overarching metaphor of the Song. See the discussion below, which argues for a historical progression in the Song, with the first part of the Song occurring before the marriage.

terms *rēʿîm* ("friends") and *dôdîm* ("lovers," RSV), used in 5:1e, are used else-where in the Song for the couple,[168] not for the companions/guests. If the terms in 5:1e refer *to* the couple, they could not be spoken *by* either bride or groom. The "omniscient" narrator/poet at this high point in the Song seems to have a ring of divine authority and power—to be able to bestow a blessing and approbation upon the consummation of the marriage of the bride and groom. In parallel with the reference to Yahweh that climaxes the other high point of the Song (8:6–7), as discussed below, most likely the voice of 5:1e is that of Yahweh himself, adding his divine blessing to the marriage, as he did at the first garden wedding in Eden. In the wedding service, only Yahweh has the ultimate authority to pronounce them husband and wife. On the wedding night, only Yahweh is the unseen guest able to express approbation of their uniting into one flesh.[169]

It is important to recognize the public nature of the wedding in the Song. It is not done in a corner but with open and elaborate display. There are attendants and witnesses—both for the bride (3:11) and for the groom (3:7). The family is involved (3:11). It is publicly sealed by God himself (5:1). The Song hereby states the social significance of marriage.

> The kind of relationship that our two lovers now have is more than a private affair. What one does with one's sexuality is from a biblical perspective always more than a private, personal thing. It has widespread social implications. Biblically, when a lover gives himself to his beloved as these two have done, the relationship of each has changed to all the rest of the human race.[170]

In Gen 2:24 the "clinging" referred not only to the formal marriage covenant but also to the inward attitudinal dimensions of the covenant bond. This is apparent also in the Song. In contrast to some of the Egyptian love literature, where promiscuity, faithlessness, and jealousy between lovers are present,[171] in the Song there are revealed the fidelity, loyalty, and devotion of the partners (3:1–5; cf. 2:16; 6:3),[172] and the steadfastness of their love (esp. 8:6–7).[173] The description of

---

[168] Song 5:16; 1:13–14, 16; 2:3, 8, 9, 10, 16, 17; 4:10, 16; 5:2, 4, 5, 6 (bis), 8, 9 (four times), 10, 16; 6:1, 2, 3; 7:10–14 (ET 7:9–13); 8:5, 14.

[169] Here I concur with Dillow, *Solomon on Sex*, 86: "The poet seems to say this is the voice of God Himself. Only the Lord could pronounce such an affirmation. He, of course, was the most intimate observer of all. Their love came from Him (Song 8:7). Thus, the Lord pronounces His full approval on everything that has taken place. He encourages them to drink deeply of the gift of sexual love." So also Glickman, *Song for Lovers*, 25: "In the final analysis this must be the voice of the Creator, the greatest Poet, the most intimate wedding guest of all, the one, indeed, who prepared this lovely couple for the night of his design."

[170] Kinlaw, "Song of Songs," 1230, on Song 5:1.

[171] See examples cited in Gordis, *Song of Songs*, 30; Fox, *Song of Songs*, 68–73.

[172] Note also the general use of the possessive pronouns and the language of ardent devotion throughout. "Underlying the Song of Songs is the basic loyalty of woman to man (Gen 2:23) and man to woman (Gen 2:24), and the mutual interdependence they enjoy (Gen 2:25)" (Bullock, *Introduction*, 207).

[173] See Phipps, *Genesis and Gender*, 94, and the discussion and references in Pope, *Song of Songs*, 195.

the "covenant partnership" between Solomon and Shulammite, like the word
dābaq, connotes a permanent attraction that transcends genital union and at the
same time gives meaning to that union.[174] The permanence of the marriage covenant is the focus of the Shulammite's imperative to Solomon and the accompanying wisdom saying that form the climatic high point of the Song (8:6–7): "Set me
as a seal upon your heart, as a seal upon your arm. For love is as strong as death,
ardent [zealous—yes, jealous] love [*qinᵓâ*][175] as relentless [*qāšeh*][176] as Sheol. . . .
Many waters cannot quench love, nor can the floods drown it" (translation
mine). A seal is a highly valued, precious item from which the bearer would never
want to part. The Shulammite wishes to be permanently over his heart, the seat of
his affections, and on his arm, the source of his strength. Just as death does not let
go of those it has claimed, so the lovers possess each other forever. Just as Sheol is
relentless in not giving up its dead, so ardent love, zealous—yes, jealous—love,
will never give up the beloved. This verse may also contain an image of the seal
actually impressed upon the heart/arm, denoting an indissolubility that not even
the powers of death, Sheol, or the cosmic waters can overcome. Carr has aptly
summarized the aspect of permanent commitment in the Song's portrait of sexuality: "The Song celebrates human sexuality as a fact of life, God-given, to be enjoyed within the confines of a permanent, committed relationship. This is no
passing fling. What is celebrated here is total dedication to the beloved other, a
permanent obligation gladly assumed."[177]

Sexuality and Intimacy

Not only is the sexual relationship between Solomon and Shulammite characterized by exclusivity and permanence; an eighth facet of sexual theology in the
Song is that their relationship is one of intimacy.[178] As in Gen 2:24 the "one flesh"

---

[174] Phipps, *Genesis and Gender,* 95, explores the evidence for "a note of moral commitment throughout the Song" that includes "an exclusive and permanent relationship":
"This monogamous bonding is 'till death do us part.'"

[175] I find "ardent love" or "ardor" to be a better translation than "jealousy" or "passion"
in this context of synonymous parallelism with the preceding poetic line, although there do
seem to be also connotations of "holy" jealousy and passionate love, in the sense that the
lover will not surrender the beloved to someone else. See Ginsburg, *Song of Songs,* 188 (who
lists numerous other commentators that concur); and Murphy, *Song of Songs,* 191, 197. Cf.
the apropos comments of Garrett, "Song of Songs," 256–57: "Those who passionately love
are passionately possessive. One cannot trifle with love or with one's lover. Yahweh himself
is a jealous God (Exod 20:5). . . . If the jealousy of Yahweh over Israel is the model, the term
refers to a proper possessiveness in the setting of a wholesome relationship."

[176] The adjective *qāšeh* in its concrete meaning denotes something "hard" but may
have abstract meanings such as "difficult," "severe," "fierce," "intense," "unyielding," or
"relentless." In the context of 8:6, the meanings "unyielding," "relentless," or "intense"
seem to fit best. See BDB 904.

[177] Carr, "Song of Songs," 294.

[178] Robert Alter proposes that the entire Song is nothing less than "an ode to intimacy"
("The Song of Songs: An Ode to Intimacy," *BR* 18, no. 4 [2002]: 24–32, 52). Alter shows that

union follows the "clinging," so in the Song of Songs sexual intercourse between the lovers occurs only within the context of the marriage covenant. Scholars who argue to the contrary have failed to take seriously the unity of the Song and the testimony of the groom regarding his bride.[179] During the wedding ceremony proper, as noted above, Solomon likens his bride to a garden. More precisely she is a locked garden (4:12): "A garden locked is my sister, my bride, a garden locked, a fountain sealed." There is a wide agreement among modern commentators that here "the locked garden denotes virginity,"[180] and the argumentation for this interpretation is persuasive.[181] If this interpretation is correct and the Song is a

---

this intimacy is highlighted in numerous ways, such as the "segue from third-person distance to second-person intimacy" (p. 26) in the very first seven words of the Song: "Let him kiss me with the kisses of his mouth! For your love is better than wine" (1:2).

[179] See, e.g., Trible, *God and the Rhetoric of Sexuality,* 162: "To the issues of marriage and procreation the Song does not speak." Cf. Foster R. McCurley, *Ancient Myths and Biblical Faith: Scriptural Transformations* (Philadelphia: Fortress, 1983), 101: "It is not even clear in the Song that the man and woman are married to each other." And LaCocque, *Romance She Wrote,* 8: "The entire Song strums the chord of 'free love,' neither recognized nor institutionalized." For other examples of recent scholars who have espoused this conclusion, see Horine, *Interpretive Images,* 5–6. Horine points out, "The superimposition of an Egyptian worldview upon the Song, vis-à-vis the priority of Egyptian literary parallels, has resulted in the identification of a stereotyped social setting for the Song which is 'secular' in nature"; he further shows that in the process "the love relationship shared by the couple in the Song has, in recent times, been effectively divorced from what may have been its original social setting which, at the same time, represents an essential ancient Near Eastern socioeconomic institution—marriage" (p. 6). Unfortunately, in his attempt to provide a "corrective to recent interpretations which view the couple's love relationship as existing apart from the theme of marriage" (7), Horine goes to the opposite extreme and reads the "bridal chamber" motif almost everywhere in the Song whereas a more balanced approach would recognize a historical progression through the Song (see the discussion below).

[180] Pope, *Song of Songs,* 458. E.g., Carr, *Song of Solomon,* 123, recognizes that the garden here is a euphemism for the female sexual organs and concludes that "*a fountain sealed* and *a garden locked* speak of virginity." Bullock, *Introduction,* 230: "That the wedding had not been consummated [before 4:16] and that the kind of love treated in the Song is not promiscuous are clear from the beloved's description of his betrothed as 'a garden locked' and 'a spring sealed up' (v. 12)." Delitzsch, *Proverbs, Ecclesiastes, Song of Solomon,* 3:84: "To a locked garden and spring no one has access but the rightful owner, and a sealed fountain is shut against all impurity." Dillow, *Solomon on Sex,* 81: "The garden refers to her vagina. When Solomon says it is locked, he is saying it has never been entered; she is a virgin." Glickman, *Song for Lovers,* 22, concurs: "The fountain is sealed and the garden is locked (4:12). This is a poetic way to praise her virginity and at the same time gently to request that she give herself to him." This interpretation already is found in the *Targum Song of Songs* and *Song of Songs Rabbah,* not to mention the numerous Christian (allegorical) interpreters down through the centuries.

[181] Bloch and Bloch, *Song of Songs,* 176, argue that the references to the "garden locked" and the "fountain sealed" refer only to the woman's inaccessibility to anyone other than her lover, in parallel to the references to water, well, and cistern in Prov 5:5, 18. But they fail to note the crucial difference between these passages: in Proverbs it is a private cistern/well, but in the Song the emphasis is upon the "garden *locked*" and "fountain *sealed*." They also fail to take into account the other various statements in the Song regarding the woman's purity and chastity, as discussed below.

unity, then the groom is clearly announcing at the wedding ceremony that his bride is still a virgin. This detail is crucial for appreciating the significance of the high point of the ceremony and of the entire Song (4:16; 5:1): the climactic invitation and acceptance on the part of virgin bride and groom to "become one flesh" with each other through sexual intercourse makes the dramatic statement that sexual union is reserved and preserved for husband and wife after marriage.[182]

The pivotal, central section of the Song, with its description of the wedding ceremony of Solomon and his virgin bride, must be given due weight in the interpretation of what precedes and follows. I have already outlined the symmetrical literary macrostructure of the Song. But the inspired poet seems to have cast the Song in a linear structure as well. Proponents of the "dramatic" theory—already suggested by Origen of Alexandria, popular especially in the eighteenth and nineteenth centuries, and with some representatives still today[183]—have argued that the Song constituted a full-scale theatrical drama to be performed in several acts. This interpretation has been almost totally abandoned today. There is a lack of precedent for drama (in its modern form) in the ancient Near East of Solomon's

---

[182] Other imagery in the first part of the Song also implies the virginal status of the woman. These images are summarized well by Garrett, "Song of Songs," 164: "The Song uses a wide variety of images to focus on the virginal status of the woman. In 1:6, she is under the care and control of her brothers. In 1:7, she does not want to be around men. In 2:9, she is behind a wall and a lattice. In 2:14, she is a dove out of reach and in the cleft of a rock. In 3:3, she is under the eyes of the watchmen. In 3:7, she is surrounded by a troop of warriors. In 4:4, her neck is like a fortified tower. In 4:8, she is in a lofty mountain lair."

[183] Origen begins the prologue to his commentary on the Song thus: "It seems to me that this little book is an epithalamium, that is to say, a marriage-song, which Solomon wrote in the form of a drama." He defines drama "as something in which certain characters are introduced who speak; and from time to time some of them arrive upon the scene, while others go or come, so that the whole action consists in interchange between the characters" (*Comm. Cant.*, prologue; 1.1 [Lawson, 21, 38]). Eighteenth- and nineteenth-century representatives of the dramatic theory include, e.g., Delitzsch, *Proverbs, Ecclesiastes, Song of Solomon*, vol. 3 (German original, 1885); S. R. Driver, *An Introduction to the Literature of the Old Testament* (9th ed.; New York: Charles Scribner, 1913; repr., Cleveland: Meridian, 1957), 438–47; Heinrich G. A. Ewald, *Das Hohe Lied Salomos* (Göttingen: R. Deuerlich, 1826); Johann Friedrich Jacobi, *Das durch eine leichte und ungekünstelte Erklärung von seinen Vorwürfen gerettete Hohe Lied* (Celle, 1772); and Ernest Renan, *Le Cantique des cantiques* (Paris: Michel Lévy Frères, 1884). Twentieth-century proponents of the dramatic interpretation include, e.g., Arvid Bruno, *Das Hohe Lied, das Buch Hiob* (Stockholm: Almquist & Wiksell, 1956); Goulder, *Song of Fourteen Songs;* Andrew Harper, *The Song of Solomon* (Cambridge Bible; Cambridge: Cambridge University Press, 1907); Albert Hazan, *Le Cantique des cantiques enfin expliqué* (Paris: Lipzschatz, 1936); Guillaume Pouget and Jean Guitton, *Le Cantique des cantiques* (Paris: Gabalda, 1934), ET: *The Canticle of Canticles* (trans. Joseph L. Lilly; Catholic Scripture Library; New York: Declan X. McMullen, 1948); Alberto Vaccari, "La Cantica," in *I libri poetici della Bibbia: Tradotti dai testi originali e annotati* (ed. Alberto Vaccari; La Sacra Bibbia 5/2; Rome: Pontifical Biblical Institute, 1925), 111–29; Waterman, *Song of Songs;* and T. E. P. Woods, *Shulammith* (Grand Rapids: Eerdmans, 1940).

time, and a lack of indicators (such as stage directions) within the Song that it is to be theatrically performed. Nevertheless, a number of recent commentaries have recognized that although not full-blown drama, the Song is indeed dramatic[184] and may have been utilized in the ancient world as a kind of dramatic poem or song with several voices.[185]

Several recent literary-critical analyses have also pointed out the presence of "narrative progression" throughout various sections of the Song. Alter shows that "narrativity is the dominant pattern in a number of the poems," and demonstrates that "in the Song of Songs there are whole poems in which all semblance of semantic equivalence between versets is put aside for the sake of narrative concatenation from verset to verset and from line to line."[186] Munro traces the narrativity in the poetic imagery of the Song, especially regarding the images of the vineyard, garden, and water and the entire constellation of courtly imagery.[187] Michael Fox recognizes a "narrative frame" to the Song.[188] Garrett speaks of "the quasi-story that stands behind the Song."[189]

---

[184] E.g., Murphy, *Song of Songs,* 58: "The Song, like the book of Job, is in many respects dramatic, but it cannot convincingly be described as the script of a drama." Cf. Provan, *Ecclesiastes, Song of Songs,* 244–45.

[185] E.g., Munro, *Spikenard and Saffron,* 47: "The role of the daughters of Jerusalem in making the lovers' dialogue live again perhaps gives us a clue as to the utilization of the Song in the ancient world, namely as a dramatic poem with several voices."

[186] Alter, *Art of Biblical Poetry,* 187. E.g., Alter examines the wedding procession scene (3:6–11), observing that it "incorporates narrative progression." Again, Alter analyzes 3:1–4 and 5:1–8, showing that "figuration is entirely displaced by the report of sequenced actions" (pp. 187–88). Klara Butting points out the intertextual links between the Song of Songs and the Abraham/Sarah narrative, with the use of the phrase "Go your way!" (Butting translation) unique to the HB in Gen 12:1; 22:1 and Song 2:10, 13 and in the same context of "seeing" the "land" ("Go Your Way: Women Rewrite the Scriptures [Song of Songs 2:8–14]," in *The Song of Songs* [ed. Athalya Brenner and Carole R. Fontaine; FCB² 6; Sheffield, Eng.: Sheffield Academic Press, 2000], 142–51). I do not subscribe to Butting's feminist interpretation of this intertextual link (that the Song subverts Genesis) but rather see in the linkage an affirmation of narrative historical flow in the Song as in the Abrahamic cycle.

[187] Munro, *Spikenard and Saffron,* 144–46, summarizes her findings regarding narrative development of the Song's poetic imagery. At the same time, Munro does not find "sufficient consistency of character, setting and tone to maintain any clear narrative line" (p. 16) throughout the Song.

[188] Fox, *Song of Songs,* 217–18. This frame includes the springtime setting throughout and the pervasive theme of leaving the city and going to the countryside; a historical development in the girl's relationship with her brothers; and the movement from personal experiences of the speakers to the climactic statements about love's power and value at the end of the Song. Fox, however, does not see a consistent plotline extending throughout the book.

[189] Garrett, "Song of Songs," 193. Although Garrett sees in the Song only "minimal plot" (p. 81), he does recognize a chronological sequence in which the first four chapters (up to 4:16) occur before the consummation of the marriage by sexual intercourse on the wedding night and the last half of the book occurs either during or after this physical consummation. See also Sigrid Eder, "Ein Happy End im Hohelied? Eine Untersuchung zu Hld 2,8–14; 3,1–5 und 5,2–8 und eine narrative Lesart," *PzB* 13 (2004): 3–24, who reads several sections of the Song (2:8–14; 3:1–5 and 5:2–8) as narrating a plot.

Moving beyond those who find some elements of narrativity in the Song, Michael D. Goulder contends that the entire Song consists of a "semi-continuous sequence, in which one scene leads on from another."[190] In his understanding of the plot, the first part of the "Song of Fourteen Songs" describes experiences before the marriage (1:2–3:5), and the second half after the wedding (5:2–8:14), with the centerpiece being the procession/wedding and consummation of the marriage with the woman's first sexual encounter (3:6–5:1). Kinlaw's outline of the Song reveals, in a similar way, his acceptance of a basic three-part historical progression consisting of three main parts: "The Courtship" (1:2–3:5), "The Bridal Procession and Wedding" (3:6–5:1), and "The Life of Love" after marriage (5:2–8:7).[191] S. Craig Glickman refines this progressive historical (narrative) development in the Song by suggesting six chronological sections: (1) courtship (1:1–3:5); (2) procession for the marriage (3:6–11); (3) consummation of the marriage (4:1–5:1); (4) marital conflict and resolution (5:2–7:1 [ET 5:2–6:13]); (5) maturation of the marriage (7:2–8:4 [ET 7:1–8:4]); and (6) concluding appendix (8:5–14). Several recent commentators have followed Glickman's proposal of this "story-line" in poetic narration.[192]

Although I reject the interpretation of the Song as a full-blown drama to be performed in successive acts and scenes (as in Delitzsch and others), analysis of the Song leads me to accept the basic linear outline of a three-part historical progression, as proposed by Goulder, Kinlaw, and others, which is at the same time intersected by a symmetrical literary structure. A close look at the matching pairs and echoing refrains of the symmetrical structure surrounding the central wedding sections (3:6–5:1) further supports the linear progression of the book.

There appears to be a consistent pattern of more restrained sexual imagery, without reference to sexual intercourse, in the scenes before the wedding and of

---

[190] Goulder, *Song of Fourteen Songs,* 2. Goulder outlines the plot as he understands it on pp. 3–4. Where Goulder goes astray is in reading sexual double entendres into almost every verse and image of the Song, which in turn leads him to see Solomon as sexually promiscuous (with other women in his harem, including with the Shulammite, whom he interprets to be Abishag) throughout the Song, and the woman as seeking (finally with success) to win her way to be Solomon's favorite queen. See the philological analysis of Stoop-van Paridon, *The Song of Songs,* 476–77, who also sees a continuous story in the Song: "On the grounds of the results of this study it can be concluded that שִׁיר הַשִּׁירִים is just one continuous story. . . . The events of the SofS take place according to a clearly recognisable plan. The scenario displays a continual construction of episodes which fit in with each other and are clearly cohesive."

[191] Kinlaw, "Song of Songs," 1214 and passim in his commentary on the Song. See Mitchell, *Song of Songs,* 137–54, who suggests a similar linear progression in the Song in which the first half of the book deals mainly with the time leading up to the wedding and consummation (in four cycles) and the last half deals with the period of married love after the wedding (in two cycles plus the conclusion).

[192] See, e.g., Jack S. Deere, "The Song of Solomon," in *The Bible Knowledge Commentary, Old Testament: An Exposition of the Scriptures* (ed. John F. Walvoord and Roy B. Zuck; Wheaton, Ill.: Victor, 1985), 1009–25; Hubbard, *Ecclesiastes, Song of Solomon,* 257–58; Tommy Nelson, *The Book of Romance: What Solomon Says about Love, Sex, and Intimacy* (Nashville: Nelson, 1998).

an intensification of sexual imagery with frequent allusions to intercourse after the wedding. For example, in sections A and B (1:2–2:7 and 2:8–17) of my proposed symmetrical structure of the book, the desire or wish (but probably not the actual experience)[193] of the woman before the wedding focuses upon kissing (1:2), embracing (2:6), and the man's lying between her breasts (1:12), with no reference to sexual intercourse,[194] whereas in sections B′ (7:11–8:2 [ET 7:10–8:2]) and A′ (8:3–14) the sexual experiences (both actual and desired) intensify to include the caressing of her breasts and nipples[195] (7:8–9 [ET 7:7–8]) and a number of references to sexual intercourse—"There I will give you my love [*dôdîm*, 'lovemaking']"[196] (7:13 [ET 7:12]); "all choice [sexual] fruits, new as well as old, which

---

[193] The verb *yiššāqēnî* in 1:2 is generally regarded as a *qal* jussive (of the verb *nāšaq*) which would express a wish or desire, "Let him kiss me" or "Oh that he would kiss me." Likewise 2:6 may be taken as a nominal sentence followed by a *piʿel* jussive (of the verb *ḥābaq* "embrace"), expressing a wish or desire ("Let his left hand be under my head, and his right hand embrace me" (NJPS) or "Oh that his left hand were under my head, and that his right hand embraced me" [RSV, NRSV]). This seems to fit the context best, with her wish being suggested as a cure for her lovesickness (see Murphy, *Song of Songs*, 133). Throughout the Song it is frequently difficult to determine whether what is being described is being wished for or being experienced. J. Cheryl Exum, "In the Eye of the Beholder: Wishing, Dreaming, and *double entendre* in the Song of Songs," in *The Labour of Reading: Desire, Alienation, and Biblical Interpretation* (ed. Fiona C. Black et al.; SemeiaSt 36; Atlanta: Society of Biblical Literature, 1999), 71–86, discusses this "slippage between anticipation and experience" (77) especially in the double entendres of the Song. Cf. idem, *Song of Songs*, 9–11.

[194] In this section, one reference that some commentators have insisted implies sexual intercourse is 1:4, where the woman states, "The king has brought me to his chambers." But one must note that the noun in the expression "his chambers" (*ḥădārāyw*) is in the plural—a "plural of generalization" (see Murphy, *Song of Songs*, 125)—and probably refers to the whole palace of the king, not just his bedchamber. Note also that this reference occurs in the context of her female companions, who are accompanying her, and further seems to be a precise intertextual parallel with Ps 45:14–16 (ET 45:13–15), where the "princess . . . in many-colored robes . . . is led to the king; behind her the virgins, her companions, follow. With joy and gladness they [the woman and her female companions] are led along as they enter the palace of the king." The immediate and intertextual contexts seem to imply a setting less intimate than the woman spending the night and having sexual intercourse with Solomon in his bedchamber. Garrett, "Song of Songs," 127–28, provides an alternative explanation—i.e., that the reference is to the "wedding chamber" but as part of the opening canto, which is "proleptic" of what is to come later in the book.

Another reference that sometimes is interpreted as implying genital contact is the refrain in 2:6 (and parallel in 8:3): "His left hand is under my head, / and his right hand embraces me" (NKJV). As noted above, however, this may constitute a wish and not reality. So translates the RSV and NRSV: "O that his left hand were under my head, and that his right hand embraced me!" Further (or alternatively), in contrast to a similarly worded Sumerian love song ("Dumuzi-Inanna Songs," translated by Yitschak Sefati [*COS* 1.169:541]), where the woman requests that the man place his left hand at her head and his right hand at her nakedness (i.e., her genitals), in the biblical Song "the right-hand–left-hand dyad only implies affection and support, not genital stimulation" (Garrett, "Song of Songs," 152).

[195] For evidence that *ʾap* (which regularly in the HB means "nose") here refers to the nipples of the woman's breasts, see the discussion and bibliography in ch. 14, below.

[196] Bloch and Bloch, *Song of Songs*, 137, point out that "the plural *dodim* is a comprehensive term for lovemaking" and the translation "love" in most versions is "too general

I have laid up for you" (7:14 [ET 7:13]; "give you . . . to drink, the juice of my pomegranates" (8:2).[197]

The paired pictures of going and coming to the countryside (sections B and B') present another historical progression in the sexual relationship: there is eagerness for (restrained) friendship (he wants to see and hear her) in the country visit before the wedding (2:8–14), but the second countryside visit, coming after the wedding, is punctuated with allusions to sexual intercourse (7:13–14 [ET 7:12–13]). In another example from these sections, Shulammite invites her lover in 2:17 to "turn . . . , be like a gazelle or a young stag on the cleft mountains [lit. 'cleavage,' very probably an allusion to her breasts],"[198] whereas the repetition of this refrain at the end of the Song (8:14) seems to intensify the imperative and omit the limitation to the breasts: "Make haste, . . . and be like a gazelle or a young stag upon the mountains of spices [now her whole body]!" Goulder rightly notes that in the former passage (2:17) "the limitation of invitation to her breasts is intentional, for they are not yet married: 'petting,' yes, 'heavy petting,' no."[199] Garrett similarly indicates that this former passage "is an invitation. The text does not indicate that the couple has already consummated their relationship with sexual intercourse."[200] By contrast with 2:17, Kinlaw points out that in the latter passage (8:14), relating to the now married couple, "restraints are gone."[201]

The matched pair of nocturnal "dream" sections C (3:1–5) and C' (5:2–8) once again, by intensification in sexual description and intimacy, show historical progression in the relationship: in dream 1 the woman wants to hold him and not let him go (3:4),[202] whereas in dream 2 the husband comes by night to her bou-

---

and evasive." Illuminating parallel texts outside the Song include Ezek 16:8; 23:17; and Prov 7:18. The immediate context must be decisive to determine whether this "lovemaking" includes sexual intercourse. The context of *dôdîm* in Song 1:2 is that of "kissing" whereas the "lovemaking" in Song 7 seems to go beyond to include sexual intercourse.

[197] Garrett, "Song of Songs," 248, recognizes that the optative mood utilized by the poet in 8:1 ("O that you were like a brother to me. . . . I would kiss you, and no one would despise me") is not found in v. 2: "The imperfect forms . . . do not continue the optative construction of the previous verse. The actions expressed here . . . are not unattainable wishes but are the kinds of things she can do with him. The use of two verbs side by side indicates determination to carry out her intention toward her lover." She is not saying that she wishes he were her brother so that she could sneak him into her mother's house. Rather, she declares that since she cannot give him any affection openly, she will more than make up for it with the affection she gives him in private. For evidence that the reference to "juice of my pomegranates" is a double entendre for sexual intercourse, see ch. 14, below.

[198] See Garrett, "Song of Songs," 163.

[199] Goulder, *Song of Fourteen Songs*, 25. Goulder further points out that the reference to "Until the day breathes and the shadows flee" (2:17) apparently indicates that Solomon spent the night with his beloved "but without sexual union"; he cites the parallel in Ruth 3:6–9 (which text he—in my view, correctly—does not think alludes to sexual intercourse).

[200] Garrett, "Song of Songs," 163.

[201] Kinlaw, "Song of Songs," 1243.

[202] Song 3:4 continues by describing her wish to bring him into her mother's house, but I do not see in this verse an implication of sexual intercourse, any more than in 1:4,

doir, clearly for the purpose of making love (5:2), probably with double entendres of lovemaking embedded in the dream description.[203]

In sections D (3:6–11) and D' (5:9–6:3), the matching praises of the groom, an intensification also seems to occur: Solomon's form does not even appear in the first, only his palanquin, whereas in the *wasf* that forms the matching section, the woman describes his body in detail from head down to his legs/feet, with a probable reference to his genitals in 5:14.[204]

Finally, in the matching praises of the bride (sections EF [4:1–7 and 8–15] and E'F' [6:4–12 and 7:1–10 (ET 6:13–7:9)]) before the consummation of the marriage, the groom describes his bride from her head down to her breasts (4:1–6) and indicates that she is a virgin (4:12), whereas in the *wasfs* after the wedding (in particular 7:2–10 [ET 7:1–9]), his praise is far more explicitly erotic and encompasses her whole body, with much of the description lingering around the area of the genitals (7:2–3 [ET 7:1–2])[205] and his fondling of her breasts (7:4, 8–9 [ET 7:3, 7–8]). In summary, there is distinct movement from somewhat restrained and reserved to more intense and intimate sexual language as one moves from the prenuptial to the postnuptial sections of the Song.

Besides the comparisons between matching pairs in the two halves of the Song, there appears to be a progression of maturity in the relationship as one moves horizontally through the various nonpaired sections of the Song. For example, Jack Deere points out a progression in the physical proximity of domicile:

---

where the king brings her into his chambers. Nowhere in these contexts is the purpose described with explicit statements or implicit imagery of sexual union. It should be noted also that the context of this passage is most likely a dream ("Upon my bed at night I sought him whom my soul loves," 3:1), not an actual occurrence of physical encounter.

[203] This section of the Song not only describes the husband's coming by night to make love but probably constitutes a sexual double entendre in which "the poetry works on two levels: in her dream world, the protagonist at once prepares to make love and engages in the sexual act as well" (Gary A. Rendsburg, "Word Play in Biblical Hebrew: An Eclectic Collection," in *Puns and Pundits: Word Play in the Hebrew Bible and Ancient Near Eastern Literature* [ed. Scott B. Noegel; Bethesda, Md.: CDL, 2000], 153). See ch. 14, below, for details.

[204] The Hebrew *mēʿeh* (always appearing in dual or plural in the HB) usually refers to the "inward parts, internal organs" (BDB 588) but here is "obviously not describing his internal organs or his emotions; it refers either to his abdominal region generally or his genitals" (Garrett, "Song of Songs," 222). For Longman, *Song of Songs*, 173, the imagery is unambiguous: "The woman's description of the man's physical beauty continues [in v. 14] with her praise of his arms and, then, his sexual organ [in v. 15]." Longman points out the allusions to a tusk of ivory, which well could have sexual connotations, and to the decoration of lapis lazuli, which indicates its preciousness (as the organ of regeneration), and the use of *mēʿeh* in an erotic sense for the woman in 5:4.

[205] Song 7:3 (ET 7:2): "Your navel [*šōr*] is a rounded bowl that never lacks mixed wine. Your belly [*beṭen*] is a heap of wheat, encircled with lilies [lotus flowers]." The word *šōr* in its two other occurrences in the HB refers to the navel or umbilical cord (Prov 3:8; Ezek 16:4), but in the sequence of descriptive movement up Shulammite's body in the Song, this term comes between the thighs and the belly/abdomen (*beṭen*) and thus here is probably a euphemism for "vulva" (see ch. 14, below, for substantiation).

during the courtship period (represented by 1:2–3:5), the couple is represented as living apart, but after the wedding night (4:1–5:1), they are living together (5:2–7; 7:12–14 [ET 7:11–13]).[206]

As another example, the thrice recurring refrain describing the Shulammite's sense of mutuality with Solomon (2:16; 6:3; 7:11) gives evidence of a developing sense of security. In the first statement of the refrain, the woman places her possession of the beloved as primary, and his as secondary: "By beloved is mine and I am his" (2:16). In the second occurrence of the refrain, she reverses the order, putting his possession of her as primary and thus apparently stressing an increased security in him: "I am my beloved's, and my beloved is mine" (6:3). In the final restatement of the refrain, the Shulammite not only puts his possession of her as primary but also underscores this by referring to his desire for her, totally omitting reference to her possession of him: "I am my beloved's, and his desire is for me" (7:11 [ET 7:10]). In this progression, "she has really lost herself in him and thereby found herself."[207]

Garrett points out the change in metaphors from *inaccessibility* in 4:1–15 (a woman high on a mountain, dwelling with lions and leopards, and her locked garden, representing her virginity) to metaphors of *awesomeness* in 6:4–10 (grand cities and the heavenly array, representing that after the wedding she is more awe-inspiring than ever).[208] Garrett also succinctly summarizes the flow of the first half of the Song, showing that the woman is consistently presented as a virgin and that there is no description of sexual intercourse until the climactic sexual union of 4:16–5:1:

> There is no indication whatsoever that she had lost her virginity prior to the consummation at Song 4:16–5:1. To review, the woman begins by singing of her longing for the man and of her self-consciousness (1:2–8). The woman and man then sing of their devotion to each other (1:9–2:7). The language is sexually charged (he is like a bundle of myrrh between her breasts, 1:13), but there is no statement to the effect that they have attained sexual union. Song 2:8–17 is the invitation to depart, and again the desire for sexual fulfillment is clear, but there is no indication that the desire has been achieved. Song 3:1–4:15 is the beginning of the "wedding night songs" that lead directly to the moment of fulfillment in 4:16–5:1. In short, the language of 1:2–4:15 is charged with sexual anticipation and as such strongly implies that the consummation has *not* occurred.[209]

By contrast to the first half of the Song up to 4:15, as pointed out above, the consummation of the marriage is clearly referred to in the central verses of 4:16–5:1 and throughout the last half of the Song.

Delitzsch, followed more recently by Joseph Dillow, Daniel Akin, and others, argued rather forcefully, and in much more detail than Kinlaw, that the Song contains a series of reflections encompassing the historical scope of the relationship between Solomon and Shulammite from the first flush of friendship and love

---

[206] Jack S. Deere, "The Meaning of the Song of Songs: An Historical and Exegetical Inquiry" (ThD diss., Dallas Theological Seminary, 1984), 253–55.

[207] Glickman, *Song for Lovers*, 87.

[208] Garrett, "Song of Songs," 230.

[209] Ibid., 214–15.

through the courtship period, reaching its climax on the wedding day and extending beyond with a depiction of married life together.[210] Although Delitzsch
should be faulted for his emphasis upon the dramatic character of the Song (six
acts, each with two scenes), for his division of some of the sections of the Song,
and for his interpretation of certain details, his overall analysis of the historical
sequence and basic "plot" of the book has much to commend it. Dillow[211] and
others[212] have shown how this approach may indeed provide in the Song a "Biblical Guide to Married Love," with practical theological principles pertaining to
each stage of the love relationship.

Our discussion thus far of the "one flesh" dimension of human sexuality has
repeatedly highlighted the motif of intimacy. A classic study of marital intimacy
by marriage and family counselors Howard and Charlotte Clinebell has isolated
at least a dozen different kinds of marital intimacy.[213] It is fascinating to compare
this list with the Song of Songs and discover that Solomon and Shulammite experience all of these kinds of intimacy in their love relationship:

1. *Physical/sexual intimacy:* kissing (1:2; 8:1); touching (1:8); cradling/embracing/
   petting (2:6; 8:3); hugging (3:4); flirtation with eyes (4:9; 6:5); fondling (2:17;
   7:8–9 [ET 7:7–8]); snuggling (8:5); sexual arousal (8:2); sexual intercourse
   (4:16; 5:1; 7:13–14 [ET 7:12–13]; 8:2; plus other possible double entendres to
   be discussed below, ch. 14); and other undisclosed [or ambiguous references
   to] physical intimacy (2:3–4, 16; 3:4; 4:5; 6:2–3; 7:10 [ET 7:9]; 8:5).

2. *Emotional intimacy:* "faint with love" (2:5; 5:8); the heart ravished and overwhelmed (4:9; 6:5); the inner being (the seat of the emotions) yearning/
   thrilling for the lover (5:4); the soul faint with love (5:6); strong emotional
   desire (*tĕšûqâ*) (7:11 [ET 7:10]).

---

[210] Delitzsch, *Proverbs, Ecclesiastes, Song of Solomon,* 3:10–11; cf. Daniel Akin, *God on
Sex: The Creator's Ideas about Love, Intimacy, and Marriage* (Nashville: Broadman &
Holman, 2003); Dillow, *Solomon on Sex,* passim; and Glickman, *Song for Lovers,* passim.

[211] In the bride's wedding day reflection of Song 1:1–14, Dillow, *Solomon on Sex,*
points to her healthy attitude toward sexuality in anticipation of the wedding night
(1:2–4): recognition of the principle of natural versus contrived beauty, and acceptance of
the special value of physical imperfections (vv. 5–6); the need for counting the cost of
commitment to the relationship (vv. 7–8); and the virtue of modesty (v. 7b). Dillow follows Delitzsch in interpreting the next section, 1:17–2:7, as describing the married couple's wedding night; it is a flashback in the mind of Shulammite as years later she is
reflecting on the night (pp. 26–31). I prefer to see the Song unfold in basic historical progression without flashbacks; nothing in this section precludes it from occurring during
the courtship stage of the love relationship.

[212] See, e.g., Nelson, *Book of Romance,* passim; and Akin, *God on Sex,* passim. Greg W.
Parsons, "Guidelines for Understanding and Utilizing the Song of Songs," *BSac* 156
(1999): 421–22, suggests (and cites others who concur) using the Song of Songs in premarital counseling as an "antidote to perversions of sexuality and to asceticism" (421), although he does not see the historical progression in the Song.

[213] Howard J. Clinebell Jr. and Charlotte H. Clinebell, *The Intimate Marriage* (New
York: Harper & Row, 1970), 23–40, and passim. Cf. Alberta Mazat, *The Intimate Marriage:
Connecting with the One You Love* (Hagerstown, Md.: Review and Herald, 2001).

3. *Intellectual intimacy:* friendship (*rēaᶜ*, "friend" [5:1, 16]; *raᶜyâ*, "[female] companion"²¹⁴ [1:9, 15; 2:2, 10, 13; 4:1, 7; 5:6; 6:4]); the wisdom statements of the Song (8:6–7).

4. *Aesthetic intimacy:* numerous references to beauty (*yāpâ* or *yāpeh*) (1:8, 15 bis, 16; 2:10, 13; 4:1 bis, 7, 10; 5:9; 6:1, 4, 10; 7:2 [ET 7:1], 7 [ET 6]); the aesthetic encounters with nature in visits to the countryside (2:10–13; 6:11; 7:12–14 [ET 7:11–13]).

5. *Creative intimacy:* the designing and building of the royal litter or palanquin (3:9–10); singing together (implied in 2:12).

6. *Recreational intimacy:* fellowship together (2:3–4); visits to the countryside (1:16–17; 2:10–14; 7:12–14 [ET 7:11–13]); invitations to run together (1:4); other allusions to physical activity (2:8, 17; 4:6; 8:14); recreation in nature (4:8; 8:5).

7. *Work intimacy:* shepherding (1:7–8); vineyard business (1:6; 8:11–12); making ornaments (1:10).

8. *Crisis intimacy:* the attack by the city watchmen (5:7–8); "many waters" and "floods" (8:6–7).

9. *Conflict intimacy:* the absence-presence conflict in the two dreams (3:1–4; 5:2–8); the "little foxes, that ruin the vineyards" (2:15).

10. *Commitment intimacy* (shared dedication to a cause): commitment to each other (2:16; 6:3; 7:11 [ET 7:10]) and the preparation for their marriage (3:6–11).

11. *Spiritual intimacy* (shared meaning of life): the wisdom statements on love, the ultimate meaning of life (8:6–7).

12. *Communication intimacy:* the active dialogues between the man and the woman throughout the Song.

The physical/sexual intimacy of the lovers the Song will be discussed further in ch. 14 below, as the wholesome and holy beauty of sexuality is explored. But here I point out how the sense of the lovers' intimacy in the Song is enhanced by various poetic techniques which give

> the illusion of immediacy, the impression that far from being simply reported, the action is taking place in the present, unfolding before the reader. . . . [The lovers] are captured in language on the brink of attaining their bliss. . . . The erotic imperative—the call to love by means of grammatical imperatives, jussives, and cohortatives—lends urgency to the moment. . . . Coupled with imperatives vocatives strengthen the impression of the lover's presence at the moment of utterance. . . . The present moment is also vividly captured by participles. . . . The lovers move effortlessly over the

---

²¹⁴BDB 946.

poetic landscape—vineyards, gardens, palaces, houses, rocky cliffs, the wilderness, Lebanon—finding pleasure wherever they materialize.[215]

Regarding the last kind of intimacy, communication, which the Clinebells identify as the source of all other intimacy, it is significant to point out how pervasively the Song is suffused with dialogue between the lovers. Fox has shown that this feature is the "one remarkable difference" between the Song and the ancient Egyptian love poetry.[216] Whereas in the Song the lovers are continually interacting in speech, the Egyptian songs consist wholly of monologues, never speaking to one another or affecting one another by their speech. In the Egyptian love poetry, love is a way of feeling, but the Song "goes beyond the expression of feelings to present the interanimation of two souls. . . . Love in Canticles is not only feeling. It is a confluence of souls, best expressed by tightly interlocking dialogue."[217]

Another element of communication intimacy is the abundant use of terms of endearment and other expressions of affirmation by the lovers in their dialogues and descriptions of each other. A list of the terms of endearment in the Song include ten different hypocorisms (pet names) for the woman:

1. "My love" (raʿyātî): nine times (1:9, 15; 2:2, 10, 13; 4:1, 7; 5:2; 6:4); usually translated "my love/darling" in the modern English versions, but it is the feminine counterpart to the masculine term rēʿâ, "companion"; only appears here in the HB.

2. "Bride" (kallâ): six times (4:8, 9, 10, 11, 12; 5:1); only in the marriage ceremony section of the Song.

3. "My sister" (ʾāḥōtî): five times (4:9, 10, 12; 5:1, 2); only in the marriage ceremony section and immediately thereafter.

4. "My dove" (yônātî): three times (2:14; 5:2; 6:9).

5. "Fairest among women" (hayyāpâ bannāšîm): three times (1:8; 5:9; 6:1).

6. "My beautiful one" (NASB, NIV) (yāpātî): twice (2:10, 13).

7. "Shulammite" (haššûlammît): twice (7:1 [ET 6:13]).

8. "My perfect one" (tammātî): twice (5:2; 6:9).

9. "Prince's daughter" (bat-nādîb): once (7:2 [ET 7:1 (NKJV, NASB, NIV)]).

10. "Loved one" (ʾahăbâ): once (7:7 [ET 7:6]).

---

[215] Exum, *Song of Songs,* 3–6.
[216] Michael V. Fox, "Love, Passion, and Perception in Israelite and Egyptian Love Poetry," *JBL* 102 (1983): 219–28; idem, *Song of Songs,* 315–18.
[217] Fox, "Love, Passion, and Perception," 222, 228.

Four epithets of endearment are used of Solomon:[218]

1. "My beloved" (*dôdî*): twenty-six times (1:13, 14, 16; 2:3, 8, 9, 10, 16, 17; 4:16; 5:2, 4, 5, 6 bis, 8, 10, 16; 6:2, 3 bis; 7:10 [ET 7:9], 11 [ET 10], 12 [ET 11], 14 [ET 13]; 8:14).

2. "Whom my soul loves" (*šeʾāhăbâ napšî*): five times (1:7; 3:1, 2, 3, 4).

3. "He who grazes among the lilies/lotus flowers" (*hārōʿeh baššôsannîm*): twice (2:16; 6:3 translation mine).

4. "My friend" (*rēʿî*): once (5:16).

Beyond these specific pet names, the Song resounds with other expressions by the lovers communicating intimate affirmation and praise for each other. Indeed, the *wasfs* of praise constitute a full half of the major sections of the Song. Outside the boundaries of these *wasfs* there are scores of additional lines bursting with affectionate, affirming praise for each other. In these many lines of loving expressions, the lovers never say, "I love you." Rather they say, "You are beautiful!" The lovers "build up and affirm and encourage the other for themselves and who they are . . . [They give] an objective affirmation of the worth and value of the other, an enthusiasm for what is good and beautiful in the other. . . . Words such as 'I love you' focus on our feelings. The song focuses on what is lovely in the other."[219] Such usage bespeaks the vital importance of loving verbal communication and especially of objective affirming complements in the love relationship.

We thus return to the holy of holies of Eden. In the fullness of ways delineated above, the Song of Songs parallels and expands upon Gen 1–3 in its portrayal of a divinely ordained multidimensional sexual relationship. With double forte volume the author orchestrates the symphony of exclusive, permanent, and intimate love.

Sexuality and Procreation

If the relational movement in the symphony of sexuality is performed double forte in the Song of Songs, the procreational movement is punctuated by deafening silence. Amid the cacophony of pagan fertility rite percussion, beating out the message that sex is solely for procreation, in the Song the procreative function of sexuality is conspicuous by its absence. The Song does not deny this

---

[218] Those who do not accept the male lover of the Song as Solomon would add two additional epithets, the name "Solomon" (1:5; 3:7, 9, 11; 8:11, 12) and the designation "king" (1:4, 12; 7:6 [ET 7:5]), which they see used by the rustic lovers in their "romantic fantasy" of royalty (see, e.g., Murphy, *Song of Songs,* 83). As argued above, I reject the view that the royal terminology is only fantasy of royalty employed in a literary fiction and take these not as epithets of endearment but as the name and title of the real historical personage who is the lover in (and author of) the Song.

[219] Payne, "Song of Songs," 333.

ninth facet of a sexual theology, but as in Gen 1, where procreation is added as a separate blessing (Gen 1:28), sexuality in the Song is freed from the common misunderstanding that its sole (or even primary) intent must be for the propagation of children.

The fertility cults of the ancient Near East exploited sexual activity—whether enacted in public mass orgies, sacred prostitution, or representations of the god and goddess by the king and priestess—as a ritual means to emulate and stimulate the gods to bring fertility to the earth.[220] But the Song of Songs "demythologizes" sexuality—or, better, restores sexuality to its original "unmythologized" meaning and thereby serves to "shear it of pragmatic overtones."[221] Although sexuality is framed in a setting bursting with fertility at springtime (e.g., 2:12–13; 6:11; 7:12–14 [ET 7:11–13]), it does not cause that fertility. "Carnal love [in the Song] is no mimetic duplication of a primordial divine archetype of copulation; hence its justification and purpose are not to be found in its generative power. All utilitarianism, even religious, is here excluded. . . . Eros does not need justification in order to be. Eros is a 'given' of creation."[222]

An implicit polemic against the pragmatic goals of sexuality in the fertility cults, the Song "also guards it [sexuality] from another sort of pragmatism, namely, the belief that sex exists solely for purposes of reproduction."[223] Although, on the one hand, the Song is not hostile to the procreative aspect of sexuality—the lovers unhesitatingly, even enthusiastically, allude to the beauty of their own conception (3:4; cf. 8:2) and birth (6:9; 8:5)—on the other hand, sexual union is given independent meaning and value. Sexuality does not need to be justified as a means to a superior (i.e., procreative) end.

Fox notes in particular that the Song does not "mention or even allude to the most essential of sexual differentia, which is not the external genitalia but the womb." Because, as he points out, women's bearing of children is "a fact of limitless social, economic, and personal consequence," it is amazing that "this quintessentially female ability, vital for the race and crucial to individual well-being and happiness, is passed over in silence in Canticles. . . . The lovers do not even *muse* about the children they will have together. In the carefully circumscribed horizon of these love poems, anatomy is not destiny."[224]

Again we have returned to the holy of holies of Eden's garden. As in the creation account of Gen 2, the sexual experience within marriage is not linked with the utilitarian intent to propagate children. Lovemaking for the sake of (married) love, not procreation, is the message of the Song.

---

[220] See ch. 3, above. See also Samuel Noah Kramer, *The Sacred Marriage Drama* (Bloomington: Indiana University Press, 1969); Tikva Frymer-Kensky, *In the Wake of the Goddesses: Women, Culture, and the Biblical Transformation of Pagan Myth* (New York: Free Press/Maxwell Macmillan, 1992), 7–80; and Pope, *Song of Songs,* passim.

[221] Whitesell, " 'Behold, Thou Art Fair, My Beloved,' " 98.

[222] LaCocque, *Romance She Wrote,* 49.

[223] Whitesell, " 'Behold, Thou Art Fair, My Beloved,' " 99.

[224] Fox, *Song of Songs,* 309.

14

Sexuality in the Song of Songs: The Flame of Yahweh

The Wholesome, Holy Beauty of Sexuality

We come now to the final symphonic movement—and the major statement—of the Song of Songs regarding the theology of sexuality. In orchestral splendor, sexuality is presented as beautiful, good, and wholesome, to be celebrated and enjoyed without fear or embarrassment. Far from being cheap, ugly, and inferior, the love of the Song is of paramount value. "If one offered for love all the wealth of one's house, it would be utterly scorned" (8:7). In the Song, as in Gen 1, sexuality, along with the rest of God's creation, is *tôb mĕʾōd,* "very good." As in Gen 2, lovers in the Song "were both naked, and were not ashamed."

Indeed, we have returned to Eden. "The Song is written as if in Paradise. Adam's song: Thou art my second self! Thou art mine own! echoes in it in speech and interchanging song from end to end."[1] Though in a sinful world, lovers after the fall may still bask in the beauty of paradise.

A plenitude of intertwining themes highlight this wholesome beauty and goodness of paradisal sexuality.[2]

1. *Paradisal love is stunningly beautiful.* We encounter beauty everywhere in the Song. It is already highlighted in the superscription, which is probably best translated, "Solomon's *most beautiful/excellent* Song" (1:1). The spectacular beauty of the natural surroundings mirrors, and often merges with, the beauty of the lovers. In myriad ways the man tells the woman, "You are beautiful, my love" (1:15), and she replies, "Ah, you are beautiful, my beloved," (1:16). By sundry means, beauty in the Song is evoked, from the structural symmetry to the elegantly crafted verbal portraits, from the dozens of rare and exotic words and objects to the subtle aesthetic puns. Even the animals cry, "Beauty!"; the word for that graceful gazelle that leaps from poem to poem—*ṣĕbî*—means both the animal and the word "beauty." "The Song is thus a cornucopia of

---

[1] K&D, 6:500, citing German philosopher and poet Johann Gottfried von Herder.

[2] I am indebted to my graduate students in seminars on the Song of Songs at Andrews University Theological Seminary, who helped germinate many of the concepts in this section amid stimulating discussion and vigorous wrestling with the Hebrew text.

nouns, of beautiful things, when to be beautiful is to be beautiful in the eyes of the beloved."[3]

2. *Paradisal love is wonderfully sensuous.*[4] References to the five senses in the Song were tabulated in chapter 13, above, but here we savor Trible's summary of the sublime sensuousness in the Song's return to Eden, the garden of love:

> Male and female first became one flesh in the garden of Eden. There a narrator reported briefly their sexual union (Gen. 2:24). Now in another garden, the lovers themselves praise at length the joys of intercourse. Possessive adjectives do not separate their lives. "My garden" and "his garden" blend in mutual habitation and harmony. Even person and place unite: the garden of eroticism is the woman.

> In this garden the sensuality of Eden expands and deepens. Emerging gradually in Gen 2–3, all five senses capitulated to disobedience through the tasting of the forbidden fruit. Fully present in the Song of Songs from the beginning, these senses saturate the poetry to serve only love. Such love is sweet to the taste, like the fruit of the apple tree (2:3; cf. 4:16; 5:1, 13). Fragrant are the smells of the vineyards (2:13), the perfumes of myrrh and frankincense (3:6), the scent of Lebanon (4:11), and the beds of spices (5:13; 6:2). The embraces of lovers confirm the delights of touch (1:2; 2:3–6; 4:10, 11; cf. 5:1; 7:6–9; 8:1, 3). A glance of the eyes ravishes the heart (4:9; 6:13), as the sound of the lover thrills it (5:2). Taste, smell, touch, sight and hearing permeate the garden of the song.[5]

3. *Paradisal love is an exuberant celebration.* Set against a backdrop where all is sensuously beautiful, the lovers in the Song celebrate the beauty of married sexual love. Indeed, the Song of Songs is nothing less than "a continuous celebration of passion and its pleasures."[6] From the first flush of friendship between the lovers to the awaking of romantic love; from the acclamation of each other's beauty to the joy of reunion after absence; from the pageantry of the wedding ceremony to the sexual consummation of the marriage and on to the laudation of the power and permanence of love itself—the Song is a nonstop symphony of exquisite celebration, exquisite and exotic and extravagant. There is the lavishly prepared palanquin (3:6–11). Expensive imported spices superabound: *mountains* of myrrh

---

[3] Nicholas Ayo. *Sacred Marriage: The Wisdom of the Song of Songs* (illustrated by Meinrad Craighead; New York: Continuum, 1997), 49.

[4] For different explorations of this theme, see Phyllis Trible, *God and the Rhetoric of Sexuality* (OBT; Philadelphia: Fortress, 1978), 155–57; Marcia Falk, *Love Lyrics from the Bible: A Translation and Literary Study of the Song of Songs* (Sheffield, Eng.: Almond, 1982), 88–106; Roland E. Murphy, "A Biblical Model of Human Intimacy: The Song of Songs," in *The Family in Crisis or in Transition: A Sociological and Theological Perspective* (ed. Andrew Greeley; Concilium 121; New York: Seabury, 1979), 64; idem, *The Song of Songs: A Commentary on the Book of Canticles or the Song of Songs* (Hermeneia; Minneapolis: Fortress, 1990), 68–70; Robert Alter, *The Art of Biblical Poetry* (New York: Basic Books, 1985), 185–203.

[5] Trible, *God and the Rhetoric of Sexuality,* 154–55. Cf. William E. Phipps, *Genesis and Gender: Biblical Myths of Sexuality and Their Cultural Impact* (New York: Praeger, 1989), for analysis of the Song of Songs as "Paradise Continual."

[6] Alter, *Art of Biblical Poetry,* 185.

and frankincense and other spices (4:6; 8:14). There is the "banqueting house" with its festive banner of love (2:4), succulent fruits (2:3, 5; 4:13, 16; 7:14 [ET 7:13]), and freely flowing spiced wine and juice of the pomegranate (7:10 [ET 7:9]; 8:2). And at the heart of the Song is the divine invitation—even command—to *celebrate with abandon:* "Eat, friends, drink, and be drunk with love" (5:1). Indeed, "the two lovers revel in the moments of union and reunion, celebrating exuberantly the sweet times of consummation."[7]

4. *Paradisal love is a thrilling adventure.* The Song of Songs is a high drama of amorous adventure. One lover excitedly beckons to the other: "let us make haste" (1:4). We then see the other lover "leaping upon the mountains, bounding over the hills" (2:8). He in turn calls her to continue the adventure: "Arise, my love, my fair one, and come away" (2:10). There is the exhilaration of springtime; the daring expedition "in the clefts of the rock, in the covert of the cliff" (2:14); and, indeed, even the excitement of catching the pesky "little foxes, that ruin the vineyards" (2:15). The adventure continues throughout the rest of the Song. From the thrill of the wedding itself (4:1–5:1), to the heart-pounding rapture in the anticipation and experience of lovemaking (5:4, 8; 6:11–12); from the energizing excursions to the countryside and electrifying sexual explorations (7:12–14 [ET 7:11–13]) to the final animated challenge—"Make haste, my beloved, and be like a gazelle or a young stag on the mountains of spices" (8:14)—the adventure never ceases for those in love.

5. *Paradisal love is an exquisite delight.* In one of the most precious experiences pictured in the Song, Shulammite says of Solomon, "As an apple tree among the trees of the wood, so is my beloved among young men. *With great delight* I sat in his shadow, and his fruit was sweet to my taste. He brought me to the banqueting house, and his intention toward me was love" (2:3–4). The intensive *piʿel* form of the Hebrew word *ḥāmad,* "to take delight in," may here denote a prolonged or continual experience. Ariel and Chana Bloch freely translate this clause, "I took delight many times, and stayed on and on."[8] What is described is not just a pause for a moment in her beloved's presence but personal contact, sitting down in joyful companionship with him. This verse encapsulates the mood of exquisite delight in the Song, a delight that emerges on the faces of the lovers and envelops their words and actions in almost every line.

6. *Paradisal love is highly erotic.* Fox does not exaggerate when he writes about the Song of Songs (as well as the Egyptian love songs), "I would like to emphasize at the outset the place of eroticism in these songs: everywhere."[9] In language that

---

[7] J. William Whedbee, "Paradox and Parody in the Song of Solomon: Towards a Comic Reading of the Most Sublime Song," in *A Feminist Companion to the Song of Songs* (ed. Athalya Brenner; FCB 1; Sheffield, Eng.: Sheffield Academic Press, 1993), 275.

[8] Ariel Bloch and Chana Bloch, *The Song of Songs: A New Translation with an Introduction and Commentary* (New York: Random House, 1995), 150.

[9] Michael V. Fox, *The Song of Songs and Ancient Egyptian Love Songs* (Madison: University of Wisconsin Press, 1985), 298. See also Jonneke Bekkenkamp, "Into Another Scene of Choices: The Theological Value of the Song of Songs," in *The Song of Songs* (ed. Athalya Brenner and Carole R. Fontaine; FCB[2] 6; Sheffield, Eng.: Sheffield Academic

is thoroughly erotic and sensual, the lovers extol each other's physical beauty and describe their sexual encounters. Sometimes this is by direct description: "Let him kiss me with the kisses of his mouth!" (1:2); "O that his left hand were under my head, and that his right hand embraced me!" (2:6; 8:3); "when I found him whom my soul loves, I held him, and would not let him go" (3:4).[10] But more often, by means of poetic metaphors, intentional ambiguities, double entendres and euphemisms that both reveal and conceal, the beauty of the beloved's physical charms and the ecstatic pleasure of sexual experiences are described.[11] Special emphasis in the Song is placed upon the sexual appeal of the woman's breasts, echoing Solomon's words in Prov 5:19: "May her breasts satisfy you at all times."[12] My own representative sampling of erotic "concealing revelations" includes the following:

1. Song 1:13—"My beloved is to me a bag of myrrh that lies between my breasts." The Hebrew grammar is ambiguous but seems to be a deliberate "delightful confusion"[13] moving from the metaphor of myrrh to reality: Solomon lying between her breasts.

2. Song 2:3–4—The "apple tree" and "banqueting house" are metaphors for Solomon himself; his "fruit" that was sweet to her taste describes sweet fellowship and probably also unspecified sexual pleasuring.

3. Song 2:16 (also 4:5; 6:2–3)—Solomon "pastures his flock [rō'eh] among the lilies/lotus blossoms [beššôšannîm]." A delightful double entendre exists here: Solomon is grazing a *flock* (the word "flock" is not in the Hebrew but

Press, 2000), 86: "This song is not 'about' eroticism and sensuality; it *is* erotic and sensual." Cf. Fiona C. Black, "What Is My Beloved? On Erotic Reading and the Song of Songs," in *The Labour of Reading: Desire, Alienation, and Biblical Interpretation* (ed. Fiona C. Black et al.; SemeiaSt 36; Atlanta: Society of Biblical Literature, 1999), 35–52; Othmar Keel, "Erotik als Amulett gegen den allgegenwärtigen Tod: Die Lebensmetaphorik des Hohenlieds im Spiegel israelitischer Siegelkunst," *JBT* 19 (2004): 49–62; and Frederic Raurell, "Erotic Pleasure in the 'Song of Songs,'" *Laur* 24 (1983): 5–45.

[10] For a comparison with the erotic love poetry of Egypt, see esp. John B. White, *The Study of the Language of Love in the Song of Songs and Ancient Egyptian Poetry* (SBLDS 38; Missoula, Mont.: Scholars Press, 1978); and Fox, *Song of Songs,* passim.

[11] For an analysis of the double entendres and especially the imagery of sexual activity, including intercourse, in the Song, see Cosby, *Sex in the Bible,* 53–81; Joseph C. Dillow, *Solomon on Sex: The Biblical Guide to Married Love* (New York: Thomas Nelson, 1977), 28–32, 72–86; J. Cheryl Exum, "A Literary and Structural Analysis of the Song of Songs," *ZAW* 85 (1973): 57–58, 71; idem, "In the Eye of the Beholder: Wishing, Dreaming, and *double entendre* in the Song of Songs," in *The Labour of Reading: Desire, Alienation, and Biblical Interpretation* (ed. Fiona C. Black et al.; SemeiaSt 36; Atlanta: Society of Biblical Literature, 1999), 71–86; Benjamin J. Segal, "Double Meanings in the Song of Songs," *Dor le-dor* 16 (1987–1988): 249–55; Trible, *God and the Rhetoric of Sexuality,* 152–53, 157; and Carey Ellen Walsh, "A Startling Voice: Woman's Desire in the Song of Songs," *BTB* 28 (1998): 129–34.

[12] So also Garrett, "Song of Songs," 191: "For the man, her breasts are a focal point of her sexuality."

[13] Alter, *Art of Biblical Poetry,* 199.

could be implied and is supplied by some modern versions) among a pasture of lilies/lotus blossoms; but no, Solomon *himself* is grazing or browsing among the "lilies/lotus blossoms" of Shulammite's body (cf. parts of her body compared to lilies/lotus blossoms—4:5; 7:3 [ET 7:2]; 5:13).

4. Song 2:17 (cf. 4:6–8; 8:14)—"Until the day breathes and the shadows flee, turn, my beloved, be like a gazelle or a young stag on the cleft ['Bether'] mountains." The word "Bether" means "cleavage," and "mountains of Bether/cleavage" probably do not refer to literal mountains but to the landscape of her body—her two breasts with cleavage. The reference to "mountain of myrrh" and "hill of frankincense" (4:6) may likewise probably allude to her two breasts.[14] Robert Alter suggests that the two mountain ranges— Mt. Lebanon and Mt. Amana (Antilebanon)—with a rift valley in between (4:8), blend actual Palestinian landscape into the landscape of her breasts. In 4:6–8 there is a play on words between *lĕbônâ* ("frankincense") and *lĕbānôn* ("Lebanon"), which then links with the verb *libbabtinî* (*pi'el* of *lbb* "ravish, make the heart beat faster") in v. 9 and thereby "triangulates the body-as-landscape, the external landscape, and the passion the beloved inspires."[15]

5. Song 4:5 (= 7:4 [ET 7:3])—"Your two breasts are like two fawns, twins of a gazelle, that feed among the lilies [lotus blossoms]." The comparison of her breasts to fawns leaves to the imagination exactly what the point of reference is. The gazelle was known for its beauty and grace; twins denote the symmetry of the breasts; add the browsing among the lilies/lotus blossoms, and a picture emerges of "the bouncing, supple, symmetrical breasts."[16]

6. Song 4:12–16; 5:1 (cf. 6:2)—The woman herself is the locked garden and sealed fountain (her inaccessibility and virginity) (v. 12). She invites her groom to come to her—now his—garden and eat its pleasant fruits (4:16), clearly an invitation to have sexual intercourse. The groom says, "I come"! (5:1). Thus, as already noted, the very apex of the book—the chiastic center (4:16, 5:1)—consists of an invitation and an acceptance of the invitation, to consummate marriage through sexual union. Alter summarizes what is transpiring in 4:1–5:1: "The poetry by the end becomes a kind of self-transcendence of *double entente:* the beloved's body is, in a sense, 'represented' as a garden,

---

[14] Garrett, "Song of Songs," 192, translates these as "Myrrh Mountain" and "Incense Hill" and sees them as "a straightforward metaphor for breasts."

[15] Alter, *Art of Biblical Poetry,* 199.

[16] Ibid., 198. Alternatively, suggests Michael D. Goulder, the comparison is with shape; the fawn's "protuberant forehead sloping steeply down to its delicate contrasted nose, bears a close likeness to the curve of a young woman's breast, sloping down to the nipple" (*The Song of Fourteen Songs* [Sheffield, Eng.: JSOT Press, 1986], 34). So also Judith Ernst, *Song of Songs: Erotic Love Poetry* (Grand Rapids: Eerdmans, 2003), 44: "Imagine two fawns feeding, their necks arched down. Something catches their attention, and their heads bob up. Seen in profile, the line of their necks, extending down to their upturned noses, is a perfect image for the upper line of the breast, dipping to the nipple."

but it also turns into a real garden, magically continuous with the mountain landscape so aptly introduced at the midpoint of the poem."[17]

7. Song 5:2–6—The woman dreams of her lover's approach to make love, but at the same time the song may allude to the lovemaking itself. "The poetry works on two levels: in her dream world, the protagonist at once prepares to make love and engages in the sexual act as well."[18] Thus 5:2 ("Listen! my beloved is knocking") may be understood both literally, as her lover's approach, and in a sexual sense, as intercourse. The phrase "I had bathed my feet" (5:3) may also be translated, "I had had intercourse" (with "feet" as a euphemism for the genitalia). In 5:4 the woman's statement "My beloved thrust his hand into the opening" may be taken literally as the man seeking to open the door, or the word "hand" (*yād*) may be regarded as a euphemism for "penis" (as in Isa 57:8) and the "opening" (*ḥôr*) may refer to her vaginal opening.

8. Song 6:1–2—"My beloved has gone down to his garden, to the beds of spices, to pasture his flock in the gardens,[19] and to gather lilies [lotus blossoms]." Here again, as in 4:12–16, the woman is no doubt the "garden," and the husband's "pasturing" and gathering "lilies/lotus blossoms" are his sexual activity with his wife.

9. Song 7:3 (ET 7:2)—"Your navel [*šōr*] is a rounded bowl that never lacks mixed wine. Your belly [*beṭen*] is a heap of wheat, encircled with lilies [lotus blossoms]." The word *šōr* in its two other occurrences in the HB refers to the navel or umbilical cord (Prov 3:8; Ezek 16:4), but in the sequence of descriptive movement up Shulammite's body in the Song, this term comes between the thighs and the belly/abdomen (*beṭen*), and thus here is probably a euphemism for the female genitals or, more specifically, the vulva.[20] The Arabic cognate terms support this interpretation.[21] The reference to not lacking in blended beverage fits the picture of the moist vulva at the time of sexual arousal. The word *beṭen*, "belly/womb," probably refers to the abdomen with

---

[17] Alter, *Art of Biblical Poetry*, 202.

[18] Gary A. Rendsburg, "Word Play in Biblical Hebrew: An Eclectic Collection," in *Puns and Pundits: Word Play in the Hebrew Bible and Ancient Near Eastern Literature* (ed. Scott B. Noegel; Bethesda, Md.: CDL, 2000), 153; the insights in this section are drawn largely from Rendsburg, 153–54.

[19] Goulder, *Song of Fourteen Songs*, 46, argues from the plural "gardens" here that Solomon has gone to have sex with others in his harem, but the use of the singular for "garden" in poetic parallelism in the same verse makes this interpretation highly unlikely. Bloch and Bloch, *Song of Songs*, 188, suggest, "The plural *gannim* probably does not refer to gardens but to a single garden or garden area, as the so-called plural of local extension."

[20] See J. A. Loader, "Exegetical Erotica to Canticles 7:2–6," *JS* 10 (1998–2001): 99, 105–6; Murphy, *Song of Songs*, 182; and Marvin H. Pope, *Song of Songs* (AB 7C; Garden City, N.Y.: Doubleday, 1977), 617–21.

[21] Murphy points out that this interpretation is supported by the Arabic cognates *sirr* (meaning "secret" and then "pudenda" or "vulva") and *surr* ("umbilical cord," "navel," or "valley"). He prefers the translation "valley" as a "metaphor for the euphemism and double meaning that is intended" (*Song of Songs*, 182).

its color of wheat, set about (below) with "lilies/lotus blossoms," an apparent euphemism for the curling pubic hair.[22]

10. Song 7:8–9 (ET 7:7–8)—Shulammite's stature is compared to a palm tree, and her breasts to its clusters; but the metaphor blends into the woman herself as Solomon describes his desire to fondle her: "I will climb the palm tree and lay hold of its branches."

11. Song 7:9–10 (ET 7:8–9)—The man says of the woman, "O may your breasts be like clusters of the vine, and the scent of your breath [ʾap, lit. 'nose'] like apples, and your kisses [lit. 'palate'] like the best wine." She interrupts and finishes his statement: "that goes down smoothly, gliding over lips and teeth (lit., 'the lips of sleepers')." The word ʾap could indicate nose kissing but in Ugaritic and Akkadian can refer to the nipple of the breast, and in parallel with "breasts" here, it probably has that meaning.[23] The palate of the mouth compared to best wine may refer to "deep kissing." The imagery of "gliding over the lips of sleepers" is unclear but probably refers to her lips and teeth in the process of kissing (as interpreted by the ancient versions).[24]

12. Song 7:12–14 (ET 7:11–13)—"Come, my beloved, let us go forth into the fields, and lodge in the villages (or 'henna bushes' [kĕpārîm]); let us go out early to the vineyards. . . . There I will give you my love [dōday]. The mandrakes [dûdāʾîm] give forth fragrance, and over our doors are all choice fruits, new as well as old, which I have laid up for you, O my beloved." Ambiguity again heightens the eroticism: are they going to stay all night in the villages, or amid the sensuous henna blossoms (since the same Hebrew word can mean both)? The clause "I will give you my love" seems clearly to describe lovemaking (including sexual intercourse). There is a clear play on words between "love" and "mandrake" (an ancient aphrodisiac whose name is etymologically linked to "love"). The various kinds of fruits denote the delicious aspects of the lovemaking process, including old and new sexual explorations and delights between the lovers.

13. Song 8:2—"I will lead you, bring you into the house of my mother, she who used to instruct me [or 'You will instruct me'].[25] I will cause you to drink of

---

[22] See Goulder, *Song of Fourteen Songs*, 56.

[23] See Duane A. Garrett, *Proverbs, Ecclesiastes, Song of Songs* (NAC 14; Nashville: Broadman, 1993), 422; idem, "Song of Songs," in Duane A. Garrett and Paul R. House, *Song of Songs, Lamentations* (WBC 23B; Nashville: Nelson, 2004), 237; Murphy, *Song of Songs*, 422; and Pope, *Song of Songs*, 636–37.

[24] For further discussion, see Murphy, *Song of Songs*, 184. Goulder, following the change of vowels implied by the LXX, translates 7:10b (ET 7:9b), "to touch my love's erectness, and my lips to kiss his sleepers" (*Song of Fourteen Songs*, 56), and sees here an allusion to oral sex.

[25] I translate following the MT here and not the LXX and the Syriac, which have the idea of "the one who bore me." The emendation of the MT is unwarranted. See Garrett, "Song of Songs," 249. I also follow Garret (ibid., 248) in recognizing that Song 8:2 does not continue the optative mood of v. 1.

spiced wine, of the juice of my pomegranate" (translation mine). It is ambiguous in the Hebrew of v. 2 who does the instruction—the mother or the beloved. This ambiguity may well be the intention on the part of the poet to connote both continuity with the home and fresh experience from her husband. The drinking of her spiced wine and her pomegranate juice seems to be a metaphor for the delights of sexual intercourse. The wordplay between ʾeššāqkā, "I would kiss you," and ʾašqěkā, "I will cause you to drink," in these verses highlights the erotic connection.

14. Song 8:5—"Under the apple tree I awakened you," says Shulammite of her beloved. The "awakening," in light of the refrains using the same term in 2:7, 3:5, and 8:4, is undoubtedly sexual arousal.

15. Song 8:9–10—The imagery of the sister as a "wall" or "door" in v. 9 seems to be a double entendre for the two paths she could choose—to be pure and inaccessible (a wall) or to be promiscuous and "available" (a door). The brothers (who presumably are the speakers here) determine to protect their sister by adding additional protection if she is a "wall," or blocking her way if she is a "door."[26] In v. 10, Shulammite makes clear that she is a "wall" and her breasts are like "towers." She is an unconquered city, impregnable to the advances of anyone but her husband. This knowledge of her faithfulness brought Solomon *shalom.*

16. Song 8:14—"Make haste [bārah], my beloved, and be like a gazelle or a young stag upon the mountains of spices." The verb bārah ("make haste") is used only here in the Song and may be part of the climatic erotic double entendre of the Song. Carr has pointed out that the root brh elsewhere in the Bible sometimes connotes the idea of "piercing" or "penetration" (Exod 36:33; Isa 27:1).[27] Is Shulammite climaxing the Song with a call for Solomon to make haste in penetrating her body ("the mountains of spices") in sexual climax?

7. *Paradisal love is unashamed and uninhibited.* The language of erotic love saturating the Song makes the eloquent statement that sexuality is wholesome and good and can be enjoyed without fear or embarrassment. Both lovers uninhibitedly and openly describe—and explore—the body of the beloved.[28] As in the

---

[26] See the discussion of this wall-and-door image by R. Lansing Hicks, "The Door of Love," in *Love and Death in the Ancient Near East: Essays in Honor of Marvin H. Pope* (ed. John H. Marks and Robert M. Good; Guilford, Conn.: Four Quarters, 1987), 153–58.

[27] G. Lloyd Carr, *The Song of Solomon: An Introduction and Commentary* (TOTC 17; Downers Grove, Ill.: InterVarsity, 1984), 175.

[28] In the Song "bodily descriptions and bodily experiences speak of uninhibited paradise-like freedom. . . . The Song's rhetoricity of the body creates a world of uninhibited freedom. It speaks openly and freely of nudity, sexuality and the equality of the sexes. The Song's erotic discourse portrays a liberated picture of how the sexes should be able to enjoy their bodies" (Hendrik Viviers, "The Rhetoricity of the 'Body' in the Song of Songs," in *Rhetorical Criticism and the Bible* [ed. Stanley E. Porter and Dennis L. Stamps; JSOTSup 195; Sheffield, Eng.: Sheffield Academic Press, 2002], 245, 252).

garden of Eden, they can stand naked and unashamed before each other. The most intimate moments of sexual pleasure are presented without any suggestion that it is somehow dirty, cheap, or ugly. Only modern readers—not the Song's lovers—are embarrassed by the eroticism in the Song.

8. *Paradisal love is restrained and in good taste.* The fact that the Song is erotic does not mean that it is obsessed with sex. Those who have seen moist vulvas and erect penises in profusion throughout the Song have read too much into the book.[29] It is not accidental that in the Song one finds no explicit mention of the male or female genitalia or any explicit description of sexual intercourse,[30] in

---

[29] A notable representative of this tendency to "oversexualize" is Goulder, *Song of Fourteen Songs.* He overtly affirms, "To be aware of these recurrent double-entendres is, on one level, to understand the Song" (pp. 18–19). Then he proceeds to find references to the genitals in scene after scene. The following are examples: The woman's "vineyard" in 1:6 is her vulva covered with pubic hair; her statement that she had not "worked" it refers to her not being impregnated by a man (13); her "spikenard" in 1:12 "implies more than personal scents"—"flowing with passion" (i.e., a moist vulva) (17). In 2:1 she is called "lily," which is chosen not only for its beauty and scent but for its likeness to the vulva with its "deep calyx" (18). The "apple tree" in 2:3 (and 8:5) evokes the image of "two fruits hanging down above the trunk" (read "penis"), and "under" the tree refers to the place on the penis where the nerves are concentrated that make for sexual arousal (7–8). "His standard" over her (2:4) refers to his erect penis on top of her as he lies above her, letting her know of his "love," or sexual arousal (19). The "raisin-cakes" of 2:5 that would "support" her, Goulder suggests, might have been shaped like a French loaf, surrounded by two apples—again evoking the shape of the penis (20). The "dove . . . in clefts of rock" (2:14) alludes to the bird flying to remote rocks to mate, with the clefts also serving as sexual symbols (i.e., the vulva, like the "lily" and the "valley"); the "foxes" (2:15)—with their "long slim muzzles ending in rounded tips"—symbolize the penis "poking up into the vines," i.e., impregnating the vulva (24). Solomon's feeding among the lilies and the plural "gardens" (2:16; 6:2) refer to his sexual encounters with the various other members of his harem (24, 46). The woman's thought of bringing Solomon to the house of her mother (3:4) is a "euphemism for her welcoming him into her womb" (27). The woman's "conduits" of her garden (4:13) refer to the conduits of the womb, i.e., the cervical canal; the "end of the pomegranate" suggests what it is shaped like, i.e., the cervix—"similarly curved, firm, and with a depression" (38). The "fountain of living waters" (4:15) is the sexually aroused woman "flooding with desire" (39). In Song 6:12 Goulder solves the famous crux by seeing a portrayal of a new sexual position: the woman is no longer the mare (as in 1:19) but the chariot, and the man the charioteer: "The Hebrews had thus already discovered that sexual union could take place in more than one position" (51). Goulder translates 7:10b (ET 7:9b), ". . . to touch my love's erectness [penis], and my lips to kiss his sleepers," and sees here (as well as 8:2) a reference to oral sex (58–59, 62). Again, the mention of "sprouting vineshoots" (7:13 [ET 7:12]) alludes to his erect penis, and "doors/gates" into the forbidden fruit (7:14 [ET 7:13]) is a sexual euphemism for the vulva (61). The final call of the woman in the Song (8:14) is for Solomon to leave the literal gardens and come partake of her "feminine delights" (69–70).

[30] This is recognized, e.g., by David M. Carr, *The Erotic Word: Sexuality, Spirituality, and the Bible* (New York: Oxford University Press, 2003), 115, who shows that the Song "describes the yearning for and celebration of lovemaking without ever clearly describing the lovemaking itself." His explanation for this technique on the part of the poet is insightful: "The Song of Songs, however explicit it will get at times about the man's

contrast to repeated references to the penis and vulva and "plowing the vulva" (sexual intercourse) in the ANE pornographic and fertility cult poetry and ico-nography.[31] "The eroticism of the Song is not genital-centered; rather it is dif-fused throughout the body and projected onto the world beyond."[32]

Nor is sexuality in the Song vulgar or cheap. Those who have viewed the Song as "soft pornography"[33] or a "poetic porn text"[34] have failed to recognize its overarching context of chastity and marital faithfulness. In stark contrast with the crude, crass, baldly pornographic depictions of sexual arousal and intercourse found in ancient Mesopotamian texts,[35] not to speak of modern pornographic

---

and woman's bodies, never attempts to tame their sexual union (or our imaginative creation of it) with language. Instead, the Song constantly approaches their love-making and fades away, or teases with double entendres. It stokes the fire of erotic imag-ination, getting explicit enough to get the flames burning, yet not dousing them with the water of description" (p. 116). J. Cheryl Exum, *Song of Songs* (OTL; Louisville, Ky.: Westminster John Knox, 2005), 24, aptly points out that even in the lover's descriptions of each other's bodies, the poet renders "our pleasure more aesthetic than erotic, by clothing the lovers' bodies in metaphors, which never quite gives access to the body being described."

[31] E.g., the goddess Inanna composes a song about her vulva, comparing it to a horn, the crescent moon, fallow land, a field, and a hillock, then ends by telling the god Dumuzi, "Plow my vulva, sweetheart" ("Prosperity in the Palace," translated by Samuel Noah Kramer [*ANET* 643]). Again, in the Sumerian Hymn to Inanna, there is a clear reference to the male erection: "At the King's lap stood the rising cedar" (Whitesell, " 'Behold, Thou Art Fair, My Beloved,' " 98). Cf. the Ugaritic text *KTU* 1.23 describing the penis erection of the god El in the Canaanite fertility cult ritual: "The organ of El grows long as the sea, Yes, the organ of El as the flood. The organ of El is as long as the sea, Yea, the organ of El as the flood" (John Gray, *Legacy of Canaan* [2d rev. ed.; VTSup 5; Leiden: E. J. Brill, 1965], 98). Again, Fox cites a Ramesside pornographic papyrus "in which a woman demands of an ithyphallic (i.e., portrayed with an erect penis) man: 'Come behind me with your love [phallus]; your penis belongs to me" (*Song of Songs,* 21). Note also the many pictures of exaggerated genitals in ANE iconography, as referred to in ch. 3, above. For Egyptian erot-ica, see esp. the reproduction and analysis of the "Turin Erotic Papyrus," P.Cair.Zen. 55001 (David O'Connor, "Eros in Egypt," *Archaeology Odyssey* 4, no. 5 [2001]: 43–51).

[32] Michael V. Fox, "Love, Passion, and Perception in Israelite and Egyptian Love Po-etry," *JBL* 102 (1983): 228.

[33] David J. A. Clines, "Why Is There a Song of Songs and What Does It Do to You If You Read It?" *Jian Dao* 1 (1994): 19. Clines's article makes the radical suggestion that the Song of Songs was a man's pornographic "wish-fulfillment dream. . . . He is a certain kind of man, who wants a certain kind of woman, a type that is not generally available in his culture. He fantasizes such a woman, he writes his dream, he finds an audience of like-minded men, his poem becomes a best-seller" (p. 14).

[34] See Roland Boer, "The Second Coming: Repetition and Insatiable Desire in the Song of Songs," *BibInt* 8 (2000): 276–301. Boer, utilizing psychoanalytic theory, reads the whole Song as hard pornography expressing perverse desire. Within the Song he finds suggestions and references to intergenerational sex, incest, pedophilia, group sex, bestial-ity, and other expressions of perverse desire, all within a context of pervasive fetishism (*Knockin' on Heaven's Door: The Bible and Popular Culture* [London: Routledge, 1999], 53–70). His reading of the text is against the grain of the Song and repugnant.

[35] In the Hymn to Inanna, the lightly veiled metaphor of male erection ("At the King's lap stood the rising cedar") leads into a "spate of bald pornography, the deliberate

literature,[36] the Song's language of lovemaking displays extraordinary restraint and delicate taste in its use of erotic metaphors, euphemisms, and double entendres (as sampled above).

The Song is restrained and in good taste not only in its use of language but in the sexual activity of its lovers. As discussed in ch. 13, above, there is a progression of intimacy in the Song, commensurate with the unfolding stages of the love relationship and climaxing in sexual intercourse only within the boundaries of the marriage covenant. This principle of appropriate restraint is emphasized by the Shulammite's thrice repeated solemn adjuration to her female companions: "I adjure, O daughters of Jerusalem, by the gazelles or the wild does: do not stir up or awaken love until it is ready" (2:7; 3:5; 8:4).[37]

The principle of appropriate restraint and good taste applies not only to time but to place. Although the lovers revel in intimate sexual experiences together,

---

intent of which is to stimulate sexual desire and thus to facilitate enactment of the sacred rites" (Whitesell, " 'Behold, Thou Art Fair, My Beloved,' " 98). For the full text, see Diane Wolkstein and Samuel N. Kramer, *Inanna, Queen of Heaven and Earth: Her Stories and Hymns for Sumer* (New York: Harper & Row, 1983), 30–49 (esp. 35, 37). See also Wilfried G. Lambert, "The Problem of the Love Lyrics," in *Unity and Diversity: Essays in the History, Literature, and Religion of the Ancient Near East* (ed. H. Goedicke and J. J. M. Roberts; Baltimore: Johns Hopkins University Press, 1975), 98–135, who presents translations of first-millennium B.C.E. Late Assyrian and Late Babylonian love lyrics between the god Marduk and his concubine Ishtar. Note, e.g., the tablet labeled BM 41005: "Into your genitals in which you trust I will make a dog enter and will tie shut the door. Into your genitals in which you trust, like your precious stone before you. Genitals of my girl-friend, why do you constantly so do? Genitals of my girl-friend, the district of Babylon is seeking a rag. Genitals with two fingers (?), why do you constantly provoke quarrels?" (pp. 104–5). Cf. the similar tablet LKA 92 (photo K212a): lines 1–23; 81-2-4, 294 obv.: lines 12–23: "[Genitals of] my girl-friend, the district of Babylon is seeking a rag, [To] wipe your vulva, to wipe your vagina. [Now] let him/her say to the women of Babylon, 'The women will not give her a rag to wipe her vulva, to wipe her vagina.' . . . Into your genitals in which you trust I will make a dog enter and will tie shut the door; I will make a dog enter and will tie shut the door; I will make a hahhuru-bird enter and it will nest" (123). For a helpful discussion of the distinction between "erotica" and "pornography," see Carey Ellen Walsh, *Exquisite Desire: Religion, the Erotic, and the Song of Songs* (Minneapolis: Fortress, 2000), 41–45. Contra Walsh's view, however, that "the Song discards punishments and a shrill insistence on monogamy" (p. 34), the Song of Songs places the erotic within the context of a chaste monogamous sexual relationship.

[36] See the forthcoming exegetical monograph on the Song of Songs by Grenville Kent, which shows how the Song explicitly provides a stark contrast to modern pornography.

[37] For defense of the interpretation of this phrase, "until she/it (Love) pleases" as "until it be ready" or "until it is the right time," see, e.g., Murphy, *Song of Songs* 137; Garrett, *Proverbs, Ecclesiastes, Song of Songs,* 392–93. Garrett, "Song of Songs," 154–55, catches the basic thrust of this statement in the Song: "In this context, the exhortation can only mean that they should avoid promiscuity and save their virginity for marriage. . . . The woman is simply telling the younger girl to wait until she finds and marries the man she loves." For a detailed study of this entire verse, see, e.g., Michael A. Eschelbach, "Song of Songs: Increasing Appreciation of and Restraint in Matters of Love," *AUSS* 42 (2004): 305–24.

this is reserved for private settings.[38] Throughout the Song there is a sustained hesitancy to engage in a public display of sexual intimacy, in stark contrast to the public sex orgies of the fertility cults.[39] In 8:1–2 the (married) Shulammite expresses a wish that Solomon were like her brother, so that it might be appropriate even to kiss him in public. Contrary to some scholarly claims that the Song's lovers are oblivious to—or even attempt to subvert and defy—the biblical/societal norms of propriety and chastity,[40] the Song presents the love relationship fully within these norms (while at the same time restoring sexuality from distortions of the biblical perspective to its place of beauty and wholesome goodness).

9. *Paradisal love is light-hearted play.* Lovemaking in the Song is described not only in uninhibited and tasteful erotic language but in playful language. The Song brims with paronomasia, or the play on words, which teases the reader into playful imagination. This play of words parallels the play of love: "There is, in other words, an odd and satisfying consonance in this teasing game of transformations between the pleasure of play with language through metaphor and pleasure of love play that is the subject of the lines."[41] The sexual playfulness is also revealed in the interactive dialogue between the lovers. For example, 1:7–8 is probably best taken as Solomon playfully teasing his beloved: "If you do not know [where I feed my flock] . . . follow in the footsteps of the flock."[42] Again, in 7:10 (ET 7:9) the woman "playfully interrupts" her beloved by completing his sentence.[43] Goulder also notices the "playful eroticism" here as well as throughout the poem.[44] The Song presents "a world of uninhibited self-delighting play, without moral conflict, without the urgent context of history and nationhood and destiny, without the looming perspectives of a theological world-view."[45] This is not to say that the Song is opposed to any of these things, but in the joy of playful love, such "mundane" matters are transcended.

---

[38] The one time where the woman describes a public prolonged embrace with her husband (3:4) is in the context of her dream (3:1). The mention of the daughters of Jerusalem in times of the couple's sexual intimacy is probably to be seen as a literary foil or the woman's inward cogitations, not a depiction of sexual intercourse in the company of others.

[39] See Whitesell, "'Behold, Thou Art Fair, My Beloved,'" 92, 98, for elaborations on the contrast with the public fertility rites.

[40] See, e.g., André LaCocque, *Romance She Wrote: A Hermeneutical Essay on Song of Songs* (Harrisburg, Pa.: Trinity Press International, 1998), 6–11, 16–21. See also Keel, *The Song of Songs: A Continental Commentary* (trans. Frederick J. Gaiser; Minneapolis: Fortress, 1994), 32, who writes, "It [the Song] ignores the claims of society that often come into conflict with spontaneous expressions of love." Keel lists "the institution of marriage" as one of these claims with which he claims the Song has nothing to do. Fox, *Song of Songs*, 307–8, on the other hand—rightly, I believe—points out that the egalitarian view of love in the Song "is no deliberate rejection of preordained sex roles, nor are the girl's assertiveness and her equality with her lover a social statement."

[41] Alter, *Art of Biblical Poetry*, 199.

[42] Tom Gledhill, *The Message of the Song of Songs* (Bible Speaks Today; Downers Grove, Ill.: InterVarsity, 1994), 249.

[43] Bloch and Bloch, *Song of Songs*, 206.

[44] Goulder, *Song of Fourteen Songs*, 58.

[45] Alter, *Art of Biblical Poetry*, 203.

Love play in the Song is even a time for light-hearted laughter and fun. While I would not agree with the overall theses of those who call for a thoroughgoing "comic reading of the Song of Songs"[46] or see one or more of the *wasf*s in the Song as full-blown parodies on the genre,[47] I cannot overlook that "the Song expresses a spirit of fun and frivolity in its poetic tale of two lovers."[48] The Song teaches us that we should not look upon sexuality with too much reverential gravity.[49]

10. *Paradisal love is a romantic love affair.* Perhaps to avoid confusion with the technical literary use of the word, most commentators seem to avoid the term "romance" in describing the Song of Songs.[50] But the Song is thoroughly romantic—it is a love affair par excellence. Many of the points made thus far in this chapter could be brought together under the heading of "romance." From the running and frolicking together (1:4) to the exhilaration and urgency of the lovers' approach to each other (2:8), to the ravished heart (4:9) and thrilled inner being (5:4) and sexual desire (7:11 [ET 7:10]), to the surprise vacation in the countryside (7:12–13 [ET 7:11–12]) and other creatively romantic occasions in married life (making love out of doors [7:13 (ET 7:12)], going on reminiscent walks together [8:5], talking about love [8:6–7], and on and on)—the Song has all the characteristics of a robust romantic relationship. It is noteworthy also that the romantic touches and expressions of endearment do not end with the wedding; if anything, they become even more prominent. Romance does not need to end on the wedding night; it can be forever.

11. *Paradisal love is powerfully passionate.* The same can be said for the intense passion in the Song as for its romantic element: it becomes more intense as

---

[46] Whedbee, "Paradox and Parody," 266–73. See Whedbee for a list of other interpreters before him who see comic elements in the Song (p. 267).

[47] Athalya Brenner, "'Come Back, Come Back the Shulammite' (Song of Songs 7:1–10): A Parody of the *wasf* Genre," in *On Humour and the Comic in the Hebrew Bible* (ed. Yehuda T. Radday and Athalya Brenner; JSOTSup 92; Sheffield, Eng.: Almond, 1990), 251–75. Brenner offers "a daring, even dazzling new interpretation" (according to Whedbee, "Paradox and Parody," 273), that in 7:1–10 (ET 6:13–7:9) sexual humor is introduced, portraying the dancer whose physical charms are a "mixed bag" calling forth jocularity and laughter: although she dances well and has some conventionally beautiful features, at the same time "her belly is fat and jumpy like her breasts (3c, 4 [ET 2c, 3]), her neck is (disproportionately?) long, her eyes by now turbid, her nose outsize (5)" (p. 267). Brenner's thesis is considerably weakened if the Song is taken as a unity and other statements by the woman's lover about her perfect beauty are taken into account (e.g., 4:7; 6:9).

[48] Whedbee, "Paradox and Parody," 277.

[49] Gledhill, *Song of Songs,* 169–71, discusses this point at some length.

[50] LaCocque is a notable exception, even entitling his hermeneutical essay on the Song *Romance She Wrote.* Kinlaw, "Song of Songs," 1216, also calls the Song "a royal romance." Exum, *Song of Songs,* 13, speaks of the "romantic vision of love" that lies behind the Song, and provides a vivid description of this romance: "Romance is more than sexual gratification. Romance transforms the way lovers look at the world around them; suddenly the whole world becomes more beautiful, more vibrant, more wonderful. This is what happens to the Song of Songs lovers." On a popular level, see Tommy Nelson, *The Book of Romance: What Solomon Says about Love, Sex, and Intimacy* (Nashville: Nelson, 1998).

the Song progresses. Indeed, in the historical progression of the Song, the most intense expressions of passion in the love relationship come during and after the wedding. Granted, the woman is "faint with love"—"faint from the intensity of erotic yearning"[51]—before the wedding (2:5), but it is in Song 4 and onward that one encounters the cascade of expressions about the ravished heart (4:9), the inner being thrilled (5:4), the soul fainting with love (5:6), and a "mind blowing," "out of this world" experience (6:12).[52] After the wedding the king is held captive by his beloved's tresses (7:5 [ET 7:4]), and his strong sexual desire is for her (7:10 [ET 7:11]).

Love is personified as an elemental power in the threefold adjuration by Shulammite (2:7; 3:5; 8:3): "do not stir up or awaken love until it is ready."[53] The passionate power of love is evident throughout the Song (especially in describing the "almost violent power"[54] of the woman's sexual attraction) and finds its quintessential expression in the climactic wisdom declaration of Song 8:6: "love is as strong as death, passion fierce as the grave." The power of death and Sheol is absolute and inexorable, but so is the power of love. Love's power, the woman of wisdom continues, is like vehement flames of fire, unquenchable by many waters or even floods (8:6–7).

12. *Paradisal love is an awe-inspiring mystery.* This characteristic of human sexual love leads naturally from the preceding. Such powerful, death-defying, flaming love as presented in the Song is awesome. When Solomon looked at Shulammite, he saw such awesomeness revealed (6:4): "You are beautiful as Tirzah, my love, comely as Jerusalem, terrible [*ʾăyummâ*] as an army with banners." Not content with one such statement, the poet repeats it as an *inclusio* to the section a few verses later (6:10): "Who is this that looks forth like the dawn, fair as the moon, bright as the sun, *terrible* [*ʾăyummâ*] as an army with banners [read probably 'bannered starry host']?" (6:10).[55] The word for "terrible"

---

[51] Bloch and Bloch, *Song of Songs,* 151.

[52] Many unsuccessful attempts have been made to discover the key for interpreting Song 6:12, perhaps the most enigmatic statement in the Song. For a survey of interpretations, see Martin J. Mulder, "Does Canticles 6,12 Make Sense?" in *The Scriptures and the Scrolls: Studies in Honour of A. S. van der Woude on the Occasion of His 65th Birthday* (ed. Florentino García Martínez, A. Hilhorst, and C. J. Labuschagne; VTSup 49; Leiden: E. J. Brill, 1992), 104–13. Mulder argues that although the exact meaning of the idiom behind the text is obscure, the context suggests a meaning equivalent to our colloquial expressions "to have a 'mindblowing' experience," "to be over the moon," "to be out of this world" (pp. 110–11).

[53] For extended discussion of love as an elemental power, see esp. Keel, *Song of Songs,* 30–37.

[54] Alter, *Art of Biblical Poetry,* 103. For discussion of this female sexual power, see the section on egalitarianism in ch. 13, above.

[55] The *nipʿal* absolute passive participle *nidgālôt,* "bannered," in 6:4 probably refers to an army (in the context of military cities) but in 6:10 may well refer to the "bannered" constellations of stars (in the context of the moon and sun). Bloch and Bloch, *Song of Songs,* 95, 193–94, provide evidence for this understanding of 6:10. They translate, "daunting as the stars in their courses" (p. 95).

(ʾăyummâ) in these passages has the connotations of "fear/dread/awe" and "majesty."[56] The beauty of Shulammite was so intense and majestic that it struck awe in the ones who looked at her.

The Song does not try to explain the awesomeness of love's sexual attraction: it is a mystery. The Song proclaims the mysterious character of love by employing many literary mystifications to portray it. "There is mystification here. The reader must delve into it, and return again and again to savour the richness of its multiple layers of meaning and to respond with all the senses to its evocation of beauty."[57] The Song of Songs is the enfleshment of the wise man's saying in the Proverbs: "the way of a man with a girl" is a mystery too wonderful for him to understand (Prov 30:18–19). Again the climactic encapsulation of the mystery of sexual love is implicit in the wisdom declaration of Song 8:6–7: love's awesome power is as mysterious as the mystery of Death and Sheol themselves; as mysterious as a vehement flame that cannot be quenched, even by floods of many waters. As mysterious as the "flame of Yahweh."[58] This leads us to the innermost and greatest mystery of love in the Song.

The Flame of Yahweh

A whole book taken up with celebrating the wholesome beauty and enjoyment of human sexual love! How can the inclusion of such a book be justified in the sacred canon? No further justification is needed. Those who have resorted to an allegorical interpretation to legitimize the existence of the Song in Scripture have missed the crucial point—the Song of Songs in its plain and literal sense is not just a "secular" love song but already fraught with deep spiritual, theological significance.[59] From the OT Hebrew perspective, God is not absent from the Song, nor does his love and concern for his creatures fail to be manifested in it. Rather,

---

[56] Two of the three occurrences of ʾāyōm in the HB are these two verses of the Song (6:4, 10); it means "awe-inspiring," with an implication of dread and also majesty; the third reference (in Hab 1:7) refers to the "dread and fearsome" Babylonian army. See BDB 33; HALOT 41.

[57] For elucidation of this "mystification" motif in the Song, see Grace I. Emmerson, "The Song of Songs: Mystification, Ambiguity, and Humour," in Crossing the Boundaries: Essays in Biblical Interpretation in Honour of Michael D. Goulder (ed. Stanley E. Porter, Paul Joyce, and David E. Orton; New York: E. J. Brill, 1994), 97, 104, 111 (quote at 111).

[58] Translation mine. Throughout the subsection below that comprises the remainder of this chapter, I supply my own translation of the Hebrew text.

[59] Even among modern scholars who accept the plain, literal sense of the Song, most fail to see any theological significance in the book. Murphy, Song of Songs, 100, notes the "striking fact that the Song of Songs has largely been neglected in studies of biblical theology." He suggests that this may be "because major contributors to the contemporary discussion have held views of the Songs's original meaning that leave little room for theological development" and because "recognition that the Song is comprised of erotic poetry has meant for some an absence of religious or theological significance."

they are clearly shown in the enjoyment and pleasure (given by God to man in the creation) that the lovers find in each other and in their surroundings.[60]

In harmony with the presentation of creation in Genesis and consonant with the high doctrine of creation in the Wisdom literature, to which this book belongs, sexuality in the Song is part of God's good creation; and since it is created by God, it speaks eloquently—perhaps most eloquently of all—of God's love for his creation as it is enjoyed in harmony with the divine intention. The affirmation of human sexual love in the Song is therefore an implicit affirmation of the Creator of love.

Many commentators find no reference to God or the sound of God's voice in the Song, and it is understandable that in a time of pagan fertility cults, when the very air was charged with the divinization of sex, the divine presence/voice would have to be muted in the context of sexuality. Nonetheless, God is clearly present in the Song—and is not silent.

A veiled but clear and striking allusion to God appears in the thrice repeated adjuration spoken by Shulammite: "I adjure you, O daughters of Jerusalem, by the gazelles or the wild does: do not stir up or awaken love until it is ready" (2:7; 3:5; 8:4). In the first two occurrences of this refrain, Shulammite binds the women to an oath, *biṣbāʾôt ʾô bĕʾaylôt haśśādeh*, "by the gazelles or the wild does." Scholars have widely recognized the play on words between this phrase and the names for God: *bēʾlōhê ṣĕbāʾôt*, "by Elohe Shabaoth, the God of hosts," and *bĕʾēl šadday*, "by El Shaddai, the Mighty God."[61] The inspired poet has substituted similar-sounding names of animals (symbolic of love) for the customary divine names used in oaths.[62] Contrary to those who see this as a "secularization" of the Song, I find this a powerful affirmation of God's presence there. Although God's name is muted, it is true, as a safeguard against any attempts to divinize sex after the order of the fertility cults, it is in fact heard even more distinctly through the animals of love that echo the divine appellations. The poet surely would not have included the oath formula that regularly throughout Scripture employs the divine name ("I adjure you/swear by . . . [divine name] . . . if you do not . . .")[63] if he did not intend to allude intertextually to the divine presence behind the Song. And he would certainly not have used verbal echoes of the divine names if he were seeking to remove any reference to God in the Song. By substituting similar-sounding names of animals, symbolizing love for the divine name, and then

---

[60] Sapp, *Sexuality, the Bible, and Science,* 26. See the more recent exploration of this theme by Camilla Burns, "Human Love: The Silent Voice of God," *TBT* 36 (1998): 159–63, although I disagree with her that God's voice is totally absent in the Song.

[61] See, e.g., Robert Gordis, *The Song of Songs and Lamentations: A Study, Modern Translation, and Commentary* (New York: Ktav, 1974), 28; Murphy, *Song of Songs,* 133; Bloch and Bloch, *Song of Songs,* 152.

[62] For discussion of the love symbolism of these animals in the Song, other biblical Wisdom literature, and in the ANE parallels, see, e.g., George M. Schwab, *The Song of Songs' Cautionary Message concerning Human Love* (New York: Peter Lang, 2002), 43, 47–48.

[63] See, e.g., Gen 24:3; cf. Gen 14:22–23; Josh 9:19; Judg 21:7; 1 Sam 24:22 (ET 24:21); 28:10; 2 Sam 19:8 (ET 19:7); 1 Kgs 1:30; 2:8, 23, 42; 2 Chr 36:13; Neh 13:25; Isa 48:1; 65:16; Jer 12:16; Zeph 1:5.

incorporating these into a divine oath formula, the refrain succeeds in inextricably linking Love (personified in the oath) with the divine presence without thereby divinizing sex.[64] George M Schwab has accurately captured the use of circumlocutions for the divine name in this verse:

> In the Bible, there is no case where one swears by zoological specimens. . . . The girl desires the daughters of Jerusalem—and the author desires the reader—to swear by God not to stir up love until it pleases. . . . The girl wants the young women to take an oath by the gazelle and doe. These terms serve as circumlocutions for God Almighty, Lord of Hosts. But they are also used as symbols throughout the Song for sexual endowment, appeal, comeliness, and fervor. The words, then, exist with three referents: animals in a symbolic forest, the divine warrior God Almighty and his Hosts, and ardent affection. . . . Thus the terms combine the concept of God with the concept of love and its power. The girl desires the daughters of Jerusalem to swear by sexuality and God—and these two concepts are fused into a single image. The Song should then be read as if love were conceived as a divine attribute of God. . . . Love is not simply a matter of feelings, social contracts, or trysts in the wood.[65]

Let us move from the dominant recurring refrain of the Song to its twin apexes. There is wide scholarly agreement that the two high points of the Song are 4:16–5:1 and 8:5–7. One is the structural/symmetrical center of the Song; the other is the thematic peak. Landy refers to these passages as "the two central foci: the centre and the conclusion."[66] Ernst Wendland calls them the "middle climax" and the "final peak" of the Song respectively and amasses a persuasive display of literary evidence to support the choice of these passages as the Song's twin summits.[67]

Chapter 13, above, points out that 4:16–5:1 comes at the very center of the symmetrical literary structure of the Song. There is was argued that it is probably the voice of God himself that resounds in the climactic last line (5:1c) of this central apex to the Song, giving his divine benediction upon the marriage and its consummation: "Eat, friends, drink, and be drunk with love" (5:1.) God's voice is the central and, indeed, the omniscient voice. God's authoritative voice here at the climax to the Song returns us to Eden, to another divine approbation upon the sexual union God already had proclaimed "very good" in the beginning. By speaking here at the focal point of the Song and to both lovers, God underscores that sexual fulfillment is in the center of the divine will for *both* partners.

The echo of God's names resonates in the dominant recurring refrain of the Song (2:7; 3:5; cf. 8:4), and the very voice of God resounds from the Song's central summit (5:1). But when one moves to the Song's thematic climax and conclusion,

---

[64] The ancient versions recognized the link with God in this verse. The LXX translates, "by the powers and forces of the field," and the Targum, "by the Lord of Hosts and by the Strength of the land of Israel."

[65] Schwab, *Song of Songs' Cautionary Message*, 43, 47–48.

[66] Francis Landy, *Paradoxes of Paradise: Identity and Difference in the Song of Songs* (Sheffield, Eng.: Almond, 1983), 51.

[67] Ernst R. Wendland, "Seeking a Path through a Forest of Symbols: A Figurative and Structural Survey of the Song of Songs," *JTT* 7, no. 2 (1995): 41–46, quote at 41.

the great paean to love (8:6), the name of Yahweh makes its single explicit appearance in the book, and his flaming theophanic presence encapsulates the entire message of the Song. Song 8:6 reads,

> For love is as strong as death,
> Ardent love as relentless/intense as Sheol;
> Its flames [*rĕšāpêyhā*] are flames of fire [*rišpêy ʾēš*]—
> *The very flame of Yah(weh)* [*šalhebetyâ*].[68]

Wendland demonstrates that "a host of Hebrew literary devices converge here [Song 8:6] to mark this as the main peak of the entire message. . . . In this verse we have the fullest, most sustained attempt to describe (or is it evoke?) the supreme subject of the Song, namely 'love.'"[69] He also points out that the Hebrew word selected by the inspired poet to occupy the "ultimate, climactic position" of this verse—and thus of the final peak of the Song—is *šalhebetyâ*, "the flame of Yah(weh)."[70]

Some have suggested that this Hebrew word be excised from the text as a gloss,[71] but there is no manuscript evidence for such emendation, and the word fits the context precisely. Murphy provides a sound assessment of the situation: "Some commentators have questioned the integrity of the text, but without substantial support from the ancient versions. Although the colon is short, with only four syllables, one need not conclude that the construction is a gloss."[72]

The word *šalhebetyâ* is a compound term, composed of the noun *šalhebet*, "flame," and the suffix -*yâ*. Although the Ben Asher text of the MT does not separate this compound term, the Ben Naphtali tradition (as well as many manuscripts and editors [BHK]) divides the term into two words, *šalhebet–yāh*.[73] The probable 3 + 2 rhythm of the poetry here may lend support to this separation of *yāh* as an independent word.[74] Whether it is separated or not, commentators are

---

[68] The discussion below will give the evidence for this original translation.

[69] Wendland, "Seeking a Path," 43–44. The literary devices include, among other things, "strict parallelism (the first two lines); syntactic placement (the utterance—final key terms, 'love' and 'ardor'); imagery (simile and metaphor); symbolism (death and fire); paradox (the compelling power of death [destructive] v. love [creative]; condensation (esp. the last line); an even rhythmic pattern (3 + 3 + 3) with variation (the last word/demi-line [?]); alliteration (the repeated *[s]* of lines 2–3) with possible onomatopoeia (imaging the hi-ss-ing of a fire); and an apocopated mention of the divine name (-*ya*) in ultimate, climactic position." Schwab, *Song of Songs' Cautionary Message*, 61, presents a conclusion similar to that of Wendland: "What is expressed in Cant 8:6–7 can serve as a lens to bring into focus the whole Song of Songs' conception of love."

[70] Wendland, "Seeking a Path," 44. Mitchell, *The Song of Songs*, 1188, concurs: "This is the single most significant phrase in the Song, and tragically most expositions downplay and mistranslate. It is the apex of the book's theological highlight (Song 8:6–7). This is the Song's sole direct reference to God, or more specifically, to 'Yah,' the short form of 'Yahweh.'"

[71] E.g., Pope, *Song of Songs*, 670, who lists various suggested emendations.

[72] Murphy, *Song of Songs*, 192.

[73] See Fox, *Song of Songs*, 170.

[74] See Tournay's note in André Robert and Raymond J. Tournay, eds., *Le Cantique des cantiques* (Paris: Gabalda, 1963), 453; Raymond J. Tournay, "Les chariots d'Aminadab (Cant. vi 12): Israël, peuple théophore," *VT* 9 (1959): 307; cf. Murphy, *Song of Songs*, 192.

generally agreed that the -yâ (or yāh) connected with šalhebet is the Hebrew for "Yah," the shortened form of the Tetragrammaton, YHWH (Yahweh).[75]

Although it is generally conceded that the name of Yah(weh) appears in this passage, many insist that this is simply another instance of the Hebrew idiom for expressing the superlative, that is, "a most vehement flame."[76] This is a theoretical possibility, although valid examples of using a divine name to express the superlative in the HB are not nearly as common as has been claimed[77] and any instance of the covenant name yāh (or the full Tetragrammaton YHWH) ever being used as a superlative has been questioned.[78] "While the generic term for god does function as a semantic device for superlatives, this [Song 8:6] verse would be the sole case where the proper name of Yahweh does. And it would be a surprising use, really. Considerable care [was] taken around the divine name in the Bible, illustrated by the Third Commandment, which prohibited the wrongful use of the divine name (Exod 20:7). . . . The reverence toward the divine name makes it unlikely that it was used as a mere stylistic device in the Song."[79]

[75] The pointing of the MT clearly suggests this conclusion. It fits the pattern of other words that have the apocopated suffix -yâ, "Yah(weh)." The apocopated form of Yahweh, Yah, often has the mappîq dot in the final hê, especially when appearing by itself (e.g., Ps 118:5) or joined by a maqqēp (e.g., Ps 117:2) but not necessarily when it is part of a longer word. See, e.g., Jer 2:31, ma'pēlyâ, "the darkness of Yah(weh)," and many names with the theophoric ending (e.g., yĕdîdyāh, Jedidiah, 2 Sam 12:25; yĕkonyâ, Jeconiah, 1 Chr 3:16; ḥizqîyâ, Hezekiah, 2 Kgs 18:1). The LXX apparently took -yâ as a third-person feminine singular pronominal suffix, but there is no good reason to abandon the MT pointing in favor of the LXX reading, especially since the Aramaic Targumim apparently understood it along the lines of the MT, as referring to the divine name.

[76] See, e.g., Bloch and Bloch, Song of Songs, 213; Gordis, Song of Songs, 26, n. 90; and a number of other commentators and various modern versions (e.g., RSV, NRSV, KJV, NKJV, NIV [although the margin reads, "like the very flame of the Lord"]). Parallel texts used to support this position include most often the following (with Yahweh or Yah): Jer 2:31 (ma'pēlyâ, "darkness of Yah" = "deep gloom"); Ps 118:5 (bammerḥāb yāh, "broad place of Yah" = "great enlargement"); 1 Sam 11:7 (paḥad yhwh, "the dread of the LORD" = "a great fear"); Gen 10:9 (gibbōr-ṣayid lipnê yhwh, "a mighty hunter before the LORD" = "an exceedingly mighty hunter"). Cf. several references to Elohim: Gen 35:5 (ḥittat 'ĕlōhîm, "terror from God" = "a dreadful terror"); Ps 36:7 (ET 36:6) (kĕharrê-'ēl, "like the mountains of God" = "mighty mountains"); Ps 80:11 (ET 80:10) ('arzê-'ēl, "cedars of God" = "mighty cedars"); Jonah 3:3 ('îr-gĕdôlâ lē'lōhîm, "a great city before God" = "an exceedingly great city"). The first example (Jer 2:31) is the only precise parallel to Song 8:6 (compound term with apocopated suffix -yâ).

[77] I concur with Landy: "While I concede that the name of God may sometimes be used idiomatically, as a vague connotation of grandeur, the instances most commonly referred to are not always convincing, e.g., Nineveh was a very great city before God (Jonah 3.3); it is the concern of God for the great city that is the point of the parable" (Paradoxes of Paradise, 315, n. 114). Landy then points to other passages (Ps 36:7 [ET 36:6] and Ps 80:11 [ET 80:10]) that he argues are not superlatives but indicate the "divine domicile."

[78] So, e.g., A. M. Harman, "Modern Discussion on the Song of Songs," RTR 37 (1978): 71: "Many modern discussions assume that 'flames of Yah' is yet another instance of the divine name being used as a superlative. It is true that 'elohim may be used in this way but not the covenant name yah which occurs here (similarly the use of yahweh in Gen. 35:5 and 1 Sam. 26:12 need not be explained as a superlative)." See the discussion of this point below.

[79] Walsh, Exquisite Desire, 205.

Several crucial considerations lead to the conclusion—shared with dozens of commentaries[80] and translations[81]—that the expression in this context moves beyond the superlative to describe "the very flame of Yahweh." First, the *šapʿel* or causative verbal root of *šalhebet* (common in Aramaic/Syriac), suggesting the meaning "causing to flame," supports the conclusion that the construct relationship here is best interpreted as a *subjective genitive*, with Yah(weh) the cause or source of the flame.[82] "This predicate does not state the flames of love are 'most

---

[80] E.g., "A flaming out of God (Yah)" (Ayo, *Sacred Marriage*, 246); "Flammen JHWHs" (Walter Bühlmann, *Das Hohelied* [Stuttgart: Katholisches Bibelwerk, 1997], 87); "A flame of Jah" (Delitzsch, *Proverbs, Ecclesiastes, Song of Solomon*, 3:144); "the very flame of Yah!" (M. Timothea Elliott, *The Literary Unity of the Canticle* [European University Studies, Series 23, 371; New York: Peter Lang, 1989], 266); "flames of Yah" (Carole R. Fontaine, "'Go Forth into the Fields': An Earth-Centered Reading of the Song of Songs," in *The Earth Story in Wisdom Traditions* [ed. Norman C. Habel and Shirley Wurst; Earth Bible 3; Cleveland: Pilgrim, 2001], 138); "The flames of the Eternal" (H. L. Ginsberg, "Introduction to the Song of Songs," in *The Five Megilloth and Jonah: A New Translation* [Philadelphia: Jewish Publication Society of America, 1969], 188; Christian David Ginsburg, *The Song of Songs and Coheleth (Commonly Called Ecclesiastes): Translated from the Original Hebrew, with a Commentary, Historical and Critical* [2 vols., 1857–1861; repr., 2 vols. in 1; Library of Biblical Studies; New York: Ktav, 1970], 188); "the flame of Yahweh" (S. Craig Glickman, *A Song for Lovers* [Downers Grove, Ill.: InterVarsity, 1976], 169); "A flame of God" (Gordis, *Song of Songs,* 74); "A very flame of the Lord" (A. F. Harper, *Beacon Bible Commentary* [Kansas City, Mo.: Beacon Hill, 1967], 633); "the very flame of the Lord" (Walter C. Kaiser Jr., *Toward Old Testament Ethics* [Grand Rapids: Zondervan, 1983], 195); "the flame of God" (Landy, *Paradoxes of Paradise,* 121); "the flame of Yah" (Mitchell, *The Song of Songs,* 1170, and discussion on pp. 1185–92); "A flame of Yah" (Murphy, *Song of Songs,* 117); "the flame of the Lord" (Iain W. Provan, *Ecclesiastes, Song of Songs* [NIVAC; Grand Rapids: Zondervan, 2001], 368); "une flamme de Yahvé" (Robert and Tournay, *Le Cantique des cantiques,* 301); "du Feu de la fille de Yah" (Carlo Suarès, *Le Cantique des cantiques* [Geneva: Mont-Blanc, 1969], 244); "A flame of YHWH" ("une flamme de YHWH") (Tournay, *Word of God, Song of Love: A Commentary on the Song of Songs* [trans. J. Edward Crowley; New York: Paulist, 1988], 28, 80); "a flame of Yah" (Walsh, *Exquisite Desire,* 205–6); "The flame of Yah[weh]!" (Wendland, "Seeking a Path," 43); "a blaze of Jehovah" (Otto Zöckler, "Song of Songs," in *A Commentary on the Holy Scriptures: Critical, Doctrinal, and Homiletical* [ed., Johann P. Lange; trans., W. Henry Green; 12 vols.; repr., Grand Rapids: Zondervan, 1960], vol. 5. sect. 3, p. 129). See also D. Buzy, *Le Cantique des cantiques* (Paris: Létouzey & Ané, 1946), 358; G. Krinetzki, *Hoheslied* (Stuttgart: Echter, 1980), 243; D. Lys, *Le plus beau chant de la création: Commentaire du Cantique des cantiques* (Paris: Cerf, 1968), 290; Tommaso Piatti, *Il Cantico dei cantici* (Rome: Edizioni Paoline, 1958), 184; G. Ravasi, *Cântico dos cânticos* (São Paulo: Edições Paulinas, 1988), 135; V. Zapeltal, *Das Hohelied* (2d ed.; Freiburg, Switz.: Universitäts Buchhandlung, 1907), 146.

[81] Modern versions that translate *šalhebetyâ* as a reference to God include, e.g., ASV ("A very flame of Jehovah"); BVME ("a very flame of the Lord"); ESV ("the very flame of the Lord"); NASB ("The very flame of the Lord"); JB and NJB ("a flame of Yahweh himself"); HCSB, margin ("the blaze of the Lord"); NIV, margin ("like the very flame of the Lord"); RV ("a very flame of the Lord"); EBR ("the flash of Yah"); French Nouvelle Edition de Geneve ("Une flamme de l'Éternel"); French Bible de Jérusalem ("une Flamme de Yahvé"); Spanish Nácar-Colunga translation ("son llamas de Yahvé"); German Luther Bible ("und eine Flamme des Herrn").

[82] See Delitzsch, *Proverbs, Ecclesiastes, Song of Solomon,* 3:147.

vehement,' but affirms that they emanate from the Eternal. . . . [*Yāh*] is the genitive of cause or origin."[83]

Second, the single occurrence of a precise *terminological parallel* to *šalhebetyâ* in the HB—*ma᾿pēlyâ*, "darkness of Yah" (Jer 2:31), also (like *šalhebetyâ*) a compound term with the apocopated suffix -*ya*—most probably should not be taken as an example of a superlative usage but rather seen as referring to darkness originated by Yahweh.[84]

Third, the *immediate context* of the term *šalhebetyâ* in Song 8:6 seems to go beyond the superlative meaning of "most vehement flame" or "lightning." "Either this is a poor choice of metaphor, or it is claiming a supernatural quality for love. We are at this moment hearing something about the divine aspect of Love."[85] "To interpret 'salhebetya' as chance lightning does not do justice to it in the context of the Song as a whole or of this verse, with its confrontation of eternal forces."[86] The "eternal forces" of love, death, ardent love, and Sheol in this passage call for reference to another "eternal force"—that is, Yahweh—not just common lightning bolts. It has also been pointed out that this passage is an implicit contrast (even polemic, I might add) between Yahweh and the other prominent Canaanite/Ugaritic "deities" over whom he shines supreme: Death (*māwet*), Sheol (*šĕ᾿ôl*), Blazes (*rešep*), and Many Waters = primeval chaos (*mayim rabbîm*).[87]

Fourth and fifth, the *structural position* of the term *šalhebetyâ* in the passage and the *heightened literary artistry* that accompanies it here point beyond a mere

---

[83] Ginsburg, *Song of Songs and Coheleth*, 188.

[84] For this point I am indebted to one of my students, Ronaldo D. Marsollier, "Cant 8:6–7—Love as a Divine Gift: The Crown and Climax of the Song of Songs" (paper presented for the class OTST668 Psalms/Wisdom Literature: Song of Songs, Andrews University Theological Seminary, winter 1999). The only other occurrence of *ma᾿apēl*, "darkness," in the HB (but without the -*yâ* suffix) is in Josh 24:7, where Yahweh reminds his people that "he put darkness [*ma᾿apēl*] between you and the Egyptians" at the time of the exodus by the Red Sea. After briefly describing the drowning of the Egyptians, the verse concludes, "and your eyes saw what I [Yahweh] did to Egypt. Afterwards you lived in the wilderness a long time." The passage in Jer 2:31, by utilizing a term used only once more in the HB, appears to be an intertextual echo of the Joshua passage: it is also set against an exodus backdrop (cf. Jer 2:2, 6, 18), and Jer 2:31 has the same terms/motifs as Josh 24:7: *midbār* "wilderness"; *ma᾿apēl*; and "Israel/my people." Both passages allude to the incident recorded in Exod 14:19–20, where God himself was the pillar of darkness to the Egyptians and a pillar of light to Israel. The Joshua passage captures this divine causation of the darkness: "your eyes saw what I [Yahweh] did to Egypt." The compressed Jeremiah allusion likewise captures the divine connotations to the darkness by adding the suffix -*yâ* to *ma᾿apēl*. The resulting compound term, *ma᾿pēlyâ*, is not just the superlative "deep darkness" but in fact "darkness of Yah," a darkness originating with, and caused by, Yahweh.

[85] Mark W. Elliott, "Ethics and Aesthetics in the Song of Songs," *TynBul* 45 (1994): 147.

[86] Landy, *Paradoxes of Paradise*, 127. Landy also points out (citing Lys) that since lightning was considered divine fire, interpreting the text as "divine fire of the divine" would be tautologous. He notes further that *šalhebet* does appear twice more in the HB (both without the prefixed divine name): Job 15:30, and Ezek 21:3 (ET 20:47), where it could refer to either lightning or a forest fire (p. 316, n. 118).

[87] See Wendland, "Seeking a Path," 44; cf. John G. Snaith, *The Song of Songs* (NCB; Grand Rapids: Eerdmans, 1993), 121–22.

superlative usage. "The clipped and suffixed reference to 'Yahweh,' while it could be a mere idiomatic substitute for the superlative (i.e., the 'hottest/brightest' flame), in this structural position [the 'ultimate, climactic position' of this verse] . . . and in conjunction with so much stylistic embellishment, definitely seems to signify something more [i.e., the flame of God]."[88] Landy shows that the structural placement of *šalhebetyâ* in the phrase *rĕšāpêhā rišpê ʾēš šalhebetyâ* ("its flames are flames of fire—the very flame of Yahweh") gives this word the role of resolving the suspense built up earlier in the credo: "Rhythmically the phrase is characterized by compression: from 'rešāpeyhā' to 'rišpê' to the monosyllable ''ēš.' . . . In fact, the double stress 'rišpê ʾēš' can only be followed by a pause, a moment of suspense, resolved in the long climactic apposition: 'šalhebetyâ.'"[89]

Sixth, the larger canonical context points to Yahweh's presence here in Song 8:6, for "fire betrays God's presence throughout the Bible; substanceless, and shapeless, it is his element, the nearest approach to his image."[90] The presence of God in theophany is connected with flames of fire in numerous places in Scripture.[91] Thus in the Song love "is portrayed here as an amorous phlogiston, an unappeasable holocaust, Yahweh's fire. Coming into love is like coming into God's presence."[92] The closest and most crucial connection between fire and God's presence concerns the sanctuary in Israel's midst. Landy grasps this connection with the sanctuary, and the application to love as the flame of God:

> For in Israel, in the dialectics of king and kingdom, the flame of God is constantly alight only on the altar at its center; it communicates between heaven and earth. . . . In the sanctuary, the union and differentiation of lovers is a collective process; there, symbolically, the wealth of the kingdom is reduced to ashes, merged with the divine flame, and renewed. God, the source of life, is indwelling in the land, and guarantees its continuance. The shine is thus the matrix, an inner confine, and the hearth, the generative flame. There the king and the Beloved participate in the creative current, that infuses the lovers at the centre of their world.[93]

Landy is on the right track in connecting the flame of Yahweh with the divine flame on the altar of the sanctuary, but he has not gone far enough. He needs to go "further up and further in" (to use C. S. Lewis's phrase)—further up to the heavenly sanctuary and further in to the inner sanctum.[94]

---

88 Wendland, "Seeking a Path," 44.

89 Landy, *Paradoxes of Paradise,* 129.

90 Ibid., 127.

91 E.g., in Gen 3:24 the use of the verb *šākan* to describe the "placement" of the cherubim with "a sword flaming and turning" may allude to the Shechinah presence in their midst; the "smoking fire pot" and "flaming torch" that passed between the pieces of the covenant sacrifices in Gen 15 clearly represents the divine presence (Gen 15:17); God appears to Moses at the burning bush (Exod 3:2); and the pillar of fire symbolizes Yahweh's presence (Exod 13:21; 40:38; Num 9:15).

92 Schwab, *Song of Songs' Cautionary Message,* 63.

93 Landy, *Paradoxes of Paradise,* 127.

94 C. S. Lewis, *The Last Battle* (New York: MacMillan, 1956), 161–77.

As a seventh and final point I call attention to *specific intertextual linkages* with Song 8:6—even closer intertextuality than alluded to by Landy. In the divine theophanies related to the sanctuary, there is fire, flames of fire, not just at the altar but also and especially in the very throne room of Yahweh. In the earthly sanctuary, the pillar of fire hovered over the "tent of the covenant" (Num 9:15; Exod 40:38). The blazing glory of God filled the tent at its inauguration (Exod 40:34), and the Shekinah dwelt between the cherubim in the holy of holies (Exod 25:22; 1 Sam 4:4; 6:2; Ps 80:1; 99:1; Isa 37:16). In the heavenly temple, the seraphim (lit., "burning ones") surrounded the throne (Isa 6:2), antiphonally singing "Holy, holy, holy," and the whole temple was filled with smoke (Isa 6:4); there on the holy mountain of God the anointed cherub walked in the midst of "stones of fire" (Ezek 28:14, 16). But beyond all this general intertextual background, one (the only one of which I am aware) OT passage equals Song 8:6 with as much concentrated references to flames/fire; this passage describes the very throne of Yahweh, the Ancient of Days. Daniel 7:9–10, the intertextual twin of Song 8:6, overflows with fiery flames. In immediate succession, three times flames/fire are mentioned, matching (in Aramaic) almost precisely the threefold (in Hebrew) mention of fiery flames in Song 8:6: (1) Dan 7:9, "his [the Ancient of Days'] throne was fiery flames" (= *rĕšāpêhā*, "its flames," of Song 8:6); (2) Dan 7:9, "its wheels were burning fire" (= *rišpê ʾēš*, "flames of fire," of Song 8:6); and (3) Dan 7:10, "A stream of fire issued and flowed out from his presence" (= *šalhebetyâ*, "flame of Yah[weh]," in Song 8:6). These texts appear to be intertextually related, with Dan 7:10 as a parallel description of the "the flame of Yahweh." In canonical perspective, the "flame of Yah" in Song 8:6 is none other than the fiery stream that comes forth from the enthroned Yahweh himself. The Song's flame of Yahweh thus brings us into the heavenly holy of holies.[95]

In light of the multidimensional evidence supporting the acceptance of *šalhebetyâ* as an integral part of the text and constituting an explicit mention of Yahweh, the various arguments against this position fall to the ground. Landy cogently summarizes the main points of opposition and diffuses them by going to the root causes for such resistance to the presence of the divine name in this passage. To those who wish to emend the text, he chides, "The postulation of glosses seems to me questionable, since it is uncomfortably like an excuse for eliminating anything inconvenient. Numerous and ungainly are the emendations proposed for 'šalhebetyâ.'" To those who do textual surgery as well as those who attenuate the divine name into hyperbole, he cuts to their unstated (and perhaps unconscious) motivation—"misguided prurience." To those who argue that this would

---

[95] In this light, Rabbi Akiba's speech at Yavneh— "All the writings [of Scripture] are holy, but the Song of Songs is the Holy of Holies!" (quoted at the beginning of ch. 13, above)—is right on the mark. "Maybe Akiba, himself a profound mystic, meant exactly what he said. Though the visible Temple be destroyed, through the medium of the Song, it is still possible for those who pray to enter the presence of 'the King'" (Ellen F. Davis, *Proverbs, Ecclesiastes, and the Song of Songs* [Westminster Bible Companion; Louisville: Westminster John Knox, 2000], 241).

be Yahweh's sole entry in the book and therefore it cannot refer to Yahweh, Landy
replies that this "is no argument. . . . It is equally as valid to say that its uniqueness
reinforces its solemnity." Those who maintain that sexuality is inconsistent with
sanctity he both reminds and reprimands: "References and comparisons to divinity are found in the love-literature of all ages. . . . It is a remarkable irony that just
those commentators who populate the Song with concealed deities refuse to
recognise his presence there when he comes to the surface."[96]

Landy has also rightly assessed the importance of *šalhebetyâ* in the wisdom
credo of 8:6–7, and of the entire book. He states it dramatically: " '*Šalhebetyâ* 'the
flame of God' is the apex of the credo, and of the Song."[97] LaCocque concurs: " 'A
flame of Yah[weh].' . . . The whole of the Canticle is encapsulated in this phrase."[98]
And Wendland summarizes the profound implication from this phrase: "YHWH
is the Source not only of love in all its power and passion, but also of the paired,
male-female (= marriage) relationship in which love is most completely and intimately experienced."[99]

If the blaze of love, ardent love, such as between a man and woman, is indeed
the flame of Yahweh, then this human love is explicitly described as originating in
God, a spark off of the Holy Flame. It is therefore, in a word, *holy* love.[100] Such a
conclusion has profound implications for the whole reading of the Song of
Songs—and for the quality and motivation of human sexual love. When the
woman adjures her companions not to awaken Love until it is ready, implicit in
this statement (and already hinted by the play on words with names of God in the
oath formula) is the reality that Love is not ready capriciously or randomly but
according to the will of him from whom this holy love originated. The love between man and woman is not just animal passion, or evolved natural attraction,
but a holy love ignited by Yahweh himself! The love relationship is not only beautiful, wholesome, and good but holy. Lovers, then, will treat each other with godly
self-giving because they are animated by a holy self-giving Love. It is perhaps no
accident that the LXX translators translated the Hebrew word for "love" throughout the Song—*ʾahăbâ*—with the Greek *agapē,* the same word chosen by the NT
writers to describe God's principled, selfless love.

To put it another way, if human love is the very flame of Yahweh, then this
human love at its best—as described in the Song—points beyond itself to the

---

96 Landy, *Paradoxes of Paradise,* 127, 315–16.

97 Ibid., 129.

98 LaCocque, *Romance She Wrote,* 172.

99 Wendland, "Seeking a Path," 44. Ayo, *Sacred Marriage,* 246, states this implication
similarly: "This verse of the Song becomes the unique mention of God and the climactic
declaration that the perduring strength of human love, strong as death itself, derives its
endurance from the boundless persevering love of God."

100 "Whilst the *Song of Songs* is certainly a celebration and endorsement of human
eroticism it is surely also in some sense a sacralization of it" (John Richardson, "Preaching
from the *Song of Songs:* Allegory Revisited," *ERT* 21 [1997]: 256). This is not in the cultic
sense, as with the sacralization of sex in fertility cults, but "holy" as God is holy—unique,
"set apart" *from* the secular and *for* relationship.

Lord of love. The human "spark off the Eternal Flame" reveals the character of that divine flame. Love between man and woman in the Song "focuses for us the love within the very being of God. Christians can discern the eternal dance (*perichōrēsis*) of divine Persons in the reciprocal love of a man and a woman."[101] Even though the Godhead is clearly above the polarity of sex,[102] yet, as already hinted in the first chapter of the Bible (Gen 1:26–27), the love relationship of male and female, made in the image of God, reflects the I-Thou love relationship inherent in the very nature of the triune God. The various characteristics and qualities of holy human love that have emerged from the Song—mutuality, reciprocity, egalitarianism, wholeness, joy of presence, pain of absence, exclusivity (yet inclusiveness), permanence, intimacy, oneness, disinterestedness, wholesomeness, beauty, goodness, and so on—all reflect the divine love within the very nature of God's being. By beholding the love relationship within the Song and within contemporary godly marriages, one may catch a glimpse of the divine holy love. These marriages preach to us of the awesome love of God.

The /ḥesed/ *agapē* love within the intradivine I-Thou relationship flows out from the divine throne—as a *šalhebetyâ*, "flame of Yahweh"—to all humanity and especially to Yahweh's covenant-keeping people.[103] In the final analysis, then, the

---

101 Robin Payne, "The Song of Songs: Song of Woman, Song of Man, Song of God," *ExpTim* 107 (1996): 331.

102 I have emphasized this point throughout this book, but once more caution against a misunderstanding of the argument in this last section of the book. Because human sexual love comes from God, is created by God, one must not conclude that God is somehow a sexual being after all, or that human sexual activity has some kind of ritual function as in the fertility cults of Canaan. Sexuality is the Flame of Yahweh because Yahweh has created sexuality, not because Yahweh is a sexual being. The relational aspects of human sexuality correspond to the I-Thou relationship within the Godhead, but do not imply sexual relationship among the members of the Godhead.

103 A number of scholars in recent years—whether critical, feminist, or evangelical—are sensing the need for this kind of reading, which unites sexuality and spirituality. See, e.g., Alicia Ostriker, "A Holy of Holies: The Song of Songs as Countertext," in *The Song of Songs* (ed. Athalya Brenner and Carole R. Fontaine; FCB² 6; Sheffield, Eng.: Sheffield Academic Press, 2000), 36–54, who explores from a feminist perspective one of the trajectories of this divine-human interaction by suggesting that the Song implies "a mutually delighting love-relationship with God" (37). Ostriker asks if the Song does not teach us about God as Lover: "What of a God as a being who yearns toward us, as we yearn back, unconditionally? The Song stares us in the face—unique among texts, a Holy of Holies!" (50). Larry L. Lyke seeks to demonstrate that "the metaphors used in the Song for human love can be understood as part of a much larger phenomenon in the Hebrew Bible in which the love of God is consistently described in sexual metaphors" ("The Song of Songs, Proverbs, and the Theology of Love," in *Theological Exegesis: Essays in Honor of Brevard S. Childs* [ed. Christopher Seitz and Kathryn Greene-McCreight; Grand Rapids: Eerdmans, 1999], 208; see his full argument in 208–23). Lyke conducts a case study of the imagery of springs and wells in the HB, finding that "the theological and human registers of these metaphors are essentially inseparable" (222). Thus the poetry of the Song of Songs, "while always the poetry of human love, . . . simultaneously can be understood in terms of the ancient idiom that understands humans' relation to God via the same metaphor." And "simultaneity of the theological and human registers" of the language of love

allegorical interpretation of the Song may be right in its *conclusion* that the Song reveals God's love for his people, although wrong in the *way* in which the conclusion is reached. The human love relationship between Solomon and Shulammite is not the worthless "husk" to be stripped away *allegorically* to find the kernel, the "true" meaning, the love between God and his covenant community. Rather the love relationship between man and woman, husband and wife, described in the Song, has independent meaning and value of its own to be affirmed and extolled, while at the same time this human love is given even greater significance as, according to the Song's climax (8:6), it *typologically* points beyond itself to the divine Lover. Far different from the *allegorical* approach, with its fanciful, externally and arbitrarily imposed meaning alien to the plain and literal sense, the Song itself calls for a *typological* approach[104] that remains faithful to, and even enhances, the literal sense of the Song by recognizing what the text itself indicates— that human love typifies the divine. Thereby human sexual love, already so highly esteemed elsewhere in Scripture, is here given its highest acclamation. The Song of Songs thus becomes the most fitting climax and conclusion to our study, the supreme statement on the theology of sexuality (and, dare I add, on the theology of God) in the OT. We have indeed reached the holy of holies, ablaze with the flame of Yahweh.

---

in the Song also provides one "of the primary vehicles for the sanctifying of human sexuality" (223). Robert W. Jenson suggests that "the canonical text of the Song posits an analogy between the relation of human lovers to each other and the relation between God and his people, precisely as both relations are—analogously—erotic" ("Male and Female He Created Them," in *I Am the Lord Your God: Christian Reflections on the Ten Commandments* [ed. Carl E. Braaten and Christopher R. Seitz; Grand Rapids: Eerdmans, 2005], 184). David M. Carr argues for reading the Song both as erotic human love poetry and as an erotic love of God ("Rethinking Sex and Spirituality: The Song of Songs and Its Readings," *Soundings* 81 [1998]: 413–35 (quote at 432); cf. idem, "Gender and the Shaping of Desire in the Song of Songs and Its Interpretations," *JBL* 119 [2000]: 233–48; idem, *Erotic Word,* 109–51). Carr, *Erotic Word,* 136, surveys in the Song various intertextual echoes of motifs from biblical stories about God and Israel, correctly noting that these echoes are not allegorizing, "an encoded description of God's relationship with Israel. . . . Instead, it is more likely that the Song uses motifs from Israel's sacred story to enrich its picture of an erotic relationship between human beings. The woman retraces Israel's steps on her way to her beloved." Although concurring with Carr's basic concern to unite sexuality and spirituality in the interpretation of the Song, I disagree with his thesis that the Song constitutes a subversion of the (abusive) message of the Prophets and consider that Carr has not grasped the key exegetical basis within the Song for linking sexuality with spirituality (i.e., in the phrase "flame of Yahweh" in 8:6).

[104] For the distinction between allegory and typology, see Richard M. Davidson, *Typology in Scripture: A Study of Hermeneutical τύπος Structures* (Andrews University Dissertation Series 2; Berrien Springs, Mich.: Andrews University Press, 1981), 20, 81, 100–101. Since the appearance of my initial article on the theology of sexuality in the Song of Songs (Richard M. Davidson, "Theology of Sexuality in the Song of Songs: Return to Eden," *AUSS* 27 [1989]: 1–19), others have (independently, it seems) pointed out the need for recognizing the typological (not allegorical) approach to the Song, based upon the *šalhebetyâ,* "flame of Yahweh," in 8:6. See esp. Mitchell, *Song of Songs,* passim; Murphy, *Song of Songs,* 104; and Wendland, "Seeking a Path," 51, 53.

Afterword: Some Implications for a New Testament Theology of Sexuality

What follows in the next few pages is not a full-orbed theology of sexuality in the NT or even a comprehensive presentation of implications from my study for such a theology. Rather, it tentatively and partially traces some of the trajectories of sexual theology from OT to NT, gives some preliminary indications of the unity, consistency, and development between the two Testaments on this theological subject, and suggests how OT insights may illuminate crucial NT passages dealing with sexuality. In order to allow the relationship between the Testaments to appear, comments are arranged under the same basic headings as in the OT study. A comprehensive NT theology of sexuality and a biblical theology synthesizing both OT and NT theology remain to be written.

Sexuality as a Creation Order

It has been widely recognized that the creation passages of Gen 1–2 are foundational to the NT as well as the OT in setting forth the basic contours of a theology of sexuality. "In several New Testament passages dealing with aspects of the relationship between men and women, we find an appeal to the Old Testament creation stories of Genesis 1 and 2. These passages are fundamental for New Testament perceptions of human sexuality. . . . The New Testament has resolutely chosen to make the revelation in Genesis 1 and 2 of human sexuality as God's good creation the measure and judge of our conduct, not the other way around."[1]

In the NT Jesus affirms the creation order of sexuality by citing Gen 1:27: "the one who made them at the beginning 'made them male and female'" (Matt 19:4). Paul likewise refers to the creation of man and woman at the beginning (1 Cor 11:8–9; 1 Tim 2:13). The NT, like the OT, contends against distortions of this

---

[1] Ulrich W. Mauser, "Creation and Human Sexuality in the New Testament," in *Biblical Ethics and Homosexuality: Listening to Scripture* (ed. Robert L. Brawley; Louisville: Westminster John Knox, 1996), 3, 13.

fundamental distinction between Creator and creation inasmuch as the mystery religions and other syncretistic cults of the first century C.E. freely borrowed from the ANE theology of the goddess worship. Paul's epistles to Timothy at Ephesus are a prime example of the apostle's polemic against the goddess worship (Artemis or Diana, Acts 19:21–41) of the first century.[2] The study of these epistles must be informed by the cultural milieu of the mother goddess theology, seen in light of its ANE roots, if one is to understand more fully the issues that the apostle is addressing. Failure to take this milieu into account can lead to distortions of Pauline theology.

Heterosexual versus Homosexual Practice

The quotation of Gen 1:27 and 2:23 by Jesus (Mark 10:6–8; cf. the quotation of only Gen 2:23 in Matt 19:5 and by Paul in 1 Cor 6:16; Eph 5:31) makes explicit the point of heterosexual relationship: "But from the beginning of creation, 'God made them *male* and *female*.' 'For this reason a *man* shall leave his father and mother and be joined to his *wife*, and the two [man and woman] shall become one flesh.'" Jesus' emphasis on the fact that "God made" this arrangement "from the beginning of creation" demonstrates his acceptance of the prescriptive nature of the creation texts and his understanding that heterosexual (not homosexual) relations as divinely ordained in Gen 1 and 2 remain normative in NT times.

Jesus' pronouncements against *porneia* (Matt 5:32; 15:19; 19:9; Mark 7:21), when viewed against the OT background, include same-sex intercourse as well as other illicit sexual practices. The nature of πορνεία (without qualifiers) as used by Jesus and the various NT writers has been the subject of considerable debate, but I believe the OT provides the key to its identification. Especially significant is its usage (again without qualifiers) in Acts 15, where intertextual allusions to Lev 17–18 are unmistakable. Acts 15 lists four prohibitions for Gentile Christians given by the Jerusalem Council: "that you abstain from what has been sacrificed to idols and from blood and from what is strangled [i.e., not drained of their blood],[3] and from fornication [*porneia*]" (15:29). Particularly striking is that this

---

[2] See, e.g., Sharon Hodgin Gritz, *Paul, Women Teachers, and the Mother Goddess at Ephesus: A Study of 1 Timothy 2:9–15 in Light of the Religious and Cultural Milieu of the First Century* (Lanham, Md.: University Press of America, 1991); and Richard Clark Kroeger and Catherine Clark Kroeger, *I Suffer Not a Woman: Rethinking 1 Timothy 2:11–15 in Light of Ancient Evidence* (Grand Rapids: Baker, 1992).

[3] The Greek adjective *pniktos*, usually translated "strangled" or "choked," in fact refers precisely to the situation described in Lev 17:13–16. H. Bietenhard, "πνικτός," *NIDNTT* 1:226: "The command [of Acts 15:20, 29] goes back to Lev. 17:13 f. and Deut. 12:16, 23. An animal should be so slaughtered that its blood, in which is its life, should be allowed to pour out. If the animal is killed in any other way, it has been 'strangled.'" The meaning of this term is stated even more clearly in H. Bietenhard, "πνίγω, ἀποπνίγω, συμπνίγω, πνικτός," *TDNT* 6:457: "The regulations in Lv. 17:13 f. and Dt. 12:16, 23 lay down that an animal should be slaughtered in such a way that all the blood drains from the carcase. If it is put to death in any other way, it 'chokes,' since the life seated in the blood remains in the body."

is the same list, in the same order, as the four major legal prohibitions stated to be applicable to the stranger/alien as well as to native Israelites in Lev 17–18. These OT chapters forbid (1) sacrificing to demons/idols (Lev 17:7–9), (2) eating blood (17:10–12), (3) eating anything that has not been immediately drained of its blood (17:13–16), and (4) various illicit sexual practices (Lev 18). In this clear case of intertextuality, the Jerusalem Council undoubtedly concluded that the practices forbidden to the alien in Lev 17–18 were what should be prohibited to Gentile Christians in the church. The parallel of the fourth prohibition in each passage is unambiguous: what Acts 15 labels *porneia* are the illicit sexual activities included in Lev 18. These activities may be summarized in general as illicit sexual intercourse—including incest, adultery, homosexual practices, and bestiality. Various scholars have recognized this intertextual connection.[4] The correlation between Acts 15 and Lev 17–18 seems to provide a solid foundation for determining what the early church understood by the term *porneia*. "No first-century Jew could have spoken of *porneiai* (sexual immoralities) without having in mind the list of forbidden sexual offenses in Leviticus 18 and 20, particularly incest, adultery, same-sex intercourse, and bestiality."[5] Jesus' denunciation of *porneia* includes all forms of homosexual practice.

Jesus also probably had in mind a condemnation of homosexual practice in his references to the sinfulness of Sodom (Matt 10:15; 11:23–24; Mark 6:11; Luke 10:12; 17:29; cf. Jude 7). He may also have alluded to male cult prostitution when he said, "Do not give what is holy to dogs" (Matt 7:6), echoing the reference to the *qādēš*, lit. "holy one," the male cult prostitute who is called a "dog" in Deut 23:18–19 (ET 23:17–18).[6] Although this allusion is not certain in the Gospels, it

---

[4] For further support for this position on the parallel of Acts 15 and Lev 17–18 and the meaning of πορνεία, see esp. H. Reisser, "πορνεύω," *NIDNTT* 1:497–501; F. Hauck and S. Schulz, "πόρνη, πόρνος, πορνεία, πορνεύω, ἐκπορνεύω," *TDNT* 6:579–95; James B. Hurley, *Man and Woman in Biblical Perspective* (Grand Rapids: Zondervan, 1981), 95–106, 129–37; and Timothy L. Wilt, "Acts 15:19–21: Some Further Discussion," *BT* 42 (1991): 234–36. This is contra those who equate the πορνεία of Acts 15 (as well as Matt 5:32 and 19:9) only with the incestuous relationships of Lev 18:6–18. The incest interpretation for these passages fails to recognize that the entire chapter of Lev 18 is a unit describing the various illicit sexual activities carried out by the Canaanites (see the *inclusio* in 18:3 and 30). Defenders of the latter view include, e.g., Samuele Bacchiocchi, *The Marriage Covenant: A Biblical Study on Marriage, Divorce, and Remarriage* (Berrien Springs, Mich.: Biblical Perspectives, 1991), 182–89; Joseph A. Fitzmyer, "The Matthean Divorce Texts and Some New Palestinian Evidence," *TS* 37 (1976): 197–226; Roger L. Omanson, "How Does It All Fit Together? Thoughts on Translating Acts 1.15–22 and 15.19–21," *BT* 41 (1990): 419–21; idem, "On Appealing to Context: A Reply," *BT* 42 (1991): 236–41; and Ben Witherington III, "Matthew 5:32 and 19:9—Exception or Exceptional Situation?" *NTS* 31 (1985): 571–76. For cogent critique of the incest interpretation (esp. in the Matthean passages), see, e.g., Craig L. Blomberg, "Marriage, Divorce, Remarriage, and Celibacy: An Exegesis of Matthew 19:3–12," *TJ* 11 (1990): 176–78.

[5] Robert A. J. Gagnon, "The Bible and Homosexual Practice: Key Issues," in Dan O. Via and Robert A. J. Gagnon, *Homosexuality and the Bible: Two Views* (Minneapolis: Fortress, 2003), 72.

[6] Ibid., 73: "Jesus' saying [Matt 7:6] would be a logical extension of the command in Deut 23:17–18 not to allow 'dogs' to give money received from abominable practices to

seems probable in the reference to "dogs" being outside the holy city in Rev 22:15: "Outside are the dogs and sorcerers and fornicators and murderers and idolaters, and everyone who loves and practices falsehood."[7]

The apostle Paul specifically denounces homosexual lust and practice in several passages: Rom 1:24–27, 1 Cor 6:9–11, and 1 Tim 1:10. All of these passages must ultimately be interpreted according to the OT context in which they are explicitly placed. Paul's whole discussion in Rom 1 is informed by the OT quotation of Hab 2:4, and the OT Scriptures are the source of authority for normative social behavior. "Paul and his audience share knowledge of God's judgement on homosexual activity on the basis of the Old Testament."[8]

It has been argued that Rom 1:24–27 speaks only of "exploitive forms of homoerotic behavior—pederasty (love of boys), sex with slaves, prostitution, and/or homoeroticism in the context of idolatrous cults—so we cannot know what Paul would have thought about committed adult relationships."[9] Others have argued that "Paul had no concept of a homosexual 'orientation'—a relatively fixed and congenitally based disposition—so we cannot know what Paul would have thought about same-sex intercourse between two people exclusively oriented toward the same sex."[10] Still others have set forth a misogyny argument, claiming that "Paul was opposed to same-sex intercourse because he feared that homoerotic unions would upset the hierarchical dominance of men over women."[11]

---

the holy place: if the temple is too holy to receive the fees from homosexual cult prostitutes, then the message of the kingdom, which was holier still, should not be entrusted to those who mock holiness through their continuance in abominable practice."

[7] See David E. Aune, *Revelation 17–22* (WBC 52C; Nashville: Nelson, 1998), 1222–23. For further, careful discussion of the witness of Jesus regarding homosexual practice, see esp. Robert A. J. Gagnon, *The Bible and Homosexual Practice: Texts and Hermeneutics* (Nashville: Abingdon, 2001), 185–228.

[8] Christopher Seitz, "Sexuality and Scripture's Plain Sense: The Christian Community and the Law of God," in *Homosexuality, Science, and the "Plain Sense" of Scripture* (ed. David L. Balch; Grand Rapids: Eerdmans, 2000), 195.

[9] Gagnon, "Bible and Homosexual Practice," 74 (summarizing, but not defending, this positon). Proponents of this view include, e.g., Robin Scroggs, *The New Testament and Homosexuality: Contextual Background for Contemporary Debate* (Philadelphia: Fortress, 1983), passim; and Dale B. Martin, "*Arsenokoitēs* and *malakos*: Meanings and Consequences," in *Biblical Ethics and Homosexuality: Listening to Scripture* [ed. Robert Brawley; Louisville: Westminster John Knox], 117–36). For further discussion, see Gagnon, *Bible and Homosexual Practice,* 347–61.

[10] This is the position of, e.g., Martti Nissinen, *Homoeroticism in the Biblical World: A Historical Perspective* [trans. Kirsi Stjerna; Minneapolis: Fortress, 1998], 103–13; and Walter Wink, "Homosexuality and the Bible," in *Homosexuality and Christian Faith: Questions of Conscience for the Churches* (ed. Walter Wink; Minneapolis: Fortress, 1999], 35–37, as summarized by Gagnon, "Bible and Homosexual Practice," 74. For extended critique, see idem, *Bible and Homosexual Practice,* 380–95.

[11] This is the view of, e.g., Bernadette J. Brooten, *Love between Women: Early Christian Responses to Female Homoeroticism* (Chicago Series on Sexuality, History, and Society; Chicago: University of Chicago Press, 1996), passim; and David E. Fredrickson, "Natural and Unnatural Use in Romans 1:24–27: Paul and the Philosophic Critique of Eros," in *Homosexuality, Science, and the "Plain Sense" of Scripture* (ed. David Balch; Grand Rapids: Eerd-

Against all of these positions, however, it has been demonstrated that Rom 1:24–27 contains strong intertextual echoes with the Genesis creation accounts, in particular with Gen 1:26–30.[12] If one recognizes the intertextual linkage between Rom 1:24–27 and its subtext of Gen 1:26–30, then the recent attempts to discount this passage as not condemning same-sex intercourse are beside the point and fall to the ground.

> With respect to the exploitation and orientation arguments: No homoerotic union could have met with Paul's approval because Paul was looking at Genesis 1 more than at the exploitative models in his culture or at a presumption of bisexuality. The main concern for Paul was what same-sex intercourse was *not*—the complementary male-female union ordained by God at creation and revealed in Scripture. A homoerotic union 'done well' or with congenital post-fall impulses at work does not satisfy that concern. As regards the misogyny argument, Gen 1:26–31 stresses gender differentiation—essential maleness and femaleness—not gender stratification.[13]

In Rom 1:26–27 Paul condemns female as well as male same-sex relations, although lesbianism is not explicitly mentioned in Lev 18. As noted in the discussion of Lev 18 in chapter 4, above, the pentateuchal legislation forbids by implication all same-sex intercourse as a distortion of the creation order; Paul makes explicit what is implicit in Lev 18.[14]

In the vice list of 1 Cor 6:9, Paul mentions the *malakoi* (lit. "soft men"), which probably refers to the passive partner described in Lev 18:22 and 20:13 who is lain with as though a woman.[15] First Corinthians 6:9 also refers to the *arsenokoitai*, "practicing homosexuals" (NAB), and this term appears again in Paul's vice list of 1 Tim 1:10. Against those who see a Greco-Roman background

---

mans, 2000), 197–241, as summarized by Gagnon, "Bible and Homosexual Practice," 75. For extended critique, see idem, *Bible and Homosexual Practice*, 361–80.

[12] See Gagnon, *Bible and Homosexual Practice*, 236, 289–93; idem, "Bible and Homosexual Practice," 77–78; and Mauser, "Creation and Human Sexuality," 10–14. There is also evidence that Rom 1:18–32 is intertextually alluding to the OT Sodom tradition. See esp. Philip F. Esler, "The Sodom Tradition in Romans 1:18–32," *BTB* 34 (2004): 4–16.

[13] Gagnon, "Bible and Homosexual Practice," 78. Cf. Mauser, "Creation and Human Sexuality," 13: "Homosexual practice cannot honor the creation of human life in the essential differentiation of male and female. Homosexual conduct is the practical, and today also the theoretical, denial that the human being is good as God's creature in the polarity of being male or female. In one form or the other, homosexual conduct fears or denies, despises or ridicules, the goodness of God's creation of male and female."

[14] For more detailed discussion of Rom 1:24–27, see esp. Gagnon, *Bible and Homosexual Practice*, 229–303; cf. James B. DeYoung, *Homosexuality: Contemporary Claims Examined in Light of the Bible and Other Ancient Literature and Law* (Grand Rapids: Kregel, 2000), 139–73; Richard B. Hays, *The Moral Vision of the New Testament: A Contemporary Introduction to New Testament Ethics* (San Francisco: Harper, 1996), 383–89; and Ronald M. Springett, *Homosexuality in History and the Scriptures: Some Historical and Biblical Perspectives on Homosexuality* (Washington, D.C.: Biblical Research Institute, 1988), 120–31.

[15] For support of this interpretation and critique of alternative views, see esp. Gagnon, *Bible and Homosexual Practice*, 306–12.

behind Paul's condemnation (and thus limit this term to something less than all same-sex intercourse), it cannot be overemphasized that this term never appears in the secular Greek of Paul's day, but only in Jewish-Christian literature. It is virtually certain that this compound term was coined by the LXX translators in their rendering of Lev 18:22 and 20:13, as they combined the words "male" (*arsēn*) and "lying" (*koitē*), corresponding to the Hebrew terms *zākār* ("male") and *miškāb* ("lying"), to denote "homosexual intercourse." The undeniable intertextual link between Paul's use of *arsenokoitai* (1 Cor 6:9 and 1 Tim 1:10) and Lev 18 and 20 indicates that Paul primarily had in mind the OT Levitical background, which forbids all same-sex intercourse (see ch. 4, above), not just issues of exploitation or orientation.[16]

Monogamy versus Polygamy

The LXX translation of Gen 2:23, followed by both Jesus (Matt 19:5) and Paul (1 Cor 6:16; Eph 5:31), not only emphasizes human heterosexual relationship but makes explicit the point of monogamy: "the *two* [man and woman] shall become one flesh."[17]

Paul clearly upholds monogamy in other passages (1 Cor 7:1–4; 1 Tim 3:2, 12; Titus 1:6) in harmony with the OT legislation. The grammar of 1 Cor 7:2 ("each man should have his own wife and each woman her own husband") implies a monogamous marriage;[18] the "Pauline privilege" of 1 Cor 7 (esp. 7:17, 20, 24) does not provide an exception to this monogamous norm and does not indicate that practicing polygamists should be allowed to remain in the church;[19] and the standard of "husband of one wife" (RSV, lit. "a one-wife husband") in Titus and Timothy implies monogamous fidelity not only for the elders and deacons but for all Christians.[20]

---

[16] For further discussion of 1 Cor 6:9 and 1 Tim 1:10 and the key Greek terms *malakoi* and *arsenokoitai,* see esp. ibid., 303–13. Gagnon rightly concludes, "A first-century Jew or Christian would regard the prohibitions in Lev 18:22 and 20:13 as absolute and affecting any male-to-male sexual intercourse, even if the primary examples of his/ her culture were confined to pederastic models" (p. 330). Cf. DeYoung, *Homosexuality,* 175–203; and Hays, *Moral Vision,* 382–83.

[17] See Ronald A. G. du Preez, *Polygamy in the Bible* (Adventist Theological Society Dissertation Series 3; Berrien Springs, Mich.: ATS, 1993), 246–50.

[18] See, e.g., F. W. Grosheide, *The First Epistle to the Corinthians* (NICNT; Grand Rapids: Eerdmans, 1953), 155: "*Each man . . . his own* implies a monogamous marriage. . . . *Let have* implies that monogamous marriage is a commandment. The same thing is then repeated with reference to *every woman.*"

[19] See, e.g., Grosheide, ibid., 167–72, who argues that these verses do not refer to external circumstances but rather to "internal circumstances involved in a Christian's vocation."

[20] See, e.g., Ralph Earle, "1 Timothy," *EBC* 11:364: "Most commentators agree that it [this phrase in Titus and Timothy] means monogamy—only one wife at one time—and that the overseer must be completely faithful to his wife." Cf. Ed Glasscock, "The Husband

Elevation versus Denigration of Women

Against the background of an ambivalent and often negative attitude toward women in first-century C.E. Judaism and other Mediterranean cultures,[21] the NT elevates women's status in radical ways.[22] This is seen in the revolutionary treatment of women by Jesus as recorded in the Gospels,[23] and in the high valuation of

---

of One Wife Requirement in 1 Timothy 3:2," *BSac* 140 (1983): 244–58. For further discussion of all these passages (1 Cor 7:1–4; 1 Tim 3:2, 12; Titus 1:6), see esp. du Preez, *Polygamy in the Bible,* 256–68.

[21] On this issue, see esp. the syntheses by John Temple Bristow, *What Paul Really Said about Women* (San Francisco: Harper & Row, 1988), 1–30; Randall D. Chesnutt, "Jewish Women in the Greco-Roman Era," in *Essays on Women in Earliest Christianity* (ed. Carroll D. Osburn; 2 vols.; Joplin: Mo.: College Press, 1993), 1:93–130; Hurley, *Man and Woman,* 58–78; and Ben Witherington III, *Women in the Earliest Churches* (SNTSMS 59; New York: Cambridge University Press, 1988), 5–23. Cf. Tal Ilan, *Integrating Women into Second Temple History* (Tübingen: Mohr Siebeck, 1999; repr., Peabody, Mass.: Hendrickson, 2001); idem, *Jewish Women in Greco-Roman Palestine* (Peabody, Mass.: Hendrickson, 1995); Amy-Jill Levine, ed., *"Women Like This": New Perspectives on Jewish Women in the Greco-Roman World* (Williston, Vt.: Society of Biblical Literature, 1991); Deborah F. Sawyer, *Women and Religion in the First Christian Centuries* (New York: Routledge, 1996); Gregory E. Sterling, "Women in the Hellenistic and Roman Worlds (323 B.C.E.–138 C.E.)," in *Essays on Women in Earliest Christianity* (ed. Carroll D. Osburn; 2 vols.; Joplin, Mo.: College Press, 1993), 1:41–92; and Chesnutt, "Jewish Women."

[22] For a general survey, see esp. Witherington, *Women in the Earliest Churches,* 128–82; cf. the summaries in Clarence Boomsma, *Male and Female, One in Christ: New Testament Teaching on Women in Office* (Grand Rapids: Baker, 1993), 21–26; Jo Ann Davidson, "Women in Scripture: A Survey and Evaluation," in *Women in Ministry: Biblical and Historical Perspectives* (ed. Nancy Vyhmeister; Berrien Springs, Mich.: Andrews University Press, 1998), 172–86; Mary Ann Getty-Sullivan, *Women in the New Testament* (Collegeville, Minn.: Liturgical Press, 2001); Margaret Y. MacDonald, "Was Celsus Right? The Role of Women in the Expansion of Early Christianity," in *Early Christian Families in Context: An Interdisciplinary Dialogue* (ed. David L. Balch and Carolyn Osiek; Grand Rapids: Eerdmans, 2003), 157–84; and Mary T. Malone, *The First Thousand Years* (vol. 1 of *Women & Christianity;* Maryknoll, N.Y.: Orbis Books, 2000), 43–85. For treatment of individual women in the NT (with bibliography), see esp. Carol Meyers, Toni Craven, and Ross S. Kraemer, eds., *Women in Scripture: A Dictionary of Named and Unnamed Women in the Hebrew Bible, the Apocryphal/Deuterocanonical Books, and the New Testament* (Boston: Houghton Mifflin, 2000), passim. Though stressing the evidence for the elevation of women's status in the NT, I do not wish to imply that such a trend toward the elevation of women was solely a Christian phenomenon. As pointed out at the end of ch. 6, above, movements toward the elevation of women's status also may be found in Judaism at the same time as the rise of Christianity. See the cautionary note against "Christian anti-Judaism" in portraying Jesus as "first-century feminist" as opposed to first-century C.E. Judaism, sounded, e.g., by Glenna Jackson, "Jesus as First-Century Feminist: Christian Anti-Judaism?" *FemT* 19 (1998): 85–98.

[23] For studies on Jesus' treatment of women and on women as presented in the Gospels and Acts, see esp. Ben Witherington III, *Women and the Genesis of Christianity* (ed. Ann Witherington; Cambridge: Cambridge University Press, 1990), 29–120, 201–36; and idem, *Women in the Ministry of Jesus: A Study of Jesus' Attitudes to Women and Their Roles as Reflected in His Earthly Life* (SNTSMS 51; Cambridge: Cambridge University Press,

women in the earliest churches as depicted in the book of Acts and the NT
Epistles[24] and in extrabiblical materials.[25]

On the question of the NT role of women in the home and church, two major
camps have become entrenched within evangelical scholarship, the egalitarian
and hierarchical complementarian positions, represented respectively by two
parachurch organizations founded in 1987, the Christians for Biblical Equality

---

1984). Cf. Judy L. Brown, *Women Ministers according to Scripture* (Minneapolis: Christians for Biblical Equality, 1996), 119–50; Colleen M. Conway, *Men and Women in the
Fourth Gospel: Gender and Johannine Characterization* (SBLDS 167; Atlanta: Society of
Biblical Literature, 1999); Kathleen E. Corley, *Private Women, Public Meals: Social Conflict
in the Synoptic Tradition* (Peabody, Mass.: Hendrickson, 1993); Davidson, "The Well
Women of Scripture Revisited," 220–28; Janeth Norfleete Day, *The Woman at the Well: In-
terpretation of John 4:1–42 in Retrospect and Prospect* (Boston: E. J. Brill, 2002); David J.
Hamilton, "Jesus Broke Down the Walls," in Loren Cunningham and David J. Hamilton
with Janice Rogers, *Why Not Women? A Fresh Look at Women in Missions, Ministry, and
Leadership* (Seattle: YWAM, 2001), 111–28; Andreas J. Köstenberger, *Studies on John and
Gender: A Decade of Scholarship* (StBL 38; New York: Peter Lang, 2001); William E. Phipps,
Assertive Biblical Women (CWS 128; Westport, Conn.: Greenwood, 1992), 105–18; Walter
F. Specht, "Jesus and Women," in *Symposium on the Role of Women in the Church* (ed. Julia
Neuffer; Washington, D.C.: General Conference of Seventh-day Adventists, 1984), 78–96;
Aída Besançon Spencer, "Jesus' Treatment of Women in the Gospels," in *Discovering Bibli-
cal Equality: Complementarity without Hierarchy* (ed. Ronald W. Pierce and Rebecca
Merrill Groothuis; Downers Grove, Ill.: InterVarsity, 2004), 126–41; Bonnie Thurston,
Women in the New Testament: Questions and Commentary (New York: Crossroad, 1998),
62–128; Ruth A. Tucker and Walter Liefeld, *Daughters of the Church: Women and Ministry
from New Testament Times to the Present* (Grand Rapids: Zondervan, 1987), 19–51; and
Satoko Yamaguchi, *Mary and Martha: Women in the World of Jesus* (Maryknoll, N.Y.:
Orbis Books, 2002). For feminist perspectives, see, e.g., Amy-Jill Levine with Marianne
Blickenstaff, eds., *A Feminist Companion to Luke* (FCNTECW 3; London: Sheffield Aca-
demic Press, 2002); idem, *A Feminist Companion to John* (2 vols.; FCNTECW 4; New York:
Sheffield Academic Press, 2003); idem, *A Feminist Companion to Matthew* (FCNTECW 1;
Sheffield, Eng.: Sheffield Academic Press, 2001); Ivoni Richter Reimer, *Women in the Acts
of the Apostles: A Feminist Liberation Perspective* (trans. Linda M. Maloney; Minneapolis:
Fortress, 1995; and Turid Karlsen Seim, *The Double Message: Patterns of Gender in Luke
and Acts* (Nashville: Abingdon, 1994).

[24] See, e.g., James Malcolm Arlandson, *Women, Class, and Society in Early Christian-
ity: Models from Luke–Acts* (Peabody, Mass.: Hendrickson, 1997); Bristow, *What Paul Re-
ally Said about Women,* passim; Brown, *Women Ministers,* 151–85; David J. Hamilton,
"Paul Turned His World Upside Down," in Cunningham and Hamilton with Rogers,
Why Not Women? 139–40; Andrew C. Perriman, *Speaking of Women: Interpreting Paul*
(Leicester, Eng.: Apollos/Inter-Varsity, 1998); Phipps, *Assertive Biblical Women,* 119–31;
Thurston, *Women in the New Testament,* 30–61, 129–55; Tucker and Liefeld, *Daughters of
the Church,* 53–87. For feminist perspectives, see Seim, *Double Message,* passim; Amy-Jill
Levine with Marianne Blickenstaff, eds., *A Feminist Companion to Paul* (FCNTECW 6;
London: T&T Clark, 2004); and idem, *A Feminist Companion to Paul: Deutero-Pauline
Writings* (JSNTSup 7; New York: Continuum, 2003).

[25] See, e.g., Ute E. Eisen, *Women Officeholders in Early Christianity: Epigraphical and
Literary Studies* (Collegeville, Minn.: Liturgical Press, 2000); and Karen Jo Torjesen, *When
Women Were Priests: Women's Leadership in the Early Church and the Scandal of Their Sub-
ordination in the Rise of Christianity* (San Francisco: Harper, 1993).

(CBE) and the Council on Biblical Manhood and Womanhood (CBMW).[26] Chapter 2, above, summarizes the main contours of these two positions.

My own published NT research in this area has focused upon the issue of headship/submission/equality in NT passages dealing with male/female relationships.[27] This is a summary of my findings concerning the use of terminology for headship and submission in NT passages. There has been much discussion regarding the meaning of "head" (*kephalē*) in its seven occurrences in a metaphorical sense in the NT,[28] with the debate polarizing into two camps. Some have vigorously argued that *kephalē* in first-century Greek (including the NT) often means "source" (as in the "head" of a river) and rarely or never "head" (as in superior rank);[29] others have just as vigorously argued for the common meaning of "head" (as in superior rank) and its rarely or never meaning "source."[30] Although the most responsible treatment of the evidence seems to favor the latter argument, the best conclusion seems to be to recognize that both meanings appear in first-century secular Greek and are possible in NT usage and thus the immediate context must be the final determiner of meaning.[31] Two occurrences of *kephalē* occur in a context of man-woman relationships: 1 Cor 11:3 and Eph 5:23.

---

[26] For a comprehensive bibliography of books and articles written by both camps (and others on the subject that do not fit into either camp), see esp. Wayne A. Grudem, *Evangelical Feminism and Biblical Truth: An Analysis of More Than One Hundred Disputed Questions* (Sisters, Ore.: Multnomah, 2004), 767–81. Grudem has helpfully designated books that clearly support one of the two main evangelical positions as either "egalitarian" or "complementarian" (hierarchical).

[27] See Richard M. Davidson, "Headship, Submission, and Equality in Scripture," in *Women in Ministry: Biblical and Historical Perspectives* (ed. Nancy Vyhmeister; Berrien Springs, Mich.: Andrews University Press, 1998), 273–95.

[28] 1 Cor 11:3; Eph 1:22; 4:15; 5:23; Col 1:18; 2:10, 14.

[29] See esp. Berkeley Mickelsen and Alvera Mickelsen, "What does *kephalē* Mean in the New Testament?" in *Women, Authority and the Bible* (ed. Alvera Mickelsen; Downers Grove, Ill.: InterVarsity, 1986), 97–110; Gilbert G. Bilezikian, *Beyond Sex Roles: What the Bible Says about a Woman's Place in Church and Family* (Grand Rapids: Baker, 1985), 215–52; Catherine Clark Kroeger, "The Classical Concept of Head as 'Source,'" in *Equal to Serve: Women and Men in the Church and Home* (ed. Gretchen G. Hull; Old Tappan, N.J.: Fleming H. Revell, 1987), 267–83; and Gordon D. Fee, *The First Epistle to the Corinthians* (Grand Rapids: Eerdmans, 1987), 502–3. The impetus for this position seems to come from the study by Stephen F. B. Bedale, "The Meaning of κεφαλή in the Pauline Epistles," *JTS* 5 (1954): 211–15.

[30] See Wayne A. Grudem, "Does ΚΕΦΑΛΗ ('Head') Mean 'Source' or 'Authority over' in Greek Literature? A Survey of 2,336 Examples," *TJ* 6 (1985): 38–59; and idem, "The Meaning of Κεφαλή ('Head'): A Response to Recent Studies," *TJ* 11 (1990): 3–72; repr. in *Recovering Biblical Manhood and Womanhood: A Response to Evangelical Feminism* (ed. John Piper and Wayne A. Grudem; Wheaton, Ill.: Crossway, 1991), 425–68; Joseph A. Fitzmyer, "Another Look at ΚΕΦΑΛΗ in 1 Corinthians 11:3," *NTS* 35 (1989): 503–11. Cf. BDAG 431, where *kephalē* is regarded, "in the case of living beings, to denote superior rank."

[31] See David M. Scholer, "The Evangelical Debate over Biblical 'Headship,'" in *Women, Abuse, and the Bible: How Scripture Can Be Used to Hurt or to Heal* (ed. Catherine Clark Kroeger and James R. Beck; Grand Rapids: Baker, 1996), 28–57; and Kenneth V. Neller, "'Submission' in Eph 5:21–33," in *Essays on Women in Earliest Christianity* (ed. Carroll D. Osburn; 2 vols.; Joplin, Mo.: College Press, 1993), 1:251–60.

The NT term for "submit" in husband-wife relationships is *hypotassō*, a verb that appears in some form about thirty-nine times in the NT (twenty-three times in Pauline epistles and six times in 1 Peter). The root verb (*tassō*) means "order, position, determine" and with the prepositional prefix *hypo*-means in the active voice "place under, subordinate, subject, submit," in the passive voice "become subject [to someone or something]," and in the middle voice "[voluntarily] submit oneself, defer to, acquiesce, surrender one's rights or will."[32] Seven occurrences of *hypotassō*—all in the middle voice—occur in the context of man-woman relationships: 1 Cor 14:34; Eph 5:21, 24; Col 3:18; Tit 2:5; 1 Pet 3:1, 5.

Ephesians 5:21–33, the foundational NT passage dealing with husband-wife relations, is the only NT passage on this issue that contains both *kephalē*, "head," and *hypotassō*, "submit." There is no question that in this passage it is the husband-wife relationship that is in view, not men-women relationships in general. Ephesians 5 is part of a series of "household codes" (*Haustafeln*) providing counsel for proper relationships between various members of domestic households: husbands and wives (5:22–33), children and parents (6:1–4), and servants and masters (6:5–9).[33] Unmistakably in Eph 5 the counsel concerns the husband as the head of his own wife, not male headship over women in general.[34]

Although attempts have been made to translate *kephalē* in this passage in the sense of "source" (or a related concept), as noted above, the pairing of *kephalē* with *hypotassō* clearly seems to indicate a ranking of authority or status, not the idea of origin or source. This parallels the similar usage of *kephalē* as "authority" or "superior rank" with reference to Christ in Eph 1:22 and Col 2:10.

It is beyond the scope of this afterword to explore in detail the nature of the headship/submission with reference to husbands and wives as set forth in Eph 5. But the following points emerge from this passage:

(1) The context of the Pauline counsel for husbands and wives (Eph 5:22–33) is one of "mutual submission" described in v. 21: "Be subject to one another out of reverence for Christ."[35]

(2) The word *hypotassō* in the middle voice in v. 22 ("Wives, be subject [lit. 'submit yourselves']") indicates that the wife's submission is a "voluntary

---

[32] See BDAG 855. Cf. James W. Thompson, "The Submission of Wives in 1 Peter," in *Essays on Women in Earliest Christianity* (ed. Carroll D. Osburn; 2 vols.; Joplin, Mo.: College Press, 1993), 1:382–85; Neller, "'Submission,'" 247–51.

[33] For a succinct discussion of the NT *Haustafeln* in recent literature and in Eph 5, see Witherington, *Women in the Earliest Churches*, 42–61. Other NT household codes include Col 3:18–4:1; 1 Tim 2:8–15; 6:1–2; Titus 2:1–10; 1 Pet 2:18–3:7.

[34] For discussion of Eph 5, see esp. Craig S. Keener, *Paul, Women, and Wives: Marriage and Women's Ministry in the Letters of Paul* (Peabody, Mass.: Hendrickson, 1992), 139–224.

[35] Scholars debate whether the phrase "Be subject to one another" means that all parties in the discussions that follow (wives-husbands, children-parents, and slaves-masters) should have an attitude of submission to one another or whether this means that in each of the relationships discussed, the one in inferior rank should submit to the one in superior rank. Regardless of what position is taken on this point, the context of Eph 5 indicates that the husband's role is one of a submissive servant leader (as noted below).

yielding in love,"[36] not forced by the husband. There is no permission given for the husband to demand that his wife submit to his "headship."

(3) The wife's submission is not a blind yielding of her individuality. She is to submit only "as you [submit] to the Lord" (v. 22).

(4) The nature of the husband's "headship" is paralleled to that of Christ, who "loved the church and gave himself up for it" (v. 25). The husband's headship is thus a loving servant leadership. It means "head servant, or taking the lead in serving,"[37] not an authoritarian rule. It consists of the husband's loving his wife as his own body, nourishing and cherishing her, as Christ does the church (vv. 28–29).

(5) The emphasis in the headship/submission relationship seems underscored in the summary of v. 33: love (of the husband for his wife) and respect (of the wife for her husband).

(6) Although mutual submission is implied between husband and wife, this does not necessitate total role interchangeableness in the marriage relation. The term "head" is used only of the husband. "There is a mutuality of submission, but this works itself out in different ways involving an ordering of relationships, and exhortations according to gender."[38]

(7) The ultimate ideal for husband-wife relations is still the partnership of equals that is set forth from the beginning in Gen 2:24: "they become one flesh" (quoted in Eph 5:31). By citing Gen 2:24 in the larger context of a call for mutual submission (Eph 5:21), Paul implicitly issues a divine redemptive invitation offering enabling power to return as much as possible to the pre-fall total egalitarianism in the marriage relationship, without denying the validity of the servant leadership principle as it may be needed in a sinful world to preserve unity and harmony in the home.

Aside from Eph 5:23, the only other NT passage utilizing *kephalē* in the context of man-woman relationships is 1 Cor 11:3. First Corinthians 11:3–16 is thematically parallel to Eph 5:22–33. First Corinthians 11 is about wives submitting to the headship of their own husbands, not about the headship of men over women in general. Even though the same Greek word, *gynē*, can mean either "woman" or "wife," and the same Greek word, *anēr*, can likewise mean either "man" or "husband," Larry Richards, among many others, indicates how the context of 1 Cor 11 makes the choice clearly in favor of the translation "wife" and "husband."[39] Recognizing this context, the RSV and the NRSV correctly translate v. 3, "the head of a woman is her husband." The wearing of the head covering described in 1 Cor 11 was a sign of the wife's submission to her husband's leadership, not to

---

[36] BDAG 855.

[37] Witherington, *Women in the Earliest Churches*, 220.

[38] Ibid., 56.

[39] W. Larry Richards, "How Does a Woman Prophesy and Keep Silence at the Same Time? (1 Corinthians 11 and 14)," in *Women in Ministry: Biblical and Historical Perspectives* (ed. Nancy Vyhmeister; Berrien Springs, Mich.: Andrews University Press, 1998), 313–33. Cf. Keener, *Paul, Women, and Wives*, 32–36; W. Harold Mare, "1 Corinthians," *EBC* 10:255.

the leadership of all men. Although this passage affirms the appropriateness of the headship principle in the marital relation as in Ephesians, it also affirms the mutuality of the marriage partners, implying an ideal situation in which there is no hierarchy: "Nevertheless, in the Lord woman is not independent of man or man independent of woman. For just as woman came from man, so man comes through woman; but all things come from God" (vv. 11–12).

The other NT passages utilizing the term *hypotassō* ("to submit") in a context of man-woman relationships—1 Cor 14:34; Col 3:18; Titus 2:5; 1 Pet 3:1, 5— likewise deal with a husband-wife relationship, not the relationship of men and women in general.

> I Cor. 14:34–35 represents the application, in a particular cultural context, of an order of the present creation concerning the conduct of a wife *vis-a-vis* her husband. It reflects a situation in which the husband is participating in the prophetic ministries of a Christian meeting. In this context the coparticipation of his wife, which may involve her publicly "testing" (*diakrinein,* 14:29) her husband's message, is considered to be a disgraceful (*aischron*) disregard of him, of accepted priorities, and of her own wifely role. For these reasons it is prohibited.[40]

William Orr and James Walther concur: "Paul is probably thinking of marital subordination rather than some kind of subordination of all females to all males. . . . The intent of the command, then, is to interdict situations in which wives publicly contradict what their husbands say or think or embarrass them by an interchange of conversation. They may thus be rejecting the authority of their husbands."[41]

The last three NT passages with occurrences of *hypotassō* (Col 3:18; Titus 2:5; 1 Pet 3:1, 5) are all part of *Haustafeln* as in Eph 5, and all undisputedly refer to the submission of wives to their husbands, not of women to men in general.[42]

---

[40] E. Earle Ellis, "The Silenced Wives of Corinth (1 Cor. 14:34–35)," in *New Testament Textual Criticism: Its Significance for Exegesis* (ed. Eldon J. Epp and Gordon D. Fee; New York: Oxford University Press, 1981), 218. For a careful, detailed analysis of this passage and a similar conclusion to that of Ellis, see Carroll D. Osburn, "The Interpretation of 1 Cor. 14:34–35," in *Essays on Women in Earliest Christianity* (ed. Carroll D. Osburn; 2 vols.; Joplin, Mo.: College Press, 1993), 1:219–42. Others who espouse the position that this verse involves a husband-wife (and not a general man-woman) issue include, e.g., Brown, *Women Ministers,* 270–73; Mary J. Evans, *Woman in the Bible: An Overview of All the Crucial Passages on Women's Roles* (Downers Grove, Ill.: InverVarsity, 1984), 100; J. Massyngberde Ford, "Biblical Material Relevant to the Ordination of Women," *JES* 10 (1973): 681; R. T. France, *Women in the Church's Ministry: A Test-Case for Biblical Interpretation* (Grand Rapids: Eerdmans, 1995), 47, 55; Gritz, *Paul, Women Teachers,* 88–90; and William F. Orr and James A. Walther, *1 Corinthians: A New Translation* (AB 32; Garden City, N.Y.: Doubleday, 1976), 312–13.

[41] Orr and Walther, *1 Corinthians,* 312–13. Cf. Daniel C. Arichea Jr., "The Silence of Woman in the Church: Theology and Translation in 1 Corinthians 14.33b–36," *BT* 46 (1995): 104–5.

[42] See the analysis of these passages in Davidson, "Headship, Submission, and Equality," 276–78. For 1 Pet 3, see esp., David L. Balch, *Let Wives Be Submissive: The Domestic Code in 1 Peter* (Chico, Calif.: Scholars Press, 1981).

This interpretation also holds for the most disputed passage in the women's ordination debate: 1 Tim 2:9–14. Already with Martin Luther, 2:11–12 was understood as referring to the husband-wife relationship, not to men and women in general.[43] A number of other commentators in the intervening centuries have contended for the marital reference in this passage.[44] In the same trajectory of understanding, the once popular Williams version of the NT, for example, renders vv. 11–12 in this way: "A married woman must learn in quiet and perfect submission. I do not permit a married woman to practice teaching or domineering over a husband. She must keep quiet."[45]

More recently a number of scholars have argued cogently and convincingly that *gynē* and *anēr* in these verses should be translated "wife" and "husband" respectively, not simply "woman" and "man."[46] Several lines of evidence strongly support this conclusion.

First, as Hugenberger demonstrates, everywhere else in the Pauline writings, and indeed throughout the whole NT, where *gynē*, and *anēr* are found paired in close proximity, the reference is consistently to wife and husband, not women and men in general.[47] Second, the movement from the plural in vv. 8–10 to the

---

[43] Martin Luther, *Commentaries on 1 Corinthians 7, 1 Cor 15, Lectures on 1 Timothy* (ed. H. C. Oswald; vol. 28 of *Works;* ed. Jaroslav Pelikan; St. Louis: Concordia, 1973), 276.

[44] These include, e.g., Gulielmus Estius, Abraham Calovius, Konrad S. Matthies, C. S. Garratt, C. R. Erdman, A. E. Burn, and H. L. Goudge. See Gordon P. Hugenberger, "Women in Church Office: Hermeneutics or Exegesis? A Survey of Approaches to 1 Tim 2:8–15," *JETS* 35 (1992): 350–51, for precise bibliographical data.

[45] Charles B. Williams, *The New Testament: A Translation in the Language of the People* (Chicago: Moody, 1937).

[46] The most comprehensive presentation of evidence for this view (and the critique of alternate positions) is Hugenberger, "Women in Church Office." See also C. K. Barrett, *The Pastoral Epistles in the New English Bible* (Oxford: Clarendon, 1963), 55–56; Ed Christian, "Women, Teaching, Authority, Silence: 1 Timothy 2:8–15 Explained by 1 Peter 3:1–6," *JATS* 10, nos. 1–2 (1999): 285–90; France, *Women in the Church's Ministry*, 60–61; Gritz, *Paul, Women Teachers*, 125, 130–35; N. J. Hommes, "'Let Women Be Silent in Church': A Message concerning the Worship Service and the Decorum to Be Observed by Women," *CTJ* 4 (1969): 13; and B. Ward Powers, "Women in the Church: The Application of 1 Tim 2:8–15," *Interchange* 17 (1975): 55–59. Cf. Michael Griffiths, *The Church and World Mission* (Grand Rapids: Zondervan, 1980), 196; Russell C. Prohl, *Woman in the Church: A Restudy of Woman's Place in Building the Kingdom* (Grand Rapids: Zondervan, 1957), 80; and Fritz Zerbst, *The Office of Woman in the Church: A Study in Practical Theology* (St. Louis: Concordia, 1955), 51.

[47] Hugenberger, "Women in Church Office," 353–54. In the Pauline writings, besides the headship and submission passages referred to above, the following passages are in view: Rom 7:2–3; 1 Cor 7:2–4, 10–14, 16, 27, 29, 33–34, 39; 1 Tim 3:2–3, 11–12; 5:9; and Titus 1:6. Regarding the Pauline writings, Hugenberger summarizes, "Apart from 1 Timothy 2, *anēr* occurs 50 times and *gynē* occurs 54 times in close proximity within eleven distinct contexts, and in each case these terms bear the meanings 'husband' and 'wife' rather than 'man' and 'woman'" (p. 354). In the rest of the NT, the only exceptions to this are where the terms occur in listings of individuals that stress the mixed nature of the group being described. Hugenberger concludes his lexical survey thus: "In summary, besides the use of *anēr* and *gynē* in lists (where the terms are generally found in the plural) there are no examples where *anēr* and *gynē* bear the meanings 'man' and 'woman' when the terms are found in close proximity."

singular in vv. 11–12 seems to highlight the focus upon the wife and her husband especially in the latter verses.[48] Third, the reference to the married couple Adam and Eve in vv. 13–14 seems to provide a marital context to the passage.

Fourth, the reference to childbirth in v. 15 and the shift back to the plural "they" (probably referring to both husband and wife as parents of the child or perhaps broadening again to speak of wives in general as in vv. 9–10) certainly provide a marital context. Fifth, as summarized above, the reference to submission (*hypotassō*) in a setting of man-woman relationships elsewhere in Paul always concerns the submission of the wife to her husband. "In the face of this established pattern of usage only the most compelling evidence should be allowed to overturn the presumption that *hypotagē* ('submission') in 1 Timothy 2 has to do with a requirement specifically for wives rather than women in general."[49]

Sixth, strong parallels with 1 Cor 14:34–36 (a passage dealing with husbands and wives, as noted above) point to a similar context of husband-wife relationships in 1 Tim 2. In particular, E. E. Ellis has noted striking verbal and conceptual similarities between the two passages: "to allow or permit" (*epitrepō*), "silence" (*sigaō, hēsychia*), "submission" (*hypotassō, hypotagē*), "learn" (*manthanō*), and the allusion to Gen 2–3.[50]

Finally, the most determinative line of evidence supporting the husband-wife context of 1 Tim 2:8–15 is found in the extensive verbal, conceptual, and structural parallels between this passage and the household code of 1 Pet 3. Various scholars have recognized that the parallels between these two passages are so impressive that either one passage depends upon the other or both go back to a common tradition.[51] But it is Hugenberger who has set forth most comprehensively the extensive parallelism.[52] In a chart displaying the two passages in parallel columns, he highlights the detailed verbal correspondences, including the rare NT terms for "adornment" (*kosmios/kosmeō/kosmos*), "quiet" (*hēsychia*), and "braided" hair (cognate terms *plegma, emplokē*), appearing only here in the NT.

Both passages have the same structural flow of logic and thought, moving from a discussion of wifely submission to the specific counsel on her proper adornment and then to an OT paradigm for proper marital relationships (Adam-Eve, Abraham-Sarah). The only significant difference in order is that Paul puts the additional counsel to husbands first (1 Tim 2:8) whereas Peter puts it last

---

[48] As argued below from the parallel passage in 1 Pet 3, the context of the entire passage seems to be that of husbands and wives, but 1 Tim 2:11–12, moving to the singular for both *gynē* and *anēr*, focuses more directly on a wife's role vis-a-vis her husband.

[49] Hugenberger, "Women in Church Office," 355.

[50] Ellis, "Silenced Wives," 214.

[51] E.g., E. G. Selwyn, *The First Epistle of St. Peter* (2d ed.; London: Macmillan, 1946), 432–35; Martin Dibelius and Hans Conzelmann, *The Pastoral Epistles* (Hermeneia; Philadelphia: Fortress, 1972), 5. The interdependence and/or commonality of these two passages should not be surprising, since, according to available evidence, both Paul and Peter wrote them about the same time (the early 60s C.E.)—Peter from Rome, and Paul just after having left Rome.

[52] Hugenberger, "Women in Church Office," 355–58. Cf. Christian, "Women, Teaching, Authority, Silence," 285–90.

(1 Pet 3:7). But even this counsel to husbands shows striking linkages between the two passages, since the shared warning of problems hindering prayer life occurs only rarely elsewhere in Scripture. Inasmuch as 1 Pet 3 is a household code unambiguously dealing with the interrelationships of husband and wives, it is difficult to escape the same conclusion for the corresponding Pauline passage in 1 Tim 2.[53]

In light of the preceding lines of evidence, it seems most probable that in 1 Tim 2:8–15 Paul is addressing the relationship of husbands and wives, not men and women in general. It would be in harmony with this conclusion to see the "submission" (*hypotagē*) called for on the part of the wife (2:11) as submission to her husband, as in all the other *hypotassō* passages dealing with man-woman relations.

Other studies of 2:8–15 have also shown that Paul is not arguing for a creation headship of man over woman, as has often been assumed. Rather he is correcting a false syncretistic theology in Ephesus that claimed that woman was created first and man fell first and that therefore women are superior to men. Because of this false theology, wives were apparently domineering over their husbands in public church meetings.[54] The thrust of Paul's counsel in this passage serves to safeguard the headship/submission principle in the marital relation between husband and wife. Paul "do[es] not permit a *wife* (*gynaiki*) to teach—that is, to boss her *husband* (*andros*); she must be *quiet* (*hesychia*)."[55] Hugenberger rightly concludes that "Paul's concern is to prohibit only the sort of teaching that would constitute a failure of the requisite wifely 'submission' to her husband."[56]

One of the most rewarding findings of this research was to discover that the NT continues the same pattern regarding headship/submission/equality in male-female relationships as appears in Gen 1–3 and throughout the OT. There is a clear distinction between counsel regarding husband-wife relationships in the nuclear family and general men-women relationships in the church. The examination of the various NT passages that employ the words "head" (*kephalē*) or "be subject to/submit" (*hypotassō, hypotagē*) in contexts of male-female relationships leads to a striking conclusion: all of these NT passages regarding headship and submission between men and women are limited to the marriage relationship

---

[53] This probably also implies that the setting of 1 Tim 2:8–15 is not primarily the church worship but the home. See the cogent argumentation by Powers, "Women in the Church"; and Hugenberger, "Women in Church Office," 357–58.

[54] See the detailed analysis supporting this conclusion in Gritz, *Paul, Women Teachers*, 123–56. Cf. Sarah Sumner, *Men and Women in the Church: Building Consensus on Christian Leadership* (Downers Grove, Ill.: InterVarsity, 2003), 258–60; and Bruce Barron, "Putting Women in Their Place: 1 Timothy 2 and Evangelical Views of Women in Church Leadership," *JETS* 33 (1990): 453–56.

[55] Translation by Hugenberger, "Women in Church Office," 356.

[56] Ibid. 358. Hugenberger shows that this interpretation also indicates another parallel with 1 Pet 3. In both passages, the apostles are counseling the wives not to "teach" their husbands. Paul explicitly uses the words "teach" and "have authority over" (1 Tim 2:12), and Peter (1 Pet 3:1) expresses the same warning with the synonymous phrase "without a word" (*aneu logou*), thus addressing "the very real danger of a wife vaunting herself over her husband with her superior knowledge" (ibid.).

between husbands and wives; never is there any widening of the Edenic pattern to include the headship of men over women in general or submission of women to men in general. The NT writers remain faithful to the OT pattern established in the garden of Eden. Just as in Gen 3 the headship/submission principle was divinely established to preserve harmony in husband-wife relationships, so the NT passages affirm this ordering of roles. But just as the equal partnership was described in Gen 2:24 as the ultimate ideal for after the fall as well as before, so the NT counsel calls husbands and wives beyond hierarchy to a loving partnership of mutual submission.

There is a headship/submission principle in the apostolic church. But it does not consist of male leaders being given this headship role and women submitting to the male headship. Rather, according to the NT witness, there is only one true Head—Jesus Christ; he is the "husband" to the church, and all the church—both men and women—as his bride, is to submit to his headship. This is the clear teaching of Eph 5.

Neither is there any earthly priestly leader in the early church, no clergy functioning as a mediator between God and the people. The NT clearly presents the priesthood of all believers (1 Pet 2:5, 9; cf. Rom 12:1; Heb 13:15; Rev 1:6), in which all Christians are priests ministering for and representing God to the world. This is a return to the Edenic model, in which both Adam and Eve were priests, and to the original plan for Israel described in Exod 19. Within this priesthood of all believers, there are various spiritual gifts involving leadership functions (Rom 12:3–8; Eph 4:11–15; 1 Cor 12:1–11), distributed by the Spirit "to each one individually just as the Spirit chooses" (1 Cor 12:11), with no mention of any restrictions based upon gender.[57]

In the NT, the Magna Carta of true biblical equality is contained in Paul's emphatic declaration: "There is no longer Jew or Greek, there is no longer slave or free, there is no longer male and female; for all of you are one in Christ Jesus" (Gal 3:28). This is not merely a statement on equal access to salvation among various groups (cf. Gal 2:11–15; Eph 2:14–15). Rather, it specifically singles out the three relationships in which the Jews had distorted God's original plan in Eden by making one group unequal to another: (1) Jew-Gentile, (2) slave-free, and (3) male-female.[58]

---

[57] See the excellent discussion of spiritual gifts and equality in Stanley J. Grenz with Denise Muir Kjesbo, *Women in the Church: A Biblical Theology of Women in Ministry* (Downers Grove, Ill.: InterVarsity, 1995), 188–92. The qualifications for elder/bishop in 1 Tim 3:2 and Titus 1:6 are also not gender exclusive, despite the claims of many hierarchicalists. Both 1 Tim 3:1 and Titus 1:6 introduce the ones eligible for this office with the pronoun *tis*, "someone," not *anēr*, "man." The phrase "husband of one wife" (RSV)—literally "of-one-wife husband," with the word "one" (*mias*) put first in the phrase—is clearly emphasizing monogamy and not gender exclusiveness (see discussion above regarding polygamy). This is confirmed a few verses later by 1 Tim 3:12, where the same phrase is used in the qualifications for a deacon, an office held by women in NT times (Rom 16:1).

[58] For a penetrating synthesis of the exegetical arguments for this conclusion, against the argumentation of hierarchical (or "traditionalist," to use his term) interpreters, see esp. David M. Scholer, "Galatians 3:28 and the Ministry of Women in the Church," *CovQ*

By using the rare terms "male-female" (*arsēn-thēlys*) instead of "husband-wife" (*anēr-gynē*), Paul establishes a link with Gen 1:27 and thus shows that the gospel calls us back to the divine ideal, which has no place for general subordination of females to males. At the same time, Paul's choice of terminology upholds the equality of men and women in the church without denying the qualified provision of Gen 3:16 for the husband to be leader of the family to preserve harmony in the home.[59]

Within the social restraints of his day, Paul and the early church, like Jesus, did not act precipitously.[60] The inequality of Gentiles was difficult to root out (even in Peter! Gal 2:11–14). Slavery was not immediately abolished in the church (Eph 6:5–9; Col 3:22; 1 Tim 6:1), and yet the principles of the gospel were set forth that began to lead back to the Edenic ideal (as evidenced in Paul's revolutionary counsel to Philemon). Likewise women did not immediately receive full and equal partnership with men in the ministry of the church. At the same time, the evidence of women in leadership roles in the early church is sufficient to demonstrate that women were not barred from positions of influence, leadership, and even headship over men in the Christian church.

Examples of women in church leadership/headship roles abound. Deacons included the woman Phoebe (Rom 16:1) and probably the women referred to in 1 Tim 3:11.[61] The evidence points toward Junia (Rom 16:7) being a female apostle.[62] The women at Philippi, including Euodia and Syntyche (Phil 4:2–3), are described as the leaders of the local congregation.[63] The "elect lady" (2 John 1)

61, no. 3 (1998): 2–18; cf. Klyne R. Snodgrass, "Galatians 3:28: Conundrum or Solution?" in *Women, Authority, and the Bible* (ed. Alvera Mickelsen; Downers Grove, Ill.: InterVarsity, 1986), 161–81.

[59] For further discussion of Gal 3:28, see Gordon D. Fee, "Male and Female in the New Creation: Galatians 3:26–29," in *Discovering Biblical Equality: Complementarity without Hierarchy* (ed. Ronald W. Pierce and Rebecca Merrill Groothuis; Downers Grove, Ill.: InterVarsity, 2004), 172–85; Jan Faver Hailey, "'Neither Male and Female' (Gal. 3:28)," in *Essays on Women in Earliest Christianity* (ed. Carroll D. Osburn; 2 vols.; Joplin, Mo.: College Press, 1993), 1:131–66; Grenz with Kjesbo, *Women in the Church*, 99–107; Witherington, *Women in the Earliest Churches*, 76–78; Boomsma, *Male and Female*, 31–41. Contra, e.g., Richard W. Hove, *Equality in Christ? Galatians 3:28 and the Gender Dispute* (Wheaton, Ill.: Crossway, 1999).

[60] Although Jesus treated women and Gentiles in a way that was revolutionary for his day, he did not ordain as one of his disciples either a Gentile or a woman. But this pattern was no more normative for the future roles of women in church leadership than for future roles of Gentiles.

[61] See Barry L. Blackburn, "The Identity of the 'Women' in 1 Tim. 3:11," in *Essays on Women in Earliest Christianity* (ed. Carroll D. Osburn; 2 vols.; Joplin, Mo.: College Press, 1993), 1:302–19.

[62] See the evidence presented by Eldon Jay Epp, *Junia: The First Woman Apostle* (Minneapolis: Fortress, 2005); cf. Bernadette J. Brooten, "Junia . . . Outstanding among the Apostles," in *Women Priests: A Catholic Commentary on the Vatican Declaration* (ed. Leonard Swidler and Arlene Swidler; New York: Paulist, 1977), 141–44; Eisen, *Women Officeholders*, 47–49; Grenz with Kjesbo, *Women in the Church*, 92–96; and Witherington, *Women in the Earliest Churches*, 114–15.

[63] See esp. A. Boyd Luter, "Partnership in the Gospel: The Role of Women in the Church at Philippi," *JETS* 39 (1996): 411–20; and J. Paul Pollard, "Women in the Earlier

may have been an ecclesiastical title, and the one bearing this title, to whom John addresses his second epistle, may have been a prominent woman church leader with a congregation under her care.[64] The woman Priscilla assumed an authoritative teaching role (over men, Acts 18),[65] and women prophetesses also carried out authoritative teaching roles in the early church.[66] Paul also mentions numerous other women who ministered together with him as coworkers (*synergoi*),[67] and his readers are instructed to "put yourselves at the service of" (*hypotassō*) such workers (see 1 Cor 16:16).

In short, there is ample NT evidence, as there was in the OT, that nothing barred women in the covenant community from holding the highest offices of leadership, including authoritative teaching roles that constitute headship over men. As chapter 2, above, pointed out, this conclusion goes beyond both hierarchicalism and egalitarianism in the modern debate over women's ordination. Throughout Scripture, both OT and NT, the headship/submission principle remains operative (though not the ultimate ideal) in husband-wife relationships (in harmony with the view of the hierarchicalists but contrary to the views of most egalitarians), but at the same time this headship/submission principle does not extend into the man-woman relationships in the covenant community, so as to bar women from positions of influence, leadership, and even headship over men (in harmony with the views of egalitarians but contrary to the views of hierarchicalists).[68]

A growing body of literature in the evangelical scholarly community recognizes this distinction between a divinely approved hierarchical relationship of husband and wife in the home and an egalitarian relationship of men and women in the church. For example, Witherington, after his comprehensive survey of the question of women in the earliest churches, concludes that the NT continues biblical patriarchy (headship) in the home, and at the same time he affirms new roles for women in the church that do not preclude women's ordination to ministry:

> The question of women's ordination is not discussed or dismissed in the New Testament, but there is nothing in the material that rules out such a possibility. If the possibilities for women in the earliest churches, as evidenced in the NT, should be seen as

---

Philippian Church (Acts 16:13–15; Phil. 4:2–3) in Recent Scholarship," in *Essays on Women in Earliest Christianity* (ed. Carroll D. Osburn; 2 vols.; Joplin, Mo.: College Press, 1993), 1:261–80.

[64] See Grenz with Kjesbo, *Women in the Church*, 91–92. It is also possible that the term "elect lady" refers symbolically to the church.

[65] See esp. Wendell Willis, "Priscilla and Aquila—Co-workers in Christ," in *Essays on Women in Earliest Christianity* (ed. Carroll D. Osburn; 2 vols.; Joplin, Mo.: College Press, 1993), 2:261–76.

[66] See Gary Selby, "Women and Prophecy in the Corinthian Church," in *Essays on Women in Earliest Christianity* (ed. Carroll D. Osburn; 2 vols.; Joplin, Mo.: College Press, 1993), 2:277–306.

[67] See, e.g., the seven women mentioned in the list of Rom 16:1–16.

[68] See, e.g., Donald G. Bloesch, *Is the Bible Sexist? Beyond Feminism and Patriarchalism* (Westchester, Ill.: Crossway Books, 1982; repr., Eugene, Ore.: Wip & Stock, 2001), 55; Witherington, *Women in the Earliest Churches*, 219–20; Gritz, *Paul, Women Teachers*, 158.

models for church practice in subsequent generations, then it should be seen that women in the NT era already performed the tasks normally associated with ordained clergy in later times. These roles seem to be clearly supported by various NT authors.

At the same time, note that there is no evidence in the NT material investigated in this study of any sort of radical repudiation of the traditional family structure. Headship comes to mean head servant, or taking the lead in serving, but this is not quite the same as some modern notions of an egalitarian marriage structure.[69]

Another example of this position is the work of Donald G. Bloesch, who sees Scripture consistently supporting the concerns of both "patriarchalism" (hierarchicalism) and "feminism" (egalitarianism): "As the wife of her husband, the woman is obliged to serve and support him as a helpmate in the Lord. But as a sister in Christ, she has equal spiritual status with her husband."[70] Bloesch elaborates on the implications of his position, which includes the continued prescription of the headship of husband over wife in the nuclear family but allows for ordination of women to ministry in the church.

As a final example, Sharon Gritz, in her monograph dealing with 1 Tim 2:9–15 in its larger religious and cultural context, concludes that this passage is dealing with husband-wife relations, not the headship of all men over all women. She then draws the broader implications:

This interpretation eliminates any contradiction between this passage and other biblical materials. It restates the teaching of 1 Cor. 14:34–36. It also permits the exercise of spiritual gifts by all women, both married and single. Thus, 1 Tim. 2:9–15 does not contradict Jesus' relation with and teachings about women nor Paul's relationship with women coworkers and his affirmation of their participation in the worship of the church (1 Cor. 11:2–16). All women do have the right to enter the ministry as God so calls and equips them. The New Testament examples verify this. The normative principle underlying 1 Tim 2:9–15 is that marriage qualifies a married woman's ministry. A wife's commitment and obligations to her husband should shape her public ministry.[71]

My conclusions coincide with these recent studies. The biblical witness is consistent regarding the divine ideal for headship/submission/equality in man-woman relationships. Before the fall there was full equality with no headship/submission in the relationship between Adam and Eve (Gen 2:24). But after the fall, according to Gen 3:16, the husband was given a servant headship role to preserve the harmony of the home while at the same time the model of egalitarian partnership was still set forth as the ideal. This postfall (qualified) prescription of husband headship and wife submission was limited to the husband-wife relationship. In the divine revelation throughout the rest of the OT and NT witness, servant headship and voluntary submission on the part of husband and wife respectively is affirmed, but this is never broadened to the covenant community

---

[69] Witherington, *Women in the Earliest Churches,* 219–20.
[70] Bloesch, *Is the Bible Sexist?* 55.
[71] Gritz, *Paul, Women Teachers,* 158.

in such a way as to prohibit women from taking positions of leadership, including headship positions over men.

The consistent OT and NT evidence on the status of women calls for reassessment on the part of both sides in the evangelical Christian debate over this topic, resulting, it is hoped, in a new consensus that will enrich the church with the leadership/teaching ministry of ordained women while at the same time affirming the servant leadership of the husband in the home where necessary and holding up the ultimate ideal for egalitarian relationships in marriage as well as in the church.[72]

Wholeness versus Fragmentation

The same concerns for wholeness appear in the NT as in the OT. There is the Hebraic understanding of anthropology, in which humans are wholistic beings: they *are* souls; they do not just have souls. There is no Greek dualism dichotomizing the things of body and soul, relegating the former to a lesser status.[73] Wholistic sexuality also emphasizes the whole family, not just the husband and wife in isolation. The household codes of the NT Epistles make this point clear.[74]

---

[72] Recent studies have sought to reconcile egalitarian and patriarchal materials in Scripture in ways approximating my own conclusion. John G. Stackhouse Jr., *Finally Feminist: A Pragmatic Christian Understanding of Gender* (Grand Rapids: Baker, 2005), argues for a "pattern of doubleness regarding gender" (66) throughout Scripture after the fall, in which both patriarchal and egalitarian positions are upheld, revealing God's accommodation to patriarchal societies that will not tolerate anything else but his steady working to bring about a day in which patriarchy will be eliminated. So, for example, Stackhouse sees in the writings of Paul that the apostle is inspired "to do two things simultaneously: (1) to give the church prudent instruction as to how to survive and thrive in a patriarchal culture that he thinks will not last long; and (2) to maintain and promote the egalitarian dynamic already at work in the career of Jesus that in due course will leave gender lines behind" (51). While I agree with Stackhouse in recognizing this pattern of doubleness, I dispute his contention that patriarchy is "fundamentally evil" (57). Though clearly not God's ideal, undistorted patriarchy (understood as servant leadership in the home—not in the church) was introduced by God after the fall as a blessing to preserve harmony in the home, while at the same time God steadily called married couples back to the Edenic egalitarian ideal as much as possible. Another recent work, written by Glen G. Scorgie, *The Journey Back to Eden: Restoring the Creator's Design for Women and Men* (Grand Rapids: Zondervan, 2005), follows the same basic contours of my study, calling for a return to Eden and the original egalitarian divine ideal for man-woman relationships, although again Scorgie differs from my conclusion by castigating all patriarchy as intrinsically evil and viewing much of the OT as non-normative for Christians in its support of gender oppression and gender privilege.

[73] See esp. Oscar Cullmann, "Immortality of the Soul or Resurrection of the Dead: The Witness of the New Testament." in *Immortality and Resurrection: Four Essays* (ed. Krister Stendahl; New York: Macmillan, 1965), 9–53.

[74] For a succinct discussion of the NT household codes in recent literature and in the NT Epistles, see Witherington, *Women in the Earliest Churches*, 42–61. NT household codes include Eph 5; Col 3:18–4:1; 1 Tim 2:8–15; 6:1–2; Titus 2:1–10; and 1 Pet 2:18–3:7.

In the NT, Paul in particular emphasizes the complementarity aspect of sexual wholeness as he underscores mutuality of man and woman in 1 Cor 11:11: "Nevertheless, in the Lord woman is not independent of man or man independent of woman." Ephesians 5 likewise indicates the mutual love and respect that is to accrue between husband and wife (see esp. Eph 5:33). And such mutuality is revealed in the concrete lives of such NT marriage partners as Priscilla and Aquila (Acts 18:18, 26; 1 Cor 16:19; 2 Tim 4:19). As in the OT, sexual wholeness is not limited to married people: singles who do not marry by choice or by divine calling are assured of empowering divine grace and a sense of fulfillment. But celibacy is not held up as an ideal of a higher plane of spirituality, as construed in the later history of Christianity.[75] Sexual wholeness is also revealed in NT recognition of various OT laws of ritual cleanness, although these laws are not seen as binding upon Christians (Acts 15:20, 29).[76]

Fragmentation of sexual wholeness in the NT, as in the OT, is particularly evidenced in the life of the prostitute (*pornē*). References are made to the OT harlot Rahab (Matt 1:5; Heb 11:31; Jas 2:25); harlots have the same low reputation as in the OT (Matt 21:31–32; Luke 15:30); men are commanded not to join themselves to a harlot, in harmony with OT counsel (1 Cor 13:16; citing Gen 2:24; cf. Luke 15:30); and the harlot metaphor is utilized to describe God's covenant community in apostasy, as in the OT (Rev 17:1, 5, 15, 16; 19:2).[77] Fragmentation of sexual wholeness through mixed (interfaith) marriages is also condemned, as in the OT (2 Cor 6:14–16), although the apostles counsel those who are married to unbelievers not to break up the marriage but rather, through an exemplary life, to win their unbelieving spouse (1 Cor 7:12–16; 1 Pet 3:1–2).[78] Divine grace will operate powerfully in the life of the believing spouse for his/her marriage partner.

---

[75] For passages dealing with singleness and celibacy, see Matt 19:12; 1 Cor 7:7, 25–40; and possibly Luke 18:29. For references to eunuchs in the NT, see Acts 8:26–40 (the Ethiopian eunuch). Jesus was, of course, unmarried, as was apparently John the Baptist; Paul was probably a widower at the time of writing 1 Cor 7:7, since, in his former status as Pharisee (and member of the Sanhedrin?), he was undoubtedly required to be married. Paul also suggests temporary celibacy or sexual abstinence (by consent of both spouses) for limited times to devote oneself to prayer (1 Cor 7:5). See, e.g., Will Deming, *Paul on Marriage and Celibacy: The Hellenistic Background of 1 Corinthians 7* (2d ed.; Grand Rapids: Eerdmans, 2004), passim; W. Edward Glenny, "1 Corinthians 7:29–31 and the Teaching of Continence in the Acts of Paul and Thecla," *GTJ* 11 (1990): 53–70; and John Richardson, *God, Sex, and Marriage: Guidance from 1 Corinthians 7* (London: MPA Books, 1995), passim.

[76] For a survey of the numerous allusions to ritual impurity in the NT (esp. in the Gospels), see, e.g., Hyam Maccoby, *Ritual and Morality: The Ritual Purity System and Its Place in Judaism* (Cambridge: Cambridge University Press, 1999), 149–64.

[77] For discussion of the NT harlotry motif, see, e.g., Kathy L. Gaca, *The Making of Fornication: Eros, Ethics, and Political Reform in Greek Philosophy and Early Christianity* (Hellenistic Culture and Society 40; Joan Palevsky Imprint in Classical Literature; Berkeley: University of California Press, 2003), 165–72.

[78] For a discussion with bibliography, see, e.g., ibid., 146–52.

Exclusivity versus Adultery

The same emphasis upon marital exclusivity is found in the NT as in the OT, with specific and abundant warnings against adultery, often citing the seventh commandment of the Decalogue.[79] The same "two ways" of morality are contrasted in the NT as in the OT: the ways of the Spirit versus the ways of the flesh (Gal 5:16–26), the ways of the new man versus the ways of the old man (Eph 4:17–24; Col 3:5), the ways of purity[80] versus sexual immorality,[81] the way of God's plan for sexuality versus the way of sexual rebellion against God.[82] The particular seriousness of sexual sins is shown in the fact that they alone are sins "against the body itself" (1 Cor 6:18). The nature of sexual faithfulness is radicalized to include purity of thoughts (Matt 5:27–30; 2 Cor 10:5; Col 3:5; Jas 4:8; 1 Pet 2:11; 2 Pet 2:14; 1 John 2:16) and modesty of dress (1 Tim 2:9–10; 1 Pet 3:2–4) as well as refraining from illicit sexual intercourse. The NT, like the OT, utilizes the metaphor of sexual adultery/fornication to describe spiritual disobedience or apostasy.[83]

Permanence versus Divorce

The permanency of the marriage bond is also emphasized in the NT, with allowance for its dissolution only in case of the death of the spouse (Rom 7:1–3)[84] or *porneia* on the part of the spouse (Matt 5:31–32; 19:3, 8–9).[85] The nature of *porneia* (used without qualifiers) has already been discussed above, with the conclusion (through Acts 15) that the term includes all illicit sexual intercourse

---

[79] For references to adultery (*moicheia/moicheuō* and other expressions from the same word-group), see the following: Matt 5:27–30; 12:39; 15:19; 19:18; Mark 7:21; 8:38; 16:4; Luke 18:11; John 8:3–4; Rom 2:22; 7:3; 13:9; 1 Cor 6:9; Gal 5:19; Heb 13:4; Jas 2:11; 4:4; 2 Pet 2:14; Rev 2:22.

[80] Matt 5:8; Phil 4:8; 1 Tim 1:5; 4:12; 5:22; 2 Tim 1:3; Titus 1:3; Jas 1:27; 3:17; 2 Pet 3:1; 1 John 3:3; Rev 14:4–5.

[81] Matt 5:27–30; Acts 15:20, 29; Rom 1:24–29; 6:12; 13:14; 1 Cor 6:9–18; 10:8; 2 Cor 7:14; 1 Thess 4:4; 2 Tim 2:22; Titus 2:11; Jas 1:21, 27; 1 Pet 1:14; 2:11; 4:3; 2 Pet 2:10–14; Jude 4–19; Rev 2:14, 20; 21:8; 22:15.

[82] For discussion of these two ways, see, e.g., Gaca, "Rival Plans for God's Sexual Program in the Pentateuch and Paul," in *Making of Fornication*, 119–59.

[83] See, e.g., John 8:39–44; 1 Cor 6:15; 10:6–12; Rev 2:20–23. Cf. ibid., 160–89.

[84] The marriage that is dissolved upon the death of the spouse allows the surviving spouse to remarry (Rom 7:1–3), as in OT practice. In 1 Cor 7:10–16 Paul also allows for separation (but not divorce) of the marriage partners in the case of incompatibility. The one further possible exception where divorce is allowed seems to be in the case where an unbelieving spouse departs: as for the believing spouse, "in such a case the brother or sister is not bound" (1 Cor 7:15, although the meaning of "is not bound" is not certain). For further discussion, see, e.g., Deming, *Paul on Marriage and Celibacy,* passim; and Richardson, *God, Sex, and Marriage,* passim.

[85] For support of the genuineness of the exception clause in Matthew, see esp. Blomberg, "Marriage, Divorce."

mentioned in Lev 18 and 20.[86] This inner-biblical definition of *porneia* seems to me to be decisive in understanding Jesus' "exception clause" regarding divorce on grounds of *porneia* in Matt 5:32; 19:9. This exception clause is stricter than the grounds for divorce presented in Deut 24:1. His exception as grounds for divorce is *porneia*, which is not the exact equivalent of *ʿerwat dābār* of Deut 24:1. The term *porneia* has a much narrower focus, referring exclusively to illicit sexual intercourse, which in the Mosaic law called for the offender being "cut off" from God's people (Lev 18:29).[87] "Jesus says that whereas Moses allowed for divorce for indecent exposure without illicit sexual relations, He permits divorce only if illicit sexual relations take place."[88]

Furthermore, in this light, Jesus' exception clause in Matt 5 and 19 is not to be seen in contradiction to the Synoptic parallel accounts in Mark (10:11–12) and Luke (16:18), which contain no exception clause. Mark and Luke do not mention any exception clause presumably because they do not consider the case of *porneia*, the penalty for which was being "cut off" or death. It was assumed that the death penalty or being "cut off" from the congregation meant a de facto dissolution of the marriage. Matthew apparently preserves the original intent of Jesus for readers after 30 C.E., when the death penalty for adultery was abolished (*b. Sanh.* 41a).[89]

---

[86] Additional support (beyond the connections with Acts 15 and Lev 18) for taking *porneia* as referring to illicit sexual intercourse (not limited to incest) is provided by Blomberg, ibid., 176–78. Cf. Dale C. Allison Jr., "Divorce, Celibacy and Joseph (Matthew 1:18–25 and 19:1–12)," *JSNT* 49 (1993): 3–10; Bruce J. Malina, "Does *porneia* Mean Fornication?" *NovT* 14 (1972): 10–17; and Joseph Jensen, "Does *porneia* Mean Fornication: A Critique of Bruce Malina," *NovT* 20 (1978): 161–84.

[87] This entailed the death penalty at least in the case of adultery (Lev 20:10), some instances of incest (v. 12), homosexual relationships (v. 13), and bestiality (vv. 15–16). By the time of Jesus, the death penalty for illicit sexual intercourse had all but died out (both the Babylonian Talmud [*b. Sanh.* 41a] and the Jerusalem Talmud [*y. Sanh.* 18a, 24b] indicate that the death penalty was abolished forty years before the destruction of the temple, i.e., about 30 C.E.), and therefore the school of Shammai could rightly include such sexual activity in the meaning of *ʿerwat dābār* while also including indecent exposure in general.

[88] Roy Gane, "Old Testament Principles Relating to Divorce and Remarriage," *JATS* 12, no. 2 (2001): 47–48. Gane further points out that "in Matt 5:32, Jesus' Greek phraseology follows the syntax of the House of Shammai formulation: *logou porneias*, 'a matter of fornication.' The difference between the two formulations is the difference between the range of meaning of *porneia*, illicit sexual intercourse, and that of the broader term *ʾerwah*, exposure in general" (pp. 48–49).

[89] For more complete discussion of this point, see R. H. Charles, *The Teaching of the New Testament on Divorce* (London: Williams & Norgate, 1921). Charles summarizes:

> When we recognise that Mark's narrative takes no cognisance of the case of adultery, but only of the other and inadequate grounds advanced for divorce, the chief apparent contradictions between Matthew and Mark cease to exist. What is implicit in Mark is made explicit in Matthew. Both gospels therefore teach that marriage is indissoluble for all offences short of adultery. . . . Now, it was impossible to misinterpret the plain words of Christ, as stated in Mark, at the time they were uttered, and so long as the law relating to the infliction of death on the adulteress and her paramour was not abrogated. But, as we know, this law was abrogated a few years later. The natural result was that to our Lord's words, which had one meaning

The OT also clarifies another aspect of Jesus' teaching on divorce. Chapter 9, above, concluded that the rare *hotpaʿal* (of *ṭāmēʾ*) in Deut 24:4, "she has been caused to defile herself" (translation mine), is an internal indicator that divorce does not meet with divine approval. The husband's putting away his wife has in effect caused her to defile herself in a second marriage in a similar way as if she were committing adultery. The best translation of Deut 24:4 ("she has been caused to defile herself") throws light on Jesus' words in Matt 5:32: "But I say to you that anyone who divorces his wife, except on the ground of unchastity [*porneia*], *causes her to commit adultery* [presumably when she remarries]; and whoever marries a divorced woman commits adultery." Just as in the other "But I say to you" sayings of Matt 5, Jesus is not changing or adding something new to the law but showing the true and deeper meaning that is already contained in the law, which had been distorted by later misinterpretation. Already in Deut 24:4 it is indicated that breaking the marriage bond on grounds less than illicit sexual intercourse causes the woman to defile herself, that is, commit what is tantamount to adultery,[90] and Jesus, the master exegete, restores the true meaning of the text.

before the abrogation of this law, a different meaning was in many quarters attached after its abrogation, and they came to be regarded as forbidding divorce under all circumstances, though really and originally they referred only to divorces procured on inadequate grounds—that is, grounds not involving adultery. Now, it was just to correct such a grave misconception, or the possibility of such a misconception, of our Lord's words, whether in Mark or other early documents, that Matthew (v. 32, xix.9) edited the narrative afresh and inserted the clause, "saving for the cause of unchastity." . . . By the insertion of these clauses Matthew preserves the meaning of our Lord's statements on this subject for all subsequent generations that had lost touch with the circumstances and limitations under which they were originally made. Matthew's additions are therefore justifiable. Without them the reader is apt to misunderstand the passages on divorce. (pp. 21–23)

It is also possible that Matthew preserves the original complete wording of Jesus (in translation, of course) and that Mark and Luke simply left out the reference to *porneia* in the Greek translation because Jesus' original intent is clear without it (since *porneia* called for death or being "cut off," which implies a de facto dissolution of the marriage in those cases). In other words, one does not have to decide on the question of the Synoptic problem (which Gospel is prior, if any) to reconcile this apparent contradiction.

[90] C. F. Keil and Franz Delitzsch recognize this when they indicate that "the second marriage of a divorced woman was placed *implicite* upon a par with adultery, and some approach made toward the teaching of Christ concerning marriage: [Matt 5:32 quoted]" (K&D, 1:951). My conclusion is in opposition to more recent analyses of the relationship between Deuteronomy 24 and Matt 5:32, which conclude that the conditions/grounds for divorce presumed in Deut 24 are still the norm for today and that Matt 5 and 19 are simply hyperbole and exaggeration and not intended to be exhaustive in providing the only guide for divorce. See esp. Joe Sprinkle, "Old Testament Perspectives on Divorce and Remarriage," *JETS* (1997): 529–50, who argues that the grounds for divorce in Deut 24:1–4 (*ʿerwat dābār*) is "behavior fundamentally in violation of the essence of the marriage covenant" (p. 531) and such behavior is still valid grounds for divorce today. For Sprinkle, this includes "wife abuse, flat refusal of conjugal rights, lack of support of the wife financially, and so forth" (549). See idem, *Biblical Law and Its Relevance: A Christian Understanding and Ethical Application for Today of the Mosaic Regulations* (Lanham, Md.: University Press of America, 2006), 129–54.

Furthermore, Jesus, in pointing the Pharisees away from the divine "concession" in Deut 24:1–4 to God's ideal "from the beginning" (Matt 19:8), was not arbitrarily shifting from the Deuteronomic law to the Edenic ideal. He was, rather,
pointing to a conclusion that was already implicit in Deut 24:4: that Deut 24:1–3
was a temporary concession to the "hard-heartedness" of Israel and did not represent God's divine ideal for marriage.

Intimacy versus Incest

In the NT, specific counsel is given for optimum marital relationships, especially in the household codes,[91] underscoring the need for husbands to love,
nourish, cherish, and seek to understand their wives and for wives to love and respect their husbands. Both husbands and wives are to ensure the continuation of
sexual intimacy in the marriage (1 Cor 7:4–5). As in the OT data, sexual intercourse is equated with "becoming one flesh," but this act by itself does not constitute marriage (1 Cor 6:16). The distortion of intimacy in incestuous relationships
is condemned (1 Cor 5:1), assuming the OT prohibitions of Lev 18 and 20.

The promise is given of divine forgiveness and cleansing from all the acts of
sexual distortion (e.g., 1 Cor 6:11), including incest and the other illicit sexual activity referred to above. At the same time, however, persistence in a lifestyle of immorality calls for discipline, even disfellowshipping, of the offender (1 Cor 5:2, 9, 11,
13), modeled on the oft-repeated OT reference cited in 1 Cor 5:13: "Drive out the
wicked person from among you."[92] Persistence in sexual sin (as with the others mentioned by the apostles) without repentance and reformation would also disqualify
one from inheriting the kingdom of God (Gal 5:21; Eph 5:5; cf. Rev 21:8; 22:15).[93]

---

[91] See the household codes of Eph 5:21–33; Col 3:18–25; 1 Tim 2:8–15; Tit 2:4–5; and
1 Pet 3:1–7; see esp. Witherington, *Women in the Earliest Churches*, 42–61.

[92] This citation alludes to Deut 13:6 (ET 13:5); 17:7, 12; 19:19; 21:21; 22:21, 24; 24:7.
Most of these Deuteronomic passages refer to capital punishment. As pointed out in ch. 8,
above, however, the use of this phrase in connection with sexually related capital crimes did
not add the phrase "Show no pity," and thus there may have been the possibility of a commutation of the death sentence for sex crimes. Evidently, in the NT covenant community, no
longer the theocracy, the equivalent to the death penalty (or, alternately, its generally accepted commutation since the abolishing of the death penalty among Jews in ca. 30 C.E. [see
above]) was to be disfellowshipped from the church. In contrast to the death penalty, which
was final, the process of church discipline could lead to salvation and restoration (1 Cor 5:5).

[93] On the homiletical level, I suggest that the NT gives similar practical steps (a biblical "twelve-step program") for preserving moral purity both in thought and action as
does the OT: (1) daily consecration and surrender of the will (Rom 6:11–13); (2) claiming
God's keeping power by faith (1 Pet 1:5); (3) focusing on pure thoughts (Phil 4:8);
(4) meditation on the character of Christ (2 Cor 3:18); (5) avoiding situations that include temptations to impurity (Rom 13:14); (6) constant watchfulness (Matt 26:41;
1 Pet 1:13–15; 2 Cor 10:5; Jas 1:14–15); (7) earnest prayer and claiming of God's promises (Matt 26:41; 2 Pet 1:4); (8) dependence upon the abiding influence of the Holy
Spirit (Rom 8:1–11); (9) diligent study of the word (Rom 10:17; 2 Tim 3:15–17); (10) cultivating a sense of God's presence and the certainty of future judgment (1 Cor 3:16–17;

Sexuality and Procreation

The NT, like the OT, gives sexual union independent meaning and value; sexual relations do not need to be justified as a means to a superior (i.e., procreative) end. Although the value of childbirth is upheld (Matt 1:18–25; Luke 1:26–28; 2:1–7; John 16:20–22; 1 Tim 2:15; 5:10, 14; Rev 12:2, 4–5), sexual intimacy is also described as honorable on its own account, independent of procreation (1 Cor 7:3–5; Heb 13:4).

Allusion is made to various issues regarding procreation, such as barrenness (Luke 1:7, 36; 23:29; Gal 4:27), levirate marriage (Matt 22:23–23; Mark 12:18–21; Luke 20:27–38), and circumcision.[94] The NT also upholds the same view of the status of the unborn fetus, treating it as fully human (e.g., Luke 1:15, 35, 41, 44).[95]

The Wholesome Beauty of Sexuality

The NT, like the OT, upholds the wholesomeness and beauty of married sexual love. "Let marriage be held in honor by all, and let the marriage bed be kept undefiled" (Heb 13:4). The divine love is affirmed and illustrated by the language of married sexual love. Paul speaks of the "great mystery" of the union between Christ and his church paralleling the one-flesh experience between husband and wife (Eph 5:21–33). On the other hand, a parody of that beautiful one-flesh experience is found in union with a harlot (1 Cor 6:16), and the spiritual parody is found in the beautifully dressed, seductive harlot of Revelation (Rev 17, 19).

The final sustained metaphor of the Bible depicts the consummation in terms of sexuality: the marriage of the Lamb and his virgin bride who has made herself ready (Rev 19:7; cf. 14:1–5), the marriage supper of the Lamb (19:8), the new Jerusalem descending as a bride adorned for her husband (21:2), the extended description of the Lamb's wife, the new Jerusalem (21:9–22:5), and the final invitation in Scripture coming from the Spirit and the bride: "Come" (22:17). The new Jerusalem, called the bride, is also depicted as a cube, the equivalent of the most holy place in the temple (21:2–3, 16). Thus, here at the climax of the Bible, as with the Song of Songs in the OT, in the marriage relation between bride and Groom, we come to the holy of holies. Here again, where the bride is illuminated by the "glory of God" and "the Lamb" (21:23), we encounter the flame of Yahweh.

6:18; Gal 5:19, 21; Heb 4:13); (11) cultivating intimacy and sexual satisfaction with one's own spouse (1 Cor 7:5; Heb 13:4); and (12) cultivating a sense of the ennobling power of pure thoughts (Matt 5:8).

[94] Passages referring to circumcision include Luke 1:59; 2:21; John 7:22–23; Acts 7:8; 10:45; 11:2; 15:1, 5, 24; 16:3; 21:1; Rom 2:25–29; 3:1, 30; 4:9–12; 15:8; 1 Cor 7:18–19; Gal 2:3, 7–9, 12; 5:2, 6, 11, 13; 6:12–13; Eph 2:11; Phil 3:3, 5; Col 2:11; 3:11; 4:11; Titus 1:10.

[95] See, e.g., John M. Frame, "Abortion from a Biblical Perspective," in *Thou Shalt Not Kill: The Christian Case against Abortion* (ed. Richard L. Ganz; New Rochelle, N.Y.: Arlington House, 1978), 43–75; John Youngberg and Millie Youngberg, eds., *The Reborn and the Unborn* (Berrien Springs, Mich.: Marriage and Family Commitment Seminars, 1988), 23–34.

Bibliography

Aaron, David H. *Biblical Ambiguities: Metaphor, Semantics, and Divine Imagery.* Brill Reference Library of Ancient Judaism 4. Boston: E. J. Brill, 2001.

Aaseng, Rolf E. "Male and Female Created He Them." *Christianity Today* 15, no. 4 (1970): 5–6.

Abba, R. "Name," Pages 500–508 in Vol. 3 of *The Interpreter's Dictionary of the Bible.* Edited by G. A. Buttrick. 4 vols. Nashville: Abingdon, 1962.

Abma, Richtsje. *Bonds of Love: Methodic Studies of Prophetic Texts with Marriage Imagery (Isaiah 50:1–3 and 54:1–10, Hosea 1–3, Jeremiah 2–3).* Assen, Neth.: Van Gorcum, 1999.

Abraham, Joseph. "Feminist Hermeneutics and Pentecostal Spirituality: The Creation Narrative of Genesis as a Paradigm." *Asian Journal of Pentecostal Studies* 6 (2003): 3–21.

Abraham, Joseph, and Gordon McConville. *Eve—Accused or Acquitted: An Analysis of Feminist Readings of the Creation Narrative Texts in Genesis 1–3.* Paternoster Biblical and Theological Monographs. Combria, Ga.: Paternoster, 2002.

Abusch, Tzvi, ed. *Riches Hidden in Secret Places: Ancient Near Eastern Studies in Memory of Thorkild Jacobsen.* Winona Lake, Ind.: Eisenbrauns, 2002.

Achtemeier, Elizabeth. *Nahum–Malachi.* Interpretation: A Bible Commentary for Teaching and Preaching. Atlanta: John Knox, 1986.

———. *Preaching from the Old Testament.* Louisville: Westminster John Knox, 1989.

———. "Why God Is Not Mother: A Response to Feminist God-Talk in the Church." *Christianity Today* 37, no. 9 (1993): 16–20, 22–23.

Ackerman, Susan. " 'And the Women Knead Dough': The Worship of the Queen of Heaven in Sixth-Century Judah." Pages 109–24 in *Gender and Difference in Ancient Israel.* Edited by Peggy L. Day. Minneapolis: Fortress, 1989.

———. "Child Sacrifice: Returning God's Gift." *Bible Review* 9, no. 3 (1993): 20–28, 56.

———. "Digging Up Deborah: Recent Hebrew Bible Scholarship on Gender and the Contribution of Archaeology." *Near Eastern Archaeology* 66 (2003): 172–84.

———. "The Queen Mother and the Cult in Ancient Israel." *Journal of Biblical Literature* 112 (1993): 385–401.

————. "The Queen Mother and the Cult in the Ancient Near East." Pages 197–209 in *Women and Goddess Traditions in Antiquity and Today.* Edited by Karen L. King. Minneapolis: Fortress, 1997.

————. "Sacred Sex, Sacrifice, and Death: Understanding a Prophetic Poem." *Bible Review* 6, no. 1 (1990): 38–44.

————. *Warrior, Dancer, Seductress, Queen: Women in Judges and Biblical Israel.* New York: Doubleday, 1998.

————. "Why Is Miriam Also among the Prophets? (and Is Zipporah among the Priests?)" *Journal of Biblical Literature* 121 (2002): 47–80.

Ackroyd, Peter R. "Goddesses, Women, and Jezebel." Pages 245–59 in *Images of Women in Antiquity.* Edited by A. Cameron and A. Kuhrt. Beckenham, Kent, Eng.: Croom Helm, 1983.

————. *The Second Book of Samuel: Commentary.* Cambridge Bible Commentary. Cambridge: Cambridge University Press, 1977.

Adams, Carol J., and Marie M. Fortune, eds. *Violence against Women and Children: A Christian Theological Sourcebook.* New York: Continuum, 1995.

Adams, Jay. *Marriage, Divorce, and Remarriage in the Bible.* Phillipsburg, N.J.: Presbyterian and Reformed, 1980.

Adams, Jay E., Paul E. Steele, and Charles C. Ryrie. "Point and Counterpoint: Are Divorce and Remarriage Ever Permissible." *Fundamentalist Journal* 3, no. 6 (1984): 16–20.

Adams, Q. M. *Neither Male nor Female: A Study of the Scriptures.* Ilfracombe, Eng.: Stockwell, 1973.

Adler, Elaine J. "The Background for the Metaphor of Covenant as Marriage in the Hebrew Bible." PhD diss., University of California, Berkeley, 1990.

Aerts, Theo. "Two Are Better Than One (Qohelet 4:10)." *Point Series* 14 (1990): 11–48.

Aichele, George, Jr., and G. Phillips, eds. *Intertextuality and the Bible.* Semeia 69–70. Atlanta: Society of Biblical Literature, 1995.

Akin, Daniel. *God on Sex: The Creator's Ideas about Love, Intimacy, and Marriage.* Nashville: Broadman & Holman, 2003.

Albright, William F. *Archaeology and the Religion of Israel.* 5th ed. Baltimore: Johns Hopkins University Press, 1968.

————. "Archaic Survivals in the Text of Canticles." Pages 1–7 in *Hebrew and Semitic Studies Presented to Godfrey Rolles Driver.* Edited by D. Winton Thomas and W. D. McHardy. Oxford: Clarendon, 1963.

————. "The Names Shaddai and Abram." *Journal of Biblical Literature* 54 (1935): 180–93.

Alcorn, Randy. *ProLIFE Answers to ProCHOICE Arguments.* Revised and enlarged edition. Sisters, Ore.: Multnomah, 2000.

Alexander, Patrick H., et al. *The SBL Handbook of Style: For Ancient Near Eastern, Biblical, and Early Christian Studies.* Peabody, Mass.: Hendrickson, 1999.

Allam, Schafik. "De l'adoption en Egypte pharaonique." *Oriens antiquus* 11 (1972): 277–95.

———. *Some Pages from Everyday Life in Ancient Egypt.* Prism Archaeology Series 1. Guizeh, Egypt: Prism, 1985.

Allen, Christine Garside. "Who Was Rebekah? 'On Me Be the Curse, My Son.'" Pages 183–216 in *Beyond Androcentrism: New Essays on Women and Religion.* Edited by Rita M. Gross. Missoula, Mont.: Scholars Press, 1977.

Allen, Leslie C. *Psalms 101–150.* World Biblical Commentary 21. Waco, Tex.: Word, 1983.

Allen, Prudence. *The Aristotelian Revolution, 750 B.C.–A.D. 1250.* Vol. 1 of *The Concept of Woman.* Montreal: Eden, 1985. Repr., Grand Rapids: Eerdmans, 1997.

Allen, Robert L. *All about Eve: Ten Selected Women of the Bible.* Lima, Ohio: CSS, 2001.

Allen, Ronald B. "Numbers." Pages 657–1008 in vol. 2 of *The Expositor's Bible Commentary.* Edited by Frank E. Gaebelein. 12 vols. Grand Rapids: Zondervan, 1976–1992.

Allen, Ronald B., and Beverly Allen. *Liberated Traditionalism: Men and Women in Balance.* Portland, Ore.: Multnomah, 1985.

Allender, Dan B., and Tremper Longman III. *Intimate Allies: Rediscovering God's Design for Marriage and Becoming Soul Mates for Life.* Wheaton, Ill.: Tyndale, 1995.

Allison, Dale C., Jr. "Divorce, Celibacy, and Joseph (Matthew 1:18–25 and 19:1–12)." *Journal for the Study of the New Testament* 49 (1993): 3–10.

Alter, Robert. *The Art of Biblical Narrative.* New York: Basic, 1981.

———. *The Art of Biblical Poetry.* New York: Basic, 1985.

———. "Biblical Type-Scenes and the Uses of Convention." *Critical Inquiry* 5 (1978): 355–68.

———. "How Convention Helps Us Read: The Case of the Bible's Annunciation Type-Scene." *Prooftexts: A Journal of Jewish Literary History* 3 (1983): 115–30.

———. "The Song of Songs: An Ode to Intimacy." *Bible Review* 18, no. 4 (2002): 24–32, 52.

———. *The World of Biblical Literature.* New York: Basic, 1992.

Amaru, Betsy Halpern. *The Empowerment of Women in the Book of Jubilees.* Journal for the Study of Judaism Supplements 60. Leiden: E. J. Brill, 1999.

Ambrose. *Hexameron, Paradise, and Cain and Abel.* Translated by John J. Savage. Fathers of the Church 42. New York: Fathers of the Church, 1961.

Amit, Yairah. "'Am I Not More Devoted to You Than Ten Sons?' (1 Samuel 1.8): Male and Female Interpretations." Pages 68–76 in *A Feminist Companion to Samuel and Kings.* Edited by Athalya Brenner. Feminist Companion to the Bible 5. Sheffield, Eng.: Sheffield Academic Press, 1994.

———. *The Book of Judges: The Art of Editing.* Translated by Jonathan Chipman. Biblical Interpretation Series 38. Leiden: Brill, 1999.

———. "Literature in the Service of Politics: Studies in Judges 19–21." Pages 28–40 in *Politics and Theopolitics in the Bible and Postbiblical Literature.* Edited by Henning G. Reventlow, Yair Hoffman, and Benjamin Uffenheimer. Journal for the Study of the Old Testament Supplement Series 171. Sheffield: Sheffield Academic Press, 1994.

————. "'Manoah Promptly Followed His Wife' (Judges 13.11): On the Place of Woman in Birth Narratives." Pages 146–50 in *A Feminist Companion to Judges*. Edited by Athalya Brenner. Feminist Companion to the Bible 4. Sheffield, Eng.: Sheffield Academic Press, 1993.

Amorim, Nilton. "Defilement and Desecration in the Old Testament." PhD diss., Andrews University, 1985.

Amram, D. W. *The Jewish Law of Divorce.* London: David Nutt, 1897. Repr., New York: Sepher-Hermon, 1975.

Anderlini, Giampaolo. "*Eset Zenuim* (Os 1:2)." *Bibbia e oriente* 30 (1988): 169–82.

Andersen, Francis I. *Job.* Tyndale Old Testament Commentaries 13. Downers Grove, Ill.: InterVarsity, 1976.

Andersen, Francis I., and David Noel Freedman. *Hosea: A New Translation with Introduction and Commentary.* Anchor Bible 24A. New York: Doubleday, 1989.

Anderson, Bernhard W. "The Biblical Circle of Homosexual Prohibition: Is Heterosexuality—the Biological Norm for Reproduction—Also the Ethical Norm for Human Sexual Relations?" *Bible Review* 9, no. 3 (1993): 10, 52.

————. "The Song of Miriam Poetically and Theologically Considered." Pages 285–302 in *Directions in Biblical Hebrew Poetry*. Edited by Elaine R. Follis. Journal for the Study of the Old Testament: Supplement Series 40. Sheffield, Eng.: Sheffield Academic Press, 1987.

Anderson, Cheryl B. *Women, Ideology, and Violence: Critical Theory and the Construction of Gender in the Book of the Covenant and the Deuteronomic Law.* Journal for the Study of the Old Testament Supplement Series 394. London: T&T Clark, 2004.

Anderson, Gary A. "Is Eve the Problem?" Pages 96–123 in *Theological Exegesis: Essays in Honor of Brevard S. Childs.* Edited by Christopher Seitz and Kathryn Greene-McCreight. Grand Rapids: Eerdmans, 1999.

————. "The Punishment of Adam and Eve in the Life of Adam and Eve." Pages 57–81 in *Literature on Adam and Eve: Collected Essays.* Edited by Gary A. Anderson, Michael Stone, and Johannes Tromp. Leiden: E. J. Brill, 2000.

Anderson, Gary M. "Celibacy or Consummation in the Garden? Reflections on Early Jewish and Christian Interpretations of the Garden of Eden." *Harvard Theological Review* 82 (1989): 121–48.

Anderson, Janice Copel. "Mapping Feminist Biblical Criticism: The American Scene, 1983–1990." Pages 21–44 in *Critical Review of Books in Religion.* Edited by Eldon Joy Epp. Atlanta, Ga.: American Academy of Religion/Society of Biblical Literature, 1991.

Anderson, John O. *Cry of the Innocents: Abortion and the Race towards Judgement.* South Plainfield, N.J.: Bridge, 1984.

Andersson, Greger. *The Book and Its Narratives: A Critical Examination of Some Synchronic Studies of the Book of Judges.* Örebro Studies in Literary History and Criticism 1. Örebro, Swed.: Universitetsbiblioteket, 2001.

Andreasen, Niels-Erik. "The Role of the Queen Mother in Israelite Society." *Catholic Biblical Quarterly* 45 (1983): 179–94.

Aquinas, Thomas. *Summa theologiae: Latin Text and English Translation, Introduction, Notes, Appendices, and Glossaries.* Edited by Thomas Gilby. 60 vols. New York: McGraw-Hill, 1964.

Arambarri, Jesus M. "Gen 1,1–2,4a: Ein Prolog und ein Programm für Israel." Pages 65–86 in *Gottes Wege suchend—Beiträge zum Verständnis der Bibel und Ihrer Botschaft: Festschrift für Rudolf Mosis zum 70. Geburtstag.* Edited by Franz Sedlmeier. Würzburg: Echter, 2003.

Archer, Gleason L. *Encyclopedia of Bible Difficulties.* Grand Rapids: Zondervan, 1982.

———. *A Survey of Old Testament Introduction.* Updated and rev. ed. Chicago: Moody, 1994.

Archer, Léonie J. "The Role of Jewish Women in the Religion, Ritual, and Cult of Graeco-Roman Palestine." Pages 273–87 in *Images of Women in Antiquity.* Edited by Averil Cameron and Amélie Kuhrt. Rev. ed. Detroit: Wayne State University Press, 1993.

Arenhoevel, Diego. "Der Bund der Versöhnung: Die Ehe zwischen Jahwe und Israel (Hos 2,4–9.16f.20–22)." Pages 117–35 in *Versöhnung—Versuche zu ihrer Geschichte und Zukunft: Festschrift für Paulus Engelhardt.* Edited by Thomas Eggensperger, Ulrich Engel, and Otto Hermann Pesch. Mainz: Grünewald, 1991.

Arichea, Daniel C., Jr. "The Silence of Woman in the Church: Theology and Translation in 1 Corinthians 14.33b–36." *The Bible Translator* 46 (1995): 101–12.

Arlandson, James Malcolm. *Women, Class, and Society in Early Christianity: Models from Luke–Acts.* Peabody, Mass.: Hendrickson, 1997.

Armenteros, Victor. "'YHWH, el Amante': Modelos de Relación Derivados de la Simbologia Matrimonial Veterotestamentaria." *DavarLogos* 3 (2004): 139–66.

Armstrong, Karen. *In the Beginning: A New Interpretation of Genesis.* New York: Knopf, 1996.

Arnold, Patrick M. "Hosea and the Sin of Gibeah." *Catholic Biblical Quarterly* 51 (1989): 447–60.

Arx, Urs von. "The Gender Aspects of Creation from a Theological, Christological, and Soteriological Perspective: An Exegetical Contribution." *Anglican Theological Review* 84 (2002): 519–54.

Ashby, Godfrey. "The Bloody Bridegroom: The Interpretation of Exodus 4:24–26." *Expository Times* 106 (1995): 203–5.

Asmussen, Jes P. "Bemerkungen zur sakralen Prostitution im Alten Testament." *Studia theologica* 11 (1957): 167–92.

Assis, Elie. "Chiasmus in Biblical Narrative: Rhetoric of Characterization." *Prooftexts: A Journal of Jewish Literary History* 22 (2002): 273–304.

Astell, Ann W. *The Song of Songs in the Middle Ages.* Ithaca, N.Y.: Cornell University Press, 1990.

Astour, Michael C. "Tamar the Hierodule: An Essay in the Method of Vestigial Motifs." *Journal of Biblical Literature* 85 (1966): 185–96.

Atkinson, David. *The Message of Genesis 1–11: The Dawn of Creation.* Leicester, Eng.: Inter-Varsity, 1990.

Atkinson, Kenneth. "Dancing at Qumran? Women and Worship at the Dead Sea." *Proceedings of the Central States Society of Biblical Literature and the American Schools of Oriental Research* 3 (2000): 39–54.

Atwell, James E. "An Egyptian Source for Genesis 1." *Journal of Theological Studies* 51 (2000): 441–77.

Aune, David E. *Revelation 17–22.* Word Biblical Commentary 52C. Nashville: Nelson, 1998.

Austin, J. L. *How to Do Things with Words.* 2d ed. Cambridge: Harvard University Press, 1975.

Avis, Paul. *Eros and the Sacred.* Harrisburg, Pa.: Moorehouse, 1989.

Avner, Uzi. "Sacred Stones in the Desert." *Biblical Archaeology Review* 27/3 (2001): 31–41.

Avraham, Nachum. "The Nature of David and Jonathan's Relationship (2 Sam 1:26: נִפְלְאַתָה אַהֲבָתְךָ לִי מֵאַהֲבַת נָשִׁים)." Hebrew. *Beit Mikra* 48 (2003): 215–22.

Ayo, Nicholas. *Sacred Marriage: The Wisdom of the Song of Songs.* Illustrated by Meinrad Craighead. New York: Continuum, 1997.

Azevedo, Joachim. "At the Door of Paradise: A Contextual Interpretation of Gen 4:7." *Biblische Notizen* 100 (1999): 45–59.

Baab, Otto J. "Sex, Sexual Behavior." Pages 296–301 in vol. 4 of *The Interpreter's Dictionary of the Bible.* Edited by George A. Buttrick. 4 vols. Nashville: Abingdon, 1962.

Babbage, Stuart B. *Christianity and Sex.* Chicago: InterVarsity, 1963.

―――. *Sex and Sanity: A Christian View of Sexual Morality.* Philadelphia: Westminster, 1965.

Bacchiocchi, Samuele. "Headship, Submission, and Equality in Scripture." Pages 65–110 in *Prove All Things: A Response to "Women in Ministry."* Edited by Mercedes H. Dyer. Berrien Springs, Mich.: Adventists Affirm, 2000.

―――. *The Marriage Covenant: A Biblical Study on Marriage, Divorce, and Remarriage.* Berrien Springs, Mich.: Biblical Perspectives, 1991.

―――. *Women in the Church: A Biblical Study on the Role of Women in the Church.* Berrien Springs, Mich.: Biblical Perspectives, 1987.

Bach, Alice. "The Pleasure of Her Text." In "Ad feminam: Fiftieth Anniversary Volume." Edited by Alice Bach. *Union Seminary Quarterly Review* 43 (1989): 41–58.

―――. "Rereading the Body Politic: Women and Violence in Judges 21," Pages 143–59 in *Judges.* Edited by Athalya Brenner; Feminist Companion to the Bible: Second Series 4. Sheffield, Eng.: Sheffield Academic Press, 1999.

Bach, Alice. ed. "Ad feminam: Fiftieth Anniversary Volume." *Union Seminary Quarterly Review* 43 (1989).

―――, ed. *Women in the Hebrew Bible: A Reader.* New York: Routledge, 1999.

Bachofen, Johann J. *Myth, Religion, and Mother Right: Selected Writings of J. J. Bachofen.* Translated by Ralph Manheim. Princeton, N.J.: Princeton University Press, 1967.

Bader, Mary Anna. "Genesis 34 and 2 Samuel 13, Dinah and Tamar: Their Brothers and Fathers." PhD diss., Lutheran School of Theology at Chicago, 2002.

———. *Sexual Violation in the Hebrew Bible: A Multi-Methodological Study of Genesis 34 and 2 Samuel 13.* Studies in Biblical Literature 87. New York: Peter Lang, 2006.

Bahnsen, L. *Homosexuality: A Biblical View.* Grand Rapids: Baker, 1978.

Bahrani, Zainab. "Performativity and the Image: Narrative, Representation, and the Uruk Vase." Pages 15–22 in *Leaving No Stones Unturned: Essays on the Ancient Near East and Egypt in Honor of Donald P. Hansen.* Edited by Erica Ehrenberg. Winona Lake, Ind.: Eisenbrauns, 2002.

Baildam, John D. *Paradisal Love: Johann Gottfried Herder and the Song of Songs.* Journal for the Study of the Old Testament: Supplement Series 298. Sheffield, Eng.: Sheffield Academic Press, 1999.

Bailey, D. S. *Homosexuality and the Western Christian Tradition.* New York: Longmans, Green, 1955. Repr., Hamden, Conn.: Archon, 1975.

Bailey, Kenneth E. "Paul's Theological Foundation for Human Sexuality: 1 Cor 6:9–20 in the Light of Rhetorical Criticism." *Theological Review* 3, no. 1 (1980): 27–41.

Bailey, Randall C. *David in Love and War: The Pursuit of Power in 2 Samuel 10–12.* Sheffield, Eng.: JSOT Press, 1990.

———. "They're Nothing but Incestuous Bastards: The Polemical Use of Sex and Sexuality in Hebrew Canon Narratives." Pages 121–38 in *Reading from This Place.* Edited by Fernando F. Segovia and Mary Ann Tolbert. Minneapolis: Fortress, 1995.

Bailey, Wilma Ann. "Black and Jewish Women Consider Hagar." *Encounter* 63 (2002): 37–44.

———. "Hagar: A Model for an Anabaptist Feminist?" *Mennonite Quarterly Review* 68 (1994): 219–28.

Baker, David L. "Last But Not Least: The Tenth Commandment." *Horizons in Biblical Theology* 27 (2005): 3–24.

Baker, James R. *Women's Rights in Old Testament Times.* Salt Lake City: Signature, 1992.

Baker, John P. "Biblical Attitudes to Romantic Love." *Tyndale Bulletin* 35 (1984): 91–128.

Bakon, Shimon. "Deborah: Judge, Prophetess, Poet." *The Jewish Biblical Quarterly* 34 (2006): 110–18.

Bal, Mieke. "Between Altar and Wondering Rock: Toward a Feminist Philology ['Virginity']." Pages 211–31 in *Anti-covenant: Counter-reading Women's Lives in the Hebrew Bible.* Edited by M. Bal. Sheffield, Eng.: Almond, 1989.

———. *Death and Dissymmetry: The Politics of Coherence in the Book of Judges.* Chicago: University of Chicago Press, 1988.

———. *Lethal Love: Feminist Literary Readings of Biblical Love Stories.* Bloomington: Indiana University Press, 1987.

———. "Lots of Writing." *Semeia* 54 (1991): 77–102.

―――. *Murder and Difference: Gender, Genre, and Scholarship on Sisera's Death.* Translated by Matthew Gumpert. Bloomington: Indiana University Press, 1988.

―――, ed. *Anti-covenant: Counter-reading Women's Lives in the Hebrew Bible.* Bible and Literature Series 22. Journal for the Study of the Old Testament: Supplement Series 81. Sheffield, Eng.: Almond, 1989.

Balch, David L. *Let Wives Be Submissive: The Domestic Code in 1 Peter.* Chico, Calif.: Scholars Press, 1981.

―――, ed. *Homosexuality, Science, and the "Plain Sense" of Scripture.* Grand Rapids: Eerdmans, 2000.

Balch, David L., and Carolyn Osiek, eds. *Early Christian Families in Context: An Interdisciplinary Dialogue.* Grand Rapids: Eerdmans, 2003.

Baldwin, Joyce G. *Haggai, Zechariah, Malachi: An Introduction and Commentary.* Tyndale Old Testament Commentaries 24. Downers Grove, Ill.: InterVarsity, 1972.

Ball, Edward, ed. *In Search of True Wisdom: Essays in Old Testament Interpretation in Honour of Ronald E. Clements.* Journal for the Study of the Old Testament: Supplement Series 300. Sheffield, Eng.: Sheffield Academic Press, 1999.

Balorda, Aron. "The Jealousy of Phinehas in Numbers 25 as the Embodiment of the Essence of Numinal Marriage." M.A. thesis, Andrews University, 2002.

Balswick, Judith K., and Jack O. Balswick. *Authentic Human Sexuality: An Integrated Christian Approach.* Downers Grove, Ill.: InterVarsity, 1999.

Balz-Cochois, Helgard. "Gomer oder die Macht der Astarte: Versuch einer feministischen Interpretation von Hos 1–4." *Evangelische Theologie* 42 (1982): 37–65.

Bar-Efrat, Shimeon. *Narrative Art in the Bible.* Journal for the Study of the Old Testament: Supplement Series 70. Sheffield, Eng.: Almond, 1989.

Bar-Ilan, Meir. *Some Jewish Women in Antiquity.* Brown Judaic Studies 317. Williston, Vt.: Society of Biblical Literature, 1998.

Barger, Lilian Calles. *Eve's Revenge: Women and a Spirituality of the Body.* Grand Rapids: Brazos, 2003.

Barker, Margaret. *The Gate of Heaven: The History and Symbolism of the Temple in Jerusalem.* London: SPCK, 1991.

Barr, James. "One Man, or All Humanity?" Pages 3–21 in *Recycling Biblical Figures: Papers Read at a NOSTER Colloquium in Amsterdam, 12–13 May 1997.* Edited by Athalya Brenner and J. W. van Hentern. Leiden: Deo, 1999. Repr. as "Adam: Single Man, or All Humanity." Pages 3–12 in *Hesed ve-Emet: Studies in Honor of Ernest S. Frerichs.* Edited by Jodi Magness and Seymour Gitin. Atlanta: Scholars Press, 1998.

―――. *The Semantics of Biblical Language.* London: Oxford University Press, 1961.

Barrett, C. K. *The Pastoral Epistles in the New English Bible.* Oxford: Clarendon, 1963.

Barron, Bruce. "Putting Women in Their Place: 1 Timothy 2 and Evangelical Views of Women in Church Leadership." *Journal of the Evangelical Theological Society* 33 (1990): 451–59.

Barth, Karl. *Church Dogmatics*. Edited by G. W. Bromiley and T. F. Torrance. Translated by J. W. Edwards et al. 5 vols. in 13. Edinburgh: T&T Clark, 1956–1969. Vol. 3.

Bartholomew, Craig G., et al., eds. *Canon and Biblical Interpretation*. The Scripture and Hermeneutics Series 7. Grand Rapids: Zondervan, 2006.

Bartlett, David L. "Biblical Perspective on Homosexuality." *Foundations* 20 (1977): 133–47.

Barton, John. "Intertextuality and the 'Final Form' of the Text." Pages 33–37 in *Congress Volume: Oslo, 1998*. Edited by André Lemaire and Magne Sæbø. Vetus Testamentum Supplements 80. Leiden: E. J. Brill, 2000.

―――, ed. *The Biblical World*. London: Routledge, 2002.

Barton, Stephen C. *Life Together: Family, Sexuality, and Community in the New Testament and Today*. New York: T&T Clark, 2001.

Bartor, Asnat. "Prophet versus King—'Juridical Dialogue': A Juridical Analysis of Three Passages." *Beit Mikra* 47 (2002): 105–32.

Basser, Herbert W. *Studies in Exegesis: Christian Critiques of Jewish Law and Rabbinic Responses*. Leiden: E. J. Brill, 2000.

Bassett, Frederick W. "Noah's Nakedness and the Curse of Canaan: A Case of Incest?" *Vetus Testamentum* 21 (1971): 232–37.

Batto, Bernard F. "The Divine Sovereign: The Image of God in the Priestly Creation Account." Pages 143–86 in *David and Zion: Biblical Studies in Honor of J.J.M. Roberts*. Edited by Bernard Frank Batto, Kathryn L. Roberts and J. J. M. Roberts. Winona Lake, Ind.: Eisenbrauns, 2004.

―――. "The Institution of Marriage in Genesis 2 and in *Atrahasis*." *Catholic Biblical Quarterly* 62 (2000): 621–31.

―――. *Studies on Women at Mari*. Baltimore: Johns Hopkins University Press, 1974.

Bauckham, Richard. "The Book of Ruth and the Possibility of a Feminist Canonical Hermeneutic." *Biblical Interpretation* 5 (1997): 29–45.

―――. *Gospel Women: Studies of the Named Women in the Gospels*. Grand Rapids: Eerdmans, 2002.

―――. *Is the Bible Male? The Book of Ruth and Biblical Narrative*. Cambridge, Eng.: Grove, 1996.

Bauer, Angela. "Dressed to Be Killed: Jeremiah 4:29–31 as an Example for the Functions of Female Imagery in Jeremiah." Pages 293–305 in *Troubling Jeremiah*. Edited by A. R. Pete Diamond, Kathleen M. O'Connor, and Louis Stulman. Journal for the Study of the Old Testament: Supplement Series 260. Sheffield, Eng.: Sheffield Academic Press, 1999.

―――. *Gender in the Book of Jeremiah: A Feminist-Literary Reading*. Studies in Biblical Literature 5. New York: Peter Lang, 1999.

―――. "Jeremiah as Female Impersonator: Roles of Difference in Gender Perception and Gender Perceptivity." Pages 199–207 in *Escaping Eden: New Feminist Perspectives on the Bible*. Edited by Harold C. Washington, Susan Lochrie Graham, and Pamela Thimmes. Biblical Seminar 65. Sheffield, Eng.: Sheffield Academic Press, 1998.

Bauer, Walter. *A Greek-English Lexicon of the New Testament and Other Early Christian Literature.* Edited by F. W. Gingrich and F. W. Danker. Translated and adapted by W. F. Arndt and F. W. Gingrich. 3d ed. Chicago: University of Chicago Press, 2000.

Bauer-Kayatz, Christa. *Studien zu Proverbien 1–9.* Wissenschaftliche Monographien zum alten und neuen Testament 22. Neukirchen-Vluyn: Neukirchener Verlag, 1966.

Baumann, Gerlinde. "A Figure with Many Facets: The Literary and Theological Functions of Personified Wisdom in Proverbs 1–9." Pages 44–78 in *Wisdom and Psalms.* Edited by Athalya Brenner and Carol Fontaine. Feminist Companion to the Bible: Second Series 2. Sheffield, Eng.: Sheffield Academic Press, 1998.

———. *Love and Violence: Marriage as Metaphor for the Relationship between YHWH and Israel in the Prophetic Books.* Translated by Linda Maloney. Collegeville, Minn.: Liturgical, 2003.

Baumert, Norbert. *Woman and Man in Paul: Overcoming a Misunderstanding.* Collegeville, Minn.: Liturgical, 1996.

Baylis, Charles P. "Naomi in the Book of Ruth in Light of the Mosaic Covenant." *Bibliotheca Sacra* 161 (2004): 413–31.

Beach, Eleanor Ferris. "Transforming Goddess Iconography in Hebrew Narrative." Pages 239–63 in *Women and Goddess Traditions in Antiquity and Today.* Edited by Karen L. King. Minneapolis: Fortress, 1997.

Beal, Timothy K. *The Book of Hiding: Gender, Ethnicity, Annihilation, and Esther.* London: Routledge, 1997.

Beale, Gregory K. *The Temple and the Church's Mission: A Biblical Theology of the Dwelling Place of God.* New Studies in Biblical Theology 17. Downers Grove, Ill.: InterVarsity, 2004.

Beattie, D. R. G. "The Book of Ruth as Evidence for Israelite Legal Practice." *Vetus Testamentum* 24 (1974): 251–67.

———, trans. *The Targum of Ruth: Translated, with Introduction, Apparatus, and Notes.* The Aramaic Bible 19. Collegeville, Minn.: Liturgical, 1994.

Bechtel, Lyn M. "Boundary Issues in Genesis 19.1–38." Pages 22–40 in *Escaping Eden: New Feminist Perspectives on the Bible.* Edited by Harold C. Washington, Susan Lochrie Graham, and Pamela Thimmes. Biblical Seminar 65. Sheffield, Eng.: Sheffield Academic Press, 1998.

———. "A Feminist Reading of Genesis 19:1–11." Pages 108–28 in *Genesis.* Edited by Athalya Brenner. Feminist Companion to the Bible: Second Series 1. Sheffield, Eng.: Sheffield Academic Press, 1998.

———. "Rethinking the Interpretation of Genesis 2:4b–3:24." Pages 77–117 in *A Feminist Companion to Genesis.* Edited by Athalya Brenner. Feminist Companion to the Bible 2. Sheffield, Eng.: Sheffield Academic Press, 1993.

———. "What If Dinah Is Not Raped? (Genesis 34)," *Journal for the Study of the Old Testament* 62 (1994): 19–36.

Beck, James R., and Craig L. Blomberg, eds. *Two Views on Women in Ministry.* Grand Rapids: Zondervan, 2001.

Beckett, Michael. *Gospel in Esther.* Carlisle, Eng.: Paternoster, 2002.

Beckman, Gary M. "Goddess Worship—Ancient and Modern." Pages 11–23 in *"A Wise and Discerning Mind": Essays in Honor of Burke O. Long*. Edited by Saul M. Olyan and Robert C. Culley. Brown Judaic Studies 325. Providence: Brown Judaic Studies, 2000.

———. *Hittite Birth Rituals: An Introduction*. Sources from the Ancient Near East 1/4. Malibu, Calif.: Undena, 1978.

Beckmann, Joachim. "Die Ehescheidung in biblisch-theologischer Beleuchtung." Pages 121–32 in *Im Kampf für die Kirche des Evangeliums: Eine Auswahl von Reden und Aufsätzen aus drei Jahrzehnten*. Edited by Joachim Beckmann. Gütersloh: G. Mohn, 1961.

Beckwith, Francis J. *Politically Correct Death: Answering Arguments for Abortion Rights*. Grand Rapids: Baker, 1993.

Bedale, Stephen F. B. "The Meaning of κεφαλή in the Pauline Epistles." *Journal of Theological Studies* 5 (1954): 211–15.

Beek, Martinus A. "Rahab in the Light of Jewish Exegesis (Josh 2:1–24; 6:17, 22–23,25)." Pages 37–44 in *Von Kanaan bis Kerala: Festschrift für J. P. M. van der Ploeg*. Edited by W. Delsman. Alter Orient und Altes Testament 211. Kevelaer, Ger.: Butzon & Bercker, 1982.

Beinert, Wolfgang. "Dogmatische Überlegungen zum Thema Priestertum und Frau." *Theologische Quartalschrift* 173 (1993): 187–204.

Bekkenkamp, Jonneke. "Into Another Scene of Choices: The Theological Value of the Song of Songs." Pages 55–89 in *The Song of Songs*. Edited by Athalya Brenner and Carole R. Fontaine. Feminist Companion to the Bible: Second Series 6. Sheffield, Eng.: Sheffield Academic Press, 2000.

Bell, Robert D. "The Theology of the Book of Numbers." *Biblical Viewpoint* 37 (2003): 39–45.

Belleville, Linda L. *Women Leaders and the Church: Three Crucial Questions*. Grand Rapids: Baker, 2000.

Bellinger, W. H., Jr. "Enabling Silent Lips to Speak: Literary Criticism in the Service of Old Testament Interpretation." Pages 53–69 in *In Search of True Wisdom: Essays in Old Testament Interpretation in Honour Of Ronald E. Clements*. Edited by Edward Ball. Journal for the Study of the Old Testament: Supplement Series 300. Sheffield, Eng.: Sheffield Academic Press, 1999.

Bellis, Alice Ogden. "Feminist Biblical Scholarship." Pages 24–32 in *Women in Scripture: A Dictionary of Named and Unnamed Women in the Hebrew Bible, the Apocryphal/Deuterocanonical Books, and the New Testament*. Edited by Carol Meyers, Toni Craven, and Ross S. Kraemer. Boston: Houghton Mifflin, 2000.

———. *Helpmates, Harlots, and Heroes: Women's Stories in the Hebrew Bible*. Louisville: Westminster John Knox, 1994.

Bellis, Alice Ogden, and Terry L. Hufford. *Science, Scripture, and Homosexuality*. Cleveland: Pilgrim, 2002.

Bellis, Alice Ogden, and Joel S. Kaminsky. *Jews, Christians, and the Theology of the Hebrew Scriptures*. Atlanta: Society of Biblical Literature, 2000.

Ben-Barak, Zifrira. "The Status and Right of the *gĕbîrâ*." *Journal of Biblical Literature* 110 (1991): 23–34.

Benjamin, Don C. "Israel's God: Mother and Midwife." *Biblical Theology Bulletin* 19 (1989): 115–20.

Bennett, Harold V. *Injustice Made Legal: Deuteronomic Law and the Plight of Widows, Strangers, and Orphans in Ancient Israel.* Grand Rapids: Eerdmans, 2002.

Bennett, Robert J. "A Summary of the Biblical Teaching concerning Male/Female Roles." M.A. thesis, Cincinnati Christian Seminary, 1985.

Benton, John. *Gender Questions: Biblical Manhood and Womanhood in the Contemporary World.* Darlington, Eng.: Evangelical Press, 2000.

Berg, Sandra Beth. *The Book of Esther: Motifs, Themes, and Structure.* Missoula, Mont.: Scholars Press, 1979.

Bergant, Dianne. *The Song of Songs.* Edited by David W. Cotter, Jerome T. Walsh, and Chris Franke. Berit Olam: Studies in Hebrew Narrative and Poetry. Collegeville, Minn.: Liturgical, 2001.

———. *The Song of Songs: The Love Poetry of Scripture.* Spiritual Commentaries. Hyde Park, N.Y.: New City, 1998.

Berger, Paul Richard. "Zum Huren bereit bis hin zu einem Rundlaib Brot: Prov 6:26." *Zeitschrift für die alttestamentliche Wissenschaft* 99 (1987): 98–106.

Bergmeier, Roland. "Zur Septuagintaübersetzung von Gen 3:16." *Zeitschrift für die alttestamentliche Wissenschaft* 79 (1967): 77–79.

Berkouwer, G. C. *Man: The Image of God.* Grand Rapids: Eerdmans, 1962.

Berlin, Adele. "Characterization in Biblical Narrative: David's Wives." *Journal for the Study of the Old Testament* no. 23 (1982): 69–85.

———. *Esther: The Traditional Hebrew Text with the New JPS Translation.* JPS Bible Commentary. Philadelphia: Jewish Publication Society, 2001.

———. "Hannah and Her Prayers." *Scriptura* 87 (2004): 227–32.

———. *Poetics and Interpretation of Biblical Narrative.* Sheffield, Eng.: Almond, 1983. Repr., Winona Lake, Ind.: Eisenbrauns, 1994.

Berlinerblau, Jacques. "'Poor Bird, Not Knowing Which Way to Fly': Biblical Scholarship's Marginality, Secular Humanism, and the Laudable Occident." *Biblical Interpretation* 10 (2002): 267–304.

Berlyn, P. J. "The Great Ladies." *Jewish Bible Quarterly* 24 (1996): 26–35.

Bernard of Clairvaux. *On the Song of Songs.* Translated by Kilian Walsh and Irene M. Edmonds. 4 vols. Spencer, Mass.: Cistercian, 1971–1980.

Berquist, Jon L. *Controlling Corporeality: The Body and the Household in Ancient Israel.* New York: Rutgers University Press, 2002.

———. "Expectations and Repeated Climax in the Rahab Story." Paper presented at the annual meeting of the AAR/SBL. San Francisco, November 23, 1992.

———. *Reclaiming Her Story: The Witness of Women in the Old Testament.* St. Louis: Chalice, 1992.

Berry, Marian G. *The Prophetic Song of Songs.* Albia, Iowa: Prophetic Song of Songs, 1985.

Beuken, William A. M. "The Human Person in the Vision of Genesis 1–3: A Synthesis of Contemporary Insights." *Louvain Studies* 24 (1999): 6–9.

———. "No Wise King without a Wise Woman (I Kings III 16–28)." Pages 1–10 in *New Avenues in the Study of the Old Testament.* Edited by Adam S. van der Woude. Oudtestamentische Studiën 25. Leiden: E. J. Brill, 1989.

Beydon, France. "Violence sous silence: À propos d'une lecture féministe de Juges 19, par Ph. Trible." *Foi et Vie* 88 (1989): 81–87.

Biale, David. *Eros and the Jews: From Biblical Israel to Contemporary America.* New York: Basic, 1992.

———. "The God with Breasts: El Shaddai in the Bible." *History of Religions* 21 (1982): 240–56.

Biddle, Mark E. "The 'Endangered Ancestress' and Blessing for the Nations." *Journal of Biblical Literature* 109 (1990): 599–611.

Bigger, Stephen F. "The Family Laws of Leviticus 18 in Their Setting." *Journal of Biblical Literature* 98 (1979): 187–203.

Bilezikian, Gilbert G. *Beyond Sex Roles: What the Bible Says about a Woman's Place in Church and Family.* Grand Rapids: Baker, 1985.

———. *Community 101: Reclaiming the Local Church as Community of Oneness.* Grand Rapids: Zondervan, 1997.

———. "Hermeneutical Bungee-Jumping: Subordination in the Godhead." *Journal of the Evangelical Theological Society* 40 (1997): 57–68.

———. "Hierarchist and Egalitarian Inculturations." *Journal of the Evangelical Theological Society* 30 (1987): 421–26.

———. "Subordination in the Godhead: A Re-emerging Heresy." Transcription of lecture given at the Christians for Biblical Equality Conference. Wheaton, Ill., August 1993.

Bilezikian, Gilbert, et al. "Men, Women, and Biblical Equality." *Christianity Today* 34, no. 6 (1990): 36–37.

Bird, Phyllis A. "The Bible in Christian Ethical Deliberation concerning Homosexuality: Old Testament Contributions." Pages 142–76 in *Homosexuality, Science, and the "Plain Sense" of Scripture.* Edited by David L. Balch. Grand Rapids: Eerdmans, 2000.

———. "'Bone of My Bone and Flesh of My Flesh.'" *Theology Today* 50 (1994): 521–34.

———. "The End of the Male Cult Prostitute." Pages 37–80 in *Congress Volume: Cambridge, 1995.* Edited by J. A. Emerton. Vetus Testamentum Supplements 66. Leiden: E. J. Brill, 1997.

———. "Genesis 1–3 as a Source for a Contemporary Theology of Sexuality." *Ex auditu* 3 (1987): 31–44. Repr., pages 155–73 in *Missing Persons and Mistaken Identities: Women and Gender in Ancient Israel.* Overtures to Biblical Theology. Minneapolis: Fortress, 1997.

———. "The Harlot as Heroine: Narrative Art and Social Presupposition in Three Old Testament Texts." *Semeia* 46 (1989): 119–39. Repr., pages 197–218 in *Missing Persons and Mistaken Identities: Women and Gender in Ancient Israel.* Overtures to Biblical Theology. Minneapolis: Fortress, 1997.

————. "Images of Women in the Old Testament." Pages 41–88 in *Religion and Sexism: Images of Woman in the Jewish and Christian Traditions.* Edited by Rosemary Radford Ruether. New York: Simon & Schuster, 1974.

————. "Male and Female He Created Them: Gen 1:27b in the Context of the Priestly Account of Creation." *Harvard Theological Review* 74 (1981): 129–59.

————. *Missing Persons and Mistaken Identities: Women and Gender in Ancient Israel.* Overtures to Biblical Theology. Minneapolis: Fortress, 1997.

————. "The Place of Women in the Israelite Cultus." Pages 397–419 in *Ancient Israelite Religion: Essays in Honor of Frank Moore Cross.* Edited by Patrick D. Miller Jr., Paul D. Hanson, and S. Dean McBride. Philadelphia: Fortress, 1987.

————. "Sexual Differentiation and Divine Image in the Genesis Creation Texts." Pages 11–34 in *Image of God and Gender Models in Judaeo-Christian Tradition.* Edited by Kari Elizabeth Børresen. Oslo: Solum, 1991.

————. "To Play the Harlot: An Inquiry into an Old Testament Metaphor." Pages 75–94 in *Gender and Difference in Ancient Israel.* Edited by Peggy L. Day. Minneapolis: Fortress, 1989.

————. "Translating Sexist Language as a Theological and Cultural Problem." *Union Seminary Quarterly Review* 42 (1988): 89–95.

————. "Women in the Ancient Mediterranean World: Ancient Israel." *Biblical Research* 39 (1994): 31–79.

Bird, Phyllis A., ed. *Reading the Bible as Women: Perspectives from Africa, Asia, and Latin America.* Semeia 78. Williston, Vt.: Society of Biblical Literature, 1997.

Black, Fiona C. *The Artifice of Love: Grotesque Bodies and the Song of Songs.* New York: Continuum, 2006.

————. "Beauty or the Beast? The Grotesque Body in the Song of Songs." *Biblical Interpretation* 8 (2000): 302–23.

————. "Unlikely Bedfellows: Allegorical and Feminist Readings of the Song of Songs 7:1–8." Pages 104–29 in *The Song of Songs.* Edited by Athalya Brenner and Carole R. Fontaine. Feminist Companion to the Bible: Second Series 6. Sheffield, Eng.: Sheffield Academic Press, 2000.

————. "What Is My Beloved? On Erotic Reading and the Song of Songs." Pages 35–52 in *The Labour of Reading: Desire, Alienation, and Biblical Interpretation.* Edited by Fiona C. Black et al. Semeia Studies 36. Atlanta: Society of Biblical Literature, 1999.

Black, James. "Ruth in the Dark: Folktale, Law, and Creative Ambiguity in the Old Testament." *Literature and Theology* 5 (1991): 20–36.

Blackburn, Barry L. "The Identity of the 'Women' in 1 Tim. 3:11." Pages 302–19 in vol. 1 of *Essays on Women in Earliest Christianity.* Edited by Carroll D. Osburn. 2 vols. Joplin, Mo.: College Press, 1993.

Blankenhorn, David, Don S. Browning, and Mary Stewart Van Leeuwen, eds. *Does Christianity Teach Male Headship? The Equal-Regard Marriage and Its Critics.* Grand Rapids: Eerdmans, 2003.

Blaschke, Andreas. *Beschneidung: Zeugnisse der Bible und verwandter Texte.* Texte und Arbeiten zum neutestamentlicher Zeitalter 28. Tübingen: Francke, 1998.

Bledstein, Adrien Janis. "The Trials of Sarah." *Judaism* 30 (1981): 411–17.

———. "Was Eve Cursed? (or Did a Woman Write Genesis?)" *Bible Review* 9, no. 1 (1993): 42–45.

———. "Was *Habbiryâ* a Healing Ritual Performed by a Woman in King David's House?" *Biblical Research* 37 (1992): 15–31.

Blenkinsopp, Joseph. "The Household in Ancient Israel and Early Judaism." Pages 169–85 in *The Blackwell Companion to the Hebrew Bible.* Edited by Leo G. Perdue. Blackwell Companions to Religion 3. Malden, Mass.: Blackwell, 2001.

———. *Sexuality and the Christian Tradition.* Dayton, Ohio: Pflaum, 1969.

Bloch, Ariel, and Chana Bloch. *The Song of Songs: A New Translation with an Introduction and Commentary.* New York: Random House, 1995.

Block, Daniel I. "Deborah among the Judges: The Perspective of the Hebrew Historian." Pages 229–53 in *Faith, Tradition, and History: Old Testament Historiography in Its Near Eastern Context.* Edited by Alan R. Millard, James K. Hoffmeier, and David W. Baker. Winona Lake, Ind.: Eisenbrauns, 1994.

———. "Marriage and Family in Ancient Israel." Pages 33–102 in *Marriage and Family in the Biblical World.* Edited by Ken M. Campbell. Downers Grove, Ill.: InterVarsity, 2003.

———. "Unspeakable Crimes: The Abuse of Women in the Book of Judges." *Southern Baptist Journal of Theology* 2, no. 3 (Fall 1998): 46–55.

———. "Why Deborah's Different." *Bible Review* 17, no. 3 (2001): 34–40,49–52.

Bloesch, Donald G. *Is the Bible Sexist? Beyond Feminism and Patriarchalism.* Westchester, Ill.: Crossway, 1982. Repr., Eugene, Ore.: Wip & Stock, 2001.

Blomberg, Craig L. "Marriage, Divorce, Remarriage, and Celibacy: An Exegesis of Matthew 19:3–12." *Trinity Journal* 11 (1990): 161–96.

———. "Neither Hierarchicalist nor Egalitarian: Gender Roles in Paul." Pages 329–72 in *Two Views on Women in Ministry.* Edited by James R. Beck and Craig L. Blomberg. Grand Rapids: Zondervan, 2001.

Blum, Georg G. "Das Amt der Frau im Neuen Testament." *Novum Testamentum* 7 (1965): 142–61.

Blum, Ruth, and Erhard Blum. "Zippora und ihr *choten damim.*" Pages 41–54 in *Die hebräische Bibel und ihre zweifache Nachgeschichte: Festschrift für Rolf Rendtorff.* Edited by Erhard Blum, Christian Macholz, and Ekkehard Stegemann. Neukirchen-Vluyn: Neukirchener Verlag, 1990.

Blumenthal, David. "The Shulamite Is Not the Woman of Valor." Pages 216–31 in *Relating to the Text: Interdisciplinary and Form-Critical Insights on the Bible.* Edited by Timothy J. Sandoval and Carleen Mandolfo. Journal for the Study of the Old Testament: Supplement Series 384. New York: T&T Clark, 2003.

Boadt, Lawrence, ed. *The Song of Solomon: Love Poetry of the Spirit.* 1st St. Martin's Griffin ed. Classic Bible Books Series. New York: St. Martin's Griffin, 1999.

Boda, Mark J. "The Delight of Wisdom." *Themelios* 30 (2004): 4–11.

———. "Haggai: Master Rhetorician." *Tyndale Bulletin* 51 (2000): 295–304.

Boer, Roland. *Knockin' on Heaven's Door: The Bible and Popular Culture.* London: Routledge, 1999.

———. "The Second Coming: Repetition and Insatiable Desire in the Song of Songs." *Biblical Interpretation* 8 (2000): 276–301.

———. "Women First? On the Legacy of 'Primitive Communism.'" *Journal for the Study of the Old Testament* 30 (2005): 3–28.

Bolger, Eric. "The Compositional Role of the Eden Narrative in the Pentateuch." PhD diss., Trinity Evangelical Divinity School, 1993.

Boling, Robert G. *Judges: A New Translation with Introduction and Commentary.* Anchor Bible 6A. Garden City, N.Y.: Doubleday: 1975.

Boman, Thorleif. *Hebrew Thought Compared to Greek.* New York: W. W. Norton, 1960.

Bonora, Antonio. "La donna eccellente, la sapienza, il sapiente (Pr 31:10–31)." *Rivista biblica* 36 (1988): 137–64.

Bontrager, G. Edwin. *Divorce and the Faithful Church.* Scottdale, Pa.: Herald, 1978.

Boomsma, Clarence. *Male and Female, One in Christ: New Testament Teaching on Women in Office.* Grand Rapids: Baker, 1993.

Borgman, Paul. *Genesis: The Story We Haven't Heard.* Downers Grove, Ill.: InterVarsity, 2001.

Borowski, Oded. *Daily Life in Biblical Times.* Archaeology and Biblical Studies 5. Atlanta: Society of Biblical Literature, 2003.

Børresen, Kari Elisabeth. "God's Image, Man's Image? Patristic Interpretation of Gen 1,27 and I Cor 11,7." Pages 188–207 in *Image of God and Gender Models in Judaeo-Christian Tradition.* Edited by Kari Børresen. Oslo: Solum, 1991.

———. *Subordination and Equivalence: The Nature and Role of Woman in Augustine and Thomas Aquinas.* Translated by Charles H. Talbot. Washington, D.C.: University Press of America, 1981.

Bos, Johanna W. H. "Out of the Shadows: Genesis 38; Judges 4:17–22; Ruth 3." *Semeia* 42 (1988): 37–67.

Boshoff, Willem. "The Female Imagery in the Book of Hosea: Considering the Marriage Metaphor in Hosea 1–2 by Listening to Female Voices." *Old Testament Essays* 15 (2002): 23–41.

Bosman, Hendrik. "Adultery, Prophetic Tradition, and the Decalogue." Pages 267–74 in *The Ten Commandments: The Reciprocity of Faithfulness.* Edited by William P. Brown. Louisville, Ky.: Westminster John Knox, 2004.

Boswell, John. *Christianity, Social Tolerance, and Homosexuality: Gay People in Western Europe from the Beginning of the Christian Era to the Fourteenth Century.* Chicago: University of Chicago Press, 1980.

Bottéro, J., and H. Petschow. "Homosexualität." Pages 459–68 in vol. 4 of *Reallexikon der Assyriologie.* Edited by Erich Ebeling et al. Berlin: de Gruyter, 1928–.

Bouit, Jean-Jacques. "A Christian Consideration of Polygamy." D.Min. project report, Andrews University, 1981.

Bowen, Nancy R. "The Daughters of Your People: Female Prophets in Ezekiel 13:17–23." *Journal of Biblical Literature* 118 (1999): 417–33.

———. "The Quest for the Historical *gĕbîrâ*." *Catholic Biblical Quarterly* 63 (2001): 597–618.

———. "Women, Violence, and the Bible." Pages 186–99 in *Engaging the Bible in a Gendered World: An Introduction to Feminist Biblical Interpretation in Honor of Katharine Doob Sakenfeld*. Edited by Linda Day and Carolyn Pressler. Louisville: Westminster John Knox, 2006.

Bowman, Ann L. "Women in Ministry: An Exegetical Study of 1 Timothy 2:11–15." *Bibliotheca sacra* 149 (1992): 193–213.

Bowman, Craig D. "Prophetic Grief, Divine Grace: The Marriage of Hosea." *Restoration Quarterly* 43 (2001): 229–42.

Boyarin, Daniel. "Are There Any Jews in the 'The History of Sexuality'?" *Journal of the History of Sexuality* 5, no. 3 (1995): 333–55.

Boyd, Ian T. E. "Galatians 3.28c: Male and Female Related in Christ." M.A. thesis, Covenant Theological Seminary, 1994.

Braaten, Laurie J. "Parent-Child Imagery in Hosea (Marriage, Legitimacy, Adoption, Disownment)." PhD diss., Boston University, 1987.

Bradshaw, Timothy, ed. *The Way Forward? Christian Voices on Homosexuality and the Church*. London: Hodder & Stoughton, 1997.

Branch, Robin Gallaher. "Athaliah, a Treacherous Queen: A Careful Analysis of Her Story in 2 Kings 11 and 2 Chronicles 22:10—23:21." *In die Skriflig* 38 (2004): 537–59.

———. "Rizpah: An Activist in Nation-building. An Analysis of 2 Samuel 21:1–14." *Journal for Semitics* 14 (2005): 74–94.

———. "Rizpah: Catalyst in King-making. An Analysis of 2 Samuel 3:6–11." *Journal for Semitics* 14 (2005): 1–16.

Braulik, Georg. "Die Abfolge der Gesetze in Deuteronomium 12–26 und der Decalog." Pages 252–72 in *Das Deuteronomium: Entstehung, Gestalt, und Botschaft*. Edited by Norbert Lohfink. Leuven: Leuven University Press, 1983.

———. "Zur Abfolge der Gesetze in Deuteronomium 16,18–21,23: Weitere Beobachtungen." *Biblica* 69 (1988): 63–92.

———. "Das Volk, das Fest, die Liebe: Alttestamentliche Spiritualität." Pages 139–55 in *Spiritualität—mehr als ein Megatrend: Gedenksschrift für Kardinal DDr. Franz König*. Edited by Paul M. Zulehner. Ostfildern: Schwabenverlag, 2004.

Brawley, Robert L., ed. *Biblical Ethics and Homosexuality: Listening to Scripture*. Louisville: Westminster John Knox, 1996.

Breja, Alexandru. "A Biblical Approach to Transcultural Analysis." Paper presented at the annual meeting of the Evangelical Theological Society. Atlanta, November 21, 2003.

———. "The Meaning and Theological Implications of *chuqqim lo tobim* ('laws that were not good') in Ezekiel 20:25." Paper presented at the annual meeting of the Evangelical Theological Society. San Antonio, Tex., November 19, 2004.

Brenner, Athalya. "'Come Back, Come Back the Shulammite' (Song of Songs 7:1–10): A Parody of the *wasf* Genre." Pages 251–75 in *On Humour and the Comic in the Hebrew Bible*. Edited by Yehuda T. Radday and Athalya Brenner. Journal for the Study of the Old Testament: Supplement Series 92. Sheffield, Eng.: Almond, 1990.

———. "Female Social Behaviour: Two Descriptive Patterns within the 'Birth of the Hero' Paradigm." *Vetus Testamentum* 36 (1986): 257–73.

———. "Gazing Back at the Shulammite, Yet Again." *Biblical Interpretation* 11 (2003): 295–300.

———. "Gendering in/by the Hebrew Bible—Ten Years Later." *Old Testament Essays* 15 (2002): 42–51.

———. *The Intercourse of Knowledge: On Gendering Desire and "Sexuality" in the Hebrew Bible*. Biblical Interpretation Series 26. Leiden: E. J. Brill, 1997.

———. "Introduction." Pages 13–24 in *A Feminist Companion to Samuel and Kings*. Edited by Athalya Brenner. Feminist Companion to the Bible 5. Sheffield, Eng.: Sheffield Academic Press, 1994.

———. *The Israelite Woman: Social Role and Literary Type in Biblical Narrative*. Sheffield, Eng.: JSOT Press, 1985.

———. "On Incest." Pages 113–38 in *A Feminist Companion to Exodus to Deuteronomy*. Edited by Athalya Brenner. Feminist Companion to the Bible 6. Sheffield, Eng.: Sheffield Academic Press, 1994.

———. "On Prophetic Propoganda and the Politics of 'Love': The Case of Jeremiah." Pages 256–74 in *A Feminist Companion to the Latter Prophets*. Edited by Athalya Brenner. Feminist Companion to the Bible 8. Sheffield, Eng.: Sheffield Academic Press, 1995.

———. "Some Reflections on Violence against Women and the Image of the Hebrew God: The Prophetic Books Revisited." Pages 69–81 in *On the Cutting Edge—the Study of Women in Biblical Worlds: Essays in Honor of Elisabeth Schüssler Fiorenza*. Edited by Jane Schagerg, Alice Bach, and Esther Fuchs. New York: Continuum, 2003.

———. "A Triangle and a Rhombus in Narrative Structure: A Proposed Integrative Reading of Judges 4 and 5." Pages 98–109 in *A Feminist Companion to Judges*. Edited by Athalya Brenner. Feminist Companion to the Bible 4. Sheffield, Eng.: JSOT Press, 1993.

———, ed. *Are We Amused? Humour about Women in Biblical Worlds*. New York: Sheffield Academic Press, 2003.

———, ed. *Exodus to Deuteronomy*. Feminist Companion to the Bible. Second Series 5. Sheffield, Eng.: Sheffield Academic Press, 2000.

———, ed. *A Feminist Companion to Esther, Judith, and Susanna*. Feminist Companion to the Bible 7. Sheffield, Eng.: Sheffield Academic Press, 1995.

———, ed. *A Feminist Companion to Exodus to Deuteronomy*. Feminist Companion to the Bible 6. Sheffield, Eng.: Sheffield Academic Press, 1994.

———, ed. *A Feminist Companion to Genesis*. Feminist Companion to the Bible 2. Sheffield, Eng.: Sheffield Academic Press, 1993.

————, ed. *A Feminist Companion to the Hebrew Bible in the New Testament.* Feminist Companion to the Bible 10. Sheffield, Eng.: Sheffield Academic Press, 1996.

————, ed. *A Feminist Companion to Judges.* Feminist Companion to the Bible 4. Sheffield, Eng.: Sheffield Academic Press, 1993.

————, ed. *A Feminist Companion to the Latter Prophets.* Feminist Companion to the Bible 8. Sheffield, Eng.: Sheffield Academic Press, 1995.

————, ed. *A Feminist Companion to Ruth.* Feminist Companion to the Bible 3. Sheffield, Eng.: Sheffield Academic Press, 1993.

————, ed. *A Feminist Companion to the Song of Songs.* Feminist Companion to the Bible 1. Sheffield, Eng.: Sheffield Academic Press, 1993.

————, ed. *A Feminist Companion to Wisdom Literature.* Feminist Companion to the Bible 9. Sheffield, Eng.: Sheffield Academic Press, 1995.

————, ed. *Genesis.* Feminist Companion to the Bible: Second Series 1. Sheffield, Eng.: Sheffield Academic Press, 1998.

————, ed. *Judges.* Feminist Companion to the Bible: Second Series 4. Sheffield, Eng.: Sheffield Academic Press, 1999.

————, ed. *Prophets and Daniel.* Feminist Companion to the Bible: Second Series 8. Sheffield, Eng.: Sheffield Academic Press, 2001.

————, ed. *Ruth and Esther.* Feminist Companion to the Bible: Second Series 3. Sheffield, Eng.: Sheffield Academic Press, 1999.

————, ed. *Samuel and Kings.* Feminist Companion to the Bible: Second Series 7. Sheffield, Eng.: Sheffield Academic Press, 2000.

Brenner, Athalya, and Carole R. Fontaine, eds. *A Feminist Companion to Reading the Bible: Approaches, Methods, and Strategies.* Sheffield, Eng.: Sheffield Academic Press, 1997.

————, eds. *Song of Songs.* Feminist Companion to the Bible: Second Series 6. Sheffield, Eng.: Sheffield Academic Press, 2000.

————, eds. *Wisdom and Psalms.* Feminist Companion to the Bible: Second Series 2. Sheffield, Eng.: Sheffield Academic Press, 1998.

Brett, Mark G. "The Future of Old Testament Theology." Pages 465–88 in *Congress Volume: Oslo, 1998.* Edited by André Lemaire and Magne Sæbø. Vetus Testamentum Supplements 80. Leiden: E. J. Brill, 2000.

————. *Genesis: Procreation and the Politics of Identity.* Old Testament Readings. New York: Routledge, 2000.

Brettler, Marc Zvi. "Women and Psalms: Toward an Understanding of the Role of Women's Prayer in the Israelite Cult." Pages 25–56 in *Gender and Law in the Hebrew Bible and the Ancient Near East.* Edited by Victor H. Matthers, Bernard M. Levinson, and Tikva Frymer-Kensky. Journal for the Study of the Old Testament: Supplement Series 262. Sheffield, Eng.: Sheffield Academic Press, 1998.

Brichto, Herbert Chanan. "The Case of the SŌṬĀ and a Reconsideration of Biblical 'Law.'" *Hebrew Union College Annual* 46 (1975): 55–70.

Bridges, Linda McKinnish. "Silencing the Corinthian Men, Not the Women (An Exegesis of 1 Corinthians 14:34–36)." Pages 40–50 in *The New Has Come:*

Emerging Roles among Southern Baptist Women. Edited by Anne Thomas Neil and Virginia Garrett Neely. Washington, D.C.: Southern Baptist Alliance, 1989.

Briggs, Richard S. "The Implied Author and the Creation of the World: A Test Case in Reader-Response Criticism." *Expository Times* 113 (2002): 264–70.

Bristow, John Temple. "St. Paul's Radical Model for Christian Marriage." *Impact* 20 (1988): 28–40.

———. *What Paul Really Said about Women.* San Francisco: Harper & Row, 1988.

———. *What the Bible Really Says about Love, Marriage, and Family.* St. Louis: Chalice, 1994.

Bromiley, Geoffrey William. *God and Marriage.* Grand Rapids: Eerdmans, 1980.

Bronner, Leila Leah. "Esther Revisited: An Aggadic Approach." Pages 176–97 in *A Feminist Companion to Esther, Judith, and Susanna.* Edited by Athalya Brenner. Feminist Companion to the Bible 7. Sheffield, Eng.: Sheffield Academic Press, 1995.

———. "Reclaiming Esther: From Sex Object to Sage." *Jewish Biblical Quarterly* 26, no. 1 (1998): 3–10.

———. *Stories of Biblical Mothers: Maternal Power in the Hebrew Bible.* Dallas: University Press of America, 2004.

Bronznick, Norman M. "More on *hlk'l.*" *Vetus Testamentum* 35 (1985): 98–99.

Brooke, George J., and Florentino García Martínez, eds. *New Qumran Texts and Studies: Proceedings of the First Meeting of the International Organization for Qumran Studies, Paris, 1992.* Studies on the Texts of the Desert of Judah 15. Leiden: E. J. Brill, 1994.

Brooks, David L. "The Ideological Relationship between Old Testament Law and the Book of Proverbs." PhD diss., Dallas Theological Seminary, 2000.

Brooten, Bernadette J. "Junia . . . Outstanding among the Apostles." Pages 141–44 in *Women Priests: A Catholic Commentary on the Vatican Declaration.* Edited by Leonard Swidler and Arlene Swidler. New York: Paulist, 1977.

———. *Love between Women: Early Christian Responses to Female Homoeroticism.* Chicago Series on Sexuality, History, and Society. Chicago: University of Chicago Press, 1996.

———. "Paul's Views on the Nature of Women and Female Homoeroticism." Pages 61–87 in *Immaculate and Powerful: The Female in Sacred Image and Social Reality.* Edited by Clarissa W. Atkinson, Constance H. Buchanan, and Margaret R. Miles. Boston: Beacon, 1985.

———. "Women and the Churches in Early Christianity." *Ecumenical Trends* 14, no. 4 (1985): 51–54.

———. *Women Leaders in the Ancient Synagogue: Inscriptional Evidence and Background Issues.* Brown Judaic Studies 36. Williston, Vt.: Society of Biblical Literature, 1982.

Brown, Ann. *Apologies to Women: Christian Images of the Female Sex.* Downers Grove, Ill.: InterVarsity, 1991.

Brown, Cheryl Anne. *No Longer Be Silent: First Century Jewish Portraits of Biblical Women.* Louisville: Westminster John Knox, 1992.

Brown, Harold O. J. *Death before Birth*. Nashville: Nelson, 1977.

Brown, Judy L. *Women Ministers according to Scripture*. Minneapolis: Christians for Biblical Equality, 1996.

Brown, W. Kennedy. *Gunethics; or, The Ethical Status of Woman*. New York: Funk & Wagnalls, 1887.

Brown, William P. "*Creatio corporis* and the Rhetoric of Defense in Job 10 and Psalm 139." Pages 107–24 in *God Who Creates: Essays in Honor of W. Sibley Towner*. Edited by William P. Brown and S. Dean McBride Jr. Grand Rapids: Eerdmans, 2000.

———. *Structure, Role, and Ideology in the Hebrew and Greek Texts of Genesis 1:1–2:3*. Atlanta: Scholars Press, 1993.

Brown, William P., and S. Dean McBride Jr., eds. *God Who Creates: Essays in Honor of W. Sibley Towner*. Grand Rapids: Eerdmans, 2000.

Bruce, Michael, and G. E. Duffield, eds. *Why Not? Priesthood and the Ministry of Women—A Theological Study*. Appleford, Eng.: Marcham Manor, 1972.

Brueggemann, Walter. "I Samuel 1: A Sense of a Beginning." *Zeitschrift für die alttestamentliche Wissenschaft* 102 (1990): 33–48.

———. *First and Second Samuel*. Interpretation: A Bible Commentary for Teaching and Preaching. Louisville: Westminster John Knox, 1990.

———. *Genesis*. Interpretation: A Bible Commentary for Preaching and Teaching 1. Atlanta: John Knox, 1982.

———. "Of the Same Flesh and Bone (Gen 2:23*a*)." *Catholic Biblical Quarterly* 32 (1970): 532–42.

Brunet, Gilbert. "L'hébreu kèlèb." *Vetus Testamentum* 35 (1985): 485–88.

Brunner, Emil. *Man in Revolt*. Philadelphia: Westminster, 1947.

Bruno, Arvid. *Das Hohe Lied, das Buch Hiob*. Stockholm: Almquist & Wiksell, 1956.

Bryan, Cyril P. *Ancient Egyptian Medicine: The Papyrus Ebers*. Chicago: Ares, 1974. Repr. of *The Papyrus Ebers*. London: G. Bles, 1930.

Bucher, Christina. "The Origin and Meaning of 'ZNH' Terminology in the Book of Hosea." PhD diss., Claremont Graduate University, 1988.

Buckley, Timothy J. *What Binds Marriage? Roman Catholic Theology in Practice*. New York: Continuum, 2002.

Budde, Karl. "Bemerkungen zum Bundesbuch." *Zeitschrift für die alttestamentliche Wissenschaft* 11 (1891): 99–114.

———. "Das Hohelied erklärt." Pages ix–48 in *Die fünf Megillot*. Edited by Karl Budde, Alfred Bertholet, and D. G. Wildeboer. Freiburg im Breisgau: Mohr, 1898.

———. "Was ist das Hohelied?" *Preussische Jahrbücher* 78 (1894): 92–117.

Bühlmann, Walter. *Das Hohelied*. Stuttgart: Katholisches Bibelwerk, 1997.

Bullock, C. Hassell. *An Introduction to the Old Testament Poetic Books*. Rev. and expanded ed. Chicago: Moody, 1988.

Bullough, Vern L., with Bonnie Bullough. *The Subordinate Sex*. Urbana: University of Illinois Press, 1973.

Bultmann, Christoph. "Luther on Gender Relations—Just One Reading of Genesis?" *Currents in Theology and Mission* 29 (2002): 424–28.

Burke, H. Dale. *Different by Design: God's Master Plan for Harmony between Men and Women in Marriage.* Chicago: Moody, 2000.

Burke, J. Ashleigh. *The X-Rated Book: Sex and Obscenity in the Bible.* Houston: J.A.B., 1983.

Burkhardt, Helmut. "Ehe und Ehescheidung in christlicher Sicht." *Theologische Beiträge* 26 (1995): 35–49.

Burnett, Stephen G. "Exegetical Notes: Hosea 9:10–17." *Trinity Journal* 6 (1985): 211–14.

Burns, Camilla. "Human Love: The Silent Voice of God." *The Bible Today* 36 (1998): 159–63.

Burns, John Barclay. "Proverbs 7,6–27: Vignettes from the Cycle of Astarte and Adonis." *Scandinavian Journal of the Old Testament* 9 (1995): 20–36.

Burns, Rita J. *Has the Lord Indeed Spoken Only through Moses? A Study of the Biblical Portrait of Miriam.* Society of Biblical Literature Dissertation Series 84. Atlanta: Scholars Press, 1987.

Burrows, Millar. "The Ancient Oriental Background of Hebrew Levirate Marriage." *Bulletin of the American Schools of Oriental Research* 77 (1940): 2–15.

———. "Levirate Marriage in Israel." *Journal of Biblical Literature* 59 (1940): 23–33.

Burrus, Virginia, and Stephen D. Moore. "Unsafe Sex: Feminism, Pornography, and the Song of Songs." *Biblical Interpretation* 11 (2003): 24–52.

Busenitz, Irvin A. "Woman's Desire for Man: Genesis 3:16 Reconsidered." *Grace Theological Journal* 7 (1986): 203–12.

Bush, George. *Notes, Critical and Practical, on the Book of Genesis.* 26th ed. New York: Ivision, Phinney, 1859. Repr., Minneapolis: James & Klock, 1976.

Bushnell, Katherine C. *God's Word to Women.* London: Women's Correspondence Bible Class, 1912. Repr., Mossville, Ill.: God's Word to Women, 1990.

Büsing, Gerhard. "Benennung in Gen 1–3—ein *Herrenrecht*?" *Biblische Notizen* 73 (1994): 42–49.

Buswell, Sara. *The Challenge of Old Testament Women.* 2 vols. Grand Rapids: Baker, 1987. Vol. 1.

Butting, Klara. "Esther: A New Interpretation of the Joseph Story in the Fight against Anti-Semitism and Sexism." Pages 239–48 in *Ruth and Esther.* Edited by Athalya Brenner. Feminist Companion to the Bible: Second Series 3. Sheffield, Eng.: Sheffield Academic Press, 1999.

———. "Go Your Way: Women Rewrite the Scriptures [Song of Songs 2:8–14]." Pages 142–51 in *The Song of Songs.* Edited by Athalya Brenner and Carole R. Fontaine. Feminist Companion to the Bible: Second Series 6. Sheffield, Eng.: Sheffield Academic Press, 2000.

———. "'Die Töchter Judas frohlocken' (Ps 48,12): Frauen beten die Psalmen." *Bibel und Kirche* 56 (2001): 35–39.

Buzy, D. *Le Cantique des cantiques.* Paris: Létouzey & Ané, 1946.

Byrne, Brendan. *Paul and the Christian Woman.* Collegeville, Minn.: Liturgical, 1988.

Cahill, Lisa Sowle. *Between the Sexes: Foundations for a Christian Ethics of Sexuality.* Philadelphia: Fortress, 1985.

Cainion, Ivory. "An Analogy of the Song of Songs and Genesis Chapters Two and Three." *Scandinavian Journal of the Old Testament* 14, no. 2 (2000): 219–59.

Caird, George B. "Paul and Women's Liberty." *Bulletin of John Rylands University Library of Manchester* 54 (1972): 268–81.

Callaway, Mary. *Sing, O Barren One: A Study in Comparative Midrash.* Society of Biblical Literature Dissertation Series 91. Atlanta: Scholars Press, 1986.

Callicott, J. Baird. "Genesis and John Muir." Pages 107–40 in *Covenant for a New Creation: Ethics, Religion, and Public Policy.* Edited by Carol S. Robb and Carl J. Casebolt. Maryknoll, N.Y.: Orbis, 1991.

Calvin, John. *Commentaries on the Four Last Books of Moses Arranged in the Form of a Harmony.* Translated by Charles William Bingham. 4 vols. Edinburgh: Calvin Translation Society, 1852–1855. Repr., 4 vols. in 2. Grand Rapids: Baker, 1989.

———. *Commentary on Genesis.* Grand Rapids.: Eerdmans, n.d.

Cambier, Jules. "Le grand mystère concernant le Christ et son église: Ephésiens 5:22–33." *Biblica* 47 (1966): 43–90, 223–42.

Camp, Claudia V. "1 and 2 Kings." Pages 96–109 in *The Women's Bible Commentary.* Edited by Carol A. Newsom and Sharon H. Ringe. Louisville: Westminster John Knox, 1992.

———. "The Female Sage in Ancient Israel and in the Biblical Wisdom Literature." Pages 185–204 in *The Sage in Israel and the Ancient Near East.* Edited by John G. Gammie and Leo G. Perdue. Winona Lake, Ind.: Eisenbrauns, 1990.

———. "Female Voice, Written Word: Women and Authority in Hebrew Scripture." Pages 97–113 in *Embodied Love: Sensuality and Relationship as Feminist Values.* Edited by Paula M. Cooey, Sharon A. Farmer, and Mary Ellen Ross. San Francisco: Harper & Row, 1987.

———. "The Three Faces of Esther: Traditional Woman, Royal Diplomat, Authenticator of Tradition." *Academy: Journal of Lutherans in Professions* 38 (1982): 20–25.

———. "What's So Strange about the Strange Woman?" Pages 17–31 in *The Bible and the Politics of Exegesis: Essays in Honor of Norman K. Gottwald.* Edited by David Jobling, Peggy L. Day, and Gerald T. Sheppard. Cleveland: Pilgrim, 1991.

———. *Wisdom and the Feminine in the Book of Proverbs.* Bible and Literature Series 11. Decatur, Ga.: Almond, 1985.

———. "Wise and Strange: An Interpretation of the Female Imagery in Proverbs in Light of Trickster Mythology." *Semeia* 42 (1988): 14–36.

———. *Wise, Strange, and Holy: The Strange Woman and the Making of the Bible.* Journal for the Study of the Old Testament: Supplement Series 320. Sheffield, Eng.: Sheffield Academic Press, 2000.

————. "The Wise Women of 2 Samuel: A Role Model for Women in Early Israel?" *Catholic Biblical Quarterly* 43 (1981): 14–29.

————. "Woman Wisdom and the Strange Woman: Where Is Power to Be Found?" Pages 85–112 in *Reading Bibles, Writing Bodies: Identity and the Book.* Edited by Timothy K. Beal and David M. Gunn. London: Routledge, 1997.

————. "Woman Wisdom as Root Metaphor: A Theological Consideration." Pages 45–76 in *The Listening Heart: Essays in Wisdom and the Psalms in Honor of Roland E. Murphy, O. Carm.* Edited by Kenneth G. Hoglund et al. Journal for the Study of the Old Testament: Supplement Series 58. Sheffield, Eng.: Sheffield Academic Press, 1987.

Campbell, Antony F. "Women Storytellers in Ancient Israel." *Australian Biblical Review* 48 (2000): 72–73.

Campbell, Iain D. "The Song of David's Son: Interpreting the Song of Solomon in the Light of the Davidic Covenant." *Westminster Theological Journal* 62 (2000): 17–32.

Campbell, K. M. "Rahab's Covenant: A Short Note on Joshua 2:9–21." *Vetus Testamentum* 22 (1972): 243–44.

Cañellas, Gabriel. "La mujer: La época patriarcal." *Biblia y fe* 78 (2000): 356–79.

Cantarella, Eva. *Pandora's Daughters: The Role and Status of Women in Greek and Roman Antiquity.* Translated by Maureen B. Fant. Baltimore: Johns Hopkins University Press, 1981.

Caplice, Richard I. *The Akkadian Namburbi Texts: An Introduction.* Sources from the Ancient Near East 1/1. Los Angeles: Undena, 1974.

Caquot, Andrâe, and Maurice Sznycer. *Ugaritic Religion.* Leiden: E. J. Brill, 1980.

Carey, George. "Women and Authority in the Scriptures." Pages 44–55 in *Feminine in the Church.* Edited by Monica Furlong. London: SPCK, 1984.

Carlson, Richard Paul. "New Testament Perspectives on Human Sexuality." *Lutheran Theological Seminary Bulletin* 73 (1993): 16–33.

Carmichael, Calum M. "A Ceremonial Crux: Removing a Man's Sandal as a Female Gesture of Contempt." *Journal of Biblical Literature* 96 (1977): 321–36.

————. "Forbidden Mixtures." *Vetus Testamentum* 32 (1982): 394–415.

————. "Law and Narrative in the Pentateuch." Pages 321–34 in *The Blackwell Companion to the Hebrew Bible.* Edited by Leo G. Perdue. Blackwell Companions to Religion 3. Malden, Mass.: Blackwell, 2001.

————. *Law, Legend, and Incest in the Bible: Leviticus 18–20.* Ithaca, N.Y.: Cornell University Press, 1997.

————. *The Laws of Deuteronomy.* Ithaca, N.Y.: Cornell University Press, 1974.

————. "'Treading' in the Book of Ruth." *Zeitschrift für die alttestamentliche Wissenschaft* 92 (1980): 248–66.

————. *Women, Law, and the Genesis Traditions.* Edinburgh: Edinburgh University Press, 1979.

Carmody, Denise Lardner. *Biblical Woman: Contemporary Reflections on Scriptural Texts.* New York: Crossroad, 1988.

————. *Feminism and Christianity: A Two-Way Reflection.* Nashville: Abingdon, 1982.

Carpenter, Holly M. Blackwelder. "A Comprehensive Narrative Analysis of the Book of Ruth." M.A. thesis, Andrews University, 2004.

Carr, Anne E., and Elisabeth Schüssler Fiorenza, eds. *Motherhood: Experience, Institution, Theology.* Edinburgh: T&T Clark, 1989.

Carr, David M. *The Erotic Word: Sexuality, Spirituality, and the Bible.* New York: Oxford University Press, 2003.

————. "Gender and the Shaping of Desire in the Song of Songs and Its Interpretations." *Journal of Biblical Literature* 119 (2000): 233–48.

————. "Passion for God: A Center in Biblical Theology." *Horizons in Biblical Theology* 23 (2001): 1–24.

————. "Rethinking Sex and Spirituality: The Song of Songs and Its Readings." *Soundings* 81 [1998]: 413–35.

Carr, G. Lloyd. "The Love Poetry Genre in the Old Testament and the Ancient Near East: Another Look at Inspiration." *Journal of the Evangelical Theological Society* 25 (1982): 489–98.

————. *The Song of Solomon: An Introduction and Commentary.* Tyndale Old Testament Commentaries 17. Downers Grove, Ill.: InterVarsity, 1984.

————. "Song of Songs." Pages 281–95 in *A Complete Literary Guide to the Bible.* Edited by Leland Ryken and Tremper Longman III. Grand Rapids: Zondervan, 1993.

Carroll, Robert P., Alastair G. Hunter, and Philip R. Davies, eds. *Sense and Sensitivity: Essays on Reading the Bible in Memory of Robert Carroll.* Journal for the Study of the Old Testament: Supplement Series 348. New York: Sheffield Academic Press, 2002.

Carson, Donald A. "Silent in the Churches: On the Role of Women in 1 Corinthians 14:33b–36." Pages 140–53, 487–90 in *Recovering Biblical Manhood and Womanhood: A Response to Evangelical Feminism.* Edited by John Piper and Wayne A. Grudem. Wheaton, Ill.: Crossway, 1991.

Caspi, Mishael Maswari. "The Story of the Rape of Dinah: The Narrator and the Reader." *Hebrew Studies* 26, no. 1 (1985): 25–45.

Caspi, Mishael Maswari, and Rachel S. Havrelock. *Women on the Biblical Road: Ruth, Naomi, and the Female Journey.* Lanham, Md.: University Press of America, 1996.

Cassin, E. M. *L'adoption à Nuzi.* Paris: Adrien-Maisonneuve, 1938.

Cassuto, Umberto. *Biblical and Oriental Studies.* Translated by Israel Abrahams. 2 vols. Jerusalem: Magnes, 1973.

————. *A Commentary on the Book of Exodus.* Translated by Israel Abrahams. Jerusalem: Magnes, 1967.

————. *A Commentary on the Book of Genesis.* Translated by Israel Abrahams. 2 vols. Jerusalem: Magnes, 1961–1964.

————. *The Documentary Hypothesis.* Jerusalem: Magnes, 1961.

Cathcart, Kevin J., Michael Maher, and Martin McNamara, eds. *Targumic and Cognate Studies: Essays in Honour of Martin McNamara.* Journal for the

Study of the Old Testament: Supplement Series 230. Sheffield, Eng.: Sheffield Academic Press, 1996.

Cerling, Charles E. "Abortion and Contraception in Scripture." *Christian Scholar's Review* 2 (1971): 42–58.

———. "Annotated Bibliography of the New Testament Teaching about Women." *Journal of the Evangelical Theological Society* 16 (1973): 47–53.

Cervin, Richard S. "Does *kephale* mean 'Source' or 'Authority over' in Greek Literature? A Rebuttal." *Trinity Journal* 10 (1989): 85–112.

Chapman, Kathryn. "Hosea 11:1–4—Images of a Loving Parent." *Review and Expositor* 90 (1993): 263–68.

Charles, R. H. *The Teaching of the New Testament on Divorce.* London: Williams & Norgate, 1921.

Charry, Ellen T. "Female Sexuality as an Image of Empowerment: Two Models." *Saint Luke's Journal of Theology* 30 (1987): 201–18.

Chave, Peter. "Towards a Not Too Rosy Picture of the Song of Songs." *Feminist Theology* 18 (1998): 41–53.

Chesnutt, Randall D. "Jewish Women in the Greco-Roman Era." Pages 93–130 in vol. 1 of *Essays on Women in Earliest Christianity.* Edited by Carroll D. Osburn. 2 vols. Joplin, Mo.: College Press, 1993.

Childs, Brevard S. *Biblical Theology in Crisis.* Philadelphia: Fortress, 1970.

———. *Biblical Theology of the Old and New Testaments.* Minneapolis: Fortress, 1992.

———. *The Book of Exodus: A Critical, Theological Commentary.* Philadelphia: Westminster, 1974.

———. *Introduction to the Old Testament as Scripture.* Philadelphia: Fortress, 1979.

———. *Old Testament Theology in a Canonical Context.* Philadelphia: Fortress, 1985.

Chirichigno, Gregory C. "Debt Slavery in the Ancient Near East and Israel: An Examination of the Biblical Manumission Laws in Exod 21:6, 7–11; Deut 15:12–18; Lev 25:39–54." PhD diss., Council for National Academic Awards, 1989.

Chisholm, Robert B., Jr. " 'Drink Water from Your Own Cistern': A Literary Study of Proverbs 5:15–23." *Bibliotheca sacra* 157 (2000): 397–409.

Chitando, Ezra. " 'The Good Wife': A Phenomenological Re-reading of Proverbs 31:10–31 in the Context of HIV/AIDS in Zimbabwe." *Scriptura* 86 (2004): 151–59.

Chittister, Joan. *Job's Daughters: Women and Power.* New York: Paulist, 1990.

———. *The Story of Ruth: Twelve Moments in Every Woman's Life.* Grand Rapids: Eerdmans, 2000.

Choksy, Jamsheed K. *Evil, Good, and Gender: Facets of the Feminine in Zoroastrian Religious History.* Toronto Studies in Religion 28. New York: Peter Lang, 2002.

Christ, Carol P. *Rebirth of the Goddess: Finding Meaning in Feminist Spirituality.* Reading, Mass.: Addison-Wesley, 1997.

———. *She Who Changes: Re-imagining the Divine in the World.* New York: Palgrave Macmillan, 2003.

Christensen, Duane L. "Huldah and the Men of Anathoth: Women in Leadership in the Deuteronomic History." Pages 399–404 in the *SBL Seminar Papers, 1984.* Society of Biblical Literature Seminar Papers 23. Atlanta: Scholars Press, 1984.

Christian, Ed. "Women, Teaching, Authority, Silence: 1 Timothy 2:8–15 Explained by 1 Peter 3:1–6." *Journal of the Adventist Theological Society* 10, nos. 1–2 (1999): 285–90.

Claassens, L. Juliana M. "Rupturing God-Language: The Metaphor of God as Midwife in Psalm 22." Pages 166–75 in *Engaging the Bible in a Gendered World: An Introduction to Feminist Biblical Interpretation in Honor of Katharine Doob Sakenfeld.* Edited by Linda Day and Carolyn Pressler. Louisville: Westminster John Knox, 2006.

Clack, Beverley. *Sex and Death: A Reappraisal of Human Mortality.* Malden, Mass.: Polity, 2002.

Clanton, Jann Aldredge. *In Whose Image? God and Gender.* New York: Crossroad, 1990.

Clark, David J. "Sex-Related Imagery in the Prophets." *The Bible Translator* 33 (1982): 409–13.

Clark, Elizabeth A. *Women in the Early Church.* Message of the Fathers of the Church 13. Collegeville, Minn.: Liturgical, 1983.

Clark, Stephen B. *Man and Woman in Christ: An Examination of the Roles of Men and Women in the Light of Scripture and the Social Sciences.* Ann Arbor, Mich.: Servant, 1980.

Clifford, Anne M. *Introducing Feminist Theology.* Maryknoll, N.Y.: Orbis, 2001.

Clinebell, Howard J., Jr., and Charlotte H. *The Intimate Marriage.* New York: Harper & Row, 1970.

Clines, David J. A. "אדם, the Hebrew for 'Human, Humanity': A Response to James Barr." *Vetus Testamentum* 53 (2003): 297–310.

———. "He-Prophets: Masculinity as a Problem for the Hebrew Prophets and Their Interpreters." Pages 310–28 in *Sense and Sensitivity: Essays on Reading the Bible in Memory of Robert Carroll.* Edited by Alastair G. Hunter and Phillip R. Davies. Journal for the Study of the Old Testament: Supplement Series 348. Sheffield, Eng.: Sheffield Academic Press, 2002.

———. "The Image of God in Man." *Tyndale Bulletin* 19 (1968): 53–103.

———. "The Significance of the 'Sons of God' Episode (Genesis 6:1–4) in the Context of the 'Primeval History' (Genesis 1–11)." *Journal for the Study of the Old Testament* no. 13 (1979): 33–46.

———. *The Theme of the Pentateuch.* Journal for the Study of the Old Testament: Supplement Series 10. Sheffield, Eng.: University of Sheffield Press, 1978.

———. "What Does Eve Do to Help? And Other Irredeemably Androcentric Orientations in Genesis 1–3." Pages 25–48 in *What Does Eve Do to Help? And Other Readerly Questions to the Old Testament.* Edited by David J. A. Clines.

Journal for the Study of the Old Testament: Supplement Series 94. Sheffield, Eng.: JSOT Press, 1990.

———. "Why Is There a Song of Songs and What Does It Do to You If You Read It?" *Jian Dao* 1 (1994): 3–27.

Clines, David J. A., and Tamara C. Eskenazi, eds. *Telling Queen Michal's Story: An Experiment in Comparative Interpretation.* Journal for the Study of the Old Testament: Supplement Series 119. Sheffield, Eng.: JSOT Press, 1991.

Clouse, Bonnidell, and Robert G. Clouse, eds. *Women in Ministry: Four Views.* Downers Grove, Ill.: InterVarsity, 1989.

Co, Adam. "The Probable Identity of the 'Sons of God' in the Literary Context of Genesis 6:1–4." Paper presented at the annual meeting of the Evangelical Theological Society. Danvers, Mass., November 17, 1999.

Coakley, Sarah. "Creaturehood before God: Male and Female." *Theology* 93 (1990): 343–54.

Coats, George W. "Widow's Rights: A Crux in the Structure of Genesis 38." *Catholic Biblical Quarterly* 34 (1972): 461–66.

Cody, Aelred. "Sin and Its Sequel in the Story of David and Bathsheba." Pages 115–26 in *Sin, Salvation, and the Spirit: Commemorating the Fiftieth Year of the Liturgical Press.* Edited by D. Durken. Collegeville, Minn.: Liturgical, 1979.

Coetzee, J. H. "The 'Outcry' of the Dissected Woman in Judges 19–21: Embodiment of a Society." *Old Testament Essays* 15 (2002): 52–63.

Coggins, Richard J. *Introducing the Old Testament.* 2d ed. Oxford Bible Series. Oxford: Oxford University Press, 2001.

Cohen, A., ed. *The Five Megilloth: Hebrew Text, English Translation, and Commentary.* London: Soncino, 1946.

Cohen, Jeffrey M. "*HATAN DAMIM*—The Bridegroom of Blood." *Jewish Bible Quarterly* 33, no. 2 (2005): 120–26.

———. "Vashti—an Unsung Heroine." *Jewish Bible Quarterly* 24 (1996): 103–6.

Cohen, Martin Samuel. "The Biblical Prohibition of Homosexual Intercourse." *Journal of Homosexuality* 19, no. 4 (1990): 3–20. Repr., pages 153–64 in *Biblical Studies Alternatively: An Introductory Reader.* Edited by Susanne Scholz. Upper Saddle River, N.J.: Prentice Hall, 2003.

Cohens, H. Hirsch. *The Drunkenness of Noah.* University: University of Alabama Press, 1974.

Coiner, Harry G. "Those Divorce and Remarriage Passages." *Concordia Theological Monthly* 39 (1968): 367–84.

Cole, R. Alan. *Exodus: An Introduction and Commentary.* Tyndale Old Testament Commentaries 2. Downers Grove, Ill.: InterVarsity, 1973.

Cole, William G. *Sex and Love in the Bible.* New York: Association, 1959.

Collins, Adela Yarbro, ed. *Feminist Perspectives on Biblical Scholarship.* Biblical Scholarship in North America 10. Chico, Calif.: Scholars Press, 1985.

Collins, C. John. "Galatians 3:16: What Kind of Exegete Was Paul?" *Tyndale Bullletin* 54, no. 1 (2003): 75–86.

————. *Genesis 1–4: A Linguistic, Literary, and Theological Commentary.* Phillipsburg, N.J.: P & R Publishing, 2006.

————. "What Happened to Adam and Eve? A Literary-Theological Approach to Genesis 3." *Presbyterion* 27, no. 1 (2001): 12–44.

Collins, Jack. "A Syntactical Note (Genesis 3:15): Is the Woman's Seed Singular or Plural?" *Tyndale Bulletin* 48 (1997): 139–48.

Collins, John J. "Marriage, Divorce, and Family in Second Temple Judaism." Pages 104–62 in Leo G. Perdue et al., *Families in Ancient Israel.* Louisville: Westminster John Knox, 1997.

Collins, John Joseph, and Robert A. Kugler. *Religion in the Dead Sea Scrolls.* Studies in the Dead Sea Scrolls and Related Literature. Grand Rapids: Eerdmans, 2000.

Collins, Raymond F. "The Bible and Sexuality." *Biblical Theology Bulletin* 7 (1977): 149–67; 8 (1978): 3–18.

Colwell, Jerry D. "A Survey of Recent Interpretations of Women in the Church." M.A. thesis, Grand Rapids Baptist Seminary, 1984.

Conolly, Tristanne J. "Metaphor and Abuse in Hosea." *Feminist Theology* 18 (May 1998): 55–66.

Conway, Colleen M. *Men and Women in the Fourth Gospel: Gender and Johannine Characterization.* Society of Biblical Literature Dissertation Series 167. Atlanta: Society of Biblical Literature, 1999.

Coogan, Michael D. "The Goddess Wisdom—'Where Can She Be Found?'" Pages 203–9 in *Ki Baruch Hu: Ancient Near Eastern, Biblical, and Judaic Studies in Honor of Baruch A. Levine.* Edited by Robert Chazan, William W. Hallo, and Lawrence H. Schiffman. Winona Lake, Ind.: Eisenbrauns, 1999.

Cook, Joan E. "Four Marginalized Foils—Tamar, Judah, Joseph, and Potiphar's Wife: A Literary Study of Genesis 38–39." *Proceedings, Eastern Great Lakes and Midwest Biblical Society* 21 (2001): 115–28.

————. "Women in Ezra and Nehemiah." *The Bible Today* 37 (1999): 212–16.

Cooke, Richard Joseph. "The Teaching of Jesus concerning Divorce." *Methodist Review* 105 (1922): 714–25.

Cooper, Alan. "Hagar in and out of Context." *Union Seminary Quarterly Review* 55 (2001): 35–46.

Cooper, Jerrold S. "Buddies in Babylonia: Gilgamesh, Enkidu, and Mesopotamian Homosexuality." Pages 73–85 in *Riches Hidden in Secret Places: Ancient Near Eastern Studies in Memory of Thorkild Jacobsen.* Edited by Tzvi Abusch. Winona Lake, Ind.: Eisenbrauns, 2002.

Corley, Kathleen E. *Private Women, Public Meals: Social Conflict in the Synoptic Tradition.* Peabody, Mass.: Hendrickson, 1993.

Cornelius, Izak. *The Many Faces of the Goddess: The Iconography of the Syro-Palestinian Goddesses Anat, Astarte, Qedeshet, and Asherah c. 1500–1000 B.C.E.* Orbis Biblicus Et Orientalis 24. Fribourg: Academic Press, 2004.

Cornelius, Sakkie. "The Goddess Qedeshet in Syro-Palestinian Iconography." *Journal of Northwest Semitic Languages* 25, no. 2 (1999): 241–55.

Cornes, Andrew. *Divorce and Remarriage: Biblical Principles and Pastoral Practice.* Grand Rapids: Eerdmans, 1993.

Corona, Mary. "Woman in Creation Story." *Jeevadhara* 21 (1991): 95–106

Cortez, Marc. "The Law on Violent Intervention: Deuteronomy 25:11–2 Revisited." *Journal for the Study of the Old Testament* 30 (2006): 431–47.

Cosby, Michael R. *Sex in the Bible: An Introduction to What the Scriptures Teach Us about Sexuality.* Englewood Cliffs, N.J.: Prentice Hall, 1984.

Cotter, Wendy. "Women's Authority Roles in Paul's Churches: Countercultural or Conventional?" *Novum Testamentum* 36 (1994): 350–72.

Cottrell, Jack W. "Abortion and the Mosaic Laws." *Christianity Today* 17, no. 12 (1973): 6–9.

———. *Gender Roles and the Bible—Creation, the Fall, and Redemption: A Critique of Feminist Biblical Interpretation.* Joplin, Mo.: College Press, 1994.

Countryman, Louis William. *Dirt, Greed, and Sex: Sexual Ethics in the New Testament and Their Implications for Today.* Philadelphia: Fortress, 1988.

Coxon, Peter W. "Was Naomi a Scold? A Response to Fewell and Gunn." *Journal for the Study of the Old Testament* 45 (1989): 25–37.

Crabb, Larry. *Men and Women: Enjoying the Difference.* Grand Rapids: Zondervan, 1991.

Craghan, John F. "Esther: A Fully Liberated Woman." *The Bible Today* 24 (1986): 6–11.

———. "Esther, Judith, and Ruth: Paradigms for Human Liberation." *Biblical Theology Bulletin* 12 (1982): 11–19.

Craigie, Peter C. *The Book of Deuteronomy.* New International Commentary on the Old Testament. Grand Rapids: Eerdmans, 1976.

———. *Ugarit and the Old Testament.* Grand Rapids: Eerdmans, 1983.

Craigie, Peter C., Page H. Kelley, and Joel F. Drinkard Jr. *Jeremiah 1–25.* Word Biblical Commentary 26. Dallas: Word, 1991.

Craven, Toni. "Women as Teachers of Torah in the Apocryphal/Deuterocanonical Books." Pages 275–89 in *Passion, Vitality, and Foment: The Dynamics of Second Temple Judaism.* Edited by Lamontte M. Luker. Harrisburg, Pa.: Trinity Press International, 2001.

———. "Women in Genesis." *The Bible Today* 35 (1997): 32–39.

Crawford, Sidnie White. "Esther: A Feminine Model for Jewish Diaspora." Pages 161–77 in *Gender and Difference in Ancient Israel.* Edited by Peggy L. Day. Minneapolis: Fortress, 1989.

———. "Esther and Judith: Contrasts in Character." Pages 61–76 in *The Book of Esther in Modern Research.* Edited by Sidnie White Crawford and Leonard J. Greenspoon. London: T&T Clark, 2003.

Crawford, Sidnie White, and Leonard J. Greenspoon, eds. *The Book of Esther in Modern Research.* Journal for the Study of the Old Testament: Supplement Series 380. New York: T&T Clark, 2003.

Crenshaw, James L. "Prolegomenon." Pages 1–60 in *Studies in Ancient Israelite Wisdom.* Edited by James L. Crenshaw. New York: Ktav, 1976. Repr., pages

90–140 in *Urgent Advice and Probing Questions: Collected Writings on Old Testament Wisdom*. Macon, Ga.: Mercer, 1995.

———. *Samson: A Secret Betrayed, a Vow Ignored*. Atlanta: John Knox, 1978.

———. "Samson Saga: Filial Devotion or Erotic Attachment?" *Zeitschrift für die alttestamentliche Wissenschaft* 86 (1974): 470–504.

———, ed. *Studies in Ancient Israelite Wisdom*. New York: Ktav, 1976.

Crompton, Louis. *Homosexuality and Civilization*. Cambridge: Belknap, 2003.

Cross, Frank M. *From Epic to Canon: History and Literature in Ancient Israel*. Baltimore: Johns Hopkins University Press, 1998.

Crüsemann, Frank. "'. . . für Salomo'? Salomo und die Interpretation des Hohenliedes." Pages 141–57 in *Das Manna fällt auch heute noch. Beiträge zur Geschichte und Theologie des Alten, Ersten Testaments. Festschrift für Erich Zenger*, ed. Frank-Lothar Hossfeld and Ludger Schwienhorst-Schönberger. Herders biblische Studien 44. Freiburg: Herder, 2004.

———. *The Torah: Theology and Social History of Old Testament Law*. Translated by Allan W. Mahnke. Minneapolis: Fortress, 1996.

Cullmann, Oscar. "Immortality of the Soul or Resurrection of the Dead: The Witness of the New Testament." Pages 9–53 in *Immortality and Resurrection: Four Essays*. Edited by Krister Stendahl. New York: Macmillan, 1965.

Culver, Robert D. "A Traditional View: Let Your Women Keep Silence." Pages 25–54 in *Women in Ministry: Four Views*. Edited by Bonnidel Clouse and Robert G. Clouse. Downers Grove, Ill.: InterVarsity, 1989.

Cunningham, Loren, and David J. Hamilton with Janice Rogers. *Why Not Women? A Fresh Look at Women in Missions, Ministry, and Leadership*. Seattle: YWAM, 2001.

Currie, Stuart D. "Biblical Studies for a Seminar on Sexuality and the Human Community." *Austin Seminary Bulletin: Faculty Edition* 87 (1971): 4–60.

Curtis, Edward M. "Genesis 38: Its Context(s) and Function." *Criswell Theological Review* 5 (1991): 247–57.

Dahood, Mitchel. *Psalms*. 3 vols. Anchor Bible 16–17A. Garden City, N.Y.: Doubleday, 1965–1970.

Dalglish, Edward R. *Psalm Fifty-One in the Light of Near Eastern Patternism*. Leiden: E. J. Brill, 1962.

Dalley, Stephanie. "Hebrew Tahaš, Akkadian Duhšu, Faience and Beadwork." *Journal of Semitic Studies* 45 (2000): 1–19.

Daly, Mary. *Beyond God the Father: Toward a Philosophy of Women's Liberation*. Boston: Beacon, 1973.

Damazio, Frank. *From Barrenness to Fruitfulness*. Ventura, Calif.: Regal, 1998.

D'Angelo, Mary Rose. "The Garden: Once and Not Again: Traditional Interpretations of Genesis 1:26–27 in 1 Corinthians 11:7–12." Pages 1–41 in *Genesis 1–3 in the History of Exegesis: Intrigue in the Garden*. Edited by Gregory A. Robbins. Lewiston, N.Y.: Mellen, 1988.

———. "Remarriage and the Divorce Sayings Attributed to Jesus." Pages 78–106 in *Divorce and Remarriage: Religious and Psychological Perspectives*. Edited by William P. Roberts. Kansas City, Mo.: Sheed & Ward, 1990.

Darr, Katheryn Pfisterer. "'Alas, She Has Become a Harlot,' but Who's to Blame? Unfaithful-Female Imagery in Isaiah's Vision." Pages 55–76 in *Passion, Vitality, and Foment: The Dynamics of Second Temple Judaism.* Edited by Lamontte M. Luker. Harrisburg, Pa.: Trinity Press International, 2001.

———. *Far More Precious Than Jewels: Perspectives on Biblical Women.* Louisville: Westminster John Knox, 1991.

———. "Like Warrior, Like Woman: Destruction and Deliverance in Isaiah 42:10–17." *Catholic Biblical Quarterly* 49 (1987): 560–71.

Dass, Maria. "The Divorce (?) Formula in Hos 2:4a." *Indian Theological Studies* 34 (1997): 56–88.

Daube, David. "*Consortium* in Roman and Hebrew Law." *Juridical Review* 62 (1950): 71–91.

———. *Studies in Biblical Law.* New York: Ktav, 1969.

Dautzenberg, Gerhard, Helmut Merklein, and Karlheinz Müller, eds. *Die Frau im urchristentum.* Quaestiones disputatae 95. Freiburg im Breisgau: Herder, 1989.

Davidson, Jo Ann. "Abraham, Akedah, and Atonement." Pages 49–72 in *Creation, Life, and Hope: Essays in Honor of Jacques B. Doukhan.* Edited by Jiří Moskala. Berrien Springs, Mich.: Old Testament Department, Seventh-day Adventist Theological Seminary, Andrews University, 2000.

———. "Genesis Matriarchs Engage Feminism," *Andrews University Seminary Studies* 40, no. 2 (2002): 169–78.

———. "Modern Feminism, Religious Pluralism, and Scripture." *Journal of the Adventist Theological Society* 10, nos. 1–2 (1999): 401–40.

———. "The Well Women of Scripture Revisited." *Journal of the Adventist Theological Society* 17, no. 1 (2006): 209–28.

———. "Women in Scripture: A Survey and Evaluation." Pages 157–86 in *Women in Ministry: Biblical and Historical Perspectives.* Edited by Nancy Vyhmeister. Berrien Springs, Mich.: Andrews University Press, 1998.

Davidson, Richard M. "The Biblical Account of Origins." *Journal of the Adventist Theological Society* 14, no. 1 (2003): 32–33.

———. "Cosmic Metanarrative for the Coming Millennium." *Journal of the Adventist Theological Society* 11, nos. 1–2 (2000): 102–19.

———. "Divorce and Remarriage in Deuteronomy 24:1–4." *Journal of the Adventist Theological Society* 10, nos. 1–2 (1999): 2–22.

———. "Headship, Submission, and Equality in Scripture." Pages 273–95 in *Women in Ministry: Biblical and Historical Perspectives.* Edited by Nancy Vyhmeister. Berrien Springs, Mich.: Andrews University Press, 1998.

———. *In the Footsteps of Joshua.* Hagerstown, Md.: Review and Herald, 1995.

———. "Interpreting Scripture: An Hermeneutical 'Decalogue.'" *Journal of the Adventist Theological Society* 4, no. 2 (1993): 95–114.

———. "The Literary Structure of the Song of Songs *redivivus.*" *Journal of the Adventist Theological Society* 14, no. 2 (2003): 44–65.

———. *A Love Song for the Sabbath.* Washington, D.C.: Review and Herald, 1988.

———. "New Testament Use of the Old Testament." *Journal of the Adventist Theological Society* 5, no. 1 (1994): 14–39.

———. "Proverbs 8 and the Place of Christ in the Trinity." *Journal of the Adventist Theological Society* 17, no. 1 (2006): 33–54.

———. "The Theology of Sexuality in the Beginning: Genesis 1–2." *Andrews University Seminary Studies* 26 (1988): 5–24.

———. "Theology of Sexuality in the Song of Songs: Return to Eden." *Andrews University Seminary Studies* 27 (1989): 1–19.

———. *Typology in Scripture: A Study of Hermeneutical τύπος Structures.* Andrews University Dissertation Series 2. Berrien Springs, Mich.: Andrews University Press, 1981.

———. "A Woman Virgin Shall Bear a Child: Isaiah 7:14." *Perspective Digest* 7, no. 2 (2002): 47–51.

Davidson, Richard M., and Skip MacCarty. "Biblical Questions on Woman and Ministry." *Spectrum* 19, no. 5 (1989): 29–32.

Davidson, Robert. *Ecclesiastes and the Song of Solomon.* Daily Bible Study Series. Philadelphia: Westminster, 1986.

Davies, Eryl W. *The Dissenting Reader: Feminist Approaches to the Hebrew Bible.* Aldershot, Eng.: Ashgate, 2003.

———. "Inheritance Rights and the Hebrew Levirate Marriage." *Vetus Testamentum* 31 (1981): 138–44, 257–68.

———. "Land: Its Rights and Privileges." Pages 349–69 in *The World of Ancient Israel: Sociological, Anthropological, and Political Perspectives.* Edited by R. E. Clements. Cambridge: Cambridge University Press, 1989.

———. "Ruth iv 5 and the Duties of the *gōʾēl.*" *Vetus Testamentum* 33 (1983): 231–34.

Davies, Philip R., ed. *First Person: Essays in Biblical Autobiography.* Biblical Seminar 81. London: Sheffield Academic Press, 2002.

Davis, Elizabeth Gould. *The First Sex.* Baltimore: Penguin, 1972.

Davis, Ellen F. *Proverbs, Ecclesiastes, and the Song of Songs.* Westminster Bible Companion. Louisville: Westminster John Knox, 2000.

Davis, Ellen F., and Margaret Adams Parker. *Who Are You, My Daughter? Reading Ruth through Image and Text.* Louisville: Westminster John Knox, 2003.

Davis, John J. *Abortion and the Christian: What Every Believer Should Know.* Philadelphia: Presbyterian and Reformed, 1984.

———. *Moses and the Gods of Egypt: Studies in the Book of Exodus.* Grand Rapids: Baker, 1971.

Davison, Lisa W. " 'My Soul Is Like the Weaned Child That Is with Me': The Psalms and the Feminine Voice." *Horizons in Biblical Theology* 23 (2001): 155–67.

Day, Janeth Norfleete. *The Woman at the Well: Interpretation of John 4:1–42 in Retrospect and Prospect.* Biblical Interpretation Series 61. Boston: E. J. Brill, 2002.

Day, John. "Asherah." Pages 485–87 in vol. 1 of *The Anchor Bible Dictionary.* Edited by David Noel Freedman. 6 vols. New York: Doubleday, 1992.

————. "Asherah in the Hebrew Bible and Northwest Semitic Literature." *Journal of Biblical Literature* 105 (1986): 385–408.

————. "Ashtoreth." Pages 491–94 in vol. 1 of *The Anchor Bible Dictionary.* Edited by David Noel Freedman. 6 vols. New York: Doubleday, 1992.

————. "Baal." Pages 545–49 in vol. 1 of *The Anchor Bible Dictionary.* Edited by David Noel Freedman. 6 vols. New York: Doubleday, 1992.

————. "Canaan, Religion of." Pages 831–37 in vol. 1 of *The Anchor Bible Dictionary.* Edited by David Noel Freedman. 6 vols. New York: Doubleday, 1992.

————. *Molech: A God of Human Sacrifice in the Old Testament.* University of Cambridge Oriental Publications 41. Cambridge: Cambridge University Press, 1989.

————. *Yahweh and the Gods and Goddesses of Canaan.* Journal for the Study of the Old Testament: Supplement Series 265. Sheffield, Eng.: Sheffield Academic Press, 2000.

Day, John, ed. *Temple and Worship in Biblical Israel.* Library of Hebrew Bible/Old Testament Studies 422. New York: T&T Clark, 2005.

Day, Linda. "Rhetoric and Domestic Violence in Ezekiel 16." *Biblical Interpretation* 8 (2000): 205–30.

————. *Three Faces of a Queen: Characterization in the Books of Esther.* Journal for the Study of the Old Testament Supplementary Series 186. Sheffield, Eng.: Sheffield Academic Press, 1995.

————. "Wisdom and the Feminine in the Hebrew Bible." Pages 114–27 in *Engaging the Bible in a Gendered World: An Introduction to Feminist Biblical Interpretation in Honor of Katharine Doob Sakenfeld.* Edited by Linda Day and Carolyn Pressler. Louisville: Westminster John Knox, 2006.

Day, Linda, and Carolyn Pressler, eds. *Engaging the Bible in a Gendered World: An Introduction to Feminist Biblical Interpretation in Honor of Katharine Doob Sakenfeld.* Louisville: Westminster John Knox, 2006.

Day, Peggy L. "Adulterous Jerusalem's Imagined Demise: Death of a Metaphor in Ezekiel XVI." *Vetus Testamentum* 50, no. 3 (2000): 285–309.

————. "The Bitch Had It Coming to Her: Rhetoric and Interpretation in Ezekiel 16." *Biblical Interpretation* 8 (2000): 231–53.

————, ed. *Gender and Difference in Ancient Israel.* Minneapolis: Fortress, 1989.

Day, Wylark. *Sex and the Bible: Creating a War between Love and Repression:* Philadelphia: Xlibris, 2002.

De Ena, Jean Emmanuel. *Sens et interprétations du Cantique des cantiques.* Paris: Cerf, 2004.

De Troyer, Kristin. "Blood: A Threat to Holiness or toward (Another) Holiness?" Pages 45–64 in *Wholly Woman, Holy Blood: A Feminist Critique of Purity and Impurity.* Edited by Kristin De Troyer et al. Studies in Antiquity and Christianity. Harrisburg, Penn.: Trinity Press International, 2003.

De Troyer, Kristin, Judith A. Herbert, Judith Ann Johnson, and Anne-Marie Korte, eds. *Wholly Woman, Holy Blood: A Feminist Critique of Purity and Impurity.* Studies in Antiquity and Christianity. Harrisburg, Pa.: Trinity, 2003.

Dearman, J. Andrew. "Interpreting the Religious Polemics against Baal and the Baalim in the Book of Hosea." *Old Testament Essays* 14 (2001): 9–25.

———. "Marriage in the Old Testament." Pages 53–67 in *Biblical Ethics and Homosexuality: Listening to Scripture.* Edited by Robert L. Brawley. Louisville: Westminster John Knox, 1996.

———. *Religion and Culture in Ancient Israel.* Peabody, Mass.: Hendrickson, 1992.

DeBerg, Betty A. *Ungodly Women: Gender and the First Wave of American Fundamentalism.* Minneapolis: Fortress, 1990.

Deckers, M. "The Structure of the Song of Songs and the Centrality of *nepes* (6:12)." Pages 172–96 in *A Feminist Companion to the Song of Songs.* Edited by Athalya Brenner. Feminist Companion to the Bible 1. Sheffield, Eng.: Sheffield Academic Press, 1993.

Deem, Ariella. "The Goddess Anath and Some Biblical Hebrew Cruces." *Journal of Semitic Studies* 23 (1978): 25–30.

Deere, Jack S. "The Meaning of the Song of Songs: An Historical and Exegetical Inquiry." ThD diss., Dallas Theological Seminary, 1984.

———. "The Song of Solomon," Pages 1009–1025 in *The Bible Knowledge Commentary, Old Testament: An Exposition of the Scriptures.* Edited by John F. Walvoord and Roy B. Zuck. Wheaton, Ill.: Victor, 1985.

Dehsen, Christian D. von. "Sexual Relationships and the Church: An Exegetical Study of 1 Corinthians 5–7." PhD diss., Union Theological Seminary, 1987.

Delaney, Carol. *Abraham on Trial: The Social Legacy of Biblical Myth.* Princeton, N.J.: Princeton University Press, 1998.

Delitzsch, Franz. *Ecclesiastes.* Grand Rapids: Eerdmans, n.d.

———. *Das Hohelied untersucht und ausgelegt.* Leipzig: Dörffling & Franke, 1851.

———. *A New Commentary on Genesis.* Translated by Sophia Taylor. New York: Scribner & Welford, 1889.

Deming, Will. *Paul on Marriage and Celibacy: The Hellenistic Background of 1 Corinthians 7.* 2d ed. Grand Rapids: Eerdmans, 2004.

DeMoss, Nancy Leigh. "Portrait of a Foolish Woman." Pages 83–100 in *Biblical Womanhood in the Home.* Edited by Nancy Leigh DeMoss. Foundations for the Family Series. Wheaton, Ill.: Crossway, 2002.

DeMoss, Nancy Leigh, ed. *Biblical Womanhood in the Home.* Foundations for the Family Series. Wheaton, Ill.: Crossway, 2002.

Dempsey, Carol J. "The 'Whore' of Ezekiel 16: The Impact and Ramifications of Gender-Specific Metaphors in Light of Biblical Law and Divine Judgment." Pages 57–78 in *Gender and Law in the Hebrew Bible and the Ancient Near East.* Edited by Victor H. Matthews, Bernard M. Levinson, and Tikvah Frymer-Kensky. Journal for the Study of the Old Testament: Supplement Series 262. Sheffield, Eng.: Sheffield Academic Press, 1998.

Dennis, Trevor. *Sarah Laughed: Women's Voices in the Old Testament.* Nashville: Abingdon, 1994.

Derby, Josiah. "The Daughters of Zelophehad Revisited." *Jewish Bible Quarterly* 25, no. 3 (1997): 169–71.

Derouchie, Jason S. "Circumcision in the Hebrew Bible and Targums: Theology, Rhetoric, and the Handling of Metaphor." *Bulletin for Biblical Research* 14 (2004): 175–203.

Derrett, J. Duncan M. "Law in the New Testament: The Story of the Woman Taken in Adultery." *New Testament Studies* 10 (1963): 1–26.

Descamps, Albert L. "The New Testament Doctrine on Marriage." Pages 217–73 in *Contemporary Perspectives on Christian Marriage: Propositions and Papers from the International Theological Commission.* Edited by Richard Malone and John R. Connery. Chicago: Loyola University Press, 1984.

Desroches-Noblecourt, Christiane. *La femme au temps des pharaons.* Paris: Pernoud, 1986.

Dever, William. *What Did the Bible Writers Know and When Did They Know It?* Grand Rapids: Eerdmans, 2001.

Devlin-Glass, Frances, and Lyn McCredden. *Feminist Poetics of the Sacred: Creative Suspicions.* American Academy of Religion Cultural Criticism Series. New York: Oxford University Press, 2001.

DeVries, Simon J. "The Scheme of Dynastic Endangerment in Chronicles." *Proceedings, Eastern Great Lakes and Midwest Bible Society* 7 (1987): 59–77.

DeWitt, Dale S. "The Jephthah Traditions: A Rhetorical and Literary Study in the Deuteronomistic History." PhD diss., Andrews University, 1986.

DeYoung, James B. "The Contributions of the Septuagint to Biblical Sanctions against Homosexuality." *Journal of the Evangelical Theological Society* 34 (1991): 157–77.

———. *Homosexuality: Contemporary Claims Examined in Light of the Bible and Other Ancient Literature and Law.* Grand Rapids: Kregel, 2000.

Di Lella, A. A. "Women in the Wisdom of Ben Sira and the Book of Judith: A Study in Contrasts and Reversals." Pages 39–53 in *Congress Volume: Paris, 1992.* Edited by J. A. Emerton. Vetus Testamentum Supplements 61. Leiden: E. J. Brill, 1995.

Di Vito, Robert A. "Questions about the Construction of (Homo) Sexuality: Same-Sex Relations in the Hebrew Bible." Pages 108–32 in *Sexual Diversity in Catholicism: Toward the Development of Moral Theology.* Edited by Patricia Bettie Jung with Joseph Andrew Coray. Collegeville, Minn.: Liturgical, 1989.

Dibelius, Martin, and Hans Conzelmann. *The Pastoral Epistles.* Hermeneia. Philadelphia: Fortress, 1972.

Dickson, Charles. "Response: Does the Hebrew Bible Have Anything to Say About Homosexuality?" *Old Testament Essays* 15 (2002): 350–67.

Dijk-Hemmes, Fokkelien van. "The Great Woman of Shunem and the Man of God: A Dual Interpretation of 2 Kings 4:8–37." Pages 218–30 in *A Feminist Companion to Samuel and Kings.* Edited by Athalya Brenner. Feminist Companion to the Bible 5. Sheffield, Eng.: Sheffield Academic Press, 1994.

———. "The Imagination of Power and the Power of Imagination: An Intertextual Analysis of Two Biblical Love Songs—the Song of Songs and Hosea 2." *Journal for the Study of the Old Testament* no. 44 (1989): 75–88.

———. "The Metaphorization of Woman in Prophetic Speech: An Analysis of Ezekiel XXIII." *Vetus Testamentum* 43 (1993): 162–70. Repr., pages 167–76 in *On Gendering Texts: Female and Male Voices in the Hebrew Bible*. Edited by Athalya Brenner and Fokkelien van Dijk-Hemmes. Biblical Interpretation Series 1. Leiden: E. J. Brill, 1993.

———. "Ruth: A Product of Women's Culture?" Pages 134–39 in *A Feminist Companion to Ruth*. Edited by Athalya Brenner. Feminist Companion to the Bible 3. Sheffield, Eng.: Sheffield Academic Press, 1993.

———. "Tamar and the Limits of Patriarchy: Between Rape and Seduction (2 Samuel 13 and Genesis 38)." Pages 135–56 in *Anti-covenant: Counter-reading Women's Lives in the Hebrew Bible*. Edited by M. Bal. Sheffield, Eng.: Almond, 1989.

Dille, Sarah J. *Mixing Metaphors: God as Mother and Father in Deutero-Isaiah*. Journal for the Study of the Old Testament Supplement Series 398. Gender, Culture, Theory 13. London: T&T Clark, 2004.

Dillmann, A. *Genesis*. Edinburgh: T&T Clark, 1897.

Dillow, Joseph C. *Solomon on Sex: The Biblical Guide to Married Love*. New York: Thomas Nelson, 1977.

Dion, Paul E. "Did Cultic Prostitution Fall into Oblivion during the Postexilic Era? Some Evidence from Chronicles and the Septuagint." *Catholic Biblical Quarterly* 43 (1981): 41–48.

Dirksen, P. B. "Song of Songs III 6–7." *Vetus Testamentum* 39 (1989): 219–25.

Dobbs-Allsopp, F. W., and Tod Linafelt. "The Rape of Zion in Thr 1,10." *Zeitschrift für die alttestamentliche Wissenschaft* 113 (2001): 77–81.

Dobson, Edward G. *What the Bible Really Says about Marriage, Divorce, and Remarriage*. Old Tappan, N.J.: Fleming H. Revell, 1986.

Dodd, C. H. *The Epistle of Paul to the Romans*. London: Hodder & Stoughton, 1954.

Donner, H. "Adoption oder Legitimation? Erwägungen zur Adoption im Alten Testament auf dem Hintergrund der altorientalischen Rechte." *Oriens antiquus* 8 (1969): 87–119.

Doorly, William J. *The Laws of Yahweh: A Handbook of Biblical Law*. New York: Paulist, 2002.

Doriani, Dan. *Women in Ministry: What the Bible Teaches*. Wheaton, Ill.: Crossway, 2003.

Dorsey, David. *The Literary Structure of the Old Testament: A Commentary on Genesis–Malachi*. Grand Rapids: Baker, 1999.

———. "Literary Structuring in the Song of Songs." *Journal for the Study of the Old Testament* no. 46 (1990): 81–96.

Douglas, Mary. *Purity and Danger: An Analysis of Concepts of Pollution and Taboo*. New York: Praeger, 1966.

———. "Responding to Ezra: The Priests and the Foreign Wives." *Biblical Interpretation* 10 (2002): 1–23.

Doukhan, Jacques B. *The Literary Structure of the Genesis Creation Story*. Andrews University Seminary Doctoral Dissertation Series 5. Berrien Springs, Mich.: Andrews University Press, 1978.

————. "Women Priests in Israel: A Case for Their Absence." Pages 29–43 in *Women in Ministry: Biblical and Historical Perspectives*. Edited by Nancy Vyhmeister. Berrien Springs, Mich.: Andrews University Press, 1998.

Dove, Mary. "Sex, Allegory, and Censorship: A Reconsideration of Medieval Commentaries on the Song of Songs." *Literature and Theology* 10 (1996): 317–28.

Dowling, Maurice. "Proverbs 8:22–31 in the Christology of the Early Fathers." *Irish Biblical Studies* 24 (2002): 99–117.

Doyle, Robert. "Created Male and Female: Sexuality, Personhood, and the Image of God." Pages 43–56 in *Personhood, Sexuality, and Christian Ministry*. Edited by B. Webb. Homebush West, N.S.W., Australia: Lancer, 1987.

Dozeman, Thomas B. "Creation and Procreation in the Biblical Teaching on Homosexuality." *Union Seminary Quarterly Review* 49 (1995): 175–76, 179, 189.

Dragga, Sam. "Genesis 2–3: A Story of Liberation." *Journal for the Study of the Old Testament* no. 55 (1992): 3–13.

Dresner, Samuel H. "Homosexuality and the Order of Creation." *Judaism* 40 (1991): 309–21.

Drey, Philip R. "The Role of Hagar in Genesis 16." *Andrews University Seminary Studies* 40 (2002): 179–95.

Drinkard, Joel. "An Understanding of Family in the Old Testament: Maybe Not as Different as We Usually Think." *Review and Expositor* 98 (2001): 485–502.

Driver, G. R., and John C. Miles. *The Assyrian Laws*. Oxford: Clarendon, 1935.

Driver, S. R. *The Book of Genesis*. London: Metheuen, 1904.

————. *A Critical and Exegetical Commentary on Deuteronomy*. International Critical Commentary. New York: Charles Scribner's Sons, 1902.

————. *An Introduction to the Literature of the Old Testament*. 9th ed. New York: Charles Scribner, 1913; Repr., Cleveland: Meridian, 1967.

Dumais, Marcel. "Couple et sexualité selon le Nouveau Testament." *Église et théologie* 8 (1977): 47–72.

Dumbrell, William J. *The End of the Beginning*. Homebush, N.S.W., Australia: Lancer, 1985.

————. "Exodus 4:24–26: A Textual Re-examination." *Harvard Theological Review* 65 (1972): 285–90.

Dunnam, Maxie D. "The Creation/Covenant Design for Marriage and Sexuality." Pages 104–14 in *Staying the Course: Supporting the Church's Position on Homosexuality*. Edited by Maxie D. Dunnam and H. Newton Malony. Nashville: Abingdon, 2003.

Dunnam, Maxie D., and H. Newton Malony, eds. *Staying the Course: Supporting the Church's Position on Homosexuality*. Nashville: Abingdon, 2003.

Durham, John I. *Exodus*. Word Biblical Commentary 3. Waco, Tex.: Word, 1987.

Dutcher-Walls, Patricia. *Jezebel: Portraits of a Queen*. Collegeville, Minn.: Liturgical, 2004.

Duty, Guy. *Divorce and Remarriage*. Minneapolis: Bethany Fellowship, 1967.

Dybdahl, Jon. *Old Testament Grace*. Boise, Idaho: Pacific, 1990.

Dyrness, William. *Themes in Old Testament Theology.* Downers Grove, Ill.: InterVarsity, 1979.

Earle, Ralph. "1 Timothy." Pages 340–90 in vol. 11 of *The Expositor's Bible Commentary.* Edited by Frank E. Gaebelein. 12 vols. Grand Rapids: Zondervan, 1976–1992.

Ecker, Ronald L. *And Adam Knew Eve: A Dictionary of Sex in the Bible.* Palatka, Fla.: Hodge & Braddock, 1995.

Edelman, Diana. "Proving Yahweh Killed His Wife (Zechariah 5:5–11)." *Biblical Interpretation* 11 (2003): 335–44.

Eder, Sigrid. "Ein Happy End im Hohelied? Eine Untersuchung zu Hld 2,8–14; 3,1–5 und 5,2–8 und eine narrative Lesart." *Protokolle zur Bibel* 13 (2004): 3–24.

Edwards, Brian, ed. *Men, Women, and Authority: Serving Together in the Church.* Kent, Eng.: Day One, 1996.

Edwards, George R. *Gay/Lesbian Liberation: A Biblical Perspective.* New York: Pilgrim, 1984.

Edwards, I. E. S., C. J. Gadd, and N. G. L. Hammonds, eds. *Early History of the Middle East.* 3d ed. Cambridge Ancient History 1/2. Cambridge: Cambridge University Press, 1971.

Efird, James M. *Marriage and Divorce: What the Bible Says.* Nashville: Abingdon, 1985.

Efthimiadis, Helen. "Is There a Place for Women in the Theology of the Psalms? Part I: An Investigation into the Female Imagery of the Ancient Hebrew Psalter." *Old Testament Essays* 12 (1999): 33–56.

Eichler, B. L. "Nuzi and the Bible: A Retrospective." Pages 107–19 in *DUMU-E2-DUB-BA-A: Studies in Honor of Åke W. Sjöberg.* Edited by Hermann Behrens, Darlene Loding, and Martha T. Roth. Philadelphia: Babylonian Section, University Museum, 1989.

Eisen, Ute E. *Women Officeholders in Early Christianity: Epigraphical and Literary Studies.* Collegeville, Minn.: Liturgical, 2000.

Eisler, Riane Tennenhaus. *Sacred Pleasure: Sex, Myth, and the Politics of the Body.* San Francisco: HarperSan Francisco, 1995.

Ellens, Deborah L. "A Comparison of the Conceptualization of Women in the Sex Laws of Leviticus and in the Sex Laws of Deuteronomy." PhD diss., Claremont Graduate University, 1998.

———. "Leviticus 15: Contrasting Conceptual Associations regarding Women." Pages 124–51 in vol. 2 of *Reading the Hebrew Bible for a New Millennium.* Edited by W. Kim et al. 2 vols. Harrisburg, Penn.: Trinity Press International, 2000.

———. "Menstrual Impurity and Innovation in Leviticus 15." Pages 29–43 in *Wholly Woman, Holy Blood: A Feminist Critique of Purity and Impurity.* Edited by Kristin De Troyer et al. Studies in Antiquity and Christianity. Harrisburg, Penn.: Trinity Press International, 2003.

———. "Numbers 5.11–31: Valuing Male Suspicion." Pages 55–82 in *God's Word for Our World, Vol. I: Theological and Cultural Studies in Honor of Simon John*

De Vries. Edited by J. Harold Ellens et al. Journal for the Study of the Old Testament: Supplement Series 388. New York: T&T Clark, 2004.

Ellens, J. Harold. *Sex in the Bible: A New Consideration*. Psychology, Religion, and Spirituality. Westport, Conn.: Praeger, 2006.

Ellens, J. Harold, ed. *God's Word for Our World I: Theological and Cultural Studies in Honor of Simon John De Vries*. Journal for the Study of the Old Testament: Supplement Series 388. New York: T&T Clark, 2004.

———, ed. *God's Word for Our World II: Theological and Cultural Studies in Honor of Simon John De Vries*. Journal for the Study of the Old Testament: Supplement Series 389. New York: T&T Clark, 2004.

Elliger, K. "Das Gesetz Leviticus 18." *Zeitschrift für die alttestamentliche Wissenschaft* 26 (1955): 1–7.

Ellingson, Stephen, and Christian Green, eds. *Religion and Sexuality in Cross-cultural Perspective*. New York: Routledge, 2002.

Ellington, John. "Miscarriage and Premature Birth." *Bible Translator* 37, no. 3 (1986): 374–77.

Elliot, Elisabeth. *The Mark of a Man*. Old Tappan, N.J.: Fleming H. Revell, 1981.

Elliott, John H. "Deuteronomy—Shameful Encroachment on Shameful Parts: Deuteronomy 25:11–12 and Biblical Euphemism." Pages 161–76 in *Ancient Israel: The Old Testament in Its Social Context*. Edited by Philip F. Esler. Minneapolis: Fortress, 2006.

Elliott, M. Timothea. *The Literary Unity of the Canticle*. European University Studies, Series 23, 371. New York: Peter Lang, 1989.

Elliott, Mark W. "Ethics and Aesthetics in the Song of Songs." *Tyndale Bulletin* 45 (1994): 137–52.

———. *The Song of Songs and Christology in the Early Church, 381–451*. Studies in Texts in Antiquity and Christianity 7. Tübingen: Mohr Siebeck, 2000.

Ellis, E. Earle. "The Silenced Wives of Corinth (1 Cor. 14:34–35)." Pages 213–20 in *New Testament Textual Criticism: Its Significance for Exegesis*. Edited by Eldon J. Epp and Gordon D. Fee. New York: Oxford University Press, 1981.

Ellis, Maria deJ. "An Old Babylonian Adoption Contract from Tell Harmal." *Journal of Cuneiform Studies* 27 (1975): 130–51.

Emerton, J. A. "'Yahweh and His Asherah': The Goddess or Her Symbol?" *Vetus Testamentum* 49 (1999): 315–37.

Emmerson, Grace I. "The Song of Songs: Mystification, Ambiguity, and Humour." Pages 97–111 in *Crossing the Boundaries: Essays in Biblical Interpretation in Honour of Michael D. Goulder*. Edited by Stanley E. Porter, Paul Joyce, and David E. Orton. New York: E. J. Brill, 1994.

———. "Women in Ancient Israel." Pages 371–94 in *The World of Ancient Israel: Sociological, Anthropological, and Political Perspectives*. Edited by R. E. Clements. Cambridge: Cambridge University Press, 1989.

Engelken, Karen. *Frauen im alten Israel: Eine begriffsgeschichtliche und sozialrechtliche Studie zur Stellung der Frau im Alten Testament*. Beiträge zur Wissenschaft vom Alten und Neuen Testament. Stuttgart: W. Kohlhammer, 1990.

Engelsman, Joan Chamberlain. *The Feminine Dimension of the Divine.* Philadelphia: Westminster, 1979.

Epp, Eldon Jay. *Junia: The First Woman Apostle.* Minneapolis: Fortress, 2005.

Epstein, Louis M. *Marriage Laws in the Bible and the Talmud.* Harvard Semitic Series 12. Cambridge: Harvard University Press, 1942.

———. *Sex Laws and Customs in Judaism.* New York: Bloch, 1948.

Erler, Mary Carpenter, and Maryanne Kowaleski, eds. *Gendering the Master Narrative: Women and Power in the Middle Ages.* Ithaca, N.Y.: Cornell University Press, 2003.

Ernst, Judith. *Song of Songs: Erotic Love Poetry.* Grand Rapids: Eerdmans, 2003.

Eschelbach, Michael A. "Song of Songs: Increasing Appreciation of and Restraint in Matters of Love." *Andrews University Seminary Studies* 42 (2004): 305–24.

Eskenazi, Tamara C. "Out from the Shadows: Biblical Women in the Postexilic Era." *Journal for the Study of the Old Testament* no. 54 (1992): 25–43.

Esler, Philip F. "The Sodom Tradition in Romans 1:18–32." *Biblical Theology Bulletin* 34 (2004): 4–16.

Eslinger, Lyle M. "The Case of an Immodest Lady Wrestler in Deuteronomy XXV 11–12." *Vetus Testamentum* 31 (1981): 269–81.

———. "More Drafting Techniques in Deuteronomic Laws." *Vetus Testamentum* 34 (1984): 221–26.

Estes, Daniel J. "Like Arrows in the Hand of a Warrior (Psalm 127)." *Vetus Testamentum* 41 (1991): 304–11.

Evans, Mary J. "The Invisibility of Women: An Investigation of a Possible Blind Spot for Biblical Commentators." *Christian Brethren Research Fellowship Journal* 122 (1990): 37–40.

———. *Woman in the Bible: An Overview of All the Crucial Passages on Women's Roles.* Downers Grove, Ill.: InterVarsity, 1984.

———. "Women." Pages 897–904 in *Dictionary of the Old Testament: Pentateuch.* Edited by T. Desmond Alexander and David W. Baker. Downers Grove, Ill.: InterVarsity, 2003.

Evans, William. *The Right and Wrong in Divorce and Remarriage.* Grand Rapids: Zondervan, 1946.

Everhart, Janet S. "The Hidden Eunuchs of the Hebrew Bible: Uncovering an Alternate Gender." PhD diss., Iliff School of Theology and University of Denver, 2003.

———. "Serving Women and Their Mirrors: A Feminist Reading of Exodus 38:8b." *Catholic Biblical Quarterly* 66 (2004): 44–54.

Ewald, George R. *Jesus and Divorce: A Biblical Guide for Ministry to Divorced Persons.* Scottdale, Pa.: Herald, 1991.

Ewald, Heinrich G. A. *Das Hohe Lied Salomos.* Göttingen: R. Deuerlich, 1826.

Exum, J. Cheryl. "The Ethics of Biblical Violence against Women." Pages 248–71 in *The Bible in Ethics: The Second Sheffield Colloquium.* Edited by John W. Rogerson, Margaret Davies, and M. Daniel Carroll R. Journal for the Study of the Old Testament: Supplement Series 207. Sheffield, Eng.: Sheffield Academic Press, 1995.

———. "Feminist Criticism: Whose Interests Are Being Served?" Pages 65–90 in *Judges and Method: New Approaches in Biblical Studies.* Edited by Gale A. Yee. Minneapolis: Fortress, 1995.

———. *Fragmented Women: Feminist (Sub)Versions of Biblical Narratives.* Journal for the Study of the Old Testament: Supplement Series 163. Sheffield, Eng.: JSOT Press, 1993.

———. "In the Eye of the Beholder: Wishing, Dreaming, and *double entendre* in the Song of Songs," Pages 71–86 in *The Labour of Reading: Desire, Alienation, and Biblical Interpretation.* Edited by Fiona C. Black et al. Semeia Studies. Atlanta: Society of Biblical Literature, 1999.

———. "Lethal Woman 2: Reflections on Delilah and Her Incarnation as Liz Hurley." Pages 254–73 in *Borders, Boundaries, and the Bible.* Edited by Martin O'Kane. Journal for the Study of the Old Testament: Supplement Series 313. New York: Sheffield Academic Press, 2002.

———. "A Literary and Structural Analysis of the Song of Songs." *Zeitschrift für die alttestamentliche Wissenschaft* 85 (1973): 47–79.

———. "Mother in Israel: A Familiar Figure Reconsidered." Pages 73–85 in *Feminist Interpretation of the Bible.* Edited by Letty M. Russell. Philadelphia: Westminster, 1985.

———. "Murder They Wrote: Ideology and the Manipulation of Female Presence in Biblical Narrative." In "Ad feminam: Fiftieth Anniversary Volume." Edited by Alice Bach. *Union Seminary Quarterly Review* 43 (1989): 19–39. Repr., pages 45–67 in *The Pleasure of Her Text: Feminist Readings of Biblical and Historical Texts.* Edited by Alice Bach. Philadelphia: Trinity Press International, 1990.

———. *Plotted, Shot, and Painted: Cultural Representations of Biblical Women.* Journal for the Study of the Old Testament: Supplement Series 215. Gender, Culture, Theory 3. Sheffield, Eng.: Sheffield Academic Press, 1996.

———. "Promise and Fulfillment: Narrative Art in Judges 13." *Journal of Biblical Literature* 99 (1980): 43–59.

———. "Prophetic Pornography." Pages 101–28 in *Plotted, Shot, and Painted: Cultural Representations of Biblical Women.* Journal for the Study of the Old Testament: Supplement Series 215. Gender, Culture, Theory 3. Sheffield, Eng.: Sheffield Academic Press, 1996.

———. "Second Thoughts about Secondary Characters: Women in Exodus 1.8–2.10." Pages 75–87 in *A Feminist Companion to Exodus to Deuteronomy.* Edited by Athalya Brenner. Feminist Companion to the Bible 6. Sheffield, Eng.: Sheffield Academic Press, 1994.

———. "Seeing Solomon's Palanquin (Song of Songs 3:6–11)." *Biblical Interpretation* 11 (2003): 301–16.

———. "Ten Things Every Feminist Should Know." Pages 24–35 in *Song of Songs.* Edited by Althaya Brenner and Carol R. Fontaine. Feminist Companion to the Bible: Second Series 6. Sheffield, Eng.: Sheffield Academic Press, 2000.

———. "Who's Afraid of 'the Endangered Ancestress'?" Pages 91–113 in *The New Literary Criticism and the Hebrew Bible.* Edited by J. Cheryl Exum and David J. A. Clines. Sheffield, Eng.: JSOT Press, 1993.

———. "'You Shall Let Every Daughter Live': A Study of Exodus 1:8–2:10." *Semeia* 28 (1983): 63–82.

Falk, Marcia. *Love Lyrics from the Bible: A Translation and Literary Study of the Song of Songs.* Bible and Literature Series 4. Sheffield, Eng.: Almond, 1982.

———. *The Song of Songs.* San Francisco: Harper & Row, 1990.

Farla, Piet. "The Two Shall Become One Flesh: Gen 1.27 and 2.24 in the New Testament Marriage Texts." Pages 67–82 in *Intertextuality in Biblical Writings: Essays in Honor of Bas van Iersel.* Edited by Sipke Draisma. Kampen, Neth.: Kok, 1989.

Farley, Margaret. "New Patterns of Relationship: Beginnings of a Moral Revolution." *Text and Studies* 36 (1975): 641–43.

Farmer, Kathleen A. "Psalms." Pages 137–44 in *The Women's Bible Commentary.* Edited by Carol A. Newsom and Sharon H. Ringe. Louisville: Westminster John Knox, 1992.

———. "Women, Symbolic Universe, and Structures of Silence: Challenges and Possibilities in Androcentric Texts." *Studia theologica* 43 (1989): 61–80.

Faulkner, Raymond O., ed. and trans. *The Ancient Egyptian Coffin Texts.* 3 vols. Warminster, Eng.: Aris & Phillips, 1973–1978.

———. *The Ancient Egyptian Pyramid Texts.* 2 vols. Oxford: Oxford University Press, 1969.

Fee, Gordon D. *The First Epistle to the Corinthians.* Grand Rapids: Eerdmans, 1987.

———. "Issues in Evangelical Hermeneutics, Part II: The Crucial Issue—Authorial Intentionality: A Proposal Regarding New Testament Imperatives." *Crux* 26 (September 1990): 35–42.

———. "Issues in Evangelical Hermeneutics, Part III: The Great Watershed—Intentionality and Particularity/Eternality: 1 Timothy 2:8–15 as a Test Case." *Crux* 26 (October 1990): 31–37.

———. "Male and Female in the New Creation: Galatians 3:26–29." Pages 172–85 in *Discovering Biblical Equality: Complementarity without Hierarchy.* Edited by Ronald W. Pierce and Rebecca Merrill Groothuis. Downers Grove, Ill.: InterVarsity, 2004.

Feinberg, Charles Lee. "The Image of God." *Bibliotheca sacra* 129 (1972): 235–45.

Feinberg, Paul D. "Homosexuality and the Bible." *Fundamentalist Journal* 4, no. 3 (1985): 17–19.

Fensham, F. Charles. *The Books of Ezra and Nehemiah.* New International Commentary on the Old Testament. Grand Rapids: Eerdmans, 1982.

———. "The Marriage Metaphor in Hosea for the Covenant Relationship between the Lord and His People (Hos 1:2–9)." *Journal of Northwest Semitic Languages* 12 (1984): 71–78.

———. "Widow, Orphan, and the Poor in Ancient Near Eastern Legal and Wisdom Literature." *Journal of Near Eastern Studies* 21 (1962): 129–39.

Fewell, Danna Nolan, and David M. Gunn. *Compromising Redemption: Relating Characters in the Book of Ruth.* Louisville: Westminster John Knox, 1990.

———. "Controlling Perspectives: Women, Men, and the Authority of Violence in Judges 4–5." *Journal of the American Academy of Religion* 58, no. 3 (1990): 389–411.

———. *Gender, Power, and Promise: The Subject of the Bible's First Story.* Nashville: Abingdon, 1993.

———. "Is Coxon a Scold? On Responding to the Book of Ruth." *Journal for the Study of the Old Testament* 45 (1989): 39–43.

———. "'A Son Is Born to Naomi!': Literary Allusions and Interpretation in the Book of Ruth." Pages 233–39 in *Women in the Hebrew Bible: A Reader.* Edited by Alice Bach. New York: Routledge, 1999.

———. "Tipping the Balance: Sternberg's Reader and the Rape of Dinah." *Journal of Biblical Literature* 110 (1991): 193–211.

Field, David. *The Homosexual Way—A Christian Option?* Downers Grove, Ill.: InterVarsity, 1979.

Fields, Weston W. "Early and Medieval Jewish Interpretation of the Song of Songs." *Grace Theological Journal* 2 (1980): 221–31.

Finkelstein, Jacob J. "Cutting the *sissiktu* in Divorce Proceedings." *Die Welt des Orients* 8 (1976): 236–40.

———. "Sex Offenses in Sumerian Law." *Journal of the American Oriental Society* 86 (1966): 355–72.

Finley, Thomas. "The Ministry of Women in the Old Testament." Pages 73–88 in *Women and Men in Ministry: A Complementary Perspective.* Edited by Robert L. Saucy and Judith K. TenElshof. Chicago: Moody, 2001.

———. "The Relationship of Woman and Man in the Old Testament." Pages 49–71 in *Women and Men in Ministry: A Complementary Perspective.* Edited by Robert L. Saucy and Judith K. TenElshof. Chicago: Moody, 2001.

Fischer, Irmtraud. "The Book of Ruth: A 'Feminist' Commentary to the Torah?" Pages 24–49 in *Ruth and Esther.* Edited by Athalya Brenner. Feminist Companion to the Bible: Second Series 3. Sheffield, Eng.: Sheffield Academic Press, 1999.

———. *Die Erzeltern Israels: Feministisch-theologische Studien zu Genesis 12–36.* Beihefte zur Zeitschrift für die alttestamentliche Wissenschaft 222. Berlin: de Gruyter, 1994.

———. "Salomo und die Frauen." Pages 218–43 in *Das Manna fällt auch heute noch: Beiträge zur Geschichte und Theologie des Alten, Ersten Testaments. Festschrift für Erich Zenger.* Edited by Frank-Lothar Hossfeld and Ludger Schwienhorst-Schönberger. Herders biblische Studien 44. Freiburg: Herder, 2004.

———. *Women Who Wrestled with God: Biblical Stories of Israel's Beginnings.* Translated by Linda M. Maloney. Collegeville, Minn.: Liturgical, 2005.

Fishbane, Michael. "Accusations of Adultery: A Study of Law and Scribal Practice in Numbers 5:11–31." *Hebrew Union College Annual* 45 (1974): 25–45.

———. *Text and Texture: Close Readings of Selected Biblical Texts.* New York: Schocken, 1979.

————. "Types of Biblical Intertextuality." Pages 39–44 in *Congress Volume: Oslo, 1998*. Edited by André Lemaire and Magne Sæbø. Vetus Testamentum Supplements 80. Leiden: E. J. Brill, 2000.

Fisher, Eugene J. "Cultic Prostitution in the Ancient Near East? A Reassessment." *Biblical Theology Bulletin* 6 (1976): 225–36.

FitzGerald, Kyriaki Karidoyanes, ed. *Orthodox Women Speak: Discerning the "Signs of the Times."* Brookline, Mass.: Holy Cross Orthodox Press, 1999.

Fitzmyer, Joseph A. "Another Look at ΚΕΦΑΛΗ in 1 Corinthians 11:3." *New Testament Studies* 35 (1989): 503–11.

————. "*Kephale* in I Corinthians 11:3." *Interpretation* 47 (1993): 52–59.

————. "The Matthean Divorce Texts and Some New Palestinian Evidence." *Theological Studies* 37 (1976): 197–226.

Flak, Ze'ev Wilhelm. *Hebrew Law in Biblical Times: An Introduction*. Winona Lake, Ind.: Eisenbrauns, 2001.

Fleishman, Joseph. "Shechem and Dinah in the Light of Non-Biblical and Biblical Sources." *Zeitschrift für die Alttestamentliche Wissenschaft* 116 (2004): 12–32.

Fleming, Joy Elasky. *Man and Woman in Biblical Unity: Theology from Genesis 2–3*. Old Tappan, N.J.: Christians for Biblical Equality, 1993.

Floyd, Michael H. "The Bible and Sex [Review Article of L. W. Countryman, *Dirt, Greed and Sex*, 1988]." *Anglican Theological Review* 72 (1990): 95–103.

————. "Can God's Name Change? A Biblical-Theological Perspective on the Feminist Critique of Trinitarian Nomenclature." Pages 144–68 in *Theological and Hermeneutical Studies*. Vol. 1 of *Reading the Hebrew Bible for a New Millennium: Form, Concept, and Theological Perspective*. Edited by Wonil Kim et al. Studies in Antiquity and Christianity. Harrisburg, Pa.: Trinity, 2000.

Foh, Susan T. "A Male Leadership View: The Head of the Woman Is the Man." Pages 69–105 in *Women in Ministry: Four Views*. Edited by Bonnidel Clouse and Robert G. Clouse. Downers Grove, Ill.: InterVarsity, 1989.

————. "What Is the Woman's Desire?" *Westminster Theological Journal* 37 (1975): 376–83.

————. *Women and the Word of God: A Response to Biblical Feminism*. Phillipsburg, N.J.: Presbyterian and Reformed, 1979.

Fokkelman, J. P. *King David (II Sam 9–20 and 1 Kings 1–2)*, Vol. 1 of *Narrative Art and Poetry in the Books of Samuel*. Assen, Neth.: Van Gorcum, 1981.

————. *Narrative Art in Genesis: Specimens of Stylistic and Structural Analysis*. 2d ed. Biblical Seminar 12. Sheffield, Eng.: JSOT Press, 1991.

————. *Reading Biblical Poetry: An Introductory Guide*. Louisville: Westminster John Knox, 2001.

Fontaine, Carole R. "'Go Forth into the Fields': An Earth-Centered Reading of the Song of Songs." Pages 126–42 in *The Earth Story in Wisdom Traditions*. Edited by Norman C. Habel and Shirley Wurst. Earth Bible 3. Cleveland: Pilgrim, 2001.

————. "A Heifer from Thy Stable: On Goddesses and the Status of Women in the Ancient Near East." In "Ad feminam: Fiftieth Anniversary Volume." Edited by Alice Bach. *Union Seminary Quarterly Review* 43 (1989): 67–91.

————. *Smooth Words: Women, Proverbs, and Performance in Biblical Wisdom.* Journal for the Study of the Old Testament: Supplement Series 356. New York: Sheffield Academic Press, 2002.

————. "The Social Roles of Women in the World of Wisdom." Pages 24–49 in *A Feminist Companion to Wisdom Literature.* Edited by Athalya Brenner. Feminist Companion to the Bible 9. Sheffield, Eng.: Sheffield Academic Press, 1995.

Ford, J. Massyngberde. "Biblical Material Relevant to the Ordination of Women." *Journal Ecumenical Studies* 10 (1973): 669–94.

Foucault, Michel. *An Introduction.* Vol. 1 of *The History of Sexuality.* Translated by Robert Hurley. New York: Pantheon, 1978.

————. *The Use of Pleasure.* Vol. 2 of *The History of Sexuality.* Translated by Robert Hurley. New York: Pantheon, 1985.

Fowler, Paul W. *Abortion: Toward an Evangelical Consensus.* Portland, Ore.: Multnomah, 1987.

Fox, Michael V. *Character and Ideology in the Book of Esther.* Columbia: University of South Carolina Press, 1991.

————. "Love, Passion, and Perception in Israelite and Egyptian Love Poetry." *Journal of Biblical Literature* 102 (1983): 219–28.

————. "The Sign of the Covenant: Circumcision in the Light of the Priestly *'ôt* Etiologies." *Revue biblique* 81 (1974): 557–96.

————. *The Song of Songs and the Ancient Egyptian Love Songs.* Madison: University of Wisconsin, 1985.

————. "Three Esthers." Pages 50–60 in *The Book of Esther in Modern Research.* Edited by Sidnie White Crawford and Leonard J. Greenspoon. London: T&T Clark, 2003.

————, ed. *Texts, Temples, and Traditions: A Tribute to Menahem Haran.* Winona Lake, Ind.: Eisenbrauns, 1996.

Fox, Robin. *Kinship and Marriage: An Anthropological Perspective.* Harmondsworth, Eng.: Penguim, 1967.

Frame, John M. "Abortion from a Biblical Perspective." Pages 43–75 in *Thou Shalt Not Kill: The Christian Case against Abortion.* Edited by Richard L. Ganz. New Rochelle, N.Y.: Arlington House, 1978.

France, R. T. *Women in the Church's Ministry: A Test-Case for Biblical Interpretation.* Grand Rapids: Eerdmans, 1995.

Frankel, Ellen. *The Five Books of Miriam: A Woman's Commentary on the Torah.* New York: G. P. Putnam's, 1996.

Franklin, Cecil L. "Sexuality and Gender in the Bible." *Iliff Review* 35 (1978): 19–27.

Frantz, Nadine Pence, and Deborah L. Silver. "Women in Leadership: A Theological Perspective." *Brethren Life and Thought* 30 (1985): 37–40.

Fredericks, Daniel C. *Qoheleth's Language: Re-evaluating Its Nature and Date.* Ancient Near Eastern Texts and Studies 3. Lewiston, N.Y.: Mellen, 1988.

Fredrickson, David E. "Natural and Unnatural Use in Romans 1:24–27: Paul and the Philosophic Critique of Eros." Pages 197–241 in *Homosexuality, Science, and the "Plain Sense" of Scripture.* Edited by David Balch. Grand Rapids: Eerdmans, 2000.

Freedman, David Noel. "Dinah and Shechem, Tamar and Amnon." *Austin Seminary Bulletin: Faculty Edition* 105 (1990): 51–63.

———. *Hosea: A New Translation with Introduction and Commentary.* Anchor Bible 24A. New York: Doubleday, 1989.

Freedman, David Noel, with Jeffrey C. Geoghegan and Michael M. Homan. *The Nine Commandments: Uncovering a Hidden Pattern of Crime and Punishment in the Hebrew Bible.* Edited by Astrid Billes Beck. New York: Doubleday, 2000.

Freedman, R. David. "Woman, a Power Equal to Man." *Biblical Archaeology Review* 9, no 1 (1983): 56–58.

Frettloeh, Magadelene Luise. "O amor é forte como a morte: Uma leitura de Cânticos dos cânticos com ohlos de mulher" [Love Is Strong as Death: A Reading of the Song of Songs with a Woman's Eyes]. *Fragmenta de cultura* 12 (2002): 633–42.

Friberg, Jöran. "Numbers and Counting." Pages 1139–46 in vol. 4 of *Anchor Bible Dictionary.* Edited by David Noel Freedman. 6 vols. New York: Doubleday, 1992.

Friedman, Mordecai A. "Israel's Response in Hosea 2:17b: 'You Are My Husband.'" *Journal of Biblical Literature* 99 (1980): 199–204.

———. "Tamar, a Symbol of Life: The 'Killer Wife' Superstition in the Bible and Jewish Tradition." *Association for Jewish Studies Review* 15 (1990): 23–61.

Friedman, Richard Elliott. *Commentary on the Torah: With a New English Translation.* San Francisco: HarperSanFrancisco, 2001.

Friedmann, Daniel. *To Kill and Take Possession: Law, Morality, and Society in Biblical Stories.* Peabody, Mass.: Hendrickson, 2002.

Frolov, Serge. "The Other Side of Jabbok: Genesis 32 as a Fiasco of Patriarchy." *Journal for the Study of the Old Testament* no. 91 (2000): 41–59.

Frymer-Kensky, Tikva. "Deuteronomy." Pages 52–62 in *The Women's Bible Commentary.* Edited by Carol A. Newsom and Sharon H. Ringe. Louisville: Westminster John Knox, 1992.

———. *In the Wake of the Goddesses: Women, Culture, and the Biblical Transformation of Pagan Myth.* New York: Free Press/Maxwell Macmillan, 1992.

———. "Law and Philosophy: The Case of Sex in the Bible." *Semeia* 45 (1989): 89–102.

———. "Patriarchal Family Relationships and Near Eastern Law." *Biblical Archaeologist* 44 (1981): 209–14.

———. "Reading Rahab." Pages 57–67 in *Tehillah le-Moshe: Biblical and Judaic Studies in Honor of Moshe Greenberg.* Edited by Mordechai Cogan, Barry Eichler, and Jeffrey Tigay. Winona Lake, Ind.: Eisenbrauns, 1997.

———. *Reading the Women of the Bible.* New York: Schocken, 2002.

———. "Sex and Sexuality." Pages 1144–46 in vol. 5 of *Anchor Bible Dictionary.* Edited by David Noel Freedman. 6 vols. New York: Doubleday, 1992.

———. "The Strange Case of the Suspected Sotah (Numbers V 11–31)." *Vetus Testamentum* 34 (1984): 11–26.

———. "Virginity in the Bible." Pages 79–96 in *Gender and Law in the Hebrew Bible and the Ancient Near East.* Edited by Victor H. Matthews, Bernard M. Levinson, and Tikva Frymer-Kensky. Journal for the Study of the Old Testament: Supplement Series 262. Sheffield, Eng.: Sheffield Academic Press, 1998.

Fuchs, Esther. "A Jewish-Feminist Reading of Exodus 1–2." Pages 307–26 in *Jews, Christians, and the Theology of the Hebrew Scriptures.* Edited by Alice Ogden Bellis and Joel S. Kaminsky. Society of Biblical Literature Symposium Series 8. Atlanta: Society of Biblical Literature, 2000.

———. "The Literary Characterization of Mothers and Sexual Politics in the Hebrew Bible." Pages 117–36 in *Feminist Perspectives on Biblical Scholarship.* Edited by Adela Yarbro Collins. Chico, Calif.: Scholars Press, 1985.

———. "Marginalization, Ambiguity, Silencing: The Story of Jephthah's Daughter." *Journal of Feminist Studies in Religion* 5 (1989): 35–45.

———. *Sexual Politics in the Biblical Narrative: Reading the Hebrew Bible as a Woman.* Journal for the Study of the Old Testament: Supplement Series 310. Sheffield, Eng.: Sheffield Academic Press, 2000.

Furman, Nelly. "His Story versus Her Story: Male Genealogy and Female Strategy in the Jacob Cycle." Pages 107–16 in *Feminist Perspectives on Biblical Scholarship.* Edited by Adela Yarbro Collins. Chico, Calif.: Scholars Press, 1985. Repr., *Semeia* 46 (1989): 141–49.

Furnish, Victor Paul. "The Bible and Homosexuality." Pages 6–21 in *Homosexuality, in Search of a Christian Understanding: Biblical, Theological-Ethical, and Pastoral Care Perspectives.* Edited by Leon Smith. Nashville: Discipleship Resources, 1981.

———. " 'The Loyal Opposition' and Scripture." Pages 33–42 in *The Loyal Opposition: Struggling with the Church on Homosexuality.* Edited by Tex Sample and Amy E. DeLong. Nashville: Abingdon, 2000.

Gaca, Kathy L. *The Making of Fornication: Eros, Ethics, and Political Reform in Greek Philosophy and Early Christianity.* Hellenistic Culture and Society 40. Joan Palevsky Imprint in Classical Literature. Berkeley: University of California Press, 2003.

Gaden, John. "For the Ordination of Women." *St Mark's Review* 125 (March 1986): 22–33.

Gage, Warren Austin. *The Gospel of Genesis: Studies in Protology and Eschatology.* Winona Lake, Ind.: Carpenter, 1984.

Gagné, Jacques. " '. . . Homme et femme il les créa' (Gn 1,27)." *Cahiers de l'oratoire saint-Joseph* 11 (2000): 91–98.

Gagnon, Robert A. J. "The Bible and Homosexual Practice: Key Issues." Pages 40–92 in Dan O. Via and Robert A. J. Gagnon, *Homosexuality and the Bible: Two Views.* Minneapolis: Fortress, 2003.

———. *The Bible and Homosexual Practice: Texts and Hermeneutics.* Nashville: Abingdon, 2001.

———. "The Old Testament and Homosexuality: A Critical Review of the Case Made by Phyllis Bird." *Zeitschrift für die alttestamentliche Wissenschaft* 117 (2005): 367–94.

_____. "Scriptural Perspectives on Homosexuality and Sexual Identity." *Journal of Psychology and Christianity* 24 (2005): 293–303.

_____. "Sexuality." Pages 739–48 in *Dictionary for Theological Interpretation of the Bible.* Edited by Kevin J. Vanhoozer et al. Grand Rapids: Baker, 2005.

Gaines, Janet Howe. "How Bad Was Jezebel?" *Bible Review* 16, no. 5 (2000): 12–23.

Galpaz-Feller, Pnina. "לא תנאף ! עיונים במקרא ובתרבות מצרים הקדומה" *Beit Mikra* 49 (2004): 159–73. [" 'You Shall Not Commit Adultery!' Adultery in the Bible and in Ancient Egypt." R.M.D.]

_____. "Private Lives and Public Censure—Adultery in Ancient Egypt and Biblical Israel." *Near Eastern Archaeology* 67 (2004): 153–61.

Gane, Roy. *Altar Call.* Berrien Springs, Mich.: Diadem, 1999.

————. "Biblical and Ancient Near Eastern Penalties for Sexual Misconduct." PhD preliminary examination in biblical law, University of California, Berkeley, November 1988, pages 139–45 in Gane's 1995 syllabus for the Andrews University Theological Seminary course Covenant-Law-Sabbath.

————. *God's Faulty Heroes.* Hagerstown, Md.: Review and Herald, 1996.

————. *Leviticus, Numbers.* NIV Application Commentary 3. Grand Rapids: Zondervan, 2004.

————. "Old Testament Principles Relevant to Divorce and Remarriage." *Journal of the Adventist Theological Society* 12, no. 2 (2001): 35–61.

————. *Ritual Dynamic Structure.* Gorgias Dissertations 14. Piscataway, N.J.: Gorgias, 2004.

Gangloff, Frédéric. "A l'ombre des déesses-arbres? (Os 4:12–14)." *Biblische Notizen* 106 (2001): 13–20.

García Martínez, Florentino, et al., eds. *Studies in Deuteronomy: In Honour of C. J. Labuschagne on the Occasion of His 65th Birthday.* Vetus Testamentum Supplements 53. New York: E. J. Brill, 1994.

Gardiner, A. H. "Adoption Extraordinary." *Journal of Egyptian Archaeology* 26 (1940): 23–29.

————. trans. *The Chester Beatty Papyri.* Oxford: Oxford University Press, 1931.

Gardner, Anne. "Genesis 2:4b–3: A Mythological Paradigm of Sexual Equality or of the Religious History of Pre-exilic Israel?" *Scottish Journal of Theology* 43 (1990): 1–18.

Gardner, Tim Alan. *Sacred Sex: A Spiritual Celebration of Oneness in Marriage.* Colorado Springs, Colo.: Waterbrook, 2000.

Garland, David E. "A Biblical View of Divorce." *Review and Expositor* 84 (1987): 419–32.

Garr, W. Randall. " 'Image' and 'Likeness' in the Inscription from Tell Fakhariyeh." *Israel Exploration Journal* 50 (2000): 227–34.

————. *In His Own Image and Likeness: Humanity, Divinity, and Monotheism.* Culture and History of the Ancient Near East 15. Leiden: E. J. Brill, 2003.

Garrett, Duane A. "Ecclesiastes 7:25–29 and the Feminist Hermeneutic." *Criswell Theological Review* 2 (1988): 309–21.

————. *Hosea, Joel.* New American Commentary 19A. Nashville: Broadman and Holman, 1997.

————. *Proverbs, Ecclesiastes, Song of Songs.* New American Commentary 14. Nashville: Broadman, 1993.

————. *Rethinking Genesis: The Sources and Authorship of the First Book of the Pentateuch.* Grand Rapids: Baker, 1991.

————. "Song of Songs." Pages 1–265 in Duane A. Garrett and Paul R. House, *Song of Songs, Lamentations.* Word Biblical Commentary 23B. Nashville: Nelson, 2004.

————. "Votive Prostitution Again: A Comparison of Proverbs 7:13–14 and 21:28–29." *Journal of Biblical Literature* 109 (1990): 681–82.

Garsiel, Moshe. "The Story of David and Bathsheba: A Different Approach." *Catholic Biblical Quarterly* 55 (1993): 244–62.

Gaster, Theodore. *The Holy and the Profane: Evolution of Jewish Folkways.* New York: W. Sloane Associates, 1955.

Gehrke, Ralph. "Biblical View of the Sexual Polarity." *Concordia Theological Monthly* 41 (1970): 195–205.

Gelernter, David. "Tsipporah's Bloodgroom: A Biblical Breaking Point." *Orim* 3 (spring 1988): 46–55.

Geller, Markham J. "The Elephantine Papyri and Hosea 2,3: Evidence for the Form of the Early Jewish Divorce Writ." *Journal for the Study of Judaism in the Persian, Hellenistic, and Roman Periods* 8 (1977–1978): 139–48.

Georgoudi, Stella. "Creating a Myth of Matriarchy." Pages 449–63 in *From Ancient Goddesses to Christian Saints.* Vol 1 of *A History of Women in the West.* Translated by Arthur Goldhammer. Cambridge, Mass.: Belknap, 1992.

Gerber, Aaron H. *Biblical Attitudes on Human Sexuality.* Great Neck, N.Y.: Todd & Honeywell, 1982.

Gerleman, Gillis. *Ruth: Das Hohelied.* Neukirchen-Vluyn: Neukirchener Verlag, 1965.

Gerstein, Beth. "A Ritual Processed: A Look at Judges 11:40." Pages 175–93 in *Anti-covenant: Counter-reading Women's Lives in the Hebrew Bible.* Edited by Mieke Bal. Sheffield, Eng.: Almond, 1989.

Gerstenberger, Erhard S. "Herrschen oder Lieben: Zum Verhältnis der Geschlechter im Alten Testament." Pages 335–47 in *Die Botschaft und die Boten: Festschrift für Hans Walter Wolff zum 70. Geburtstag.* Edited by Joachim Jeremias and Lothar Perlitt. Neukirchen-Vluyn: Neukirchener Verlag, 1981.

————. "Sexualidade, homossexualismo e convivência" (Sexuality, Homosexual Behavior, and Life with Others). *Estudos teológicos* 39 (1999): 5–26.

————. *Yahweh the Patriarch: Ancient Images of God and Feminist Theology.* Minneapolis: Fortress, 1996.

Gerstenberger, Erhard S., and Wolfgang Schrage. *Woman and Man.* Translated by D. W. Stott. Biblical Encounter Series. Nashville: Abingdon, 1981.

Getty-Sullivan, Mary Ann. *Women in the New Testament.* Collegeville, Minn.: Liturgical, 2001.

Gevirtz, Stanley. "Of Patriarchs and Puns: Joseph at the Fountain, Jacob at the Ford." *Hebrew Union College Annual* 46 (1975): 33–54.

Geyer, Marcia L. "Stopping the Juggernaut: A Close Reading of 2 Samuel 20:13–22." *Union Seminary Quarterly Review* 41 (1986): 33–42.

Gieschen, Charles A., ed. *The Law in Holy Scripture: Essays from the Concordia Theological Seminary Symposium.* St. Louis: Concordia, 2003.

Giguère, Paul André. "Trois textes bibliques sur le plaisir sexuel." *Église et théologie* 17 (1986): 311–20.

Giles, Kevin. "Response." Pages 65–87 in *The Bible and Women's Ministry: An Australian Dialogue.* Edited by Alan Nichols. Wanniassa, Australia: Acorn, 1990.

———. *The Trinity and Subordinationism: The Doctrine of God and the Contemporary Gender Debate.* Downers Grove, Ill.: InterVarsity, 2002.

Ginsberg, Harold L. *The Five Megilloth and Jonah: A New Translation.* Philadelphia: Jewish Publication Society of America, 1969.

Ginsburg, Christian David. *The Song of Songs and Coheleth (Commonly Called Ecclesiastes): Translated from the Original Hebrew, with a Commentary, Historical and Critical.* 2 vols. 1857–1861. Repr., 2 vols. in 1. Library of Biblical Studies. New York: Ktav, 1970.

Ginzberg, Louis. *The Legends of the Jews.* 7 vols. Philadelphia: Jewish Publication Society of America, 1909–1928.

Gitay, Yehoshua. "Prophetic Criticism—'What Are They Doing?': The Case of Isaiah—a Methodological Assessment." *Journal for the Study of the Old Testament* no. 96 (2001): 101–27.

Gitay, Zefira. "Esther and the Queen's Throne." Pages 136–48 in *A Feminist Companion to Esther, Judith, and Susanna.* Edited by Athalya Brenner. Feminist Companion to the Bible 7. Sheffield, Eng.: Sheffield Academic Press, 1995.

Gladson, Jerry A. "The Role of Women in the Old Testament outside the Pentateuch." Pages 46–61 in *Symposium on the Role of Women in the Church.* Edited by Julia Neuffer. Washington, D.C.: General Conference of Seventh-day Adventists, 1984.

Glasscock, Ed. "The Biblical Concept of Elder." *Bibliotheca sacra* 144 (1987): 66–78.

———. "The Husband of One Wife Requirement in 1 Timothy 3:2." *Bibliotheca sacra* 140 (1983): 244–58.

Glatt-Gilad, David A. "Yahweh's Honor at Stake: A Divine Conundrum." *Journal for the Study of the Old Testament* no. 98 (2002): 63–74.

Glazier-McDonald, Beth. "Intermarriage, Divorce, and the *bat'-el nekar:* Insights into Mal 2:10–16." *Journal of Biblical Literature* 106 (1987): 603–11.

Gledhill, Tom. *The Message of the Song of Songs.* Bible Speaks Today. Downers Grove, Ill.: InterVarsity, 1994.

Glenny, W. Edward. "1 Corinthians 7:29–31 and the Teaching of Continence in the Acts of Paul and Thecla." *Grace Theological Journal* 11 (1990): 53–70.

Glezerman, M., B. Piura, and V. Insler. "Cervical Cancer in Jewish Women." *American Journal of Obstetrics and Gynecology* 161, no. 5 (1989): 1186–90.

Glickman, S. Craig. *A Song for Lovers.* Downers Grove, Ill.: InterVarsity, 1976.

Godfrey, W. Robert. "Headship and the Bible." Pages 82–91 in *Does Christianity Teach Male Headship? The Equal-Regard Marriage and Its Critics.* Edited by David Blankenhorn, Don S. Browning, and Mary Stewart Van Leeuwen. Grand Rapids: Eerdmans, 2003.

Gold, Michael. *And Hannah Wept: Infertility, Adoption, and the Jewish Couple.* Philadelphia: Jewish Publication Society, 1988.

Goldenberg, Naomi R. *Changing of the Gods: Feminism and the End of Traditional Religions.* Boston: Beacon, 1979.

Goldingay, John. "The Bible and Sexuality." *Scottish Journal of Theology* 39 (1986): 175–88.

———. "Divine Ideals, Human Stubbornness, and Scriptural Inerrancy." *Transformation* 2, no. 4 (1985): 1–4.

———. "Hosea 1–3, Genesis 1–4, and Masculist Interpretation." *Horizons in Biblical Theology* 17 (1995): 37–44.

———. "The Significance of Circumcision." *Journal for the Study of the Old Testament* no. 88 (2000): 3–18.

Gollaher, David L. *Circumcision: A History of the World's Most Controversial Surgery.* New York: Basic, 2000.

Gonnet, Hatice. "Hittite Religion." Translated by Stephen Rosoff. Pages 225–28 in vol. 3 of *The Anchor Bible Dictionary.* Edited by David Noel Freedman. 6 vols. New York: Doubleday, 1992.

Good, Edwin M. "Deception and Women: A Response." *Semeia* 42 (1988): 116–32.

Good, Robert M. "Exodus 32:18." Pages 137–42 in *Love and Death in the Ancient Near East: Essays in Honor of Marvin H. Pope.* Edited by John H. Marks and Robert M. Good. Guilford, Conn.: Four Quarters, 1987.

Goodfriend, Elaine A. "Adultery." Pages 82–86 in vol. 1 of *Anchor Bible Dictionary.* Edited by David Noel Freedman. 6 vols. New York: Doubleday, 1992.

———. "Prostitution (OT)." Pages 505–10 in vol. 5 of *Anchor Bible Dictionary.* Edited by David Noel Freedman. 6 vols. New York: Doubleday, 1992.

Gordis, Robert. "The Knowledge of Good and Evil in the Old Testament and Qumram Scrolls." *Journal of Biblical Literature* 76 (1957): 114–20.

———. "Love, Marriage, and Business in the Book of Ruth: A Chapter in Hebrew Customary Law." Pages 241–64 in *A Light unto My Path: Old Testament Studies in Honor of Jacob M. Myers.* Edited by Howard N. Bream, Ralph D. Heim, and Carey A. Moore. Philadelphia: Temple University Press, 1974.

———. *The Song of Songs and Lamentations: A Study, Modern Translation, and Commentary.* New York: Ktav, 1974.

Gordon, Cynthia. "Hagar: A Throw-away Character among the Matriarchs?" Pages 271–77 in the *SBL Seminar Papers, 1985.* Society of Biblical Literature Seminar Papers 24. Atlanta: Scholars Press, 1985.

Gordon, Cyrus H. *Before the Bible: The Common Background of Greek and Hebrew Civilisations.* New York: Harper & Row, 1962.

———. "Biblical Customs and the Nuzi Tablets." *Biblical Archaeologist* 3 (1940): 1–12.

———. *Ugaritic Literature: A Comprehensive Translation of the Poetic and Prose Texts.* Rome: Pontifical Biblical Institute, 1949.

Gossai, Hemchand. *Power and Marginality in the Abraham Narrative.* Lanham, Md.: University Press of America, 1995.

Gottwald, Norman K. *The Tribes of Yahweh: A Sociology of the Religion of Liberated Israel, 1250–1050 B.C.E.* Maryknoll, N.Y.: Orbis, 1979.

Goulder, Michael D. "Ruth: A Homily on Deuteronomy 22–25?" Pages 307–19 in *Of Prophets' Visions and the Wisdom of Sages: Essays in Honour of R. Norman Whybray on His Seventieth Birthday.* Edited by Heather A. McKay and David J. A. Clines. Journal for the Study of the Old Testament: Supplement Series 162. Sheffield, Eng.: Sheffield Academic Press, 1993.

———. *The Song of Fourteen Songs.* Sheffield, Eng.: JSOT Press, 1986.

Gous, Ignatius G. P. "Proverbs 31:10–31—the A to Z of Woman Wisdom." *Old Testament Essays* 9 (1996): 35–51.

Grabbe, Lester L. *Ezra-Nehemiah.* New York: Routledge, 1998.

Grabowski, John S. *Sex and Virtue: An Introduction to Sexual Ethics.* Catholic Moral Thought. Washington, D.C.: Catholic University of America Press, 2003.

Graetz, Naomi. "Dinah the Daughter." Pages 306–17 in *A Feminist Companion to Genesis.* Edited by Athalya Brenner. Feminist Companion to the Bible 2. Sheffield, Eng.: Sheffield Academic Press, 1993.

———. "God Is to Israel as Husband Is to Wife: The Metaphoric Battering of Hosea's Wife." Pages 126–45 in *A Feminist Companion to the Latter Prophets.* Edited by Athalya Brenner. Feminist Companion to the Bible 8. Sheffield, Eng.: Sheffield Academic Press, 1995.

———. *S/He Created Them: Feminist Retellings of Biblical Tales.* Piscataway, N.J.: Gorgias, 2003.

Gravett, Sandra L. "That All Women May Be Warned: Reading the Sexual and Ethnic Violence in Ezekiel 16 and 23." PhD diss., Duke University Press, 1994.

Gray, John. *The Legacy of Canaan.* 2d rev. ed. Vetus Testamentum Supplements 5. Leiden: E. J. Brill, 1965.

Grayson, A. Kirk, and Donald B. Redford. *Papyrus and Tablet.* Englewood Cliffs, N.J.: Prentice Hall, 1973.

Green, A. R. W. *The Role of Human Sacrifice in the Ancient Near East.* American Schools of Oriental Research Dissertation Series 1. Missoula, Mont.: Scholars Press, 1975.

Green, Lyn. "In Search of Ancient Egyptian Virgins." *The Journal of the Society for the Study of Egyptian Antiquites* 28 (2001): 90–98.

Green, M. Christian, and Paul D. Numrich. *Religious Perspectives on Sexuality: A Resource Guide.* Chicago: Park Ridge Center, 2001.

Greenberg, David F. *The Construction of Homosexuality.* Chicago: University of Chicago Press, 1988.

Greenberg, Moshe. *Ezekiel 1–20: A New Translation with Introduction and Commentary.* Anchor Bible 22. Garden City, N.Y.: Doubleday, 1983.

———. "Ezekiel 16: A Panorama of Passions." Pages 143–50 in *Love and Death in the Ancient Near East: Essays in Honor of Marvin H. Pope*. Edited by Jon H. Marks and Robert M. Good. Guilford, Conn.: Four Quarters, 1987.

———. *Ezekiel 21–37: A New Translation with Introduction and Commentary*. Anchor Bible 22A. Garden City, N.Y.: Doubleday, 1997.

———. "More Reflections on Biblical Criminal Law." Pages 3–17 in *Studies in Bible, 1986*. Edited by Sara Japhet. Scripta hierosolymitana 31. Jerusalem: Magnes, 1986.

———. "Some Postulates of Biblical Criminal Law." Pages 5–28 in *Yehezkel Kaufmann Jubilee Volume*. Edited by M. Haran. Jerusalem: Magnes, 1960.

Greengus, Samuel. "The Old Babylonian Marriage Contract." *Journal of the American Oriental Society* 89 (1969): 505–32.

———. "Redefining 'Inchoate Marriage' in Old Babylonian Contexts." Pages 123–39 in *Riches Hidden in Secret Places: Ancient Near Eastern Studies in Memory of Thorkild Jacobsen*. Edited by Tzvi Abusch. Winona Lake, Ind.: Eisenbrauns, 2002.

Greenstein, E. L. "Recovering 'the Women Who Served at the Entrance.'" Pages 165–73 in *Studies in Historical Geography and Biblical Historiography: Presented to Zechariah Kallai*. Edited by Gershon Galil and Moshe Weinfeld. Vetus Testamentum Supplements 81. Boston: E. J. Brill, 2000.

Grenz, Stanley J. "Is God Sexual? Human Embodiment and the Christian Conception of God." Pages 196–208 in *This Is My Name Forever: The Trinity and Gender Language for God*. Edited by Alvin F. Kimel Jr. Downers Grove, Ill.: InterVarsity, 2001.

———. *Sexual Ethics: An Evangelical Perspective*. Louisville: Westminster John Knox, 1997.

———. "Theological Foundations for Male-Female Relationships." *Journal of the Evangelical Theological Society* 41 (1998): 615–30.

———. *Welcoming but Not Affirming: An Evangelical Response to Homosexuality*. Louisville: Westminster John Knox, 1998.

Grenz, Stanley J., with Denise Muir Kjesbo. *Women in the Church: A Biblical Theology of Women in Ministry*. Downers Grove, Ill.: InterVarsity, 1995.

Griffiths, Michael. *The Church and World Mission*. Grand Rapids: Zondervan, 1980.

Grisanti, Michael A. "Old Testament Poetry as a Vehicle for Historiography." *Bibliotheca Sacra* 161 (2004): 163–78.

Gritz, Sharon Hodgin. *Paul, Women Teachers, and the Mother Goddess at Ephesus: A Study of 1 Timothy 2:9–15 in Light of the Religious and Cultural Milieu of the First Century*. Lanham, Md.: University Press of America, 1991.

———. "The Role of Women in the Church." Pages 299–314 in *The People of God: Essays on the Believers' Church*. Edited by Paul Basden and David S. Dockery. Nashville: Broadman, 1991.

Groothuis, Rebecca Merrill. *The Feminist Bogeywoman: Questions and Answers about Evangelical Feminism*. Grand Rapids: Baker, 1995.

———. *Good News for Women: A Biblical Picture of Gender Equality*. Grand Rapids: Baker, 1997.

Grosheide, F. W. *The First Epistle to the Corinthians*. New International Commentary on the New Testament. Grand Rapids: Eerdmans, 1953.

Gross, Rita M. "Steps toward Feminine Imaging of Deity in Jewish Theology." Pages 234–47 in *On Being a Jewish Feminist: A Reader*. Edited by Susannah Heschel. New York: Schocken, 1983.

Gross, Rita M., and Rosemary Radford Ruether, eds. *Religious Feminism and the Future of the Planet: A Christian-Buddhist Conversation*. New York: Continuum, 2001.

Groß, Walter. "Jiftachs Tochter." Pages 273–93 in *Das Manna fällt auch heute noch: Beiträge zur Geschichte und Theologie des Alten, Ersten Testaments. Festschrift für Erich Zenger*. Edited by Frank-Lothar Hossfeld and Ludger Schwienhorst-Schönberger. Herders biblische Studien 44. Freiburg: Herder, 2004.

Grossberg, Daniel. *Centripetal and Centrifugal Structures in Biblical Poetry*. Atlanta: Scholars, 1989.

———. "Sexual Desire: Abstract and Concrete." *Hebrew Studies* 22 (1981): 59–60.

———. "Two Kinds of Sexual Relations in the Hebrew Bible." *Hebrew Studies* 34 (1994): 7–25.

Grossman, Susan, and Rivka Haut, eds. *Daughters of the King—Women and the Synagogue: A Survey of History, Halakhah, and Contemporary Realities*. Philadelphia: Jewish Publication Society, 1992.

Gruber, Mayer I. "Hebrew *qĕdēšāh* and Her Canaanite and Akkadian Cognates." *Ugarit-Forschungen* 18 (1986): 133–48.

———. *The Motherhood of God and Other Studies*. South Florida Studies in the History of Judaism 57. Atlanta: Scholars Press, 1992.

———. "The Motherhood of God in Second Isaiah." *Revue biblique* 90 (1983): 351–59.

———. "A Re-examination of the Charges against Shechem Son of Hamor," *Beit Mikra* 157 (1999): 119–27.

———. *Women in the Biblical World: A Study Guide*. American Theological Library Association Bibliography Series 38. Lanham, Md.: Scarecrow, 1995.

Grudem, Wayne A. *Countering the Claims of Evangelical Feminism: Biblical Responses to the Key Questions*. Colorado Springs, Colo.: Multnomah, 2006.

———. "Does ΚΕΦΑΛΗ ('Head') Mean 'Source' or 'Authority over' in Greek Literature? A Survey of 2,336 Examples." *Trinity Journal* 6 (1985): 38–59.

———. *Evangelical Feminism: A New Path to Liberalism?* Wheaton, Ill.: Crossway, 2006.

———. *Evangelical Feminism and Biblical Truth: An Analysis of More Than One Hundred Disputed Questions*. Sisters, Ore.: Multnomah, 2004.

———. "The Meaning of Κεφαλή ('Head'): A Response to Recent Studies." *Trinity Journal* 11 (1990): 3–72. Repr., pages 425–68 in *Recovering Biblical Manhood and Womanhood: A Response to Evangelical Feminism*. Edited by John Piper and Wayne A. Grudem. Wheaton, Ill.: Crossway, 1991.

————. "Should We Move beyond the New Testament to a Better Ethic? An Analysis of William J. Webb, *Slaves, Women and Homosexuals: Exploring the Hermeneutics of Cultural Analysis.*" *Journal of the Evangelical Theological Society* 47 (2004): 299–346.

————, ed. *Biblical Foundations for Manhood and Womanhood.* Foundations for the Family Series. Wheaton, Ill.: Crossway, 2002.

Gruenwald, Ithamar. *Rituals and Ritual Theory in Ancient Israel.* Brill Reference Library of Ancient Judaism 10. Leiden: E. J. Brill, 2003.

Gründwaldt, Klaus. *Exil und Identität: Beschneidung, Passa, und Sabbat in der Preisterschrift.* Bonner biblische Beiträge 85. Frankfurt am Main: Anton Hain, 1992.

Guenther, Allen. "A Typology of Israelite Marriage: Kinship, Socio-Economic, and Religious Factors." *Journal for the Study of the Old Testament* 29 (2005): 387–407.

Guillaume, Philippe. "The Demise of Lady Wisdom and of *Homo Sapiens:* An Unwise Reading of Genesis 2 and 3 in Light of Job and Proverbs." *Theological Review* 25, no. 2 (November 2004): 20–38.

Guinness, Michele. *Woman—the Full Story: A Dynamic Celebration of Freedoms.* Grand Rapids: Zondervan, 2003.

Gundry, Patricia. *Woman Be Free! The Clear Message of Scripture.* Grand Rapids: Zondervan, 1977.

Gunkel, Hermann. *Genesis.* Handkommentar zum Alten Testament, Abteilung 1, no. 1. 3d ed. Göttingen: Vandenhoeck & Ruprecht, 1910.

Gunn, David M. "Samson of Sorrows: An Isaianic Gloss on Judges 13–16." Pages 225–53 in *Reading between Texts: Intertextuality and the Hebrew Bible.* Edited by Danna Nolan Fewell. Louisville: Westminster John Knox, 1992.

Guy, Fritz. "The Disappearance of Paradise." Pages 137–53 in *The Welcome Table: Setting a Place for Ordained Women.* Edited by Patricia A. Habada and Rebecca Frost Brillhart. Langley Park, Md.: Team, 1995.

Haacker, Klaus. "Exegetische Gesichtspunkte zum Thema Homosexualität." *Theologische Beiträge* 25 (1994): 173–80.

Haas, Guenther. "Patriarchy as an Evil That God Tolerated: Analysis and Implications for the Authority of Scripture." *Journal of the Evangelical Theological Society* 38 (1995): 321–36.

Haase, Ingrid J. "Cult Prostitution in the Hebrew Bible?" M.A. diss., University of Ottawa, 1990.

Habel, Norman C., and Shirley Wurst, eds. *The Earth Story in Genesis.* Earth Bible 2. Sheffield, Eng.: Sheffield Academic Press, 2000.

————, eds. *The Earth Story in Wisdom Traditions.* Earth Bible 3. Cleveland: Pilgrim, 2001.

Haberman, Bonna Devora. "Foreskin Sacrifice." Pages 18–29 in *The Covenant of Circumcision: New Perspectives on an Ancient Jewish Rite.* Edited by Elizabeth Wyner Mark. Lebanon, N.H.: Brandeis University Press, 2003.

Hackett, Jo Ann. "In the Days of Jael: Reclaiming the History of Women in Ancient Israel." Pages 15–38 in *Immaculate and Powerful: The Female in Sacred*

Image and Social Reality. Edited by Clarissa W. Atkinson, Constance H. Buchanan, and Margaret R. Miles. Boston: Beacon, 1985.

———. "Rehabilitating Hagar: Fragments of an Epic Pattern." Pages 12–27 in *Gender and Difference in Ancient Israel.* Edited by Peggy L. Day. Minneapolis: Fortress, 1989.

———. "Women's Studies in the Hebrew Bible." Pages 141–64 in *The Future of Biblical Studies: The Hebrew Scriptures.* Edited by Richard E. Friedman and H. G. M. Williamson. Atlanta: Scholars Press, 1987.

Hadley, Judith M. *The Cult of Asherah in Ancient Israel and Judah: Evidence for a Hebrew Goddess.* New York: Cambridge University Press, 2000.

Haerich, Donna Jeane. "Genesis Revisited." Pages 93–111 in *The Welcome Table: Setting a Place for Ordained Women.* Edited by Patricia A. Habada and Rebecca Frost Brillhart. Langley Park, Md.: Team, 1995.

Hailey, Jan Faver. "'Neither Male and Female' (Gal. 3:28)." Pages 131–66 in vol. 1 of *Essays on Women in Earliest Christianity.* Edited by Carroll D. Osburn. 2 vols. Joplin, Mo.: College Press, 1993.

———. "'Not Male and Female': The Interpretation and Scope of Meaning of Galatians 3:28 in the Context of the Galatian Epistle." Master of Arts thesis, Abilene Christian University, 1995.

Hall, Gary H. "The Marriage Imagery of Jeremiah 2 and 3: A Study of Antecedents and Innovations in a Prophetic Metaphor." Th.D. diss., Union Theological Seminary in Virginia, 1980.

———. "Origin of the Marriage Metaphor." *Hebrew Studies* 23 (1982): 169–71.

Hall, Robert G. "Circumcision." Pages 1025–31 in vol. 1 of *Anchor Bible Dictionary.* Edited by D. N. Freedman. 6 vols. New York: Doubleday, 1992.

Halperin, David J. *Seeking Ezekiel: Text and Psychology.* University Park: Pennsylvania State University Press, 1993.

Hals, Ronald M. *Grace and Faith in the Old Testament.* Minneapolis: Augsburg, 1980.

Hamilton, Victor P. *The Book of Genesis: Chapters 1–17.* New International Commentary on the Old Testament. Grand Rapids: Eerdmans, 1990.

———. *The Book of Genesis: Chapters 18–50.* New International Commentary on the Old Testament. Grand Rapids: Eerdmans, 1995.

———. *Handbook on the Pentateuch.* Grand Rapids: Baker, 1982.

———. "Marriage: Old Testament and Ancient Near East." Pages 559–69 in vol. 4 of *Anchor Bible Dictionary.* Edited by David Noel Freedman. 6 vols. New York: Doubleday, 1992.

Hammer, Jill. *Sisters at Sinai: New Tales of Biblical Women.* Philadelphia: Jewish Publication Society, 2001.

Hanko, Herman, ed. *Far above Rubies: Today's Virtuous Woman.* Grand Rapids: Reformed Free Publishing Association, 1992.

Hannay, James Ballantyne, with an appreciation by George Birdwood. *Sex Symbolism in Religion.* 2 vols. London: Religious Evolution Research Society, 1922. Repr., Amsterdam: Fredonia, 2002.

Hanselman, Stephen W. "Narrative Theory, Ideology, and Transformation in Judges 4." Pages 95–112 in *Anti-covenant: Counter-reading Women's Lives in the Hebrew Bible.* Edited by Mieke Bal. Sheffield, Eng.: Almond, 1989.

Hansen, Tracy. "My Name Is Tamar." *Theology* 95 (1992): 370–76.

Harbach, Robert C. *Studies in the Book of Genesis.* Grandville, Mich.: Reformed, 2001.

Hardesty, Nancy. "When Does Life Begin?" *Eternity* 22, no. 2 (1971): 19, 43.

Harland, P. J. "Menswear and Womenswear: A Study of Deuteronomy 22:5." *Expository Times* 110, no. 3 (1998): 73–76.

Harman, A. M. "Modern Discussion on the Song of Songs." *Reformed Theological Review* 37 (1978): 66–72.

Harper, A. F. *Beacon Bible Commentary.* Kansas City, Mo.: Beacon Hill, 1967.

Harper, Andrew. *The Song of Solomon.* Cambridge Bible. Cambridge: Cambridge University Press, 1907.

Harper, Michael. *Equal and Different: Male and Female in Church and Family.* London: Hodder & Stoughton, 1994.

Harris, J. Gordon, Cheryl Anne Brown, and Michael S. Moore. *Joshua, Judges, Ruth.* New International Biblical Commentary: Old Testament series 5. Peabody, Mass.: Hendrickson, 2000.

Harris, Kevin. *Sex, Ideology, and Religion: The Representation of Women in the Bible.* Totowa, N.J.: Barnes & Noble, 1984.

Harris, Paul R. *Why Is Feminism So Hard to Resist?* Decator, Ill.: Repristination, 1998.

Harris, R. Laird. "Leviticus." Pages 501–654 in vol. 2 of *The Expositor's Bible Commentary.* Edited by Frank E. Gaebelein. 12 vols. Grand Rapids: Zondervan, 1976–1992.

Harris, Rivkah. "Women (Mesopotamia)." Pages 947–51 in vol. 6 of *Anchor Bible Dictionary.* Edited by David Noel Freedman. 6 vols. New York: Doubleday, 1992.

Harris, Scott L. "Hannah's Vow to Yahweh in I Samuel 1: An Issue of Faithfulness." *Lutheran Forum* 26 (May 1992): 28–33.

———. "Proverbs 1–9: A Study of Inner-biblical Interpretation." PhD diss., Union Theological Seminary, 1988.

Harris, Timothy J. "Why Did Paul Mention Eve's Deception? A Critique of P. W. Barnett's Interpretation of 1 Timothy 2." *Evangelical Quarterly* 62 (1990): 335–52.

Harrison, R. K. *Introduction to the Old Testament.* Grand Rapids: Eerdmans, 1969.

———. *Leviticus: An Introduction and Commentary.* Tyndale Old Testament Commentaries 3. Downers Grove, Ill.: InterVarsity, 1980.

———. *Numbers.* Wycliffe Exegetical Commentary. Chicago: Moody, 1990.

Hartley, John E. *Leviticus.* Word Biblical Commentary 4. Dallas: Word, 1992.

Harvey, Anthony E. "Marriage, Sex, and the Bible." *Theology* 96 (1993): 364–72, 461–68.

Hasel, Gerhard F. *Biblical Interpretation Today.* Washington, D.C.: Biblical Research Institute, 1985.

———. "Clean and Unclean Meats in Leviticus 11: Still Relevant?" *Journal of the Adventist Theological Society* 2, no. 2 (1991): 91–125.

———. "Divine Inspiration and the Canon of the Bible." *Journal of the Adventist Theological Society* 5, no. 1 (1994): 68–105.

———. "Equality from the Start: Woman in the Creation Story." *Spectrum* 7, no. 2 (1975): 21–28.

———. "Health and Healing in the Old Testament." *Andrews University Seminary Studies* 21 (1983): 191–202.

———. "Man and Woman in Genesis 1–3." Pages 10–27 in *Symposium on the Role of Women in the Church*. Edited by Julia Neuffer. Washington, D.C.: General Conference of Seventh-day Adventists, 1984.

———. "The Meaning of 'Let Us' in Gen 1:26." *Andrews University Seminary Studies* 13 (1975): 58–66.

———. *Old Testament Theology: Basic Issues in the Current Debate*. 4th ed. Grand Rapids: Eerdmans, 1991.

———. "The Polemic Nature of the Genesis Cosmology." *Evangelical Quarterly* 46 (1974): 81–102.

———. *Understanding the Living Word of God*. Mountain View, Calif.: Pacific, 1980.

Hausmann, Jutta. "Beobachtungen zu Spr 31,10–31." Pages 261–66 in *Alttestamentlicher Glaube und biblische Theologie: Festschrift für Horst Dietrich Preuss zum 65. Geburtstag*. Edited by Jutta Hausmann and Hans-Jürgen Zobel. Stuttgart: Kohlhammer, 1992.

Hawk, L. Daniel. "Strange Houseguests: Rahab, Lot, and the Dynamics of Deliverance." Pages 89–97 in *Reading between Texts: Intertextuality and the Hebrew Bible*. Edited by Danna Nolan Fewell. Louisville: Westminster John Knox, 1992.

Hawkins, Tom R. "The Wife of Noble Character in Proverbs 31:10–31." *Bibliotheca sacra* 153 (1996): 12–23.

Hays, J. Daniel. "Applying the Old Testament Law Today." *Bibliotheca sacra* 158 (2001): 21–35.

Hays, Richard B. "Awaiting the Redemption of Our Bodies: The Witness of Scripture concerning Homosexuality." Pages 3–17 in *Homosexuality in the Church: Both Sides of the Debate*. Edited by Jeffrey S. Siker. Louisville: Westminster John Knox, 1994.

———. "The Biblical Witness concerning Homosexuality." Pages 65–84 in *Staying the Course: Supporting the Church's Position on Homosexuality*. Edited by Maxie D. Dunnam and H. Newton Malony. Nashville: Abingdon, 2003.

———. *The Moral Vision of the New Testament: A Contemporary Introduction to New Testament Ethics*. San Francisco: Harper, 1996.

Hayter, Mary. *The New Eve in Christ: The Use and Abuse of the Bible in the Debate about Women in the Church*. Grand Rapids: Eerdmans, 1987.

Hazan, Albert. *Le Cantique des cantiques enfin expliqué*. Paris: Lipzschatz, 1936.

Healey, Joseph P. "Fertility Cults." Pages 791–93 in vol. 2 of *Anchor Bible Dictionary*. Edited by David Noel Freedman. 6 vols. New York: Doubleday, 1992.

Heath, William A., and Gordon J. Wenham. *Jesus and Divorce: The Problem with the Evangelical Consensus.* Nashville: T. Nelson, 1985.

Heering, S. L., et al. "A Cohort Analysis of Cervical Cancer in Israeli Jewish Women." *Gynecologic Oncology* 39, no. 3 (1990): 244–48.

Heider, George C. *The Cult of Molek: A Reassessment.* Journal for the Study of the Old Testament: Supplement Series 43. Sheffield, Eng.: University of Sheffield Press, 1985.

———. "Molech." Pages 895–98 in vol. 4 of *Anchor Bible Dictionary.* Edited by D. N. Freedman. 6 vols. New York: Doubleday, 1992.

———. "Molech." Pages 1090–97 in *Dictionary of Deities and Demons in the Bible.* Edited by Karel van der Toorn, Bob Becking, and Pieter Willem van der Horst. Leiden: E. J. Brill, 1995.

Heijst, Annelies van. "Beyond Dividing Thinking: Solomon's Judgment and the Wisdom-Traditions of Women." *Louvain Studies* 19 (1994): 99–117.

Heimbach, Daniel R. *Pagan Sexuality: At the Center of the Contemporary Moral Crisis.* Wake Forest, N.C.: Southeastern Baptist Theological Seminary Press, 2001.

———. *True Sexual Morality: Recovering Biblical Standards for a Culture in Crisis.* Wheaton, Ill.: Crossway, 2004.

Heller, Jan. "Die Priesterin Raab." *Communio viatorum* 8 (1965): 113–17.

Helminiak, Daniel A. *What the Bible Really Says about Homosexuality.* San Francisco: Alamo Square, 1994.

Helton, Stanley N. "Titus 2:5—Must Women Stay at Home?" Pages 367–76 in vol. 1 of *Essays on Women in Earliest Christianity.* Edited by Carroll D. Osburn. 2 vols. Joplin, Mo.: College Press, 1993.

Hendel, Ronald S. "King David Loves Bathsheba; Is What the Historical David Did or Said More Important Than What the Bible Relates?" *Bible Review* 17, no. 1 (2001): 6.

———. "Of Demigods and the Deluge: Toward an Interpretation of Genesis 6:1–4." *Journal of Biblical Literature* 106 (1987): 13–26.

———. "Of Sacred Leopards and Abominable Pigs: How Common Practice Becomes Ritual Law." *Bible Review* 16, no. 5 (2000): 8.

Henry, Matthew. *Commentary on the Whole Bible.* 6 vols. Old Tappan, N.J.: Fleming H. Revell, n.d.

Henshaw, Richard A. *Female and Male—the Cultic Personnel: The Bible and the Rest of the Ancient Near East.* Allison Park, Pa.: Pickwick, 1994.

Henten, Jan Willem van, and Athalya Brenner, eds. *Families and Family Relations, as Represented in Early Judaisms and Early Christianities—Texts and Fictions: Papers Read at a NOSTER Colloquium in Amsterdam, June 9–11, 1988.* Studies in Theology and Religion 2. Leiden: Deo, 2000.

Hentrich, Thomas. "Qui était Gomer, ʾēšèt zᵉnûnîm (Os 1,2–3)?" *Science et esprit* 55 (2003): 5–22.

Hepner, Gershon. "Abraham's Incestuous Marriage with Sarah: A Violation of the Holiness Code." *Vetus Testamentum* 53 (2003): 143–55.

———. "Verbal Resonance in the Bible and Intertextuality." *Journal for the Study of the Old Testament* no. 96 (2001): 3–27.

Herbert J., and Fern Miles. *Husband-Wife Equality*. Old Tappan, N.J.: Fleming H. Revell, 1978.

Herodotus, *Histories*. Translated by A. D. Godley, 4 vols. Loeb Classical Library. Cambridge, Mass.: Harvard University Press, 1946.

Herr, Denise Dick. "How a Modern Bestseller Illuminates the Book of Ruth." *Bible Review* 14, no. 4 (1998): 34–41, 54–55.

Hertzberg, H. W. *I and II Samuel: A Commentary*. Old Testament Library. London: SCM, 1964.

Heschel, Abraham. *The Sabbath*. New York: Harper & Row, 1951.

Heskett, Randall J. "Proverb 23:13–15." *Interpretation* 55 (2001): 181–84.

Hess, Richard S. "Equality with and without Innocence: Genesis 1–3." Pages 79–95 in *Discovering Biblical Equality: Complementarity without Hierarchy*. Edited by Ronald W. Pierce and Rebecca Merrill Groothuis. Downers Grove, Ill.: InterVarsity, 2004.

———. *Joshua: An Introduction and Commentary*. Tyndale Old Testament Commentaries 6. Downers Grove, Ill.: InterVarsity, 1996.

———. "The Roles of the Woman and the Man in Genesis 3." *Themelios* 18 (1993): 15–19.

———. *Song of Songs*. Baker Commentary on the Old Testament Wisdom and Psalms. Grand Rapids: Baker, 2005.

———. "Splitting the Adam: The Usage of *ʾādām* in Genesis I–V." Pages 1–15 in *Studies in the Pentateuch*. Edited by J. A. Emerton. Vetus Testamentum Supplement 41. Leiden: E. J. Brill, 1990.

Hess, Richard S., M. Daniel, and R. Carroll, eds. *Family in the Bible: Exploring Customs, Culture, and Context*. Grand Rapids: Baker, 2003.

———, eds. *Israel's Messiah in the Bible and the Dead Sea Scrolls*. Grand Rapids: Baker, 2003.

Heth, William A. "The Changing Basis for Permitting Remarriage after Divorce for Adultery: The Influence of R. H. Charles." *Trinity Journal* 11 (1990): 143–59.

———. "Divorce and Remarriage." Pages 219–39 in *Applying the Scriptures*. Edited by Kenneth S. Kantzer. Grand Rapids: Academie, 1987.

———. "Divorce and Remarriage: The Search for an Evangelical Hermeneutic." *Trinity Journal* 16 (1995): 63–100.

Heth, William A., and Gordon J. Wenham. *Jesus and Divorce: The Problem with the Evangelical Consensus*. Nashville: T. Nelson, 1985.

Hewett, John H. "Genesis 2:4b–3:31; 4:2–16; 9:20–27; 19:30–38." *Review and Expositor* 86 (1989): 237–41.

Heywood, Leslie, and Jennifer Drake, eds. *Third Wave Agenda: Being Feminist, Doing Feminism*. Minneapolis: University of Minnesota Press, 1997.

Hicks, R. Lansing. "The Door of Love." Pages 153–58 in *Love and Death in the Ancient Near East: Essays in Honor of Marvin H. Pope*. Edited by John H. Marks and Robert M. Good. Guilford, Conn.: Four Quarters, 1987.

———. "Onan." Page 602 in vol. 3 of *The Interpreter's Dictionary of the Bible.* Edited by George A. Buttrick. 4 vols. Nashville: Abingdon, 1962.

Hidal, Sten. "The Land of Cush in the Old Testament." *Svensk exegetisk årsbok* 41–42 (1976–1977): 97–106.

Hiebert, Paula S. " 'Whence Shall Help Come to Me?' The Biblical Widow." Pages 125–41 in *Gender and Difference in Ancient Israel.* Edited by Peggy L. Day. Minneapolis: Fortress, 1989.

Hill, Andrew E. "Abortion in the Ancient Near East." Pages 31–48 in *Abortion: A Christian Understanding and Response.* Edited by James K. Hoffmeier. Grand Rapids: Baker, 1987.

———. "On David's 'Taking' and 'Leaving' Concubines (2 Sam 5:13; 15:16)." *Journal of Biblical Literature* 125 (2006): 129–50.

Hillers, Delbert R. "The Bow of Aqhat: The Meaning of a Mythological Theme." Pages 71–80 in *Orient and Occident: Essays Presented to Cyrus H. Gordon on the Occasion of His Sixty-Fifth Birthday.* Edited by Harry A. Hoffner Jr. Alter Orient und Altes Testament 22. Neukirchen-Vluyn: Neukirchener Verlag, 1973.

Hillman, Eugene. *Polygamy Reconsidered: African Plural Marriage and the Christian Church.* Maryknoll, N.Y.: Orbis, 1975.

Hitchens, Robert J. *Multiple Marriage: A Study of Polygamy in Light of the Bible.* Elkton, Md.: Doulos, 1987.

Hobbs, T. R. "Jeremiah 3:1–5 and Deuteronomy 24:1–4." *Zeitschrift für die alttestamentliche Wissenschaft* 86 (1974): 23–29.

Hoehner, Harold W. "A Response to Divorce and Remarriage." Pages 240–46 in *Applying the Scriptures: Papers from ICBI Summit III.* Edited by Kenneth Kantzer [a paper read by Willam A. Heth]. Grand Rapids: Zondervan, 1987.

Hoekema, Anthony A. *Created in God's Image.* Grand Rapids: Eerdmans, 1986.

Hoerth, Alfred. *Archaeology and the Old Testament.* Grand Rapids: Baker, 1998.

Höffken, Peter. "Das Hohelied und Salomoliteratur." Pages 125–35 in *Verbindungslinien: Festschrift für Werner H. Schmidt zum 65. Geburtstag.* Edited by Axel Graupner, Holger Delkurt, and Alexander Ernst. Neukirchen-Vluyn: Neukirchener Verlag, 2000.

Hoffmeier, James K. "Abortion and the Old Testament Law." Pages 49–63 in *Abortion: A Christian Understanding and Response.* Edited by James K. Hoffmeier. Grand Rapids: Baker, 1987.

———. "Zipporah." Page 1201 in vol. 4 of *International Standard Bible Encyclopedia.* Edited by G. W. Bromiley. 4 vols. Grand Rapids: Eerdmans, 1979–1988.

Hoffner, Harry A., Jr. *Hittite Myths.* 2d ed. Society of Biblical Literature Writings from the Ancient World 2. Atlanta: Scholars Press, 1998.

———. "Incest, Sodomy, and Bestiality in the Ancient Near East." Pages 83–90 in *Orient and Occident: Essays Presented to Cyrus H. Gordon on the Occasion of His Sixty-Fifth Birthday.* Edited by Harry A. Hoffner Jr. Alter Orient und Altes Testament 22. Neukirchen-Vluyn: Neukirchener Verlag, 1973.

———. "Symbols for Masculinity and Femininity: Their Use in Ancient Near Eastern Sympathetic Magic Rituals." *Journal of Biblical Literature* 85 (1966): 326–34.

Hoftijzer, Jacob. "David and the Tekoite Woman." *Vetus Testamentum* 20 (1970): 419–44.

Høgenhaven, Jesper. "The Opening of the Psalter: A Study in Jewish Theology." *Scandinavian Journal of the Old Testament* 15, no. 2 (2001): 169–80.

Holben, L. R. *What Christians Think about Homosexuality: Six Representative Viewpoints.* North Richland Hill, Tex.: Bibal, 1999.

Holbrook, Frank B. "A Brief Analysis and Interpretation of the Biblical Data regarding the Role of Woman." Pages 107–37 in *Symposium on the Role of Women in the Church.* Edited by Julia Neuffer. Washington, D.C.: General Conference of Seventh-day Adventists, 1984.

Holladay, William L. "Jeremiah xxxi 22b Reconsidered: 'The Woman Encompasses the Man.'" *Vetus Testamentum* 16 (1966): 236–39.

Hollis, Harry, Jr. *Thank God for Sex: A Christian Model for Sexual Understanding and Behavior.* Nashville: Broadman, 1975.

———, ed. "Christianity and Sexuality: Annotated Bibliography." *Review and Expositor* 68 (1971): 169–74.

Holloway, Steven W. "Distaff, Crutch, or Chain Gang: The Curse of the House of Joab in 2 Samuel 3:29." *Vetus Testamentum* 37 (1987): 370–75.

Hollyday, Joyce. "Voices out of the Silence: Recovering the Biblical Witness of Women." *Sojourners* 15, no. 6 (1986): 20–23.

Holmes, Michael W. "The Text of the Matthean Divorce Passages: A Comment on the Appeal to Harmonization in Textual Decisions." *Journal of Biblical Literature* 109 (1990): 651–64.

Holmyard, Harold R., III. "Solomon's Perfect One." *Bibliotheca sacra* 155 (1998): 164–71.

Holst, Robert "Polygamy and the Bible." *International Review of Missions* 56 (1967): 205–13.

Homan, Michael M. "Date Rape: The Agricultural and Astronomical Background of the Sumerian Sacred Marriage and Genesis 38." *Scandinavian Journal of the Old Testament* 16 (2002): 283–92.

Hommes, N. J. "'Let Women Be Silent in Church': A Message concerning the Worship Service and the Decorum to Be Observed by Women." *Calvin Theological Journal* 4 (1969): 5–22.

Hook, Donald D., and Alvin F. Kimel Jr. "The Pronouns of Deity: A Theolinguistic Critique of Feminist Proposals." Pages 62–87 in *This Is My Name Forever: The Trinity and Gender Language for God.* Edited by Alvin F. Kimel Jr. Downers Grove, Ill.: InterVarsity, 2001.

Hooke, S. H. "Genesis." Pages 175–207 in *Peake's Commentary on the Bible.* Edited by Matthew Black and H. H. Rowley. New York: Thomas Nelson, 1962.

Hooks, S. M. "Sacred Prostitution in the Bible and the Ancient Near East." PhD diss., Hebrew Union College, 1985.

Horine, Steven C. *Interpretive Images in the Song of Songs: From Wedding Chariots to Bridal Chambers.* Studies in the Humanities: Literature-Politics-Society 55. New York: Peter Lang, 2001.

Horner, Thomas M. *Jonathan Loved David: Homosexuality in Biblical Times.* Philadelphia: Westminster, 1978.

———. *Sex in the Bible.* Rutland, Vt.: C. E. Tuttle, 1974.

Horst, Pieter W. van der. "Celibacy in Early Judaism." *Revue biblique* 109 (2002): 390–402.

Horton, Fred L. "Form and Structure in Laws Relating to Women: Leviticus 18:6–18." Pages 20–33 in the *SBL Seminar Papers, 1973.* Society of Biblical Literature Seminar Papers 1. Missoula, Mont.: Scholars Press, 1973.

Hosch, Harold E. "Psalms 1 and 2: A Discourse Analysis." *Notes on Translation* 15, no. 3 (2001): 4–12.

Hossfeld, Frank-Lothar and Ludger Schwienhorst-Schönberger, eds. *Das Manna fällt auch heute noch: Beiträge zur Geschichte und Theologie des Alten, Ersten Testaments. Festschrift für Erich Zenger.* Herders Biblische Studien 44. Freiburg: Herder, 2004.

Hostetter, Edwin C. "Mistranslation in Cant 1.5." *Andrews University Seminary Studies* 34 (1996): 35–36.

House, H. Wayne. "Miscarriage or Premature Birth: Additional Thoughts on Exodus 21:22–25." *Westminster Theological Journal* 41 (1978): 105–23.

———. *The Role of Women in Ministry Today.* Nashville: Nelson, 1990. Repr., Grand Rapids: Baker, 1996.

Houten, Christian van. "The Rape of the Concubine." *Perspectives* 12, no. 8 (October 1997): 12–14.

Houtman, Cornelis. "Another Look at Forbidden Mixtures." *Vetus Testamentum* 34 (1984): 226–28.

———. "Exodus 4:24–26 and Its Interpretation." *Journal of Northwest Semitic Languages* 11 (1983): 81–105.

Houwink ten Cate, Philo H. J. "Hittite History." Pages 219–25 in vol. 3 of *The Anchor Bible Dictionary.* Edited by David Noel Freedman. 6 vols. New York: Doubleday, 1992.

Hove, Richard W. *Equality in Christ? Galatians 3:28 and the Gender Dispute.* Wheaton, Ill.: Crossway, 1999.

Howard, J. Keir. "Neither Male nor Female: An Examination of the Status of Women in the New Testament." *Evangelical Quarterly* 55 (1982): 31–42.

Hsu, Albert Y. *Singles at the Crossroads: A Fresh Perspective on Christian Singleness.* Downers Grove, Ill.: InterVarsity, 1997.

Hubbard, David A. *Ecclesiastes, Song of Solomon.* Communicator's Commentary 15. Dallas: Word, 1991.

Huffmon, Herbert B. "The Covenant Lawsuit in the Prophets." *Journal of Biblical Literature* 78 (1959): 285–95.

Hugenberger, Gordon P. *Marriage as a Covenant: Biblical Law and Ethics as Developed from Malachi.* Vetus Testamentum Supplements 52. Leiden: E. J. Brill, 1994. Repr., Grand Rapids: Baker, 1998.

———. "Women in Church Office: Hermeneutics or Exegesis? A Survey of Approaches to 1 Tim 2:8–15." *Journal of the Evangelical Theological Society* 35 (1992): 341–60.

Hull, Gretchen Gaebelein. *Equal to Serve: Women and Men in the Church and Home.* Old Tappan, N.J.: Fleming H. Revell, 1987.

Humann, Roger J. "1 Corinthians 11:2–16: Exegesis Case Study." *Consensus* 7 (January 1981): 17–30.

Humbert, Paul. *Études sur le récit du paradis et de la chute dans la Genèse.* Neuchâtel: Secrétariat de l'Université, 1940.

Humphreys, Lee W. "A Life-style for Diaspora: A Study of the Tales of Esther and Daniel." *Journal of Biblical Literature* 93 (1973): 211–23.

Hunt, Angela E. "All's Not Wrong with Women's Rights." *Fundamentalist Journal* 2, no. 10 (1983): 14–15.

Hunt, Susan. *By Design.* Wheaton, Ill.: Crossway, 1994.

———. The True Woman: The Beauty and Strength of a Godly Woman. Wheaton, Ill.: Crossway, 1997.

Hunt, Susan, and Barbara Thompson. *The Legacy of Biblical Womanhood.* Wheaton, Ill.: Crossway, 2003.

Hunter, Jannie H. "The Song of Protest: Reassessing the Song of Songs." *Journal for the Study of the Old Testament* no. 90 (2000): 109–24.

Hurley, James B. "Did Paul Require Veils or the Silence of Women? A Consideration of 1 Cor 11:2–16 and 14:33b–36." *Westminster Theological Journal* 35 (1973): 190–220.

———. *Man and Woman in Biblical Perspective.* Grand Rapids: Zondervan, 1981.

Hwang, Andrew. "The New Structure of the Song of Songs and Its Implications for Interpretation." *Westminster Theological Journal* 65 (2003): 97–111.

Hyatt, J. Philip. "Circumcision." Pages 629–31 in vol. 1 of *The Interpreter's Dictionary of the Bible.* Edited by George A. Buttrick. 4 vols. Nashville: Abingdon, 1962.

———. *Commentary on Exodus.* New Century Bible. London: Oliphants, 1971.

Hyman, Ronald T. "Final Judgment: The Ambiguous Moral Question That Culminates Genesis 34." *Jewish Bible Quarterly* 28 (2000): 93–101.

Ide, Arthur Frederick. *Women in the Ancient Near East.* Mesquite, Tex.: Ide House, 1982.

Ilan, Tal. "The Daughters of Zelophehad and Women's Inheritance: The Biblical Injunction and Its Outcome." Pages 176–86 in *A Feminist Companion to Exodus to Deuteronomy.* Edited by Athalya Brenner. Feminist Companion to the Bible 6. Sheffield, Eng.: Sheffield Academic Press, 1994.

———. *Integrating Women into Second Temple History.* Tübingen: Mohr Siebeck, 1999. Repr., Peabody, Mass.: Hendrickson, 2001.

———. *Jewish Women in Greco-Roman Palestine.* Peabody, Mass.: Hendrickson, 1995.

Impson, Beth. *Called to Womanhood: A Biblical View for Today's World.* Focal Point. Wheaton, Ill.: Crossway, 2001.

Ind, Jo. *God Is Sexy.* London: SCM, 2002.

Instone-Brewer, David. "Deuteronomy 24:1–4 and the Origin of the Jewish Divorce Certificate." *Journal of Jewish Studies* 49 (1998): 230–43.

———. *Divorce and Remarriage in the Bible: The Social and Literary Context.* Grand Rapids: Eerdmans, 2002.

———. "Nomological Exegesis in Qumran 'Divorce' Texts." *Revue de Qumran* 18 (1998): 561–79.

Isaac, Erich. "Circumcision as a Covenant Rite." *Anthropos* 59 (1964): 444–56.

Isaksson, Abel. *Marriage and Ministry in the New Temple: A Study with Special Reference to Matt. 19.13[sic]–12 and 1 Cor. 11.3–16.* Translated by N. Tomkinson with J. Gray. Acta seminarii neotestamentici upsaliensis 24. Lund, Swed.: Gleerup, 1965.

Ishida, Tomoo. "Solomon." Pages 105–13 in vol. 6 of *The Anchor Bible Dictionary.* Edited by David Noel Freedman. 6 vols. New York, Doubleday, 1992.

Isserlin, B. S. J. "Song of Songs IV,4: An Archaeological Note." *Palestine Exploration Quarterly* 90 (1958): 59–60.

Jackson, Bernard S. "Liability for Mere Intention in Early Jewish Law." *Hebrew Union College Annual* 42 (1971): 197–225.

———. "The Problem of Exod. xxi 22–25 (*ius talionis*)." *Vetus Testamentum* 23 (1973): 292–93.

Jackson, Glenna. "Jesus as First-Century Feminist: Christian Anti-Judaism?" *Feminist Theology* 19 (1998): 85–98.

Jackson, Melissa. "Lot's Daughters and Tamar as Tricksters and the Patriarchal Narratives as Feminist Theology." *Journal for the Study of the Old Testament* no. 98 (2002): 29–46.

Jacob, B. *Das erste Buch der Tora: Genesis.* Berlin: 1934.

Jacob, Edmond. *Theology of the Old Testament.* New York: Harper, 1958.

Jacobi, Johann Friedrich. *Das durch eine leichte und ungekünstelte Erklärung von seinen Vorwürfen gerettete Hohe Lied.* Celle, 1772.

Jacobson, Diane. "Biblical Perspectives on Sexuality." *Word and World* 10 (1990): 156–60.

Jaeggli, J. Randolph. "Ruth—the Ideal Woman." *Biblical Viewpoint* 35, no. 2 (2001): 5–10.

Jagendorf, Zvi. "In the Morning, Behold, It Was Leah: Genesis and the Reversal of Sexual Knowledge." *Prooftexts: A Journal of Jewish Literary History* 4 (1984): 187–92. Repr., pages 51–60 in *Biblical Patterns in Modern Literature.* Edited by D. Hirsch and N. Aschkenasy. Brown Judaic Studies 77. Chico, Calif.: Scholars Press, 1984.

James, Sharon. *God's Design for Women: Biblical Womanhood for Today.* Darlington, Eng.: Evangelical Press, 2002.

Janssen, Claudia, Ute Ochtendung, and Beate Wehn, eds. *Transgressors: Toward a Feminist Biblical Theology.* Collegeville, Minn.: Liturgical, 2002.

Jantzen, Grace M. *Becoming Divine: Towards a Feminist Philosophy of Religion.* Bloomington: Indiana University Press, 1999.

Janzen, David. "Why the Deuteronomist Told about the Sacrifice of Jephthah's Daughter." *Journal for the Study of the Old Testament* 29 (2005): 339–57.

Janzen, J. Gerald. "Song of Moses, Song of Miriam: Who Is Seconding Whom?" *Catholic Biblical Quarterly* 54, no. 2 (1992): 211–20.

Japhet, Sara. "Law and 'the Law' in Ezra-Nehemiah." Pages 99–115 in *Proceedings of the Ninth World Congress of Jewish Studies*. Edited by Moshe Goshen-Gottstein. Jerusalem: Magnes, 1988.

Japinga, Lynn. *Feminism and Christianity: An Essential Guide*. Abingdon Essential Guides. Nashville: Abingdon, 1999.

Jarrell, R. H. "The Birth Narrative as Female Counterpart to Covenant." *Journal for the Study of the Old Testament* 97 (2002): 3–18.

Jasper, Gerhard. "Polygyny in the Old Testament." *Africa Theological Journal* 2 no. 2 (February 1969): 27–57.

Jeansonne, Sharon Pace. *Old Testament Women*. Storyteller's Companion to the Bible 4. Nashville: Abingdon, 1993.

———. *The Women of Genesis: From Sarah to Potiphar's Wife*. Minneapolis: Fortress, 1990.

Jensen, Anne. *God's Self-Confident Daughters: Early Christianity and the Liberation of Women*. Translated by O. C. Dean Jr. Louisville: Westminster John Knox, 1996.

Jensen, Joseph. "Does *porneia* Mean Fornication? A Critique of Bruce Malina." *Novum Testamentum* 20 (1978): 161–84.

———. "Human Sexuality in the Scriptures." Pages 15–35 in *Human Sexuality and Personhood*. Edited by J. Gill. St. Louis: Pope John XXIII Medical-Moral Research and Education Center, 1981.

———. "The Relevance of the Old Testament." Pages 1–20 in *Dimensions of Human Sexuality*. Edited by Dennis Doherty. Garden City, N.Y.: Doubleday, 1979.

Jenson, Robert W. "Male and Female He Created Them." Pages 175–88 in *I Am the Lord Your God: Christian Reflections on the Ten Commandments*. Edited by Carl E. Braaten and Christopher R. Seitz. Grand Rapids: Eerdmans, 2005.

Jepson, Dee. *Women: Beyond Equal Rights*. Waco, Tex.: Word, 1984.

Jeremias, Joachim. *The Prayers of Jesus*. Translated by John Reumann. Bible Series 8. Philadelphia: Fortress, 1964.

Jewett, Paul K. *Man as Male and Female: A Study of Sexual Relationships from a Theological Point of View*. Grand Rapids: Eerdmans, 1975.

Jobling, David. *1 Samuel*. Berit Olam: Studies in Hebrew Narrative and Poetry. Collegeville, Minn.: Liturgical, 1998.

———. "A Deconstructive Reading of Hosea 1–3." Pages 206–15 in *Relating to the Text: Interdisciplinary and Form-Critical Insights on the Bible*. Edited by Timothy J. Sandoval and Carleen Mandolfo. Journal for the Study of the Old Testament: Supplement Series 384. New York: T&T Clark, 2003.

———. *The Sense of Biblical Narrative: Structural Analysis in the Hebrew Bible*. 2 vols. Journal for the Study of the Old Testament: Supplement Series 39. Sheffield, Eng.: JSOT Press, 1986. Vol. 2.

Jobling, David, Peggy L. Day, and Gerald T. Sheppard, eds. *The Bible and the Politics of Exegesis: Essays in Honor of Norman K. Gottwald on His Sixty-Fifth Birthday*. Cleveland: Pilgrim, 1991.

Jobling, J'annine. *Feminist Biblical Interpretation in Theological Context: Restless Reading.* Burlington, Vt.: Ashgate, 2002.

Johnson, E. Elizabeth. "Biblical and Historical Perspectives on Human Sexuality." *Church and Society* 80 (1989): 6–25.

Johnson, Elizabeth A. *She Who Is: The Mystery of God in Feminist Theological Discourse.* New York: Crossroad, 1992.

Johnson, James R. "Toward a Biblical Approach to Masturbation." *Journal of Psychology and Theology* 10 (1982): 137–46.

Johnson, L. D. *Proverbs, Ecclesiastes, Song of Solomon.* Layman's Bible Book Commentary 9. Nashville: Broadman, 1982.

Johnson, S. Lewis. "Role Distinctions in the Church: Galatians 3:28." Pages 154–64, 490–92 in *Recovering Biblical Manhood and Womanhood: A Response to Evangelical Feminism.* Edited by John Piper and Wayne A. Grudem. Wheaton, Ill.: Crossway, 1991.

Johnston, George F. *Abortion from the Religious and Moral Perspective: An Annotated Bibliography.* Bibliographies and Indexes in Religious Studies 53. Westport, Conn.: Praeger, 2003.

Johnston, Robert K. "Biblical Authority and Interpretation: The Test Case of Women's Role in the Church & Home Updated." Pages 30–41 in *Women, Authority, and the Bible.* Edited by Alvera Mickelsen. Downers Grove, Ill.: InterVarsity, 1986.

Joiner, E. Earl. *A Christian Considers Divorce and Remarriage.* Nashville: Broadman, 1983.

Jones, Alan W. "Male and Female Created He Them." *Anglican Theological Review* 57 (1975): 423–45.

Jones, Peter. *The God of Sex: How Spirituality Defines Your Sexuality.* Colorado Springs, Colo.: Victor, 2006.

Jones, Stanton L., and Mark A. Yarhouse. *Homosexuality: The Use of Scientific Research in the Church's Moral Debate.* Downers Grove, Ill.: InterVarsity, 2000.

Jongsma-Tieleman, P. E. "The Creation of Eve and the Ambivalence between the Sexes." Pages 97–113 in *God, Biblical Stories, and Psychoanalytic Understanding.* Edited by Rainer Kessler and Patrick Vendermeersch. Frankfurt am Main: Peter Lang, 2001.

Jónsson, Gunnlaugur A. *The Image of God: Genesis 1:26–28 in a Century of Old Testament Research.* Conjectanea Biblica. Old Testament Series 26. Lund: Almquist & Wiksell, 1988.

Joosten, Jan. "La non-mention de la fille en Lévitique 18." *Etudes théologiques et religieuses* 75 (2000): 415–20.

Jordan, Mark, ed. *Authorizing Marriage? Canon, Tradition, and Critique in the Blessing of Same-Sex Unions.* Princeton, N.J.: Princeton University Press, 2006.

Jost, Renate. "Von 'Huren und Heiligen': Ein sozialgeschichtlicher Beitrag." Pages 126–37 in *Feministische Hermeneutik und erstes Testament: Analysen und Interpretation.* Edited by Hedwig Jahnow. Stuttgart: Kohlhammer, 1994.

Jung, Patricia Beattie, and Joseph Andrew Coray. *Sexual Diversity and Catholicism: Toward the Development of Moral Theology*. Collegeville, Minn.: Liturgical, 2001.

Jung, Patricia Beattie, Mary E. Hunt, and Radhika Balakrishnan, eds. *Good Sex: Feminist Perspectives from the World's Religions*. New Brunswick, N.J.: Rutgers University Press, 2001.

Jüngling, Hans-Winfried. *Richter 19: Ein Plädoyer für das Königtum*. Rome: Biblical Institute Press, 1981.

Juschka, Darlene M., ed. *Feminism in the Study of Religion: A Reader*. Controversies in the Study of Religion. New York: Continuum, 2001.

Kähler, Else. *Die Frau in den paulinischen Briefen*. Frankfurt am Main: Gotthelf, 1960.

Kaiser, Otto. "Von der Schönheit des Menschen als Gabe Gottes." Pages 153–63 in *Verbindungslinien: Festschrift für Werner H. Schmidt zum 65. Geburtstag*. Edited by Axel Graupner, Holger Delkurt, and Alexander Ernst. Neukirchen-Vluyn: Neukirchener Verlag, 2000.

Kaiser, Walter C., Jr. "Divorce in Malachi 2:10–16." *Criswell Theological Review* 2 (1987): 73–84.

———. "Exodus." Pages 287–497 in vol. 2 of *The Expositor's Bible Commentary*. Edited by Frank E. Gaebelein. 12 vols. Grand Rapids: Zondervan, 1976–1992.

———. *Toward an Exegetical Theology: Biblical Exegesis for Preaching and Teaching*. Grand Rapids: Baker, 1981.

———. *Toward an Old Testament Theology*. Grand Rapids: Zondervan, 1978.

———. *Toward Old Testament Ethics*. Grand Rapids: Zondervan, 1983.

———. "True Marital Love in Proverbs 5:15–23 and the Interpretation of the Song of Songs." Pages 106–16 in *The Way of Wisdom: Essays in Honor of Bruce K. Waltke*. Edited by J. I. Packer and Sven K. Soderlund. Grand Rapids: Zondervan, 2000.

Kaiser, Walter C., Jr., and Bruce Waltke. "Shared Leadership or Male Headship?" *Christianity Today* 30, no. 14 (1986): 121–31.

Kalland, Earl S. "Deuteronomy." Pages 3–235 in vol. 3 of *The Expositor's Bible Commentary*. Edited by Frank E. Gaebelein. 12 vols. Grand Rapids: Zondervan, 1976–1992.

Kalugila, Leonidas. "Women in the Ministry of Priesthood in the Early Church: An Inquiry." *Africa Theological Journal* 14, no. 1 (1985): 35–45.

Kam, Rose. *Their Stories, Our Stories: Women of the Bible*. New York: Continuum, 1995.

Kamionkowski, S. Tamar. "Gender Reversal in Ezekiel 16." Pages 170–85 in *Prophets and Daniel*. Edited by Athalya Brenner. Feminist Companion to the Bible: Second Series 8. New York: Sheffield Academic Press, 2001.

Karant-Nunn, Susan, and Merry Wiesner-Hanks. *Luther on Women: A Sourcebook*. Cambridge: Cambridge University Press, 2003.

Kass, Leon R. "Man and Woman: An Old Story." *First Things* 17 (November 1991): 14–26.

————. "Regarding Daughters and Sisters: The Rape of Dinah." *Commentary* 93, no. 4 (1992): 29–38.

————. "Seeing the Nakedness of His Father." *Commentary* 93, no. 6 (1992): 41–47.

Kassian, Mary A. *The Feminist Gospel: The Movement to Unite Feminism with the Church.* Wheaton, Ill.: Crossway, 1992.

————. *Woman, Creation, and the Fall.* Westchester, Ill.: Crossway, 1990.

Kates, Judith A., and Gail Twersky Reimer, eds. *Reading Ruth: Contemporary Women Reclaim a Sacred Story.* New York: Ballantine, 1994.

Kaufman, Steven A. "The Structure of the Deuteronomic Law." *Maarav* 1–2 (1978–1979): 105–58.

Kaye, Bruce N. "One Flesh and Marriage." *Colloquium* 22 (May 1990): 46–57.

Keefe, Alice A. "Rapes of Women/Wars of Men." *Semeia* 61 (1993): 79–97.

————. *Woman's Body and the Social Body in Hosea.* Journal for the Study of the Old Testament Supplement Series 358. London: Sheffield, 2001.

————. "Women, Community, and Conflict: Rethinking the Metaphor of Female Adultery in Hosea 1–2." PhD diss., Syracuse University, 1996.

Keel, Othmar. *Deine Blicke sind Tauben: Zur Metaphorik des Hohen Liedes.* Stuttgart: Katholisches Bibelwerk, 1984.

————. "Erotik als Amulett gegen den allgegenwärtigen Tod: Die Lebensmetaphorik des Hohenlieds im Spiegel israelitischer Siegelkunst." *Jahrbüch für Biblische Theologie* 19 (2004): 49–62.

————. *The Song of Songs: A Continental Commentary.* Translated by Frederick J. Gaiser. Minneapolis: Fortress, 1994.

————. "Die Stellung der Frau in der Erzählung von Schöpfung und Sündenfall," *Orientierung* 39 (1975): 74–76.

Keener, Craig S. *And Marries Another: Divorce and Remarriage in the Teaching of the New Testament.* Peabody, Mass.: Hendrickson, 1991.

————. *Paul, Women, and Wives: Marriage and Women's Ministry in the Letters of Paul.* Peabody, Mass.: Hendrickson, 1992.

————. "Some Biblical Reflections on Justice, Rape, and an Insensitive Society," Pages 117–30 in *Women, Abuse, and the Bible: How Scripture Can Be Used to Hurt or to Heal.* Edited by Catherine Clark Kroeger and James R. Beck. Grand Rapids: Baker, 1996.

Kegler, Jürgen. "Debora: Erwägungen zur politischen Funktion einer Frau in einer patriarchalischen Gesellschaft." Pages 37–59 in *Traditionen der Befreiung: Sozialgeschichtliche Bibelauslegungen.* Edited by Willy Schottroff and Wolfgang Stegemann. Munich: Kaiser, 1980.

Keil, Carl F., and Franz Delitzsch. *Biblical Commentary on the Old Testament.* Translated by J. Martin et al. 25 vols. Edinburgh, 1857–1878. Reprint, 10 vols., Peabody, Mass.: Hendrickson, 1996.

Keita, Shadrac, and Janet W. Dyk. "The Scene at the Threshing Floor: Suggestive Readings and Intercultural Considerations on Ruth 3." *The Bible Translator* 57 (2006): 17–32.

Kelle, Brad E. "Hosea 2: Metaphor and Rhetoric in Historical Perspective." PhD diss., Emory University, 2003.

Kessler, John. "Sexuality and Politics: The Motif of the Displaced Husband in the Books of Samuel." *Catholic Biblical Quarterly* 62 (2000): 409–23.

Kevers, Paul. "Etude littéraire de Genèse 34." *Revue biblique* 87 (1980): 38–86.

Key, Steven R. "A Virtuous Woman." Pages 3–15 in *Far above Rubies: Today's Virtuous Woman*. Edited by Herman Hanko. Grand Rapids: Reformed Free Publishing Association, 1992.

Kidner, Derek. *Ezra and Nehemiah: An Introduction and Commentary*. Tyndale Old Testament Commentaries 11. Downers Grove, Ill.: InterVarsity, 1979.

———. *Genesis: An Introduction and Commentary*. Tyndale Old Testament Commentaries 1. Downers Grove, Ill.: InterVarsity, 1967.

———. *Love to the Loveless: The Message of Hosea*. Bible Speaks Today. Downers Grove, Ill.: InterVarsity, 1981.

———. *The Proverbs: An Introduction and Commentary*. Tyndale Old Testament Commentaries 15. Downers Grove, Ill.: InterVarsity, 1964.

Kikawada, I. M., and A. Quinn. *Before Abraham Was: The Unity of Genesis 1–11*. Nashville: Abingdon, 1985.

Kim, Hyun Chul Paul. "Gender Complementarity in the Hebrew Bible." Pages 263–91 in *Theological and Hermeneutical Studies*. Vol. 1 of *Reading the Hebrew Bible for a New Millennium: Form, Concept, and Theological Perspective*. Edited by Deborah Ellens et al. Studies in Antiquity and Christianity. Harrisburg, Pa.: Trinity Press International, 2000.

Kim, Hyun Chul Paul, and M. Fulgence Nyengele, "Murder S/He Wrote? A Culture and Psychological Reading of 2 Samuel 11–12." Pages 95–116 in *Pregnant Passion: Gender, Sex, and Violence in the Bible*. Semeia Studies 44. Atlanta: Society of Biblical Literature, 2003.

Kimberley, David R. "1 Tim 2:15: A Possible Understanding of a Difficult Text." *Journal of the Evangelical Theological Society* 35 (1992): 481–86.

Kimmerling, Ben. "Celibacy and Intimacy." Pages 429–37 in *Christian Perspectives on Sexuality and Gender*. Edited by Adrian Thatcher and Elizabeth Stuart. Grand Rapids: Eerdmans, 1996.

King, Karen L., ed. *Women and Goddess Traditions: In Antiquity and Today*. Studies in Antiquity and Christianity. Minneapolis: Fortress, 1997.

King, Philip J., and Lawrence E. Stager. *Life in Biblical Israel*. Louisville: Westminster John Knox, 2001.

———. "Of Fathers, Kings, and the Deity." *Biblical Archaeology Review* 28, no. 2 (2002): 42–45, 62.

Kinlaw, Dennis F. "A Biblical View of Homosexuality." Pages 104–16 in *The Secrets of Our Sexuality: Role Liberation for the Christian*. Edited by Gary R. Collins. Waco, Tex.: Word, 1976.

———. "Song of Songs." Pages 1201–44 in vol. 5 of *The Expositor's Bible Commentary*. Edited by Frank E. Gaebelein. Grand Rapids: Zondervan, 1976–1992.

Kirk-Duggan, Cheryl A. "Slingshots, Ships, and Personal Psychosis: Murder, Sexual Intrigue, and Power in the Lives of David and Othello." Pages 37–70 in

Pregnant Passion: Gender, Sex, and Violence in the Bible. Edited by Cheryl A. Kirk-Duggan. Semeia Studies 44. Atlanta: Society of Biblical Literature, 2003.

———, ed. *Pregnant Passion: Gender, Sex, and Violence in the Bible.* Semeia Studies 44. Atlanta: Society of Biblical Literature, 2003.

Kirsch, Jonathan. "What Did Sarah See?" *Bible Review* 14, no. 5 (1998): 2, 49.

Kitchen, Kenneth A. *Ancient Orient and Old Testament.* Chicago: InterVarsity, 1966.

———. *The Bible in Its World.* Downers Grove, Ill.: InterVarsity, 1978.

———. *The Third Intermediate Period in Egypt, 1100–650 B.C.* 2d ed. with suppl. Warminster, Eng.: Aris & Phillips, 1986.

Klawans, Jonathan. *Impurity and Sin in Ancient Judaism.* New York: Oxford University Press, 2000.

———. "The Impurity of Immorality in Ancient Judaism." *Journal of Jewish Studies* 48 (1997): 1–16.

Klee, Deborah. "Menstruation in the Hebrew Bible." PhD diss., Boston University, 1998.

Klein, Jacob. "Sacred Marriage." Pages 856–70 in vol. 5 of *Anchor Bible Dictionary.* Edited by D. N. Freedman. 6 vols. New York: Doubleday, 1992.

———, ed., *Three Šulgi Hymns.* Tel Aviv: Bar-Ilan University Press, 1982.

Klein, Joel T. "A Comment on You Shall Not Boil a Kid in Its Mother's Milk." *Jewish Bible Quarterly* 33 (2005): 196–97.

Klein, Lillian R. "Achsah: What Price This Prize?" Pages 18–26 in *Judges.* Edited by Athalya Brenner. Feminist Companion to the Bible: Second Series 4. Sheffield, Eng.: Sheffield Academic Press, 1999.

———. "Bathsheba Revealed." Pages 47–64 in *Samuel and Kings.* Edited by Athalya Brenner. Feminist Companion to the Bible: Second Series 7. Sheffield, Eng.: Sheffield Academic Press, 2000.

———. "The Book of Judges: Paradigm and Deviation in Images of Women." Pages 55–71 in *A Feminist Companion to Judges.* Edited by Athalya Brenner. Feminist Companion to the Bible 4. Sheffield, Eng.: Sheffield Academic Press, 1993.

———. *From Deborah to Esther: Sexual Politics in the Hebrew Bible.* Minneapolis: Fortress, 2003.

———. "Hannah: Marginalized Victim and Social Redeemer." Pages 77–92 in *A Feminist Companion to Samuel and Kings.* Edited by Athalya Brenner. Feminist Companion to the Bible 5. Sheffield, Eng.: Sheffield Academic Press, 1994.

———. "Michal, the Barren Wife," Pages 37–46 in *Samuel and Kings.* Edited by Athalya Brenner. Feminist Companion to the Bible: Second Series 7. Sheffield, Eng.: Sheffield Academic Press, 2000.

———. "A Spectrum of Female Characters in the Book of Judges." Pages 24–33 in *A Feminist Companion to Judges.* Edited by Athalya Brenner. Feminist Companion to the Bible 4. Sheffield, Eng.: Sheffield Academic Press, 1993.

———. *The Triumph of Irony in the Book of Judges.* Bible and Literature Series 14. Sheffield, Eng.: Almond, 1988.

Kline, Meredith G. *By Oath Consigned.* Grand Rapids: Eerdmans, 1968.

———. "Divine Kingship in Genesis 6:1–4." *Westminster Theological Journal* 24 (1962): 187–204.

———. *Kingdom Prologue.* South Hamilton, Mass.: M. G. Kline, 1989.

———. "*Lex talionis* and the Human Fetus." *Journal of the Evangelical Theological Society* 20 (1977): 193–201.

———. *Treaty of the Great King—the Covenant Structure of Deuteronomy: Studies and Commentary.* Grand Rapids: Eerdmans, 1963.

Klingbeil, Gerald A. "Altars, Ritual and Theology—Preliminary Thoughts on the Importance of Cult and Ritual for a Theology of the Hebrew Scripture." *Vetus Testamentum* 54 (2004): 495–515.

Klopper, F. "Women, Monotheism, and the Gender of God." *In die Skriflig* 36 (2002): 421–37.

Knierim, Rolf P. "On Punishment in the Hebrew Bible." Pages 216–32 in *God's Word for Our World, Vol. II: Theological and Cultural Studies in Honor of Simon John De Vries.* Edited by J. Harold Ellens et al. Journal for the Study of the Old Testament: Supplement Series 389. New York: T&T Clark, 2004.

———. "Role of the Sexes in the Old Testament." *Lexington Theological Quarterly* 10 (1975): 1–10.

Knight, George A. F. *Servant Theology: A Commentary on the Book of Isaiah 40–45.* International Theological Commentary. Grand Rapids: Eerdmans, 1984.

Knight, George W., III. "*Authenteô* in Reference to Women in I Timothy 2:12." *New Testament Studies* 30 (1984): 143–57.

———. "Husbands and Wives as Analogues of Christ and the Church: Ephesians 5:21–33 and Colossians 3:18–19." Pages 165–78, 492–95 in *Recovering Biblical Manhood and Womanhood: A Response to Evangelical Feminism.* Edited by J. Piper and Wayne A. Grudem. Wheaton, Ill.: Crossway, 1991.

———. "The New Testament Teaching on the Role Relationship of Male and Female with Special Reference to the Teaching/Ruling Functions in the Church." *Journal of the Evangelical Theological Society* 18 (1975): 81–91.

———. *The Role Relationship of Men and Women: New Testament Teaching.* Chicago: Moody, 1985.

Knobloch, Frederick W. "Adoption." Pages 76–79 in vol. 1 of *Anchor Bible Dictionary.* Edited by D. N. Freedman. 6 vols. New York: Doubleday, 1992.

———, ed. *Biblical Translation in Context.* Studies and Texts in Jewish History and Culture 10. Bethesda, Md.: University Press of Maryland, 2002.

Koch, Klaus. "Aschera als Himmelskönigin in Jerusalem." *Ugarit-Forschungen* 20 (1988): 97–120.

Kochalunkal, Peter. "God Is the God of Justice." *Bible Bhashyam* 29 (2003): 67–84.

Koenen, Klaus. "Sexuelle Zweideutigkeiten und Euphemismen in Jes 57:8." *Biblische Notizen* 44 (1988): 46–53.

Koptak, Paul E. *Proverbs.* NIV Application Commentary. Grand Rapids: Zondervan, 2003.

Kornfeld, Walter J. "L'adultère dans L'Orient Antique." *Revue biblique* 57 (1950): 92–109.

Korpel, Marjo Christina Annette, and Josef M. Oesch, eds. *Delimitation Criticism: A New Tool in Biblical Scholarship.* Pericope: Scripture as Written and Read in Antiquity 1. Assen, Neth.: Van Gorcum, 2000.

Korsak, Mary Phil. "Genesis: A New Look." Pages 39–52 in *A Feminist Companion to Genesis.* Edited by Athalya Brenner. Feminist Companion to the Bible 2. Sheffield, Eng.: JSOT Press, 1993.

———. "Hebrew Word Patterns Retained in English in Genesis 2:4b–3:24." *Amsterdamse cahiers voor exegese en bijbelse theologie* 15 (1996): 9–21.

———. "Translating the Bible: Bible Translations and Gender Issues." Pages 132–46 in *Bible Translation on the Threshold of the Twenty-First Century: Authority, Reception, Culture, and Religion.* Edited by Athalya Brenner and Jan Willem van Henten. Journal for the Study of the Old Testament: Supplement Series 353. London: Sheffield Academic Press, 2002.

Kosmala, Hans. "Bloody Husband." *Vetus Testamentum* 12 (1962): 14–28.

Kosnik, Anthony, et al. *Human Sexuality: New Directions in American Catholic Thought.* New York: Paulist, 1977.

Köstenberger, Andreas J. "Gender Passages in the New Testament: Hermeneutical Fallacies Critiqued." *Westminster Theological Journal* 56 (1994): 259–83.

———. "The Mystery of Christ and the Church: Head and Body, 'One Flesh.'" *Trinity Journal* 12 (1991): 79–94.

———. *Studies on John and Gender: A Decade of Scholarship.* Studies in Biblical Literature 38. New York: Peter Lang, 2001.

Köstenberger, Andreas J., with David W. Jones. *God, Marriage, and Family: Rebuilding the Biblical Foundation.* Wheaton, Ill.: Crossway, 2004.

Köstenberger, Andreas J., Thomas R. Schreiner, and H. Scott Baldwin, eds. *Women in the Church: A Fresh Analysis of 1 Timothy 2:9–15.* Grand Rapids: Baker, 1995.

Kraeling, Emil G. H. "The Significance and the Origin of Genesis 6:1–4." *Journal of Near Eastern Studies* 6 (1947): 193–208.

———, ed. *The Brooklyn Museum Aramaic Papyri.* New Haven: Yale University Press, 1953.

Kraemer, Ross Shepard, ed. *Women's Religions in the Greco-Roman World: A Sourcebook.* New York: Oxford University Press, 2004.

Kraemer, Ross Shepard, and Mary Rose D'Angelo, eds. *Women and Christian Origins.* New York: Oxford University Press, 1999.

Kramer, Phyllis Silverman. "Miriam." Pages 104–33 in *Exodus to Deuteronomy.* Edited by Athalya Brenner. Feminist Companion to the Bible: Second Series 5. Sheffield, Eng.: Sheffield Academic Press, 2001.

Kramer, Samuel Noah. *From the Poetry of Sumer: Creation, Glorification, Adoration.* Berkeley: University of California Press, 1979.

———. *History Begins at Sumer.* Garden City, N.Y.: Doubleday, 1959.

———. *The Sacred Marriage Drama.* Bloomington: Indiana University Press, 1969.

———. *The Sacred Marriage Rite: Aspects of Faith, Myth, and Ritual in Ancient Sumer.* Bloomington: Indiana University Press, 1969.

———. *The Sumerians: Their History, Culture, and Character.* Chicago: University of Chicago Press, 1963.

Krause, Deborah. "A Blessing Cursed: The Prophet's Prayer for Barren Womb and Dry Breasts in Hosea 9." Pages 191–202 in *Reading between Texts: Intertextuality and the Hebrew Bible.* Edited by Danna Nolan Fewell. Louisville: Westminster John Knox, 1992.

Krause, Martin. "2 Sam 11:4 und das Konzeptionsoptimum." *Zeitschrift für die alttestamentliche Wissenschaft* 95 (1983): 434–37.

Krebs, W. "Zur kultischen Kohabitation mit Tieren im alten Orient." *Forschungen und Fortschritte* 37 (1963): 19–21.

Krinetzki, G. *Hoheslied.* Stuttgart: Echter, 1980.

Kroeger, Catherine Clark. "1 Timothy 2:12: A Classicist's View." Pages 225–44 in *Women, Authority, and the Bible.* Edited by Alvera Mickelsen. Downers Grove, Ill.: InterVarsity, 1986.

———. "The Classical Concept of Head as 'Source.'" Pages 267–83 in *Equal to Serve: Women and Men in the Church and Home.* Edited by Gretchen G. Hull. Old Tappan, N.J.: Fleming H. Revell, 1987.

Kroeger, Catherine Clark, and James R. Beck, eds. *Women, Abuse, and the Bible: How Scripture Can Be Used to Hurt or to Heal.* Grand Rapids: Baker, 1996.

Kroeger, Catherine Clark, and Mary J. Evans, eds. *The IVP Women's Bible Commentary.* Downers Grove, Ill.: InterVarsity, 2002.

Kroeger, Catherine Clark, and Tina J. Ostrander, eds. *Reflections: Biblical and Otherwise about Sexuality.* Lenoir, N.C.: Reformation, 2001.

Kroeger, Richard Clark, and Catherine Clark Kroeger. *I Suffer Not a Woman: Rethinking 1 Timothy 2:11–15 in Light of Ancient Evidence.* Grand Rapids: Baker, 1992.

Kruger, Paul A. "Israel, the Harlot (Hos 2:4–9)." *Journal of Northwest Semitic Languages* 11 (1983): 107–16.

———. "The Marriage Metaphor in Hosea 2:4–17 against Its Ancient Near Eastern Background." *Old Testament Essays* 5 (1992): 7–25.

———. "Promiscuity or Marriage Fidelity? A Note on Prov 5:15–18." *Journal of Northwest Semitic Languages* 13 (1987): 61–68.

Krüger, Thomas. "Frau Weisheit in Koh 7:26?" *Biblica* 73 (1992): 394–403.

Kruijf, T. *The Bible on Sexuality.* De Pere, Wis.: St. Norbert Abbey, 1966.

Kubo, Sakae. *Theology and Ethics of Sex.* Washington, D.C.: Review and Herald, 1980.

Kugel, James L. "The Story of Dinah in the Testament of Levi." *Harvard Theological Review* 85 (1992): 1–34.

———. *Traditions of the Bible: A Guide to the Bible as It Was at the Start of the Common Era.* Cambridge: Harvard University Press, 1998.

———. "Why Was Lamech Blind?" *Hebrew Annual Review* 12 (1990): 91–103.

Kunz, Andreas. "Die Vorstellung von Zeugung und Schwangerschaft im antiken Israel." *Zeitschrift für die alttestamentliche Wissenschaft* 111 (1999): 561–82.

Kvam, Kristen E., Linda S. Schearing, and Valarie H. Ziegler, eds. *Eve and Adam: Jewish, Christian, and Muslim Readings on Genesis and Gender*. Bloomington: Indiana University Press, 1999.

La Rondelle, Hans K. *Perfection and Perfectionism: A Dogmatic-Ethical Study of Biblical Perfection and Phenomenal Perfectionism*. Berrien Springs, Mich.: Andrews University Press, 1975.

La Verdiere, Eugene A. "The Witness of the New Testament." Pages 21–38 in *Dimensions of Human Sexuality*. Edited by Dennis Doherty. Garden City, N.Y.: Doubleday, 1979.

LaCocque, André. *The Feminine Unconventional: Four Subversive Figures in Israel's Tradition*. Overtures to Biblical Theology. Minneapolis: Fortress, 1990.

———. *Romance She Wrote: A Hermeneutical Essay on Song of Songs*. Harrisburg, Pa.: Trinity Press International, 1998.

Laffey, Alice L. *An Introduction to the Old Testament: A Feminist Perspective*. Philadelphia: Fortress, 1988.

Lafont, Sophie. *Femmes, droit, et justice dans l'antiquité orientale: Contributions à l'étude du droit pénal au Proche-Orient ancien*. Orbis biblicus orientalis 165. Göttingen: Vandenhoeck & Ruprecht, 1999.

Lambe, Anthony J. "Judah's Development: The Pattern of Departure-Transition-Return." *Journal for the Study of the Old Testament* no. 83 (1999): 53–68.

Lambert, Wilfried G. "Morals in Ancient Mesopotamia." *Jaarbericht van het Vooraziatisch-Egyptisch Gezelschap (Genootschap) Ex oriente lux* 15 (1957–1958): 184–96.

———. "The Problem of the Love Lyrics." Pages 98–135 in *Unity and Diversity: Essays in the History, Literature, and Religion of the Ancient Near East*. Edited by H. Goedicke and J. J. M. Roberts. Baltimore: Johns Hopkins University Press, 1975.

———. "Prostitution." Pages 127–57 in *Aussenseiter und Randgruppen: Beiträge zu einer Sozialgeschichte des alten Orients*. Edited by Volkert Haas. Xenia: Konstanzer althistorische Vorträge und Forschungen 32. Constance: Universitätsverlag, 1992.

Lancaster, Sarah Heaner. *Women and the Authority of Scripture: A Narrative Approach*. Harrisburg, Pa.: Trinity, 2002.

Landsberger, Benno. *Die Serie ana ittišu*. Vol. 1 of *Materialien zum sumerischen Lexikon*. Edited by Benno Landsberger; Rome: Pontificium Institutum Biblicum, 1937–.

Landy, Francis. "Misneh Torah: A Response to Myself and Phyllis Trible." Pages 260–65 in *A Feminist Companion to the Song of Songs*. Edited by Athalya Brenner. Feminist Companion to the Bible 1. Sheffield, Eng.: Sheffield Academic Press, 1993.

———. *Paradoxes of Paradise: Identity and Difference in the Song of Songs*. Sheffield, Eng.: Almond, 1983.

———. "Prophetic Intercourse." Pages 261–79 in *Sense and Sensitivity: Essays on Reading the Bible in Memory of Robert Carroll*. Edited by Alastair G. Hunter and Philip R. Davies. Journal for the Study of the Old Testament: Supplement Series 348. London: Sheffield Academic Press, 2002.

———. "The Song of Songs." Pages 305–19 in *The Literary Guide to the Bible.* Edited by Robert Alter and K. Kermode. Cambridge, Mass.: Belknap, 1987.

———. "The Song of Songs and the Garden of Eden." *Journal of Biblical Literature* 98 (1979): 513–28.

Laney, J. Carl. "Deuteronomy 24:1–4 and the Issue of Divorce." *Bibliotheca sacra* 149 (1992): 3–15.

Lang, Bernhard. "The Hebrew Wife and the Ottoman Wife: An Anthropological Essay on Proverbs 31:10–31." Pages 140–57 in *Anthropology and Biblical Studies: Avenues of Approach.* Edited by Louise J. Lawrence and Mario I. Aguilar. Leiden: Deo, 2005.

———. "Women's Work, Household and Property in Two Mediterranean Societies: A Comparative Essay on Proverbs xxxi 10–31." *Vetus Testamentum* 54 (2004): 188–207.

Langdon, Stephen. *Sumerian Liturgical Texts.* Philadelphia: University Museum, University of Pennsylvania, 1917.

Lange, Armin, Hermann Lichtenberger, and K. F. Diehard Römheld, eds. *Die Dämonen: Die Dämonologie der israelitisch-jüdischen und frühchristlichen Literatur im Kontext ihrer Umwelt = Demons: The Demonology of Israelite-Jewish and Early Christian Literature in Context of Their Environment.* Tübingen: Mohr (Siebeck), 2003.

Laniak, Timothy S. *Shame and Honor in the Book of Esther.* Atlanta: Scholars Press, 1998.

Lanoir, Corinne. *Femmes fatales, filles rebelles: Figures féminines dans le livre des Juges.* Sciences Bibliques. Geneva: Labor et Fides, 2005.

Lanser, Susan. "(Feminist) Criticism in the Garden: Inferring Genesis 2–3." *Semeia* 41 (1988): 69–72.

Lapsley, Jacqueline E. "Seeing the Older Woman: Naomi in High Definition." Pages 102–13 in *Engaging the Bible in a Gendered World: An Introduction to Feminist Biblical Interpretation in Honor of Katharine Doob Sakenfeld.* Edited by Linda Day and Carolyn Pressler. Louisville: Westminster John Knox, 2006.

———. "The Voice of Rachel: Resistance and Polyphony in Gen 31:14–35." Pages 233–48 in *Genesis.* Edited by Athalya Brenner. Feminist Companion to the Bible: Second Series 1. Sheffield, Eng.: Sheffield Academic Press, 1998.

———. *Whispering the Word: Hearing Women's Stories in the Old Testament.* Louisville: Westminster John Knox, 2005.

Larue, Gerald A. *Sex and the Bible.* Buffalo: Prometheus, 1983.

Lattey, Cuthbert. *The Old Testament: The Book of Ruth.* London: Longmans, Green, 1935.

Laurin, R. B. "The Life of True Love: The Song of Songs and Its Modern Message." *Christianity Today* 6, no. 22 (1962): 10–11.

Lawler, Michael G. *Marriage and Sacrament: A Theology of Christian Marriage.* Collegeville, Minn.: Liturgical, 1993.

————. *Marriage and the Catholic Church: Disputed Questions.* Collegeville, Minn.: Liturgical, 2002.

Lawler, Michael G., and William P. Roberts. *Christian Marriage and Family: Contemporary Theological and Pastoral Perspectives.* Collegeville, Minn.: Liturgical, 1996.

Lawrence, Michael. "A Theology of Sex." Pages 135–41 in *Sex and the Supremacy of Christ.* Edited by John Piper and Justin Taylor. Wheaton, Ill.: Crossway, 2005.

Lawton, Robert B. "Genesis 2:24: Trite or Tragic?" *Journal of Bible Literature* 105 (1986): 97–98.

Layton, Scott C. "A Chain Gang in 2 Samuel 3:29? A Rejoinder." *Vetus Testamentum* 39 (1989): 81–86.

Lee, Eunny P. "Ruth the Moabite: Identity, Kinship, and Otherness." Pages 89–101 in *Engaging the Bible in a Gendered World: An Introduction to Feminist Biblical Interpretation in Honor of Katharine Doob Sakenfeld.* Edited by Linda Day and Carolyn Pressler. Louisville: Westminster John Knox, 2006.

Leeb, Carolyn S. *Away from the Father's House: The Social Location of the Na'ar and Na'arah in Ancient Israel.* Journal for the Study of the Old Testament: Supplement Series 301. Sheffield, Eng.: Sheffield Academic Press, 2000.

————. "The Widow: Homeless and Post-menopausal." *Biblical Theology Bulletin* 32 (2002): 160–62.

————. "The Widow in the Hebrew Bible: Homeless and Post-menopausal." *Proceedings, Eastern Great Lakes and Midwest Biblical Society* 21 (2001): 61–67.

Leggett, Donald A. *The Levirate and Goel Institutions in the Old Testament, with Special Attention to the Book of Ruth.* Cherry Hill, N.J.: Mack, 1974.

Leick, Gwendolyn. *Sex and Eroticism in Mesopotamian Literature.* London: Routledge, 1994.

Leith, Mary Joan Winn. "Back to the Garden." *Bible Review* 18, no. 2 (2002): 10–11, 46.

————. "First Lady Jezebel." *Bible Review* 20, no. 4 (August 2004): 8, 46.

Lemaire, André, ed. *Congress Volume: Basel, 2001.* Vetus Testamentum Supplements 92. Leiden: E. J. Brill, 2002.

Lemaire, André, and Magne Sæbø, eds. *Congress Volume: Oslo, 1998.* Vetus Testamentum Supplements 80. Leiden: E. J. Brill, 2000.

Lerner, Berel Dov. "Rahab the Harlot and Other Philosophers of Religion." *Jewish Bible Quarterly* 28 (2000): 52–55.

Lerner, Gerda. *The Creation of Patriarchy.* Woman and History 1. New York: Oxford University Press, 1986.

Lesètre, Henri. "Lévirat." Col. 213–16 in vol. 4 of *Dictionnaire de la Bible.* Edited by Fulcran Vigouroux. 5 vols. Paris: Letouzey & Ané, 1895–1912.

Lesko, Leonard H. "Women and Priests in Two Egyptian Stories" Pages 217–29 in *Hesed Ve-Emet: Studies in Honor of Ernest S. Frerichs.* Edited by Jodi Magness and Seymour Gitin. Brown Judaic Studies 320. Atlanta: Scholars Press, 1998.

Leupold, H. C. *Exposition of Genesis.* Columbus, Ohio: Wartburg, 1942.

Levenson, Jon D. "1 Samuel 25 as Literature and as History." *Catholic Biblical Quarterly* 40 (1978): 11–28.

———. *Sinai and Zion: An Entry into the Jewish Bible.* Minneapolis: Winston, 1985.

Levenson, Jon D., and Baruch Halpern. "The Political Import of David's Marriages." *Journal of Biblical Literature* 99 (1980): 507–18.

Levine, Amy-Jill. "Ruth." Pages 78–84 in *The Women's Bible Commentary.* Edited by Carol A. Newsom and Sharon H. Ringe. Louisville: Westminster John Knox, 1992.

———. "Settling at Beer-lahai-roi." Pp. 12–34 in *Daughters of Abraham: Feminist Thought in Judaism, Christianity, and Islam.* Edited by Yvonne Yazbeck Haddad and John L. Esposito. Gainesville, Fla: University Press of Florida, 2001.

———, ed. *"Women Like This": New Perspectives on Jewish Women in the Greco-Roman World.* Williston, Vt.: Society of Biblical Literature, 1991.

Levine, Amy-Jill, with Marianne Blickenstaff, eds. *A Feminist Companion to John.* 2 vols. Feminist Companion to the New Testament and Early Christian Writings 4. New York: Sheffield Academic Press, 2003.

———, eds. *A Feminist Companion to Luke.* Feminist Companion to the New Testament and Early Christian Writings 3. London: Sheffield Academic Press, 2002.

———, eds. *A Feminist Companion to Mark.* Feminist Companion to the New Testament and Early Christian Writings 2. Sheffield, Eng.: Sheffield Academic Press, 2001.

———, eds. *A Feminist Companion to Matthew.* Feminist Companion to the New Testament and Early Christian Writings 1. Sheffield, Eng.: Sheffield Academic Press, 2001.

———, eds. *A Feminist Companion to Paul.* Feminist Companion to the New Testament and Early Christian Writings 6. London: T&T Clark, 2004.

———, eds. *A Feminist Companion to Paul: Deutero-Pauline Writings.* Journal for the Study of the New Testament: Supplement Series 7. New York: Continuum, 2003.

Levine, Baruch A. "Priests," Pages 687–790 in *Interpreter's Dictionary of the Bible: Supplementary Volume.* Edited by K. Crim. Nashville: Abingdon, 1976.

Lewis, Alan E., ed. *The Motherhood of God: A Report by a Study Group Appointed by the Woman's Guild and the Panel on Doctrine on the Invitation of the General Assembly of the Church of Scotland.* Edinburgh: Saint Andrew, 1984.

Lewis, C. S. *The Last Battle.* New York: MacMillan, 1956.

Lewis, Jack P. "The Capable Wife (Prov 31:10–31)." Pages 125–54 in vol. 2 of *Essays on Women in Earliest Christianity.* Edited by Carroll D. Osburn. 2 vols. Joplin, Mo.: College Press, 1995.

———. "Jamnia Revisited." Pages 146–63 in *The Canon Debate.* Edited by Lee Martin McDonald and James A. Sanders. Peabody, Mass.: Hendrickson, 2002.

Lewis, T., and C. E. Armerding. "Circumcision." Pages 701–2 in vol. 1 of *International Standard Bible Encyclopedia*. Edited by G. W. Bromiley. 4 vols. Grand Rapids: Eerdmans, 1979–1988.

Lichtenstein, M. H. "Chiasm and Symmetry in Proverbs 31." *Catholic Biblical Quarterly* 44 (1982): 202–11.

Lichtenwalter, Larry. *Behind the Seen: God's Hand in Esther's Life . . . and Yours*. Hagerstown, Md.: Review and Herald, 2001.

Liefeld, Walter L. "Women, Submission, and Ministry in 1 Corinthians." Pages 134–54 in *Women, Authority, and the Bible*. Edited by Alvera Mickelsen. Downers Grove, Ill.: InterVarsity,1986.

Lightfoot, N. R. *The Role of Women: New Testament Perspectives*. Memphis: Student Association, 1978.

Lim, Johnson T. K. *Grace in the Midst of Judgment: Grappling with Genesis 1–11*. Beihefte zur Zeitschrift für die alttestamentliche Wissenschaft 314. Berlin: de Gruyter, 2002.

———. *A Strategy for Reading Biblical Texts*. Studies in Biblical Literature 29. New York: Peter Lang, 2002.

———. "Towards a Final Form Approach to Biblical Interpretation." *Stulos Theological Journal* 7, nos. 1–2 (1999): 1–11.

Limburg, J. "The Root *RÎB* and the Prophetic Lawsuit Speeches." *Journal of Biblical Literature* 88 (1969): 291–304.

Linafelt, Tod. "Taking Women in Samuel: Readers/Responses/Responsibility." Pages 99–113 in *Reading between Texts: Intertextuality and the Hebrew Bible*. Edited by Danna Nolan Fewell. Louisville: Westminster John Knox, 1992.

Lindboe, Inger Marie. *Women in the New Testament: A Select Bibliography*. Bibliography Series 1. Oslo: University of Oslo, Faculty of Theology, 1990.

Lipinski, E. "The Wife's Right to Divorce in the Light of an Ancient Near Eastern Tradition." *Jewish Law Annual* 4 (1981): 9–27.

Lipka, Hilary B. *Sexual Transgression in the Hebrew Bible*. Sheffield: Sheffield Phoenix, 2006.

———. "'Such a Thing Is Not Done in Israel': The Construction of Sexual Transgression in the Hebrew Bible." PhD diss., Brandeis University, 2004.

Litke, John D. "The Daughters of Zelophehad." *Currents in Theology and Mission* 29 (2002): 207–18.

Ljung, Inger. *Silence or Suppression: Attitudes towards Women in the Old Testament*. Acta Universitatis Upsaliensis: Uppsala Women's Studies A, Women in Religion 2. Uppsala: S. Academiae Upsaliensis, 1989.

Loader, James Alfred. "Exegetical Erotica to Canticles 7:2–6." *Journal for Semitics* 10 (1998–2001): 98–111.

———. "A Woman Praised by Women Is Better Than a Woman Praised by Seven Men." *Harvard Theological Studies* 60 (2004): 687–701.

Loader, William. *The Septuagint, Sexuality, and the New Testament: Case Studies on the Impact of the LXX in Philo and the New Testament*. Grand Rapids: Eerdmans, 2004.

Locher, Clemens. *Die Ehre einer Frau in Israel: Exegetische und rechtsvergleichende Studien zu Deuteronomium 22, 13–21.* Orbis biblicus et orientalis 70. Freiburg, Switz.: Universitätsverlag, 1986.

Lockwood, Peter F. "Tamar's Place in the Joseph Cycle." *Lutheran Theological Journal* 26 (1992): 35–43.

———. "Zipporah in the Account of Exodus: Literary and Theological Perspectives on Exodus 4:24–26." *Lutheran Theological Journal* 35 (2001): 116–27.

Loewenstamm, Samuel E. *Comparative Studies in Biblical and Ancient Oriental Literatures.* Neukirchen-Vluyn: Neukirchener Verlag, 1980.

Lohfink, Norbert. *In the Shadow of Your Wings: New Readings of Great Texts from the Bible.* Translated by L. Maloney. Collegeville, Minn.: Liturgical, 2003.

Long, Burke O. "The Shunammite Woman: In the Shadow of the Prophet?" *Bible Review* 7, no. 1 (1991): 12–19, 42.

Long, Burke O., Saul M. Olyan, and Robert C. Culley. *"A Wise and Discerning Mind": Essays in Honor of Burke O. Long.* Brown Judaic Studies 325. Providence: Brown Judaic Studies, 2000.

Long, V. Philips. "One Man among a Thousand, but Not a Woman among Them All: A Note on the Use of *māṣā'* in Ecclesiastes vii 28." Pages 101–9 in *"Lasset uns Brücken bauen . . ."* Edited by Klaus-Dietrich Schunck and Matthias Augustin. Beiträge zur Erforschung des Alten Testaments und des antiken Judentums 42. Frankfurt am Main: Peter Lang, 1998.

Longenecker, Richard N. "Authority, Hierarchy, and Leadership Patterns in the Bible." Pages 66–85 in *Women, Authority, and the Bible.* Edited by Alvera Mickelsen. Downers Grove, Ill.: InterVarsity, 1986.

Longman, Tremper, III. *The Song of Songs.* New International Commentary on the Old Testament. Grand Rapids: Eerdmans, 2001.

———. "Song of Songs." Pages 339–93 in August H. Konkel and Tremper Longman III, *Job, Ecclesiastes, Song of Songs.* Cornerstone Biblical Commentary 6. Carol Stream, Ill.: Tyndale House, 2006.

Longstaff, Thomas R. W. "Ordination of Women: A Biblical Perspective." *Anglican Theological Review* 57 (1975): 316–27.

Loughlin, Gerard. *Alien Sex: The Body and Desire in Cinema and Theology.* Challenges in Contemporary Theology. Malden, Mass.: Blackwell, 2004.

Louth, Andrew. *Discerning the Mystery: An Essay on the Nature of Theology.* Oxford: Clarendon, 1983.

———, with Marco Conti, eds. *Genesis 1–11.* Ancient Christian Commentary on Scripture: Old Testament 1. Downers Grove, Ill.: InterVarsity, 2001.

Lowe, Stephen Douglas. "Rethinking the Female Status/Function Question: The Jew/Gentile Relationship as Paradigm." *Journal of the Evangelical Theological Society* 34 (1991): 59–75.

Lubac, Henri de. *Medieval Exegesis: The Four Senses of Scripture.* 2 vols. Translated by E. M. Macierowski (vol. 1) and Mark Sebanc (vol. 2). Grand Rapids: Eerdmans, 2000.

Lubitch, Rivkah. "A Feminist's Look at Esther." *Judaism* 42 (1993): 438–46.

Luc, Alex. "The Titles and Structure of Proverbs." *Zeitschrift für die alttesta-mentliche Wissenschaft* 112 (2000): 252–55.

Luck, William F. *Divorce and Remarriage: Recovering the Biblical View.* San Francisco: Harper & Row, 1987.

Luker, Lamontte M., ed. *Passion, Vitality, and Foment: The Dynamics of Second Temple Judaism.* Harrisburg, Pa.: Trinity Press International, 2001.

Lundbom, Jack R. "What about Divorce?" *Covenant Quarterly* 36, no. 3 (November 1978): 21–27.

Lundy, Daniel G. *Women, the Bible, and the Church: Currents of Change in the Evangelical World.* Richmond Hill, Ont.: Canadian Christian Publications, 1993.

Luter, A. Boyd. "Partnership in the Gospel: The Role of Women in the Church at Philippi." *Journal of the Evangelical Theological Society* 39 (1996): 411–20.

Luther, Martin. *Commentaries on 1 Corinthians 7, 1 Corinthians 15, Lectures on 1 Timothy.* Edited by Hilton C. Oswald. Translated by Edward Sittler, Martin H. Bertram, and Richard J. Dinda. Vol. 28 of *Works.* Edited by Jaroslav Pelikan. St. Louis: Concordia, 1973.

———. *Lectures on Genesis: Chapters 1–5.* Translated by George V. Schick. Vol. 1 of *Works.* Edited by Jaroslav Pelikan. St. Louis: Concordia, 1958.

———. *Lectures on Genesis: Chapters 38–44.* Translated by Paul D. Pahl. Vol. 7 of *Works.* Edited by Jaroslav Pelikan. St. Louis: Concordia, 1965.

———. *Lectures on Ecclesiastes, Song of Solomon, and Last Words of Daniel.* Translated by Ian Siggins. Vol. 15 of *Works.* Edited by Jaroslav Pelikan; St. Louis: Concordia, 1972.

Luttikhuizen, Gerard P., ed. *The Creation of Man and Woman: Interpretations of the Biblical Narratives in Jewish and Christian Traditions.* Themes in Biblical Narrative 3. Boston: E. J. Brill, 2000.

Lyke, Larry L. *King David with the Wise Woman of Tekoa: The Resonance of Tradition in Parabolic Narrative.* Journal for the Study of the Old Testament: Supplement Series 255. Sheffield, Eng.: Sheffield Academic Press, 1997.

———. "The Song of Songs, Proverbs, and the Theology of Love." Pages 208–23 in *Theological Exegesis: Essays in Honor of Brevard S. Childs.* Edited by Christopher Seitz and Kathryn Greene-McCreight. Grand Rapids: Eerdmans, 1999.

Lyons, Ellen Louise. "A Note on Proverbs 31:10–31." Pages 237–45 in *The Listening Heart: Essays in Wisdom and the Psalms in Honor of Roland E. Murphy.* Edited by Kenneth G. Hoglund et al. Journal for the Study of the Old Testament: Supplement Series 255. Sheffield, Eng.: JSOT Press, 1987.

Lyons, William John. " 'Outing' Qoheleth: On the Search for Homosexuality in the Wisdom Tradition." *Theology and Sexuality* 12 (2006): 181–202.

Lys, D. *Le plus beau chant de la création: Commentaire du Cantique des cantiques.* Paris: Cerf, 1968.

Maberly, Clifton R. "The Polygamous Marriage variant: The Perspective of Sacred History." Term Paper, Adventist Heritage Center, Andrews University, 1975.

Maccoby, Hyam. "Holiness and Purity: The Holy People in Leviticus and Ezra-Nehemiah." Pages 153–70 in *Reading Leviticus: A Conversation with Mary Douglas*. Edited by John F. A. Sawyer. Journal for the Study of the Old Testament: Supplement Series 227. Sheffield, Eng.: Sheffield Academic Press, 1996.

———. *Ritual and Morality: The Ritual Purity System and Its Place in Judaism.* Cambridge: Cambridge University Press, 1999.

MacDonald, Margaret Y. "Was Celsus Right? The Role of Women in the Expansion of Early Christianity." Pages 157–84 in *Early Christian Families in Context: An Interdisciplinary Dialogue*. Edited by David L. Balch and Carolyn Osiek. Grand Rapids: Eerdmans, 2003.

Macht, David I. "A Scientific Appreciation of Leviticus 12:1–2." *Journal of Biblical Literature* 52 (1933): 253–60.

Macintosh, A. A. *A Critical and Exegetical Commentary on Hosea*. Edinburgh: T&T Clark, 1997.

Madvig, Donald. "Joshua." Pages 239–371 in vol. 3 of *The Expositor's Bible Commentary*. Edited by Frank E. Gaebelein. Grand Rapids: Zondervan, 1976–1992.

Magliola, Robert. "Differential Theology and Womankind: On Isaiah 66:13." Pages 211–25 in *Shadow of Spirit: Postmodernism and Religion*. Edited by Philippa Berry and Andrew Wernick. London: Routledge, 1992.

Magonet, Jonathan. " 'But If It Is a Girl She Is Unclean for Twice Seven Days . . .': The Riddle of Leviticus 12:5." Pages 144–52 in *Reading Leviticus: A Conversation with Mary Douglas*. Edited by John F. A. Sawyer. Journal for the Study of the Old Testament Supplementary Series 227. Sheffield, Eng.: Sheffield Academic Press, 1996.

Makujina, John. "Additional Considerations for Determining the Meaning of 'A case of 'ĂNÔT and 'ANNÔT in Exod. XXXII 18." *Vetus Testamentum* 55 (2005): 39–46.

Malchow, Bruce V. "Scripture as a Norm of Moral Deliberation and Its Application to Homosexuality." *Currents in Theology and Mission* 31 (2004): 465–72.

Malcolm, Kari Torjesen. *Women at the Crossroads: A Path beyond Feminism and Traditionalism*. Downers Grove, Ill.: InterVarsity, 1982.

Malick, David E. "The Condemnation of Homosexuality in 1 Corinthians 6:9." *Bibliotheca sacra* 150 (1993): 479–92.

———. "The Condemnation of Homosexuality in Romans 1:26–27." *Bibliotheca sacra* 150 (1993): 327–40.

Malina, Bruce J. "Does *porneia* Mean Fornication?" *Novum Testamentum* 14 (1972): 10–17.

Malone, Mary T. *The First Thousand Years*. Vol. 1 of *Women and Christianity*. Maryknoll, N.Y.: Orbis, 2000.

———. *From 1000 to the Reformation*. Vol. 2 of *Women and Christianity*. Maryknoll, N.Y.: Orbis, 2001.

Malphurs, Aubrey. *Biblical Manhood and Womanhood: Understanding Masculinity and Femininity from God's Perspective*. Grand Rapids: Kregel, 1996.

Malul, Meir. "Adoption of Foundlings in the Bible and Mesopotamian Documents: A Study of Some Legal Metaphors in Ezekiel 16–17." *Journal for the Study of the Old Testament* no. 46 (1990): 97–126.

———. *Knowledge, Control, and Sex: Studies in Biblical Thought, Culture, and Worldview.* Tel Aviv–Jaffa: Archaeological Center, 2002.

———. *Studies in Mesopotamian Legal Symbolism.* Kevelaer, Ger.: Butzon & Bercker, 1988.

Mankowski, Paul. "The Gender of Israel's God." Pages 35–61 in *This Is My Name Forever: The Trinity and Gender Language for God.* Edited by Alvin F. Kimel Jr. Downers Grove, Ill.: InterVarsity, 2001.

Manniche, Lise. "Goddess and Woman in Ancient Egypt." *The Journal of the Society for the Study of Egyptian Antiquites* 29 (2002): 1–7.

———. *Sexual Life in Ancient Egypt.* London: Kegan Paul, 1987.

———. "Some Aspects of Ancient Egyptian Sexual Life," *Acta orientalia* 38 (1977): 11–23.

March, W. Eugene. "Father as a Metaphor for God in the Psalms." *Austin Seminary Bulletin: Faculty Edition* 97 (1981): 5–12.

Marcus, David. "The Bargaining between Jephthah and the Elders (Judges 11:4–11)." *Journal of Near Eastern Studies* 19 (1989): 95–100.

———. "The Legal Dispute between Jephthah and the Elders." *Hebrew Annual Review* 12 (1990): 105–13.

Mare, W. Harold. "1 Corinthians." Pages 173–297 in vol. 10 of *The Expositor's Bible Commentary.* Edited by Frank E. Gaebelein. 12 vols. Grand Rapids: Zondervan, 1976–1992.

Mark, Elizabeth Wyner, ed. *The Covenant of Circumcision: New Perspectives on an Ancient Jewish Rite.* Lebanon, N.H.: Brandeis University Press, 2003.

———. "Wounds, Vows, Emanations." Pages 3–17 in *The Covenant of Circumcision: New Perspectives on an Ancient Jewish Rite.* Edited by Elizabeth Wyner Mark. Lebanon, N.H.: Brandeis University Press, 2003.

Marrow, Stanley B. "Marriage and Divorce in the New Testament." *Anglican Theological Review* 70 (1988): 3–15.

Marrs, Rick R. "In the Beginning: Male and Female (Gen 1–3)." Pages 1–36 in vol. 2 of *Essays on Women in Earliest Christianity.* Edited by Carroll D. Osburn. 2 vols. Joplin, Mo.: College Press, 1995.

Marsman, Hennie J. *Women in Ugarit and Israel: Their Social and Religious Position in the Context of the Ancient Near East.* Boston: E. J. Brill, 2003.

Marsollier, Ronaldo D. "Cant 8:6–7—Love as a Divine Gift: The Crown and Climax of the Song of Songs." Paper presented for the class OTST668 Psalms/Wisdom Literature: Song of Songs, Andrews University, winter 1999.

Martin, Dale B. "*Arsenokoitēs* and *malakos*: Meanings and Consequences." Pages 117–36 in *Biblical Ethics and Homosexuality: Listening to Scripture.* Edited by Robert Brawley. Louisville: Westminster John Knox, 1996.

———. *Sex and the Single Savior: Gender and Sexuality in Biblical Interpretation.* Louisville, Ky.: Westminster John Knox, 2006.

Martin, Faith McBurney. *Call Me Blessed: The Emerging Christian Woman*. Grand Rapids: Eerdmans, 1988.

Martin, Francis. *The Feminist Question: Feminist Theology in the Light of Christian Tradition*. Grand Rapids: Eerdmans, 1994.

Martin, James D. "Forensic Background to Jeremiah 3:1." *Vetus Testamentum* 19 (1969): 82–92.

Martin, Troy W. "The Covenant of Circumcision (Genesis 17:9–14) and the Situational Antitheses in Galatians 3:28." *Journal of Biblical Literature* 122 (2003): 111–25.

Marx, Alfred. "Rahab, prostituée et prophétesse: Josue 2 et 6." *Études théologiques et religieuses* 55 (1980): 72–76.

Mathews, Kenneth A. *Genesis 1–11:26*. New American Commentary 1A. Nashville: Broadman & Holman, 1996.

Mathewson, Steven D. "An Exegetical Study of Genesis 38." *Bibliotheca sacra* 146 (1989): 373–92.

Matlock, Michael D. "Disobeying or Obeying the First Part of the Tenth Commandment: Alternative Meanings from Deuteronomy 25:5–10." *Proceedings, Eastern Great Lakes and Midwest Biblical Society* 21 (2001): 91–103.

Matter, E. Ann. *The Voice of My Beloved: The Song of Songs in Western Medieval Christianity*. Philadelphia: University of Pennsylvania Press, 1990.

Matthews, Victor H. "Female Voices: Upholding the Honor of the Household." *Biblical Theology Bulletin* 24 (1994): 8–15.

———. "Honor and Shame in Gender-Related Legal Situations in the Hebrew Bible." Pages 97–112 in *Gender and Law in the Hebrew Bible and the Ancient Near East*. Edited by Victor H. Matthews, Bernard M. Levinson, and Tikva Frymer-Kensky. Journal for the Study of the Old Testament: Supplement Series 262. Sheffield, Eng.: Sheffield Academic Press, 1998.

———. "Hospitality and Hostility in Genesis 19 and Judges 19." *Biblical Theology Bulletin* 22 (1992): 3–11.

———. "Hospitality and Hostility in Judges 4." *Biblical Theology Bulletin* 21 (1991): 13–21.

———. "Marriage and Family in the Ancient Near East." Pages 1–32 in *Marriage and Family in the Biblical World*. Edited by Ken M. Campbell. Downers Grove, Ill.: InterVarsity, 2003.

Matthews, Victor H., and Don C. Benjamin. *Old Testament Parallels: Laws and Stories from the Ancient Near East*. Rev. and expanded ed. New York: Paulist, 1997.

———. *The Social World of Ancient Israel, 1250–587 B.C.E.* Peabody, Mass.: Hendrickson, 1993.

Matthews, Victor H., Bernard M. Levinson, and Tikva Simone Frymer-Kensky, eds. *Gender and Law in the Hebrew Bible and the Ancient Near East*. Journal for the Study of the Old Testament: Supplement Series 262. Sheffield, Eng.: Sheffield Academic Press, 1998.

Mattox, Mickey Leland. *"Defender of the Most Holy Matriarchs": Martin Luther's Interpretation of the Women of Genesis in the "Enarrationes in Genesin," 1535–45*. Studies in Medieval and Reformation Thought 92. Leiden: E. J. Brill, 2003.

Mauser, Ulrich W. "Creation and Human Sexuality in the New Testament." Pages 3–15 in *Biblical Ethics and Homosexuality: Listening to Scripture.* Edited by Robert L. Brawley. Louisville: Westminster John Knox, 1996.

Maxnes, Halvar. "Social Integration and the Problem of Gender in St. Paul's Letter." *Studia theologica* 43 (1989): 99–113.

Maxwell, Marcus. "Creation, Redemption, and Sexuality in 1 Corinthians." Pages 257–77 in *Women in the Biblical Tradition.* Edited by George J. Brooke. Lewiston, N.Y.: Mellen, 1992.

Mayes, A. D. H. *Judges.* Old Testament Guides 8. Sheffield, Eng.: JSOT Press, 1985.

Mays, James Luther. *Amos: A Commentary.* Old Testament Library. Philadelphia: Westminster, 1969.

———. *Hosea: A Commentary.* Old Testament Library. Philadelphia: Westminster, 1969.

Mazar, Amihai. *Archaeology of the Land of the Bible, 10,000–586 B.C.E.* New York: Doubleday, 1990.

Mazat, Alberta. *The Intimate Marriage: Connecting with the One You Love.* Hagerstown, Md.: Review and Herald, 2001.

———. *That Friday in Eden: Sharing and Enhancing Sexuality in Marriage.* Mountain View, Calif.: Pacific, 1981.

Mazor, Yair. "The Song of Songs or the Story of Stories? 'The Song of Songs'— between Genre and Unity." *Scandinavian Journal of the Old Testament* 1 (1990): 1–29.

Mazzinghi, Luca. "La sapienza dell_oriente antico: il canto degli arpisti." *Parole di Vita* 48, no. 3 (2003): 50–51.

Mbiti, John S. *Love and Marriage in Africa.* Essex, Eng.: Longman, 1973.

Mbuwayesango, Dora Rudo. "Can Daughters Be Sons? The Daughters of Zelophehad in Patriarchal and Imperial Society." Pages 251–62 in *Relating to the Text: Interdisciplinary and Form-Critical Insights on the Bible.* Edited by Timothy J. Sandoval and Carleen Mandolfo. Journal for the Study of the Old Testament: Supplement Series 384. New York: T&T Clark, 2003.

———. "Childlessness and Woman-To-Woman Relationships in Genesis and African Patriarchal Society: Sarah and Hagar from a Zimbabwean Woman's Perspective (Gen. 16:1–16; 21:8–21)." *Semeia* 78 (1997): 27–36.

McBride, S. Dean, Jr., "Divine Protocol: Genesis 1:1–2:3 as Prologue to the Pentateuch." Pages 3–41 in *God Who Creates: Essays in Honor of W. Sibley Towner.* Edited by William P. Brown and S. Dean McBride Jr. Grand Rapids: Eerdmans 2000.

McCann, J. Clinton, Jr. "The Hermeneutics of Grace: Discerning the Bible's 'Single Plot.'" *Interpretation* 57 (2003): 5–15.

McCartney, Dan, and Charles Clayton. *Let the Reader Understand: A Guide to Interpreting and Applying the Bible.* Wheaton, Ill.: Victor, 1994.

McClenney-Sadler, Madeline G. "Re-covering the Daughter's Nakedness: A Formal Analysis of Israelite Kinship Terminology and the Internal Logic of Leviticus 18." PhD diss., Duke University, 2001.

McComiskey, Thomas Edward. *The Covenants of Promise: A Theology of the Old Testament Covenants.* Grand Rapids: Baker, 1985.

———. "Hosea." Pages 1–237 in *Hosea, Joel, and Amos.* Volume 1 of *The Minor Prophets: An Exegetical and Expository Commentary.* 3 vols. Edited by Thomas Edward McComiskey. Grand Rapids: Baker, 1992–1998.

McConville, J. G. *Deuteronomy.* Apollos Old Testament Commentary 5. Downers Grove, Ill.: InterVarsity, 2002.

———. *Grace in the End: A Study of Deuteronomic Theology.* Studies in Old Testament Biblical Theology. Grand Rapids: Zondervan, 1993.

McCreesh, Thomas P. "Wisdom as Wife: Proverbs 31:10–31." *Revue biblique* 92 (1985): 25–46.

McCurley, Foster R. *Ancient Myths and Biblical Faith: Scriptural Transformations.* Philadelphia: Fortress, 1983.

McDonald, Elizabeth Mary. *The Position of Women as Reflected in Semitic Codes of Law.* Toronto: University of Toronto Press, 1931.

McFague, Sallie. *Models of God: Theology for an Ecological, Nuclear Age.* Philadelphia: Fortress, 1987.

McGovern, Thomas. "John Paul II on the Millennium and God as Father." *Homiletical and Pastoral Review* 99, no. 7 (1999): 8–17.

McKeating, Henry. "Sanctions against Adultery in Ancient Israelite Society, with Some Reflections on Methodology in the Study of Old Testament Ethics." *Journal for the Study of the Old Testament* no. 11 (1979): 57–72.

McKenzie, John L. "The Literary Characteristics of Genesis 2–3." *Theological Studies* 15 (1954): 541–72.

———. *Second Isaiah: A New Translation with Introduction and Commentary.* Anchor Bible 20. Garden City, N.Y.: Doubleday, 1968.

McKinlay, Judith E. *Gendering Wisdom the Host: Biblical Invitations to Eat and Drink.* Journal for the Study of Old Testament Supplement Series 216. Gender, Culture, Theory 4. Sheffield: Sheffield Academic Press, 1996.

McLay, R. Timothy. "Beyond Textual Criticism: The Use of the Septuagint in NT Research." *Journal of Northwest Semitic Languages* 28, no. 1 (2002): 68–85.

———. *The Use of the Septuagint in New Testament Research.* Grand Rapids: Eerdmans, 2003.

McMahon, Gregory. "Anatolia." Pages 236–39 in vol. 1 of *Anchor Bible Dictionary.* Edited by D. N. Freedman. 6 vols. New York: Doubleday, 1992.

Meacham, Tirzah. "The Missing Daughter: Leviticus 18 and 20." *Zeitschrift für die alttestamentliche Wissenschaft* 109 (1997): 254–59.

Meek, T. J. "Canticles and the Tammuz Cult." *American Journal of Semitic Languages and Literature* 39 (1922–1923): 1–14.

———. "The Song of Songs: Introduction and Exegesis." Pages 89–148 in Vol. 5 of *The Interpreter's Bible.* Edited by G. A. Buttrick et al. 12 vols. New York: Abingdon, 1956.

Meeser, Spenser Byron. "Divorce and Remarriage." *Methodist Review* 110 (1927): 853–70.

Meilaender, Gilbert. "Marriage in Counterpoint and Harmony." *First Things* 24 (June–July 1992): 30–36.

Meiselman, Moshe. *Jewish Women in Jewish Law.* New York: Ktav, 1978.

Melcher, Sarah J. "The Holiness Code and Human Sexuality." Pages 87–102 in *Biblical Ethics and Homosexuality: Listening to Scripture.* Edited by Robert L. Brawley. Louisville: Westminster John Knox, 1996.

———. "Lacan, the Phallus and the Construal of Intergenerational Kinship in Genesis-Numbers." Pages 191–205 in *Relating to the Text: Interdisciplinary and Form-Critical Insights on the Bible.* Edited by Timothy J. Sandoval and Carleen Mandolfo. Journal for the Study of the Old Testament: Supplement Series 384. New York: T&T Clark, 2003.

Melville, Sarah C. "Neo-Assyrian Royal Women and Male Identity: Status as a Social Tool." *Journal of the American Oriental Society* 124 (2004): 37–57.

Menn, Esther Marie. *Judah and Tamar (Genesis 38) in Ancient Jewish Exegesis: Studies in Literary Form and Hermeneutics.* Journal for the Study of Judaism Supplements 51. Leiden: E. J. Brill, 1997.

———. "Sexuality in the Old Testament: Strong as Death, Unquenchable as Fire." *Currents in Theology and Mission* 30 (2003): 37–45.

Mercadante, Linda A. *Gender, Doctrine, and God: The Shakers and Contemporary Theology.* Nashville: Abingdon, 1990.

Merideth, Betsy. "Desire and Danger: The Drama of Betrayal." Pages 63–78 in *Anti-covenant: Counter-reading Women's Lives in the Hebrew Bible.* Edited by Mieke Bal. Sheffield, Eng.: Almond, 1989.

Merkin, Daphne. "The Woman in the Balcony: On Rereading the Song of Songs." Pages 238–55 in *Out of the Garden: Women Writers on the Bible.* Edited by Christina Büchmann and Celine Spiegel. New York: Fawcett Columbine, 1994.

Merling, David. "Rahab: The Woman Who Fulfilled the Words of YHWH." *Andrews University Seminary Studies* 41, no. 1 (2002): 31–44.

Merrill, Eugene H. *Deuteronomy.* New American Commentary 4. Nashville: Broadman & Holman, 1994.

Metlitzki, Dorothée. "'A Woman of Virtue': A Note on *eshet hayil.*" *Orim* 1 (spring 1986): 23–26.

Metti, A. "The Female Body in Hebrew Scriptures: A Critique." *Vidyajyoti* 68 (2004): 177–95.

Meyers, Carol. *Discovering Eve: Ancient Israelite Women in Context.* New York: Oxford University Press, 1988.

———. "Discovering Women in Scripture." *Bible Review* 16, no. 4 (2000): 8, 59.

———. "From Household to House of Yahweh: Women's Religious Culture in Ancient Israel." Pages 277–303 in *Congress Volume: Basel, 2001.* Edited by André Lemaire. Vetus Testamentum Supplements 92. Leiden: E. J. Brill, 2002.

———. "Gender Imagery in the Song of Songs." *Hebrew Annual Review* 10 (1986): 209–23.

———. "Gender Roles and Gen 3:16 Revisited." Pages 337–54 in *The Word of the Lord Shall Go Forth: Essays in Honor of David Noel Freedman in Celebration of*

His Sixtieth Birthday. Edited by Carol L. Meyers and M. O'Connor. Winona Lake, Ind.: Eisenbrauns, 1983.

———. "Hannah and Her Sacrifice: Reclaiming Female Agency." Pages 93–104 in *A Feminist Companion to Samuel and Kings.* Edited by Athalya Brenner. Feminist Companion to the Bible 5. Sheffield, Eng.: Sheffield Academic Press, 1994.

———. "The Hebrew Bible." Pages 4–11 in *Women in Scripture: A Dictionary of Named and Unnamed Women in the Hebrew Bible, the Apocryphal/Deuterocanonical Books, and the New Testament.* Edited by Carol Meyers, Toni Craven, and Ross S. Kraemer. Boston: Houghton Mifflin, 2000.

———. "Miriam the Musician." Pages 207–30 in *A Feminist Companion to Exodus to Deuteronomy.* Edited by Athalya Brenner. Feminist Companion to the Bible 6. Sheffield, Eng.: Sheffield Academic Press, 1994.

———. "Returning Home: Ruth 1:8 and the Gendering of the Book of Ruth." Pages 85–114 in *A Feminist Companion to Ruth.* Edited by Athalya Brenner. Feminist Companion to the Bible 3. Sheffield, Eng.: Sheffield Academic Press, 1993.

———. "The Roots of Restriction: Women in Early Israel." *Biblical Archaeologist* 41 (1978): 91–103.

———. "To Her Mother's House: Considering a Counterpart to the Israelite *bêt 'ab.*" Pages 39–51 in *The Bible and the Politics of Exegesis.* Edited by David Jobling, Peggy L. Day, and Gerald T. Sheppard. Cleveland: Pilgrim, 1991.

———. "Woman of Thebez." Pages 241–42 in *Women in Scripture: A Dictionary of Named and Unnamed Women in the Hebrew Bible, the Apocryphal/Deuterocanonical Books, and the New Testament.* Edited by Carol Meyers, Toni Craven, and Ross S. Kraemer. Boston: Houghton Mifflin, 2000.

Michel, Walter L. "BTWLH, 'Virgin' or 'Virgin (Anat)' in Job 31:1?" *Hebrew Studies* 23 (1982): 59–66.

Mickelsen, Alvera. "An Egalitarian View: There Is Neither Male nor Female in Christ." Pages 173–206 in *Women in Ministry: Four Views.* Edited by Bonnidell Clouse and Robert G. Clouse. Downers Grove, Ill.: InterVarsity, 1989.

———, ed. *Women, Authority, and the Bible.* Downers Grove, Ill.: InterVarsity, 1986.

Mickelsen, Berkeley, and Alvera Mickelsen. "What Does *kephalē* Mean in the New Testament?" Pages 97–110 in *Women, Authority, and the Bible.* Edited by Alvera Mickelsen. Downers Grove, Ill.: InterVarsity, 1986.

Middlekoop, Pieter. "Significance of the Story of the Bloody Husband, Ex 4:24–26." *South East Asia Journal of Theology* 8 (1967): 34–38.

Mies, Françoise. " 'Dame Sagesse' en Proverbes 9: Une personification féminine?" *Revue biblique* 108 (2001): 161–83.

Mikaelsson, Lisbeth. "Sexual Polarity: An Aspect of the Ideological Structure in the Paradise Narrative, Genesis 2:4–3:24." *Temenos* 16 (1980): 84–91.

Miles, Carrie A., and Laurence R. Iannaccone. *Male and Female in Christ: Discover What the Bible Really Says about Women—and about Men.* 3d ed. Minneapolis: Christians for Biblical Equity, 2000.

Miles, Jack. *God: A Biography.* London: Simon & Schuster, 1995.

Miletic, Stephen Francis. *One Flesh: Ephesians 5:22–24; 5:31: Marriage and the New Creation.* Analecta biblica 115. Rome: Biblical Institute Press, 1988.

Milgrom, Jacob. "The Betrothed Slave-Girl, Lev 19:20–22." *Zeitschrift für die alttestamentliche Wissenschaft* 89 (1977): 43–50.

———. "The Case of the Suspected Adulteress, Numbers 5:11–31: Redaction and Meaning." Pages 69–75 in *The Creation of Sacred Literature: Composition and Redaction of the Biblical Text.* Edited by Richard Elliott Friedman. Berkeley: University of California Press, 1981.

———. "Does the Bible Prohibit Homosexuality?" *Bible Review* 9, no. 6 (1993): 11.

———. "How Not to Read the Bible." *Bible Review* 10, no. 2 (1994): 14, 48.

———. "A Husband's Pride, a Mob's Prejudice: The Public Ordeal Undergone by a Suspected Adulteress in Numbers 5 Was Meant Not to Humiliate Her but to Protect Her." *Bible Review* 12, no. 4 (1996): 21.

———. "Impurity Is Miasma: A Response to Hyam Maccoby." *Journal of Biblical Literature* 119 (2000): 729–33.

———. *Leviticus 1–16: A New Translation with Introduction and Commentary.* Anchor Bible 3. New York: Doubleday, 1991.

———. *Leviticus 17–22: A New Translation with Introduction and Commentary.* Anchor Bible 3A. New York: Doubleday, 2000.

———. *Leviticus 23–27: A New Translation with Introduction and Commentary.* Anchor Bible 3B. New York: Doubleday, 2001.

———. "The Nature and Extent of Idolatry in Eighth–Seventh Century Judah." *Hebrew Union College Annual* 69 (1998): 1–13.

———. *Numbers: The Traditional Hebrew Text with the New JPS Translation.* JPS Torah Commentary. Philadelphia: Jewish Publication Society, 1990.

———. "On the Suspected Adulteress (Numbers 5:11–31)." *Vetus Testamentum* 35 (1985): 368–69.

———. "Sex and Wisdom: What the Garden of Eden Story Is Saying." *Bible Review* 10, no. 6 (1994): 21, 52.

Millard, Alan R. "The Position of Women in the Family and Society in Ancient Egypt with Special Reference to the Middle Kingdom." PhD diss., University of London, University College, 1976.

Miller, James E. "Notes on Leviticus 18." *Zeitschrift für die alttestamentliche Wissenschaft* 112 (2000): 401–3.

———. "Sexual Offences in Genesis." *Journal for the Study of the Old Testament* no. 90 (2000): 41–53.

Miller, John W. *Calling God "Father": Essays on the Bible, Fatherhood, and Culture.* 2d ed. New York: Paulist, 1999.

———. "God as Father in the Bible and the Father Image in Several Contemporary Ancient Near Eastern Myths: A Comparison." *Studies in Religion/ Sciences religieuses* 14 (1985): 347–54.

Miller, Patrick D. *Deuteronomy.* Interpretation: A Bible Commentary for Teaching and Preaching. Louisville: John Knox, 1990.

———. "Yeled in the Song of Lamech." *Journal of Biblical Literature* 85 (1966): 477–78.

Miller, Patrick D., Jr., Paul D. Hanson, and S. Dean McBride, eds. *Ancient Israelite Religion: Essays in Honor of Frank Moore Cross.* Philadelphia: Fortress, 1987.

Mills, Mary E. *Biblical Morality: Moral Perspectives in Old Testament Narratives.* Heythrop Studies in Contemporary Philosophy, Religion & Theology. Burlington, Vt.: Ashgate, 2001.

Milne, Pamela. "Feminist Interpretation of the Bible: Then and Now." *Bible Review* 8 (October 1992): 38–43, 52–54.

———. "The Patriarchal Stamp of Scripture: The Implications of Structuralist Analyses for Feminist Hermeneutics." *Journal of Feminist Studies in Religion* 5 (1989): 17–34.

Mitchell, Christopher W. *The Song of Songs.* Concordia Commentary: A Theological Exposition of Sacred Scripture. Saint Louis: Concordia, 2003.

———. "The Song of Songs: A Lutheran Perspective." Pages 79–110 in *"Hear the Word of Yahweh": Essays on Scripture and Archaeology in Honor of Horace D. Hummel.* Edited by Dean O. Wenthe, Paul L. Schrieber, and Lee A. Maxwell. St. Louis: Concordia, 2002.

Mitchell, Patrick. *The Scandal of Gender: Early Christian Teaching on the Man and the Woman.* Salisbury, Mass.: Regina Orthodox Press, 1998.

Mitchell, Stephen. *The Book of Job.* San Francisco: North Point, 1987.

Mohrmann, Doug C. "Making Sense of Sex: A Study of Leviticus 18." *Journal for the Study of the Old Testament* 29, no. 1 (September 2004): 57–79.

Moingt, Joseph. "Le divorce 'pour motif d'impudicité.'" *Recherches de science religieuse* 56 (1968): 337–84.

Moiser, Jeremy. "A Reassessment of Paul's View of Marriage with Reference to 1 Cor 7." *Journal for the Study of the New Testament* 18 (1983): 103–22.

Molldrem, Mark J. "A Hermeneutic of Pastoral Care and the Law/Gospel Paradigm Applied to the Divorce Texts of Scripture." *Interpretation* 45 (1991): 43–54.

Mollenkott, Virginia Ramey. *The Divine Feminine: The Biblical Imagery of God as Female.* New York: Crossroad, 1988.

———. *Godding: Human Responsibility and the Bible.* New York: Crossroad, 1988.

———. *Women, Men, and the Bible.* Nashville: Abingdon, 1977.

Montet, Pierre. *Everyday Life in Egypt in the Days of Ramesses the Great.* London: Edward Arnold, 1958.

Moo, Douglas J. "1 Timothy 2:11–15: Meaning and Significance." *Trinity Journal* 1 (1980): 62–83.

———. "The Interpretation of 1 Timothy 2:11–15: A Rejoinder." *Trinity Journal* 2 (1981): 198–222.

———. "What Does It Mean Not to Teach or Have Authority over Men? 1 Timothy 2:11–15." Pages 179–93, 495–99 in *Recovering Biblical Manhood and Womanhood: A Response to Evangelical Feminism.* Edited by J. Piper and Wayne A. Grudem. Wheaton, Ill.: Crossway, 1991.

Moor, Johannes C. de. "The Duality in God and Man: Gen 1:26–27." Pages 112–25 in *Intertextuality in Ugarit and Israel: Papers Read at the Tenth Joint Meeting of the Society for Old Testament Study and Het Oudtestamentisch Werkgezelschap in Nederland en België, Held at Oxford, 1997.* Edited by Johannes C. de Moor. Oudtestamentische Studiën 40. Leiden: E. J. Brill, 1998.

―――, ed. *The Elusive Prophet: The Prophet as a Historical Person, Literary Character, and Anonymous Artist.* Oudtestamentische Studiën 45. Boston: E. J. Brill, 2001.

Moore, G. F. *Judges.* International Critical Commentary. Edinburgh: T&T Clark, 1895.

Moore, Michael S. " 'Wise Women' in the Bible: Identifying a Trajectory." Pages 87–104 in vol. 2 of *Essays on Women in Earliest Christianity.* Edited by Carroll D. Osburn. 2 vols. Joplin, Mo.: College Press, 1995.

Moran, William L. "The Conclusion of the Decalogue." *Catholic Biblical Quarterly* 95 (1967): 543–54.

―――. *The Most Magic Word: Essays on Babylonian and Biblical Literature.* Catholic Biblical Quarterly Monograph Series 35. Washington, D.C.: Catholic Biblical Association, 2002.

―――. "New Evidence from Mari on the History of Prophecy." *Biblica* 50 (1969): 15–56.

―――. "The Scandal of the 'Great Sin' at Ugarit." *Journal of Near Eastern Studies* 18 (1959): 280–81.

Morfino, Mauro Maria. "Il Cantico dei cantici e il patto elettivo: Possibili connessioni." *Theologica & historica* 5 (1996): 7–42.

Morgenstern, Julian. "The 'Bloody Husband' (?) (Exod 4:24–26) Once Again." *Hebrew Union College Annual* 34 (1963): 35–70.

Moskala, Jiří. *The Laws of Clean and Unclean Animals of Leviticus 11: Their Nature, Theology, and Rationale (an Intertextual Study).* Adventist Theological Society Dissertation Series 4. Berrien Springs, Mich.: Adventist Theological Society, 2000.

Motyer, J. Alec. *The Prophecy of Isaiah: An Introduction and Commentary.* Downers Grove, Ill.: InterVarsity, 1993.

Motyer, Stephen. "The Relationship between Paul's Gospel of 'All One in Christ Jesus' (Galatians 3:28) and the 'Household Codes.'" *Vox evangelica* 19 (1989): 33–48.

Mueller, E. Aydeet. *The Micah Story: A Morality Tale in the Book of Judges.* New York: Peter Lang, 2001.

Muilenburg, James. "Form Criticism and Beyond." *Journal of Biblical Literature* 88 (1969): 1–18.

Mulder, Martin J. "Does Canticles 6,12 Make Sense?" Pages 104–13 in *The Scriptures and the Scrolls: Studies in Honour of A. S. van der Woude on the Occasion of His 65th Birthday.* Edited by Florentino García Martínez, A. Hilhorst, and C. J. Labuschagne. Vetus Testamentum Supplements 49. Leiden: E. J. Brill, 1992.

Müller, Hans-Peter. "Zur Frage nach dem 'Wesen' früher Lyrik—Am Beispiel des Hohenliedes." Pages 817–32 in *Gott und Mensch im Dialog. Festschrift für Otto Kaiser zum 80. Geburtstag.* Edited by Markus Witte. BZAW 345/1–2. New York: de Gruyter, 2005.

Mullins, Patrick. "The Public, Secular Roles of Women in Biblical Times." *Milltown Studies* 43 (1998): 79–111.

———. "The Religious Roles of Women among Israel's Neighbors." *Milltown Studies* 45 (2000): 81–113.

Müllner, Ilse. "Lethal Differences: Sexual Violence as Violence against Others in Judges 19." Pages 126–42 in *Judges.* Edited by Athalya Brenner. Feminist Companion to the Bible: Second Series 4. Sheffield, Eng.: Sheffield Academic Press, 1999.

Mulzac, Ken. "Hannah: The Receiver and Giver of a Great Gift." *Andrews University Seminary Studies* 40, no. 2 (2002): 207–17.

———. "The Role of Abigail in 1 Samuel 25." *Andrews University Seminary Studies* 41, no. 1 (2003): 45–53.

Munro, Jill M. *Spikenard and Saffron: The Imagery of the Song of Songs.* Journal for the Study of the Old Testament: Supplement Series 203. Sheffield, Eng.: Sheffield Academic Press, 1995.

Murken, Todd. "Hath God Said . . . ?" *Currents in Theology and Mission* 32 (2005): 195–203.

Murphy, Cullen. *The Word according to Eve: Women and the Bible in Ancient Times and Our Own.* Boston: Houghton Mifflin, 1998.

Murphy, Roland E. "A Biblical Model of Human Intimacy: The Song of Songs." Pages 61–66 in *The Family in Crisis or in Transition: A Sociological and Theological Perspective.* Edited by Andrew Greeley. Concilium 121. New York: Seabury, 1979.

———. *The Song of Songs: A Commentary on the Book of Canticles or the Song of Songs.* Hermeneia. Minneapolis: Fortress, 1990.

———. "The Symbolism of the Song of Songs." Pages 229–34 in *The Incarnate Imagination: Essays in Theology, the Arts, and Social Sciences in Honor of Andrew Greeley—a Festschrift.* Edited by Ingrid H. Shafer. Bowling Green, Ohio: Bowling Green State University Popular Press, 1988.

———. *The Tree of Life: An Exploration of Biblical Wisdom Literature.* 2d ed. Grand Rapids: Eerdmans, 1996.

———. "The Unity of the Song of Songs." *Vetus Testamentum* 29 (1979): 436–43.

———. "Wisdom and Creation." *Journal of Biblical Literature* 104 (1985): 3–11.

———. "Wisdom and Eros in Proverbs 1–9." *Catholic Biblical Quarterly* 50 (1988): 600–603.

———. *Wisdom Literature: Job, Proverbs, Ruth, Canticles, Ecclesiastes, Esther.* Forms of the Old Testament Literature 13. Grand Rapids: Eerdmans, 1981.

Murray, John. *Divorce.* Grand Rapids: Baker, 1961.

———. *Principles of Conduct.* Grand Rapids: Eerdmans, 1957.

Myers, Charles D. "What the Bible Really Says about Homosexuality." *Anima* 19 (fall 1992): 47–56.

Myers, Jacob M. *II Chronicles*. Anchor Bible 13. Garden City, N.Y.: Doubleday, 1965.

Ndoga, S. S., and Hendrik Viviers. "Is the Woman in the Song of Songs Really That Free?" *Hervormde teologiese studies* 56, no. 4 (2000): 1286–1307.

Neall, Beatrice S. "A Theology of Woman." *Spectrum* 19, no. 5 (1989): 14–28.

Neff, David. "The Battle of the Lexicons: Scholars Debate Biblical Roles of Men and Women." *Christianity Today* 31, no. 1 (1987): 44–46.

Negbi, Ora. *Canaanite Gods in Metal: An Archaeological Study of Ancient Syro-Palestinian Figurines*. Tel Aviv: Tel Aviv University, Institute of Archaeology, 1976.

Neller, Kenneth V. " 'Submission' in Eph 5:21–33." Pages 243–60 in vol. 1 of *Essays on Women in Earliest Christianity*. Edited by Carroll D. Osburn. 2 vols. Joplin, Mo.: College Press, 1993.

Nelson, James B. *Embodiment: An Approach to Sexuality and Christian Theology*. Minneapolis: Augsburg, 1978.

Nelson, James B., and Sandra P. Longfellow, eds. *Sexuality and the Sacred: Sources for Theological Reflection*. Louisville: Westminster John Knox, 1994.

Nelson, Tommy, *The Book of Romance: What Solomon Says about Love, Sex, and Intimacy*. Nashville: Nelson, 1998.

Nembach, Ulrich. "Ehescheidung nach alttestamentlichem und jüdischem Recht." *Theologische Zeitschrift* 26 (1970): 161–71.

Nemet-Nejat, K. R. *Daily Life in Ancient Mesopotamia*. Westport, Conn.: Greenwood, 1998.

Nepi, Antonio. "La stanza del figlio: La Sunammita converte Eliseo." *Parole di vita* 46, no. 5 (2001): 33–38.

Neudecker, Reinhard, "Das 'Ehescheidungsgesetz' von Dtn 24,1–4 nach altjüdischer Auslegung: Ein Beitrag zum Verständnis der neutestamentlichen Aussage zur Ehescheidung." *Biblica* 75 (1994): 350–87.

Neuer, Werner. *Man and Woman in Christian Perspective*. Translated by G. Wenham. Wheaton, Ill.: Crossway, 1991.

Neufeld, Ephraim. *Ancient Hebrew Marriage Laws: With Special References to General Semitic Laws and Customs*. New York: Longmans, 1944.

Neusner, Jacob. *Israel's Love Affair with God: Song of Songs*. Bible of Judaism Library. Valley Forge, Pa.: Trinity Press International, 1993.

Newsom, Carol A. "Common Ground: An Ecological Reading of Genesis 2–3." Pages 60–72 in *The Earth Story in Genesis*. Edited by Norman C. Habel and Shirley Wurst. Sheffield, Eng.: Sheffield Academic Press, 2000.

———. "Job." Pages 130–36 in *The Women's Bible Commentary*. Edited by Carol A. Newsom and Sharon H. Ringe. Louisville: Westminster John Knox, 1992.

———. "Woman and the Discourse of Patriarchal Wisdom: A Study of Proverbs 1–9." Pages 142–60 in *Gender and Difference in Ancient Israel*. Edited by Peggy L. Day. Minneapolis: Fortress, 1989.

Ngun, Richard. "Theological Implications of the Concept of *nephesh* in the Pentateuch." *Stulos Theological Journal* 7 (1999): 13–25.

Nicholls, Bruce J., and Kathleen D. Nicholls. "How Biblical Is Your View on Divorce and Remarriage?" *Evangelical Review of Theology* 6 (1982): 115–17.

Nicol, George G. "Bathsheba, a Clever Woman?" *Expository Times* 99 (1988): 360–63.

———. "David, Abigail and Bathsheba, Nabal and Uriah: Transformations within a Triangle," *Scandinavian Journal of the Old Testament* 12 (1998): 130–45.

Nicole, Jacques, and Marie-Claire Nicole. "Sara, soeur et femme d'Abraham." *Zeitschrift für die alttestamentliche Wissenschaft* 112 (2000): 5–23.

Nicole, Roger. "Biblical Authority and Feminist Aspirations." Pages 42–50 in *Women, Authority, and the Bible.* Edited by Alvera Mickelsen. Downers Grove, Ill.: InterVarsity, 1986.

Niditch, Susan. "Eroticism and Death in the Tale of Jael." Pages 43–57 in *Gender and Difference in Ancient Israel.* Edited by Peggy L. Day. Minneapolis: Fortress, 1989.

———. "Esther: Folklore, Wisdom, Feminism, and Authority." Pages 26–46 in *A Feminist Companion to Esther, Judith, and Susanna.* Edited by Athalya Brenner. Feminist Companion to the Bible 7. Sheffield, Eng.: Sheffield Academic Press, 1995.

———. "Portrayals of Women in the Hebrew Bible." Pages 25–42 in *Jewish Women in Historical Perspective.* Edited by Judith R. Baskin. Detroit: Wayne State University Press, 1991.

———. "Short Stories: The Book of Esther and the Theme of Women as a Civilizing Force." Pages 195–209 in *Old Testament Interpretation Past, Present, and Future: Essays in Honor of Gene M. Tucker.* Edited by James Luther Mays, David L. Petersen, and Kent Harold Richards. Nashville: Abingdon, 1995.

———. "The 'Sodomite' Theme in Judges 19–20: Family, Community, and Social Disintegration." *Catholic Biblical Quarterly* 44 (1982): 365–78.

———. *Underdogs and Tricksters: A Prelude to Biblical Folklore.* San Francisco: Harper & Row, 1987.

———. "The Wronged Woman Righted: An Analysis of Genesis 38." *Harvard Theological Review* 72 (1979): 143–49.

Niederwimmer, Kurt. *Askese und Mysterium: Über Ehe, Ehescheidung, und Eheverzicht in den Anfängen des christlichen Glaubens.* Forschungen zur Religion und Literatur des Alten und Neuen Testaments 113. Göttingen: Vandenhoeck & Ruprecht, 1975.

Nielsen, Kirsten. *Yahweh as Prosecutor and Judge: An Investigation of the Prophetic Lawsuit (ríb-Pattern).* Translated by Frederick Cryer. Journal for the Study of the Old Testament: Supplement Series 9. Sheffield, Eng.:Department of Biblical Studies, Unversity of Sheffield, 1978.

Niemann, Hermann M. "Choosing Brides for the Crown-Prince: Matrimonial Politics in the Davidic Dynasty." *Vetus Testamentum* 60 (2006): 225–38.

Nikaido, Scott K. "Hagar and Ishmael as Literary Figures: An Intertextual Study." *Vetus Testamentum* 51, no. 2 (2001): 219–42.

Nissinen, Martti. "Akkadian Rituals and Poetry of Divine Love." Pages 93–136 in *Mythology and Mythologies: Methodological Approaches to Intercultural Influences*. Edited by R. M. Whiting. Helsinki: Neo-Assyrian Text Corpus Project, 2001.

———. *Homoeroticism in the Biblical World: A Historical Perspective*. Translated by Kirsi Stjerna. Minneapolis: Fortress, 1998.

———. "Die Liebe von David und Jonatan als Frage der modernen Exegese." *Biblica* 80 (1999): 250–63.

Nissinen, Martti, and Risto Uro, eds. *Sacred Marriages in the Ancient World*. Winona Lake, Ind.: Eisenbrauns, 2006.

Noble, Paul R. "A 'Balanced' Reading of the Rape of Dinah: Some Exegetical and Methodological Observations." *Biblical Interpretation* 4 (1996): 173–204.

———. "Esau, Tamar, and Joseph: Criteria for Identifying Inner-biblical Allusions." *Vetus Testamentum* 52 (2002): 219–52.

———. "Synchronic and Diachronic Approaches to Biblical Interpretation." *Literature and Theology* 7 (1993): 130–48.

Noegel, Scott B., ed. *Puns and Pundits: Word Play in the Hebrew Bible and Ancient Near Eastern Literature*. Bethesda, Md.: CDL, 2000.

Noordtzij, Arie. *Leviticus*. Translated by Raymond Togtman. Bible Student's Commentary. Grand Rapids: Zondervan, 1982.

Noort, Edward. "The Creation of Man and Woman in Biblical and Ancient Near Eastern Traditions." Pages 1–18 in *The Creation of Man and Woman: Interpretations of the Biblical Narratives in Jewish and Christian Traditions*. Edited by Gerard P. Luttikhuizen. Themes in Biblical Narrative 3. Leiden: E. J. Brill, 2000.

———. "Genesis 22: Human Sacrifice and Theology in the Hebrew Bible." Pages 1–20 in *The Sacrifice of Isaac: The Aqedah (Genesis 22) and Its Interpretations*. Edited by Edward Noort and Eibert Tigchelaar. Leiden: E. J. Brill, 2002.

Noort, Edward, and Eibert J. C. Tigchelaar, eds. *The Sacrifice of Isaac: The Aqedah (Genesis 22) and Its Interpretations*. Themes in Biblical Narrative 4. Leiden: E. J. Brill, 2002.

Norrback, Anna. *The Fatherless and the Widows in the Deuteronomic Covenant*. Åbo, Finland: Åbo Akademis Forlag, 2001.

Norris, Richard A., Jr., ed. and trans. *The Song of Songs: Interpreted by Early Christian and Medieval Commentators*. Church's Bible 1. Grand Rapids: Eerdmans, 2003.

North, Robert. "Flesh, Covering, a Response, Ex. xxi 10." *Vetus Testamentum* 5 (1955): 204–6.

Noth, Martin. *Das dritte Buch Mose: Leviticus*. Das Alte Testament Deutsch 6. Göttingen: Vandenhoeck & Ruprecht, 1966.

———. *Leviticus*. Old Testament Library. Philadelphia: Westminster, 1963.

Nowell, Irene. *Women in the Old Testament*. Collegeville, Minn.: Liturgical, 1997.

Nunnally-Cox, Janice. *Foremothers: Women of the Bible*. New York: Seabury, 1981.

O'Brien, Julia M. "Judah as Wife and Husband: Deconstructing Gender in Malachi." *Journal of Biblical Literature* 115 (1996): 241–50.

Ochshorn, Judith. *The Female Experience and the Nature of the Divine.* Bloomington: Indiana University Press, 1981.

O'Connell, Robert H. "Proverbs VII 16–17: A Case of Fatal Deception in a 'Woman and the Window' Type-Scene." *Vetus Testamentum* 41 (1991): 235–41.

O'Connor, David. "Eros in Egypt." *Archaeology Odyssey* 4, no. 5 (2001): 43–51.

O'Connor, Kathleen M. "Jeremiah." Pages 169–77 in *The Women's Bible Commentary.* Edited by Carol A. Newsom and Sharon H. Ringe. Louisville: Westminster John Knox, 1992.

———. "The Tears of God and Divine Character in Jeremiah 2–9." Pages 387–401 in *Troubling Jeremiah.* Edited by A. R. Pete Diamond, Kathleen M. O'Connor, and Louis Stulman. Journal for the Study of the Old Testament: Supplement Series 260. Sheffield, Eng.: Sheffield Academic Press, 1999.

O'Connor, Michael Patrick. "The Women in the Book of Judges." *Hebrew Annual Review* 10 (1987): 277–93.

O'Day, Gail R. "Singing Woman's Song: A Hermeneutic of Liberation." *Currents in Theology and Mission* 12, no. 4 (1985): 203–10.

Odell-Scott, David W. "Let the Women Speak in Church: An Egalitarian Interpretation of 1 Cor 14:33b–36." *Biblical Theology Bulletin* 13 (1983): 90–93.

Oden, Robert A., Jr. *The Bible without Theology: The Theological Tradition and Alternatives to It.* San Francisco: Harper & Row, 1987.

O'Grady, Kathleen. "The Semantics of Taboo: Menstrual Prohibitions in the Hebrew Bible." Pages 1–28 in *Wholly Woman, Holy Blood: A Feminist Critique of Purity and Impurity.* Edited by Kristin De Troyer et al. Studies in Antiquity and Christianity. Harrisburg, Penn.: Trinity Press International, 2003.

Ojewole, Afolarin. "The Seed in Genesis 3:15: An Exegetical and Intertextual Study." PhD diss., Andrews University, 2002.

O'Leary, Dale. *The Gender Agenda: Redefining Equality.* Lafayette, La.: Vital Issues, 1997.

Olley, John W. "Pharaoh's Daughter, Solomon's Palace, and the Temple: Another Look at the Structure of 1 Kings 1–11." *Journal for the Study of the Old Testament* 27, no. 3 (March 2003): 355–69.

Olmo Lete, Gregorio del. *Canaanite Religion according to the Liturgical Texts of Ugarit.* Translated by Wilfred G. E. Watson. Bethesda, Md.: CDL, 1999.

———. "Nota sobre Prov 30:19 (wuederek geber buecalmah)." *Biblica* 67 (1986): 68–74.

Olson, Dennis T. *Deuteronomy and the Death of Moses: A Theological Reading.* Overtures to Biblical Theology. Minneapolis: Fortress, 1994.

Olyan, Saul M. "'And with a Male You Shall Not Lie the Lying Down of a Woman': On the Meaning and Significance of Leviticus 18:22 and 20:13." *Journal of the History of Sexuality* 5, no. 2 (1994): 179–206.

———. *Asherah and the Cult of Yahweh in Israel.* Society of Biblical Literature Monograph Series 34. Atlanta: Scholars Press, 1988.

Olyan, Saul M., and Robert C. Culley, eds. *"A Wise and Discerning Mind": Essays in Honor of Burke O. Long.* Brown Judaic Studies 325. Providence: Brown Judaic Studies, 2000.

Omanson, Roger L. "How Does It All Fit Together? Thoughts on Translating Acts 1.15–22 and 15.19–21." *Bible Translator* 41 (1990): 419–21.

———. "On Appealing to Context: A Reply." *Bible Translator* 42 (1991): 236–41.

Origen. *The Song of Songs: Commentary and Homilies.* Edited and translated by R. P. Lawson. Ancient Christian Writers 26. Westminster, Md.: Newman, 1957.

Orlinsky, Harry. "The Hebrew Root ŠKB." *Journal of Biblical Literature* 63 (1944): 19–44.

Ormanty, Stanislaw. "Fenomen Biblijnego Spojrezenia na Człowieka." *Collectanea theologica* 73, no. 3 (2003): 41–50. ["The Biblical View of the Human Person" R.M.D.]

Orr, William F., and James A. Walther. *1 Corinthians: A New Translation.* Anchor Bible 32. Garden City, N.Y.: Doubleday, 1976.

Ortlund, Jani. *Fearlessly Feminine: Boldly Living God's Plan for Womanhood.* Sisters, Ore.: Multnomah, 2000.

Ortlund, Raymond C., Jr. "Male-Female Equality and Male Headship: Genesis 1–3." Pages 95–112, 479–83 in *Recovering Biblical Manhood and Womanhood: A Response to Evangelical Feminism.* Edited by John Piper and Wayne A. Grudem. Wheaton, Ill.: Crossway, 1991.

———. *Whoredom: God's Unfaithful Wife in Biblical Theology.* Grand Rapids: Eerdmans, 1996. Repr. as *God's Unfaithful Wife: A Biblical Theology of Spiritual Adultery.* New Studies in Biblical Theology 2. Downers Grove, Ill.: InterVarsity, 2002.

Osborn, Noel D. "Circumspection about Circumcision in Exodus 4:24–26." Pages 247–64 in *Issues in Bible Translation.* Edited by Philip C. Stine. London: United Bible Societies, 1988.

Osborne, Grant R. *The Hermeneutical Spiral: A Comprehensive Introduction to Biblical Interpretation.* Downers Grove, Ill.: InterVarsity, 1991.

———. "Hermeneutics and Women in the Church." *Journal of the Evangelical Theological Society* 20 (1977): 337–52.

Osburn, Carroll D. "The Interpretation of 1 Cor. 14:34–35." Pages 219–42 in vol. 1 of *Essays on Women in Earliest Christianity.* Edited by Carroll D. Osburn. 2 vols. Joplin, Mo.: College Press, 1993.

———. *Women in the Church: Reclaiming the Ideal.* Abilene, Tex.: Abilene Christian University Press, 2001.

Osiek, Carolyn. "The Feminist and the Bible: Hermeneutical Alternatives." Pages 93–105 in *Feminist Perspectives on Biblical Scholarship.* Edited by Adela Yarbro Collins. Atlanta: Scholars Press, 1985.

Ostriker, Alicia. "The Book of Ruth and the Love of the Land." *Biblical Interpretation* 10 (2002): 343–59.

———. "A Holy of Holies: The Song of Songs as Countertext." Pages 36–54 in *The Song of Songs.* Edited by Athalya Brenner and Carole R. Fontaine. Feminist Companion to the Bible: Second Series 6. Sheffield, Eng.: Sheffield Academic Press, 2000.

———. Preface to *The Five Scrolls.* Vintage Spiritual Classics. New York: Vintage, 2000.

Oswalt, John N. *The Book of Isaiah, Chapters 1–39.* New International Commentary on the Old Testament. Grand Rapids: Eerdmans, 1986.

———. *The Book of Isaiah, Chapters 40–66.* New International Commentary on the Old Testament. Grand Rapids: Eerdmans, 1998.

Ottermann, Mônica. "Antropologia bíblica: Uma leitura feminista e de gênero" [Biblical Anthropology: A Feminist and Gender Reading]. *Fragmenta de cultura* 11 (2001): 815–22.

Ottosson, Magnus. "Rahab and the Spies." Pages 419–27 in *DUMU-E2–DUB-BA-A: Studies in Honor of Åke W. Sjöberg.* Edited by Hermann Behrens, Darlene Loding, and Martha T. Roth. Philadelphia: Babylonian Section, University Museum, 1989.

Otwell, John H. *And Sarah Laughed: The Status of Women in the Old Testament.* Philadelphia: Westminster, 1977.

Ouellette, Lucien. "Woman's Doom in Genesis 3:16." *Catholic Biblical Quarterly* 12 (1950): 389–99.

Owens, John Joseph. *Numbers.* Broadman Bible Commentary 1. Nashville: Broadman, 1970.

Owusu, Samuel. "Marriage and Polygamy: A Biblical and Theological Analysis against the Background of the Akan Christian Church of Ghana." PhD diss., Trinity Evangelical Divinity School, 2000.

Padgett, Alan G. "Feminism in First Corinthians: A Dialogue with Elisabeth Schüssler Fiorenza." *Evangelical Quarterly* 58 (1986): 121–32.

———. "The Pauline Rationale for Submission: Biblical Feminism and the *hina* Clauses of Titus 2:1–10." *Evangelical Quarterly* 59 (1987): 39–52.

———. "Wealthy Women at Ephesus: 1 Timothy 2:8–15 in Social Context." *Interpretation* 41 (1987): 19–31.

Padilla, C René. "The Human Couple: A Biblical Perspective." *Evangelical Review of Theology* 8 (1984): 275–88.

Page, Sydney. "Marital Expectations of Church Leaders in the Pastoral Epistles." *Journal for Study of the New Testament* 50 (1993): 105–20.

Pagels, Elaine H. *Adam, Eve, and the Serpent.* New York: Random House, 1988.

———. "Paul and Women: A Response to Recent Discussion." *Journal of the American Academy of Religion* 42, no. 3 (1974): 538–49.

Pahk, Johan Yeong Sik. "A Syntactical and Contextual Consideration of *'šh* in Qoh. ix 9." *Vetus Testamentum* 51 (2001): 370–80.

Pantel, Pauline Schmitt, ed. *From Ancient Goddesses to Christian Saints.* Vol. 1 of *A History of Women in the West.* Translated by Arthur Goldhammer. Cambridge, Mass.: Belknap, 1992.

Paolantino, Marguerite. "God as Husband." *The Bible Today* 27 (1989): 299–303.

Pape, Dorothy R. *In Search of God's Ideal Woman: A Personal Examination of the New Testament.* Downers Grove, Ill.: InterVarsity, 1976.

Pardee, Dennis. *Ritual and Cult at Ugarit.* Edited by Theodore J. Lewis. Society of
    Biblical Literature Writings from the Ancient World 10. Atlanta: Society of
    Biblical Literature, 2002.

Pardes, Ilana. "Beyond Genesis 3: The Politics of Maternal Naming." Pages
    173–93 in *A Feminist Companion to Genesis.* Edited by Athalya Brenner. Fem-
    inist Companion to the Bible 2. Sheffield, Eng.: Sheffield Academic Press,
    1993.

———. *Countertraditions in the Bible: A Feminist Approach.* Cambridge: Harvard
    University Press, 1992.

Park, Chun Sik. "Theology of Judgment in Genesis 6–9." PhD dissertation, An-
    drews University, 2005.

Park, David M. "The Early Traditions of Jesus' Sayings on Divorce." *Theology* 96
    (1993): 372–83.

———. "The Structure of Authority in Marriage: An Examination of *hupotasso*
    and *kephale* in Ephesians 5:21–33." *Evangelical Quarterly* 59 (1987): 117–24.

Parker, Harold M., Jr. "Solomon and the Queen of Sheba." *Iliff Review* 24 (1967):
    17–23.

Parker, Simon B. "The Hebrew Bible and Homosexuality." *Quarterly Review* 11
    (fall 1991): 4–19.

Parpola, Simo, and Robert M. Whiting, eds. *Sex and Gender in the Ancient Near
    East: Proceedings of the 47th Rencontre assyriologique internationale, Hel-
    skinki, July 2–6, 2001.* Helsinki: Neo-Assyrian Text Corpus Project, 2002.

Parry, Donald W. "Garden of Eden: Prototype Sanctuary." Pages 126–51 in
    Temples of the Ancient World: Ritual and Symbolism. Edited by Donald W.
    Parry. Salt Lake City: Deseret, 1994.

Parry, Robin. "Feminist Hermeneutics and Evangelical Concerns: The Rape of
    Dinah as a Case Study." *Tyndale Bulletin* 53 (2002): 1–28.

———. *Old Testament Story and Christian Ethics.* Waynesboro, Ga.: Paternoster,
    2004.

Parsons, Greg W. "Guidelines for Understanding and Utilizing the Song of
    Songs." *Bibliotheca sacra* 156 (1999): 399–422.

Parsons, Michael. "Luther and Calvin on Rape: Is the Crime Lost in the Agenda?"
    Evangelical Quarterly 74 (2002): 123–42.

Passamaneck, Stephen M. "Notes on Violence and Combative Behavior in Jewish
    Law." Pages 87–107 in *The Oxford Conference.* Edited by Abraham M. Fuss.
    Vol. 3 of *Jewish Law Association Studies.* Atlanta: Scholars Press, 1987.

Passno, Diane. *Mystique or Mistake? Rediscovering God's Liberating Plan for
    Women.* Wheaton, Ill.: Tyndale House, 2000.

Patai, Raphael. *The Hebrew Goddess.* New York: Ktav, 1967.

———. *Sex and Family in the Bible and the Middle East.* Garden City, N.Y.:
    Doubleday, 1959.

Patella, Michael. "Women of Mystery." *The Bible Today* 44 (2006): 94–97.

Patterson, Dorothy Kelley. "Nurturing Mothers." Pages 161–70 in *Biblical Wom-
    anhood in the Home.* Edited by Nancy Leigh DeMoss. Foundations for the
    Family Series. Wheaton, Ill.: Crossway, 2002.

————. "Why I Believe Southern Baptist Churches Should Not Ordain Women." *Baptist History and Heritage* 23 (July 1988): 56–62.

Patton, Corrine L. "'Should Our Sister Be Treated Like a Whore?' A Response to Feminist Critiques of Ezekiel 23." Pages 221–38 in *The Book of Ezekiel: Theological and Anthropological Perspectives.* Edited by Margaret S. Odell and John T. Strong. Society of Biblical Literature Symposium Series 9. Atlanta: Society of Biblical Literature, 2000.

Paul, Martin. "Die 'fremde Frau' in Sprichwörter 1–9 und die 'Geliebte' des Hohenliedes: Ein Beitrag zur Intertextualität." *Biblische Notizen* 106 (2001): 40–46.

Paul, Shalom M. "Adoption Formulae: A Study of Cuneiform and Biblical Legal Clauses." *Maarav* 2 (1979–1980): 173–85.

————. "Biblical Analogues to Middle Assyrian Law." Pages 333–50 in *Religion and Law: Biblical-Judaic and Islamic Perspectives.* Edited by Edwin B. Firmage, Bernard G. Weiss, and John W. Welch. Winona Lake, Ind.: Eisenbrauns, 1990.

————. "Exod. 21:10: A Threefold Maintenance Clause." *Journal of Near Eastern Studies* 28 (1969): 48–53.

————. *Studies in the Book of the Covenant in the Light of Cuneiform and Biblical Law.* Leiden: E. J. Brill, 1970.

————. "Two Cognate Semitic Terms for Mating and Copulation." *Vetus Testamentum* 32 (1982): 492–94.

Pawson, J. David. *Leadership Is Male.* Nashville: Oliver-Nelson, 1990.

Payne, J. Barton. "1, 2 Chronicles." Pages 301–562 in vol. 4 of *The Expositor's Bible Commentary.* 12 vols. Grand Rapids: Zondervan, 1976–1992.

Payne, Philip B. "Libertarian Women in Ephesus: A Response to Douglas J. Moo's Article, '1 Timothy 2:11–15: Meaning and Significance.'" *Trinity Journal* 2 (1981): 169–97.

Payne, Robin. "The Song of Songs: Song of Woman, Song of Man, Song of God." *Expository Times* 107 (1996): 329–33.

Pedersen, Johannes. *Israel: Its Life and Culture.* 4 vols. in 2. London: Oxford University Press, 1926–1940. Repr., Atlanta: Scholars Press, 1991.

Peleg, Yaron. "Love at First Sight? David, Jonathan, and the Biblical Politics of Gender." *Journal for the Study of the Old Testament* 30 (2005): 171–89.

Pelikan, Jaroslav, ed. *Luther's Works.* 55 vols. St. Louis: Concordia, 1972.

Penchansky, David. "Staying the Night: Intertextuality in Genesis and Judges." Pages 77–88 in *Reading between Texts: Intertextuality and the Hebrew Bible.* Edited by Danna Nolan Fewell. Louisville: Westminster John Knox, 1992.

Penner, Carol, ed. *Women and Men: Gender in the Church.* Waterloo, Ont.: Herald, 1998.

Perdue, Leo G., et al. *Families in Ancient Israel.* Louisville: Westminster John Knox, 1997.

————. *Wisdom and Creation: The Theology of Wisdom Literature.* Nashville: Abingdon, 1994.

Perriman, Andrew C. *Speaking of Women: Interpreting Paul.* Leicester, Eng.: Apollos/Inter-Varsity, 1998.

Perry, F. L. *Sex and the Bible.* Atlanta: John Knox, 1982.

Petersen, John. *Reading Women's Stories: Female Characters in the Hebrew Bible.* Minneapolis: Fortress, 2004.

Pfeiffer, R. H. *The Hebrew Iliad.* New York: Harper, 1957.

Philip, Tarja S. *Menstruation and Childbirth in the Bible: Fertility and Impurity.* Studies in Biblical Literature 88. New York: Peter Lang, 2006.

Phillips, Anthony. *Ancient Israel's Criminal Law: A New Approach to the Decalogue.* Oxford: Basil Blackwell, 1970.

———. "Another Look at Adultery." *Journal for the Study of the Old Testament* no. 20 (1981): 3–25.

———. "The Book of Ruth—Deception and Shame." *Journal of Jewish Studies* 37, no. 1 (1986): 1–17.

———. *Deuteronomy.* Cambridge Bible Commentary. Cambridge: Cambridge University Press, 1973.

———. "Nebalah—a Term for Serious Disorderly and Unruly Conduct." *Vetus Testamentum* 25 (1975): 237–42.

———. "A Response to Dr McKeating." *Journal for the Study of the Old Testament* no. 22 (1982): 142–43.

———. "Uncovering the Father's Skirt." *Vetus Testamentum* 30 (1980): 38–43.

Phillips, Elaine A. "Serpent Intertexts: Tantalizing Twists in the Tales." *Bulletin for Biblical Research* 10 (2000): 233–45.

Phillips, John A. *Eve: The History of an Idea.* New York: Harper & Row, 1984.

Phipps, William E. *Assertive Biblical Women.* Classics of Western Spirituality 128. Westport, Conn.: Greenwood, 1992.

———. *Genesis and Gender: Biblical Myths of Sexuality and Their Cultural Impact.* New York: Praeger, 1989.

———. "Is Paul's Attitude toward Sexual Relations Contained in 1 Cor 7:1?" *New Testament Studies* 28 (1982): 125–31.

———. *Recovering Biblical Sensuousness.* Philadelphia: Westminster, 1975.

Piatti, Tommaso. *Il Cantico dei cantici.* Rome: Edizioni Paoline, 1958.

Pierce, Ronald W. "Contemporary Evangelicals for Gender Equality." Pages 58–75 in *Discovering Biblical Equality: Complementarity without Hierarchy.* Edited by Ronald W. Pierce and Rebecca Merrill Groothuis. Downers Grove, Ill.: InterVarsity, 2004.

———. "Evangelicals and Gender Roles in the 1990s: 1 Timothy 2:8–15—A Test Case." *Journal of the Evangelical Theological Society* 36 (1993): 343–55.

———. "From Old Testament Law to New Testament Gospel." Pages 98–109 in *Discovering Biblical Equality: Complementarity without Hierarchy.* Edited by Ronald W. Pierce and Rebecca Merrill Groothuis. Downers Grove, Ill.: InterVarsity, 2004.

Pierce, Ronald W., and Rebecca Merrill Groothuis, eds. *Discovering Biblical Equality: Complementarity without Hierarchy.* Downers Grove, Ill.: InterVarsity, 2004.

Pigott, Susan M. "Wives, Witches, and Wise Women: Prophetic Heralds of Kingship in 1 and 2 Samuel." *Review and Expositor* 99 (2002): 145–74.

Pilch, John A. "A Window into the Biblical World: Adultery." *The Bible Today* 41 (2003): 117–22.

Pilch, John J. "Who Is a Virgin?" *The Bible Today* 40 (2002): 248–52.

———. "A Window into the Biblical World: The Family—Status and Roles." *The Bible Today* 40 (2002): 386–91.

Piper, John. *What's the Difference? Manhood and Womanhood Defined according to the Bible.* Westchester, Ill.: Crossway, 1990.

Piper, John, and Wayne A. Grudem. "An Overview of Central Concerns: Questions and Answers." Pages 60–92 in *Recovering Biblical Manhood and Womanhood: A Response to Evangelical Feminism.* Edited by John Piper and Wayne A. Grudem. Wheaton, Ill.: Crossway, 1991.

———, eds. *Recovering Biblical Manhood and Womanhood: A Response to Evangelical Feminism.* Wheaton, Ill.: Crossway, 1991.

Piper, John, and Justin Taylor, eds. *Sex and the Supremacy of Christ.* Wheaton, Ill.: Crossway, 2005.

Piper, Otto A. *The Biblical View of Sex and Marriage.* New York: Charles Scribner's Sons, 1960.

Pippin, Tina. "Jezebel Re-vamped." *Semeia* 69–70 (1995): 221–33.

Plaskow, Judith. *Standing Again at Sinai: Judaism from a Feminist Perspective.* San Francisco: HarperSanFrancisco, 1991.

Plaskow, Judith, and Carol P. Christ. *Weaving the Visions: New Patterns in Feminist Spirituality.* San Francisco: Harper & Row, 1989.

Plekker, Robert J. *Divorce and the Christian: What the Bible Teaches.* Wheaton, Ill.: Tyndale, 1980.

Polan, Gregory J. "Hosea's Interpretation of Israel's Traditions." *The Bible Today* 39 (2001): 329–34.

Polaski, D. C. "'What Will Ye See in the Shulamite?' Women, Power, and Panopticism in the Song of Songs." *Biblical Interpretation* 5 (1997): 64–81.

Pollard, J. Paul. "Women in the Earlier Philippian Church (Acts 16:13–15; Phil. 4:2–3) in Recent Scholarship." Pages 261–80 in vol. 1 of *Essays on Women in Earliest Christianity.* Edited by Carroll D. Osburn. 2 vols. Joplin, Mo.: College Press, 1993.

Pope, Marvin H. "A Divine Banquet at Ugarit." Pages 170–203 in *The Use of the Old Testament in the New and Other Essays: Studies in Honor of William Franklin Stinespring.* Edited by James M. Efird. Durham, N.C.: Duke University Press, 1972.

———. *El in the Ugaritic Texts.* Leiden: E. J. Brill, 1955.

———. Review of John Gray, *The Legacy of Canaan. Journal of Semitic Studies* 11 (1966): 235.

———. *Song of Songs.* Anchor Bible 7C. Garden City, N.Y.: Doubleday, 1977.

Popović, M. "Bibliography of Recent Studies." Pages 211–23 in *The Sacrifice of Isaac: The Aqedah (Genesis 22) and Its Interpretations.* Edited by Edward Noort and Eibert Tigchelaar. Leiden: E. J. Brill, 2002.

Porteous, Norman W. "Image of God." Pages 682–85 in vol. 2 of *The Interpreter's Dictionary of the Bible*. Edited by George A. Buttrick. 4 vols. Nashville: Abingdon, 1962.

Porter, Stanley E. "What Does It Mean to Be 'Saved by Childbirth' (1 Timothy 2:15)?" *Journal for the Study of the New Testament* 49 (1993): 87–102.

Porter, Stanley E., and Paul Buchanan. "On the Logical Structure of Matt 19:9." *Journal of the Evangelical Theological Society* 34 (1991): 335–39.

Porter, Stanley E., and Dennis L. Stamps, eds. *Rhetorical Criticism and the Bible*. Journal for the Study of the New Testament: Supplement Series 195. New York: Sheffield Academic Press, 2002.

Pouget, Guillaume, and Jean Guitton. *Le Cantique des cantiques*. Paris: Gabalda, 1934. English translation: *The Canticle of Canticles*. Translated by Joseph L. Lilly. Catholic Scripture Library. New York: Declan X. McMullen, 1948.

Powers, B. Ward. *Marriage and Divorce: The New Testament Teaching*. Petersham, N.S.W., Australia: Jordan, 1987.

———. "Women in the Church: The Application of 1 Tim 2:8–15." *Interchange* 17 (1975): 55–59.

Poythress, Vern S., and Wayne A. Grudem. *The Gender-Neutral Bible Controversy: Muting the Masculinity of God's Words*. Nashville: Broadman & Holman, 2000.

Preez, Ronald A. G. du. "The God-Given Marital Mandate: Monogamous, Heterosexual, Intrafaith." *Journal of the Adventist Theological Society* 10, nos. 1 & 2 (1999): 23–40.

———. *Polygamy in the Bible*. Adventist Theological Society Dissertation Series 3. Berrien Springs, Mich.: ATS, 1993.

———. "The Status of the Fetus in Mosaic Law." *Journal of the Adventist Theological Society* 1, no. 2 (1990): 5–21.

Pressler, Carolyn. "The 'Biblical View' of Marriage." Pages 200–11 in *Engaging the Bible in a Gendered World: An Introduction to Feminist Biblical Interpretation in Honor of Katharine Doob Sakenfeld*. Edited by Linda Day and Carolyn Pressler. Louisville: Westminster John Knox, 2006.

———. *Joshua, Judges, and Ruth*. Westminister Bible Companion. Louisville: Westminster John Knox, 2002.

———. "Sexual Violence and Deuteronomic Law." Pages 102–12 in *A Feminist Companion to Exodus to Deuteronomy*. Edited by Athalya Brenner. Feminist Companion to the Bible 6. Sheffield, Eng.: Sheffield Academic Press, 1994.

———. *The View of Women Found in the Deuteronomic Family Laws*. Beihefte zur Zeitschrift für die alttestamentliche Wissenschaft 216. Berlin: de Gruyter, 1993.

Pritchard, James B. *Solomon and Sheba*. London: Phaidon, 1974.

Prohl, Russell C. *Woman in the Church: A Restudy of Woman's Place in Building the Kingdom*. Grand Rapids: Zondervan, 1957.

Propp, William H. "Circumcision: The Private Sign of the Covenant." *Bible Review* 20, no. 4 (August 2004): 22–29.

———. "Is Psalm 45 an Erotic Poem?" *Biblical Research* 20, no. 2 (2004): 33–42.

————. "Kinship in 2 Samuel 13." *Catholic Biblical Quarterly* 55 (1993): 39–53.

————. "That Bloody Bridegroom (Exodus iv 24–6)." *Vetus Testamentum* 43 (1993): 495–518.

Provan, Iain W. *Ecclesiastes, Song of Songs.* NIV Application Commentary. Grand Rapids: Zondervan, 2001.

Province, Diana. "An Examination of the Purity Laws regarding Childbirth and Menstruation in Leviticus." M.A. thesis, Denver Conservative Baptist Seminary, 1995.

Quasten, Johannes. *Patrology.* 4 vols. Westminster: Newman, 1953–1986.

Rabin, Chaim. "The Origin of the Hebrew Word *Pīlegeš*." *Journal of Jewish Studies* 25 (1974): 353–64.

Rabinowitz, Jacob J. "The 'Great Sin' in Ancient Egyptian Marriage Contracts." *Journal of Near Eastern Studies* 18 (1959): 73.

Raccah, William. "Close Kin Relationships and Economical Dimensions in the Stipulations of the Law of the Levirate as Articulated in Deuteronomy 25:5–10." PhD diss., Université Laval, 2003.

Rad, Gerhard von. *Deuteronomy: A Commentary.* Translated by Dorothea Barton. Old Testament Library. Philadelphia: Westminster, 1966.

————. *Genesis: A Commentary.* Translated by John H. Marks. Old Testament Library. Philadelphia: Westminster, 1961.

————. *Old Testament Theology.* Translated by D. M. G. Stalker. 2 vols. New York: Harper, 1962–1965.

Radcliffe, Timothy. "Paul and Sexual Identity: 1 Corinthians 11:2–16." Pages 62–72 in *After Eve.* Edited by Janet Martin Soskice. London: Marshal Pickering, 1990.

Radday, Yehuda T. "Chiasm in Samuel," *Linguistica biblica* 9–10, no. 3 (1973): 21–31.

————. "Chiasmus in Biblical Hebrew Narrative," Pages 50–117 in *Chiasmus in Antiquity: Structures, Analyses, Exegesis.* Edited by John W. Welch. Hildesheim: Gerstenberg, 1981.

Ramras-Rauch, Gila. "Fathers and Daughters: Two Biblical Narratives." Pages 158–69 in *Mappings of the Biblical Terrain: The Bible as Text.* Edited by Vincent L. Tollers and John R. Maier. Lewisburg, Pa.: Bucknell University Press, 1990.

Ramsey, George W. "Is Name-Giving an Act of Domination in Genesis 2:23 and Elsewhere?" *Catholic Biblical Quarterly* 50 (1988): 24–35.

Raney, Donald C., II. "Does YHWH Naham? A Question of Openness." Pages 105–15 in *Society of Biblical Literature Seminary Papers 2003.* Edited by Varii. Atlanta: Society of Biblical Literature, 2003.

Rankin, John. "Power and Gender at the Divinity School." Pages 199–204 in *Finding God at Harvard: Spiritual Journeys of Thinking Christians.* Edited by Kelly Monroe. Grand Rapids: Zondervan, 1996.

Rapp, Ursula. *Mirjam: Eine feministisch-rhetorische Lektüre der Mirjamtexte in der hebräischen Bibel.* Beihefte zur Zeitschrift für die alttestamentliche Wissenschaft 317. New York: de Gruyter, 2002.

Rashkow, Ilona N. "Daddy-Dearest and the 'Invisible Spirit of Wine.'" Pages 98–107 in *Genesis*. Edited by Athalya Brenner. Feminist Companion to the Bible: Second Series 1. Sheffield, Eng.: Sheffield Academic Press, 1998.

———. *Taboo or Not Taboo: Sexuality and Family in the Hebrew Bible*. Minneapolis: Fortress, 2000.

———. *Upon the Dark Places: Anti-Semitism and Sexism in English Renaissance Biblical Tradition*. Sheffield, Eng.: Sheffield Academic Press, 1990.

Rasmussen, Rachel C. "Deborah the Woman Warrior." Pages 79–93 in *Anti-covenant: Counter-reading Women's Lives in the Hebrew Bible*. Edited by Mieke Bal. Sheffield, Eng.: Almond, 1989.

Rattray, Susan. "Marriage Rules, Kinship Terms, and Family Structure in the Bible." Pages 537–44 in the *SBL Seminar Papers, 1987*. Society of Biblical Literature Seminar Papers 26. Atlanta: Scholars Press, 1987.

Raurell, Frederic. "Erotic Pleasure in the 'Song of Songs.'" *Laurentianum* 24 (1983): 5–45.

Ravasi, G. *Cântico dos cânticos*. São Paulo: Edições Paulinas, 1988.

Rawlinson, George. *Ezra and Nehemiah: Their Lives and Times*. New York: Randolph, 1890.

Rea, John. "Zipporah." Pages 1848–49 in vol. 2 of *The Wycliffe Bible Encyclopedia*. Edited by Charles F. Pfeiffer, Howard F. Vos, and John Rea. Chicago: Moody, 1975.

Redditt, Paul L., and Aaron Schart, eds. *Thematic Threads in the Book of the Twelve*. Beihefte zur Zeitschrift für die alttestamentliche Wissenschaft 325. Berlin: de Gruyter, 2003.

Redekop, Gloria Neufeld. "Let the Women Learn: 1 Timothy 2:8–15 Reconsidered." *Studies in Religion/Sciences religieuses* 19 (1990): 235–45.

Redford, Donald. *Egypt, Canaan, and Israel in Ancient Times*. Princeton, N.J.: Princeton University Press, 1992.

Reed, William L. "Asherah." Pages 250–52 in vol. 1 of *The Interpreter's Dictionary of the Bible*. Edited by George A. Buttrick. 4 vols. Nashville: Abingdon, 1962.

Rees, Thomas. "Adoption." Pages 53–55 in vol. 1 of *International Standard Bible Encyclopedia*. Edited by G. W. Bromiley. 4 vols. Grand Rapids: Eerdmans, 1979–1988.

Reimer, Ivoni Richter. *Women in the Acts of the Apostles: A Feminist Liberation Perspective*. Translated by Linda M. Maloney. Minneapolis: Fortress, 1995.

Reinhartz, Adele. "Anonymous Women and the Collapse of the Monarchy: A Study in Narrative Technique." Pages 43–65 in *A Feminist Companion to Samuel and Kings*. Edited by Athalya Brenner. Feminist Companion to the Bible 5. Sheffield, Eng.: Sheffield Academic Press, 1994.

———. "Samson's Mother: An Unnamed Protagonist." Pages 157–70 in *A Feminist Companion to Judges*. Edited by Athalya Brenner. Feminist Companion to the Bible 4. Sheffield, Eng.: Sheffield Academic Press, 1993.

Reis, Pamela Tamarkin. "Cupidity and Stupidity: Woman's Agency and the 'Rape' of Tamar." *Journal of Near Eastern Studies* 25 (1997): 43–60.

———. "Hagar Requited." *Journal for the Study of the Old Testament* no. 87 (2000): 75–109.

———. *Reading the Lines: A Fresh Look at the Hebrew Bible.* Peabody, Mass.: Hendrickson, 2002.

———. "Uncovering Jael and Sisera: A New Reading." *Scandinavian Journal of the Old Testament* 19 (2005): 24–47.

Reisenberger, Azila Talit. "The Bridegroom of Blood: A New Reading." *Judaism* 40 (1991): 324–31.

———. "The Creation of Adam as Hermaphrodite and Its Implications for Feminist Theology." *Judaism* 42 (1993): 447–52.

Reiss, Moshe. "The Women Around Moses." *Jewish Bible Quarterly* 33 (2005): 127–30.

Renan, Ernest. *Le Cantique des cantiques.* Paris: Michel Lévy Frères, 1884.

Rendsburg, Gary A. "Unlikely Heroes: Women as Israel." *Bible Review* 19, no. 1 (2003): 16–23, 52–53.

———. "Word Play in Biblical Hebrew: An Eclectic Collection." Pages 137–62 in *Puns and Pundits: Word Play in the Hebrew Bible and Ancient Near Eastern Literature.* Edited by Scott B. Noegel. Bethesda, Md.: CDL, 2000.

Reno, R. R. "Feminist Theology as Modern Project." Pages 161–89 in *This Is My Name Forever: The Trinity and Gender Language for God.* Edited by Alvin F. Kimel Jr. Downers Grove, Ill.: InterVarsity, 2001.

Reventlow, Henning Graf, and Yair Hoffman, eds. *Creation in Jewish and Christian Tradition.* Journal for the Study of the Old Testament: Supplement Series 319. New York: Sheffield Academic Press, 2002.

Richards, W. Larry. "How Does a Woman Prophesy and Keep Silence at the Same Time? (1 Corinthians 11 and 14)." Pages 313–33 in *Women in Ministry: Biblical and Historical Perspectives.* Edited by Nancy Vyhmeister. Berrien Springs, Mich.: Andrews University Press, 1998.

Richardson, John. *God, Sex, and Marriage: Guidance from 1 Corinthians 7.* London: MPA, 1995.

———. "Preaching from the *Song of Songs:* Allegory Revisited." *Evangelical Review of Theology* 21 (1997): 250–57.

Richardson, Peter. "Judgment in Sexual Matters in 1 Corinthians 6:1–11." *Novum Testamentum* 25 (1983): 37–58.

Richter, Hans-Friedemann. *Geschlechtlichkeit, Ehe, und Familie im Alten Testament und seiner Umwelt.* Beiträge zur biblischen Exegese und Theologie 10. Frankfurt am Main: Peter Lang, 1978.

Ridderbos, Jan. *Deuteronomy.* Translated by Ed M. van der Maas. Grand Rapids: Zondervan, 1984.

———. *Isaiah.* Bible Student's Commentary. Grand Rapids: Zondervan, 1985.

Riddle, J. M. *Contraception and Abortion from the Ancient World to the Renaissance.* Cambridge: Harvard University Press, 1992.

Ridout, George. "The Rape of Tamar: A Rhetorical Analysis of 2 Sam 13:1–22." Pages 75–84 in *Rhetorical Criticism: Essays in Honor of James Muilenberg.*

Edited by Jared J. Jackson and Martin Kessler. Pittsburgh Theological Monograph Series 1. Pittsburgh: Pickwick, 1974.

Riegner, Irene E. "The Vanishing Hebrew Harlot: A Diachronic and Synchronic Study of the Root *znh*." PhD diss., Temple University, 2001.

Riley, Patrick G. D. *Civilizing Sex: On Chastity and the Common Good.* Edinburgh: T&T Clark, 2000.

Ringgren, Helmer. "The Marriage Motif in Israelite Religion." Pages 421–28 in *Ancient Israelite Religion: Essays in Honor of Frank Moore Cross.* Edited by Patrick D. Miller Jr., Paul D. Hanson, and S. Dean McBride. Philadelphia: Fortress, 1987.

Robarts, Charme E. "Deborah—Judge, Prophetess, Military Leader, and Mother in Israel." Pages 69–86 in vol. 2 of *Essays on Women in Earliest Christianity.* Edited by Carroll D. Osburn. 2 vols. Joplin, Mo.: College Press, 1995.

Robbins, Gregory Allen, ed. *Genesis 1–3 in the History of Exegesis: Intrigue in the Garden.* Lewiston, N.Y.: Mellen, 1988.

Robert, André, and Tournay, Raymond J., eds. *Le Cantique des cantiques.* Paris: Gabalda, 1963.

Roberts, J. J. M., and Kathryn L. Roberts. "Yahweh's Significant Other." Pages 176–85 in *Engaging the Bible in a Gendered World: An Introduction to Feminist Biblical Interpretation in Honor of Katharine Doob Sakenfeld.* Edited by Linda Day and Carolyn Pressler. Louisville: Westminster John Knox, 2006.

Robertson, O. Palmer. *The Genesis of Sex: Sexual Relationships in the First Book of the Bible.* Phillipsburg, N.J.: Presbyterian and Reformed, 2002.

Robins, Gay. *Women in Ancient Egypt.* London: British Museum, 1993.

Robinson, Bernard P. "The Story of Jephthah and His Daughter: Then and Now." *Biblica* 85 (2004): 331–48.

———. "Zipporah to the Rescue: A Contextual Study of Exodus 4:24–6." *Vetus Testamentum* 36 (1986): 447–61.

Roche, Carole. "Daily Life: The Lady of Ugarit." *Near Eastern Archaeology* 63, no. 4 (2000): 214–15.

Roddy, Lee. *Women in the Bible.* Chappauqua, N.Y.: Christian Herald, 1980.

Rodríguez, Angel. "Sanctuary Theology in the Book of Exodus." *Andrews University Seminary Studies* 24, no.2 (1986): 131–37.

Rofé, Alexander. "Family and Sex Laws in Deuteronomy and the Book of the Covenant." *Beth Mikra* 68 (1976): 19–36. [Hebrew with English summary. R.M.D.]

———. "Family and Sex Laws in Deuteronomy and the Book of the Covenant." *Henoch* 9, no 2 (1987): 131–59. [English translation of *Beth Mikra* 68 (1976): 19–36 article above. R.M.D.]

———. "The Tenth Commandment in the Light of Four Deuteronomic Laws." Pages 45–65 in *Ten Commandments in History and Tradition.* Edited by Ben-Zion Segal. Jerusalem: Magnes, 1990.

Rogers, Cleon L., III. "The Meaning and Significance of the Hebrew Word *'āmōn* in Proverbs 8,30." *Zeitschrift für die alttestamentliche Wissenschaft* 109 (1997): 208–21.

Rogers, Eugene F. *Theology and Sexuality: Classic and Contemporary Readings.* Blackwell Readings in Modern Theology. Oxford: Blackwell, 2001.

Rogers, Jack Bartlett. *Jesus, the Bible, and Homosexuality: Explode the Myths, Heal the Church.* Louisville, Ky.: Westminster John Knox, 2006.

Ron, Zvi. "The Daughters of Zelophehad." *Jewish Bible Quarterly* 26, no. 4 (1998): 260–62.

Roncace, Mark. "Elisha and the Woman of Shunem: 2 Kings 4:8–37 and 8:1–6 Read in Conjunction." *Journal for the Study of the Old Testament* no. 91 (2000): 109–27.

Ronson, Barbara L Thaw. *The Women of the Torah: Commentaries from the Talmud, Midrash, and Kabbalah.* Northvale, N.J.: Jason Aronson, 1999.

Rook, John. "Making Widows: The Patriarchal Guardian at Work." *Biblical Theology Bulletin* 27 (1997): 10–15.

———. "When Is a Widow Not a Widow? Guardianship Provides the Answer." *Biblical Theology Bulletin* 28 (1998): 4–6.

Rosenblatt, Naomi H., and Joshua Horwitz. *Wrestling with Angels: What the First Family of Genesis Teaches Us about Our Spiritual Identity, Sexuality, and Personal Relationships.* New York: Delacorte, 1995.

Rösener, Christiane. " 'Your People Shall Be My People, and Your God My God': The Shared Life of Ruth and Naomi as a Model for Women Transgressing Intercultural Boundaries." Pages 1–8 in *Transgressors: Toward a Feminist Biblical Theology.* Edited by Claudia Janssen, Ute Ochtendung, and Beate Wehn. Collegeville, Minn.: Liturgical, 2002.

Rosenzweig, Michael L. "A Helper Equal to Him." *Judaism* 35 (1986): 277–80.

Ross, Allen P. "Proverbs." Pages 890–1134 in vol. 5 of *The Expositor's Bible Commentary.* Edited by Frank E. Gaebelein. 12 vols. Grand Rapids: Zondervan, 1976–1992.

Ross-Burstall, Joan. "Leah and Rachel: A Tale of Two Sisters." *Word and World* 14 (1992): 162–70.

Roth, Martha T. *Babylonian Marriage Agreements: 7th–3rd Centuries B.C.* Alter Orient und Altes Testament 222. Kevelaer, Ger.: Butzon & Bercker, 1989.

———. "The Slave and the Scoundrel: CBS 10467, a Sumerian Morality Tale?" *Journal of the American Oriental Society* 103 (1983): 275–82.

Rowe, Arthur. "Hermeneutics and 'Hard Passages' in the NT on the Role of Women in the Church: Issues from Recent Literature." *Epworth Review* 18 (1991): 82–88.

Rowley, Harold H. "The Meaning of 'The Shulammite.'" *American Journal of Semitic Languages and Literatures* 56 (1939): 84–91.

———. *Men of God: Studies in Old Testament History and Prophecy.* London: Nelson, 1963.

———. *The Servant of the Lord and Other Essays on the Old Testament.* London: Lutterworth, 1952. Repr., Oxford: Blackwell, 1965.

Rudman, Dominic. "Reliving the Rape of Tamar: Absalom's Revenge in 2 Samuel 13." *Old Testament Essays* 11 (1998): 326–39.

Rudolph, W. *Das Buch Ruth, das Hohe Lied, die Klagelieder*. Kommentar zum Alten Testament. Gütersloh: Gerd Mohn, 1962.

Ruether, Rosemary Radford. *Sexism and God-Talk: Toward a Feminist Theology*. Boston: Beacon, 1983.

———. *Woman-Church: Theology and Practice of Feminist Liturgical Communities*. San Francisco: Harper & Row, 1985.

———, ed. *Gender, Ethnicity, and Religion: Views from the Other Side*. Minneapolis: Fortress, 2002.

———, ed. *Religion and Sexism: Images of Woman in the Jewish and Christian Traditions*. New York: Simon & Schuster, 1974.

Rulon-Miller, Nina. "Hagar: A Woman with an Attitude." Pages 60–89 in *The World of Genesis: Persons, Places, Perspectives*. Edited by Philip R. Davies and David J. A. Clines. Journal for the Study of the Old Testament Supplementary Series 257. Sheffield, Eng.: Sheffield Academic Press, 1998.

Runions, Erin. *Changing Subjects: Gender, Nation, and Future in Micah*. Playing the Text 7. New York: Sheffield Academic Press, 2001.

———. "Violence and the Economy of Desire in Ezekiel 16:1–45." Pages 156–69 in *Prophets and Daniel*. Edited by Athalya Brenner. Feminist Companion to the Bible: Second Series 8. New York: Sheffield Academic Press, 2001.

Runzo, Joseph, and Nancy M. Martin, eds. *Love, Sex, and Gender in the World Religions*. Oxford: Oneworld, 2000.

Russell, Letty M. *Human Liberation in a Feminist Perspective: A Theology*. Philadelphia: Westminster, 1974.

———, ed. *Feminist Interpretation of the Bible*. Philadelphia: Westminster, 1985.

———, ed. *The Liberating Word: A Guide to Nonsexist Interpretation of the Bible*. Philadelphia: Westminster, 1976.

Russouw, Tiana. "'I Will Greatly Increase Your Toil and Your Pregnancies': Alternative Perspectives on Genesis 3:16." *Old Testament Essays* 15 (2002): 149–63.

Rutter, Peter. *Sex in the Forbidden Zone: When Men in Power—Therapists, Doctors, Clergy, Teachers, and Others—Betray Women's Trust*. Los Angeles: Jeremy P. Tarcher, 1989.

Ryken, Leland. *Words of Delight: A Literary Introduction to the Bible*. 2d ed. Grand Rapids: Baker, 1992.

Ryrie, Charles C. "Biblical Teaching on Divorce and Remarriage." *Grace Theological Journal* 3 (1982): 177–92.

Sæbø, Magne. "On the Canonicity of the Song of Songs." Pages 267–77 in *Texts, Temples, and Traditions: A Tribute to Menahem Haran*. Edited by Michael V. Fox et al. Winona Lake, Ind.: Eisenbrauns, 1996.

Saggs, H. W. F. *Everyday Life in Babylonia and Assyria*. London: B. T. Batsford, 1965.

———. *The Greatness That Was Babylon*. New York: Hawthorn, 1962.

Sailhamer, John. *Genesis Unbound: A Provocative New Look at the Creation Account*. Sisters, Ore.: Multnomah, 1996.

———. *The Pentateuch as Narrative: A Biblical-Theological Commentary*. Grand Rapids: Zondervan, 1992.

Sakenfeld, Katharine Doob. "How Hosea Transformed the Lord of the Realm into a Temperamental Spouse." *Bible Review* 20, no. 1 (February 2004): 28–33, 52.

———. *Just Wives? Stories of Power and Survival in the Old Testament and Today.* Louisville: Westminster John Knox, 2003.

———. "Naomi's Cry: Reflections on Ruth 1:20–21." Pages 129–43 in *A God So Near: Essays on Old Testament Theology in Honor of Patrick D. Miller.* Edited by Brent A. Strawn and Nancy R. Bowen. Winona Lake, Ind.: Eisenbrauns, 2003.

———. *Ruth.* Interpretation: A Bible Commentary for Teaching and Preaching. Louisville: John Knox, 1999.

———. "Zelophehad's Daughters." *Perspectives in Religious Studies* 15 (1988): 37–47.

Salkin, Jeffrey K. "Dinah, the Torah's Forgotten Woman." *Judaism* 35 (1986): 284–89.

Sample, Tex, and Amy E. DeLong, eds. *The Loyal Opposition: Struggling with the Church on Homosexuality.* Nashville: Abingdon, 2000.

Sánchez, Jorge Piedad. "El rol político de las mujeres en el Antiguo Testamento." *Qol* 28 (2002): 49–60.

Sandberg, Ruth N. *Development and Discontinuity in Jewish Law.* Lanham, Md.: University Press of America, 2002.

Sanders, James A. "The Family in the Bible." *Biblical Theology Bulletin* 32 (2002): 117–28.

Sandoval, Timothy J. and Carleen Mandolfo, eds. *Relating to the Text: Interdisciplinary and Form-Critical Insights on the Bible.* Journal for the Study of the Old Testament: Supplement Series 384. New York: T&T Clark, 2003.

Saporetti, Claudio. *The Status of Women in the Middle Assyrian Period.* Monographs on the Ancient Near East 2/1. Malibu, Calif.: Undena, 1979.

Sapp, Stephen. "Biblical Perspectives on Human Sexuality." *Duke Divinity School Review* 41 (1977): 105–22.

———. *Sexuality, the Bible, and Science.* Philadelphia: Fortress, 1977.

Sarna, Nahum M. *Exodus.* JPS Torah Commentary. Philadelphia: Jewish Publication Society, 1989.

———. *Genesis.* JPS Torah Commentary. Philadelphia: Jewish Publication Society, 1989.

Sasson, Jack M. "Circumcision in the Ancient Near East." *Journal of Biblical Literature* 85 (1966): 473–76.

———. "Of Time and Immortality." *Bible Review* 21, no. 3 (Summer 2005): 32–41, 52, 54.

———. "The Ravishing of Dinah: A Commentary on Genesis, Chapter 34." Pages 143–56 in *Studies in Jewish Education and Judaica in Honor of Lewis Newman.* Edited by Alexander M. Shapiro and Burton Cohen. New York: Ktav, 1984.

———. "Unlocking the Poetry of Love in the Song of Songs." *Bible Review* 1, no. 1 (1985): 10–19.

Sasson, Victor. "King Solomon and the Dark Lady in the Song of Songs." *Vetus Testamentum* 39 (1989): 407–14.

Satlow, Michael L. *Jewish Marriage in Antiquity.* Princeton, N.J.: Princeton University Press, 2001.

Saucy, Robert L. "The Negative Case against the Ordination of Women." Pages 277–86 in *Perspectives on Evangelical Theology: Papers from the Thirtieth Annual Meeting of the Evangelical Theological Society.* Edited by Kenneth S. Kantzer and Stanley N. Gundry. Grand Rapids: Baker, 1979.

Saucy, Robert L., and Judith K. TenElshof, eds. *Women and Men in Ministry: A Complementary Perspective.* Chicago: Moody, 2001.

Sawyer, Deborah F. "Gender-Play and Sacred Text: A Scene from Jeremiah." *Journal for the Study of the Old Testament* no. 83 (1999): 99–111.

———. *God, Gender, and the Bible.* Biblical Limits. London: Routledge, 2002.

———. *Women and Religion in the First Christian Centuries.* New York: Routledge, 1996.

Saxegaard, Kristin Moen. " 'More Than Seven Sons': Ruth as Example of the Good Son." *Scandinavian Journal of the Old Testament* 15, no. 2 (2001): 257–75.

Scalise, Pamela J. "Women in Ministry: Reclaiming Our Old Testament Heritage." *Review and Expositor* 83, no. 1 (1986): 7–13.

Scanzoni, Letha Dawson, and Nancy A. Hardesty. *All We're Meant to Be: Biblical Feminism for Today.* 3d rev. ed. Grand Rapids: Eerdmans, 1992.

Scanzoni, Letha Dawson, and Virginia Ramey Mollenkott. *Is the Homosexual My Neighbor? Another Christian View.* San Francisco: Harper & Row, 1978.

Schaberg, Jane, Alice Bach, and Esther Fuchs, eds. *On the Cutting Edge—the Study of Women in Biblical Worlds: Essays in Honor of Elisabeth Schüssler Fiorenza.* New York: Continuum, 2004.

Schaeffer, Francis A. *Genesis in Space and Time.* Downers Grove, Ill.: InterVarsity, 1975.

Schäfer-Lichtenberger, Christa. "JHWH, Hosea, und die drei Frauen im Hoseabuch." *Evangelische Theologie* 55 (1995): 114–40.

Scharbert, Josef. "Ehe und Eheschliessung in der Rechtssprache des Pentateuch und beim Chronisten." Pages 213–25 in *Studien zum Pentateuch: Walter Kornfeld.* Edited by Georg Braulik. Vienna: Freiberg, 1977.

Scharen, Christian Batalden. *Married in the Sight of God: Theology, Ethics, and Church Debates over Homosexuality.* Lanham, Md.: University Press of America, 2000.

Scheffler, Eben. "In Praise of Canticles: a (Male) Reaction to the Second Feminist Companion to the Song of Songs." *Old Testament Essays* 18 (2005): 309–22.

Schelkle, Karl Hermann. *The Spirit and the Bride: Woman in the Bible.* Collegeville, Minn.: Liturgical, 1979.

Schiff, Daniel. *Abortion in Judaism.* New York: Cambridge University Press, 2002.

Schleicher, Marianne. "Døtre, skøger, og mødre i Jahves Haender" [Daughters, Harlots, and Mothers in Yahweh's Hands]. *Dansk teologisk tidsskrift* 63 (2000): 161–80.

Schloen, J. David. *The House of the Father as Fact and Symbol: Patrimonialism in Ugarit and the Ancient Near East.* Studies in the Archaeology and History of the Levant 2. Winona Lake, Ind.: Eisenbrauns, 2001.

Schmidt, Ludwig. "Bemerkungen zu Hosea 1,2–9 und 3,1–5." Pages 155–65 in *Alttestamentlicher Glaube und biblische Theologie: Festschrift für Horst Dietrich Preuss zum 65. Geburtstag.* Edited by Jutta Hausmann and Hans-Jürgen Zobel. Stuttgart: Kohlhammer, 1992.

Schmidt, Thomas E. *Straight and Narrow? Compassion and Clarity in the Homosexuality Debate.* Downers Grove, Ill.: InterVarsity, 1995.

Schmitt, John J. "Like Eve, Like Adam: *Mšl* in Gen 3:16." *Biblica* 72 (1991): 1–22.

———. "The Motherhood of God and Zion as Mother." *Revue biblique* 92 (1985): 557–69.

———. "Virgin." Pages 853–54 in vol. 6 of *Anchor Bible Dictionary.* Edited by D. N. Freedman. 6 vols. New York: Doubleday, 1992.

———. "The 'Virgin' of Israel: Referent and Use of the Phrase in Amos and Jeremiah." *Catholic Biblical Quarterly* 53 (1991): 365–87.

———. "The Wife of God in Hosea 2." *Biblical Research* 34 (1989): 5–18.

Schneemann, Gisela. "Die Deutung und Bedeutung der Beschneidung nach Exodus 4:24–26." *Communio viatorum* 32 (1989): 21–38.

Schneider, Tammi J. *Sarah: Mother of Nations.* New York: Continuum, 2004.

———. "Sarah: The Chosen Mother." *The Bible Today* 44 (2006): 76–80.

Scholer, David M. "1 Timothy 2:9–15 and the Place of Women in the Church's Ministry. Pages 193–224 in *Women, Authority, and the Bible.* Edited by Alvera Mickelsen. Downers Grove, Ill.: InterVarsity, 1986.

———. "The Evangelical Debate over Biblical 'Headship.'" Pages 28–57 in *Women, Abuse, and the Bible: How Scripture Can Be Used to Hurt or to Heal.* Edited by Catherine Clark Kroeger and James R. Beck. Grand Rapids: Baker, 1996.

———. "Feminist Hermeneutics and Evangelical Biblical Interpretation." *Journal of the Evangelical Theological Society* 30 (1987): 407–20.

———. "Galatians 3:28 and the Ministry of Women in the Church." *Covenant Quarterly* 61, no. 3 (1998): 2–18.

Scholz, Susanne. *Rape Plots: A Feminist Cultural Study on Genesis 34.* Studies in Biblical Literature 13. New York: Peter Lang, 2000.

———. "Through Whose Eyes? A 'Right' Reading of Genesis 34." Pages 150–71 in *Genesis.* Edited by Athalya Brenner. Feminist Companion to the Bible: Second Series 1. Sheffield, Eng.: Sheffield Academic Press, 1998.

———. "Was It Really Rape in Genesis 34? Biblical Scholarship as a Reflection of Cultural Assumptions." Pages 182–98 in *Escaping Eden: New Feminist Perspectives on the Bible.* Edited by Harold C. Washington, Susan L. Graham, and Pamela Thimmes. Biblical Seminar 65. Sheffield, Eng.: Sheffield Academic Press, 1998.

———, ed. *Biblical Studies Alternatively: An Introductory Reader.* Upper Saddle River, N.J.: Prentice Hall, 2003.

Schoors, Antoon. "Bitterder dan de dood is de vrouw (Koh 7,26)." *Bijdragen* 54 (1993): 121–40.

Schottroff, Luise, Silvia Schroer, and Marie-Theres Wacker. *Feminist Interpretation: The Bible in Women's Perspective.* Translated by Martin and Barbara Rumscheidt. Minneapolis: Fortress, 1998.

Schottroff, Luise, and Marie-Theres Wacker, eds. *Kompendium feministische Bibelauslegung.* Gütersloh: Christian Kaiser/Gütersloher Verlagshaus, 1998.

Schramm, Gene M. "Ruth, Tamar, and Levirate Marriage." Pages 191–200 in *Studies in Near Eastern Culture and History: In Memory of Ernest T. Abdel-Massih.* Edited by James A. Bellamy. Michigan Series on the Middle East 2. Ann Arbor: Center for Near Eastern and North African Studies, University of Michigan, 1990.

Schreiner, Thomas R. "Head Coverings, Prophecies, and the Trinity: 1 Corinthians 11:2–16." Pages 124–39 in *Recovering Biblical Manhood and Womanhood: A Response to Evangelical Feminism.* Edited by John Piper and Wayne A. Grudem. Wheaton, Ill.: Crossway, 1991.

———. "Women in Ministry." Pages 177–235 in *Two Views on Women in Ministry.* Edited by James R. Beck and Craig L. Blomberg. Grand Rapids: Zondervan, 2001.

Schroeder, Joy A. "The Rape of Dinah: Luther's Interpretation of a Biblical Narrative." *Sixteenth Century Journal* 28, no. 3 (1997): 775–91.

Schroer, Silvia. *Wisdom Has Built Her House: Studies on the Figure of Sophia in the Bible.* Translated by Linda M. Maloney and William McDonough. Collegeville, Minn.: Liturgical, 2000.

———. "Wise and Counseling Women in Ancient Israel: Literary and Historical Ideals of Personified *ḥokmâ.*" Pages 67–84 in *A Feminist Companion to Wisdom Literature.* Edited by Athalya Brenner. Feminist Companion to the Bible 9. Sheffield, Eng.: Sheffield Academic Press, 1995.

Schroer, Silvia, and Sophia Bietenhard, eds. *Feminist Interpretation of the Bible and the Hermeneutics of Liberation.* Journal for the Study of the Old Testament: Supplement Series 374. New York: Sheffield Academic Press, 2003.

Schroer, Silvia, and Thomas Staubli. "Saul, David, and Jonathan—the Story of a Triangle? A Contribution to the Issue of Homosexuality in the First Testament." Pages 22–36 in *Samuel and Kings.* Edited by Athalya Brenner. Translated by Barbara and Martin Rumscheidt. Feminist Companion to the Bible: Second Series 7. Sheffield, Eng.: Sheffield Academic Press, 2000.

Schuller, Eileen. "Feminism and Biblical Hermeneutics: Gen 1–3 as a Test Case." Pages 31–46 in *Gender, Genre, and Religion: Feminist Reflections.* Edited by Morny Joy and Eva K. Neumaier-Dargyay. Waterloo, Ont.: Wilfrid Laurier University Press, 1995.

Schulman, Alan R. "Diplomatic Marriage in the Egyptian New Kingdom." *Journal of Near Eastern Studies* 38 (1979): 177–93.

Schulze, Peter H. *Frauen im alten Ägypten.* Bergisch Gladbach: Gustav Lübbe, 1987.

Schumacher, Michele M., ed. *Women in Christ: Toward a New Feminism.* Grand Rapids: Eerdmans, 2004.

Schüngel-Straumann, Helen. "Feministische Exegese ausgewählter Beispiele aus der Urgeschichte: Rückblick auf ein Vierteljahrhundert feministische Auslegung von Gen 2 und 3." Pages 205–23 in *Congress Volume: Basel, 2001.* Edited by André Lemaire. Vetus Testamentum Supplements 92. Leiden: E. J. Brill, 2002.

———. "On the Creation of Man and Woman in Genesis 1–3: The History and Reception of the Texts Reconsidered." Pages 53–76 in *A Feminist Companion to Genesis*. Edited by Athalya Brenner. Feminist Companion to the Bible 2. Sheffield, Eng.: Sheffield Academic Press, 1993.

———. "Zwei Weibliche Gegensatzpaare: Ester und Waschti—Lilit und Eva." Pages 511–31 in *Das Manna fällt auch heute noch. Beiträge zur Geschichte und Theologie des Alten, Ersten Testaments. Festschrift für Erich Zenger*. Edited by Frank-Lothar Hossfeld and Ludger Schwienhorst-Schönberger. Herders biblische Studien 44. Freiburg: Herder, 2004.

Schüssler Fiorenza, Elizabeth. "Interpreting Patriarchal Traditions." Pages 39–61 in *The Liberating Word: A Guide to Nonsexist Interpretation of the Bible*. Edited by Letty M. Russell. Philadelphia: Westminster, 1976.

———. "Neutestamentlich-frühchristliche Argumente zum Thema Frau und Amt." *Theologische Quartalschrift* 173 (1993): 173–86.

———. *Wisdom Ways: Introducing Feminist Biblical Interpretation*. Maryknoll, N.Y.: Orbis, 2001.

Schwab, George M. *The Song of Songs' Cautionary Message concerning Human Love*. Studies in Biblical Literature 41. New York: Peter Lang, 2002.

———. "Woman as the Object of Qohelet's Search." *Andrews University Seminary Studies* 39 (2001): 73–84.

Schwartz, Baruch J. "The Bearing of Sin in the Priestly Literature." Pages 3–21 in *Pomegranates and Golden Bells: Studies in Biblical, Jewish, and Near Eastern Ritual, Law, and Literature in Honor of Jacob Milgrom*. Edited by David P. Wright, David Noel Freedman, and Avi Hurvitz. Winona Lake, Ind.: Eisenbrauns, 1995.

———. *The Holiness Legislation: Studies in the Priestly Code*. Jerusalem: Magnes, 1999.

Schwartz, Katherine, and Paul Michael Yedwab, eds. *Sex in the Texts:* Union of American Hebrew Congregations, 2001.

Schwartz, Regina M. "Adultery in the House of David: The Metanarrative of Biblical Scholarship and the Narratives of the Bible." *Semeia* 54 (1991): 35–55.

———. *The Curse of Cain: The Violent Legacy of Monotheism*. Chicago: University of Chicago Press, 1997.

Schweizer, Eduard. "Scheidungsrecht der jüdischen Frau? Weibliche Jünger Jesu?" *Evangelische Theologie* 42 (1982): 294–300.

Scorgie, Glen G. *The Journey Back to Eden: Restoring the Creator's Design for Women and Men*. Grand Rapids: Zondervan, 2005.

Scroggs, Robin. *The New Testament and Homosexuality: Contextual Background for Contemporary Debate*. Philadelphia: Fortress, 1983.

Sedlmeier, Franz, ed. *Gottes Wege suchend—Beiträge zum Verständnis der Bibel und ihrer Botschaft: Festschrift für Rudolf Mosis zum 70. Geburtstag*. Würzburg: Echter, 2003.

Segal, Benjamin J. "Double Meanings in the Song of Songs." *Dor le-dor* 16 (1987–1988): 249–55.

Segal, M. H. *The Pentateuch: Its Composition and Its Authorship.* Jerusalem: Magnes, 1967.

Seibert, Ilse. *Women in the Ancient Near East.* New York: Abner Schram, 1974.

Seim, Turid Karlsen. *The Double Message: Patterns of Gender in Luke and Acts.* Nashville: Abingdon, 1994.

Seitz, Christopher. "Sexuality and Scripture's Plain Sense: The Christian Community and the Law of God." Pages 177–96 in *Homosexuality, Science, and the "Plain Sense" of Scripture.* Edited by David L. Balch. Grand Rapids: Eerdmans, 2000.

Selby, Gary. "Women and Prophecy in the Corinthian Church." Pages 277–306 in vol. 2 of *Essays on Women in Earliest Christianity.* Edited by Carroll D. Osburn. 2 vols. Joplin, Mo.: College Press, 1993.

Selling, Joseph A., ed. *Embracing Sexuality: Authority and Experience in the Catholic Church.* Burlington, Vt.: Ashgate, 2001.

Selman, Martin J. *2 Chronicles: A Commentary.* Tyndale Old Testament Commentaries 10B. Downers Grove, Ill.: InterVarsity, 1994.

———. "Comparative Customs and the Patriarchal Age." Pages 93–138 in *Essays on the Patriarchal Narratives.* Edited by A. R. Millard and D. J. Wiseman. Winona Lake, Ind.: Eisenbrauns, 1983.

Selms, A. van. *Marriage and Family Life in Ugaritic Literature.* Pretoria Oriental Series 1. London: Luzac, 1954.

Selvidge, Marla J. "Mark 5:25–34 and Leviticus 15:19–20: A Reaction to Restrictive Purity Regulations." *Journal of Biblical Literature* 103 (1984): 619–23.

———. *Woman, Cult, and Miracle Recital: A Redactional Critical Investigation on Mark 5:24–34.* Lewisburg, Pa.: Bucknell University Press, 1990.

Selwyn, E. G. *The First Epistle of St. Peter.* 2d ed. London: Macmillan, 1946.

Selz, Gebhard J. "Sex, Crime, and Politics: Zur Interpretation Sumerischer Literaturwerke—Überlegungen zu Inana-K und Sukaletuda." *Journal of Ancient Civilizations* 16 (2001): 37–58.

Sèolle, Dorothee. *Great Women of the Bible in Art and Literature.* Translated by Joe H. Kirchberger. Grand Rapids: Eerdmans, 1994.

Seow, Choon-Leong. "A Heterotextual Perspective." Pages 14–27 in *Homosexuality and Christian Community.* Edited by Choon-Leong Seow. Louisville: Westminster John Knox, 1996.

———. "Job's Wife." Pages 141–50 in *Engaging the Bible in a Gendered World: An Introduction to Feminist Biblical Interpretation in Honor of Katharine Doob Sakenfeld.* Edited by Linda Day and Carolyn Pressler. Louisville: Westminster John Knox, 2006.

———. "Textual Orientation." Pages 17–34 in *Biblical Ethics and Homosexuality: Listening to Scripture.* Edited by Robert L. Brawley. Louisville: Westminster John Knox, 1996.

———, ed. *Homosexuality and Christian Community.* Louisville: Westminster John Knox, 1996.

Setel, T. Drorah. "Prophets and Pornography: Female Sexual Imagery in Hosea." Pages 86–95 in *Feminist Interpretation of the Bible.* Edited by Letty M. Russell. Philadelphia: Westminster, 1985.

Shaner, Donald W. *A Christian View of Divorce: According to the Teachings of the New Testament.* Leiden: E. J. Brill, 1969.

Shanks, Hershel, ed. *Feminist Approaches to the Bible.* Washington, D.C.: Biblical Archaeological Society, 1995.

Shapira, Amnon. "On the Equal Status of Women in the Bible." Hebrew. *Beit Mikra* 159 (1999): 309–37. English abstract by Christopher T. Begg, *Old Testament Abstracts* 23 (2000): 195–96.

Sharp, Donald B. "The Courting of Rebecca: A Yahwist Portrait of the Ideal 'Bride-to-Be.'" *Irish Biblical Studies* 22 (2000): 26–37.

———. "On the Motherhood of Sarah: A Yahwistic Theological Comment." *Irish Biblical Studies* 20 (1998): 2–14.

Shaw, Jane. "Constructions of Woman in Readings of the Story of Deborah." Pages 113–32 in *Anti-covenant: Counter-reading Women's Lives in the Hebrew Bible.* Edited by Mieke Bal. Sheffield, Eng.: Almond, 1989.

Shea, William H. "The Chiastic Structure of the Song of Songs." *Zeitschrift für die alttestamentliche Wissenschaft* 92 (1980): 378–96.

———. "Literary Structural Parallels between Genesis 1 and 2." *Origins* 16 (1989): 49–68.

Shepherd, David. "Violence in the Fields? Translating, Reading, and Revising in Ruth 2." *Catholic Biblical Quarterly* 63, no. 3 (2001): 444–63.

Shepherd, Loraine MacKenzie. *Feminist Theologies for a Postmodern Church: Diversity, Community, and Scripture.* American University Studies, Series 7: Theology and Religion 219. New York: Peter Lang, 2002.

Sherwood, Yvonne. *The Prostitute and the Prophet: Hosea's Marriage in Literary-Theoretical Perspective.* Journal for the Study of the Old Testament: Supplement Series 212. Sheffield, Eng.: Sheffield Academic Press, 1996.

Shibayama, Sakae. "Notes on *yarad* and *alah:* Hints on Translating." *Journal of Bible and Religion* 34 (1966): 358–62.

Shideler, Mary McDermott. *The Theology of Romantic Love: A Study in the Writings of Charles Williams.* New York: Harper, 1962.

Shields, Martin. "Syncretism and Divorce in Malachi 2, 10–16." *Zeitschrift für alttestamentliche Wissenschaft* 111 (1999): 68–86.

Shields, Mary E. "Circumcision of the Prostitute: Gender, Sexuality, and the Call to Repentance in Jeremiah 3:1–4:4." Pages 121–33 in *Prophets and Daniel.* Edited by Athalya Brenner. Feminist Companion to the Bible: Second Series 8. New York: Sheffield Academic Press, 2001.

———. "Circumscribing the Prostitute: The Rhetorics of Intertextuality, Metaphor, and Gender in Jeremiah 3:1–4:4." PhD diss., Emory University, 1996.

———. "Multiple Exposures: Body Rhetoric and Gender in Ezekiel 16." Pages 137–53 in *Prophets and Daniel.* Edited by Athalya Brenner. Feminist Companion to the Bible: Second Series 8. New York: Sheffield Academic Press, 2001.

————. "Subverting a Man of God, Elevating a Woman: Role and Power Reversals in 2 Kings 4." *Journal for the Study of the Old Testament* no. 58 (1993): 59–69.

Shoemaker, Thomas P. "Unveiling of Equality: 1 Corinthians 11:2–16." *Biblical Theology Bulletin* 17 (1987): 60–63.

Sickenberger, Joseph. "Zwei neue Ausserungen zur Ehebruchklausel bei Mattäus." *Zeitschrift für die neutestamentliche Wissenschaft und die Kunde der älteren Kirche* 42 (1949): 202–9.

Siebert-Hommes, Jopie. "But If She Be a Daughter . . . She May Live! 'Daughters' and 'Sons' in Exodus 1–2." Pages 62–74 in *A Feminist Companion to Exodus to Deuteronomy*. Edited by Athalya Brenner. Feminist Companion to the Bible 6. Sheffield, Eng.: Sheffield Academic Press, 1994.

————. "The Widow of Zarephath and the Great Woman of Shunem: A Comparative Analysis of Two Stories." Pages 98–114 in *Samuel and Kings*. Edited by Athalya Brenner. Feminist Companion to the Bible: Second Series 7. Sheffield, Eng.: Sheffield Academic Press, 2000.

————. " 'With Bonds of Love': Hosea 11 as 'Recapitulation' of the Basic Themes in the Book of Hosea." Pages 167–73 in *Unless Some One Guide Me . . . : Festschrift for Karel A. Deurloo*. Edited by J. W. Dyk et al. Amsterdamse cahiers voor exegese van de Bijbel en zijn tradities: Supplement Series 2. Maastricht: Shaker, 2001.

Sigal, Phillip. *The Halakah of Jesus of Nazareth according to the Gospel of Matthew*. Lanham, Md.: University Press of America, 1986.

Sigountos, James G., and Myron Shank. "Public Roles for Women in the Pauline Church: A Reappraisal of the Evidence." *Journal of the Evangelical Theological Society* 26 (1983): 283–95.

Sigvartsen, Jan Åge. "The Biblical Law of *Niddah* and Its Muslim Parallel." Paper presented at the fifty-fourth annual meeting of the ETS. Toronto, November 21, 2002.

Silva, Aldina da. "Ruth, plaidoyer en faveur de la femme." *Studies in Religion* 27 (1998): 252–57.

Simkins, Ronald A. "Gender Construction in the Yahwist Creation Myth." Pages 32–51 in *Genesis*. Edited by Athalya Brenner. Feminist Companion to the Bible: Second Series 1. Sheffield, Eng.: Sheffield Academic Press, 1998.

Simon, Uriel. *Reading Prophetic Narratives*. Translated by Lenn J. Schramm. Indiana Studies in Biblical Literature. Bloomington: Indiana University Press, 1997.

Simons, Louise. "An Immortality Rather Than a Life: Milton and the Concubine of Judges 19–21." Pages 144–73 in *Old Testament Women in Western Literature*. Edited by Raymond-Jean Frontain and Jan Wojcik. Conway, Ariz.: UCA Press, 1991.

Simpson, A. B. *The Love-Life of the Lord*. Harrisburg, Pa.: Christian Alliance, n.d.

Simpson, Cuthbert A. "The Book of Genesis: Introduction and Exegesis." Pages 439–829 in vol. 1 of *The Interpreter's Bible*. Edited by G. A. Buttrick et al. 12 vols. New York: Abingdon, 1951–1957.

Simpson, William K. *The Literature of Ancient Egypt.* New Haven: Yale University Press, 1972.

Singer, Graciela N. Gestoso. "Notes About Children in the Pentateuch." *Davar-Logos* 5 (2006): 67–73.

Sjöö, Monica, and Barbara Mor. *The Great Cosmic Mother: Rediscovering the Religion of the Earth.* San Francisco: Harper&Row, 1987.

Skehan, Patrick W. "Structures in Poems on Wisdom: Proverbs 8 and Sirach 24." *Catholic Biblical Quarterly* 41 (1979): 365–79.

Skinner, John. *A Critical and Exegetical Commentary on Genesis.* 2d ed. International Critical Commentary 1. Edinburgh: T&T Clark, 1930.

Sly, Dorothy I. "Changes in the Perception of the Offence in Numbers 25:1." *Proceedings, Eastern Great Lakes and Midwest Biblical Society* 11 (1991): 200–209.

Small, Dwight Hervey. "The Prophet Hosea: God's Alternative to Divorce for the Reason of Infidelity." *Journal of Psychology and Theology* 7 (1979): 133–40.

———. *The Right to Remarry.* Old Tappan, N.J.: Fleming H. Revell, 1975.

Smith, Bryan. "The Role of Judah in Genesis 37–50: Tangential or Central?" *Biblical Viewpoint* 37, no. 1 (2003): 73–90.

Smith, Carol. "Delilah: A Suitable Case for (Feminist) Treatment?" Pages 93–116 in *Judges.* Edited by Athalya Brenner. Feminist Companion to the Bible: Second Series 4. Sheffield, Eng.: Sheffield Academic Press, 1999.

———. "Samson and Delilah: A Parable of Power?" *Journal for the Study of the Old Testament* no. 76 (1997): 45–57.

———. "Stories of Incest in the Hebrew Bible: Scholars Challenging Text or Text Challenging Scholars?" *Henoch* 14 (1992): 227–42.

———. "The Story of Tamar: A Power-Filled Challenge to the Structures of Power." Pages 16–28 in *Women in the Biblical Tradition.* Edited by George J. Brooke. Lewiston, N.Y.: Mellen, 1992.

Smith, David L. "The Case for Clergy Divorce." *Didaskalia* 2 (April 1991): 12–15.

Smith, Don T. "The Matthean Exception Clauses in the Light of Matthew's Theology and Community." *Studia biblica et theologica* 17 (1989): 55–82.

Smith, Jenny. "The Discourse Structure of the Rape of Tamar (2 Samuel 13:1–22)." *Vox evangelica* 20 (1990): 21–42.

Smith, Paul R. *Is It Okay to Call God "Mother": Considering the Feminine Face of God.* Peabody, Mass.: Hendrickson, 1993.

Smith, Ralph. *Micah–Malachi.* Word Biblical Commentary 32. Waco, Tex.: Word, 1984.

Smith, S. H. " 'Heel' and 'Thigh': The Concept of Sexuality in the Jacob-Esau Narratives." *Vetus Testamentum* 40 (1990): 464–73.

Snaith, John G. *The Song of Songs.* New Century Bible. Grand Rapids: Eerdmans, 1993.

Snaith, N. H. *Leviticus and Numbers.* New Century Bible. London: Nelson, 1967.

Snell, Daniel C. "Notes on Love and Death in Proverbs." Pages 165–68 in *Love and Death in the Ancient Near East: Essays in Honor of Marvin H. Pope.* Edited by John H. Marks and Robert M. Good. Guilford, Conn.: Four Quarters, 1987.

Snodgrass, Klyne R. "Galatians 3:28: Conundrum or Solution?" Pages 161–81 in *Women, Authority, and the Bible*. Edited by Alvera Mickelsen. Downers Grove, Ill.: InterVarsity, 1986.

Soden, Wolfram von. "Zum hebräischen Wörterbuch." *Ugarit-Forschungen* 13 (1981): 157–65.

Soggin, J. Alberto. "The Equality of Humankind from the Perspective of the Creations Stories in Genesis 1:26–30 and 2:9, 15, 18–24." *Journal of Northwest Semitic Languages* 23 (1997): 21–33.

———. *Judges*. Old Testament Library. Philadelphia: Westminster, 1981.

Sohn, Seock-Tae. "'I Will Be Your God and You Will Be My People': The Origin and Background of the Covenant Formula." Pages 255–372 in *Ki Baruch Hu: Ancient Near Eastern, Biblical, and Judaic Studies in Honor of Baruch A. Levine*. Edited by Robert Chazan, William W. Hallo, and Lawrence H. Schiffman. Winona Lake, Ind.: Eisenbrauns, 1999.

Solà, Teresa. *Jahvè, Espòs d'Israel: Poderosa Metàfora Profètica*. Barcelona: Claret, 2006.

Solomon, Lewis D. *The Jewish Tradition, Sexuality, and Procreation*. Lanham, Md.: University Press of America, 2002.

Solvang, Elna K. *A Woman's Place Is in the House: Royal Women of Judah and Their Involvement in the House of David*. Journal for the Study of the Old Testament: Supplement Series 349. New York: Sheffield Academic Press, 2003.

Soskice, Janet Martin, ed. *After Eve*. London: Marshal Pickering, 1990.

———, and Diana Lipton, eds. *Feminism and Theology*. Oxford Readings in Feminism. New York: Oxford University Press, 2001.

Soulen, Richard N. "The '*wasfs*' of the Song of Songs and Hermeneutic." *Journal of Biblical Literature* 86 (1967): 183–90. Repr., pages 214–24 in *A Feminist Companion to the Song of Songs*. Edited by Athalya Brenner. Feminist Companion to the Bible 1. Sheffield, Eng.: Sheffield Academic Press, 1993.

Spanier, Ktziah. "The Queen Mother in the Judean Royal Court: Maacah—a Case Study." Pages 186–95 in *A Feminist Companion to Samuel and Kings*. Edited by Athalya Brenner. Feminist Companion to the Bible 5. Sheffield, Eng.: Sheffield Academic Press, 1994.

Specht, Walter F. "Jesus and Women." Pages 78–96 in *Symposium on the Role of Women in the Church*. Edited by Julia Neuffer. Washington, D.C.: General Conference of Seventh-day Adventists, 1984.

Speiser, E. A. *Genesis*. Anchor Bible 1. Garden City, N.Y.: Doubleday, 1964.

———. "New Kirkuk Documents Relating to Family Laws." *Annual of the American School of Oriental Research* 10 (1930): 1–73.

———. "Notes to Recently Published Nuzi Texts." *Journal of the American Oriental Society* 55 (1935): 432–50.

———. "The Stem *pll* in Hebrew." *Journal of Biblical Literature* 82 (1963): 301–6.

Spencer, Aída Besançon. *Beyond the Curse: Women Called to Ministry*. Nashville: Nelson, 1985.

———. "Eve at Ephesus." *Journal of the Evangelical Theological Society* 17 (1974): 215–22.

———. "God's Order Is Truth." *Brethren in Christ History and Life* 13 (1990): 51–63.

———. "Jesus' Treatment of Women in the Gospels." Pages 126–41 in *Discovering Biblical Equality: Complementarity without Hierarchy.* Edited by Ronald W. Pierce and Rebecca Merrill Groothuis. Downers Grove, Ill.: InterVarsity, 2004.

Spencer, Aída Besançon, with Donna F. G. Hailson, Catherine Clark Kroeger, and William D. Spencer. *The Goddess Revival.* Grand Rapids: Baker, 1995.

Spielman, Larry W. "David's Abuse of Power." *Word and World* 19 (1999): 251–59.

Spieth, Susan Ives. "Divorce: Under No Circumstances?" *Ashland Theological Journal* 24 (1992): 73–79.

Springett, Ronald M. "Homosexual Activity: Does Romans 1 Condone or Condemn It?" *Journal of the Adventist Theological Society* 1, no. 2 (1990): 51–69.

———. *Homosexuality in History and the Scripture: Some Historical and Biblical Perspectives on Homosexuality.* Washington, D.C.: Biblical Research Institute, 1988.

Sprinkle, Joe M. *Biblical Law and Its Relevance: A Christian Understanding and Ethical Application for Today of the Mosaic Regulations.* Lanham, Md.: University Press of America, 2006.

———. "The Interpretation of Exodus 21:22–25 (*Lex Talionis*) and Abortion." *Westminster Theological Journal* 55 (1993): 233–53.

———. "Old Testament Perspectives on Divorce and Remarriage." *Journal of the Evangelical Theological Society* 40 (1997): 529–50.

———. "Sexuality, Sexual Ethics." Pages 741–53 in *Dictionary of the Old Testament: Pentateuch.* Edited by T. Desmond Alexander and David W. Baker. Downers Grove, Ill.: InterVarsity, 2003.

Spronk, Klaas. "Deborah, a Prophetess: The Meaning and Background of Judges 4:4–5." Pages 232–42 in *The Elusive Prophet: The Prophet as a Historical Person, Literary Character, and Anonymous Artist.* Edited by Johannes C. DeMoor. Oudtestamentische Studiën 45. Leiden: E. J. Brill, 2001.

Stackhouse, John G., Jr. *Finally Feminist: A Pragmatic Christian Understanding of Gender.* Grand Rapids: Baker, 2005.

Stadelmann, Luis. *Love and Politics: A New Commentary on the Song of Songs.* New York: Paulist, 1989.

Stanton, Elizabeth Cady. *The Woman's Bible.* New York: European, 1895. Repr., Boston: Northeastern University Press, 1993.

Starr, Lee Anna. *The Bible Status of Woman.* New York: Fleming H. Revell, 1926. Repr., New York: Garland, 1987.

Staton, Julia. *What the Bible Says about Women.* Joplin, Mo.: College Press, 1980.

Steck, Odil Hannes. *Old Testament Exegesis: A Guide to the Methodology.* 2d ed. Resources for Biblical Study 39. Atlanta: Scholars Press, 1998.

Stegemann, Wolfgang. "Zu ihrem Gedächtnis . . . eine feministisch-theologische Rekonstruktion der christlichen Ursprünge." *Evangelische Theologie* 51 (1991): 383–95.

Stein, Robert H. "Is It Lawful for a Man to Divorce His Wife?" *Journal of the Evangelical Theological Society* 22 (1979): 115–21.

Steinberg, Naomi. *Kinship and Marriage in Genesis: A Household Economics.* Minneapolis: Fortress, 1993.

———. "Romancing the Widow: The Economic Distinctions between the *'ALMĀNÂ,* the *IŠŠÂ 'ALMĀNÂ,* and the *'ŠET-HAMMEˉT.*" Pages 327–46 in *God's Word for Our World, Vol. I: Theological and Cultural Studies in Honor of Simon John De Vries.* Edited by J. Harold Ellens et al. Journal for the Study of the Old Testament: Supplement Series 388. New York: T&T Clark, 2004.

Steinmann, Andrew E. "Proverbs 1–9 as a Solomonic Composition." *Journal of the Evangelical Theological Society* 43 (2000): 659–74.

Stendahl, Krister. *The Bible and the Role of Women: A Case Study in Hermeneutics.* Translated by E. T. Sander. Facet Books, Biblical Series 15. Philadelphia: Fortress, 1966.

Sterling, Gregory E. "Women in the Hellenistic and Roman Worlds (323 B.C.E.– 138 C.E.)." Pages 41–92 in vol. 1 of *Essays on Women in Earliest Christianity.* Edited by Carroll D. Osburn. 2 vols. Joplin, Mo.: College Press, 1993.

Stern, Ephraim. "What Happened to the Cult Figurines? Israelite Religion Purged after the Exile." *Biblical Archaeology Review* 15, no. 4 (1989): 22–29, 53–54.

Sternberg, Meir. "Biblical Poetics and Sexual Politics: From Reading to Counter-reading." *Journal of Biblical Literature* 111 (1992): 463–88.

———. *The Poetics of Biblical Narrative: Ideological Literature and the Drama of Reading.* Bloomington: Indiana University Press, 1987.

Sterring, Ankie. "The Will of the Daughters." Pages 88–99 in *A Feminist Companion to Exodus to Deuteronomy.* Edited by Athalya Brenner. Feminist Companion to the Bible 6. Sheffield, Eng.: Sheffield Academic Press, 1994.

Stewart, David T. "Ancient Sexual Laws: Text and Intertext of the Biblical Holiness Code and Hittite Laws." PhD diss., University of California, Berkeley, 2000.

Stiebert, Johanna. "Homosexuality in Botswana and in the Hebrew Bible: An Impression." *Verbum et ecclesia* 23 (2002): 196–208.

———. "Shame and Prophecy: Approaches Past and Present." *Biblical Interpretation* 8 (2000): 255–75.

———. "The Woman Metaphor of Ezekiel 16 and 23: A Victim of Violence, or Symbol of Subversion?" *Old Testament Essays* 15 (2002): 200–208.

Stiebert, Johanna, and J. T. Walsh. "Does the Hebrew Bible Have Anything to Say about Homosexuality?" *Old Testament Essays* 14 (2001): 119–52.

Stiefel, Jennifer H. "Women Deacons in 1 Timothy: A Linguistic and Literary Look at 'Women Likewise . . .' (1 Tim 3.11)." *New Testament Studies* 41 (1995): 442–57.

Stitzinger, Michael F. "Genesis 1–3 and the Male/Female Role Relationship." *Grace Theological Journal* 2 (1981): 23–44.

Stock, Augustine. "Matthean Divorce Texts." *Biblical Theology Bulletin* 8 (1978): 24–33.

Stocker, Margarita. "Biblical Story and the Heroine." Pages 81–102 in *The Bible as Rhetoric: Studies in Biblical Persuasion and Credibility*. Edited by Martin Warner. London: Routledge, 1990.

Stolper, Pinchas. "The Man-Woman Dynamic of HA-ADAM: A Jewish Paradigm of Marriage." *Tradition* 27 (1992): 34–41.

Stone, Elizabeth C., and David I. Owen. *Adoption in Old Babylonian Nippur and the Archive of Mannum-mešu-lissur*. Winona Lake, Ind.: Eisenbrauns, 1991.

Stone, Kenneth A. *Sex, Honor, and Power in the Deuteronomistic History*. Journal for the Study of the Old Testament: Supplement Series 234. Sheffield, Eng.: JSOT Press, 1996.

Stone, Merlin. *When God Was a Woman*. San Diego: Harcourt Brace Jovanovich, 1978.

Stoop-van Paridon, P. W. T. *The Song of Songs: A Philological Analysis of the Hebrew Book* שִׁיר הַשִּׁירִים. Ancient Near Eastern Studies Supplement Series 17. Louvain: Peeters, 2005.

Stordalen, Terje. *Echoes of Eden: Genesis 2–3 and Symbolism of the Eden Garden in Biblical Hebrew Literature*. Contributions to Biblical Exegesis and Theology 25. Leuven: Peeters, 2000.

Storkey, Elaine. *Origins of Difference: The Gender Debate Revisited*. Grand Rapids: Baker, 2001.

Stott, John R. W. "Biblical Teaching on Divorce." *Churchman* 85 (1971): 165–74.

———. "Does Life Begin before Birth?" *Christianity Today* 24, no. 15 (1980): 50–51.

Strabo. *Geography*. Translated by Horace Leonard Jones. 8 vols. Loeb Classical Library. New York: G. P. Putnam's Sons, 1917–1933.

Stratton, Beverly J. *Out of Eden: Reading, Rhetoric, and Ideology in Genesis 2–3*. Journal for the Study of the Old Testament: Supplement Series 208. Sheffield, Eng.: Sheffield Academic Press, 1995.

Štrba, Blažej. "שׁוֹשַׁנָּה of the Canticle." *Biblica* 85 (2004): 475–502.

Streete, Gail Corrington. *The Strange Woman: Power and Sex in the Bible*. Louisville: Westminster John Knox, 1997.

Stroes, H. R. "Does the Day Begin in the Evening or Morning? Some Biblical Observations." *Vetus Testamentum* 16 (1966): 460–75.

Strotmann, Angelika. "Frau Weisheit, der Gott Israels und die Frauen: Eine kleine Forschungsgeschichte zur personifizierten göttlichen Weisheit in der feministischen Exegese." *Bibel und Kirche* 59 (2004): 203–8.

Stuart, Douglas. *Hosea-Jonah*. Word Biblical Commentary 31; Nashville: Thomas Nelson, 1987.

———. "Malachi." Pages 1245–1396 in *Zephaniah, Haggai, Zechariah, and Malachi*. Vol. 3 of *The Minor Prophets: An Exegetical and Expository Commentary*. Edited by Thomas Edward McComiskey. Grand Rapids: Baker, 1998.

Stuckey, Johanna H. "The Great Goddesses of the Levant." *The Journal of the Society for the Study of Egyptian Antiquites* 29 (2002): 28–57.

Stuhlmiller, Wayne J. H. "'One Flesh': In the Old and New Testaments." *Consensus* 5 (January 1979): 3–9.

Stuhlmueller, Carroll. "Prophetic Ideals and Sexual Morality." Pages 8–16 in *Dimensions of Human Sexuality.* Edited by Dennis Doherty. Garden City, N.Y.: Doubleday, 1979.

Suarès, Carlo. *Le Cantique des cantiques.* Geneva: Mont-Blanc, 1969.

Suderman, W. Derek. "Modest or Magnificent? Lotus versus Lily in Canticles." *Catholic Biblical Quarterly* 67 (2005): 42–58.

Sumner, Sarah. *Men and Women in the Church: Building Consensus on Christian Leadership.* Downers Grove, Ill.: InterVarsity, 2003.

Sundberg, Walter. "Jephthah's Daughter: An Invitation to Non-lectionary Preaching." *Word and World* 13 (1993): 85–90.

Swartley, Willard M. *Slavery, Sabbath, War, and Women: Case Issues in Biblical Interpretation.* Conrad Grebel Lectures, 1982. Scottdale, Pa.: Herald, 1983.

Sweeney, Marvin A., and Ehud Ben Zvi, eds. *The Changing Face of Form Criticism for the Twenty-First Century.* Grand Rapids: Eerdmans, 2003.

Swidler, Arlene. "In Search of Huldah." *The Bible Today* 98 (1978): 1780–85.

Swidler, Leonard. *Biblical Affirmations of Woman.* Philadelphia: Westminster, 1979.

Szpek, Heidi M. "Achsah's Story: A Metaphor for Societal Transition." *Andrews University Seminary Studies* 40 (2002): 245–56.

Taber, Charles R. "Sex, Sexual Behavior." Pages 817–20 in *Interpreter's Dictionary of the Bible: Supplementary Volume.* Edited by Keith Crim. Nashville: Abingdon, 1962.

Tadmor, Miriam. "Female Cult Figurines in Late Canaan and Early Israel: Archaeological Evidence." Pages 139–74 in *Studies in the Period of David and Solomon and Other Essays.* Edited by Tomoo Ishida. Winona Lake, Ind.: Eisenbrauns, 1982.

Taitz, Emily, Sondra Henry, and Cheryl Tallan. *The JPS Guide to Jewish Women: 600 B.C.E.–1900 C.E.* Philadelphia: Jewish Publication Society, 2003.

Tal, Ilan. "The Daughters of Zelophehad and Women's Inheritance: The Biblical Injunction and Its Outcome." Pages 176–86 in *A Feminist Companion to Exodus to Deuteronomy.* Edited by Athalya Brenner. Feminist Companion to the Bible 6. Sheffield, Eng.: Sheffield Academic Press, 1994.

Tapp, Anne Michele. "An Ideology of Expendability: Virgin Daughter Sacrifice in Genesis 19:1–11, Judges 11:30–39 and 19:22–26." Pages 157–74 in *Anti-covenant: Counter-reading Women's Lives in the Hebrew Bible.* Edited by Mieke Bal. Sheffield, Eng.: Almond, 1989.

Tarwater, John K. "The Covenantal Nature of Marriage in the Order of Creation in Genesis 1 and 2." PhD diss., Southeastern Baptist Theological Seminary, 2002.

Tasker, David R. *Ancient Near Eastern Literature and the Hebrew Scriptures about the Fatherhood of God.* Studies in Biblical Literature 69. New York: Peter Lang, 2004.

———. "The Fatherhood of God: An Exegetical Study from the Hebrew Scriptures." PhD diss., Andrews University, 2001.

Tate, Marvin E. "An Exposition of Psalm 8." *Perspectives in Religious Studies* 28 (2001): 343–59.

Taylor, J. Glen. "The Song of Deborah and Two Canaanite Goddesses." *Journal for the Study of the Old Testament* no. 23 (1982): 99–108.

Tenney, Merril C. *Zondervan Pictorial Encyclopedia of the Bible.* 5 vols. Grand Rapids: Zondervan, 1975.

Tennis, Diane. *Is God the Only Reliable Father?* Philadelphia: Westminster, 1985.

Terblanche, M. D. "Ter wille van 'n stabiele familie: Die literêre konteks van Levitikus 18:22 en 20:13 ["For the sake of a stable family: The literary context of Lev 18:22 and 20:13" R.M.D.]." *Acta Theologica Sup* 6 (2004): 142–56.

Terrien, Samuel. *The Elusive Presence: The Heart of Biblical Theology.* San Francisco: Harper & Row, 1978.

———. *Till the Heart Sings: A Biblical Theology of Manhood and Womanhood.* Philadelphia: Fortress, 1985.

———. "Toward a Biblical Theology of Womanhood." Pages 17–23 in *Male and Female: Christian Approaches to Sexuality.* Edited by Ruth T. Barnhouse and Urban T. Holmes III. New York: Seabury, 1976.

Tetlow, Elisabeth Meier. *The Ancient Near East.* Vol. 2 of *Women, Crime, and Punishment in Ancient Law and Society.* New York: Continuum, 2004.

———. *Women and Ministry in the New Testament.* New York: Paulist, 1980.

Teubal, Savina J. *Hagar the Egyptian: The Lost Tradition of the Matriarchs.* San Francisco: Harper & Row, 1990.

———. *Sarah the Priestess: The First Matriarch of Genesis.* Athens, Ohio: Swallow, 1984.

Teugels, Lieve. " 'A Strong Woman Who Can Find?' A Study of Characterization in Genesis 24 with Some Perspectives on the General Presentation of Isaac and Rebekah in the Genesis Narrative." *Journal for the Study of the Old Testament* no. 63 (1994): 89–104.

Thatcher, Adrian, and Elizabeth Stuart, eds. *Christian Perspectives on Sexuality and Gender.* Grand Rapids: Eerdmans, 1996.

Thielicke, Helmut. *The Ethics of Sex.* New York: Harper & Row, 1964.

Thistlethwaite, Susan B., and Toinette M. Eugene. "A Survey of Contemporary Global Feminist, Womanist, and Muherista Theologies." Pages 1–20 in *Critical Review of Books in Religion.* Edited by Eldon Jay Epp. Atlanta, Ga.: American Academy of Religion/Society of Biblical Literature, 1991.

Thomas, Kenneth J. "Husband-Wife Relations: A Hermeneutical Case Study." *Theological Review* 3, no. 2 (1980): 20–30.

Thompson, James A. *The Book of Jeremiah.* New International Commentary on the Old Testament. Grand Rapids: Eerdmans, 1980.

———. *Deuteronomy: An Introduction and Commentary.* Tyndale Old Testament Commentaries 5. Downer's Grove, Ill.: InterVarsity, 1974.

Thompson, James W. "The Submission of Wives in 1 Peter." Pages 382–85 in vol. 1 of *Essays on Women in Earliest Christianity.* Edited by Carroll D. Osburn. 2 vols. Joplin, Mo.: College Press, 1993.

Thompson, Thomas L. *The Historicity of the Patriarchal Narratives: The Quest for the Historical Abraham.* Beihefte zur Zeitschrift für die alttestamentliche Wissenschaft 133; Berlin: de Gruyter, 1974.

———. "Preaching Texts of Terror in the Book of Judges: How Does the History of Interpretation Help?" *Calvin Theological Journal* 37 (2002): 49–61.

———. *Writing the Wrongs: Women of the Old Testament among Biblical Commentators from Philo through the Reformation.* Oxford Studies in Historical Theology. Oxford: Oxford University Press, 2001.

Thompson, Thomas, and Dorothy Thompson. "Some Legal Problems in the Book of Ruth." *Vetus Testamentum* 18 (1968): 79–99.

Thurston, Bonnie. *Women in the New Testament: Questions and Commentary.* New York: Crossroad, 1998.

Tigay, Jeffrey H. *Deuteronomy.* JPS Torah Commentary. Philadelphia: Jewish Publication Society, 1996.

Tinder, Glenn E. *The Political Meaning of Christianity: An Interpretation.* Baton Rouge: Louisiana State University Press, 1989.

Todd, Judith A. "Can Their Voices Be Heard? Narratives about Women in 1 Samuel 16 through 1 Kings 2." PhD diss., Graduate Theological Union, 1990.

Toews, John E. "Paul's Radical Vision for the Family." *Direction* 19 (1990): 29–38.

Toews, John E., Valerie Rempel, and Katie Funk Wiebe, eds. *Your Daughters Shall Prophesy: Women in Ministry in the Church.* Winnipeg: Kindred, 1992.

Tolbert, Mary Ann. "Defining the Problem: The Bible and Feminist Hermeneutics." *Semeia* 28 (1983): 113–26.

Tomasino, Anthony J. "History Repeats Itself: The 'Fall' and Noah's Drunkenness." *Vetus Testamentum* 42 (1992): 128–30.

Toorn, Karel van der. "Cultic Prostitution." Pages 510–13 in vol. 5 of *Anchor Bible Dictionary.* Edited by David Noel Freedman. 6 vols. New York: Doubleday, 1992.

———. *Family Religion in Babylonia, Ugarit, and Israel: Continuity and Change in the Forms of Religious Life.* Studies in the History and Culture of the Ancient Near East 7. Leiden: E. J. Brill, 1996.

———. "Female Prostitution in Payment of Vows in Ancient Israel." *Journal of Biblical Literature* 108 (1989): 193–205.

———. *From Her Cradle to Her Grave: The Role of Religion in the Life of the Israelite and the Babylonian Woman.* Translated by Sara J. Denning-Bolle. Biblical Seminar 23. Sheffield, Eng.: JSOT Press, 1994.

———. "Torn between Vice and Virtue: Stereotypes of the Widow in Israel and Mesopotamia." Pages 1–13 in *Female Stereotypes in Religious Traditions.* Edited by Ria Kloppenborg and Wouter J. Hanegraaff. Studies in the History of Religions 66. Leiden: E. J. Brill, 1995.

Torjesen, Karen Jo. *When Women Were Priests: Women's Leadership in the Early Church and the Scandal of Their Subordination in the Rise of Christianity.* San Francisco: Harper, 1993.

Törnkvist, Rut R. *The Use and Abuse of Female Sexual Imagery in the Book of Hosea: A Feminist Critical Approach to Hosea 1–3.* Acta Universitatis

Upsaliensis: Uppsala Women's Studies A, Women in Religion 7. Uppsala: Uppsala University Library, 1998.

Torrance, David W., ed. *God, Family, and Sexuality.* Carberry, Scotland: Handsel, 1997.

Tosato, Angelo. "The Law of Leviticus 18:18: A Reexamination." *Catholic Biblical Quarterly* 46 (1984): 199–214.

——. "On Genesis 2:24." *Catholic Biblical Quarterly* 52 (1990): 389–409.

Tournay, Raymond J. "Les chariots d'Aminadab (Cant. vi 12): Israël, peuple théophore." *Vetus Testamentum* 9 (1959): 288–309.

——. *Word of God, Song of Love: A Commentary on the Song of Songs.* Translated by J. Edward Crowley. New York: Paulist, 1988.

Tov, Emanuel. "The Textual Basis of Modern Translations of the Hebrew Bible: The Argument against Eclecticism." *Textus* 20 (2000): 193–211.

——. *Textual Criticism of the Hebrew Bible.* 2d rev. ed. Minneapolis: Fortress, 2001.

Tracy, Steven. "Headship with a Heart: How Biblical Patriarchy Actually Prevents Abuse." *Christianity Today* 47, no. 2 (2003): 50–54.

Trenchard, Warren C. *Ben Sirah's View of Women: A Literary Analysis.* Brown Judaic Studies 38. Chico, Calif.: Scholars Press, 1982.

Trible, Phyllis. "Bringing Miriam out of the Shadows." *Bible Review* 5, no. 1 (1989): 14–25, 34.

——. "Depatriarchalizing in Biblical Interpretation." *Journal of the American Academy of Religion* 41, no. 1 (1973): 30–48.

——. "Eve and Adam: Genesis 2–3 Reread." *Andover Newton Quarterly* 13 (1973): 251–58. Repr., pages 94–100 in *Biblical Studies Alternatively: An Introductory Reader.* Edited by Susanne Scholz. Upper Saddle River, N.J.: Prentice Hall, 2003.

——. "Genesis 22: The Sacrifice of Sarah." Pages 170–91 in *Not in Heaven: Coherence and Complexity in Biblical Narrative.* Edited by Jason P. Rosenblatt and Joseph C. Sitterson. Bloomington: Indiana University Press, 1991.

——. *God and the Rhetoric of Sexuality.* Overtures to Biblical Theology. Philadelphia: Fortress, 1978.

——. "If the Bible's So Patriarchal, How Come I Love It?" *Bible Review* 8, no. 5 (1992): 44–47, 55.

——. "Not a Jot, Not a Tittle: Genesis 2–3 after Twenty Years." Pages 101–5 in *Biblical Studies Alternatively: An Introductory Reader.* Edited by Susanne Scholz. Upper Saddle River, N.J.: Prentice Hall, 2003.

——. "The Odd Couple: Elijah and Jezebel." Pages 166–79, 340–41 in *Out of the Garden: Women Writers on the Bible.* Edited by Christina Büchmann and Celina Spiegel. New York: Fawcett Columbine, 1994.

——. "Ominous Beginnings for a Promise of Blessing." Pp. 33–69 in *Hagar, Sarah, and their Children: Jewish, Christian, and Muslim Perspectives.* Edited by Phyllis Trible and Letty M. Russell. Louisville, Ky.: Westminster John Knox, 2006.

————. "The Other Woman: A Literary and Theological Study of the Hagar Narratives." Pages 221–46 in *Understanding the Word: Essays in Honor of Bernhard W. Anderson.* Edited by James T. Butler, Edgar W. Conrad, and Ben C. Ollenburger. Journal for the Study of the Old Testament: Supplement Series 37. Sheffield, Eng.: JSOT Press, 1985.

————. *Texts of Terror: Literary-Feminist Readings of Biblical Narratives.* Overtures to Biblical Theology. Philadelphia: Fortress, 1984.

————. "Women in the Old Testament." Pages 963–66 in *Interpreter's Dictionary of the Bible: Supplementary Volume.* Edited by Keith Krim. Nashville: Abingdon, 1976.

Trible, Phyllis, and Letty M. Russell, eds. *Hagar, Sarah, and their Children: Jewish, Christian, and Muslim Perspectives.* Louisville, Ky.: Westminster John Knox, 2006.

Trobisch, Walter. *I Married You.* New York: Harper & Row, 1971.

Trombley, Charles. *Who Said Women Can't Teach?* South Plainfield, N.J.: Bridge, 1985.

Tromp, Nico. "De twee sleutels van het Hooglied: Het wek-en sjaloom-motief." *Nederlands theologisch tijdschrift* 39 (1985): 89–101.

Tsevat, Matitiahu. "Hagar and the Birth of Ishmael." Pages 53–76 in *The Meaning of the Book of Job and Other Biblical Studies: Essays on the Literature and Religion of the Hebrew Bible.* Edited by Matitiahu Tsevat. New York: Ktav, 1980.

————. "The Husband Veils a Wife (Hittite Laws, 197–198)." *Journal of Cuneiform Studies* 27 (1975): 235–40.

————. "Marriage and Monarchical Legitimacy in Ugarit and Israel." *Journal of Semitic Studies* 3 (1958): 237–43.

Tuana, Nancy. *The Less Noble Sex: Scientific, Religious, and Philosophical Conceptions of Woman's Nature.* Race, Gender, and Science. Bloomington: Indiana University Press, 1993.

Tucker, Ruth A. *Women in the Maze: Questions and Answers on Biblical Equality.* Downers Grove, Ill.: InterVarsity, 1992.

Tucker, Ruth A., and Walter Liefeld. *Daughters of the Church: Women and Ministry from New Testament Times to the Present.* Grand Rapids: Zondervan, 1987.

Tull, Patricia. "Intertextuality and the Hebrew Scriptures." *Currents in Research: Biblical Studies* 8 (2000): 59–60.

Turner, Laurence A. *Genesis.* Readings: A New Biblical Commentary. Sheffield, Eng.: Sheffield Academic Press, 2000.

Turner, Mary Donovan. "Rebekah: Ancestor of Faith." *Lexington Theological Quarterly* 20, no. 2 (1985): 42–49.

Ulrich, Dean R. "The Framing Function of the Narratives about Zelophehad's Daughters." *Journal of the Evangelical Theological Society* 41 (1998): 529–38.

United Church of Christ. *Human Sexuality: A Preliminary Study of the United Church of Christ.* New York: United Church, 1977.

Vaccari, Alberto. "La Cantica." Pages 111–29 in *I libri poetici della Bibbia: Tradotti dai testi originali e annotati.* Edited by Alberto Vaccari. La Sacra Bibbia 5/2. Rome: Pontifical Biblical Institute, 1925.

Vall, Gregory. "Hosea and 'Knowledge of God.'" *The Bible Today* 39 (2001): 335–41.

Valler, Shulamit, and Judith Hauptman. *Women and Womanhood in the Talmud.* Translated by Betty Sigler Rozen. Brown Judaic Studies 321. Atlanta: Scholars Press, 1999.

Van Den Eynde, Sabine M. L. "If Esther Had Not Been That Beautiful: Dealing with a Hidden God in the (Hebrew) Book of Esther." *Biblical Theology Bulletin* 31 (2001): 145–50.

———. "Taking Broken Cisterns for the Fountain of Living Water: On the Background of the Metaphor of the Whore in Jeremiah." *Biblische Notizen* 110 (2001): 86–96.

Van der Broek, Lyle. "Women and the Church: Approaching Difficult Passages." *Reformed Review* 38 (1985): 225–31.

Van Kooten, Robert. "The Song of Miriam." *Kerux* 16, no. 3 (2001): 35–41.

Van Leeuwen, Mary Stewart. *Gender and Grace: Love, Work, and Parenting in a Changing World.* Downers Grove, Ill: InterVarsity, 1990.

———. *My Brother's Keeper: What the Social Sciences Do (and Don't) Tell Us about Masculinity.* Downers Grove, Ill.: InterVarsity, 2002.

Van Rensburg, J. F. "Intellect and/or Beauty: A Portrait of Women in the Old Testament and Extra-biblical Literature." *Journal for Semitics* 11, no. 1 (2002): 112–25.

Van Wieringen, Willien C. G. "De wederwaardigheden van de dochters in het boek Richteren als teken van verval" (The Experiences of the Daughters in Judges as a Sign of Decline). Pages 125–38 in *Richteren.* Edited by Klaas Spronk et al. Amsterdamse cahiers voor exegese van de Bijbel en sijn tradities 19. Maastricht: Shaker, 2001.

Van Wijk-Bos, Johanna W. H. *Ruth and Esther: Women in Alien Lands.* Nashville: Abingdon, 2001.

Van Zyl, A. H. "1 Sam 1:2–2:11—a Life-World Lament of Affliction." *Journal of Northwest Semitic Languages* 12 (1984): 151–61.

Vancil, Jack W. "Sarah—Her Life and Legacy." Pages 37–68 in vol. 2 of *Essays on Women in Earliest Christianity.* Edited by Carroll D. Osburn. 2 vols. Joplin, Mo.: College Press, 1995.

VanderKam, James C. *No One Spoke Ill of Her: Essays on Judith.* Early Judaism and Its Literature 2. Atlanta: Scholars Press, 1992.

VanGemeren, Willem A. "'Abba' in the Old Testament?" *Journal of the Evangelical Theological Society* 31 (1988): 385–98.

———. "The Sons of God in Genesis 6:1–4: An Example of Evangelical Demythologization?" *Westminster Theological Journal* 43 (1981): 320–48.

Vasholz, Robert Ivan. "'He (?) Will Rule over You': A Thought on Genesis 3:16." *Presbyterion* 20 (1994): 51–52.

———. "You Shall Not Covet Your Neighbor's Wife." *Westminster Theological Journal* 49 (1987): 397–403.

Vaux, Roland de. *Ancient Israel: Its Life and Institutions.* Translated by John McHugh. New York: McGraw-Hill, 1961.

Vawter, Bruce. "Divorce Clauses in Matthew 5:32 and 19:9." *Catholic Biblical Quarterly* 16 (1954): 155–67.

Verhey, Allen D. "The Holy Bible and Sanctified Sexuality: An Evangelical Approach to Scripture and Sexual Ethics." *Interpretation* 49 (1995): 31–45.

Verhoef, Peter A. *The Books of Haggai and Malachi.* New International Commentary on the Old Testament. Grand Rapids: Eerdmans, 1987.

Vermes, Geza. "Leviticus 18:21 in Ancient Jewish Bible Exegesis." Pages 108–24 in *Studies in Aggadah, Targum, and Jewish Liturgy in Memory of Joseph Heinemann.* Edited by Jakob J. Petuchowski. Jerusalem: Magnes, 1981.

Villalobos, Manuel. "La Prohibición de la Homosexualidad en Lev 18,22 y 20,13." *Qol* 34 (2004): 41–72.

Vincent, Mark A. "The Song of Deborah: A Structural and Literary Consideration." *Journal for the Study of the Old Testament* no. 91 (2000): 61–82.

Vine, Kenneth L. "The Legal and Social Status of Women in the Pentateuch." Pages 28–45 in *Symposium on the Role of Women in the Church.* Edited by Julia Neuffer. Washington, D.C.: General Conference of Seventh-day Adventists, 1984.

Visotzky, Burton L. *The Genesis of Ethics.* New York: Crown, 1996.

Viviers, Hendrik. "The 'Body' and Lady Wisdom (Proverbs 1–9)." *Old Testament Essays* 18 (2005): 879–90.

———. "Clothed and Unclothed in the Song of Songs." *Old Testament Essays* 12 (1999): 609–22.

———. "The Rhetoricity of the 'Body' in the Song of Songs." Pages 237–54 in *Rhetorical Criticism and the Bible.* Edited by Stanley E. Porter and Dennis L. Stamps. Journal for the Study of the Old Testament: Supplement Series 195. Sheffield, Eng.: Sheffield Academic Press, 2002.

Voelz, James W. *What Does This Mean? Principles of Biblical Interpretation in the Post-modern World.* 2d ed. St. Louis: Concordia, 1997.

Vogels, Walter. "Hosea Gift to Gomer (Hos 3:2)." *Biblica* 69 (1988): 412–21.

———. "It Is Not Good That the 'Mensch' Should Be Alone; I Will Make Him/Her a Helper Fit for Him/Her." *Église et théologie* 9 (1978): 9–35.

———. "Man and Woman—Their Dignity, Mutuality, and Fidelity in Marriage: A Biblical Perspective (Gn 1–3)." *Bible Bhashyam* 23 (1997): 205–27.

———. "The Parallel-Chiastic Structure of the Christian Bible." *Theoforum* 32 (2001): 203–21.

———. "The Power Struggle between Man and Woman (Gen 3,16b)." *Biblica* 77 (1996): 197–209.

Vogger, David. "Yhwh gab Rut Empfängnis und sie gebar einen Sohn (Rut 4, 13): Zur Interpretation der Rut-Erzählung." *Biblische Notizen* 100 (1999): 85–100.

Vollebregt, G. N. *The Bible on Marriage.* Translated by R. A. Downie. London: Sheed & Ward, 1965.

Vos, Clarence J. *Woman in Old Testament Worship.* Amsterdam: Judels & Brinkman, 1968.

Vriezen, Theodorus C. *An Outline of Old Testament Theology.* 2 ed. rev. and enlarged. Oxford: Blackwell, 1970.

Wacker, Marie-Theres. "God as Mother? On the Meaning of a Biblical God-Symbol for Feminist Theology." Pages 103–11 in *Motherhood: Experience, Institution, Theology*. Edited by Anne E. Carr and Elizabeth Schüssler Fiorenza. Edinburgh: T&T Clark, 1989.

———. "Tödliche Gewalt des Judenhasses—mit tödlicher Gewalt gegen Judenhass? Hermeneutische Überlegungen zu Est 9" Pages 609–37 in *Das Manna fällt auch heute noch: Beiträge zur Geschichte und Theologie des Alten, Ersten Testaments. Festschrift für Erich Zenger*. Edited by Frank-Lothar Hossfeld and Ludger Schwienhorst-Schönberger. Herders biblische Studien 44. Freiburg: Herder, 2004.

Wade, Theodore E., Jr. *The Song of Songs: Tracing the Story of the Church*. Auburn, Calif.: Gazelle, 1992.

Wadsworth, Tom. "Is There a Hebrew Word for Virgin? *Bethulah* in the Old Testament." *Restoration Quarterly* 23 (1980): 161–71.

Waegeman, Maryse. "The Perfect Wife of Proverbia, 10–31." Pages 101–7 in *Goldene Äpfel in silbernen Schalen: Collected Communications to the XIIIth Congress of the International Organization for the Study of the Old Testament, Leuven, 1989*. Edited by Klaus-Dietrich Schunck and Matthias Augustin. Frankfurt am Main: Peter Lang, 1992.

Waetjen, Herman C. "Same-Sex Relations in Antiquity and Sexuality and Sexual Identity in Contemporary American Society." Pages 103–16 in *Biblical Ethics and Homosexuality: Listening to Scripture*. Edited by Robert L. Brawley. Louisville: Westminster John Knox, 1996.

Waightman, G. J. *The Walls of Jerusalem: From the Canaanites to the Mamluks*. Mediterranean Archaeological Supplement 4. Sydney, Australia: Meditarch, 1993).

Wainwright, Elaine Mary. *New Testament Women*. Storyteller's Companion to the Bible 13. Edited by Dennis E. Smith and Michael E. Williams. Nashville: Abingdon, 1991.

Wakefield, Norm, and Jody Brolsma. *Men Are from Israel, Women Are from Moab: Insights about the Sexes from the Book of Ruth*. Downers Grove, Ill.: InterVarsity, 2000.

Walker, L. L. "Barren, Barrenness." Page 479 in vol. 1 of *Zondervan Pictorial Encyclopedia of the Bible*. 5 vols. Grand Rapids: Zondervan, 1979.

Wallace, Ronald S. *The Story of Joseph and the Family of Jacob*. Grand Rapids: Eerdmans, 2001.

Walls, Neal H. *The Goddess Anat in Ugaritic Myth*. Society of Biblical Literature Dissertation Series 135. Atlanta: Scholars Press, 1992.

Walsh, Carey Ellen. *Exquisite Desire: Religion, the Erotic, and the Song of Songs*. Minneapolis: Fortress, 2000.

———. "A Startling Voice: Woman's Desire in the Song of Songs." *Biblical Theology Bulletin* 28 (1998): 129–34.

Walsh, Jerome T. "Genesis 2:4b–3:24: A Synchronic Approach." *Journal of Biblical Literature* 96 (1977): 161–77.

———. "'You Shall Cut Off Her . . . Palm'? A Reexamination of Deuteronomy 25:11–12." *Journal of Semitic Studies* 49 (2004): 47–58.

Waltke, Bruce K. "1 Corinthians 11:2–16: An Interpretation." *Bibliotheca sacra* 135 (1978): 46–57.

———. "The Old Testament and Birth Control." *Christianity Today* 13, no. 8 (1968): 3–6.

———. "Old Testament Texts Bearing on the Issues." Pages 5–23 in *Birth Control and the Christian.* Edited by Walter O. Spitzer and Carlyle L. Saylor. Wheaton, Ill.: Tyndale House, 1969.

———. "Reflections from the Old Testament on Abortion." *Journal of the Evangelical Theological Society* 19 (1976): 3–13.

———. "The Relationship of the Sexes in the Bible." *Crux* 19 (September 1983): 10–16.

———. "The Role of the 'Valiant Wife' in the Marketplace." *Crux* 35 (September 1999): 25–29.

Walton, John H. "The Place of the *hutqattel* within the D-Stem Group and Its Implications in Deuteronomy 24:4." *Hebrew Studies* 32 (1991): 7–17.

Ward, Roy Bowen. "Porneia and Paul." Pages 219–28 in *Proceedings, Eastern Great Lakes and Midwest Bible Society* 6 (1986): 219–28.

Ward, William A. "Reflections on Some Egyptian Terms Presumed to Mean 'Harem, Harem-Woman, Concubine." *Berytus* 31 (1983): 67–74.

Ware, Bruce A. "Male and Female Complementarity and the Image of God." Pages 73–92 in *Biblical Foundations for Manhood and Womanhood.* Edited by Wayne A. Grudem. Foundations for the Family Series. Wheaton, Ill.: Crossway, 2002.

Warren, Andrew. "Did Moses Permit Divorce? Modal *wĕqāṭal* as Key to New Testament Readings of Deuteronomy 24:1–4." *Tyndale Bulletin* 49 (1998): 39–56.

Washburn, David L. "Perspective and Purpose: Understanding the Josiah story." *Trinity Journal* 12 (1991): 59–78.

Washington, Harold C. "Israel's Holy Seed and the Foreign Women of Ezra-Nehemiah: A Kristevan Reading." *Biblical Interpretation* 11 (2003): 427–38.

———. "'Lest He Die in the Battle and Another Man Take Her': Violence and the Construction of Gender in the Laws of Deuteronomy 20–22." Pages 185–213 in *Gender and Law in the Hebrew Bible and the Ancient Near East.* Edited by Victor H. Matthers, Bernard M. Levinson, and Tikva Frymer-Kensky. Journal for the Study of the Old Testament: Supplement Series 262. Sheffield, Eng.: Sheffield Academic Press, 1998.

———. "Violence and the Construction of Gender in the Hebrew Bible: A New Historicist Approach." *Biblical Interpretation* 5 (1997): 324–63.

Washington, Harold C., Susan Lochrie Graham, and Pamela Thimmes, eds. *Escaping Eden: New Feminist Perspectives on the Bible.* Biblical Seminar 65. Sheffield, Eng.: Sheffield Academic Press, 1998.

Waterman, Leroy. *The Song of Songs, Translated and Interpreted as a Dramatic Poem.* Ann Arbor: University of Michigan Press, 1948.

Waters, John. "Who Was Hagar?" Pages 187–205 in *Stony the Road We Trod: African American Biblical Interpretation*. Edited by Cain H. Felder. Minneapolis: Fortress, 1991.

Watson, Natalie K. *Feminist Theology*. Guides to Theology. Grand Rapids: Eerdmans, 2003.

Webb, Barry G. *Five Festal Garments: Christian Reflections on the Song of Songs, Ruth, Lamentations, Ecclesiastes, and Esther*. New Studies in Biblical Theology 10. Downers Grove, Ill.: InterVarsity, 2000.

———. "The Song of Songs: A Love Poem and as Holy Scripture." *Reformed Theological Review* 49 (1990): 96–97.

Webb, William J. "The Limits of a Redemptive-Movement Hermeneutic: A Focused Response to T. R. Schreiner." *Evangelical Quarterly* 75 (2003): 327–42.

———. "A Redemptive-Movement Hermeneutic: The Slavery Analogy." Pages 382–400 in *Discovering Biblical Equality: Complementarity without Hierarchy*. Edited by Ronald W. Pierce and Rebecca Merrill Groothuis. Downers Grove, Ill.: InterVarsity, 2004.

———. *Slaves, Women, and Homosexuals: Exploring the Hermeneutics of Cultural Analysis*. Downers Grove, Ill.: InterVarsity, 2001.

Weber, Linda. *Woman of Splendor: Discovering the Four Facets of a Godly Woman*. Nashville: Broadman & Holman, 1999.

Weber-Han, Cindy. "Sexual Equality according to Paul: An Exegetical Study of 1 Corinthians 11:1–16 and Ephesians 5:21–33." *Brethren Life and Thought* 22 (1977): 167–70.

Webster, Edwin C. "Pattern in the Song of Songs." *Journal for the Study of the Old Testament* no. 22 (1982): 73–93.

Weems, Renita J. *Battered Love: Marriage, Sex, and Violence in the Hebrew Prophets*. Overtures to Biblical Theology. Minneapolis: Fortress, 1995.

———. "Gomer: Victim of Violence or Victim of Metaphor?" *Semeia* 47 (1989): 87–104.

———. *Just a Sister Away: A Womanist Vision of Women's Relationships in the Bible*. San Diego: LuraMedia, 1988.

Weiler, Gerda. *Das Matriarchat im alten Israel*. Stuttgart: Kohlhammer, 1989.

Weinfeld, Moshe. "Berit—Covenant vs. Obligation." *Biblica* 56 (1975): 120–28.

———. *Deuteronomy 1–11: A New Translation with Introduction and Commentary*. Anchor Bible 5; New York: Doubleday, 1991.

Weis, Richard D. "Stained Glass Window, Kaleidoscope, or Catalyst: The Implications of Difference in Readings of the Hagar and Sarah Stories." Pages 253–73 in *A Gift of God in Due Season: Essays on Scripture and Community in Honor of James A. Sanders*. Edited by Richard D. Weis and David M. Carr. Journal for the Study of the Old Testament: Supplement Series 225. Sheffield, Eng.: Sheffield Academic Press, 1996.

Weisberg, Dvora E. "The Widow of Our Discontent: Levirate Marriage in the Bible and Ancient Israel." *Journal for the Study of the Old Testament* 28, no. 4 (June 2004): 403–29.

Weiss, Charles. "Motives for Male Circumcision among Preliterate and Literate People." *Journal of Sex Research* 2 (1966): 76–84.

Weitzman, Steven. *Song and Story in Biblical Narrative: The History of a Literary Convention in Ancient Israel.* Indiana Studies in Biblical Literature. Bloomington: Indiana University Press, 1997.

Wells, Bruce. "Adultery, Its Punishment, and the Nature of Old Testament Law." Paper presented at the annual meeting of the Evangelical Theological Society. Orlando, Fla., November 21, 1998.

Wendland, Ernst R. "Seeking a Path through a Forest of Symbols: A Figurative and Structural Survey of the Song of Songs." *Journal of Translation and Textlinguistics* 7, no. 2 (1995): 13–59.

Wenham, Gordon J. "*Beṯûlah,* 'a Girl of Marriageable Age.'" *Vetus Testamentum* 22 (1972): 326–48.

———. *The Biblical View of Marriage and Divorce.* London: Third Way, 1982.

———. "Genesis: An Authorship Study and Current Pentateuchal Criticism." *Journal for the Study of the Old Testament* no. 42 (1988): 3–18.

———. *Genesis 1–15.* Word Biblical Commentary 1. Waco, Tex.: Word, 1987.

———. "Gospel Definitions of Adultery and Women's Rights." *Expository Times* 95 (1984): 330–32.

———. *Leviticus.* New International Commentary on the Old Testament. Grand Rapids: Eerdmans, 1979.

———. "Marriage and Divorce in the Old Testament." *Didaskalia* 1 (November 1989): 6–17.

———. "Matthew and Divorce: An Old Crux Revisited." *Journal for the Study of the New Testament* 22 (1984): 95–107.

———. *Numbers: An Introduction and Commentary.* Tyndale Old Testament Commentaries 4. Downers Grove, Ill.: InterVarsity, 1981.

———. "The Old Testament Attitude to Homosexuality." *Expository Times* 102 (1991): 359–63.

———. "The Restoration of Marriage Reconsidered." *Journal of Jewish Studies* 30 (1979): 36–40.

———. "Sanctuary Symbolism in the Garden of Eden Story." Pages 399–404 in "*I Studied Inscriptions from before the Flood*": *Ancient Near Eastern, Literary, and Linguistic Approaches to Genesis 1–11.* Edited by Richard S. Hess and David T. Tsumara. Vol. 4 of *Sources for Biblical and Theological Studies.* Edited by David W. Baker. Winona Lake, Ind.: Eisenbrauns, 1994.

———. *Story as Torah: Reading the Old Testament Ethically.* London: T&T Clark, 2000.

———. "The Syntax of Matthew 19:9." *Journal for the Study of the New Testament* 28 (1986): 17–23.

———. "Why Does Sexual Intercourse Defile (Lev 15:18)?" *Zeitschrift für die alttestamentliche Wissenschaft* 95 (1983): 432–34.

Wénin, André. "Saraï, Hagar, et Abram: Une approche narrative et contextuelle de Gn 16, 1–6." *Revue théologique de Louvain* 32 (2001): 24–54.

Wente, Edward Frank. "Egyptian Religion." Pages 408–12 in vol. 2 of *Anchor Bible Dictionary*. Edited by David Noel Freedman. 6 vols. New York: Doubleday, 1992.

Wente, Edward Frank, and Edmund S. Meltzer. *Letters from Ancient Egypt*. Writings from the Ancient World 1. Atlanta: Scholars Press, 1990.

Wenthe, Dean O., Paul L. Schrieber, and Lee Maxwell, eds. *"Hear the Word of Yahweh": Essays on Scripture and Archaeology in Honor of Horace D. Hummel*. St. Louis: Concordia, 2002.

Wernik, Uri. "Will the Real Homosexual in the Bible Please Stand Up?" *Theology and Sexuality* 11 (2005): 47–64.

Wesley, John. *Explanatory Notes upon the Old Testament*. 3 vols. Bristol, Eng.: William Pine, 1765.

Wesselius, J. W. "De wijze vrouwen in 2 Samuël 14 en 20." *Nederlands theologisch tijdschrift* 45 (1991): 89–100.

Wessels, Francois. "Exegesis and Proclamation: Ephesians 5:21–33." *Journal of Theology for Southern Africa* 67, no. 1 (June 1989): 67–75.

West, Angela. "Sex and Salvation: A Christian Feminist Study of I Corinthians 6:12–7:39." *Modern Churchman* 29, no 3 (1987): 17–24.

West, Gerald. "Reading Abused Female Bodies in the Bible: Interpretative Strategies for Recognising and Recovering the Stories of Women Inscribed by Violence but Circumscribed by Patriarchal Text (2 Kings 5)." *Old Testament Essays* 15 (2002): 240–58.

Westbrook, Raymond. "Adultery in Ancient Near Eastern Law," *Revue biblique* 97 (1990): 542–80

———. "Biblical and Cuneiform Law Codes." *Revue biblique* 92 (1985): 247–64.

———. "*Lex talionis* and Exodus 21,22–25." *Revue biblique* 93 (1986): 52–69.

———. *Old Babylonian Marriage Law*. Archiv für Orientforschung 23. Horn, Austria: Berger und Söhne, 1988.

———. "The Prohibition on Restoration of Marriage in Deuteronomy 24:1–4." Pages 387–405 in *Studies in Bible, 1986*. Edited by Sara Japhet. Scripta hierosolymitana 31. Jerusalem: Magnes, 1986.

———. *Property and the Family in Biblical Law*. Journal for the Study of the Old Testament: Supplement Series 113. Sheffield, Eng.: Sheffield Academic Press, 1991.

———. *Studies in Biblical and Cuneiform Law*. Paris: J. Gabalda, 1988.

Westbrook, Raymond, and Gary M. Beckman. *A History of Ancient Near Eastern Law*. 2 vols. Handbook of Oriental Studies, 1: The Near and Middle East 72, nos. 1–2. Boston: E. J. Brill, 2003.

Westenholz, Joan Goodnick. "Great Goddesses in Mesopotamia: The Female Aspect of Divinity." *The Journal of the Society for the Study of Egyptian Antiquites* 29 (2002): 9–27.

———. "Tamar, QĔDĒŠÂ, QADIŠTU, and Sacred Prostitution in Mesopotamia." *Harvard Theological Review* 82 (1989): 245–65.

Westermann, Claus. *Creation*. London: SPCK, 1974.

———. *Genesis.* 3 vols. Biblischer Kommentar, Altes Testament 1. Neukirchen-Vluyn: Neukirchener Verlag, 1974.

———. *Genesis 1–11.* Minneapolis: Augsburg, 1974.

———. *The Genesis Accounts of Creation.* Philadelphia: Fortress, 1964.

———. "Structure and Intention of the Book of Ruth." *Word and World* 19 (1999): 285–302.

Westminster Assembly. *Annotations upon All the Books of the Old and New Testaments.* 2d ed. London: John Legatt, 1651.

Westphal, Carol J. "Coming Home." *Reformed Review* 42 (1989): 177–88.

Wetzstein, J. G. "Die syrische Dreschtafel." *Zeitschrift für Ethnologie* 5 (1873): 270–302.

Whedbee, J. William. "Paradox and Parody in the Song of Solomon: Towards a Comic Reading of the Most Sublime Song." Pages 266–78 in *A Feminist Companion to the Song of Songs.* Edited by Athalya Brenner. Feminist Companion to the Bible 1. Sheffield, Eng.: JSOT Press, 1993.

White, Ellen G. *Patriarchs and Prophets.* Mountain View, Calif.: Pacific, 1890. Repr., 1958.

———. *The Story of Prophets and Kings.* Mountain View, Calif.: Pacific, 1917. Repr., 1943.

White, James R., and Jeffrey D. Niell. *The Same Sex Controversy: Defending and Clarifying the Bible's Message about Homosexuality.* Minneapolis: Bethany House, 2002.

White, John B. *The Study of the Language of Love in the Song of Songs and Ancient Egyptian Poetry.* Society of Biblical Literature Dissertation Series 38. Missoula, Mont.: Scholars Press, 1978.

White, Leland J. "Does the Bible Speak about Gays or Same-Sex Orientation? A Test Case in Biblical Ethics, Part I." *Biblical Theology Bulletin* 25 (1995): 14–23.

White, Sidnie Ann. "Esther: A Feminine Model for Jewish Diaspora." Pages 161–77 in *Gender and Difference in Ancient Israel.* Edited by Peggy L. Day. Minneapolis: Fortress, 1989.

———. "In the Steps of Jael and Deborah: Judith as Heroine." Pages 570–78 in the *SBL Seminar Papers, 1989.* Society of Biblical Literature Seminar Papers 28. Atlanta: Scholars Press, 1989. Repr., pages 5–16 in *No One Spoke Ill of Her: Essays on Judith.* Edited by James C. VanderKam. Atlanta: Scholars Press, 1992.

Whitekettle, Richard. "Levitical Thought and the Female Reproductive Cycle: Wombs, Wellsprings, and the Primeval World." *Vetus Testamentum* 46 (1996): 376–91.

———. "Leviticus 15:18 Reconsidered: Chiasm, Spatial Structure, and the Body." *Journal for the Study of the Old Testament* no. 49 (1991): 31–45.

Whitesell, Connie J. "'Behold, Thou Art Fair, My Beloved.'" *Parabola* 20 (1995): 92–99.

Whitt, William D. "The Divorce of Yahweh and Asherah in Hos 2:4–7,12ff." *Scandinavian Journal of the Old Testament* 6 (1992): 31–67.

Whybray, Roger N. *Isaiah 40–66.* New Century Bible. London: Oliphants, 1975.

———. *The Making of the Pentateuch: A Methodological Study.* Sheffield, Eng.: JSOT Press, 1987.

———. *Wisdom in Proverbs.* Studies in Biblical Theology 45. Naperville, Ill.: Allenson, 1965.

Wiebe, Phillip H. "Jesus' Divorce Exception." *Journal of the Evangelical Theological Society* 32 (1989): 327–33.

———. "The New Testament on Divorce and Remarriage: Some Logical Implications." *Journal of the Evangelical Theological Society* 24 (1981): 131–38.

Wightman, G. J. *The Walls of Jerusalem: From the Canaanites to the Mamluks.* Mediterranean Archaeological Supplement 4. Sydney, N.S.W.: Meditarch, 1993.

Wijngaard, Marianne van den. *Reinventing the Sexes: The Biomedical Construction of Femininity and Masculinity.* Race, Gender, and Science. Bloomington: Indiana University Press, 1997.

Wijngaards, J. N. M. *The Ordination of Women in the Catholic Church: Unmasking a Cuckoo's Egg Tradition.* New York: Continuum, 2001.

Wilcke, C. "Die Anfänge des akkadischen Epen." *ZA* 67 (1977): 200–211.

Wilfong, Marsha M. "Human Creation in Canonical Context: Genesis 1:26–31 and Beyond." Pages 42–52 in *God Who Creates: Essays in Honor of W. Sibley Towner.* Edited by William P. Brown and S. Dean McBride Jr. Grand Rapids: Eerdmans, 2000.

Willey, Patricia K. "The Importunate Woman of Tekoa and How She Got Her Way." Pages 115–31 in *Reading between Texts: Intertexuality and the Bible.* Edited by Dana Nolan Fewell. Louisville: Westminster John Knox, 1992.

Williams, Charles B. *The New Testament: A Translation in the Language of the People.* Chicago: Moody, 1937.

Williams, Delores S. *Sisters in the Wilderness: The Challenge of Womanist God-Talk.* Maryknoll, N.Y.: Orbis, 1993.

Williams, Jacqueline. "And She Became 'Snow White': Numbers 12:1–16." *Old Testament Essays* 15 (2002): 259–68.

Williams, James G. "The Beautiful and the Barren: Conventions in Biblical Type-Scenes." *Journal for the Study of the Old Testament* no. 17 (1980): 107–19.

———. *Women Recounted: Narrative Thinking and the God of Israel.* Bible and Literature Series 6. Sheffield, Eng.: Almond, 1982.

Williams, John. *For Every Cause? The Question of Divorce.* Neptune, N.J.: Loizeaux Brothers, 1981.

Williams, Prescott H. "Who Came First, Man or Woman?" *Austin Seminary Bulletin: Faculty Edition* 97 (1981): 21–27.

Williams, Ronald J. *Hebrew Syntax, an Outline.* Toronto: University of Toronto Press, 1967.

Williamson, Paul R. *Abraham, Israel, and the Nations: The Patriarchal Promise and Its Covenantal Development in Genesis.* Journal for the Study of the Old Testament: Supplement Series 315. Sheffield, Eng.: Sheffield Academic Press, 2000.

———. "Circumcision." Pages 122–25 in *Dictionary of the Old Testament Penta-teuch*. Edited by T. Desmond Alexander and David W. Baker. Downers Grove, Ill.: InterVarsity, 2003.

Willis, John T. *Genesis*. Living Word Commentary. Austin: Sweet, 1979.

———. "Symbolic Names and Theological Themes in the Book of Isaiah." *Horizons in Biblical Theology* 23 (2001): 72–92.

Willis, Wendell. "Priscilla and Acquila—Co-workers in Christ." Pages 261–76 in vol. 2 of *Essays on Women in Earliest Christianity*. Edited by Carroll D. Osburn. 2 vols. Joplin, Mo.: College Press, 1993.

Wilshire, Leland Edward. "1 Timothy 2:12 Revisited: A Reply to Paul W. Barnett and Timothy J. Harris." *Evangelical Quarterly* 65 (1993): 43–55.

———. "The TLG Computer and Further Reference to *authenteô* in 1 Timothy 2:12." *New Testament Studies* 34 (1988): 120–34.

Wilson, P. Eddy. "Deuteronomy xxv 11–12—One for the Books." *Vetus Testamentum* 47 (1997): 220–35.

Wilt, Timothy L. "Acts 15:19–21: Some Further Discussion." *Bible Translator* 42 (1991): 234–36.

Wink, Walter. "Homosexuality and the Bible." Pages 33–49 in *Homosexuality and Christian Faith: Questions of Conscience for the Churches*. Edited by Walter Wink. Minneapolis: Fortress, 1999.

Winkler, Gershon. *Sacred Secrets: The Sanctity of Sex in Jewish Law and Lore*. Northvale, N.J.: Jason Aronson, 1998.

Winter, Paul. "Genesis 1:27 and Jesus' Saying on Divorce." *Zeitschrift für die alttestamentliche Wissenschaft* 70 (1958): 260–61.

Wire, Antoinette Clark. "Theological and Biblical Perspective: Liberation for Women Calls for a Liberated World." *Church and Society* 76, no. 3 (1986): 7–17.

Wirt, Sherwood Eliot. "Some New Thoughts about the Song of Solomon." *Journal of the Evangelical Theological Society* 33 (1990): 433–36.

Witherington, Ben, III. "Matthew 5:32 and 19:9—Exception or Exceptional Situation?" *New Testament Studies* 31 (1985): 571–76.

———. "Rite and Rights for Women: Galatians 3.28." *New Testament Studies* 27 (1981): 593–604.

———. "Women (NT)." Pages 957–61 in vol. 6 of *Anchor Bible Dictionary*. Edited by David Noel Freedman. 6 vols. New York: Doubleday, 1992.

———. *Women and the Genesis of Christianity*. Edited by Ann Witherington. Cambridge: Cambridge University Press, 1990.

———. *Women in the Earliest Churches*. Society for New Testament Studies Monograph Series 59. New York: Cambridge University Press, 1988.

———. *Women in the Ministry of Jesus: A Study of Jesus' Attitudes to Women and Their Roles as Reflected in His Earthly Life*. Society for New Testament Studies Monograph Series 51. Cambridge: Cambridge University Press, 1984.

Wojciech, Kowalski. "Female Subjection to Man: Is It a Consequence of the Fall?" *African Ecclesial Review* 35 (1993): 274–76, 284.

Wold, Donald J. "The Meaning of the Biblical Penalty *Kareth*." PhD diss., University of California, Berkeley, 1978.

———. *Out of Order: Homosexuality in the Bible and the Ancient Near East.* Grand Rapids: Baker, 1998.

Wolde, Ellen van. "Deborah and Ya'el in Judges 4." Pages 283–95 in *On Reading Prophetic Texts: Gender-Specific and Related Studies in Memory of Fokkelien van Dijk-Hemmes.* Edited by Bob Becking and Meindert Dijkstra. Leiden: E. J. Brill, 1996.

———. "The Dinah Story: Rape or Worse?" *Old Testament Essays* 15 (2002): 225–39.

———. "Does '*innâ* Denote Rape? A Semantic Analysis of a Controversial Word." *Vetus Testamentum* 52 (2002): 528–44.

———. "A Leader Led by a Lady: David and Abigail in 1 Samuel 25." *Zeitschrift für die Alttestamentliche Wissenschaft* 114 (2002): 355–75.

———. "The Story of Cain and Abel: A Narrative Study." *Journal for the Study of the Old Testament* no. 52 (1991): 25–41.

———. *Words Become Worlds: Semantic Studies of Genesis 1–11.* Biblical Interpretation Series 6. Leiden: E. J. Brill, 1994.

Wolf, Herbert M. *An Introduction to the Old Testament: Pentateuch.* Chicago: Moody, 1991.

———. "Judges." Pages 373–506 in vol. 3 of *The Expositor's Bible Commentary.* Edited by Frank E. Gaebelein. Grand Rapids: Zondervan, 1976–1992.

Wolff, Hans Walter. *Anthropology of the Old Testament.* London: SCM, 1974.

Wolfson, Harry Austryn. *The Philosophy of the Church Fathers: Faith, Trinity, Incarnation.* Cambridge: Harvard University Press, 1970.

Wolkstein, Diane, and Samuel N. Kramer. *Inanna, Queen of Heaven and Earth: Her Stories and Hymns from Sumer.* New York: Harper & Row, 1983.

Wolters, Albert M. "Cross-Gender Imagery in the Bible." *Bulletin for Biblical Research* 8 (1998): 217–28.

———. "Nature and Grace in the Interpretation of Proverbs 31:10–31." *Calvin Theological Journal* 19 (1984): 153–66.

———. "Proverbs XXXI 10–31 as Heroic Hymn: A Form-Critical Analysis." *Vetus Testamentum* 38 (1988): 456–57.

———. *The Song of the Valiant Woman: Studies in the Interpretation of Proverbs 31:10–31.* Waynesboro, Ga.: Paternoster, 2001.

Wood, James R. *Where the Spirit Leads: The Evolving Views of United Methodists on Homosexuality.* Nashville: Abingdon, 2000.

Woods, T. E. P. *Shulammith.* Grand Rapids: Eerdmans, 1940.

World Commission on Human Sexuality, "An Affirmation of God's Gift of Sexuality," October 1997. Pages 5–6 in *God's Good Gift of Sexuality: A Seventh-day Adventist Curriculum Framework for Sexual Education.* Silver Spring, Md.: Department of Family Ministries, General Conference of Seventh-day Adventists, 2002.

Woude, Adam S. van der. "Malachi's Struggle for a Pure Community: Reflections on Malachi 2:10–16." Pages 65–71 in *Tradition and Re-interpretation in Jewish and Early Christian Literature: Essays in Honor of Jürgen C. H. Lebram.* Edited by Jan Willem van Henten et al. Studia post-biblica 36. Leiden: E. J. Brill, 1986.

Wright, Christopher J. H. *Deuteronomy.* New International Biblical Commentary: Old Testament Series 4. Peabody, Mass.: Hendrickson, 1996.

———. "The Israelite Household and the Decalogue: The Social Background and Significance of Some Commandments." *Tyndale Bulletin* 30 (1979): 102–24.

Wright, David F. "Homosexuality: The Relevance of the Bible." *Evangelical Quarterly* 61 (1989): 291–300.

———. "Women before and after the Fall: A Comparison of Luther's and Calvin's Interpretation of Genesis 1–3." *Churchman* 98, no. 2 (1984): 126–35.

Wright, David P. *The Disposal of Impurity: Elimination Rites in the Bible and in Hittite and Mesopotamian Literature.* Society of Biblical Literature Dissertation Series 101. Atlanta: Scholars Press, 1987.

Wright, David P., and Richard N. Jones. "Discharge." Pages 204–7 in vol. 2 of *Anchor Bible Dictionary.* Edited by David Noel Freedman. 6 vols. New York: Doubleday, 1992.

Wright, John. "Sexuality within the Old Testament." *St Mark's Review* 106 (June 1981): 3–12.

Wurst, Shirley. "Retrieving Earth's Voice in Jeremiah: An Annotated Voicing of Jeremiah 4." Pages 172–84 in *The Earth Story in the Psalms and the Prophets.* Edited by Norman C. Habel. Sheffield, Eng.: Sheffield Academic Press, 2001.

———. "Woman Wisdom's Ways: Ecokinship." Pages 48–64 in *The Earth Story in Wisdom Traditions.* Edited by Norman C. Habel and Shirley Wurst. Earth Bible 3. Cleveland: Pilgrim, 2001.

Wyatt, Nicolas. "Araunah the Jebusite and the Throne of David." *Studia theologica* 39 (1985): 39–53.

———. "Dennis Pardee, *Les textes rituels* (Rso 12, Paris 2000), an Appraisal." *Ugarit-Forschungen* 33 (2001): 697–706.

———. *Religious Texts from Ugarit: The Words of Ilimilku and His Colleagues.* Biblical Seminar 53. Sheffield, Eng.: Sheffield Academic Press, 1998.

———. "The Story of Dinah and Shechem." *Ugarit-Forschungen* 22 (1990): 433–58.

Wyler, Bea. "Esther: The Incomplete Emancipation of a Queen." Pages 111–35 in *A Feminist Companion to Esther, Judith, and Susanna.* Edited by Athalya Brenner. Feminist Companion to the Bible 7. Sheffield, Eng.: Sheffield Academic Press, 1995.

Yadin, Yigael. *The Temple Scroll: The Hidden Law of the Dead Sea Sect.* New York: Random House, 1985.

———, ed. *The Temple Scroll.* 3 vols. Jerusalem: Israel Exploration Society, 1983.

Yamaguchi, Satoko. *Mary and Martha: Women in the World of Jesus.* Maryknoll, N.Y.: Orbis, 2002.

Yamauchi, Edwin M. *Africa and the Bible.* Grand Rapids: Baker, 2004.

———. "Cultic Prostitution: A Case Study in Cultural Diffusion." Pages 213–22 in *Orient and Occident: Essays Presented to Cyrus H. Gordon on the Occasion of*

His Sixty-Fifth Birthday. Edited by Harry A. Hoffner Jr. Alter Orient und Altes Testament 22. Neukirchen-Vluyn: Neukirchener Verlag,1973.

———. "Cultural Aspects of Marriage in the Ancient World." *Bibliotheca sacra* 135 (1978): 241–52.

———. "Ezra–Nehemiah." Pages 563–771 in vol. 4 of *The Expositor's Bible Commentary*. Edited by Frank E. Gaebelein. 12 vols. Grand Rapids: Zondervan, 1976–1992.

Yancey, Philip. "Holy Sex: How It Ravishes Our Souls." *Christianity Today* 47, no. 10 (2003): 46–51.

———. *Rumors of Another World*. Grand Rapids: Zondervan, 2003.

Yaron, Reuven. *Introduction to the Law of the Aramaic Papyri*. Oxford: Clarendon, 1962.

———. *The Laws of Eshnunna*. 2d rev. ed. Jerusalem: Magnes, 1988.

———. "On Divorce in Old Testament Times." *Revue internationale des droits de l'antiquité* 4 (1957): 357–62.

———. "The Restoration of Marriage." *Journal of Jewish Studies* 17 (1966): 1–11.

Yaron, Shlomith. "The Politics of Sex—Woman's Body as an Instrument for Achieving Man's Aims." *Old Testament Essays* 15 (2002): 269–92.

———. "Sperm Stealing: A Moral Crime by Three of David's Ancestresses." *Bible Review* 17, no. 1 (2001): 34–38, 44.

Yee, Gale A. "An Analysis of Prov 8:22–31 according to Style and Structure." *Zeitschrift für alttestamentliche Wissenschaft* 94 (1982): 64–65.

———. "By the Hand of a Woman: The Metaphor of the Woman Warrior in Judges 4." *Semeia* 61 (1993): 99–132.

———. "Hosea." Pages 195–202 in *The Women's Bible Commentary*. Edited by Carol A. Newsom and Sharon H. Ringe. Louisville: Westminster John Knox, 1992.

———. " 'I Have Perfumed My Bed with Myrrh': The Foreign Woman (*'issâ zarâ*) in Proverbs 1–9." *Journal for the Study of the Old Testament* no. 43 (1989): 53–68. Repr., pages 110–30 in *A Feminist Companion to Wisdom Literature*. Edited by Athalya Brenner. Feminist Companion to the Bible 9. Sheffield, Eng.: Sheffield Academic Press, 1995.

———. "Ideological Criticism: Judges 17–21 and the Dismembered Body." Pages 146–70 in *Judges and Method: New Approaches in Biblical Studies*. Edited by Gale A. Yee. Minneapolis: Fortress, 1995.

———. *Poor Banished Children of Eve: Woman as Evil in the Hebrew Bible*. Minneapolis: Fortress, 2003.

———. " 'She Is Not My Wife and I Am Not Her Husband': A Materialist Analysis of Hosea 1–2." *Biblical Interpretation* 9 (2001): 345–83.

Yoder, Christine Elizabeth. *Wisdom as a Woman of Substance: A Socioeconomic Reading of Proverbs 1–9 and 31:10–31*. Beihefte zur Zeitschrift für die alttestamentliche Wissenschaft 304. New York: de Gruyter, 2001.

Young, Edward J. *The Book of Isaiah*. 3 vols. New International Commentary on the Old Testament. Grand Rapids: Eerdmans, 1972.

———. *Genesis 3*. London: Banner of Truth, 1966.

———. *An Introduction to the Old Testament.* Revised edition. Grand Rapids: Eerdmans, 1960.

Young, Ian. *Diversity in Pre-exilic Hebrew.* Tübingen: Mohr (Siebeck), 1993.

Young, William A. "Wisdom, Nature, and the Feminine: Proverbs 8 in Cross-cultural Perspective." *Proceedings of the Central States Society of Biblical Literature and the American Schools of Oriental Research* 4 (2001): 219–35.

Youngberg, John, and Millie Youngberg, eds. *The Reborn and the Unborn.* Berrien Springs, Mich.: Marriage and Family Commitment Seminars, 1988.

Youngblood, Ronald F., ed. *The Genesis Debate.* Grand Rapids: Baker, 1990.

Younger, K. Lawson, Jr. *Judges and Ruth.* NIV Application Commentary. Grand Rapids: Zondervan, 2002.

Younker, Randall W. "The Emergence of the Ammonites: Socio-cultural Transformation on the Transjordanian Plateau during the Late Bronze/Iron Age Transition." PhD diss., University of Arizona, 1997.

Zakovitch, Yair. *"For Three . . . and for Four": The Pattern for the Numerical Sequence Three-Four in the Bible.* Hebrew. 2 vols. Jerusalem: Makor, 1979.

———. *Das Hohelied.* Herders theologischer Kommentar zum Alten Testament. Freiburg: Herder, 2004.

Zannoni, Arthur E. "Feminine Language for God in the Hebrew Scriptures." *Dialogue and Alliance* 2, no. 3 (1988): 3–15.

Zapletal, V. *Das Hohelied.* 2d ed. Freiburg, Switz.: Universitäts Buchhandlung, 1907.

Zehnder, Markus. "A Fresh Look at Malachi II 13–16." *Vetus Testamentum* 53 (2003): 224–59.

Zenger, Erich. "Die Erschaffung des Menschen als Mann und Frau: Eine Lesehilfe für die sogenannte Paradies-und Sündenfallgeschichte Gen 2,4b–3,24." *Bibel und Kirche* 58 (2003): 12–15.

Zerbst, Fritz. *The Office of Woman in the Church: A Study in Practical Theology.* St. Louis: Concordia, 1955.

Zimmermann, Ruben. *Geschlechtermetaphorik und Gottesverhältnis: Traditionsgeschichte und Theologie eines Bildfelds in Urchristentum und antiker Umwelt.* Wissenschaftliche Untersuchungen zum Neuen Testament: 2. Reihe, 122. Tübingen: Mohr (Siebeck), 2001.

Ziskind, Jonathan R. "Legal Rules on Incest in the Ancient Near East." *Revue internationale des droits de l'antiquité* 35 (1988): 79–107.

———. "The Missing Daughter in Leviticus xviii." *Vetus Testamentum* 46 (1996): 125–30.

Zlotnick, Helena. *Dinah's Daughters: Gender and Judaism from the Hebrew Bible to Late Antiquity.* Philadelphia: University of Pennsylvania Press, 2002.

Zöckler, Otto. "From Jezebel to Esther: Fashioning Images of Queenship in the Hebrew Bible." *Biblica* 82, no. 4 (2001): 477–95.

———. "The Rape of Cozbi (Numbers XXV)." *Vetus Testamentum* 51 (2001): 69–80.

———. "The Silent Women of Yehud: Notes on Ezra 9–10." *Journal of Jewish Studies* 51, no. 1 (2000): 3–18.

———. "Song of Songs." Pages 1–135 in Vol. 5, Sect. 3 of *A Commentary on the Holy Scriptures: Critical, Doctrinal, and Homiletical.* Edited by Johann P. Lange. Translated by W. Henry Green. 12 volumes. Reprint, Grand Rapids: Zondervan, 1960.

Zornberg, Avivah Gottlieb. *The Beginning of Desire: Reflections on Genesis.* New York: Doubleday, 1996.

Zuck, Roy B. *Precious in His Sight: Childhood and Children in the Bible.* Grand Rapids: Baker, 1996.

Index of Modern Authors

Index of Ancient Sources

19:23   9, 154
19:29   306, 437
19:31   327
20   145, 150, 153–55, 158,
   163, 174–75, 196–98,
   244, 333, 346–47, 398,
   430, 432–33, 436–41,
   471–72, 635, 638, 655,
   657
20:1–3   327
20:2–21   155
20:3–4   453
20:5   102, 153
20:5–6   114
20:6   102
20:9   250
20:10   178, 346, 655
20:10–11   446
20:10–16   158
20:10–18   391
20:10–21   243
20:11   440
20:11–12   434
20:11–13   11
20:11–21   391
20:12   174, 440, 655
20:13   viii, 150–51,
   156–57, 159, 162–63,
   171, 637–38, 655
20:14   164, 195, 434, 440
20:14–16   152
20:15   9, 11
20:15–16   655
20:16   10, 11
20:17   10, 11, 142, 196, 391,
   429–30, 434, 440–41, 445
20:17–18   196
20:17–21   9
20:18   11, 196, 244, 328,
   332, 333, 334, 335, 441
20:19   11, 429, 440–41
20:19–21   434
20:20–21   441
20:21   441
20:23   318
20:24   318
20:26   443
20:27   243
20:20–21   142
20:22–23   154
20:22–26   153
20:30   9
21   406
21:1   395

21:1–4   335
21:2   437
21:3   340
21:3–4   395
21:7   xiv, 307, 384, 406
21:9   307
21:10–12   340
21:11   395
21:13   178
21:13–14   340
21:14   xiv, 384, 406
21:20   9, 11
22:4   9
22:4–6   328
22:12–13   407
22:13   384
23:10   154
23:19   152
25:2   154
25:18   123
25:19   123
25:39–54   193
25:49   47, 437
26   352
26:9   199
27:1–8   x, 247
27:20   446
27:33   362

Numbers
3:7   251
3:7–8   47
3:8   251
3:38   251–52
3:40   12
3:43   12
4:23   255
4:30   255
4:35   255
4:39   255
4:43   255
5   x, xi, 214, 245, 349, 353,
   396
5:2   10
5:6   254
5:8   254
5:11–31   245, 349, 350, 353
5:12   178
5:12–14   350
5:13   9, 11, 351, 396
5:13–14   396
5:14   396, 350
5:15   350, 351
5:15–18   350

5:16   350
5:17   351
5:18   350–51
5:19   11, 214, 350
5:19–20   213
5:19–24   350–51
5:20   9, 11, 352, 396
5:21   8, 350, 353
5:21–22   352
5:21–29   8, 188
5:22   8, 10
5:24   350
5:25–26   351
5:25–28   350
5:27   350, 352, 396
5:28   9
5:29   214
5:29–30   350
5:31   353
6   255
6:2–21   243, 255
6:7   395
7:12   259
8:24–25   255
9:15   628–29
11   264
11:12   120
11:15   120, 129
11:16–17   123
12   190
12:1   177, 190–91, 239, 317
12:1–8   255
12:1–16   190
12:2   191
12:4   239
12:5   239
12:10   239
12:12   495
12:15   239
13   256, 257
14:4   194
14:24   192
14:29–34   100
14:33   99
15:14   43
18:2–7   251
18:3–7   47
18:7   252
18:18   254
18:24   43
19:9   472
19:13   472
19:20   472
19:21   472